THE
SCOTS LAW TIMES

1994

General Editor: PETER A NICHOLSON, LLB

EDINBURGH
PUBLISHED BY W GREEN, THE SCOTTISH LAW PUBLISHER
21 ALVA STREET

ISBN This Volume only: 0 414 01095 7
As a set: 0 414 01096 5

TYPESETTING BY MACDONALD LINDSAY PINDAR PLC, EDGEFIELD ROAD, LOANHEAD, MIDLOTHIAN

Printed and bound in Great Britain by
Hartnolls Limited, Bodmin, Cornwall

INDEX OF CASES

ACCORDING TO NAMES OF PARTIES

REPORTS

SHERIFF COURT REPORTS

SCOTTISH LAND COURT REPORTS

LANDS TRIBUNAL FOR SCOTLAND REPORTS

LYON COURT REPORTS

THE
SCOTS LAW TIMES

NEWS

1994

EDINBURGH
PUBLISHED BY W GREEN, THE SCOTTISH LAW PUBLISHER
21 ALVA STREET

INDEX

NEWS PORTION

Extension of land register, 327
Fife and Kinross Solicitors Property Centre, 118
Liability as occupier to user of a right of way
  (J Blackie), 349
Possession: Nine tenths of the law (R Rennie), 261
Property certificates:
  Edinburgh, 88
  Grampian, 134
  Highland, 88
  Inverclyde, 119
  Moray, 134
  Nairn, 119
Rate of interest on landed securities, 190, 393
Sharp cases make good law (G L Gretton), 313, 371
Hooligan's game — played by gentlemen (A M Duff),
  277
Housebreaking with intent (J Ross), 315
HOUSING —
Shelter housing advice service, 89
HUMAN RIGHTS —
Rewriting the European Convention on Human
  Rights (W Finnie), 389

Impact of the new regulatory framework on Scottish
charities (C R Barker, R C Elliot and S R Moody),
331
INCOME TAX —
Access to government information, 363, 394
Approved employee share schemes, 119
Approved pension schemes, 35
Banks and building societies: payment of gross
  interest, 90
Benefits in kind:
  cheap loans, 35, 156, 220, 257, 363, 381
  company vans, 120
  transfers of assets, 173
Business economic notes, 290
Charitable unit trust schemes, 220
Collection of tax:
  codes of practice, 394
Company cars, 135
Disclosure of information to DSS, 311
Double taxation:
  companies: booklet, 135
  future negotiating priorities, 408
  Spain, 271
  Switzerland, 19
  United States, 271
Enterprise Investment Scheme: 211, 327
  approved investment funds, 284
European Economic Area, 89
Excess payments, handling of, 145
Extra-statutory concessions booklet, 256
Fees to professional bodies, 135
Foreign exchange gains and losses, 56, 90
Fundraising for charity, 134
Inland Revenue information powers: 134, 156
  inquiry, 271
Interest on unpaid tax and repayments, 36, 327
Interest paid by government departments, 79
Interest relief, 240
Loss relief, 407
MIRAS: qualifying lenders, 257

Non-statutory redundancy payments, 101
PAYE: 145
  counter avoidance, 110, 179
Payments out of discretionary trusts, 344
Payments to relocated employees, 229
Pension schemes:
  loss of tax approval, 381
Personal residence rules, 35
Private medical insurance, 229
Profit related pay, 270
Publication of internal guidance on tax, 290
Remission of arrears, 172
Self assessment, 270, 353, 381
  anti-avoidance provisions, 144
Share options, 119
Subcontractors in the construction industry, 90
Tax appeals, 48
Tax returns:
  1994 returns, 101
  electronic lodgement service, 119
Venture capital trusts, 135
Vocational training, 19
INSURANCE —
Limited interests in property, covenants to insure
  and subrogation (F P Davidson), 1
Traded endowment policies, 48
It's a wise testator who knows his own great grand-
children (E Crawford), 225

LANDLORD AND TENANT —
Recent development in English law: the politics of
  leasehold reform (R C Elliot), 97
LAW REFORM —
Company law, 133
Criminal procedure review, 78
Metric units of measurement legislation, 17
Right to silence:
  consultation, 311, 327, 352
Scottish Law Commission:
  confiscation and forfeiture, 302
  contract law, 142
  multi-party actions, 368
Security over moveables, 133
Sentencing and appeals, 100
LAW SOCIETY OF SCOTLAND —
ACCORD ADR service, 210
New President, 47
Review of solicitors' training, 405
LEGAL AID —
research report, 201
LEGAL BODIES AND SOCIETIES —
Advocates Criminal Law Group, 290
Advocates, Faculty of, 17, 48, 133, 210, 251, 368,
  393
  consultation centres, 100
  pagers, 99
Crofting Law Group, 119
Dunfermline District Faculty of Solicitors, 18, 405
Edinburgh Bar Association, 144
Faculty of Procurators and Solicitors in Dundee,
  134
Faculty of Solicitors of Dunbartonshire, 56
Glasgow Bar Association, 5
Glasgow University Law Society, 363

APPENDIX

EUROPEAN COURT CASE NOTES

INDEX ACCORDING TO NAMES OF PARTIES

INDEX ACCORDING TO SUBJECT MATTER

ARTICLES

Limited Interests in Property, Covenants to Insure and Subrogation

Fraser P Davidson,
Senior Lecturer in Law,
University of Dundee.

Can an owner of property recover damages from a negligent tenant or subcontractor where the owner has contracted to insure the property? Dr Davidson examines recent case law in various jurisdictions which suggests a developing policy against such recovery, albeit for differing reasons.

Introduction

Increasingly it is the case that a single insured in respect of a given property decides or (more frequently) is contractually obliged to cover the interests of others within his insurance. This short article considers how the courts in a variety of jurisdictions have dealt with the way in which such contractual arrangements affect the question of delictual liability between those parties, and the consequent availability of subrogation to the insurer.

Commercial convenience and co-insurance

It is trite law that one cannot insure property in which one has no insurable interest. Equally, the amount recoverable under a policy reflects the nature of the insured's interest. So, for example, a tenant cannot recover the full value of the property leased unless he is liable for that value by virtue of an obligation to insure or reinstate. Yet it has always been recognised, at least in English law, that a custodier has an insurable interest in the full value of the goods, despite his limited interest. Having recovered from the insurer, the custodier holds the moneys in trust for the owner.

The justification for this has simply been commercial convenience, and recent years have witnessed the English courts extending this principle by analogy to other situations. Thus in *Petrofina (UK) Ltd v Magnaload Ltd* [1984] QB 127, it was accepted that both the main contractor and any subcontractor on a building project ought to be able to insure the entire contract works. Lloyd J opined (at pp 136E-137A): "a head contractor ought to be able to insure the entire contract works in his own name and the name of all his sub-contractors . . . and . . . a sub-contractor ought to be able to recover the whole of the loss insured, holding the excess over his own interest

in trust for the others . . . the position of a sub-contractor in relation to the contract works as a whole is sufficiently similar to that of a bailee . . . to hold, by analogy, that he is entitled to insure the entire contract works".

It might be suggested that neither the convenience of allowing a subcontractor to insure the entire contract works nor the similarity of a subcontractor to a bailee (custodier) is immediately obvious. However, by so finding Lloyd J was able to regard each subcontractor as a co-insured in respect of the whole works. Thus where, as in *Petrofina*, the contract works were damaged by a subcontractor's negligence, that subcontractor being a co-insured, the principle of circuity of action would prevent the insurer being subrogated to the rights of any other co-insured in respect of the damage. This result is in line with US and Canadian authority (see, e g *Louisiana Fire Insurance Co v Royal Indemnity Co* (1949) 38 So 2d 801). In *Commonwealth Construction Co v Imperial Oil Co* (1977) 69 DLR (3d) 558, a case involving the Supreme Court of Canada, de Grandpre J observed (at p 561): "the basic principle [is] that subrogation cannot be obtained against the insured himself. . . . In a case of true joint insurance . . . the interests of the joint insured are so inseparably connected that the several insureds are to be considered as one with the obvious result that subrogation is impossible. In the case of several insurance, if the different interests are pervasive and if each relates to the entire property, albeit from different angles, again there is no question that the several insureds must be regarded as one and that no subrogation is possible."

This conclusion is significant as it has by no means been universally accepted that a bailee (custodier), for instance, is to be treated as co-insured with the bailor. This was emphasised by the following (obiter) remarks of Lloyd J in *The "Yasin"* [1979] 2 Lloyd's Rep 45 at pp 54-55: "It is said to be a fundamental rule in the case of joint insurance that the insurer cannot exercise a right of subrogation against one of the co-insured in the name of the other. I am not satisfied that there is any such fundamental principle. . . . The reason why an insurer cannot exercise a right of subrogation against a co-insured rests . . . on ordinary rules about circuitry. In the present case, a claim in the name of the plaintiffs might well have been defeated by circuity if the insurance had purported to protect the defendants against third party liability. . . . [But the] submission was that the insurance protected the defendants' proprietary interest as bailees. That being so, I do not see how circuitry can help the defendants. . . . They cannot fasten ultimate liability on the insurers; for any sum they might, as bailees, have recovered from the insurers they would have been bound to hold as trustees for the plaintiffs, who, already having received full indemnity, would be bound to pass it back to the insurers."

In other words, a custodier may choose to insure his own interest in the goods or to insure against any liability he may incur in respect of those goods. If he chooses the former course, there remains a potential liability towards the owner of the goods. If the goods are lost through the custodier's negligence, the owner will have a right of action against him. The custodier, of course, will be able to recover the whole value of the goods from the insurer, holding the excess above his own interest for the owner. The owner will, therefore, be effectively indemnified by the insurer, who will then be subrogated to the owner's rights against the custodier. There is, admittedly, a certain tortuous logic in this analysis. However, it requires one to proceed on the supposition that in insuring the goods for their full value the custodier intends primarily to benefit the owner, while leaving himself in a vulnerable position. It also overlooks the argument that, since the owner is not, strictly speaking, insured under the contract, the insurer is not entitled to be subrogated to his rights in the first place.

Yet, whatever the strengths and weaknesses of the analysis, Lloyd J had lost enthusiasm for it by the time of the *Petrofina* case. He observed (at p 140A-B): "in *The 'Yasin'* I went on to contrast the position where the bailee had insured, not his liability to the bailor, but the goods themselves. . . . I have come to the conclusion that the contrast I was seeking to draw is fallacious. Whatever be the reason why an insurer cannot sue one co-insured in the name of another . . . it seems to me now that it must apply equally . . . whether it is the goods which the bailee has insured, or his liability in respect of the goods."

Of course it begs the whole question to describe the bailor and bailee in this situation as co-insured. Nor does the learned judge advance any reason why the "*Yasin*" analysis is fallacious save for the fact that it is not consistent with the conclusion reached in *Petrofina* and the North American decisions which *Petrofina* follows. Yet the situations in *The "Yasin"* and *Petrofina* are, arguably, not strictly comparable. Unlike the relationship of a custodier to the property, a subcontractor rarely has a proprietary interest in the contract works as a whole. Accordingly, if he is insured in respect of the entire contract works,

the only sensible conclusion is that he intends to protect himself against liability for causing damage to those works. On the other hand, where there are a number of different interests in the whole property, it is still possible to see an insured person as seeking merely to insure his proprietary interest, rather than seeking to protect himself against potential liability to others interested in the property. Logically, the distinction drawn in the *The "Yasin"* remains as supportable as ever.

The remarks of Lloyd J in *Petrofina*, then, should be construed as signalling a shift of policy towards the construction of insurance contracts in such situations on the part of English courts.

Landlord and tenant and covenants to insure

The above tendency is not confined to the types of relationship which feature in *The "Yasin"* and *Petrofina*. In *Mark Rowlands Ltd v Berni Inns Ltd* [1986] QB 211, by the terms of the lease the landlord was obliged to insure the premises while the tenant was obliged to pay insurance rent. The tenant was relieved of liability to make repairs and the landlord was bound to use the insurance moneys to effect repairs. The premises had burned down due to the tenant's negligence. The landlord had insured exclusively in his own name and had been compensated by the insurer. It was an established principle that the fact that A has promised B that certain subjects will be insured does not prevent A suing B, should those subjects be damaged by B's negligence (*Airforce Steamship Co v Christie* (1892) 9 TLR 104). What was to prevent the insurer being subrogated to the landlord's rights in respect of the loss?

Some assistance was derived from the case of *Mumford Hotels Ltd v Wheler* [1964] Ch 117, where there had been similar obligations on the part of the landlord and tenant. It was held that in such circumstances there was an inference that the insurance enured for their joint benefit. However, that served only to establish that the landlord in such a case was obliged to apply the insurance moneys towards reinstatement if called on to do so. It still left open the question of whether the insurer might be subrogated to the landlord's rights should the damage occur through the tenant's negligence, and thus be able to recover from the latter. In other words, the conclusion that the landlord had impliedly agreed that the insurance should enure for the joint benefit of himself and the tenant does not necessitate the further conclusion that he has also impliedly agreed that the tenant should also not be liable for the consequences of his negligence.

There was then no English authority directly on the point, but there was a wealth of US and Canadian cases. The tendency of the US cases (see, e g *General Mills Inc v Goldman* (1950) 184 F 2d 359) is summed up by Laskin CJC in the Canadian Supreme Court in *Agnew-Surpass Shoe Stores Ltd v Cummer-Yonge Investments Ltd* (1975) 55 DLR (3d) 676 at p 686: "Where, in the American cases, the exception from liability for fire in the tenant's repairing covenants . . . is reinforced by a covenant on the lessor's part to insure, or to pay for insurance, the weight of authority appears to be that the tenant is not liable for loss or damage from fire caused by its negligence".

As far as Canadian authority was concerned, a series of Supreme Court decisions had followed the US line, albeit by a majority in each case. The essence of the debate between majority and minority was thus articulated by Kerr LJ in the *Berni* case (at p 977): "The minority view, in effect, was that sufficient content could be given to the landlords' covenant to insure . . . by concluding that the purpose of the covenant was to assure the tenants that funds for the reinstatement of the premises would be available, and that in these circumstances the provisions of the lease did not go far enough to exclude the tenants' liability in negligence since there was no provision to this effect . . . the majority view was that there was no need for any such provision, since it was sufficiently clear from the terms of the leases and the landlords' covenant to insure . . . that the landlord could not maintain an action for negligence against the tenants and the landlords' insurers' right of subrogation could therefore equally not be enforced."

Thus in *Eaton & Co Ltd v Smith* (1977) 92 DLR (3d) 425, Laskin CJC observed (at pp 429-430): "the covenant to insure . . . must be given effect against liability for fires arising from the tenant's negligence because otherwise, as a covenant expressly running to the benefit of the tenant, it would have no subject-matter. . . . This is not a case where one has to consider whether there is some provision exonerating one contracting party from liability to the other for the former's negligence. Rather is it a case where a supervening covenant has been given . . . to cover by an insurance policy the risk of loss . . . caused by negligence. An insurer could not refuse to pay a claim for loss of fire merely because a fire arose from the insured's negligence. I can see no reason why its position can be any better against a tenant, whose negligence caused loss by fire, if the lease . . . makes it clear that a policy was to be taken out by the landlord to cover such fires".

Yet the other side of the coin is represented by de Grandpre J who speaks in the *Agnew-Surpass* case (at p 695) of: "the principle that the undertaking by the landlord [to insure] does not constitute the tenant a co-insured so as to permit it to escape liability for fire damage caused by its negligence."

Indeed, in *Ross Southward Tire Ltd v Pyrotech Products Ltd* (1975) 57 DLR (3d) 248, the same judge (at p 255) went so far as to suggest that the tenant was not impliedly relieved of liability for negligence when he covenanted to pay the insurance premiums directly to the insurer: "It made good sense for the lessor to obtain a certain return on his investment; one way of achieving that result was to put on the shoulders of the lessee the payment of all those items which were still to be determined when the lease was signed . . . no importance from the point of view of the tenant's liability should be attached to the fact that one or other of the parties to the lease pays the insurance rates."

There were then two diametrically opposed approaches to this question, and a reasonable case could be made out for either of them. Understandably, the Court of Appeal in *Berni* chose to adopt the majority view. Kerr LJ observed (at p 979): "I would respectfully follow and adopt the reasoning which has prevailed in this impressive series of North American authorities. . . . The intention of the parties, sensibly construed, must therefore have been that . . . the landlord's loss was to be recouped from the insurance moneys and that in that event they were to have no further claim against the tenant in damages for negligence."

It can be noted that although the same result vis-à-vis the insurer's right of subrogation is reached in these landlord and tenant cases, in cases involving other limited interests in property, the route is different. Whereas these other cases stress the fact that the principle of circuity of action prevents the insurer proceeding against a negligent co-insured, cases such as *Berni* indicate that the proper construction of the agreement between landlord and tenant is that the tenant is not to be liable to the landlord for its negligence, so that there is no right of action against the tenant to which the insurer may be subrogated.

This difference was stressed when the issue arose for the first time in Scotland in the case of *Barras v Hamilton*, 1993 SLT 1301. The only Scottish authorities quoted before the court in that case concerned the tenant's right to share in insurance moneys when he had contributed towards the premium, or the right of the tenant to demand that the landlord applied those moneys towards reinstatement. As the judge (McEwan, QC) observes (at p 1305G): "this point is not what was decided in the Scottish cases and no obiter remarks were made about it . . . I have to regard the point as an open question on which there is no Scottish authority", so: "Having regard to the case of *Berni* I am of the view that it is sound in principle and should be followed."

However, *Berni* was invoked not to defeat a claim by the insurer, but to defeat a claim by the landlord for losses not covered by the policy. It follows logically from *Berni* that a tenant might resist a claim from a landlord by insisting that the landlord observe the implied agreement between them by claiming from the insurer. *Barras* goes a stage further by suggesting that the arrangement between landlord and tenant precludes the former proceeding against the latter in respect of losses attributable to the latter's negligence, which losses lie beyond the scope of the insurance policy. It cannot be stated with any certainty whether this is intended to be a point of general principle or simply the construction to be imposed on the arrangement between the parties in this particular case. In support of this latter interpretation it may be observed that some emphasis was placed on the fact that the landlord arranged the insurance and that therefore the scope of the policy was a "matter of deliberate choice". Unfortunately, there is no guarantee that this point will arise in the future, so that clarification is not likely.

Conclusions
This article has examined the trend in England and North America towards interpreting covenants to insure between landlord and tenant as impliedly relieving tenants of liability towards their landlords in respect of negligence, and thus preventing insurers being subrogated to the landlord's rights against those tenants. This analysis seems to apply whether the tenant leases the whole or only part of the property. It was seen that this approach had been followed and perhaps developed in Scotland.

There was identified an associated trend towards allowing those with a limited interest in property, such as custodiers and subcontractors, to insure the entire property for its full value, again whether or not their interest embraced the entire property. They were then seen as co-insured, so that the principle of circuity of action prevented the insurer being subrogated to the rights of other parties interested in the property in the event of the property being damaged through the negligence of the custodier or sub-contractor. Whether this approach would similarly be adopted in Scotland is so far untested, but there is no reason to suppose that it would not.

Finally, a couple of points may be made. First, as the questions are essentially ones of construction, the matter might be put beyond doubt by explicit provision in the covenant or the insurance policy. Secondly, these are doctrines which were adopted into English law from North America, and which are coming to be adopted in Scots law from English law. It is an interesting example of how a growing congruence is developing between legal systems on commercial matters.

◆

NEWS

Court

Sheriffdoms: Grampian, Highland and Islands
The Sheriff Principal of Grampian, Highland and Islands, by virtue of the powers conferred by rules 12.1 and 15.4 (2) of the Rules contained in the First Schedule annexed to the Act of Sederunt (Sheriff Court Ordinary Cause Rules) 1993, has directed:

1. For the purpose of said rules 12.1 and 15.4 (2) "the sheriff clerk" shall not include a sheriff clerk below the rank of higher executive officer save that, in any sheriff court within the Sheriffdom where the resident sheriff clerk in charge of a court holds the rank of executive officer, it shall include that sheriff clerk or his temporary replacement provided he is of the same or higher rank.

2. The classes of interlocutor which a sheriff clerk may write and sign in terms of the said rule 12.1 shall not include any final interlocutor or any interlocutor which the sheriff concerned directs to be written or signed by him or her. Subject to the foregoing, an interlocutor dealing with a motion which has been determined by a sheriff clerk in terms of the said rule 15.4 (2)

shall be written and signed by that sheriff clerk.

3. The classes of unopposed motions which a sheriff clerk may determine in terms of the said rule 15.4 (2) are set out in the appendix to this direction. However, if the granting of any such motion might also involve any order relating to expenses, it shall be referred to the sheriff who shall deal with it in accordance with rule 15.4 (1).

4. This direction shall take effect from 1 January 1994.

Appendix

Classes of motion which may be determined by a sheriff clerk in terms of rule 15.4 (2):

(a) A motion to authorise re-service of an initial writ in terms of rule 5.9.

(b) A motion to recall a sist and to re-enrol a cause for further procedure.

(c) A motion, made under rule 10.3 (1), to close the record before the expiry of the adjustment period provided by rule 10.1 (1).

(d) A motion to allow an amendment of a kind specified in rule 18.1.

(e) A motion to allow a minute of amendment to be received and answered within a specified period in terms of rule 18.3 (1) (a) and (b) (ii).

(f) A motion for an order for service of a third party notice, made under rule 20.1 (1) and (2).

General

Glasgow Bar Association
The Glasgow Bar Association's executive committee for 1993-94 is: *President*, W S S Ireland; *vice president*, P D Langan; *secretary*, T L Ross; *treasurer*, Mrs M M Galbraith; *past president*, David C Clapham, SSC; *country member*, Crawford Mason; *committee*, Miss C A Kelly, A L Miller, E G Savage, Ian Fleming, Andrew Pollock and Albert Thomson.

WS Society
The following have been admitted to the Society of Writers to Her Majesty's Signet: I J Anderson, N J Atkins, J Baxter, A S Biggart, A A Boyd, A D Buchanan, J Carlin, A S Chalmers, F J Chalmers, F J Cooper, J T Cunningham, R J C Gardner, D I Johnston, S A Kerr, K C Lauder, G S Lockerbie, M C MacGregor, C Mackay, A M McKenzie, A Mackie, E A Malcolm, I D Mason, D C Mitchell, D O C Mitchell, F I Moore, R J C Morton, F M Mundy, P D Peddie, S C Pottinger, A L Renton, J W Robertson, M Sales, C A S Smith.

Taxation

Corporation tax: interest payable by banks and similar businesses
The Inland Revenue have published an extra statutory concession which applies to annual interest paid by banks and similar concerns. Under the concession, which reflects an existing practice applied to banks, annual interest will not be treated as a charge on total profits but may be deducted as a trading expense in arriving at the trading profit.

The new concession is published as a transitory measure pending the outcome of a wider review of the tax treatment of interest which the Inland Revenue is commencing and on which there will be consultation with interested parties. That review will encompass the matters covered by the concession.

Building societies: trading income
The Inland Revenue have published an extra statutory concession relating to the timing of tax relief for dividends and interest payable by building societies. Under the concession, which reflects existing practice, the gross amount of the dividends and interest charged in a building society's annual accounts, rather than the actual amount paid or credited in the period, may be deducted as an expense in computing its trading income for that accounting period.

The new concession is published as part of the Inland Revenue's continuing review of their administrative practices to identify those which should properly be classified and published as extra statutory concessions.

Business changes

McGrigor Donald announce the appointment of five new associates. They are Richard Masters, who specialises in mergers and acquisitions and joint ventures; Eleanor Kerr, who specialises in tax planning and trust and executory administration; Eilidh Cameron, a Court of Session litigator with a particular expertise in employment law; Vincent Connor, a commercial litigator who specialises in contentious construction law; and Elspeth Campbell, who has wide experience of acquisitions and mergers, joint ventures and share holder disputes.

Messrs Montgomerie & Co, solicitors, Apsley House, 29 Wellington Street, Glasgow, intimate the retiral from the partnership of Mr John Gilfillan Luscombe Robinson and Mr Edward Goodman with effect from 31 December 1993. Mr Robinson and Mr Goodman continue to be associated with the firm as consultants.

Parliamentary News

Royal Assent

17 December 1993

Consolidated Fund (No 3) Act 1993 (c 52).

New Bills

HOUSE OF LORDS

23 November 1993

Intelligence Services (Amendment)—To make provision about the Secret Intelligence Service and the Government Communications Headquarters, including provision for the issue of warrants and authorisations enabling certain actions to be taken and for the issue of such warrants and authorisations to be kept under review; to make further provision about warrants issued on applications by the Security Service; to establish a procedure for the investigation of complaints about the Secret Intelligence Service and the Government Communications Headquarters; to make provision for the establishment of an Intelligence and Security Committee to scrutinise all three of those bodies; and for connected purposes. (Government)

Education—To make provision about teacher training and related matters; to make provision with respect to the funding and conduct of students' unions; and for connected purposes. (Government)

Dangerous Dogs (Amendment)—To amend the law relating to dangerous dogs; and for connected purposes. (Introduced by Lord Houghton of Sowerby)

Dog Control and Welfare—To establish a Dog Control and Welfare Council and to amend section 2 of the Dangerous Dogs Act 1991. (Introduced by Lord Houghton of Sowerby)

24 November 1993

Trademarks—To make new provision for registered trade marks, implementing Council Directive No 89/104/EEC of 21st December 1988 to approximate the laws of the Member States relating to trade marks; to make provision in connection with the Council Regulation (EEC) on the Community trade mark; to give effect to the Madrid Protocol Relating to the International Registration of Marks of 27th June 1989, and to certain provisions of the Paris Convention for the Protection of Industrial Property of 20th March 1883, as revised and amended; and for connected purposes. (Government)

British Nationality (Hong Kong)—To provide for the acquisition of British citizenship by certain of the British nationals in Hong Kong. (Introduced by Lord Bonham-Carter)

Inshore Fishing (Scotland)—To amend the Inshore Fishing (Scotland) Act 1984 to make provision for the control of fishing in Scottish inshore waters by vehicles or equipment. (Introduced by Lord Campbell of Croy)

25 November 1993

New Towns (Amendment)—To amend Schedule 9 to the New Towns Act 1981. (Introduced by Lord Finsberg)

30 November 1993

Local Government (Wales)—To make provision with respect to local government in Wales. (Government)

HOUSE OF COMMONS

7 December 1993

Finance—To grant certain duties, to alter other duties, to amend the law relating to the national debt and the public revenue, and to make further provision in connection with finance. (Government)

9 December 1993

Local Government etc (Scotland)—To make provision with respect to local government and the functions of local authorities; to make amendments in relation to local government finance, local authority accounts and the records of local authorities; to establish a Strathclyde Passenger Transport Authority for the purposes of the Transport Act 1968; to provide for the establishment of new water and sewerage authorities; to provide for the establishment of a council to represent the interests of customers and potential customers of those new authorities; to provide for the vesting of those new authorities of the property, rights and liabilities of the Central

Scotland Water Development Board and of such property, rights and liabilities of regional and islands councils as those councils have as water authorities, as providers of sewerage and in relation to dealing with the contents of sewers; to provide for the dissolution of that Board; to cancel certain obligations to contribute towards expenses which have been incurred by local authorities in making provision for sewerage or disposal of sewage in rural localities; to create an office of Principal Reporter and transfer to him the functions of reporters to children's hearings; to establish a body to facilitate the performance by the Principal Reporter of his functions; to amend the Social Work (Scotland) Act 1968 in relation to reports made with a view to and for the purposes of children's hearings; to amend section 21 of the Self-Governing Schools etc (Scotland) Act 1989; to amend the law relating to roads and the placing of traffic signs on roads; to make amendments in relation to valuation and rating; to abolish the Scottish Valuation Advisory Council; to empower local authorities to make grants to ethnic minorities; to confer on local authorities the function of promoting economic development; to provide for the establishment of area tourist boards; to make amendments in relation to lieutenancies; all as respects Scotland; and for conncected purposes. (Government)

13 December 1993

Consolidated Fund—To apply certain funds out of the Consolidated Fund to the service of the years ending on 31 March 1994 and 1995. (Government)

16 December 1993

Non-Domestic Rating—To make further provision with respect to non-domestic rating for the financial year beginning in 1994 and subsequent financial years; and for connected purposes. (Government)

Criminal Justice and Public Order—To make further provision with respect to the treatment, and certain services connected with the treatment, of offenders; to amend the law relating to bail; to amend the law relating to the proceedings of criminal courts, including the law relating to evidence and the law relating to juries, and the law relating to the collection of fines; to amend the law relating to the publication of reports or pictures relating to proceedings in which children or young persons are concerned; to penalise intimidatory or harmful conduct towards witnesses, jurors and others; to confer new powers on the police to take samples from or search persons and to make further provision in relation to samples and fingerprints; to create new offences and make further provision in relation to persons unlawfully or without authorisation on land or causing a public nuisance by noise on land or otherwise affecting public order, including offences in relation to the recovery of possession of land from squatters and to make related amendments and repeals in certain enactments relating to gipsy caravan sites; to create further powers and offences for the prevention of terrorist activities; to amend the law relating to obscenity and pornography and the enforcement of the Video Recordings Act 1984; to make further provision in relation to prisons, the provision of prison services and employment in the prison service; to amend the law relating to the transfer of detainees; to increase certain penalties; to extend the powers of the Serious Fraud Office; to penalise the sale of tickets for designated football matches by unauthorised persons; to authorise the payment of grants for expenditure on measures for the prevention of crime or reduction of the fear of crime or for security at party conferences; and for purposes connected with those purposes. (Government)

Progress of Bills

Inshore Fishing (Scotland) [HL] — Second reading, 7 December 1993.

Statutory Sick Pay — Commons: all stages, 15 December 1993.

Social Security (Contributions) — Commons: all stages, 16 December 1993.

Questions answered

HOUSE OF COMMONS

6 December 1993

ADVOCATES

Dr Goodman: To ask the Secretary of State for Scotland how many advocates there are in practice at the present moment; and how many are women.

Lord James Douglas-Hamilton: There are 323 advocates currently in practice, 54 of whom are women.

8 December 1993

PREVENTION OF TERRORISM (TEMPORARY PROVISIONS) ACT 1989

Sir Ivan Lawrence: To ask the Secretary of State for the Home Department what arrangements he has made for the current year's review of the Prevention of Terrorism (Temporary Provisions) Act 1989; and how observations from interested persons or organisations should be submitted for consideration.

Mr Howard: I am glad to say that Mr J J Rowe, QC, this year's chairman of the Bar Council, has accepted my invitation to succeed Viscount Colville of Culross, QC, in carrying out this annual review. Viscount Colville has performed this task with great dedication and integrity and has deservedly won widespread respect. I am extremely grateful to him for this invaluable public service.

Written observations about the operation of the Act should be submitted to Mr Rowe, c/o Room 647, Home Office, 50 Queen Anne's Gate, London SW1H 9AT, by 15 January 1994.

9 December 1993

COURT SERVICE

Mr Raymond S Robertson: To ask the Secretary of State for Scotland if he will make a statement about the future of the Scottish court service.

Mr Lang: After consultation with the senior judiciary, I have decided that the Scottish court service, part of the Scottish Courts Administration, should be considered as a candidate for executive agency status, under the Next Steps initiative.

◆

ACT OF SEDERUNT

ACT OF SEDERUNT (Summary Suspension) 1993
(SI 1993/3128) [10 DECEMBER 1993]

The Lords of Council and Session, under and by virtue of the powers conferred on them by section 32 of the Sheriff Courts (Scotland) Act 1971 (c 58) and of all other powers enabling them in that behalf, having approved, with modifications, draft rules submitted to them by the Sheriff Court Rules Council in accordance with section 34 of that Act, do hereby enact and declare:

Citation and commencement
1.—(1) This Act of Sederunt may be cited as the Act of Sederunt (Summary Suspension) 1993 and shall come into force on 1st January 1994.

(2) This Act of Sederunt shall be inserted in the Books of Sederunt.

Summary application for suspension of charge
2. Where a charge for payment has been executed on any decree to which section 5 (5) of the Sheriff Courts (Scotland) Act 1907 applies the person so charged may apply to the sheriff in the sheriff court having jurisdiction over him for suspension of such charge and diligence.

Sist of diligence
3.—(1) On sufficient caution being found or other security given for—
(a) the sum charged for with interest and expenses, and
(b) a further sum to be fixed by the sheriff in respect of expenses to be incurred in the suspension process,
the sheriff may sist diligence, order intimation and answers, and proceed to dispose of the cause in a summary manner.

(2) The following rules of the Ordinary Cause Rules 1993 shall, with the necessary modifications, apply to an applicant under paragraph 2:—
rule 27.4 (methods of finding caution or giving security)
rule 27.5 (cautioners and guarantors)
rule 27.6 (forms of bonds of caution and other securities)
rule 27.7 (sufficiency of caution or security and objections)
rule 27.8 (insolvency or death of cautioner or guarantor).

Objections
4. Where objections are taken to the competency or regularity of suspension proceedings, the decision of the sheriff on such objections may be appealed to the sheriff principal whose decision shall be final and not subject to appeal.

Savings for proceedings arising out of causes already commenced
5. Nothing in this Act of Sederunt shall affect suspension proceedings arising out of causes commenced before the date of coming into force of this Act of Sederunt, which shall proceed according to the law and practice in force immediately before that date.

J A D HOPE, LORD JUSTICE GENERAL, *IPD*

[Acts of Sederunt are reproduced with the permission of the Controller of Her Majesty's Stationery Office.]

ARTICLES

Better Heard and not Seen

Child Witnesses, Competency and Hearsay

Lilian Edwards,
Lecturer in Private Law,
University of Edinburgh.

A series of recent cases have posed problems for the courts in determining the extent to which hearsay evidence of children should be admitted to establish grounds of referral to a children's hearing. Ms Edwards highlights the danger of upsetting, in either direction, the difficult balance between the interests of the child and the interests of natural justice, but suggests that the most recent decision, in which the court allowed a new hearing of the evidence, has helped to restore equilibrium.

In that halcyon age when the ink was barely dry on the Kilbrandon report and the overwhelming majority of referrals to the children's panel were on uncomplicated grounds of offence and truancy, it would have been difficult to envisage that issues of evidence and procedure would come to be so prominent within the jurisprudence of the children's hearing system. The structure of the children's hearings procedure has always represented a compromise, increasingly perhaps an unhappy one, between the interests of the child who is in need of compulsory measures of care, and the interests of natural justice, particularly as it relates to the claims of the child's family. As is well known, this compromise is implemented by a division of proceedings between the children's hearing itself, in which forum the rules of evidence and procedure are substantially relaxed, and the courts, wherein any dispute about the truth of the ground of referral to the hearing is resolved by something near normal methods of proof.

But this simple dichotomy of almost absent rules of procedure in the hearing and almost normal rules of proof in the sheriff court is not wholly satisfactory. Proofs in the sheriff court, brought under s 42 of the Social Work (Scotland) Act 1968, face unusual difficulties since they inherently involve the evidence of children, sometimes very young, increasingly often the victims or alleged victims of abuse, who are not at their most forthcoming in a courtroom. In the past it has been recognised repeatedly that proceedings under Pt III of the 1968 Act are proceedings sui generis, notably in *Macgregor v D*, 1977 SLT 182; 1977 SC 330, wherein Lord Cameron (at p 187) opposed the importation of "the more elaborate

and technical rules of formal process in the courts, be they civil or criminal" into the hearing process, and the then Lord President Emslie opined (at p 185) that "although the basic rules of evidence must be observed in applications before the sheriff, the ordinary codes of civil and criminal procedure do not apply".

These opinions were reinforced more recently in *W v Kennedy*, 1988 SLT 583, wherein Lord Sutherland, in relation only to the rules excluding hearsay, went so far as to formulate a principle that the normal rules should be relaxed where "it is clear that the purpose and intention of the 1968 Act would [otherwise] be thwarted and the interests of the child would be prejudiced" (at p 586E). Since *W v Kennedy* we have seen a rash of cases dealing with particular issues of evidence relating to the child witness and s 42 proofs. The optimistic sweep of Lord Sutherland's dictum has largely been replaced by a more parsimonious attitude to detail which is informed by the increasingly adversarial tone of child protection cases. Some of the outstanding themes arising out of these cases are discussed below. The context addressed throughout is that of the children's hearing system, although it is clear that there are implications here also for the law of evidence beyond this domain.

(1) Competency of child witnesses

The starting point here is found in the two leading cases of *Rees v Lowe*, 1990 SLT 507; 1989 SCCR 664 and *Kelly v Docherty*, 1991 SLT 419; 1991 SCCR 312. These two cases make it plain that before a child who is too young to be sworn can be admitted to give evidence, the judge or sheriff must carry out a preliminary examination of the child to see whether the child knows the difference between truth and lies. The child must then be admonished to tell the truth.

This seemed unexceptionable until the rule was considered in conjunction with the new rules on hearsay in civil proceedings introduced by the Civil Evidence (Scotland) Act 1988. Section 2 (1) of the Act provides that: "In any civil proceedings . . . (b) a statement made by a person otherwise than in the course of the proof shall be admissible as evidence of any matter contained in the statement of which direct oral evidence would be admissible."

Hearings by the sheriff under s 42 of the Social Work (Scotland) Act 1968 — that is, proofs of grounds for referral to the children's hearing — count as civil proceedings (s 9 of the 1988 Act). (The only exception to this is where they relate to a s 32 (2) (g) ground, which is where it is alleged that the child has committed an offence.) In practice most problems are arising where the child is alleged to have been the victim of an offence (s 32 (2) (d) ground) — particularly the offence of sexual abuse — where the proceedings are still characterised as civil for purposes of proof but in reality criminal allegations are being made and bitterly contested.

The case then arose of *F v Kennedy (No 1)*, 1993 SLT 1277. Here, three children were referred to the hearing on the ground that they had been sexually abused. The father refused to accept the reference and it went to the sheriff where some grounds were found proven. The father appealed to the Inner House on the basis that the sheriff in reaching his decision had admitted hearsay evidence by one of the children (aged three at the time) concerning the abuse. The father's case was that the Civil Evidence Act does not make hearsay admissible unless the witness's evidence would have been admissible if given directly. Thus it had to be established by the *Rees* test that the child was a competent witness. But in fact when the child was called as a witness he refused to say anything to the sheriff at all. Hence as the child had not been examined as to his ability to tell truth from lies, he could not be a competent witness and the evidence he gave earlier to social workers could not be admitted as hearsay under s 2 (1) (b).

The problem here — from the point of view of social work and the child — is that it means every child witness, however young or traumatised, must be brought to court for preliminary examination, and if that child is too intimidated to give evidence of his or her competency, as here, then their previous evidence, however well documented (and however much taken conform to interviewing guidelines) is inadmissible. The suggestion made by counsel for the reporter that a non-rigid application of the rule against hearsay should be adopted in children's proceedings (as previously recommended in *W v Kennedy*) was rejected on the ground that this dictum had been replaced by the specific statutory provisions of the 1988 Act. Rather oddly then, it seems that the 1988 Act may have liberalised the use of hearsay in ordinary civil proceedings but effectively restricted it in child protection cases.

This decision was all the more unfortunate in view of the decision in *O v Rae*, 1993 SLT 570, two months later. This cleared up a longstanding dispute as to whether the children's panel are allowed in formulating their disposal of a case to consider all the circumstances of the case or merely those proven or accepted as part of the

grounds for referral. It was held, overruling *K v Finlayson*, 1974 SLT (Sh Ct) 51, that the panel are entitled to consider information beyond that in the grounds for referral and that the test of relevancy is whether the information is relevant to the consideration of what course should be taken in the child's best interests. This result was drawn from an examination of the duty of the children's panel as stated in s 43 of the 1968 Act. That duty is to proceed, once grounds have been established or accepted, to decide on a course in the best interests of the child, and to do this it is stated that they must consider not only the grounds as accepted or established, but also a social background report and "such other relevant information as may be available to them". The Lord President in his judgment rejected the view that this was inherently unfair since that disposal might be based on allegations which had not formed part of the grounds for referral and had therefore not been judicially tested. Instead he endorsed the view that "the principles of natural justice must yield to the best interests of the child".

Thus it seems that hearsay evidence such as that found in *F v Kennedy (No 1)* is inadmissible to establish a ground of referral, but would be relevant, and admissible, information to help formulate a disposal if another ground was proven by admissible evidence. If no such ground existed, the child could not be brought under the protection of the children's hearing even though there were circumstances indicated by the hearsay evidence which indicated a need for measures of care. Though this is conform to strict principles of natural justice, it may seem somewhat unhelpful in the context of child protection and may encourage reporters to bring multiple or spurious grounds of referral, resulting in longer proofs at the sheriff court stage.

Strangely enough, in *K v Kennedy*, 1993 SLT 1281, decided by yet another division of the Inner House in the month between *F v Kennedy (No 1)* and *O v Rae*, we have the statement of Lord Sutherland (at p 388C) that "hearings before a sheriff under the Social Work (Scotland) Act are sui generis and that the purpose of the hearing is to consider what is in the best interests of the child. Strict rules of evidence and procedure which might be appropriate in adversarial cases are not necessarily appropriate in such hearings".

This is of course just the approach which Lord Ross said had been overtaken by the introduction of the specific rules of the Civil Evidence Act in *F v Kennedy (No 1)*. So we have some patent conflict here which may provide a last gasp of hope for the admissibility of hearsay by incompetent witnesses.

Finally we have another unusually difficult witness in the case of *M v Kennedy*, 1993 SCLR 69. Here again a child V, aged 12 at the date of referral, was referred on the ground that she had been the subject of sexual abuse by her father. The parents did not accept the grounds and the matter went to the sheriff. The aspect of the case that concerns us here was that V for some time prior to the proof had become an elective mute. This is a rare condition in which in emotional reaction to a major trauma (such as sexual abuse) a person uses social withdrawal to indicate distress. The practical question arising was how V could be tested to see if she was a competent witness, and indeed, if a person in such a state of non-communication could ever be a competent witness. Of course, following *F v Kennedy (No 1)*, supra, if V was not established to be a competent witness then her earlier statements, which were consistent with a conclusion that she had suffered abuse (to which there was other medical and psychiatric evidence) would be inadmissible. What transpired was that the sheriff conducted a very long preliminary investigation of V in which he established to his own satisfaction that she knew the difference between telling truth and telling lies. He then admonished her to tell the truth and took evidence from her by dint of asking what can only be presumed to be leading questions, to which she responded by nodding or shaking her head. This evidence was taken to confirm the statements she had made earlier and the ground of referral was found established.

The parents appealed. The Inner House rejected the appeal. In a long and careful judgment which examines a range of authorities, the Lord President found that the requirements for a child to be a competent and admissible witness are simply that the child is likely to give trustworthy evidence. It was not part of the test of competency that the child could give a spontaneous account of his or her testimony. That went instead to the quality of the evidence, and might affect the value given to it overall. In the instant case, this was of course useful since although the direct evidence given by V might be given little weight, her competency opened the gates to the admission of her earlier statements as hearsay.

The distinction drawn here between factors affecting competency and factors affecting quality of evidence is an interesting one which reduces the requirements for competency to a fairly basic level and thus allows a wide role for hearsay. In the interests of the child, this seems correct.

The question raised by *M v Kennedy*, but not answered by the court, is how to deal with supervening incompetency. What if V had not been found to be competent (as might have been the case with a less patient sheriff)? Could her previous statements have been accepted as valid hearsay on the grounds that at the time she made them, though not at the date of proof, she was a competent witness? If so, what evidence would need to be led to prove this, since the sheriff would be unable to establish it by his own direct assessment? The 1988 Act does not make it clear whether competency at the date of making the statement, or at the date of proceedings, was intended. The Scottish Law Commission memorandum no 46 which preceded the 1988 Act prefers the latter. The Lord President's comments (at p 78F) seem to lean towards accepting with caution the evidence of a superveningly incompetent child but do not resolve the issue: "If [this point] is to be raised, careful attention will need to be given to the leading of evidence about the child's ability to give a trustworthy account at the time when he made the statement and as to the reason or reasons why that test cannot be satisfied when the time comes for the child to give evidence."

(2) Hearsay and the "best evidence"
In some of the recent cases on child witnesses, the issue is not their competency per se but other factors affecting the reliability or worth of their evidence. In some cases, the issues of competency, hearsay and reliability are not easily separable.

The first case in the recent sequence is perhaps *K v Kennedy*, supra, where a 14 year old girl was referred on the ground of having been sexually abused by her father. The girl initially made statements to a police officer which supported this. Before the sheriff she retracted her statement. The sheriff did not accept the girl's retraction, and found her earlier statement, even though uncorroborated, admissible evidence to found the ground. The Inner House affirmed the sheriff, stating that in a social work referral, he was not bound to refrain from relying on the hearsay evidence just because there might have been other, more direct, evidence before him that would also have been helpful.

Oddly enough, there was little comment sparked by *K v Kennedy* as to the tension it highlighted between the extensive use of hearsay in social work proceedings and its traditional role in civil proceedings as not the "best evidence". It was not until *F v Kennedy (No 2)*, 1993 SLT 1284; 1992 SCLR 751, that these issues really came into focus. Here, similar allegations of sexual abuse came before the sheriff. One of the children involved, J, had made certain relevant statements in a long series of interviews prior to the hearing. At the proof itself, J gave evidence in person but was not questioned as to the matters contained in those previous statements. The father appealed. His argument was principally that if a witness is available to give direct evidence, then that evidence should be taken and should take precedence over hearsay statements as to the same facts. That hearsay evidence should be displaced. This is a result of the familiar "best evidence" rule.

It was generally thought when the Civil Evidence Act 1988 was introduced that although s 2 (1) (b) legitimised the use of hearsay, it did not displace wholly the rule that the best evidence should be led. There would still then be a restriction on s 2 to the effect that the direct evidence of an available witness should exclude his hearsay evidence on the same point (for substance not credibility — see s 3 of the Act). David Field, for example, comments in his *Current Law* annotation to the Act that although the Act allows all hearsay to be admissible without judicial discretion, the operation of the "best evidence" rule should allow the court to make adverse assumptions if the maker of the statement was available but not called (or, as here, not interrogated on the material in question). Another point made was that if s 2 allowed all hearsay without reservation to be admissible then s 3 of the Act, which allows some hearsay statements to be admissible for credibility but not for substance, would be redundant (see for a fuller report of this argument Sheldon, "I Heard It On The Grapevine" (1993) 38 JLS 292).

However it seems after all that the more cautious interpretations of the effect of s 2 have been swept away by the courts. The Lord Justice Clerk took the view in *F v Kennedy (No 2)* that the rule allowing hearsay in s 2 (1) (b) did not become applicable only where a witness had not given direct oral evidence. He based this on the definition of "statement" in s 9 which refers to "any representation . . . of fact or opinion" not made in a precognition. Any such "statement" is admissible by s 2 (1) (b) providing it would be admissible if given as direct oral evidence. There was nothing in this that restricted s 2 to statements made only by witnesses who do not go on to give direct evidence in court. Thus the sheriff was entitled to rely on the witness's previous statements even though she had been available for direct interrogation on the same material. Lord

Ross stated (at p 1287F): "Accordingly, reading s 2 and s 9 together, I am satisfied that the fact that the maker of the statement has given oral evidence does not prevent hearsay evidence being given of what he has said upon another occasion. In this connection the effect of these two sections is that the best evidence rule is overridden."

The last statement is certainly a far reaching one. In the children's context, this seems to mean that hearsay is acceptable even if direct evidence could have been made available (the case here) or even if direct evidence was led and actually contradicts the hearsay (as in *K v Kennedy*). From a child protection point of view this is probably positive, since it minimises the number of times a child must be exposed to the trauma of appearing in court, perhaps, in a sexual abuse case, in the presence of her alleged abuser. It seems to mean that a witness like J who had been thoroughly interviewed before the proof (and about whom there was no issue of competency) need theoretically not be called at all. This point of policy was certainly in the contemplation of the Lord Justice Clerk, who commented that "It is plain that . . . the evidence of children will be critical, and there may well be occasions when it will be difficult to take the whole of a child's evidence in court. It may therefore be important for the sheriff to be able to rely to some extent at least on hearsay evidence of what the child has said on other occasions" (at p 1287G).

From the point of view of a father defending himself against allegations of abuse it may seem less fair. What has come out of Orkney about pressurised interviewing techniques seems rather relevant here. However it must be remembered that these cases are about child protection and not about convicting fathers (or other named abusers) of a criminal offence. In any ensuing criminal proceedings, of course, hearsay would not be available. Even if this interpretation of the dicta in *F v Kennedy (No 2)* is correct, furthermore, there is no guarantee that a sheriff would look in a kindly fashion on a case presented wholly as hearsay evidence, unless there was good reason why it would not be in the interests of the child concerned to give direct evidence. As we have seen above, the issue of the quality of the evidence, and the weight it is to be given, can be severed from the initial question of admissibility.

While outwith the scope of the article, it has to be noted that the significance of this case goes well beyond child protection cases. It seems the effect of s 2 is to override the best evidence rule, not just in children's hearings referrals, but in all civil cases, since s 2 applies to all civil cases, with s 42 proofs merely a subset of this category. This would mean, as Sheriff Johnston comments in his note to *F v Kennedy (No 2)* in *Scottish Civil Law Reports*, that it is now the law in all civil proceedings that direct evidence given in court has no higher status than hearsay evidence of what the witness said on another occasion. For further comment on these wider issues, see Sheldon's useful survey of the developing law on hearsay, op cit supra.

Two final points in this case are important to children's hearings jurisprudence. One is the finding that statements obtained in the course of interviews with social workers preparing their case are not equivalent to "precognitions", which are excluded from s 2 by s 9 and are thus not admissible hearsay. The reason for the exclusion of precognitions is that they are prepared by one side for use against the other and are therefore unreliably tainted by the self interest natural in an adversarial process (see the classic statement on this in *Kerr v HM Advocate*, 1958 SLT 82; 1958 JC 14). The statements collected by social work were not for use in adversarial proceedings but in a tribunal whose interest was the welfare of the child. Furthermore their main purpose was to establish whether the children were in need of measures of compulsory care, not to prepare for litigation. Though the policy issue here in terms of child protection is again clear, this seems a mite naîve. It is true that information gathered by social work may never be used in court if both child and parents accept the grounds of referral. However it is often clear at an early stage, certainly in most sex abuse cases, that grounds will be disputed. (And of course if the child is below the age of understanding, the case must go to the sheriff for proof.) Some of the evidence referred to in *F v Kennedy (No 2)* had been gathered after the case had already been referred to the sheriff for proof. In strict law, it is true that such referrals are sui generis proceedings, not adversarial litigation, but again the spectre of Orkney reminds us just how adversarial such proceedings can truly be.

Finally, the suggestion was made that since evidence had been acquired in interviews that had not been conducted in accordance with the recommendations in the Cleveland report, that evidence was fatally flawed and inadmissible. This was firmly repelled. The Lord Justice Clerk was sceptical of attempts to elevate the report to the status of "something approaching gospel", preferring instead to respect the sheriff's own assessment of the material before him.

These comments must be treated with some care now though, following the recent First Division case of *L, Petrs (No 2)*, 1993 SLT 1342 (see section (4) below also) in which the father from *F v Kennedy (Nos 1 and 2)*, with other petitioners, succeeded in applying to the nobile officium for a rehearing of the evidence in this case (which was in fact the well known Ayrshire child abuse case). Although no further direct appeal from *F v Kennedy (No 2)* was competent, it is clear that in *L* we have some very relevant comments catalysed by the publication of the Clyde report on Orkney subsequent to the proof in *F v Kennedy (No 2)*. In *L*, the Lord President, in allowing the new hearing, emphasised that since the Clyde report a greater understanding had arisen of the fundamental importance of the issues raised by the Rochdale and Orkney cases concerning the proper evaluation of evidence. In particular he commented that "it is highly unlikely that criticisms of social workers for seeking what they thought were the right answers from children in matters of sexual abuse could now be treated as lightly as they appear to have been treated in [*F v Kennedy (No 2)*]". These are stern words. On the other hand he clearly affirmed the line of the Lord Justice Clerk that the sheriff was not compelled to reject evidence just because it had been gathered in contravention of the Cleveland guidelines. For more guidance on this very difficult area we shall have to await the outcome of the rehearing itself of the Ayrshire child abuse cases.

(3) What evidence is available to the children's panel to formulate its disposal once grounds are proven?

As mentioned above, the case of *O v Rae*, 1993 SLT 570, makes it clear that the panel are entitled to consider all relevant information in deciding how to dispose of a case, and not just that information which has been judicially tested as part of the grounds of referral. As said in the unreported sheriff court case of *M v Finlayson* (1981), the grounds once proven "act as a kind of trigger which releases the activity of the hearing, but once that has happened, the activity is not confined to an attempt to solve the particular problems raised by the ground for referral, but is concerned with the whole welfare of the child".

However there is an important caveat to this in the case of *M v Kennedy*, 1993 SLT 431. *O v Rae* allows a panel to take account of any relevant facts even if not proven in court as part of the grounds. However *M v Kennedy* seems to say that even given this, the panel are *excluded* from considering any allegations which have been expressly *disproven* in court. The background here is a textbook example of linguistic ambivalence. The ground of referral was that sexual abuse of a girl M had occurred "within the family home or elsewhere in Glasgow". The sheriff found this established under deletion of the particular words of locality above. On remission back to the panel, a supervision requirement was made which required M to live with foster parents on the basis that the family home might have been the setting for abuse. It was argued that it could not be assumed the sheriff had excluded the family home as a locus for abuse, just that he had not found it proven. On appeal, the matter went back to the original sheriff for clarification. He reported that he *had* found it established that abuse had *not* taken place in the home. Given that, the Inner House found that it was not legitimate for the panel to make a disposal which was based on the belief that sexual abuse *might* have taken place within the family home — and so the case was remitted back to the hearing for them to reconsider their disposal on that basis.

Those representing parents in s 42 referrals may note that this may mean it is to their benefit to have more matters tested in the sheriff court, rather than deleted by agreement, since if any allegations are found not proven it then seems the panel cannot consider these allegations even as part of the whole background to the case.

(4) Discredited grounds of referral

What if a ground of referral is established, a disposal is made in respect of the case in the interests of the child and then the evidence which purported to prove the grounds is revised or discredited? This has recently become a topic of some controversy which is by no means yet resolved. The first reported case where this was explored was *R, Petr*, 1993 SLT 910. Here it was established on her own testimony that a girl S had been the victim of sexual abuse by her father. On that basis, not only she but also her two siblings were put under supervision and the father was excluded from the family home. Then S confessed she had fabricated the story to protect her boyfriend. The father sought to have the grounds of referral quashed. However in terms of s 50 of the 1968 Act, there is an appeal from a sheriff only on a point of law or irregularity of procedure. There is no provision for an appeal on the facts, nor for the hearing of new evidence. Neither does the Secretary of State under s 52 have power to discharge a referral, only to terminate a supervision requirement. Finally the father approached the nobile officium as a last resort.

The Court of Session refused to allow this final possible remedy. While the use of the nobile officium might sometimes be appropriate, given the lack of other remedy, it was not here, said the First Division. The lack of any machinery in the statute to review new evidence was not coincidental but was intended to allow the panel to dispose of the case secure in the knowledge that the grounds had been irrevocably proven. Following *O v Rae*, supra, the particular ground of referral proven did not blind the panel to a specific course of action; it might have been that another ground of referral would have been proven if that one had not been at the time. The correct course for the father was to ask for a review of the supervision requirement, since there had been a change of circumstances, and that remedy was available to him without using the nobile officium. (In fact, the panel charged with this review had already decided that the time had come for the father to be "reintegrated fully" into the family home — that is, allowed to go home. Thus in functional terms the end result of the father's petition — the discharge of the supervision requirement — had already been achieved. However, clearly there is also a point of justice and reputation at issue here.)

Superficially this scenario resembles an earlier case, *Kennedy v B*, 1992 SCLR 55, where a father accused of sexual abuse of his daughter was found not guilty on trial, and then questioned in the Inner House the supervision orders which had been made on the basis of his alleged abuse. Then too it might be said that the substance fell out of the supposedly proven ground, leaving the disposal of the panel in a precarious state. But the situation was actually quite different. In *Harris v F*, 1991 SLT 242, it was recognised that since a s 32 ground of referral has only to be proved to the civil standard of probabilities, while criminal proceedings work on a standard of beyond reasonable doubt, it was perfectly possible that a ground that a child was a victim of an offence might be proven for the benefit of the hearing process and then "disproven" in a subsequent criminal trial. There is nothing anomalous about such a result, since protection of the child is a justification for a lower standard of proof. This reasoning was followed in *Kennedy v B*, where the court held that the acquittal of the father had no effect per se on the supervision orders, and that the real question was whether their continued existence was in the interests of the child (s 47 (1) of the 1968 Act).

In *R, Petr*, there was no question of differing standards of proof. The problem is far more akin to that in criminal cases which are reheard on grounds of new evidence. Would the grounds have been established if the girl had told her new story at the time of the proof? Should there not have been an opportunity for judicial consideration of the new evidence? Such a right exists, on certain criteria, in criminal proceedings. However the Inner House were not disposed to allow such a rehearing. The thrust of their judgment seemed to be that once the child is in the remit of the panel, however the grounds were proved, the panel is entitled to retain jurisdiction over that child. Although in this case this may have been in accordance with the girl's immediate welfare (there were doubts about the reliability of her retractions), it is very thin natural justice. (Her new version of events, even if admitted, would in any case not necessarily have compelled an alteration to the finding at proof — as we saw in *K v Kennedy*, 1993 SLT 1281, discussed supra, the sheriff is not compelled by the best evidence rule to accept the later evidence in displacement of the earlier story.)

The point that other grounds of referral might have been raised by the reporter at the same time as the subsequently discredited ground seems irrelevant. If such alternative grounds exist to the knowledge of social work, then it should be their duty to make a new referral and go to a new proof — not to depend on an old ground of referral whose reliability has been discredited. Alternatively they should originally have brought multiple grounds of referral. The Lord President stated that once the child was before the panel, it might be clear for other reasons than the ground established that the child was in need of compulsory measures of care, and then he "ought not to be deprived of them for even the short time that might be needed for the case to begin again on other grounds". But this is surely an invitation to establish grounds by any means and with no reference to any restraining principles of evidence, if to do so seems "in the child's best interest". Such an approach would make all the other cases discussed so far redundant.

It must be emphasised that, especially since *O v Rae*, the establishment of the grounds is crucial. It is, as we have seen, the trigger that entitles the panel to leave behind in their disposal the restrictive ambit of what facts have been judicially proven and turn their attention on the whole facts, whether proven, alleged or assumed. To proceed on a discredited ground is to abandon the principal procedural safeguard in the system.

Luckily events have moved on rather swiftly since *R, Petr*. In *L, Petrs (No 1)*, 1993 SLT 1310, the parents of eight children taken into care under supervision orders following the Ayrshire child abuse cases sought recourse to the nobile officium in order to gain a rehearing of the grounds established before the sheriff, on the grounds that new evidence was now available. This evidence included, inter alia, new medical and psychological reports, but the most important piece of "fresh evidence" which they wished to bring to judicial consideration was the advent of the Clyde report on the Orkney inquiry which had brought about a new and greater awareness of the importance of collecting children's evidence in the fashion approved by the Cleveland report guidelines. This might shed new light on the evidence presented by the social work authorities whose behaviour even at the original hearing had been described as "over zealous". Here as in *R, Petr*, no procedure was available to expedite a rehearing except application to the nobile officium.

The issue of whether such an application was in principle competent was considered at length in *L, Petrs (No 1)*. The Lord President, delivering the judgment of the First Division, made the following statements about when application to the nobile officium can be competent:

(1) The circumstances leading to review must be "exceptional or unforeseen". This seems to be a first hurdle, familiar in the jurisprudence of the nobile officium, which was not surmounted in *R, Petr*, hence the relative lack of explicit discussion in that judgment. It is not exceptional or unforeseen that a witness changes his or her story after the hearing.

(2) The nobile officium cannot be exercised when to do so is in conflict with an express provision of a statute. The Lord President found that there was no such conflict in respect of Pt III of the 1968 Act. To seek a rehearing is not the same as to seek an appeal on the facts (which was expressly excluded by s 50 (1)); the former requires the sheriff to hear new evidence not brought to his attention first time around; the latter involves the substitution of the view of a higher court on the facts for that of the sheriff. If Parliament intended to exclude the possibility of a rehearing of the facts it should have used a formulation such as that "the sheriff's decision on the facts is to be final and conclusive".

(3) The nobile officium cannot be exercised when it is in conflict with the implicit statutory intention (*Anderson v HM Advocate*, 1974 SLT 239). Looking at the 1968 Act, this raised a clear conflict in argument between the view that the implicit intention of Pt III is to secure the welfare of children, which requires that children not in

need of measures of compulsory care be not subjected to them if a wrong decision has been made at proof, and the narrower view that s 50 (1) clearly intends that the panel be able to proceed on the basis that the sheriff has finally adjudged the facts (which was very much the view espoused by the court in *R, Petr*). This latter argument was bolstered by the fact that the "extraordinary" remedy the Act does provide is the power of the Secretary of State to terminate a supervision requirement (s 52), not to order a rehearing.

This argument was resolved by taking another standpoint. Did Parliament truly contemplate when formulating the 1968 Act that circumstances might occur which demanded an extraordinary remedy to allow the hearing of fresh evidence? If it did, the absence of express provision is fatal. If it did not, the application to the nobile officium is appropriate since its function is to fill lacunae within a statutory framework. The fundamental distinction is whether the new remedy sought amends the statute, in which case it is inappropriate, or whether it merely provides a procedural framework to facilitate a remedy implicit in the existing statute. Lord Hope's finding was that the recent phenomenon of highly complex group child abuse cases involving numerous parties and the associated acute evidential problems had not been contemplated by Parliament — this was especially apparent by reference to the Kilbrandon report which preceded the 1968 Act. Therefore the exceptional need for the hearing of fresh evidence had not been in contemplation and was not impliedly excluded by omission.

This resolved in principle the point that application to the nobile officium to allow a hearing of fresh evidence is competent. In *L, Petrs (No 2)*, 1993 SLT 1342, the Court of Session also gave some guidance as to when an application might be successful. It was recognised that it was not appropriate in proceedings whose purpose was to protect the interests of the child to allow a rehearing only where fresh evidence had arisen which was not reasonably available at the time of the original hearing (although the court would still have "regard" to this standard). The additional evidence need only meet the high standard of materiality and significance demanded by the nobile officium. This is an interesting and sensible diversion from the usual rule in criminal and civil rehearings, given the fact that those who suffer the disposal of the panel, i e the children, are not the original litigants and should not be held responsible for the failure of their parents to collect evidence at the right time.

For the Ayrshire parents this was also welcome news, as it will allow them to have their day in court to present evidence concerning the nonconformity of the Ayrshire social workers to Cleveland and Orkney report standards. Since it was admitted that many of the Orkney recommendations can be traced back to Cleveland, and the Cleveland report predated the original Ayrshire proofs, they would have otherwise been in difficulties.

This article began with sketching out the commonplace that the structure of the current system represents a compromise between natural justice and the welfare of the child. *L, Petrs (No 1)* is an important exercise of judicial responsibility which extends the procedural framework of the children's hearings system so as to maintain this fine and difficult compromise, and is to be welcomed.

[The author would like to thank David Sheldon for his helpful comments on an earlier draft of this article.]

♦

NEWS

Appreciation

David Evans

David Evans, chairman of W Green and Sweet & Maxwell, died after a short illness on 10 December 1993 at the early age of 56.

A native Welshman, David Evans joined Sweet & Maxwell soon after he was called to the Bar in 1960 and served the company in many capacities over the following 33 years, one of his great strengths being that he had first hand experience of all aspects of the company's operations. He first became managing director in 1975; by the time of the company's acquisition by The Thomson Corporation in 1987 he was managing director designate of Associated Book Publishers plc, with responsibilities for ABP's Commonwealth as well as UK legal publishing. After assisting Thomson to assimilate the ABP organisation he resumed the chief executive role at Sweet & Maxwell.

His involvement with W Green dates from 1973. Despite his many other commitments he always took a close interest in Greens' business and its people. Those who knew him will remember with affection a constantly inquiring mind hiding a very private family man beneath, one equally at home with strategic board decisions and a private heart to heart talk with an individual employee.

A memorial service will be held at 12 noon on Tuesday, 25 January in St Bride's Church, Fleet Street, London.

— ◊ —

Appointments

New Court of Session judge
The Queen, on the recommendation of the Secretary of State for Scotland, has approved the appointment of Mr Alan Charles Macpherson Johnston, QC, to be an additional Senator of the College of Justice with effect from 10 January 1994.

— ◊ —

Court

Sheriffdoms: South Strathclyde, Dumfries and Galloway
The Sheriff Principal of South Strathclyde, Dumfries and Galloway, by virtue of the powers conferred by rules 12.1 and 15.4 (2) of the Rules contained in the First Schedule annexed to the Act of Sederunt (Sheriff Court Ordinary Cause Rules) 1993 has directed in relation to any cause to which these rules apply:

1. For the purpose of said rules 12.1 and 15.4 (2) and notwithstanding the definition of "Sheriff Clerk" in s 3 (f) of the Sheriff Courts (Scotland) Act 1907 "the sheriff clerk" shall not include a sheriff clerk below the rank of higher executive officer save that, in any sheriff court within the sheriffdom where the senior resident sheriff clerk holds the rank of executive officer, it shall include that sheriff clerk or his temporary replacement provided he is of the same or higher rank.

2. The classes of interlocutor which a sheriff clerk may write and sign in terms of the said rule 12.1 shall not include any final interlocutor or any interlocutor which the sheriff concerned directs to be written or signed by him or her. Subject to the foregoing, any interlocutor dealing with a motion which has been determined by a sheriff clerk in terms of the said rule 15.4 (2) shall be written and signed by that sheriff clerk.

3. The classes of unopposed motions which a sheriff clerk may determine in terms of the said rule 15.4 (2) are set out in the Appendix to this direction.

Appendix
Classes of motion which may be determined by a sheriff clerk in terms of rule 15.4 (2):

(a) A motion to authorise re-service of an initial writ in terms of rule 5.9.

(b) A motion to recall a sist and to re-enrol a cause for further procedure.

(c) A motion, made under rule 10.3 (1), to close the record before the expiry of the adjustment period provided by rule 10.1 (1).

(d) A motion to allow an amendment of a kind specified in rule 18.1.

(e) A motion to allow a minute of amendment to be received and answered within a specified period in terms of rule 18.3 (1) (a) and (b) (ii).

(f) A motion for an order for service of a third party notice, made under rule 20.1 (1) and (2).

◊

Faculty of Advocates
Mr Alastair Murray Learmont, BA(Bristol), Mr Maurice Jamieson, LLB(Strathclyde), Mr Michael Jack Miller, LLB(Glasgow), Miss Louise Janet Milligan, LLB, MBA(Edinburgh), Mr Dale William Alexander Hughes, LLB(Aberdeen), Mr John Speir, LLB(Edinburgh) and Miss Isobel Fiona Mackie Davies, MA, LLB(Edinburgh), have been admitted to the Faculty of Advocates.

— ◊ —

Law reform

Metric units of measurement legislation
In November 1989, the EC Council adopted an amending directive (89/617/EEC) which set out dates for ending the use of imperial units of measurement for economic, public health, public safety and administrative purposes and for the construction and use of weighing and measuring instruments.

Because of difficulties in identifying all the relevant legislation (including private and local legislation), the Department of Trade and Industry intends to introduce generic legislation to amend all references to imperial measurements in UK legislation which are not otherwise amended by specific regulations. To this end DTI has drawn up detailed proposals for such legislation, on which comments are sought before instructing parliamentary counsel to draw up generic legislation under the European Communities Act 1972, to come into force on 1 January 1995.

It is proposed to retain the original imperial references on the face of legislation, not so as to constitute a requirement, but to provide information to the user of the legislation as to what the imperial reference was (and in the case of primary legislation, the intention of Parliament).

In the case of references to a particular quantity, the legislation will make the conversion of the imperial reference (e g of 2 pounds weight) by (a) multiplying and or dividing the quantity in the reference by the appropriate conversion factor or factors (e g 2 × 0.4536 pounds to the kilogram = 0.9072) and (b) substituting the metric unit or units corresponding to the imperial unit or units (e g kilogram for pound). It is proposed that the metric quantity should be rounded to the smallest number of significant figures to which the relevant conversion factors are given — e g for the conversion factor of 0.4536 kilogram which is given for the pound (which is to four significant figures) a figure of 112 lbs should be replaced by 50.80 kilograms (rounded to four significant figures) and not 50.8032 (0.4536 × 112) kilograms (which is to six significant figures). The normal convention will be followed whereby, if the least significant digit is 1 to 4 the number is rounded down, and if it is 5 to 9 it is rounded up (e g 48.275 becomes 48.28 but 48.274 becomes 48.27).

Where there is only a reference to an imperial unit this unit should be replaced by the corresponding metric unit (e g kilogram for pound). Similarly where there is a reference to quantity expressed in imperial units by means of a noun such as "chainage", "tonnage" or "acreage" it is proposed to replace this by a reference to the corresponding unit. Thus "acreage" will be translated into "number of square metres".

The government intend generally to take maximum advantage of the transitional arrangements and derogations in the 1989 Directive, and accordingly to:

(i) cease to authorise, after 31 December 1994, imperial units used for economic, public health, public safety and administrative purposes except for the units used for the purposes set out in (ii) and (iii) below;

(ii) cease to authorise after 31 December 1999: (a) the pound and ounce for goods sold loose from bulk; (b) the pint and fluid ounce for beer, cider, waters, lemonades and fruit juices in returnable containers; (c) the fathom for marine navigation; and (d) the therm for gas supply;

(iii) authorise the continued use, without time limit, of: (a) the mile, yard, foot and inch for road traffic signs and related distance and speed measurement; (b) the pint for dispensing draught beer and cider and for milk in returnable containers; (c) the troy ounce for transactions in precious metals; and (d) the acre for land registration purposes.

Metric units will continue to be authorised for use in the UK for economic, public health, public safety and administrative purposes.

Because it is necessary to have the legislation in force as far in advance of 1 January 1995 as possible, comments are requested by 10 February 1994. These should be addressed to Mrs L G Belfall, Room 239, St Andrew's House, Edinburgh EH1 3DG.

In order to help informed debate on this proposal the department would like (as is normal practice) to make available to the public on request, copies of responses to this letter. The department will assume therefore that responses can be made publicly available in this way. If respondents indicate that they wish all, or part, of their reply excluded from this arrangement, its confidentiality will be strictly respected.

General

Dunfermline District Society of Solicitors
At the annual general meeting of the Dunfermline District Society of Solicitors, the following office bearers and members of the Dean's council were elected: *Dean*, Tom G Johnston; *vice dean*, David A Harkess; *secretary/treasurer*, Caroline J Flanagan, 10 Viewfield Terrace, Dunfermline KY12 7JH; *council members*, John R Bain, Craig Bennet (librarian), Keith S Mason, Kyle A D Peddie, Douglas J C Thomson, Valerie Waddell.

Crown Office relocation
The Crown Office will be moving as from 31 January 1994 to new premises at 25 Chambers Street, Edinburgh EH1 1LA (tel 031-226 2626; fax 031-226 6564). The address for the Lord Advocate and Solicitor General from 31 January will be Lord Advocate's Chambers, 25 Chambers Street, Edinburgh EH1 1LA (tel 031-226 2626; fax 031-226 6910).

Taxation

Income tax: vocational training

The Inland Revenue have laid regulations before the House of Commons amending the detailed arrangements for administering the tax relief for vocational training available to those paying for their own training towards national and Scottish Vocational Qualifications. The new regulations require trainees to confirm from 1 January 1994 that they have attained school leaving age and, if under the age of 19, are not in full time education at a school, and that they are undertaking the course neither wholly nor mainly for recreational purposes or as a leisure activity.

◊

Corporation tax: Pay and File

The Inland Revenue have issued three statements of practice (SP9/93, SP10/93 and SP11/93) dealing with the procedure under Pay and File for making and amending corporation tax returns and claims to group relief, and the circumstances under which late claims for capital allowances and group relief claims may be accepted.

The first two statements provide an opportunity for companies to deal with amended returns and group relief claims on a more informal basis which should help reduce compliance costs.

Statement of practice 9/93 explains that, under Pay and File, an amended corporation tax return for an accounting period may be made by completing and delivering to the inspector an amended official corporation tax return form. Alternatively, a form or letter can be substituted which gives clear and sufficient information about the change, shows the tax effect of the change and includes a declaration that the information is correct and complete.

Statement of practice 10/93 provides an opportunity for companies to use a similar procedure under Pay and File for making or revising claims to group relief, and for giving and receiving notices of consent to surrender relief, where a group of companies is dealt with mainly in one tax district.

Statement of practice 11/93 explains the criteria the Board of Inland Revenue adopts in exercising its power to admit claims to capital allowances or group relief which are made outside the normal time limit.

Copies of the statements may be obtained by sending an s a e to the Public Inquiry Room, West Wing, Somerset House, Strand, London WC2R 1LB.

◊

Double taxation

Switzerland

Agreements between the United Kingdom and Switzerland were signed in Berne on 17 December which will replace the existing death duties convention signed in 1956 by a double taxation convention covering taxes on estates and inheritances, and amend, by protocol, the double taxation convention covering taxes on income signed in 1977. The texts will be published as a schedule to a draft order in council.

Obituaries

On 23 December 1993, Andrew Dunlop Ralston, formerly senior partner in the firm of Messrs Macnair Clyde and Ralston, solicitors, Paisley.

On 24 December 1993, Alexander Jackson Ambrose, WS, formerly senior partner in the firm of Messrs Gillespie, MacAndrew & Co, WS, Edinburgh.

On 24 December 1993, Robert Currie Wright, formerly senior partner in and subsequently consultant to the firm of Messrs Alex L Wright & Co, solicitors, Motherwell.

On 26 December 1993, Roger George Manson, formerly senior partner in the firm of Messrs Lowndes, Renwick & Manson, solicitors, Glasgow.

On 1 January 1994, William Dickson, WS, Edinburgh.

On 2 January 1994, the hon Lord Maxwell, formerly Senator of the College of Justice.

Business changes

Messrs Carruthers Gemmill, solicitors, 81 Bath Street, Glasgow, announce that with effect from 1 January 1994 they have assumed their associate, Mr Charles Wilson Hay, as a partner.

Messrs Carlton Gilruth, solicitors, 30 Whitehall Street, Dundee, and 77 High Street, Lochee, Dundee, intimate the retiral of their senior partner, Dennis Ferguson Collins, with effect from 31 December 1993. The business is carried on by the remaining partners.

Messrs Mair Matheson, solicitors, Newmilns and Stewarton, intimate that with effect from 1 January 1994 their associate, Mr William Meechan, has been assumed as a partner of the firm.

Caesar & Howie, solicitors and estate agents, Bathgate and elsewhere, announce the retiral of Miss Elvyne Kathleen Struthers as a partner in the firm with effect from 31 December 1993 and the assumption of Gordon McNeil Henderson and Gordon Addison as partners in the firm with effect from 1 January 1994.

— ◇ —

Parliamentary News

New Bills

HOUSE OF COMMONS

16 December 1993

The following bills were presented by members successful in the Private Members' ballot:

Bank of England (Amendment) — Mr Nicholas Budgen
Energy Conservation — Mr A J Beith
Tobacco Advertising — Mr Kevin Barron
Chiropractors — Mr David Lidington
Antarctic — Mr Michael Jopling
Road Traffic Regulation (Special Events) — Mr Peter Atkinson
Civil Rights (Disabled Persons) — Dr Roger Berry
Water (Domestic Disconnections) — Mr Stanley Orme
Nursery Education (Assessment of Need) — Mr Nigel Spearing
Protection of Dogs — Mr Alan Williams
Race Relations (Remedies) — Mr Keith Vaz
Parliamentary Commissioner — Mr Gerald Malone
Sale and Supply of Goods — Mr David Clelland
Racial Hatred and Violence — Mr Hartley Booth

Merchant Shipping (Salvage and Pollution) — Mr David Harris
Insolvency — Mr John Butterfill
Building Conversion and Energy Conservation — Mr John McAllion
Small Business — Sir Michael Grylls
Women into Parliament — Mrs Teresa Gorman
Safety in Schools — Mr David Porter.

Questions answered

HOUSE OF COMMONS

14 December 1993

JUDGES

Mr McFall: To ask the Secretary of State for Scotland what consideration is being given to methods of making the appointment of judges more open and democratic; and if he will make a statement.

Lord James Douglas-Hamilton: The procedures adopted for making judicial appointments are kept under constant review. These procedures are designed to identify in respect of each vacancy the best fitted candidate. They were recently extended, on a trial basis, by inviting applications for two current vacancies on the shrieval bench through an intimation in the *Scots Law Times*.

15 December 1993

LEGAL SERVICES

Mr Phil Gallie: To ask the Secretary of State for Scotland what progress is being made towards the extension of compulsory competitive tendering to legal services.

Mr Stewart: Since we announced in November 1992 our intention to further extend CCT we have been in discussion with local authority associations about the details of implementation. We are now in a position to consult more widely and have today issued a consultation paper on the Government's implementation plans. Comments are invited by 18 March on a detailed package of measures which will bring the benefits of CCT to local authority legal services. Copies of the consultation paper will be placed in the House Library.

ACT OF SEDERUNT

ACT OF SEDERUNT (Sheriff Court Summary Application Rules) 1993
(SI 1993/3240) [14 DECEMBER 1993]

The Lords of Council and Session, under and by virtue of the powers conferred on them by section 32 of the Sheriff Courts (Scotland) Act 1971 (c 58) and of all other powers enabling them in that behalf, having approved, with modifications, draft rules submitted to them by the Sheriff Court Rules Council in accordance with section 34 of that Act, do hereby enact and declare:

Citation and commencement

1.—(1) This Act of Sederunt may be cited as the Act of Sederunt (Sheriff Court Summary Application Rules) 1993 and shall come into force on 1st January 1994.

(2) This Act of Sederunt shall be inserted in the Books of Sederunt.

Summary application rules

2. The provisions of Schedule 1 to this Act of Sederunt shall have effect for the purpose of providing rules for summary applications within the meaning of section 3 (p) of the Sheriff Courts (Scotland) Act 1907 (c 51).

Revocations

3. The Acts of Sederunt specified in column 1 of Schedule 2 to this Act of Sederunt are revoked to the extent specified in column 3 of that Schedule.

Savings for summary applications already commenced

4. Nothing in this Act of Sederunt shall affect any summary application commenced before the date of the coming into force of this Act of Sederunt and any such summary application shall proceed according to the law and practice in force immediately before that date.

J A D HOPE, LORD JUSTICE GENERAL, *IPD*

SCHEDULE 1   Paragraph 2
SHERIFF COURT SUMMARY APPLICATION RULES 1993
ARRANGEMENT OF RULES

Citation and application

1.—(1) These Rules may be cited as the Sheriff Court Summary Application Rules 1993.

(2) These Rules apply to a summary application within the meaning of section 3 (p) of the Sheriff Courts (Scotland) Act 1907.

Interpretation

2.—(1) In these Rules, unless the context otherwise requires—

"decree" includes any judgment, deliverance, interlocutor, act, order, finding or authority which may be extracted;

"defender" means any person other than the pursuer who is a party to a summary application;

"pursuer" means any person making a summary application;

"sheriff clerk" includes a sheriff clerk depute;

"summary application" has the meaning given by section 3 of the Sheriff Courts (Scotland) Act 1907.

(2) Where there is a reference to a form in these Rules, that form in the Appendix to these Rules or a form substantially to the same effect shall be used with such variation as circumstances may require.

Relief from failure to comply with rules

3.—(1) The sheriff may relieve a party from the consequences of failure to comply with a provision in these Rules which is shown to be due to mistake, oversight or other excusable cause, on such conditions as he thinks fit.

(2) Where the sheriff relieves a party from the consequences of a failure to comply with a provision in these Rules under paragraph (1), he may make such order as he thinks fit to enable the summary application to proceed as if the failure to comply with the provision had not occurred.

The initial writ

4.—(1) Unless otherwise prescribed by any other enactment, a summary application shall be commenced by initial writ in Form 1.

(2) The initial writ shall be written, typed or printed on A4 size paper of durable quality and shall not be backed or folded.

(3) Where the pursuer has reason to believe that an agreement exists prorogating jurisdiction over the subject-matter of the summary application to another court, the initial writ shall contain details of that agreement.

(4) Where the pursuer has reason to believe that proceedings are pending before another court involving the same cause of action and between the same parties as those named in the instance of the initial writ, the initial writ shall contain details of those proceedings.

(5) An article of condescendence shall be included in the initial writ averring—
(a) the ground of jurisdiction; and
(b) the facts upon which the ground of jurisdiction is based.

(6) Where the residence, registered office or place of business, as the case may be, of the defender is not known and cannot reasonably be ascertained, the pursuer shall set out in the instance that the whereabouts of the defender are not known and aver in the condescendence what steps have been taken to ascertain his present whereabouts.

(7) The initial writ shall be signed by the pursuer or his solicitor (if any) and the name and address of that solicitor shall be stated on the back of every service copy of that writ.

(8) The initial writ shall include averments about those persons who appear to the pursuer to have an interest in the application and in respect of whom a warrant for citation is sought.

Order for intimation to interested persons by sheriff

5. The sheriff may make an order for intimation to any person who appears to him to have an interest in the summary application.

Time limits

6.—(1) This rule applies to a summary application where the time within which the application may be made is not otherwise prescribed by the enactment under which it is made.

(2) An application to which this rule applies shall be lodged with the sheriff clerk within 21 days after the date on which the decision, order, scheme, determination, refusal or other act complained of was intimated to the pursuer.

(3) On special cause shown, the sheriff may hear an application to which this rule applies notwithstanding that it was not lodged within the period prescribed in paragraph (2).

Warrants, forms and certificate of citation

7.—(1) Subject to paragraph (2), a warrant for citation, intimation or arrestment on the dependence may be signed by the sheriff or sheriff clerk.

(2) A warrant containing a period of notice shorter than the period of notice to be given to a defender under rule 3.6 (1) (a) or (b), as the case may be, of the Ordinary Cause Rules 1993 or any other warrant which the sheriff clerk may not sign shall be signed by the sheriff.

(3) Where the sheriff clerk refuses to sign a warrant which he may sign, the party presenting the summary application may apply to the sheriff for the warrant.

(4) Where citation is necessary—
(a) the warrant of citation shall, subject to paragraph (5) of this rule, be in Form 2; and
(b) citation shall, subject to paragraph (7) of this rule and rule 13 (service where address of person is not known), be in Form 3.

(5) Where a time to pay direction under the Debtors (Scotland) Act 1987 (c 18) may be applied for by the defender, the warrant of citation shall be in Form 4.

(6) Where a warrant of citation in accordance with Form 4 is appropriate, there shall be served on the defender (with the initial writ and warrant) a notice in Form 5.

(7) Where a time to pay direction under the Debtors (Scotland) Act 1987 may be applied for by the defender, citation shall be in Form 6 which shall be attached to a copy of the initial writ and warrant of citation.

(8) Where citation is necessary, the certificate of citation shall be in Form 7 which shall be attached to the initial writ.

(9) Where citation is by a sheriff officer, one witness shall be sufficient for the execution of citation.

(10) Where citation is by a sheriff officer, the certificate of citation shall be signed by the sheriff officer and the witness and shall state—
(a) the method of citation; and
(b) where the method of citation was other than personal or postal citation, the full name and designation of any person to whom the citation was delivered.

(11) Where citation is executed under paragraph (3) of rule 11 (depositing or affixing by sheriff officer) the certificate shall include a statement—
(a) of the method of service previously attempted;
(b) of the circumstances which prevented such service being executed; and
(c) that a copy was sent in accordance with the provisions of paragraph (4) of that rule.

Orders against which caveats may be lodged

8. A person may lodge a caveat against an interim order (other than an order under section 1 of the Administration of Justice (Scotland) Act 1972 (c 59) (orders for inspection of documents and other property, etc)) sought before service of the initial writ.

Form, lodging and renewal of caveats

9.—(1) A caveat shall be in Form 8 and shall be lodged with the sheriff clerk.

(2) A caveat shall remain in force for a period of one year from the date on which it was lodged and may be renewed on its expiry for a further period of one year and yearly thereafter.

(3) Where a caveat has been lodged and has not expired, no order in respect of which the caveat was lodged may be pronounced unless the sheriff is satisfied that all reasonable steps have been taken to afford the person lodging the caveat an opportunity of being heard; and the sheriff may continue the hearing on such an order until he is satisfied that such steps have been taken.

Postal service or intimation

10.—(1) In any summary application in which service or intimation of any document or citation of any person may be by recorded delivery, such service, intimation or citation shall be by the first class recorded delivery service.

(2) Notwithstanding the terms of section 4 (2) of the Citation Amendment (Scotland) Act 1882 (c 77) (time from which period of notice reckoned), where service or intimation is by post, any period of notice contained in the warrant of citation shall run from the beginning of the day after the date of posting.

(3) On the face of the envelope used for postal service or intimation under this rule there shall be written or printed the following notice:—
"This envelope contains a citation to or intimation from (specify the court). If delivery cannot be made at the address shown it is to be returned immediately to:— The Sheriff Clerk (insert address of sheriff clerk's office).".

(4) The certificate of citation or intimation in the case of postal service shall have attached to it any relevant postal receipts.

Service within Scotland by sheriff officer

11.—(1) An initial writ, decree, charge, warrant or any other order or writ following upon such initial writ or decree served by a sheriff officer on any person shall be served—
(a) personally; or
(b) by being left in the hands of a resident at the person's dwelling place or an employee at his place of business.

(2) Where service is executed under paragraph (1) (b), the certificate of citation or service shall contain the full name and designation of any person in whose hands the initial writ, decree, charge, warrant or other order or writ, as the case may be, was left.

(3) Where a sheriff officer has been unsuccessful in executing service in accordance with paragraph (1), he may,

after making diligent inquiries, serve the document in question—
(a) by depositing it in that person's dwelling place or place of business; or
(b) by affixing it to the door of that person's dwelling place or place of business.

(4) Subject to rule 18 (service of schedule of arrestment), where service is executed under paragraph (3), the sheriff officer shall, as soon as possible after such service, send a letter containing a copy of the document by ordinary first class post to the address at which he thinks it most likely that the person on whom service has been executed may be found.

Service on persons furth of Scotland

12.—(1) Subject to the following provisions of this rule, an initial writ, decree, charge, warrant or any other order or writ following upon such initial writ or decree served on a person furth of Scotland shall be served—
(a) at a known residence or place of business in England, Wales, Northern Ireland, the Isle of Man, the Channel Islands or any country with which the United Kingdom does not have a convention providing for service of writs in that country—
(i) in accordance with the rules for personal service under the domestic law of the place in which service is to be executed; or
(ii) by posting in Scotland a copy of the document in question in a registered letter addressed to the person at his residence or place of business;
(b) in a country which is a party to the Hague Convention on the Service Abroad of Judicial and Extra-Judicial Documents in Civil or Commercial Matters dated 15th November 1965 or the Convention in Schedule 1 or 3C to the Civil Jurisdiction and Judgments Act 1982 (c 27)—
(i) by a method prescribed by the internal law of the country where service is to be executed for the service of documents in domestic actions upon persons who are within its territory;
(ii) by or through the central, or other appropriate authority in the country where service is to be executed at the request of the Secretary of State for Foreign and Commonwealth Affairs;
(iii) by or through a British Consular Office in the country where service is to be executed at the request of the Secretary of State for Foreign and Commonwealth Affairs;
(iv) where the law of the country in which the person resides permits, by posting in Scotland a copy of the document in a registered letter addressed to the person at his residence; or
(v) where the law of the country in which service is to be executed permits, service by an *huissier*, other judicial officer or competent official of the country where service is to be executed; or
(c) in a country with which the United Kingdom has a convention on the service of writs in that country other than the conventions mentioned in sub-paragraph (b), by one of the methods approved in the relevant convention.

(2) Any document which requires to be posted in Scotland for the purposes of this rule shall be posted by a solicitor or a sheriff officer; and on the face of the envelope there shall be written or printed the notice set out in rule 10 (3).

(3) In the case of service by a method referred to in paragraph (1) (b) (ii) and (iii), the pursuer shall—
(a) send a copy of the writ and warrant of service with citation attached, or other document, as the case may be, with a request for service by the method indicated in the request to the Secretary of State for Foreign and Commonwealth Affairs; and
(b) lodge in process a certificate signed by the authority which executed service stating that it has been, and the manner in which it was, served.

(4) In the case of service by a method referred to in paragraph (1) (b) (v), the pursuer or the sheriff officer shall—
(a) send a copy of the writ and warrant for service with citation attached, or other document, as the case may be, with a request for service by the method indicated in the request to the official in the country in which service is to be executed; and
(b) lodge in process a certificate of the official who executed

service stating that it has been, and the manner in which it was, served.

(5) Where service is executed in accordance with paragraph (1) (a) (i) or (1) (b) (i) other than on another party in the United Kingdom, the Isle of Man or the Channel Islands, the party executing service shall lodge a certificate by a person who is conversant with the law of the country concerned and who practices or has practised law in that country or is a duly accredited representative of the Government of that country, stating that the method of service employed is in accordance with the law of the place where service was executed.

(6) Every writ, document, citation or notice on the face of the envelope mentioned in rule 10 (3) shall be accompanied by a translation in an official language of the country in which service is to be executed unless English is an official language of that country.

(7) A translation referred to in paragraph (6) shall be certified as correct by the person making it; and the certificate shall—
(a) include his full name, address and qualifications; and
(b) be lodged with the execution of citation or service.

Service where address of person is not known

13.—(1) Where the address of a person to be cited or served with a document is not known and cannot reasonably be ascertained, the sheriff shall grant warrant for citation or service upon that person—
(a) by the publication of an advertisement in Form 9 in a specified newspaper circulating in the area of the last known address of that person; or
(b) by displaying on the walls of court a copy of the instance and crave of the initial writ, the warrant of citation and a notice in Form 10;
and any period of notice contained in the warrant of citation shall run from the date of publication of the advertisement or display on the walls of court, as the case may be.

(2) Where service requires to be executed under paragraph (1), the pursuer shall lodge a service copy of the initial writ and a copy of any warrant of citation with the sheriff clerk from whom they may be uplifted by the person for whom they are intended.

(3) Where a person has been cited or served in accordance with paragraph (1) and, after the summary application has commenced, his address becomes known, the sheriff may allow the initial writ to be amended subject to such conditions as to re-service, intimation, expenses or transfer of the summary application as he thinks fit.

(4) Where advertisement in a newspaper is required for the purpose of citation or service under this rule, a copy of the newspaper containing the advertisement shall be lodged with the sheriff clerk by the pursuer.

(5) Where display on the walls of court is required under paragraph (1) (b), the pursuer shall supply to the sheriff clerk for that purpose a certified copy of the instance and crave of the initial writ and any warrant of citation.

Persons carrying on business under trading or descriptive name

14.—(1) A person carrying on a business under a trading or descriptive name may be designed in the instance of the initial writ by such trading or descriptive name alone; and an extract—
(a) of a decree pronounced in the sheriff court, or
(b) of a decree proceeding upon any deed, decree arbitral, bond, protest of a bill, promissory note or banker's note or upon any other obligation or document on which execution may proceed, recorded in the sheriff court books,
against such person under such trading or descriptive name, shall be a valid warrant for diligence against such person.

(2) An initial writ, decree, charge, warrant or any other order or writ following upon such initial writ or decree in a summary application in which a person carrying on business under a trading or descriptive name is designed in the instance of the initial writ by that name shall be served—
(a) at any place of business or office at which such business is carried on within the sheriffdom of the sheriff court in which the cause is brought; or

(b) where there is no place of business within that sheriffdom, at any place where such business is carried on (including the place of business or office of the clerk or secretary of any company, corporation or association or firm).

Endorsation unnecessary

15. An initial writ, decree, charge, warrant or any other order or writ following upon such initial writ or decree may be served, enforced or otherwise lawfully executed anywhere in Scotland without endorsation by a sheriff clerk; and, if executed by a sheriff officer, may be so executed by a sheriff officer of the court which granted it or by a sheriff officer of the sheriff court district in which it is to be executed.

Re-service

16. Where it appears to the sheriff that there has been any failure or irregularity in citation or service on a person, he may order the pursuer to re-serve the initial writ on such conditions as the sheriff thinks fit.

No objection to regularity of citation, service or intimation

17.—(1) A person who appears in a summary application shall not be entitled to state any objection to the regularity of the execution of citation, service or intimation on him; and his appearance shall remedy any defect in such citation, service or intimation.

(2) Nothing in paragraph (1) shall preclude a party from pleading that the court has no jurisdiction.

Service of schedule of arrestment

18. If a schedule of arrestment has not been personally served on an arrestee, the arrestment shall have effect only if a copy of the schedule is also sent by registered post or the first class recorded delivery service to—
(a) the last known place of residence of the arrestee, or
(b) if such a place of residence is not known, or if the arrestee is a firm or corporation, to the arrestee's principal place of business if known, or, if not known, to any known place of business of the arrestee;
and the sheriff officer shall, on the certificate of execution, certify that this has been done and specify the address to which the copy of the schedule was sent.

Arrestment on dependence before service

19.—(1) An arrestment on the dependence of a summary application used before service shall cease to have effect if the initial writ is not served within 20 days from the date of arrestment and either—
(a) in the case where the pursuer is entitled to minute for decree in absence on the expiry of a period of notice contained in the warrant of citation, decree in absence has not been pronounced within 20 days after the expiry of the period of notice; or
(b) in the case where the pursuer is not entitled to minute for decree in absence prior to the first hearing of the summary application, there is no appearance by the pursuer at the first hearing and the summary application drops from the roll.

(2) After such an arrestment has been executed, the party who executed it shall forthwith report the execution to the sheriff clerk.

Movement of arrested property

20.—(1) Any person having an interest may apply by motion for a warrant authorising the movement of a vessel or cargo which is the subject of an arrestment to found jurisdiction or on the dependence of a summary application.

(2) Where the court grants a warrant sought under paragraph (1), it may make such further order as it thinks fit to give effect to that warrant.

Transfer to another sheriff court

21.—(1) The sheriff may, on cause shown, remit a summary application to another sheriff court.

(2) Subject to paragraph (4), where a summary application in which there are two or more defenders has been brought in the sheriff court of the residence or place of business of one of them, the sheriff may transfer the summary application to any other sheriff court which has jurisdiction over any of the defenders.

(3) Subject to paragraph (4), where a plea of no jurisdiction is sustained, the sheriff may transfer the summary application to the sheriff court before which it appears to him the summary application ought to have been brought.

(4) The sheriff shall not transfer a summary application to another sheriff court under paragraph (2) or (3) except—
(a) on the motion of a party; and
(b) where he considers it expedient to do so having regard to the convenience of the parties and their witnesses.

(5) On making an order under paragraph (1), (2) or (3), the sheriff—
(a) shall state his reasons for doing so in the interlocutor; and
(b) may make the order on such conditions as to expenses or otherwise as he thinks fit.

(6) The court to which a summary application is transferred under paragraph (1), (2) or (3) shall accept the summary application.

(7) A transferred summary application shall proceed in all respects as if it had been originally brought in the court to which it is transferred.

(8) An interlocutor transferring a summary application may, with leave of the sheriff, be appealed to the sheriff principal but shall not be subject to appeal to the Court of Session.

Applications for time to pay directions

22.—(1) This rule applies to a summary application in which a time to pay direction may be applied for under the Debtors (Scotland) Act 1987 (c 18).

(2) A defender may apply for a time to pay direction and, where appropriate, for recall or restriction of an arrestment—
(a) by appearing and making the appropriate motion at a diet fixed for hearing of the summary application;
(b) except where the warrant of citation contains a shorter period of notice than the period of notice to be given to a defender under rule 3.6 (1) (a) or (b), as the case may be, of the Ordinary Cause Rules 1993 by completing and returning the appropriate portion of Form 5 to the sheriff clerk at least seven days before the first diet fixed for hearing of the summary application or the expiry of the period of notice or otherwise, as the case may be, in the warrant of citation; or
(c) by application to the court at any stage before final decree.

(3) The sheriff may determine an application under paragraph (2) (b) or (c) without the defender having to appear.

Remuneration of assessors

23. Where an assessor is appointed by the sheriff to assist him in determining the summary application the remuneration to be paid to such assessor shall be part of the expenses of the application.

Deposits for expenses

24. Where, under any enactment, the sheriff requires the pursuer to deposit a sum of money to cover the expenses of an appeal under the enactment, such sum shall, subject to the provisions of that enactment, not exceed an amount which is twenty five times the amount of the fee payable at the time in respect of lodging the initial writ.

When decrees extractable

25.—(1) Subject to the following paragraphs—
(a) subject to sub-paragraph (c) a decree in absence may be extracted after the expiry of 14 days from the date of decree;
(b) subject to sub-paragraph (c) any decree pronounced in a defended summary application may be extracted at any time after whichever is the later of the following:—
(i) the expiry of the period within which an application for leave to appeal may be made and no such application has been made;
(ii) the date on which leave to appeal has been refused and there is no right of appeal from such refusal;
(iii) the expiry of the period within which an appeal may be marked and no appeal has been marked; or

(iv) the date on which an appeal has been finally disposed of; and

(c) where the sheriff has, in pronouncing decree, reserved any question of expenses, extract of that decree may be issued only after the expiry of 14 days from the date of the interlocutor disposing of the question of expenses unless the sheriff otherwise directs.

(2) The sheriff may, on cause shown, grant a motion to allow extract to be applied for and issued earlier than a date referred to in paragraph (1).

(3) In relation to a decree referred to in paragraph (1) (b) or (c), paragraph (2) shall not apply unless—

(a) the motion under that paragraph is made in the presence of the parties; or

(b) the sheriff is satisfied that proper intimation of the motion has been made in writing to every party not present at the hearing of the motion.

(4) Nothing in this rule shall affect the power of the sheriff to supersede extract.

Form of extract decree

26. The extract of a decree shall be in Form 11.

Form of warrant for execution

27. An extract of a decree on which execution may proceed shall include a warrant for execution in the following terms:— "This extract is warrant for all lawful execution hereon.".

Date of decree in extract

28.—(1) Where the sheriff principal has adhered to the decision of the sheriff following an appeal, the date to be inserted in the extract decree as the date of decree shall be the date of the decision of the sheriff principal.

(2) Where a decree has more than one date it shall not be necessary to specify in an extract what was done on each date.

Decrees in absence where defender furth of United Kingdom

29.—(1) Where a defender if domiciled in another part of the United Kingdom or in another Contracting State, the sheriff shall not grant decree in absence until it has been shown that the defender has been able to receive the initial writ in sufficient time to arrange for his defence or that all necessary steps have been taken to that end; and for the purposes of this paragraph—

(a) the question whether a person is domiciled in another part of the United Kingdom shall be determined in accordance with sections 41 and 42 of the Civil Jurisdiction and Judgments Act 1988;

(b) the question whether a person is domiciled in another Contracting State shall be determined in accordance with Article 52 of the Convention in Schedule 1 or 3C to that Act, as the case may be; and

(c) the term "Contracting State" has the meaning assigned in section 1 of that Act.

(2) Where an initial writ has been served in a country to which the Hague Convention on the Service Abroad of Judicial and Extra-Judicial Documents in Civil or Commercial Matters dated 15th November 1965 applies, decree shall not be granted until it is established to the satisfaction of the sheriff that the requirements of Article 15 of that Convention have been complied with.

Applications under the Administration of Justice (Scotland) Act 1972

30.—(1) An application for an order under section 1 (1) of the Administration of Justice (Scotland) Act 1972 (orders for inspection of documents and other property, etc) shall be made by summary application where the proceedings in respect of which the application is made have not been commenced.

(2) An application for an order under section 1 (1A) of the Administration of Justice (Scotland) Act 1972 (order on person to disclose information as to the identity of any person who might be a witness or defender in any civil proceedings which are likely to be brought) shall be made by summary application.

Motion Roll procedure

31. Except where the sheriff otherwise directs, any motion relating to a summary application shall be made in accordance with, and regulated by, Chapter 15 of the Ordinary Cause Rules 1993.

Power of sheriff to make orders

32. The sheriff may make such order as he thinks fit for the progress of a summary application in so far as it is not inconsistent with section 50 of the Sheriff Courts (Scotland) Act 1907.

APPENDIX

FORM 1   Rule 4 (1)

Form of initial writ

SUMMARY APPLICATION UNDER (title and section of statute or statutory instrument)

INITIAL WRIT

SHERIFFDOM OF (*insert name of sheriffdom*)
AT (*insert place of sheriff court*)

[A.B.] (*design and state any special capacity in which the pursuer is suing*). Pursuer.

Against

[C.D.] (*design and state any special capacity in which the defender is being sued*). Defender.

The Pursuer craves the Court (*here state the specific decree, warrant or order sought*)

CONDESCENDENCE
(*State in numbered paragraphs the facts which form the ground of action*)

PLEAS-IN-LAW
(*State in numbered sentences*)

Signed
[A.B.], Pursuer

or [X.Y.], Solicitor for the pursuer (*state designation and business address*)

FORM 2   Rule 7 (4) (a)

Form of warrant of citation

(*Insert place and date*) Grants warrant to cite the defender (*insert name and address*) by serving upon him [*or her*] a copy of the writ and warrant [on a period of notice of (*insert period of notice*) days], [and ordains him [*or her*] to answer within the Sheriff Court House (*insert place of sheriff court*) at [in Room No., or in Chambers, *or otherwise, as the case may be*] on the day of   at   o'clock noon] [*or otherwise, as the case may be*] [and grants warrant to arrest on the dependence].

Signed
Sheriff [or sheriff clerk]

FORM 3   Rule 7 (4) (b)

Form of citation for summary application

CITATION FOR SUMMARY APPLICATION

SHERIFFDOM OF (*insert name of sheriffdom*)
AT (*insert place of sheriff court*)

[A.B.], (*insert designation and address*), Pursuer, against [C.D.], (*insert designation and address*), Defender.
Court ref. no.
(*Insert place and date*). You [C.D.], are hereby served with this copy writ and warrant, and are required to answer it.

> **IF YOU ARE UNCERTAIN AS TO WHAT ACTION TO TAKE** you should consult a solicitor. You may be eligible for legal aid depending on your income, and you can get information about legal aid from a solicitor. You may also obtain advice from any Citizens' Advice Bureau or other advice agency.
>
> **PLEASE NOTE THAT IF YOU DO NOTHING IN ANSWER TO THIS DOCUMENT** the court may regard you as admitting the claim made against you and the pursuer may obtain decree against you in your absence.

ACT OF SEDERUNT (SHERIFF COURT SUMMARY APPLICATION RULES) 1993

Signed
[P.Q.], Sheriff officer,
or [X.Y.] (*add designation and business address*)
Solicitor for the pursuer

FORM 4 — Rule 7 (5)
Form of warrant of citation where time to pay direction may be applied for

(*Insert place and date*) Grants warrant to cite the defender (*insert name and address*) by serving a copy of the writ and warrant, together with Form 5, [on a period of notice of (*insert period of notice*) days] and ordains him [*or her*] if he [*or she*]—

(a) intends to defend the action or make any claim [to answer within the Sheriff Court House (*insert place and address of sheriff court*) at [in Room No., or in Chambers, *or otherwise, as the case may be*] or

(b) admits the claim and intends to apply for a time to pay direction (and where appropriate apply for recall or restriction of an arrestment) [either to appear at that diet and make such application or] to lodge the appropriate part of Form 5 duly completed with the sheriff clerk at (*insert place of sheriff court*) at least seven days before [the diet *or* the expiry of the period of notice *or otherwise, as the case may be*] [and grants warrant to arrest on the dependence].

Signed
Sheriff [or sheriff clerk]

FORM 5 — Rules 7 (6) and 22 (2) (b)
Form of notice to be served on defender in summary application where time to pay direction may be applied for
ACTION IN SUMMARY APPLICATION BY

PURSUER   DEFENDER

AT   SHERIFF COURT
(Including address)

COURT REF. NO.

/   [DATE OF FIRST HEARING]
[EXPIRY OF PERIOD OF NOTICE]

THIS SECTION MUST BE COMPLETED BY THE PURSUER BEFORE SERVICE

The Debtors (Scotland) Act 1987 gives you the right to apply to the court for a 'time to pay direction' which is an order permitting you to pay any sum of money you are ordered to pay to the pursuer (which may include interest and court expenses) either by way of instalments or deferred lump sum. A deferred lump sum means that you must pay all the amount at one time within a period specified by the court.

When making a time to pay direction the court may recall or restrict an arrestment made on your property by the pursuer in connection with the action or debt (for example your bank account may have been frozen).

HOW TO APPLY FOR A TIME TO PAY DIRECTION WHERE YOU ADMIT THE CLAIM AND YOU DO NOT WANT TO DEFEND THE ACTION

1 Attached to this notice at pages 3 and 4 is an application for a time to pay direction, and for recall or restriction of an arrestment, if appropriate. If you want to make an application you should lodge the completed application with the sheriff clerk at the above address at least seven days before the date of the first hearing or expiry of the period of notice or otherwise, as the case may be in the warrant of citation given above. No court fee is payable when lodging the application.

2 Before completing the application please read carefully the notes overleaf on page 2. In the event of difficulty you may contact the court's civil department at the address above or any sheriff clerk's office, solicitor, Citizens' Advice Bureau or other advice agency.

HOW TO COMPLETE THE APPLICATION
PLEASE WRITE IN INK USING BLOCK CAPITALS
PART A of the application will have been completed in advance by the pursuer and gives details of the pursuer and you as the defender.

PART B — If you wish to apply to pay by instalments enter the amount and tick the appropriate box at B3 (1). If you wish to apply to pay the full sum due in one deferred payment enter the period of deferment you propose at B3 (2).

PART C — Give full details of your financial position in the space provided.

PART D — If you wish the court, when making the time to pay direction to recall or restrict an arrestment made in connection with the action, enter the appropriate details about what has been arrested and the place and date of the arrestment at D5, and attach the schedule of arrestment or copy.

Sign the application where indicated and detach pages 3 and 4. Retain the copy initial writ and pages 1 and 2 of this form as you may need them at a later stage. You should ensure that your application arrives at the court at least seven days before the date of the first hearing or expiry of the period of notice or otherwise, as the case may be in the warrant of citation.

WHAT WILL HAPPEN NEXT

If the pursuer objects to your application the court will advise you in writing and you will be required to attend the first hearing given in the warrant of citation or other hearing fixed for that purpose.

If the pursuer does not object to your application, a copy of the court order for payment (called an extract decree) will be served on you by the pursuer's solicitor advising when instalment payments should commence or deferred payment be made.

Court ref. no.

APPLICATION FOR A TIME TO PAY DIRECTION UNDER THE DEBTORS (SCOTLAND) ACT 1987

*PART A

By _____

_____

_____

DEFENDER

*(This section must be completed by pursuer before service)

In an action raised by

_____

_____

_____

PURSUER

PART B

1 The applicant is a defender in the action brought by the above named pursuer.

2 The defender admits the claim and applies to the court for a time to pay direction.

3 The defender applies   (1) To pay by instalments of £

(Tick one box only)

EACH WEEK ☐   FORTNIGHT ☐   MONTH ☐

OR

(2) To pay the sum ordered in one payment within WEEKS/MONTHS

PART C

4 Defender's financial position

My	weekly	fortnightly	monthly
outgoings are:	☐	☐	☐

Rent/mortgage £
Heating £
Food £
HP £
Other £

Total £

My	weekly	fortnightly	monthly
income is:	☐	☐	☐

Wages/pensions £
Social security £
Other £

Total £

Dependants: Dependent relatives:
Children — how many ☐   —how many ☐

Here list all capital (if any) eg value of house; amounts in bank or building society accounts; shares or other investments:

Here list any outstanding debts:

PART D

5 The defender seeks to recall or restrict an arrestment of which the details are as follows (_please state, and attach the schedule of arrestment or copy_):—

6 This application is made under sections 1 (1) and 2 (3) of the Debtors (Scotland) Act 1987.

Therefore the defender asks the court

*a. to make a time to pay direction.

*b. to recall the above arrestment.

*c. to restrict the above arrestment (_in which case state restriction wanted_):—

* Delete what does not apply

Date (_insert date_)   Signed

Defender

FORM 6   Rule 7 (7)

Form of citation where time to pay direction may be applied for in summary application

SHERIFFDOM OF (_insert name of sheriffdom_)

AT (_insert place of sheriff court_)

[A.B.], (_insert designation and address_) Pursuer against [C.D.], (_insert designation and address_) Defender

Court ref. no.

(_Insert place and date_). You [C.D.], are hereby served with this copy writ and warrant, together with Form 5 (application for time to pay direction in summary application).

Form 5 is served on you because it is considered that you may be entitled to apply for a time to pay direction [and for the recall or restriction of an arrestment used on the dependence of the action or in security of the debt referred to in the copy writ]. See Form 5 for further details.

IF YOU ADMIT THE CLAIM AND WISH TO APPLY FOR A TIME TO PAY DIRECTION, you must complete Form 5 and return it to the sheriff clerk at the above address at least 7 days before the hearing or the expiry of the period of notice or otherwise, as the case may be in the warrant of citation.

IF YOU ADMIT THE CLAIM AND WISH TO AVOID A COURT ORDER BEING MADE AGAINST YOU, the whole sum claimed including interest and any expenses due should be paid to the pursuer or his solicitor by the court date.

IF YOU ARE UNCERTAIN AS TO WHAT ACTION TO TAKE you should consult a solicitor. You may be eligible for legal aid depending on your income, and you can get information about legal aid from a solicitor. You may also obtain advice from any Citizens' Advice Bureau, or other advice agency.

PLEASE NOTE THAT IF YOU DO NOTHING IN ANSWER TO THIS DOCUMENT the court may regard you as admitting the claim made against you and the pursuer may obtain decree against you in your absence.

Signed

[P.Q.], Sheriff officer

or [X.Y.], (_add designation and business address_) Solicitor for the pursuer

FORM 7   Rule 7 (8)

Form of certificate of citation

CERTIFICATE OF CITATION

(_Insert place and date_) I,   hereby certify that upon the   day of   I duly cited [C.D.], Defender, to answer to the foregoing writ. This I did by (_state method of service; if by officer and not by post, add: in the presence of_ [L.M.], (_insert designation_), witness hereto with me subscribing; *and where service executed by post state whether by registered post or the first class recorded delivery service*).

In actions in which a time to pay direction may be applied for, state whether Form 4 and Form 5 were sent in accordance with rule 7 (5) and (6).

    Signed
        [P.Q.], Sheriff officer
        [L.M.], witness
        or [X.Y.], (*add designation and business address*)
        Solicitor for the pursuer

FORM 8	Rule 9 (1)

Form of Caveat

SHERIFFDOM OF (*insert name of sheriffdom*)
AT (*insert place of sheriff court*)

CAVEAT for [A.B.] (*insert designation and address**)

Should any application be made for (*here specify the nature of the application(s) to which this caveat is to apply*) prior to service of the initial writ, it is requested that intimation be made to the caveator before any order is pronounced.

Date (*insert date*)

        Signed
        [A.B.]
        or [X.Y.], Solicitor for [A.B.] (*add designation and business address*)

Caveator's telephone and fax number (*insert where caveat is not lodged by solicitor*)
Solicitor (*insert name and address, telephone and fax number and reference*)
Out of hours contacts:
    1. (*insert name and telephone number*)
    2. (*insert name and telephone number*)
  *State whether the caveat is lodged in an individual capacity, or a specified representative capacity (eg as trustee of a named trust) or both. Where appropriate, state also the nature of the caveator's interest (eg shareholder, debenture holder).

FORM 9	Rule 13 (1) (a)

Form of advertisement

NOTICE TO [C.D.]   Court ref. no.
An action has been raised in   Sheriff Court by [A.B.], Pursuer calling as a Defender [C.D.], whose last known address was (*insert last known address of defender*).
If [C.D.] wishes to defend the action he [*or she*] should immediately contact the sheriff clerk (*insert address*) from whom the service copy initial writ may be obtained. If he [*or she*] fails to do so decree may pass against him [*or her*] [when the case calls in court on (*date*) *or* on the expiry of the period of notice or *otherwise, as the case may be in the warrant of citation*].

        (Signed)
        [X.Y.], (*add designation and business address*)
        Solicitor for the pursuer
        or [P.Q.], (*add business address*)

FORM 10	Rule 13 (1) (b)

Form of notice for walls of court

NOTICE TO [C.D.]   Court ref. no.
An action has been raised in   Sheriff Court by [A.B.], Pursuer calling as a Defender [C.D.], whose last known address was (*insert last known address of defender*).
If [C.D.] wishes to defend the action he [*or she*] should immediately contact the sheriff clerk at (*insert address*) from whom the service copy initial writ may be obtained. If he [*or she*] fails to do so decree may pass against him [*or her*] [when the case calls in court on (date) *or* on the expiry of the period of notice *or otherwise, as the case may be in the warrant of citation*].

Date (*insert date*)
        (Signed)
        Sheriff clerk (depute)
        Telephone no. (*insert telephone number of sheriff clerk's office*)

FORM 11

Form of extract decree
EXTRACT DECREE

Sheriff court	Court ref. no.
Date of decree	*In absence
Pursuer(s)	Defender(s)

The sheriff

and granted decree against the   for payment of expenses of £

    This extract is warrant for all lawful execution hereon.

Date   Sheriff clerk (depute)
* Delete as appropriate

	SCHEDULE 2	Paragraph 3
	REVOCATIONS	

Column 1	Column 2	Column 3 Extent of
References	Acts of Sederunt	Revocation
SR & O 1937/1016	Act of Sederunt Regulating Appeals to the Sheriff under the Methylated Spirits (Sale by Retail) (Scotland) Act 1937	The whole Act of Sederunt
SI 1961/1018	Act of Sederunt (Caravan Sites Appeals) 1961	The whole Act of Sederunt
SI 1964/817	Act of Sederunt (Building Appeals) 1964	The whole Act of Sederunt
SI 1970/1984	Act of Sederunt (Firearms Appeals) 1970	The whole Act of Sederunt
SI 1981/1591	Act of Sederunt (Statutory Appeals) 1981	The whole Act of Sederunt
SI 1983/747	Act of Sederunt (Ordinary Cause Rules, Sheriff Court) 1983	Paragraph 5
SI 1988/1978	Act of Sederunt (Amendment of Sheriff Court Ordinary Cause and Summary Cause Rules) 1988	Paragraph 36

[Acts of Sederunt are reproduced with the permission of the Controller of Her Majesty's Stationery Office.]

ARTICLES

Delictual Liability Between Parties to a Contract

Joe Thomson,
The School of Law,
University of Glasgow.

In a revised version of a paper delivered at Glasgow Caledonian University in September 1993, Professor Thomson explores the extent to which the courts have permitted one party to a contract to claim a remedy in delict against another, and the differences between, and respective advantages of, the two types of claim.

In this paper, I wish to explore a seemingly simple situation. A and B have a contract between them. If B breaks the contract, A will have a remedy for breach of contract. If, however, B's breach has been the result of conduct by B intended to harm A, or conduct by B which would otherwise constitute negligence, does A have, in addition or as an alternative to his remedy in contract, the right to sue B in delict?

Contractual obligations arise from the voluntary agreement of the parties to a contract. Delictual obligations arise ex lege as a result of (a) conduct intended to cause harm or (b) careless conduct resulting in harm where the defender owes the pursuer a duty of care, i e negligence. Contract and delict are therefore based on quite separate principles; yet, as we shall see, recent developments in the law of delict which allow recovery for pure economic loss may necessitate redrawing the boundary between contract and delict.

It is well settled that the mere fact that A and B are parties to a contract does not prevent A being liable to B in delict provided the criteria for delictual liability are established. Thus, for example, if A and B are employer and employee, there exists a contract of employment between them. It is, of course, an implied term of the contract of employment that the employer owes his employee an obligation to take reasonable care for the safety of the employee; if the employer fails to take such care and the employee is injured, an action lies for breach of contract.

That said, injury to the employee is not essential before an action would lie in contract; if, for example, the employer failed to take reasonable care, they would be in material breach of the contract, justifying the employee before he or she is injured to refuse further performance of his/her obligations and entitling the employee to sue in contract for loss of earnings. However, independently of the contract of employment, the employer owes a duty of care to anyone whom they could reasonably foresee would suffer injury as a probable consequence of the employer's acts or omissions which fall short of the standards of the reasonable person; in establishing the reasonable foreseeability criterion the contractual relationship between the parties is one of the relevant factors so that an employee is obviously a person to whom such a duty is owed. Accordingly, if the employer is negligent and as a result the employee is injured, the employee can sue the employer in delict; this right to sue in delict is independent of the employee's contractual rights. And, unlike the position in contract, it is only available if the employee suffers injury, because physical injury to the pursuer's person or property is an essential criterion for liability in delict. Thus contractual liability and delictual liability are prima facie separate and distinct legal concepts, albeit that a contractual relationship is a relevant factor in determining whether injury to the pursuer or his property is reasonably foreseeable by the defender.

However, these principles were laid down in the halcyon days before there was delictual liability for pure economic loss — i e economic loss arising to the pursuer other than that deriving from any physical injuries to the pursuer or damage to his property. As we all know, the criteria for a duty of care to prevent unintentional economic loss are problematic. Reasonable foreseeability of economic loss to the pursuer arising from the defender's conduct is not sufficient: there must be additional factors which create a degree of "proximity" between the parties. I would like en passant to emphasise that these difficulties of proximity only arise in relation to delictual liability for unintentional wrongs — in fraud, for example, pure economic loss is the paradigm of the type of damages recovered by the pursuer, because the essential element of the defender's intention to deceive the pursuer prevents potential indeterminate liability; and it is to prevent such liability for careless conduct that the courts have been reluctant to extend liability for negligent conduct resulting in pure economic loss unless there is a sufficient degree of proximity between the parties.

In certain areas, we can now discern factors which indicate that a sufficient degree of proximity exists to create a duty of care to prevent economic loss arising from careless as opposed to intentional conduct. Thus, for example, it was settled in *Hedley Byrne v Heller* [1964] AC 465 that A will be liable in delict in respect of pure economic loss arising from a negligent misrepresentation made to B, if A gave advice to B with the knowledge that B would rely on that advice for a specific purpose and B acted upon that advice to B's detriment, though it is still arguable whether A must have given the advice in a professional capacity. We shall return to the problems of the interrelationship between delictual liability for misrepresentation and contract later in this paper.

More problematic is the degree of proximity required to create a duty of care to prevent pure economic loss in what I might call a *Junior Books v Veitchi* situation: 1982 SLT 492. There, it will be remembered, the House of Lords held that there was a sufficient degree of proximity between an employer in a building contract and a nominated subcontractor, to allow the employer to recover for pure economic loss resulting from the subcontractor's negligence in laying a floor.

From the speech of Lord Roskill the major factors which, apart from reasonable foreseeability of loss, constituted the relevant degree of proximity were the facts that (a) Veitchi were subcontractors nominated by the pursuer's architect; (b) Veitchi were specialists in flooring and knew that the pursuers relied on their expertise, and (c) their relationship was as close as it could be short of being parties to a contract.

As is well known, *Junior Books* has proved to be a plant which has not blossomed among the tares and thistles of the English law of torts. As Lord Bridge said in *D & F Estates v Church Commissioners for England* [1988] 3 WLR 368 at p 381: "The consensus of judicial opinion, with which I concur, seems to be that the decision of the majority [in *Junior Books*] is so far dependent upon the unique, albeit non-contractual, relationship between the pursuer and the defender in that case and the unique scope of the duty of care owed by the defender to the pursuer arising from that relationship that the decision cannot be regarded as laying down any principle of general application in the law of tort or delict."

Thus where parties are linked by a series of contracts the approach of the English courts is to encourage the parties to pursue contractual remedies and, in spite of *Junior Books,* to deny an action in delict by refusing to find sufficient proximity to establish a duty of care.

However, the approach of the Scottish courts to *Junior Books* has been less negative. This is hardly surprising as *Junior Books* is a decision of the House of Lords which is binding on a humble Lord Ordinary.

In *Scott Lithgow Ltd v GEC Electrical Projects Ltd,* 1992 SLT 244, the question arose whether a subcontractor and sub-subcontractor owed a duty of care towards the main contractor and/or the employer in a contract to build a ship, to prevent economic loss arising from careless conduct. The issue was, of course, whether the relationships were sufficiently proximate for the duty of care to arise. In his judgment, the Lord Ordinary (Clyde) took the view that for a *Junior Books* duty of care to arise, first, it was not necessary for the subcontractor to be nominated — though it would be a factor pointing to a relationship of proximity if in fact there was nomination or at least approval by the employer or main contractor (pp 251L-252B); secondly, the fact that the parties were linked by contractual structures was an important factor in deciding whether a duty of care existed between the parties who had no contractual link inter se (p 252K-L). So, for example, if A contracts with B who contracts with C who contracts with D, the contractual structure is relevant in determining whether there is sufficient proximity between A and C or A and D to give rise to a duty of care, for the purposes of the law of delict. But in reaching any decision the terms of the various contracts will be important, particularly the presence or absence of exemption clauses. Thus the existence of contractual structures does not prevent a duty of care arising and, indeed, contrary to the approach in England, could be a factor suggesting sufficient proximity, though the terms of the contracts would have to be carefully considered, particularly exemption clauses. Thirdly, Lord Clyde (at p 252E-G) considered that reliance by the pursuer was important, but it was neither necessary nor sufficient to establish proximity.

Similarly, in *Comex Houlder Diving Ltd v Colne Fishing Co Ltd (No 2),* 1992 SLT 89, the Lord Ordinary (Prosser) considered that contractual structures between the parties could be a factor indicating a sufficient degree of proximity for a *Junior Books* duty of care to arise. This was important in this case as the pursuers were the assignees of co-defenders in an earlier litigation, who had had a contract of indemnity with the defender in the current action. Accordingly, in their capacity as assignees, the pursuers had a direct contractual relationship with the defenders. In spite of this, Lord Prosser maintained that it was still possible to argue that the defenders owed the pursuers a duty of care: "In general again, I think it true that in the law of Scotland there is no fundamental difference between claims arising from physical damage and claims where the damage is purely monetary and economic. The problem with the latter category of claims will be the difficulty of establishing proximity in the absence of any physical damage to person or property. It may be, moreover, that the undertaking of indemnity obligations might be seen as demonstrating proximity or reliance, although the very fact of a contractual obligation of indemnity might rather be seen as indicating the absence of any other right of recovery, and as overlaying and replacing any right there might be" (at p 96F-G).

This, with respect, might also be said to be a judicial attempt to have one's cake and eat it!

While the pursuer in *Comex Houlder Diving Ltd v Colne Fishing Co Ltd (No 2)* was technically a party to the defender's contract because of the assignation, the point of the case was whether the defender owed him a duty of care inter alia because of the defender's original contract with the cedent: i e the pursuer in *Comex* was originally not a party to the defender's contract. This is important. For what these cases illustrate is that where there is a contractual structure between A and B, B and C and C and D, the contractual arrangements can be a factor in determining that there is sufficient proximity between A and C or A and D to give rise to a duty of care: persons who do not have direct privity of contract. In other words, insofar as *Junior Books* liability for economic loss survives, the duty of care to prevent primary economic loss arises between parties who are not in a direct contractual relationship — though the existence of a series of contractual relationships interconnecting them could, in Scotland at least, be regarded as a factor indicating a sufficient degree of proximity. This delictual duty is independent of contract — even if the contractual relationship is a relevant factor in determining whether or not the proximity criterion is satisfied.

If then the existence of contracts between A and B and B and C could give rise to a duty of care on C to prevent A suffering economic loss as a result of C's conduct, i e is a factor from which sufficient proximity can be ascertained, does it not follow a fortiori that such a duty exists between B and A or B and C who have direct privity of contract? The answer would appear to be a resounding "no". In *Scott Lithgow Ltd v GEC Electrical Projects Ltd,* Lord Clyde maintained that direct privity of contract will exclude delictual liability for economic loss unless what the Lord Ordinary describes as the "quasi-delictual" duty is simply a different formulation of an existing duty under the contract. But with respect, it is difficult to understand Lord Clyde's "rider". What we are seeking to establish is whether there is an independent duty of care to perform a contract which could give rise to a

claim for pure economic loss in delict if the failure to perform was due to the fault of one of the contracting parties. The Lord Ordinary appears to suggest that if there is a term of the contract that X will be done with reasonable care, the innocent party can sue in delict as an alternative to contract if the term is breached. But that goes against the fundamental principle that when the parties have a direct contractual relationship, an action in delict must lie independently of the contract per se. (On the other hand, in *Comex Houlder Diving Ltd,* the fact that the parties technically had direct privity of contract did not per se prevent a duty of care arising, but that, as we have seen, was an exceptional case.)

The issue was explored in greater depth by the Lord Ordinary (Marnoch) in *Middleton v Douglass,* 1991 SLT 726. In this case A entered into a contract with B under which A undertook to have a survey carried out on a piece of property. A used the services of an architectural technician rather than a chartered surveyor. B purported to sue A in delict as well as for breach of contract. Lord Marnoch took the view that there was no duty of care on A to take reasonable care to ensure that the survey was carried out by a chartered surveyor as opposed to an architectural technician. In other words, even if it had been a term of the contract that a chartered surveyor should be used, A, while guilty of a breach of contract, would not be liable in delict because he did not owe an independent duty of care to B to perform his contractual obligations. Lord Marnoch accepted that a party to a contract could owe the other contracting party a duty of care to prevent physical injury or harm to his property. This was independent of and distinct from the contractual relationship — though the contractual relationship is a factor to be taken into account in deciding whether the harm is reasonably foreseeable. But in cases of recovery for pure economic loss, there is no general duty of care or any other duty other than the duties in the contract itself. In other words, in determining whether there is a duty of care between the parties to prevent physical injury or harm to the property, the reasonable foreseeability criterion is used and the contractual relationship is only one — if sometimes an important — factor in determining whether the harm to the pursuer is reasonably foreseeable; therefore the pursuer may be able to sue in both contract and delict, i e the delictual obligation arises simply on reasonable foreseeability of physical harm. In determining whether there is a duty of care to prevent pure economic loss, as we have seen, the contractual links between the parties can be essential in determining whether a sufficient degree of proximity exists, but if the parties have direct privity of contract, there is nothing except the contract upon which to find the necessary proximity.

In these circumstances the courts appear to be taking the view that there is no room for an action in delict independent of the contract, and accordingly the parties are to be left to their contractual obligations. Thus failure to perform a contract does not per se constitute a delict — contract and delict remain separate concepts and the traditional categorisation of obligations remains intact.

Given the current approach of the House of Lords to recovery in delict for pure economic loss, it would appear that the citadel will remain unassailable for the foreseeable future. However, there is another possible challenge to the dichotomy between contract and delict which I have already mentioned, viz misrepresentation. A misrepresentation can give rise to two sets of remedies. The first set I shall call contractual. If B induces A to enter into a contract with B under material error, as a result of a misrepresentation by B, then A can rescind/reduce the contract provided inter alia restitutio in integrum is possible. In a contract of sale, for example, A will recover the price under general principles of restitution. This remedy is available regardless of B's mens rea, i e whether B's misrepresentation is fraudulent, negligent or innocent. In addition, the facts which have been misrepresented may have been incorporated as a term of contract, in which case A can sue B for breach of contract. This is, of course, an alternative remedy to rescission/reduction as the effect of rescission/reduction is retrospectively to annul the contract. The choice will depend on whether or not A would have made a good or bad bargain if the contract had been fulfilled: if it would have been a good bargain then A will sue for breach of contract in order to recover his expectation interest; if it would have been a bad bargain, then A will rescind/reduce in order to recover his restitution interests.

The second set of remedies I shall call delictual. These depend on the mens rea of B, the misrepresentor. It is long settled that if the misrepresentation is fraudulent, A can recover damages in delict. As the defender is liable for all losses directly arising from the fraudulent conduct, these could in my view include expectation interests under the contract — thus, in this respect, destroying the contract/delict dichotomy. If the misrepresentation is innocent, there is no delictual remedy.

However, if the misrepresentation is negligent,

then it would appear that A could sue if the *Hedley Byrne v Heller* criteria for liability are established. There it will be remembered that X was liable to Y for inducing Y by a negligent misrepresentation to enter into a contract with Z; the case did not deal with the situation where X induced Y by a negligent misrepresentation to enter into a contract with X. For many years, Scots law was unable to develop potential delictual liability between contracting parties for negligent misrepresentation because of the decision of the Inner House in *Manners v Whitehead* (1898) 6 SLT 199; (1898) 1 F 171, which held that a person who had been induced to enter into a contract as a result of a misrepresentation made by the other party to the contract could not sue in delict unless the misrepresentation was made fraudulently. After *Hedley Byrne v Heller* was accepted into Scots law, we then had the anomalous situation that X could be liable for negligent misrepresentation if it induced Y to enter into a contract with Z but not if it induced Y to enter into a contract with X, the misrepresentor. A parallel with potential *Junior Books* liability where, as we have seen, X can be liable in delict to Y for breach of his contract with Z but not if X breaches his contract with Y, is, I think, obvious. However, the rule in *Manners v Whitehead* was abolished by s 10 of the Law Reform (Miscellaneous Provisions) (Scotland) Act 1985 so that, provided the *Hedley Byrne v Heller* criteria are satisfied, A can sue B in delict if he enters into a contract with B as a result of B's negligent misrepresentation. Interestingly enough the writer has not come across any decision since 1985 where an action for negligent misrepresentation had been brought against the other party to the contract: an attempt to do so in *Palmer v Beck*, 1993 SLT 485, failed on the ground that s 10 was not retrospective. Nor is it clear whether damages for negligent misrepresentation would include A's expectation interest under the contract.

If the misrepresentation were also a term of the contract, A could sue B for breach of contract as well as in delict, as the delictual claim is independent of the contract. Often this will only be of academic interest as a pursuer cannot be compensated twice for the same loss. However, if A exercises his right to rescind/reduce the contract, while any possibility of suing in contract disappears as the contract is retrospectively null, A still retains his right to sue B in delict if the misrepresentation was made fraudulently or, since 1985, negligently.

This, of course, presupposes that the misrepresentation was made in pre-contractual negotiations. But, as we have seen, a statement which is a misrepresentation can sometimes also be a term of the contract. Can it not be argued that some terms of a contract, at least, could constitute implied misrepresentations? If this were so, then the contract/delict dichotomy would seriously be undermined. If, for example, in missives of sale, the seller warranted that the central heating system was in good working order, could it not be argued that this impliedly induced the purchaser to agree to the missives, thus opening up the possibility of an action in delict if there was no non-supersession clause or if the period of non-supersession had expired before the faults in the system were discovered?

It might be asked why we should be concerned about breaking down the contract/delict dichotomy, apart from its obvious, I trust, academic interest. There are several reasons. First, an action in delict might be useful when an action in contract cannot succeed because of a valid exemption clause. In *Golden Sea Produce Ltd v Scottish Nuclear plc*, 1992 SLT 942, the parties were landlord and tenant; the Lord Ordinary (MacLean) held that the landlord was under a delictual obligation not to supply water which could harm the fish in the tenant's fish farm. By suing in delict, the tenants were able to avoid an exemption clause, which construed contra proferentem could be restricted to damage caused without negligence. In the course of his opinion, Lord MacLean said at p 946E-F: "Whether it is just and reasonable to hold that certain duties, whether they be duties of care or of any other kind, were incumbent upon parties who are in a contractual relationship will, in my opinion, depend upon the nature and terms of that relationship. It will probably be of additional significance that parties are in the relationship of landlord and tenant. Clearly, also, it will be easier to infer such duties in law in cases where the loss sustained is not purely economic in nature".

Not only does this case illustrate the practical advantages of a delictual action but it also provides an example of how in the case of a duty of care to prevent physical harm, the contractual relationship between the parties is relevant in determining whether the defender could reasonably foresee harm to the pursuer's property.

Secondly, as we have seen, a delictual action for misrepresentation, at least, can be important if the contract has been retrospectively annulled as a result of rescission/reduction with the consequence that an action for breach of contract no longer exists.

Thirdly, the heads of loss recoverable in delict

may be different from those recoverable for breach of contract. If actions are available in both contract and delict, then the pursuer may be able to recover for losses not available in an action in contract per se. This is illustrated by the decision of the Lord Ordinary (Osborne) in *Black v Gibson*, 1992 SLT 1076. There the pursuer brought an action for breach of a building contract and also an action in delict for personal injuries sustained as a result of the defender's negligence. Lord Osborne held that the claim for damages in respect of the diminution in the value of the building and the cost of repairs etc was relevant to the claim in contract, and that a claim for solatium for anxiety, distress, worry and resultant illness was relevant as the pursuer was also suing in delict. Of course, the pursuer would have to establish that the defender owed him a duty of care under the general law of delictual liability for physical harm, and as we have seen the contractual relationship between the parties would be a relevant factor in establishing the reasonable foreseeability of harm criterion. A similar approach was taken by the Lord Ordinary (Kirkwood) in *Palmer v Beck*.

Finally, the measure of damages and remoteness tests are different in contract and delict. Sometimes it may be desirable for a pursuer to sue in contract to obtain damages for loss of his expectation interest; sometimes it will be advantageous to sue in delict to recover damages in order to return the pursuer to his/her position before the delict. Indeed, it is not clear whether, for example, in suing for fraudulent misrepresentation both of these interests can be recovered. Moreover, there may be advantages in suing in delict rather than contract — or vice versa — in relation to the remoteness of damages rules.

In short, there appear to be sound practical reasons why the possibility of delictual liability should be explored even if there is a direct contractual relationship between the parties.

Conclusion

At the outset of this paper, the question was posed whether parties to a contract may also have delictual remedies where the conduct giving rise to the breach has caused harm to the pursuer. The answer to that question is not simple.

The mere fact that A has a contract with B does not prevent B being liable in delict for personal injuries to A or harm to A's property, provided the reasonable foreseeability of harm criterion is satisfied. While this delictual obligation is independent of the parties' contract, the fact that the parties have a direct contractual relationship is a relevant — and, indeed, may be a crucial —

factor in deciding whether or not the reasonable foreseeability of harm criterion is satisfied, thus giving rise to a duty of care. Where, however, the delictual claim is for pure economic loss, while contractual structures may be important in creating a sufficient degree of proximity to give rise to a duty of care where the parties have no direct contractual nexus, if the parties have direct privity of contract there appears to be no room for delictual liability as there is no obligation — apart from the contract itself — to prevent economic loss arising as a result of a failure to take reasonable care to perform a contract. However, there is a duty of care not to cause economic loss as a result of fraudulent or negligent misrepresenta-

tion and this does apply between parties who have direct privity of contract: hitherto, a misrepresentation has been restricted to a pre-contractual statement, but if it could be argued that at least some terms of the contract are implied misrepresentations the dichotomy between contract and delict would be seriously undermined. But whatever the difficulties in relation to pure economic loss where the parties have a direct contractual relationship, it is important always to consider whether there is potential delictual liability for personal injury or harm to property, as there may be important practical advantages in being able to sue in delict in addition, or as an alternative, to an action for breach of contract.

◆

NEWS

Court

Sheriffdoms: North Strathclyde
Sessions in the sheriff courts for the disposal of civil business during 1994 will be held as follows: 6 January to 25 March; 25 April to 1 July; 29 August to 23 December.

Court days and times remain as previously published except that sittings at Campbeltown will begin at 10.30 am and not 9.30 am.

◇

Admission of solicitor advocates
The following solicitor advocates with rights of audience in the High Court of Justiciary have been admitted:

John Martin, procurator fiscal service, Dumfries; Roderick Williamson Urquhart, procurator fiscal service, Kilmarnock; Malcolm Macdonald Macleod, procurator fiscal service, Dumbarton; Patrick Wheatley of Patrick Wheatley & Co, Edinburgh; Elizabeth Cumming Munro, procurator fiscal service, Glasgow; George Edward Pollock of Pollock Stewart & Co, Stirling; Alexander Prentice of McCourts, Edinburgh; Francis Mulholland, Crown Office; Desmond John Finnieston of Franchi Finnieston, Glasgow; Anthony Quinn of Gordon & Smyth, Glasgow; Kenneth Maclean MacIver, procurator fiscal service, Edinburgh; Frank Richard Crowe, procurator fiscal service, Kirkcaldy, and John Stewart Fraser McInnes of Gilfedder & McInnes, Edinburgh.

— ◇ —

Coming events

Legal Services Agency seminars
Leasing legally, 17 February 1994; Race discrimination: the law, 25 February 1994; Disability appeal tribunals, 4 March 1994; Guardianship and the law, 17 March 1994; Criminal Injuries Compensation Board: the future, 28 March 1994 (Edinburgh); Community care: the law, one year on, 14 April 1994 (Edinburgh); Head injury, trauma and the law, 16 May 1994 (Edinburgh).

Seminars will be held at the Hospitality Inn, Cambridge Street, Glasgow, unless otherwise stated. Most seminars will last all day. Further details and booking forms can be obtained from Jamie Carrick, 11th Floor, Fleming House, 134 Renfrew Street, Cowcaddens, Glasgow G3 6ST (tel 041-353 3354; fax 041-353 0354).

— ◇ —

General

New year honours
Knights Bachelor — James Brown Highgate, CBE, consultant to Messrs Miller Beckett & Jackson, solicitors, Glasgow, for political and public service; Alexander Stone, OBE, consultant to Messrs Alexander Stone & Co, solicitors, Glasgow, for charitable services to the community in Scotland.

CB — Gordon Murray, Director, Scottish Courts Administration.

CBE — Douglas Reith, QC, lately deputy social security commissioner.

OBE — Hugh Findlay, regional sheriff clerk, Sheriffdom of South Strathclyde, Dumfries and Galloway; Alexander Lindsay Ingram, procurator fiscal, Forfar; Andrew Ogilvie Robertson, partner in Messrs T C Young & Son, solicitors, Glasgow, for legal services to the local housing movement; David Bruce Boyter Smith, chief executive, Dunfermline Building Society, for services to housing and to public life in Scotland.

◇

Scottish Law Librarians Group

Elections for the new Scottish Law Librarians Group committee (convener, secretary, treasurer plus four committee members) will take place at the 1994 a g m. Members are invited to submit nominations for the 1994-95 committee by 31 January 1994 to Christine Wilcox, Secretary, SLLG, c/o SSC Library, 11 Parliament Square, Edinburgh EH1 1RF, DX ED 209 Edinburgh 1 (tel 031-225 6268).

— ◇ —

Taxation

Income tax: personal residence rules

The Inland Revenue have published a revised edition of booklet IR20, "Residents and non-residents — liability to tax in the United Kingdom". This includes changes to take account of the amendment of the residence rules in the Finance Act 1993.

◇

Income tax: approved pension schemes

Regulations have been made by the Inland Revenue which will remove differences between tax and social security rules for occupational pension schemes.

The regulations ease the effect of legislation introduced by the 1987 and 1989 Finance Acts which overrides the trust deeds and rules of approved pension schemes. The main changes allow schemes to: (i) give people who retire because of ill health, pensions based on the length of service that could have been completed if they had not been forced to retire early; (ii) increase pensions to take account of the movements in the cost of living even where that would take the pension above the normal two thirds of final salary limit.

These are common features of occupational pension schemes and are allowed under the normal conditions for tax approval. The regulations therefore restore consistency between the tax approval rules for existing pension schemes and those that apply to new schemes.

The overriding legislation in the Finance Acts could also, in exceptional cases, cause problems for pension schemes in complying with social security rules. In particular, it could prevent schemes from complying with the arrangements for contracting out of the State Earnings Related Pension Scheme (SERPS), and the rules protecting the pensions of early leavers, which require the purchasing power of deferred pensions to be maintained. The regulations will remove this disparity between tax and social security rules. This accords with one of the recommendations of the recent report of the Pension Law Review Committee.

◇

Income tax: benefits in kind: cheap loans

Regulations came into force on 6 January 1994 to set the official rate of interest at 7.5 per cent from that date. This brings the official rate more closely into line with typical mortgage rates following their response to the fall in the bank base rate to 5.5 per cent on 23 November 1993.

◇

Capital gains tax: extra-statutory concessions

The Inland Revenue have published two new extra-statutory concessions relating to capital gains tax (CGT). These deal with rollover relief on depreciating assets, and relief for capital losses against income on the disposal of shares in an unquoted trading company, and take effect from 16 December 1993 for both new and open cases.

Roll over into depreciating assets
When an asset used in a trade is disposed of, roll-over relief allows tax on any gain made on the asset to be deferred if a new non-depreciating qualifying asset is purchased. The gain is not chargeable to tax until the new asset is disposed of. But, where a taxpayer rolls over a gain into a new asset, and subsequently dies still owning that asset, there is no CGT charge.

The rules for rolling over gains into depreciating assets — broadly those with a working life of 60 years or fewer — are different. In these cases, the gain which is rolled over is chargeable to capital gains tax on the earliest of one of three events: disposal of the asset; the point at which the asset ceases to be used in a trade by the claimant; and 10 years after the asset is acquired (s 154 of the Taxation of Chargeable Gains Act 1992).

The current rules mean that there will be a charge to tax when the taxpayer dies, since the asset will necessarily cease to be used in a trade by him or her. The new concession exempts these gains from tax.

Relief against income for capital losses on the disposal of unquoted shares in a trading company
Shareholders who have subscribed for unquoted shares in trading companies may be able to claim relief under ss 573-575 of the Income and Corporation Taxes Act 1988 if capital losses arise when they dispose of the shares. Among the conditions for the relief are that the disposal is made on a distribution in the course of the winding up or dissolution of the company, or involves an arms length bargain or a claim that the shares have negligible value under s 24 (2) of the Taxation of Chargeable Gains Act 1992. In some cases, none of the conditions will be satisfied, and relief will not be due. Similarly, relief for the original cost of shares may be restricted where a number of interim distributions are made as part of a winding up or dissolution, but no final distribution is made.

The concession will allow relief to run under ss 573-575 in cases where a company without assets is dissolved, and either no distribution is made during winding up or no final distribution is made, provided the other conditions for relief in ss 573 and 574 are met.

◇

Inland Revenue interest regulations
An order of the Board of Inland Revenue was issued on 15 December 1993 specifying that in accordance with the relevant regulations the rate of interest charged on tax paid late and paid in respect of tax overpaid has decreased from 6.25 to 5.5 per cent. The rate in respect of inheritance tax has decreased from 5 per cent to 4 per cent.

The rate of interest charged (under s 87A of the Taxes Management Act 1970) on unpaid corporation tax is 5.5 per cent; and the rate of interest paid (under s 826 of the Income and Corporation Taxes Act 1988) on overpaid corporation tax is 2.5 per cent. The rate of interest on tax paid late and overpaid tax takes account of the tax treatment of interest and repayment supplement.

The new rates will take effect from 6 January 1994 whether or not interest has already started to run before that date.

— ◇ —

Parliamentary News

Questions answered
HOUSE OF COMMONS

16 December 1993
SHERIFF COURT FEES
Sir David Steel: To ask the Secretary of State for Scotland if he will reconsider the proposed increases in sheriff court fees; and what representations he has received from the Law Society on this matter.

Mr Lang: The changes to sheriff court fees, which are projected to lead to an overall 12 per cent increase in income, are included in the Sheriff Court Fees Amendment (No 2) Order 1993 which was laid before Parliament on 10 December.

My noble and learned Friend has received a number of representations from the Law Society of Scotland to which he has responded clarifying the basis of the changes.

17 December 1993
SHRIEVAL BENCH VACANCIES
Mr McFall: To ask the Secretary of State for Scotland how many applications were received following the intimation for two judicial vacancies on the shrieval bench in the *Scots Law Times*; and how many applicants were female.

Lord James Douglas-Hamilton: Applications specifically resulting from the intimation in the *Scots Law Times* numbered 11, of which four were from female candidates.

 — ◇ —

Book Review

Business FactSheets
A new series has been launched providing basic information and advice on small business needs in 36 selected areas, grouped under the headings Starting up, Marketing, Buying and Selling, Tax, Finance, Premises, Management, Computers, and Law (with the titles "Business Law and using a solicitor", and "Employment"). Each factsheet contains a structured set of key points to be borne in mind before embarking on a course of action.

The complete series costs £100 including p & p, reduced to £72 until 28 February 1994. The publishers are Business Hotline Publications Ltd, 120-126 Lavender Avenue, Mitcham, Surrey CR4 3HP (tel 081-640 7806).

ARTICLES

Adoption: The Child's View

Elaine E Sutherland,
Senior Lecturer,
The School of Law,
University of Glasgow.

Both in Scotland and in England a court has approved the withholding of information as to parentage from a child in the course of adoption. Ms Sutherland argues that the courts should not sanction such deception, which may be more detrimental to the child in the longer term.

At first sight, Scots law appears to take a reasonable approach to the role of the child concerned in consenting to or expressing views about his or her own adoption. Where the child is 12 years old or over, his or her consent to the adoption must be obtained if the adoption is to proceed. Where the child is incapable of giving consent, the court can dispense with it (Age of Legal Capacity (Scotland) Act 1991, s 2 (3)), but, that special case aside, the child's right to consent to or veto his or her own adoption from the age of 12 is absolute. Unlike that of the parents (Adoption (Scotland) Act 1978, s 16 (2) (b): see *P v Lothian Regional Council*, 1989 SLT 739; *Lothian Regional Council v A*, 1992 SLT 858), the child's refusal to consent cannot be overridden by the court on the basis of a reasonableness test.

Where the child is below the age of 12, the court is directed to ascertain the child's wishes and feelings about the proposed adoption, so far as that is practicable, and to "give due consideration to them, having regard to [the child's] age and understanding" (1978 Act, s 6). Similar provisions apply to consent to an application freeing the child for adoption.

On the face of it, all of this is in accordance with the requirement found in art 12 of the United Nations Convention on the Rights of the Child, that:

"1. States Parties shall assure to the child who is capable of forming his or her own views the right to express those views freely in all matters affecting the child, the views of the child being given due weight in accordance with the age and maturity of the child.

"2. For this purpose the child shall in particular be provided the opportunity to be heard in any judicial and administrative proceedings affecting the child, either directly or through a representative or an appropriate body, in a manner consistent with the procedural rules of national law."

However, two points raise questions about the extent to which we take the matter of children's views seriously. The first concerns the practice of how the child's consent or wishes and feelings are ascertained. The second, more fundamental problem, concerns children giving views or consent based on erroneous facts, where the error is a product of deception by the adults and the court involved in the particular case.

The practice

Prior to the petition coming before the court, a report from the local authority or adoption agency will be prepared (1978 Act, ss 22 and 23) and a curator ad litem and reporting officer will be appointed and report (1978 Act, s 58). This provides an opportunity for those reporting to discuss the matter with the child alone and ascertain the child's views. When the case gets to court, the child will be seen in chambers by the sheriff and it is apparently the practice of some sheriffs to allow the applicants to be present throughout the interview with the child. Clearly, the intention here is to avoid upsetting the child by placing him or her alone in a room with a complete stranger, but how freely can a child express opposition to the adoption in such circumstances? It can be argued that it places the child in an impossible position and one which denies him or her an effective opportunity to express a view. Take, for example, the common case of a joint adoption application by a birth parent and stepparent. If the child were to express opposition to the adoption, he or she would face the prospect of returning to live in a household with both applicants who would then be aware of what the child had said.

Many sheriffs do see children alone in adoption and other proceedings and, so far as the writer is aware, the children do not suffer undue distress. Failing an interview alone, it must be possible to find someone other than the applicants to be present and with whom the child (and the sheriff) would feel comfortable. It is imperative that the child be given the opportunity to discuss the whole matter freely and openly.

Consent in a climate of deception

Perhaps greater concern should focus on the cases where a child is invited to express views about the prospective adoption, but is misled about crucial background information. In 1988, the Court of Appeal had the opportunity to consider the prospect of adoption taking place in a climate of deception. In *Re S (a minor)* [1988] 1 FLR 418, the application concerned a 13 year old girl, S, who had been born and previously adopted as a baby in California. In accordance with Californian law, a new birth certificate showing the adopters as parents was issued and S grew up unaware of the adoption. The adopters' marriage was dissolved and S and her adoptive mother moved to England where the latter remarried. S's adoptive father took no further interest in her. S believed her adoptive mother to be her birth mother, that woman's first husband to be her birth father, and treated the second husband as a stepfather. The adoption application before the English courts was made by the adoptive mother and her second husband and the applicants made it clear that they had no intention of telling S the truth about the first adoption unless she sought to trace the first husband or some third party threatened to disclose the truth.

At first instance, the application was refused by the judge because of the applicants' refusal to tell S the truth, although he took no steps to ascertain S's wishes. It is submitted that this was the correct approach. It was not possible to ascertain S's wishes since she was being denied crucial information on which to base them. However, on appeal, the application was granted. The Court of Appeal took the view that S's interests were best served by the adoption and that, while the county court judge was entitled to find it in her best interests that she should know the truth, the adoptive mother was entitled to take a different point of view and, furthermore, the judge had erred in failing to consult S. With respect, this smacks of woolly thinking. If S's wishes mattered, and it is submitted that they did, then what they were in the light of the true facts is what should have been sought.

This writer expressed the hope that the Scottish courts would not have taken the same view as did the Court of Appeal (*The Laws of Scotland: Stair Memorial Encyclopaedia*, Vol 10, "Family Law", para 1197). While in England and Wales it was only the child's wishes and feelings that had to be taken into account, in Scotland, at the time, a minor had the right to consent to or to veto his or her own adoption (Adoption (Scotland) Act 1978, s 12 (8)), just as all young people of or over the age of 12 have that power now. It is hard to imagine that a Scottish court would interpret "consent" in the context of adoption as meaning anything other than what it means in the general law, but the effect of error on consent in adoption has at least two possible parallels. On the one hand, induced error is a ground for avoiding a contract. On the other hand, error only renders a marriage void where it relates to the identity and not the quality of the other party (*Lang v Lang*, 1920 2 SLT 353; 1921 SC 44; see Clive, *Husband*

and Wife (3rd ed), at pp 86-90). It can be argued that error as to one's relationship with an adopter is one of quality and not identity. This provides for interesting academic debate about reduction, but the practical point is that courts are not being asked to consider reduction, they are being asked to participate in deception. That is something they can and should avoid doing.

What one Scottish court was prepared to do when required to take a child's wishes and feelings into account was made clear in the recent decision in *C, Petrs*, 1993 SLT (Sh Ct) 8. The case concerned the adoption of a six year old boy, C, and the applicants were his mother and her husband, who was not C's father. C's mother and the male applicant had had a relationship prior to his conception and had married two weeks after his birth. In between, C's mother had had a brief relationship with C's father but had not seen him since she was two months pregnant and had no contact with him. C believed the applicants to be his birth parents and they had no intention of ever telling him the truth. The social work department felt unable to provide the report required by s 22 of the 1978 Act because the refusal to disclose the true facts to C made it impossible to ascertain his wishes and feelings. The court appointed a reporting officer and curator ad litem who duly submitted a report dealing with the family circumstances and the applicants' reasons for not wishing to disclose the truth to the child. The court found that it was not practicable to ascertain the wishes and feelings of the child and granted the adoption petition.

To grant a petition in such circumstances is a regrettable reflection on taking the views of children seriously. To say that it is not practicable to ascertain a child's views simply because adults with an interest choose to deceive the child is, it is submitted, to misunderstand the statutory provisions. These words are intended to cover cases where the child is too young to form or express a view. It may be considered naïve to say so, but courts are about trying to get to the truth and should not become parties to deception, however good the motive. Nor was the court without another avenue in this case. It would have been quite possible to deal with the situation by using the Children Act 1975, s 53 (1). That provides that, in refusing an adoption petition, the court can award custody to the applicants instead. Usually, its advantage lies in the recognition given to the step-parent's role in the child's life without the termination of the child's legal link with the other parent. Here it could simply recognise the step-parent's role without further muddying the waters and deceiving the child.

It is submitted that the correct course for any court faced with the sort of case described above is to refuse the petition and consider whether or not an award of custody is appropriate. If the applicants do not feel that this meets their needs adequately, the solution is in their hands. They can always tell the child the truth, a truth that he or she will inevitably discover later on when birth records are required.

But what of the case of a child conceived in the course of rape or incest? Can it be in a child's interests to know the truth in such a case? It would be too easy to reply that hard cases make bad law. However, such cases would not necessarily give rise to assertions that someone was a parent when that was not so. The mother is hardly likely to be applying to adopt along with the father in such a case. Nonetheless, there could be a desire by the mother to withhold information about paternity. That she should try to do so is no less a denial of the child's right to be informed. In any event, the problematic information is known to the mother and probably other individuals. Skeletons of that kind have an unhappy knack of coming out of cupboards, often in the course of an argument, and that risk can hardly serve a child's interests. Recent evidence suggests that, at least in the context of incest, it is the deception rather than the facts which causes the child distress when the truth is discovered later (McWhinnie and Batty, *Children of Incest: Whose secret is it?* (BAAF, 1993)).

Opportunity not to be missed

In their *Report on Family Law* (Scot Law Com no 135, 1992), the Scottish Law Commission made the following general recommendations on the place of a child's views: that rules of court should provide a mechanism for the views of a child involved being put before the court; that the court should take those views into account in reaching its decision in the light of the child's age and understanding; and that there should be a statutory presumption that every child of or above the age of 12 is capable of expressing his or her own views (draft Family Law (Scotland) Bill, cl 12 (5) and (6)). The implementation of these recommendations would go some way towards addressing the first, procedural, problem highlighted here, by ensuring that whatever mechanism is devised affords every child the opportunity to express views freely and honestly. It might not solve the second problem if courts persist in believing that a child's views can be ascertained where these apparent views are based on falsehood.

The most thoroughgoing examination of adoption law since the concept of adoption was introduced in 1930 is currently nearing completion. The white paper for England and Wales, *Adoption: The Future* (Cm 2288, 1993) has just been published and, while it recognises that the child's wishes and feelings should be ascertained, it does not address the point about deception (para 2.6). Equivalent proposals for Scotland can be expected shortly. The most recent consultation document, *The Future of Adoption Law in Scotland*, issued by the Social Work Services Group last year, recommended no change to the current law on a child's consent in the context of adoption (para 6.6).

Given the approach taken by courts north and south of the border, it is imperative that future legislation should make clear that, in the context of adoption, consent means the same as it does in other areas of the law: that is, consent based on the truth. In the case of a younger child, where it is simply the child's wishes and feelings which are being assessed, the same principle applies and we must stop insulting children by suggesting that something less will do.

◆

NEWS

Editorial

Readers will have noticed that the weekly cumulative index ("the blue index") now includes a section covering the News/articles to date as well as the Reports.

This is only one aspect of a more fundamental change to the blue index required as a result of the massive expansion of the Reports in line with the growth in reportable case law.

With over 1,350 pages of decisions from the Supreme Courts published in 1993 (plus sheriff court, Land Court and Lands Tribunal reports), maintaining a weekly cumulative index covering the full year to date has become a very cumbersome exercise. We therefore propose in 1994 to publish a separate cumulative index after every tenth issue and index only those issues published thereafter in the blue index.

Thus after 25 issues a reader wishing to search the year to date would consult the separate cumulative index covering issues 1-20 and the blue index in issue 25 for issues 21-24, using, as at present, the contents page of issue 25 for material in that issue. The News section will now be indexed from week to week in the same way, the change described above enabling us to provide a more comprehensive indexing service in the course of the year, to the benefit, we hope, of all our readers.

General

Data protection: code of practice
The Association of British Insurers has produced a data protection code of practice. The code refers to personal information covered by the Data Protection Act 1984. It has been developed following detailed discussions with the Data Protection Registrar. The registrar will take into account the manner in which insurers have complied with the code in looking at any complaints received against insurance companies.

The 1984 Act gave people who have information about them held on computers a right of access to that information, and the right to have inaccurate information corrected or erased. Insurance companies are required to keep the Data Protection Registrar informed on how they use the information they have about their policyholders.

Further information can be obtained from the Association of British Insurers, 51 Gresham Street, London EC2V 7HQ (tel 071-600 3333; fax 071-696 8999).

Obituaries

On 14 January 1994, John Kenneth Finlayson, WS, formerly senior partner in the firm of Messrs Bonar Mackenzie, WS.

On 16 January 1994, Ian Stewart McCall, WS, Edinburgh.

Business changes

The Society of Messengers at Arms and Sheriff Officers will move to new premises at 54 Carlton Place (ground floor), Glasgow, on Tuesday, 1 February 1994. The society's telephone number from that date will be 041-420 3926 and its fax number will change to 041-420 3927. With effect from 1 February 1994, solicitors requiring the

services of an officer of court for urgent business outwith normal hours can make contact with a society representative by telephoning the new number.

Messrs Murray Beith & Murray, WS, 39 Castle Street, Edinburgh, intimate that Mr Michael Gordon Robson, SSC, has been assumed a partner of the firm with effect from 1 February 1994. The firm also announce that Andrew Douglas Stewart Lothian, solicitor, and Sandra Elizabeth Taylor, solicitor, have been appointed as associates in the litigation and personal law departments respectively, also with effect from 1 February 1994.

Messrs Miller Samuel & Co, solicitors, RWF House, 5 Renfield Street, Glasgow, announce that Christine McMenamin and John McQuillan have been assumed as partners of the firm with effect from 1 January 1994.

Pagan Osborne Grace & Calders, Cupar, St Andrews, Anstruther and Dundee, intimate that with effect from 1 February 1994 the firm name will change to "Pagan Osborne".

Parliamentary News

New Bills
HOUSE OF COMMONS

11 January 1994

Human rights—To provide protection to individuals and in the courts of the United Kingdom for the rights and freedoms specified in the European Convention of Human Rights and Fundamental Freedoms; to entrench those rights and freedoms; to establish a Human Rights Commission; to make further provision with regard to the protection of civil, political, economic and social rights; and for connected purposes. (Private Member's Bill introduced by Mr Graham Allen)

Hedgerows—For the protection and maintenance of boundary hedges, hedges bordering footpaths, bridleways and highways and other hedgerows and thorn fences. (Private Member's Bill introduced by Mr Peter Hardy)

12 January 1994

Social Security (Incapacity for Work)—To provide for incapacity benefit in place of sickness benefit and invalidity benefit; to make provision as to the test of incapacity for work for the purposes of that benefit and other social security purposes; to make provision as to the rate of statutory sick pay; to make other amendments as to certain allowances payable to a person who is or has been incapable of work; and for connected purposes. (Government)

Progress of Bills

Criminal Justice and Public Order — Commons: second reading, 11 January 1994.

Non-Domestic Rating — Commons: second reading, 12 January 1994. Remaining stages, 13 January 1994.

Licensing of Domiciliary Care Agencies — Lords: Second reading, 17 January 1994.

Local Government Etc (Scotland) — Commons: Second reading, 17 January 1994.

Coal Industry — Commons: Second reading, 18 January 1994.

Police and Magistrates' Courts — Lords: Second reading, 18 January 1994.

Inshore Fishing (Scotland) — Lords: Third reading, 20 January 1994.

Local Government (Wales) — Lords: Committee stage concluded, 20 January 1994.

Mental Health (Amendment) — Lords: Second reading, 20 January 1994.

New Towns (Amendment) — Lords: Third reading, 20 January 1994.

Book Reviews

How to Apply for a Legal Aid Franchise

By Martin Davies. 1993. London: Blackstone Press. Paperback, £14.95. ISBN 1 85431 303 7.

Relax — it is an English book. But just as someone must have said in a wine bar somewhere in London — "Poll tax — Na . . . it'll never come 'ere", this book could be a harbinger.

Relax, but do not be complacent, for if franchising "works" it might come here. Even if it does not, many of the things required of the potential franchisee are very good things that would help a legal business. This may be the first time some readers have been provoked to think of these issues. Already reviews have appeared of some similar books (see 1992 SLT (News) 176) and a review has also appeared of the first management book for solicitors written with the Scottish solicitor in mind (Mill and Allingham): see 1993 SLT (News) 73. Solicitors in the company commercial sector have been aware of the need for similar management controls through BS5750 and ISO9000. This is the first time the ordinary little firm (in England just now) doing lots of legal aid is faced with the issue of management as a survival rather than an educational issue.

Optimistically the book tells us that the franchise requirements are reasonable, imposing management standards that should have been adopted anyway. An overall business plan is required as is an office manual. All this work for a franchise which turns out not to be anything like a car dealership. It is not exclusive in area and there is no fixed number of franchisees (yet?). It is not (yet?) compulsory. There are however carrots and sticks. If you become a franchisee then you get devolved powers (strictly controlled, supervised and recorded) to award legal aid yourself and much more money "up front". It is thus as empowering as it is apparently threatening. The improvements in structure may themselves mean twice as much profit per partner, according to a report in the book of a study by accountants, and avoidance of the wasted 20 per cent of time most non-managed firms spend on correcting errors. There is a variety of the kite mark — the franchising logo. To have it will be a plus, not to have it may have to be explained to the more consumerist clients.

The burdens are considerable, just as with BS5750 or TQM. There has to be a franchise partner who may in turn become the franchise representative. It will be essential to have an employee suitably qualified to recognise the need for welfare benefits advice. Sometimes thought a Cinderella subject, if franchising comes to Scotland welfare law will soon be at the ball. To your reviewer's knowledge, one Glasgow law firm already offers free welfare benefits advice.

The author spends a long time justifying the business plan requirement, not just because you have to have one for the franchise but because a firm should have one anyway. He does this brilliantly, but it would certainly be worth looking at the more detailed treatment of many of these issues in Mill and Allingham as well. These issues will include management, finance, technology, people (the term "human resource management" used in the graduate business schools is avoided, no doubt because it smacks of the jargon that experienced lawyers becoming tyro managers loathe) and marketing (of which advertising is but a small aspect). You will have to buy the book to read all the helpful hints. Staff appraisal is required, but not that of partners. It probably should be introduced for partners as well. It would assist one of the other useful management objectives mentioned by Mr Davies in relation to partners: "If someone is underperforming then they need to be told and given the opportunity to do something about the situation.

If nothing can be done then they should be asked to leave" (p 9). This sort of statement puts a certain kind of person off the whole idea of management, let alone appraisal.

One of the crafty things about the management quality movement is its cascading momentum. Some of the company commercial firms have investigated BS5750 and the like because their clients are committed to using only those services that offer these standards. And so it is with the franchise. A register of experts and counsel must be kept and the entries regularly assessed. There will ultimately be implications, perhaps, even for the bar whose members would appear on these registers.

The meat is in the 10 rules for handling legal aid files. Many Scottish legal aid firms would meet these as systems stand. In the same way the detailed rules on taking instructions, progressing and concluding cases will not be considered onerous by many firms. Transaction criteria are a little more worrying. The aim is to produce criteria that a non-lawyer could check to see if things generally in the firm as a whole are moving properly. All the systems must actually be applied and will be independently audited — it is not just a "paper" system.

It might never happen here.

W J STEWART.

Constitutional and Administrative Law

(Wade & Bradley)

Eleventh edition. By A W Bradley and K D Ewing. 1993. London: Longman. Paperback, £25. ISBN 0582 082 390.

The appearance of the 11th edition of Wade and Bradley is to be welcomed. Since the 10th edition was published in 1985 there have been several significant developments and the 11th edition covers most of these.

The constitutional relationship between the EC and the UK rightly receives a fuller treatment than in the 10th edition. Also, with many developments in the field of state security and official secrecy since the last edition, the thorough treatment of the Interception of Communications Act 1985, the Security Service Act 1989, the Official Secrets Act 1989 and the Prevention of Terrorism (Temporary Provisions) Act 1989 in chaps 24 and 25 is welcome. However, virtually nothing is said about the constitutional position of the Secret Intelligence Service, which is disappointing given the coverage devoted to the other security agencies.

Some changes in the 11th edition are disappointing. There is no longer a chapter on local government, as there was in the 10th edition. This is perhaps an inevitable reflection of the changing face of public administration, with privatised bodies and non-governmental organisations (which merit a separate chapter) having increased responsibility for public administration.

From a Scottish perspective, the discussion in chap 5, "Parliamentary Supremacy", of the recent cases which challenged the community charge on the basis that it contravened the Act of Union is regrettably limited. Devolution, which merited a separate chapter in the 10th edition, is now included in chap 3, "The Structure of the UK". While this may be more logical, it is disappointing that the treatment of devolution remains virtually unchanged from the 10th edition given the proposals of the Scottish Constitutional Convention, which merit no more than a footnote. This perhaps reflects a waning interest in the subject following the Conservative election victory in 1992.

While the discussion of administrative law is still from an English perspective, the substantive grounds of judicial review are essentially the same in Scotland. The discussion of proportionality and legitimate expectations as grounds of judicial review in chap 29 is welcome. Chapter 30 almost exclusively deals with English administrative law remedies, although Scots remedies do receive a longer treatment than they did in the 10th edition as a result of the introduction of the new judicial review procedure in 1985 and the important case *West v Secretary of State for Scotland*, 1992 SLT 636, which is welcome.

This edition has a partly changed structure. Part I, previously entitled "General Constitutional Law", has been divided in this edition into Part I, "General Principles of Constitutional Law", and Part II, "The Institutions of Government". The other Parts remain the same. While this division improves the overall formal structure, the allocation of chapters within it is less satisfactory. For example, the treatment of the police is puzzling. While it is logical to include a discussion of police powers in Part III, "The Citizen and the State", it is less logical to discuss the police as an institution there. On this basis it is hard to see why the armed forces are discussed in Part II rather than Part III where the use of troops in Northern Ireland and martial law is covered.

The new edition remains an invaluable work especially for students of constitutional and administrative law.

MARK POUSTIE,
University of Strathclyde.

ARTICLES

Recovery of Documents — New Rules?

William Holligan,
Brodies, WS,
Edinburgh.

In Scottish litigation the conventional method of recovery of documents has been by way of commission and diligence following approval by the court of a specification setting out certain classes of documents of which recovery is sought. For the last few years, Court of Session procedure has, in the case of commercial causes and optional procedure, seen an innovation on the existing rules of procedure. The purpose of this article is to explore some of the issues raised by these rules.

It has always been a significant distinction between Scottish and common law procedures that the Scottish practitioner is relieved of the burden of discovery of documents. In English procedure, a party to a litigation is, in general, obliged to disclose (discover) to all other parties to the litigation all documents in his possession which are relevant to the issues in the litigation. Indeed, it is the obligation of that party's solicitor, as an officer of court, to ensure that full disclosure of relevant documents is made by his client.

The procedure itself requires that a party produce a list of documents setting out the various documents which he has to produce. The other parties to the litigation are then entitled to inspect the documents referred to in the list (see Halsbury (4th ed), sub nom "Discovery").

Such a procedure is foreign to the Scottish practitioner. Certainly, a party usually lodges in process documents incorporated into the pleadings as part of that party's case (Rule of Court 78 (d) was amended in 1990 to omit the obligation to lodge documents; this was re-enacted in rule 134E), but, until forced to do so, after commission procedure, a Scottish litigant is not obliged to offer up his own documents. (For a discussion of commission procedure see Walkers on *Evidence*, chap 32.)

Clearly, rules 151C (commercial causes) and 188K (optional procedure) call for a new approach (see also rule 260B (8): judicial review). It is worth setting out the relevant parts of these rules in full:

Rule 151C (1): "Within 28 days of an interlocutor allowing a proof or proof before answer, each party to a commercial action shall intimate to every other party a list of the documents relating to the matters at issue between them which are, or to the best of his knowledge have been, in his possession or control."

Rule 188K (1): "Without prejudice to Rule 188M, within 14 days of the interlocutor pronouncing an order for a proof or proof before answer, each party to the action shall intimate to every other party and lodge in process— (a) a list of the documents which are, or to the best of his knowledge have been, in his possession or control relating to the matters in issue between them; (b) a note stating the whereabouts so far as known to him of any such documents which have been but are no longer in his possession."

Reference has already been made to the English practice of discovery. When one examines the relevant English rule of practice (Order 24, rule 1) the similarity between rules 151C and 188K is obvious: "After the close of pleadings in an action begun by writ there shall, subject to and in accordance with the provisions of this Order, be discovery by the parties to the action of the documents which are or have been in their possession, custody or power relating to matters in question in the action."

So far as the writer has been able to establish, there are no Court of Session authorities giving guidance as to what the Scottish rules envisage. A few obvious points emerge.

(a) What are matters in or at issue?

As both rules apply after any adjustment of the pleadings has taken place, determining what constitute the matters at issue will, presumably, be done by reference to the pleadings. Matters which are expressly denied are clearly an issue; conversely matters the subject of admission are not. Something which is stated to be not known and not admitted ought to be treated as an issue in dispute, at least for the purposes of production of documents.

However, once one identifies the issues by reference to the pleadings, how far is a party obliged to go, bearing in mind that he carries the obligation of disclosing his documents?

Take the following example. Assume a commercial dispute concerning a sale of goods case. A sells to B a quantity of goods which B then fails to pay for, alleging that they are not fit for their purpose. There will probably have been many letters, telexes, faxes, notes of meetings concerning the alleged failure of the goods. The seller will have technical data concerning the goods' manufacture and possibly other quality control information. In short, there is likely to be a lot of documentation which is "relevant" in a broad sense to the whole dispute. It may be inconvenient for the unpaid seller to disclose it — it may damage his case — but it is certainly useful and relevant to the conduct of the litigation. To the English practitioner there is little room for doubt, the matter being clearly set out in the judgment of Brett LJ in the case of *Compagnie Financiere du Pacifique v Peruvian Guano Co* (1882) 11 QBD 55 (see also *O'Rourke v Darbishire* [1920] AC 851).

The plaintiffs in *Compagnie Financiere* sued the defendants for breach of contract arising out of an alleged contract for the supply of guano. The defendants denied that agents acting on their behalf had the authority to reach any agreement and claimed that, in any event, negotiations had continued beyond the date relied upon by the plaintiffs as being the date upon which the negotiations were concluded. The plaintiffs made discovery but the defendants sought further and better discovery, seeking recovery of documents created subsequent to the date of the alleged breach of contract. It is clear that the plaintiffs' documents, postdating the alleged conclusion of the contract, would do nothing to advance the plaintiffs' own case and, if produced, could only help the defendants' case in showing that the alleged contract was truly the subject of continuing negotiation. In upholding the defendants' argument for further and better discovery from the plaintiffs Brett LJ said (at p 62):

"The doctrine seems to me to go farther than that and to go as far as the principle which I am about to lay down. It seems to me that every document relates to the matters in question in the action, which not only would be evidence upon any issue, but also which, it is reasonable to suppose, contains information which may — not which must — either directly or indirectly enable the party requiring the affidavit either to advance his own case or to damage the case of his adversary. I have put in the words 'either directly or indirectly' because, as it seems to me, a document can properly be said to contain information which may enable the party requiring the affidavit either to advance his own case or to damage the case of his adversary, if it is a document which may fairly lead to a train of enquiry, which may have either of these two consequences".

If a similar approach in Scotland is adopted then two consequences follow. First, a party complying with the rule is obliged to produce all documents whether or not these specifically advance his case. He may not "fillet" files and select only those documents which he considers are in his best interest to produce. Secondly, the concept of "matters in issue" is broad. On one view, using the above example, every document which relates to the transaction in question is relevant. The crucial point is a document which

may lead to a train of inquiry — a very broad test. In the example of the sale of goods case, it may cover a great deal of documentation.

(b) What is possession or control?
The rules predicate a distinction between "possession" and "control". A document may not be in the possession of a party but yet may be under his control. The rules suggest that the party must do more than look upon himself as being a "haver" in the sense of holding the documents personally. For example, the employer may have to search for documents within his employee's possession which relate to "matters in issue". There may be documents in the hands of a third party (an agent or adviser) which may have to be obtained on the basis that the relationship between the party and that agent or adviser places the documents under the former's "control".

(c) What of documents no longer in the party's control?
Although slightly differently phrased, both rules 188K and 151C impose an obligation to disclose relevant documents which are no longer in the party's possession. Rule 188K makes this expressly clear — rule 151C is less clear but it is submitted that the use of the words "are . . . or have been" must include documents which the party no longer has.

At first blush it does seem rather odd to require a party to identify something he does not have. However, there may well be circumstances where owing to some misfortune a crucial document no longer exists, or, alternatively, the document may now have been put beyond the possession or control of the party who once had it. Yet its existence may be essential to the case.

That places upon the solicitor advising the party a responsibility to ensure that his client realises that this is not simply a question of disclosing documents which the client has at present. The rules themselves do not show how such documents should be described, but it is suggested that the most appropriate way to deal with it is to set aside a separate part of the list of documents, identifying the documents which were but are no longer in the party's possession or control which are relevant to the matters in issue.

(d) Enforcement
One of the most curious features of both rules is their silence on the question of enforcement. One might be forgiven for thinking that, considering the relative innovation brought about by these rules, there ought to be an express provision to secure their compliance.

Up to now the Scottish rules have been contrasted with their English equivalent, if only because of the clear similarities between the particular rules themselves and as a useful comparison to show the way in which a similar rule has been interpreted in England. However, there is a limit to which analogies can be drawn. The conceptual origins of the rules of discovery in England are entirely different from Scotland. Although the English rules envisage a solicitor of the court ensuring his client's compliance with the rules of discovery, there is nothing expressly stated in the Scottish rules to that effect.

If one party to the litigation suspects that the other has not made full disclosure of all relevant documents there are two possibilities: (a) a motion brought pursuant to the relevant rule itself, or (b) a more traditional specification of documents.

In the case of the former it could be argued that the recovering party is doing nothing other than asking the court to secure compliance with its own rules. Procedure would be by way of motion seeking an order that the other party intimate a list of documents relating to certain specific classes of documents referred to either in the motion itself or in a separate document. The matter would then be argued by reference to those documents already intimated in the list and the closed record.

The alternative method is expressly preserved in both rules but there is one important issue. Does one determine the extent of the recovery by reference to the relevant rules themselves, or does one do so by reference to the more restrictive test which relates to commission and diligence for the recovery of documents? (For an interesting comparison see *Campbell v John Laing Construction Ltd*, 1992 GWD 36-2146, and *McInally v John Wyeth & Brother Ltd*, 1992 SLT 344.) It would certainly seem odd if one were to find that the demand for the recovery of documents under (b) was to be determined more restrictively than a demand under (a).

(e) Procedure

The rules provide (as do their counterparts in England) that the documents should be set out in a list. The other parties are entitled to copies of the documents referred to in the list. If one party insists upon production of an original rather than a copy then he can proceed by way of a traditional commission and diligence, lodging the recovery in process as a production.

Another curious blank in the Scottish procedure is the use to which any recoveries may be put. In the ordinary course of events the documents may be used as productions either relied on by witnesses in their evidence in chief or as cross examination material.

Sheriff Macphail states: "The documents cannot be used as productions in another process, or for any other purposes than those of the action in which they are produced" (*Sheriff Court Practice*, para 15-80). No authority is cited in support of the proposition but, as a statement in principle, it certainly ought to be correct.

However, there may be circumstances in which a party may legitimately wish to use a document in commencing other proceedings. There is no clear authority to state what sanction exists for use of a document outwith the particular proceedings nor whether, and in what circumstances, the court has power to release a party from any such obligations which may be incumbent upon parties and their advisers.

Perhaps the most obvious illustration of this issue concerns intellectual property actions. It is not uncommon for the holder of intellectual property rights to mount an exercise to seize documents and property in the hands of an alleged infringer pursuant to s 1 of the Administration of Justice (Scotland) Act 1972 (see, e g *British Phonographic Industry Ltd v Cohen*, 1983 SLT 137). Such a procedure is done by way of petition. The principal purpose of the exercise is to preserve the evidence pending further proceedings between the same parties. But what happens if the petitioner discovers documents which involve the infringement of other parties' rights? Can he disclose the content of the documents to that party — can he report the matter to the prosecuting authorities if the conduct is criminal?

An interesting example of this arose in the case of *EMI Records Ltd v Spillane* [1986] 1 WLR 967; [1986] 2 All ER 1016. A firm of solicitors was in possession of certain documents following the carrying out of a "search and seize" order against certain defendants. The plaintiffs alleged breach of copyright. Shortly thereafter the solicitors received a demand from the Commissioners of Customs and Excise calling upon the solicitors to produce the documents seized by the civil action to enable the commissioners to conduct an inquiry as to the defendant's liability to VAT. The solicitors refused and brought the matter before the court seeking directions. The court held that the solicitors were correct in not handing over the documents on the grounds that where documents are recovered pursuant to the court's procedure for discovery, the solicitor is under an implied obligation, personal to the solicitor, not to use the documents for any purpose not connected with the action in which discovery is given.

The point of the personal liability of the solicitor is further emphasised by the leading case of *Harman v Home Office* [1983] 1 AC 280. The action concerned proceedings for contempt of court against a solicitor for breach inter alia of the implied undertaking not to use documents for any purpose other than the particular litigation. The main case involved an action by a plaintiff against the Home Office during his treatment in an experimental "control unit". Certain confidential documents produced by the Home Office were read out in open court. The solicitor later handed copies of the documents to a journalist who had been present during the hearing. The journalist was preparing a feature article. By a majority, the House of Lords held that the solicitor was in contempt, notwithstanding the fact that the documents had been read out in open court.

The Scottish position is not clear. The courts have recently taken a strict view of the use of s 1 procedures (*Dominion Technology Ltd v Gardner Cryogenics Ltd (No 2)*, 1993 SLT 832) and the use to which confidential reports may be put (*Hunter v Douglas Reyburn & Co Ltd*, 1993 SLT 637). In the latter case Lord Penrose held that if confidentiality existed in a report prepared for a particular litigation, such a quality did not fly off on completion of the litigation. However, the rules themselves seem curiously silent on this issue.

(f) Sheriff court rules

The new Ordinary Cause Rules are a fairly radical departure from previous Scottish practice and reflect the court's determination to take a much more interventionist role in the conduct of litigation.

The new rules anticipate a standard procedure which will apply to the majority of cases unless the alternative procedure in chap 10 is held to apply.

Rule 9.13 (1) provides: "Each party shall, within 14 days after the date of the interlocutor allowing a proof or proof before answer, intimate to every other party a list of the documents, which are or have been in his possession or control which he intends to use or put in evidence at the proof, including the whereabouts of those documents."

The odd thing about the rule (which applies to standard procedure) is that it appears to limit the obligation to list documents to those which that party intends to use at the proof. It is in markedly different terms from Court of Session rules 151C and 188K. The obligation is only to disclose documents which the party intends to use or put in evidence at the proof. If that is correct then it is hard to see just what purpose falls to be served by rule 29.11 which requires that, once a proof has been allowed, all productions to be used thereat should be lodged not less than 14 days before the diet. If the requirements of rule 9.13 (1) have been satisfied there ought to be nothing which has yet to be lodged. One possible explanation for this may be that rule 9.13 applies only to standard procedure and not additional procedure, in which case rule 29.11 continues to have a role to play.

Conclusion

The rules discussed above clearly do provide a new procedure in Scotland — and, if the sheriff court rules are anything to go by, then it is likely that further, similar, innovations may follow to other actions. It is submitted that the rules need expansion and clarification as to what obligations are incumbent upon parties and what sanctions may follow for breach or non-compliance. Although English procedure provides an interesting comparison, if only to show the issues which can arise, the historical origins of this aspect of English procedure are quite different and provide an unsafe guide.

◆

NEWS

Appreciation

Lord Maxwell

Peter Maxwell, the Hon Lord Maxwell, who was the third Chairman of the Scottish Law Commission, died on 2 January 1994. His period of office at the Commission from 1981 until 1988 marked the final phase of a career notable for many outstanding contributions to the Law of Scotland. He was admitted to the Faculty of Advocates in 1951, took silk in 1961 and was appointed a Senator of the College of Justice in 1973.

To the task of advocacy he brought a mature and incisive legal mind, prodigious industry and a magnificent court presence. As a junior counsel the thoroughness of his preparation was formidable; in one complicated case he was not satisfied that he had done justice to his note on the line of evidence until he had covered 100 pages of foolscap. In court he was restrained, almost diffident, in his handling of witnesses, as if anxious not to seem overbearing. No such inhibitions were apparent in his legal submissions to the bench. After a slow, even leisurely, start he developed his argument with growing confidence and power to its climax; whereupon, if he did not consider that the reaction of the judge was sufficiently enthusiastic, he was known to add, with a hint of menace, "Do you see what I mean?"

As a judge Peter Maxwell found greater scope to display his profound perception of character, robust common sense and human sympathy. Although many of the cases that came before him posed little intellectual challenge, he was invariably patient, courteous and attentive, some of his interventions being designed to relieve the tedium of the proceedings as much as to seek enlightenment. Fortunately the law reports record the bulk of his important decisions. Even on a superficial reading they are characterised by depth, balance and clarity.

Before he went to the Commission he was familiar with the pitfalls and restraints that beset the law reformer, having been a member of the Scottish Law Reform Committee throughout its active life. In addition, as a serving judge he was chairman of the Scottish Committee on Jurisdiction and Enforcement. The radical recommendations of that committee were enacted in the Civil Jurisdiction and Judgments Act 1982. His approach to law reform was simple and direct. He sought practical solutions which were based on sound principles. Utopian proposals were subjected to rigorous analysis before being dismissed as "piffle". He was bold or cautious as the occasion required. The Commission's Memorandum on *The Mental Element in Crime* rejected refined concepts about the nature of intention in favour of tested principles which a Scottish jury could readily understand. On the other hand his long experience of presenting and hearing evidence in the Court of Session had convinced him that the then current corroboration requirements and restraints upon hearsay were unduly demanding for proof on balance of probabilities and should be relaxed.

Peter Maxwell served the law as advocate, judge and reformer with high distinction. He will be sorely missed by many in Parliament House and Causewayside who had the privilege of working with him and of enjoying his friendship.

CKD

Appointments

New sheriff
The Queen, on the recommendation of the Secretary of State for Scotland, has appointed Mr R A Davidson, solicitor, Glasgow, to be a sheriff for the Sheriffdom of Tayside, Central and Fife based at Dundee. Mr Davidson, who is 46, has held a commission as a temporary sheriff since 1988. He will take up his appointment on a date to be announced.

New Law Society President
The next President of the Law Society of Scotland is to be Kenneth Ross, a partner with Gillespie, Gifford & Brown (formerly McGowans), Dumfries. He will take office in succession to Ian Dunbar at the end of May. The next vice president is to be Alan Boyd, legal adviser at Irvine Development Corporation.

Court

Training of judiciary in sheriff courts
The Secretary of State for Scotland has announced that he is setting up a group to coordinate the provision of training for the judiciary in the sheriff courts. Lord Cameron of Lochbroom has agreed to chair the group, the membership of which will be as follows: Sheriff Iain Macmillan, President, Temporary Sheriffs' Association; Mr Gordon Murray, director, Scottish Courts Administration; Sheriff Principal Gordon Nicholson, QC, convener, Sheriffs Principal; and Sheriff Gordon Shiach, acting President, Sheriffs' Association.

Tape recording of court proceedings
The Prisoners and Criminal Proceedings (Scotland) Act 1993 and the new Ordinary Cause Rules made provision, with effect from 1 January 1994, for the use of tape recorders to record certain court proceedings. In the immediate term, this covers criminal jury trials and fatal accident inquiries. It has now been decided, after extensive consultation, to introduce tape recording of these proceedings in a planned programme over the next few years.

Initially, tape recorders will be introduced in all courts within the sheriffdoms of Tayside, Central and Fife and Grampian, Highland and Islands. The installations will be completed by mid-March so that they may be brought into use with effect from Monday, 4 April 1994. From that date, in these courts, all such proceedings will be recorded by tape recorder. Intimation will be given once dates have been agreed to introduce tape recording in the other sheriffdoms and the supreme courts.

Until otherwise advised, it is intended that the High Court of Justiciary will continue to use shorthand writers. Accordingly, when the High Court sits in a sheriff court which normally uses tape recorders, a shorthand writer will continue to be provided.

Court clerks will operate the tape recorders in court and will make the necessary arrangements for transcription of the proceedings, where this is authorised.

Solicitors wishing to view the equipment can contact their local sheriff clerk (in the two sheriff-doms immediately affected) after mid-March. Sheriff clerks will provide a short checklist for the guidance of solicitors prior to the start of any proceedings which are to be recorded by tape recorder.

◊

Faculty of Advocates
The Faculty of Advocates has announced the appointment of Mr John G Sturrock, advocate, as its first director of training and education. Mr Sturrock, who was called to the bar in 1986, will remain in full time practice during his three year term of office apart from a period between April and October this year when he will be engaged in setting up a training programme for intrants and a programme of continuing education and training for practising members.

— ◊ —

General

Prisons ombudsman
The Secretary of State for Scotland has announced in Parliament plans to introduce an independent element to the prisoner complaints system by appointing a prisons ombudsman: see Parliamentary News below, p 50.

◊

University of Edinburgh
Simpson & Marwick, WS, have agreed to fund for a three year period the establishment of a new specialist lectureship in delict in the University of Edinburgh's Faculty of Law. Dr Douglas Brodie, a lecturer within the Department of Private Law, is to become the first holder of the lectureship.

The funding will enable the university to make a second lecturer grade appointment — preferably of another person with special experience in this field — to provide a special focus for professional teaching and research in this area.

◊

Traded endowment policies
Many solicitors find that, due to a change in some clients' circumstances, they frequently own an endowment policy which is no longer required for its original purpose. Traditionally, the only course of action is to surrender the policy to the life assurance company which issued it.

Solicitors may not be aware that there exists a traded endowment market, through which the client can often obtain up to 30 per cent more than the surrender value, with a 3 per cent commission being paid to the solicitor who introduces the business. The figures come from Policy Portfolio plc, which has now published an information leaflet "Surrendering?", available from the company at 5 Dancastle Court, Arcadia Avenue, London N3 2JU (tel 081-343 4567).

— ◊ —

Taxation

Tax appeals
The 1994 Finance Bill contains provisions which extend powers given to the Lord Chancellor to make regulations about the practice and procedure for the hearing of tax appeals by the general and special commissioners. The changes will allow the Lord Chancellor, with the consent of the Lord Advocate, to make regulations giving the commissioners a power to seek information that is even handed in its treatment of the revenue and other parties to an appeal. Such a power, which is not available in current legislation, would enable the general or special commissioners, or both, to require the revenue to produce information relating to the taxpayer's liability to tax.

◊

Corporation tax: capital allowances

The government intend to bring forward provisions in the 1994 Finance Bill to amend the capital allowances legislation applying to expenditure on industrial buildings and buildings constructed in enterprise zones. The provisions will rectify a defect in the legislation which enables the owner of a building effectively to dispose of his interest in it through the granting of a long lease without there being any recovery of excess tax allowances given.

— ◇ —

Business changes

Messrs John G Gray & Co, SSC, 24 York Place, Edinburgh, intimate that Mr Michael Gordon Robson retired as a partner of the firm with effect from 31 December 1993. The partnership continues under the remaining partners at the same address (tel 031-557 4452, fax 031-556 7677, DX ED 14 Edinburgh).

H M Love & Co, messengers at arms and sheriff officers, announce the opening of a new office on 14 February 1994 at Parliament House Building, 120 Cowgate, Edinburgh EH1 1JN, DX ED 173 Edinburgh (tel 031-557 0100; fax 031-225 8411). This will be the principal office now dealing with citation and diligence. 19 Heriot Row, Edinburgh EH3 6JR, will remain as the head office.

Mr K J B S MacLeod intimates that as from 23 December 1993 he has resigned from MacLeod and Co, WS, Inverness, and has commenced practice from 13 Lombard Street, Inverness, under the firm name of MacLeod, Mackay, WS, incorporating Mackay & Co of 17 Queensgate, Inverness, where Thomasina Mackay continues to operate. His telephone number is 0463 242222; fax number 0463 711606; Rutland Exchange/DX number is IN 41. The branch office at 26 Argyle Street, Ullapool, continues under the new firm name; the telephone and fax numbers remain the same.

— ◇ —

Parliamentary News

New Bills

HOUSE OF COMMONS

19 January 1994

Conscientious Objection (Public Expenditure)—To reform the system of taxation so that taxpayers are enabled to hypothecate on grounds of conscience a proportion of taxation to purposes which they nominate. (Private Member's Bill introduced by Mr Neil Gerrard)

20 January 1994

Northern Ireland Termination of Jurisdiction—To terminate British jurisdiction in Northern Ireland, and for purposes connected therewith. (Private Member's Bill introduced by Mr Tony Benn)

Questions answered

HOUSE OF COMMONS

17 January 1994

FINE DEFAULTERS

Mr William Ross: To ask the Secretary of State for Scotland what is the average prison sentence imposed for defaulting on a fine; what is the average period actually spent in prison by such a defaulter in Scotland; and what is the average cost of such a person's imprisonment.

Lord James Douglas-Hamilton: The average sentence imposed in 1992 for defaulting on a fine was 23 days. The average time spent in prison by a fine defaulter was an estimated 13 days and the estimated average cost of the person's imprisonment was £970.

18 January 1994

GOVERNMENT PAPERS

Mr McFall: To ask the Secretary of State for Scotland what plans he has to introduce legislation applying to Scotland similar to the 30-year rule regarding the release of Government and Cabinet papers.

Lord James Douglas-Hamilton: Scottish Office papers have for many years been released as a matter of course under arrangements which mirror administratively those which apply statutorily in England and Wales. I have no plans at present to place the system on a statutory footing.

20 January 1994

ENVIRONMENTAL PROTECTION ACT 1990

Mr Foulkes: To ask the Secretary of State for Scotland what advice he has given Scottish councils concerning compliance with the Environmental Protection Act 1990.

Sir Hector Monro: Guidance has been issued to local authorities accompanying orders, codes of practice and regulations made under the Environmental Protection Act 1990. Specific guidance has been issued on recycling, in the form of a waste management paper on the compilation of waste recycling plans and on the environmental standards that should normally be applied to industrial processes covered by local authority air pollution control. The hazardous waste inspectorate, as an ongoing part of its responsibility, gives advice to local authorities with respect to their duties under relevant legislation on waste management matters including Pt II of the Environmental Protection Act 1990. Further advice is given at meetings of the Scottish Pollution Control Co-ordinating Committee.

JURY SYSTEM

Mr Kynoch: To ask the Secretary of State for Scotland what progress he has made with his review of the jury system and the not proven verdict.

Mr Lang: I am today publishing a consultation paper seeking views on a number of proposals for improving the jury system and on the future of our system of verdicts, including the not proven verdict. The proposals in relation to juries are aimed at more effective selection of juries which are representative and willing to serve, and at a reduction in the inconvenience suffered by those cited to attend court for jury service. The paper also sets out the case for and against the retention of the three verdict system. I hope that the proposals made and questions raised in this paper will stimulate the widest possible debate.

This consultation paper is the third in a series seeking views on proposals for improving the delivery of justice in Scotland. We are inviting comments by 15 April. A copy of the consultation paper has been placed in the library.

25 January 1994

PRISONS OMBUDSMAN

Mr Gallie: To ask the Secretary of State for Scotland what plans he has to create a post of prisons ombudsman and if he will make a statement.

Mr Lang: Proposals to revise the procedures under which prisoners in Scotland are able to make requests and complaints and to air grievances in relation to the Scottish Prison Service were contained in the report of a Scottish Prison Service working group entitled "Right and Just", which was published for comment in September 1992. The consultation exercise indicated a general consensus in favour of introducing an independent element to the system,

and we have taken the view that this can best be achieved by the appointment of an external complaints adjudicator — an independent person on a fixed term contract, with advisory functions. This will fulfil the commitment in the Justice Charter for Scotland to introduce an independent element in the new procedures. Officials in the Scottish Office have been asked to start the process of advertising for such a person with a view to an appointment later this year.

In advance of that, however, proposals for revised internal grievance procedures have been fully worked up for implementation in establishments next month. The main features are that requests or complaints will be resolved as close as possible to the source of the matter at issue; those who take decisions will be accountable for them; prisoners will receive reasoned responses with a set timescale; and accurate and sufficiently detailed records will be maintained. Gallery officers and hall managers will have a key role to play in the day-to-day handling of requests and complaints, but issues which they cannot resolve will be referred to an internal complaints committee. Prisoners will be given the opportunity to appeal against the committee's decisions to the governor in charge. If they remain dissatisfied, they will have the right of appeal to the external complaints adjudicator. (Under transitional arrangements there will be a right of appeal to Scottish Prison Service headquarters.)

The external complaints adjudicator will take a case on board only when all previous stages in the procedure have been exhausted. He or she will review both the merits of decisions and the way in which requests and complaints have been handled in the internal system. Where the complaints adjudicator disagrees with a decision, he or she will have the power to recommend the questioning of any finding of guilt or remission of any punishment. The complaints adjudicator will make a report to the chief executive of the Scottish Prison Service on each case with a reasoned recommendation.

I believe that this new appointment, taken with the overhauled internal procedures, will represent a significant advance in the way in which prisoners' requests and complaints are handled.

ARTICLES

Common Law Contempt: The Story So Far

Alistair J Bonnington,
The Law School,
University of Glasgow.

Mr Bonnington argues that recent English decisions have opened up a field of contempt jurisdiction hitherto precluded in Scotland since Hall v Associated Newspapers, *1978 SLT 241, and argues that sooner or later the Scottish courts will want to reconsider* Hall.

Clarence Darrow, the eminent American lawyer, reflecting on his long life in the courts, wryly observed that often the most important legal principles came out of cases involving the most unattractive people. So too it is, it would appear, in the law of contempt of court where two of the landmark judgments have been issued in cases against these twin jewels in the crown of our national press, the *Sun* and the *Daily Sport*. The latter publication, which Sir David Calcutt's committee noted "was regarded by most who gave evidence to us as not being a real newspaper", now has its name firmly established in the corpus juris on contempt at common law.

It is important, first, to define the precise area of contempt law which was being examined by the English courts in *Att Gen v News Group Newspapers* [1989] QB 110; [1988] 3 WLR 163; [1988] 2 All ER 906, and *Att Gen v Sport Newspapers Ltd* [1991] 1 WLR 194; [1992] 1 All ER 503.

There was no question in either case of a finding of contempt under the statutory provisions which are found in the Contempt of Court Act 1981. On both occasions the courts were dealing with the law applicable to publications made *before* the strict liability rule set out in s 2 of the 1981 Act became "active" under the timetable set out in Sched 1.

While in a case under the statute the court has to do no more than apply the test laid down in s 2 (substantial risk of serious prejudice), in a common law case the task is infinitely more complex. Since the *Sport* case, it seems that the courts of Scotland and those of England will apply different tests in determining common law contempt cases. The purpose of this article is to examine the law of the two countries and question what problems might be caused by their different approaches.

It is sometimes believed that since 1981 the whole of the law of contempt of court, insofar as it relates to the media, has been set out in the Contempt of Court Act of that year. That is not so. There is a saving provision in s 6 (c) allowing cases at common law to continue to be brought. For the newspapers, TV and radio this raises a number of questions, the principal of which are:

(1) From what time does the court claim to have jurisdiction on common law contempt in "publication" cases?

(2) What standard does the court apply in testing for the existence of common law contempt?

To answer these questions, it is first necessary to understand the nature of contempt at common law. The fundamental point to appreciate is that common law contempt is an offence sui generis. It is not a crime and does not require mens rea — see *Hall v Associated Newspapers*, 1978 SLT 241; 1979 JC 1.

Further, it is not even necessary for a finding of contempt that the publication had a prejudicial effect on the proceedings in question. The creation of a risk of prejudice is enough. Again, see *Hall.*

The 1981 Act, when creating a statutory form of contempt in publication cases, preserved this approach. The "strict liability" rule of s 2 does not require any element of intent on the part of the contemnor. Nor is it a prerequisite that the publication created any actual prejudice — the creation of *substantial* risk of *serious* prejudice is enough.

To put the matter in context, the sort of conduct which might amount to common law contempt could also constitute the crime of attempting to pervert the course of justice. The latter is, of course, a crime and, accordingly, for a conviction to be secured the Crown require to prove mens rea.

Common law contempt and attempt to pervert

Let us take as a starting point a case which illustrates the possible overlap between the two, the sheriff court decision of *Skeen v Farmer*, 1980 SLT (Sh Ct) 133.

The case arose out of an alleged assault by Billy Connolly, the comedian, on Hugh Farmer, news editor of the *Sunday People* when Farmer called at Connolly's house to interview him about his marital problems. The libel was to the effect that Farmer, knowing that the police were investigating his own complaint of assault, wrote an article on the incident in the newspaper and that this was prejudicial to the administration of justice (both the investigation and the prospective trial of Connolly were specified). Kenneth Cohn, the editor of the *Sunday People*, was charged as a second accused for publishing Farmer's article.

The sheriff dismissed the complaint as being of insufficient specification for a libel of attempting to pervert the course of justice. He pointed out that there was no allegation that the newspaper article was inaccurate, false or misleading. There was no specification as to how either the investigation and/or the possible prosecution might be prejudiced. Mere publication, said the sheriff, was not enough. Full details of his criticisms of the lack of specification in the complaint are set out at pp 135 and 136.

But he contrasted the crime charged with the offence of contempt of court. In such a case, he observed, it would not have been necessary for the Crown to libel and prove mens rea. Nor would it have been necessary for them to libel and prove a prejudicial effect on the relevant proceedings (p 135). However in the particular circumstances of the *Farmer* case, applying the contempt "timetable" (explained below), a charge of contempt could not lie.

In reaching these conclusions Sheriff Stone relied on the recently decided five judge case of *Hall v Associated Newspapers*. (*Hall* is widely and wrongly believed by the press to overrule entirely Lord Clyde's decision in *Stirling v Associated Newspapers*, 1960 SLT 5; 1960 JC 5. See Lord Emslie's judgment, at p 250 (p 15): "although the reasons on which the Court proceeded or appeared to proceed in Stirling are not sound, the decision at which the Court arrived was correct and represents accurately the law of Scotland"). In *Hall* the judges found the publishers guilty of contempt although they accepted "that there was no deliberate intention . . . to interfere with the course of the administration of justice" (p 250 (p 16)).

Further, the *Hall* court accepted that prejudice might well be caused to the administration of justice by publications made at a time before the court's special contempt jurisdiction arose. That sort of publication "is left to the control of the general criminal law and cannot constitute contempt of court which is a matter *sui generis*". Reference was made to a criminal charge of attempting to pervert the course of justice (p 246 (p 9)).

Chronology is of the essence in the law of contempt. Indeed, the judges in *Hall* saw it as a large part of their task in that case to set down guidelines on the "trigger points" which would cause the law of contempt to operate. It is a standing tribute to their work that when Parliament came to pass the 1981 Act they basically adopted the timetable set out by the Scots court in *Hall*: arrest, granting of an arrest warrant or service of a summons in a summary case are the starting times for contempt jurisdiction.

Now, it might be thought that despite its impressive credentials, *Hall* now can be completely ignored as it was decided before Parliament intervened in the shape of the 1981 Act. That cannot be so because, as noted above, Parliament specifically preserved in s 6 (c) the possibility of contempt being committed at common law.

Since the 1981 Act became law, to the writer's knowledge there have been no Scottish "publications" contempt cases at common law. It is, however, in the writer's view, possible to draw certain tentative conclusions for Scots law from the two decisions in England mentioned at the outset, i e, the *Sun* and the *Sport* cases, particularly that of the divisional court in the *Sport* case. (We shall ignore the purist's point that a decision of the English divisional court has no authority as a precedent in Scotland. Judgments of the range and quality of those given by Bingham LJ and Hodgson J could well be of considerable influence north of the border.)

Parliament laid down certain qualifications for a finding of common law contempt in s 6 (c). A publication contempt will occur only if the alleged contemnor's conduct is "intended to impede or prejudice the administration of justice". In short, there is now a requirement of mens rea in common law contempt cases: something which was unnecessary before the 1981 Act, and something which is clearly unnecessary in the sort of conduct struck at by the strict liability rule of s 2. But note that there is no change on the question of causing actual prejudice. As observed above it was not necessary at common law before the 1981 Act that the conduct complained of caused actual prejudice; and that remains the position today. So the *Hall* approach, in this respect, remains correct.

Further, the qualifying words "*substantial* risk of *serious* prejudice" have no application in the common law context (it may be wondered what value is to be put on such words after the House of Lords' judgment in *Att Gen v English* [1983] AC 116; [1982] 3 WLR 278; [1982] 2 All ER 903, where Lord Diplock defined "substantial" as meaning "not remote"). In this respect common law contempt seems, on the face of it, easier to prove than its statutory counterpart.

The English approach

So what have the English courts said about post-1981 common law contempt, and what may Scots lawyers take from these decisions?

In *Att Gen v News Group* [1988] 2 All ER 906, they were dealing with the articles in the *Sun* newspaper which vigorously and repeatedly accused a doctor of raping an eight year old girl. The Crown had refused to proceed with a prosecution against the doctor on the ground that there was insufficient evidence. Proceedings, therefore, were not "active" under the 1981 Act, so the strict liability rule of s 2 did not apply.

Contemporaneously with publishing their accusatory articles, the *Sun* were offering to fund the child's family to pursue a private prosecution of the doctor. In these circumstances the court found that the *Sun* had "intended to impede or prejudice the administration of justice" (as s 6 (c) required) and so were guilty of contempt at common law. A fine of £75,000 was imposed.

It would be wrong to leave that case without quoting a particularly purple passage from Watkins LJ: "The need for a free press is axiomatic, but the press cannot be allowed to charge about like a wild unbridled horse. It has, to a necessary degree, in the public interest, to be curbed. The curb is in no circumstance more necessary than when the principle that every man accused of crime shall have a fair trial is at stake."

So the principle was established. The courts would in extreme cases be willing to use the common law to protect the administration of justice from interference from the media.

But the *Sun* case was particularly extreme, effectively concerning an attempt to poison the minds of the public (who will make up the jury) against a man, on the one hand, while trying to arrange his arraignment before the court on the other.

That is why the more usual circumstances found in *Att Gen v Sport Newspapers* [1992] 1 All ER 503, make it more instructive for everyday guidance. The background to the case was the disappearance of a 15 year old schoolgirl. Initial inquiries led the police to believe that she may have been abducted. There the court was dealing again with a publication made when proceedings were not active. Police, however, were following a definite line of inquiry and it is perhaps surprising they had not arranged for an arrest warrant from a court. They revealed the name of the man they suspected and asked for the media's help in finding him — a very common procedure nowadays. Seizing on the prurient aspect of the case, the *Sport* published details of the suspect's criminal record (he had served 10 years for raping a 17 year old girl), calling him a "sex monster" and "a vicious evil rapist". Two days later magistrates granted a warrant for his arrest.

The Attorney General contended that common law contempt could be committed *before* a criminal defendant had been arrested or a warrant granted for his arrest, whether or not criminal proceedings were imminent. The Attorney General accepted that for his case to succeed: (1) the publication had to create a real risk of prejudice (note the lack of the qualifying words "substantial" and "serious"); and (2) the publisher had specifically to intend to create such a risk. In reply, the *Sport*'s lawyers contended that a common law contempt could not be committed before criminal proceedings had been instituted.

The court would have none of it. They firmly rejected the defence submission and found the Attorney General's interpretation of the law correct. From the Scots viewpoint the interesting aspect of this decision is the full review of *Hall v Associated Newspapers* made by the divisional court. Bingham LJ and Hodgson J noted the *Hall* court's approval of the Australian case of *James v Robinson* (1963) 109 CLR 593, a case which decided that in Australian law contempt could not be committed before any proceedings were in existence. The *Hall* "timetable" for the operation of the law of contempt was noted and the fact that the Scots court seemed to be saying that before contempt jurisdiction arose the Crown must rely on the general criminal law, i e, the crime of attempting to pervert the course of justice.

Hall, of course, came in 1979 before the 1981 Act divided the law of contempt in publication cases into statutory and common law cases. The English judges decided that *Hall*, if it were still the law of Scotland, was not the law of England. In England, it was quite possible for the media to be guilty of common law contempt when there were no proceedings in existence. *James v Robinson*, too, was disapproved. In disapproving these weighty precedents, the court noted that in the *Sun* case in 1988 the English court had been well aware of the fact that in reaching its decision it was extending the boundaries of contempt as previously understood.

The "imminence" test

It was said above that chronology is of the essence in the law of contempt and in that area the *Sport* case is confused. There was unanimity that common law contempt could exist if, as the

Attorney General had submitted, (1) the publication had created a real risk of prejudice, and (2) the publisher had specifically intended to create such a risk. But on the crucial point of timetable (the point which so exercised the Scots judges in *Hall*) there was disagreement.

Hodgson J decided that for the law of contempt to bite, proceedings must be "imminent" (see p 535). In so doing, he followed the judgment of Watkins LJ in *Att Gen v News Group* [1988] 2 All ER at p 919. Watkins LJ accepted that "imminence" was a vague and uncertain concept, but found that one of its attractions — presumably as it allows the court to take an "each case is decided on its own particular facts" approach.

Watkins LJ in adopting the "imminence" approach for common law contempt jurisdiction's starting point, was following a line of English precedent going back to the House of Lords case *Att Gen v Times Newspapers* [1973] 3 All ER 54, Lord Reid at p 65 and Lord Diplock at p 71 ([1974] AC 273; [1973] 3 WLR 298).

In contrast, Bingham LJ at p 516 was willing to accept that common law contempt could be committed even if proceedings were neither in existence nor imminent. Now, if that is the law of England it would appear that events have come full circle and the draconian aspects of *Stirling v Associated Newspapers*, 1960 SLT 5, are with us (or at least with the English) once again.

Differences between England and Scotland

Stirling's case still holds terrors for Scottish editors. Lord Clyde's judgment in the case is taught to trainee journalists as an example of how things were in the dark ages of Scots contempt law. That is because the High Court decided there that contempt jurisdiction could bite from the time a crime was suspected. In *Hall*, the five judges decided that this part of the judgment in *Stirling*'s case was wrong. They accepted that just as much damage could be done to the interests of justice by prejudicial publication at such an early stage as by later publications. But that sort of publication was a matter for the general criminal law, i e, the Crown could prosecute for attempt to pervert: 1978 SLT at p 250 (1979 JC at p 15).

The *Hall* approach is now clearly disapproved by the English courts. The unfortunate result of the *Sport* case is that the law on common law contempt, as Bingham LJ observed at p 515, may be different north and south of the Tweed. The amazing news for Scots lawyers is that in this area

at least it would appear that the law of England is more restrictive towards the media than the law of Scotland.

To give the full picture, however, we have to report that in their prosecution of the *Sport*, the Crown, having successfully established the existence of a body of contempt law which could operate from a time before proceedings had begun, fell at the final hurdle. They failed to prove to the satisfaction of the court that the editor of the *Sport* had the "specific intent" required. The court accepted the Attorney General's submission that intent could be inferred from all the circumstances, including the foreseeability of the consequences of publication, but the judges concluded that the probability of the consequences being foreseen had to be little short of overwhelming before it was sufficient to establish the necessary intent. On the facts of this case the court was not so satisfied.

Scots law now?

Scots editors and their legal advisers must take comfort from the fact that even if we should at some later date import this particular bit of law from over the border, it brings with it a high standard of proof for the Crown to discharge before a finding of contempt (with its attendant risk of fines and imprisonment) can be made. It is interesting to note that the English court did lay some store on the fact that in England only the Attorney General can bring contempt proceedings. That, of course, is not the case in Scotland where an accused or the judge ex proprio motu can raise an issue of contempt: 1981 Act, s 7.

When all is said and done, the writer does not believe he will be alone in thinking that our High Court would find it difficult to accept that they had no jurisdiction to deal with the media in situations such as the *Sun* and *Sport* cases described above. A five judge case may be a bit of an obstacle to overcome, but the explanation that *Hall* was before the 1981 Act is available. In matters of contempt the court allows itself the luxury of making up the rules to meet the problem, although the judges would never admit to that unscientific approach.

For example, if the media had published grossly prejudicial material about the Lockerbie bombing, after the case reverted to a common law situation when the warrants for the two suspects became one year old in November 1992 (1981 Act, Sched 1, para 11) it is not really credible that our High Court would have stood idly by and said they could do nothing because of their decision in *Hall*. (The question of the high standard of "specific intent" is a separate issue.) Might they not have taken the view that the existence of a valid arrest warrant (albeit over a year old) would have allowed them to draw an inference of the specific intent required by s 6 (c) of the 1981 Act much more readily than in the situation where there was no such warrant?

In any event it would be open to the Lord Advocate to bring proceedings against the media on a charge of attempting to pervert the course of justice, i e use "the control of the general criminal law" as envisaged in *Hall*.

In relation to Lockerbie no such problem has arisen because the media have been properly circumspect in their reporting, knowing that the two Libyan suspects might possibly turn up in Scotland at some future time for trial by jury.

But if the Scots courts follow the English precedents in the *Sun* and *Sport* cases, the obvious effect will be that it will be extremely difficult for the most responsible of editors to ascertain when he is working subject to the law of contempt and when he is not. As the English judges cannot even agree on the applicability of the imminence test (and it is accepted on all sides that such a test is itself very vague) then how on earth are the editors and their lawyers to work out what rules they must obey? Surely ascertainability is of the essence in a sophisticated and fair legal system. Now in England the law cannot be clearly ascertained in the area of common law contempt and our judges should think long and hard before importing such law to Scotland. If they go down the English road, the ghost of *Stirling* walks once again. If we take that path it is possible that the sort of investigative journalism which is aimed at exposing a wrongdoer and aimed at suggesting that he should be prosecuted by the authorities might become too risky to contemplate except for the wealthiest sections of the media. It is something of a paradox that it is precisely this type of journalism which often best serves the interest of justice.

Let Hodgson LJ, speaking at the end of his judgment in *Att Gen v Sport Newspapers*, be given the last word. Commenting on the Queen's Bench decision in the *Sun* case he made an observation which applies equally to his own court's decision on the *Sport*. In a classic English understatement he said, "It is also a decision which has implications for the media which I am not sure have yet been appreciated."

How very true!

Caveat editor.

◆

NEWS

Coming events

The Society of Solicitors in the Supreme Courts of Scotland will be holding their triennial dinner on Friday 25 February 1994 in the Playfair Library within the Old College, University of Edinburgh, South Bridge, Edinburgh at 6.30 for 7 pm. The principal speakers will be Mrs Doris Littlejohn, president of the Industrial Tribunals and Mr Andrew Hardie, QC, the newly elected Dean of the Faculty of Advocates. Tickets are £35 each and can be obtained from Alistair Brownlie, secretary of the SSC Society, 2 Abercromby Place, Edinburgh, EH3 6JZ (tel 031-556 4116; DX ED 195).

General

Register Office: fees
The fee payable for a certificate of birth, death or marriage issued for special purposes under certain statutory provisions is increased to £7 by SI 1993 No 3151; the fee payable for the solemnisation of a civil marriage is increased to £40 by SI 1993 No 3152; and certain fees payable to the Registrar General and district registrars for services provided under the Registration of Births, Deaths and Marriages (Scotland) Act 1965 are increased by SI 1993 No 3153, all with effect from 1 April 1994.

— ◇ —

◇

Faculty of Solicitors of Dunbartonshire

The Faculty of Solicitors of Dunbartonshire elected the following office bearers at its a g m on Wednesday 26 January 1994: *Dean,* John Steele; *vice dean,* Brian Adair; *honorary secretary,* Roderick Boag; *honorary treasurer,* Peter Young.

Taxation

Foreign exchange gains and losses

The Inland Revenue have published draft regulations which will supplement the provisions on exchange gains and losses contained in Chap II of Pt II of the Finance Act 1993 as they apply in relation to assets and liabilities held or owed by insurance companies, and draft regulations which will enable companies to use currencies other than sterling, in specified circumstances, for computing and expressing their trading profits and losses before computation of any capital allowances. The regulations are to be made under enabling powers included in provisions on exchange gains and losses of companies which are contained in the Finance Act 1993. Draft regulations dealing with other aspects of these provisions will be published over the next few months.

Further information can be obtained from, and comments on the draft regulations (before 30 April 1994) sent to: Inland Revenue (Financial Institutions Division), Foreign Exchange Consultations, Room 510, 22 Kingsway, London WC2B 6NR.

Alterations to pension funds

The Inland Revenue have published a new extra-statutory concession relaxing the conditions under which some pension funds may commute very small pensions to a lump sum or alter their rules for increasing pensions already being paid. The concession will allow these funds to amend their rules without losing entitlement to tax reliefs.

The text of the concession is as follows:

Where an alteration is made to the terms on which benefits are payable by a fund to which s 608 of the Income and Corporation Taxes Act 1988 applies, exemption from tax shall continue to be allowed in respect of the income, commissions, profits and gains applied for the purposes of the fund if: (i) the alteration provides for

pensions in payment to be increased by an amount not exceeding the rise in the Retail Prices Index or at a fixed rate of up to 3 per cent a year compound (whether or not the increase in the Retail Prices Index reaches that level); (ii) subject to the conditions below, the alteration allows for pensions to be commuted in full to a lump sum where the total benefit payable under all schemes in respect of the employment does not exceed the value of a pension of £260 a year.

The conditions applying to limb (ii) of this concession are that either: (a) the administrator of the fund should make no reduction in the amount of commutation payment made to the employee on account of any income tax borne by the administrator when making the payment; or (b) the employee, having been made aware of the tax consequences, has agreed to the commutation payment.

Parliamentary News

New Bills

HOUSE OF COMMONS

26 January 1994

Leasehold Law Reform—To amend the law regarding privity of contract and estate for future but not existing leases; and for connected purposes. (Private Member's Bill introduced by Mr Richard Page)

1 February 1994

Regulation of Political Funding—To regulate the system of funding of political parties; and for connected purposes. (Private Member's Bill introduced by Mr John Spellar)

Questions answered

26 January 1994

SHERIFFS

Mr McFall: To ask the Secretary of State for Scotland what proportion of a sheriff's time is taken on (a) civil and (b) criminal and other work.

Lord James Douglas-Hamilton: It is estimated that, on average, 30 per cent of a sheriff's time is spent on civil work and 70 per cent on criminal and other work.

28 January 1994

PROCURATORS FISCAL

Mr McFall: To ask the Secretary of State for Scotland what procedures are in operation to monitor the way in which procurators fiscal deal with cases reported to them by the police; and what account is taken of the results of such monitoring in the rewarding or career patterns of procurators fiscal and in the allocation of financial resources.

Lord James Douglas-Hamilton: Procurators fiscal prepare monthly reports of workload and performance. The information is analysed centrally in Crown Office for senior management. The work of local offices is monitored regularly by regional procurators fiscal and by the management services group in the Crown Office, which is engaged in a continuing programme of review.

Procurators fiscal are subject to the directors of my noble and learned Friend, the Lord Advocate and must report serious cases for the instructions of his deputes.

Financial resources are allocated on the basis of the workload of each office and the allocation takes account of the demands made by different types of case. A procurator fiscal is a civil servant. His competence is systematically appraised each year and he has the opportunity to earn performance pay. His performance is not measured in terms of results in court or by the number of convictions he obtains. The development of a procurator fiscal's career depends on how well he carries out a wide range of duties, and to advance he must be successful at promotion boards, which form part of the service's rigorous selection process.

◆

ACT OF SEDERUNT

ACT OF SEDERUNT (Fees of Solicitors in the Sheriff Court) (Amendment and Further Provisions) 1993

(SI 1993/3080) [3 DECEMBER 1993]

The Lords of Council and Session, under and by virtue of the powers conferred on them by section 40 of the Sheriff Courts (Scotland) Act 1907 (c 51) and of all other powers enabling them in that behalf, do hereby enact and declare:

Citation and commencement

1.—(1) This Act of Sederunt may be cited as the Act of Sederunt (Fees of Solicitors in the Sheriff Court) (Amendment and Further Provisions) 1993 and shall come into force on 1st January 1994.

(2) This Act of Sederunt shall be inserted in the Books of Sederunt.

Fees for solicitors

2.—(1) Subject to sub-paragraph (2), Schedule 1 to this Act of Sederunt shall apply to work done and expenses or outlays incurred on or after the date on which this Act of Sederunt comes into force.

(2) Schedule 1 to this Act of Sederunt shall not apply to fees for work done, expenses or outlays incurred or to the taxation of accounts for which the Secretary of State may make regulations under and by virtue of section 14A of the Legal Aid (Scotland) Act 1967 or section 33 of the Legal Aid (Scotland) Act 1986.

Revocation and saving

3.—(1) The Acts of Sederunt specified in Schedule 2 to this Act of Sederunt are hereby revoked.

(2) Notwithstanding the revocation in sub-paragraph (1), the provisions of the Act of Sederunt (Fees of Solicitors in the Sheriff Court) 1989 shall continue to have effect in respect of work done and expenses or outlays incurred before the coming into force of this Act of Sederunt.

J A D HOPE, LORD PRESIDENT, *IPD*

SCHEDULE   Paragraph 2 (1)

GENERAL REGULATIONS

1. The Table of Fees in this Schedule shall regulate the taxation of accounts between party and party; and shall be subject to the aftermentioned powers of the court to increase or modify such fees.

2. The pursuer's solicitor's account shall be taxed by reference to the sum decerned for unless the court otherwise directs.

3. Where an action has been brought under summary cause procedure, only expenses under Chapter IV of the Table of Fees shall be allowed unless the court otherwise directs.

4. Fees for work done under the Social Work (Scotland) Act 1968 and summary applications shall be chargeable under Chapter III of the Table of Fees.

5. The court shall have the following discretionary powers in relation to the Table of Fees:—

(a) In any case the court may direct that expenses shall be subject to modification.

(b) The court may, on a motion made not later than seven days after the date of any interlocutor disposing of expenses, pronounce a further interlocutor regarding those expenses allowing a percentage increase in the fees authorised by the Table of Fees to cover the responsibility undertaken by the solicitor in the conduct of the cause. Where such an increase is allowed a similar increase may, if the court so orders, be chargeable by each solicitor in the cause against his own client. In fixing the amount of the percentage increase the following factors shall be taken into account:—

(i) the complexity of the cause and the number, difficulty or novelty of the questions raised;

(ii) the skill, time and labour, and specialised knowledge required, of the solicitor;

(iii) the number and importance of any documents prepared or perused;

(iv) the place and circumstances of the cause or in which the work of the solicitor in preparation for, and conduct of, the cause has been carried out;

(v) the importance of the cause or the subject-matter of it to the client;

(vi) the amount or value of money or property involved in the cause;

(vii) the steps taken with a view to settling the cause, limiting the matters in dispute or limiting the scope of any hearing.

(c) Where a party or his solicitor abandons, fails to attend or is not prepared to proceed with any diet of proof, debate, appeal or meeting ordered by the court, the court shall have power to decern against that party for payment of such expenses as it considers reasonable.

6. The expenses to be charged against an opposite party shall be limited to proper expenses of process without any allowance (beyond that specified in the Table of Fees) for preliminary investigations, subject to this proviso that precognitions, plans, analyses, reports, and the like (so far as relevant and necessary for proof of the matters in the Record between the parties), although taken or made before the bringing of an action or the preparation of defences, or before proof is allowed, and although the case may not proceed to trial or proof, may be allowed.

7. Except as otherwise provided in the Table of Fees, a solicitor may charge an account either on the basis of the inclusive fees of Chapters I and II or on the basis of the detailed fees of Chapter III of the Table of Fees, but he may not charge partly on one basis and partly on the other.

8. In order that the expense of litigation may be kept within proper and reasonable limits only such expenses shall be allowed in the taxation of accounts as are reasonable for conducting it in a proper manner. It shall be competent to the auditor to disallow all charges for papers, parts of papers or particular procedure or agency which he shall judge irregular or unnecessary.

9. Notwithstanding that a party shall be found entitled to expenses generally yet if on the taxation of the account it appears that there is any particular part of the cause in which such party has proved unsuccessful or that any part of the expenses has been occasioned through his own fault he shall not be allowed the expense of such part of the proceedings.

10. When a remit is made by the court regarding matters in the Record between the parties to an accountant, engineer, or other reporter the solicitors shall not, without special agreement, be personally responsible to the reporter for his remuneration, the parties alone being liable therefor.

11. In all cases, the solicitor's outlays reasonably incurred in the furtherance of the cause shall be allowed. Those outlays shall include a charge in respect of posts and sundries of 12 per cent of the taxed amount of fees.

12. In the taxation of accounts where counsel is employed—

(a) counsel's fees and the fees for instruction of counsel in Chapter II and Chapter III of the Table of Fees are to be allowed only where the court has sanctioned the employment of counsel; and

(b) except on cause shown, fees to counsel and solicitor for only two consultations in the course of the cause are to be allowed.

13. Where work done by a solicitor constitutes a supply of services in respect of which value added tax is chargeable by him, there may be added to the amount of fees an amount equal to the amount of value added tax chargeable.

14. In Chapter IV of the Table of Fees—

(a) necessary outlays, including—

(i) in relation to Part II only, a charge in respect of post and sundries of 12 per cent of the fees allowed, and

(ii) fees for witnesses calculated as provided by Act of Sederunt, are allowed in addition to the fees allowed under this Chapter;

(b) in Parts I and II, sheriff officers' fees and the costs of advertising are allowable as outlays;

(c) in Parts I and II, in respect of paragraph 3 (attendance at court), no fee is allowable for attendance at a continuation of the first calling, unless specially authorised by the court;

(d) in Part II, in respect of paragraph 7 (precognitions), in a case where a skilled witness prepares his own precognition or report, half of the drawing fee is allowable to the solicitor for revising and adjusting it;

(e) in Part II, in respect of paragraph 15, no fees shall be allowed in respect of accounts of expenses when the hearing on the claim for expenses takes place immediately on the sheriff or sheriff principal announcing his decision;

(f) all fees chargeable under this Chapter in respect of the actions mentioned in the left-hand column of the following table shall, unless the sheriff, on a motion in that behalf, otherwise directs, be reduced by the amount of the percentage specified opposite those actions in the right-hand column of the following table:—

TABLE

Actions	Percentage reduction
1. of a value* from £50 to £250	25%
2. of a value* of less than £50	50%
3. for recovery of possession of heritable property, if not defended	50%

* "value" in relation to any action in which a counterclaim has been lodged, is the total of the sums craved in the writ and the sum claimed in the counterclaim.

(g) in Part I, in respect of paragraph 1 (instruction fees), in relation to actions for reparation there are allowable such additional fees for precognitions and reports as are necessary to permit the framing of the writ and necessary outlays in connection therewith; and

(h) in Part II, the fee allowable in respect of paragraph 14 (supplementary note of defence) is a fixed fee allowable only when a supplementary note of defence is ordered by the court.

ACT OF SEDERUNT (FEES OF SOLICITORS IN THE SHERIFF COURT) 1993

TABLE OF FEES
CHAPTER I
PART I — UNDEFENDED ACTIONS
(other than actions of divorce or separation and aliment (affidavit procedure))

1. *Actions (other than those specified in paragraph 2 of this Chapter) in which decree is granted without proof—*
(a) Inclusive fee to cover all work from taking instructions up to and including obtaining extract decree £100.00
(b) In cases where settlement is effected after service of a writ but before the expiry of the *induciae* £80.00
(c) If the pursuer's solicitor elects to charge this inclusive fee he shall endorse a minute to that effect on the initial writ before ordering extract of decree. Outlays such as court dues for deliverance and posts shall be chargeable in addition and taxation shall be unnecessary.

2. *Actions of separation and aliment, adherence and aliment and custody and aliment where proof (other than by way of affidavit evidence) takes place—*
(a) Inclusive fee to cover all work from taking instructions up to and including obtaining extract decree £349.40
(b) If the pursuer's solicitor elects to charge this inclusive fee he shall endorse a minute to that effect on the initial writ after the close of the proof and before extract of the decree is ordered; and when the option is so exercised decree for expenses shall be granted against the defender for said sum together with the shorthand writer's fee actually charged as provided by Act of Sederunt and of other outlays up to £60 without the necessity of taxation. If outlays in excess of £60, excluding the shorthand writer's fee, are claimed, an account of such outlays shall be remitted to the auditor of court for taxation and the sum allowed for outlays shall be the amount of the account as taxed.

3. *Petition for appointment or discharge of a curator bonis*
(a) Inclusive fee to cover all work enquiring into estate and taking instructions up to and including obtaining extract decree £312.00
(b) (i) If the solicitor elects to charge the inclusive fee and to recover only the normal outlays as set out in head (ii) of this sub-paragraph, he shall endorse on the petition before ordering extract of the decree a minute setting out the said fee and the outlays. Taxation of charges so specified shall not be necessary.
(ii) The normal outlays referred to in head (i) of this sub-paragraph are:—
reasonable fees for medical reports;
court dues for deliverance;
sheriff officers' fees for service;
advertising costs incurred;
posts and incidents; and
value added tax chargeable on solicitors' fees and posts.

PART II

UNDEFENDED ACTIONS OF DIVORCE AND OF SEPARATION AND ALIMENT
(affidavit procedure)

1. In any undefended action of divorce or separation and aliment where—
(a) the facts sets out in section 1 (2) (b) (unreasonable behaviour) of the Divorce (Scotland) Act 1976 ("the 1976 Act") are relied on;
(b) there is no crave relating to any ancillary matters; and
(c) the pursuer seeks to prove those facts by means of affidavits, the pursuer's solicitor may, in respect of the work specified in column 1 of Table A, charge the inclusive fee specified in respect of that work in column 2 of that Table.

TABLE A

Column 1 Work done	Column 2 Inclusive fee £
1. All work to and including the period of notice	245.80
2. All work from the period of notice to and including swearing affidavits	174.70
3. All work from swearing affidavits to and including sending extract decree	53.70
4. All work to and including sending extract decree	474.20
Add process fee	of 10%

2. In any undefended action of divorce or separation and aliment where—
(a) the facts set out in sections 1 (2) (a) (adultery), 1 (2) (c) (desertion), 1 (2) (d) (two years' non-cohabitation and consent) and 1 (2) (e) (five years' non-cohabitation) of the 1976 Act are relied on;
(b) there is no crave relating to any ancillary matters; and
(c) the pursuer seeks to prove those facts by means of affidavits, the pursuer's solicitor may, in respect of work specified in column 1 of Table B, charge the inclusive fee specified in respect of that work in column 2 of that Table.

TABLE B

Column 1 Work done	Column 2 Inclusive fee £
1. All work to and including the period of notice	202.10
2. All work from the period of notice to and including swearing affidavits	97.30
3. All work from swearing affidavits to and including sending extract decree	53.70
4. All work to and including sending extract decree	353.10
Add process fee	of 10%

3. If—
(a) the pursuer's solicitor charges an inclusive fee under either paragraph 1 or paragraph 2 of this Part; and
(b) the action to which the charge relates includes a crave relating to an ancillary matter,
in addition to that fee he may charge, in respect of the work specified in column 1 of Table C, the inclusive fee specified in respect of that work in column 2 of that Table.

TABLE C

Column 1 Work done	Column 2 Inclusive fee £
1. All work to and including the period of notice	97.30
2. All work from the period of notice to and including swearing affidavits	57.00
3. All work under items 1 and 2	154.30
Add process fee	of 10%

4. If the pursuer's solicitor elects to charge an inclusive fee under this Part he shall endorse a minute to that effect on the initial writ before extract of the decree is ordered; and when the option is so exercised decree for expenses shall be granted against the defender for said sum together with outlays up to £85 inclusive of VAT without the necessity for taxation. If outlays in excess of £85 are claimed, an account of such outlays shall be remitted to the auditor of court for taxation and the sum allowed for outlays shall be the amount of the account as taxed.

CHAPTER II

PART I

DEFENDED ACTIONS COMMENCED ON OR BEFORE 31ST DECEMBER 1993

1. *Instruction fee—*
(a) To cover all work (except as hereinafter otherwise specially provided for in this Chapter) to the lodging of defences including copyings — £162.20
(b) Where separate statement of facts and counterclaim and answers lodged, additional fee of — £56.10
2. *Adjustment fee* — To cover all work (except as hereinafter otherwise specially provided for in this Chapter) in connection with the adjustment of the Record including (when appropriate) closing thereof, making up and lodging Closed Record and copyings—
(a) Agent or any party — £240.80
(b) If action settled before Record is closed — each original party's agent — £162.20
(c) If additional defender brought in before closing of Record — additional fee to each original party's agent — £27.50
(d) If additional defender brought in after closing of Record — additional fee to each original party's agent — £40.50
3. *Affidavit fee* — To framing affidavits, per sheet — £10.00
4. (a) *Debate fee* — To include preparation for and conduct of any hearing or debate other than on evidence, inquiring for cause at avizandum and noting interlocutor—
(i) When debate does not exceed 1 hour — £121.10
(ii) For every quarter hour engaged after the first hour — £14.90
(iii) Waiting time — per quarter hour — £13.50
(b) *Interim Interdict Hearings—*
(i) Pursuer's solicitor — the same fees as for debate fee above, but to include both the appearance at lodging of writ and the hearing at second diet
(ii) Defender's solicitor's fee where the debate does not exceed 1 hour — £71.10
(iii) Waiting time — per quarter hour — £13.50
5. *Precognitions* — Taking and drawing — per sheet — £24.30
Note. Where a skilled witness prepares his own precognition or report, the solicitor shall be allowed half of the above drawing fee for revising and adjusting it.
6. *Custody reports obtained under order of court—*
(a) Fee for all work incidental thereto — £53.70
(b) Additional fee per sheet of report to include all copies required (maximum £25) — £7.40
7. *Commissions to take evidence—*
(a) *On interrogatories—*
(i) Fee to solicitor applying for commission to include drawing, intimating and lodging motion, drawing and lodging interrogatories, instructing commissioner and all incidental work (except as otherwise specially provided for in this Chapter) but excluding attendance at execution of commission — £149.80
(ii) Fee to opposing solicitor if cross-interrogatories prepared and lodged — £101.10
(iii) If no cross-interrogatories lodged — £30.00
(b) *Open Commissions—*
(i) Fee to solicitor applying for commission to include all work (except as otherwise specially provided for in this Chapter) up to lodging report of commission but excluding attendance thereat — £90.40
(ii) Fee to solicitor for opposing party — £49.90
(iii) Fee for attendance at execution of commission — per quarter hour — £14.90
(iv) Travelling time — per quarter hour — £13.50
8. *Specification of documents—*
(a) Fee to cover drawing, intimating and lodging specification and relative motion and attendance at court debating specification — £62.40
(b) Inclusive fee to opposing solicitor — £40.50

(c) Fee for citation of havers, preparation for and attendance before commissioner at execution of commission—

(i) Where attendance before commissioner does not exceed 1 hour	£56.10
(ii) For each additional quarter hour after the first hour	£14.90

(d) If commission not executed — fee for serving each party with copy of specification to include recovering and examining documents or productions referred to therein £13.70

9. *Amendment of Record*—

(a) fee to cover drawing, intimating and lodging minute of amendment and relative motion and relative attendances at court—

(i) Where answers lodged	£68.70
(ii) Where no answers lodged	£44.80

(b) Inclusive fee to opposing solicitor—

(i) Where answers lodged	£56.10
(ii) Where no answers lodged	£37.40

(c) Fee for adjustment of minute and answers where applicable to be allowed in addition to each party £49.90

10. *Motions and minutes*—

(a) Fee to cover drawing, intimating and lodging any written motion or minute, including a reponing note, and relative attendances at court (except as otherwise provided for in this Chapter)—

(i) Where opposed	£71.10
(ii) Where unopposed (including for each party a joint minute other than under paragraph 15 (b))	£49.90

(b) Fee to cover considering opponent's written motion, minute or reponing note, and relative attendances at court—

(i) Where motion, minute or reponing note opposed	£40.50
(ii) Where motion, minute or reponing note unopposed	£30.00

11. *Procedure preliminary to proof*—

(a) Fee to cover fixing diet of proof, citation of witnesses, and generally preparing for trial or proof and if necessary instructing shorthand writer—

(i) If action settled or abandoned not later than 14 days before the diet of proof	£174.70
(ii) In any other case	£293.30

(b) Fee to cover preparing for adjourned diet and all incidental work as in (a) if diet postponed for more than 6 days, for each additional diet £61.20

(c) Drawing and lodging an inventory of productions, lodging the productions specified therein, and considering opponent's productions (to be charged once only in each process) £30.00

(d) Where only one party lodges productions, opponent's charges for considering same £14.90

12. *Conduct of proof or trial*—

(a) Fee to cover conduct of proof or trial and debate on evidence if taken at close of proof — per quarter hour	£14.90
(b) If counsel employed, fee to solicitor appearing with counsel — per quarter hour	£13.50
(c) Waiting time — per quarter hour	£13.50

13. *Debate on evidence*—

(a) Where debate on evidence not taken at conclusion of proof, preparing for debate	£49.90
(b) Fee for conduct of debate — per quarter hour	£14.90
(c) If counsel employed, fee to solicitor appearing with counsel — per quarter hour	£13.50
(d) Waiting time — per quarter hour	£13.50

14. *Appeals*—

(a) *To sheriff principal*—

(i) Fee to cover instructions, marking of appeal or noting that appeal marked, noting diet of hearing thereof and preparation for hearing	£93.60
(ii) Fee to cover conduct of hearing — per quarter hour	£14.90
(iii) If counsel employed, fee to solicitor appearing with counsel per quarter hour	£13.50
(iv) Waiting time — per quarter hour	£13.50

(b) *To Court of Session*—

Fee to cover instructions, marking appeal or noting that appeal marked and instructing Edinburgh correspondents £46.90

15. *Settlements*

(a) *Judicial tender*—

(i) Fee for preparation and lodging or for consideration of minute of tender	£56.10
(ii) Fee on acceptance of tender, to include preparation and lodging or consideration of minute of acceptance and attendance at court when decree granted in terms thereof	£41.80

(b) *Extra-judicial settlement*—

Fee to cover negotiations resulting in settlement, framing or revising joint minute and attendance at court when authority interponed thereto £93.60

16. *Final procedure*—

(a) Fee to cover settling with witnesses, enquiring for cause at avizandum, noting final interlocutor £74.80

(b) Fee to cover drawing account of expenses, arranging, intimating and attending diet of taxation and obtaining approval of auditor's report and adjusting account with opponent where necessary, ordering, procuring and examining extract decree £61.20

(c) Fee to cover considering opponent's account of expenses and attending diet of taxation or adjusting account with opponent £21.70

17. *Copying fees*—

Copying all necessary papers by any means—

(a) First copy — per sheet	£1.00
(b) Additional copies — per sheet	£0.40

Note. A sheet shall be 250 words. When copied by photostatic or similar process, each page shall be charged as one sheet.

18. *Process fee—*

Fee to cover all consultations between solicitor and client during the progress of the cause and all communications, written or oral, passing between them — 10 per cent on total fees and copyings allowed on taxation.

19. *Fee for instruction of counsel—*

(a) Fee for instructing counsel to revise record	£30.00
(b) Fee for instructing counsel to conduct debate, proof or trial	£62.40
(c) Fee for instructing counsel to conduct appeal to sheriff principal	£62.40

Note.

1. In each case to cover all consultations, revisal of papers and all incidental work.
2. Fee to counsel to be allowed as outlay.

CHAPTER II
PART 2
DEFENDED ORDINARY CAUSES AND FAMILY ACTIONS COMMENCED ON OR AFTER 1ST JANUARY 1994

1. *Instruction fee—*

(a) To cover all work (except as otherwise specially provided for in this Chapter) to the lodging of defences including copyings	£275.00
(b) Where separate statement of facts and counterclaim and answers lodged, additional fee of	£50.00
2. *Precognitions* — Taking and drawing — per sheet	£25.00

Note. Where a skilled witness prepares his own precognition or report, the solicitor shall be allowed half of above drawing fee for revising and adjusting it.

3. *Productions—*

(a) For lodging productions — each inventory	£30.00
(b) For considering opponent's productions — each inventory	£15.00

4. *Adjustment fee* — To cover all work (except as otherwise specially provided for in this Chapter) in connection with the adjustment of the Record including making up and lodging certified copy Record—

(a) Agent or any party	£125.00
(b) If action settled before Options Hearing, each original party's agent	£75.00
(c) If additional defender brought in before Options Hearing, additional fee to each original party's agent	£30.00
(d) If additional defender brought in after Options Hearing, additional fee to each original party's agent	£40.00
5. *Affidavits* — To framing affidavits, per sheet	£10.00

6. (a) *Options Hearing* — To include preparation for and conduct of Options Hearing (or First Hearing in defended family actions) and noting interlocutor—

(a) Where hearing does not exceed one half hour	£100.00
(b) Where hearing exceeds one half hour — for every extra quarter hour	£15.00
(c) For lodging and intimating or for considering note of basis of preliminary plea — for each note lodged	£25.00

7. *Additional Procedure* — for all work subsequent to Options Hearing including preparation for and attendance at procedural hearing—

where hearing does not exceed one half hour	£100.00
for every extra quarter hour	£15.00

8. *Debate (other than on evidence)—*

(a) Where counsel not employed	
(i) To include preparation for and all work in connection with any hearing or debate other than on evidence	£80.00
(ii) For every quarter hour engaged	£15.00
(b) Where counsel employed, fee to solicitor appearing with counsel per quarter hour	£13.50
(c) Waiting time — per quarter hour	£13.50

9. *Interim Interdict Hearings—*

(a) Preparation for each hearing — each party	£50.00
(b) Fee to conduct hearing — per quarter hour	£15.00
(c) If counsel employed, fee to attend hearing per quarter hour	£13.50
(d) Waiting time — per quarter hour	£13.50

10. *Reports obtained under order of court—*

(a) Fee for all work incidental thereto	£55.00
(b) Additional fee per sheet of report to include all copies required (maximum £35)	£7.00

11. *Commissions to take evidence—*

(a) On Interrogatories—	
(i) Fee to solicitor applying for commission to include drawing, intimating and lodging motion, drawing and lodging interrogatories, instructing commissioner and all incidental work (except as otherwise specially provided for in this Chapter) but excluding attendance at execution of commission	£150.00
(ii) Fee to opposing solicitor if cross-interrogatories prepared and lodged	£100.00
(iii) If no cross-interrogatories lodged	£30.00
(b) Open Commissions—	
(i) Fee to solicitor applying for commission to include all work (except as otherwise specially provided for in this Chapter) up to lodging report of commission but excluding attendance thereat	£100.00
(ii) Fee to opposing solicitor	£50.00
(iii) Fee for attendance at execution of commission — per quarter hour	£15.00
(iv) If counsel employed, fee for attendance of solicitor — per quarter hour	£13.50
(v) Travelling time — per quarter hour	£13.50

12. *Specification of documents—*
(a) Fee to cover drawing, intimating and lodging specification and relative motion
(i) Where motion unopposed   £55.00
(ii) Where motion opposed — additional fee per quarter hour   £13.50
(b) Fee to opposing solicitor—
(i) Where motion not opposed   £30.00
(ii) Where motion opposed — additional fee per quarter hour   £13.50
(c) Fee for citation of havers, preparation for and attendance before commissioner at execution of commission—
(i) Where attendance before commissioner does not exceed one hour   £55.00
(ii) For each additional quarter hour after the first hour   £15.00
(d) If optional procedure adopted — fee per person upon whom order is served   £13.50
(e) Fee for perusal of documents recovered per quarter hour   £13.50

13. *Amendment of Record—*
(a) (i) Fee to cover drawing, intimating and lodging minute of amendment and relative motion   £50.00
(ii) Fee for perusal of answers   £20.00
(iii) Fee for any court appearance necessary per quarter hour   £13.50
(b) (i) Fee to opposing solicitor — for perusing minute of amendment   £40.00
(ii) Fee for preparation of answers   £20.00
(iii) Fee for any court appearance necessary per quarter hour   £13.50
(c) Fee for adjustment of minute and answers where applicable to be allowed in addition to each party   £50.00

14. *Motions and minutes—*
(a) Fee to cover drawing, intimating and lodging any written motion or minute, including a reponing note, and relative attendances at court (except as otherwise specially provided for in this Chapter)—
(i) Where opposed   £70.00
(ii) Where unopposed (including for each party a joint minute other than under paragraph 20 (b))   £30.00
(b) Fee to cover considering opponent's written motion, minute or reponing note, and attendance at court—
(i) Where opposed   £70.00
(ii) Where unopposed   £30.00

15. *Hearing Limitation—*
Fee to include work (except as otherwise specially provided for in this Chapter) undertaken with a view to limiting the scope of any hearing, and including the exchange of documents, precognitions and expert reports, agreeing any fact, statement or document not in dispute, preparing and intimating any Notice to Admit or Notice of Non-Admission and preparing and lodging any Joint Minute, not exceeding   £250.00

16. *Procedure preliminary to proof—*
(a) Fee to cover all work preparing for proof (except as otherwise specially provided for in this Chapter)
(i) If action settled or abandoned not later than 14 days before the diet of proof   £160.00
(ii) In any other case   £290.00
(b) Fee to cover preparing for adjourned diet and all incidental work as in (a) if diet postponed for more than 6 days, for each additional diet   £65.00
(c) Fee for attendance inspecting opponent's documents per quarter hour   £15.00

17. *Conduct of proof—*
(a) Conduct of proof and debate on evidence if taken at close of proof — per quarter hour   £15.00
(b) If counsel employed, fee to solicitor appearing with counsel — per quarter hour   £13.50
(c) Waiting time — per quarter hour   £13.50

18. *Debate on evidence—*
(a) Where debate on evidence not taken at conclusion of proof, preparing for debate   £50.00
(b) Fee for conduct of debate — per quarter hour   £15.00
(c) If counsel employed, fee to solicitor appearing with counsel — per quarter hour   £13.50
(d) Waiting time — per quarter hour   £13.50

19. *Appeals—*
(a) To sheriff principal—
(i) Fee to cover instructions, marking of appeal or noting that appeal marked, noting diet of hearing thereof and preparation for hearing   £150.00
If counsel employed—   £85.00
(ii) Fee to cover conduct of hearing — per quarter hour   £15.00
(iii) If counsel employed, fee to solicitor appearing with counsel — per quarter hour   £13.50
(iv) Waiting time — per quarter hour   £13.50
(b) To Court of Session—
Fee to cover instructions, marking appeal or noting that appeal marked and instructing Edinburgh correspondents   £50.00

20. *Settlements*
(a) Judicial tender—
(i) Fee for preparation and lodging or for consideration of each minute of tender   £55.00
(ii) Fee on acceptance of tender, to include preparation and lodging or consideration of minute of acceptance and attendance at court when decree granted in terms thereof   £45.00
(b) Extra-judicial settlement—
Fee to cover negotiations resulting in settlement, framing or revising joint minute and attendance at court when authority interponed thereto   £100.00
(c) Whether or not fees are payable under (a) or (b) above where additional work has been undertaken with a view to effecting settlement, including offering settlement, although settlement is not agreed — not exceeding   £100.00

21. *Final procedure—*

(a) Fee to cover settling with witnesses, enquiring for cause at avizandum, noting final interlocutor £75.00

(b) Fee to cover drawing account of expenses, arranging, intimating and attending diet of taxation and obtaining approval of auditor's report and where necessary, ordering, procuring and examining extract decree or adjusting account with opponent £65.00

22. *Copying—*

Copying all necessary papers by any means—

(a) First copy — per sheet £1.00

(b) Additional copies — per sheet £0.40

Note. A sheet shall be 250 words. When copied by photostatic or similar process, each page shall be charged as one sheet.

23. *Process fee—*

Fee to cover all consultations between solicitor and client during the progress of the cause and all communications, written or oral, passing between them — 10 per cent on total fees and copyings allowed on taxation.

24. *Instruction of counsel*

(a) Fee for instructing counsel to revise pleadings £30.00

(b) Fee for instructing counsel to attend court £65.00

(c) Fee for attending consultation with counsel—

(i) where total time engaged does not exceed one hour £65.00

(ii) for each additional quarter hour £13.50

(c) Fee for attending consultation with counsel—

(i) where total time engaged does not exceed one hour £65.00

(ii) for each additional quarter hour £13.50

CHAPTER III

CHARGES FOR TIME, DRAWING OF PAPERS, CORRESPONDENCE ETC

1. Attendance at court conducting trial proof or formal debate or hearing — per quarter hour £14.90

2. Time occupied in the performance of all other work including attendances with client and others and attendances at court in all circumstances, except as otherwise specially provided—

(a) Solicitor — per quarter hour £13.50

(b) Allowance for time of clerk — one half of above

Note. Time necessarily occupied in travelling to such to be chargeable at these rates.

3. Drawing all necessary papers (other than affidavits) (the sheets throughout this Chapter to consist of 250 words or numbers) — per sheet £6.80

4. Framing affidavits — per sheet £10.10

5. Revising papers where revisal ordered — for each five sheets £2.80

6. Copying all necessary papers by any means—

(i) First copy — per sheet £1.00

(ii) Additional copies — per sheet £0.40

Note. When copies by photostatic or similar process each page shall be charged as one sheet

7. Certifying or signing a document £2.80

8. Perusing any document — per quarter hour £13.50

9. Lodging in process—

Each necessary lodging in or uplifting from process; also for each necessary enquiry for documents due to be lodged £2.80

10. Borrowing process—

Each necessary borrowing of process to include return of same £2.80

11. *Extracts—*

Ordering, procuring and examining extracts, interim or otherwise £13.50

12. *Correspondence, intimations, etc—*

(a) Formal letters and intimations £1.00

(b) Letters other than above — per page of 125 words £6.80

(c) Telephone calls except under (d) £2.80

(d) Telephone calls (lengthy) to be treated as attendances or long letters.

13. *Citations—*

Each citation of party or witness including execution thereof £6.80

14. *Instructions to officers—*

(a) Instructing officer to serve, execute or intimate various kinds of writs or diligence including the examination of executions £2.80

(b) For each party after the first on whom service or intimation is simultaneously made £2.80

(c) Agency accepting service of any writ £6.80

(d) Reporting diligence £6.80

15. *Personal diligence—*

(a) Recording execution of charge £6.80

(b) Procuring fiat £6.80

(c) Instructing apprehension £6.80

(d) Framing state of debt and attendance at settlement £8.20

16. *Sales—*

(a) Obtaining warrant to sell £6.80

(b) Instructing auctioneer or officer to conduct sale £6.80

(c) Perusing report of sale	£6.80
(d) Reporting sale under poindings or sequestrations or any other judicial sales	£6.80
(e) Noting approval of roup roll	£6.80
(f) Obtaining warrant to pay	£6.80

CHAPTER IV
SUMMARY CAUSES
PART I — UNDEFENDED ACTIONS

1. To include taking instructions, framing summons and statement of claim, obtaining warrant for service, instructing service as necessary by sheriff officer (where appropriate), attendance endorsing minute for and obtaining decree in absence and extract decree and including posts and sundries — £49.90

2. *Service*—

(a) citation by post wheresoever after the first citation for each party — £5.50

(b) framing and instructing service by advertisement — for each party — £16.20

3. Attendance at court — £16.20

PART II — DEFENDED ACTIONS

1. Instructions fee, to include taking instructions (including instructions for a counterclaim), framing summons and statement of claim, obtaining warrant for service, enquiring for notice of intention to defend, attendance at first calling, noting defence — £68.70

2. Service—

(a) Citation by post within United Kingdom, Isle of Man, Channel Islands, or the Republic of Ireland — for each party — £5.60

Citation by post elsewhere — for each party — £12.50

(b) Instructing service or reservice by sheriff officer including perusing execution of citation and settling sheriff officer's fee — for each party — £5.60

(c) Framing and instructing service by advertisement — for each party — £18.10

3. Attendance at court—

Attendance at any diet except as otherwise specially provided — £18.10

4. Preparing for proof, to include all work in connection with proof not otherwise provided for — £62.40

5. Free to cover preparing for adjourned diet and all incidental work if diet for more than six days — for each adjourned diet — £30.00

6. (a) Drawing and lodging inventory of productions, lodging the productions specified therein and considering opponent's productions (to be charged only once in each process) — £27.50

(b) Where only one party lodges productions, opponent's charges for considering same — £12.50

7. Precognitions—

(a) Drawing precognitions, including instructions, attendances with witnesses and all relative meetings and correspondence — per witness — £27.50

(b) Where precognitions exceed 2 sheets — for each additional sheet — £12.50

8. Motions and minutes—

Fee to cover drawing, intimating and lodging of any written motion or minute, excluding a minute or motion to recall decree, and relative attendance at court (except as otherwise provided in this Chapter)—

(a) Where opposed — £37.40

(b) Where unopposed (including for each party a joint minute or joint motion) — £23.10

9. Fee to cover considering opponent's written motion or minute (excluding minute of motion to recall decree) and relative attendance at court—

(a) Where motion or minute opposed — £30.00

(b) Where motion or minute unopposed — £18.10

10. Conduct of proof—

(a) Fee to cover conduct of proof or trial and debate on evidence taken at close of proof — per half hour — £18.10

(b) Waiting time — per half hour — £9.40

11. Settlements—

(a) Judicial tender, fee for consideration of, preparing and lodging minute of tender — £37.40

(i) Fee for consideration and rejection of tenders — £27.50

(ii) Fee on acceptance of tender — to include preparing and lodging, or consideration of minute of acceptance and attendance at court when decree granted in terms thereof — £27.50

(b) Extra judicial settlement — fee to cover negotiations resulting in settlement, framing or revising joint minute and attendance at court when authority interponed thereto — £62.40

12. Specification of documents—

(a) Fee to cover drawing, intimating and lodging specification of documents and relative motion and attendance at court — £31.20

(b) Inclusive fee to opposing solicitor — £28.10

(c) Fee for citation of havers, preparation for and attendance before commissioner, to each party — for each half hour — £18.10

(d) If alternative procedure adopted, a fee per person upon whom order served — £12.50

13. Commissions to take evidence—

(a) Fee to cover drawing, lodging and intimating motion and attendance at court—

(i) Where opposed — £37.40

(ii) Where unopposed — £23.10

(b) Fee to cover considering such motion and attendance at court—
(i) Where opposed £30.00
(ii) Where unopposed £18.10
(c) Fee to cover instructing commissioner and citing witness £18.10
(d) Fee to cover drawing and lodging interrogatories and cross-interrogatories — per sheet £12.50
(e) Attendance before commissioner — per hour £17.50
(f) Travelling time — per hour £12.50
  14. Supplementary note of defence (when ordered) £12.50
  15. Appeals—
(a) fee to cover instructions, marking of appeal or noting that appeal marked, noting of diet of hearing thereof and preparation for hearing £84.30
(b) Fee to cover conduct of hearing — per half hour £18.10
  16. Final procedure—
(a) Fee to cover settling with witnesses, inquiring for cause at avizandum, noting final interlocutor £37.40
(b) Fee to cover drawing account of expenses, arranging, intimating and attending hearing on expenses, and obtaining approval of sheriff clerk's report £37.40
(c) Fee to cover considering opponent's account of expenses and attendance at hearing on expenses £18.10

CHAPTER V
MERCANTILE SEQUESTRATION

Charge according to Chapter III.

CHAPTER VI
EXECUTRY BUSINESS — INTESTATE MOVEABLE SUCCESSION

  1. Taking instructions to present petition for decree-dative, drawing petition and making necessary copies, lodging and directing publication, attendance at court, moving for decree-dative, extracting decree where necessary, and all matters incidental to petition — inclusive fee £74.80
  2. Preliminary investigation and confirmation of executors—
To be charged for according to general table of fees for conveyancing and general business in testate succession in force from time to time.
  3. Bonds of caution—
(a) Taking out bond of caution, getting it signed and lodged with clerk of court, and procuring attestation of cautioner's sufficiency £21.20
(b) Where caution is found through the medium of a guarantee company for all the work in connection therewith £21.20
  4. Restriction of caution—
Taking instructions to prepare petition for restriction of caution, drawing petition and making necessary copies, instructing advertisement and all matters incidental to petition — inclusive fee £42.40

SCHEDULE 2   Paragraph 3 (1)
REVOCATIONS

Column 1 Acts of Sederunt Revoked	Column 2 References	Column 3 Extent of revocation
Act of Sederunt (Fees of Solicitors in the Sheriff Court) 1989	SI 1989/434	The whole Act of Sederunt
Act of Sederunt (Fees of Solicitors in the Sheriff Court) (Amendment) 1990	SI 1990/716	The whole Act of Sederunt
Act of Sederunt (Fees of Solicitors in the Sheriff Court) (Amendment) 1991	SI 1991/848	The whole Act of Sederunt
Act of Sederunt (Fees of Solicitors in the Sheriff Court) (Amendment) 1992	SI 1992/748	The whole Act of Sederunt
Act of Sederunt (Solicitor and Client Accounts in the Sheriff Court) 1992	SI 1992/1434	Paragraph 4
Act of Sederunt (Fees of Solicitors in the Sheriff Court) (Amendment) 1993	SI 1993/898	The whole Act of Sederunt

[Acts of Sederunt are reproduced with the permission of the Controller of Her Majesty's Stationery Office.]

ARTICLES

Design Right: Some Recent Developments

Hector L MacQueen,
Senior Lecturer,
Department of Private Law,
University of Edinburgh.

Dr MacQueen describes the nature of the new unregistered design right created by the Copyright, Designs and Patents Act 1988, and analyses the extent to which the first judicial pronouncements on the subject conform to the statutory scheme. He concludes with a brief critique of the recent EC Regulation and Directive on industrial designs.

Unregistered design right

One of the major innovations of the Copyright, Designs and Patents Act 1988 was the creation of the unregistered design right (Copyright, Designs and Patents Act 1988, Pt III (ss 213-264)). It was invented to replace the design copyright which had been judicially developed under the Copyright Act 1956, culminating in the famous case of *British Leyland v Armstrong Patents* [1986] AC 577. In that case the House of Lords felt compelled to hold that the design of the exhaust pipe of a Morris Marina car enjoyed copyright for the lifetime of the designer plus the usual 50 year period after death. This enabled British Leyland, the manufacturers of the exhaust pipe, to take control of the independent spare parts market by insisting that the operators in that market required a copyright licence to do so. The House of Lords perceived a threat to consumer interests in this result, in that the monopoly achieved through the copyright in the design meant that there were no competitive restraints on the price of spare parts. It therefore held British Leyland's copyright to be limited by the principle prohibiting derogation from grant. This was obviously unsatisfactory, and the 1988 legislation effectively removed copyright from product design, replacing it with unregistered design right. (See generally the writer's *Copyright, Competition and Industrial Design* (David Hume Institute, 1989).)

The main features of unregistered design right are as follows. It covers the design of any three dimensional product so long as that design is original in the sense of not being commonplace in the design field in question (1988 Act, s 213). The design must be recorded in a design document (s 213 (6)). Spare parts of the *British Leyland* type are excluded from protection, however, by means of the "must fit" and "must match" exceptions (s 213 (3)). This means that any aspect of a design which enables the article to which it applies to be fitted to or matched with another article is not protected. Design right belongs to the designer unless it is created under a commission or in the course of employment, in which case it belongs to the commissioner or the employer as the case may be (s 215). The period of protection is much shorter than in copyright. It lasts for 15 years from the date the design was recorded, unless during the period of five years after the date of recording an article made to the design is put on the market by or with the licence of the design right owner. The right then expires 10 years later (s 216). As it is put in Vol 18 of the *Stair Memorial Encyclopaedia*, "the fifteen-year period is a maximum which will be reduced by commercial exploitation of the design during the first five years of its existence" (para 1223). The right is infringed by copying the design for commercial purposes, either by making articles to the design or by making design documents to enable such articles to be made (s 226).

There are various limitations on unregistered design right which are supposed to prevent its use to stifle competition. The extent of these is so great that the right has been seen by some as merely a fair weather friend; the person wishing to reproduce an unregistered design for commercial purposes has several means by which to impede the enforcement of the right against him. It is therefore of some interest to examine the first three cases discussing unregistered design right to see whether it is capable of effective use.

C & H Engineering Ltd v F Klucznik & Sons Ltd

The first case, *C & H Engineering Ltd v F Klucznik & Sons Ltd* [1992] FSR 421, is a decision of Aldous J in the English High Court. It dealt with the design rights in pig fenders. Pig fenders stop piglets leaving the sty while enabling the sow to step over into the field outside the sty. It is important that the fender be shaped so that the sow's teats are not scratched as she steps over it. The first fender in the case solved this problem by having a two inch rounded metal tube placed around its top edge. The second, allegedly infringing, fender also had a rounded tube or roll bar on top but it differed from the first fender in having flaring sides which enabled it to be stacked with other fenders.

The claim of infringement failed. First, the evidence on whose idea was the design incorporating a tube on top was unclear. Aldous J therefore held that the claimant had not established that he was the owner of the design right. In any event he thought that the second fender did not infringe the design right of the first. Although there was substantial similarity in respect of the roll bars, the overall designs of the fenders were different. Aldous J argued that the test for infringement of unregistered design right was different from that for infringement of copyright. Whereas with copyright, only copying of the work or of a substantial part of it had to be shown, with unregistered design right, it had to be shown that articles had been produced exactly or substantially to the design (s 226 (2)). The judge went on (at p 428): "Whether or not the alleged infringing article is made substantially to the plaintiff's design must be an objective test to be decided through the eyes of the person to whom the design is directed. Pig fenders are purchased by pig farmers and I have no doubt that they purchase them taking into account price and design. In the present case, the plaintiff's alleged infringing pig fenders do not have exactly the same design as shown in the defendant's design document. Thus it is necessary to compare the plaintiff's pig fenders with the defendant's design drawing and, looking at the differences and similarities through the eyes of a person such as a pig farmer, decide whether the design of the plaintiff's pig fender is substantially the same as the design shown in the drawing."

Although it is probably right to say that the comparison between a design and an allegedly infringing article must be objective (see further B Turner [1993] 1 EIPR 24), the "pig farmer" test appears to be an unjustified gloss on the statutory provisions. It is true that copying by producing articles to the design is not the same as copying a work in the copyright sense, namely, reproducing it or any substantial part thereof in any material form (ss 16 (3) and 17 (2)). But the real significance of the statutory words "making articles to that design" lies elsewhere in the 1988 Act, in s 51's exclusion of making articles to a design from the ambit of copyright in the design (see further below). There is no reason to go on to test whether or not the article is made to the design by reference to the person to whom the design is directed. The question is simply whether a design has been copied — that is, whether there is a causal link between a design and a subsequent article. It was established that the designer of the second fender had seen the first one and had used it towards his own design (see [1992] FSR at p 429). "I have no doubt," said Aldous J, "that the idea of having a tube as

the roll bar came from the defendant's pig fender and therefore copying did take place" (p 429). That, it is submitted, should have been enough to establish a prima facie case of infringement of the design right in the first fender (see further Copinger & Skone James on *Copyright* (13th ed), para 20-124).

A second doubtful point is a lack of clarity about whether or not the case was about the whole of the pig fender rather than just the roll bar. Under s 213 design right subsists in designs, and a design may be the design of the whole *or part* of an article. Design right could therefore have subsisted in the roll bar alone. It is doubtful whether the rest of the pig fender had any design right. Aldous J himself noted (at p 428): "By 1990 pig fenders were commonplace and had been made in metal and wood. In essence [the farmer] wanted a commonplace pig fender with a metal roll bar on the top . . . the only part of the pig fender shown in the drawing which was not commonplace was the 2 inch tube on the top." Given his own careful recognition earlier that design right did not subsist in commonplace designs, it is puzzling that he nonetheless went on to treat these commonplace elements as of significance in judging whether or not the design right in the roll bar had been infringed. (See also B Turner [1993] 1 EIPR at p 25.)

A final difficulty with Aldous J's judgment is a comment that originality in design right is the same as in copyright. (See the same point also made in C Tootal, *The Law of Industrial Designs* (1990), pp 187-188.) The test means that the design must not be copied from another design but be the independent work of the designer ([1992] FSR at p 427). Aldous J then refers to the statutory provision in s 213 (4) that "a design is not 'original' for the purposes of [unregistered design right] if it is commonplace in the design field in question at the time of its creation". Aldous J concludes that "For the design to be original it must be the work of the creator *and* that work must result in a design which is not commonplace in the relevant field" (p 428, emphasis supplied). This is correct and, it is submitted, means that the test of originality in unregistered design right is *not* the same as in copyright. As the writer commented some years ago, the test "is certainly more restrictive than the copyright originality concept, where banality and the rehashing of old ideas have never been held unoriginal so long as an independent skill, labour and mode of expression was used" (*Copyright, Competition and Industrial Design*, p 70; see also Copinger & Skone James on *Copyright* (13th ed), para 20-76).

Squirewood Ltd v H Morris & Co Ltd

The second design right case, *Squirewood Ltd v H Morris & Co Ltd*, Outer House, 1 April 1993, unreported (1993 GWD 20-1239), is a decision of Lord Clyde. By contrast with the *C & H Engineering* case, he upheld the design right and granted interim interdict. Because the decision was one on interim interdict, Lord Clyde's opinion contains little substantive discussion of unregistered design right. But the averments disclosed an interesting situation in which the interaction between unregistered design right and copyright was an important issue.

Squirewood designed office furniture. Their designs were contained in drawings (design documents in the language of the 1988 Act). They also produced brochures in which their furniture was described and illustrated by photographs and drawings. Squirewood claimed that Morris were manufacturing and selling office furniture which was in substance a reproduction of the designs. Lord Clyde refused an interim interdict in respect of the drawings because these were not produced by the pursuers at the hearing but granted the remedy in respect of the brochure. He said: "I was satisfied that the pursuers had a prima facie right to the copyright in the brochure and all other intellectual property rights including design right in the designs there shown" (transcript, pp 2-3).

This view appears to be basically correct so far as concerns unregistered design right. Design right does not subsist unless and until the design has been recorded in a design document or an article has been made to the design (1988 Act, s 213 (6)). A design document is any record of a design, whether in the form of a drawing, a written description, a photograph, data stored in a computer or otherwise (1988 Act, s 263 (1)). A brochure of the kind found in the *Squirewood* case clearly falls within this definition. But it should be emphasised that design right does not subsist in the brochure as such or as a design document. Design right subsists in the design, of which the design document is a record only. It is not necessary to refer to any design document to determine whether infringement of a design right has taken place. As already indicated, all that is needed is to establish the causal link of copying between the original design and subsequent commercial reproduction of articles exactly or substantially to that design (1988 Act, s 226).

The brochure also had copyright. Lord Clyde held it to be a literary work also containing artistic works in the form of the photographs and drawings (transcript, p 2). But was the copyright infringed by the manufacture and sale of office furniture? The answer is that there was almost certainly no copyright infringement. While the copyright in a two dimensional artistic work may be infringed by making a copy in three dimensions (1988 Act, s 17 (3)), this is limited by s 51 of the 1988 Act as part of the legislative policy of excluding industrial designs from copyright. The section provides that "It is not an infringement of any copyright in a design document or model recording or embodying a design for anything other than an artistic work or a typeface to make an article to the design or to copy an article made to the design". Thus to make furniture to someone else's design without permission is not an infringement of copyright unless the furniture is an artistic work in its own right. Furniture can constitute artistic work: as a sculpture or a work of artistic craftsmanship, for example. But this is not very likely when the work is intended for mass industrial production, as was probably the situation in the *Squirewood* case. The copyright in the brochure only prevented other parties from making two dimensional reproductions of its contents.

It may finally be noted that unregistered design right also gives its owner the right to stop other persons making a design document recording the design for the purpose of enabling articles to be made to the design. So here the copyright and the unregistered design right march together, the crucial difference being that there is no need to show any purpose other than copying to establish infringement of copyright.

Ford Motor Co Ltd and Iveco Fiat SpA's Applications

The first two cases on unregistered design right suggest a degree of judicial uncertainty about the subject, but they also show that the right can be a useful form of protection in some situations. Neither case raised the difficult issues of "must fit" and "must match", the limits of which will surely prove the ultimate test of the right's utility to commerce. The exceptions were considered for the first time in *Ford Motor Co Ltd and Iveco Fiat SpA's Design Applications* [1993] RPC 399, a decision of Julian Jeffs, QC, sitting in the registered designs appeal tribunal as a deputy High Court judge of the Chancery Division. The case was concerned with applications to register designs rather than unregistered design right as such; but since the 1988 Act registered designs are also subject to a "must match" exclusion (Registered Designs Act 1949, s 1 (1) (b) (ii), substituted by the Copyright, Designs and Patents Act 1988, s 265 (1)). The exception is stated in exactly the same terms as for unregistered designs, so that cases in either field are authoritative in both. It was held that motor vehicle body panels could not be registered as a result of the "must match" exception. In addition, it was also held that such parts had no reality as articles of commerce apart from the vehicle itself and so, not being articles to which a design had been applied, there could be no registration of the design. (On this point, see *Stair Memorial Encyclopaedia*, Vol 18, paras 1173, 1174.) But applications in respect of the designs of a wing mirror, a lamp, a vehicle seat, a steering wheel, wheels and wheel covers were allowed to proceed.

Deputy Judge Jeffs found the amended provisions of the 1949 Act "undoubtedly ambiguous and obscure" ([1993] RPC at p 421). Like the registrar at first instance, he invoked the ruling of the House of Lords in *Pepper v Hart* [1992] 3 WLR 1032 and found guidance in the parliamentary debates on the legislation ([1993] RPC at pp 413-414, 421-422). The debates made it quite clear that the intention of Parliament had been to deny design protection to car body panels. (See also *Copyright, Competition and Industrial Design*, pp 70-73; *Stair Memorial Encyclopaedia*, Vol 18, paras 1181 and 1216.) While such panels might be sold as independent items, they had necessarily to be the same in appearance as those which they replaced. The design of the panel was subordinate to the design of the vehicle as a whole. The other items were, however, ones where an owner of a vehicle might choose between alternatives, for example, to give a car a sportier appearance or increase its comfort. Thus the appearance of parts such as these was not integral to the appearance of the vehicle as a whole, and the designs fell outwith the scope of the "must match" exception.

The Registered Designs Act as amended contains no "must fit" exception. Deputy Judge Jeffs thought that s 7 (6) of the 1949 Act as amended, providing that "The right in a registered design is not infringed by the reproduction of a feature of the design which, by virtue of section 1 (1) (b), is left out of account in determining whether the design is registrable", had the same effect as the "must match" exception ([1993] RPC at p 422). Section 1 (1) (b) refers not only to the "must match" exception but also to the exclusion from registrability of "features of shape or configuration . . . dictated solely by the function which the article has to perform". "Must fit" aspects of a design seem clearly to be features dictated by function, and hence not registrable (*Stair Memorial Encyclopaedia*, Vol 18, para 1182; see also the judgment

of the registrar (Mr B G Harden) [1993] RPC at p 406).

The decision appears to be a correct view of the intended effect of the exceptions, whatever one may think of the policy which underlies them. But it is important to note that a number of motor vehicle accessories were held to fall outwith the exceptions. The accessories would therefore receive protection from unregistered design right if registration was for any other reason not used or achieved. Again then the right can be seen to have a worthwhile function from the point of view of the producer of the design.

European Commission's draft regulation and directive

The European Commission has been interested in the protection of industrial designs for some time, and played a not insignificant background role in the formulation of the unregistered design right of the 1988 Act (see *Copyright, Competition and Industrial Design*, pp 44, 58, 76). In June 1991 it published a green paper, *The Legal Protection of Industrial Design* (111/F/5131/91-EN). Following consultation, on 3 December 1993 the Commission published proposals for a regulation to set up a Community design right (COM(93) 342 final) and a directive on the legal protection of designs (COM(93) 344 final). The draft directive seeks the harmonisation of the law of member states upon a registration basis, although this is to be without prejudice to any system of unregistered design rights such as exists in the UK. Designs may also be protected by copyright, although the extent of such protection can be determined by each member state.

The tests of registrability will be novelty and possession of an "individual character", meaning that it produces a significantly different overall impression upon the informed user by comparison with any previous design in the Community. "Must fit" and functional elements are to be excluded from protection. The design of a product which constitutes part of a complex item shall only be considered to be new and of an individual character so far as the design applied to the part as such fulfils those criteria. Protection is to last for five years in the first instance but will be renewable for five year periods up to a maximum overall of 25 years. Three years after the first marketing of the product to which a protected design has been applied, third parties may reproduce the design to effect repairs of complex products.

The regulation is a complex affair involving the creation of both a registered and an unregistered design right at Community level. It therefore requires the establishment of a Community Designs Registry. For both registered and unregistered designs the criteria of protection are like those laid down for national laws in the draft directive. Thus the Community unregistered design will offer less coverage than the UK unregistered design, which extends to designs dictated by function so long as they are not "must fit", "must match", or commonplace. The Community unregistered design right will also last for only three years from the time at which the designer first makes the design available to the public, a period significantly shorter than that provided for unregistered designs in the UK. But like the UK unregistered design right, the protection will not give an absolute monopoly over commercial reproduction of the design, but will instead prevent only copying of the design. The Community registered design, which will last for a maximum of five five-year periods, will however enable the proprietor to prevent any application of the design to a commercial product whether or not that is the result of copying.

It is difficult to see how the UK unregistered design right can live alongside the proposed Community system, and one or other will certainly have to change if there is to be an accommodation between the two. The Community proposal seems the less useful of the two from a commercial point of view. The objection to registration systems has always been cost and bureaucratic uncertainty for the applicants. If the aim is really as so often stated by the Commission, that is, to offer small and medium sized enterprises convenient and low-cost access to intellectual property protection, unregistered protection along the lines of the UK model seems, in the light of the cases to date, to go some way in that direction. Three years' worth of protection, as in the Community model, seems too short to be of commercial value. The attraction of registration is that it gives certainty as to the existence of rights; but the argument may be countered with the point that a broadly conceived unregistered design right, including functional designs, means that users and would be competitors have to start on the basis that producer rights exist. The Commission, like the UK Government in the debates preceding the 1988 Act, is much concerned that intellectual property should not inhibit competition, in particular in the spare parts market where the consumer stands to benefit from lower prices. But the right can be framed, and indeed in the draft regulation is framed, to limit the protection of spare parts, without also, as in the draft regulation, so limiting the right in general as to make it next to useless for all those who, for whatever reason, choose not to register their designs. If there is still room for discussion on these matters, the UK Government should press for reconsideration of all the implications of protecting unregistered industrial designs at Community level.

◆

NEWS

Court

Auditor of the Court of Session

The Auditor of the Court of Session has now taken delivery of a fax machine. The number is 031-220 0137.

— ◇ —

General

Small ships register of consultants and surveyors

A register of consultants and surveyors specialising in small vessels has been formed by the small ships group of the Institute of Marine Engineers. It will give insurers and others requiring technical support, as well as owners and operators, access to well qualified and experienced practitioners, many of whom will have experience of expert witness and litigation work.

The register lists members who are all highly experienced in working with marine vessels up to approximately 45 m (146 ft) in length — whether power or sail, used commercially or for leisure purposes. Registrants are either fellows, members or associate members of the Institute of Marine Engineers and are registered with the Engineering Council as either chartered or incorporated engineers. They are required to comply with a code of professional conduct and undertake to keep themselves abreast of developments within their field of competence.

Further information about the register may be

obtained from: David L Morgan, Manager, Professional Affairs, Institute of Marine Engineers, 76 Mark Lane, London EC3R 7JN (tel 071-481 8493; fax 071-488 1854).

— ◇ —

Obituaries

On 15 November 1993, James Douglas MacNaughton, retired solicitor and former chief executive of Grampian Regional Council.

On 4 February 1994, George Barclay, formerly partner in the firm of Messrs Marshall, Hunter & Dean, solicitors, Falkirk.

— ◇ —

Parliamentary News

New Bills

HOUSE OF COMMONS

2 February 1994

Professions Supplementary to Medicine (Amendment)—to amend the Professions Supplementary to Medicine Act 1960 for the purpose of permitting the title of podiatrist to be used as an alternative to that of state registered chiropodist under the terms of that Act. (Private Member's Bill introduced by Mr Alfred Morris)

Registration of Small Children's Homes—to provide for the registration of a children's home where accommodation is provided for one or more children, and for connected purposes. (Private Member's Bill introduced by Ms Ann Coffey)

Horses (Protective Headgear for Young Riders) (Amendment)—to amend s 1 (1) of the Horses (Protective Headgear for Young Riders) Act 1990 so as to increase the age set out therein. (Private Member's Bill introduced by Mr Harry Greenway)

Progress of Bills

Social Security (Incapacity for Work) — Commons second reading, 24 January 1994.

Finance — Commons second reading, 25 January 1994.

Merchant Shipping (Salvage and Pollution) — Commons second reading, 28 January 1994.

Inshore Fishing (Scotland) — Lords second reading, 4 February 1994.

Deregulation and Contracting Out — Commons second reading, 8 February 1994.

Dangerous Dogs (Amendment) — Lords second reading, 9 February 1994.

Questions answered

HOUSE OF COMMONS

3 February 1994

LOCKERBIE

Mr Dalyell: To ask the Secretary of State for Scotland from which legally qualified persons he has had requests to see the evidence which he alleges he has in respect of two Libyans, alleged to be involved in the crash of Pan Am 103.

Lord James Douglas-Hamilton: My noble and learned Friend, the Lord Advocate, has received requests from one Justice Zawi of the Libyan Supreme Court and from the noble Lord, Lord Macaulay of Bragar QC and Mr Alistair Duff, solicitor, acting on behalf of the two Libyan accused. My noble and learned Friend Lord Fraser of Carmyllie, the then Lord Advocate, made a full statement of facts available to the Libyan authorities when the arrest warrants were issued in November 1991. That statement contained more detail than would be required for extradition in most European countries.

The Lord Advocate has received a number of private requests from lawyers representing different interests, in the main civil, for information concerning the case and he has, in accordance with normal practice, declined to make evidence relating to the case against the two Libyans available to third parties.

7 February 1994

LOCAL GOVERNMENT REORGANISATION

Mr Dewar: To ask the Secretary of State for Scotland if the Transfer of Undertakings (Protection of Employment) Regulations 1981 will apply to employees of regional and district authorities affected by the reorganisation of local government if they transfer to the employment of the proposed new authorities; and if he will make a statement.

Mr Lang: The question of the extent to which the Transfer of Undertakings (Protection of Employment) Regulations 1981 as amended will apply in the context of local government reorganisation is a matter of law. It is not for the Government to determine whether and how the law applies; that must be a matter for the courts. Whether the regulations apply in any particular case will depend on the detailed circumstances, and it will be for local authorities as employers to take a view on the likelihood of the regulations applying where a new authority appears to have taken over a function of an existing authority.

PLANNING APPLICATIONS

Mr Donohoe: To ask the Secretary of State for Scotland if he will make it his policy not to implement the changes proposed to the Scottish Office's revised fee scale for applications for planning permission.

Mr Allan Stewart: My right hon Friend has no plans at present to alter his policy on revised fees scales approved by Parliament in December 1993.

TREASURE TROVE

Mr Kynoch: To ask the Secretary of State for Scotland if he will make a statement on the administration arrangements relating to treasure trove in Scotland.

Mr Lang: With the agreement of the Prime Minister and the Chancellor of the Exchequer, formal responsibility for the administration of treasure trove in Scotland has been transferred from HM Treasury to the Scottish Office. This is a further step in developing the policies set out in the White Paper *Scotland in the Union: A Partnership for Good.*

I have taken this opportunity to make some changes to the membership of the advisory panel on treasure trove. I have increased the membership of the advisory panel from three to four members, and I am pleased to announce that Dr Barbara Crawford has agreed to be its first independent expert chairperson. At the same time a number of procedural changes are being introduced.

This package of measures will improve the effectiveness and standing of the advisory panel and open up the treasure trove procedures in general.

PRISONERS

Dr Godman: To ask the Secretary of State for Scotland how many prisoners originally sentenced for murder had their sentences (a) subsequently reduced or (b) quashed on appeal while serving their sentences since 1970; and what sums of money were paid, by way of compensation, to those released from prison in such circumstances.

Lord James Douglas-Hamilton: The mandatory sentence to be imposed on a person convicted of murder is imprisonment for life. Information prior to 1981 is not held centrally, nor is information on the results of retrials, but since 1981 three prisoners originally sentenced for murder had their sentence subsequently reduced, a further four had their sentence quashed on appeal and a retrial was authorised for two prisoners.

Compensation is not payable in cases where a conviction for murder is reduced or quashed on appeal within the normal time limits. Since 1970, two payments of compensation of £77,000 and £50,415 have been made to persons originally convicted of murder and whose sentences were subsequently quashed or reversed outside the normal time limits.

HOMOSEXUALS

Dr Godman: To ask the Secretary of State for Scotland what guidelines have been recently issued by the Lord Advocate to procurators fiscal, sheriffs and judges concerning consenting homosexual relationships amongst males aged 16 years or more; and if he will make a statement.

Lord James Douglas-Hamilton: My noble and learned Friend the Lord Advocate does not issue guidelines to sheriffs and judges. Since December 1991 procurators fiscal have been directed by the Lord Advocate to report to the Crown Office for Crown counsel's consideration cases of consensual homosexual acts where both of the participants are over 16 ycars but one or both are under 18 years.

Where both the participants are over 18 years but one or both are under 21 years and there are circumstances pointing to exploitation, corruption or breach of trust, the direction to procurators fiscal is that prosecution would be appropriate and that such cases need not be reported to the Crown Office unless none of those circumstances is present but the procurator fiscal considers that there are other circumstances which would justify proceedings.

Book Reviews

Delict

(Greens Concise Scots Law)
Second edition. By William J Stewart. 1993.
Edinburgh: W Green. Paperback, £26.
ISBN 0 414 01051 5.

Stewart's *Introduction to the Scots Law of Delict*

was first published in 1989. Two reprints followed by the appearance of this second edition pay eloquent testimony to the warm welcome which the book has received from students and practitioners alike.

After an introductory chapter on the theory and history of the subject, the book has separate chapters on "Delicts with Names", Liability for Unintentional Harm, Statutory Duty, Special Areas of Activity (such as occupiers' liability, product liability, liability for animals and employers' liability), Verbal Injuries, Parties, Vicarious Liability, Practical Matters, Immunities, Defences, Transfer and Extinction, and concludes with a new chapter on Restitution which, together with Woolman's *Contract*, means that the Scots law of obligations is now covered in the Greens Concise Scots Law series. A new section on Eurorep liability deals with the potential liability in tort/delict of a member state for a breach of Community law. The treatment, in the context of employers' liability, of such measures as the Workplace (Health, Safety and Welfare) Regulations 1992, the Health and Safety (Display Screen Equipment) Regulations 1992 and the Manual Handling Operations Regulations 1992 serves as a timely warning that the health and safety professional, with his expertise in risk assessment and safety audits, may become as familiar a figure as the medical expert in personal injuries litigation. This edition includes more detailed consideration of Scottish Law Commission recommendations, and a number of sections, for example those on economic loss and the defence of illegality, have been rewritten.

The author's style is one which surely commends itself to the student reader. He writes with a lightness of touch and explains simply yet effectively difficult concepts such as causation and economic loss. Academic divisions on particular points are explained and the author is not afraid to speculate as to the future direction of the law, as witness his suggestion that the double liability problem in cases of secondary economic loss (e g *Blackburn v Sinclair*, 1984 SLT 368) might be resolved by a Rule of Court requiring a person claiming such loss to aver the identity of the owner at the time of the damage and to show evidence of intimation of proceedings.

This reviewer did think that the first edition would have been improved by the inclusion of a separate chapter on damages. However, this edition continues to treat these under the heading of "Practical Matters", along with matters of

evidence, pleading and choice of law. A separate chapter might permit mention of interim awards of damages under Rule of Court 89A. It would also allow damages for services to be dealt with in one place, whereas at present they are considered at pp 100-101 under Economic Loss, 183-184 under Families: Married Women, and at 220-221 under Relatives. On the subject of damages, recoupment of benefits (p 234) is now dealt with by the Social Security Administration Act 1992, ss 81-103, which came into force on 1 July 1992, and, for a complete understanding, mention should also be made of the Social Security (Recoupment) Regulations 1990. In that context too, only "small payments", i e those not exceeding £2,500, remain subject to the Law Reform (Personal Injuries) Act 1948, s 2 (1), as amended. This provides for the deduction from such payments of half of all "relevant benefits" received, not just those formerly listed in the 1948 Act. Such deductions can be made against all heads of damages awarded, not merely loss of earnings (p 233).

However the blemishes are de minimis. Some 100 pages longer than its predecessor, this new edition represents excellent value for money and can with confidence be recommended to the ever increasing ranks of law students in universities and colleges.

J BLAIKIE,
University of Aberdeen.

Bill Stewart, the Book Review Editor, is keen that books, and especially, books written with the practitioner in mind should be reviewed by practitioners. Accordingly, members of Faculty and solicitors who consider that they could competently review books, are invited to write with a note of their name and address, indicating upon what subjects they would be prepared to write reviews, to him c/o the Law School, University of Strathclyde, Stenhouse Building, 173 Cathedral Street, Glasgow G4 0RQ.

ARTICLES

Alluvio, Avulsio and Fluvial Boundaries

D L Carey Miller,
University of Aberdeen.

Professor Carey Miller examines the effect on title where changes occur in the course of a river making a boundary, in light of the recent case of Stirling v Bartlett. *He suggests that the fundamental factor is that of the parties' consent to a boundary being determined by natural changes.*

In *Stirling v Bartlett*, 1993 SLT 763 the Outer House was concerned with a boundary dispute involving riparian proprietors, the course of the River Orrin having been affected by flooding over a period of years. The parties were in agreement that the medium filum was the boundary but were in dispute as to the proper position at which the middle line should be drawn.

The relevant part of the Orrin is subject to periodic flooding but the dispute centred on the direct effect of two particular floods and on subsequent restorative and remedial work. In 1966 the deposits brought down by a major flood caused the river to widen out appreciably and divide itself into a number of shallow channels — a likely contributing factor being the gravel extraction works of both proprietors. The then affected parties caused a clear channel to be excavated. In the subsequent litigation the pursuer claimed that this channel was the medium filum and, as such, the proper boundary. The defender, it may be noted, took possession of his land in 1969 and claimed to be under the impression that the boundary was to the west of the new channel. When, subsequently, he established a fish farm the works involved caused the main channel of the Orrin to move some distance to the west. A severe flood in 1989 damaged the fish farming facility and caused the defender to commence major works on both sides of the channel. These works were interdicted by the pursuer and the boundary dispute followed. The essential issue between the parties was whether the boundary was the present position of the channel excavated in 1966 or a line representing the main course of the river prior to 1966.

Lord Coulsfield, having noted that there was no previous decision precisely in point, stated the principles of alluvio and avulsio in the following terms: "It is, I think, well established that where the course of a river, which constitutes the boundary between two properties, changes by the gradual and imperceptible addition or subtraction of soil on one bank or the other, the boundary shifts in accordance with the movement of the river. That is an application of the principle of alluvio. On the other hand, where the course of a river changes in a sudden and violent way, whether by the operation of natural forces or with human assistance, the boundary does not change. That is an application of the principle of avulsio" (1993 SLT at p 767I-J).

The learned Lord Ordinary went on to quote the relevant sections of *Institutes* of Justinian (II i 20, 21) on alluvio and avulsio.

In problems of fluvial accretion an eclectic attitude to authority is probably justifiable in view of the wide influence of what was developed in Roman law as a matter of ius gentium (see *Inst* II i 20). Acknowledging this, Lord Coulsfield (at p 767L) placed some reliance on the American case of *Nebraska v Iowa* (143 US 359 (1892)). This decision was to do with the flooding of the Missouri — an event which, of course, has reoccurred recently with devastating consequences. The American case is authority, inter alia, for the proposition that the imperceptible change of alluvio need not be over a protracted period but can, indeed, occur by a rapid process involving flooding. This was seen as an important aspect of the decision: "The significance of this case is that it indicates that although the changes which constitute accretion must be gradual and imperceptible in the sense that at any given time they cannot be seen to occur, they need not be gradual in the sense of occurring slowly over a period of years, or even months; it is sufficient if [the changes] occur in such a way that the transfer of soil cannot be seen to happen before the eyes of the observer" (p 768D).

As Lord Coulsfield pointed out, Stair (II i 35) supports this conclusion. The following excerpt is relevant: "though the adjection may be perceivable and considerable in a tract of time, it maketh no difference, if at no particular instant the adjection be considerable". Stair (ibid) goes on to illustrate the point on the analogy of the movement of the hands of a clock: "as the motion of the palm of a horologe is insensible at any instant, though it be very perceivable when put together, in less than the quarter of an hour".

It may be noted that Stair (ibid) identifies as a policy factor behind the alluvio principle the consideration that "the frequent questions that would arise betwixt the proprietors upon the opposite banks of rivers, are prevented". This could be seen as a cue to the point that, in practice, disputes are likely to be between riparian proprietors — in effect boundary disputes as in *Stirling* — rather than unlikely questions of alluvio or avulsio between upper and lower fluvial proprietors. Does this suggest that the focus should be on the boundary issue rather than on the less specific question of accession through water-borne accretion?

In Justinian's *Institutes* the texts on alluvio and avulsio are followed by one concerned with the change of a river's channel (alveus derelitus). The text states that if a river leaves its channel and takes a new course the old bed belongs to the riparian owners (*Inst* II i 23). Both this text and a similar *Digest* one (41 1 7 5) make clear that the river must actually abandon its former channel and the importance of this is confirmed by subsequent texts which are specific in noting that flooding does not in itself lead to any change in the proprietary status quo (*Inst* II i 24; *D* 41 1 7 6). As to how ownership in an abandoned river bed is determined the relevant texts (*Inst* II i 23; *D* 41 1 7 5) provide for the same approach as that applying in the case of insula nata, the rule on this being that an island formed in midstream belongs to the riparian owners on either side (*Inst* II i 22). As Lee in *Elements of Roman Law* (4th ed), para 194 shows, this implies the notional drawing of a line between the two banks and, of course, the result may be that a riparian owner has exclusive entitlement because the island is wholly on his side of the line. Applied to an abandoned river bed this means that the critical factors are the direction and distance of movement from the middle line which constituted the boundary prior to the change. This would appear to be consistent with the decision in *Wedderburn v Paterson* (1864) 2 M 902, concerned with the tidal River Tay. In this case the First Division regarded a sand bank — which, at low water, produced a division in the river's channel — as an obstruction to be dealt with, from a boundary point of view, by joining the middle line points above and below the bank.

Does the abandoned river bed rule have any basis in an established principle of the law of property or is it simply a matter of recognising that where a boundary defining river has made a permanent deviation from its former course the boundary necessarily changes? If the rule is seen as an adjunct of the concept of alluvio then, of course, one would tend to assume that its basis, in common with alluvio, is accession. The issue of the basis of the rule that a change in the course of a river leads to a change of boundary is raised in the *Stair Memorial Encyclopaedia* under the subheading of "Retreat of non-tidal waters". The relevant text reads: "When non-tidal waters retreat, so that the river or loch alters its course, the land reclaimed accedes to the immediately adjacent bank. This process is sometimes referred to as *alvei mutatio*."

Kenneth G C Reid, the learned author of the section in question, states in a footnote that "Bell . . . disputes that accession takes place" (*The Laws of Scotland: Stair Memorial Encylopaedia*, Vol 18 (1993), para 594). Bell's text, cited by Reid, identifies alvei mutatio with avulsio and defines the former as "the change frequently occasioned by a river which bounds the property of conterminous heritors deviating from its course" (Bell, *Principles*, s 936). According to Bell this case is analogous to avulsio, as a case which may be distinguished from the gradual process of alluvio, and in neither "is there an acquisition by accession; unless, by acquiescence on the part of the proprietor whose land is diminished, a right shall be conferred on the other". In the final part of this text it would appear that Bell is not saying merely that it is inappropriate to think of this as an instance of accession but he is, rather, pointing to the conclusion that a sudden, and thus perceivable, change in the course of a river — as is "frequently occasioned" through flooding — does not, in itself, produce any change of ownership. It is significant that Bell does not state the qualification which Stair (II i 35, supra) makes — that "perceivable and considerable" change "in a tract of time" may occur, provided that "at no particular instant the adjection be considerable".

The case of *Marquis of Tweeddale v Kerr* (1822) 1 S 397 was concerned with a change in the course of the River Kale which occurred over a 40 year period. It was not in dispute that the change was a gradual one but the owner of the estate which was diminished as a result of the change maintained that the other owner had to satisfy the requirements of acquisitive prescription. Plainly, any acceptance of this contention would undermine the concept of a change of ownership on the basis of a lateral change in the course of a river. In the event the Lords' opinion did not mention the point but supported the view that the case of a change of fluvial boundary may be distinguishable from the accession case: "A majority of their Lordships were of opinion that this was not a case of alluvio, but of alvei mutatio; — that as the river was the boundary, so any change in its course must be held to be consented to by the parties, as they were entitled to restrain it by embankments."

The notion that the basis of the rule that the boundary changes with any permanent changes in the course of the river is tacit consent, inferred from a failure to build retaining structures, is consistent with the premise that a change may occur through flooding. This said, it may be noted that Professor W M Gordon (*Scottish Land Law*, para 4.23), having observed that alvei mutatio "does not necessarily lead to a change in ownership of the property added to one, or lost by another", goes on to comment as follows: "When the change is gradual it would seem that the proprietor who loses land is to be treated as acquiescing in the loss of his land and to the gain made by the other, who will normally acquire title to it."

The significance of this modern juristic opinion is that it limits the application of the doctrine of tacit consent to cases of gradual change. This would appear to exclude a change caused by a flood because while such a change — brought about, at any rate, by a single flood — might be imperceptible, in the sense identified by Stair, it would not be gradual.

Rankine, *The Law of Land-ownership in Scotland* (4th ed), states the law in a manner which appears to support Gordon. Having dealt with alluvio and avulsio the author (at p 113) notes that "The same principles apply to cases where the change takes the shape of a shifting of the bed of a stream laterally from natural causes". Rankine goes on to say that in the case of a gradual change the doctrine of alluvio is "further justified by the acquiescence of the landlord who loses by it". In the case of a change caused by a sudden flood, however, "no alteration is made on ownership; nor has a temporary inundation any such result" (pp 113-114).

It is submitted that acquiescence should, logically and necessarily, only have force in respect of a boundary which, on the basis of the parties' agreement, is open to possible change. Otherwise one would expect the requirements of acquisitive prescription to have to be satisfied. But, of course, agreement can be taken to be the basis of a medium filum boundary: whether by reference to one or other of the respective titles (see *Wedderburn v Paterson* (1864) 2 M at p 909), or on the basis of an inference from the common law presumption (see Gordon, op cit, para 4.34) that the medium filum is the boundary. The case of *Annandale and Eskdale District Council v North West Water Authority*, 1979 SLT 266, would

appear to support the idea that the parties' agreement is the fundamental basis of the proposition that a change in the course of a boundary river by accretion gives a change of boundary. In this case, concerned with the boundary between England and Scotland, Lord Dunpark (at p 269) declined to follow American cases (including *Nebraska v Iowa*) because in the cases concerned — in contrast to the matter before the court — the river boundaries had been fixed by agreement. A medium flumen boundary does not have the fixed and final character of a boundary based upon measurements. By its nature it is open to change. This said, a fluvial boundary must, of course, be determinable. Where a change occurs it must always be possible to establish the medium flumen on the basis of the river's new channel — even if, in the last resort, "the line must be fixed on equitable principles" (per Lord Deas in *Wedderburn v Paterson*). Gradual imperceptible accretion is hardly likely to produce a dispute. But imperceptible accretion in the much wider sense of what cannot be perceived at any instant — possibly a result of flooding — is an entirely different proposition. The decision in *Stirling v Bartlett*, giving effect to Stair's extended notion of imperceptible accretion, is, with respect, a sound one. It is consistent with the basic nature of a river boundary in an environment in which it is not uncommon for flooding to produce a change of course. In tending towards the resolution of boundary approach Stair's interpretation of "imperceptible" gives priority to the fundamental factor of the parties' agreement to a medium flumen boundary. Arguably this is more logical than to proceed on the basis of whether accession has occurred. Why, after all, should original acquisition rule when the parties can be said to have consented to their boundary being determined by natural changes?

♦

NEWS

Appointments

New sheriff
The Queen, on the recommendation of the Secretary of State for Scotland, has appointed Mr Michael John Fletcher, solicitor, Dundee, to be a sheriff for the Sheriffdom of South Strathclyde, Dumfries and Galloway at Dumfries from a date to be announced.

◇

Industrial tribunals
The Lord President of the Court of Session has appointed Mr Robin M Webster to be a full time chairman of the industrial tribunals in Scotland with effect from 1 May 1994.

— ◇ —

Court

Dundee sheriff court
As from Monday, 21 February 1994, the regional

sheriff clerk and the civil and commissary offices have been relocated to a sheriff court annex in premises in Courthouse Square, Dundee, during the refurbishment/extension to the building at West Bell Street.

Courts will continue to be held in, and the criminal and fines offices will continue to operate from, the sheriff courthouse at West Bell Street.

The current telephone number for the courthouse at West Bell Street, 0382 29961, has been reassigned to the annex at Courthouse Square. The courthouse at West Bell Street has been assigned a new number — 0382 26513.

All mail should continue to be addressed to DX DD33.

— ◇ —

Coming events

David Hume Institute conference
The David Hume Institute is holding a conference on the topic "The Costs of Justice", at the Scandic Crown hotel in Edinburgh on 9 May 1994. It is hoped that the speakers will include the Lord Chancellor, Lord Mackay of Clashfern; the Lord Advocate, Lord Rodger of Earlsferry; Professor Sir Alan Peacock; Professor Karl Mackie of the Centre for Dispute Resolution; Professor Alan Paterson of the University of Strathclyde; and Professor Charles Rowley of the John Locke Institute, Washington DC. The cost of attending the conference will be £98 per person. Further details can be obtained from Mike Fenwick, In Conference Ltd, 22 Great King Street, Edinburgh EH3 6QH (tel 031-556 9245, fax 031-556 9638).

— ◇ —

Law reform

Criminal procedure review
The Scottish Law Commission have submitted to the Scottish Office some critical comments on certain proposals in the *Review of Criminal Evidence and Criminal Procedure* published by the government last year (1993 SLT (News) 227).

The object of the *Review* was to consider and make recommendations for changes in the rules of evidence and procedure in criminal cases which would reduce the inconvenience caused to witnesses and jurors by the late cancellation or adjournment of criminal trials and by the length of certain trials. The commission agree that changes are urgently necessary but consider that certain reforms should be undertaken only after careful research and should be founded on principle and workable in practice.

The commission consider that the *Review* has been handicapped by inadequate information about the reasons for late guilty pleas, adjournments and the increasing length of trials, and does not address such questions as the proper function of the judge in the criminal process and the extent of the legitimate rights of the accused. The commission express the view that the *Review's* proposals, if implemented, would bring about an unintended drift from traditional principles and an unsatisfactory blurring of the function of the judge and the rights of the accused.

The *Review* proposes that there should be a pretrial hearing at which the judge would establish the state of preparation of the prosecution and defence cases and take an active role in ascertaining whether the case was likely to go to trial and in encouraging the agreement of undisputed evidence. The commission comment that the judge would be a domineering figure and the procedure is clearly intended to exert pressure on the defence to agree evidence. In the commission's view it prejudices the impartiality of the judge, the relationship between the court and the Crown, and the rights of the accused to reserve his defence and to examine the witnesses against him at the trial. They also doubt whether it would be possible to enforce the proposed duties on the Crown and the defence to agree evidence before the trial.

The commission suggest that depending upon the results of further independent research, a case might be made for the modification or restatement of the traditional principles of Scottish criminal justice in such a way that the period between the institution of the proceedings and the trial would become an important stage in the criminal process when the issues to be contested at the trial would be clarified. The Crown and the defence could be required to disclose their cases, and the scope and nature of the evidence at the trial could be decided at a preliminary hearing before the judge. Such procedures might secure a more efficient presentation of the case in court and the most effective use of the time of witnesses and jurors.

The commission are opposed to the *Review's* proposals to introduce "sentence discounting" whereby an accused person who pleaded guilty would receive a reduced sentence. The commission comment that if the accused's right to be presumed innocent until proved guilty is to remain unqualified, it is unacceptable that an accused who is convicted after trial should be punished more severely simply because he had not pled guilty. They also express serious concern that innocent people would be pressurised into pleading guilty. It points out that in any event there is no evidence that sentence discounting encourages early pleas of guilty.

The commission generally welcome the recommendations in the report by the steering group and working group on court programming, but suggest that further work should be undertaken on the timing of court sittings.

Taxation

Interest paid by government departments
In reply to a parliamentary question about the consequences of the decision in *Esso Petroleum Co Ltd v Ministry of Defence* for the tax treatment of interest paid by government departments, the effect of which is that the provisions of Sched C of the Taxes Acts apply only to interest on government securities and do not extend to other types of interest payments made by government departments, the Financial Secretary to the Treasury has confirmed that payments of interest, other than on government securities, made by government departments after the decision have not been subject to deduction of tax at source under Sched C. In the light of legal advice, the Inland Revenue and the government departments concerned are not taking any steps to seek out, nor make further payments to, the recipients of earlier payments of interest who would then require to be assessed to tax.

Obituary

On 13 February 1994, Ronald MacDonald Kelman, former law secretary of the Clydesdale Bank.

On 16 February 1994, Charles Alastair Findlay, WS, formerly partner in and subsequently consultant to the firm of Messrs Thomson & Baxter, WS, Edinburgh.

Business change

The partners of Pagan Osborne, Cupar, St Andrews, Anstruther and Dundee, and the partners of Macbeth Currie & Co, Dunfermline, Edinburgh, Dalgety Bay and Kinross, intimate that with effect from 14 February 1994 they have formed a business law partnership "Pagan Macbeth". The partners of Pagan Macbeth will be J P Barnet, C W Pagan, J B Clarke and S M Cotton, all of whom will also remain as partners in the respective partnerships of Pagan Osborne or Macbeth Currie & Co. The partners of Pagan Macbeth and Pagan Osborne announce the appointment of Alison Green as an associate of both firms.

Parliamentary News

Royal Assent

10 February 1994

Social Security (Contributions) Act 1994 (c 1).
Statutory Sick Pay Act 1994 (c 2).

New Bills

HOUSE OF LORDS

18 January 1994

Hereditary Peerages—To amend the law relating to hereditary peerages. (Introduced by Lord Diamond)

7 February 1994

Treasure—To make provision in relation to treasure which is not treasure trove and to amend the law relating to treasure trove. (Introduced by the Earl of Perth)

HOUSE OF COMMONS

14 February 1994

European Parliamentary Elections (Gibraltar)—To entitle residents of Gibraltar to vote as electors in an English constituency in elections to the European Parliament; to amend the European Parliamentary Elections Act 1978; and for connected purposes. (Private Member's Bill introduced by Mr Jeff Rooker)

Progress of Bills

Merchant Shipping (Salvage and Pollution)—Commons committee, 9 February 1994.

British Nationality (Hong Kong)—Lords third reading, 14 February 1994.

Intelligence Services—Lords third reading, 14 February 1994.

Book Reviews

Scottish Contract Cases

Second edition. By Enid A Marshall.
1993. Edinburgh: W Green. Paperback, £25.
ISBN 0 414 01052 3.

This is the second edition of Dr Marshall's collection of cases on contract. The first edition made its appearance in 1978 and the work was then reprinted on three occasions. The issue of a second edition is most welcome and Dr Marshall is to be congratulated on the systematic way in which she has organised her material. Her preface indicates that her book has proved to be of value to students, both law students and others, but the book in fact should be attractive even to a professional readership.

The book consists of extracts from reported cases with a division into chapters. Chapter 1 deals with the nature of contract and such matters as the unilateral voluntary obligation or promise, proof thereof, the gratuitous contract without consideration, intention to create legal relationship and sponsiones ludicrae. The cases used there are now fairly elderly: the most recent was reported in 1940. However, it is very helpful to have the essentials of the nature of the contract set out.

Chapter 2 deals with the formation of contract and the favourite examiners' questions of offer and acceptance, consensus in idem, timeous acceptance, revocation of offer or of acceptance and of course the ticket cases. Chapter 3 goes on to deal with the formalities for constitution of a contract and proof thereof and the matter of obligationes literis. Perhaps one day there will be a reported decision dealing with the validity of a faxed copy of an offer.

Chapter 4 deals with grounds on which a contract may be invalid.

Chapter 5 goes on to deal with interpretation and scope. The 1883 case of *Lee v Alexander* is quoted and then the author in her note thereon goes on to discuss *Winston v Patrick, Pena v Ray*, etc. The conveyancing practitioner might perhaps look for a fuller discussion of the problem of the extent to which the missives are superseded by the disposition, but of course this is not intended to be a conveyancing textbook but is intended as a work for students. An examination of the author's note will disclose the citations of the most recent authorities.

Chapter 6 deals with breach of contract and chap 7 with termination. Appendix A reproduces the relevant sections of the Unfair Contract Terms Act 1977, and the sections of the Law Reform (Miscellaneous Provisions) (Scotland) Act 1985 affecting leases and the question of irritancy in particular, as well as the Age of Legal Capacity (Scotland) Act 1991. Appendix B is a glossary of Latin words and phrases used in this book.

This book is clearly not an exhaustive reference work on the law of contract, but neither is it intended to be. It is, however, an extremely useful collection of cases which will provide a ready guide to the practitioner who wishes to refresh his memory as regards the basics of the subject. Many of the reported cases go back to the early part of this century or to the last century. Access to the relevant law reports may not always be obtained immediately and this collection of cases will therefore be a welcome addition to the office library.

DAVID C CLAPHAM, SSC,
Glasgow.

Textbook on Constitutional and Administrative Law

By Brian Thompson. 1993. London:
Blackstone Press. Paperback, £16.95.
ISBN 1 85431 286 3.

I can think of few reasons why a student, practitioner or teacher of law in Scotland (or in Northern Ireland) would want to buy a book in the preface to which the author states: "Unfortunately, I have had to concentrate upon the position in England and Wales, and consequently the coverage of the other jurisdictions, Scotland and Northern Ireland, is much less than it deserves to be and I would wish". It is unfortunate that such material that does relate to Scotland contains some errors. For example, the reference to the departments of the Scottish Office (p 24) is out of date and does not take account of the departmental reorganisation of St Andrews House in 1991. The author also believes that the Conservatives won 12 (and not 11) seats in Scotland in the 1992 general election (p 35).

Large parts of some chapters, for example chap 10 on local government and chap 17 on the remedies of judicial review of administrative action, are set firmly in an English and Welsh context and make no reference to the major differences in the law in Scotland. The index is also disappointing for those looking for information on the Scottish dimension. Nevertheless, the chapter on the fundamental principles and doctrines of constitutional law (chap 3) deals quite well with "revisionist views" of legislative supremacy, the Acts of Union and the Scottish cases arising thereunder, including some of the "poll tax" cases.

A compact book like this (only 408 pages of text, compared with 758 in the new edition of Wade and Bradley's *Constitutional and Administrative Law* and 674 in de Smith's) cannot do full justice to all of the topics covered. It is, however, tightly yet lucidly written, and packed with information. It has a detailed paragraph numbering system which makes it easy to pinpoint essential references for students.

The materials on the European Communities and quasi-government are useful, well presented and up to date. Various chapters stimulate thoughts about reform of government institutions.

This is a book directed at the student market. It is attractively priced, and no doubt students in England and Wales will find it invaluable. Students in Scotland will find it useful in certain respects but should beware of using it as their only aid in a course in constitutional and administrative law at a Scottish university.

JEAN MCFADDEN,
University of Strathclyde.

Conveyancing

(Greens Concise Scots Law)

By George L Gretton and Kenneth G C Reid. 1993. Edinburgh: W Green. Paperback, £35. ISBN 0 414 01054 X.

It has been remarked that the sheer majestic unreadability of Burns' *Conveyancing Practice* has had much to do with conveyancing being regarded as a difficult subject over the years.

This is not a criticism that could be fairly levelled against Gretton and Reid. Take for instance the statement at p 105: "The purchaser's solicitor receives an unappetising bundle of deeds, many of which may turn out to be irrelevant. Conveyancers traditionally never throw anything away." Precisely so, but does one detect a faint, underground, rotating sound? The book is written throughout in this same humorous vein, and contains many of the throwaway lines that Messrs Gretton and Reid have delighted their audiences with in their many public appearances.

The book sets out to be of use both to practitioners and to students, and by and large it achieves this very difficult task. Probably only Gloag and Henderson is used equally by both students and practitioners, but it does not set out to be a practical book, as does Gretton and Reid. This makes the task doubly difficult.

The book covers not only the conveyancing process in great detail, but such ancillary (if the authors will forgive me using such a dreaded word in conveyancing circles) matters as mortgages, trusts and executries, companies, and insolvency.

The authors state in their preface that they have included almost no styles, to keep the book within a reasonable compass. This is understandable, but regrettable, as the topics can be highlighted for students by the inclusion of styles, and many practitioners acquire books mainly for the styles that they contain.

There are only 21 (out of 456) pages on registration of title, which seems a bit on the meagre side, considering that roughly 40 per cent of potentially registerable titles lie in operational counties.

My only real disappointment with this splendid book was the lack of coverage of environmental aspects of conveyancing. It may be argued that environmental considerations are not the concern of the conveyancer, but not I think convincingly. The environment concerns us all, and I think conveyancers are at the sharp end with the other professions. Environmental law is dismissed in six lines on the grounds that the subject is complex and is mainly concerned with commercial conveyancing, which is not dealt with in this book by design. There is a further short treatment of the now aborted registers of contaminated land.

Admittedly the problems are at their worst in the west of Scotland, where for instance it is estimated that 1.2 million cubic metres of carcinogenous chromium waste has been dumped over the years. Houses, schools and playing fields may be constructed on chrome tips. There are many other horrors, such as housing estates built on landfill sites, which are leaking methane gas.

The identification of contaminated land is not, I think, a conveyancing duty, but the conveyancer can help from a knowledge of the site gained from a knowledge of past uses gleaned from the title deeds. Ironically the Land Register, while splendid in so many ways, completely wipes out this history, and recourse to the old sasine search may have to be had!

Such minor grumbles aside, this book is a welcome addition to the range of conveyancing materials.

JOHN H SINCLAIR,
University of Strathclyde.

Offenders Aged 16-18

Report of a Working Party for the Scottish Association for the Study of Delinquency SASD, November 1993.

The SASD is an independent Scottish body with the objective of promoting research into the causes, prevention and treatment of crime and delinquency. This study reports the findings of a working party set up at the end of 1990 to examine the arrangements for dealing with offenders aged between 16 and 18 in Scotland. Currently these offenders may be referred to the hearings system at the discretion of the procurator fiscal, but most are dealt with in the courts. The working party comprised representatives from the agencies involved: procurators fiscal, police, social work, reporters to the children's hearings, prisons, schools, the voluntary sector and the judiciary. Most of the working party members either hold or have recently retired from senior positions in these organisations.

Against a background of the findings of the Child Care Law Review published by the Scottish Office in 1990, the United Nations Convention of the Rights of the Child adopted in 1989, and a discussion of the way in which Scots law defines "children", the report describes how offenders aged 16-18 are dealt with by both the children's hearing system and the courts in Scotland. The most significant difference between the systems is that the courts punish convicted offenders whereas the hearings system makes provisions which are in the best interests of the child and does not punish children.

The report contains a considerable number of practical recommendations, but the most significant is that, with the exception of those serious cases coming within the Lord Advocate's direction, and some minor road traffic offences dealt with in the district court, all offenders aged 16-18 should come before the hearings system rather than the courts. The report provides a well argued case for this policy. The main justifications are first, that most young people grow out of offending in spite of, rather than because of, the efforts made to curb their offending behaviour; secondly, that the recommendation has the potential to reduce the high numbers of "children" detained in custody; and thirdly, that, by transferring this substantial amount of work to the hearings system, it ensures that the courts have the opportunity to deal with those cases where the public require protection.

This recommendation is unlikely to be popular with the present government, although the recent speech by Minister of State Lord Fraser to the Howard League suggests that there are some differences between criminal justice policy in Scotland and England and Wales. Critics of the report may argue that it is "soft" to move 16-18 year olds from the courts to the hearings system. However, this report, based on the deliberations of experienced practitioners, presents a rational and considered case to support the argument that the public interest would be best served by dealing with all young persons under the age of 18 in the hearings system. The members of the working party are well aware that some offenders will go on to become hardened adult offenders. However, since it is impossible to predict accurately who these individuals will be, it is both more cost effective and more humane to try to keep young offenders out of custodial institutions for as long as possible.

This short report is well structured and clearly expressed and should be read by all who are interested in developing an effective and positive way of responding to the major social problem caused by the offending behaviour of young people.

DR NEIL HUTTON,
University of Strathclyde.

Bill Stewart, the Book Review Editor, is keen that books, and especially, books written with the practitioner in mind should be reviewed by practitioners. Accordingly, members of Faculty and solicitors who consider that they could competently review books, are invited to write with a note of their name and address, indicating upon what subjects they would be prepared to write reviews, to him c/o the Law School, University of Strathclyde, Stenhouse Building, 173 Cathedral Street, Glasgow G4 0RQ.

ARTICLES

Data Protection: Brussels Takes Over?

Ian Lloyd,
Deputy Director,
Centre for Law, Computers and Technology,
University of Strathclyde.

Dr Lloyd explains the effect that a proposed EU directive would have on the UK's Data Protection Act 1984.

Introduction

The EEC's involvement in the field of data protection dates back to the early 1970s when a number of initiatives were proposed, principally by the European Parliament. These efforts foundered upon a sea of Commission indifference. In 1981 the Commission recommended (OJ 1981 L246/31) that member states should sign and ratify the then recently negotiated Council of Europe Convention for the Protection of Individuals with Regard to the Automatic Processing of Personal Data. Such action would involve the implementation of national data protection statutes.

Compliance with the recommendation was patchy. It was only in 1993 that Belgium enacted a data protection statute and action is still awaited in Greece, Italy and Spain. Even where data protection statutes are in force, significant discrepancies exist between first generation statutes such as the UK's Data Protection Act 1984 and second and even third generation measures such as the German Data Processing and Data Protection Act of 1990. The latter is based upon the concept of "informational self determination", a notion which gives the individual a much enhanced right to object to the processing of personal data. Although the Council of Europe Convention guarantees free movement of data between signatory states, the existence of differing national requirements was seen as an impediment to the establishment of the Single Market. Data protection returned to the Community's agenda towards the end of the decade and in July 1990 the Commission transmitted a set of proposals for a directive harmonising national laws to ensure "a high level of protection" to the Council. Following comments in the Economic and Social Committee and the Parliament, these proposals were amended and the revised text is currently progressing through the EEC's legislative processes (COM(92) 422 final — SYN 287. Given the significance of the proposed directive, it is surprising that its text has not been published

in the *Official Journal*). This article seeks to outline the major elements of the Community proposals and assess their likely impact upon the United Kingdom's present data protection regime.

Data protection and the Treaty of Rome

Constitutionally, the basis for Community intervention in the field of data protection lies in art 100A of the Treaty. This article, which was added to the original Treaty by the Single European Act of 1987, requires the Community, in the course of establishing the Single Market, to ensure that consumers are granted a "high level of protection". The preamble to the proposed directive recites the reasons justifying legislative intervention in general and in terms of Community law and policy. Thus it is asserted that "data-processing systems are designed to serve society; whereas they must respect the fundamental freedoms and rights of individuals, notably the right to privacy, and contribute to economic and social progress, trade expansion and the well-being of individuals", whilst "the difference in levels of protection of the rights and freedoms of individuals, notably the right to privacy, with regard to the processing of personal data afforded in the member States may prevent the transmission of such data from the territory of one Member State to that of another Member State".

One significant point to note is the use of the word "privacy" in the EEC proposals. This is in marked contrast to the Council of Europe Convention on the Automated Processing of Personal Data which makes no specific reference to the concept of privacy. The preamble, however, makes express reference to the earlier instrument, commenting that "the principles of the rights and freedoms of individuals, notably the right to privacy, which are contained in this Directive, give substance to and amplify those contained in the [Convention]".

The emphasis placed upon privacy considerations has prompted the Data Protection Registrar to comment that the implement of the directive's proposals in the United Kingdom would provide the first occasion where a right to privacy was enshrined in legislation.

The scope of the directive

With one exception, the scope of the directive is broadly similar to that of the Data Protection Act. Article 2 defines "personal data" as "any information about an identified or identifiable natural person". One change from the Act's definition of the term is the absence of any distinction between statements of opinion (included in the UK's definition) and statements of intention (excluded). The basis for such a distinction has never been entirely clear and its practical implementation has proved difficult. Few will mourn its passing, although problems may remain in determining when data relates to a data subject. In relation to the other key definitions, although the directive uses the term "controller" in preference to the Act's "data user", there appear to be no differences of substance and no call for amendment of the existing UK legislation.

One significant limitation upon the directive's application arises because of the limitations upon the Community's own law making powers. Article 3 confirms that the directive is not to apply "to the processing of data in the course of an activity which falls outside the scope of Community law". On this basis it may be argued that at least some national security and police operations may be excluded from the implementing legislation. It may be unlikely, however, that the traditional refusal of United Kingdom governments to essay any definition of national security will be acceptable to the Commission, and one effect of the directive may be to provide a more precise definition.

The major difference between the scope of the Act and the directive is that whilst the former applies only in respect of automated processing, the latter is proposed to extend to "the processing of personal data wholly or partly by automated means, and to the processing otherwise than by automatic means of personal data which forms part of a file or is intended to form part of a file" (art 3). This marks an important extension into the area of paper based records. Whilst the legislation will apply, as with the present Data Protection Act, to any automated processing of personal data, the manual application will be restricted to more extensive applications with the concept of a file being restricted to a "structured set of personal data, whether centralized or geographically dispersed, which is accessible according to specific criteria and whose object or effect is to facilitate the use or alignment of data relating to the data subject or subjects" (art 2 (c)). Although this definition would exclude items such as a letter containing personal data, even a telephone directory would appear to be covered.

This extension of the scope of the legislation has been the source of criticism. In the course of a House of Lords debate upon the proposal, estimates were quoted that the cost of implementing the proposals would be in the region of £100 million in the banking sector alone. Similar horror stories were common at the time of the Data Protection Act's enactment, but few have been borne out in reality. Given that the directive confers extensive discretion upon member states to determine the extent to which the controllers of manual files will be required to notify the supervisory authority of their activities, it seems unlikely that conformity with the other requirements should prove so burdensome, especially as these provisions prescribe what might be regarded as fair data handling practices, i e those which should be followed without there being need for legislative intervention.

Data quality
Where activities are of such a nature as to fall within the above definitions, the proposal states that processing will be lawful only if it conforms with the substantive requirements of the legislation. Article 6 contains a number of provisions relating to data quality which correspond in large measure to the data protection principles which constitute a key component of the UK Act. Building on this, art 7 introduces an important innovation, providing that informed subject consent is to be a key element in determining the legitimacy of processing. This is particularly important where data are collected from the data subject and in this context art 11 provides that notification is to be given of the purpose for which the data are sought, whether the subject is obliged to supply the information and, if so, the consequences of any refusal. The subject must be given details of the controller's name and address and must also be informed of the parties to whom the data may be disclosed and of the existence of a right of access. Exceptions to this provision may be made where the requirement to inform the subject would prejudice the maintenance of public order or what is described as the "supervision and verification functions of a public authority".

Although it may often be necessary for data users to seek the specific consent of subjects to proposed forms of data processing, art 7 provides a number of additional justifications for processing. Thus, processing may be carried out in the performance of a contract with the data subject or where it is necessary to protect the subject's vital interests, is required by law, is necessary for the performance of a task in the public interest or in pursuit of either the general interest or the legitimate interest of the controller or of a third party to whom the data may be disclosed. These interests have to be weighed against those of the data subject.

In the case of sensitive data, defined as that relating to racial or ethnic origin, political opinions, religious beliefs, philosophical or ethical persuasion or trade union membership and the subject's health or sexual life, it is provided that processing may occur only in accordance with specified conditions. It is also proposed that details of criminal convictions should be held only by judicial or law enforcement agencies (art 8). Although provision is made for member states to legislate for exceptions to the prohibition, the approach is to be contrasted with that adopted in the Data Protection Act which permits sensitive data to be processed whilst empowering the government to prescribe additional safeguards (s 2 (3)), a power which has not been utilised to date.

The proposal also requires as a general principle that the data subject be notified when personal data are disclosed to a third party and of the identity, or at least the categories, of recipients involved. Where data are to be transferred to a third party for the purposes of direct mailing, it is specifically provided that the subject must be informed and given the opportunity to require that the data be erased. No fee may be levied for such erasure (art 15). The impact of this provision upon data users may be limited by the fact that subject notification may be made at any time. Thus, notification of the intended transfer at the time the data are collected will suffice.

The principle of notification is, almost inevitably, subject to exceptions. Some relate to the situation where the subject has been informed, presumably at the time of collection, that the data may be transferred or where the disclosure is required by law or is for specified purposes including national security, revenue protection or criminal proceedings (see art 14 (1)). It is provided also that the subject need not be informed where this would be impossible, would involve a "disproportionate effort" or would run "counter to the overriding legitimate interests of the controller or similar interests of a third party". Once again, the exceptions may prove more important than the rule, but it is a significant feature that the onus throughout will be on the data user or the member state concerned to justify their application.

Automated decision making

One of the more significant innovations in the directive concerns the proposal that limits should be placed upon the use of data processing equipment in order to make decisions which may adversely affect an individual. A general prohibition is proposed upon the use of automatic processing as the sole basis for making such a decision (art 16). An example might be where credit scoring techniques are utilised in order to

determine whether credit facilities should be extended to a particular applicant. It is unclear, however, how influential the automatic element may be. Exceptions are proposed where the process occurs in the course of entering into a contract with the data subject. Although the directive proposes that "any request" by the data subject must be satisfied or that there be "suitable measures to safeguard his legitimate interests" including "arrangements allowing him to defend his point of view", the imbalance of power that frequently exists in such situations may render the protection of limited value. A further exception to the prohibition against total reliance upon automatic processing arises where such practices are authorised by law, subject to the condition that this should prescribe measures to safeguard the data subject's legitimate interests.

Subject access

The right of a data subject to obtain access to data held concerning them — and rectification of any errors discovered therein — is one of the key elements of any data protection regime. The directive's proposals are broadly in line with those currently operating in the United Kingdom. A number of significant differences may be noted. First, although member states are empowered to provide that access to medical data should be obtained through the medium of a medical practitioner (art 13), there is no provision for refusal of access to such data as is presently the case under the Data Protection Act. More significantly, where access may be denied under specified exemptions such as national security, criminal proceedings or revenue protection, the directive provides that "the supervisory authority shall be empowered to carry out the necessary checks, at the data subject's request, so as to verify the lawfulness of the processing". If implemented, the effect of this will be to empower the Data Protection Registrar to inspect the data processing activities of national security agencies, a sector which is at present excluded totally from supervision.

A further novelty in the directive is a provision intended to guard against misuse of the access provisions. Article 13 (2) states that a data subject shall be entitled to "refuse any demand by a third party that he should exercise his right of access in order to communicate the data in question to that third party or to another party, unless the third party's request is founded on national or Community Law". Although the intention of the provision is clear, it may be queried how effective it could be in practice. A typical case might concern the situation where a party seeking employment is asked to obtain and supply a copy of their criminal record — or confirmation that no such record exists. Although the employer will not be entitled to demand this information, the imbalance of power which frequently exists in such situations may leave the individual concerned with little choice but to adhere to the request.

Supervisory agencies
Reference has been made on a number of occasions to the actions of supervisory agencies. The existing United Kingdom structure of a Data Protection Registrar and Registry would not be affected by the proposed directive. As has been stated in a number of contexts, implementation of the proposals would extend the registrar's powers. A further consequence would be to diminish significantly the workload associated with registration, although the directive retains the concept of registration and requires the provision of information of the nature and extent currently required (art 18). In one respect the obligation imposed on data users appears even more extensive in that it requires a description of measures which have been taken to ensure the security of any processing activities. Against this, the directive talks in terms of notification to the supervisory agency and makes no mention of the agency having any power to reject any submission, although it is provided that where processing is proposed which "poses specific risks to the rights and freedoms of individuals", the supervisory authority shall examine the proposed activity. In this situation, national laws may require that those proposing processing of the kind described above should obtain authorisation prior to its commencement.

The information supplied by the data user is to be included in a publicly available register. It is provided, however, that sections of the register may be excluded from public access where they relate to national security, criminal proceedings, revenue protection or similar specified purposes (art 21).

The application of a registration requirement to literally hundreds of thousands of small scale data users has been a much criticised feature of the Data Protection Act. The directive proposes what would amount to a significant change by empowering the modification or exclusion of the obligation to notify in respect of "processing operations which do not adversely affect the rights and freedoms of data subjects" (art 19). Decisions on any modification are to be made by, or in consultation with, the supervisory authority.

A point of novelty lies in the provision that exclusion from the requirement to notify will not release the user from the obligation to comply with the substantive provisions of the directive. Such a result is one which has previously been recommended by the Data Protection Registrar.

Codes of conduct
The proposed directive envisages a role for both national and Community wide codes of practice. In a number of respects, this will be more extensive than is the case under current UK legislation. In particular, the directive proposes that the contents of national codes should be scrutinised by the supervisory authority which may both indicate approval of their contents and arrange for their "official publication" (art 28). In the case of codes which will operate on a Community wide basis, it is provided that the Commission may arrange for their publication in the *Official Journal* (art 29). Although these changes might enhance the evidential value of codes, it is not proposed to confer any formal legal status upon the documents themselves.

Transnational data flows
The initial proposal submitted by the Commission contained a provision prohibiting the transfer of data to third countries which did not provide for an "adequate" level of protection. This approach was criticised as being excessively ambiguous. If it were interpreted in the sense of "equivalent", it would, in particular, have threatened data transfers to countries such as the United States which have favoured a sectoral approach to the problems of data processing rather than the omnibus model adopted within Europe. The amended directive contains more detailed provisions describing when third party provisions are to be considered "adequate". Article 26 provides that in determining the adequacy of the level of protection provided by a third country, account is to be taken of "all the circumstances surrounding a data transfer operation". Particular reference is to be made to "the nature of the data, the purpose or purposes and duration of the proposed processing operation . . . the legislative provisions, both general and sectoral, in force in the third country in question and the professional rules which are complied with in that country". Where legislative provisions are not considered adequate, member states may authorise a transfer if safeguards are provided in other ways. Here, the directive makes specific reference to the possibility that the subject's interests may be safeguarded by the terms of a contract between the data users con-

cerned (art 27). Model terms for such a contract have been devised by the International Chamber of Commerce acting in conjunction with the Council of Europe.

Conclusions

The prognosis for the proposed directive is unclear. In some quarters it is considered that it will be enacted in 1994; other opinions envisage a longer delay. It is noteworthy that one of the reasons given by the Data Protection Registrar for his early retiral was the likelihood of the directive's enactment and the wish to allow a successor to be appointed in time to deal with all stages of its implementation.

In the case of the United Kingdom, the need for reform of the existing Data Protection Act is clear. As far back as 1989 the registrar conducted a review of its operation and recommended significant changes. The presence of the EC proposals has undoubtedly served as a factor blocking domestic reform in the intervening years.

It seems clear that implementation of the directive will reduce significantly the scale of registration. Few would object to this. In other areas, the role of the supervisory authority will be extended and the rights of data subjects increased. In many respects, the proposals are not incompatible with UK provisions; what may be more significant is that the tenor of the document is more positive throughout. Rights are given generously whilst exceptions are closely circumscribed and require to be specifically adopted by the member states. All too often in the Data Protection Act, the exception appears to be closer to the rule and there is a sense that individual rights are given reluctantly. Implementation of the directive may move the data subject closer to the centre of the data processing stage.

Foreign Consensual Marriages

R D Leslie,
Senior Lecturer in Private Law,
University of Edinburgh.

Dr Leslie discusses the private international law aspects of consensual marriage without a ceremony in the light of a recent Court of Appeal decision.

Under some legal systems a marriage may be consensual, requiring no ceremony or similar formality for its validity. This was, of course, the position in Scotland until 1940. This raises the question: which legal system, according to international private law, determines whether consent without a ceremony can constitute marriage?

A recent English case, *McCabe v McCabe, The Independent*, 3 September 1993, is relevant here. In *McCabe* it was argued for the wife that her Ghanaian marriage was viewed as valid in England. It was claimed that the marriage had been entered into under Akan custom, a customary legal system in Ghana, and was valid under the law of Ghana. The trial judge held that the formalities of the marriage were governed by Akan law and that the essential formality of publicity of the marriage was absent, rendering the marriage void. The Court of Appeal disagreed, ruling that the requirement of publicity appeared to have a probative function and that there was ample credible evidence of the marriage. The marriage was thus valid.

This customary law marriage appears to have been an example of a consensual marriage not requiring, for its validity, a ceremony or some other similar formalities. Akan custom would appear to require for a marriage only the consent of the parties and their families. A ceremony, though usual, was not legally required. Consummation by cohabitation was also envisaged, as an essential of the marriage. The question for consideration here is: which legal system or systems determines whether consent or agreement alone can constitute a marriage? This must be distinguished from the question of which legal system or systems determine whether there is consent. Here we are concerned with the legal effect of the consent or, more specifically, with which system determines whether consent without formalities can constitute marriage. The essential formalities of a marriage are determined by the lex loci celebrationis. On the face of it, if that system requires no formalities, then none are required. But, if no formalities are observed, where is the locus celebrationis? In *McCabe* the man was Irish, the woman Ghanaian. They had been living together in England since 1984. There were non-essential marriage celebrations in Ghana, but both spouses were in England at the time and neither attended these celebrations. Why then should the law of Ghana determine whether their consent to marriage should constitute marriage?

This point was not, it seems, canvassed in *McCabe*, and it is suggested, on general principles, that the question whether agreement without a ceremony can constitute marriage should be determined by the law of the place where the agreement was reached; the lex loci contractus should be the lex loci celebrationis.

Authority for this is not easy to find, but there is support for the view in the following statement from Collins, *Dicey and Morris on the Conflict of Laws* (12th ed), p 644): "If no ceremony is required, but a marriage can be concluded by an exchange of promises (*per verba de praesenti*), difficulties may arise in identifying the *lex loci celebrationis* if the parties are in different countries when they exchange their promises. Probably the English courts would require to be satisfied that a marriage could be concluded in this manner by the laws of each of the two countries; but it is just

possible that they might apply the rules as to contracts made by correspondence or over the telephone." In *McCabe* no problem of offer and acceptance arises as both parties were in England when "they exchanged their promises". Thus their purported marriage took place in England and English law should determine whether or not a consensual marriage is possible in these circumstances. It would seem that it is not. On this basis, the *McCabe* marriage would seem to be void and the English courts' excursus into Ghanaian law to have been unnecessary.

◆

NEWS

Court

Bar Group directory
The Scottish Planning, Local Government and Environmental Bar Group has published its directory for 1994.

The directory contains details of members and guidance on the ways in which they may be instructed, in particular the arrangements for direct professional access to advocates by members of the professional bodies listed.

Copies are available from the chairman, Roy Martin, QC, or the secretary, Laura Dunlop.

— ◇ —

General

Commission for Racial Equality
The Commission for Racial Equality have produced the following publications: *Aiming High for Equality: The Commission for Racial Equality Statement of Charter Standards*, the commission's response to the citizen's charter; *Advice and Assistance from the CRE*, guidance for those seeking the commission's help with complaints of racial discrimination; *What is the Commission for Racial Equality?*, a new introductory leaflet; *Criminal Justice and Racial Discrimination: How to make a complaint*, a new guide to an area much of which is not covered by the Race Relations Act; and *Job Advertisements and the Race Relations Act: A guide to section 5 for advertisers and publishers*, a handbook for those in the trade and those offering employment covering some important areas of the Act. Further information

can be obtained from the Commission for Racial Equality, Elliot House, 10/12 Allington Street, London SW1E 5EH (tel 071-828 7022).

Property certificates
Edinburgh
Edinburgh District Council are increasing the fee for property inquiry certificates to £70, with effect from 1 April 1994.

Highland
Highland Regional Council are increasing the charges for property clearance certificates with effect from 1 April 1994, as follows: planning: £24; roads and transport: £20; water and sewerage: £15.

◇

Further success in environmental moot
For the second year running a Scottish team has won the mooting competition run by the UK Environmental Law Association. This year the Dundee University students Eunice Cameron and Richard Goodfellow were successful in a final also involving the Universities of Strathclyde (last year's winners) and Nottingham Trent, and the College of Law at York. All law schools in the UK were invited to take part, and the four finalists were chosen on the basis of the written skeleton arguments which they had submitted. The moot was argued at Lincoln's Inn before, and judged by, Lord Slynn of Hadley, who praised the quality of all the finalists.

Royal Faculty of Procurators

The Royal Faculty of Procurators in Glasgow announce that, with effect from 1 March 1994, their clerk, treasurer and fiscal is Alastair James Campbell of Messrs Mitchells Roberton, solicitors, George House, 36 North Hanover Street, Glasgow G1 2AD; DX GW77, Glasgow (tel 041-552 3422; fax 041-552 2935). The library of the Royal Faculty will continue to be at 12 Nelson Mandela Place, Glasgow G2 1BT (DX GW197).

◇

Kincardine and Deeside Faculty of Solicitors

At a meeting held in Stonehaven on 21 February 1994 Kincardine and Deeside Faculty of Solicitors was formed. Membership is open to all solicitors who practise and/or reside in Kincardine and Deeside District. The faculty officials are as follows: *chairman*, Janet H Hood; *vice chairman*, Ernest K Barbour; *honorary secretary*, Alan J Bisset; *honorary treasurer*, D Russell Spence; *committee*, Ronald C Forbes, Torquil M McLeod, Hamish M Forbes.

Any solicitor wishing to obtain further information can contact the honorary secretary (tel 0569 762971). The former Faculty of Kincardineshire Solicitors ceased to function some 30 years ago.

◇

Shelter housing advice service

Shelter Scotland has announced an expansion of its service to homeless people in Scotland with the launch of a specialist housing law service.

The service will provide advice and consultancy on individual cases and training on housing law issues, and will produce publications for tenants, housing providers and advisers.

The Scottish Housing Law Service will provide a daily consultancy service to Shelter housing aid centres, represent clients referred by the centres in court and at housing benefit review boards, and where appropriate initiate judicial review proceedings. A tenants' representation service has been started at Edinburgh sheriff court.

A leaflet "Stopping Harassment", the first of a programme of publications planned for the coming year, is now available.

The first national conference takes place in Glasgow on 21 March 1994 and will be free to enable as many organisations as possible to participate and benefit.

Legal work is undertaken by the Legal Services Agency of Glasgow.

—— ◇ ——

Taxation

European Economic Area

The European Economic Area (EEA) Agreement which came into force on 1 January 1994 extends the principles of the Single Market to five states of the European Free Trade Association (Austria, Finland, Iceland, Norway and Sweden). The agreement covers the free movement of goods, services, capital and people and rules on competition and state aids. There are a number of direct tax consequences concerning private medical insurance, maintenance payments, European Economic Interest Groupings, company migrations and deposit takers.

Private medical insurance

Tax relief is available on premiums paid under certain private medical insurance contracts for the over 60s. One condition for relief is that the insurer must be authorised to carry on insurance business either in the United Kingdom or in another European Union member state of which it is a national. From 1 January 1994 this will be extended to include all states within the European Economic Area.

Maintenance payments

The agreement extends tax relief to maintenance payments under new or existing EEA court orders or written agreements made and enforceable under the law of an EEA state. Relief will be available for payments due and made on or after 1 January 1994.

As with maintenance payments made under United Kingdom and other EU court orders or written agreements, to qualify for relief payments must be made to a divorced or separated husband or wife who has not remarried, and for his or her own maintenance or for the maintenance by him or her of a child of the family aged under 21. There is no relief for payments made directly to children.

Relief is available on maintenance payments up to a limit equal to the married couple's allowance (£1,720 for 1993-94, 1994-95 and 1995-96). The Finance Bill now before Parliament provides for the restriction of the relief to 20 per cent for 1994-95 and to 15 per cent for 1995-96 in line with similar restrictions in the married couple's allowance. Anyone wishing to claim relief should contact their tax office and provide a copy of the court order or written agreement under which payments are made.

European Economic Interest Groupings

EEIGs may be set up under Council Regulation (EEC) No 2137/85 which came into effect on 1

July 1989. For tax purposes EEIGs are fiscally transparent in that profits are taxable and losses allowable only in the hands of their members. The relevant legislation was introduced by s 69 of and Sched 11 to the Finance Act 1990. As a result of the extension of the 1985 Regulation under the agreement, these provisions will apply to all EEIGs established within the European Economic Area.

Company migrations
Section 765A of the Income and Corporation Taxes Act 1988 removed the requirement under s 765 to obtain Treasury consent before carrying out certain transactions in securities where the transaction was a movement of capital between persons resident in member states of the European Community, within the meaning of Council Directive No 88/361/EEC. The company is required instead to provide information to the Board of Inland Revenue within six months of carrying out the transaction, as set out in the Movements of Capital (Required Information) Regulations 1990 (SI 1990/1671). As a result of the agreement, these provisions will apply to movements of capital between persons resident in member states of the EEA made on or after 1 January 1994.

◊

Corporation tax: capital allowances
Under s 10B of the Capital Allowances Act 1990, capital allowances at the 100 per cent enterprise zone rate remain available for a period of two years after a building is brought into use, so long as the building was brought into use on or after 16 December 1991.

As already announced (1994 SLT (News) 69), the government will be bringing forward legislation during the committee stage of the Finance Bill to amend a defect in the capital allowances legislation as it affects long leases given in return for a capital sum. The government are conscious that, until the legislation is published, there will inevitably be some uncertainty for investors about the detailed conditions under which capital allowances will be available. In cases where entitlement to capital allowances under s 10B's two year rule was shortly to expire at the time of the announcement, this uncertainty may have had the effect of preventing some investors from making a claim under the rule. Accordingly, they propose to bring forward a provision which will give until 31 August 1994 for qualifying expenditure to fall within the s 10B rule. This will apply to cases where, under this section, the two year period would have expired on or after 13 January 1994 and not later than 31 August 1994.

◊

Subcontractors in the construction industry
The government have announced plans for changes to the construction industry tax deduction scheme, implementing some of the recommendations the 1991 consultative document "Taxation of Subcontractors in the Construction Industry". Its main proposal was that eligibility for exemption from the requirement that tax should be deducted should be restricted. Only subcontractors whose business turnover exceeded a certain figure and who met the existing criteria would be eligible for gross payment. Legislation is likely to be included in the next Finance Bill.

◊

Banks and building societies: payment of gross interest
The Commissioners of Inland Revenue have laid regulations before the House of Commons extending the circumstances in which bank and building society interest can be paid without deduction of tax. The regulations will make it easier for people who are unable to act for themselves to get the benefit of the scheme under which non-taxpayers can register to receive their bank or building society interest without deduction of tax.

From 4 March 1994 banks, building societies and other deposit takers will be able to accept registration forms signed by people appointed by the Department of Social Security to receive benefits on behalf of someone who is incapable of managing their own affairs.

The regulations also cover two other circumstances in which from 4 March 1994 building society interest can be paid without deduction of tax: on investments held at a branch situated outside the United Kingdom; and on an investment by a pension scheme which has applied to the Board of Inland Revenue for recognition as an exempt approved scheme.

◊

Foreign exchange gains and losses
The Inland Revenue have published draft regulations which provide rules for identifying amounts to be left out of account in applying the provisions on exchange gains and losses in the Finance Act 1993, and which supplement, for

loans which vary in amount, the provisions for "ring fencing" exchange losses on loans which are not on arms length terms. Further draft regulations will be published separately in the near future.

Further information can be obtained from, and comments on the draft regulations (by 30 April 1994) sent to: Sue Cooper, Inland Revenue (Financial Institutions Division), Foreign Exchange Consultations, Room 510, 22 Kingsway, London WC2B 6NR.

— ◊ —

Business change

Messrs West Anderson & Co, solicitors, 92 Bath Street, Glasgow, intimate the resignation of Mrs Fiona Quirk as a partner of the firm with effect from 4 February 1994. Mrs Quirk will continue to be associated with the firm as a consultant.

— ◊ —

Parliamentary News

New Bills

HOUSE OF COMMONS

15 February 1994

Referendum (Scotland)—To make provision for the holding of a referendum, for all persons eligible to vote, on Scotland's future constitutional status. (Private Member's Bill introduced by Mrs Ray Michie)

Marriage (Amendment)—To amend the Marriage Act 1949. (Private Member's Bill introduced by Mr David Clelland)

Representation of the People (Amendment)—To extend and improve methods of electoral registration and to allow disabled people to gain access to polling stations. (Private Member's Bill introduced by Mr Harry Barnes)

16 February 1994

Assistance For Local Authority Leaseholders—To require local authorities to identify residential properties of which the authority owns the freehold and which the leaseholders find hard

to sell; to require local authorities to make available mortgage guarantees to assist the sale of certain local authority leaseholds of residential property; to enable local authorities to repurchase the leases of certain leaseholds of residential properties; and for connected purposes. (Private Member's Bill introduced by Mr John Denham)

22 February 1994

Eggs From Foetuses (Prohibition of Use)—To prohibit the use of eggs taken from aborted human foetuses for fertilisation procedures; and for connected purposes. (Private Member's Bill introduced by Dame Jill Knight)

Progress of Bills

Intelligence Services — Commons second reading, 22 February 1994.

Sunday Trading — Commons remaining stages, 23 February 1994.

Trade Marks — Lords report stage, 24 February 1994.

Sale and Supply of Goods — Commons second reading, 11 February 1994.

Tobacco Advertising — Commons second reading, 11 February 1994.

Question answered

HOUSE OF COMMONS

16 February 1994

CRIMINAL JUSTICE

Mr Kynoch: To ask the Secretary of State for Scotland what further proposals he has for improving the Scottish criminal justice system.

Mr Lang: I am today publishing a consultation paper entitled "Sentencing and Appeals", which seeks views on a number of proposals for improving the ability of our system of justice to deal with crime effectively and fairly. The paper seeks views on possible changes of the system of fiscal fines and the sentencing powers of the sheriff courts and invites views on the case for introduction of sentencing guidelines. It proposes revised procedures for dealing with criminal appeals and invites views on whether there is a need for change to the criteria by which criminal appeals are determined. The paper also seeks views on whether the current arrangements for dealing with alleged miscarriage of justice in Scotland are satisfactory and sets out a number of possible options for change.

The consultation paper is the fourth in a series

seeking views on proposals for improving the delivery of justice in Scotland. We are inviting comments by 16 April. Copies of the consultation paper have been placed in the library.

[A copy of the paper has been obtained and will be summarised in the next issue—*Editor*.]

Book Reviews

Post-Construction Liability and Insurance

International Council for Building Research Studies and Documentation
Edited by Jens Knocke. 1993. London: E & F N Spon. Hardback £49.95.
ISBN 0 419 15350 0.

Despite the well known and much discussed decision of the House of Lords in *Murphy v Brentwood District Council*, the issue of liability for defective buildings and works of civil engineering has not gone away. It can still arise as a matter of contract, whether through the principal ones under which the project was originally completed or under later "collateral warranties" and "duty of care" agreements. Statutory liabilities and guarantee schemes such as that of the National House Building Council play an important and insufficiently studied role in providing compensation for losses arising from construction defects. Ahead lies the possibility of European harmonisation through the medium of directives on construction liability.

The work under review has been produced by a commission set up by the Conseil International du Bâtiment (the International Council for Building Research). Its aim appears to be the provision of a general structure of concepts and institutions for the international development of law and insurance arrangements relating to construction defects. The first part provides a survey of the concepts and institutions, dealing with buildings, clients and successive owners, producers, building codes, delivery, post-delivery, failure and damage, errors and omissions, defect, damage, law and contract, and the role of national governments in risk reduction. The second part provides a wide ranging series of accounts of national laws, each of which has been drawn up by local experts in response to a questionnaire derived from the preceding general structure and in accordance with a common format. This section includes several of the member states of the European Union (although, perhaps sur-

prisingly, not Germany), the United States and Japan. There is also a response for Scotland which is happily quite separate from that for England, Wales and Northern Ireland. It is to be hoped that the word "fashery", which appears at p 281 of the Scottish chapter, will become an internationally accepted term of art in relation to the collateral warranties which it is used to describe.

The book is expressly not intended to provide information to assist lawyers and insurance companies advising clients on cross frontier building transactions. To that extent it is not aimed directly at practitioners in law, insurance or the construction industry. Instead it draws attention to both common patterns and divergences in the various national laws. A general trend towards increasing liability emerges, which the editor attributes to the growth of consumerism and to the new risks arising from the deployment of new technologies and the shrinking availability of "buildable" land. The book can therefore be best seen as an interesting attempt to provide some sort of framework within which liability and its concomitant of insurance provision can most rationally be discussed and developed by legislatures, insurers and, in legal systems where this can happen, by the courts.

There is nonetheless a considerable amount of information here which is not readily discoverable in any other source, not only about law but also about building technology and the nature of insurance cover for construction projects. The authors are a mixture of lawyers, economists, and construction and insurance professionals, and the tone throughout reflects practical experience of the material under discussion. So far as the Scottish chapter goes, it generally states the law accurately enough insofar as severely compressed space allows, although the effect of *Murphy* on earlier decisions seems to be understated at p 278. Specialists and policymakers in the field of construction law and practice will probably be those with most to gain from this book, but it should also find a place in the general library as a useful source of comparative and economic information on contractual and delictual obligations in general.

HECTOR L MACQUEEN,
University of Edinburgh.

ARTICLES

Controlling Creditors' Rights under Standard Securities

Tom Guthrie,
Lecturer in Law,
University of Glasgow.

Recent decisions of the Scottish courts, with the exception of one dictum, have taken a restrictive line on attempts to regulate the exercise by creditors of their rights under standard securities on the debtor's default. Mr Guthrie argues that this is difficult to justify whether in terms of the current legislation or of the earlier case law.

What protection is enjoyed by debtors in Scotland where creditors seek to exercise their rights under standard securities, and what powers do the courts have to control such exercise by the creditor? This latter question arose in *Halifax Building Society v Gupta*, 1994 SLT 339, where the view of the Inner House appeared to be that the court's powers to control the creditor are very limited. It will be argued that this view is not justified by authority or equity. Before going on to consider this, it is worth briefly restating the ways in which the creditor under a standard security can acquire the right to exercise his/her remedies.

By virtue of the Conveyancing and Feudal Reform (Scotland) Act 1970 a creditor's rights can arise in three ways. Failure by a debtor to comply with a calling up notice served by the creditor immediately confers on the creditor the right to exercise all the remedies provided for by standard condition 10 of Sched 3 to the 1970 Act, together with any other remedies deriving from the agreement between creditor and debtor. These remedies include sale, foreclosure (if sale proves impossible), entering into possession, and entry to carry out repairs. Court action may, of course, be necessary to allow the exercise of these rights. For example, an action of ejection may be necessary to remove the debtor and permit the creditor to enter into possession, perhaps as a precursor to sale.

The second way in which a creditor can acquire the right to exercise remedies is failure to comply with a notice of default. Such failure immediately confers on the creditor the right to exercise all the standard condition 10 remedies aside from those requiring entry into possession. Power to enter into possession can only be obtained by applying to the sheriff court for a warrant to exercise this remedy under s 24 of the 1970 Act.

Finally, default by the debtor allows the creditor to apply to court under s 24 for warrant to exercise any of the standard condition 10 remedies. Such an application need not, though usually will, be preceded by service of a notice of default and is the appropriate way to proceed when the debtor becomes insolvent.

Answering our initial question involves addressing two further questions:

(a) What discretion do courts have in relation to applications under s 24?

(b) What powers does the court have to regulate the exercise of the creditor's remedies?

(a) This question has arisen in two cases. In *United Dominions Trust Ltd v Site Preparations Ltd (No 1)*, 1978 SLT (Sh Ct) 14, it was suggested in the sheriff court that the court had no discretion but was obliged to grant an application by a creditor. The justification for this conclusion was the wording of s 24. "Section 24 provides that the creditor *may* apply for a warrant: it does not provide that the sheriff *may* grant it. On the contrary, the wording of s. 24 (1) 'for warrant to exercise any of the remedies [to] which he is entitled,' makes it clear to me that the only discretion which exists is that of the creditor" (at p 17).

In the more recent case of *Halifax Building Society v Gupta* this question was briefly discussed. The Inner House approved of the *UDT* decision and rejected the defender's argument that this approach rendered any court proceedings under s 24 entirely mechanical. The court took the view that questions as to title to enforce and default by the debtor might still have to be considered by the court even if, once they are established, the remedy must be granted. In addition, in considering the crave for ejection which accompanied the application for warrant under s 24 in *Gupta* the Inner House appeared to suggest that the court has no discretion but to grant such an associated application if the warrant is granted.

(b) The modern basis for the suggestion that the courts have power to prevent the exercise of certain powers by the creditor is found in an obiter dictum from Lord Jauncey in the Outer House case of *Armstrong, Petr*, 1988 SLT 255. Since this statement has been the subject of comment by Cusine, *Standard Securities*, para 8.25, and in *Gupta*, it is worth quoting in full: "However, while I consider that the petitioner is not disabled from exercising the rights of a heritable creditor, he must exercise those rights civiliter and with proper regard for the interests of the debtors. A creditor's primary interest will normally be the recovery of the debt due to him and I do not consider that he has unlimited discretion as to which one or more of the powers he exercises. If the value of the heritage is likely to exceed the sum of the debt, his interest is to have the heritage sold and thereafter to account for the surplus to the debtor. If in such a situation he elected to exercise the powers in condition 10 in a manner which did not result in money being made available for the debtor he might very well be restrained from so acting. A heritable creditor cannot use his powers for the primary purpose of advancing his own interests at the expense of the debtor when he has the alternative of proceeding in a more equitable manner" (at p 258B-D).

The most obvious reading of these comments suggests two things: (i) that the courts have power to prevent a creditor from exercising certain powers to which he/she is entitled under a standard security; and (ii) more specifically, that where sale of the security subjects will produce a surplus the court has the power to prevent the exercise of the power of taking possession, which would not have the effect of satisfying the interests of both parties.

Commenting on the passage quoted above, Cusine makes three points. First, he suggests that the consequence of applying the dictum would be to prevent a creditor from selling where sale would not produce a surplus. It is difficult to see that this interpretation is justified by the words used by Lord Jauncey.

Secondly, he suggests that the creditor is put in an impossible position by the implicit requirement stated here both to obtain the best price and to consider the best interests of the debtor. He suggests that these requirements conflict and cannot both be fulfilled. The nature of the conflict is not further specified, but if it does exist, which the present author doubts, then the creditor is put in this position by clearly stated and accepted legal requirements. Section 25 of the 1970 Act requires the creditor to "take all reasonable steps to ensure that the price at which all or any of the security subjects are sold is the best that can reasonably be obtained". The second requirement is also backed up by authority, examples being *Rimmer v Thomas Usher & Son Ltd*, 1967 SLT 7 and *Dick v Clydesdale Bank plc*, 1991 SLT 678. In the latter case Halliday's view (*The Conveyancing and Feudal Reform (Scotland) Act 1970* (2nd ed), at para 5-11, repeated in *Conveyancing Law and practice* (Vol III), at para 33-27) that a creditor is in the position of quasi-trustee for the debtor is quoted with approval (at p 681B), and the point is also made that "it has always been understood that the creditor in a heritable security must pay due regard to the interests of the debtor when he

comes to sell the security subjects" (pp 680L-681A). It is in any event difficult to see that any conflict arises in the scenario envisaged by Lord Jauncey. Here, where sale would produce a surplus, it is clearly in the interests both of the creditor (who is repaid) and of the debtor (who has the debt discharged and receives a surplus) for sale to take place.

Finally, Cusine objects to the first suggestion, arguing that the courts have no power to prevent a creditor exercising his/her power of sale, but that they have a power to direct the way in which that is done: "In other words, the heritable creditor may be directed in the manner of the sale but not prevented from selling." This point will be returned to.

It is perhaps worth noting that Cusine's interpretation may stem from an apparent misunderstanding of what *Armstrong, Petr* was about. He presents it as an application by a judicial factor on an estate including the security subjects to prevent the heritable creditor from exercising his right of sale. In fact, the reverse was the case; it concerned an application for interdict by the heritable creditor to prevent the judicial factor exercising his right of sale. The reported case is, however, only one stage in a protracted dispute (and accompanying litigation: see *G Dunlop & Son's JF v Armstrong*, 1994 SLT 199), and it is true that at an earlier stage the judicial factor had applied to Stranraer sheriff court for an interdict to prevent the heritable creditor exercising any of his standard condition 10 remedies. The interdict was granted and apparently remained in force until 1992.

A second case which is relevant here is *Associated Displays Ltd v Turnbeam Ltd*, 1988 SCLR 220, where the debtors sought to prevent a creditor proceeding with a sale which they claimed was below the market value of the property (and therefore in breach of the creditor's duty under s 25 of the 1970 Act). The mechanism they chose for this was a crave which sought to prevent the sale until the court was satisfied that the sale price was the best which could be obtained. Two reasons were given for rejecting the pursuers' application. In the first place, s 25 makes no provision for the creditor satisfying the court as to the sufficiency of the price. This seems a rather narrow ground given that the debtor was simply seeking to enforce the creditor's statutory duty. It seems rather unsatisfying to suggest, as the court did, that the only remedy in cases like this is to wait until after the sale has taken place and then claim damages for breach of that duty. Secondly, by the time of the challenge missives had already been concluded and so the purchaser had a personal right, which could be enforced by court action, to require a disposition to be granted. In his *Conveyancing Manual* (5th ed), para 22.33, McDonald comments on the rather unhelpful nature of the court's views, particularly in light of the earlier dictum in *Armstrong, Petr.*

Finally, there is a brief treatment of *Armstrong* in *Gupta*. Here it is suggested, in an echo of Cusine's views, that the courts will not intervene to prevent the exercise by the creditor of his/her remedies but may intervene to regulate such exercise. Commenting on the dictum in *Armstrong*, the Inner House suggest first that it relates to the very unusual situation where two parties have the right of sale in respect of a property, though it is far from clear from the context that Lord Jauncey was restricting his comments to this scenario. Secondly, they appear to view it as a simple restatement and reminder of the creditor's statutory duty to account for any surplus on a sale to the debtor. Again, with respect, it is difficult to see how that interpretation is arrived at. Finally, and rather curiously in light of what has gone before, they seem to suggest that courts, in granting warrant for exercise of remedies by a creditor, will rarely have to concern themselves with the sorts of considerations to which Lord Jauncey refers. This suggests, of course, that in some circumstances they will, though arguably the Inner House considered that this would only be the case where there were two parties with right of sale.

Having briefly considered the relevant cases, let us now consider the correctness of the position which the court adopted in *Gupta* and look at what precisely the distinction might be between preventing and controlling (or regulating or directing) the exercise of the creditor's remedies.

It is certainly the case, as Cusine notes, that the courts have the power to control the exercise of the creditor's powers. An example is the case of *Kerr v McArthur's Trs* (1848) 11 D 301, where interdict was granted to prevent the creditor under a bond and disposition in security from selling below the true value of the land. The case cited by Cusine in support of his position, *Beveridge v Wilson* (1829) 7 S 279, contains dicta which can also be read as suggesting a power to control the exercise of the creditor's powers. It is notable, however, that in older texts, and in the headnote to the case itself, it is read as supporting the view that the exercise of the power of sale could be prevented rather than simply controlled (Gloag and Irvine, *Law of Rights in Security*, p 120; Craigie, *Scottish Law of Conveyancing* (3rd ed), p 971).

There is also support for the view that the courts can prevent a creditor from exercising his/her powers. In *Lucas v Gardner* (1876) 4 R 194, an interdict was granted to prevent a creditor holding an ex facie absolute disposition from exercising his power of sale. The reasons were, admittedly, similar to those on which a court could refuse an application under s 24, namely that the sums due by the debtor were not properly specified. In *Glas v Stewart* (1830) 8 S 843, both the Lord Ordinary and the Inner House appear to indicate that they would have been prepared to grant interdict to prevent the exercise of the power of sale by a creditor under a bond and disposition in security if the pursuer had been in a position to grant caution. In *Davidson v Scott*, 1915 2 SLT 55; 1915 SC 838, a creditor's action for maills and duties over part of security subjects was refused on the grounds that the remainder of the security subjects had been sold off in breach of his obligations.

More recently, in the sheriff court case referred to in *Armstrong*, interdict was granted to prevent the creditor from exercising any of his standard condition 10 remedies, including sale. Finally, the dictum of Lord Jauncey in *Armstrong* seems, on its most obvious interpretation, to support the proposition that in appropriate circumstances the creditor can be prevented from exercising remedies.

At this point it may be suggested that what in fact exists here is an entirely illusory difference, so that when Cusine, for example, speaks of directing he means the same as others when they talk of preventing. This hinges on what the distinction, if any, is between directing or controlling the exercise of remedies and preventing the exercise of remedies.

There are a number of ways in which each of these can be looked at. Preventing the exercise may refer to blanket prevention of the exercise of a creditor's powers, or it may refer to preventing a particular exercise of these powers, e g a sale at below market value in breach of the creditor's s 25 obligations. Controlling the exercise of powers may mean making directions about how a power is to be exercised, e g regulating the conditions under which a property is sold by public auction (from the selection of quotations from *Beveridge v Wilson* this is the view which Cusine appears to take, at least as far as sale is concerned; it would seem to rule out either of the other two stronger senses of control); it may mean preventing a particular exercise of a power, as in *Kerr v McArthur's Trs*; or it may mean controlling the type of power which can be used, for example the instance suggested by Lord Jauncey where it might be appropriate to prevent exercise of the power of entry into possession but to permit exercise of the power of sale. These last two senses of control seem akin to the second sense of prevention and suggest an overlap in meaning between the two.

It is suggested that these distinctions offer a way of understanding the powers of the courts which resolves the tension between the decisions noted above and which allows the courts certain powers to prevent/control the exercise of creditors' powers.

As far as preventing the exercise of powers in general is concerned, it would seem that the courts have no power. This accords with the *UDT* decision that if application is made in general terms to exercise the powers of a creditor under standard condition 10, the courts have no discretion, provided they are satisfied as to title and default, to refuse the application. That, however, is a different matter from saying that the courts have no power to prevent the exercise of a specific power, or the specific exercise of a specific power. In such cases it clearly makes sense for the courts to prevent an exercise of powers which would put the creditor in breach of his obligations to the debtor or to other creditors of the debtor, rather than waiting for the breach of duty to occur and expecting the injured party to raise a later action for damages. The circumstances in which interdict would be granted to prevent the exercise of powers would be likely to be rare; the court would have to weigh up very carefully the claimed disadvantages to the debtor as against the potential damage to the creditor by delaying the exercise of his/her remedies.

It is also possible to suggest that the use of such prevention/control may vary with the type of remedy and whether there is a specific exercise of the power which is sought to be prevented. One might suggest that while, as in *Armstrong*, the court might grant a ban on entry into possession (partly, of course, because it might be regarded as a specific exercise of a power), it would not impose a blanket ban on sale (with the possible exception of the type of situation which arose in *Armstrong* and in *Beveridge v Wilson* of there being two people with the right of sale). The reason for this is connected with the court's analysis of the interests of the creditor and of the debtor, which can be seen, for example, in *Armstrong* and in *G Dunlop & Son's JF v Armstrong*. Where a sale will generate a surplus it is regarded as being in the interests both of the creditor and the debtor. The creditor's interest is served because sale secures repayment of the debt and that, at least in the context of default in repayment, is regarded by the courts as the creditor's primary interest. This, incidentally, also

explains why, at least in cases of surplus, and probably in certain other cases, the creditor will be prevented from entering into possession per se: to do so would be to act against his/her judicially determined best interests. (It is a different matter when entry into possession is sought as a precursor to sale.) The interests of the debtor also indicate sale in this situation — the debt is paid off and the debtor benefits from the surplus.

In the situation where sale does not generate a surplus it is still, unless the deficit is great, in the interests of the creditor to sell. Sale will recoup most of the outstanding debt, which can then be used for other purposes, and relieves the creditor of the need to manage property etc which would be involved if possession was entered into. In such circumstances sale clearly operates to the detriment of the debtor — he/she loses accommodation and is still faced with the repayment of the amount of the loan which is outstanding. Even though this is the case it does not outweigh the interest of the creditor, because this detriment is precisely the sort of situation to which the debtor has consented in advance by granting the standard security. In addition, it is difficult to see that exercise of the power of sale in general could be in breach of the creditor's statutory and common law obligations.

When it comes to specific exercise of the creditor's remedies, different considerations arise. As has already been noted, it may be more correct to view a prohibition on the use of the power of entry as a bar on a specific exercise of that power, in that the court may only intervene where that is a concrete possibility. For the power of sale it is easy to see that a proposed specific exercise might involve the creditor in breach of his statutory or common law obligations and therefore merit prevention by way of interdict. This possibility is supported by *Kerr*, where interdict was granted to prevent a proposed sale at below the true value of the property, with the Inner House recognising that this did not prevent the creditor proceeding to advertise the property at an adequate price. It is also supported by dicta in *Glas* and in *Beveridge v Wilson*, where it was noted that although the creditor cannot be derived of his power of sale it is a power subject to control, and "If he acted nimiously, the Court would certainly interfere in the exercise of this right of sale" ((1829) 7 S at p 281). As suggested earlier, the proper interpretation of this is that the interference referred to would extend to preventing a particular proposed sale. This view also receives some support from the views of Lords Glenlee and Pitmilly, ibid at pp 283-284. Finally, a creditor acting in a prejudicial fashion is not only acting in breach of his/her obligations, but is also doing something to which the debtor has not consented in advance (an analogy might possibly be drawn here with volenti non fit injuria).

It is hoped that this analysis shows that the elaboration of the meanings of control and prevention sheds some light on the powers of the courts to intervene. It allows statements to the effect that courts have no discretion but to grant warrant for exercise of powers in general to stand, while, at the same time, and consistent with authority, it allows the courts to intervene in respect of specific exercises of powers, whether such intervention is described as preventing or controlling.

The protection which the above analysis suggests can be afforded to debtors is, however, limited. It seems only to be available in cases where the creditor is acting against the debtor's best interests and, in cases involving sale, where the creditor will be in breach of his/her common law or statutory obligations. In the latter context the failure of the pursuers in *Associated Displays Ltd v Turnbeam Ltd* should not be seen as disentitling debtors. All that is necessary is that the petition for interdict is framed in a more appropriate form, setting out in detail the facts which will result in a breach of the creditor's obligations. The denial of discretion to the courts where application is made for remedies under s 24 and, deriving from the views of the Inner House in *Gupta*, associated remedies such as ejection, does not allow the court to adjourn proceedings or to defer execution of decree to allow for repayment of arrears or to require the creditor to offer the debtor the same rescheduling facilities as are offered to other debtors. This last argument was floated without any success in *Gupta*.

In contrast, in England and Wales the courts are given discretion as to how to act where a creditor seeks possession because of mortgage arrears and the debtor offers to pay the amount of the arrears. The statutory provisions are found in the Administration of Justice Act 1970, s 36 and the Administration of Justice Act 1973, s 8. (For a discussion of these provisions, see *Bank of Scotland v Grimes* [1985] 1 QB 1179.) The combined effect of these is that a court hearing an application for possession of a dwellinghouse by a creditor can adjourn proceedings, stay or suspend the execution of the judgment or order made, or postpone the date for delivery of possession. The precondition for granting such a delay to the debtor is that the court is satisfied that he/she is likely to be able to repay the arrears within a reasonable time, or in cases where there has been some other default, remedy that default within a reasonable time.

It might be argued that such protections are not needed because creditors will not seek to enforce their remedies where such repayment or remedy could be made and will make strenuous efforts to avoid resorting to repossession and sale. This view did not, however, prevent the Payne committee (*Report of the Committee on the Enforcement of Judgment Debts*, Cmnd 3909 (1969), especially paras 1379-1387) recommending the reintroduction of this protection after it had been negated by the judgment in *Birmingham Citizens' Permanent Building Society v Caunt* [1962] Ch 881. The reasons they gave then have a resonance today, particularly their comment that "Under present day economic difficulties it seems not unlikely that an increasing number of mortgagors . . . may find themselves temporarily unable to keep up their mortgage instalments" (para 1386 (c)). It is therefore unfortunate that, as appeared to be the case with non-contractual disclaimers of liability in survey reports (see *Robbie v Graham & Sibbald*, 1989 SLT 870; *Melrose v Davidson & Robertson*, 1993 SLT 611), Scottish consumers find themselves in a less favourable position than those south of the border.

Recent Developments in English Law
The Politics of Leasehold Reform

Robert C Elliot,
Course Leader,
Qualifying English Law Degree,
University of Dundee.

The Leasehold Reform, Housing and Urban Development Act 1993 revealed fundamental divisions both within and between the political parties in the course of its passage through Parliament. Mr Elliot reflects on the philosophical debate and examines the practical problems facing leaseholders of flats in exercising their new right to buy the freehold.

Leasehold reform has come to be synonymous with giving lessees the right to purchase the freehold of the property they lease or the right to extend their lease. It has a history of political motivation dating back at least to 1967 when the Leasehold Reform Act of that year was passed under a Labour Government in response to pressure from voters, especially in south Wales where leasehold tenure of houses was the norm, but it did not extend to flats and maisonettes, partly because of conveyancing problems relating to the enforcement of positive covenants for mutual responsibilities such as stairs and the roof.

These problems were supposed to be solved by the development of commonhold — a strata title alternative for flat ownership being considered by the Law Commission. However, the Conservatives promised to extend the right to buy the freehold to lessees in blocks of flats in the 1992 General Election, and pressed ahead with this legislation with the result that the 1993 Act contains very complex and problematic provisions governing the relationship of enfranchising tenants and minority continuing tenants (e g s 2 (3), providing that common parts should be treated as included in the enfranchisement only if it is reasonably necessary for their management and maintenance). As predicted in earlier articles (1992 SLT (News) 343 and 1993 SLT (News) 23), the legislation ran into stormy waters in its passage through Parliament, but came into force with important amendments on 1 November 1993.

The legislation was supported in the House of Commons by Conservative members for marginal constituencies such as Kensington and Westminster North, but opposed in the House of Lords by Conservative (now ex-Conservative in some cases) peers including the Duke of Westminster who owns some 300 acres of Mayfair and Belgravia. Obviously, it would be easy to account for this split on the grounds of electoral and proprietary vested interests respectively, but the debate raised fundamental issues of political philosophy between those who regarded property rights including contractual obligations as sacrosanct and those who believed that they should be sacrificed when they impaired the efficient working of free market forces. This central issue was often obscured by a number of side issues, such as the alleged superiority of the leasehold system in preserving the visual quality of townscapes, and *The Times* in an editorial supporting the Bill on 10 March 1993 resorted to Lord Lawson's vision of "a nation of inheritors", apparently without realising that the measure was at the same time disinheriting the heirs of the landlords.

This paradox is inherent in almost all natural law based defences of the sanctity of property rights such as Locke's theoretical underpinning of the Whig theory of government, which was developed in a period of transition from an agrarian society dominated by status to a mercantile economy regulated by contract, and at a time when the English courts had begun to develop the complex rule against perpetuities to ensure a less restricted flow of land coming onto the market. Traditional property rights stemming from status can now be varied or extinguished by contract or statute, but leasehold enfranchisement involves the destruction of both real (i e common law estates in land) and contractual rights, insofar as a lease is the embodiment of a contract allowing land to be occupied by a person who does not own the freehold estate.

Translating this philosophical conundrum into practical terms, the political choice is the perennial one in a capitalist economy of adjudicating between inherited property and recently acquired wealth, with traditional conservatives favouring the former category and radical liberals the latter. The new Act is the latest indication that the present government comes down against traditional property and/or contractual rights when it becomes necessary to make a choice. This is confirmed by the powers to undo "clean break" divorce settlements given to the Child Support Agency, and its failure to repeal Labour's Inheritance (Provision for Family Dependants) Act 1975 with its wide powers for courts to set aside the provisions of a will (see 1992 SLT (News) 228). There is, after all, little point in dedicating one's life to the acquisition of property if it is to be controlled by government via taxation or other legislation and by the courts on divorce or death, although many people prefer to discount the possibility of the latter events happening to them.

However, the government may have ended up with the worst of both worlds since there are likely to be many frustrated leaseholders unable to buy their flats because of important restrictions contained in the Act, which gives two new rights for "qualifying tenants" — a new collective right to acquire the freehold of the buildings in which their flats are located (ss 1-38), and a new right for individual tenants of flats to acquire an extension of 90 years to their existing leases (ss 39-62). A "qualifying tenant" may be an individual or a company, but must have a "long lease" (i e over 21 years: s 7).

The main restrictions apply to the collective right to buy the freehold, and require that at least two thirds of the flats are let on long leases (s 3 (1)), that at least 90 per cent of the floor space is residential (s 4 (1)), and that 50 per cent or more of the flats have been used as a principal residence for the previous 12 months or three of the previous 10 years, the ground rent is "low" and at least two thirds of leaseholders of flats in the building agree to enfranchise. Section 8 defines "low rent" as nil rent during the first year of the term, or an initial rent of not more than two thirds of the initial letting value of the flat (leases entered before 1 August 1963), not more than two thirds of the rateable value of the flat (leases entered into between 1 April 1963 and 1 April 1990) or (in any other case) not more than £1,000 per annum in Greater London or £250 per annum elsewhere.

Although the flat itself need not be self contained, it has to be in a building which is or is capable of independent redevelopment or the provision of services independently (s 3 (2)). The collective right to buy does not extend to conversions with a resident landlord of less than five flats (s 4 (4)). Many larger blocks in central London may not satisfy the principal residency test as companies frequently use flats as an alternative to hotels for visitors and staff. Another problem is likely to be the cost of acquiring the freehold, since landlords will be entitled to the value of their freehold interest plus at least 50 per cent of the "marriage value" (i e the difference between present market value and its value on extension or acquisition of the freehold). The high market values existing in central London may discourage individual lessees from buying and the cumulative effect of that may mean that the two thirds minimum requirement will not be met, particularly as the leaseholders have to pay the freeholder's fees. Other lessees may be deterred by the prospect of entering into a legal relationship with neighbours. Once the initial notice to purchase has been served, those "qualifying tenants" participating in it become what is termed "participating tenants" (s 14), although other "qualifying tenants" may join in the enfranchisement process at a subsequent stage with the agreement of the "participating tenants" or continue to hold their existing leases.

Many lessees may find the alternative right granted by the 1993 Act of extending the lease for 90 years at a peppercorn rent more attractive unless they are experiencing problems with their landlords, although even then they should wait to see if the code of management practice covering areas such as service charges, buildings insurance and repairs, which s 87 empowers the housing minister to authorise, will resolve these problems when it appears.

The Act extends also to lessees of higher value houses (i e a rateable value of over £1,500 in London or £750 elsewhere) not covered by earlier legislation, although in this case the length of time as a principal residence is three years, but the "low rent" rules are the same as for flats (s 65). Disputes as to price go in the first instance to leasehold valuation tribunals but large estates may wish to establish useful precedents by taking key cases to the High Court. It will be interesting to discover the extent of the exercise of these rights in the light of all these hurdles and whether it was worthwhile for the government to alienate the Duke of Westminster and other traditional supporters.

Ironically, Pt II of the Act, relating to the formerly highly controversial "right to buy" for public sector tenants, met with only routine opposition from the Labour Party and very little debate outside of Parliament as the main ideological battle had been fought successfully in the previous decade. The Act abolishes the right of a public sector tenant to a mortgage, the right to defer completion and the right to be granted a shared ownership lease. These rights have been replaced by a new scheme — the right to acquire on rent to mortgage terms. Sections 104-116 allow a secure tenant to translate the amount of rent payments into the purchase of the home together with a right to purchase the remaining proportion. Section 121 strengthens the tenant's right to deal with disrepair, s 122 grants a right to compensation for improvements made by the tenant, and other provisions extend the delegation of housing management. Chapter II of Pt II (ss 141-157) applies similar provisions to Scotland. The new scheme is given detailed implementation by the Housing (Preservation of Right to Buy) Regulations 1993 (SI 1993/2241; the Scottish equivalent is SI 1993/2160) and the Housing (Extension of Right to Buy) Order 1993 (SI 1993/2240).

◆

NEWS

Appointments

Keeper of the Rolls
Mr T M Thomson has been appointed Keeper of the Rolls at the Court of Session with effect from 14 March 1994 in succession to Mr M G Bonar, who has been transferred to Scottish Courts Administration.

Court

Faculty of Advocates: pagers
The Faculty of Advocates is introducing a paging system into its properties in Edinburgh on 14 March 1994. It is hoped that this will improve the speed with which advocates respond to solicitors' calls. Each practising member of the

bar will be issued with a pager, and callers to the Faculty, wishing to talk to an advocate, will be directed past the switchboard direct to the paging operator. In addition, each advocate has a paging number and a list of these numbers will be circulated to all solicitors who have current dealings with the Faculty. By dialling 031-260 5685, any advocate can be paged out of hours, and providing he or she is in, or near, Parliament Hall he or she will receive a message to ring the caller's number back.

It is hoped that this system will substantially reduce the time solicitors spend in making telephone contact with an advocate. The Faculty would welcome any feedback on how successful the system is or how it might be improved upon. Comments should be sent to Mrs R Stein, administration manager (031-226 5071).

Faculty of Advocates: consultation centre
The Faculty of Advocates' Consultation Centre will open for business on Tuesday, 26 April 1994. It is located at 142 High Street in New Assembly Close. There are consultation rooms of varying sizes and comfortable waiting facilities. Disabled access has been installed as have specially equipped toilets. Solicitors arranging consultations from this date will be asked to inform all parties involved to proceed direct to the centre for the appointed time to be met by counsel.

Law reform

Sentencing and appeals
The Scottish Office have published a further consultation paper on the criminal justice system, seeking views on a number of issues related to sentencing and appeals.

Chapter 2 proposes the extension of the scope of fiscal fines from the present fixed sum of £25 to a sliding scale (with or without instalments), in line with the views of the majority of the Stewart committee, with a maximum equivalent to level 1 on the standard scale (currently £200): s 56 of the Criminal Justice (Scotland) Act 1987. It is further suggested that the range of offences for which such fines may be offered should be increased, either by making it competent to prosecute all statutory offences in the district courts, or by removing the restriction of fiscal fines to offences triable in a district court, which currently bars the possibility of a fiscal fine for many offences low on the scale of gravity.

Commenting on proposals in the recent English Royal Commission report, the paper confirms that it is already prosecution policy that the attitude of the victim and the possibility of a compensation order are taken into account before deciding on the disposal of a case.

Chapter 3, "Sentencing Powers", considers that the present distribution of business between the different courts does not appear to make the best use of available resources. The paper acknowledges that the evidence suggests an increase in the level of sentences passed following the extension of the sheriff's sentencing power in solemn cases to three years, and that any change would need to be carefully considered and implemented, but suggests that there are reasons for further extending the sheriff's powers to four or even five years. The Crown allocate the most serious cases to the High Court in any event, and have to consider the most severe sentence that would be likely to be imposed (even allowing for the sheriff's power to remit to the High Court), but for a variety of reasons around half of the sentences actually passed in the High Court in recent years could have been passed in the sheriff court, and it is not always easy to programme High Court sittings in the different towns in Scotland.

Further questions ask whether the maximum powers in summary cases should be doubled to six months (or 12 where six months is already competent for a common law offence), and whether the powers of stipendiary magistrates should be correspondingly increased.

Chapter 4 tackles the subject of sentencing guidelines, pointing out that wide variations in sentencing appear to exist between similar courts in different areas, which seem difficult to justify on an objective basis. And since about 20 per cent of appeals against sentence which come to a hearing result in a reduction of sentence, there may be some incentive for convicted persons to try their luck. It is also the case that the inappropriate or excessive use of custody for less serious offences continues to cause concern, and that the proportion of offenders given custodial sentences (especially short ones) remains higher in Scotland than elsewhere. The new power of the appeal court to increase a sentence on a reference by the Lord Advocate may lead to cases emerging which are regarded as laying down the acceptable minimum for certain types of offence. The government would therefore welcome views on whether the development of guidelines should be considered for, in particular, summary cases (where there are a larger number of sentencers), and if so whether these might be drawn up by the appeal court, or by the Sheriffs' Association and the District Courts Association and endorsed by the appeal court. Views are also canvassed on whether there could be a sentencing commission for Scotland.

Chapter 5 deals with appeals procedures, the present arrangements by which the appeal court determines appeals not having been designed to deal with the current volume of appeals, dominated as it is by summary sentence only appeals. The government consider that there should be no change to the current procedures whereby the appeal court receives all appeals and takes a view on their merits, and ask for views on whether greater efforts should be made to filter out poorly specified appeals at an early stage, whether appeals from the district court should be devolved to the sheriff principal (or heard by a smaller court), whether a single judge sift should be introduced and, if so, whether legal aid should be refused for appeals pursued after rejection in the sift, and whether two judge benches should be introduced for sentencing appeals and for appeals against conviction in summary cases.

Chapter 6 looks at the powers of the appeal court, in particular dealing with changes of evidence by a witness as additional evidence and a possible change to the test for admission of additional evidence to allow evidence available at the time of the trial where there is a reasonable explanation for the failure to adduce the evidence. Views are also invited on whether the appeal court should be expressly empowered to reconsider a jury's verdict, even in the absence of fresh evidence, where it appears that there has been a miscarriage of justice; whether it should be possible for an accused to be reindicted following an appeal on a higher charge than that on which he was originally convicted (as in *HM Advocate v Boyle*, 1993 SLT 1079); and whether (though the paper does not support the idea) there should be a Crown right of appeal against acquittal where there has been an attempt to subvert the role of the jury.

The final chapter of proposals, chap 7, asks whether there is any need to change the current procedures for handling alleged miscarriages of justice in Scotland, in the light of the English Royal Commission report. Possible options are an ombudsman to consider complaints about the handling of cases by the Secretary of State; an inspector to oversee the handling of such cases; independent advisers to assist with such cases; a new investigatory arm of the appeal court; and a new review authority as recommended by the Royal Commission.

Comments on all the proposals outlined should be submitted by 16 April.

Taxation

1994 tax returns
Advance copies of the major 1994 return forms are now available for professional bodies and software houses who wish to produce substitute forms. A specimen copy of each return form and an information sheet, "Tax returns: guidelines for production of substitute forms" can be obtained from: Inland Revenue, Corporate Communications Office, 6th Floor (KB), North West Wing, Bush House, London WC2B 4PP.

The wording and design of substitute return forms must be approved before tax offices can accept them. Applications for approval of substitute 1994 return forms should be sent to: Inland Revenue, Corporate Communications Office, Room 9/3A, 9th Floor, North West Wing, Bush House, London WC2B 4PP. All applications for approval will be considered as quickly as possible.

◇

Non-statutory redundancy payments
The Inland Revenue have issued a statement of practice (SP 1/94) which sets out their approach to non-statutory payments following the decision of the House of Lords in *Mairs (Inspector of Taxes) v Haughey* [1993] 3 WLR 393. The new statement replaces SP 1/81. The text of the statement is as follows:

(1) Sections 579 (1) and 580 (3) of the Income and Corporation Taxes Act 1988 provide that statutory redundancy payments shall be exempt from income tax under Sched E, with the exception of any liability under s 148 of that Act.

(2) Lump sum payments made under a non-statutory scheme, in addition to, or instead of statutory redundancy pay, will also be liable to income tax only under s 148 provided they are genuinely made solely on account of redundancy as defined in s 81 of the Employment Protection (Consolidation) Act 1978. This will be so whether the scheme is a standing one which forms part of the terms on which the employees give their services or whether it is an ad hoc scheme devised to meet a specific situation such as the imminent closure of a particular factory.

(3) However, payments made under a non-statutory scheme which are not genuinely made to compensate for loss of employment through redundancy may be liable to tax in full. In particular, payments which are, in reality, a form of terminal bonus will be chargeable to income tax under Sched E as emoluments from the employment under s 19 (1) ICTA. Payments made for meeting production targets or doing

extra work in the period leading up to redundancy are examples of such terminal bonuses. Payments conditional on continued service in the employment for a time will also represent terminal bonuses if calculated by reference to any additional period served following issue of the redundancy notice.

(4) The Revenue is concerned to distinguish between payments under non-statutory schemes which are genuinely made to compensate for loss of employment through redundancy and payments which are made as a reward for services in the employment or more generally for having acted as or having been an employee. As arrangements for redundancy can often be complex and provide for a variety of payments, it follows that each scheme must be considered on its own facts. The Revenue's practice, in these circumstances, is to allow employers to submit proposed schemes to their inspectors of taxes for advance clearance.

(5) An employer or any other person operating a redundancy scheme, who wishes to be satisfied that lump sum payments under a scheme will be accepted as liable to tax only under s 148 should submit the full facts to the inspector for consideration. Applications for clearance should be made in writing and should be accompanied by the scheme document together with the text of any intended letter to employees which explains its terms.

— ◊ —

Business change

W & J Burness, WS, 16 Hope Street, Edinburgh, and 242 West George Street, Glasgow, intimate that with effect from 1 March 1994 Andrew F Sleigh has been assumed as a partner practising from the firm's Glasgow office.

— ◊ —

Parliamentary News

Royal Assent

24 February 1994

Non-Domestic Rating Act 1994 (c 3)

New Bills

HOUSE OF COMMONS

23 February 1994

Hare Coursing—To make hare coursing illegal; to prohibit the use of any place for or in connection with hare coursing; to provide for the confiscation of any animal or equipment used or to be used for or in connection with hare coursing; and for connected purposes. (Private Member's Bill introduced by Mr Colin Pickthall)

Pensions Reform—To make provision for employers' and employees' pension contributions to be paid into personally owned funds registered for the purpose of future pension payment. (Private Member's Bill introduced by Mr Robert B Jones)

28 February 1994

Parliamentary Elections—To repeal the Septennial Act 1715 and to introduce a fixed term for the House of Commons; to bring the age of nomination for election to the House of Commons into line with the age of voting by amending the Parliamentary Elections Act 1695; to improve electoral registration and absent voting procedures, to introduce weekend voting and increase the number of signatures for nomination of candidates by amending the Representation of the People Acts 1983 and 1985; to change expense limits for candidates; to introduce early voting; to set up an Electoral Commission to administer and monitor all elections in the United Kingdom and to allow that commission to register political parties and set limits to the expenditure nationally of registered political parties in the period prior to the fixed term elections; and for connected purposes. (Private Member's Bill introduced by Mr Jeff Rooker)

Progress of Bills

Chiropractors — Commons: second reading, 18 February 1994.

Race Relations (Remedies) — Commons: all stages, 18 February 1994.

Local Government (Wales) — Lords: report stage, 28 February 1994.

Licensing of Domiciliary Care Agencies — Lords: committee stage, 28 February 1994.

Photography and Films (Unauthorised Use) — Lords: second reading, 28 February 1994.

Police and Magistrates' Courts — Lords: committee stage concluded, 1 March 1994.

Question answered

HOUSE OF COMMONS

24 February 1994

COURT OF SESSION

Mr McFall: To ask the Secretary of State for Scotland what plans he has to ensure that the dues of court paid in the Court of Session are directly referable to the civil element of the judicial work of Lords of Council and Session.

Lord James Douglas-Hamilton: The Government plan to include the costs of the civil element of the judicial work of Lords of Council and Session in the calculation of dues of court paid in the Court of Session. These costs will be phased into the fees structure over a three year period.

Book Reviews

Goff and Jones: The Law of Restitution

Fourth edition. By Professor G Jones. 1993. London: Sweet & Maxwell. Hardback, £98. ISBN 0 421 42560 1.

Unjustified Enrichment: A Casebook

By S Eiselen and G Pienaar. 1993. Durban: Butterworth. Paperback, £33. ISBN 0 409 02692 1.

At a time when the Scottish Law Commission are doing much work on the topic of unjustified enrichment (Discussion Paper no 95), there is a tendency to look around to see what others do about problems that are common to most modern societies. "The proper place of comparative law" is too big a topic for these reviews but, done properly, most lawyers can find an investigation of other legal systems of value. The two legal systems investigated in these two books are both rather special for Scots lawyers. Goff and Jones deals with cases that may be very persuasive before a Scots court; Eiselen and Pienaar deals with an uncodified system with civilian roots and a common law influence. The South African book is mainly in English but there are passages in Afrikaans making parts less accessible. The commentary is, however, in English.

Lord Goff has retired from his authorial duties in this edition of what can properly be called a "classic" work. The book deals with the major changes that have taken place since the third edition: *Lipkin Gorman v Karpnale* [1991] AC 548; *Woolwich v Inland Revenue* [1993] AC 70. It also deals exhaustively with all the other restitutionary cases decided in the interval. New statutory provisions are considered in detail — some of the statutes apply to Scotland. The academic literature is fully noted and discussed where appropriate. There are organisational changes, particularly in "ineffective transactions" and in the dropping of the foreign sounding (to Scots) "waiver of tort". The new title "tort and restitutionary claims" is more approachable for the Scots reader and the issues of principle are clearly brought out.

A casebook with a good commentary really allows the reader from one jurisdiction to "feel" the law of another jurisdiction. The puzzles that come to mind when reading a condensed statement in a textbook are frequently evaporated by reading a few well selected extracts. Naturally, no matter how good the commentary it is as well to read some ordinary prose before embarking on a casebook and Butterworth's own *Jouberts Encyclopaedia* is one useful starting place in English. The most significant case for the comparatist at the present time may well be *Willis Faber Enthoven Pty Ltd v Receiver of Revenue*, 1992 (4) SA 202 (A), treated at p 158. Those who cherish Scotland's civilian heritage and wish that it were more a part of the ius commune will look in envy at the passage in the judgment which begins: "For present purposes a brief résumé of the main texts of the Corpus Juris Civilis and how they were applied by the Jurists of the sixteenth and seventeenth centuries will suffice." Not an everyday occurrence at Parliament House. The outcome of the analysis is that it is understood that the condictio indebiti is but one name for an equitable action preventing a person being unjustifiably enriched at another's expense. The snappy, punchy maxim "ignorantia juris" is examined in other areas of the law to test its true applicability and it is found to be much less than universally applied. The conclusion is that there should be no distinction between the two types of error, error of law and error of fact, but that it should be a requirement that the payment should not be "slack nor studied" or "inexcusably slack" — that being the rule in relation to mistakes of fact in South Africa. English authority is considered as well as the ius commune. It is an excellent judgment and proof enough of the value of this book that if it it were required to find authority for a proposition unvouched in Scots law, recourse to cases from a jurisdiction very similar in many respects to our own, both in terminology and approach, would pay dividends.

Two wonderful books (both with full bibliographies), aimed at different markets, but useful to any lawyer anywhere, both being clear and full expositions of how a legal system deals with the universal issue of unjust enrichment. Readers who buy either book and wish to keep up to date between editions will be happy to know that in the *Restitution Law Review*, the English law is summarised annually by William Swadling and the South African law by Prof Daniel Visser.

W J Stewart,
MacMillans, Solicitors,
Glasgow.

Mayson, French & Ryan on Company Law

Tenth edition. By Stephen Mayson, Derek French and Christopher Ryan. 1993.
London: Blackstone Press. Paperback, £24.95.
ISBN 1 85431 270 7.

The student or practitioner of company law is well served by the publishers of textbooks. There is a range of student texts dealing with the subject according to the needs of students on various kinds of courses, as well as several well known practitioner works. Mayson is aimed principally at the degree level student market but also the practitioner wishing to refresh her or his memory on some point.

It meets the needs of students by combining full discussion of the legislation and case law with useful citation of periodical and other literature. In this respect one quibble might be that there is no reference to the Cadbury report, so important in the current debate on corporate governance. This deserves to have been mentioned in the discussions of directors' duties and audit. Mayson is not, and does not purport to be, in the same category as the magisterial Gower's *Principles of Modern Company Law*, happily now in a fifth edition. But that is not to disparage it, as Gower with its author's firm imprint has become a classic.

A special characteristic of Mayson is that a new edition is produced each year in time for the start of the academic year. Students therefore have a textbook which is as up to date as it is possible to be. Unfortunately, the legislative year is not organised in a way which assists the authors, so the important changes in insider dealing legislation made by Pt IV of the Criminal Justice Act 1993 can only be mentioned without any discussion. In this case there is as yet no indication when that Part of the Act will be brought into force [since implemented on 1 March 1994 — *Editor*].

From a Scottish point of view there is a major reservation about this book in that it does not pay sufficient attention to Scottish aspects of the subject. There is no reference, for example, to the Scottish legislation on floating charges or to the uncertain state of the law on corporate criminal liability in Scotland. Just over 30 Scottish cases are referred to, which compares unfavourably with the range of citations of Commonwealth authorities. In this respect it suffers in comparison with Charlesworth and Morse which has a Scottish editor and, incidentally, is rather cheaper.

W C H ERVINE,
University of Dundee.

◆

ACT OF SEDERUNT

ACT OF SEDERUNT (Solicitor's Right of Audience) 1994
(SI 1994/221) [6 JANUARY 1994]

The Lords of Council and Session, under and by virtue of the powers conferred on them by sections 5 and 48 of the Court of Session Act 1988, and of all other powers enabling them in that behalf, do hereby enact and declare:

Citation and commencement

1.—(1) This Act of Sederunt may be cited as the Act of Sederunt (Solicitor's Right of Audience) 1994 and shall come into force on 7th January 1994.

(2) This Act of Sederunt shall be inserted in the Books of Sederunt.

Interpretation

2. In this Act of Sederunt—
"the Secretary" means the Secretary of the Society for the time being, in his capacity as an office bearer of the Society;
"a right of audience by virtue of section 25A of the Solicitors (Scotland) Act 1980" (c 46) means a right of audience in, on the one hand, the Court of Session, the House of Lords and the Judicial Committee of the Privy Council or, on the other hand, the High Court of Justiciary; and
"the Society" means the Law Society of Scotland established under the Solicitors (Scotland) Act 1980.

Right of audience

3. The Secretary shall have a right of audience in the Outer House of the Court of Session on 7th January 1994 for the purpose only of introducing to the court solicitors who have acquired a right of audience by virtue of section 25A of the Solicitors (Scotland) Act 1980 and inviting the Lord Ordinary to administer the appropriate declaration.

J A D HOPE, LORD PRESIDENT, *IPD*

[Acts of Sederunt are reproduced with the permission of the Controller of Her Majesty's Stationery Office.]

ARTICLES

Sequestration and Pension Rights

Iain J S Talman,
Bishop and Robertson Chalmers,
Glasgow.

Mr Talman examines the effect of bankruptcy on a debtor's rights under pension arrangements, a subject which gives rise to difficult problems including those of vesting, upkeep of contributions, and rights of transfer on re-vesting, particularly in view of Inland Revenue rules.

Part V.2 of the Notes of Guidance of Interim and Permanent Trustees issued by the Accountant in Bankruptcy on 1 October 1990 gives guidance in relation to retirement annuity contracts and other forms of pension entitlement. Although some time has passed since this was first issued in the form of a letter of 28 February 1990, little has happened to explain or clarify the legal issues involved.

Pension arrangements

Perhaps the commonest form of pension arrangement is the employer's scheme known as an occupational pension scheme. A member of such a scheme may simultaneously make a separate individual arrangement for paying additional voluntary contributions. That is known as a free standing additional voluntary contributions scheme. A member who has ceased to be in pensionable service under an occupational pension scheme may have the right (and for those leaving after 1 January 1986 there is a statutory right under the Pension Schemes Act 1993, Pt IV, Chap IV) to have his benefit entitlement bought out into an annuity contract or insurance policy. This is known as a "section 32 buyout". A tax approval regime exists for all these arrangements in the form of Chap I of Pt XIV of the Income and Corporation Taxes Act 1988, which is further explicated by the Inland Revenue Booklet IR12, re-issued in October 1991. For an occupational pension scheme the full benefits for tax purposes are derived not simply from approval but from exempt approval which under s 592 (1) of the 1988 Act would mean that the scheme will be set up in trust. There are also statutory schemes (under e g the Superannuation Act 1972) which under s 594 have the same privileges. This article principally examines rights constituted by contract or trust. For statutory schemes the individual statute and/or regulations should be examined, but it might be noted in passing that s 5 (1) of the 1972 Act,

while making an assignation or charge void, is expressed without prejudice to the Bankruptcy (Scotland) Act 1985.

Those who have earnings to which an employer's scheme does not relate (including self employed people) may effect a personal pension scheme. That is capable of approval under Chap IV of Pt XIV of the 1988 Act. This is explicated by Inland Revenue Booklet IR76. The Inland Revenue have also issued model rules, IR/PP/88, for personal pension schemes. Personal pensions have been available only since 1 July 1988. Prior to that the Inland Revenue might approve a retirement annuity contract which complied with the requirements of Pt XIV, Chap III. A personal pension scheme or retirement annuity contract might simply be a contract or might be framed as a trust.

Broadly, all these arrangements have the purpose of providing a pension at a prescribed normal pension date, although usually also with provision for the pension to be taken earlier or later. In the case of occupational pension schemes after "two years' qualifying service" the member must nevertheless remain entitled to his pension even if he leaves before the normal pension date. This is the basic premise of the preservation requirements in Pt IV, Chap I of the Pension Schemes Act 1993. Often it is permitted to commute part of the pension for a tax free lump sum at the time of retirement.

On death a lump sum may be payable, although after retirement this will usually be restricted to the balance of a guaranteed period of payment of pension. Generally, the tax rules will permit a lump sum to be distributed by what is known as "discretionary distribution". No person has an absolute entitlement to the money; this is a useful inheritance tax saving. There may also be survivors' pensions, particularly for the widow(er).

Under Pt III of the 1993 Act, an occupational pension scheme may be used to contract-out members from the earnings related portion of the state pension scheme. One of the requirements is that the scheme must provide either a guaranteed minimum pension or protected rights for the member and his widow/her widower.

An "appropriate" personal pension scheme may, again by providing protected rights, be used to contract out by virtue of the 1993 Act, ss 26 to 33 and Sched 2. Again there are model rules in the form of IMR/APP/88. Contracting-out is a complex area which has been the subject of innumerable regulations and Occupational Pensions Board memoranda.

A further mode by which a person may make pension provision is by using a lump sum to purchase a bond (or contract) of annuity. As to the tax treatment of these, see ss 656 to 658 of the Income and Corporation Taxes Act 1988. The tax regime has, however, a lighter touch and need not detain us long. On bankruptcy the bond (or contract) vests in the permanent trustee, largely untrammelled by special considerations.

Vesting of the estate and the debtor's pension rights

The Bankruptcy (Scotland) Act 1985, s 31, vests the whole estate of the debtor, with certain exceptions, in the permanent trustee. The estate includes the capacity to exercise powers "in respect of any property as might have been exercised by the debtor for his own benefit" if exercisable on a relevant date, i e before the debtor's discharge.

However, something which is not already vested in the debtor cannot vest in the permanent trustee: *Christie's Tr v Leith, Hull, and Hamburg Steam Packet Co Ltd*, 1915 1 SLT 455; 1915 SC 848. If the right may, subject to a contingency, vest in the debtor, the trustee is in the position as if he had an intimated assignation of it: s 31 (5). That deemed assignation does not appear to override a provision making the right non-assignable. If the right is assignable, and (since it is not even vested in the debtor) would not, without s 31 (5), vest in the trustee, the debtor could assign it to a third party which would be effective by accretion when the contingency is fulfilled. If the right is non-assignable, there can be no fear of a competing assignation to a third party (see Lord Guthrie in *Christie's Tr*, supra, at 1915 SC, p 859; 1915 1 SLT, p 460). One of the main requirements of tax approval is that the annuities be non-assignable. Therefore, the statutory assignation is not effective. The practical difference is when the contingency happens and the non-vested right vests. If the right is assignable and therefore deemed assigned by the statute, it will automatically vest in the trustee. If it has not been assigned, then it will only vest in the trustee as an acquirendum if by then the debtor has not been discharged (see s 32 (6) and (10)).

Under s 32 income other than that derived from estate vesting in the permanent trustee falls to the debtor, although the trustee may make an application in respect of it. In none of this is any distinction specially made for alimentary rights. The question does, however, arise whether rights under a pension arrangement are "estate" of the debtor. In the case of contractual pension arrange-ments it can hardly be doubted that they must be part of the estate of the debtor. The guidance of the Accountant in Bankruptcy would appear to proceed upon that assumption. The position, however, is much less clear in relation to arrangements set up under trust, and these have not been fully examined by judges or jurists. While the case of *Officers' Superannuation and Provident Fund of the Union Bank of Scotland Trustees v Cooper*, 1976 SLT (Sh Ct) 2, in treating all pensions as alimentary, might suggest that they are purely income, they can also be regarded as rights under trust and therefore part of the estate of the debtor which would consequently vest in the permanent trustee. The differences are:

(1) If the right is an item of estate, and (a) is vested in the debtor, whether or not it is assignable, it vests in the permanent trustee under s 31; but (b) if it is not yet vested in the debtor, it will not vest in the permanent trustee under s 31, nor (if non-assignable) will it be treated as assigned under s 31 (5). However, if and when it vests in the debtor, it will vest in the permanent trustee as an acquirendum, but only if this happens before the debtor's discharge. In either case, once this right is vested in the permanent trustee, everything following therefrom, including all income, falls to the permanent trustee.

(2) If the right is not an item of estate but merely income, under s 32 an application must be made to the court, and even if it is successful, only income actually due before the debtor's discharge will fall to the permanent trustee.

In the case of (1) (b) or (2) (meaning really in any case until the law is clarified), the permanent trustee should consider application to postpone the debtor's discharge.

Assuming the rights are "estate", the question then becomes one of when the right under the trust vests in the debtor. The law of vesting has hitherto not been concerned with its application to rights under an occupational pension scheme. The examination must, therefore, proceed by way of general principles. In doing so, it has to be borne in mind that these principles have been derived from wills and inter vivos trusts which have been gratuitous. The extent to which a contract of employment, a right to a pension, and any existing pension scheme overlap each other and affect each other is still developing. (See such cases as *Christie's Tr* (supra); *Mettoy Pension Trs v Evans* [1990] 1 WLR 1587; [1991] 2 All ER 513; *Barber v Guardian Royal Exchange* [1991] 1 QB 344; [1991] 2 WLR 72; *Mihlenstedt v Barclays Bank International* [1989] IRLR 522; and *Imperial Group Pension Trust Ltd v Imperial*

Tobacco Ltd [1991] 1 WLR 589; [1991] 2 All ER 597.)

Early vesting is presumed even when payment is delayed. Vesting cannot be delayed beyond payment. This suggests that a person who becomes entitled to payment of a pension has a vested right to it. That right would, therefore, pass to the trustee on sequestration. This is contrary to what the Accountant suggests in his guidance notes but supports the proposition that the right to a pension would be a part of the debtor's estate.

If the vesting of a right is delayed to a dies incertus or is subject to a contingency, vesting is delayed until the contingency happens. It is suggested that vesting is accordingly delayed in respect of pension rights. Survival to a retirement date or even a date at which early retirement *could* be taken must be uncertain contingencies, as must surviving a relative in order to receive a pension.

Reverting to contractual arrangements, it is suggested that while these must be vested in the debtor, the position is different in respect of claims for dependants' benefits. Here the dependant is a tertius and it is suggested the position is more akin to that under a trust.

Contracted-out benefits do not vest in a trustee in bankruptcy: Pension Schemes Act 1993, s 159 (5).

Lump sum at retirement
In some schemes there is at retirement a right to a pension and a right to a lump sum. This applies in some statutory schemes. More commonly, there is a right to a pension and also a right to opt to commute part of that pension for a lump sum, subject to Inland Revenue limits.

In the case of an arrangement constituted by contract, the debtor's interest, including these rights, will have vested in the permanent trustee.

In relation to an arrangement constituted by trust, if the above analysis is correct, the rights will vest in the permanent trustee only if they vest in the debtor before the debtor's discharge. If they do so vest, however, it will be for the permanent trustee to opt for a lump sum. Even if the debtor's interest under the trust is not estate, the permanent trustee should, by virtue of s 31 (8) (b) of the 1985 Act, be able to exercise the option to take a lump sum.

Dependants' annuities or pensions
Most pension arrangements have provision for pension to be paid to a dependant, principally a surviving spouse. Such a pension may arise as of right or may be capable of arising by virtue of a partial surrender of the member's own entitlement.

Two principal questions arise: First, whether a debtor can exercise a right of surrender which would thereby reduce his pension and other benefits eventually vesting in him and thus in the permanent trustee in order to provide pension benefits for his family; and secondly, what the position is where the debtor is, in fact, not the member but one of those dependants.

As to the first of those questions, it is suggested that notwithstanding the debtor and thus the permanent trustee not having vested rights, it is the permanent trustee and not the debtor who has the right to exercise such options (see Bankruptcy (Scotland) Act 1985, ss 31 (8) (b) and 32 (8)).

It is suggested that a dependant's annuity must be a right which is non-vested until the contingency actually arises. Therefore, it will only vest in the bankrupt dependant's permanent trustee if vesting (i e becoming payable) before the debtor's discharge.

Contracted out benefits for the surviving spouse are similarly protected from passing to that surviving spouse's permanent trustee.

Lump sum death benefits
While the death of a person is something which is eventually certain to happen, it will not necessarily happen while that person is in pensionable service or before retiral. Therefore, the accrual of a particular lump sum benefit is in most if not all cases going to be subject to deferred vesting and subject to similar considerations as above.

In relation to pension arrangements constituted by contract, these will have vested in the permanent trustee. Generally speaking, there is no Inland Revenue requirement that the death benefit should be non-assignable. However, such arrangements may be written in trust under the Married Women's Policies of Assurance (Scotland) Acts 1880 to 1980 and would therefore not vest in the permanent trustee. (See s 2 of the 1880 Act in respect of challenges to such a policy in fraud of creditors.)

In pension arrangements constituted by trust, the tax advantages of discretionary distribution will usually have been taken. The permanent trustee of a bankrupt potential beneficiary, therefore, only has the right to ensure that the trustee of the pension arrangement in exercising that discretion does so properly.

Payment of premiums/contributions
The Accountant in Bankruptcy in his guidance notes has suggested that the permanent trustee

might wish to continue the payment of premiums to a retirement annuity contract. Many contracts allow flexibility as to payments and so the continuation of premiums may not be necessary.

It is suggested, however, that there are difficulties in the way of this. A "qualifying premium" must under s 620 (1) of the 1988 Act be paid by an individual. The real problem is that invariably such policies or contracts will be with an insurer who invests the premiums through his tax exempt "pension business" fund (see 1988 Act, s 438). Pension business is defined in s 431 (3) and (4). It is suggested that an insurer would, as a result of those provisions, be unwilling to accept a premium from a trustee in bankruptcy.

The position for an occupational pension scheme is somewhat different. A "member" has a statutory right under the 1993 Act, s 111 to pay additional voluntary contributions. Nowhere is there a pertinent definition of "member" but it is suggested that the permanent trustee cannot be regarded as the member and cannot pay ordinary or additional contributions in place of the bankrupt member.

Transfers
Can a debtor transfer his entitlement out of one pension arrangement into another? It is suggested that generally he cannot. Whether the arrangement be constituted by a contract or a trust, it would seem that the same considerations apply as apply to the taking of a commutation lump sum as discussed above.

The same cannot, with certainty, be stated also in relation to the statutory right to transfer the cash equivalent of benefits from an occupational pension scheme to another scheme or arrangement. This, as mentioned above, arises under Pt IV, Chap IV of the 1993 Act and is a statutory right of the member. It might be argued that, being a statutory right, it is not one which passes to the permanent trustee by virtue of the provisions discussed above.

Information
The Occupational Pension Schemes (Disclosure of Information) Regulations 1986 (SI 1986/1046, as amended) give members and beneficiaries certain rights to information about certain occupational pension schemes and benefits. Even if a permanent trustee cannot be said to be a member (not defined), it would appear he could be a beneficiary who is a "person, other than a member of the scheme, who is entitled to payment of benefit under the scheme". The scheme registration requirements of the 1993 Act, s 8 may assist permanent trustees in tracing schemes

which the debtor has lost touch with. Tracing request forms can be obtained from the Registrar of the Occupational Pensions Board in Newcastle.

In the case of arrangements constituted by contract, inquiries can be made of the other contracting party, the insurer concerned. Often this requires a considerable deal of kindly, and not so kindly, explanation (etc!) by the permanent trustee or his agents.

Scheme provisions and other dangers
It should be borne in mind that a scheme's documents may direct or empower the scheme trustees to exercise a lien for debts due to an employer (perfectly possible in a bankruptcy) over, or (in the event of bankruptcy or diligence being done) to forfeit, the entitlements of a member. In the latter case, the benefits may be directed to be applied to dependants. Such provisions are acceptable in Revenue terms and (within certain limitations) in terms of the preservation requirements, although generally they cannot apply to guaranteed minimum pensions or protected rights.

An examination of the use and effects of diligence in relation to pension rights would make an article in itself. Suffice to say at present that prior effective diligence can affect the rights of the permanent trustee.

Surplus
If Revenue limits on contributions to a personal pension scheme are exceeded the excess must be refunded to the member. This right of receipt, being part of the estate of the debtor, will vest in the permanent trustee.

The English case of *Davis v Richards & Wallington Industries Ltd* [1990] 1 WLR 1151; [1991] 2 All ER 563, decided among many other things that a surplus in an occupational pension scheme would only be refundable to members in the highly unlikely event that the surplus would have arisen even if the employer had not contributed. (Contributions from the employer are a condition of Revenue approval.) However, where the member has paid additional voluntary contributions and his benefits turn out to be excessive, the excess contributions (calculated as prescribed in regulations — see Retirement Benefits Schemes (Restriction on Discretion to Approve) (Additional Voluntary Contributions) Regulations 1993 (SI 1993/3016)).

Re-vesting
The Accountant in Bankruptcy has said in his guidance notes that eventually a retirement annuity contract should be re-vested in the debtor. If the above analysis (that other rights

may also vest in the permanent trustee) is correct, then a similar consideration applies to them. Rights to annuities and pensions are required by Inland Revenue approval requirements to be non-assignable, and when many other benefits are also declared by the scheme rules to be non-assignable, it is difficult to see how re-vesting can be achieved. Presumably the permanent trustee should execute an assignation and give intimation of that to the insurers or pension scheme trustees — and then wait to see what happens.

Voluntary trust deeds
By reason of the non-assignability requirements just referred to, a trustee under a voluntary trust deed will generally be precluded from having pension benefits vested in him. The deed may convey acquirenda, and so payments (e g of surplus) out of a scheme or arrangement may fall to the trustee, provided he has intimated his conveyance to the other party. In many cases the non-assignability may also be expressed to extend to such payments. Intimation of the trust deed

also holds the danger that the scheme trustees may forfeit benefits.

Challenge of payments
The extent to which payments by a debtor to a pension arrangement may be paid in fraud of his creditors is another area which has not been fully examined and which, for reasons of space, cannot be examined in detail here. The debtor could significantly alter his estate if he were able in the time leading up to sequestration freely to put funds into a tax exempt environment, subject to strict Revenue controls — particularly so if, contrary to what is argued above, contingent rights under a pension scheme are not "estate". This is rendered all the more piquant for the creditors when in so many insured arrangements huge front-ended charges and commissions (often more than 50 per cent of the premium) are levied. McBryde, *Bankruptcy*, pp 145 et seq, gives a wide meaning to transactions in fraud of creditors reducible at common law. Who will be brave enough first to try?

NEWS

Court

Court of Session: practice note
No 1 of 1994 (10 March 1994): Note of objections to auditor's report

As from this date, practitioners are advised that, when attending at the office of the Keeper of the Rolls to fix a diet for a hearing on a note of objections to a report by the Auditor of Court, they will require to indicate whether or not the diet should be assigned to a particular judge and, if so, the reason for it.

◇

Dumfries sheriff court
As from 28 March 1994 Dumfries sheriff court will be located at the following address: Sheriff Court House, Buccleuch Street, Dumfries DG1 2AN (DX 580617). The phone and fax numbers remain unchanged.

◇

Sheriffdoms: South Strathclyde, Dumfries and Galloway
The Sheriff Principal of South Strathclyde has prescribed the following revised sessions for disposal of civil business in 1994, to permit the flexibility required by the new Ordinary Cause Rules:

Spring session, 10 January to 31 March 1994. Summer session, 6 April to 15 July 1994. Winter session, 21 July to 23 December 1994. The sheriff principal has also fixed 5 April 1994 as a day upon which civil business can be disposed of.

— ◇ —

General

WS Society educational scholarship
The WS Society has established a scholarship to assist suitably qualified applicants in the study of, and research into, law or the practice of law. In establishing the scholarship the society identified in particular the need to promote a greater understanding of the law and institutions of the European Union. While preference will be given,

where appropriate, to members of the society, their qualified assistants or trainees, applications will be considered from anyone wishing to pursue a course of study or research, particularly in European law or European institutions. Applications are now invited for a grant or grants to be awarded in September or October 1994.

Application forms can be obtained from: Commander J R C Foster RN (Rtd), General Manager, The WS Society, Signet Library, Parliament Square, Edinburgh EH1 1RF. Completed application forms should be lodged by 31 May 1994.

— ◇ —

Taxation

Foreign exchange gains and losses
The Inland Revenue have published draft regulations setting out detailed rules on certain aspects of the provisions on exchange gains and losses of companies ("the Forex provisions") contained in Finance Act 1993. The draft Forex (Deferral of Gains and Losses) Regulations 1994 will supplement provisions in the Finance Act 1993 which allow companies to defer recognition of certain unrealised exchange gains. The draft Forex (Excess Exchange Gains and Losses) Regulations 1994 will provide for a balancing adjustment to restrict, in certain circumstances, the amount taxed or relieved in respect of exchange gains and losses so as to take account of the overall gain or loss on an asset or liability.

Further information can be obtained from, and comments on the drafts (by 30 April 1994) sent to: Sue Cooper, Inland Revenue (Financial Institutions Division), Foreign Exchange Consultations, Room 510, 22 Kingsway, London WC2B 6NR.

◇

Counter avoidance of PAYE
The Inland Revenue have published draft regulations which provide the rules to be operated by employers, who will in the future be required to operate the Pay As You Earn (PAYE) system if they pay their staff in assets or via certain intermediaries.

The regulations are to be made under enabling powers included in the current Finance Bill. They will complete the legislation announced in the Budget to prevent employers avoiding their PAYE responsibilities.

The regulations exclude certain transactions from the scope of PAYE as extended by the Finance Bill, i e shares acquired by the exercise of a share option granted by reason of the person's employment where the tax charge is calculated

according to special rules; and use of a credit token (e g a credit card) or a cash voucher to meet expenses.

The regulations also provide rules for employers so that they know when, and how, to account for PAYE tax when making payments to employees via intermediaries or in the form of certain types of assets (defined as "notional payments"). The rules for accounting for PAYE tax on notional payments provide that if possible the employer should deduct the tax from other cash pay paid at the same time as, or after, the notional payment in the same income tax period; to the extent that this is not possible, the employer should in any event account for the balance of the tax, alongside his PAYE tax deducted from other pay, 14 days after the end of that income tax period.

In addition, the regulations make various amendments to the PAYE regulations to ensure that they work for tax on notional payments. Further information can be obtained from, and comments on the draft regulations (by 30 April 1994) sent to: Michael Gordon-Brown, Personal Tax Division, Inland Revenue, Somerset House, London WC2R 1LB.

— ◇ —

Business change

Messrs MacMillans, solicitors, Glasgow, intimate that Mr William J Stewart, the firm's consultant, formerly senior lecturer at the University of Strathclyde, has been assumed as a partner. The firm's premises at Gordon Street closed as at 14 March and new larger premises at 78 Springfield Road, Glasgow, opened that day. The address, telephone and fax numbers of the 328 Tollcross Road office remain the same. The telephone number for Springfield Road is 041-556 4225; the modem line is 041-554 2539 and the fax number is 041-556 4311. The Glasgow Rutland Box GW350 has been closed and DX1283 Rutherglen has been opened. Mr Di Emidio has resigned from the firm to train for the Scottish bar.

— ◇ —

Parliamentary News

New Bills
HOUSE OF COMMONS
2 March 1994

Severn Bridges Act 1992 (Amendment)—To amend the Severn Bridges Act 1992. (Private Member's Bill introduced by Mr Roy Hughes)

8 March 1994

Energy Conservation (Lighting)—To promote more efficient lighting and the consequent beneficial effects on the environment. (Private Member's Bill introduced by Mr Keith Mans)

Progress of Bills

Social Security (Incapacity for Work)— Commons: remaining stages, 8 March 1994.

Sunday Trading — Lords: second reading, 8 March 1994.

Treasure — Lords: second reading, 8 March 1994.

Education — Lords: committee stage, 10 March 1994.

Questions answered

HOUSE OF COMMONS

2 March 1994

COMPUTER DISCS

Mr McAllion: To ask the Secretary of State for Scotland if he will introduce early legislation making illegal the production, manufacture and distribution of computer discs containing sexually explicit material.

Lord James Douglas-Hamilton: It is already an offence, under s 51 (2) of the Civic Government (Scotland) Act 1982, for any person to publish, sell or distribute or, with a view to its eventual sale or distribution, make, print, have or keep any obscene material. The definition of material includes any "disc or other kind of recording (whether of sound or visual images or both)". For the avoidance of doubt, a Government amendment has been tabled to the Criminal Justice and Public Order Bill to ensure that computer transmissions are covered by s 51. The need for further legislation will be assessed in the light of the recently published report of the Home Affairs Select Committee on computer pornography.

3 March 1994

PUBLIC BODIES

Mr Gordon Prentice: To ask the Secretary of State for Scotland what steps he is taking to secure greater transparency in the affairs of non-elected bodies whose membership in whole or in part is appointed by him or who exercise functions previously carried out by local authorities.

Mr Lang: Such action as is necessary has already been taken or is in hand. All the bodies to which I appoint members and which undertake expenditure directly either produce audited accounts or, in some minor cases, have their expenditure included in the accounts prepared by my Departments. Most also produce annual reports. These reports and accounts are laid before Parliament and they may be examined by the Committee of Public Accounts.

In addition, the Comptroller and Auditor General may conduct inquiries into the economy, efficiency and effectiveness with which bodies to which I appoint members and which receive more than half of their income from public funds, have used their resources. Reports by the Comptroller and Auditor General may be submitted to Parliament and the Committee of Public Accounts may question senior officials both of my Department and, in many cases, of the bodies themselves.

Management statements have been, or will be, prepared for most executive NDPBs. These will be published and will define the role and responsibilities of the body, its relationship with its sponsor departments, its accountability, aims and objectives. In addition, executive NDPBs are expected to meet the charter standards of the citizens' charter and the principles of the Government's White Paper, "Open Government". A code of conduct for NHS boards which encourages transparency about NHS activities has already been issued for consultation. It is also planned to produce a code of practice to follow up steps already taken as part of the patients' charter initiative to incorporate into the NHS the principles of the Government's White Paper, "Open Government".

The only bodies which carry out functions formerly undertaken by local authorities, are the colleges of further education for which I became responsible on 1 April 1993. The colleges produce annual reports and audited accounts and the Comptroller and Auditor General has a right to inspect their books and records and to carry out value for money studies. Again, he may report the results of these studies to Parliament and the Committee of Public Accounts can question relevant officials. This year, for the first time, each college will also be required to publish a shortened development plan, describing its forward objectives and its performance in meeting past objectives.

7 March 1994

PRISONERS (CRIMINAL PROCEEDINGS)

Dr Godman: To ask the Secretary of State for Scotland in how many cases a commissioner has been appointed under s 33 of the Prisoners and Criminal Proceedings (Scotland) Act 1993 in (a) the sheriff court and (b) the High Court to date; and if he will make a statement.

Lord James Douglas-Hamilton: There have been no appointments in either sheriff court or High Court proceedings to date.

Book Review

Textbook on Labour Law

Third edition by Bowers and Honeyball. 1993. London: Blackstone Press. Paperback, £17.95. ISBN 1 85431 302 9.

This textbook is intended for students as opposed to practitioners and has commendably been produced in paperback at a realistic price. The text follows the usual format of books on labour law in that the initial chapters deal with individual employment law issues while the later ones concentrate on collective matters. In view of the book's intended readership it could have spent some time setting the institutions of labour law in perspective by, for example, dealing somewhere with the roles and competences of industrial tribunals and the employment appeal tribunal; according to the index "Industrial tribunal" is mentioned only at p 145 and on examination that occurs in the context of a discussion of the potentially fair reasons for dismissal. Similarly an explanation of the relationship between these specialist tribunals and the ordinary courts would be helpful to students, unless of course their course structure has ensured coverage of that in an earlier component — something which, in the light of "modularisation", cannot always be guaranteed, but that is another issue! Also the institutions of collective law could have been dealt with before reference is made to them in dealing with the law of collective bargaining (this is true particularly of ACAS and the certification officer).

The text is very readable; there are no footnotes but many parenthetical references to cases and, more importantly from the student's point of view, to articles in industrial law periodicals, and it would have been advantageous to have these collated into a bibliography arranged under particular topics. There are the usual tables of cases, statutes, statutory instruments and abbreviations. The index, which is generally helpful (cf "Council for Racial Equality") and table of contents refer to page numbers; the level of detail in the latter could be considerably expanded and harmonised.

There is no doubt that the text, which seeks to state the law as at 1 August 1993, is generally up to date and incorporates changes introduced by the Trade Union Reform and Employment Rights Act 1993, although the authors seem to have overlooked the fact that EPCA ss 64A and 94 have been repealed (Trade Union Reform and Employment Rights Act 1993, Sched 10). In some places the text could be more user friendly. Thus at p 142 (e), after reference to suspension on maternity grounds, the reader is merely advised "(see below)". It would also have been helpful to have made a link between the coverage of shop stewards at p 339 and their ability to bind the union by calling industrial action (p 388). Similarly it is not correct to deal with dismissals under EPCA ss 62 and 62A as "automatically fair" dismissals, nor to suggest that the dismissal of an employee for a spent conviction is "automatically unfair". Indeed the Trade Union Reform and Employment Rights Act 1993 has resurrected the concept of "inadmissible" reasons for certain dismissals.

It is a book written for the English market — this is particularly important with regard to the chapter on industrial action — with scant reference to Scots decisions. Thus *Prestwick Circuits Ltd v McAndrew*, 1990 SLT 654, is mentioned only in the context of mitigation of loss, and the interesting issues relating to the application of Unfair Contract Terms Act 1977 raised in *Chapman v Aberdeen Construction Group plc*, 1993 SLT 1205 are not covered; nor are the matters discussed by Lords Caplan and Penrose respectively in *Malden Timber Ltd v McLeish*, 1992 SLT 727 and *Malden Timber Ltd v Leitch*, 1992 SLT 757, or for that matter the related Court of Appeal decision in *Morris Angel & Son Ltd v Hollande* [1993] IRLR 169 (Transfer of Undertakings (Protection of Employment) Regulations 1981 and restrictive covenants).

With these reservations *Textbook on Labour Law* is a helpful, economically priced guide to students of employment law, pointing the way to interesting further reading as appropriate.

V CRAIG,
Heriot-Watt University.

ARTICLES

Undercover Law Enforcement in Scots Law

Weir v Jessop, 1992 SLT 533

Colin J Fraser,
Trainee Solicitor,
Tindal Oatts,
Glasgow.

Mr Fraser discusses the leading case of Weir, *where a plain clothes policeman induced a drugs transaction, and suggests that the law would be put on a sounder footing if it recognised a defence of entrapment based on accepted standards of police conduct, rather than relying on an exclusionary rule where evidence is judged to have been unfairly obtained.*

"What's this? What's this? Is this her fault or mine?
The tempter or the tempted, who sins the most?"

(Shakespeare, *Measure for Measure*)

Many crimes require undercover methods of detection on the part of the police. The use of such tactics has become increasingly more prevalent in recent years, a trend which is set to continue. Although unobjectionable in principle, strict legal safeguards are necessary to prevent unjust convictions, safeguard the integrity of the administration of justice, and to exert an influence on operational police conduct.

The problems of entrapment have come to be treated more seriously of late, with 1991 witnessing the first High Court case to deal comprehensively with the issues thrown up by proactive police work. It is this very important case, *Weir v Jessop*, 1992 SLT 533; 1991 SCCR 636, which forms the subject matter of this article.

The history of entrapment in Scots law

The origins of the law applied in *Weir* can be seen in earlier cases dealing with entrapment. Such cases show that Scots courts have relied on the discretion to exclude unfair evidence in entrapment cases. This procedural defence means that where the evidence is found to be that of an agent provocateur it is held inadmissible. "Agent provocateur" has been defined as "a person who entices another to commit an express breach of the law which he would not otherwise have committed, and then proceeds or informs against him in respect of such offence" (*Report of the Royal Commission on Police Powers*, Cmd 3297 (1929)).

The legal implications of police initiated "buying" situations were judicially examined as long ago as the turn of the century in *Southern Bowling Club Ltd v Ross* (1902) 4 F 405, where the court recognised the need for such methods

and affirmed the propriety of their use. The judicial policy in this civil case was followed in the High Court in *Marsh v Johnston*, 1959 SLT (Notes) 28 and *Cook v Skinner*, 1977 SLT (Notes) 113; 1977 JC 9. In these two licensing cases, undercover police officers were served alcoholic drinks outside licensed hours. The evidence of these officers was held to be admissible to prove that the accused persons were supplying alcohol contrary to the Licensing Acts. The test applied by the court in both cases was one of fairness.

In *Cook*, the court endeavoured to explain exactly what conduct was to be regarded as unfair: "It is clear, however, on the decided cases to which we were referred, that where the Court has held that evidence has been obtained unfairly there has been established, on the part of the police officers concerned, conduct which clearly amounted to a trick upon the accused, and, in particular, a trick which involved positive deception and pressure, encouragement or inducement to commit an offence which, but for that pressure, encouragement or inducement, would never have been committed at all" (1977 JC at p 13).

The first time a Scottish court considered the legal implications of "buying" situations in relation to persons suspected of drugs offences was in *Harper v HM Advocate*, 1989 SCCR 472. In this case, Sheriff Spy, having applied the licensing cases already referred to, considered such methods a legitimate use of police power. However, the matter was not considered in any great detail by the High Court until the case of *Weir*.

Weir v Jessop

Having reason to suspect that Weir was engaged in the supply of drugs contrary to the Misuse of Drugs Act 1971, the police considered that the only effective means at their disposal to gain evidence against Weir was for a plain clothes officer to approach the accused and to attempt to purchase drugs from him.

At trial, objection was taken on Weir's behalf to the evidence of the transaction between the constable and himself on the ground that it had been obtained unfairly. The High Court held that although the true test required to be satisfied for admissibility is indeed one of fairness, the situation in this case did not fall foul of that test. The evidence had not been unfairly obtained, because "apart from representing that he would like to obtain cannabis, [the police officer] applied no pressure, encouragement or inducement to incite the appellant to commit an offence which he would otherwise not have committed. It might be different if the appellant had appeared reluctant to carry out the transaction and the police officer had pleaded with him to do so. Again it might have been different if the appellant had indicated that he was not in the habit of carrying out such transactions or that he had never sold drugs before in this way. But there was no such suggestion in the evidence" (per Lord Justice Clerk Ross at p 538B-C).

The exclusion of evidence

The High Court make it clear in their judgment in *Weir* that where evidence against an accused has been obtained unfairly against him by way of entrapment, that particular evidence may be excluded by the trial judge in the exercise of his discretion to exclude unfairly obtained evidence. It is thought that the correct final judgment was reached in this case, but the writer contends that the principles applied by the High Court do not withstand close scrutiny, and that had the facts of the case been different, injustice could have resulted from the application of the approach in *Weir*. Furthermore, the principles applied in that case are likely to lead to arbitrary results, because the subsequent success or failure of a case will depend on the availability of additional prosecution evidence. If the only evidence the prosecution has is that of the agent provocateur, and this evidence is excluded, then the case will fail, whereas if there is independent evidence of the commission of a crime, then provided this evidence is sufficient, the accused will be prosecuted. In arriving at his conclusion that the exclusion of evidence was the best way of dealing with entrapment, this is the most important point that Professor Heydon failed to address (Heydon, "The Problems of Entrapment" [1973] CLJ 268).

In an entrapment case, the accused is not denying his factual guilt. Notwithstanding this, the evidence should be excluded because the whole incident is one manufactured by the law enforcement officer. The exclusion of the evidence directly connected to the actions of that officer does not address the fact that without his illegitimate instigation, there would have been no crime. In a case where the discretion to exclude evidence could be used to better effect, such as an unlawful search case, if there is no unfairly obtained evidence, there is still an offence, and the other evidence, if sufficient, goes to prove this. However, in an entrapment case, any other evidence would not arise were it not for the actings of the agent provocateur, as there would be no crime in the first place.

It is essential to distinguish between the unfair conduct of the police following the commission of an offence, and the unfair conduct of the police causing the commission of a crime. The former can be adequately dealt with by the discretion to exclude evidence, but if this same criterion is used in relation to the latter type of case, the remedy will be unsatisfactory, as the approach fails to focus on the central point that but for the unfairness of the police, there would have been no offence. This distinction was reaffirmed by the Law Commission in their *Report on Defences of General Application* (Law Com no 83, para 5.9) where they concluded that the exclusionary discretion properly applies only to the former type of case: "Although there are a variety of situations in which the discretion to exclude evidence may be exercised, they are all cases where the excluded evidence is evidence which has been obtained or elicited at some stage after the commission of the offence; it is always the mode of obtaining the evidence or the consequence of admitting this evidence which are judged to be unfair or unduly prejudicial. In entrapment cases, however, the conduct about which complaint is made takes place before, indeed is the cause of, the commission of the offence." (While the report provisionally recommended an *offence* of entrapment, it considered that the issue should be fully examined by a dedicated committee.)

It has been argued academically that the exclusion of evidence is the appropriate way of dealing with entrapment: "The primary aim of an *agent provocateur* is precisely to obtain incriminating evidence against a suspect; the fact that in doing so he encourages the commission of an offence is, in this respect, strictly irrelevant, as this is only the means by which he achieves his end" (M J Allen, "Entrapment: Time for Reconsideration" [1984] Anglo Am LR 57 at p 62).

However, this side effect of his unfair action cannot be regarded as irrelevant — if we were to adopt this viewpoint, there would be little protection afforded to the administration of justice. The fact that the accused has been induced into crime is not irrelevant from his point of view; neither can it be said that it has no bearing on the administration of justice, so although it may not be of particular importance to the police officer provided he obtains the required incriminating evidence, it cannot be said that it is irrelevant in the general sense. Apt reference can be made to the dissenting judgment of Brandeis J in the American case of *Olmstead v US*, 277 US 438 (1928), at p 485, in answer to Mr Allen's assertion that the commission of crime is irrelevant as it is "only the means by which he achieves his end": "Therefore any attempt by the government to introduce into the administration of the criminal law the doctrine that the end justifies the means . . . would bring terrible retribution. Against this pernicious doctrine, courts should resolutely set their faces."

It could also be argued that as Scots courts have decided not to afford an entrapped accused a substantive defence, why should his acquittal be ordered in certain circumstances under a procedural defence? If it is thought appropriate to let the defence of entrapment in "through the back door", what possible objection could there be to the provision of a substantive defence? If it is thought that a factually guilty accused should be acquitted by reason of his entrapment, as would be the case where the only evidence against him is excluded, then why should this protection not be extended to all entrapped accused persons by way of a substantive defence, which would result in a more uniform treatment of entrapped persons and would add to certainty in the application of the law?

Indeed, one of the problems of the present system is that the rule permitting the exclusion of evidence is a discretionary power, and therefore of necessity depends to some extent on how the individual judge subjectively views the facts of the case. It was the view of the Law Commission that the discretionary element inherent in the power to exclude evidence might lead to uncertainty and inconsistency (Law Com no 83, para 5.30). This will be especially so where, as is the current position, the judiciary have only brief and skeletal directions as to when they must exclude the evidence as being that of an agent provocateur, and when the evidence is acceptable as the involvement of the police officer has not gone beyond a tolerable level. It is inappropriate that as the procedural entrapment defence rests on a discretionary power, under strict legal theory no account need be taken of the entrapment defence as it currently stands.

Confession cases and *Weir*

The criterion of fairness previously referred to has also been used in cases involving the admissibility of confessions to the police. In the case of *Chalmers v HM Advocate*, 1954 SLT 177; 1954 JC 66, it was decided that where the police are questioning someone and they reach the point of suspicion, they must caution the accused. As suspicion of involvement in a particular crime is always present before the police engage in a "buying" situation, the question arises — why should the police in that situation not also have to caution the suspect? Obviously, if this was the legal requirement, the police would find themselves unable to use such methods of crime detection, because they would be wholly ineffective if they had to be preceded by an official caution. The High Court addressed this question in *Weir*. Lord Morison did not regard the analogy made by defence counsel between the

"buying situation" in the instant case, and cases involving inadmissible confessions, as a valid one:

"Cases in which evidence of a self incriminating statement has been held inadmissible have proceeded on the basis that the statement could not be affirmed as a truly voluntary one: *Tonge v HM Advocate*, 1982 SLT 509. This may be either because the circumstances or pressure were such as to induce the making of the statement, or because the accused's decision to make it was taken in the absence of a caution which would have made it clear to him that he had a right to remain silent, and that if he did not do so evidence of what he said might be used against him. . . . It is unfair to elicit a statement from a suspect, if he had not been cautioned that he is not required to make it.

"But it is well established that it is not unfair for a policeman to question a suspect if he has observed the safeguards which are necessary for securing that the statement is truly voluntary. . . . The considerations which apply to the questioning of a suspect therefore have no application to the circumstances of the present case. . . . There is no unfairness on the part of the police in their failing to point out the obvious, and cases dealing with the absence of a caution in the terms in which it is usually given are not therefore in point. The analogy proceeds upon a misunderstanding of the nature of the caution which fairness requires should be given before a statement is elicited" (1992 SLT at p 539D-H).

The specific legal requirements relating to the administration of cautions have grown up as a response to the particular problems which this area of the law raises. They are applicable only to confessions in the course of normal investigations, and should not be necessary in the course of "buying" situations. The whole point in providing safeguards on the police obtaining confessions is to ensure that a confession by an accused is voluntary. Within the "buying" situation, there is no question of the accused's actions or statements having been cajoled or forced out of him by the police officer intimidating him. Within the setting of a police station, the accused is naturally intimidated, and unfair pressure exerted on him by police officers in order to get him to break down and confess will render the subsequent confession inadmissible. However, in the domain of the outside world, the police officer is not in a superior position to the criminal; in fact, the reverse may be the case as the transaction is likely to be taking place on the accused's terms and chosen location. Also, the police officer, since he must of necessity keep his true identity unknown, cannot bring his official capacity to bear on the suspect. It cannot easily be argued that a suspect in this position gives an admission of his guilt involuntarily — he does so spontaneously and of his own accord. The only "underhand" inducement offered by the police officer lies in his concealment of his true identity, and this is insufficient to render an otherwise valid admission of guilt inadmissible.

It is therefore apparent that *Weir* represents clear and authoritative Scottish authority in support of a distinction between the confession and licensing cases. It is submitted that the decision is correct in this respect, and that the issue of a common law caution should not be a prerequisite to undercover tactics.

Predisposition and Scots law
American courts have upheld a substantive defence of entrapment for most of this century. Academic and judicial controversy there, is not as to the existence of such a defence, but as to its form. The majority of the Supreme Court have consistently focused upon the predisposition of the accused to commit the crime in question before deciding the matter of his guilt or innocence. The decision of the High Court in *Weir* shows that although the court did not consider a substantive approach, they did apply principles similar to those which prevail in the USA. The test favoured by the High Court focuses on the predisposition of the accused to commit the crime in question, as well as the conduct of the officer involved. This is shown by the preoccupation of the court with the finding on the evidence that the appellant's actions showed that he was already involved in the supply of drugs and that this was not the first occasion on which he had broken the law in this manner. For example, Lord Justice Clerk Ross stated: "[The police] applied no pressure, encouragement or inducement to incite the appellant to commit an offence which he would otherwise not have committed. . . . There is nothing at all in the findings to suggest that supplying drugs was something which the appellant would never have done but for the approach made to him by the police officer" (at p 538B-D).

Because a thorough inquiry into the accused's actual predisposition would be extremely difficult if not impossible, a showing of prior criminal inclination is often deemed sufficient to meet the evidentiary burden in the USA (see generally, *Sherman v US*, 356 US 369 (1958)). At first glance this rule seems inconsistent with the existing law. The criminal law nowhere else entitles a prosecutor to demonstrate culpability for an act on the basis of the accused's previous inclinations towards criminality. In fact, this is the underlying rationale behind the rules relating to similar fact evidence in Scots law.

Predisposition to commit crime can sustain at least four meanings in this context. First, it could be construed as a predisposition to commit crime in general. Secondly, it could be to commit crimes of the same general type as the one in question, for instance the supply of illegal drugs. Thirdly, it could be to commit the specific type of crime charged, such as the supply of cannabis. Lastly, it could be a predisposition to commit the exact offence charged, that is, the supply of cannabis to a police officer.

The first and last of these possibilities can be discounted as being too wide and too narrow respectively. It therefore remains to be decided whether the High Court intend predisposition to be construed in accordance with the second or the third of the above possibilities. In *Weir*, Lord Ross stated that "the only reasonable inference from the evidence is that the appellant was prepared to supply controlled drugs to callers" (p 538C).

Lord Morison likewise opined: "although deception as to the policeman's true identity was involved, that deception cannot reasonably be regarded as having induced the commission of the crime of supply, if the supply was one which would in any event have taken place as a result of a request by a genuine customer" (p 538K).

Lord Caplan added: "The investigation should be designed to discover whether or not as a matter of course the suspected person is engaging in a particular category of illegal transaction" (p 540L).

It would appear, then, that the meaning attached to this question of predisposition, or willingness to commit crime, by the High Court is that an accused will not be able to have the evidence of an agent provocateur excluded as being unfairly obtained by entrapment, if there is other evidence that he was predisposed to commit a crime of a similar nature to the specific offence charged.

It is not immediately clear how such predisposition is to be proved in the absence of a developed system of similar fact evidence. Section 141 (1) (f) (i) of the Criminal Justice (Scotland) Act 1975 states that evidence of the accused's previous criminal convictions or bad character will not be allowed unless such proof is admissible evidence to show that he is guilty of the offence with which he is then charged.

It is at least arguable that s 141 (1) (f) (i) is applicable in entrapment cases and constitutes a statutory exception to the rule that an accused's character and previous criminality are inadmissible. This would mean that the prosecution could lead evidence to show the accused's predisposition, and hence his guilt of the present offence. It is, however, hoped that this interpretation will be recognised as being contrary to the parliamentary intent behind this provision. It is submitted that this section was intended to constitute an exception to the inadmissibility of similar fact evidence in only very limited circumstances, and that Parliament did not intend to allow the prosecution to show that the accused was of bad character, and thus would commit the same type of crime charged whenever given the opportunity to do so. An application of the mischief rule of statutory interpretation would thereby bar the prosecution from leading evidence of the accused's previous character or criminality.

Unfortunately, it is not known whether s 141 will be held to be applicable in entrapment cases. No enlightenment is to be found in relation to this question from the High Court, because in *Weir*, the court found that the appellant was predisposed on the circumstantial evidence surrounding the incident — the way in which Weir dealt with the police and the findings of cannabis in his flat during the subsequent search. As this evidence was sufficient to prove predisposition this difficult question was not required to be considered. However, it is hoped that in future cases, the courts will only allow circumstantial evidence to prove predisposition, and if the prosecution attempt to go further than this, the court should not entertain such an action. This approach would be more consistent with judicial pronouncements on the admissibility of similar fact evidence (cf *Slater v HM Advocate*, 1928 SLT 602; 1928 JC 94).

One consequence of the overemphasis placed by the courts upon the accused's predisposition to commit crime is that the extent to which a law enforcement officer can engage in deception and trickery in encouraging someone to commit a crime is not particularly clear from the case law. Rather than laying down rules regarding the extent to which police officers may induce others to commit crime, the judges presiding over the relevant cases have stated that the methods employed by the police are legitimate unless they cause the accused to commit a crime which he would not otherwise have committed. For instance, in *Weir*, Lord Justice Clerk Ross stated: "apart from representing that he would like to obtain cannabis, he applied no pressure, encouragement or inducement to incite the appellant to commit an offence *which he would not otherwise have committed*" (p 538B, emphasis added).

The judgments in other Scots cases follow a similar vein. It would appear, therefore, that where someone is predisposed to commit the type of crime in question, the police may employ any means of encouragement, persuasion or trickery they choose, provided the crime he eventually commits is one which he would have committed anyway. By contrast, where there is no evidence that the crime would have been committed were it not for the involvement of the police, even slight encouragement or deception would be held unfair.

This argument highlights another drawback in the current approach to the problem of entrapment. This problem relates to the circularity of the predisposition argument. If the accused is in a position to require the protection of the defence, he must have committed the offence in question. Ironically, the prosecution may be able to use this fact as evidence of predisposition, so the defence would lose all effect.

It is hoped that the inadequacies inherent in a test which focuses on the predisposition of the accused to commit the crime in question are apparent at this stage. The question remains unanswered however, if a substantive defence were created, what test should be applied in order to decide whether an accused should be acquitted?

The main issue remains the decision whether the accused would have committed the crime were it not for the involvement of the police officer. However, it is suggested that the inquiry necessary to resolve this question fairly is not one relating to the accused's predisposition, but rather a test analysing the conduct of the police officer involved. Whereas the test favoured by the majority of the Supreme Court in the USA rests on the predisposition question, that of the minority in all the entrapment cases decided at that level, while upholding the defence, looks at the actions of the police rather than the accused. (Supreme Court cases on this issue include *Sorrells v US*, 287 US 435 (1932); *Sherman v US*, 356 US 369 (1958); *US v Russell*, 411 US 423 (1973); *Hampton v US*, 425 US 484 (1976); *Mathews v US*, 485 US 58 (1988).) On this analysis, the defence should prohibit the conviction of an accused for a crime which was the product of the creative activity of the police. As Frankfurter J stated in *Sherman v US*, supra, at p 383: "The courts refuse to convict an entrapped defendant, not because his conduct falls outside the proscription of statute, but because, even if his guilt be admitted, the methods employed on behalf of the government to bring about conviction cannot be countenanced. . . . The crucial question is whether the police conduct revealed in the particular case falls below standards, to which common feelings respond, for the proper use of governmental power. . . . No matter what the defendant's past record and present inclinations to criminality, or the depths to which he has sunk in the estimation of society, certain police conduct to ensnare him into further crime is not to be tolerated."

It is thought that much can be learned from the reasoning applied by the judges in the minority in the American case law on entrapment. It is more appropriate that where it is the allegedly unacceptable conduct of the police which gives rise to the question of entrapment in the first place, it is this conduct which should form the basis of the court's inquiry rather than the tangential issue of the character of the person who has been the subject of this unfair behaviour.

Conclusion

It is hoped that this article will have afforded the reader an insight into the way Scots law has chosen to deal with entrapment. It has been shown that the courts have implemented the discretionary exclusion of evidence as their reaction to the unfairness and inherent dangers which entrapment cases represent. (It is of interest to note that Scotland is not alone in using the discretion to exclude evidence as a solution to the entrapment problem. New Zealand courts also employ this method. However, it remains to be settled whether the discretion in that jurisdiction is only to exclude the evidence of the agent provocateur, as in Scotland, or whether the court will have the power to exclude the entire case of the prosecution on the ground of unfairness. On the New Zealand approach, see *R v O'Shannessy*, CA 70/73, 8 October 1973, unreported; *R v Capner* [1975] NZLR 411.) It is the aspiration of the author that the arbitrary nature and the short-

comings of this procedural defence will be clear at this stage. The fact that the Scottish courts have elected to distinguish between the cases relating to the admissibility of confessions and entrapment cases can only be praised, but represents one example of the inconsistencies which result when this judicial discretion is applied to a category of cases which call for a newly formulated approach. The principles applied, although they operate satisfactorily in other areas of the law, are inadequate and ill suited to the entrapment issue.

Within the Scottish entrapment cases there can be found a tendency to look for the predisposition of the accused to commit the crime in question. It has been argued that this search is inappropriate and inconsistent with the long established presumption of innocence, and that even if it were not, it would be difficult to know just how this predisposition could be proved given the current adherence of Scots law to a system of strict controls on similar fact evidence.

In summary, the Scots reaction to the entrapment controversy has been to provide the accused with a procedural defence. This is inappropriate, inadequate and at odds with the current protection given to the accused by way of the law of evidence. It is also apt to produce arbitrary results, and represents a paltry force of dissuasion to an officer faced with a particularly "slippery" suspect.

[The author wishes to thank the criminal law staff at the University of Strathclyde, Jenifer Ross and Andrew Phillips, for looking over earlier drafts of this article, and Natasha Arnold, for her patience and helpful comments. While he is indebted to these lawyers, any errors and views expressed herein remain his.]

NEWS

Appointment

Industrial Tribunals (Scotland)
Mr Colin M Milne has been appointed as a regional chairman of the Industrial Tribunals in Scotland with effect from 1 May 1994.

— ◇ —

Court

Perth sheriff court
With effect from 1 May 1994 the telephone and

fax numbers of Perth sheriff court will change to the following: tel 0738-620546; fax 0738-623601.

— ◇ —

General

Fife and Kinross SPC
Nine solicitors' firms in Fife and Kinross have combined to launch Fife and Kinross Solicitors Property Centres Ltd. Each of the firms, who between them have 19 offices in seven towns throughout the area, is linked to a specialised computer network which means that clients can

instantly receive visual display of properties available through the 19 centres. A free matching service will allow buyers to view either a wide selection of property or an exact match, tailor made to their requirements.

The group is chaired by Paul Denholm, a partner at Drummond, Cook & Mackintosh.

◇

Crofting Law Group
Recent years have seen an increase in the interest of the legal profession, land agents, landowners, crofters and others in crofting law. It is proposed that a Crofting Law Group be formed to create a forum for discussion of common problems, related UK and EC legislation, to allow fresh procedures to be developed and to permit easier access to this unique branch of law. Membership of the group will be open to all interested persons, who are invited to write to Keith Graham, c/o Scottish Land Court, 1 Grosvenor Crescent, Edinburgh EH12 5ER (DX ED 259) for further details.

◇

Property certificates
Nairn
Nairn District Council are increasing the fee for property clearance certificates to £40, with effect from 1 April 1994.

◇

Inverclyde
Inverclyde District Council are increasing the charge for property inquiry certificates to £39 with effect from 1 April 1994.

 ◇ ——

Taxation

Electronic lodgement service
As part of the changes to the system for assessing personal tax, as proposed in the 1994 Finance Bill, the Inland Revenue are planning to provide a service to enable tax returns to be filed electronically. A consultative document has been issued setting out proposals for the Electronic Lodgement Service (ELS).

A feasibility study concluded that an ELS system could be in place for tax returns under the self assessment arrangements from April 1997. The proposed system will utilise standard electronic mail facilities.

The Revenue will approve accountants and other agents who wish to be involved to prepare and/or transmit returns electronically and will approve the software products which match the specified return form.

A trial exercise using the corporation tax return will run from November 1994, and could lead to a national service for CT returns in 1995.

Copies of the consultative document can be obtained from: Adrian Pearce, Room E1, Bradley House, c/o Matheson House, Grange Central, Telford TF3 4ER (tel: 0952-294426).

◇

Income tax: share options
The Inland Revenue have announced that two practices relating to the income tax treatment of share options are to be withdrawn and will not apply for options exercised on or after 6 April 1994. The practices are set out in paras 5.3 and 5.5 of the 1991 edition of the booklet IR16 — share acquisitions by directors and employees, and are as follows: where an option is exercised by an employee who is not resident or ordinarily resident in the United Kingdom when the option is exercised income tax has, in certain circumstances, not been charged; and where the earnings of an employee qualify for a foreign earnings deduction, the gain on the exercise of a share option has, in certain circumstances, been treated as attracting a similar deduction.

◇

Corporation tax: capital allowances
The government have announced further details of proposals to amend the capital allowances legislation applying to expenditure on buildings constructed in enterprise zones (see 1994 SLT (News) 69 and 90).

The legislation will provide for a balancing charge to be imposed when a long lease is disposed of within seven years. This seven year limit on balancing charges will not apply to artificial tax avoidance schemes which include guaranteed exit arrangements. For those schemes a balancing charge will apply if the building is sold within the first 25 years of its life. The draft legislation will cover buildings in enterprise zones qualifying for 100 per cent capital allowances, but not other buildings.

◇

Approved employee share schemes
The Inland Revenue have published revised versions of the leaflets and booklets IR95 to IR100, which explain the tax reliefs available for the acquisition of shares and share options through approved employee share schemes and provide guidance on each type of scheme, and a revised version of booklet IR16 and a new simple

leaflet, IR17, which explain the taxation of shares and options over shares acquired by directors and employees outside approved employee share schemes.

Benefits in kind: company vans

The Inland Revenue have published a guide for employees and employers explaining how company vans are taxed. The leaflet (IR136 in the Personal Taxpayer series) sets out for both employees and employers the new rules contained in the Finance Act 1993 for taxing the benefit in kind of vans available to employees for private use.

— ◊ —

Obituary

On 11 March 1994, Arthur Renwick McIlwraith, formerly partner in the firm of Messrs Lowndes Renwick, Glasgow, and latterly sheriff at Airdrie.

On 14 March 1994, William Adam Wilson, Lord President Reid Professor of Law, University of Edinburgh.

Business changes

James Smith & Valentine, solicitors, Girvan, and McCormick & Nicholson, solicitors, Newton Stewart, intimate the resignation from the partnership of Alistair S Lambert with effect from 18 March 1994. Margo Sheddon, solicitor, has been appointed an associate with effect from that date.

Shepherd & Wedderburn, WS, Edinburgh, intimate that their senior partner, Ivor Reginald Guild, WS, retires from the partnership with effect from 31 March 1994.

Parliamentary News

New Bills

HOUSE OF COMMONS

9 March 1994

Decorations for Gallantry (Display)—To regulate the public display or exhibition of decorations for gallantry, and for connected purposes. (Private Member's Bill introduced by Mr Nick Hawkins)

15 March 1994

Contaminated Land—To require those who were responsible for polluting land to be responsible for its restoration and decontamination; and for connected purposes. (Private Member's Bill introduced by Mr Robert Ainsworth)

Progress of Bills

Trade Marks — Lords: third reading, 15 March 1994.

Local Government (Wales) — Commons: second reading, 15 March 1994.

Race Relations (Remedies) — Lords: second reading, 15 March 1994.

National Parks — Lords: second reading, 16 March 1994.

Police and Magistrates' Courts — Lords: report stage concluded, 17 March 1994.

◆

ACTS OF SEDERUNT

ACT OF SEDERUNT (FEES OF MESSENGERS-AT-ARMS) 1994
(SI 1994/391) [18 FEBRUARY 1994]

The Lords of Council and Session, under and by virtue of the powers conferred on them by section 6 of the Execution of Diligence (Scotland) Act 1926 (c 16), section 5 of the Court of Session Act 1988 (c 36) and of all other powers enabling them in that behalf, do hereby, with the concurrence of the Lord Lyon King of Arms, enact and declare:

Citation and commencement

1.—(1) This Act of Sederunt may be cited as the Act of Sederunt (Fees of Messengers-at-Arms) 1994 and shall come into force on 23rd March 1994.

(2) This Act of Sederunt shall be inserted in the Books of Sederunt.

Fees of messengers-at-arms

2. Schedule 1 to this Act of Sederunt shall have effect in respect of work carried out by a messenger-at-arms in relation to causes in, or work authorised by, the Court of Session, and the fees specified are the fees payable to a messenger-at-arms in respect of that work.

Application, revocation and saving

3.—(1) Schedule 1 to this Act of Sederunt applies to work done on or after the date on which this Act of Sederunt comes into force.

(2) The Acts of Sederunt specified in Schedule 2 to this Act of Sederunt are hereby revoked.

(3) Notwithstanding the revocation in sub-paragraph (2), the Act of Sederunt (Fees of Messengers-at-Arms) 1990 shall continue to have effect in respect of work done before the date on which this Act of Sederunt comes into force.

J A D HOPE, LORD PRESIDENT, *IPD*

SCHEDULE 1   Paragraph 2
GENERAL REGULATIONS

1. Subject to the following paragraphs, the fees payable to a messenger-at-arms shall be calculated in accordance with the Table of Fees in this Schedule and shall be payable in respect of all forms of service or intimation of a document, citation of a person or execution of diligence and all other work authorised by the court and executed by a messenger-at-arms during the normal business hours of 9.00 am to 5.00 pm.

2. Fees in relation to service or intimation of a document, citation of a person or diligence which, of necessity, is executed outwith normal business hours shall be surcharged by the levying of an additional fee of—

(a) 33⅓ per cent of the fee specified in the Table of Fees, where it is executed on a week day between the hours of 5.00 pm and 10.00 pm; and

(b) 75 per cent of the fee specified in the Table of Fees, where it is executed on a week day after 10.00 pm or before 9.00 am or on a Saturday, Sunday or a public holiday.

3.—(1) There shall be three bands of charge in the Table of Fees in accordance with which fees shall be payable.

(2) The three bands of charge shall be—

(a) Band 1 — up to 12 miles;

(b) Band 2 — over 12 miles and up to 18 miles; and

(c) Band 3 — over 18 miles.

(3) A fee is payable in respect of one band of charge only for any item.

(4) Unless by special arrangements between a messenger-at-arms and the instructing agent, the bands of charge shall be calculated according to the distance from the place of business of the nearest messenger-at-arms to the place of execution.

4. An additional fee may be negotiated between the messenger-at-arms and the instructing agent by prior agreement in the following circumstances:—

(a) where the messenger-at-arms is standing by awaiting the delivery or uplifting of a document for immediate service;

(b) where the messenger-at-arms has to instruct an huissier or other officer of court outwith Scotland to serve a document; or

(c) where there is no prescribed fee and the importance, urgency and value of the work involved necessitates an additional fee.

5. All reasonable outlays, excluding postage, but including any recorded delivery costs exclusive of postage in respect of items 1 (b) and 1 (c) in the Table of Fees, necessarily incurred by a messenger-at-arms carrying out lawful instructions, shall be charged in addition to a fee specified in the Table of Fees.

6. Every fee note rendered by a messenger-at-arms shall be so detailed that the fees charged by him may be easily checked against the Table of Fees; and any fees agreed under paragraph 4 above and any allowable outlays shall be clearly narrated as such. The fee note shall be reviewed by the messenger-at-arms to ensure that it is fair and reasonable in the circumstances and shall be adjusted by him if necessary.

7. Discounting of fees is permitted only between messengers-at-arms.

8. Any restriction or modification made by a messenger-at-arms of fees recoverable from a person shall be passed on to that person only.

9. Time shall be charged in units of 30 minutes or part thereof and, except in relation to time under paragraphs 10, 11 or 12 below—

(a) time shall apply from the end of the first hour at the place of execution until completion; or

(b) time shall apply after the messenger-at-arms has travelled a distance of 30 miles from his place of business until he returns to a distance of 30 miles from that place.

10. Where a messenger-at-arms has to use a ferry, he and any witness shall be allowed the necessary cost of the ferry, all reasonable subsistence and the time for boarding, crossing and returning, which shall be charged on a time basis.

11. Where a messenger-at-arms is required to attend before a notary public, commissioner or other person or as a witness, a fee for such attendance by the messenger-at-arms and any witness shall be chargeable on a time basis.

12. Where inquiries are necessary in order to execute service, intimation, citation, diligence or any other work authorised by the court, a fee for such inquiries shall be chargeable on a time basis.

13.—(1) Where, in a poinding, the appraised value of an article exceeds the sum recoverable, the fee specified in the Table of Fees shall be calculated in accordance with the sum recoverable and not the appraised value.

(2) Where, in a poinding, a debtor or other occupier of the premises claims that goods are subject to a hire purchase agreement, or are otherwise the property of someone other than the debtor, but refuses, or is unable, to produce evidence to that effect, the messenger-at-arms may poind the goods and shall add a note on the schedule of the poinding stating that the debtor has claimed that the goods are subject to a hire purchase agreement or are otherwise the property of someone other than the debtor, as the case may be.

14. A messenger-at-arms supplying services to any person in respect of which fees are payable to him under this Schedule shall—

(a) if he is a taxable person within the meaning of the Value Added Tax Act 1983; and

(b) if the supply is a taxable supply within the meaning of that Act,

make charges to that person in addition to the charges in respect of that fee, being such additional charge as amounts to the value added tax payable under that Act in respect of the supply of those services.

15. In this Schedule, unless the context otherwise requires—

"the Act of 1987" means the Debtors (Scotland) Act 1987;

"apprehension" means apprehending, detaining and taking to and from court or prison;

"arranging" means accepting instructions, checking for competency, reserving time, advising instructing agent, making all necessary arrangements, intimation and service (where necessary) prior to execution;

"possession" means searching, taking possession and delivery;

"postal diligence" means service of any diligence, which may be served by post, by registered post or the first class recorded delivery service;

ACT OF SEDERUNT (FEES OF MESSENGERS-AT-ARMS) 1994

"postal service" means service or intimation by registered post or the first class recorded delivery service; "service" means service or intimation of any document under a rule of court or an order of the court and includes accepting instructions, preparation, postage and service or intimation of any ancillary form or other ancillary document.

TABLE OF FEES

Item	Band 1 £	Band 2 £	Band 3 £
1. *Service or intimation of a document*			
(a) Service			
(i) each person at a different address	31.50	53.40	67.40
(ii) each additional person at the same address or additional copy required to be served or intimated under the Act of 1987	10.50	10.50	10.50
(b) Postal service	15.45	15.45	15.45
(c) Postal diligence	23.30	23.30	23.30
2. *Inhibitions*			
(a) Inhibition only			
(i) each person at a different address	33.10	53.40	67.35
(ii) each additional person at the same address	17.15	17.15	17.15
(b) Inhibition and service			
(i) each person at a different address	43.55	63.85	78.10
(ii) each additional person at the same address	27.70	27.70	27.70
(c) Inhibition, service and interdict			
(i) each person at a different address	105.80	105.80	105.80
(ii) each additional person at the same address	44.90	44.90	44.90
3. *Interdicts*			
(a) Interdict only			
(i) each person at a different address	78.10	78.10	78.10
(ii) each additional person at the same address	17.15	17.15	17.15
(b) Interdict and service			
(i) each person at a different address	88.60	88.60	88.60
(ii) each additional person at the same address	27.70	27.70	27.70
(c) Interdict, service and inhibition			
(i) each person at a different address	105.80	105.80	105.80
(ii) each additional person at the same address	44.90	44.90	44.90
4. *Poindings*			
(a) Serving notice of entry	5.85	5.85	5.85
(b) Arranging poinding and endeavouring but being unable to execute same for whatever reason	44.25	44.25	44.25
(c) Arranging and executing poinding where appraised value is—			
(i) £364 or under	51.80	51.80	51.80
(ii) over £364 and up to £1,464	80.20	80.20	80.20
(iii) over £1,464 and up to £14,742 — 10% of the appraised value only			
(iv) over £14,742 and up to £73,702 — 10% of the first £14,742, 5% thereafter up to £73,702 of the appraised value			
(v) over £73,702 — 10% of the first £14,742, 5% thereafter up to £73,702 and 1% of the appraised value over £73,702			
(d) Reporting poinding	5.00	5.00	5.00
5. *Poindings of motor vehicles, heavy plant or machinery*			
(a) Arranging and executing poinding where appraised value is—			
(i) £364 or under	51.80	51.80	51.80
(ii) over £364 and up to £1,619	80.20	80.20	80.20
(iii) over £1,619 and up to £73,702 — 5% of the appraised value only			
(iv) over £73,702 — 5% of the first £73,702 and 1% thereafter of the appraised value			
(b) Reporting poinding	5.00	5.00	5.00
6. *Sequestrations for rent, poinding of the ground*			
(a) Arranging for the sequestration or poinding of the ground and endeavouring but being unable to execute same for whatever reason	42.25	42.25	42.25
(b) Arranging and effecting sequestration or poinding of the ground	78.10	78.10	78.10
7. *Sales*			
(a) (i) Application for warrant of sale or variation of a warrant of sale	9.80	9.80	9.80
(ii) Intimating application — as in item 1 (a) and (b) above, as the case may be			
(b) (i) Arranging warrant sale, preparing advertisement and giving public notice	12.75	12.75	12.75
(ii) Serving copy of warrant of sale and intimating the place and date of sale and if necessary the date of removal of poinded effects — as in item 1 (a) or (b) above, as the case may be			
(c) Attending warrant sale alone conducted by auctioneer	22.25	37.60	47.55
(d) (i) Attending warrant sale with witness and being unable to execute same for whatever reason	42.25	42.25	42.25

(ii) Conducting warrant sale with witness where the appraised value is—			
£364 or under	49.75	49.75	49.75
Over £364	78.10	78.10	78.10
8. *Ejections*			
(a) Arranging ejection	42.25	42.25	42.25
(b) Arranging and executing ejection	65.65	65.65	65.65
9. *Taking possession of effects*			
(a) Arranging possession	42.25	42.25	42.25
(b) Arranging and effecting possession	78.10	78.10	78.10
10. *Apprehensions*			
(a) Arranging apprehension	42.25	42.25	42.25
(b) Arranging and apprehending	78.10	78.10	78.10
11. *Taking possession of children*			
(a) Arranging to take possession	42.25	42.25	42.25
(b) Taking possession of each child	78.10	78.10	78.10
12. *Arresting vessels, aircraft and cargo*			
(a) Arranging to arrest	42.25	42.25	42.25
(b) Arranging and effecting arrestment	129.15	129.15	129.15
13. *Miscellaneous*			
(a) Making any report or application under the Act of 1987 with the exception of reporting a poinding	9.75	9.75	9.75
(b) Granting any receipt required to be issued under the Act of 1987	5.00	5.00	5.00
(c) Arranging locksmith or tradesman to be in attendance	3.15	3.15	3.15
(d) Granting certificate of displenishment or providing any other certificate or report, registering any document or making any application to a court or the creditor	9.75	9.75	9.75
(e) Executing warrant to open lockfast places	9.75	9.75	9.75

(f) Time
(i) with witness — £15.65 per unit
(ii) without witness — £11.70 per unit
(g) Photocopies
(i) first sheet of document — £1.05
(ii) subsequent copies, per sheet — £0.50

SCHEDULE 2	Paragraph 3 (2)
REVOCATIONS	

Acts of Sederunt revoked	*References*
Act of Sederunt (Fees of Messengers-at-Arms) 1990	1990/379
Act of Sederunt (Fees of Messengers-at-Arms) 1991	1991/291
Act of Sederunt (Fees of Messengers-at-Arms) 1992	1992/87
Act of Sederunt (Fees of Messengers-at-Arms) (Amendment) 1992	1992/529
Act of Sederunt (Fees of Messengers-at-Arms) 1993	1993/118

ACT OF SEDERUNT (FEES OF SHERIFF OFFICERS) 1994

(SI 1994/392) [18 FEBRUARY 1994]

The Lords of Council and Session, under and by virtue of the powers conferred on them by section 40 of the Sheriff Courts (Scotland) Act 1907 (c 51), section 6 of the Execution of Diligence (Scotland) Act 1926 (c 16) and of all other powers enabling them in that behalf, do hereby enact and declare:

Citation and commencement

1.—(1) This Act of Sederunt may be cited as the Act of Sederunt (Fees of Sheriff Officers) 1994 and shall come into force on 23rd March 1994.

(2) This Act of Sederunt shall be inserted in the Books of Sederunt.

Fees of sheriff officers

2. Schedule 1 to this Act of Sederunt shall have effect in respect of work carried out by a sheriff officer in relation to causes in, or work authorised by, the sheriff court, and the fees specified are the fees payable to a sheriff officer in respect of that work.

Application, revocation and saving

3.—(1) Schedule 1 to this Act of Sederunt

applies to work done on or after the date on which this Act of Sederunt comes into force.

(2) The Acts of Sederunt specified in Schedule 2 to this Act of Sederunt are hereby revoked.

(3) Notwithstanding the revocation in sub-paragraph (2), the Act of Sederunt (Fees of Sheriff Officers) 1990 shall continue to have effect in respect of work done before the date on which this Act of Sederunt comes into force.

J A D HOPE, LORD PRESIDENT, *IPD*

SCHEDULE 1   Paragraph 2
GENERAL REGULATIONS

1. Subject to the following paragraphs, the fees payable to a sheriff officer in relation to an ordinary cause or a summary cause, as the case may be, shall be calculated in accordance with the Table of Fees in this Schedule and shall be payable in respect of (a) all forms of service or intimation of a document, citation of a person or execution of diligence and all other work authorised by the court and (b) recovery of rates, charges or taxes by summary warrant, any of which is executed by a sheriff officer during the normal business hours of 9.00 am to 5.00 pm.

2. Fees in relation to service or intimation of a document, citation of a person or diligence which, of necessity, is executed outwith normal business hours shall be surcharged by the levying of an additional fee of—
(a) 33⅓ per cent of the fee specified in the Table of Fees, where it is executed on a week day between the hours of 5.00 pm and 10.00 pm; and
(b) 75 per cent of the fee specified in the Table of Fees, where it is executed on a week day after 10.00 pm or before 9.00 am or on a Saturday, Sunday or a public holiday.

3.—(1) There shall be three bands of charge in the Table of Fees in accordance with which fees shall be payable.
(2) The three bands of charge shall be—
(a) Band 1 — up to 12 miles;
(b) Band 2 — over 12 miles and up to 18 miles; and
(c) Band 3 — over 18 miles.
(3) A fee is payable in respect of one band of charge only for any item.
(4) Unless by special arrangements between a sheriff officer and the instructing agent, the bands of charge shall be calculated according to the distance between the court house where the warrant was granted and the place of execution or the distance from the place of business of the nearest sheriff officer within the district to the place of execution, whichever is the lesser.

4. An additional fee may be negotiated between a sheriff officer and the instructing agent by prior agreement in the following circumstances:—
(a) where the sheriff officer is standing by awaiting the delivery or uplifting of a document for immediate service;
(b) where the sheriff officer has to instruct an huissier or other officer of court outwith Scotland to serve a document; or
(c) where there is no prescribed fee and the importance, urgency and value of the work involved necessitates an additional fee.

5. All reasonable outlays, excluding postage, but including any recorded delivery costs exclusive of postage in respect of items 1 (b) and 1 (c) in the Table of Fees, necessarily incurred by a sheriff officer in carrying out lawful instructions, shall be charged in addition to a fee specified in the Table of Fees in this Schedule.

6. Every fee note rendered by a sheriff officer shall be so detailed that the fees charged by him may be easily checked against the Table of Fees; and any fees agreed under paragraph 4 above and any allowable outlays shall be clearly narrated as such. The fee note shall be reviewed by the sheriff officer to ensure that it is fair and reasonable in the circumstances and shall be adjusted by him if necessary.

7. Discounting of fees is permitted only between sheriff officers.

8. Any restriction or modification made by a sheriff officer of fees recoverable from a person shall be passed on to that person only.

9. Time will be charged in units of 30 minutes or part thereof; and, in respect of the folowing items in the Table of Fees, shall apply from the end of the first hour at the place of execution until completion:— 2, 5 (c), 6 (c), 6 (d) (i), 7 (b), 8 (b), 9 (b), 10 (b) and 11 (b).

10. Where a sheriff officer has to use a ferry, he and any witness shall be allowed the necessary cost of the ferry, all reasonable subsistence and the time for boarding, crossing and returning, which shall be charged on a time basis.

11. Where a sheriff officer is required to attend before a notary public, commissioner or other person or as a witness, a fee for such attendance by the sheriff officer and any witness shall be chargeable on a time basis.

12. Where inquiries are necessary in order to execute service, intimation, citation, diligence or any other work authorised by the court, a fee for such inquiries shall be chargeable on a time basis.

13.—(1) Where personal service is to be carried out under item 1 (a) (i) in the Table of Fees and more than one visit is required, each additional visit shall be charged at 50 per cent of the fee specified in that item.

14.—(1) Where, in a poinding, the appraised value of an article exceeds the sum recoverable, the fee specified in the Table of Fees in this Schedule shall be calculated in accordance with the sum recoverable and not the appraised value.
(2) Where, in a poinding, a debtor or other occupier of the premises claims that goods are subject to a hire purchase agreement or are otherwise the property of someone other than the debtor, but refuses or is unable to produce evidence to that effect, the sheriff officer may poind the goods and shall add a note on the schedule of the poinding stating that the debtor has claimed that the goods are subject to a hire purchase agreement or are otherwise the property of someone other than the debtor, as the case may be.

15. The fees payable to a sheriff officer in respect of recovery of rates, charges or taxes by summary warrant shall be calculated in accordance with the fees specified in the Table of Fees for ordinary causes.

16. A sheriff officer supplying services to any person in respect of which fees are payable to him under this Schedule shall—
(a) if he is a taxable person within the meaning of the Value Added Tax Act 1983; and
(b) if the supply is a taxable supply within the meaning of that Act,
make charges to that person in addition to the charges in respect of that fee, being such additional charge as amounts to the value added tax payable under that Act in respect of the supply of those services.

17. In this Schedule, unless the context otherwise requires—
"the Act of 1987" means the Debtors (Scotland) Act 1987;
"apprehension" means apprehending, detaining and taking to and from court or prison;
"arranging" means accepting instructions, checking for competency, reserving time, advising instructing agent, making all necessary arrangements, intimation and service (where necessary) prior to execution;
"possession" means searching, taking possession and delivery;
"postal diligence" means service of any diligence, which may be served by post, by registered post or the first class recorded delivery service;
"postal service" means service or intimation by registered post or the first class recorded delivery service;
"service" means service or intimation of any document under a rule of court or an order of the court and includes accepting instructions, preparation, postage and service or intimation of any ancillary form or other ancillary document.

ACT OF SEDERUNT (FEES OF SHERIFF OFFICERS) 1994

TABLE OF FEES

Item	Summary Cause			Ordinary Cause		
	Band 1 £	Band 2 £	Band 3 £	Band 1 £	Band 2 £	Band 3 £
1. *Service or intimation of a document*						
(a) Service						
(i) each person at a different address	17.40	26.80	34.65	28.45	41.75	54.35
(ii) each additional person at the same address or additional copy required to be served or intimated under the Act of 1987	5.80	5.80	5.80	9.50	9.50	9.50
(b) Postal service	8.40	8.40	8.40	14.00	14.00	14.00
(c) Postal diligence	12.80	12.80	12.80	21.10	21.10	21.10
2. *Interdicts*						
(a) Interdict only						
(i) each person at a different address				78.10	78.10	78.10
(ii) each additional person at the same address				17.15	17.15	17.15
(b) Interdict and service						
(i) each person at a different address				87.65	87.65	87.65
(ii) each additional person at the same address				26.70	26.70	26.70
3. *Poindings*						
(a) Serving notice of entry	3.85	3.85	3.85	5.85	5.85	5.85
(b) Arranging poinding and endeavouring but being unable to execute same for whatever reason	30.20	30.20	30.20	44.25	44.25	44.25
(c) Arranging and executing poinding where appraised value is—						
(i) £364 or under	51.80	51.80	51.80	51.80	51.80	51.80
(ii) Over £364 and up to £1,464	80.20	80.20	80.20	80.20	80.20	80.20
(iii) Over £1,464 and up to £14,742 — 10% of the appraised value only						
(iv) Over £14,742 and up to £73,702 — 10% of the first £14,742, 5% thereafter up to £73,702 of the appraised value						
(v) Over £73,702 — 10% of the first £14,742, 5% thereafter up to £73,702 and 1% of the appraised value over £73,702						
(d) Reporting poinding	5.00	5.00	5.00	5.00	5.00	5.00
4. *Poindings of motor vehicles, heavy plant or machinery*						
(a) Arranging and executing poinding where appraised value is—						
(i) £364 or under	51.80	51.80	51.80	51.80	51.80	51.80
(ii) Over £364 and up to £1,619	80.20	80.20	80.20	80.20	80.20	80.20
(iii) Over £1,619 and up to £73,702 — 5% of the appraised value only						
(iv) Over £73,702 — 5% of the first £73,702 and 1% thereafter of the appraised value						
(b) Reporting poinding	5.00	5.00	5.00	5.00	5.00	5.00
5. *Sequestrations for rent, poinding of ground*						
(a) Arranging for the sequestration or poinding of the ground and endeavouring but being unable to execute same for whatever reason	28.15	28.15	28.15	42.25	42.25	42.25
(b) Arranging and effecting sequestration where the appraised value is—						
(i) £364 or under	49.70	49.70	49.70			
(ii) Over £364 and up to £1,464	78.10	78.10	78.10			
(iii) Over £1,464 as 3 (c) (iii) above						
(c) Arranging and effecting ordinary sequestration or poinding of the ground				78.10	78.10	78.10
(d) Service — as in item 1 (a) or (b) above, as the case may be						
6. *Sales*						
(a) (i) Application for warrant of sale or variation of warrant of sale	8.10	8.10	8.10	8.10	8.10	8.10
(ii) Intimating application — as in item 1 (a) or (b) above, as the case may be						
(b) (i) Arranging warrant sale, preparing advertisement and giving public notice	12.75	12.75	12.75	12.75	12.75	12.75

(ii) Serving copy of warrant of sale and intimating the place and date of sale and if necessary the date of removal of poinded effects, as in item 1 (a) or (b) above, as the case may be

(c) Officer attending warrant sale conducted by auctioneer	22.25	37.60	47.55	22.25	37.60	47.55
(d) (i) Officer and witness attending warrant sale and being unable to execute same for whatever reason	28.15	28.15	28.15	42.25	42.25	42.25
(ii) Officer and witness conducting sale where the appraised value is £364 or under	49.70	49.70	49.70	49.70	49.70	49.70
(iii) Over £364	78.10	78.10	78.10	78.10	78.10	78.10
7. Ejections						
(a) Arranging ejection	28.15	28.15	28.15	42.25	42.25	42.25
(b) Arranging and executing ejection	57.80	57.80	57.80	65.60	65.60	65.60
8. Taking possession of effects						
(a) Arranging possession	28.15	28.15	28.15	42.25	42.25	42.25
(b) Arranging and effecting possession	57.80	57.80	57.80	78.10	78.10	78.10
9. Apprehensions						
(a) Arranging apprehension				42.25	42.25	42.25
(b) Arranging and apprehending				78.10	78.10	78.10
10. Taking possession of children						
(a) Arranging to take possession				42.25	42.25	42.25
(b) Arranging and taking possession of each child				78.10	78.10	78.10
11. Arresting vessels, aircraft and cargo						
(a) Arranging to arrest	28.15	28.15	28.15	42.25	42.25	42.25
(b) Arranging and effecting arrestment	71.00	71.00	71.00	129.15	129.15	129.15
12. Miscellaneous						
(a) To making any report or application under the Act of 1987 with exception of reporting a poinding	9.75	9.75	9.75	9.75	9.75	9.75
(b) To granting any receipt required to be issued under the Act of 1987	5.00	5.00	5.00	5.00	5.00	5.00
(c) To arranging locksmith or tradesman to be in attendance	3.15	3.15	3.15	3.15	3.15	3.15
(d) To granting certificate of displenishment or providing any other certificate or report, registering any document or making any application to a court or the creditor	9.75	9.75	9.75	9.75	9.75	9.75
(e) Executing warrant to open lockfast places	9.75	9.75	9.75	9.75	9.75	9.75

(f) Time
(i) with witness — £15.65 per unit
(ii) without witness — £11.70 per unit
(g) Photocopies
(i) first sheet of document — £1.05
(ii) subsequent copies, per sheet — £0.50

SCHEDULE 2   Paragraph 3 (2)

REVOCATIONS

Acts of Sederunt revoked	References
Act of Sederunt (Fees of Sheriff Officers) 1990	1990/381
Act of Sederunt (Fees of Sheriff Officers) 1991	1991/290
Act of Sederunt (Fees of Sheriff Officers) 1992	1992/82
Act of Sederunt (Fees of Sheriff Officers) (Amendment) 1992	1992/773
Act of Sederunt (Fees of Sheriff Officers) 1993	1993/120

[Acts of Sederunt are reproduced with the permission of the Controller of Her Majesty's Stationery Office.]

ARTICLES

Sex Discrimination and the Burden of Proof

Enderby v Frenchay Health Authority

(Dr) Angus Campbell,
(Ms) Meropi Voyatzi,
Lecturers in Public Law,
University of Aberdeen.

The authors explain how the Frenchay *decision represents something of a new departure for the European Court in equal pay cases, in that it is enough for the pursuer to establish a prima facie case of sex discrimination (rather than any particular requirements for "direct" or "indirect" discrimination) for the onus to shift to the employer to justify the difference.*

A. Introduction

One of the most difficult areas of sex discrimination is that of indirect discrimination. The case of *Enderby v Frenchay Health Authority* (C-127/92) [1994] 1 CMLR 8 raises once again this problem within the context of art 119 of the Treaty of Rome, which enshrines the principle of equal pay for equal work within the EC.

Article 119 provides: "Each Member State shall during the first stage ensure and subsequently maintain the application of the principle that men and women should receive equal pay for equal work."

According to a firm line of decisions of the European Court of Justice it is established that the principle of "equal pay for work for equal value" applies to both direct and indirect discrimination. Direct discrimination is easier to prove, as Advocate General Lenz pointed out in *Danfoss* (109/88) [1989] ECR 3199; [1991] 1 CMLR 8). The pursuer must prove the existence of equal work or work of equal value for which a man and a woman in the same firm are paid different wages. The pay of two employees of different sex must be specifically compared; proof of unequal pay in only a single case is enough to prove that there is wrongful discrimination in pay. In cases of indirect discrimination, he observed, the pursuer's burden of proving discriminatory treatment was harder, since he/she had to show that a neutral criterion which is applied in like manner to men and women has in practice an adverse impact on substantially more members of one or other sex. If this is proved, there is discrimination contrary to art 119, unless the employer shows that the discriminatory result is based on compelling reasons unrelated to sex,

or on "objectively justified" factors (see also Advocate General Lenz in the present case; *Bilka* (170/84) [1986] ECR 1607; [1986] 2 CMLR 701; *Kowalska* (C-33/89) [1990] ECR I-2591; *Nimz* (C-184/89) [1991] ECR I-297; [1992] 3 CMLR 699).

Until the present case, the focus of the Court of Justice has been on the burden of proof rather than on a definition of the legal concept of "indirect discrimination".

B. The facts of the case

The present case arose out of proceedings brought by Dr Enderby against the Frenchay Health Authority (hereinafter called "FHA") and the Secretary of State for Health. Dr Enderby was employed as a speech therapist by the FHA. She claimed that she was a victim of sex discrimination. The ground of her complaint was that at her level of seniority within the NHS (Chief III), members of her profession, which is overwhelmingly female, were paid appreciably less than members of comparable professions which at the same level of seniority were predominantly male.

It was established that the pay of each group had been determined by separate collective bargaining processes and that there had been no sex discrimination in either process either in connection with pay or in connection with entry, transfer or promotion in either group. It appears that prima facie the case turns on two questions: (a) Is there discrimination contrary to art 119 of the Treaty of Rome? If the answer to this is positive, does the principle of equal pay require the employer to justify objectively the difference in pay between two jobs assumed to be of equal value, one of which is carried out almost exclusively by women and the other predominantly by men? (b) What are the justifications which may be used by the employer in order to justify objectively a difference in pay? In particular, could the employer rely on the fact that the pay of the respective jobs had been determined by distinct bargaining processes which themselves separately were not discriminatory? In addition, could the difference in pay be justified — and to what extent — by market forces and in particular the shortage of candidates for one job and the need to pay them more to attract them?

C. The judgment of the Court

(i) The concept of discrimination and the burden of proof

The first question of the Court of Appeal related to the burden of proof, namely whether art 119 of the Treaty of Rome required the health authority to justify objectively the difference in pay between a principal speech therapist and a principal pharmacist. However, the main preliminary question was whether there was some form of illegal discrimination, and in particular indirect discrimination. It should be noted that the Court of Appeal assumed for the purpose of these proceedings that the two posts were comparable and of equal value (in order to examine the question of objective justification of the difference in pay before that of the equivalence of the jobs in issue, which may require more complex investigation).

There are two different approaches as to the factual ingredients of indirect sex discrimination. According to the first approach, the concept of indirect discrimination presupposes a requirement or a hurdle which is more difficult for members of one sex to meet or to overcome; this criterion or hurdle, according to this view, has to be proved by the pursuer. This was the position adopted by the defendants and the UK government in the present case. In fact, it was argued by the UK before the Court of Justice that the European Court's own case law had established that a hurdle or criterion linked to sex must be deployed to the disadvantage of women for a claim of indirect discrimination. According to the second approach, attention should be directed less (or not at all) to the existence of such a requirement or hurdle and more to the discriminatory effect itself. This was the position adopted by the plaintiff and Advocate General Lenz. According to the latter position, therefore, it would seem that disparate impact without such a hurdle is enough to find discrimination contrary to art 119; apparently, it would be possible to do so by comparing the two groups concerned by using valid statistics.

It could be noted that a similar debate (process v result) has raged in the field of equal protection in the USA (see Gunther, *Cases and Materials on Constitutional Law* (12th ed, 1991), p 709, with 1993 Supplement, p 135). In fact Dr Enderby claimed that the US Civil Rights Act 1991 is entirely consistent with the case law of the Court of Justice, establishing that a pay policy or practice having an adverse impact on a group consisting wholly or substantially of women is indirect discrimination if the employer cannot objectively justify the difference in pay.

Faced with the question on the burden of proof the Court of Justice first restated the principles involved in previous cases of discrimination, namely that while normally the burden of proof lies with the pursuer who alleges the facts, the onus of proof shifts to the employer when this is

necessary to avoid depriving workers who appear to be victims of discrimination of any effective means of enforcing the principle of equal pay. The Court referred to two established possible circumstances where the burden of proof may shift: de facto discrimination arising from a particular arrangement, as might apply in the case of part time workers, and lack of transparency in a system of pay which seems to have a discriminatory effect. The Court was fully conscious of the fact that these two cases could be distinguished from the present one. However, applying its previous case law by analogy to the present case, the Court stated that if the pay of speech therapists is significantly lower than that of pharmacists and if the former are almost exclusively women while the latter are predominantly men, there is a prima facie case of sex discrimination, at least where the two jobs in question are of equal value and the statistics describing that situation are valid.

A first reading of this conclusion of the Court reveals that it refers to a finding of a "prima facie case of sex discrimination", thus appearing to abandon or at least ignore the previous distinction between "direct" and "indirect" discrimination. It is submitted that the use of this general conceptual approach is deliberate so as to cover all cases of discrimination which do not clearly fall under either "direct" or "indirect" discrimination. The Court appears to accept implicitly the Commission's assessment that disparate impact is sufficient without it being shown that the discrimination arises from a "rule" properly so called, there being no distinction to be made between discriminatory rules and discriminatory assumptions or historical accident. Most importantly, the Court is obviously influenced by the analysis of Advocate General Lenz who urged a pragmatic rather than a formalistic approach in an overall categorisation of discrimination. In particular, the Advocate General's opinion put emphasis on the discriminatory result and maintained that a rebuttable presumption of discrimination can be raised by comparison of two groups, each doing work of equal value, which then places the onus on the employer to adduce evidence in the rebuttal of that presumption or to produce a justification. This new approach is perhaps endorsed because the Court shared the Advocate General's unease with the clarity of distinction between direct and indirect discrimination (apparent also in *Danfoss* (109/88) [1989] ECR 3199; [1991] 1 CMLR 8), and was inclined to accept his view that even in cases of direct discrimination there might be a defence of objective justification.

Having disposed of the formalism presented by the defenders, the Court then applied and, apparently, extended the philosophy of reversing the burden of proof on the employer. It held that where there is a prima facie case of discrimination, it is for the employer to show that there are objective reasons for the difference in pay. In reversing the burden of proof, the Court applied the principle of effectiveness. As the Court went on to say, workers would be unable to enforce the principle of equal pay before the national courts if evidence of a prima facie case of discrimination did not shift the onus to the employer. The Court, therefore, shifts the burden of proof to the employer thereafter in an attempt to allow employees an effective means of enforcing the principle of equal pay. In doing so, the Court is fully aware of the fact that discrimination is often an action or activity which is suspected rather than established and notoriously difficult to prove. The information on which claims can be based is almost always exclusively in the employer's hands and applicants are frequently left only with circumstantial evidence which in the ordinary course of legal proceedings will not suffice to discharge the burden of proof (see *Evaluation report on the Implementation of the Equality Directives*, 1987, Office for Official Publications of the European Communities, para 7.21).

(ii) The employer's defence: objective justification
The second question submitted to the Court was effectively whether the employer could justify discrimination on the "objective" ground of the existence of two separate collective agreements, neither being discriminatory in itself. The Court did not have any problem in concluding that the existence of separate collective agreements could not constitute an objective justification for the discrimination. The Court accepted the German Government's argument that if it were otherwise, the employer could easily, by using separate bargaining processes with the same parties and within the same establishment, circumvent the principle of equal pay.

(iii) The effect of market forces
Finally, the third question, that is whether "market forces", such as the need to attract suitable candidates, could objectively justify the difference in pay, was again answered in the affirmative. Obviously it cannot be disputed that an employer may be compelled by the state of the labour market to offer higher remuneration for members of a particular professional group in order to attract suitable applicants. The difficulty lies in establishing whether these "market forces"

justify the whole difference in pay or only that part which is immediately attributable to these factors.

The UK Government and the FHA suggested that the only realistic solution lay in attribution of the whole of the pay, a view echoing comments made by the UK employment appeal tribunal. The FHA argued partly that it is unrealistic, illogical and artificial to expect an employer to apportion the proportion of pay which is attributable to market forces. Since such forces constrain an employer to agree to a particular level of pay in order to attract candidates it is that total amount which is entirely explained by the state of the employment market. In the Advocate General's opinion, however, if one factor, which is not the cause of the whole of the difference in pay, were allowed to justify the whole difference in pay, that would leave open the door to potential discrimination.

The Court accepted the opinion of the Advocate General and held that if an increase in pay is attributable to market forces, the pay differential is objectively justified to the extent of that proportion. It is for the national court to assess the role of the market forces and whether their role was sufficiently significant to provide objective justification for part or all of the difference.

D. Conclusions
Although it is still early to assess the implications of the judgment, it seems that the decision is representative of the current trend of the Court of Justice in the field of sex discrimination, namely the focus on a result oriented rather than a formalistic approach and the pursuit of the principle of effectiveness.

Obviously the crux of the matter is a finding of equivalent work, which is a matter for the national court. But a rather formalistic approach endorsed by the UK Government and the EAT has been replaced by an emphasis on underlying principles. First, the Court refers to a finding of prima facie discrimination — apparently loosening or rethinking the conceptual apparatus employed beforehand. Then the Court accepts that there is a prima facie case of sex discrimination where significant and valid statistics disclose an appreciable difference in pay between jobs of equal value, one of which is carried out by members of predominantly one sex and the other by members of the other. The acceptance of a general principle that an adverse impact on a group of women is enough may, as the Commission suggested, address situations where by tradition or assumption, rather than a formal rule, one group of women earn less than men. Lastly, in this case, the Court shifts to the employer the onus of proof thereafter to allow employees an effective means of enforcing the principle of equal pay.

There are, however, areas of uncertainty. The Court dealt with a situation where a group was "overwhelmingly" female. But what of less overwhelming majorities? Could it not be argued, as the employment appeal tribunal suggested, that too much could depend on chance both in the size of majority and the particular group chosen? This approach, therefore, leads to the need to compare the objective worth of various jobs and to justify pay differences only on the basis of statistics which may or may not be stable. The Court left to the national court an assessment of the significance of statistics, including whether they cover enough individuals and whether they are fortuitous or short term. This is definitely the right

approach as national courts are in the best position to assess local conditions and practices.

As regards what constitutes objective justification for the difference in pay, it is submitted that the Court was quite right to accept that market forces are an objective factor which could be invoked by the employer. It is difficult not to regard "market forces" as objective and certainly something that the employer is entitled, perhaps obliged for the sake of the company, to have regard to. The danger here is that this may perpetuate discrimination. A great deal of uncertainty may also be caused in practice as to what proportion of pay is attributable to market forces. However, the Court's solution seems acceptable and inescapable in principle. It is submitted that the decision of the Court of Justice is totally acceptable and justifiable in view of the difficulties involved in this sensitive area.

◆

NEWS

Appreciation

Professor W A Wilson, MA, LLB, FRSE

[The following tribute to Professor Wilson was delivered at his thanksgiving service on 19 March 1994 by Matthew Clarke, QC, and is reproduced with permission.]

William Adam Wilson was born on 28 July 1928. He was educated at Hillhead High School, Glasgow and Glasgow University, taking the degrees of MA and LLB. He remained immensely proud throughout his life, of having attended both Hillhead High and Glasgow University. It, indeed, gave him really great pleasure during his last illness, to know that the University of Glasgow proposed to confer on him, at the forthcoming summer graduation, the degree of Doctor of Laws *Honoris Causa*. The degree was never, in the event, conferred, but Bill, a man who disliked any fuss and ceremonial, if he was to be the centre of it, was more than satisfied to know that the university, his university, had taken the decision to honour him in this way.

After completing his education he qualified as a solicitor in 1951. Following his National Service he practised as a procurator in various firms, mainly in Glasgow, until 1960, when he gave up practice and was appointed lecturer in Scots law

at the University of Edinburgh. He was soon appointed senior lecturer and in 1972 became the first incumbent of the Lord President Reid Chair of Law in the university, an appointment he held, with great distinction, until his death. From 1980 to 1989 he held the post of Director of the Scottish Universities Law Institute. For many years he was chairman of the Joint Standing Committee on legal education. In 1991 he was elected a Fellow of the Royal Society of Edinburgh.

Those bare biographical details fail to reveal adequately the greatness of the man, for Bill was truly a great man. Teaching was in his blood and, when he gave up the practice of law, to devote the rest of his life to the Faculty of Law in Edinburgh University, and to legal education in Scotland, the university and Scotland were gifted with a great teacher of law, certainly the greatest of his age. He was a natural teacher, a richly gifted communicator in lecture, tutorial, or more informal setting, who adored his students and who saw his main function as passing on to them his enjoyment of, and enthusiasm for, the law, which he retained until his death. Generations of students, many of them now distinguished members of the judiciary, both branches of the legal profession, and academic life owe so much to the inspiration of Bill. For many of them, the law was never again so interesting or stimulating as it had been when he presented it to them. His influence as a teacher was not restricted to this country but spread far beyond its borders. For the many foreign students, from all parts of the world, whom he taught, especially latterly in the MBA and LLM courses, he provided a truly unique experience. That fact is borne out by the Aladdin's cave which he had of gifts, often exotic and peculiar, from every corner of the world, which were the tangible expressions of gratitude from those whose lives he had touched deeply.

Bill had a love affair with the law of Scotland, but it was not a sentimental kind of love, based on romantic and wishful notions of what Scots law's origins and principles were. Rather it was based on an admiration for both its philosophical basis and its pragmatic approach, which he identified as its true genius. It was not without significance that Bill, before studying law, studied philosophy and that he was, indeed, something of an expert in formal logic. His modestly titled article "A Note on the Hohfeld Analysis", published in the 1972 *Juridical Review*, was a mind bending intellectual tour de force dealing with the analysis of rights in the light of deontic logic. In his essay "The Study of Scots Law", Bill wrote: "English lawyers evince a positive hostility to philosophy. . . . In Scotland," he continued, "the tradition is different. Viscount Stair, the architect of Scots law, was a regent in philosophy at Glasgow University before he became an advocate and his philosophical approach to law is clearly apparent in his *Institutions*. Many eminent Scottish judges — Lord Shaw of Dunfermline, Lord Macmillan, Lord Justice Clerk Aitchison, to name only three — studied philosophy before they turned to the law." In my view Professor W A Wilson holds a worthy place among those he named.

Bill's scholarship was immense. Throughout his life his lively and acute mind embraced new ways of thinking and doing. He was well ahead of the field in his early study of European Community law and the impact of computers on the law. He experienced great delight, which he passed on to others, in his rigorous research of some of the more recondite areas of the law. His lifetime's fondness for walking and travel allowed him to cultivate a particular interest, which he titled "Legal Geography", which involved focusing on particular places where events had occurred which had influenced the law, or which themselves were a reason for a law. His search for these places took him from Morrison's Haven to San Marino, with many locations between and beyond. It was, for example, obvious that a highlight of what proved to be one of his most

rewarding trips abroad, his trip some years ago to Australia, was that he was able to visit the actual location where the events occurred which led to the controversial decision of the Privy Council in *The "Wagon Mound"* [1961] AC 388. By the same token I am sure that it was a secret regret that he never managed actually to land on Rockall — that indeed would have been a sight and an event!

His deep love for the law was, of course, always conveyed with that lightness of touch and with wit and humour never far away. He took great pleasure out of the absurd in life. For most of us, no doubt, the fondest memories we shall retain of Bill will involve his sense of humour, as often as not employed at the expense of himself.

In the earliest times of my acquaintanceship with him he first told me the following story, which to my mind sums up perfectly the nature of the man. When he applied for the Lord President Reid Chair of Law there was another candidate, who, on paper, at that time, might have been seen by some misguided persons as a stronger candidate than Bill. Let us call this person "XY". Bill told me that some short time after he had been appointed to the chair, he found himself at a social function which was attended by the then Principal of the university. Bill also found himself in the same group as the Principal. The name of "XY" came up in conversation. The Principal said "Oh yes, XY, if ever anybody talked himself out of a Chair it was him! Who was it by the way, that we ended up appointing to that Chair?". Bill took a short step forward and indicated the answer, without words, but with a characteristic gesture. That Bill told that story, as often as he did, and every time with great glee, and no loss of dignity, to my mind speaks to his greatness as a human being.

As well as all the fun he gave us I know that many would agree with me that we will always treasure his shining integrity. That integrity made him someone to whom generations of students, colleagues and friends would go to for counsel and support, knowing that these would be given unhesitatingly and that no confidence would be betrayed. That integrity also meant that he was quick to detect intellectual or moral dishonesty which he would attack in his own quiet but effective way. On the other hand, as far as other human foibles were concerned he was the most tolerant of men. No one would ever be expelled from his circle simply because of some human frailty which others might have readily condemned.

Bill was a single man, but he was not, in any

material sense, a lonely or unfulfilled man. He had several deep love affairs in his life. His love affair with the law and his love affair with his students I have mentioned. But he also, I think, had a love affair with the University of Edinburgh. He served it, with total commitment, for almost 34 years in many capacities from lecturer to member of the University Court. He was in love with the *idea* of the university on the lines that John Henry, Cardinal Newman discussed that idea, in his work of that name, and the fire in his belly really came alight when he detected anything that appeared to compromise that idea or to devalue it. I think it was one of his few real disappointments in life to see how governmental and other policies, over the years, had succeeded in damaging that idea and, when he considered it appropriate, he spoke out courageously against such developments.

Bill has left us, but it falls to few of us to leave so many rich legacies. These include his important publications — Wilson and Duncan on *Trusts, Trustees and Executors*, his *Introductory Essays on Scots Law*, his many articles embracing a huge range of topics, the editions of Gloag and Henderson's *Introduction to the Law of Scotland* which he edited, and especially his quite excellent work on the *Law of Debt*, now in its second edition, where with his usual economy of language, he regularly provides exactly the answer to the tricky problem which many other more prolix works have failed to deliver. Then there is the inspiration he has given to generations of lawyers at home and abroad, and his service to the university and public life in Scotland.

But most of all there are the wonderful memories he has left all of us with of a decent, brilliant, amusing and lovely man.

These imperfect words of mine have been an attempt to describe a man who, in my view, is described perfectly by the words of one of Bill's favourite poets, Alfred, Lord Tennyson when he wrote as follows:

"And thou art worthy; full of power,
As gentle; liberal minded, great,
Consistent; wearing all that weight
of learning lightly like a flower".

— ◊ —

Appointments

Scottish Legal Aid Board
The Secretary of State for Scotland has made the following appointments to the Scottish Legal Aid Board, with effect from 1 April 1994.

Mrs Christine Davis, who has been chairman of the Board for the past three years, has been re-appointed for a further period of four years. Mr Alexander F Wylie, QC, Mrs Sheila Campbell, Mrs A Kay Blair and Mrs Jean Couper have been appointed as members of the Board. These appointments will run from 1 April 1994 to 31 March 1998. Mr Robert J Livingstone and Mr Colin N McEachran, QC, who were first appointed to the Board in 1988 and 1990 respectively, have been re-appointed from 1 April 1994 to 31 March 1998. Mr Archibald Gilchrist and Mr George Barrie, who were first appointed to the Board in 1986, have been re-appointed from 1 April 1994 to 31 March 1996.

— ◊ —

Court

House of Lords: practice directions
The following amendments to the House of Lords practice directions applicable to civil appeals have been made.

Judicial fees
As from 12 April 1994, the judicial fees in appendix H (*Parliament House Book*, p B529) will be increased. The new figures are:

	£
Petition of appeal	68
Appearance	8
Waiver of security for costs	17
Petition not referred to appeal committee (incidental petition to conjoin or consolidate)	34
Petition referred to appeal committee (including report thereon)	40
Joint petition (from each party thereto)	17
Application to set down for hearing	363
Final judgment	40

Security for costs
The sum to be lodged as security for costs by appellants in appeals to the House of Lords presented on or after 12 April 1994 is increased to £18,000. Agents are reminded that in accordance with direction 11.2 "No interest is payable on security monies".

Speeches of the Lords of Appeal
The charge for an individual set of opinions is increased to £5 from 12 April 1994. The annual subscription will remain unchanged.

◊

High Court of Justiciary: practice note
18 March 1994: Applications for bail pending the determination of an appeal
Although s 238 (3) of the Criminal Procedure

(Scotland) Act 1975 enables an appellant to apply for bail when he has lodged written intimation of his intention to appeal, an application for interim liberation in the case of an appeal against conviction can normally be considered only when the note of appeal containing grounds of appeal has been lodged. It is therefore at that stage that an application for bail should normally be made.

The court may consider an application for bail by a person who has lodged an intimation of intention to appeal, but in such cases the written application for bail must state clearly why bail is being applied for at that stage. The court may refuse to entertain an application for bail at that stage in the absence of any such statement in the written application.

◇

Paisley sheriff court
As from 16 May 1994 Paisley sheriff court will be located at the following address: 106 Renfrew Road, Paisley PA3 4DD. The phone and fax numbers remain unchanged.

◇

Queen's Counsel
The Queen, on the recommendation of the Secretary of State for Scotland, to whom the names were submitted by the Lord Justice General, has approved the rank and dignity of Queen's Counsel in Scotland being conferred on: Sidney Neil Brailsford, advocate; and Leeona June Dorrian, advocate.

◇

Faculty of Advocates
Mr James Noel Kennedy, LLB(Edinburgh), and Mr Alastair Mackie MacMillan Clive, LLB(Edinburgh), have been admitted to the Faculty of Advocates.

◇

Scottish Land Court Reports 1993
The *Scottish Land Court Reports 1993*, detailing all the leading legal as opposed to factual decisions of the court last year, have now been printed and copies are available, priced £19 each, from the Principal Clerk, Scottish Land Court, 1 Grosvenor Crescent, Edinburgh EH12 5ER (tel 031-225 3595).

—— ◇ ——

Law reform

Company law
Company law covering small private companies

and the law on the execution of documents is to be looked at by the Law Commission, in consultation with the Scottish Law Commission. A working group consisting of members of the business, legal and accountancy professions and DTI officials has identified private companies with a small number of shareholders actively involved in running the business as the type which might most benefit from simplification of company law.

The options for reform studied by the group include a completely new corporate form more like an incorporated partnership which would dispense with some of the existing concepts of company law (e g the distinction between shareholders and directors) while retaining other key features such as separate legal personality and limited liability. The group also looked at simplification of the Companies Act 1985, either by amending and dropping some of the existing requirements and if appropriate drawing the remaining provisions together in a self contained statute, or by allowing companies to opt out of some provisions by extending the elective regime introduced in the Companies Act 1989. Changes to the law would not diminish the protection provided for creditors and others.

The Law Commissions will carry out a feasibility study and will advise the DTI by 31 July 1994.

◇

Panel on security over moveables
A special advisory panel has been appointed to assist the Department of Trade and Industry in the preparation of a Bill to amend Scots law on security interests in moveable property.

The current inability under Scots law to create an adequate and workable fixed security over moveable property without the creditor taking possession inhibits the ability of Scottish business to raise working capital, and the government believe there is unanimous support for reform.

The panel are: Professor John Murray, QC, of the University of Edinburgh; Professor W W McBryde, of the University of Dundee; James G Birrell, of Dickson Minto, WS, Edinburgh; Jane Ryder, consultant to Davidson Chalmers, WS, Edinburgh; and Kevin Sweeney, of McGrigor Donald, Glasgow.

The draft Bill prepared by the department, with assistance from the advisory panel, will be for public consultation.

◇

NEWS

General

Faculty of Procurators and Solicitors in Dundee

At a general meeting of the Faculty of Procurators and Solicitors in Dundee held on 23 March 1994, the following were elected: *Dean*, Dennis J Young; *vice dean*, David A Brand; *secretary/treasurer*, Donald N Gordon, 30 Whitehall Street, Dundee; *council members*, Mrs Ellenore Foulis, Mr George C Donnelly, Mr Ian R Steven, and Mr Kenneth H Wood; *library convener*, David J Wallace; *librarian*, Mrs Alison Gordon.

Property certificates

Grampian

Grampian Regional Council have increased their charge for property clearance certificates to £54 with effect from 1 April 1994.

Moray

Moray District Council have increased the fee for property clearance certificates to £35 with effect from 1 April 1994.

Taxation

Inland Revenue information powers

The government have tabled an amendment to the Finance Bill to ensure that an officer seeking the papers of a tax accountant must first obtain the approval of a member of the Board of Inland Revenue. Clause 241 of the Finance Bill extends the existing power of the Inland Revenue to obtain the papers of an accountant who has been involved in the perpetration of tax offences. Subject to the consent of a special commissioner, the power will be available where the Revenue have reasonable grounds for believing that the accountant has knowingly assisted in a tax offence. Under the clause the consent of a special commissioner can be sought by any officer of the board who is authorised to do so. The amendment will provide that a member of the board has to be satisfied that there are reasonable grounds for proceeding. This further safeguard is an indication of the seriousness attached to the use of this power. In addition the Inland Revenue intend to publish guidance on the way in which they will interpret and operate this power, and are consulting the various professional bodies concerned.

Corporation tax: capital allowances

The government have proposed a number of amendments to the Finance Bill clauses on capital allowances.

Clarification of the boundary between structures and plant (cl 110)

As drafted, the clause would mean that a number of assets which under existing tax law may qualify as plant for capital allowances purposes would no longer do so. The assets involved are test beds for aero engines, fixed structures in amusement parks, fixed zoo cages, water service reservoirs and indoor swimming pools. The amendments ensure that these assets will continue to qualify as plant if they meet the existing case law tests. Under the existing rules, for investment expenditure on certain industrial structures which qualify as plant, capital allowances may be claimed as the expenditure is incurred. As drafted, the clause would delay the availability of allowances until these assets are brought into use. The amendment is to ensure that the existing rules continue to apply.

Notification of expenditure on machinery and plant (cl 111)

The amendments would extend the proposed time limit for notifying expenditure on machinery and plant from two to three years for chargeable periods ending prior to 30 November 1993. For accounting periods ending on or after 1 December 1990 they would also extend the notification period to the date of Royal Assent where the three year period would otherwise have expired at an earlier date. A further amendment proposes that a power be given to the Board of Inland Revenue to extend the notification period, in particular circumstances which have delayed the giving of any notice or computation. Subject to this proposal being enacted the board would issue a statement of practice setting out how this power would be used.

Transfers of assets between connected persons (cl 112)

Clause 112 would give retrospective effect to a change made by s 158 of the Finance Act 1993, which allowed enterprise zone buildings and hotels to be transferred between connected persons at their tax written down value. The amendment extends this also to scientific research assets.

Fundraising for charity

The Inland Revenue have issued a booklet which contains guidance on how fundraising activities for charity are treated for tax purposes. Under an existing extra-statutory concession (C4), the Revenue do not seek to tax the profits from certain types of events arranged to raise funds for charity. The booklet explains the circumstances in which the concession applies. A small amendment has also been made to the text of the concession.

The guidance supersedes any earlier advice which charities may have received from the Inland Revenue. In particular, it replaces paras 27 and 28 of the booklet "Guidelines on the Tax Treatment of Disaster Funds" issued jointly by the Inland Revenue and Customs and Excise in 1989. The booklet, entitled "Fund-Raising for Charity" is available free of charge from: Inland Revenue Claims (Scotland), Trinity Park House, South Trinity Road, Edinburgh EH5 3SD (tel 031-551 8127).

◇

Capital gains tax: capital loss buying
The government has tabled a new clause in the 1994 Finance Bill to amend the rules which restrict the set off of pre-entry capital losses. Two defects in the provisions have been corrected. The first allowed groups of companies to sidestep the provisions by transferring within the group any assets with unrealised losses which had been brought into the group. The second may have allowed one group to avoid the provisions of buying a company with an unrealised loss, carrying out a series of transactions within the group and then selling the company to a second group before the loss was realised. The new rules will apply to disposals made on or after 11 March 1994.

◇

Venture capital trusts
The Inland Revenue have published a consultative document outlining the government's proposals for introducing venture capital trusts, a new scheme for investment in small unquoted companies. Investors' dividends and gains on shares held in a venture capital trust would be free from income and capital gains tax. Copies of the document (price £2) are available from the Reference Room, Inland Revenue Library, Room 8, New Wing, Somerset House, Strand, London WC2R 1LB.

Comments on the draft proposals (by 16 May 1994) should be sent to: Peter Fawcett, Inland Revenue, Room 232, South West Wing, Bush House, Strand, London WC2B 4RD.

◇

Foreign exchange gains and losses
The Inland Revenue have published draft regulations which will provide transitional rules for assets, currency contracts and liabilities held or owed on the date the tax rules on exchange gains and losses in the Finance Act 1993 first apply to a company.

Further information can be obtained from, and comments on the draft (by 20 May 1994) sent to: Sue Cooper, Inland Revenue (Financial Institutions Division), Foreign Exchange Consultations, Room 510, 22 Kingsway, London WC2B 6NR.

◇

Double taxation relief
The Inland Revenue have published a revised edition of booklet IR6, "Double taxation relief for companies". Whenever a UK company does business abroad through a branch in the other country, or by setting up a subsidiary there, the question arises how the right to tax the profits arising from those operations will be split between the two countries. A similar question arises when a foreign company does business in the UK. Booklet IR6 explains how double taxation arises and how relief is given for it in the UK. Where the other country is one of the 90 or so with which the UK has negotiated a double taxation agreement, a company's tax position will depend on the provisions of the relevant agreement. The booklet includes guidance on how typical agreements apply to particular types of income.

◇

Fees and annual subscriptions to professional bodies
Tax relief is available for fees and annual subscriptions paid by employees to certain professional bodies and learned societies. A new edition of the list of these bodies is now available. The relief is available where the organisation is approved by the Board of Inland Revenue, and the activities of the organisation are relevant to the employee's job.

The new edition replaces the list published on 29 March 1993 and contains details of all organisations approved by the Board up to 31 October 1993. Copies of the list are available, price £5.00 (post free) from: Inland Revenue Library Reference Room, Room 8, New Wing, Somerset House, Strand, London WC2R 1LB.

◇

Income tax: company cars
The Treasury have laid regulations before the House of Commons to simplify the treatment of replacement cars provided while an employee's

normal company car is not available, and replacement accessories which take the place of equipment already fitted to a car. The Inland Revenue have also laid amendments to the Pay As You Earn regulations, setting out details of the quarterly return to be completed by employers for changes in company cars.

— ◊ —

Letter to the Editor

School of Art History
University of St Andrews
St Andrews KY16 9AL

5 April 1994

Sir,

The School of Art History at the University of St Andrews is making a survey of disappearing Scottish furniture types and would be very grateful to hear from any lawyers' offices where these survive. Our aim is to record good examples of office furniture such as counting house desks, pigeonholes, bookcases, letter racks, filing cabinets, deed box racks, boardroom furniture and the like before these items completely disappear in the face of modern computerisation and the removal of premises. If any of your readers have such items I would be delighted to hear from them. Any offer of such help will be most keenly received.

Yours sincerely,
DAVID JONES,
Lecturer in Furniture History.

— ◊ —

Obituaries

On 17 March 1994, John Paterson, formerly senior partner in the firm of Messrs Squair Middleton & Co, solicitors, Nairn.

On 29 March 1994, John Bayne, advocate, formerly sheriff at Dumfries.

On 29 March 1994, Douglas James Forbes, partner in the firm of Messrs Beltrami & Co, solicitors, Glasgow.

— ◊ —

Business changes

Messrs Park & MacRae, solicitors, 26 Carden Place, Aberdeen, announce that with effect from

4 April 1994 Rory Cradock has joined the firm as an associate.

Messrs Borland Johnston & Orr, Messrs Montgomerie & Co and Messrs Keyden Strang & Co, all solicitors, Glasgow, announce the amalgamation of their practices with effect from 1 April 1994. The name of the amalgamated firm is Messrs Borland Montgomerie Keyden and the firm will initially practise from offices at Apsley House, 29 Wellington Street, Glasgow G2 6JA (tel 041-221 8004; fax 041-221 8088; DX GW55 Glasgow), and 53 Bothwell Street, Glasgow G2 6TH (tel 041-221 9762; fax 041-221 2407; DX GW108 Glasgow). The partners of Borland Montgomerie Keyden are Colin W R Gemmill, Alastair Garland, Hugh M K Hopkins, Ronald S Alexander, Alan L Grassick, Brian E Scoullar, Anthony J Barber-Fleming, Iain C Dunn, Colin W Pettigrew, Finlay J McKendrick, Anne M Blackstock, Andrew Smith and Keith H Mackenzie. J Loudon Downs, John G L Robinson and Edward Goodman are consultants to the firm and Anthony G Hunter is an associate. The amalgamated firm will also practise as T J & W A Dykes from 105 Cadzow Street, Hamilton ML3 6HJ (tel 0698 282726; fax 0698 425892; DX HA4 Hamilton).

Messrs Barlas & Sharpe, WS, 33a Westgate, North Berwick, intimate that Mr Robin Francis Murray has been assumed as a partner of the firm with effect from 1 April 1994.

Mr Richard Godden was readmitted to the Faculty of Advocates on 25 March 1994, and has resumed practice.

— ◊ —

Parliamentary News

Royal Assent

24 March 1994

Consolidated Fund Act 1994 (c 4).
New Towns (Amendment) Act 1994 (c 5).
Mental Health (Amendment) Act 1994 (c 6).
Insolvency Act 1994 (c 7).
Transport Police (Jurisdiction) Act 1994 (c 8).

— ◊ —

ARTICLES

Procedure in Children's Hearings

Joan Rose,
Centre for Continuing Education,
University of Edinburgh.

Ms Rose, a former children's panel member and now an assistant training organiser for children's panels, challenges the assertion that panel hearings are unstructured compared with those of the courts and unburdened with procedural requirements.

In a recent article in the *Scots Law Times*, "Better Heard and not Seen: Child Witnesses, Competency and Hearsay", 1994 SLT (News) 9, Lilian Edwards states that there appears to be an increasingly unhappy compromise between the interests of the child who is in need of compulsory measures of care and the interests of natural justice, particularly as it relates to the claims on the child's family. She refers to this compromise being "implemented by a division of proceedings between the children's hearing itself, in which forum the rules of evidence and procedure are substantially relaxed, and the courts, wherein any dispute about the truth of the ground of referral to the hearing is resolved by something near normal methods of proof". Ms Edwards then states that, in her opinion, the "simple dichotomy of almost absent rules of procedure in the hearing and almost normal rules of proof in the sheriff court is not wholly satisfactory".

What is, indeed, entirely unsatisfactory is perpetuation of the myth that children's hearings are totally unstructured and informal, as well as the inference that, because panel members are lay volunteers, the hearings system is inferior to a wholly court based system. Although there are a number of matters in Ms Edwards' article with which one could take issue, we shall confine ourselves to the question of procedure in order to challenge, and hopefully dispel, the illusion that there is an absence of procedure in hearings, by illustrating the standard processes that the legislation requires panel members to follow. There is a distinction between the relative informality of the setting of hearings and the procedures which must be followed, procedural irregularity being a ground for appeal against the decision of a hearing. Moreover, in addition to mandatory procedure, panel members have over the years developed considerable expertise in identifying and implementing good practice, the purpose of which is to ensure that children and parents are afforded the most enabling and responsive opportunity to participate in hearings.

We should at the outset refer to the Kilbrandon principles. It was concluded, after careful deliberation, that court procedure was not appropriate when the needs of children (troubled or troublesome) required to be determined, and that decisions as to disposal should be made by people with special interest in, and knowledge of, children (Kilbrandon Report, Cmnd 2306). The separation of adjudication on disputed matters of fact and disposal of the case of the child has been described by the Lord President as "the genius of this reform, which has earned it so much praise" (*Sloan v B*, 1991 SLT 530 at p 548E). So far as the compromise between the interests of the child and natural justice is concerned, in *Kennedy v A*, 1986 SLT 358, the Lord Justice Clerk stated at p 362B that "the principles of natural justice must yield to the best interests of the child".

Panel members may be lay volunteers; they are not unskilled. They are appointed following a rigorous selection process. Nationally, in the pre-service period following their appointment in early January until 16 May when they are entitled to commence service on hearings, panel members undergo between 70 and 85 hours of induction training. This is followed by a second stage of new member training, which includes reviewing and extending knowledge of particularly complex legal procedures, including specific chairmanship training, as well as issues relating to children and families — such as sexual abuse or offending. Furthermore, all panel members are required to make an ongoing commitment to in-service training, whether organised locally or regionally.

In the *Report of the Inquiry into Child Care Policies in Fife*, it is stated (at p 625, para 11): "More generally we believe that the Children's Panel on the one hand and the Reporter on the other hand because their concerns are principally with children may sometimes be regarded as less significant in our legal system than they might be. We suspect our equating . . . of the responsibilities of the Reporter with those of an Advocate Depute or Regional Procurator Fiscal may have struck some readers as *prima facie* surprising: but we feel sure that on reflection our observation will be seen to have some validity. A similar observation might be made of Panel Members: they have responsibilities for disposal of cases which present equal difficulties to those facing High Court Judges, Sheriffs and District Justices".

Sheriff Kearney, one of the authors of the Fife report, has an extensive knowledge of the hearings system and his book *Children's Hearings and the Sheriff Court* is widely used by lawyers. His recognition of the onerous nature of the responsibilities of panel members is, therefore, heartening.

Robert Black, Professor of Scots Law in the University of Edinburgh, who is a very experienced temporary sheriff and who has observed children's hearings, considers that the procedure in hearings is only relatively informal when compared with a summary criminal court. Moreover, he has indicated (in personal conversation with the writer) that, as a sentencer, he is bound by fewer formal procedural constraints than are panel members and, in particular, the chairman of the hearing, in reaching decisions as to how the case should be disposed of. In addition, he has commented on the fact that, unlike sheriffs and senior members of the judiciary, panel members must not only attempt to involve the family in the decision making process, they must announce — and justify — the reasons for that decision in the presence of the child and parents.

What then actually happens when a children's hearing considers the case of a child?

Preparation: stage 1

The law requires that panel members should have received from the reporter not later than three clear days before the hearing (and preferably earlier), a copy of a report from the local authority on the child and his social background; a copy of the statement of the grounds of referral; a copy of any judicial remit or reference, or reference by a local authority (where relevant); if the child is already subject to a supervision requirement, a copy of that requirement; and where a safeguarder has been appointed, a copy of any report which the safeguarder may have prepared (Children's Hearings (Scotland) Rules 1986 (SI 1986/2291), rule 6 (1) (e)). In addition there might be complex psychiatric, medical or assessment reports to be considered. Panel members are required, in terms of the same rule, to keep any documents secure and to return them to the reporter immediately upon the conclusion of the hearing. The contents are to be treated as strictly confidential.

Citizens Serving Children: a study of the Children's Panel in Scotland on behalf of the Children's Panel Chairmen's Group (Scottish Office, 1992) found that panel members spent, on average, between four and six hours preparing for a session of hearings. This may well be an underestimate in areas where four hearings per session are common and where very complex care and protection cases are being considered. Panel members can be faced with a pile of papers two to three inches high. They may not have seen a particular family before and must therefore familiarise themselves with the background to the case. As families do not have

access to the documents available to panel members and only the substance of reports must be disclosed in a hearing (see below, "The discussion", and *Kennedy v A*, supra), panel members must be able to sift fact from opinion, and be able to identify areas of substance for disclosure and discussion in the hearing.

Preparation: stage 2

There are considerable variations between regions as to when decisions are made as to who should chair particular hearings. The system with which the writer is most familiar, and which the writer considers to be good practice, is for all panel members to prepare on the basis that they might be called upon to chair any of the hearings in a particular session. While panel members must clearly not prejudge a case before the hearing, practice has developed over the years regarding what can and should happen, and this is entirely legitimate in order that the best possible use can be made of the limited time available for a hearing — the average time scheduled being 45 minutes. Members should, as a team:

(a) clarify the purpose of the hearing;

(b) check that everyone has received the same information and that no one is missing any of the reports;

(c) clarify any legal issues, amongst themselves or with the reporter, including the range of disposals available to the panel (Social Work (Scotland) Act 1968, ss 43 and 44): this does not mean considering specific resources but is merely consideration of what their legal duties and powers are, for example, in relation to issuing or extending warrants (ss 37 and 40), placing a child in secure accommodation (s 58A), or whether they may impose conditions in a supervision requirement, and what those conditions might be;

(d) check who will be at the hearing, and consider if, say, a child should be present for only part of the hearing, or at all (ss 40 (1) and (2)); or, perhaps, whether someone like a guidance teacher might be asked to leave once the panel have had an opportunity to discuss the child's progress at school and before matters deeply private to the family are considered by the hearing. They should also consider seating arrangements — particularly important when it is known that there is dissension between members of the family or if an alleged abuser is likely to be present;

(e) identify and note significant issues, flagging those of particular concern, and agreeing who might take initial responsibility for ensuring that particular subjects are raised. This ensures that, whenever possible, all relevant matters will be raised. However, any framework must be sufficiently flexible to allow panel members to respond to altered circumstances in the hearing.

Once the hearing commences

(1) Procedure

Unless there is specific provision in the legislation, the procedure of a hearing is determined by the chairman (rule 9 (1)). The chairman may at any time during the hearing adjourn, provided that the adjournment will enable the children's hearing to sit again on the same day as the adjournment was made (rule 9 (2)). This can be helpful if, for example, during the course of a hearing a particular resource is identified as being in the best interests of a child and the social worker is requested to investigate immediately the possibility of a place being available because the matter is urgent and it would not be appropriate to continue the hearing to a later date for further information (s 43 (3)), or if a short interval is required to allow distressed or angry children or parents to recover. In fact, given the time constraints, and the number of specific provisions, the chairman does not have much leeway regarding procedure.

The panel must attempt to create a welcoming atmosphere: considerable skill is required to strike the right note between providing an encouraging ambience whilst not losing sight of the fact that the proceedings are those of a legally constituted tribunal with extensive powers, and that, for the family, the whole event is likely to be extremely traumatic.

(2) Attendance

The chairman of a hearing is required in terms of the Act (s 35 (1)) to ensure that no person other than someone whose presence is necessary for the proper consideration of the case being heard, or whose presence is permitted by the chairman, may be present. The principle of hearings being conducted in private is included in the same section. It is self evident that there will be three panel members present, at least one of whom must be a man and one a woman (s 33 (2)), and there is an implicit expectation that a reporter will be present throughout as the reporter is required to keep a record of the proceedings (rule 30).

(a) The child. The question of the attendance of the child, or the panel dispensing with the child's attendance for all or part of the hearing, must be dealt with. Normally, panels would — or should — expect children to be present, but see *Sloan v B*, supra, "*Sloan v B* — The Legal Issues", Joe Thomson, 1991 SLT (News) 421, and "Excluding Children from Children's Hearings", Kenneth

McK Norrie, 1993 SLT (News) 67. If the child's attendance is dispensed with, the reasons for this should be relayed to the parents when the hearing commences. The panel are obliged to ascertain that the person appearing before them is a child within the meaning of the legislation (s 55).

(b) The parents. The attendance of parents must then be considered, including the issue of who is a parent or guardian — this in itself can be a complex issue. The parents may not be married, in which case the natural father, unless he can be considered to be a guardian (*C v Kennedy*, 1991 SLT 735), may not be entitled to attend as a parent but might be entitled to attend as either the mother's or the child's representative (see (c) below), or may be excluded if he is not attending in either of these capacities. A child may consider a particular man to be its parent and the panel may have been advised in a report that this is not so: an example of the type of information it would be detrimental to reveal in the course of a hearing if the child were present. Indeed, the man himself may not know that he is not the child's father! If a parent or parents do not attend, and it is considered that in order to reach a decision their attendance is required, the panel must be aware of what steps might be taken to bring about a parent's attendance (s 41 (3)). Parents have an absolute right to be present at all stages of a hearing (s 41 (1)), unless the hearing is satisfied that it would be unreasonable to require attendance or that attendance would be unnecessary to consideration of the case (s 41 (2)).

(c) Representative(s). Although the child and parents have a statutory right to have a representative present (and it may be the same person for both), the chairman may exclude the representative if satisfied that he or she is persisting in behaviour which is disruptive to the hearing, or which is likely to be detrimental to the interests of the child (rule 11 (3)).

(d) Other parties with statutory or discretionary rights of attendance. The chairman of the hearing must also be aware of other parties who have statutory rights to attend hearings (s 35 (3) and rules 12 and 13). The chairman may exercise discretionary powers so far as other parties are concerned (rule 14), but must take all reasonable steps to ensure that the number of persons present at any one time is kept to a minimum (s 35 (2)). The chairman must impress upon all parties the confidentiality of the proceedings (s 35 (1)).

(3) Purpose of the hearing

Unless a hearing is considering the case of a child in the absence of the child, his parent and any representative, the chairman is obliged to explain the purpose of the hearing before the children's hearing proceed to consider the case (rule 19 (1); see also "Excluding Children from Children's Hearings", Kenneth McK Norrie, supra).

(4) Grounds of referral

If there are grounds of referral — normally at a first hearing but possibly also at review hearings when there may be new or further grounds — it is the chairman's duty to explain to the child and .the parents the grounds of referral and establish which grounds are accepted by all of them (s 42 (1)). Care must be taken that the family understand the grounds, and it is not sufficient for grounds merely to be read. Legal terms such as "art and part" may need to be explained and panel members may, when grounds relating to sexual abuse have been formulated, have to elucidate in simple language the meaning of phrases such as "lewd and libidinous behaviour" or establish if the child understands the parts of the body which are being referred to, or what the family euphemism for such parts might be. The hearing must then establish if all, or any, of the grounds are accepted. If so, the hearing may proceed to consider the case of the child (s 41 (2) (a)). If the grounds are accepted in part, the hearing may proceed on the grounds (or parts of the grounds) which are accepted, or refer the matter to the sheriff for proof, or discharge the case (s 42 (2) (b)). If the grounds are not accepted, the hearing may either send the matter to the sheriff or discharge the referral (s 42 (2) (c)).

Clearly, the grounds of referral, which form the basis of the panel's jurisdiction over the child, are crucial, and panel members must have a very clear understanding of the issues relating to acceptance or denial of grounds. If some grounds are accepted and others denied, there may be problematic issues relating to the manner in which the case is then discussed. While the Court of Session has decided that the whole circumstances of a child may be considered (*O v Rae*, 1993 SLT 570), panel members must endeavour to ensure that if they have discharged certain grounds that have been denied, those grounds do not inform their consideration of the case.

When a case is sent for proof, the chairman of the hearing must explain to the child and parents the purpose of the referral to the sheriff and inform the child that he is obliged to attend unless his or her attendance has been dispensed with by a sheriff (s 42 (3)). It is good practice to advise the family to consult a solicitor as soon as possible, if they wish to be legally represented, and also to inform them that they may be entitled to legal aid.

Panel members must also be aware that if the child is not capable of understanding the grounds of referral, then — even if the grounds are accepted by the parents — the hearing cannot proceed and panel members may either discharge or refer to the sheriff (s 42 (7)). The hearing must also know that if a parent is not present and the grounds of referral are accepted by the child, the hearing may proceed, although consideration should be given as to whether that would be the best course of action in the long run (s 42 (8)) and whether it might not be preferable to continue the hearing and request the reporter to endeavour to contact the parent and encourage attendance.

(5) The discussion

The 1986 Rules state that "The chairman shall inform the child and parents of the substance of any reports, documents and information" if it seems material to the manner in which the case is disposed of, and its disclosure would not be detrimental to the interests of the child (rule 19 (3)). It is, in fact, good practice for this duty to be shared by the panel members as a team (see "Preparation: Stage 2", above). The hearing must endeavour to obtain the views of the child, parents and any safeguarder who may be appointed and attending the hearing, on what arrangements with respect to the child would be in the child's best interests (rule 19 (2) (d)). The disposal decision should not, therefore, come as a surprise to the family as options should have been considered by the hearing.

If there is informality in the procedure at hearings, it is manifested only at the discussion stage when panel members must exercise very considerable skills in questioning and listening (and being aware of non-verbal communication signals). In meeting their legal obligations, they must try to open up discussion with what may be very reluctant family members, deal with strong emotions, and keep their own feelings in check. They must attempt to be non-judgmental about family practices which they may well abhor, and they must try to understand the context of the particular family's life. Most families who attend hearings are likely to be suffering from multiple disadvantage and there may be problems with, for example, relationships, housing, employment, alcohol or drug abuse, to be taken into account. Panel members must also be aware of the consequences of removal of children from home, the likelihood of rehabilitation being a possibility, and whether the standard of parenting — while perhaps not meeting their own standards — is "good enough". They must also — crucially — be able to challenge constructively the opinions of professionals and must be seen not to be "rubber stamping" recommendations but using their independent judgment to determine the child's best interests.

The chairman is required to consider whether it is necessary to appoint a safeguarder, for the purpose of safeguarding the interests of the child because there is or may be a conflict between the interests of the child and parents, on any matter relevant to the proceedings (s 34A). Any safeguarder so appointed is entitled to be present throughout the duration of any hearing until the disposal of the child's case. Hearings must also consider whether they have sufficient information to make a decision, or whether they wish to continue the hearing (and this may include removal of the child from home for a period of assessment (s 34 (4)).

Panels must understand what legal disposals are available and what conditions, if any, may be attached thereto (ss 43 and 44). It must be clear that the supervision relates to the child, not the parents, however much the parents' behaviour may be "the problem". If a panel wishes a social worker to undertake a particular programme of work with a child or family, the plan and the reasons therefor should be clearly spelt out when the decision is announced. Unlike judges, panel members may not make avizandum or withdraw to discuss their decisions amongst themselves.

(6) The decision
When a hearing has reached a decision, having followed all the necessary procedures in the discussion stage, but before the proceedings are concluded, the chairman must (rule 19 (4)) inform the child, parents and any safeguarder, of the decision, the reasons for the decision, the right of the child and of the parent to appeal to the sheriff against the decision (s 49 (1)), and of the right to receive a statement in writing of the reasons for the decision (rule 20). It is good practice to make a positive offer to send reasons to the family. If the child or parents seem to be at all unhappy with the decision — and that is, of course, an inevitable possibility given the nature of the matters which hearings are considering — it is also good practice for the chairman, in advising them of their right to appeal against the decision within three weeks, to indicate that they may be entitled to legal aid and should consult a solicitor if they so wish.

As soon as possible after a children's hearing, the chairman "shall make or cause to be made" a report of the decision and a statement in writing of the reasons for the decision, and shall sign the statement and report (rule 9 (3)). It is good practice for all three panel members to contribute to the writing of the reasons, particularly after a long and complex hearing. Written reasons must not vary

from the verbal decision communicated to the family. They must be capable of being a record for the family (and be comprehensible to them), be a guide for a future hearing and, at the same time, fulfil the requirement that, in the event of an appeal, a sheriff will be able to understand what the hearing's thinking was in reaching the decision. In the early days of the hearings system, panel members were less skilled in this respect (see *K v Finlayson*, 1974 SLT (Sh Ct) 51).

(7) Review procedure
The final stage in a hearing is for the chairman to advise the family that a supervision requirement may be reviewed (s 48) and to spell out the details of the process. The hearing must also be aware that there is an automatic review after three months where a supervision requirement with a condition of secure accommodation has been made (s 58 (c)) and explain this to the family.

The procedures outlined above relate to "standard" hearings. Panel members must also be aware of and carry out legal requirements in relation to emergency hearings, transfers of children, boarding out and fostering regulations, and a host of other provisions. They may also be called upon by sheriffs and, indeed, the High Court of Justiciary, for advice on disposal of the case of a child who has offended. While the reporter is always present and can be consulted, it is incumbent upon panel members to have a thorough basic knowledge of the legislation and to be competent in implementing it.

The government have indicated in the white paper *Scotland's Children* their intention of strengthening the powers of the hearing system. The children's hearing system — with whatever flaws it may have — is still regarded worldwide as an enlightened system. A children's hearing is not a forum wherein a bunch of do-gooders get together with a family to have a blether about what to do about their difficulties. It is a legally constituted tribunal which has a clear structure and which conforms to a complex set of procedural requirements. Panel members are skilled and committed people who undertake an unenviable and not always appreciated task in dealing with some of the most intractable problems facing children in our society.

[The writer is grateful to Professor Robert Black and Dr Kenneth Norrie for their comments on an earlier draft of this article. The views expressed in it are entirely her own.]

Design Right and Artistic Works — Transitional Provisions

The writer would reply to the article on unregistered design rights (1994 SLT (News) 67). That article illustrates the nature and recent development of unregistered design rights created by s 213 of the Copyright, Designs and Patents Act 1988. It also suggests, in the context of *Squirewood Ltd v H Morris & Co Ltd*, OH, 1 April 1993, unreported (1993 GWD 20-1239) a limitation contained in s 51 of that Act to the use of copyright in artistic works in the field of design and manufacture.

Design rights per se only apply to designs recorded or articles made in accordance with the design after 1 August 1989: see s 213 (6) and (7) of the 1988 Act. So the continuing but temporary importance of copyright in "artistic" works in the design field should not be overlooked. The importance of this stems from the argument which prevailed in *British Leyland v Armstrong Patents* [1986] AC 577, which was that original engineering drawings of purely functional objects nevertheless had copyright as artistic works. This copyright was infringed, albeit indirectly, by the manufacture of the items depicted in the drawings. The process of manufacture of those items by copying the relevant articles, described

as reverse engineering, inevitably reproduced the original drawings of the articles in material form in three dimensions. This involved a restricted act: see ss 2, 3, 9 (8) and 48 of the Copyright Act 1956 and equivalent provisions, namely ss 4, 16 and 17 (3) of the 1988 Act.

Under s 51 of the 1988 Act, the right to prevent reverse engineering by means of copyright in artistic works (inasmuch as these happen to be design documents) is abolished. That section is only partially in force. It does not yet apply to such design documents in existence before 1 August 1989. Under transitional provisions, its effect in relation to these documents is suspended for 10 years until 1 August 1999. Thus there is still considerable scope for the use of copyright in design cases until then: see para 19 (1) of Sched 1 to the 1988 Act and SI 1989/816.

It should also be noted, however, that the usual terms of copyright in artistic works, namely life of author plus 50 years, is limited in the foregoing industrial cases under s 52 of the 1988 Act. The term is reduced to 25 years from first marketing of relevant articles in certain circumstances where articles have been marketed after 1 August 1989: see para 20 (2) of Sched 1 to the 1988 Act and the Copyright (Industrial Process and Excluded Articles) (No 2) Order 1989 (SI 1989/1070).

R A S

♦

NEWS

Appointment

New Keeper of the Registers

The Secretary of State for Scotland, with the consent of the Lord President of the Court of Session, has appointed Mr Alan W Ramage to be Keeper of the Registers of Scotland from 1 July. He succeeds Mr James W Barron who is retiring. Since 1990 Mr Ramage, who has spent his working life in the Registers of Scotland, has occupied the post of (Senior) Director of Central Services (Principal Establishment and Finance Officer) in the Registers.

— ◇ —

Law reform

Scottish Law Commission: contract law

The Scottish Law Commission in a new discussion paper (no 97), *Extrinsic Evidence, Supersession, and the Actio Quanti Minoris* ask for comments on a number of provisional proposals for reform of Scottish contract law.

Restrictive rules of evidence
(a) Extrinsic evidence to prove additional term of contract. Under the present law, when a document has been drawn up which appears to contain the terms of a contract, no evidence of anything outside the document itself can be led to prove an additional term. This can cause

injustice. One party may have refused to sign a document setting out the contract unless the other agreed that there was an additional term not mentioned in the document. The other party may have agreed to this additional term before witnesses, or may have acknowledged it in an informal writing, but if a dispute arises as to what are the contract terms a court, under the existing law, may refuse to allow evidence of the additional term to be led.

The commission suggest that the rule which disallows extrinsic evidence to prove an additional term of a contract in such circumstances should be replaced by a presumption that a document which appears to contain all the express terms of a contract does contain all those terms and that this presumption should be capable of being rebutted, extrinsic evidence being admissible for that purpose.

(b) Extrinsic evidence in the interpretation of contracts. It is widely recognised that the existing Scottish rules on the admissibility of extrinsic evidence in the interpretation of written contracts are unsatisfactory. The general rule is that extrinsic evidence is not admissible but there are numerous vague and overlapping exceptions, with the result that the law is very difficult to state and apply. The commission seek views on proposals which would (a) tighten up the substantive law on the process of interpretation, by making it even more clear than it is already that the subjective uncommunicated intentions of the parties are irrelevant, and (b) make all *relevant* evidence admissible.

The effect would be a simplification and rationalisation of the law but, because of the scope of the existing exceptions, the main change of substance would be in relation to *relevant* evidence of prior negotiations and subsequent actings.

Supersession of contract by conveyance
In recent years a great deal of difficulty has been caused by the rule that, where a contract is followed by a conveyance which is intended to implement it, the contract is entirely superseded by the conveyance. In practice solicitors attempt to get round this difficulty by various methods, but there are doubts about the effectiveness of some of these methods and, at best, they require provisions which may be elaborate and ought to be unnecessary.

The commission suggest that it should be provided by statute that (a) any rule of law whereby, regardless of the intentions of the parties, terms of a contract are superseded by the

execution or delivery of a conveyance or other deed intended to implement or give effect to that contract in whole or in part should cease to have effect, but that (b) the conveyance or other deed should supersede the contract insofar as (but only insofar as) it implements or gives effect to the contract.

No damages unless property returned
There is a general rule that a buyer of property cannot, while keeping the property, successfully claim damages for breach by the seller of a contractual term relating to the property which results in a diminution in its value. The law of Scotland, it is said, does not allow an actio quanti minoris. This rule, which probably crept into Scots law as a result of a confusion between two rules of Roman law, was changed over 100 years ago in relation to the sale of goods, but in relation to property other than moveables it remains in operation and is harmful in its operation. There are many cases where the buyer of a house would be most unwilling to reconvey the house and start looking for another one. It is unrealistic to make the return of the property a condition of claiming damages for a breach of contract by the seller. The commission therefore suggest that this rule of law should cease to have effect.

Time for comments
Comments on the provisional proposals in the discussion paper are invited by 30 September 1994.

General

City Disputes Panel
A new dispute resolution body offering arbitration and mediation in financial services disputes became operational on 18 April 1994.

Entitled the City Disputes Panel (CDP), the new body, which has been supported by the Corporation of London, will provide the wholesale financial services industry with its own, specialist, arbitral organisation. Until now there has been no such body specifically to serve the needs of parties in dispute over financial matters, whether the disputes were between market professionals themselves or between market professionals and their clients.

The CDP will function outside the consumer areas served by the arbitration and conciliation schemes administered by the regulatory bodies for the benefit of small investors.

CDP members will have the opportunity of resolving disputes otherwise than through the courts, and will benefit from a private, speedy, adaptable, more economic and wholly modern system of arbitration and dispute resolution designed specifically for the banking and financial services industry. Membership is open, for an annual subscription of £400 plus VAT for corporate members and £100 plus VAT for individuals, to financial institutions, corporations, firms and individuals.

A set of model arbitration rules, incorporating many up to date features in the interests of practicality and speed, has been prepared by John Hall, QC, in consultation with a working party comprising Lord Ackner, Arthur Marriott and Richard Freeman.

A link with Scotland has been established through sponsorship by the Faculty of Advocates. Other organisations in the City have given monetary and advisory assistance towards the project.

A handbook has been published by the panel, whose current (temporary) address is 32 Farringdon Street, London EC4A 4HT (tel 071-212 1590; fax 071-212 1638).

◊

Edinburgh Bar Association
The following office bearers for the Edinburgh Bar Association have been elected for 1994: *President*, Alex Prentice; *vice president*, Alasdair Loudon; *secretary*, Fergus Christie, Burnett Christie, 53 George IV Bridge, Edinburgh; *treasurer*, Fiona Cooper; *librarian*, Alastair Milne.

◊

Sottish Law Librarians Group
The Scottish Law Librarians Group have published a Union List of Overseas Material comprising information on the collections of primary foreign jurisdiction legal materials held in Scotland. The Union List, compiled and edited by Susan Mansfield and Kathleen Davidson, is indexed by jurisdiction and provides a list of contributors with a key to lending restrictions. Copies are available, priced £10 plus £1.50 p & p, from Kathleen Davidson, Fyfe Ireland, WS, Orchard Brae House, 130 Queensferry Road, Edinburgh EH4 2HG.

— ◊ —

Taxation

Income tax: self assessment anti-avoidance provisions
The Financial Secretary to the Treasury has announced the broad scope of provisions that the government intend to introduce in the next Finance Bill to counter avoidance of tax through manipulation of the rules for the transition from the preceding year basis to the current year basis of income tax.

At present income taxed under Sched D is assessed on a preceding year basis except in the first and last years of trading. Under the rules in the Finance Bill 1994, such income will from 1997-98 be taxed on a current year basis. Businesses commencing after 5 April 1994 — or deemed to commence under s 113 (1) ICTA 1988 following a change after that date in the membership of a partnership — will be immediately taxed on the new current year basis.

1996-97 will be a transitional year for which the rules for computation are set out in Sched 19 to the Finance Bill 1994. Tax for this year will normally be assessed on the profits from the end of the 1995-96 basis period (the accounting date ending in 1994-95) to the latest accounting date ending in 1996-97 (the "transitional basis period"). In the normal cases that will be a 24 month period, and one half of the profits will be taxed. In cases where the accounting date is changed, the period may be longer or shorter.

Under the new rules, the 1997-98 assessment will normally be based on the 12 months' accounts ending in that year. That proportion of the profits which arises before 5 April 1997 will be available — as transitional relief — for deduction from the profits of the final period of trading, or, if earlier, when the accounting date of the business moves to 5 April. This means that eventually the profits arising in the period immediately preceding 5 April 1997 (the "transitional relief period") will drop out of account.

The proposed anti-avoidance provisions will cancel any tax advantage that might accrue from artificial movement of profits into periods of account that form the transitional basis period or the transitional relief period. In certain circumstances such counteraction will extend to taxing in full, as well as in a proportionate amount, profits which are artificially moved into the 1996-97 period. Similarly the amount of transitional relief may be reduced by the full amount of the profits shifted into the basis period for 1997-98 of which the transitional relief period forms a part.

In some circumstances, businesses will be taxed for 1996-97 on the actual profits arising in the year to 5 April 1997. Such businesses will not be affected by the proposed provisions.

The legislation will take a four step approach. The first step is to identify the type of transaction, event or change in practice — referred to collectively as "triggers" — which may bring taxpayers within the scope of the anti-avoidance rules. Those triggers are: (a) a change of one accounting policy for another or a modification within one policy; (b) transactions with persons with whom the taxpayer has some family or proprietorial link (typically "connected" persons) including partnerships; (c) arrangements with unconnected persons which are wholly or partly reciprocal or self cancelling, for example the sale of stock immediately before the end of the transitional basis period and repurchase immediately afterwards; (d) changes in business behaviour, which need not involve any changes in accounting policy. This would mean any change in a settled practice of a trade, profession or vocation as to the timing of any of the following: on the incoming side of a business — the supply of goods or services, the invoicing of customers or clients and the collection of debts (including payments on account); on the expenditure side of a business — the obtaining of goods or services, the incurring of business expenses and the settlement of outstanding debts (including making payments on account).

Any case that falls into one of these four categories will be regarded as raising a prima facie case for challenge that avoidance has taken place unless either: (a) the obtaining of a tax advantage arising from an increase in the profits of the transitional basis period, or as the case may be of the transitional relief period, is not the main benefit or one of the main benefits that can reasonably be expected to arise from the trigger; or (b) the business can show that the triggering transaction was undertaken solely for bona fide commercial reasons. Obtaining a tax advantage will not be such a reason; or (c) the absolute and relative amounts of profits shifted into particular periods fall below a prescribed limit, or the turnover of the business is less than a prescribed amount. The legislation will provide powers to make regulations to set these amounts which will be announced by 5 April 1997. The government's intention is to deter people from undertaking triggering transactions; it is therefore not appropriate at this stage to indicate the level at which these limits will be set.

If the business is not excluded by any one of the tests in the preceding paragraph, the increase in profits identified for the transitional basis period will be charged in full in addition to the profits averaged down, without any adjustments to the profits for any other year of assessment. For the transitional relief period, the transitional relief will be reduced by the full amount of the profits moved into the basis period for 1997-98.

Income taxed under cases III-V of Sched D on the preceding year basis will, under the transitional rules, be assessed for 1996-97 on half of the income arising in the two years to 5 April 1997. Broadly similar rules to those applying for trades, professions and vocations will apply to income — other than interest — which is artificially moved into these periods. Such income is not subject to transitional relief.

Further provisions will deal with interest received and paid.

◊

Income tax: handling of excess payments

The Inland Revenue have announced the introduction of new computer support for handling certain overpayments from 5 April 1994, relating to income tax, Scheds A and D, capital gains tax, higher rate tax, national insurance contributions (class 4) and associated interest.

Under the new arrangements, the majority of overpayments due to be set against other liabilities for the same taxpayer or repaid will be handled automatically by computer in the accounts offices at Cumbernauld and Shipley. Any interest and/or repayment supplement will be likewise automatically calculated.

Taxpayers will receive computer printed letters setting out details of the overpayment and the way it has been dealt with. Where appropriate, a computer printed payable order will be attached to the letter. In line with normal Inland Revenue policy and procedures, detailed computations of revised and repaid interest and repayment supplement will not be issued automatically. However, should a taxpayer require a computation showing how any revised interest or repayment supplement has been calculated, this information will be provided on request.

Under the new system, taxpayers may continue to authorise accountants or other nominees to receive repayment. The taxpayer's authority should be sent to the tax office in the same way as in the past. The tax office will then arrange for the repayment to be sent to the authorised person.

◊

Income tax: PAYE

The Chancellor of the Exchequer has tabled two new clauses to the Finance Bill and a number of related drafting amendments which introduce measures to ensure that PAYE can continue to be operated in particular circumstances.

One of the measures is intended to apply when employees who are not resident or, if resident, not ordinarily resident, in the UK come to work in the UK. This measure will ensure that, where such an employee's liability to tax in the UK is, or may be, limited to the emoluments for work done in the UK, and at the time the emoluments are paid the proportion liable to tax under Sched E in the UK is uncertain, the tax can continue to be collected under PAYE. The measure will remove doubts that have arisen that PAYE should be operated in such circumstances. It will also confirm the validity of PAYE collection in the past.

A second measure aims to put beyond doubt the power of the Inland Revenue in certain circumstances to collect PAYE tax from the people for whom employees of another person work if their employer does not operate PAYE on payments made to them. This can apply in circumstances where all the parties involved are based in the UK.

— ◇ —

Obituary

On 13 April 1994, Robert Holms, formerly partner in the firm of Messrs Paterson, Holms & Co, solicitors, Glasgow.

— ◇ —

Business changes

Messrs Johnston & Herron, solicitors, Lochgelly and Cowdenbeath, announce the appointment of Alexander R F Baxter as a consultant with effect from 6 April 1994.

L & L Lawrence, 18 Woodside Terrace, Glasgow, intimate that Fiona D McKeracher ceased to be a partner of the firm with effect from 24 March 1994.

— ◇ —

Parliamentary News

New Bills

HOUSE OF COMMONS

16 March 1994

Social Security Regulations (Chronic Bronchitis and Emphysema) Amendment—To amend the Social Security (Industrial Injuries) (Prescribed Diseases) Regulations to reduce to 10 years the aggregate period of underground work required to qualify for benefits in cases of chronic bronchitis and emphysema; to amend the rules relating to medical assessment of percentage levels of disablement in people suffering from these conditions; and for connected purposes. (Private Member's Bill introduced by Mr Michael Clapham)

22 March 1994

Freedom to Roam (Access to Countryside)—To provide for codification of law to ensure public access to the countryside and to define obligations and responsibilities for the public and landowners alike; and for connected purposes. (Private Member's Bill introduced by Mrs Margaret Ewing)

23 March 1994

Withdrawal of Medical Treatment—To prescribe circumstances in which medical treatment and nutrition can be withdrawn and to secure the continued provision in such circumstances of palliative care; and for connected purposes. (Private Member's Bill introduced by Mr Gary Waller)

29 March 1994

Stray Dogs—To allow local authorities to identify permanently a stray dog before returning it to its owner; and for connected purposes. (Private Member's Bill introduced by Ms Jean Corston)

30 March 1994

Picture Manipulation—To require news media to prepare a code of practice to cover the principles by which pictures may be edited, altered or changed using computer techniques and to record clearly when old film is being used and when the person presenting the film was not present during its filming. (Private Member's Bill introduced by Mr Andrew F Bennett)

18 April 1994

Social Security Regulations (Chronic Bronchitis And Emphysema) Amendment (No 2)—To reduce to 10 years the aggregate period of underground work required to qualify for benefits in cases of chronic bronchitis and emphysema; to amend the regulations relating to medical examinations for these diseases; to amend provisions relating to the percentage levels of disablement required to qualify for benefits in respect of these diseases; and for connected purposes. (Private Member's Bill introduced by Mr Michael Clapham)

19 April 1994

Water Charge (Amendment)—To amend the Water Act 1989 to prohibit the use by water undertakers of rateable values as a basis for charging from 31 March 1995; to provide for charging by water undertakers in accordance with council tax bands; and for connected purposes. (Private Member's Bill introduced by Mr Paul Tyler)

19 April 1994

Public Conveniences—To remove any discrimination on grounds of gender in the provision of public conveniences and to place a statutory duty on local authorities to provide a minimum level of public conveniences; and for connected purposes. (Private Member's Bill introduced by Mr Jon Owen Jones)

Progress of Bills

Criminal Justice and Public Order — Commons: third reading, 13 April 1994.

Merchant Shipping (Salvage and Pollution) — Commons: third reading, 15 April 1994.

Antarctic — Commons: third reading, 15 April 1994.

Parliamentary Commissioner — Commons: third reading, 15 April 1994.

Trade Marks — Commons: second reading, 18 April 1994.

Finance — Commons: remaining stages, 19 and 20 April 1994.

Treasure — Lords: report, 20 April 1994.

National Parks — Lords: report, 20 April 1994.

Questions answered

HOUSE OF COMMONS

23 March 1994

BAIL

Mr Gallie: To ask the Secretary of State for Scotland what steps are being taken to stop perceived abuse of bail in Scotland.

Lord James Douglas-Hamilton: Reducing bail abuse is a high priority for us. We have commissioned major research into bail decision making and the report of the research should be available in the next few weeks. We have also taken steps to improve statistical information on

bail abuse so that we have a better understanding of both the nature and the scale of the problem.

We are considering with the Crown Office, the police and the courts what further legislative and administrative action may be necessary for Scotland.

30 March 1994

ADOPTION

Mr David Marshall: To ask the Secretary of State for Scotland (1) what future arrangements he plans for adoption agencies and prospective adopters; and if he will make a statement; (2) what specific proposals he has to ensure that adoption services are part of the full range of child care services which will require to be provided by each of the new local authorities; (3) what assessment he has made of the adequacy of the arrangements for adoption following local government reorganisation; what co-ordination there will be; who will provide funding; and if he will make a statement; (4) what arrangements he intends making to ensure that children have the opportunity of adoption in each of the new local authority areas.

Mr Allan Stewart: Adoption is, and will continue to be, an important part of the range of services available for the care of children. Adoption law has been subject to extensive review and consultation in Scotland over the last few years and we propose to publish a policy statement shortly.

Reorganisation of local government will clearly involve some restructuring of services and every care will be taken to ensure that services available now will be maintained, including those provided by adoption agencies. The strategic child care plans which are to be developed from the proposals in the White Paper "Scotland's Children" are of direct relevance in this context. Scottish Office officials have had preliminary discussions about reorganisation with the British Agencies for Adoption and Fostering which are grant aided by the Government and which have an important national role to play in the development of adoption services.

14 April 1994

MINERAL WORKINGS

Mr Kynoch: To ask the Secretary of State for Scotland whether he has yet set a date for publication of the national planning policy guideline on land for mineral working; and if he will make a statement.

Mr Lang: I have today published the national planning policy guideline — NPPG — on land for mineral working. Copies are available in the Library.

This is the first comprehensive planning policy statement on the working of minerals in Scotland. It seeks to promote economic activity without compromising Scotland's important environmental assets. In so doing, it introduces a general presumption in favour of properly assessed and controlled mineral extraction, cautions against such activity in particularly sensitive locations, and requires high standards of environmental care. It also commends a greater reliance on renewable and recycled materials, in line with our undertakings in the recently published "UK Sustainable Development Strategy", Cm 2426.

In addition, the NPPG provides explicit guidance on coastal superquarries. I have concluded that such developments have a potentially important contribution to make to the economy at both national and local level, but that their scale and potential impact require them to be controlled carefully. Based on previous research and a preference for a dispersed geographical pattern, I have therefore stipulated preferred search areas on the north coast of Highland Region, in the Shetland Isles and in the Western Isles. In the first instance, I have also chosen to limit numbers, allowing for no more than four such developments, including the existing superquarry at Glensanda, over the 15-year period to 2009. Proposals will be notified to me accordingly.

This will be subject to review in the normal manner. In the meantime, I believe it represents a realistic strategy that will allow a sensible balance to be struck between social and economic benefits on the one hand and environmental care on the other.

15 April 1994

COURTS SERVICE

Mr Meacher: To ask the Parliamentary Secretary, Lord Chancellor's Department what are his plans for privatisation in the courts service; what plans he has to achieve them within the terms of the Deregulation and Contracting Out Bill; and what plans he has to seek the repeal of s 27 of the Courts Act 1971 before the contracting out or privatising of the courts service.

Mr John M Taylor: There are no plans either to privatise any part of the court service in the sense of the private sector taking over responsibility for ensuring the provision of court services or to repeal s 27 of the Courts Act 1971. However, the Deregulation and Contracting Out Bill would amend that section to enable the Lord Chancellor to contract with others to provide staff to carry out administrative work in the Supreme Court and county courts and hence enable him to market test any such work where doing so was likely to improve the value for money of the services concerned and would not risk impugning the independence or probity of the judicial process. The Government has decided, however, that there will be no market testing in the court service at least until it has been launched as an executive agency in April 1995.

AGGRAVATED TRESPASS

Mr McFall: To ask the Secretary of State for Scotland what representations he has received in respect of the aggravated trespass clause in the Criminal Justice and Public Order Bill with regard to Scotland.

Lord James Douglas-Hamilton: My right hon friend has received representations to the effect that the provisions of the clause will be used to obstruct lawful outdoor activity in Scotland, such as hill walking. There has also been some support for the clause.

Replies to those who have expressed concern about the clause have made it clear that its purpose is to ensure that those engaging in lawful activities, whoever and whatever they may be, are provided with protection from trespassers who intend to intimidate them or otherwise intend to obstruct or disrupt those activities.

19 April 1994

TAXES MANAGEMENT ACT 1970

Mr Wallace: To ask the Chancellor of the Exchequer what proposals he has to consult interested parties regarding any future amendment of s 20A of the Taxes Management Act 1970; and if he will make a statement.

Mr Dorrell: The Inland Revenue is at present consulting the accountancy and legal professions over its draft guidance notes on the use of s 20A. The Government will be considering how to take the matter forward in the light of any responses to the draft guidance notes and the points made in committee.

PRISON CAPACITY

Dr Godman: To ask the Secretary of State for Scotland if he will make a statement about capacity limits for prison accommodation.

Lord James Douglas-Hamilton: Responsibility for the subject of the question has been delegated to the Scottish Prison Service under its chief executive, Mr E W Frizzell. I have asked him to arrange for a reply to be given.

Letter from E W Frizzell to Dr Norman A Godman, dated 19 April 1994:

"Lord James Douglas-Hamilton has asked me to reply to your Question about capacity limits for prison accommodation.

"As at 1 April 1994, the design capacity of the prisons estate in Scotland was 5,736, largely in the form of single cell accommodation. Allowing for cells not available because of redecoration or damage repair work, refurbishment (including in some cases to provide night sanitation) or for other policy reasons (including being retained in the event of an emergency), a total of 5,159 places were in use at that time."

Book Reviews

Common Market Law of Competition

By Christopher Bellamy and Graham Child.
Fourth edition by Vivien Rose. 1993.
London: Sweet & Maxwell. Hardback, £165.
ISBN 0 421 48930 8.

This long awaited fourth edition was published exactly 20 years after the appearance of the first, and six years after the third. Its size in itself indicates the enormous expansion of EC competition law during the intervening years. Compared with the last edition, the substantive text has increased from 634 to 953 pages, while the appendices now cover some 395 pages as opposed to 217 in 1987. The main structure of the previous edition has been largely retained, although there have been some changes reflecting the growth of the materials in particular areas. Thus, there is now a fuller treatment of mergers and acquisitions, and each of the "special sectors" (public undertakings, agriculture, transport, energy and coal and steel) is discussed in a separate chapter.

The cut off date of the new edition is stated to be generally 1 January 1993, but some important materials appearing after that date have been incorporated, such as the *Wood Pulp* and *BPB Industries* judgments; Regulation 151/93 amending four block exemption regulations; and the Commission's notices on co-operative joint ventures and on co-operation between national courts and the Commission in applying EC competition law.

The very high standard of the previous editions is fully maintained. Major decisions of the European Court and of the Commission are thoroughly discussed in an analytical manner, while others are either summarised or listed in the footnotes. The treatment of the subject is as full as is reasonably possible and is wholly reliable. In addition to academic writings, there are very useful references to the Commission's annual *Reports on Competition Policy* which contain invaluable information, some of which is unavailable elsewhere in a published form. Although contributed to by no less than 13 contributors, the style is clear and consistent throughout, and this makes the book suitable for use not only by competition law experts but by virtually anyone possessing a basic grasp of Community law. The typographical presentation is also of an extremely high standard, there being very few errors either in the print or in the references (one such error occurs at the top of p 540 where the last five lines of the previous page have been reprinted, together with the relevant footnotes).

The present reviewer has been using this book since its first edition, both for private research and as a compulsory text for more advanced (honours and LLM) students. Over this long period, he has hardly ever come across any significant gap, mistake or misinterpretation of the law. In his opinion, this is one of the best overall presentations of EC competition law that is available in the English language. Hopefully, successive new editions will keep the book alive for many more years to come.

A G TOTH,
University of Strathclyde.

Labour Legislation and Public Policy

By Paul Davies and Mark Freedland. 1993.
Oxford: Clarendon Law Series. Paperback,
£19.95. ISBN 0 198 76060 4.

Law of Employment

Eighth edition. By Norman Selwyn. 1993.
London: Butterworth. Paperback, £18.95.
ISBN 0 406 02437 5.

It is difficult to imagine two more contrasting textbooks. The work by Davies and Freedland is a description as to how labour law has evolved since 1945. It explains the ways in which economic, political and social forces have influenced the development of the subject. The book is intended as a student text. However, it eschews the traditional approach of labour law textbooks, which is to provide an accurate snapshot of the law at a particular moment in time. In contrast, the very strength of Selwyn's work is its attempt to state the law of employment in a manner which is readable, accurate and up to date.

The work by Davies and Freedland is a masterly and scholarly analysis of the way that labour law has developed and the different pressures and policy considerations which have influenced that development. It is one of the most authoritative works that this reviewer has had the privilege to read. It not only taps into the ongoing debate about the modern philosophies of labour law but actually raises the issues to a new level by sustaining this philosophical approach over the entire post-war period in 667 pages of text. This reviewer has often felt that one of the potential weaknesses of labour law teaching is that there is a tendency to concentrate too much upon an explanation of the current legal rules with insufficient emphasis being placed upon public policy considerations. There can be no doubt that the Davies and Freedland book eradicates this weakness. However, the book goes further by enabling the reader to ascertain the policy considerations and political pressures which have influenced the shape of labour law at a particular period in the post-war era.

Given the thrust of the book it is not surprising that the bulk of the material is statute based. As the authors themselves admit, the book is a legislative history of employment law since 1945. From this perspective Davies and Freedland present the development of labour law as a political process and in this sense they challenge the orthodox approach of legal education that the law develops through the operation of the common law. There can be no doubt that common law principles do play an important role in labour law, but given the wealth of legislative intervention it is appropriate that a book such as this should concentrate exclusively on statutory developments. However, this does not mean that the book is simply a statement of the contents of the major labour law statutes which have been enacted since 1945. The authors appreciate the importance of administrative and other political factors in assessing the development of the subject. They also make it clear that labour law statutes are the products of the particular policy objectives pursued by the government of the day. In this way the book is also a fascinating account of how the various post-war governments have pursued their own particular agendas for labour law reform.

Even allowing for the quality of the work of Davies and Freedland, students will still want to know what is the content of the current rules of labour law. Norman Selwyn's book seeks to provide this service. It is a comprehensive and readable description of the body of statutory provisions and case law which constitute modern employment law. It is very much a rule based book and there is no attempt to describe the context in which these rules apply. Selwyn was criticised in this journal by the reviewer of the previous edition for failing to explain the application and coverage of the law in Scotland. The author has sought to take into account the differences in the law in Scotland. Thus the most glaring omissions have undoubtedly been remedied (though the statutory offences in the Public Order Act 1986 do not apply in Scotland — para 15.122). However, the problem is that although, by and large, the statutory rules of labour law are identical in the two jurisdictions, they are applied in the context of the two different legal systems. Obviously this means that the principles of the common law can diverge and in this regard the author should be applauded for seeking to explain, for example, how the legal basis for judicial review is different in Scotland. Equally, as Selwyn also points out, separate rules of procedure apply to industrial tribunals in Scotland.

But the real problem for the Scottish reader is that the book adopts a unitary view of labour law. As the author himself admits, the book is written from the general principle that the law is the same in both countries, and when Scottish cases are discussed the legal terminology has been transposed into English form. Thus a reader of this book would be entitled to assume that in the context of a restrictive covenant the appropriate remedy is an injunction based upon the principles laid down in *American Cyanamid v Ethicon Ltd* or that an *Anton Piller* order may be available, neither of which is the case in Scotland. Equally, in statutory areas there is no clear recognition that the Scottish courts and tribunals sometimes reach different interpretations from their English counterparts. Thus although Selwyn points out on the strength of *Meikle v McPhail* (a Scottish case) that the principles for redundancy set out in *Williams v Compair Maxam Ltd* do not apply to small firms or where there is no union, he is unable to convey the fact that the Scottish courts have generally been uneasy about the *Compair Maxam* case. The same point can also be made about the author's treatment of some of the case law associated with the transfer of an undertaking.

These points mean that it is still the case that the book must be used with care as far as Scotland is concerned.

KENNETH MILLER,
University of Strathclyde.

ARTICLES

The Fiscal Fine

Peter Duff, Kenneth Meechan, Michael
Christie and David Lessels,
Faculty of Law,
University of Aberdeen.

In the light of recent proposals for reform of criminal justice in Scotland, the authors outline the findings of their research study on fiscal fines, undertaken on behalf of the Crown Office.

Introduction

The fiscal fine, which came into existence at the beginning of 1988, has recently become an object of much interest. The latest Scottish Office consultation paper, forming part of the current review of criminal justice, has suggested that the scope of the fiscal fine might be extended (*Improving the Delivery of Justice in Scotland: Sentencing and Appeals*, chap 2: see 1994 SLT (News) 100). Furthermore, the recent Royal Commission on Criminal Justice in England and Wales recommended that, following the success of the fiscal fine in Scotland, a similar device should be introduced south of the border (Cm 2263 (1993), p 83).

At present, the Criminal Justice (Scotland) Act 1987, s 56 empowers a procurator fiscal to issue a "conditional offer" to an alleged offender in respect of any offence which could competently be tried in the district court, excluding those traffic offences already covered by the "fixed penalty" scheme. The Lord Advocate has directed that various other categories of offence are not suitable for a conditional offer, for example, cases where a compensation order would be appropriate and TV licence evasion cases (Crown Office Circulars nos 1933/3 and 1933/8).

The substance of a conditional offer is that if the alleged offender accepts, by paying a specified sum to the clerk of the relevant district court within 28 days (or such longer period as may be specified by the procurator fiscal), criminal proceedings are not brought. At present, the specified sum is set at £25 (SI 1987/2025). This is payable as a lump sum or in five instalments of £5. In the latter eventuality, the first payment constitutes acceptance and, thereafter, instalments must be paid on a fortnightly basis. Outstanding instalments may be pursued only through civil debt procedure and, consequently, failure to pay cannot lead to imprisonment. Finally, it is crucial to note that the acceptance of a conditional offer does not amount to a criminal conviction.

The Scottish Office consultation paper canvasses the possibility of expanding the fiscal fine mechanism to cover a wider range of offences. Two related — but not necessarily interdependent — options are suggested. First, the paper discusses whether the possibility of offering a fiscal fine might be extended to all statutory offences, perhaps by making the prosecution of all such offences competent in the district court (para 2.13). Secondly, it is suggested that the present fixed penalty of £25 might be replaced by some sort of sliding scale of penalties, possibly between £25 and £100 (paras 2.15-2.20).

At this stage, it ought to be noted that the Stewart committee, which originally recommended the introduction of the fiscal fine, envisaged the use of a variable penalty, subject to a maximum of £50, because of the flexibility this would provide (*Keeping Offenders Out of Court: Further Alternatives to Prosecution*, Second Report, Cmnd 8958 (1983), paras 4.36, 5.18). Ultimately, a sliding scale was not adopted because it was thought to involve too great a usurpation of the judicial function. It should also be emphasised that the Royal Commission recommended that if the device were to be adopted in England and Wales, "an appropriate range of fines" should be incorporated (p 83). Finally, it is worth pointing out that in continental jurisdictions, where the prosecutor fine is common, a sliding scale of penalties is the norm (see Stewart committee, paras 4.01-4.15).

Given the current interest in the fiscal fine, this is an opportune time to summarise the main findings of a large scale research exercise which sought to discover the way in which the mechanism operates in practice. The research was funded by the Crown Office and carried out by the authors between 1 April 1989 and 31 March 1991. (A full report is shortly to be published by the Scottish Office Central Research Unit.) The purpose of this article is simply to describe some of the main research findings, particularly those which are relevant to the issues canvassed in the Scottish Office consultation paper. The theoretical issues raised by the prosecutor fine — for instance, the implications of this type of "administrative justice", and whether its advent leads to "net-widening" by the criminal justice process rather than diversion — are explored at some length elsewhere, as is the most advanced form of the prosecutor fine, namely the Dutch "transaction" (P Duff, "The Prosecutor Fine and Social Control: The Introduction of the Fiscal Fine to Scotland" (1993) 33 *British Journal of Criminology* 481-503; and P Duff, "The

Prosecutor Fine", 1994 *Oxford Journal of Legal Studies* (forthcoming)).

Pattern of use

Since the introduction of the fiscal fine, fiscals have used it as follows:

	Number of fiscal fines	Percentage of all disposals
1988	9,304	2.7
1989	15,556	4.2
1990	16,985	4.5
1991	15,532	4.5
1992	17,777	4.6

Judging by these figures, it might well seem that the fiscal fine, as presently constituted, has reached about the limit of its use. Obviously, only a certain — and, as a result of inflation, probably decreasing — proportion of cases is likely to be thought suitable for a fixed penalty of £25: hence the suggestion in the Scottish Office consultation paper that a more flexible penalty be considered.

A detailed analysis of the Crown Office annual returns for the three years before and after the introduction of the fiscal fine — 1985 to 1990 inclusive — was carried out by the authors of this article. The exercise proved informative. First, it revealed that there were considerable variations in the use of the fiscal fine in different procurator fiscals' offices. In 1990, for instance, the proportion of crime reports disposed of by fiscal fine in the 10 largest offices — all dealing with over 10,000 cases annually — ranged from 2.2 to 12.3 per cent. Indeed, the latter rate was not exceeded in any of the other 39 offices. At the other end of the scale, one medium sized office — dealing with around 5,000 cases annually — offered only five fiscal fines, a usage rate of 0.1 per cent. Thus, the range of fiscal fine use is sufficiently great to mean that the national figures provide no more than a crude indication of what is happening across the country.

Secondly, the analysis exposed the pattern of use. As a preliminary, it must be noted that a fiscal has various options for the disposal of minor cases. A file may be marked for: no proceedings — known as a "no pro"; the issue of a warning letter; diversion for treatment by psychiatric or social work services or for reparation; a fiscal fine; or prosecution in the district court. To what extent has the introduction of the fiscal fine affected the use of these other disposals? In theory, only the number of district court prosecutions ought to have dropped because the reason for introducing the fiscal fine was to ease the pressure upon both the court system and the prosecution service. Further, the first Crown

Office Circular (1933/3) upon the subject makes it very clear that a fiscal fine should only be issued in a case which would otherwise merit prosecution.

Instead, the study revealed that, at the national level, it was the use of the "no pro" and the warning letter which had dropped, rather than the rate of prosecution in the district court. The pattern was one of "net-widening": more cases were being dragged further into the criminal justice process. This phenomenon probably represents to some extent the use of the fiscal fine in cases which previously fiscals would have liked to prosecute but refrained because of the pressure of business upon the district court. Nevertheless, the fiscal fine does appear to be used as an intermediate disposal, between district court prosecution and the "no pro" or warning letter. Despite this general conclusion, the pattern of use varied considerably between different offices. In brief, in 24 of the 49 offices, there was a statistically significant movement of cases from the "no pro" disposal to the fiscal fine; and in a further two offices, there was a movement from the warning letter to the fiscal fine. In 10 offices, there was a movement of cases from district court prosecution to the fiscal fine. In seven of these, there was also a move from the "no pro" or the warning letter to the fiscal fine (thus these offices also appear in the earlier figures). In eight offices, the only statistically significant movement of cases involved disposals other than the fiscal fine — e g from "no pro" to district court prosecution — and, in the remaining 12 offices, all with low fiscal fine usage rates, there was no statistically significant movement of cases at all. (For further interpretation of these figures and suggestions as to why the pattern was primarily one of "net-widening", see P Duff, 1993, op cit.)

Offences and offenders

A sample of cases where a fiscal fine was offered was monitored in six procurator fiscals' offices, producing a total of almost 600 cases. The relevant offices covered a wide geographical spread, and comprised four of the 10 busiest offices in the country and two of medium size.

The various offences in respect of which a fiscal fine was offered were:

172 breaches of the peace;
134 cases of urinating to public annoyance (Civic Government (Scotland) Act 1982, s 47);
76 thefts — of which 59 involved shoplifting;
54 offences under the various Railways Acts (primarily involving trespass on a railway line);
40 assaults;

35 cases of drunkenness at sports grounds (Criminal Justice (Scotland) Act 1980, s 74);

29 offences of being drunk and incapable (Civic Government (Scotland) Act 1982, s 50 (1); and small numbers of a variety of other offences, ranging from reset to a breach of the Litter Act 1983.

The pattern of offences was relatively similar in each office, subject to two qualifications. First, the bulk of the assault cases stemmed from one office, although it must be emphasised that fiscal fines were occasionally used in respect of assaults elsewhere. Nevertheless, this phenomenon did seem to represent a difference in "marking" policy. Secondly, most of the offences involving drunkenness at sports grounds derived from another office. There were probably two reasons for this: first, the fact that drinking associated with football matches is probably more common in this office's jurisdiction than elsewhere; and, secondly, the time of year at which the samples were gathered from the various offices.

As regards the four larger offices (the samples gathered from the two smaller offices being too small to allow much in the way of further analysis), the age and sex of those offered a fiscal fine did not vary greatly. The average age ranged between 27 and 30, and around half of each sample were under 25. Only a small minority of alleged offenders were female. In terms of occupation, the most interesting finding was that many of those offered a fiscal fine were unemployed. This is significant because there were fears that the benefits of the mechanism might be denied to the unemployed, as a result of a possible perception amongst fiscals that such persons would be unable to pay the fixed amount and should thus be prosecuted ab initio. In fact, the proportion of unemployed ranged from 22.3 to 61.2 per cent. These variations probably reflected regional differences in unemployment rates rather than any divergence in policy between offices. The proportion of professional persons offered a fiscal fine was around 5 per cent in each sample.

The proportion of those offered a fiscal fine who had no previous convictions varied from slightly under one third in one office to just over one half in two others. Further, the proportion of alleged offenders with 15 or more previous convictions ranged from 14 per cent in the former office to 5 per cent in one of the latter. The variation in these figures did seem to represent a difference in policy, in that fiscals from the first office confirmed that fiscal fines were often used in "hopeless cases" where yet another court appearance was seen as a waste of everybody's time. It was also interesting — but not surprising — that this office had a higher proportionate use of fiscal fines than the other offices.

For purposes of comparison, a sample of cases marked for prosecution in the district court was collected from one office. This group proved broadly similar in terms of age, sex and occupation to those offered a fiscal fine. However, around one half of those offered a fiscal fine had no previous convictions compared to just under one third of those who were prosecuted. Fiscals from this office confirmed that they were more likely to offer a first time offender a fiscal fine.

A final point about the alleged offences and offenders is worth emphasising. Out of a grand total of almost 600 offers of a fiscal fine, very few seemed to be inappropriate. In one assault case, however, the accused forced his way into his ex-girlfriend's home and repeatedly punched and kicked her on the face and legs while she tried to eject him. The offence seemed rather serious for the offer of a fiscal fine. Similarly, in a case of shoplifting, the nature of the offender seemed to render a fiscal fine somewhat inappropriate: the accused had no fixed abode; no income; was undergoing psychiatric treatment; had made no attempt to disguise the act in question; and, upon arrest, was obviously mentally disturbed. It must be emphasised, however, that such questionable cases were very rare.

Acceptance, payment and refusal
A high proportion of those offered a fiscal fine accepted this chance to avoid prosecution. The take-up rate in the four larger offices was remarkably consistent at around 70 per cent (and it reached 90 and 100 per cent in the two smaller offices). It ought to be noted that both district court clerks and fiscals were flexible in their application of the 28 day time limit for acceptance. In the majority of cases, recipients paid their fiscal fine as a lump sum (i e £25) and this action ended their contact with the criminal justice system.

The minority who opted to pay by instalments ranged, in the four larger offices, from one quarter to almost one half. The unemployed, unsurprisingly, were more likely to pay in this fashion and, thus, payment by instalment was more common in the offices in economically depressed areas. Few of those paying by instalments followed the required timetable of five fortnightly payments of £5. Instead, the pattern of payment tended to be irregular. District court clerks adopted various methods to collect outstanding instalments, frequently resorting to warning letters and citations to the means inquiry court (despite the latter's lack of power to impose an alternative period of imprisonment). Civil diligence was not used against anyone during the period of the research and district court clerks thought it extremely unlikely that it ever would be used to secure the outstanding instalments of a fiscal fine. Nevertheless, district court clerks managed to secure full payment in most cases. Furthermore, they commented that the introduction of the fiscal fine had caused them little extra work because the task of collection was dwarfed by the effort required to secure payment of fixed penalties and court imposed fines.

What of those who failed to accept the offer of a fiscal fine? The proportion prosecuted was high, ranging in the four larger offices from 73 to 87 per cent. Of course, the logic of the process dictates this outcome: a fiscal fine should be offered only in cases which merit prosecution and, thus, if the offer is refused, prosecution should automatically follow. In fiscals' opinions, the main reasons for not prosecuting were the disappearance of the alleged offender and time bar. It was relatively unusual for an alleged offender to refuse an offer in order to plead not guilty (21 such pleas out of 101 refusals) and even rarer for this plea to be successful (two acquittals out of the 17 trials which had taken place by the end of the research period). Of those convicted, around two thirds had previous convictions compared with about one half for the sample as a whole. Thus, as one might anticipate, people with a clean record were more likely to accept the offer of a fiscal fine and, consequently, avoid a criminal conviction. Finally, a fine was the almost invariable outcome of a court appearance. For the four larger samples, the average fine was £59, £46, £42 and £40 — considerably higher than the fiscal fine of £25.

Expansion of the fiscal fine?

In addition to the sampling exercise, a questionnaire about the fiscal fine was sent to all members of the procurator fiscal service. The overwhelming majority of respondents thought it a useful device. There was clearly some support for extending the fiscal fine to the bottom range of sheriff court cases. In particular, it was suggested that the possession of small amounts of cannabis should be dealt with in this way. Further, it was pointed out that various offences relating to the use of tachographs had recently been rendered ineligible for a fiscal fine when the maximum penalty had been increased, and it was thought that the previous position ought to be restored. Other offences mentioned in this con-

nection were: careless driving; TV licence evasion; and failure to pay vehicle excise duty (although the fact that a court order is needed to collect the arrears was considered to make this problematic).

The questionnaire also requested fiscals to consider whether the fiscal fine would be more useful if a sliding scale were to be introduced. The majority (60 per cent) of the 164 fiscals who responded to this question favoured such a move. Those fiscals were further asked what should be the maximum and minimum points upon a sliding scale. The median figures suggested were £25 as a minimum and £100 as a maximum — precisely the figures now mooted in the Scottish Office consultation paper (paras 2.15-2.20). It is worth noting that some fiscals thought that a £25 minimum was too high, making it difficult to deal with the unemployed, for instance.

A significant minority (40 per cent) of respondents were opposed to the introduction of a sliding scale. All but one gave explanations for their view, several providing more than one reason. In brief, 36 fiscals raised various practical difficulties, principally, that a lack of consistency would result, that it would take too much time to decide upon an appropriate amount, and that such a system would be too complicated to operate. (It is anticipated that these fears will be met, to some extent, by the issuing of detailed guidelines by the Lord Advocate on the use of fiscal fines.) Further, 40 respondents voiced theoretical or philosophical objections, primarily that determining the precise level of a fine smacked too much of a usurpation of the judicial role, and that the present system had already reached about the right level because more serious cases ought to be dealt with by a court.

Conclusion

The fiscal fine, as presently constituted, works well. Although it was introduced to provide an alternative to prosecution in the district court, it has inevitably come to be used, to some extent, as a halfway house between a "no pro" or warning letter and prosecution. If, however, the mechanism were extended in the way suggested, it would bite almost exclusively into court workloads. Further, there would be few administrative problems. It is significant that in several continental jurisdictions, the prosecutor fine covers a wide range of offences and the public prosecutor is empowered to vary the level of penalty, often to a considerable degree. While most fiscals would welcome an expansion of the fiscal fine, some might have reservations about this.

NEWS

Court

Admission of solicitor advocates

The following solicitors have been granted extended rights of audience in the High Court of Justiciary: Branislav Sudjic of Baird & Co, Kirkcaldy, Cameron Ritchie, Procurator Fiscal's Office, Hamilton, Michael John Bell, Procurator Fiscal's Office, Edinburgh, Petra Margaret Collins, Procurator Fiscal's Office, Falkirk, Peter Black Watson of Levy & McRae, Glasgow, James Douglas Keegan of Keegan Walker & Co, Livingston, Gordon Fleetwood of Fleetwood & Robb, Inverness, Andrew Berry of Berry Scullion, Glasgow, Daniel Scullion of Berry Scullion, Glasgow, Nigel Wilson Orr, Crown Office, Edinburgh and Liam Robertson of Liam Robertson & Co, Glasgow.

The following solicitors have been granted extended rights of audience in the Court of Session, House of Lords and Judicial Committee of the Privy Council: Derek Colin Wilson Pyle of Henderson Boyd Jackson, WS, Edinburgh, George Moore of Hamilton Burns & Moore, Glasgow, Andrew Grant McCulloch of Drummond Miller, WS, Edinburgh, Robert James Livingstone of Livingstone Brown, Glasgow, William Henry Holligan of Brodies, WS, Edinburgh, Susan Ann Fraser or Craig of Brodies, WS, Edinburgh, Peter Gillam of Gillam Mackie, SSC, Edinburgh, Francis Thomas Maguire of Robin Thompson & Partners, Glasgow, and Robert Carr of Anderson Strathern, WS, Edinburgh.

— ◊ —

Appointments

W Green/Sweet & Maxwell

The Thomson Corporation plc have appointed Stephen White, currently the Group Vice President Europe/Canada of the Professional Publishing Group of McGraw-Hill Inc, as managing director of Sweet & Maxwell Ltd (including W Green & Son and ESC Publishing), in succession to the late David Evans. Stephen White will also become the group managing director of the newly created Legal and Professional Division of Thomson Corporation Publishing, which will include Professional Publishing Ltd, and UB Media in Germany, as well as Sweet & Maxwell.

In both roles his priorities will be the develop-

ment of existing businesses and expansion throughout Europe.

◊

Shrieval vacancy

There is at present a vacancy for a resident sheriff at Glasgow. Advocates and solicitors of appropriate standing who are interested in this appointment are invited to write in confidence, providing their curriculum vitae and the names of two referees, to the Director of the Scottish Courts Administration, 26-27 Royal Terrace, Edinburgh EH7 5AH, by 25 May 1994.

◊

Temporary sheriff vacancies

There are at present vacancies for temporary sheriffs. Advocates and solicitors of appropriate standing who are interested in these appointments are invited to write in confidence for an application form to the Director of the Scottish Courts Administration, 26-27 Royal Terrace, Edinburgh EH7 5AH, by 25 May 1994.

— ◊ —

Coming events

David Hume Institute conference

In cooperation with the Department of Private Law, University of Edinburgh, the David Hume Institute announces a lecture by Professor Marc Steinberg of the Southern Methodist University, Dallas, Texas, entitled "Directors' Fiduciary Duties in the USA". Professor Steinberg is a distinguished American lawyer who has worked for the Securities & Exchange Commission as well as being responsible for numerous publications in the fields of company and commercial law. The lecture will take place on Thursday 9 June 1994 at 5.30 pm in the Court Room, Old College, Edinburgh. There will be no charge for admission.

Further information can be obtained from Kathryn Mountain, The David Hume Institute, 21 George Square, Edinburgh EH8 9LD (tel 031-650 4633; fax 031-667 9111).

◊

Scottish Child Law Centre

The Scottish Child Law Centre will hold its combined a g m and conference on Friday 24 June 1994. The venue will be the Senate Room, Old College, Edinburgh University. The conference is entitled "New Horizons" and will look

NEWS

at how child law is operated in other parts of the world. Alison Cleland, who is an advice worker and legal assistant with the centre, has just concluded an extensive study tour covering the United States, Australia and New Zealand following the award of a scholarship from the English Speaking Unit. This has allowed her the opportunity to study juvenile justice in these countries and to compare it with practices in Scotland. Professor Stewart Asquith, who has carried out work in Eastern and Central Europe for the Centre for the Study of the Child & Society, will give a presentation on how child law operates in these areas. The conference will also be addressed by Lord Rodger of Earlsferry, the Lord Advocate.

Further information and booking forms can be obtained from the Scottish Child Law Centre, Lion Chambers, 170 Hope Street, Glasgow G2 2TU (tel 041-331 2244; fax 041-353 3861).

— ◇ —

Taxation

Inland Revenue information powers
The Government have tabled an amendment to the Finance Bill which removes the specific reference to "evasion or avoidance of tax" in the conditions under which a general or special commissioner may direct that information should be withheld from the taxpayer. Clause 253 (formerly 240) of the Finance Bill provides additional protection for a taxpayer where a tax inspector has applied for consent to issue a notice requiring information or documents relevant to that person's tax liability. Except in certain circumstances the inspector will be required to give to the taxpayer a summary of his reasons for applying for the notice. The amendment simplifies the definition of one such circumstance and brings the provision into line with other statutory references to the Revenue's information powers. This circumstance is where the commissioner is satisfied that there are reasonable grounds for believing the disclosure of the inspector's reasons "would prejudice the assessment or collection of tax". The words "evasion or avoidance of tax" have been removed so that straightforward tax planning will not be covered.

◇

Benefits in kind: loans to employees
The average "official rate" of interest used to calculate the taxable benefit from a loan made by an employer to an employee in terms of the Income and Corporation Taxes Act 1988, ss 146 and 160, is 7.688 per cent for 1993-94.

◇

Capital gains tax: retirement relief
The Inland Revenue have published the following extra-statutory concession relating to capital gains tax:

This concession applies where a taxpayer is unable to take advantage of the extended qualifying period for retirement relief in para 14 of Sched 6 to the Taxation of Chargeable Gains Act 1992 because the relevant disposal was not a qualifying disposal for retirement relief purposes, and it was not a qualifying disposal only because the requirement of a one year minimum qualifying period was not met. In these circumstances the Board will be prepared to treat the disposal as a qualifying disposal for the purposes of para 14 of Sched 6 to the Act. As a result, any final business period can be aggregated with earlier business periods irrespective of the length of the final business period. The concession applies for these purposes only. It does not mean that a qualifying period of less than one year will be treated as a one year period in calculating the extended qualifying period.

The concession takes effect from 14 April 1994 for all new and open cases.

◇

Capital gains tax: indexation losses
The Government have tabled an amendment to the Finance Bill which will provide transitional relief for indexation on capital losses. Each individual will be able to use up to £10,000 of indexation allowance on losses realised in the period 30 November 1993 to 5 April 1995. Trustees of settlements made before 30 November 1993 will also qualify for this transitional relief. The transitional relief does not apply to losses realised by companies.

— ◇ —

Obituary

On 29 March 1994, John Bayne, advocate, formerly sheriff at Glasgow. [Correction to intimation published at p 136.]

— ◇ —

Business changes

Patrick P Davies, Nigel R Wood, William H Summers and Gillian E Summers intimate that with effect from 1 May 1994 they have commenced practice together in the name of Davies

Wood Summers, 4 Carden Terrace, Aberdeen AB1 1US (tel 0224-622101, fax 0224-622126).

Macleod & MacCallum, solicitors, 28 Queensgate, Inverness, intimate that with effect from 30 April 1994, John Francis Matheson Macleod retired from the partnership.

Naftalin Duncan & Co, 534 Sauchiehall Street, Glasgow, announce that Doreen P Sevitt Collins retired from the partnership with effect from 1 May 1994. She continues to be associated with the firm as a consultant. They also intimate that their associate, Anne Dickson, has been assumed as a partner with effect from the same date.

— ◇ —

Book Reviews

Cases and Materials in Employment Law

By Gwyneth Pitt. 1993. London: Pitman Publishing. Paperback, £23.95.
ISBN 0273 600389.

Gwyneth Pitt has produced this book to complement her textbook *Employment Law*, published in 1992 by Sweet & Maxwell. The latter was aimed principally at undergraduates but was written with a view to it being useful to anyone studying employment law for the first time and, quite fairly, the bulk of the materials reflect that market. The structure of *Cases and Materials* follows that of the textbook, except that there is no section on occupational safety which forms chap 14 of the textbook. However that area of law has been subject to so many recent changes (principally due to the passage of many European directives), and of course is an area of law difficult to separate from other developments in the field of delict (tort), that it would be difficult to include even the most elementary materials without making the book unwieldy; indeed arguably a book about employment law, which in the United Kingdom is essentially a matter of private law, could legitimately eschew much if not all reference to that area of law now known as health and safety at work which requires a solid appreciation of the principles of delict (torts), breach of statutory duty and, to an extent, the criminal law.

Cases and Materials in Employment Law comprises 13 chapters, of which the first nine are mainly about individual employment law and the last four about collective labour law. Chapter 1 quite sensibly deals with institutional matters although the reader is advised that it may be convenient to defer reading about many of these until they are brought into focus by a substantive issue, but unless this reviewer has misunderstood the purpose of the book such advice would seem unnecessary. In view of the strategic role of conciliation officers they might have merited fuller treatment and, in the context of the powers of the discrimination commissions, the non-discrimination notice could have been mentioned. Chapter 5 deals with collective bargaining generally but might have been better divided into two sections, one being confined to the incorporation of the collective agreement and the other dealing with truly collective matters and located in chap 9 (freedom of association).

The book is essentially a compendium of selected extracts from cases domestic and European, although occasional reference is made to other sources of employment law, interspersed with comments some of which are helpful like those at p 21 on the significance of the Single European Act, while others may merit greater elucidation like that at p 22 to the effect that "European Community law prevails over inconsistent British law, whether subsequent or prior to the EC rule". While the comment on the EC Equal Treatment Directive indicates that the enforcement of the directive will be considered later in the chapter, a fuller statement of the relationship between UK and EC law would have been helpful in view of the book's intended readership. Some mention could have been made of *Francovich v Italian Republic* [1992] IRLR 84 and *Emmott v Minister for Social Welfare* [1991] IRLR 387, while the important decision of the European Court of Justice in *Marshall v Southampton and South West Hampshire Area Health Authority (No 2)* [1993] IRLR 445, was published too late for inclusion.

There is a list of contents with tables of cases, legislation and abbreviations but, regrettably, no index. Helpfully, the tables of cases and legislation highlight the places where there is more than just passing reference to the material. Where appropriate the book has incorporated the important changes introduced by the Trade Union Reform and Employment Rights Act 1993, although the section (pp 167-168) dealing with the revised s 60 of the Employment Protection (Consolidation) Act 1978 suggests that the new maternity rights are now in force whereas the new rights will not become effective until October 1994.

In summary, *Cases and Materials in Employment Law* contains many useful extracts from important cases, but its "total quality" very much depends on its being effectively combined with a complementary text or course of lectures.

V CRAIG,
Heriot-Watt University.

Missives

By D J Cusine and Robert Rennie.
1993. Edinburgh: Butterworths/Law Society of Scotland. Hardback, £28. ISBN 0 406 00593 1.

Thirty years ago a book devoted solely to the subject of missives would have seemed an eccentric and an unnecessary enterprise. But times, alas, have a-changed. Today offers for the purchase of heritable property run routinely to 30 or more clauses; and the offer is then mutilated to the point almost of incomprehensibility by a sequence of qualifying missives. Little attempt is made to scale effort to value, so that even wee flats command big contracts.

The reasons for this change in practice are not clear. Some have detected the arrival in Scotland of a new breed of super conveyancer — over-educated, over-paranoid and (in most cases) under 40. Doubtless word processors have played their part also, offering their users prolixity without pain. But whatever the reasons, it seems unlikely that the trend towards gargantuan missives will now be reversed.

A jungle needs a guide, and Professors Cusine and Rennie are confident guides through the jungle of modern missives. The emphasis of their book is firmly on domestic conveyancing, although a final chapter (omitted from the table of contents) gives a brief account of some of the issues which may arise in commerical and agricultural missives. The book begins with an introductory chapter, and there are five other chapters, dealing respectively with constitution of missives, conclusion of missives, content of missives, the relationship of missives to the disposition, and breach of missives.

The heart of the book, and its longest section, is the account of the content of missives. Although plainly not uncritical admirers of the Law Society Standard Clauses, the authors use the clauses as a convenient peg on which to hang their commentary. This works well enough for the moment, although it carries the risk that the book will become less useful in the future if the clauses do not survive on the market place (as they may not). In their account of the individual clauses, the authors display a sound command both of theory and of practice. There is much sensible and pertinent advice. This reviewer particularly enjoyed the discussion of reservation of minerals (para 4.14) and the homily on drafting (paras 4.73 et seq) with its sequence of exhortatory slogans ("don't tell stories — impose or remove obligations", and so on). However, the use throughout of "resile" (the conveyancer's friend) or, more puzzlingly, "repudiate" (para 4.79), instead of the politically correct "rescind", may earn the authors the censure of the Second Division. See *Zemhunt Holdings Ltd v Control Securities plc*, 1992 SLT 151, and *Lloyds Bank plc v Bamberger*, 1994 SLT 424.

An important merit of the book is its full citation of recent case law. Occasionally, however, the authors are over zealous in their exposition of the latest case, forgetting perhaps that the glamour of today's case becomes all too soon the tedium of yesterday's. An example is the treatment of rectification of defectively expressed documents. Roughly speaking, what the courts seem to be saying here is that while dispositions and other deeds may often be rectified, contracts usually may not be, because with contracts it is difficult to show the existence of an earlier "common intention". But this message does not emerge from the meticulous examination of the facts of recent cases given at paras 3.43 et seq.

A book of this size (209 pages) cannot hope to provide comprehensive coverage of what is now a very large area of law and practice. But the authors have written a valuable work which is more than merely introductory and which deserves considerable success in the profession.

KENNETH G C REID,
University of Edinburgh.

Bill Stewart, the Book Review Editor, is keen that books, and especially, books written with the practitioner in mind should be reviewed by practitioners. Accordingly, members of Faculty and solicitors who consider that they could competently review books, are invited to write with a note of their name and address, indicating upon what subjects they would be prepared to write reviews, to him c/o MacMillans, Solicitors, 78 Springfield Road, Glasgow G40 3ET.

ARTICLES

Belated Acceptance of Judicial Tender and Defender's Expenses

Angus Stewart, QC.

Mr Stewart considers the recent authorities holding as incompetent motions seeking expenses after the date of a tender where such expenses have not been reserved in an interlocutor disposing of the merits, and suggests that the statutory basis supporting such a ruling in earlier decisions no longer exists.

Every trainee knows that a pursuer who delays in accepting a judicial tender gets his expenses to the date of the tender but has to pay the defender's expenses from the date of the tender to the date of acceptance. There is a qualification: the pursuer is allowed a reasonable time to consider the tender and for taking advice, but after that expenses run against the pursuer.

It must have come as a shock therefore to the defenders in two recent cases when their applications for expenses from the date of tender were opposed and then thrown out as incompetent.

In the first case, *Davis v British Coal Corporation*, 1993 SLT 697, the defenders lodged a tender for £45,000 with expenses on 18 October 1991. The proof started on 22 October. At 12.35 pm on 23 October, while the pursuer was under cross examination, pursuer's counsel lodged a minute of acceptance of tender. Temporary Judge Horsburgh, on the pursuer's motion in respect of the tender and acceptance, granted decree for the sum of £45,000 and found the defenders liable to the pursuer in the expenses of the action to the date of the tender.

On 30 October the defenders enrolled a motion to find the pursuer liable to them in the expenses of the second, third and fourth days of the diet of proof (the proof having terminated at lunchtime on the second day). The motion did not call before the temporary judge until 6 December 1991. After hearing submissions the temporary judge made avizandum. On 10 January 1992 he refused the defenders' motion as incompetent.

In the second case, *Wilson v Pilgrim Systems plc*, 1993 SLT 1252, a judicial tender of £20,000 with expenses was lodged on 13 September 1991. On 30 March 1992 the pursuer accepted the tender. On 6 April 1992 the pursuer enrolled a motion for decree in terms of the tender and acceptance. The motion was not opposed. On 8 April the vacation judge granted the motion finding the defenders liable to the pursuer in the expenses of the action to the date of the tender.

On 26 October 1992 the defenders enrolled a motion for expenses from the date of the tender to the date of acceptance. The motion called before Lord Cameron of Lochbroom on 28 October 1992. His Lordship made avizandum and on 13 November 1992 refused the defenders' motion as incompetent.

Similar reasoning was applied in each case (though the report does not disclose that the *Davis* decision — then unreported — was brought to the attention of the court in *Wilson*). The common ratio was that when the merits of an action are disposed of, whether or not all questions of entitlement to expenses are explicitly disposed of at the same time, it is afterwards too late to get any award of expenses unless the matter has been expressly reserved.

Both decisions followed *Henderson v Peeblesshire County Council*, 1972 SLT (Notes) 35, an Outer House decision of Lord Robertson. The circumstances of *Henderson* were essentially similar to those of *Wilson*. Lord Robertson said: "The general rule is that expenses must be expressly awarded or reserved. If the interlocutor exhausting the merits is silent on expenses, the court has no power thereafter to award them. An interlocutor disposing of the merits but silent as to expenses exhausts the cause (see Thomson and Middleton, *Court of Session Practice*, p. 304). In the present case the final interlocutor of 9th February 1971 exhausted the merits and dealt with expenses up to a certain date. No reservation of expenses was made. In my view the court cannot re-open the matter a year later and make a further finding of expenses for a different period. The defenders had ample opportunity to make the necessary motion at the proper time and failed to do so. It may be that their failure to do so was due to a mistake induced perhaps by reliance upon communings between the respective solicitors. But such a mistake could only be rectified de recenti. . . . This motion comes too late. I shall refuse the motion."

The present article does not offer criticism of the decision in *Henderson*. The *Henderson* decision may find its justification in the statutory regulation of Court of Session procedure as it stood in 1972.

The more interesting question is whether it can now be right to take the same course given the procedural changes of recent years.

The decision in *Henderson* followed a substantial tract of case law concerned with the meaning and application of s 17 of the Judicature Act 1825. The section provided: "In pronouncing judgment on the merits of the cause, the Lord Ordinary shall also determine the matter of expences, so far as not already settled, either giving or refusing the same in whole or in part; and".

Maxwell's *Practice of the Court of Session* at p 609 summarises the effect of the cases thus: "this provision of statute has been authoritatively construed as disentitling the Lord Ordinary from dealing with expenses after the merits have been disposed of unless the question of expenses has been expressly reserved or the parties have been appointed to be heard upon it".

The authorities referred to by Maxwell are *Wilson's Trs v Wilson's Factor* (1869) 7 M 457, *Bannatine's Trs v Cunninghame* (1872) 10 M 317, *Campbell v Campbell*, 1934 SLT 45, and of course *Henderson v Peeblesshire County Council*.

To Maxwell's qualification about express reservation etc might be added the further qualification "or unless the matter is the subject of an application de recenti for the correction of an error or omission" (*Ranken v Kirkwood* (1855) 18 D 31).

Lest the rule should seem utterly arbitrary, it is proper to have in mind some of the context, in particular the provision (as it was until 1990) of a right, for the extended period of 21 days, to reclaim (appeal) without leave against Outer House decisions. This, the most generous provision for appeal, was confined by Rule of Court 264 to the case of "an interlocutor disposing either by itself, or taken along with a previous interlocutor or interlocutors, of the whole subject-matter of the cause" — in other words a "final interlocutor" as defined by the Court of Session Act 1868, s 53. What opened up the right of appeal was finality in the sense of disposal not just of the whole merits but of the *whole subject-matter* of the proceedings including expenses. Unless and until expenses were dealt with — or were deemed to have been dealt with — finality (and along with it the right of appeal under these provisions) could be elusive (*Caledonian Railway Co v Glasgow Corporation* (1900) 2 F 871; *McGuinness v Bremner plc*, 1988 SLT 340; 898).

From this evolved what can only be called the fiction that when the merits of the case were disposed of with no mention of expenses, this was tantamount to disposing of the whole subject matter of the action with an express finding of no expenses due to or by either party. In the case of *Bannatine's Trs v Cunninghame* (supra) Lord President Inglis said: "[section 17 of the Judicature Act] provides that the Lord Ordinary in pronouncing judgment on the merits 'shall also

determine the matter of expenses,' from which I think the meaning of the Legislature was that the Lord Ordinary, in his judgment disposing of the merits, should also deal finally with the question of expenses. I do not mean that this implies that he should finally decern for expenses, but that in his judgment on the merits he should give or refuse them in whole or in part . . . the 17th section of the Judicature Act has been made the subject of construction in several decided cases. It has been held that if the Lord Ordinary, in disposing of the merits of the cause, makes no mention of expenses, that is tantamount to an express finding that neither party is entitled to expenses . . . everything depends on the meaning of the 53d section [of the Court of Session Act 1868], which provides that 'It shall be held that the whole cause has been decided in the Outer-House when an interlocutor has been pronounced by the Lord Ordinary which either by itself or taken along with a previous interlocutor disposes of the whole subject-matter of the cause or of the competition between the parties in a process of competition, although judgment shall not have been pronounced on all the questions of law or fact raised in the cause.' Now, so far, I do not think that any of the provisions of this section of the statute affect the question of expenses, but the present question depends rather on the words immediately following, which appear to me to have had specially in view the 17th section of the Judicature Act, — 'But it shall not prevent a cause from being held as so decided,' *i.e.*, it shall not prevent it from being held that the whole cause has been decided, 'that expenses, if found due, have not been taxed, modified, or decerned for.' Now, I think that in using these words the framer of the Act had only two alternatives in view, first, the case where expenses have been found due, and second, the case where expenses have been refused, and these are just the two cases contemplated by the 17th section of the Judicature Act, which directs the Lord Ordinary, in giving judgment on the merits of the cause, to determine the matter of expenses by 'either giving or refusing the same in whole or in part.' Well then, under the 53d section of the statute of 1868 the judgment so pronounced shall be final, although where expenses have been found due the account may not have been taxed; but where they have been found not to be due, nothing more is to be done, the whole cause being exhausted in every possible sense, so that, the alternative being, as I have stated, the Legislature leaves the case where no expenses have been awarded to work itself out, and in the other alternative provides that it shall not prevent the whole cause from being held to be decided, that expenses if found due have not been taxed, modified, or decerned for."

This was part of the line of authority which justified the decision in *Henderson v Peeblesshire County Council*, it being a small step from saying (a) no finding of expenses equals an express finding of none due "to or by", to saying (b) no finding as to part of the expenses equals an express finding of none due "to or by" in that part of the case.

What does not appear to have been drawn to the attention of the court in either *Davis* or *Wilson* was that the statutory foundation for the line of authority culminating in *Henderson* had been swept away by the Court of Session Act 1988. The 1988 Act, s 52 (2) says that Pt III of Sched 2 shows the extent to which certain enactments are repealed without re-enactment "as being no longer of practical utility or being spent or unnecessary". The non-re-enacted repeals include, in the Act of 1825, s 17 "the words from the beginning to 'in part; and'" (i.e. the words quoted supra); and the Act of 1868, ss 52 and 53.

These provisions of the 1825 and 1868 Acts apart, and now in their absence, it is open to argue that there is no incompetency in the court returning to deal with some part of the expenses of proceedings left untouched at the time the merits are disposed of. For example where the court finds a pursuer entitled to the expenses of the action "to the date of the tender" (as in *Davis* and *Wilson*) there remains outstanding the question of the expenses of the action subsequent to the date of the tender — something which arguably the court is not now precluded from dealing with at a later stage.

Support for this proposition can be found in the way the rule dealing with the 21 day period for reclaiming without leave has been redrawn. Up till 1990 Rule of Court 264 (a) provided: "An interlocutor disposing either by itself, or taken along with a previous interlocutor or interlocutors, of the whole subject-matter of the cause, pronounced in any cause initiated in the Outer House either by summons or by petition, may be reclaimed against, without leave, not later than the twenty-first day . . . after the day on which the said interlocutor is pronounced".

As amended by SI 1990/705 the rule now reads: "An interlocutor disposing either by itself, or taken along with a previous interlocutor or interlocutors of — (i) the whole subject-matter of the cause; or (ii) the whole merits of the cause but reserving, or not disposing of, the question of expenses, pronounced in any cause initiated in the Outer House either by summons or by petition may be reclaimed against, without leave, not later than 21 days . . . after the day on which the interlocutor was pronounced".

The reference now introduced to reclaimability under this provision of interlocutors "disposing . . . of . . . the whole merits . . . but . . . not disposing of, the question of expenses", tends to support the view that such interlocutors are no longer deemed to be exhaustive of the whole subject matter. It may be noted that *non-disposal* of expenses is grouped along with *reservation* of expenses in case (ii). Had the erstwhile fiction still prevailed, such interlocutors would be deemed to fall into case (i) where the "whole subject-matter" is disposed of. Disposing of the merits without disposing of expenses does not now seem to mean that the whole subject matter of the proceedings is exhausted. And while the Lord Ordinary is still seised of part of the subject matter, it is competent for him to adjudicate on that part.

If this is correct the question arises: when, if ever, does it become too late to deal with issues about entitlement to expenses? In the case of *Wilson's Trs v Wilson's Factor* (supra) Lord Deas (dissenting on the question of competency) opined at p 460 that it was a question of circumstances: "If there was such a lapse of time that the circumstances of the case were apt to be forgotten or misunderstood, or if there were any fair grounds for supposing that expenses were not mentioned in the interlocutor because the Court did not mean to give them, then there might be incompetency in raising the question afterwards. . . . I take that to be the only kind of incompetency which can be pleaded here".

If the court has (as it does have) power, not regarded as problematic even though unlimited in time, to return to certain questions of quantum in relation to expenses (questions such as allowance of additional fees and, prior to decerniture, modification), it is not easy to see immediately why its power to return to unresolved questions of entitlement should be arbitrarily restricted. And what substantive difference is there between dealing at leisure with a question of entitlement which has been expressly reserved — which is competent — and dealing with a question of entitlement which has not been expressly reserved — hitherto said to be incompetent? Whether the matter is raised a few days or several months, even a year after the event, provided the process is still in court it is suggested that there should be no argument about a defender being entitled to expenses incurred after the date of a tender belatedly accepted.

Postscript
The defenders' application for expenses in *Davis* was probably not good on the merits anyway. The decision in *Wilson* involves a conundrum. The Lord Ordinary was persuaded by the pursuer's submissions that "It is now too late to seek to raise the matter of expenses, since the court has now no power to make any further award" (p 1254F). The pursuer then moved the Lord Ordinary to make a further award of expenses by giving the pursuer the expenses of the hearing of 28 October 1992. The motion was granted.

◆

NEWS

Court

Court of Session: sessions of court
The Lord President under Rules of Court 68B, 68C (2), 68D (2) and 68E (2), has directed that the ordinary sessions of the Court of Session for 1995 shall be Thursday 5 January to Friday 24 March; Tuesday 25 April to Friday 14 July; Tuesday 26 September to Wednesday 20 December; and shall be extended to include every Wednesday and Thursday in vacation in 1995.

Subject to rule 68D (3), no Division, Lord Ordinary or Vacation Judge shall sit on the following days in 1995: 2 and 3 January, 10, 14 and 17 April, 1 and 22 May, 18 September, 22 (afternoon), 25 and 26 December.

— ◊ —

Coming events

Scottish Law Teachers Conference
The 1994 Scottish Law Teachers Conference is being held at the Robert Gordon University, Aberdeen, on 6 and 7 September 1994. The principal speakers will be Judge David Edward of the European Court of Justice, Lord Davidson, Chairman of the Scottish Law Commission, and Professor Brownsword of the Higher Education Funding Council.

Further information about the conference, which is open to all interested persons, is available from Lynne Turnbull at the School of Public Administration and Law, 352 King Street, Aberdeen AB9 2TQ.

— ◊ —

Taxation

Stamp duty: exchanges of property
Clause 239 of the Finance Bill introduces new rules for stamp duty on exchanges of interests in land or buildings. Under the new rules duty is charged on each transfer. The duty in each case is calculated by reference to the consideration given for the transfer; where the consideration consists of property, its open market value will be taken. For example, if one house worth £100,000 is exchanged for another house worth £100,000, duty of £1,000 (1 per cent of £100,000) is charged on each transfer. The £60,000 threshold is applied separately to each side of the exchange. For example, if there is a straightforward exchange of one house worth £50,000 for another worth £50,000, both transfers are within the threshold and so no duty would be payable on either.

Where the market values of the two properties being exchanged are not equal, a payment of money (or some other consideration) may often be given with the lower value property, so as to equalise the bargain. The treatment of such cases for stamp duty purposes will depend on the facts and the effect of the relevant documents.

Representations have been made that in many cases the wording of the conveyance of the cheaper property may not fully reflect the consideration expressed in the initial contract or agreement. It has been suggested that where the contract provides for an exchange and also provides for money to be paid as equality money by one party to the other, the equality money should be taken into account in deciding how much of the more expensive property is regarded as consideration for the cheaper property (even though the equality money has not been mentioned in the conveyance of the cheaper property).

The Inland Revenue have taken legal advice on this. The conclusion is that where it is clear from the contract that the intention of the parties to the transaction is that the cheaper property should be transferred for the more expensive property *less* the equality money, the Stamp Office will limit the charge to duty accordingly. For example, if the initial contract provided for an £80,000 house to be exchanged for a £100,000 house, and for £20,000 to be paid as equality money, the amount charged to duty on the transfer of the £80,000 property would be limited to £80,000. The result in an individual case will depend on the facts of the case and the relevant documents. The Stamp Office will need to see the relevant contract with the conveyance which is to be stamped.

Where there is a multiple exchange of properties, an apportionment on similar lines may be made to determine how much of the consideration is attributable to each of the transfers. For example, two or more properties may be exchanged for one larger property, with or without a payment of equality money. Here again, the precise result will depend on the facts of the case.

Where the transfer of a cheaper property has already been stamped by reference to the full value of a more expensive property, but the person who has paid the duty thinks that the duty would be reduced on the basis explained above, the Stamp Office will be prepared to review the case. Applicants should resubmit the relevant conveyance, and the contract (or a certified copy of the contract). (If it is not possible to obtain the original stamped document from the relevant Registrar, the Stamp Office should be consulted about alternative arrangements.) Where appropriate, excess duty will be repaid provided the claim is made within the two year time limit laid down by s 10 of the Stamp Duties Management Act 1891. Claims for repayment should be made to the Stamp Office at Worthing (for England, Wales and Northern Ireland), or Edinburgh (for Scotland).

Sales of property (other than shares) for a price not exceeding the £60,000 threshold are exempted from duty, provided that a certificate of value is given stating that the transfer is not part of a larger transaction, or a series of transactions, for a total price of more than £60,000. The threshold is applied separately to each side of an exchange of properties. If in a particular case the threshold has not been applied separately to each side of an exchange (or to two sales where the purchase prices have been set off against each other), and the person who paid the duty believes that too much duty was paid, the documents (with the certificate of value) may be returned for reconsideration to the Stamp Office on the basis set out above.

Where there is a multiple exchange — for example, properties A and B are exchanged for property C — the transfers of properties A and B would be regarded as parts of a larger transaction, and the threshold would not apply to either of them if the total consideration for both was more than £60,000. The threshold would be applied separately to the transfer of property C.

Sales

In many cases, transactions which in the past have been structured and documented as exchanges could equally well be carried out as sales for a price which may be partly satisfied in kind. For example, when a builder offers a property for sale, he may receive the price from the buyer in the form either of money, or partly of money and partly of the buyer's old house. Such a transaction can be carried out and documented (commencing with the initial contract) as a sale. Stamp duty is charged on the consideration for the sale. So if, for example, the buyer is buying a new house for £100,000, and pays for it with £30,000 in cash plus his old house worth £70,000, duty of £1,000 (1 per cent of £100,000) would be charged on the transfer of the £100,000 house. The house which the builder accepts as part payment for the sale would not be regarded as a separate sale for stamp duty purposes. It would be charged only to the fixed duty of 50p. The threshold would not be of relevance to this transfer as it is not a conveyance on sale.

In cases of doubt about how a particular document of the types mentioned above would be treated by the Stamp Office for stamp duty purposes, the Technical Section, The Stamp Office, Ridgeworth House, Liverpool Gardens, Worthing BN11 1XP, will be willing to help.

◇

Shipping: capital allowance balancing charges
The Chancellor of the Exchequer has announced a new tax relief for shipping which will allow capital allowance balancing charges on disposals of ships to be rolled over for a period of up to three years, to be set against subsequent expenditure on ships within that period. The new relief will be introduced in the next Finance Bill and would be effective from 21 April 1994.

— ◇ —

Letters to the Editor

Department of Private Law,
The University of Edinburgh,
Old College,
South Bridge,
Edinburgh EH8 9YL.
29 April 1994

Sir,

Design Right and Copyright
RAS is of course quite correct in what he says about the important transitional provisions

regarding design protection in the Copyright, Designs and Patents Act 1988 (1994 SLT (News) 142), and indeed I have therefore discussed them myself in Vol 18 of the *Stair Memorial Encyclopaedia* (see paras 1152-1156 and 1161). My own article (1994 SLT (News) 67), to which RAS replies, was intended to supplement and update my *Encyclopaedia* contribution, and accordingly I did not touch on the matters referred to by RAS. In any case, their relevance to *Squirewood Ltd v H Morris & Co Ltd,* OH, 1 April 1993, unreported (1993 GWD 20-1239), is not certain, since Lord Clyde's opinion (the only material available to me) says nothing of whether or not the designs were created before 1 August 1989.

Two points may be added to RAS's note: (1) s 9 (8) of the Copyright Act 1956 has no equivalent in the 1988 Act and has no continuing effect in relation to design copyright; (2) design copyrights which existed before 1 August 1989 and survive the 1988 Act in the way described by RAS are subject to licences of right during their last five years. Finally, I would add to my own article that the decision in *Ford Motor Co Ltd and Iveco Fiat SpA's Applications* [1993] RPC 399 has now been affirmed by the Queen's Bench Divisional Court (*The Times,* 9 March 1994).

Yours faithfully,

HECTOR L MacQUEEN.

◊

Imperial Cancer Research Fund,
Scottish Centre,
Wallace House,
Maxwell Place,
Stirling FK8 1JU.
29 April 1994

Sir,

Used Laser Toner Cartridges

May I make an appeal to your readers on behalf of the Imperial Cancer Research Fund?

The Fund's Scottish centre is asking law firms to donate used laser toner cartridges for recycling.

Over £6,000 has been raised in Scotland through ICRF's laser toner scheme so far. This money helps fund life saving research into the causes, treatment and prevention of cancer at our Scottish research centres at the Western General hospital in Edinburgh and the Biomedical Research Centre, Ninewells, Dundee.

Laser cartridges already wing their way to our Scottish Centre in Stirling from companies as far afield as Sullom Voe. By saving cartridges from laser printers you can help directly in the fight against cancer — and also clean up the environment.

Please contact Kate Paxton at the above address, tel (0786) 479137, for further details or to arrange collection, if you would like to help.

Yours sincerely,

HAZEL WILSON,
Scottish Appeals Executive.

— ◊ —

Business change

Anderson Fyfe, solicitors, Glasgow, have appointed their associate Kenneth Meldrum as a partner from 1 May 1994.

— ◊ —

Parliamentary News

Royal Assent

3 May 1994

Finance Act 1994 (c 9).
Race Relations (Remedies) Act 1994 (c 10).
Road Traffic Regulation (Special Events) Act 1994 (c 11).

New Bills

HOUSE OF COMMONS

12 April 1994

Newly Qualified Drivers—To require newly qualified drivers to display on the vehicles they are driving an indication that they are newly qualified: and for connected purposes. (Private Member's Bill introduced by Mr David Amess)

13 April 1994

Fair Treatment of Widowers—To ensure fair treatment of widowers. (Private Member's Bill introduced by Mr Hartley Booth)

20 April 1994

Regulators of Privatised Utilities—To reform the accountability and other objectives of the privatised utility regulators. (Private Member's Bill introduced by Mr Peter Hain)

26 April 1994

Insolvency—To make the holder of a floating

charge liable for the fees of any administrative receiver appointed by him, such fees to be recoverable by the chargeholder from the assets of the debtor company, the debt ranking pari passu with unsecured creditors; to introduce a lien system into contract law so that contractor, sub-contractors and suppliers in the construction and building industry can register a lien against an employer's interest in the land or property, ensuring that, in the case of the employer failing, such contractors, subcontractors and suppliers are repaid before any floating charge on the develop-ment project; and for connected purposes. (Private Member's Bill introduced by Mr Julian Brazier)

27 April 1994

Company Accounts (Payments to Creditors)—To ensure the publication of information relating to the payment of company creditors and to encourage prompt settlement; and for connected purposes. (Private Member's Bill introduced by Mr Anthony Coombs)

3 May 1994

Employment Protection (Amendment)— To prevent discrimination in employment against persons solely on grounds that they are over-weight. (Private Member's Bill introduced by Mr Tony Banks)

4 May 1994

Trade Descriptions (Amendment)—To amend the Trade Descriptions Act 1968 to har-monise liabilities for misdescription of services and of goods; to impose strict liability for mis-description of services; and for connected purposes. (Private Member's Bill introduced by Mr John Hutton)

Progress of Bills

Police and Magistrates' Courts — Commons: second reading, 26 April 1994.

Intelligence Services — Commons: remaining stages, 27 April 1994.

Education — Commons: second reading, 3 May 1994.

Questions answered

HOUSE OF COMMONS

21 April 1994

POLICE COMPLAINTS

Mr McMaster: To ask the Secretary of State for Scotland what plans he has to establish an independent body to investigate and take action on complaints against police officers; and if he will make a statement.

Lord James Douglas-Hamilton: There are no plans to establish such a body. The Police and Magistrates' Courts Bill includes a new power for Her Majesty's inspectorate of constabulary to review how a complaint has been handled by the police and, in certain circumstances, to direct the chief constable to reconsider the complaint.

28 April 1994

MALE RAPE

Mr Redmond: To ask the Secretary of State for the Home Department what is now his proposed timescale for the introduction of an offence of male rape; and if he will make a statement.

Mr Maclean: The Government have no plans to create such an offence.

JUDGES

Mr Boateng: To ask the Parliamentary Secretary, Lord Chancellor's Department, how many advertisements and in which publications, and at what cost, the Lord Chancellor has placed for new judges since his speech at the Lord Mayor's dinner for judges on 7 July 1993; and how many responses he has received to these advertisements.

Mr John M Taylor: No advertisements have so far been placed for judges. However, eight advertisements have been placed for other judicial appointments since 7 July 1993, details of which are shown in the table. The total cost was £663.54.

Work is currently in progress on the develop-ment of detailed proposals for the introduction of the measures announced in the Lord Chancellor's speech to Her Majesty's judges, and an announcement will be made soon.

Advertisements placed for judicial appointments since 7 July 1993

Office	Publication	Number of applications received
Deputy Social Security Commissioners/Deputy Child Support Com-missioners (Scotland)	Journal of the Law Society of Scotland Scots Law Times	38
Deputy Taxing Masters	The Law Society Gazette Bar News	25

REGISTER OF SCOTLAND EXECUTIVE AGENCY

Mr Raymond S Robertson: To ask the Secretary of State for Scotland if he has completed the review of the Register of Scotland executive agency; and if he will make a statement.

Mr Lang: I have reviewed the registers of Scotland at the end of its first three years as an executive agency and have concluded that agency status should continue. ROS's performance has been evaluated, and the following main conclusions reached:

despite some difficulties in 1990-91, ROS has had a successful first three years;

substantial improvements in quality of service to customers have been achieved in line with the principles of the citizens charter;

backlogs of work have been largely eliminated;

the extension of the Land Register is now proceeding to an agreed timetable; and

a major information systems strategy is being successfully implemented.

The satisfactory introduction of accrual accounts for the year 1992-93 will allow consideration of ROS moving to trading fund status in the near future.

ROS's framework document has been revised and I have placed a copy in the Libraries of both Houses.

I have set ROS the following key targets for 1994-95:

to reduce turnround times for recording writs on the Sasines register from eight to seven weeks;

to reduce turnround times for dealings on the Land Register not attached to a first registration or transfer of part from 12 to 11.5 weeks;

to implement the agreed Land Register extension programme;

to contain any increase in unit costs in real terms for each of its main categories of work to 1 per cent.

4 May 1994

TEMPORARY SHERIFFS

Mr McMaster: To ask the Secretary of State for Scotland how many temporary sheriffs hold commissions to serve in sheriff courts in Scotland; how many sessions were undertaken by temporary sheriffs in each of the past five years; how many temporary sheriffs were employed in the Scottish courts for more than 80 per cent of the available court sitting days in each of the past five years; what is the current daily rate paid to a temporary sheriff; what was the total cost to his Department of temporary sheriffs during the same period; and if he will make a statement.

Lord James Douglas-Hamilton: One hundred and seven temporary sheriffs hold commissions to serve in sheriff courts in Scotland. The current daily fee paid to temporary sheriffs is £246. Information is provided on the number of sitting days undertaken, the usage made of temporary sheriffs and the total costs.

Court sitting days provided by temporary sheriffs

	Number
1989	4,046
1990	4,236
1991	5,147
1992	6,093
1993	6,660

Number of temporary sheriffs who sat for more than 80 per cent of available sitting days

	Number
1989	0
1990	3
1991	3
1992	5
1993	4

	Total costs (£)
1989-90	950,000
1990-91	952,000
1991-92	1,512,000
1992-93	2,041,000
1993-94	2,308,000

The services of temporary sheriffs have contributed significantly to reducing inconvenience to court users resulting from cancellation of court sittings and to avoiding increases in court delays due to increases in workloads. The average waiting period for summary criminal trials at the end of 1993 was the lowest recorded over the past five years.

ARTICLES

Personal Injuries Claims: The Valuation of "Services"

Dr James Blaikie,
Senior Lecturer in Law,
University of Aberdeen.

Dr Blaikie examines the approach of the Scottish courts to the problem of assessing the value of services in terms of the Administration of Justice Act 1982, ss 7-9, and analyses the merits and demerits of the commercial cost of purchasing the services and the earnings which have been lost by their provider as indicators of that value.

It is a common feature of modern personal injuries actions that the pursuer, in addition to the usual claim in respect of loss of earnings or loss of support, makes a further claim which seeks to recover the cost of various services which have been rendered to him by his relatives. Alternatively, or in addition, the pursuer may seek a sum in respect of the services which, by reason of his injuries, the pursuer is no longer able to render to his relatives. A statutory right to claim damages in respect of services was introduced by the Administration of Justice Act 1982, ss 7-9, which implemented recommendations of the Scottish Law Commission on this subject. (See Scot Law Com no 51 (1978), *Damages for Personal Injuries*, for analysis of the problems which such claims presented at common law and of the proposals for reform. For discussion of the present law, see McEwan and Paton, *Damages in Scotland* (2nd ed), chap 12.)

Section 8 (1) of the 1982 Act provides: "Where necessary services have been rendered to the injured person by a relative in consequence of the injuries in question, then, unless the relative has expressly agreed in the knowledge that an action for damages has been raised or is in contemplation that no payment should be made in respect of those services, the responsible person shall be liable to pay to the injured person by way of damages such sum as represents reasonable remuneration for those services and repayment of reasonable expenses incurred in connection therewith."

In *Forsyth's CB v Govan Shipbuilders Ltd*, 1988 SLT 321; 1989 SLT 91, it was held that s 8, as it then stood, contemplated remuneration for past services only and did not extend to services which might be rendered by a relative in the future. Although the wording of s 8 was unambiguous, this raised the anomaly that, at least under the 1982 Act, no account could be taken of future services, the cost of which might far outstrip the cost of those provided in the past. (The problem could be surmounted by the pursuer entering into a formal contract for the provision of future services by the relative: *Edgar v Lord Advocate*, 1965 SLT 158; 1965 SC 67; *McMillan v McDowall*, 1993 SLT 311 at p 316 per Temporary Judge T G Coutts, QC.) However, the Law Reform (Miscellaneous Provisions) (Scotland) Act 1990, s 69 (1) inserted new subss (2)-(4) in s 8 and subs (3) now provides for the recovery of the cost of necessary services likely to be rendered by a relative after the date of an award of damages in favour of the injured person.

A wide range of "necessary services" have attracted compensation under s 8: for example, the wife who assisted her husband with washing and dressing (*Gripper v British Railways Board*, 1991 SLT 659); the wife who walked her husband's dog and drove his car (*Miller v Fife Regional Council*, 1990 SLT 651); the husband who took over the running of the household (*Smith v Chief Constable, Central Scotland Police*, 1991 SLT 634); the cohabitee who "effectively performed the services of a nursing auxiliary" (*Lynch v W Alexander & Sons (Midlands) Ltd*, 1987 SCLR 780).

All such claims in respect of services are channelled through the injured person (see s 8 (1) and (4)), but the combined effect of subss (2) and (3) is that the injured person is under an obligation to account to the relative for any damages recovered under subs (1), i e the cost of past services, but not for those recovered under subs (3), i e the cost of future services.

Section 9 of the 1982 Act deals with the cost of services which the injured person is no longer able to render to his relatives. Section 9 (1) provides that the responsible person shall be liable to pay to the injured person a reasonable sum by way of damages in respect of the inability of the injured person to render these "personal services". And, where the injured person has died, s 9 (2) provides that any relative of his entitled to damages in respect of loss of support under s 1 (3) of the Damages (Scotland) Act 1976 shall be entitled to include as a head of damage under that section a reasonable sum in respect of the loss to him of these "personal services".

"Personal services" are defined by s 9 (3) as those: "(a) which were or might have been expected to have been rendered by the injured person before the occurrence of the act or omission giving rise to liability, (b) of a kind which, when rendered by a person other than a relative, would ordinarily be obtainable on payment, and (c) which the injured person but for the injuries in question might have been expected to render gratuitously to a relative".

Under s 9 there have been compensated, for example, the loss of the housekeeping and child care services which were formerly provided by a deceased wife and mother (*Brown v Ferguson*, 1990 SLT 274; the cost of the gardening, household maintenance and DIY tasks performed by a deceased husband (*Ingham v John G Russell (Transport) Ltd*, 1991 SLT 739; 1991 SCLR 596); and the cost of the pursuer's inability to decorate his cohabitee's flat (*Lynch*, supra). As with claims under s 8, s 9 (4) confirms that all such claims are to be channelled through the injured person or, in the case of death, the relative, by providing that the relative is to have no direct right of action in delict in respect of these services.

The problem to be addressed in this article concerns the yardstick which is used by the court in determining what, under s 8, constitutes a "reasonable remuneration" for the services provided, and, under s 9, a "reasonable sum" to compensate for the loss of such personal services. The Act itself gives no guidance as to the precise content of these phrases. The only comment by the Scottish Law Commission as to the basis on which compensation should be payable is the remark that a court would not permit, say, an injured husband to recover the lost earnings of his wife in excess of the cost of appropriate domestic help, and that it would reach this result on the basis of the injured person's duty, in an action of damages, to minimise his losses as far as possible (Scot Law Com no 51, supra, para 26). And although, as already noted, s 9 (3) (b) defines "personal services", inter alia, as those which "would ordinarily be obtainable on payment", this may not be an indication that their commercial value is to be used in quantifying their value, but a means rather of delimiting the range of services in contemplation.

The attitude of the courts is that a "broad approach" should be taken to the assessment of this head of claim, and expression is frequently given to this view, sometimes where the evidence of loss is scant, and often whether the sum claimed is large or relatively small, although in the latter case the award is often described as a "token" (e g *Watts v Russell*, 1993 SLT 1227; 1993 SCLR 608; *Campbell v Campbell & Isherwood Ltd*, 1993 SLT 1095; 1993 SCLR 597; *McGowan v Air Products (UK) Ltd*, 1991 SLT 591; 1991 SCLR 963; *Prentice v William Thyne*,

1989 SLT 336; *McWilliam v British Coal Corporation*, 1990 SLT 679). However, as a very general rule, the greater the sum sought in name of services and the more detailed the evidence of loss, the greater is the tendency for either of two particular measures of value to feature in argument. It should be stressed that neither of these measures has been treated as conclusive, the tendency being to use them only as a guide in pursuit of the "broad approach".

The "commercial rate"

The first of these measures is the "commercial rate" approach, which looks to the cost of purchasing on the open market the lost services. In *Forsyth's CB*, Lord Clyde remarked that the only evidence he had with which to quantify a claim for the cost of services of a wife to her husband was the level of her prior earnings. His view was that he would have preferred to have the additional guidance of levels of charges imposed for the kind of help required in this case, and that in future such evidence should be led to allow the court to assess more accurately what a "reasonable remuneration" should be. However, in *Clark v Chief Constable, Lothian and Borders Police*, 1993 SLT 1299 at p 1300K per Lord Morison, the Inner House, while agreeing with this view, noted that the effect of a failure to lead such precise evidence was not to exclude altogether consideration of the claim, "but to restrict the court's assessment to an amount, if any, which represents the minimum that can reasonably be inferred as appropriate on the basis of such evidence as there is".

Thus, evidence has been heard of the commercial cost of, for example, gardening services (*Wotherspoon v Strathclyde Regional Council*, 1992 SLT 1090; 1992 SCLR 806; *Harrison v R B Tennent Ltd*, 1992 SLT 1060), and of the cost of employing a nursing auxiliary (*Denheen v British Railways Board*, 1988 SLT 320). However in *Fowler v Greater Glasgow Health Board*, 1990 SLT 303, where a baby, born with a serious heart condition, and who later sustained severe brain damage, was given constant care by his parents for the last 10 months of his life, Lord Morison felt that in these special circumstances the calculation of the cost of services ought not to be made on the basis of providing commercial nursing assistance.

In *Gordon v Wilson*, 1992 SLT 849, in considering the cost of past care, the point was made that assessment of the price for any service must take account of the quality of the service provided and the qualifications of and the demands on the person providing it. Thus, the mere fact that some or even all of the care provided by a husband for his wife was of a kind which would otherwise have been provided by a qualified nurse did not entitle the pursuer to damages on that hypothetical basis, and according to scale rates published by the British Nursing Association. Lord Penrose thought it relevant to have regard to the fact that the husband did not have the qualifications of a nursing auxiliary, and indeed held that, on the evidence, the nearest equivalent to the services provided by the husband was those of a home help. The sum arrived at on the basis of a home help figure was further reduced by the commission and tax and insurance percentages. However, an argument that a further deduction should be made to reflect the fact that the services were provided in the home, and not in another person's house, was rejected on the ground that this factor was offset by the additional stress associated with the care of a loved one.

In *McMillan v McDowall*, supra, Temporary Judge T G Coutts thought it important to refer to equivalent hourly rates for similar services by outside agencies, and that such comparative rates provided material against which a court could check its impression of the sum to be given as appropriate remuneration. He did not think that the use of the word "remuneration" meant that the carer should be paid as if she were an independent employee: "indeed there is something repugnant about the idea of a caring relative being awarded an hourly wage rate". He added: "It appears to me that except in cases involving 24 hour care, there must always be some variation in the amount of time spent, the time at which it is spent and the amount of effort required from the relative providing care which means that no accurate calculation of a precise sum of money can ever be made in this regard." Indeed, the pursuer in this case required an emergency standby service which, in the court's view, was "virtually unquantifiable".

Claims under s 9 for the cost of services which the victim is no longer able to render to relatives have similarly been assessed under reference to the commercial rate. Thus in *Worf v Western SMT Co Ltd*, 1987 SLT 317, improvements, repairs and DIY work which the deceased, a US citizen, had carried out in the family home were assessed by reference to a rate of between $25 and $40 per hour. And in *Lenaghan v Ayrshire and Arran Health Board*, 1993 SLT 544; 1993 SCLR 158, where a catering assistant had hurt her back in a fall and claims for services were made under

both s 8 and s 9, regard was had to a figure based on a local authority hourly home care rate.

In *Brown v Ferguson*, 1990 SLT 274, a claim was made under s 9 by the surviving husband and three year old child of a woman who had been killed in a road accident. Lord Sutherland thought that if in fact a husband was in a financial position to employ someone to act as housekeeper and look after any children, the cost of that employment could be used as a measure of the loss of services provided that the wage paid was not unreasonable. However, in the present case the husband was looking after himself with assistance from the deceased's mother with whom the child lived most of the time. Although, to make this arrangement, the mother had had to give up her job as a school cook, that loss of earnings, it was acknowledged, could not form part of any claim against the defender (cf *Howie v Upper Clyde Shipbuilders Ltd*, infra, where the wages lost by the pursuer from the employment she had given up were used to quantify the cost of services the pursuer had provided). The husband was paying the mother some £2,000 per annum for these services and for the running costs of a car, albeit this sum included the cost of maintenance of the child. The court held that it would be reasonable to make an award in respect of loss of services on the basis of what it would cost to provide a living out housekeeper, the cost being spoken to by the proprietrix of a domestic catering agency on the basis of hiring a housekeeper who was prepared to look after a child.

In this context the words of Croom-Johnson LJ in *Spittle v Bunney* [1988] 1 WLR 847 at p 858D are apposite. While recognising that in the early years the services rendered by a mother to her small child may be valued by reference to the cost of a hired nanny, he remarked: "As the child grows older, and reaches school age, the valuation by commercial standards becomes less and less appropriate, and to use them is . . . not comparing like with like. Once the child has begun school, at least by the age of six, the extent of the services decreases in amount. She needs, for a time, to be taken to and from school. Later on, she may go there by herself. Not only is the yardstick of a nanny's wage less appropriate, but the services rendered by the mother change in nature."

A "commercial rate" approach to the valuation of services does however have its deficiencies. In *Ingham*, supra, the deceased had carried out extensive plumbing, joinery, electrical and house maintenance, DIY, babysitting and gardening services, and the defenders argued that there would be problems in quantification since the pursuers were silent on the hourly rate to be applied to such work. However the court reiterated the view that the assessment of a "reasonable sum" should be approached very broadly, and Lord McCluskey remarked that any other approach would involve extremely complicated pleadings with, in a case such as the present, detailed averments of the rates charged by a great variety of tradesmen. Indeed some of the implications of using the "commercial rate" as the sole measure of value have been noted by American commentators (see, e g Komesar (1974) 3 *Journal of Legal Studies* 457 at p 480). An accurate measure of the loss would necessitate a careful enumeration of all services. (For a flavour of the problems this might create, see Speiser, *Recovery for Wrongful Death* (1966, Rochester NY), cited in Clarke and Ogus (1978) 5 British Jo Law & Society 1 at p 9, who lists nine conventional functions of the housewife and the equivalent occupations, the hiring rate for which might be used as a basis for calculation: (i) housekeeper = household worker/domestic help; (ii) nurse = registered nurse; (iii) counsellor = teacher/psychotherapist; (iv) money manager = bookkeeper/accountant/home economist; (v) family chauffeur = chaffeur/taxi driver; (vi) "Mr Fixit" = carpenter/plumber/electrician; (vii) cook = cook/chef/dietitian; (viii) dishwasher = dishwasher; (ix) clothes washer = launderer/laundry worker). Each service would require to be adjusted to reflect the quality of performance (cf *Gordon v Wilson*, supra, per Lord Penrose). And further, it would require the identification in the case of each service of a substitute market service.

Often too the lost individual will have unique qualities which a mere market replacement will never possess. As was remarked in *Pennsylvania Railroad Co v Goodman*, 62 Pa 329 at p 339 (1869), cited in Pottick (1978-79) 50 Univ Colorado LR 59 at p 58: "The frugality, industry, usefulness, attention and tender solicitude of a wife and the mother of children, surely make her services greater than those of an ordinary servant, and therefore worth more."

American experience has noted that where a housewife's time has been broken down into many different occupations, this can induce a negative jury response from, in particular, jurywomen who perform these tasks and who know that many of them can be done simultaneously or that they do not require the degree of education, or the experience, required of the market equivalent (Pottick, op cit at p 66).

Indeed there is evidence that the Scottish judges are alert to the possibility of such exaggeration in a claim for services. For example, in *Worf*, supra, Lord Mayfield remarked, at p 318K, that the deceased husband had perhaps been "exceptionally active in household matters"; in *McMillan*, supra, it was noted, at p 315, that a mother's devotion will far exceed that of her commercial counterpart and may lead to an unnecessary and excessive provision of services; and in *Johnstone v Hardie*, 1990 SLT 744, Lord Morton of Shuna, at p 745, thought that the six hours per day spent on housework by an otherwise unemployed husband were exaggerated and partly explained by the fact that he had nothing else with which to occupy himself.

The "lost earnings"

The other measure which has been used as an indicator of "reasonable remuneration" in claims made under s 8 is the "lost earnings" approach, in terms of which the court looks to the earnings which the carer/provider of services has foregone in order to provide the necessary services to the victim. This is obviously not an approach which is appropriate in assessing the value of claims made under s 9 in respect of the services which the victim is no longer able to provide for his relatives. However in *Forsyth's CB*, although Lord Clyde would have preferred to have had, in addition, evidence of the commercial charges made for the services being provided by a wife for her injured husband, he thought that the prior earnings of the relative were a relevant consideration where employment had been given up in order to provide services: "If one was to envisage a negotiation between the injured person and the relative to agree a reasonable remuneration for the services required to be performed by the latter for the former it seems reasonable to suppose that in such a discussion notice would be taken of the level of wages which the relative would require to surrender in order to perform the services in question" (1988 SLT at pp 326L-327A).

In *Howie v Upper Clyde Shipbuilders Ltd*, 1991 SLT 2; 1990 SCLR 381, where a wife had given up work as a domestic assistant to look after her husband who subsequently died from asbestos related mesothelioma, and where the rates charged for such services by a nursing agency would have been substantially greater, Lord Cameron of Lochbroom thought that the earnings which would otherwise have been received by the widow were a "useful measure" of what amounted to "reasonable remuneration". And in *Housecroft v Burnett* [1986] 1 All ER 332 at p 343e, O'Connor LJ remarked: "in cases where the relative has given up gainful employment to look after the plaintiff, I would regard it as natural that the plaintiff would not wish the relative to be the loser and the court would award sufficient to enable the plaintiff to achieve that result. The ceiling would be the commercial rate". (See too *Mehmet v Perry* [1977] 2 All ER 529, where, after the death of his wife, the husband gave up work in order to render services to his children. Two of them suffered from a rare blood disorder, no other relative was available to take charge of the children and there was no room in the house for a resident housekeeper. Damages were assessed by reference to the husband's loss of wages and not the reasonable cost of employing a housekeeper.)

The advantage of this "lost earnings" or "opportunity costs" approach is that it allows a high degree of certainty in assessing the value of services in that the pursuer can establish the loss against a clear market measure, namely the possible wage. It also allows the law to refute the charge that it is discouraging self help, a charge which might be laid if, say, a wife were to receive only the commercial cost of the services provided and was required thereby to forego an income which would otherwise have been received. However, where the provider of the services is unskilled or has been out of the workforce for some time, the "lost earnings" measure of damages may not be very helpful. If a carer has recently been employed or has a substantial history of recent employment, as in *Howie*, this will provide the court with evidence as to lost earnings. But, if the carer has never been employed, or never employed to the full extent of her qualifications and abilities, such evidence will

be difficult to generate. Valuing the carer's services by reference to lost earnings seems also to imply that a more highly educated mother is a better mother since she will recover a higher award, based on lost earnings more lucrative than those of a less well educated mother. And of course, these earnings which have been foregone in order to provide caring services may in fact have no correlation to the skills required by a carer. Further, where the job which has been surrendered has some relevance to caring, the lost earnings approach may produce a smaller award for the carer, since the tasks which constitute the carer's job have a tendency to be on the lower end of the income scale when sold on the commercial market.

Conclusion

The two yardsticks of value as discussed above have never, in Scotland, been presented in any reported case as competing alternatives, capable of producing widely disparate results dependent on which of them is selected. Their role appears restricted to that of supporting evidence and subordinate to that of the "broad approach". Although, in a case under s 8, where there is evidence of both commercial costs and lost earnings, the Scottish courts may yet be asked to choose between the two measures, the reported cases so far have not raised this issue since, clearly, not every case will involve both types of evidence. This serves to demonstrate the wisdom of enacting a general test of "reasonableness" which the courts are then able to apply by reference to such particular evidence as there may be of the commercial cost of services and/or the foregone earnings.

◆

NEWS

Coming events

Association of Pension Lawyers

The Scottish Group of the association will hold a seminar on 25 May 1994, given by Andrew Holehouse, head of the Pensions Group at Shepherd & Wedderburn.

The seminar will be from 5.30 to 6.30 pm and will be on the topic of "Discretionary Powers and Pension Security". The seminar will include suggested wording for scheme documents and a handout. There will be an opportunity for discussion.

The venue will be the offices of Shepherd & Wedderburn, Saltire Court, 20 Castle Terrace, Edinburgh. The cost will be £10 for non-members. For members, there is no charge. Those interested in attending should contact Colin Browning, Scottish Life Assurance Co, 19 St Andrew Square, Edinburgh EH2 1YE.

— ◇ —

General

WS Society

The following were admitted to the Society of

Writers to HM Signet on 11 May 1994: Pamela Abernethy; E G A Allan; M P Anderson; D W J Bell; D M Black; N H R Bogie; J G Brophy; A J Burleigh; A E C Campbell; V I Campbell; R M Clephane; M M Dawson; A E Donaghy; S P Dougherty; G J M Dunlop; D R G Flint; C T Graham; John Grant; L M Gray; I D Haigh; D J F Halliday; G Hamilton; C A Heggie; M M Herd; David Hossack; F S Jackson; A C Jarosz; Ian Kennedy; G F Maclean; R G Macphail; J R M MacQueen; A D MacRae; S M Masterton; J G Mathieson; Lisa McCreadie; A F McDonald; A R Y McInnes; R M S Milne; S M Murray; S R Murray; Peter Paterson; Gretta Pritchard; Andrew Purdie; T G Reid; M G Robson; P F A Roper; K A Ross; J M Scott; G E M Seaton; David Semple; F B Smart; J E G Thomson; E E Towns; K M Watt; Lindsay Wood; J D G Young.

Taxation

Capital gains tax: private residence exemption

The Inland Revenue have published the following revised version of extra-statutory concession D37 relating to relocated employees:

Where work is being relocated, the employer may set up arms length arrangements under which an employee, who moves home because of the relocation, can sell his or her home to a relocation company or to the employer and have a right to a share in any later profit made when the relocation company or the employer later sells the home. Such arrangements may also exist where employees are required by their employer to transfer within an organisation and as a result have to move home. In such circumstances, if the home is fully exempt from capital gains tax, the employee's right to the share in any later profit will be exempt too. Some employees' homes may be only partially exempt (for example they may have been used partly for business purposes, or may not have been the main home throughout an employee's period of ownership). In such cases, a corresponding proportion of any gain relating to the right to later profits will also be exempt. The concession does not apply when the right is held by the employee for more than three years. Where an employee owns his or her home jointly with others and moves home in the circumstances described above, the concession will apply to the other joint holders in the same way as to the employee. The concession applies to office

holders in the same way as to employees, and to arrangements involving unincorporated relocation businesses in the same way as to those involving relocation companies.

Income tax: remission of arrears

The Inland Revenue have published the following revised text of extra-statutory concession A19, amended in respect of taxpayers in receipt of a retirement or widow's pension from the DSS:

Arrears of income tax or capital gains tax may be wholly or partly waived if they have arisen through the failure of the department to make proper and timely use of information supplied by: a taxpayer about his or her own income, gains or personal circumstances; an employer, where the information affects a taxpayer's coding; or the Department of Social Security, where the information affects a taxpayer's entitlement to a retirement or widow's pension.

The concession will be given only where: the taxpayer could reasonably have believed that his or her tax affairs were in order; and he or she was notified of the arrear after the end of the tax year following that in which it arose, unless exceptionally the revenue had made repeated errors within that period or the arrear had built up over two whole years in succession as a direct result of the department's failure to make proper and timely use of information.

The proportion of arrears waived varies according to the size of the taxpayer's gross income (before personal allowances, deductions etc) in the year in which the actual, or likely, amount of an arrear of tax is first notified. The current scale, which applies to arrears of tax which are first notified to the taxpayer or his or her agent on or after 17 February 1993, is:

Gross Income — £	Remission
15,500 or less	All
15,501 — 18,000	3/4
18,001 — 22,000	1/2
22,001 — 26,000	1/4
26,001 — 40,000	1/10
40,001 or more	None

A measure of relief may be given if the taxpayer's gross income marginally exceeds the limit set out above and he or she has large or exceptional family responsibilities.

Since the introduction of independent taxation on 6 April 1990 these income limits apply just to the person assessed regardless of whether or not he or she is married.

The revised concession takes effect from 26 April 1994.

Income tax: benefits in kind: transfers of assets

The Inland Revenue have published the following extra-statutory concession relating to transfers of assets by employees and directors to employers and others:

Where: (a) an employee sells or transfers an asset; (b) the opportunity to do so arises from the employment; and (c) the employee has earnings at a rate of £8,500 or more a year or is a director, he or she receives a benefit by reason of the employment. The cash equivalent of the benefit may be chargeable to income tax.

The cash equivalent is equal to the cost of the benefit less any amount made good by the employee to those providing the benefit. The cost of the benefit is the expense incurred in or in connection with the provision. But in the circumstances set out above: (a) the cost for the purposes of the cash equivalent (s 156 ICTA 1988) will be taken as (i) the price paid for the asset by the purchaser and any other valuable consideration given for it; plus (ii) any costs which would normally be met by a vendor but are borne by someone other than the employee; and (b) other costs incurred by the person(s) providing the benefit in connection with the transfer will be ignored.

Normal vendor's costs arising in connection with the transfer which are borne by someone other than the director or employee are not within the scope of this concession and are chargeable to tax in the normal way.

The concession applies for 1994-95 and subsequent years. For years up to and including 1993-94 the Inland Revenue will not seek tax on more than the benefit computed on the basis of this concession where the tax liability had not been settled at 27 April 1994.

— ◇ —

Obituaries

On 19 March 1994, Donald Mackay Macarthur, OBE, formerly senior partner in the firm of Messrs Kidstons & Co, solicitors, Glasgow.

On 10 May 1994, James Allan Wark, MC, senior partner in the firm of Messrs Wilson, Chalmers & Hendry, solicitors, Glasgow.

On 12 May 1994, the rt hon John Smith, QC, MP.

— ◇ —

Parliamentary News

New Bills
HOUSE OF COMMONS

6 May 1994

Water Charges (Amendment) (No 2)—To amend the Water Industry Act 1991 to prohibit the use by water undertakers of rateable values as a basis for charging from 31 March 1995; to provide for charging by water undertakers in accordance with council tax bands; and for connected purposes. (Private Member's Bill introduced by Mr Paul Tyler)

10 May 1994

Security Industry (Licensing)—To provide for the licensing of the security industry and for connected purposes. (Private Member's Bill introduced by Mr Michael Stern)

Progress of Bills
Social Security (Incapacity for Work) — Lords: report, 10 May 1994.

Insolvency Bill — Lords: committee, 11 May 1994.

Photographs and Films (Unauthorised Use) — Lords: report, 11 May 1994.

Questions answered
HOUSE OF COMMONS

6 May 1994

REGISTRY OF SCOTLAND AGENCY

Mr Shersby: To ask the Secretary of State for Scotland what information he has concerning the level of fees charged by the Keeper of the Registers in the Registry of Scotland Agency; and what percentage increases there have been in the past 12 months.

Lord James Douglas-Hamilton: Fees charged by the Keeper of the Registers of Scotland are mainly specifically listed in SI 1991/2093 and these have not changed since coming into force on 16 October 1991, and where they are not so listed the keeper is required to charge fees on a full cost recovery basis.

Mr Shersby: To ask the Secretary of State for Scotland what is his policy for ensuring competition in the supply of land registry reports to solicitors as between those supplied by the

Keeper of the Register in the Registry of Scotland Agency and members of the Society of Scottish Searchers.

Lord James Douglas-Hamilton: In principle, the policy is to encourage competition from the private sector. The Scottish Office Home and Health Department is chairing a working group involving a wider spectrum of those interested in extending access to the databases held by the keeper.

Mr Shersby: To ask the Secretary of State for Scotland what information he has concerning the level of charges made by the Keeper of the Register in the Registry of Scotland Agency to members of the Society of Scottish Searchers for a form 12 or 13 report; whether the same charges are being made by the keeper to his report section for similar reports supplied to solicitors; and if he will make a statement.

Lord James Douglas-Hamilton: The fees for charges in the Registers of Scotland Agency are set out in SI 1991/2093 and this provides for a fee of £16.50 for each form 12 and a fee of £10 for each form 13 irrespective of whether supplied to a member of the Society of Scottish Searchers or to a solicitor.

10 May 1994

IMMIGRATION APPEALS

Mr Simon Hughes: To ask the Parliamentary Secretary, Lord Chancellor's Department what is the average length of time it takes from an application being made to the Immigration Appellate Authority to the date of the determination; and if he will make a statement.

Mr John M Taylor: Once an application is made to the Immigration Appellate Authority, it is for the parties to signify when they are ready for hearing. The time taken to reach this stage varies between two and eight months. The first available hearing date at each of the IAA's centres as at 6 May 1994 is set out in the table.

Centre	Long appointment	Short appointment
Hatton Cross, West London	9 September 1994	27 July 1994
Thanet House, London	10 July 1994	1 June 1994
Birmingham	18 August 1994	17 August 1994
Manchester	17 August 1994	17 August 1994
Leeds	1 July 1994	21 June 1994
Glasgow	July 1994	30 June 1994

Once the case has been heard, the adjudicator's determination normally issues to the parties within six to eight weeks.

SPIRITS

Mr Nicholls: To ask the President of the Board of Trade what legislative changes he intends to propose to amend the quantities in which spirits may be sold for consumption on licensed premises.

Mr McLoughlin: My noble Friend Lord Strathclyde has today laid before Parliament the Weights and Measures (Intoxicating Liquor) (Amendment) Order 1994 and the Measuring Equipment (Capacity Measures) (Amendment) Regulations 1994. The order has been laid for approval by resolution of each House of Parliament. The regulations have been made before laying and are subject to the negative resolution procedure.

Current legislation provides that gin, rum, vodka and whisky may be served in a quantity of ¼ gill, ⅕ gill, ⅙ gill or 25 ml and that the three imperial quantities be phased out by the end of this year. The new legislation will allow a second metric quantity of 35 ml and thereby allow those licensees — principally in Scotland — who, at present, sell spirits in either ¼ or ⅕ gill to continue to serve a more generous measure.

SCOTTISH COURT SERVICE

Mr Raymond S Robertson: To ask the Secretary of State for Scotland what plans he has to implement his decision to establish the Scottish Court Service as an executive agency.

Mr Lang: I have decided that the Scottish Court service will be established as an executive agency under the "next steps" initiative, with a vesting day of 3 April 1995. Arrangements are now being made to recruit a chief executive for the agency, and advertisements will appear in the national press in the course of this week.

VALUE ADDED TAX

Mr David Nicholson: To ask the Chancellor of the Exchequer what representations he has received suggesting that the charging of VAT on company cars should be rescinded on legal grounds; and if he will make a statement.

Sir John Cope: None, although I understand that a number of businesses have challenged the current United Kingdom VAT regime for cars on legal grounds. Taxation of the private use of business cars is mandatory under Community law. Since the inception of the tax in April 1973, the United Kingdom has achieved this through restricting tax recovery on the purchase of cars. The current legal basis for this simplified procedure is article 17 (6) of the sixth directive (77/388/EEC).

ARTICLES

Civil Actions and Sporting Injuries Sustained by Professional Footballers

Alistair Duff,
Henderson Boyd Jackson,
Edinburgh.

This article is concerned with the recent upsurge in civil actions between professional footballers as a result of injuries received on the playing field. In addition to tracing the development of such actions, Mr Duff discusses in particular the issues of volenti non fit injuria, vicarious liability and quantification of damages.

Introduction

As of 1980, no cases involving professional footballers had reached the civil courts in either England or Scotland. In 1976, in Scotland, David Wells, an Ayr United defender, did contemplate a civil action as a result of sustaining a fractured jaw in a match against Aberdeen but, apparently following legal advice, decided not to proceed (1981 SLT (News) 157). Since then, however, three Scottish cases have reached the courts: in 1982, *J Brown v J Pelosi and St Johnstone Football Club*; and in 1993, *I Durrant v N Simpson and Aberdeen Football Club* and *S Murray v J Dolan and Motherwell Football Club*.

None of these actions ran its full course. It is believed that *Brown* settled after issuing a summons, *Durrant* settled on the morning of a civil proof and *Murray* (for whom the writer was acting) settled on the morning of a jury trial scheduled to last six days. Consequently, no Scottish judge has yet applied his mind to the standard of care to be exercised by footballers towards each other. In the cases of both *Durrant* and *Murray*, a condition of settlement was the non-disclosure of the settlement figure.

In the *Murray* case, the issue as lodged and allowed was in the following terms: "Whether the accident to the pursuer on or about 7 September at Fir Park, Motherwell was caused through the fault of the first defender in the course of his employment with the second defenders." Objection was expected inter alia on the question of vicarious liability and on the specification of damages being imprecise (see *McKeown v Sir William Arrol and Co*, 1974 SLT 143, *Timoney v Dunnery*, 1984 SLT 151 and *Shearer v Bevan's Exrx*, 1986 SLT 226). It is interesting to note however that there was no objection at any point in the court action to the pursuer's request for a jury trial which was intended to exert pressure upon the defender's insurers. It is believed that this tactic was successful in bringing about a satisfactory settlement. In England, there is no such right to demand a jury trial and, in this respect, pursuers in Scotland might be at an advantage because, given that juries are liable to award higher damages than a judge, there is greater pressure upon insurance companies to offer higher settlements.

There are not, to the writer's knowledge, any further cases before the Scottish courts, but it seems that, at present, there are three cases before the players' union where legal action is being considered. The Scottish Football Association is worried by the increasing litigation between players and clubs and feels that, in some circumstances, solicitors are promoting litigation (as occurs in the USA). Obviously, players have become more aware of their legal rights, and if they are incapacitated by foul tackles or challenges which are outwith the rules of the game, they should be fully entitled to litigate. At present, the SFA is particularly concerned about injuries caused by elbows, such as those suffered by Gary Mabbutt in a clash with John Fashanu in a premier division game in England. In a recent game, the Aberdeen defender, Brian Irvine, was rendered unconscious for around a minute after being elbowed in the face by the Kilmarnock striker, Bobby Williamson, who was sent off.

In England, there has been no case involving professional footballers as yet. At present, however, Paul Elliot of Chelsea (formerly Celtic) is bringing an action against Dean Saunders of Liverpool (now with Aston Villa) and this has been scheduled for a High Court trial on 23-27 May of this year. It appears that this hearing is purely to deal with the merits of the case and, if appropriate, the damages hearing would be at a later date. It is possible that Elliot would receive well over £1 million but no exact figure has been sought as this is not done in English proceedings of this type. Elliot's legal advisers (who have been in touch with the writer) are interested in such issues as the merits of the claim, quantification of damages and possible sources of evidence other than eyewitnesses, for example medical experts and model reconstructions which show the results of tackles of varying degrees of force and impact.

The standard of care

The only case, to the writer's knowledge, involving the standard of care owed to each other by footballers is *Condon v Basi* [1985] 2 All ER 453.

In the appeal court, Sir John Donaldson observed: "It is said there is no authority as to what is the standard of care which governs the conduct of players in competitive sports generally and, above all, in a competitive sport whose rules and general background contemplate that there will be physical contact between the players, but that appears to be the position. This is somewhat surprising but appears to be correct."

Edward Grayson, in his book *Sport and the Law*, points out (at p 140) that what was said about there being no authority was incomplete as on four earlier occasions a standard of care which governs the conduct of players in competitive sport could be gauged and was clearly identifiable.

Be that as it may, the facts in *Condon* were simple and arose from a Sunday League football match. The plaintiff, thinking that he was about to be challenged, pushed the ball away but the defendant tackled him late and in a reckless and dangerous manner, sliding in from a distance of three or four yards and lunging with his boot studs showing 12 to 18 inches above the ground. The plaintiff suffered a broken leg and the defendant was sent off for serious foul play. In the county court, the judge concluded: "[The tackle] was made in a reckless and dangerous manner not with malicious intent towards the plaintiff but in an 'excitable manner without thought of the consequences'."

The judge further observed: "It is not for me to attempt to define exhaustively the duty of care between players in a soccer football game. Nor, in my judgment, is there any need because there was here such an obvious breach of the defendant's duty of care towards the plaintiff. He was clearly guilty, as I find the facts, of serious and dangerous foul play which showed a reckless disregard of the plaintiff's safety and which fell far below the standards which might reasonably be expected of anyone pursuing the game."

In the Court of Appeal, Sir John Donaldson concurred totally with this view.

In the case of *Brown*, his counsel pled the case on the following basis in the summons: "The said accident was caused by the fault and negligence of the first defender for whose actings and omissions in the course of his employment with them the second defenders are liable. It was his duty to take reasonable care for the safety of other players such as the pursuer. It was his duty to take reasonable care to tackle such other players in an accepted manner and not by means of a foul. It was his duty to attempt to capture the said ball from the pursuer during the said tackle and not

to strike the pursuer as averred with both feet. In any event, it was his duty to take reasonable care not to leap at the pursuer with both feet. He knew or ought to have known that if he leapt at the pursuer with both feet there was a likelihood of his injuring the pursuer. In particular it was his duty to take reasonable care to tackle in accordance with the accepted rules and convention of football, to keep control of his feet so as not to endanger other players such as the pursuer and to avoid striking the pursuer on the right leg with both feet. In the said duties the first defender failed and his said failure caused the said accident. Had he fulfilled the said duties incumbent on him, the said accident would not have occurred."

The *Murray* case was pled in the closed record as follows: "The said accident was caused by fault on the part of the first defender for whose actings and omissions in the course of his employment with them the second defenders are liable. It was the first defender's duty to take reasonable care for the safety of other players in the said match including the pursuer. It was his duty to take reasonable care in tackling opposing players such as the pursuer and to do so within the rules and conventions of the game. It was his duty to take reasonable care to avoid striking the pursuer after the pursuer had played the ball. He knew or ought to have known that there was a likelihood of causing injury to the pursuer if he lunged at the pursuer with his foot high and his studs of his boot visible. It was his duty to take reasonable care to avoid striking the pursuer with his foot. In the exercise of the aforesaid duties, the first defender failed and thus caused the accident. He failed to take reasonable care to avoid striking the pursuer with his foot. In the exercise of the aforesaid duties, the first defender failed and thus caused the accident. He failed to take reasonable care for the pursuer. He failed to tackle the pursuer within the rules and convention of the game. He failed to attempt to gain possession of the ball or to dispossess the pursuer of the ball. He struck the pursuer after the pursuer had played the ball, and with his foot high. But for the first defender's failures in duty, the accident would have been avoided."

There should be noted, with regard to both cases, the averments that play should be "within the rules and conventions of the game".

Volenti non fit injuria

The apparent reluctance of players to proceed to litigation might well have resulted from their legal advisers' understanding of the doctrine of volenti non fit injuria, but it is now probably accepted that such a defence would not prevail.

Competitors must accept the risks inherent in their sport but they are not bound to accept the risk that fellow competitors might act in flagrant disregard of the rules and practice of the sport (Walker, *Delict* (2nd ed), p 630). Even if it were known that a fellow competitor was in the habit of indulging in foul play, continuing to play against such a competitor would not establish per se that the victim accepted that he would bear the risk of injury.

Vicarious liability

The *Brown* case also raised, for the first time, the issue of vicarious liability because St Johnstone football club were sued as second defenders, responsible for the actings and omissions of the first defender in the course of his employment. Basically, the position is that if a player is acting "within the scope of his employment", the club as his employer will be liable. The meaning of this phrase is discussed by Lord President Clyde in *Kirby v National Coal Board*, 1959 SLT 7 at pp 10-11; 1958 SC 514 at pp 532-533. Essentially, there is an important distinction between, on the one hand, an improper mode of doing an authorised act and, on the other, an act outside the scope of the works for which an employee has been employed — in other words, an independent act. The master is liable for the former but not the latter. (See also *Angus v Glasgow Corporation*, 1977 SLT 206, *Park v Tractor Shovels*, 1980 SLT 94, and *Williams v A & W Hemphill Ltd*, 1966 SLT 259.)

What then is the work for which a professional footballer is employed? Is the club vicariously liable for a foul tackle? A somewhat cynical view might be that the player is employed to return to the dressing room at the end of the game having acquired two points (or three in England) for his team. If this is achieved, there will be little concern about the method of acquisition. One only has to look at the bonus structure of most leading clubs to gain support for this view.

There is authority however for the view that a deliberate assault would fall outwith the employee's scope of employment and, consequently, that an employer is not responsible for an employee's criminal act unless the employer incited, induced or commanded it (*Woodhead v Gartness Mineral Co* (1877) 4 R 469 at p 504). In that passage, however, it is pointed out that what is required to elide responsibility is that the employee's act should have been intentional and malicious, and it is accepted that the employer's responsibility will extend to acts done recklessly or in momentary anger.

Thus in *Dyer v Mundy* [1895] 1 QB 742 an employee of a furniture store assaulted a householder while attempting to repossess furniture hired to a lodger, and it was held that he was acting within the scope of his employment, rendering his employer vicariously liable. A contrasting example is *Warren v Henlys* [1948] 2 All ER 935, where, after a dispute about payment for petrol, a forecourt attendant struck a customer. It was held that the assault was unconnected with any work the attendant was employed to do and, accordingly, that the employers were not liable. It would appear unlikely however that a footballer's foul tackle was motivated by personal spite or vengeance, as opposed to attempting to advance his employer's aims, and thus the writer cannot foresee football clubs avoiding liability.

Every professional football club is required to carry indemnity insurance and indeed it is the insurers who would have to settle any claim if the club were vicariously liable. It is a fair assumption that premiums have been reasonable to date. They will certainly increase if there is an upsurge in claims and this possibility is no doubt of concern to the SFA. One would like to hope that clubs now have a financial interest in ensuring that their employees play within the rules of the game and will discipline players accordingly.

Quantification of damages

Clearly, awards of damages to professional footballers at the top of the profession could be very high because a foul tackle can cause serious injuries which prevent a player from ever playing again. In any such case, the quantification of damages is likely to be more difficult than in the normal reparation claim as a result of the speculation involved in assessing future earnings. In the *Murray* case, for example, the writer's firm was dealing with a reserve team player who, it was suggested, would have gone on to make the grade, but, inevitably, this was disputed by the defenders. The action was for £900,000 and it is believed that in the *Durrant* case the amount claimed was similar. Nevertheless, footballers injured in the course of their employment should be treated no differently from other workers pursuing reparation actions as a result of industrial or work related injuries.

A further difficulty is that a normal multiplier is not appropriate given the average retiral age of a professional footballer. An examination of the cases involving divers has proved useful because they will quite often only continue to dive until around the age of 40. For instance, in *Howard v Comex Houlder Diving Ltd*, 1987 SLT 344, a multiplier of 3 was considered appropriate for someone aged 25 at the time of the accident and

30 at the date of the proof. Consideration has also been given to some of the arbitration awards following on the Piper Alpha disaster.

Conclusion
In both Scotland and England, judicial opinion is eagerly awaited as to the standard of care to be exercised by professional footballers towards each other. It is obvious that this would be equally applicable to other sports such as rugby (about which a separate article could be written). Until such a judgment is forthcoming, some players who have perfectly good grounds of action might not proceed because of the perceived uncertainty over the standard of care and the necessary finding of negligence to support an award of damages. Nowadays, most top league matches are recorded on video tape, thus difficulties regarding evidence of the tackle or challenge should not be difficult to obtain even although interpretation may vary.

◆

NEWS

Court

Sheriff courts: programming of business
The Secretary of State for Scotland has set up a working group to implement recommendations on programming of business and bring further aspects under review: see Parliamentary News, p 180.

Coming events

Association internationale des jeunes avocats
The annual congress of the International Association of Young Lawyers will take place in Vichy from 30 August to 2 September 1994. Working sessions include: environmental protection; Europe after Maastricht; NAFTA; and force majeure in international contracts. Registration fees, excluding accommodation, are 4,400 French francs for under 30s, and 4,800 French francs for over 30s, if booking before 30 June 1994.

For further details, contact Lindy Patterson, Bird Semple, Napier House, 27 Thistle Street, Edinburgh EH2 1BS (tel 031-459 2345).

General

Bail: Scottish Office report
The Scottish Office have published a report into the workings of the Bail etc (Scotland) Act 1980. *Operating Bail* is the result of a two year study into the decision making processes surrounding bail. The study examined bail decisions in detail as they were made by the police, prosecutors and the courts in three areas of Scotland. The researchers observed decisions being made, questioned those involved in the criminal justice system about their decisions, and followed cases through to their final disposal. The study included interviews with members of the High Court about their role in bail appeals.

The research was undertaken by Dr Fiona Paterson and Ms Claire Whittaker of the central research unit of the Scottish Office. It was found that the nature of bail decisions varies in different areas of the country. Practices of police, prosecutors and courts differed noticeably between the areas studied. The research found that relationships between criminal justice agencies in each of the study areas led to the creation of distinctive local criminal justice "cultures" involving a propensity towards greater use of one of bail, remand or "liberation" (i e release pending further action without any of the conditions associated with bail): in a "bail culture" the category of persons released on bail takes in those who in other cultures may either have been liberated without conditions or remanded; in the "bail culture" areas, 30 per cent of alleged bail offences in the sample were not proved, whereas 10 per cent of bail offences were not proved in the sample from the other areas; and in the "remand culture" area, a greater proportion of those who were ultimately found not guilty had spent time in prison during the course of their case (52 per cent of this group compared to around 20 per cent of the same group in the bail and liberation culture areas).

Unlike liberation without conditions, bail establishes a means of identifying that any alleged further offences are associated with those who have current contact with the criminal justice system. The study sample in the low bail area were found on arrest to be just as likely to have cases pending as those in the high bail area though they were less likely to be on bail. The implication of this is that in a "bail culture" area more "further offences" are recorded as such than would be the case in other cultures.

Where bail predominates rather than liberation, bail records are more likely to be generated for individual offenders, leading to an increased likelihood of remand should these offenders come before the courts in future. Accused involved in the same type of behaviour in areas where bail does not predominate will not have a similar past record of bail abuse and therefore are less likely to be remanded for this reason. A high use of bail therefore has the potential to lead over time to an increase in the remand population. The research did not find evidence that a high use of bail placed the public at increased risk from large scale serious further offending. Nor was there evidence that, in the area with a higher use of remand, this was providing greater protection to the public.

The research also found that there is confusion over the current application of the Wheatley guidelines on bail. Some procurators fiscal and sheriffs do not regard them as relevant. The researchers found that the lack of information about High Court decisions on bail appeals contributed to this uncertainty. Further, the statistics of recorded breaches of bail are mistakenly seen as an indicator of recidivism, since the statistics on offending on bail only record those alleged offences on bail reported by the police. No account is taken of the eventual outcome of any proceedings. These statistics are often misinterpreted as indicating risk to the public from people who might otherwise, it is assumed, be held on remand.

Copies of the report are available from HMSO, price £15.95.

◇

Child witnesses

Strathclyde University has published the results of a two year study of the interviewing of child witnesses. The research was intended to examine the skills and strategies needed for improving the testimony of child witnesses, and indicates that young children, particularly those between the ages of five and six, are most responsive to a direct and businesslike approach from adult interviewers, provided such an approach is not intimidating. This suggests that "rapport building" may be ineffective in certain circumstances, and that a flexible approach is required. Further information can be obtained from Dr Jim Baxter, Department of Psychology, University of Strathclyde (tel 041-552 4400, ext 2242).

Socio-legal research

The Scottish Office central research unit has published Vol 3 of its report entitled *Socio-Legal Research in the Scottish Courts*. The report brings together papers presented at a conference in 1993 of the same name organised by the Centre for Criminology and the Social and Philosophical Study of Law at Edinburgh University. Included are papers entitled "Sexual evidence reformed?", "A research evaluation of programmes for violent men", "Small claims — the court perspective", "A consumer perspective on small claims", "Bail decisions: risk, uncertainty, choice", "Criminal appeals", and comments on and responses to each paper by other participants in the conference. Copies of the report are available, priced £5, from the Librarian, Scottish Office, Room 1/44, New St Andrew's House, Edinburgh EH1 3TG (tel 031-244 4806).

— ◇ —

Taxation

Counter avoidance of PAYE

The Inland Revenue have now made regulations, following the draft noted at 1994 SLT (News) 110, which provide the rules for employers to operate the PAYE system if they pay their staff in assets or via certain intermediaries.

The most important change from the draft provides an exclusion from PAYE for shares (as well as for options over shares) in an employee's company. Ministers approved this change in response to representations from employers and their representatives that the original proposal would have created difficulties for some existing employee share schemes entered into for genuine commercial reasons.

The regulations came into effect for payments on or after 25 May 1994.

— ◇ —

Obituaries

On 16 May 1994, Alexander James Ramsay Bisset, WS, formerly senior partner in the firm of Messrs Biggart, Baillie & Gifford, WS, Edinburgh.

On 18 May 1994, Iain William Noble, formerly partner in the firm of Messrs Dundas & Wilson, CS, Edinburgh, and Professor Emeritus of Scots Law at Edinburgh University.

On 19 May 1994, Robert Martin, MC, formerly senior partner in the firm of Messrs Wright & Crawford, solicitors, Paisley.

— ◇ —

Business changes

Melrose & Porteous, Kelso and Coldstream; G R Wood & Muir, Eyemouth; Andersons, Duns; and Wallace & Menzies, North Berwick, intimate that with effect from 5 April 1994 Sara Louise Birnie has been appointed as an associate.

McClure Naismith Anderson & Gardiner intimate that with effect from 1 May 1994 George W Frier, Nicholas P Naddell and Andrew S C Macmillan have been assumed as partners in the firm, G Paul Gilks, an English solicitor, has been appointed as a consultant and Steven G Edgecombe has been appointed an associate. With effect from 30 April 1994 Thomas Gardiner retired as a consultant.

Semple Fraser, WS, 130 St Vincent Street, Glasgow, announce that with effect from 16 May 1994 Alan Stewart has joined the firm as a partner.

— ◇ —

Parliamentary News

New Bills

HOUSE OF COMMONS

13 May 1994

Firearms (Amendment)—To create a new offence of possessing a firearm or imitation firearm with intent to cause fear of violence; to apply certain provisions of the Firearms Act 1968 to imitation firearms; and for connected purposes. (Private Member's Bill introduced by Mr Richard Shersby)

16 May 1994

Landlord and Tenant (Covenants)—To make provision for persons bound by covenants of a tenancy to be released from such covenants on the assignment of the tenancy, and to make other provision with respect to rights and liabilities arising under such covenants; to restrict in certain circumstances the operation of rights of re-entry, forfeiture and disclaimer; and for con-

nected purposes. (Private Member's Bill introduced by Mr Peter Thurnham)

17 May 1994

Homicide (Defence of Provocation)—To amend the Homicide Act 1957 in respect of the defence of provocation. (Private Member's Bill introduced by Mr Harry Cohen)

18 May 1994

Pardon for Soldiers of the Great War—To provide for the granting of pardons to soldiers of the British Empire Forces executed during the Great War of 1914-18 following conviction for offences of cowardice, desertion or attempted desertion, disobedience, quitting post, violence, sleeping at post, throwing away arms or striking a superior officer; and for connected purposes. (Private Member's Bill introduced by Mr Andrew Mackinlay)

Education (Admission to Higher Education)—To reform the admission procedure to United Kingdom institutions of higher education for all school leavers by holding the relevant public examinations in mid-April to mid-May; to allow applicants to more than one institution to disclose to each institution the application relevant to that institution alone and to offer to applicants the right to see references given on their behalf to higher education institutions; and for connected purposes. (Private Member's Bill introduced by Mr Jeff Rooker)

Progress of Bills

Local Government etc (Scotland) — Commons: remaining stages completed, 19 May 1994.

Insolvency — Lords: third reading, 19 May 1994.

Social Security (Incapacity for Work) — Lords: third reading, 19 May 1994.

Sunday Trading — Lords: third reading, 19 May 1994.

Questions answered

HOUSE OF COMMONS

11 May 1994

SHERIFFS' COURTS

Mr Gallie: To ask the Secretary of State for Scotland what proposals he has to improve the programming of business in the sheriffs' courts.

Mr Lang: Consultations with interested

parties indicated general support for the recommendations in the first report on court programming prepared by groups under the chairmanship of Sheriff Principal Gordon Nicholson, QC and Sheriff Principal, then Sheriff Graham Cox, QC. Following consultation with the sheriffs principal, I have decided to set up a group under the chairmanship of Sheriff Principal Gordon Nicholson, QC, to facilitate the implementation of the recommendations in the first report and to bring under review other aspects of court programming. The membership of the group will be as follows:

Sheriff Principal Gordon Nicholson, QC (Chairman), Lothian and Borders

Mr Roy Cameron, QPM, Chief Constable, Dumfries and Galloway

Sheriff Robert Dickson, Airdrie

Mr James Friel, Regional Procurator Fiscal, North Strathclyde

Mr Andrew Gallen, Solicitor, Glasgow

Mr Duncan Lowe, Crown Agent

Mr Gordon Murray, CB, Director, Scottish Courts Administration

Ms Alison Paterson, Director, Victim Support

Ms Marilyn Riddell (Secretary), Edinburgh Sheriff Court

Mr John Robertson, Regional Sheriff Clerk, Grampian, Highland and Islands

Book Reviews

Textbook on Torts

Fourth edition by Michael G Jones. 1993.
London: Blackstone Press Ltd. Paperback, £15.95.
ISBN 1 85431 268 5.

The market for textbooks on the subject of Torts is a competitive one, with both a large range and variable quality. The fact that the text presently under review is now in its fourth edition (in only seven years — such is the pace of change in this area of the law) suggests that it has successfully found a niche in that market and an examination of the work suggests that such success is well deserved.

As one may surmise from the title, this book is aimed squarely at the student market and is an excellent example of its genre. However, it is not only the student who is likely to find the book useful, as the harried practitioner looking for an up to date summary of the key points and judicial decisions in areas such as the law relating to negligence is almost certainly bound to find some assistance here. The book provides excellent, accurate summaries of the state of the law in the areas which it covers, along with concise critical comment on the manner in which the law is developing. Those seeking guidance on such areas as the current law on economic loss and nervous shock could certainly do worse than start here. While, since this is a general text, some matters are not dealt with in as much detail as one would perhaps wish, those wishing to take their research further further will find plentiful citation of authority, along with references to relevant articles and parts of other textbooks. In accordance with the emerging practice (at least of the House of Lords and textbook writers) the cross references include references not only to English cases, but also where appropriate to cases from Commonwealth jurisdictions. However, one will search almost in vain for cross references to Scottish cases (other than the usual references to the leading cases which made it to the House of Lords), a fact which diminishes the usefulness of the book to Scottish readers.

Given this point, it is worth stating that, as with similar texts, some care has to be exercised in the use of the book by Scottish readers. While there are some instances where the English law of torts and the Scots law of delict are identical or virtually identical (most obviously in the case of negligence), there are still significant differences between the two and when reading the book these differences must be borne in mind. In this respect, it is worth noting that even some of the chapter headings should be treated with caution — the question of occupiers' liability is, in this book, treated as being a sub-set of negligence ("Negligence V: Dangerous Premises") rather than as a separate issue of (largely) statutory liability.

However, these difficulties are by no means insurmountable — use of the book along with an appropriate Scots law text should obviate most of them. As a companion to such a text, and/or treated with appropriate caution, this is an excellent text not only for students but, as I have suggested above, also for practitioners.

James G Logie,
Office of the Solicitor to the
Secretary of State for Scotland.

Conveyancing Manual

Fifth edition. By A J McDonald. 1993.
Edinburgh: T & T Clark. Paperback, £25.
ISBN 0 567 29230 4.

For the student in the mid-1970s (as I then was), there may have been an abundance of desert boots in shoe shops but there was a considerable dearth of texts on conveyancing in bookshops. Since the late 1970s several books have appeared on this subject. One of the earliest of the modern textbooks on the subject was McDonald's *Conveyancing Practice*, the first edition of which came out in 1982.

The fourth edition is about four years old and although there have been no major conveyancing innovations since that edition emerged with registration of title creeping across Scotland (affecting both the student and the practitioner) this is a good time to bring out a fifth edition.

The preface states that the book is a student text. That is an important market to cover and as a student text it succeeds. Writing a student text is probably more difficult than writing a practitioner's text in the sense that, with a student text, what is left out is often as important as what is put in. For instance while the realistic representation of plans, searches and land registration forms would give the student a taste of the real thing and is therefore an excellent advantage, it was not perhaps so necessary to give so many specific styles of deeds (which can be found elsewhere).

In a student text, layout is often important, if only to encourage its use, and this edition has been laid out well. The general introduction is helpful and cases are put beside the statements they vouch rather than in footnotes.

The book is split into five different parts which form a natural progression around the conveyancing system in Scotland.

A lot of time is spent on registration of title. While this is justified, the subject is dealt with under "Feus". I wondered if it would not have been more comfortable with "Completion of Title".

It might not be necessary in such a book to deal with commercial leases and agricultural leases in great detail, whereas the section on residential leases is perfect because it gives a brief but adequate understanding of the subject. On the other hand the detail given on contracts of sale and examination of title is quite justified as that is a specific area of study in the diploma. But the chapter on a typical conveyancing transaction may be a bit beyond the student.

The authors have also, very commendably, highlighted certain areas that one would not automatically think had conveyancing implications, such as the sections on VAT, council tax and environmental protection.

This particular edition is more user friendly than previous editions. The print is larger, there is a good use of bold print with headings and there is an excellent reading list and digest of cases, although we are not given the name of the defender in most cases.

Some things have changed their position. In the fourth edition there was a chapter on "Infeftment", but this has been replaced by one on "Registration". In the fourth edition there was a section on "Reform". That section has gone and while in various places there is passing mention of reform, as a student textbook it might have been appropriate to mention reform specifically. This is an area where the student would be particularly interested and which is perhaps of less immediate interest to the practitioner.

While the number of texts on conveyancing may be on the increase, quality texts are still few and far between. This is one of the quality ones, at least from the student's standpoint. Although it is not, as the author admits, specialised, this book should be the first stop on the (former) student's shopping trip when he (hopefully) does move into practice (having abandoned his desert boots for training shoes), to find the answer to his particular practical problem.

L D Most,
Alexander Stone & Co,
Glasgow.

Bill Stewart, the Book Review Editor, is keen that books, and especially, books written with the practitioner in mind should be reviewed by practitioners. Accordingly, members of Faculty and solicitors who consider that they could competently review books, are invited to write with a note of their name and address, indicating upon what subjects they would be prepared to write reviews, to him c/o MacMillans, Solicitors, 78 Springfield Road, Glasgow G40 3ET.

ARTICLES

Dead on Delivery
Sharp v Thomson, 11 May 1994

Robert Rennie,
University of Glasgow.

Professor Rennie describes the Sharp *case, which appears to put at risk the holder of any unrecorded title, and suggests what practical measures may require to be implemented to counteract its effects.*

Cases relating to conveyancing topics appear with ever increasing frequency every year in the courts. Many cases are dealt with as a matter of routine, but occasionally a decision throws the profession into a state of confusion and uncertainty. *Winston v Patrick*, 1981 SLT 41; 1980 SC 246, was such a case in relation to the supersession of missives. *Rutterford v Allied Breweries*, 1990 SLT 249 and *Findlater v Maan*, 1990 SLT 465; 1990 SC 150, were cases of this type in relation to the conclusion of missives and the withdrawal of formal letters. More recently, *Lloyds Bank v Bamberger*, 1994 SLT 424, was such a case in relation to the question of penalty interest. There may well be a feeling among those who practise conveyancing that the courts should simply leave them alone. Unfortunately, the courts require to decide such matters as are brought before them and in the recent Outer House decision in the case of *Sharp and Souter (Receivers of Albyn Construction Ltd) v Thomson and Woolwich Building Society*, 11 May 1994, 1994 GWD 19-1181, another large boulder has been thrown into the already rippling conveyancing pool.

The case relates to delivery of deeds and what rights in the property (if any) are transferred on delivery of a disposition to the disponee on settlement of a transaction. It is perhaps well to look at what was thought, by some at least, to be the effect of delivery of a deed before looking at the case itself. Professor Halliday (*Conveyancing Law and Practice*, Vol I, para 9-05) states: "If rights conferred by the deed are such that they will become real rights of property only upon further procedure such as registration in an appropriate register, although the rights are created real only when registration has been effected, the personal right to the property is completed on delivery of the deed."

In *Sharp v Thomson* the pursuers were joint receivers appointed by the Bank of Scotland on 10 August 1990 in respect of a floating charge dated 2 July and registered 16 July 1984, covering the whole property of the company from time to

time. By missives concluded on 23 May 1989 the company sold a basement flat in Aberdeen to Mr and Mrs Thomson with a date of entry of 14 April 1989. On 9 August 1990 the company executed a feu disposition of the property and this was delivered to Mr and Mrs Thomson's solicitors on that date. The feu disposition was recorded in the Register of Sasines on 21 August 1990. The deed contained a date of entry of 14 April 1989. Mr and Mrs Thomson granted a standard security in favour of Woolwich Building Society on 31 July 1990 and that deed was also recorded on 21 August 1990.

The receivers argued that the property remained in the ownership of the company as at 10 August 1990 and was therefore attached by the floating charge which crystallised on that date. Further, the receivers argued that the floating charge operated by law as a fixed security from the date of crystallisation, having priority over the standard security in favour of Woolwich Building Society. The receivers sought a declarator that they were entitled to take possession of the subjects and sell or otherwise dispose of them. Not unnaturally the purchasers and their building society contended that on the date the feu disposition was delivered, the company was effectively divested of the beneficial ownership of the subjects and the floating charge did not attach to the property in question.

The case was well argued before Lord Penrose in the Outer House. It was debated on the procedure roll and thereafter his Lordship put the case out by order so that further authorities might be discussed. On 11 May 1994 his Lordship repelled the pleas in law for both defenders, sustained the receivers' fourth plea in law and granted decree de plano in their favour, holding that despite delivery of the feu disposition the floating charge attached to the subjects and the receivers took priority over the purchasers and their building society.

The significance of the decision
It will not take conveyancers long to realise the significance of this decision. The cheque for the purchase price had been handed over in exchange for delivery of the feu disposition. In most conveyancing transactions there is normally a gap while the disposition is completed and stamped and sent to the appropriate register. If a purchaser is buying from a limited company such as a builder or developer, the purchaser may now be at risk until such time as the title is recorded or registered. The decision however may not just affect purchases from limited companies. If the

decision is correct in its wider aspects, then it may affect purchases even from individuals who may of course go bankrupt in the intervening period.

It must be remembered however that *Sharp v Thomson* itself relates to the competition between a crystallised floating charge which has become a fixed security and the title of a purchaser and that purchaser's lender. It may not affect ordinary sales by individuals, although this must be regarded as uncertain.

The arguments in the case revolved round the differences between a ius crediti, ius ad rem and ius in re. A ius crediti is, of course, simply a personal right which exists between purchaser and seller at the date of conclusion of missives. It has always been accepted that if the seller goes bankrupt or into liquidation or receivership prior to delivery of the disposition or other title, then the purchaser has no rights in the property whatsoever and will be at the mercy of the trustee in bankruptcy, liquidator or receiver (*Gibson v Hunter Home Designs Ltd*, 1976 SLT 94; 1976 SC 23). A ius ad rem was generally supposed, by some at least, to be a personal right in the property obtained after delivery of the deed which would be good at least against the seller and any representative of the seller such as a trustee, trustee in bankruptcy or liquidator. A ius in re was regarded as being a real right in the property good against all parties and this of course was only achieved on infeftment. Infeftment was originally obtained by taking sasine, but following various land registration statutes is now obtained by recording the deed in the Register of Sasines or effecting registration in the Land Register of Scotland.

The purchasers' case

The defenders argued:

(1) That delivery of the deed removed the flat from the whole property of the company and therefore from the grasp of the floating charge.

(2) That on delivery of the deed the purchasers had at least a ius ad rem or personal right to the subjects which could only be defeated if another party recorded or registered a title before the purchaser.

(3) That although after delivery the company remained infeft, this was a bare title which would disappear as soon as the purchaser recorded the title, there being nothing which the company could lawfully do after delivery in respect of the property to prevent this.

(4) That after delivery no competing party had any right to the property and the company had no

vestige of residual beneficial interest in the property as an asset.

(5) That on delivery the seller required to do no more and indeed could do no more to transfer the flat as an asset to the purchaser.

In summary, the argument was that the heritable property comprised in the feu disposition was no longer the property of the company on 10 August 1990 when the floating charge crystallised and accordingly could not be subject to that floating charge which had then become a fixed security.

As an alternative argument, senior counsel for the building society focused on the interpretation of s 462 (1) of the Companies Act 1985 and s 53 (7) of the Insolvency Act 1986. This argument centred round whether or not the flat could be said to be part of the "property" of the company as at the date of crystallisation. In his argument senior counsel adopted a broad view of the concept of "property", as distinct from the narrow view of a real right in feudal property constituted only by infeftment. Senior counsel adopted Erskine's definition of property, namely that it was a right recognised by law to use and dispose of a thing as one's own.

In many ways this type of broad definition of a right of property is similar to the opinion of Lord Macnaghten in *Heritable Reversionary Co v Millar* (1892) 19 R (HL) 43 when his Lordship spoke generally of something belonging to a person in relation to ownership. Senior counsel's view was that in the context of the companies legislation and floating charges, the word "property" was to be defined in that general sense and not in the strict narrow sense of infeftment or perfected feudal title.

Senior counsel also made much of the fact that there was no question of a race to the register. There was no question of the receivers having been able to complete a title in any sense. This was not a competition between two purchasers where a second purchaser had obtained later delivery of a deed but had been able to record or register it first. This was purely a competition between the rights of a creditor under a floating charge and a purchaser with a delivered deed. Senior counsel submitted that, applying Erskine's definition of property as something which simply belonged to a party, it followed that the floating charge did not attach to anything after delivery because after delivery there was no right to use the land, no right to make grants of or connected with the land, and no right in law to do anything in relation to the subjects remaining with the company. The floating charge holder was, after all, never vested in the subjects themselves. That was not the nature of a charge.

Alternatively counsel for the purchasers argued that there was a constructive trust in favour of the purchasers from the date of delivery of the deed which was good against the rights of the floating charge holder. This perhaps was the most difficult of all the arguments to put forward because the doctrine of constructive trust came in for some criticism by Lord Cameron in the *Gibson v Hunter Home Designs* case.

In support of their arguments the various counsel for the two defenders referred inter alia to the following cases: *Heritable Reversionary Co v Millar* (1892) 19 R (HL) 43 especially at pp 49 and 53; *Hawking v Hafton House Ltd*, 1990 SLT 496; *Thomas v Lord Advocate*, 1953 SC 151 especially at pp 158 and 161 (1953 SLT 119); *Embassy Picture House (Troon) Ltd v Cammo Developments Ltd*, 1971 SC 25 especially at p 28 (1970 SLT (Notes) 85); *Gibson v Hunter Home Designs*, 1976 SC 23 and in particular the opinions of the Lord President at p 26 and Lord Cameron at pp 30-31 (1976 SLT 94); *Margrie Holdings Ltd v Commissioners of Customs and Excise*, 1991 SLT 38 and in particular the opinion of Lord President Hope at p 42; *Lombardi's Tr v Lombardi*, 1982 SLT 81; *James Grant & Co v Moran*, 1948 SLT (Sh Ct) 8; and *The Life Association of Scotland v Black's Leisure Group*, 1989 SLT 674.

The receivers' case

Counsel for the receivers submitted quite simply that the subjects were attached by the floating charge in terms of the Insolvency Act 1986, ss 53, 55 and 70. Counsel adopted the simple argument that on crystallisation on 10 August 1990 the floating charge took effect as if it were a standard security recorded on 10 August 1990. In a sense therefore counsel was stating that the holders of the floating charge were already in the register by statutory fiction and the only issue was whether delivery of the feu disposition on 9 August had divested the company of the property so that it could not have been attached. Counsel for the receivers made the following points:

(1) That Scots law initially required sasine to divest the seller of the real right in the property and that sasine was eventually effected by recording or registration.

(2) That there was a fundamental distinction between real and personal rights and that recording or registration was necessary to complete the transfer of a real right.

(3) That both ius crediti and ius ad rem were

personal rights, the only difference being that in the latter case the disponee who held the delivered title could obtain a real right in the property without any further act of the disponer.

(4) That a ius ad rem or personal right to property was virtually meaningless as a property right.

(5) That even after delivery, the disponee was exposed to the risk that the disponer might grant a subsequent disposition which if recorded or registered first could defeat the purchaser's right.

In his submission counsel for the receivers made great play of the fact that the recording or registration of a title was merely the equivalent to the ancient system of taking sasine and that no one could divest themselves of their right of feudal ownership before sasine was taken by the purchaser. Counsel referred to the following cases: *Forth & Clyde Construction Co Ltd v Trinity Timber and Plywood Co Ltd*, 1984 SLT 94; 1984 SC 1; *Edmond v Gordon* (1857) 3 Macq 116 especially at pp 122 and 129; *Young v Leith* (1847) 9 D 932 especially at pp 932-944; *Cameron's Tr v Cameron*, 1907 SC 407 especially at pp 413, 421 and 425 ((1907) 14 SLT 719); *Mitchell v Ferguson* (1781) Mor 10296; *Gibson v Hunter Home Designs*, supra, especially the judgment of Lord Cameron at 1976 SC, pp 29 and 30; *Cormack v Anderson* (1829) 7 S 868 especially at pp 870-871; *Melville v Paterson* (1842) 4 D 1311 especially at p 1315; *Heritable Reversionary Co v Millar* especially at pp 49-50; *Rodger (Builders) v Fawdry*, 1950 SLT 345; 1950 SC 483; and *Clark Taylor & Co v Quality Site Development (Edinburgh) Ltd*, 1981 SLT 308; 1981 SC 111.

Perhaps the most interesting discussion in the case surrounded the previous decision of *Gibson v Hunter Home Designs*. Most practitioners will have assumed from that decision, and in particular the judgment of the Lord President, that a purchaser is safe at least from the sellers and creditors, trustees in bankruptcy, liquidators or receivers of the sellers if delivery of the deed has taken place. Not surprisingly, counsel for the defenders referred to the case and in particular the judgment of the Lord President. Counsel for the pursuers however referred to the judgment of Lord Cameron.

Lord Penrose's judgment

In his judgment Lord Penrose stated that two requirements fell to be met if the receivers were to succeed: (a) the subjects must fall within the expression "the property . . . comprised in the property and undertaking" of the company on 10

August 1990; and (b) the interest of the company in the subjects on that date must have been such that as between the company and the floating charge creditor there could then attach to the subjects a standard security assumed to have been duly recorded without any act of the company being required (transcript, pp 34-35).

In relation to the *Heritable Reversionary Co v Millar* case, Lord Penrose took the view that it dealt with matters of trust and had no bearing on the matter in hand. His Lordship did however pay particular attention to the case of *Young v Leith* which had gone to the House of Lords and then been remitted back to the Court of Session for a hearing before the whole court. In his Lordship's opinion it was clear from that case that what was required to divest the grantor and invest the acquirer of heritage with a real right of property was registration and that in the absence of registration the property was not transferred.

In his Lordship's view the result of the authorities was: "that in a question with third parties the grantor of an unrecorded disposition remains fully vested with feudal right and title notwithstanding delivery of the deed until it is recorded in the Register of Sasines" (transcript, p 65).

His Lordship accepted that more difficult and substantial questions arose from the decision in *Gibson v Hunter Home Designs* and the related authorities. In that case the Lord President had stated (at p 27): "In the law of Scotland no right of property vests in a purchaser until there has been delivered to him the relevant disposition. On delivery of the disposition the purchaser becomes vested in a personal right to the subjects in question and his acquisition of a real right to the subjects is dependent on recording the disposition in the appropriate Register of Sasines. Putting the matter in another way, the seller of subjects under missives is not, in a question with the purchaser, divested of any part of his right of property in the subjects of sale until, in implement of his contractual obligation to do so, he delivers to the purchaser the appropriate disposition. Until the moment of delivery, the purchaser, even if he has paid the price and obtained occupation of the subjects, has no more than a right under the contract of sale, the missives, to demand performance by the seller of his contractual obligation to convey. Such right as the purchaser has, accordingly, is no more than a *ius crediti* until delivery of the disposition for which he contracted has been made to him."

In the *Gibson* case Lord Johnston concurred with the Lord President but Lord Cameron's opinion was slightly different. He likened the position of the liquidator to the position of a person with a decree of adjudication in terms of the old s 327 (1) (b) of the Companies Act 1948 and stated (p 30): "Thus if the debtor is the beneficial owner his personal obligation to convey the subjects to a third party even for onerous causes will not affect an adjudger. Even if the obligation has been so far implemented as by delivery of a conveyance or disposition, an adjudger infeft before the disponee will be preferred."

There is a suggestion here that delivery of itself may not convey any sort of right in the property. Lord Penrose concedes in his judgment that Lord President Emslie's opinion in *Gibson v Hunter Home Designs* reflects an established view of the effect of delivery of a disposition of heritage and also accepts that the view has been accepted in later cases as accurate — see the opinion of Lord Jauncey in *Lombardi's Tr v Lombardi* where he states: "It is trite law that a disponer of subjects does not divest himself of any right of property in those subjects until he delivers actually or constructively to the disponee a disposition thereof".

Lord Penrose also accepts that the current Lord President applied Lord Emslie's dictum in *Gibson* in the case of *Margrie Holdings Ltd v Commissioners of Customs and Excise* where he states (1991 SLT at p 41E-F): "there was no divestiture by Muirfield . . . until they delivered the disposition".

Lord Penrose brushes aside the comments of both Lord Presidents and Lord Jauncey as "wider comments". It is fair to state that the facts of *Sharp v Thomson* relate precisely to a competition between a floating charge which had become a fixed security and a delivered but unrecorded feu disposition. However Lord Penrose argues very much on a conceptual basis and not just on the particular circumstances. In contrasting a personal right to property with a real right in property, he makes the point that the notion of a partial transfer of property is fraught with difficulty. He states (transcript, p 76): "At best it must consist in a combination of incidents which asserts the transfer of beneficial ownership derived from, and wholly dependent on, the disposition, and divorced from obligation founded on the contract, with retention of formal title pending recording of the disposition."

Lord Penrose lays great stress on the majority decision in *Young v Leith* and rejects an intermediate position between a ius crediti and an absolute right in re. He states, having considered the case of *Young v Leith* in some detail: "In my opinion it follows that until recording, a disposition is not effective to divest the grantor and the subjects remain comprised in his property in circumstances such as the present. The alternative view necessarily implies a right of property in heritable subjects not only without infeftment, but while the grantor of the disposition remains infeft. In other words, it implies that the feudal fee in the undivided subjects has come to be shared between disponer and disponee on the delivery of the disposition. . . . Any analysis of 'property' in heritable subjects in such terms appears to be inconsistent with principle and to be impossible to reconcile with the majority opinion in *Young v Leith*."

Finally Lord Penrose had no difficulty in disposing with the "constructive trust" type argument which had also been rejected in *Gibson v Hunter Home*.

Is the decision correct?
Looking at the decision critically, it is easy to see both sides of this argument from a conceptual point of view. Anyone who has had to lecture students on the effect of the delivery of a disposition always finds it most difficult to put across the difference between the personal right or ius crediti which arises when missives are concluded, the personal right to the property which is supposed to arise on delivery of the disposition and the right in re which arises only on infeftment by recording or registration. There is no doubt that it is easier, conceptually, to have only a personal right against a person and real right in a thing arising on infeftment. The intermediate stage which was thought to follow delivery of a disposition is no easy matter to explain. However Lord Penrose in giving judgment has courageously disapproved the dictum of the Lord President in the *Gibson* case and it remains to be seen what will be made of this matter if the case reaches the Inner House. It is necessary to examine the decision in the narrow context of the particular case and in the wider context of the law relating to delivery in general.

(a) The case itself
It must be borne in mind that the case relates to a competition between a delivered but unrecorded feu disposition and a crystallised floating charge. The statutory provision states that on the appointment of a receiver the floating charge attaches to the property "as if the charge was a fixed security over the property" (Insolvency Act 1986, s 53 (7)). At the time of the crystallisation there is no doubt that the company still had a recorded title to the property. If a fixed security in relation to heritable property is deemed to

mean a recorded security in favour of a third party (the receivers) one can easily see why Lord Penrose took the view that the receivers were to be preferred. The problem however is what is to be regarded as the "property" of the company in terms of the section given the fact that the company had executed and delivered a feu disposition *and* received the price. Can it really be the case that the floating charge becomes a fixed security on both the property *and* the price of the property in circumstances where the title had been delivered and could be recorded by the grantee without any further help from the grantor? Is it not the case that the "property" is no longer part of the assets of the company on delivery of the deed and receipt of the price? This type of interpretation is of course to apply a commercial rather than strictly legal definition to the word "property", but this interpretation does seem to accord with the opinions of the Lord Presidents Emslie and Hope in the *Gibson* and *Margrie* cases.

(b) Delivery in general
Whatever conceptual arguments exist between a ius ad rem and a ius in re, it is difficult to see how Lord Penrose has been able to ignore the judgment of the Lord President in *Gibson*. It has to be said, however, that others have disagreed with the Lord President's dictum. There have been various articles on this topic (see K G C Reid, "Ownership on Delivery", 1982 SLT (News) 149; G L Gretton, "Delivery of Deeds and the Race to the Register" (1984) 29 JLS 400; A J McDonald, "Bankruptcy, Liquidation and Receivership and the Race to the Register" (1985) 30 JLS 20; G L Gretton and K G C Reid, "Insolvency and Title: a reply" (1985) 30 JLS 109; K G C Reid, "Ownership on Registration", 1985 SLT (News) 280).

When considering the question in relation to the bankruptcy proposals, the Scottish Law Commission took the view that the law was uncertain. They did however recommend that the trustee should not be entitled to any heritable property after delivery of the deed to someone who had acquired for value (*Report on Bankruptcy and Related Aspects of Insolvency on Liquidation* (Scot Law Com no 68), para 11.29). Unfortunately this recommendation was not enacted in the Bankruptcy (Scotland) Act 1985.

Among academics, there is a fairly clear division of view. Kenneth Reid and George Gretton take the simple but firm view that there can be no right in the property as such until recording or registration. Professor McDonald, Professor Burgess and some others take the view that the matter is either uncertain or that some sort of right in or to the property passes on delivery.

The arguments which passed to and fro between 1982 and 1985 are well set out in the articles already cited. In summary however the Reid/Gretton position is that there are only two stages where rights accrue in a conveyancing transaction. On conclusion of missives a personal right accrues to the purchaser against the seller and this personal right remains on delivery of the disposition, although insofar as the disposition supersedes the missives, it then depends on the disposition. Only on infeftment by recording or registration is there any type of real right in the property. On this basis a floating charge holder whose charge has crystallised will always succeed against the grantee in a disposition because by statutory fiction the floating charge becomes an effective fixed security on the heritable property which presumably is deemed to be recorded or registered. Insofar as ordinary bankruptcies are concerned, the Reid/Gretton view appears to be that there will be a race to the register and if the liquidator or trustee cannot get a title on the register before the grantee in the disposition, the grantee will prevail.

The alternative view, as advanced by one former keeper and other academics, is that delivery in some way divests the granter of the substance of ownership, if not the bare title, and accordingly the grantee will succeed against trustees in bankruptcy, receivers with crystallised floating charges and liquidators, provided, presumably, the grantee records a title to the property immediately and in priority to any of the others. This theory is, it appears to the writer, not so much based on the notion of feudal title or infeftment having passed to the grantee, but on the notion of the grantor having divested himself of all the essentials of ownership in the wider sense of that word. For those who support the delivery theory, the critical question is not so much what type of ownership has been received by the grantee, but what (if any) type of ownership has been left with the grantor.

Conclusion

Messrs Gretton and Reid advance the theory that registration is the only thing which transfers ownership with authority and, it has to be said, with all the benefits which attach to a clear cut academic proposition. Those who advance the delivery theory face the problem that their views appear to run counter to the principle of ownership by infeftment on registration on which our land tenure system is based. However Messrs Gretton and Reid (like Lord Penrose) do brush aside a clutch of cases including *Gibson* and others which contain pronouncements clearly in favour of the delivery theory.

Furthermore, Messrs Gretton and Reid do not allow or admit the possibility that the question of what "property" is left with a grantor may depend on the context of the transaction. In the writer's view it is perfectly possible to adopt a particular definition of "property" in circumstances where the grantor has gone bankrupt or been put into liquidation or receivership which is different from the notion of full feudal ownership. The rules surrounding insolvency have always been characterised by a certain amount of equity. There can be no other reason for the latitude allowed to latent trusts in insolvency situations. Indeed the latent trust argument was put forward in the *Gibson* case and has been supported by Professor Burgess, although it probably has to be said that it has now been roundly rejected in the context of transfers of heritable property.

In relation to the present case it is submitted that Lord Penrose has not given sufficient weight to the arguments surrounding the definition of the company's "property" for the purpose of crystallisation, and in particular to the fact that there is a clear inequity if the floating charge can attach both to the property itself and to the proceeds of the property where a deed has been delivered. Furthermore, it is suggested that Lord Penrose, and indeed Messrs Gretton and Reid before him, all tend to overlook the fact that the dicta in the most recent case law in the Inner House tend to support the delivery theory no matter what the illogicality of that may be in the system where final ownership is dependent on recording or registration.

Suggestions for practice

On a practical level, there are now clear difficulties in relation to the settlement of a transaction, especially where the seller is a limited company. It must be obvious that very specific letters of non-crystallisation will be required from the holders of floating charges whereby they consent to the sale and bind themselves not to take steps to crystallise the floating charge within a set period of time. Fourteen days would appear to the writer to be an appropriate period.

Where the purchase is from an individual seller or a firm, it can be argued that the decision itself will not apply. However given the breadth of Lord Penrose's reasoning, it is not safe to assume that the same dangers do not exist in sales by individuals or firms. (See McBryde, *Bankruptcy*, p 104.) Consideration must now be given to asking the seller (whether a corporate entity or a firm) to sign a deed of trust confirming that the property is truly held in trust for the purchaser pending recording or registration. Practitioners will recall that this method of dealing with settlements of transactions was used during the industrial disputes at Register House. Such a deed of trust would, it is submitted, protect the purchaser even on the bankruptcy of the seller because the seller would only hold the bare title subject to the trust, and the trustee in bankruptcy would take tantum et tale (*Heritable Reversionary Co v Millar*). There would seem to be no good reason why the declaration of trust should not be included as an extra clause in the disposition itself.

The future

The practice of conveyancing has been bedevilled with uncertainties and worries of various kinds for more than a decade. The Scottish Law Commission have produced, or are in the process of producing, reports on the requirements of probative writing, the law of the tenement, the abolition of the feudal system and the supersession of missives and actio quanti minoris. Of these reports one has been outstanding since 1988. There surely must be a good argument for having a comprehensive Conveyancing (Scotland) Bill to deal not only with specific areas of law reform but also the type of problem thrown up by cases which, although of great interest to academics, bring in their wake the threat of catastrophe to ordinary practitioners and their clients.

◆

NEWS

Appreciation

Sir Allan Walker, QC, LLD

Sir Allan Grierson Walker QC, LLD, who was Sheriff Principal of Lanarkshire from 1963 to 1974, died on 22 May aged 87.

Sir Allan Walker was one of the finest lawyers of his time. Born on 1 May 1907 and educated at Whitgift School, Croydon and Edinburgh University, he practised at the Scottish bar from 1931 to 1939 when he became a sheriff. He served in Selkirk, Peebles and Dumbarton before being appointed to Glasgow in 1950. In 1963, when he was the senior sheriff in Glasgow, he was promoted to Sheriff Principal of Lanarkshire at a time when sheriffs principal were almost invariably appointed from the practising senior bar in the Parliament House.

Allan Walker's appointment was an outstanding success. Both on and off the bench his manner was courteous and unassuming. He never paraded the depth of his knowledge or the acuteness of his mind, but his few interventions in debate were pointed and his decisions, invariably expressed in measured and lucid terms, were founded on principle, learning and common sense. The confidence which the legal profession placed in his judgment was reflected in his large weekly roll of appeals from his sheriffs in civil cases. There was seldom any further appeal from his decision to the Court of Session, and few such appeals were successful. His judgments, which illuminated many areas of law and practice, form the most outstanding series of sheriff court decisions to have been reported since the regular reporting of such decisions began in 1885. His profound knowledge of the law and his exemplary judicial temperament fitted him for the highest office, and it was widely believed that he declined promotion to the bench of the High Court and the Court of Session.

As sheriff principal Sir Allan did not sit in criminal trials, over which he had attained an unobtrusive mastery in his years as senior sheriff, but he presided over several important fatal accident inquiries including that which followed the Ibrox disaster in 1971 when 66 people died and many were injured.

He also paid scrupulous attention to the administrative, social and ceremonial duties which form an essential part of a sheriff principal's responsibilities. Not the least of his problems was the management of the growing volume of business in Glasgow in the increasingly inadequate court house in Ingram Street. He was nevertheless a meticulous administrator, and he handled his sometimes difficult team of sheriffs with patience and tact. The success of the large annual dinners of the Glasgow Juridical Society owed much to his careful advice and quietly adroit chairmanship as the society's honorary president.

In addition to his burdens as sheriff principal Sir Allan was the first chairman of the Sheriff Court Rules Council from 1972 to 1974 after its establishment by the Sheriff Courts (Scotland) Act 1971. He was also a member of the Law Reform Committee for Scotland from 1964 to 1970. He wrote excellent articles on oral and written pleading, and edited the seventh and eighth editions of Purves' *Scottish Licensing Laws.* Glasgow University awarded him the honorary degree of LLD in 1967 and he was knighted in 1968.

Perhaps Sir Allan's most lasting memorial will be *The Law of Evidence in Scotland* (1963), which he wrote with another exceptionally fine scholar-sheriff, the late Norman M L Walker. Their formidable scholarship and industry produced an exhaustive and accurate work, fresh in approach and felicitous in expression, which is often cited with approval in the supreme courts and remains an invaluable resource for modern practitioners and scholars.

In retirement Sir Allan enjoyed walking and gardening at his home in Dumfriesshire until his health began to fail in later years. He is survived by his wife and son.

IAIN MACPHAIL.

General

Ombudsman's annual report
In his Annual Report for 1993, the Scottish Legal Services Ombudsman, Mr David Morrell, calls upon the Law Society of Scotland to use their powers to promote high quality professional services and to take effective action to reduce the number of occasions when clients receive unpleasant shocks over costs.

The Ombudsman again expresses concern over the failure of solicitors to give clients guidance on the likely level of costs. He points out that practice is inconsistent and confusing and that unless clients know that they will be given adequate information at first contact with a solicitor, complaints will continue to arise and members of the public will continue to be reluctant to consult solicitors in good time.

The report makes it clear that although serious differences of view still arise in a small number of cases, it is the Ombudsman's view that the attitudes and procedures of the Law Society are changing in response to the expectations of modern clients and in recognition that a good

service at a reasonable price is the best basis for professional success.

Temporary Sheriffs' Association
At the first annual general meeting of the Temporary Sheriffs' Association held in Edinburgh on 23 April 1994 the following office bearers were elected: *President,* Iain Macmillan, CBE; *vice president,* Alexander E McIlwain, CBE; *secretary,* Jamie H C Gilmour; *treasurer,* David T Crowe; *council members,* Alexander Bolland, QC, John C Morris, Marcus Green.

Correspondence course on Chinese commercial laws
The Wuhan University in the People's Republic of China will offer a correspondence course in Chinese commercial laws for people living outside China. Participants can choose to study either in English or Chinese.

The course consists of two parts, namely four core and four from 12 optional subjects. At the end, a postgraduate diploma in Chinese commercial laws will be awarded by the Wuhan University.

For more information, contact the liaison office, GPO box 12705, Hong Kong (fax (852) 544 9377 or 538 0914).

Rate of interest on landed securities
The commissioners on the rate of interest on landed securities in Scotland have resolved that the rate of interest on such first class securities shall be 7½ per cent per annum for the six months from and after the term of Whitsunday (28 May) 1994.

Obituary

On 22 May 1994, Frederick Hemming McClintock, Professor Emeritus of the University of Edinburgh.

Business change

Bennetts, solicitors, Cupar intimate that Isla J Ashcroft has been appointed as an associate.

Parliamentary News

New Bills

HOUSE OF COMMONS

24 May 1994

Fine Defaulters (Restriction of Power to Imprison)—To restrict the power of magistrates' courts to impose imprisonment for default of the payment of fines. (Private Member's Bill introduced by Dr Lynne Jones)

24 May 1994

Television Licences (Reduction for Poor Reception)—To give television licence holders a reduction in their licence fee when it is recognised that the household is unable to enjoy good television reception. (Private Member's Bill introduced by Mr Charles Hendry)

Progress of Bills

Deregulation and Contracting Out — Commons: remaining stages, 23 May 1994.

Value Added Tax — Lords: second reading, 23 May 1994.

Local Government (Scotland) — Commons: third reading, 24 May 1994.

Merchant Shipping (Salvage and Pollution) — Lords: second reading, 24 May 1994.

Antarctic — Lords: second reading, 25 May 1994.

Vehicle Excise and Registration — Lords: third reading, 26 May 1994.

Land Drainage — Lords: second reading, 26 May 1994.

Chiropractors — Lords: second reading, 26 May 1994.

Questions answered

HOUSE OF COMMONS

19 May 1994

RESIDENCE ARRANGEMENTS

Sir Teddy Taylor: To ask the Secretary of State for the Home Department if he will take steps to clarify the arrangements whereby persons of independent means are admitted to reside in the United Kingdom.

Mr Charles Wardle: We are planning to lay consolidated Immigration Rules before the House, which will create a new category of investor, designed to attract investment into the country without weakening the immigration control. The category of persons of independent means will continue but with a minimum age limit of 60.

EUROPEAN UNION ANTI-DISCRIMINATION LAW

Mr Wigley: To ask the Prime Minister if he will make a statement on the competence of the European Union in regard to the adoption of European law against discrimination whether on the basis of sex, race, age or disablement following the entry into force of the Maastricht treaty.

The Prime Minister: The entry into force of the treaty on European Union has not altered the European Community's competence to legislate in respect of the principles under article 119 of the treaty of Rome against discrimination on the basis of sex, or its lack of specific competence to legislate against discrimination on the basis of race, age or disablement.

20 May 1994

DNA TESTING

Mr Butcher: To ask the Parliamentary Secretary, Lord Chancellor's Department what is the accuracy of DNA tests; and if he will now introduce legislation to make blood tests compulsory in cases of disputed paternity.

Mr John M Taylor: DNA profiling evidence may be conclusive in eliminating a putative father from being the natural father of a child. It is also a technique which can provide extremely strong evidence of positive association and in most instances of dispute is the most accurate way to determine paternity. Courts already have the power to order such tests in appropriate cases. I have no plans to amend the law to make blood tests compulsory in cases of disputed paternity.

EU RESIDENCE RIGHTS

Mr Allen: To ask the Secretary of State for the Home Department (1) in what United Kingdom legislation provision is made for retired self-employed citizens of the European Union entitled to the benefits set out in Council directive 75/34 EC relating to residence rights;

(2) in what United Kingdom legislation provision is made to give effect to article 5 of Council directive 75/34 relating to the period within which a retired self-employed citizen of the European Union may exercise the right of residence.

Mr Charles Wardle: The draft (European

Economic Area) Order 1994, which was approved by the House on 9 May 1994, makes full provision to transpose the EC rights of residence directives, including Directive 75/34/EEC, into the United Kingdom law. Hitherto, the directives have been implemented either by way of the Immigration Rules (HC 251) or administratively.

— ◇ —

Book Reviews

Judicial Remedies in Public Law

By Clive Lewis. 1992 (with 1993 Supplement). London: Sweet & Maxwell. Hardback, £123 (Supplement £18). ISBN 0 421 51380 2 (Supplement 0 421 50230 4).

Given the fundamental differences between the Scots and English law of judicial remedies, particularly in the area of what English law terms "public law", the relevance of Mr Lewis's book in Scotland may not be apparent. However, important as the differences between the two systems are, there are also many points of contact ranging from the grounds of judicial review, through the jurisdictional difficulties of remedies against the Crown to the developing remedies available under European Union law. In these respects it is important for Scots lawyers to keep abreast of developments in England, especially when even the House of Lords fails to keep abreast of developments in Scotland, as the recent decision in *M v Home Office* allowing injunctions against the Crown forcibly indicates. For this purpose, Mr Lewis's book is an excellent place to look.

The book is published in Sweet & Maxwell's 'Litigation Library series and possesses the structural quality of the other books in the series. It does not set out to be a book on administrative law in the strict sense. Rather, it assumes a degree of knowledge about the usual subjects of administrative law, such as the rules of natural justice, and aims to discuss these in the context of the law relating to the remedies through which judicial review is exercised. In this regard, the book follows a logical pattern with discussion of the jurisdiction and powers of the High Court in public law cases coming in the early chapters, followed by a very detailed discussion of the particular remedies available in English public law proceedings such as the prerogative orders, declarations and injunctions. The last two chapters are given over to European law, chapter 15 looking at the enforcement of European law

before national courts and chapter 16 discussing the law relating to art 177 references from national courts to the European Court of Justice. These are matters that are difficult to find discussed in the context of national judicial remedies and since they are common to Scots law, should be of some interest to those involved in European law.

More generally, Mr Lewis makes occasional references to Scots law, discussing, for example, *British Medical Association v Greater Glasgow Health Board*, 1989 SLT 493; [1989] AC 1211 and its importance in defining "the Crown" for the purposes of s 21 of the Crown Proceedings Act. The discussion of "public law issues" in chapter 3 is relevant in highlighting the technicality of the public/private distinction that has evolved in English administrative law since the introduction of the new judicial review procedure. Some support for the Court of Session's refusal to take Scots law down a similar path can be derived from the author's conclusion that the "procedural issues have distorted the substantive law" (p 90), which is ironic, not to say rather sad given the historic development of administrative law in England during the last 30 years. Overall, it is only possible to praise this book. Only the breathtaking speed of developments in judicial review challenges the author's quest for completeness, but there can be no doubt that a second edition will be just as worthwhile as the first.

DENIS J EDWARDS,
University of Strathclyde.

Law of Restitution

By Andrew Tettenborn. 1993. London: Cavendish Publishing Ltd, Corporate and Commercial Law Series. Paperback, £17.95. ISBN 1 874242 88 0.

On the back cover there is a picture of a man in casual jacket, shirt unbuttoned and wearing a flat cap. He looks off to the middle distance as if contemplating who will win the 3.15 at Doncaster. But if this is indeed a picture of the author, then it is more likely that he is musing over how many more words can be deleted from his text to keep it clear and concise.

The existence of three textbooks and two recent House of Lords judgments means that the necessary background for a brief treatment of the law of restitution in England is possible. There is no copious citation of authority, very little reference to periodical literature and almost no verbatim extracts from other texts. These can be found in other publications. What this book does successfully is set out the whole ambit of the modern English law of restitution in small compass in a readable way.

It is, it is submitted, often more difficult to write a good small book than a mediocre large one. The more words available, the more tendency to quotation, deviation, digression or downright obfuscation. This book succeeds in saying all the major things that need be said. Not only that, it argues with some of the prevalent doctrine and dogma: the notion of "incontrovertible benefit" is not accepted, albeit perhaps too much is put onto the use of the word "reasonable" in the "no reasonable man test" in this critique. Significantly, the book offers serious respect for contract — something which restitution scholars are often challenged (unfairly?) with neglecting. The principle against forced exchange is introduced and utilised in a number of discussions to argue against restitutionary remedies. On this point Scotland has had many hundreds of years' experience and a recent case, *Bryce Houston Ltd v Glass's Fruit Markets Ltd*, 1992 SCLR 1019, illustrates that respect well.

The best for last. Almost every point of principle is illustrated by a very brief hypothetical, making difficult concepts clearer: like an excellent university seminar or exchange with an appellate court. The book deals with the issues of restitution rather than simply setting out the English law and thus is an excellent introduction to the subject for anyone.

W J STEWART,
MacMillans, Solicitors,
Glasgow.

Butterworths Employment Law Handbook

Sixth edition. Edited by Peter Wallington. 1994. London: Butterworths. Paperback, £29.95. ISBN 0 406 02234 8.

Blackstone's Statutes on Employment Law

Third edition. Edited by Richard Kidner. 1994. London: Blackstone Press Ltd. Paperback, £10.95. ISBN 1 85431 877 2.

The amount of recent legislative activity in the field of employment law is reflected in the contents of both of these books. The Wallington book, for example, has been extended in length from just over 1,000 pages for the previous edition to nearly 1,330 pages for the new edition.

This has enabled the editor to accommodate not only at least three important new statutes but also the increasing number of European directives and the ensuing British regulations, particularly in the field of health and safety law. The most significant change since the previous edition has been the enactment of the Trade Union and Labour Relations (Consolidation) Act 1992 which places all of collective labour law in the one statute. As the editor himself admits, no edition of the handbook has had to incorporate such a volume of change in legislation, both in form and substance.

It is also noteworthy that Wallington has reorganised his presentation of the statutory and associated material. Thus whereas in the previous edition the editor covered the statutory material in a thematic way by having a section on the collective framework, a section dealing with individual employment law and separate sections on discrimination and health and safety, the new edition in Part 1 deals with all statutes on a chronological basis. Thus statutes appear in the handbook on the basis of their year of enactment rather than their subject matter. As well as Part 1 dealing with statutes, Part 2 contains statutory instruments, Part 3 covers European materials, Part 4 is concerned with statutory codes of practice and Part 5 contains miscellaneous materials.

I must say that this reviewer will find it difficult to adjust to the new ordering of material. In particular, the fact that statutory instruments are now in a different section from their statutory parents can be inconvenient. Thus whereas the Health and Safety at Work Act 1974 starts at para 34, one has to turn to para 1057 for the Safety Representatives and Safety Committees Regulations 1977. Apart from this, a new edition of the handbook is to be welcomed. It is unfailingly accurate and the notes which indicate the source of changes to statutory material are very useful. The destination table for the provisions of the Trade Union and Labour Relations (Consolidation) Act 1992 is most helpful. Any practitioner who is seeking an up to date and accurate collection of statutory and other quasi-statutory materials on employment law should buy this new edition.

The collection of statutes edited by Richard Kidner is a much slimmer volume, running to some 350 pages. The print is very small and Blackstones have been able to get a great many words on to a page. The collection is very competitively priced at £10.95. It is somewhat of a misnomer to title this book *Statutes on Employment Law* since the collection also contains such non-statutory material as codes of practice, European Community materials and international obligations. The compass of the collection is more modest since, for example, there are no materials on health and safety law. Equally, the book does not provide notes on the sources for additions to or deletions from the provisions, nor is there any indication of the statutory basis for repeals. But perhaps this would be asking for too much in a book which is so reasonably priced.

Kidner's collection constitutes a useful first source for employment law materials but those embarking on more detailed research may find it frustrating to have to refer to other sources for information on the statutory basis for amendments and repeals.

KENNETH MILLER,
University of Strathclyde.

Environmental Law

The Law and Policy relating to the Protection of the Environment
Second edition. By S Ball and S Bell. 1994. London: Blackstone Press Ltd. Paperback, £21.95. ISBN 1 85431 287 1.

On the whole this is an excellent book which will be of use to students and practitioners alike. A better introduction to environmental law would be hard to find. It is divided into two parts. The first covers general issues including sources of environmental law, agencies involved in environmental protection, the EC and the environment, the regulation of environmental protection, enforcement, access to environmental information and the common law. The second deals with the law relating to specific issues including planning, integrated pollution control, waste management, water pollution and nature conservation.

Since it is a book about domestic law, international environmental law is not covered. Other areas including genetically modified organisms and radioactive substances law are also omitted. The latter exclusion is somewhat disappointing, although the authors justify it partly on the basis of the complexity of the law and partly on the basis that the book is about environmental protection whereas radioactive substances law is largely concerned with protecting humans rather than the environment per se. Moreover, since the book is about environmental protection it does not deal with environmental liability issues in depth. For that reason commercial practitioners may not find the book particularly useful.

The style is eminently readable. This helped by the fact that the text is unencumbered by foot-notes. Full references are given where appropriate in the text.

Environmental law is a fast moving subject and it is hard to remain abreast of developments. Much has changed in the law since the first edition appeared in 1991. However, the second edition deals with the changes well. New legislation such as the Water Industry Act 1991, the Water Resources Act 1991, the Clean Air Act 1993 and the Environmental Information Regulations 1992 is fully covered.

The coverage of recent case law is generally very good. For example, the important House of Lords decision in *Cambridge Water Co v Eastern Counties Leather plc* [1994] 1 All ER 53 is discussed in chap 8. However, while most recent waste law cases are discussed in chap 13, "Waste Management", this is not true in relation to the duty of care for waste. Hardly any of the significant number of reported cases including, e g *West Yorkshire WRA v Pudsey Skip Hire & Station Maintenance* [1993] 220 ENDS Report 39 and *Greater Manchester WRA v ICI* [1993] 223 ENDS Report 42 are mentioned and no citations are provided. These cases provide additional guidance on how the courts are interpreting the duty of care legislation and their inclusion would have enhanced the chapter.

There is a new chapter on environmental assessment which received only a very brief mention in the chapter on planning in the first edition. There are also new chapters on the protection of the countryside and the protection of trees and woodlands, in addition to the chapter on nature conservation which appeared in the first edition. These are all welcome additions.

Given the problems ascertaining the current position of many environmental law issues, the authors have usefully included in their preface a summary of the present state of play on various issues including the government's deregulation initiative, the new waste management licensing system, the proposed environmental protection agencies and contaminated land proposals.

From a Scottish perspective the book is disappointing. While there is a recognition in chap 14, "Water pollution", of the different Scottish dimension in terms of the institutional structure and applicable legislation, there is little elsewhere. Scots nuisance law is not discussed. However, because environmental law is largely similar in the two jurisdictions this sparse coverage should not pose an insurmountable problem for Scottish readers.

MARK POUSTIE,
University of Strathclyde.

ARTICLES

Can Scots Law Cope with the Sale of Incorporeal Moveables?

D P Sellar,
Lecturer in Private Law,
University of Edinburgh.

In a revised version of a seminar paper given at the University of Dundee, Mr Sellar argues that Scots law as it stands is ill suited to regulate a sale of incorporeal rights, and that it is likely to remain so unless practitioners and judges give more weight to commercial considerations when arguing and deciding cases in court.

The subject of this paper was suggested particularly by a reference in the listing particulars for the flotation of Stagecoach Holdings plc. The reference was to the remedies for breach of contract available under Scots law to a purchaser of the existing shares which were being sold in the flotation. The reference was, of course, not developed. It seems, therefore, useful to consider both (1) the seller's obligations implied into a sale of incorporeal rights and also (2) his remedies (or secondary rights) arising from a breach of either those implied terms or an express term of the contract of sale. The paper deals primarily with sales of shares because of their economic importance.

The theme of this paper is that in this area both the substantive Scots law and the law of remedies are unsatisfactory. The relevant law is old and undeveloped, or sometimes inconsistent, and often impractical in its application to modern transactions. More generally, these difficulties in the law seem to arise from basic features of the legal system in Scotland.

Turning first to the seller's implied obligations in a sale of incorporeal moveables, Scots law's traditional approach to these implied obligations is best seen in the late Professor Halliday's *Conveyancing Law and Practice* (Vol 1). These obligations are dealt with as part of the law of warrandice, so familiar to conveyancers. There are five relevant passages, namely (1) para 4.31 on warrandice in general, including warrandice in sales of heritage, although the word "warranty" is also used, (2) para 4.41 on the warrandice on the assignation of a debt, (3) and (4) paras 7.05 and 7.12 on the warrandice on a sale of a traditional Scottish personal bond, and (5) para 7.29 on warrandice on the sale of a life policy.

The descriptions of these passages show that the law is undeveloped. Although Professor Halliday treats transfers of shares and assig-

nations of intellectual property rights as part of his whole subject of conveyancing, he nowhere discusses the question of warranties in relation to those transfers. The case law which Professor Halliday cites is also very old, namely *Barclay v Liddel* (1671) Mor 16591, *Houston v Corbet* (1771) Mor 16619, *Ferrier v Graham's Trs* (1828) 6 S 818 and *Reid v Barclay* (1879) 6 R 1007). These are in fact the only significant authorities, except for the case of *Sinclair v Wilson & McLellan* (1829) 7 S 401 and the relevant institutional authorities such as Stair, II iii 46, Erskine, II iii 25 and Bell's *Principles*, para 1469.

Professor Halliday's discussion is also not entirely clear or consistent. In three of these four passages it is stated that the implied warrandice is that of debitum subesse, that is that the obligation is due, although it does not warrant that debtor's ability (or willingness) to pay. It is, however, also stated in two of the passages that the warrandice is both debitum subesse and warrandice from fact and deed (see paras 4.31 (b) and 7.29). Professor Halliday appears to have appreciated the difficulty that warrandice debitum subesse is inconsistent with warrandice from fact and deed and is arguably the same as absolute warrandice (para 7.29). Professor Halliday appears to go on to suggest a distinction that warrandice debitum subesse, in contrast to absolute warrandice, would not protect the purchaser against remedial defects. This is not, however, convincing.

From the earlier authorities which Professor Halliday cites the solution appears to be that it was only in the 19th century that the rule became clear that implied warrandice was debitum subesse. That rule was in fact not challenged in *Reid v Barclay* (supra) (see, also, for example, Gloag and Henderson (9th ed), para 38.3). The passages in Professor Halliday's work seem to continue the earlier uncertainty.

In any event, there remains the striking fact of a complete absence of authority on, or even discussion of, the seller's implied obligations in the sale of any incorporeal right other than a debt or a life policy. One is left to derive from the authorities that in the sale of any incorporeal right there is an implied obligation (1) that the right is enforceable and (2) that the seller's title is free from what may be usefully described as any adverse right, such as a security right or an arrestment.

In a sale of a share in a limited company it should, therefore, follow that the seller is under an implied obligation not only as to his title but also that the share has been validly issued. The latter obligation should also extend to the company not being in liquidation, which is a general bar to transfers (see the Insolvency Act 1986, s 88 for a voluntary winding up, and s 127 for a compulsory winding up). There is, however, only limited authority to support this argument from principle. The seller requires to deliver a valid transfer and a certificate or equivalent (see, for example, *London Founders Association v Clarke* (1888) 20 QBD 576, which is accepted for Scots law in *Green's Encyclopedia of the Laws of Scotland*, Vol 4, para 190).

The implied obligations on a vendor in a sale of an intellectual property right are no clearer. It would appear, indeed, that there is not even an implied obligation of validity in the sale of a patent (see Bell's *Principles* (10th ed), s 1355, following English case law in the 19th century). There may be only some broadly equivalent obligation to that of "fact and deed" warrandice, namely that the vendor has not deliberately allowed the patent to lapse (*Re Railway and Electric Appliances Co* (1888) 38 ChD 597).

The obvious question is whether it matters in practice that the implied obligations of a vendor in sales of incorporeal rights are so undeveloped. Do practitioners not set out a vendor's implied obligations in considerable (not to say excessive) detail, particularly in the sale of the whole share capital of a private company? There seem two basic reasons why the present state of the law does matter in practice. The first, and most direct, is that it is not unknown for some institutional shareholders simply to refuse to give any express warranties. One solicitor of a local authority once claimed to the writer that his authority had, in fact, no power to give express warranties on the sale of shares. These examples seem important enough by themselves to justify concern.

The second reason is, however, of even greater practical significance. The law on the remedies (or secondary rights arising on breach of an express obligation on the sale of incorporeal right) seems at least as unsatisfactory as the substantive law.

At first sight that might seem a surprising contention to many practitioners in this area. The experienced practitioner's view of the law is succinctly stated in the commentary by A Pairman, WS, on the Scottish Forms of Share Purchase Agreement and Business Sale Agreement in *Butterworths Company Law Service* (Vol 2). The practitioner's view is that the word "warranty" has no technical meaning in Scots, as opposed to English, law. In particular, the use of the word "warranty" does not restrict the remedy

for its breach to damages as opposed to rescission in the sense of termination on breach. The legal right to terminate depends on the materiality of the breach. There is an argument that any breach other than a trivial one is material in this context. It is, therefore, both prudent and common to state expressly in an agreement that the only remedy on a breach of a warranty is damages. This analysis essentially follows the remedies under Scots law for breaches of the implied terms in the Sale of Goods Act 1979 and in particular s 11 (5) (see, however, Gloag, *Contract* (2nd ed), pp 602 and 603, and the obiter comments in *Millars of Falkirk Ltd v Turpie*, 1976 SLT (Notes) 66, which suggest that the right to terminate may be more restricted).

It is crucial in the present context to appreciate that the practitioner's approach to express contractual terms (invariably called warranties, following the English usage) differs from what can be called the traditional approach described by Professor Halliday. As we have seen, express obligations on sale have traditionally been seen as examples of warrandice in an assignation, a form of conveyance (see also Halliday (supra), para 4.29, which seems to go as far as to treat warranties on the sale of goods as part of the general law of warrandice). It seems significant that in Burns' *Conveyancing* (4th ed) the style of agreement for the sale of shares at p 138 is utterly different from the modern form of sale agreement. The former assumes an auction and excludes any obligations on the vendors (see also the terms of the sale in *Stevenson v Wilson*, 1907 SC 445, on which the style in Burns may well be based).

It is, therefore, not surprising that the application of traditional rules to the present forms of share and business sale agreements creates difficulties which can lead to unfair and unrealistic results. Two of the difficulties are only potential. The third has, however, already arisen very starkly in practice.

The first possible difficulty is that the execution of the conveyance, whether in the form of the transfer of shares or the assignation of an intellectual property right, may supersede the detailed contract. It is, therefore, not surprising that share and business sale agreements commonly err on the side of caution and include a non-supersession clause (see Butterworth's Scottish Forms of Agreement (supra)). The risk is greater for assignations of intellectual property rights. It is not possible to repeat pages of warranties on a share transfer form. It is however quite common to repeat contractual warranties in assignations of intellectual property rights.

The difficulty arises from the potential application of the well known, or arguably notorious, case of *Winston v Patrick*, 1981 SLT 41; 1980 SC 246, beyond heritable conveyancing. In that case the court held that the rule on supersession could not be disapplied by implication, although that decision meant that the contractual obligations became after settlement merely scrap paper. The decision becomes all the more remarkable when one recalls that the contractual obligation which was superseded related to the physical condition of the house. The *Winston* case seems, therefore, a striking example of the courts not merely continuing to apply what might be described as traditional rules but extending them without any apparent consideration of the result.

It is far beyond the scope of this paper to embark on a consideration of the subsequent case law on this area (see the useful analysis by K G C Reid (1988) 33 JLS 7). It is, however, relevant to notice that in three cases it has been held that a "non-supersession clause" must be in the disposition (see *Wood v Edwards*, 1988 SLT (Sh Ct) 17, *Greaves v Abercromby*, 1989 SCLR 11 and *Porch v Macleod*, 1992 SLT 661). These cases may be said, ironically, to apply the logic of the *Winston* case further than that case itself did. Again, there was no discussion in any of these cases as to the commercial sense of the decision. This silence is in stark contrast to the emphatic comments of the House of Lords on the possible adverse commercial consequences of their being forced to uphold irritancy of a commercial lease in the case of *CIN Properties Ltd v Dollar Land (Cumbernauld) Ltd*, 1992 SLT 669. The recent English decision of *Re Maxwell Communications Corporation plc (No 3)* [1993] 1 WLR 1402, in which contractual subordination of a debt was recognised, goes one stage further since commercial considerations seem to have been the principal justification for the decision.

The second potential difficulty arises from an application to share and business sale agreements of the traditional view that express warranties are part of the law of warrandice. If that rule is applied, then the only remedy on a breach of warrandice is clearly damages (see, for example, *Welsh v Russell* (1894) 21 R 769). There is no right to termination for breach, as the practitioner's approach assumes.

The argument is plausible and a court might accept it, although it seems without substance. It is quite clear that Scots common law accepts that breach of the seller's implied obligations in the sale of moveables, commonly called warranties, results in a right to terminate. Professor Halliday's treatment of warranties on sale of goods as part of the whole law of warrandice seems potentially misleading. In addition to this analysis, one case on the sale of a debt appears expressly consistent with the purchaser's right to rescission and repayment (or repetition) of the price (see *Reid v Barclay*, supra, especially per Lord Deas at p 1010). In that case the right was, however, wholly unenforceable. The damages would have been the whole price and there was, therefore, no practical difference between damages and repayment of the price.

The third difficulty is ironically the converse of the second and has arisen in two recent decisions, in which it was held in the sale of a business that the only remedy for a breach of an express warranty was termination (*Widdowson v Hunter*, 1989 SLT 478, a decision of Lord Sutherland, and *Fortune v Fraser*, 1993 SLT 68, a decision of Sheriff Principal Nicholson, a former Scottish Law Commissioner). This exclusion of the remedy of damages is clearly of immense practical significance. The reasoning clearly applies to sales of shares, as accepted by Professor McBryde in his *Contract*, para 20.9. In addition, damages are usually the remedy which the purchaser will wish and may indeed be the only feasible remedy. The commentary in Butterworth's Scottish Forms, supra, emphasises the latter point. Again, the difficulty appears to arise from a judicial willingness to apply 19th century rules further than the cases themselves either did or justify.

The case of *Widdowson* appears not to have attracted the attention of commercial practitioners, but that of *Fortune* certainly has, probably because certain dicta go far beyond this particular issue.

Both cases apply the rule so trenchantly expressed in relation to the sale of goods by Lord President Inglis in *McCormick & Co v Rittmeyer & Co* (1869) 7 M 854 that the Scots common law of sale does not accept the actio quanti minoris of Roman law (see also the approval by the House of Lords in *Pollock & Co v Macrae*, 1922 SC (HL) 192, per Lord Dunedin at p 200). It has, however, been very persuasively argued that the courts in the *McCormick* case and subsequent cases misunderstood the relevant Roman law and institutional authority (see Stewart (1966) 11 JLS 124 and Evans-Jones, 1991 JR 190). The two articles were in fact referred to by the sheriff principal.

The significant point for this paper is, however, that both Lord Sutherland and Sheriff Principal Nicholson were prepared to apply the rule, despite these cogent doubts over its basic validity, in situations in which it was very doubtful, to say the least, that the 19th century authorities actually required them to do so. It is significant that in the 1930s Professor Burns could state in *Green's Encyclopedia of the Laws of Scotland*, Vol 13, para 431, that it was still not clear how far Scots law accepted the so called actio quanti minoris in relation to the sale of heritage.

The simpler case seems to be that of *Fortune v Fraser*, which there was a detailed offer and an unqualified acceptance. The offer apparently contained detailed warranties, one of which was typically as to the accuracy of the accounts, but no limitations on damages for breach on any of the warranties.

Apart from the *Widdowson* case, the sheriff principal relied on the Outer House case of *Bryson & Co Ltd v Bryson*, 1916 1 SLT 361, in which Lord Anderson applied the general rule against damages to a breach of an agreement for the sale of a business. *Bryson* is, however, hardly a strong case. Lord Anderson stated frankly that the authorities were conflicting as to how far the general rule applied to the seller's implied obligations (at p 363). More significant points may, however, be (1) that the *Bryson* case did not involve an express warranty and (2) that Lord Anderson also cited, with apparent approval, a passage in Bell's *Principles*, s 893, in which it is arguably implicit that the general rule did not apply to an express warranty, a passage approved by the Lord Chancellor in *Brownlie v Miller* (1879) 7 R (HL) 66 at p 71. There is indeed an unreported modern decision in which Lord Allanbridge applied that passage in Bell and refused to follow the *Bryson* case in relation to an express warranty in a share purchase agreement (see *Herd & Mackenzie (Buckie) Ltd v Mackenzie*, OH, 21 October 1987, unreported (1987 GWD 32-1176). It is most unfortunate that the case has never been reported, although it is referred to in the writer's article in (1990) 35 JLS 34).

A related point is that the breach of warranty in the *Fortune* case was latent. The sheriff principal, and to a lesser extent, Lord Anderson in the *Bryson* case, did not take account of the line of 19th century cases in which it was accepted that there was an exception in cases of latent defect to the general rule against damages (see the acceptance in *Pollock & Co v Macrae* at p 201). The exception may in fact have also applied where there was difficulty in rescinding the sale (see the dictum of Lord McLaren in *Louttit's Trs v Highland Railway Co* (1892) 19 R 791 at pp 799 and 800, to which Lord Anderson referred in the *Bryson* case).

A further point in the sheriff principal's approach also seems unfortunate. That is the short rejection of the purchaser's argument that the parties should reasonably be assumed to have contracted for damages on breach of a warranty and not only for a right of termination. The sheriff principal merely asked rhetorically whether the parties would have contracted to exclude the rule against the obscure actio quanti minoris. That seem to put the question in an unrealistic way, giving insufficient weight to the substance rather than the possible title of the remedy.

If one turns to the *Widdowson* case, it was curiously both wider and narrower than that of *Fortune* in its application of the general rule against damages. The decision was wider because it applied not only to an express warranty as to its turnover but also to obligations on the conduct of the business between the conclusion date of the missives and the date of entry. The decision was, however, narrower in that it accepted that the general rule did not apply where the breach was alleged to be fraudulent, provided that the breach was latent.

On the apparent extension of the general rule to the obligations up to the date of entry the basic criticism already made of the *Fortune* decision seems to apply all the more strongly. It seems irrelevant to that criticism that the breach was patent by the time of entry. On the exception to the general rule based on fraud, this does seem illogically to confuse an action based on breach of contract with one based on the delict of fraud (*Smith v Sim*, 1954 SC 357). The sheriff principal in the *Fortune* case refused for this reason to follow Lord Sutherland in applying this exception.

The *Fortune* case has been appealed, the purchaser having prudently amended his pleadings. The appeal has been only partly heard but the grounds of appeal do not apparently suggest that the purchaser advanced the fundamental criticisms of the sheriff principal's reasoning suggested in this paper.

What is clear at this stage is the alarm which the decision of the sheriff principal has caused among company practitioners. Advice has apparently been given in transactions in which one party is not Scottish that the contract should be governed by English law, with the consequent implied submission to the English courts. It is also understood that the Scottish Law Commission is now considering this area of law as its most urgent priority in the whole field of contract law. While the commission's attention is welcomed, it must be doubtful when proper legislation can be passed.

In the meantime, it is only common sense for a share or business sale agreement to state expressly that a purchaser has a right to damages for a breach of warranty (see the suggestion to this effect in the Butterworth's Scottish Forms (supra at p 689), although they preceded the *Fortune* case). It would, however, seem better to state this in good plain English rather than to refer to the actio quanti minoris which the Scottish Forms do, following conveyancing practice. English practitioners are already sufficiently patronising about what they see as the archaic nature and language of Scots law.

The unreported decision of the Second Division in *Colgan v Mooney*, 19 November 1993 (1994 GWD 1-43) may also support the use of plain English. That case involved missives which gave an express right to the actio. All three judges accepted that the purchaser would have had a right to damages if she could have established a breach of the missives. Lord Clyde seems, however, to have doubted whether the purchaser's claim was one under the actio. It is remarkable how much difficulty the three Latin words "actio quanti minoris" have caused to the Scots law of sale.

It is also worth adding here that the *Fortune* case includes further controversial statements by the sheriff principal, which extend to breach of contracts beyond sales of incorporeal rights. The most important is that the sheriff principal doubted whether a breach of a warranty could ever cause loss because the warranty related to something which preceded the contract or existed at the time the contract was concluded.

This simply cannot be correct. Such a term as to the quality of the goods at the time of sale is, for example, implied by the Sale of Goods Act into every sale of goods. The sheriff principal accepted that a breach of contract meant that the other party failed to obtain the benefit of at least one of its terms. There is no reason why that term should not be one which vouches (to use a neutral word) a present or past state of facts.

From this brief consideration of the case law, the remedies for breach of the seller's express obligations seems, therefore, as unsatisfactory as the substantive obligations implied on him. That seems ironically far more dangerous in practice.

Having suggested that Scots law in this area is unsatisfactory, what are the reasons for this? It is suggested that they seem to arise from structural features of the Scottish legal system in its widest sense, including its judges, both branches of its legal profession and its teachers of law.

Certain reasons seem fairly clear. The most basic is that Scots law inevitably suffers from a lack of authoritative case law in this area of law because the Scottish economy is small and now only a branch of a larger British economy. To many businessmen, including many based in Scotland, the existence of a separate Scots law is often an anachronistic inconvenience. The lack of case law is increased by the less inevitable fact that, as we have seen, some of the few relevant cases are not reported.

A further reason is that the judiciary in both the Court of Session and the sheriff courts is generalist. The present forms of commercial agreements are also of fairly recent adoption. Understandably, most judges, and even more so most sheriffs, are unfamiliar with these documents and the commercial rationale behind their terms.

Furthermore, the judiciary must proceed on the submissions addressed to them. It may well be that litigation practitioners have insufficiently emphasised the practical consequences of the application of certain rules, especially the effect on standard form agreements. That failure may derive in turn from a still largely generalist bar. Even more perhaps, it may be the result of a lack of co-ordination between litigation solicitors and their colleagues who deal with, and in particular draft, commercial agreements.

In addition, a further reason for the present state of the law in this field is the historic emphasis in the solicitors' branch on heritable conveyancing. Until very recently there has been, for example, a corresponding lack of specialisation in the fields of company law, banking law and intellectual property work. These historic features will presumably become progressively less important.

The law faculties of our universities are also to some extent responsible for the state of this area of law. Sales of incorporeal rights, including shares, have perhaps been given insufficient attention. Law courses have also and for obvious reasons emphasised the law as illustrated in cases. This emphasis has applied even in company law or intellectual property law, which have, as already mentioned, only relatively recently been accepted as distinct subjects. Case law, by definition, involves litigation rather than the more constructive task of using the law to implement transactions without subsequent disputes. The avoiding of disputes involves, it is suggested, legal issues which are at least as intellectually demanding as the solving of disputes.

Ironically, the only course in which there has been any real emphasis on transactions and their documents has been conveyancing, although this has meant primarily heritable conveyancing.

The Diploma in Legal Practice has probably improved this imbalance in legal education but only to a limited extent. The diploma may indeed cause its own problem by encouraging the notion, to which too many practitioners seem sympathetic, that the law in the cases and textbooks is distinct from the application of the law in practice. The diploma may also not survive in its present form.

In conclusion, Scots law does not seem to deal adequately with sales of incorporeal rights such as shares or intellectual property rights. The substantive law on the seller's implied obligations can be described as at best undeveloped. The law on remedies is no better and often difficult to justify in terms of commercial sense. These difficulties seem to be exacerbated by a conservatism and lack of co-ordination within the Scottish legal process, which make Scots law even less useful to the business community.

Postscript
Since this paper was first written, there have been two significant and welcome developments. The first is that the Scottish Law Commission have recommended in their consultation paper on aspects of contract law that "the rule against the actio quanti minoris" should be abolished. The second is that, following the report of Lord Coulsfield's committee on commercial litigation in the Court of Session, the Lord President has appointed Lord Penrose to be, in effect, a full time commercial judge.

◆

NEWS

Court

Court of Session: practice note
No 2 of 1994 (26 May 1994): Judicial factors — caution

(1) Practitioners are reminded that a judicial factor (a) is an officer of court and (b) requires to obtain a certified copy interlocutor of his/her appointment *without delay.*

(2) As a certified copy interlocutor is not issued until the judicial factor finds caution, the practitioner before presenting a petition for appointment should reach agreement with the nominees as to whose responsibility it will be to arrange caution.

(3) If such responsibility lies with the nominee then the practitioner should advise the nominee of his/her appointment within 24 hours thereof and the nominee should proceed to find caution without delay.

(4) If such responsibility lies with the practitioner, then the practitioner should proceed to find caution without delay.

(5) The foregoing is of particular importance where such an appointment is made ad interim.

◇

Rules of the Court of Session 1994
On 31 May 1994 the Lord President signed the Act of Sederunt (Rules of the Court of Session) 1994 (SI 1994/1443), consolidating with amendments the Rules of Court 1965, as amended to date, as well as certain enactments and practice notes.

The new provisions include a procedure for a party litigant to bring an action or raise a petition without the signature of a counsel or solicitor, a reduction in the period of time for lodging defences from 14 to seven days, a formal procedure for application for early disposal of a reclaiming motion or appeal, a new procedure for family actions after defences have been lodged, and a requirement that accounts of expenses be lodged within four months after a final interlocutor in which a finding for expenses is made.

It is intended to make the rules available to subscribers to the *Parliament House Book*, annotated by a team led by Nigel Morrison, QC, the principal draftsman of the rules, in time for their commencement on 5 September 1994.

—— ◇ ——

General

Breast implants
A worldwide settlement on behalf of women who may now or at a later date have claims against certain manufacturers of breast implants and their suppliers is being considered by a United States district court in Alabama. A hearing will take

place at the court in the state capital Birmingham, on 18 August 1994 to decide whether the settlement proposed is "fair, reasonable, and adequate" and should be approved. The district court's chief judge, Sam C Pointer, has begun an international notification programme to inform all potential claimants of the proposed agreement and their rights and obligations under it. The settlement if approved will provide benefits to women who before 1 June 1993 had one or more breast implants manufactured by a United States manufacturer.

Women living outside the United States but who are US citizens or women who have had the implant operations in the United States are eligible to receive full benefits from the settlement. Women who are not US citizens and who had their operations outside the United States are eligible to receive limited benefits. Five Scottish law firms have already been approached by potential claimants. Any woman who believes she may have a claim should contact her solicitor immediately and if unable to do so should contact Iona Cockburn at the Law Society of Scotland by phoning 031-226 7411.

◇

Scottish Law Directory 1994
The publishers of the *Scottish Law Directory* have intimated the following corrections:

On p C79, in the entry for Fyfe Ireland, WS, the names of Shona M Frame, Rosalind MM McInnes and A G A Walker should be deleted. They should be added to the entry for Bird Semple which appears on p C73.

On p C170, the telephone and fax number for MacArthur Stewart, Tobermory, should be 0688-2300.

◇

Legal aid: research report
A research report which deals with the distribution of the supply of legal aid in Scotland is available from the Scottish Legal Aid Board.

This research generally concludes that there is an adequacy of outlets supplying legal aid services throughout Scotland and that the pattern of supply over the two year period which ended in December 1992 has shown little change — there is certainly no indication of a fall in the number of providers, civil or criminal.

The research does, however, indicate certain geographical areas of the country where there may be problems of access and others where services covering specific fields, such as social welfare law, may be more difficult to obtain.

Legal aid outlets are highly concentrated, with 20 per cent of law firms being responsible for 60 per cent of the work in civil cases and 75 per cent of the work in criminal cases. The majority of the providers are situated in the central belt of Scotland and this could potentially lead to problems of access in rural areas.

The report recommends further research into the extent of any unmet needs, particularly in rural areas, and in the field of social welfare law; the monitoring of levels of rejection and refusals of civil legal aid on the grounds of insufficient paperwork and inadequate information in order to identify whether the responsible firms are likely to be those which deal only infrequently with such applications; and the carrying out of research into enhancing the quality of legal aid work based on case studies of the management structures and systems of selected suppliers of legal aid.

Copies of the report, written jointly by Professor Alan Paterson of the University of Strathclyde and Malcolm Turner-Kerr, the board's director of finance and administration, can be obtained by writing to: Mrs Sandra McMillan, Executive Assistant, The Scottish Legal Aid Board, 44 Drumsheugh Gardens, Edinburgh EH3 7SW.

Obituaries

On 26 May 1994, John T Porter, solicitor, formerly with Borders Regional Council.

On 27 May 1994, James Aitken, formerly Town Clerk of Paisley.

On 28 May 1994, George Lovat Fraser Henry, former partner in the firm of Messrs Shepherd & Wedderburn, WS, and Professor Emeritus of Conveyancing at Edinburgh University.

Business change

Thorntons, WS, Dundee, announce that Christina Baillie, Gillian Buchanan, Iain Hutcheson, Graeme Kelly and Bruce Renfrew have been appointed associates of the firm with effect from 1 June 1994.

Book Reviews

Contract

(Greens Concise Scots Law)
Second edition. By Stephen Woolman. 1994.
Edinburgh: W Green. Paperback, £27.
ISBN 0 414 01058 2.

The author in his preface to this new edition notes that it is intended to be a "short, understandable introduction to the subject". It is all of these things, although some 10 per cent longer than the first edition, which appeared in 1987. As with that edition it is also much more. It contains a succinct formulation of the rules, principles and concepts of the law of contract, which are invaluable to anyone seeking to analyse contractual situations. At a number of points this is even more the case in this edition. An example is the new statement with regard to the incorporation of an exemption (or limitation) clause by course of dealing: do "the circumstances yield the inference that both parties proceeded on the basis that the exemption clause was a term of the contract"? Another is with regard to the role of equity in determining public policy in cases of alleged "illegality".

The process of updating has not obscured this clarity by overloading the text. At the same time a discriminating approach to selecting new material has enabled the text to develop ideas in the framework of today's world, which is a help to the teacher of contract, since many of the factual situations in the older cases involve long superseded ways of dealing. So the text benefits now, for example, from the Outer House cases of *British Coal Corporation v South of Scotland Electricity Board* (for the economic impact of contract on the mining industry), *Dawson International plc v Coats Paton plc* (for what in a commercial context is appropriately treated as not binding though someone says they will do something — in connection with takeovers), and the cases involving missives for the analysis of "qualified acceptances".

The same goes for statutes. The Timeshare Act 1992 now appears to exemplify a particular statutory requirement for writing, and its rationale of protecting the consumer. The English law is not left behind either, even where different. The useful brief treatment of consideration is very well illustrated by a case reported in 1991 concerning a contractor agreeing to pay a subcontractor in financial difficulties in order to get the subcontracted work done.

A small criticism from the teacher's point of view is that often, though not always, cases that were designated "recent" at the time of the first edition are still "recent", and the hypothetical examples still have the same monetary values (£50,000 for going round Scotland in a kayak etc) and "fax" at one point has reverted to the formal "facsimile". One new feature is a small selective bibliography which highlights the importance of Professor McBryde's work amongst the "Works of Reference". The teacher would want this in the footnotes and/or text as well; say, in dealing with "intention to enter into legal relations".

There are two parts which, as before, stand out as being especially original: the treatment of error and the treatment of restrictive covenants. The author has largely stuck to his guns in his approach to error. His conclusion on the unimportance of "uninduced error" is, indeed underlined by now emphasising the word "uninduced". There is a small shift in that in the first edition misrepresentation was described as an idea that "may have eclipsed error entirely", and this has changed to being something that has "substantially eclipsed the role of error". *Spook Erection* is slotted in as an ordinary unsuccessful unilateral error argument. *Angus v Bryden* is slotted in as a "snatching at a bargain" case. All appears simple. It might have been a good idea to point out that there is new controversy to which an article in the bibliography will lead the student. The error part, which was admirably clear before, has been rephrased in parts; the subheadings used and the layout have been changed which enhances those features.

The treatment of restrictive covenants has been very carefully adjusted to take account of shifts of emphasis in recent cases, for example on the approach to the relevance of seeking to preserve a business connection. Significantly there is a new subsection relating to court procedure. This perhaps signifies a shift from the teaching to the practising role. By contrast the bar charts on examples of spatial and temporal restrictions — an enterprising teaching method — have not been updated.

It is inevitable that in a book of this size some things will be left out. The role of personal bar where there is no concluded agreement in writing in connection with heritage is one major point of dispute that has not been followed up by consideration of a range of cases that have been decided since 1987. However, as it happens it would have been premature anyway as a new leading case has been reported from the Inner

House since this book was printed (*Stewart's Exrs v Stewart*, 1994 SLT 466).

Contract law of course marches on. For example one case relied on with regard to "intention to enter into legal relations" has recently been overturned (*Avintair Ltd v Ryder Airline Services Ltd*). So has the Inner House decision on remoteness, *Balfour Beatty Construction (Scotland) Ltd v Scottish Power plc*, which is noted in a footnote as being on appeal to the House of Lords.

The publishers have given the book a much more user friendly layout. Typographical errors are absent. There is one delight of an associated sort, though. Page 179 refers to "Council for the respondent". This reviewer sympathises. Word processor spelling checkers do not pick these things up.

This is altogether a model for this type of book. Practitioners as well as students and teachers would be well advised to go out and buy it right away.

J W G BLACKIE,
University of Strathclyde.

The Scottish Legal System

By Robin M White and Ian D Willock. 1993. Edinburgh: Butterworths. Paperback, £24. ISBN 0 406 00571 0.

The Legal System of Scotland: Cases and Materials

Third edition. By Alan A Paterson and T St John N Bates. 1993. Edinburgh: W Green. Paperback, £22.50. ISBN 0 414 01069 8.

One need only scan the catalogues of the Scottish law publishers to see that there are now laudable attempts to meet the expanding needs of the Scottish legal market. Where once there were few texts and little or no choice, there are now a greater number of books available to both students and practitioners. While it is true that books on Scots law are still relatively expensive in comparison to their English counterparts, the situation is improving and can only continue to improve with a widening of choice.

Against this background the arrival of a new book and the updating of another well known text in the most fundamental of law subjects — the Scottish legal system — is to be welcomed. Where previously students could only resort to work of David Walker there is now the opportunity to acquire a more reasonably priced book from White and Willock. The scholarly thoroughness of Walker's *The Scottish Legal System* did not and does not always commend itself to students. White and Willock on the other hand have shown real understanding of and greater empathy towards the student reader. In so doing they are likely to be rewarded by substantial sales in what by the nature of the topic must be the biggest market for a Scottish legal text. Scottish legal system is a core subject and not just in the traditional LLB degree course but in a plethora of other courses as well. Moreover it is invariably taught in the first year of study when arguably the new enthusiastic student is more amenable to spending scarce resources on books.

As for the book itself, it contains all that one would expect in a book on the legal system: institutions of the legal system, sources of Scots law, the personnel and legal services and a chapter on law reform. The influence of the European Community on the Scottish legal system is also discussed. One thing which could be improved is the contents page which this reviewer found sparse and not particularly "user friendly". This though is more a criticism of aesthetics than substance.

The back cover of the book contends that "it is an ideal introduction of the Scottish legal system". Obviously readers will be reflecting on the old adage that "one cannot judge a book by its cover", but in this instance the claims of the publisher are vindicated by the reading of the text. Other books will undoubtedly follow on the Scottish legal system, but for the moment White and Willock can be content that they have produced a book which is likely, because of the level at which it is pitched and the price at which it is sold, to reach a broader audience than its main rival.

Paterson and Bates are in a somewhat different position from White and Willock. Their book has long held the market place as the only text of its kind. Though the writers would undoubtedly dispute the fact, their book is primarily a supplemental text providing further material for the student who has read either Walker's book or the new book by White and Willock. In fairness to the authors it is also a good reference book, containing many interesting statistics. By issuing a third edition updating the text to 1993, the writers have at one re-established the marketability of a book which was last updated in 1986, and also ensured that any competing publication is going to have to attain a very high standard indeed if it is to supplant what is a fine textbook.

To the consumer it must seem as though books of this nature are relatively easy to put together; they are after all a collection of materials of others rather than the authors' own original thoughts and analysis. However there is a skill in the selectivity of the material and its presentation. *The*

Legal System of Scotland — Cases and Materials is an excellent illustration of how it should be done.

RICHARD MAYS,
The Robert Gordon University,
Aberdeen.

◆

ACTS OF SEDERUNT

ACT OF SEDERUNT (RULES OF THE COURT OF SESSION AMENDMENT NO 1) (FEES OF SOLICITORS) 1994

(SI 1994/1139) [21 APRIL 1994]

The Lords of Council and Session, under and by virtue of the powers conferred on them by section 5 of the Court of Session Act 1988 (c 36) and of all other powers enabling them in that behalf, do hereby enact and declare:

Citation and commencement

1.—(1) This Act of Sederunt may be cited as the Act of Sederunt (Rules of the Court of Session Amendment No. 1) (Fees of Solicitors) 1994 and shall come into force on 24th May 1994.

(2) This Act of Sederunt shall be inserted in the Books of Sederunt.

Amendment of Table of Fees

2. In Chapters I and III of the Table of Fees in rule 347 of the Rules of the Court of Session, for the fees and outlays set out in column 2 of the Schedule to this Act of Sederunt, as applying to the paragraphs set out in column 1 of that Schedule, there shall be substituted the fees and outlays set out in column 3 of that Schedule; and the fees and outlays so substituted shall apply to work done and outlays incurred, for which those fees and outlays are chargeable, on or after the date on which this Act of Sederunt comes into force.

Saving

3. The fees and outlays set out in column 2 of the Schedule to this Act of Sederunt shall continue to apply to work done and outlays incurred before this Act of Sederunt comes into force.

J A D HOPE, LORD PRESIDENT, *IPD*

SCHEDULE   **Paragraph 2**

Column 1 (paragraph)	Column 2 (old fee) £	Column 3 (new fee) £
Chapter I:—		
1 (a)	6.80	7.00
(b)	2.80	2.90
(c)	10.00	10.30
2	1.00	1.03
	0.40	0.41
3	2.80	2.90
4	6.80	7.00
	6.80	7.00
	6.80	7.00
5 (a)	13.50	13.90
(b)	13.50	13.90
(d)	2.80	2.90
	6.80	7.00
	6.80	7.00
6	6.80	7.00
	2.80	2.90
Chapter III:— Part I		
(Inclusive Fee)	121.10	124.70
(Maximum Outlays)	160.00	200.00
Part II		
1	170.60	175.70
2	97.30	100.20
3 (a)	24.90	25.70
(b)	36.10	37.20
(c)	44.80	46.10
4 (a)	43.70	45.00
(b)	13.50	13.90
(c)	7.40	7.60
5 (a)	40.50	41.70
(b)	13.50	13.90
7	121.10	124.70
8	37.40	38.50
Part IIA 1. Table A		
1	245.80	253.20
	280.70	289.10
2	174.70	179.90
	212.10	218.50

Column 1 (paragraph)	Column 2 (old fee) £	Column 3 (new fee) £
3	53.70	55.30
	78.70	81.10
4	474.10	488.40
	571.60	588.70
2. Table B		
1	202.10	208.20
	237.10	244.20
2	97.30	100.20
	123.50	127.20
3	53.70	55.30
	78.70	81.10
4	353.20	363.70
	439.30	452.50
3. Table C		
1	49.90	51.40
2	56.00	57.70
3	106.00	109.10
Part III		
1	252.10	259.70
	349.40	359.90
2	170.90	176.00
4 (a)	30.50	31.40
5	28.80	29.70
Part IV		
1 (a)	237.10	244.20
(b)	25.50	26.30
(c)	49.90	51.40
2 (a)	252.10	259.70
(b)	155.90	160.60
(c) (i)	25.50	26.30
(ii)	13.50	13.90
(d)	74.80	77.00
(e)	111.10	114.40
3 (a)	49.90	51.40
(b)	13.50	13.90
(c)	37.40	38.50
4 (a)	47.40	48.80
(b)	13.50	13.90
(c)	6.80	7.00
(d)	47.40	48.80
(e)	13.50	13.90
(f)	6.80	7.00
5	24.30	25.00
6 (a)	53.70	55.30
(b)	7.40	7.60
(Maximum Fee)	25.00	38.00

Column 1 (paragraph)	Column 2 (old fee) £	Column 3 (new fee) £
7 (a)	49.90	51.40
(b)	24.30	25.00
(c)	13.50	13.90
(d)	19.90	20.50
8 (a)	101.10	104.10
(b)	81.20	83.60
(c)	30.00	30.90
(d)	7.40	7.60
9 (a)	111.10	114.40
(b)	49.90	51.40
(c)	13.50	13.90
10 (a)	13.50	13.90
(b)	37.40	38.50
(c)	13.50	13.90
(d)	37.40	38.50
11	141.10	145.30
12 (a)	37.40	38.50
(b)	13.50	13.90
(c)	54.90	56.50
(d)	25.20	26.00
(e)	127.80	131.60
(f)	71.10	73.20
13 (a)	343.20	353.50
(b)	30.50	31.40
(c)	62.40	64.30
15 (a) (i)	74.80	77.00
(ii)	49.90	51.40
(iii)	49.90	51.40
(b)	124.80	128.50
(c)	212.00	218.40
16	265.00	273.00
17	13.50	13.90
18	90.40	93.10
19	19.90	20.50
20 (a)	101.10	104.10
(b)	30.50	31.40
Part V		
1 (a)	74.80	77.00
(b)	37.40	38.50
(c)	31.30	32.20
2 (a)	90.40	93.10
(b)	44.80	46.10
(c)	30.50	31.40
3 (a)	74.80	77.00
(b)	13.50	13.90
6	30.50	31.40

ACT OF SEDERUNT (RULES OF THE COURT OF SESSION AMENDMENT NO 2) (SHORTHAND WRITERS' FEES) 1994

(SI 1994/1140) [21 APRIL 1994]

The Lords of Council and Session, under and by virtue of the powers conferred on them by section 5 of the Court of Session Act 1988 (c 36), and of all other powers enabling them in that behalf, do hereby enact and declare:

Citation and commencement

1.—(1) This Act of Sederunt may be cited as the Act of Sederunt (Rules of the Court of Session Amendment No 2) (Shorthand Writers' Fees) 1994 and shall come into force on 24th May 1994.

(2) This Act of Sederunt shall be inserted in the Books of Sederunt.

Amendment of Table of Fees

2. In Chapter IV of the Table of Fees in rule 347 of the Rules of the Court of Session, for the fees set out in column 2 of the following table, as applying to the paragraphs set out in column 1 of that table, there shall be substituted the fees set out in column 3 of that table; and the fees so substituted shall apply to work, for which those fees are chargeable, done on or after the date on which this Act of Sederunt comes into force:—

Column 1 (paragraph)	Column 2 (old fees) £	Column 3 (new fees) £
1 (minimum fee per day)	53.15	54.75
1 (per hour)	17.71	18.25
2	3.78	3.90
2	4.54	4.70
5	0.29	0.30

Saving

3. The fees set out in column 2 of the table in paragraph 2 above shall continue to apply to work done before this Act of Sederunt comes into force.

J A D HOPE, LORD PRESIDENT, *IPD*

ACT OF SEDERUNT (FEES OF SHORTHAND WRITERS IN THE SHERIFF COURT) 1994

(SI 1994/1141) [21 APRIL 1994]

The Lords of Council and Session, under and by virtue of the powers conferred on them by section 40 of the Sheriff Courts (Scotland) Act 1907 (c 51), and of all other powers enabling them in that behalf, do hereby enact and declare:

Citation and commencement

1.—(1) This Act of Sederunt may be cited as the Act of Sederunt (Fees of Shorthand Writers in the Sheriff Court) 1994 and shall come into force on 24th May 1994.

(2) This Act of Sederunt shall be inserted in the Books of Sederunt.

Amendment of Table of Fees

2. In the Table of Fees in Schedule 2 to the Act of Sederunt (Fees of Witnesses and Shorthand Writers in the Sheriff Court) 1992, for the fees set out in column 2 of the following table, as applying to the paragraphs set out in column 1 of that table, there shall be substituted the fees set out in column 3 of that table; and the fees so substituted shall apply to work, for which those fees are chargeable, done on or after the date on which this Act of Sederunt comes into force:—

TABLE

Column 1 (paragraph)	Column 2 (old fees) £	Column 3 (new fees) £
1 (a)	17.71	18.25
(b) (i)	53.15	54.75
(ii)	63.20	65.10
4 (a)	3.78	3.90
(b)	4.54	4.70
5	0.29	0.30

Saving

3. The fees set out in column 2 of the table in paragraph 2 above, shall continue to apply to work done before the date on which this Act of Sederunt comes into force.

J A D HOPE, LORD PRESIDENT, *IPD*

[Acts of Sederunt are reproduced with the permission of the Controller of Her Majesty's Stationery Office.]

ARTICLES

Assignations of All-Sums Standard Securities

George L Gretton, WS,
Reader in Law,
University of Edinburgh.

Mr Gretton explores the little charted, but potentially important, area of the extent to which an assigned standard security may cover further advances by the assignee.

Heritable securities are, of course, assignable by the creditor. Such assignations are not uncommon where the lender is an individual or a family trust, but rarer in the case of a financial institution. With the decline in secured lending by individuals and family trusts (which can perhaps be dated from about 1940), assignations of heritable securities accordingly became rarer. But in recent years institutions have become more involved in the trading of debt assets, and there are accordingly signs that the practice of assigning heritable securities is reviving. The sale of mortgage portfolios has become more common in recent years. Sometimes such sales are purely contractual, so that the selling institution remains legally the heritable creditor, and will collect payments and manage and enforce the security on behalf of the buyer, with whom the borrower has no direct connection or concern. Such sales are what the Bank of England calls sub-participations. But sometimes the sale of a secured debt does involve a formal assignation.

A standard security can be for a fixed sum, or for a maximum sum, or for all sums. In practice almost all standard securities are of the last type. Even in the familiar "tabular" standard security used in domestic mortgages, where a definite figure is entered into the "amount of loan" box, there is almost always wording later on to say that the security covers not only the loan but all other sums due or to become due.

The assignation of a standard security will thus usually be the assignation of an all-sums security. And that may cause problems. Two main problems arise. The first is the form which the assignation should take. The second, and connected problem, is whether such an assigned security will secure advances made thereafter by the assignee to the borrower. Thus suppose X borrows £60,000 from the Bank of Pictavia and grants to the bank an all-sums standard security. The Bank of Pictavia then assign the security to the Bank of Dalriada. At this stage the debt due by X is £65,000. The latter bank then lend X £10,000. Does the security, which is now vested in the Bank of Dalriada, secure the whole £75,000? In principle there would seem to be three main positions which could be taken. The first is that an assigned standard security cannot cover future advances by the assignee, and that if such future advances are to be secured, a new standard security is required. There are some dicta in the *Ambion* case, below, which can be read as supporting this position. The second is that such future advances can be secured on the original security, though only if there is a deed of variation. This is Halliday's position. The third is that future advances by the assignee are automatically secured, a position which seems not to have attracted support.

The conveyancing literature has little on the subject. Professor J M Halliday has one paragraph in his *Conveyancing and Feudal Reform (Scotland) Act 1970* (2nd ed, 1977), para 9-07. This paragraph is repeated in his *Conveyancing Law and Practice*, Vol III (1987), para 40-19, and there is also one paragraph in Professor D J Cusine's *Standard Securities* (1991), para 6-11. Both authors choose the same word about assignations of all-sums standard securities: "undesirable". Both say that new advances by the assignee will not be covered unless there has been a variation of the standard security. Halliday recommends that it is advisable, if a new advance is to be made, to have a new security. Professor Cusine mentions assignation by the *debtor*, but with respect a debtor cannot assign a standard security. If the debtor transfers his interest subject to the security, that will be by disposition not by assignation. Neither author comments on the form of an assignation of an all-sums standard security.

Hitherto it had been supposed that there was no case law on the matter. But now the 1977 decision of Lord Dunpark in *Sanderson's Trustees v Ambion Scotland Ltd* has been reported at 1994 SLT 645. Given the increased frequency of assignations of standard securities, this decision is of some importance.

Ambion Scotland Ltd were house builders. They needed loan finance. For some unexplained reason, a convoluted financing mechanism was adopted. The lender, a trust, lent not to Ambion Scotland Ltd but to the latter's holding company, which then lent the funds to its subsidiary. (The holding company is called "Ambion" in the documentation but in the judgment it is called "Holdings".) Ambion Scotland gave Ambion Holdings a standard security, which the latter then assigned to the trust. The original contract, which was tripartite, seems to have made both Ambion Scotland and Ambion Holdings jointly and severally liable to the trust for all sums due or to become due. Needless to say, Ambion Scotland and Ambion Holdings became insolvent.

There are two main questions for decision. The first was whether the assignation was valid at all, inasmuch as it was disconform to the style in Sched 4 to the Conveyancing and Feudal Reform (Scotland) Act 1970. In particular, note 2 to the Schedule provides that where an all sums security is assigned, the assignation must contain the words: "to the extent of £ . . . being the amount now due thereunder". The actual assignation did not contain any such words. Lord Dunpark held that the omission of this formula was not fatal in the admittedly unusual facts of the case. He says that if the assignee were a "stranger" (i e the ordinary case where the assignee was not party to the original contract), then the required wording would have been necessary. He does not however say clearly whether its omission would invalidate the assignation.

He also opines that the need for stating the amount outstanding derived from the Bankruptcy Act 1696. This however may be questioned. The 1696 Act invalidated heritable securities for future advances, but there seems to be nothing in it to require an assignation to state the amount then due. But as Lord Dunpark observes, the 1696 Act was disapplied to standard securities, and it may be mentioned that it was wholly repealed by the Bankruptcy (Scotland) Act 1985.

The other main question was whether the trust's security was good only for the sum outstanding at the date of the assignation, or whether it also covered subsequent advances. Lord Dunpark held that subsequent advances were indeed covered, given the terms of the original security documentation, which contemplated that such further advances by the trust would be secured. This seems reasonable.

However, the question arises as to what the position would have been if the original documentation had made no provision about future advances by the assignee. As mentioned above, Halliday says that such advances will be secured if, but only if, there is a deed of variation. While Lord Dunpark does not directly contradict this, he seems to do so indirectly. In the first place, he says that where an assignation is to a "stranger" (i e someone not a party to the initial security) the amount outstanding must be inserted in the assignation. In the second place, he says that if, in the actual case, the amount outstanding had been inserted in the assignation, then "it would have been necessary for two new deeds to have been executed and also recorded . . . namely, the discharge of the standard security . . . and the grant of a new standard security by Scotland directly to

the pursuers" (p 651A-B). If I understand this correctly, he is saying that where an all sums security is assigned, and the amount outstanding is stated, as required by the Act, then new advances by the assignee to the debtor will be covered only if there is a new standard security. That is the first of the three possible positions mentioned earlier. Though I think that such a position is wrong, these dicta may in practice make assignees of standard securities reluctant to rely on deeds of variation to cover new advances.

One argument which seems not to have been canvassed is that s 14 (1) of the 1970 Act provides that upon assignation the security "shall be vested in the assignee as effectually as if the security . . . had been granted in his favour". If the security had been granted directly in favour of the assignee, it would of course cover new advances made by the assignee (assuming that it was for all sums). This argument would mean that not even a deed of variation would be required. However, I doubt whether much weight can be placed on the words quoted. Schedule 4, note 2, requires an assignation of an all-sums security to contain the words: "to the extent of £ . . . being the amount now due thereunder". This wording suggests that such an assignation converts an all-sums security into a fixed sum security, for it does not merely narrate the amount then outstanding, but suggests that the security is assigned only to that extent. However, I know of no reason why a fixed sum security should not be converted, or reconverted, by a deed of variation, into an all-sums security. Hence I think that Halliday's view, that a deed of variation can secure new advances by an assignee, is correct.

Another practical problem arises where the statutory style is adopted but the amount stated as outstanding is too low. This can happen surprisingly easily. Thus suppose that X has a mortgage with the Bank of Pictavia. The amount outstanding on the mortgage account is £65,000. However, X also has a personal loan account, on which £7,000 is outstanding. Since the security is for all sums, the £7,000 is also secured, unless otherwise agreed. When the Bank of Pictavia assigns the security to the Bank of Dalriada, the figure in the mortgage account is inserted in the assignation. This will mean that the Bank of Dalriada is now the creditor of X for that sum, and that the Bank of Pictavia remains X's creditor for the £7,000. So far so good. But it may well be that the security itself is now split into two. At common law it is competent to have a partial assignation of a heritable security, and the 1970 Act provides that this is equally true for standard securities. Accordingly, a possible — and in my view a probable — interpretation of what has happened is that the security originally held by the Bank of Pictavia has been partially assigned. The result is that the standard security is now held pro parte by the one bank and pro parte by the other. Very likely this was not what was intended, but, worse than that, the law of partial assignation is obscure, especially as to ranking and enforcement. (See W M Gloag and J M Irvine, *Rights in Security*, p 126.) The position is even more obscure than it was for the old bond and disposition in security, in that for standard securities there is the possibility of further lending, by either the cedent or the assignee or, horror of horrors, both. It should be noted that the above example is far from the only type of case where the problem might arise. For instance, X might own a company with overdraft facilities with the Bank of Pictavia, and have guaranteed those facilities. His guarantee is a contingent debt which would be, unless otherwise agreed, secured by the all-sums standard security.

To avoid such dangers, it is suggested that where an all-sums standard security is assigned, words should be included declaring that the cedent will retain no title in the security itself in the event that the cedent is owed other debts, including contingent debts, by the debtor. This will make it clear that the assignation of the *security* is not a partial assignation, even if it turns out that the assignation of the *debt* is partial.

Halliday's view, that an assigned standard security will not cover future advances unless there is a deed of variation, might be criticised as being too formalistic. But, in addition to the inferences which can be drawn from the wording of the 1970 Act, there is another argument in favour of Halliday's view. Take the following case. X has granted a standard security to the Bank of Pictavia, for all sums. The debt secured has mostly been paid off, and now stands at just £1,000. X also owes £100,000 to the Bank of Dalriada, unsecured. The Bank of Dalriada are worried at the lack of security. They approach the Bank of Pictavia, and the latter assign their standard security. The debt due by X to the Bank of Dalriada is now £101,000. Does the security cover the whole of this sum, or just £1,000? If Halliday's view were incorrect, the security would presumably cover the whole £101,000, for if an assigned standard security is good for all sums then it is good for all sums. The logic is inescapable. But the consequences would be absurd. For example, X might have been about to sell the property in question. He would have been able to do so simply by paying off the last slice (£1,000) of the debt, which would have entitled him to a discharge of the security. But now, without his consent, his property is burdened by

a debt of £101,000. He may be unable to pay this off at short notice. Indeed, if he has already concluded missives, the assignation would probably force him into breach of contract. This simply cannot be the law. His property cannot be burdened by the extra £100,000 without his consent. Another odd consequence, if Halliday's view were wrong, could arise in the law of insolvency. Suppose that X is sequestrated shortly after the assignation. The Bank of Dalriada will have leapfrogged: the £100,000 debt has magically changed from unsecured to secured, to the prejudice of X's other creditors. This ought to be challengeable as an unfair preference. But the law of unfair preferences strikes only at *acts of the debtor*. The assignation would not be an act of X. Hence it would be unchallengeable. That cannot be the law. (If X had signed a deed of variation, agreeing that the security now held by the Bank of Dalriada would cover the £100,000, that would be an act of the debtor, and so open to challenge in the event of insolvency.)

It might be replied that while X's consent is required, that consent can fairly be presumed, in respect of future advances by the assignee, because X has consented to such advances, whereas it cannot be presumed that X has agreed that the existing advances by the Bank of Dalriada should be secured. Hence, it might be argued, a deed of variation is required to make the existing advances secured, but not future advances. But this argument is circular. It presupposes the very point in question, namely whether future advances by the assignee will be secured. It could equally well be argued that X, in borrowing further sums from the Bank of Dalriada, is assuming that such advances will be on the same footing as the existing advances — namely unsecured. And he may have a legitimate interest in this. There may be many reasons why an owner of heritable property may not wish a particular debt to be secured on that property. One such reason has already been mentioned. Another might be, in a commercial situation, a breach of a negative pledge clause.

Hence it seems reasonably clear that an assigned standard security cannot cover debts already due to the assignee, unless the debtor so agrees. Since it is difficult to draw any logical distinction, in relation to an all-sums security, between existing debts and future debts, one is led to the conclusion that an assigned standard security covers only the debt assigned, unless and until its scope is widened by a deed of variation.

Lastly, the facts of the *Ambion* case would seem to raise another important issue, though it seems not to have been canvassed. It appears that whilst the assignation by Ambion Holdings to the trust was to some extent intended as an outright assignation, it was also to some extent intended as an assignation in security. In other words, to some extent the trust was securing its advances to Ambion Holdings by taking the assignation of the security. Now s 9 (8) (b) of the 1970 Act makes it clear that a standard security is an "interest in land". Section 9 (4) provides that any security over an interest in land is void unless in the form of a standard security. Hence a security over a standard security is void unless it is itself a standard security. It would thus seem to have been open to argument that the assignation to the trust was void. Of course, the concept of a standard security over a standard security is an odd one. But it can be made to work and indeed piggyback standard securities are sometimes used in modern commercial practice. It would have been interesting to see this issue aired in the *Ambion* case. But notwithstanding that omission, and notwithstanding some unclarities in the judgment, *Ambion*, being apparently the only case on a subject of growing importance, should not be overlooked by conveyancers and commercial practitioners.

◆

NEWS

Coming events

Lawyers' Christian Fellowship
The annual weekend UK conference of the LCF will take place at Glasgow Caledonian University, Gibson Hall of Residence, from Friday 9 to Sunday 11 September 1994. The principal speaker on the theme of "Family, Taught and Contract — A view from the bench" will be His Honour Judge Mark Hedley from Liverpool, and various other practising lawyers from all over the UK will also be participating. There will be opportunity for prayer, fellowship and discussion and a ceilidh on the Saturday evening. A creche and children's programme for those of primary school age will also be provided. The standard cost for the weekend will be £70 per head with a reduced rate of £49 for students and unemployed.

Booking forms for the conference, as well as other information about the activities and publications of the LCF, are available from Alan and Joyce Holloway, The Lawyers Christian Fellowship, 20 Waterside Drive, Mearns Park, Newton Mearns, Glasgow G77 6TL (tel 041-616 0522). Prompt bookings will be especially appreciated as these help in conference organisation.

— ◇ —

General

Faculty of Advocates
The following have been admitted to the Faculty of Advocates: John Park Robertson, LLB(Edinburgh); John Charles Buchanan Hipwell, LLB (Edinburgh); Celia Louise McLean or Sanderson, LLB(Edinburgh); Alan Andrew Summers, LLB (Dundee), BCL(Oxford); Jane Mary Porter, LLB(Edinburgh); Martin Jones, LLB, MPhil (Glasgow); Alison Margaret Innes, LLB(Aberdeen); Gary James Allan, LLB(Aberdeen); Brian McConnachie, LLB(Glasgow); and Jamie Gilchrist, MA(Cambridge), LLB(Edinburgh).

◇

Law Society of Scotland: ACCORD ADR service
The Law Society of Scotland have launched ACCORD, the society's own ADR service, which offers both guidance on the suitability of a dispute for ADR (and on the most appropriate form of ADR for an individual dispute) and a panel of trained and accredited solicitor mediators.

ACCORD has been developed in response to the growing demand for disputes to be settled by ADR, and in particular mediation, as an alternative to the expense, delay and time required to pursue traditional litigation or arbitration.

Parties can either make a joint application to ACCORD to appoint a mediator or else approach the approved mediator direct. The Law Society also offer to assist by approaching another party to explain the advantages of mediation and encourage him or her to try it. The process does not result in any binding obligations (other than the mediator's fees) until the conclusion of an agreement following mediation.

ACCORD deals with most kinds of disputes except family related ones, for which there is a separate panel of accredited family law mediators.

The charges, which require to be paid in advance, are: an administrative charge of £100 on submission of a joint application for mediation; £40 for an assessment of the suitability of a dispute for mediation or for an approach to another party (£10 for each further party); the mediator's fee of between £250 and £1,000 depending on the value of the claim; £50 for each mediation session after the first and £150 (or the actual costs of premises other than 26 Drumsheugh) for provision of premises, all plus VAT.

The eight solicitor mediators so far accredited are David Semple of Semple Fraser Haniford Di Ciacca, Glasgow, David Kidd of Biggart Baillie Gifford, Edinburgh, Martin Sales of W & J Burness, Edinburgh, Gordon Hollerin of Bird Semple, Edinburgh, Douglas Russell of Simpson & Marwick, Edinburgh, Leonard Mair of Morton Fraser Milligan, Edinburgh, Kenneth Cumming of Dundas & Wilson, Edinburgh, and Vincent Connor of McGrigor Donald, Glasgow. The Law Society hope that up to 75 solicitors will be accredited within 12-18 months, from all parts of Scotland.

A series of seminars are now taking place to explain the benefits of the service to the profession. Those still to take place are: Moat House hotel, Glasgow, 21 June; Kingsmill hotel, Inverness, 23 June; Earl Grey hotel, Dundee, 28 June, and Amatola hotel, Aberdeen, 30 June, all from (6 for) 6.30 to 8 pm.

For further information on ACCORD contact Iona Campbell or Bruce Ritchie at 26 Drumsheugh Gardens.

— ◊ —

Taxation

Capital gains tax: assets of negligible value
The Inland Revenue have published the following revised version of extra-statutory concession D28, which deals with the treatment of claims that assets have become of negligible value for capital gains tax purposes:

Where an asset has become of negligible value, s 24 (2) of the Taxation of Chargeable Gains Act 1992 allows the owner to claim to be treated as though the asset had been sold and immediately re-acquired at the specified value. If the claim is accepted, this will normally give rise to an allowable loss. Strictly, s 24 (2) requires the deemed sale and re-acquisition to be treated as taking place when the claim is made. In practice, the Inland Revenue will accept that a claim by the owner to be treated as having sold and re-acquired the asset at a particular date may be made not later than 24 months after the end of the tax year

(or accounting period in the case of a company) in which that date fell. This will apply provided that the asset is of negligible value both at the date the claim is made and at that earlier date.

For negligible value claims made on or after 30 November 1993, the computation on the disposal will be made on the basis of the legislation in force at the date of claim, not at the date of the deemed disposal. Where the benefit of the concession is claimed in respect of a negligible value claim made in the period from 30 November 1993 to 5 April 1995, the indexation loss for transitional relief purposes will be computed under Sched 12 to the Finance Act 1994 on the assumption that any available indexation is calculated up to the date of the deemed disposal only. Chargeable gains will be reduced first by any allowable loss. The taxpayer may then use the indexation loss, under this concession, to reduce any gains (before any allowable losses carried forward) on which liability would arise in the year of the deemed disposal or any later year up to and including 1994-95. Relief remains subject to the limit of £10,000 in Sched 12 on the total amount of indexation losses which any taxpayer may use, and subject to the taxpayer qualifying for transitional relief. Any indexation loss unused will not be available to set against gains arising on disposals made on or after 6 April 1995.

In the case of unquoted shares, where this extra-statutory concession applies, relief under ss 573-576 of the Income and Corporation Taxes Act 1988 will be available if the conditions for such relief are satisfied both at the date the claim to negligible value is made and the date at which the owner is treated as having sold and re-acquired the shares. Loss relief under s 574 may include any appropriate amount of indexation loss.

◊

Income tax: Enterprise Investment Scheme
The Inland Revenue have published two statements of practice (SP2/94 and SP3/94) relating to the Enterprise Investment Scheme (EIS) and a revised text of extra-statutory concession A76. These apply to the EIS similar practices and a concession which apply to the Business Expansion Scheme (BES).

The EIS replaces the BES, which came to an end for new investment at the end of 1993. Relief under the new scheme is available in respect of qualifying investments in eligible shares issued on or after 1 January 1994.

Statement of practice SP2/94 gives the Inland Revenue's interpretation of the requirement that qualifying trades for which money is raised through the EIS should be carried on "wholly or mainly in the United Kingdom". An existing statement of practice (SP4/87) gives the Inland Revenue's interpretation of a similar BES rule; this will continue to apply in respect of the BES.

Statement of practice SP3/94 gives the Inland Revenue's interpretation of the rule that relief under the BES or EIS is not available in respect of investments in eligible shares which are linked to loans. The loans affected by the rule are those where there is a specific connection, as far as the lender is concerned, between the loan and shares. The provision does not extend to loans which are not made specifically on the security of the shares or otherwise on terms which are affected by the borrower's, or one of his or her associate's ownership of them.

The text and title of concession A76 have been slightly amended so that it applies both to BES relief and to EIS relief; no changes of substance have been made. Under the terms of the concession, an investor who acquires a subscriber share in a company from company formation agents will not be prevented from qualifying for relief simply because, for the period until further shares are issued, that investor will hold 50 per cent of the issued share capital of the company.

Copies of the statements of practice can be obtained from the Public Inquiry Room, West Wing, Somerset House, Strand, London WC2R 1LB.

— ◇ —

Obituary

On 10 June 1994, John Gibb, CBE, OBE, formerly senior partner in and subsequently consultant to the firm of Messrs J & W Buchan, solicitors, Peebles and Innerleithen.

— ◇ —

Parliamentary News

Royal Assent

26 May 1994

Insolvency (No 2) Act 1994 (c 12).
Intelligence Services Act 1994 (c 13).

— ◇ —

Book Review

Blackstone's EC Legislation

Fourth edition. By Nigel Foster. 1993.
London: Blackstone Press. Paperback, £11.95.
ISBN 1 85431 283 9.

Nearly all of the major law publishing houses have sought to produce books of this type. It is perhaps indicative of not just the need for primary materials but also of the prohibitive cost of acquiring individual statutes and other forms of legislation from HMSO. By bringing all the relevant legislation into the confines of one book at a modest price, publishers such as Blackstone are undoubtedly meeting the needs of students and practitioners alike. Naturally publishers are not doing this for altruistic reasons but rather because there is a substantial market.

This present text under review joins a growing series of such books by Blackstone, encompassing a broad range of law areas. Given the number of students now studying European Community law, *Blackstone's EC Legislation* is likely to appeal to a larger market than some other books which collate the main legislation in a particular field. The fourth edition includes the now renowned Maastricht Treaty. The author explains, in classic understatement, that "uncertainty over Masstricht prevented me from including the amended EC Treaty". Obviously the confines of space restrict what can be included, but the author appears to have given some thought as to what should be included and has produced a book that will address the needs of most of those who have to source EC legislation. All in all a useful purchase but with ever evolving European Community law, one with a limited shelf life.

RICHARD MAYS,
The Robert Gordon University,
Aberdeen.

Bill Stewart, the Book Review Editor, is keen that books, and especially, books written with the practitioner in mind should be reviewed by practitioners. Accordingly, members of Faculty and solicitors who consider that they could competently review books, are invited to write with a note of their name and address, indicating upon what subjects they would be prepared to write reviews, to him c/o MacMillans, Solicitors, 78 Springfield Road, Glasgow G40 3ET.

ARTICLES

Written Fee Charging Agreements

Roderick C McKenzie,
Harper Macleod,
Glasgow.

Mr McKenzie considers the effect of s 61A of the Solicitors (Scotland) Act 1980 against the background of the common law and the equivalent English rules. He argues that care must be taken in drafting to achieve an enforceable agreement, and suggests forms which might be used. He also speculates that the section may have unintended effects in relation to the validity of contingency fee arrangements.

The existing Scots law

The common law position in relation to remuneration for professional services is that if there is an express agreement for remuneration for the services then that determines the remuneration to be paid: *Arthur Duthie and Co Ltd v Merson and Gerry*, 1947 SLT 81; 1947 SC 43. An express agreement will be preferred even against a scale of fees laid down by a professional institution: *Wilkie v Scottish Aviation Ltd*, 1956 SLT (Notes) 25; 1956 SC 198.

However in the case of solicitors' fees the rule is that no decree will be granted, whether in absence or in foro, in an action by a solicitor seeking payment of his fees unless the account has been taxed by the relevant auditor of court.

The principle which underlies this rule appears to be founded upon the view that as solicitors are in a particular position of trust they should not be seen to be in a position of potential abuse of that trust and therefore their accounts, where an action for payment is required, must be scrutinised by an independent person who has been appointed by the court, inter alia for the purpose of scrutinising such accounts.

The matter was thoroughly reviewed by Sheriff Principal R D Ireland, QC, in *Lyall and Wood v Thomson*, 1993 SLT (Sh Ct) 21. In that case the sheriff refused to grant decree in absence in a small claim without taxation and the pursuers appealed to the sheriff principal, who held that it was incompetent to grant decree in an action for payment of a solicitor's account without taxation, irrespective of the form of process or forum. Sheriff Principal Ireland followed Sheriff Principal Taylor in the case of *W and A S Bruce v Ewans*, 1986 SLT (Sh Ct) 20 and did not follow the decision in *Alex Morison and Co, WS v McCulloch*, 1984 SLT (Sh Ct) 88. For a full discussion of the matter see Richard Mays, "A Taxing Time for Solicitors", 1993 SLT (News) 249.

The English position

The earliest recorded statutory provision relating to taxation of costs in England is a 1729 Act (2 Geo II, c 23) (Attorneys and Solicitors). The matter is now governed by the Solicitors Act 1974, ss 69, 70 and 71, as amended. The effect of these provisions is that where an account has been issued by a solicitor, a client has a period of 12 months in which to require the solicitor to refer the account for taxation.

In *Harrison v Tew* [1990] 2 AC 523; [1990] 2 WLR 210; [1990] 1 All ER 321, the House of Lords held that the inherent jurisdiction of the court to require taxation of a solicitor's account had been ousted and replaced by s 70 of the 1974 Act, and that if a solicitor's account had not been referred to taxation by a client within 12 months then the court had no power to require the account to be taxed.

Sections 57 and 59-66 of the 1974 Act respectively provide for non-contentious and contentious business agreements in relation to fees.

In the case of non-contentious business (i e non-litigation), s 57 (1) provides that a solicitor may enter into an agreement with a client as to the solicitor's remuneration in respect of any particular piece of non-contentious business. The agreement may provide for remuneration to be paid by way of a gross sum, or by commission, or by a percentage, or by salary or otherwise, and may also provide as to whether or not disbursements are to be included: s 57 (2). Section 57 (3) provides that the agreement shall be in writing and must be signed by the client or by his agent. The agreement is capable of being set aside or the amount payable reduced where a court finds that the amount charged is unfair or unreasonable: s 57 (4) and (5).

In the case of contentious business s 59 (1) provides that a solicitor and client "may make an agreement in writing" as to the remuneration to be paid to the solicitor for contentious business done or to be done by him. The agreement may provide for remuneration by gross sum, or by a salary or otherwise. Where a contentious business agreement has been entered into, the court may not refer the amount of the solicitors' account for taxation except pursuant to ss 60 and 61, which provide that the court may enforce or set aside the agreement and determine the validity or effect of the agreement, or may refuse to enforce the agreement if it considers it to be unfair or unreasonable. The court may set aside the agreement and/or order that the costs incurred under it be taxed if it is of the opinion that the agreement is in any respect unfair or unreasonable.

The provisions of s 59 of the 1974 Act were considered in *Chamberlain v Boodle & King (a firm)* [1982] 3 All ER 188. In that case, solicitors had been retained to act in a complex litigation. A letter from the solicitors to the client indicated that the solicitors' charges would be calculated on the basis of standard hourly rates depending upon the attorney or solicitor involved at any particular stage in the litigation. The range of specified charges for partners was from £60 to £80 an hour and for associates from £30 to £45 per hour.

Eventually the litigation was settled, and whilst Mr Chamberlain had paid the first three solicitors' accounts he declined to pay the fourth. He required the fourth account to be referred to taxation pursuant to s 70 (1) of the 1974 Act. The solicitors contended that the letter which had been sent to Mr Chamberlain constituted a "contentious business agreement" for the purposes of ss 59 and 60 of the 1974 Act and accordingly could not be referred to taxation except in the circumstances set out in ss 60 and 61.

The Court of Appeal held that a letter could only be a contentious business agreement if it was specific in its terms and signed with some form of acceptance by the client. Whilst Mr Chamberlain had replied to the letter sent by the solicitors notifying him of the charging rates, that reply was by no means an explicit acceptance of the terms proposed by the solicitors. In any event the letter from the solicitors was imprecise in its terms as regards the amount which Mr Chamberlain might be expected to be liable to pay and the letter was silent as regards the question of disbursements.

Lord Denning MR at p 191 stated that a contentious business agreement could be constituted by an exchange of letters, but that there had to be explicit acceptance by the client of the proposals made by the solicitors and the agreement had to be explicit as to the charges which would be made. Lord Denning appears, from the decision, to have been invited to hold that a contentious business agreement could not be constituted in circumstances where the agreement only related to the hourly rates which might be applied by the solicitors, but he declined to express a decided view on the matter since it was not necessary for him to do so to determine the case. He holds however that where a range of charges are specified for solicitors of the same status, it could not be said to be an agreement on charges since the actual amount charged could fall anywhere within the range.

Whilst the court was not required to state a decided view on the issue of whether a contentious business agreement could be constituted by specification of hourly rates of charge only, the impression is obtained from Lord Denning's opinion that he was not impressed by the methodology adopted in the purported agreement.

Section 98 of the Courts and Legal Services Act 1990 amended ss 57 and 59 of the 1974 Act by providing that contentious and non-contentious business agreements could provide that the remuneration of the solicitors concerned was to be calculated under reference to hourly rates.

Scottish proposals for law reform

In *Public Protection: Professional Independence*, the response by the Law Society of Scotland to the Scottish Home and Health Department's consultation paper, *The Legal Profession in Scotland: The Way Forward*, June 1989 at para 7.C.4, the Law Society proposed that a solicitor and his client "should be entitled to enforce the terms of a contract made with respect to legal fees, whether a fixed sum, a percentage or scale relating to value, or an hourly rate". The Law Society went on to propose that only in the absence of a fee charging agreement should the matter of the amount of a solicitors' account be determined by reference to the auditor of court.

The government agreed to this proposal and Parliament enacted the relevant primary legislation in s 36 (3) of the Law Reform (Miscellaneous Provisions) (Scotland) Act 1990, amending the Solicitors (Scotland) Act 1980 by inserting a new s 61A.

Section 61A (1) of the 1980 Act provides, deceptively simply: "[W]here a solicitor and his client have reached an agreement in writing as to the solicitor's fees in respect of any work done or to be done by him for his client it shall not be competent, in any litigation arising out of any dispute as to the amount due to be paid under any such agreement, for the court to remit the solicitor's account for taxation."

It is to be noted that the section does not provide that it shall be competent for either of the parties to ask for the auditor of court to tax an account; the provision simply makes it incompetent for the court to remit the account for taxation. The relevant English legislation extends over a number of (amended) sections of the 1974 Act and the Scottish legislation is in effect encompassed in a single subsection of s 61A of the amended 1980 Act. Whilst, in general, brevity is laudable, s 61A (1) provides no guidance as to what constitutes an "agreement in writing" for the purposes of the Act.

WRITTEN FEE CHARGING AGREEMENTS

The Law Society of Scotland has promulgated practice rules, entitled the Solicitors (Scotland) (Written Fee Charging Agreements) Practice Rules 1993. The only requirement in the rules is a negative provision which prohibits a written fee charging agreement containing a clause for consent to registration for preservation and execution (rule 4) and the rules are accordingly of little practical assistance.

Following the decision in *Chamberlain* (supra) it is suggested that there is no reason why a written fee charging agreement should not be constituted in the form of either an exchange of letters or alternatively a written acceptance by a client endorsed on a letter addressed by the solicitors to the client or vice versa. The writer would envisage that in most circumstances the most convenient method of constituting a written fee charging agreement would be by a letter from the solicitor to the client with an appropriate docquet of acceptance endorsed thereon which the client would sign and return. Readers are referred to the suggested styles which accompany this article.

Leaving aside the question of the form of the agreement, the most significant question that arises out of the terms of s 61A (1) of the 1980 Act is, what constitutes an agreement as to solicitors' fees in respect of work done or to be done?

There should be no difficulty in concluding that an agreement which provides for a fixed charge or a percentage charge in respect of any particular piece of work would be a valid fee charging agreement for the purposes of the section. An agreement to the effect that £500 (for example), exclusive of disbursements and VAT, would be charged for the conveyance of a particular property, or alternatively a charge of 1 per cent (for example), exclusive of disbursements and VAT of the selling or buying price of a property, would be valid.

However in many matters it will not be possible to arrive at a set charge for the work that will be undertaken, and in such matters the work is typically charged out on the basis of the time spent on the matter, the charging rate being multiplied by the units of time spent working on the matter.

The difficulty is that s 61A (1) does not specifically provide for the right to charge at a rate per unit of time. Since the agreement must be in respect of fees for work done or to be done, a "fee charging agreement" would not be constituted by a provision, where in respect of a particular litigation or transaction, the solicitor's time would be charged at a rate per unit of time. In the writer's opinion that is not an agreement *in respect of fees for work done or to be done*: it is an agreement in

relation to the hourly rate which will be charged per unit of time spent doing legal work. The distinction may be a narrow one but its significance is obvious. If an agreement is not a written fee charging agreement for the purposes of the subsection then the existing law requiring a remit to taxation of a solicitor's account, in all actions for recovery of professional charges, will apply whatever may be the terms of the agreement.

How then may a written fee charging agreement be constituted where it is intended to charge on the basis of an amount per unit of time? The writer would suggest that it is possible so to do, but not under direct reference to a simple time based rate for a particular litigation or transaction. If the agreement narrates that the solicitor is to provide legal services, without specifying what that work would be in respect of, and the legal services are to be provided in units of time, and that a specific amount will be charged for each unit of time spent providing those legal services, such a form of agreement would appear to meet the terms of s 61A.

What, in effect, is being proposed is an agreement which will provide for an indefinite (as to number) series of fixed charge, time based, units of legal work. The parties to such an agreement are contracting whereby the solicitor provides units of legal work at a fixed charge per unit. The suggested style B is intended to apply to a client who instructs, has instructed or will instruct a particular firm in a number of matters. With appropriate (but careful) modification the style could be referenced to a specific matter, but only so long as the "core" of the contract remains payment for time based units of legal service provided, and not a simple agreement as to the hourly rate to be charged for work on the particular matter to which the agreement related.

The author of the article "Written Fee Charging Agreements", Walter G Semple (1993) 38 JLS 395, in the paragraph entitled "Enforceable Agreements", suggests that a "written fee charging agreement" that "related only to hourly or daily rates" would meet the terms of s 61A (1). It follows from the observations above that the learned author is correct, but *only* if the agreement is drawn in such a way as to avoid the trap of the agreement being one as to hourly rates only. The hourly rate or daily rates must be "related" to legal work done or to be done. To constitute an effective written fee charging agreement the crucial connection is between the work and the charge to be made for that work, and not the rate to be charged for a particular unit of time.

If a fee charging agreement meets the terms of the subsection then that ousts the right of the court to remit the account for taxation and in effect provides that the court cannot refer to taxation either the amount charged per unit of time or the time claimed to have been spent on any particular matter to which the agreement relates. In such circumstances, where the amount of time is disputed, it would be for the pursuer to prove that the amount of time claimed had actually been spent carrying out the work claimed to have been done. It would be open to the defender to challenge, for determination by the judge or sheriff, that the work claimed to have been done was done and/or that the time claimed to have been spent was spent and/or that the amount of time spent was necessary and/or reasonable. The onus would of course be on the solicitor to establish these matters. In the case of a time based charging system it would be necessary to record accurately, and in some detail, the time expended on work carried out for the client and what that time was expended in doing.

The style letters which follow adopt a minimalist approach. In the writer's opinion it is not advisable to include any extraneous material of an explanatory or other nature in the agreement itself. To include such material is to risk creating ambiguities in the core contract that is intended to be created. Information about particular instructions given, interim billing, identification of persons who will be carrying out particular pieces of work and explanations as to the terms of the proposed agreement etc are more appropriately contained in a separate letter or other communication.

Contingency fees

In *The Scottish Legal Profession: The Way Forward*, the Secretary of State for Scotland indicated that a system of contingency fees was not to be permitted in Scotland. Whilst the Law Society's response in *Public Protection: Professional Independence*, at para 7.L and chap 7: appendix, was somewhat lukewarm, there is an argument that the provisions of s 61A (1) have by the back door allowed the introduction of contingency fee arrangements.

The rule that contingency fee agreements (or *pacta de quota litis*) are illegal and void is, historically, closely allied to the rule that any solicitor's account required to be referred for taxation before a decree was granted, as opposed to any express public policy considerations attendant on such agreements.

An arguable case may be made out that s 61A (1) may have rendered, unintentionally, contingency fee arrangements lawful. The decision in *Johnston v Rome* (1831) 9 S 364 at p 369 was

given at a time when taxation was mandatory in all cases. It is not entirely clear that if taxation had not been mandatory, a contingency fee agreement would have been unlawful. The writer speculates, however, that the courts would now consider that public policy considerations alone would ensure that the courts would still regard such agreements as unenforceable.

The requirement of taxation has always afforded de facto protection on the basis that a contingency fee agreement could never be directly enforceable. It should be noted that the Scottish legislation does not contain a prohibition against contingency fee arrangements such as that contained in s 59 (2) (b) of the 1974 Act. It would however be a brave lawyer who would be the first to take on the issue by attempting to enforce a contingency fee arrangement through the operation of a written fee charging agreement said to be constituted in terms of s 61A (1) of the 1980 Act, where the basis of charge was expressed as a percentage of any sum recovered in a litigation contingent upon success in that litigation.

Appendix A

Draft fee charging agreement for fixed fee (particular matter specified):

Dear [   ]

With reference to our recent discussions this firm offers to act on your behalf in connection with [here detail the piece of work, transaction, litigation or other matter with which the agreement is concerned] ("the matter").

The fee charged by us in connection with the matter shall be £

You shall in addition be liable to indemnify us in respect of all disbursements incurred or liable to be incurred by us on your behalf in connection with the matter. You shall be liable to pay VAT on the fee.

Where we are instructed by two or more persons in the matter those persons are jointly and severally liable for the fee, disbursements and the VAT.

This offer is open for your acceptance. If you accept this offer please sign the original of this letter in the space provided below and return it to us in the (reply paid/stamped addressed) envelope enclosed.

Yours sincerely,

I/We,   residing at   hereby accept the offer on the terms set out above and instruct   , Solicitors, to act on my/our behalf in the matter on those terms.

Signature(s)................ Date ....

Appendix B

Draft fee charging agreement for time based work (no reference to any specific matter).

Dear [   ]

With reference to our recent discussions this firm offers to provide you with professional legal services. The services will be provided in [here insert length of unit] units of time. The charge per unit of time will depend upon the status within the firm, of the solicitor or legal executive who expends the time providing the legal services in each instance.

The charging rate per unit of time for the legal services which we offer to provide are:

Partner : [rate per unit]
Associate : [rate per unit]
Assistant solicitor : [rate per unit]
Trainee : [rate per unit]
Legal executive —
          paralegal : [rate per unit]

[Here insert if desired hourly unit rate equivalents, for information, if length of unit is not one hour and/or provision for mechanism for uprating of rates, e g annually for inflation.]

You shall in addition be liable to indemnify us in respect of all disbursements made or liable to be made by us on your behalf. You shall be liable to pay VAT on our charges.

Where we are instructed by two or more persons those persons are jointly and severally liable for our charges, disbursements and VAT.

This offer is open for your acceptance. If you accept this offer please sign the original of this letter in the space provided below and return it to us in the (reply paid/stamped addressed) envelope enclosed.

Yours sincerely,

I/We,   residing at   hereby accept the offer on the terms set out above and instruct   , Solicitors, to provide legal services to me/us on those terms.

Signature(s)................. Date ......

Still No Interdicts Against the Crown

I S Dickinson,
Senior Lecturer in Law,
University of Strathclyde.

A striking disparity in the availability of remedies under the Crown Proceedings Act 1947 as between England and Scotland as a result of the House of Lords decision in M v Home Office *has been con-firmed by the Inner House in* McDonald v Secretary of State for Scotland. *This article examines the decision together with the background to the law in the two jurisdictions and supports a legislative change to remove the disparity.*

In the Reith Lectures for 1986, "Law Justice and Democracy", Lord McCluskey observed that "Courts do not choose what disputes come before them. . . . It is largely a matter of chance whether or not the courts get the opportunity to answer any particular legal question" (p 5). Fortuitously or otherwise, hard on the heels of *M v Home Office* [1993] 3 WLR 433 (see 1993 SLT (News) 311 for discussion of the case), the Scottish courts were recently called upon to answer an identical question, whether or not interim relief was available to a litigant against a minister of the Crown: *McDonald v Secretary of State for Scotland*, 1994 SLT 692. Whereas the House of Lords ruled that injunctive relief could be granted on an application for judicial review in England, the Scottish courts have concluded that they lack the power to grant interdict in any civil proceedings against the Crown.

Before examining the decision it may be helpful to trace briefly the different paths followed by the law in England and Scotland. In England no injunctions (interim or otherwise) were available against the Crown prior to the passing of the Crown Proceedings Act 1947. Moreover the Act by s 21 precluded all forms of such relief against the Crown in "civil proceedings" (*Merricks v Heathcoat-Amory* [1955] Ch 567 and *Harper v Secretary of State for the Home Department* [1955] Ch 238), providing only for the making, in the discretion of the court, of a declaratory order. Significantly, however, proceedings invoking the supervisory jurisdiction of the High Court — begun since 1978 by way of an application for judicial review — were excluded from the definition of "civil proceedings" by s 38 (2) of the Act.

The full impact of this exclusion did not apparently surface till 1986 when, against the background of both the 1947 Act and the Supreme Court Act 1981, Hodgson J in *R v Secretary of State for the Home Department, ex p Herbage* [1987] QB 872 expressed the opinion that a court of the Queen's Bench Division had jurisdiction under Order 53, rule 10 (3) (b) of the Rules of the Supreme Court to grant an injunction against an officer of the Crown. He declined in the exercise of his discretion to grant the particular order sought, but made it plain that in the light of s 31 of the 1981 Act the court had jurisdiction in an application for judicial review to award interim relief against the prison governor and the Secretary of State. The correctness of Hodgson J's interpretation of s 31 of the 1981 Act was eventually upheld in *M v Home Office*, supra.

In Scotland, on the other hand, in two reported cases prior to the 1947 Act (*Russell v Magistrates of Hamilton* (1897) 25 R 350 and *Bell v Secretary of State for Scotland*, 1933 SLT 519) interdicts had been granted against a minister of the Crown. However from the inception of the Crown Proceedings Act in 1948 this remedy ceased to be available in Scotland (see, e g *MacCormick v Lord Advocate*, 1953 SLT 255; 1953 SC 396).

Had proceedings invoking the supervisory jurisdiction of the Court of Session been expressly excluded by an appropriate form of words in the 1947 Act, those proceedings would not have been categorised as "civil proceedings" for purposes of the Act. A petition for interim interdict against a minister of the Crown would thus have remained a competent procedure in Scotland after the commencement of the Act. That is to say the law of Scotland would not have suffered the regressive change, which ran counter to the reforming purpose of the legislation as a whole, brought about by s 21 (1).

That section, as applied to Scotland and so far as relevant to the *McDonald* appeal, is in the following terms:

"(1) In any civil proceedings by or against the Crown the court shall, subject to the provisions of this Act, have power to make all such orders as it has power to make in proceedings between subjects, and otherwise to give such appropriate relief as the case may require: Provided that: (a) where in any proceedings against the Crown any such relief is sought as might in proceedings between subjects be granted by way of interdict or specific performance, the court shall not grant an interdict or make an order for specific performance, but may in lieu thereof make an order declaratory of the rights of the parties; . . .

"(2) The court shall not in any civil proceedings grant any interdict or make any order against an officer of the Crown if the effect of granting the interdict or making the order would be to give any relief against the Crown which could not have been obtained in proceedings against the Crown."

Turning to the appeal itself, the appellant sought interim interdict against the Secretary of State or those acting on his instructions from repeatedly searching the appellant without lawful authority, warrant or justifiable cause. In support of his application he relied on s 21 of the 1947 Act and on the opinion of Lord Woolf in *M v Home Office*. He also claimed damages totalling £300,000 in respect of some 3,000 searches which

he alleged had been wrongfully carried out within Glenochil prison.

Both the sheriff and the sheriff principal on appeal had refused the appellant's motion for interim interdict on the ground that, notwithstanding the decision in *M v Home Office*, in the light of s 21 of the 1947 Act the remedy sought was not one which a Scottish court could competently grant. The appellant appealed to the Inner House. As the appellant was unrepresented, and on account of the importance of the issues raised by the appeal, the Second Division ordered the appointment of a senior member of the bar to act as amicus curiae.

The crucial questions for the Second Division were, first, whether the proceedings were civil proceedings against the Crown in the sense of s 21 of the 1947 Act, and secondly, assuming they were, whether the liberalising judgment of the House of Lords had any impact on the restrictive provisions of s 21 as it applied to Scotland. The court had no difficulty in answering the first of these questions in the affirmative, but encountered problems in attempting to apply the reasoning of Lord Woolf in *M v Home Office*, especially in reference to s 21 (2), to Scotland.

After examining s 21 Lord Justice Clerk Ross pointed out that *M v Home Office* had been decided under English law and that caution had to be exercised in relying on English decisions on the 1947 Act where those decisions turned upon rules of procedure which differed from those applying in Scotland — *Smith v Lord Advocate*, per Lord Avonside, 1980 SC 227 at p 231; 1981 SLT 19 at p 22; and *British Medical Association v Greater Glasgow Health Board*, 1989 SLT 493 per Lord Jauncey at p 497. As regards s 21 (2) the Lord Justice Clerk, while confessing difficulty in determining the content to be given to it in a Scottish context, held that it was not necessary to make such a determination because the present action plainly fell under s 21 (1), the terms of which were unambiguous (p 698D-E). In a similar vein Lord Sutherland observed: "Because of the nature of the Scottish procedure it is not necessary to invoke s 21 (2), whatever its meaning may be" (p 700H).

The other distinguishing feature which Lord Ross noted was that in England the jurisdiction to grant injunctions against ministers or other officers of the Crown in proceedings for judicial review derived from s 31 of the Supreme Court Act 1981. Accordingly in the light of the different legal systems and procedures for suing the Crown as between England and Scotland, the Second Division concluded that *M v Home Office* was not binding in Scotland. The result was that the rule introduced in 1948 barring the award by a Scottish court of interim relief against a minister of the Crown remained intact.

Before leaving the judgment, brief reference should be made to the contribution of the amicus curiae. The court heard submissions by the amicus, who found himself unable to advance any fresh submissions on the pursuer's behalf because the proceedings before the court were plainly civil proceedings governed by s 21 (1). He did however submit that had an application for judicial review been made by the pursuer in which he sought interim interdict, it might have been open to him to argue that, being an application to the supervisory jurisdiction under Rule of Court 260B, it did not constitute civil proceedings against the Crown within the meaning of s 21 (1). However, given the unqualified terms in which that expression is used in s 21 (1), the court was content to observe that there were formidable difficulties in the way of that submission and that in any event it was unnecessary to decide the question in the present appeal.

To conclude, the failure of this appeal was not the result of resorting to an inappropriate procedure. Indeed if an application for judicial review of the kind posited by the amicus had been presented, the outcome would almost certainly have been identical. Rather it was a reflection of the manner in which s 21 of the 1947 Act was applied and continues to apply to Scotland. The absence of a provision on similar lines to that found in s 38 (2) for England, coupled with the fact that the machinery for judicial review in Scotland has not been placed on a statutory footing, means that a Scottish litigant is denied a valuable remedy against the Crown available to those south of the border. Following *M v Home Office* the case for reform of the law of Scotland was clear, strong and pressing. In the light of the unanimity on the part of the Second Division demonstrated in *McDonald v Secretary of State for Scotland*, the argument for amending the law to remove the disparity between the two jurisdictions is even more cogent.

◆

NEWS

Appointments

W Green
Anthony Kinahan, currently commercial director of Sweet & Maxwell, has been appointed as managing director of W Green with effect from 4 July 1994 in succession to Steven Mair, who has been appointed director of professional publishing with John Wiley & Sons Ltd of Chichester.

Anthony Kinahan has been with Sweet & Maxwell for 18 years, for much of that time as marketing director as well as a director of Greens. He is already thoroughly familiar with Greens' business and with legal publishing on both sides of the border, and is keen to continue the development strategy which has been pursued by Greens in recent years.

◇

Rotary International
John Kenny, senior partner in the firm of Messrs Tait & Mackenzie, Grangemouth, has been elected a director of the worldwide service organisation, Rotary International, and will serve from 1995 to 1997.

— ◇ —

Coming events

Centre for Professional Legal Studies
The Centre for Professional Legal Studies at the University of Strathclyde is offering the following one day courses in 1994. *Civil Litigation:* Edinburgh, 15 September; Glasgow, 22 September. *Commercial and Corporate:* Dundee, 27 October; Edinburgh, 29 September; Glasgow, 6 September. *Conveyancing:* Aberdeen, 28 September; Edinburgh, 21 September; Glasgow, 31 August and 26 October; Inverness, 14 September; Perth, 19 October. *Criminal Law:* Edinburgh, 24 September; Glasgow, 10 September. *Executries:* Edinburgh, 20 September; Glasgow, 13 September. *Management:* Edinburgh, 14 September; Glasgow, 7 September, 21 September and 19 October; Perth, 28 September; Aberdeen, 5 October; Inverness, 12 October; Dundee, 26 October. *Pensions:* Glasgow, 5 September and 5 October. Fees for all courses are £195 including materials and lunch. For enrolments and further information contact Ms Shirley Betts or Mrs Jane Hutton, CPLS, University of Strathclyde, Stenhouse Building, 173 Cathedral Street, Glasgow G4 0RQ.

— ◇ —

General

Birthday honours
CBE — Charles Milne Glennie, Registrar General, General Register Office for Scotland.

OBE — Colin Alexander Bell Crosby, chairman, Grampian Housing Association, for services to the housing association movement in Scotland; Donald Andrew Stirling, regional reporter to the children's panel, Lothian Region, for services to young people.

◇

Winston Churchill Memorial Trust: travelling fellowships
The Winston Churchill Memorial Trust offers travelling fellowships to British citizens to undertake study projects related to their trade, profession or interests. The fellowship grant covers return air fare, travel and living expenses, essential equipment and insurance, and usually covers a stay overseas of about eight weeks. The categories of award offered for 1995 are as follows: the rural economy, agriculture, forestry and conservation; opera — producers and designers; training and education in industry; multi-media aids to secondary, higher and further education; agricultural pollution; ancient remedies and alternative medicine; OPEN — for projects in China; the investigation and prosecution of fraud; schoolchildren and drugs; contributions to the success of a multi-ethnic society; and individual exploration and adventure. About 100 awards are made annually. For an application form write to the Winston Churchill Memorial Trust, 15 Queen's Gate Terrace, London SW7 5PR. The closing date for applications is 24 October 1994.

◇

Trust fund in honour of the late Professor W A Wilson
The Faculty of Law at Edinburgh University has established a trust fund in honour of the late Professor W A Wilson. The fund will be used (1) to establish an annual public lecture, to be known as the W A Wilson Lecture, and to be given by a person of distinction from the UK or abroad in an area of law which was of particular interest to Professor Wilson; (2) to commission and publish a volume of essays in honour of Professor Wilson; and (3) to purchase books for the law library at Edinburgh University. Donations, large or small, are invited to this trust fund. They should be in form of a cheque made payable to "University of Edinburgh Development Trust" and sent to Professor R Black, QC, c/o the Development Office, Old College, South Bridge, Edinburgh

EH8 9YL. Donations will be acknowledged by the publication of a list of donors and by a personal invitation to the first W A Wilson lecture.

 ◇

Taxation

Charitable unit trust schemes
The Treasury have laid regulations before the House of Commons extending the definition of charitable unit trust schemes to cover funds established under the Church of Scotland (Properties and Investments) Order 1994. The regulations will come into force on 27 June 1994.

◇

Benefits in kind: cheap loans
Regulations made under s 88 (2) of the Finance Act 1994 came into force on 6 June 1994 to set "official rates" of interest with effect from 6 June 1994 for some loans in foreign currencies: 3.9 per cent for Japanese yen; and 5.7 per cent for Swiss francs. These separate "official rates" will apply to loans made in the currency of a country or territory outside the United Kingdom, to an employee who normally lives in that country or territory, and who has actually lived in that country or territory at some time in the tax year or in the previous five years.

Income tax is charged based on the difference between the official rate and any interest paid by the employee. The official rate of 7.5 per cent continues to apply to all other employer provided loans.

 ◇

Obituary

On 16 June 1994, Robert Dalglish Hunter, former Town Clerk of Cumnock, formerly senior partner in the firm of R D Hunter & Co, Cumnock, and honorary sheriff.

 ◇

Business changes

Warden Bruce & Co, WS, Edinburgh, intimate the retiral from the partnership of their senior partner Roy McWhirter with effect from 11 June 1994. Mr McWhirter continues to be associated with the firm as a consultant.

Alistair S Lambert intimates that with effect from 18 March 1994 he resigned as a partner of the firm of James Smith & Valentine, Girvan and McCormick and Nicholson, Newton Stewart, and that with effect from 21 March 1994 he commenced practice on his own account under the firm name of Lambert & Co, with offices at 12 Cathcart Street, Ayr KA7 1BJ (tel 0292 282811), and 1 Hamilton Street, Girvan KA26 9EY (tel 0465 5434).

— ◊ —

Letter to the Editor

Harper Macleod,
Solicitors,
The Ca'd'oro,
45 Gordon Street,
Glasgow G1 3PE.
10 June 1994

Sir,

Sporting Injuries

In his article *Civil Actions and Sporting Injuries Sustained by Professional Footballers* (1994 SLT (News) 175) Alistair Duff, in studying two Scottish cases involving civil liability for alleged assault on the field of play, emphasises the averments that play should be "within the rules and conventions of the game". That is a less helpful test than the principle volenti non fit injuria, which requires consideration of what risks a player is deemed to accept.

Every football player knows as he takes the field that he may leave on a stretcher. Equally players know that mistimed and late tackles occur in every match because, apart from anything else, skills and abilities differ. And so, a late tackle may be outwith the rules and conventions of the game but it would still not automatically be actionable for that reason.

The English Law Commission in their consultation paper *Consent and Offences Against the Person* (no 134) capture this difficulty with the suggestion: "[I]n assessing whether the player's conduct has been reckless, the conformity of his conduct to the rules of the game, will be *persuasive but not conclusive* as to the reasonableness of his conduct" (p 65, my emphasis). That paper is open for comment until 30 June 1994 and anyone seeking a workable test before the English Law Commission report on their consultation will find one in Lord Denning's judgment in *Lane v Holloway* [1968] 1 QB 379. That case involved a punch up between neighbours in which the younger participant put his elder opponent in hospital for a month with one blow.

The action being one arising from an illegal fight, Lord Denning required to consider the principle ex turpi causa non oritur actio as well as volenti non fit injuria. In his approach to the latter principle Lord Denning suggested (at pp 386-387) that a participant in a fight (or for that matter a football match or any other contact sport) "does not take on himself the risk of a savage blow out of all proportion to the occasion".

When our own sports unit was launched early last year Tony Higgins, the secretary of the Scottish Players' Football Association, described the increase of lawyers in his sport as a "major concern".

I think, however, that the real concern in professional sport today is indiscipline. It is inarguable that high profile civil and criminal cases have forced participants to become more conscious of their rights and responsibilities on the field of play, and I hope that, as a result, we see a decrease in the number of careers prematurely ended by injury.

Yours sincerely,

STEPHEN C MILLER,
Partner.

— ◊ —

Parliamentary News

New Bills

HOUSE OF COMMONS

14 June 1994

Regulation of Cosmetic Surgery—To establish registration procedures for cosmetic surgeons in order to set minimum standards of training and practice; and for connected purposes. (Private Member's Bill introduced by Mrs Ann Clwyd)

Book Review

Criminal Sentences

By Daniel Kelly. 1994. Edinburgh: T & T Clark. Paperback, £28. ISBN 0 567 29240 1.

In this book Mr Kelly examines the decisions of the court of criminal appeal over the past 10 years or so in an attempt to draw out some principles which might be said to provide guidance for sentencers in Scotland.

The first part of the book deals with principles of sentencing, sentencing procedure, appeals, and the various penalties available to the court. He describes what the court of criminal appeal has had to say about these various topics. This section includes references to the relevant statutory provisions on sentencing. The first chapter lists 23 "general sentencing provisions, rulings and practices" gleaned from appeal decisions. These are diverse and while they do offer guidance to sentencers on a range of specific matters, they do not amount to a systematic statement of sentencing policy, as Mr Kelly himself admits.

The second part of the book deals with a wide range of specific offences. This contains decisions of the court of criminal appeal both where sentence was upheld and when sentence was altered. Mr Kelly does not explain the criteria he used to select these cases and thus the selection appears idiosyncratic. For example, the section on rape contains only two cases. This is disappointingly brief given current public debate about sentencing for sexual offences.

In the introduction to part 2 of the book, Mr Kelly expresses the hope that his examination of the decisions of the court of criminal appeal will aid consistency. There are however no reasons given for the sentences being excessive or inappropriate where that is held to be the case, and there is no reference to sentences passed for similar cases, or to what factors about the case make the sentence inappropriate. Mr Kelly

presents brief information about the offence and the offender, but there is no attempt to define more generally what might be meant by a "similar case". The pursuit of consistency in sentencing requires a rather more sophisticated attempt to provide guidance as to what constitutes a similar case.

The book will be of interest to sentencers and other criminal law practitioners, as well as to sentencing scholars. It is well organised and indexed and is easy to use. However I am less convinced that it will do much to aid consistency in sentencing. This is not the fault of the author. It is simply that because the court of criminal appeal has assiduously avoided passing "guideline judgments" in the English manner, it is not possible, as Sheriff Principal Nicholson has argued in his *Sentencing* (2nd edition), to discern a coherent sentencing policy by examining the decisions of the court.

This is a most useful addition to the sparse literature on sentencing in Scotland, even if one of the conclusions which might be reached from reading the book is that there is a real need for more systematic provision of information and guidance for sentencers in Scotland.

(Dr) NEIL HUTTON,
School of Law,
University of Strathclyde.

ACT OF SEDERUNT

ACT OF SEDERUNT (FEES OF SOLICITORS IN THE SHERIFF COURT) (AMENDMENT) 1994

(SI 1994/1142) [21 APRIL 1994]

The Lords of Council and Session, under and by virtue of the powers conferred on them by section 40 of the Sheriff Courts (Scotland) Act 1907 (c 51), and of all other powers enabling them in that behalf, do hereby enact and declare:

Citation, commencement and interpretation

1.—(1) This Act of Sederunt may be cited as the Act of Sederunt (Fees of Solicitors in the Sheriff Court) (Amendment) 1994 and shall come into force on 24th May 1994.

(2) This Act of Sederunt shall be inserted in the Books of Sederunt.

(3) In this Act of Sederunt, "the Act of Sederunt 1993" means the Act of Sederunt (Fees

of Solicitors in the Sheriff Court) (Amendment and Further Provisions) 1993.

Amendment of General Regulations

2.—(1) The General Regulations contained in Schedule 1 to the Act of Sederunt 1993 shall be amended in accordance with the following subparagraphs.

(2) At the beginning of paragraph 11 of the General Regulations there shall be inserted "Subject to paragraph 14 of these General Regulations,".

(3) In sub-paragraphs (a) and (f) of paragraph 14 of the General Regulations, for the words "this Chapter" there shall be substituted the words "that Chapter".

Amendment of Table of Fees

3. In Chapters I, II, III, IV and VI of the Table of Fees in the Schedule to the Act of Sederunt 1993, for the fees set out in column 2 of the Schedule to this Act of Sederunt as, applying to the paragraphs set out in column 1 of that Schedule, there shall be substituted the fees set out in column 3 of that Schedule; and the fees so substituted shall apply to work, for which those fees are chargeable, done on or after the date on which this Act of Sederunt comes into force.

Saving

4. The fees set in column 2 of the Schedule to this Act of Sederunt shall continue to apply to work done before this Act of Sederunt comes into force.

J A D HOPE, LORD PRESIDENT, *IPD*

SCHEDULE		Paragraph 2

Column 1 (paragraph)	Column 2 (old fee) £	Column 3 (new fee) £
Chapter I:—		
Part I		
1 (a)	100.00	103.00
(b)	80.00	82.40
2 (a)	349.40	359.90
3 (a)	312.00	321.40
Part II		
1 Table A1	245.80	253.20
2	174.70	179.90
3	53.70	55.30
4	474.20	488.40
2 Table B1	202.10	208.20
2	97.30	100.20
3	53.70	55.30
4	353.10	363.70
3 Table C1	97.30	100.20
2	57.00	58.70
3	154.30	158.90
Chapter II:—		
Part I		
1 (a)	162.20	167.10
(b)	56.10	57.80
2 (a)	240.80	248.00
(b)	162.20	167.10
(c)	27.50	28.30
(d)	40.50	41.70
3	10.00	10.30
4 (a) (i)	121.10	124.70
(ii)	14.90	15.30
(iii)	13.50	13.90
(b) (ii)	71.10	73.20
(iii)	13.50	13.90
5	24.30	25.00
6 (a)	53.70	55.30
(b)	7.40	7.60
(maximum fee)	25.00	38.00
7 (a) (i)	149.80	154.30
(ii)	101.10	104.10
(iii)	30.00	30.90
(b) (i)	90.40	93.10
(ii)	49.90	51.40
(iii)	14.90	15.30
(iv)	13.50	13.90
8 (a)	62.40	64.30
(b)	40.50	41.70
(c) (i)	56.10	57.80
(ii)	14.90	15.30
(d)	13.70	14.10
9 (a) (i)	68.70	70.80
(ii)	44.80	46.10
(b) (i)	56.10	57.80
(ii)	37.40	38.50
(c)	49.90	51.40
10 (a) (i)	71.10	73.20
(ii)	49.90	51.40
(b) (i)	40.50	41.70
(ii)	30.00	30.90
11 (a) (i)	174.70	179.90
(ii)	293.30	302.10
(b)	61.20	63.00
(c)	30.00	30.90
(d)	14.90	15.30
12 (a)	14.90	15.30
(b)	13.50	13.90
(c)	13.50	13.90
13 (a)	49.90	51.40
(b)	14.90	15.30
(c)	13.50	13.90
(d)	13.50	13.90
14 (a) (i)	93.60	96.40
(ii)	14.90	15.30
(iii)	13.50	13.90
(iv)	13.50	13.90
(b)	46.90	48.30
15 (a) (i)	56.10	57.80
(ii)	41.80	43.10
(b)	93.60	96.40
16 (a)	74.80	77.00
(b)	61.20	63.00
(c)	21.70	22.40
17 (a)	1.00	1.03
(b)	0.40	0.41
19 (a)	30.00	30.90
(b)	62.40	64.30
(c)	62.40	64.30
Part II		
1 (a)	275.00	283.30
(b)	50.00	51.50
2	25.00	25.80
3 (a)	30.00	30.90
(b)	15.00	15.50
4 (a)	125.00	128.80
(b)	75.00	77.30
(c)	30.00	30.90
(d)	40.00	41.20
5	10.00	10.30
6 (a)	100.00	103.00
(b)	15.00	15.50
(c)	25.00	25.80
7	100.00	103.00
	15.00	15.50
8 (a) (i)	80.00	82.40
(ii)	15.00	15.50
(b)	13.50	13.90
(c)	13.50	13.90
9 (a)	50.00	51.50
(b)	15.00	15.50
(c)	13.50	13.90
(d)	13.50	13.90
10 (a)	55.00	56.70
(b)	7.00	7.20
(maximum fee)	35.00	36.00

ACT OF SEDERUNT (FEES OF SOLICITORS IN THE SHERIFF COURT) (AMENDMENT)

Column 1 (paragraph)	Column 2 (old fee) £	Column 3 (new fee) £
11 (a) (i)	150.00	154.50
(ii)	100.00	103.00
(iii)	30.00	30.90
(b) (i)	100.00	103.00
(ii)	50.00	51.50
(iii)	15.00	15.50
(iv)	13.50	13.90
(v)	13.50	13.90
12 (a) (i)	55.00	56.70
(ii)	13.50	13.90
(b) (i)	30.00	30.90
(ii)	13.50	13.90
(c) (i)	55.00	56.70
(ii)	15.00	15.50
(d)	13.50	13.90
(e)	13.50	13.90
13 (a) (i)	50.00	51.50
(ii)	20.00	20.60
(iii)	13.50	13.90
(b) (i)	40.00	41.20
(ii)	20.00	20.60
(iii)	13.50	13.90
(c)	50.00	51.50
14 (a) (i)	70.00	72.10
(ii)	30.00	30.90
(b) (i)	70.00	72.10
(ii)	30.00	30.90
15	250.00	257.50
16 (a) (i)	160.00	164.80
(ii)	290.00	298.70
(b)	65.00	67.00
(c)	15.00	15.50
17 (a)	15.00	15.50
(b)	13.50	13.90
(c)	13.50	13.90
18 (a)	50.00	51.50
(b)	15.00	15.50
(c)	13.50	13.90
(d)	13.50	13.90
19 (a) (i)	150.00	154.50
	85.00	87.60
(ii)	15.00	15.50
(iii)	13.50	13.90
(iv)	13.50	13.90
(b)	50.00	51.50
20 (a) (i)	55.00	56.70
(ii)	45.00	46.40
(b)	100.00	103.00
(c)	100.00	103.00
21 (a)	75.00	77.30
(b)	65.00	67.00
22 (a)	1.00	1.03
(b)	0.40	0.41
24 (a)	30.00	30.90
(b)	65.00	67.00
(c) (i)	65.00	67.00
(ii)	13.50	13.90
Chapter III:—		
1	14.90	15.30
2 (a)	13.50	13.90
3	6.80	7.00
4	10.10	10.40
5	2.80	2.90
6 (i)	1.00	1.03
(ii)	0.40	0.41
7	2.80	2.90
8	13.50	13.90
9	2.80	2.90
10	2.80	2.90
11	13.50	13.90
12 (a)	1.00	1.03
(b)	6.80	7.00
(c)	2.80	2.90
13	6.80	7.00
14 (a)	2.80	2.90
(b)	2.80	2.90
(c)	6.80	7.00
(d)	6.80	7.00
15 (a)	6.80	7.00
(b)	6.80	7.00
(c)	6.80	7.00
(d)	8.20	8.40
16 (a)	6.80	7.00
(b)	6.80	7.00
(c)	6.80	7.00
(d)	6.80	7.00
(e)	6.80	7.00
(f)	6.80	7.00
Chapter IV:—		
Part I		
1	49.90	51.40
2 (a)	5.50	5.70
(b)	16.20	16.70
3	16.20	16.70
Part II		
1	68.70	70.80
2 (a)	5.60	5.80
	12.50	12.90
(b)	5.60	5.80
(c)	18.10	18.60
3	18.10	18.60
4	62.40	64.30
5	30.00	30.90
6 (a)	27.50	28.30
(b)	12.50	12.90
7 (a)	27.50	28.30
(b)	12.50	12.90
8 (a)	37.40	38.50
(b)	23.10	23.80
9 (a)	30.00	30.90
(b)	18.10	18.60
10 (a)	18.10	18.60
(b)	9.40	9.70
11 (a)	37.40	38.50
(i)	27.50	28.30
(ii)	27.50	28.30
(b)	62.40	64.30
12 (a)	31.20	32.10
(b)	28.10	28.90
(c)	18.10	18.60
(d)	12.50	12.90
13 (a) (i)	37.40	38.50
(ii)	23.10	23.80
(b) (i)	30.00	30.90
(ii)	18.10	18.60
(c)	18.10	18.60
(d)	12.50	12.90
(e)	17.50	18.00
(f)	12.50	12.90
14	12.50	12.90
15 (a)	84.30	86.80
(b)	18.10	18.60
16 (a)	37.40	38.50
(b)	37.40	38.50
(c)	18.10	18.60
Chapter VI:—		
1	74.80	77.00
3 (a)	21.20	21.80
(b)	21.20	21.80
4	42.40	43.70

ARTICLES

It's a Wise Testator Who Knows His Own Great Grandchildren

Wright's Trustees v Callender, 1992
SLT 498 (Ex Div); 1993 SLT 556 (HL)

Elizabeth Crawford,
Lecturer in Private Law,
University of Glasgow.

Dr Crawford considers the conflict of laws aspect of Wright's Trs, *in which claimants to an estate were legitimated after the testator's death and in a different jurisdiction.*

Wright's Trs promised at the outset, in the Court of Session, to provide a useful Scottish conflict case within the fields of wills, succession, status and choice of law, but became, in the House of Lords, a purely domestic authority upon interpretation of a testator's intention, where a relevant change in the law has occurred after the testator's death.

It raised (and then perforce abandoned) a subtle point upon which conflict rules of England and Scotland, now in most areas so close, differ. However, there remains a useful point of interpretation, probably welcome to testators and their advisers, if not to the trusters' legitimated great grandchildren, who were ultimately the unsuccessful parties in the case.

The background

The problem first presented is this: it may be that a testator, drawing up a trust many years ago (when convention was less often flouted, and legitimacy of descendants was to be presumed) has directed that, e g on the death of the liferenter, the fee of his estate shall pass to the "next of kin", "heirs", or "surviving children" of the liferenter or that, on the predecease of a legatee, his share should be taken by person(s) fulfilling such qualification. Who then is the legatee's heir?

These questions arise: What did the testator mean by the use of such terms? Did he intend to benefit only the legitimate (or legitimated), or may the succession open also to the illegitimate and the adopted? These are matters which should be referred, it is generally thought, to the law governing the interpretation of the testament, and this law often will be the law of the testator's last domicile, although it may be a different law, if a different intention of the testator can be identified from the terms and language of the will (*Philipson-Stow v IRC* [1961] AC 272).

If the conclusion should be reached that the testator intended to benefit only the legitimate, or at most the legitimate and the legitimated, it becomes necessary for the forum to adjudicate upon the status of claimants. In order to do so, should the forum refer to the personal law of the testator, or the personal law of the liferenter or legatee?

The authorities principally relevant with regard to the last point are *Re Fergusson's Will* [1902] 1 Ch 483; *Mitchell's Tr v Rule* (1908) 16 SLT 189; *Smith's Trs v Macpherson*, 1926 SLT 669; 1926 SC 983, and *Spencer's Trs v Ruggles*, 1982 SLT 165.

English law has favoured a reference to the law of the testator (*Fergusson's Will*), while the Scots courts have preferred the application of the personal law of the legatee (as in *Mitchell's Tr v Rule*, where the question of identifying Walter Rule's "heirs" was referred to the English law of Walter Rule's last domicile; and in the later case of *Smith's Trs v Macpherson*, referred to by Lord Allanbridge in his opinion in *Wright's Trs*). In the modern example (*Spencer's Trs v Ruggles*), we are deprived of our discussion because it was held that the trust, in directing that the liferenter's surviving lawful children should succeed to the fee, did not intend to extend the succession to adopted children, and hence it was not necessary to consider by which law to judge the validity of the adoption.

The decision at first instance in *Wright's Trs* is a decision by a Scottish court on the Scottish approach taken in *Smith's Trs*. It is gratifying that the late Dr J H C Morris tended to the view that the Scottish line on this nice problem is preferable (*The Conflict of Laws* (3rd ed), p 399; and see 4th ed (J D McLean), p 357). However, in the House of Lords closer attention was paid to the first question above (what did the testator intend?), and the conclusion was reached that, in the absence of express indication, it was more natural to presume that the trusters did not contemplate legislative changes on the subject of legitimation such as would widen the class of entitled beneficiaries.

Wright's Trs — the facts

The dispute concerned the succession, upon the death of the liferentrix in 1989, to the trust estates of the claimants' great grandfather (whose trust was dated and came into operation in 1917) and great grandmother (whose trust was dated 1925 and came into operation in 1932). Suffice it to say that from one branch of the tree sprang the single claimant (the second party), the legitimate issue of his parents; from another came the third parties, who all were born while their mother was unmarried and their father was married to a third person. Their parents married each other in 1954.

Great grandfather's trust declared that those persons entitled to succeed were the "issue" of the liferentrix; great grandmother's trust stated that her "great-grandchildren" should succeed. The liferentrix, Mrs Holmes, was the granddaughter of the trusters and the mother of the claimants the third parties.

It was agreed that Scots law governed the interpretation of both trusts, and that, on a proper construction, "issue" and "great-grandchildren" denoted legitimate and (in principle) legitimated issue.

Mrs Holmes was domiciled at all material times in England. It was agreed that vesting in the fee was suspended until her death, and it could not be ascertained until that date who were her issue or her children.

Legitimation per subsequens matrimonium
Clearly, the hopes of the third parties rested on the concept and rules (of which law?) concerning legitimation.

By the law of England, the children, all having been born when their father was married to a third person, could not have the benefit of the Legitimacy Act 1926, which belatedly introduced legitimation into the law of England, but they did benefit from the Legitimacy Act 1959, and were regarded, by the law of England, as legitimated from 29 October 1959.

Legitimation has been part of the law of Scotland since the 12th century, but by Scots common law, the children could not be legitimated by the subsequent marriage of their parents, because their parents were not free to marry at their conception. However, the law of Scotland on this point was altered by the Legitimation (Scotland) Act 1968, s 4, with effect from 8 June 1968.

The second party argued that the words "issue" and "great-grandchildren" meant children who were legitimated according to Scots law at the date of the coming into effect of the respective trusts in 1917 and 1932. The opposing argument was that the words in question meant children (of grandchildren) who were in life at the death of Mrs Holmes in 1989, and whose legitimacy was recognised by Scots law at that date.

In the Court of Session, much attention was paid to the choice of law question: "Which law shall determine the status of parties who claim to be entitled to succeed in a destination, the destination being not to the children of the testator, but to the children of a third party?"

The court noted at the outset the "clearly appropriate" application of the (English) domicile of Mrs Holmes. He appreciated the doubtful nature of the argument that a testator must be assumed to know the law, but maintained that, if we are to go down this road, we must assume the testator to be familiar with Scots conflict law. It is a far sighted testator who foresees that, three generations down, there is likely to be a conflict problem, and a well informed one who knows the answer. Nevertheless, on this view, we conclude that we must apply — as the testator, Mr Wright, must be assumed to have foreseen — the law of the ultimate domicile of Mrs Holmes to determine the class of persons entitled to succeed, such being the conflict rule of Scots law, as seen in *Smith's Trs v Macpherson* (Anton with Beaumont, *Private International Law* (2nd ed, 1990), p 693). It is submitted that this is the best approach in any event, leaving aside fictions about the testator's knowledge.

Picking and choosing or ducking and weaving
Sometimes it happens in conflict cases that matters turn out particularly well for one side in that, by picking a careful way through the pitfalls, that side has the best of both legal systems. So it turned out for the third parties until appeal was taken (successfully) by the second party to the House of Lords. In October 1991, the Court of Session found in favour of the third parties.

Had they been required to rely on Scots law to determine their status, they would have been precluded from taking a share of the residue by reason of s 7 of the Legitimation (Scotland) Act 1968 (saving provision of the Act, excluding the operation of its substantive terms, if the deed came into operation before the commencement of the Act). On the other hand, the choice of Scots law to govern the interpretation of the trusts avoided the (similar) saving provisions of the English Legitimacy Act 1959, which the court held were intended to affect only the construction of deeds where the law governing the interpretation was English law.

Hence, it was the (temporary) good fortune of the third parties to have their status determined by English law, but to have the trusts construed by Scots law.

Whether or not the word "dépeçage" springs to mind, one can certainly see that it was lucky for some. The luck did not hold: it happened that in the House of Lords, the point was not necessary for decision, but the effect of the picking and choosing reasoning did not find favour with Lord Keith (at p 560A-C) nor with Lord Jauncey who took care to express his disapproval (at p 563D-E): "It is clear from the terms of the Acts of 1926, 1959 and 1968 that Parliament was concerned that deeds throughout Scotland and England which were already in operation should not be affected by the emergence of newly legitimated persons. If the arguments for the third parties were correct it would mean that domiciled English persons legitimated under the 1959 Act could not benefit under an English deed prior to their legitimation but could benefit under a Scottish one et e contra, a result which would certainly not appear to accord with the general intention of Parliament as expressed in the English and Scottish Acts."

The decision in the House of Lords

The ground on which four out of the five judges in the House of Lords allowed the appeal of the second party, however, was essentially on the basis of the testator's intention, viz that it was reasonable to attribute to the testator the intention that succession to his estate be regulated by the law as it stood at the time of his death, and that the testator should not be held to have had in contemplation that persons might be entitled to gain admission to the category "lawful" through changes in the law occurring after the coming into operation of the instrument (albeit before the opening of the succession). Lord Keith noted the absence of authority. Some help is to be derived from *Cockburn's Trs v Dundas* (1864) 2 M 1185. The question is whether the "mind and will" of the testator is to have the law at the earlier date apply (which he must be held to have known and accepted) or whether to let the law as it may stand at the (perhaps much later) death of the liferenter, do as it will with the will. Lord Justice-Clerk Inglis said at p 1190: "When the testator directs the distribution of his estate without saying expressly that the law at the period of distribution, whatever that law may be, shall regulate the distribution of the fee of the residue of my estate, was it not more natural that he should have in his mind the law as it then stood . . .?"

Hence, the House of Lords considered that the trusters were not to be taken to have contemplated that changes would take place in the domestic law of succession. Such a conclusion is in agreement with domestic cases in which it was held that a testator, having in view the age of majority, was not to be held to foresee that the

age would be lowered. Probably this is the reasonable view.

It is a different case if a change in the law occurs after testing but before death, because then the view can reasonably be taken that the testator should have taken steps to avoid the operation of the new law, if he wished to do so and if avoidance were possible (*Nimmo v Murray's Trs* (1864) 2 M 1144). (See also *Salvesen's Trs* infra, at p 1332E-F.)

Their Lordships' conclusion, therefore, was that it was not sufficient that the claimant should possess the status of legitimacy at the date of vesting. The court must follow as nearly as possible the "mind and will" of the testator (Lord Justice Clerk Inglis, *Cockburn's Trs v Dundas* at p 1189), and must estimate his intention "by the law he knew of, rather than by the law he knew nothing of" (Lord Benholme at p 1193). This is a persuasive view from which it might be thought that few would dissent, and which has been approved by the First Division on 2 March 1994, in *Wemyss's Trs v Wemyss*, 1994 GWD 11-702. But the reader may care to consider a nice variation on the theme, to different effect (dependent on the interpretation of the Succession (Scotland) Act 1964), to be found in the First Division decision in *Salvesen's Trs, Petrs*, 1993 SLT 1327. There, children adopted by overseas adoption were entitled to the benefit of the rules of construction in the case of adopted children contained in the 1964 Act, on the basis that on the construction of relevant statutory provisions, the date of the effecting of the overseas adoption was immaterial (see further p 1330K-L); and that it mattered not that the deed had been executed prior to the making of the adoption orders. The decision is one of statutory interpretation.

Conclusion

From a conflict of laws viewpoint, the case of *Wright's Trs* loses much of its interest in the House of Lords. All that can be noted is that the Inner House gave its support to the Scottish preference on the conflict point, that is, that the status of claimants as issue or children of a third party, is a matter for decision by the law of the domicile of the third party. However (per Lord Jauncey in the House of Lords, at p 562J-K) that class of beneficiaries is not necessarily to be determined by the domicile of the parent of the potential class member at the date of death of the parent or when the succession opens to the members — which is, it is submitted, another way of saying that choice of law must wait upon interpretation.

The House of Lords decision is concerned with, and confined to, interpretation of the trusters' intentions; a restrictive view having been taken, the further point of choice of law to decide status becomes redundant. *Smith's Trs v Macpherson* is not a relevant authority, and the claims falls at the first hurdle, as happened in *Spencer's Trs v Ruggles*.

But the journey was interesting, and the authoritative decision on an important point of interpretation, on which there had been no recent guidance, is of note.

The Arrestment of Earnings of Merchant Seamen — A Postscript

Professor Gerry Maher,
The Law School,
University of Strathclyde.

Professor Maher draws attention to the coming into force of a provision correcting a repeal in the Debtors (Scotland) Act 1987 which had unintended consequences for merchant seamen.

Prior to the Debtors (Scotland) Act 1987 there existed various restrictions on the use of the common law diligence of arrestment and furthcoming against the earnings of merchant seamen. Statutory provisions in the Merchant Shipping Acts of 1970 and 1979 had the effect that that particular diligence was completely competent if used against the earnings of merchant seamen who were fishermen. However the earnings of merchant seamen who were not fishermen could be attached by arrestment only for maintenance debts.

Part III of the Debtors (Scotland) Act 1987 abolished the diligence of arrestment and furthcoming as used against earnings and replaced it with a number of new diligences. In a paper published at 1989 SLT (News) 340 it was argued that the provisions of the 1987 Act had the effect of permitting the use of the common law diligence of arrestment and furthcoming to attach the earnings of non-fishermen merchant seamen, thus reversing the previous statutory policy. Such a change was not part of the recommendations of the Scottish Law Commission on which the 1987 Act was based and if anything was inconsistent with the arguments underlying the commission's proposals. Indeed the change in the law came about by what appears to have been a per incuriam repeal of part of s 11 of the Merchant Shipping Act 1970 by Sched 8 to the 1987 Act.

This situation has now been altered by a provision of a recent statute. Paragraph 9 of Sched 4 to the Merchant Shipping (Registration, etc) Act 1993, which came into effect on 1 May 1994, now further amends s 11 of the Merchant Shipping Act 1970. As amended that section provides that the wages of a merchant seaman shall not in Scotland be subject to any diligence other than those provided for in s 46 (1) of the 1987 Act. The general consequence of these statutory changes is that the situation prior to the 1987 Act has now been adapted in full to take account of the provisions relating to the new diligences against earnings introduced by that Act.

The overall effect of the various provisions is that the earnings of merchant seamen who are fishermen are subject to the diligence of earnings arrestment for all types of debt which may be competently recovered by that diligence (and this includes arrears of maintenance). The earnings of such merchant seamen are also subject to the diligence of current maintenance arrestment to recover (current) maintenance. In respect of the earnings of merchant seamen who are not fishermen, an earnings arrestment may be used to recover arrears of maintenance but no other form of debt; but those earnings are fully open to the diligence of current maintenance arrestment to recover (current) maintenance. The common law diligence of arrestment and furthcoming cannot be used at all against the earnings of merchant seamen, whether or not fishermen.

◆

NEWS

Court

Rules of the Court of Session 1994
The Act of Sederunt (Rules of the Court of Session) 1994 (SI 1994/1443) is now available from HMSO, price £20.40.

Admission of solicitor advocate
Robert James Livingstone of Livingstone Brown, Glasgow, who holds extended rights of audience in the High Court of Justiciary, has been granted extended rights of audience before the Court of Session, House of Lords and Judicial Committee of the Privy Council.

General

Will Aid

November will be Will Aid month. Will Aid is the biennial fundraising event when solicitors' firms throughout the UK draft straightforward wills free of charge and clients make a donation to Will Aid. The suggested minimum is £35. Will Aid is supported by the TSB and past experience of participating firms has shown that it is good for business in that it increases the client bank.

The benefiting charities are Action Aid, Christian Aid, Oxfam, Save the Children and the Scottish Catholic International Aid Fund.

For advance information about participating in this year's event, telephone 0865 313102 or contact Graeme Pagan, Hosack and Sutherland, Oban (tel 0631 62308). From September members of the public will be able to call the TSB Will Aid helpline on 091-417 6688 to receive mailed details of local Will Aid solicitors.

— ◊ —

Taxation

Income tax: private medical insurance

The Treasury and the Board of Inland Revenue have laid new regulations covering tax relief for private medical insurance premiums for people aged 60 or over. These regulations amend the current rules to reflect changes made in the Finance Act 1994. They also make some other minor amendments to the relief. The regulations will take effect on 1 July 1994.

Individuals who pay private medical insurance premiums for someone aged 60 or over can receive 25 per cent tax relief on the premium payments they make. Relief is only due on contracts which meet certain conditions. The person who pays the premiums may, but need not, be insured under the contract.

The Finance Act 1994 lifts the administrative requirement on insurers to have such medical contracts certified by the Inland Revenue before they can qualify for relief. This provision comes into effect on 1 July 1994. The new regulations update the rules to cater for this change. They also make some other minor administrative amendments.

An insurer can offer contracts that qualify for tax relief only if the Board of Inland Revenue have approved it to do so. The new rules allow three types of insurer to offer such contracts for the first time. These are trade unions and employers' associations; incorporated friendly societies; and insurers from other states within the European Economic Area who from 1 July 1994 will be able to carry on business in the United Kingdom without authorisation by the Department of Trade and Industry.

The new regulations lift the current restrictions on medical treatment and services outside the United Kingdom.

The regulations set out the medical and other benefits that may be provided under a contract that attracts tax relief. They list the medical services that may be offered as part of, or following, an approved treatment. The new rules extend this list to include occupational therapy and orthopty, and make it clear that podiatry is allowed. They also allow another person to accompany a patient in an ambulance or air ambulance where this is medically necessary.

The regulations are the Private Medical Insurance (Disentitlement To Tax Relief And Approved Benefits) Regulations 1994 and the Private Medical Insurance (Tax Relief) (Amendment) Regulations 1994.

◊

Income tax: payments to relocated employees

The Inland Revenue have published a guide for employees explaining how relocation packages are taxed. The leaflet (IR 134 in the personal taxpayer series) sets out the new rules contained in the Finance Act 1993 for the taxation of relocation assistance provided by some employers when employees move home for job purposes.

Copies can be obtained from any tax office or tax inquiry centre and, if anyone has any difficulty getting them locally, from the Public Inquiry Room, West Wing, Somerset House, London WC2R 1LB.

— ◊ —

Obituaries

On 15 June, David Rodger, formerly sole partner in the firm of David Rodger & Co, solicitors, Hamilton.

On 16 June 1994, Sir John Alexander Dick, MC, QC, formerly Sheriff Principal of Glasgow and Strathkelvin.

— ◊ —

Business changes

Biggart Baillie & Gifford, solicitors, Glasgow and Edinburgh, intimate the retiral of John Harold Mutch and Alan Maitland Dewar McWilliam from the partnership with effect from 1 July 1994. Colin Beaton McKay, currently an associate with the firm, has been assumed as a partner also from that date.

Bonar Mackenzie, WS, Edinburgh, intimate that with effect from 10 June 1994 they have assumed their associate, Claire Lucy Cowell, as a partner of the firm and appointed their assistants, Lisa Anne Irvine Girdwood, Linda Anne Forbes and Gary George Thomas, as associates of the firm. It is further intimated that Robert Desmond Oliphant Chill has retired as a partner with the firm with effect from 10 June 1994.

Tods Murray, WS, Edinburgh, intimate the retiral from the partnership of their senior partner John Robin Sinclair Bell with effect from 30 June 1994.

Seagrave & Co, solicitors, 75 Buccleuch Street, Dumfries, announce the appointment of Nigel Stephen Kenny as an associate of the firm with effect from 16 May 1994.

Parliamentary News

New Bills

HOUSE OF COMMONS

15 June 1994

Marriage—To amend the Marriage Act 1949 so as to enable civil marriages to be solemnised on premises approved for the purpose by local authorities and so as to provide for further cases in which marriages may be solemnised in registration districts in which neither party to the marriage resides; and for connected purposes. (Private Member's Bill introduced by Mr Gyles Brandreth)

21 June 1994

Sports (Discrimination)—To make it unlawful for any rule making body for a sport to dis-

criminate against persons who have participated, are participating or are expected to participate in any other lawful sport, and for connected purposes. (Private Member's Bill introduced by Mr David Hinchliffe)

Progress of Bills

Local Government (Wales) — Commons: remaining stages completed, 16 June 1994.

Trade Marks — Commons: remaining stages, 20 June 1994.

Value Added Tax — Lords: third reading, 20 June 1994.

Criminal Justice and Public Order — Lords: committee stage completed, 21 June 1994.

Law of Property (Miscellaneous Provisions) — Lords: report, 20 June 1994.

Social Security (Incapacity for Work) — Commons: Lords amendments, 21 June 1994.

Sunday Trading — Commons: Lords amendments, 21 June 1994.

Chiropractors — Lords: third reading, 21 June 1994.

Coal Industry — Lords: third reading, 21 June 1994.

Civil Rights (Disabled Persons) (No 2) — Lords: second reading, 22 June 1994.

Merchant Shipping (Salvage and Pollution) — Lords: report, 23 June 1994.

Questions answered

HOUSE OF COMMONS

14 June 1994

LAW STUDENTS

Mr McFall: To ask the Secretary of State for Scotland how many students are currently studying for a diploma in legal practice at each Scottish university.

Lord James Douglas-Hamilton: Information collected by the Law Society of Scotland for the academic year 1993-94 is as follows:

University	Number of Students
Aberdeen	92
Dundee	75
Edinburgh	116
Glasgow	113
Strathclyde	102
Total Scotland	498

Mr McFall: To ask the Secretary of State for Scotland what estimate he has of the total cost involved in funding a law student who completes an LLB and diploma in legal practice at a Scottish university.

Lord James Douglas-Hamilton: The estimated cost of full public funding for a student completing a four-year LLB and a one-year diploma in legal practice is £28,550. This estimate assumes full funding of tuition by the Scottish Higher Education Funding Council and full student support based on elsewhere maintenance rates, no parental/spouse contribution and no excess travel.

Mr McFall: To ask the Secretary of State for Scotland how many students currently studying for a diploma in legal practice at Scottish universities have not yet secured a legal traineeship place.

Lord James Douglas-Hamilton: The latest available estimate is 230.

Mr McFall: To ask the Secretary of State for Scotland how many Scottish Education Department funded places there are for the diploma in legal practice each year.

Lord James Douglas-Hamilton: Institutional grant funding for teaching at Scottish higher education institutions is now the responsibility of the Scottish Higher Education Funding Council. There is no separate category or allocation of funded or fees-only places for the diploma in legal practice. Taught undergraduate and postgraduate courses in law and legal studies are included but not specified by SHEFC in the broader category of "Social Sciences". The number of postgraduate student awards available for Scottish-domiciled students undertaking the diploma course in 1993-94 is 390. Other students may finance their own costs of tuition and maintenance.

20 June 1994

PRISONS

Mr Kirkwood: To ask the Secretary of State for Scotland what proposals he has to amend the Prison (Scotland) Rules 1952; and if he will make a statement.

Lord James Douglas-Hamilton: The draft revised Prisons and Young Offenders Institutions (Scotland) Rules were issued for consultation last September. Consideration of the comments received has almost been completed and it is intended to lay the new rules before Parliament in the next few weeks.

— ◇ —

Book Reviews

Fair Employment Case Law

Religious and Political Discrimination in Employment

Edited by Michael Rubenstein. 1993. Belfast: Fair Employment Commission for Northern Ireland. Paperback, £10.

While there is debate about introducing an explicit prohibition against religious discrimination in Britain, there already is such a law in Northern Ireland. The Fair Employment (Northern Ireland) Act 1976 prohibits discrimination in relation to employment on grounds of religious belief or political opinion, the major mischief being tackled being less favourable treatment of Roman Catholics and Nationalists in employment, but applying (as do the sex and race discrimination statutes here in relation to their spheres) impartially to less favourable treatment of any person on the prohibited grounds. The law is enforced so far as individual complaints are concerned in front of the Fair Employment Tribunal, a body unique to Northern Ireland, and is monitored by the Fair Employment Commission.

The Fair Employment Commission have published a casebook edited by Michael Rubinstein, who is the editor of *Industrial Relations Law Reports* and co-editor of the *Equal Opportunities Review*. The book uses the same format as the well established Industrial Relations Services Discrimination Guides by the same author, that is on a subject by subject basis it summarises (sometimes in one sentence) principles which are derived from decided cases. It includes many decisions of the Fair Employment Tribunal, although these decisions do not have the status of precedents.

The structure of the Fair Employment Act and the Sex Discrimination and Race Relations Acts (and the Sex Discrimination (Northern Ireland) Order, the Northern Irish equivalent of the Sex Discrimination Act) are very similar, the basic concepts of direct and indirect discrimination and victimisation being identically defined, and thus decisions in respect of all these statutes are of importance in understanding each. This book deals only with the Fair Employment Act; the reader who wishes to follow up decisions of the UK courts in these related areas (including decisions of the Northern Ireland Court of Appeal in sex discrimination cases) is referred to the Industrial Relations Services Guide.

The book is a useful resource book, although access to the relevant case reports would be necessary to utilise it properly. The Fair Employment Act does not apply in Scotland, but the principles are relevant to anyone with an interest in discrimination law generally. The judgment of the Northern Ireland Court of Appeal, for example, in *McAusland v Dungannon District Council* [1993] IRLR 583 (referred to on p 4) makes an important contribution to the law on the meaning of "considerably smaller proportion" in establishing indirect discrimination under all the statutes.

JENIFER M ROSS,
University of Strathclyde.

Ethnic Minorities Benefits Handbook

By Paul Morris, Inderpal Rahal and Hugo Storey; edited by Janet Gurney. 1993. London: Child Poverty Action Group. Paperback, £8.95. ISBN 0 946744 50 5.

Council Tax Handbook

By Martin Ward. 1993. London: Child Poverty Action Group. Paperback, £7.95. ISBN 0 946744 53 X.

These are two publications from the Child Poverty Action Group joining an established list of handbooks to social security benefits. Social security legislation is extremely complex, changing frequently, usually with complex transition provisions. Expertise in advising in this area is not generally found in the legal profession, and CPAG publications are aimed at advisers of claimants and claimants themselves.

For people who are of an ethnic minority origin, who may not be British citizens or who are but who wish to bring into the country members of their families or their spouses, problems in finding their way through the benefits minefield may be compounded by their or their families' immigration status. The first of these books is a guide to the benefits system where immigration status raises a complicating factor. There is a lengthy introduction to immigration itself, with an interesting and critical discussion of the primary purpose rule in relation to spouses and fiancés entering the country, although this is not the main purpose of the handbook.

The book also contains a substantial section on EC immigration law and its impact on EC rules on social security benefits. Its major function,

however, is to look systematically at the range of social security benefits and how claims are affected by immigration status and by entering and leaving the country.

It is extremely readable. Many case examples are incorporated into the text, with footnotes to enable further research, as well as a bibliography and list of useful names and addresses. While there is little room for discussion of the social issues raised by the immigration rules and their effects, the book takes a critical approach where appropriate, particularly in the section on immigration. In that context one of the few judges singled out for praise (at p 51) is Lord Prosser in *Saftar v Secretary of State for the Home Department* [1992] Imm AR 1, for his "refreshing" view that immigration rules "do not merely have a preventative role. They are protecting or preserving for the sponsor, a UK citizen, the ability to marry and live permanently with the man she wants to marry".

The handbook does not stand alone: for a comprehensive understanding of the benefits a claimant or adviser would have to refer to the handbooks on the benefits themselves. As an aid to those advising in the field it is an excellent addition to the material available. It is also a good starting point for the legal professional who wants to become familiar with this area.

The *Council Tax Handbook* is a comprehensive guide to the new tax, which takes account of differences between the English and Scottish systems.

JENIFER M ROSS,
University of Strathclyde.

Bill Stewart, the Book Review Editor, is keen that books, and especially, books written with the practitioner in mind should be reviewed by practitioners. Accordingly, members of Faculty and solicitors who consider that they could competently review books, are invited to write with a note of their name and address, indicating upon what subjects they would be prepared to write reviews, to him c/o MacMillans, Solicitors, 78 Springfield Road, Glasgow G40 3ET.

ARTICLES

"Amicable Composition" in Minor Building Disputes

Sinclair Gauldie, CBE, FRIBA, PPRIAS.

Mr Gauldie brings his experience as an architect to advising on the best way of resolving building disputes involving private individuals without resort to litigation.

Contractual disputes between builders and their customers commonly involve technicalities which may require costly exposition by expert witnesses to make them intelligible to a court. Hence the normal styles of formal building contract include a clause binding the parties to arbitration, the assumption being that the arbiter will be a man of skill who needs no such instruction.

However, most of the ordinary builder's workload consists of jobs which are put in hand with no such formality as a probative deed — often on the strength of a simple telephone call. In such an informal agreement there will be no obligation to submit to arbitration. Nor is arbitration necessarily the best way to settle disputes over building works which, although high in cost relative to the customer's resources, are, in absolute terms of capital committed, "minor works".

Albeit extracurial, an arbitration is none the less a process of adjudication in which the essential question before the arbiter is whether or not one of the parties is in breach of contract. Where that contract contains few, if any, recorded express terms it is possible that the dispute arises from innocent misunderstanding of what was required, or from a layman's ignorance of what is technically practicable, rather than from a deliberate attempt to evade a contractual obligation. In such a situation an objective and patient examination of the parties' contentions, without the purpose of assigning blame, can save a good deal of expense and much acrimony by effecting a compromise acceptable to both. The contriving of such a compromise is the antithesis of adjudication and is no part of the role proper to an arbiter as established in the law of Scotland. So disputants who wish to avoid litigation may usefully look at the various other modes of alternative dispute resolution which are currently gaining in popularity.

All of these aim to take the heat out of the dispute by interposing a third party not as an arbiter but rather as a "candid friend". He may operate as:

a *mediator*, sitting down with the parties and helping them to whittle down their differences in a three cornered exchange of views;

a *conciliator*, carrying out a similar operation but with the parties kept physically apart — a useful expedient if confrontation is likely to produce more heat than light;

a *consultant* engaged, either by both parties or unilaterally, to look at the problem in the round, as a man of skill, and to offer an unbiased opinion;

a *negotiator* engaged by one or other of the parties — usually by the customer, who naturally feels disadvantaged by technical ignorance — to save him the ordeal of eyeball to eyeball personal conflict.

The distinctions between these functions are important, because the best method of resolving one kind of dispute will not necessarily be appropriate to another. The temperaments of the disputants and the state of their relationship, as well as the grounds of the dispute itself, have to be taken into account: moreover, an individual who is perfectly suited to one of these intermediary roles may be quite inept in another. Consequently generalisations are dangerous. However it is worth attempting a rough order of preference for each of the main classes of building dispute, if only to aid a realistic appraisal of the alternatives in any given case.

Inevitably, what follows must be read as suggestive only, rather than as prescriptive. If the suggestions have any weight, it is simply that they are those of an architect whose experience extends beyond the contractual problems of his own clients into the field of arbitrating upon the disputes of others and, on occasion, assisting the lower and higher courts as an expert witness. As such, they may be of some value to those for whom the peculiar problems of building contracts are unexplored territory.

A builder and his customer may fall out over the time taken to complete the works, over the quality of the works, or over payment for the works. Often the dispute will embrace more than one of these, sometimes all three. But if so it will generally be found that the real source of the trouble lies in one alone, the others being accretions which have gathered in the course of a deteriorating relationship. Whoever has to advise a disputant must first probe to find the root of the matter: this is a skill of the practised lawyer which needs no exposition here.

Disputes over delay

Delay may be inflicted by either party upon the

other. Recognising this, formal building contracts are at pains not only to specify the grounds which absolve the contractor from failure to meet the completion date but also to allow him to recoup direct loss and expense caused to him by the other party's vacillation or obstruction. As far as the latter is concerned, no such precision can be expected in an informal agreement; but, given the relatively short timespan of such contracts, the amount of injury which can be inflicted by an uncooperative customer is not likely to occasion serious argument and it can be ignored for present purposes. Much more likely are the consequences of similar imprecision about the builder's liability for his own delays — and, most likely, about the contract period itself.

This is a much commoner casus belli, if only because "having the builders in" can be an exasperating business at the best, and prolonging it can build up resentment to the point of provoking a deduction from the amount which the builder claims as his due. If litigation ensues, it is easier for the builder to quantify the work for which he seeks payment than for the customer to quantify his injury. Moreover an allegation of unreasonable delay — involving, as it well may, all sorts of technicalities — is not simple either to substantiate or to rebut without expert evidence. These are solid reasons for trying to settle the dispute extracurially.

The aggrieved customer will have assumed an unqualified right of offset in respect of the builder's failure to meet a (probably uncovenanted) completion date. He will also have assumed that the failure results solely from fecklessness of one kind or another, a belief crystallised in the familiar phrase, "I'm not interested in excuses". The first of these assumptions is for his lawyer to correct: the second may require help of a more technical kind.

The Scottish Building Contract embodies 13 identifiable "relevant events" which excuse late completion. Not all of these would be held as implied in an informal contract, but the length of the list does illustrate the unpredictable course of building operations and hence the imprudence of dogmatising on what constitutes "reasonable despatch". It is almost certain that consultation with an expert in trade practice, who can assess the validity of the builder's excuses, will be less expensive than having them argued back and forth in court. Admittedly the consultant will be hearing less than the full story, unless his client permits him to listen also to the builder. But even so he may detect conclusive arguments in the latter's favour which could spell failure for the

putative defender; and if he were to proceed further and undertake the role of negotiator, he would at least be able to suggest a reasonable figure to tender should litigation become inevitable, even if he failed to arrange a compromise which would stay the hands of both parties.

If a dispute of this kind cannot be settled by consultation or negotiation it can be assumed that the builder is too sure of his ground to accept mediation or conciliation, and the customer must either face litigation or cut his losses.

Preference order: (1) consultation
(2) negotiation.

Disputes over quality

A quality dispute (as opposed to mere argument) materialises when the customer calls for a defect (real or imagined) to be made good free of charge and the contractor refuses to do so. Theoretically, the former might seek a decree for specific implement, but this would be a monstrously cumbersome way of dealing with the situation, and a very uncertain one. In some kinds of work, referral to the appropriate trade organisation — for instance, the National Federation of Roofing Contractors or the Scottish and Northern Ireland Plumbing Employers' Federation — can achieve the same result without expense, and the very first step should be to ascertain whether such a scheme is available.

It may be that the work is being so abjectly bungled that the customer feels entitled to rescind and bar the contractor from the site, and it may also be that the contractor's sense of guilt will lead him to accept such treatment. If he resists it, the parties face the prospect of legal argument over whether the breach is so material and irremediable that rescission is legitimate: and where the contract is informal that argument can be prolonged and costly. Rescission should therefore be avoided if at all possible.

More commonly, the customer will simply look for reimbursement, either for the cost of having the defect remedied or for the vexation of having to live with it, and will be hoping to obtain this with minimal expense and trouble. The contractor will be equally keen to avoid expense and trouble, but not at the price of making a loss on the job: this last consideration is particularly acute when the customer is withholding payment of some or all of the final balance due. How far the expense and trouble can actually be minimised depends upon a number of considerations. The most important of these is the degree of informality of the parties' agreement, for upon this depends the ease or difficulty of proving that the work is disconform to contract.

The documentation annexed to a formal building contract aims at telling the builder, as precisely as possible, what is expected of him. If the architect feels that his expectations are being disappointed and his intentions frustrated, any argument can be conducted in the light of these express and specific requirements. In proportion as an agreement departs from formality, such requirements are fewer, greater reliance has to be placed on implied terms and the risk of disappointment and dispute — and the difficulty of resolving such dispute — increases correspondingly. At the extreme of informality, the only standard is "sound trade practice", a criterion which has been fruitful of dispute throughout the centuries. (Ruling upon such disputes was in fact a major function of the medieval craft incorporations in Scotland.)

In such a situation the parties are likely to find themselves in territory which is the profitable province of the expert witness. This is perhaps less hazardous where the disconformity can be substantiated objectively, e g by measurement. If, for instance, a roof leaks because the contractor has laid the tiles with less overlap than the minimum prescribed by their manufacturer, the departure from sound practice speaks for itself. It is a different matter where the disconformity is a matter of subjective opinion — for instance, acceptability of appearance. Difference of opinion here opens the door to debate over what the customer was entitled to expect in all the circumstances, including the amount he was prepared to pay and the time he was willing to allow.

It is necessary to take a coldly realistic view of the parties' chances of achieving satisfaction through litigation or even arbitration. The aggrieved customer will be looking for his pound of flesh in full measure, and it can be assumed that this claim will be contested by the builder's lawyer as being grossly excessive even if there were a breach of contract. For example, the customer may have asked for a particular proprietary product — say a named brand of paint — and been provided with a different one. While the disconformity may be demonstrable, the injury suffered thereby may well exist only in the complainer's mind, for there is little to choose between one reputable paint and another. A court or arbiter could be persuaded without difficulty that the customer benefited to the extent of a paint job which is indistinguishable from what he expected, and the damages awarded would certainly fall far short of his hopes.

This is an extreme case, but it is common experience that the courts are reluctant to assume that the benefit conferred by building works, even when imperfect, is negligible: thus the customer ends up paying more than he thinks the job was worth and the builder ends up with less than he considers his due. Common sense indicates that the same result, or a more acceptable one, could have been achieved without invoking the majesty of the law.

The alternative which suggests itself as most obvious is negotiation between the parties' lawyers before, rather than after, they reach the door of the sheriff court. This will be achieved more readily if the builder knows himself to be to some extent at fault (as in the paintwork example above) but is prepared to face the court simply because he objects to the damages claimed. It will not recommend itself to lawyers if the builder stands foursquare on the technical issue of sound trade practice.

If negotiation is ruled out, the remaining non-adjudicative alternatives are mediation and conciliation. Neither of these will put the question of conformity to tests as severe as those which an arbiter, conscious of the conclusive nature of his final award, would find it necessary to apply. On the other hand, they allow the parties an exchange of views, and so whatever reimbursement is finally agreed will probably seem fairer than a figure plucked from the air by a judge or an arbiter.

Here there is little to choose between mediation and conciliation — apart from the state of the parties' personal relationship — but a factor in the choice will be the availability of a suitable intermediary. To sit equally in the crossfire of two disputants while retaining firm control of the proceedings calls for certain temperamental qualities which a conciliator, operating at one remove, need not possess. However the first essential is to persuade the parties into the process at all and, having done so, to find a third party, be he mediator or conciliator, acceptable to both. This may be easier than to find an arbiter, since an arbiter's final award, if valid, is unappealable and disputants are sometimes wary of putting themselves irreversibly in the hands of an amateur judge possessed of such awesome powers.

There is one class of quality complaint which may not yield to any of the treatments outlined above. Where there are patent defects and the builder's account has not been paid in full, both parties have an interest in reaching a quick and inexpensive settlement. The position is rather different where the defect comes to light long after the bill has been paid — as, for example, where it takes really bad weather to show up a roofing defect. In such a case, a cautious contractor may feel that his position would be prejudiced by anything short of a flat denial of liability. If so, he is unlikely to agree to negotiation, mediation or conciliation — at least until a court action is imminent, and then only if he has had second thoughts.

Preference order: (1) referral to a trade organisation (if available);
(2) negotiation;
(3) mediation/conciliation.

Disputes over payment

Apart from disagreement over moneys withheld because of delay or defective quality, the builder's account may be disputed because it looks like an overcharge. This may be due to rascality on his part (the explanation which occurs most readily to the customer) but is more likely to be due to simple misunderstanding.

Formal styles of building contract have been refined over generations in the knowledge of how easily such misunderstandings arise. Hence they attempt to define precisely the extent of the works contracted for; the sum to be paid for those works or, at least, how that sum is to be calculated; how the contract sum is to be adjusted when the work is varied; the percentages to be applied to the prime costs of materials and labour; fluctuations in rates of VAT and national insurance contributions; and — most importantly — when and by what instalments payment is to be made.

With one possible exception, none of these precautions is likely to figure in an informal contract. That exception is the contract sum, which — if the work is undertaken on a lump sum basis — will appear as an offer by the builder which may or may not receive written acceptance by the customer. Even that provision is likely to be sadly deficient since any building job is likely to be subject to unforeseen circumstances or changes of instruction, and lack of prior agreement on how — or even whether — the contract sum is to be adjusted to reflect these is a recipe for contention. Moreover, the nature of the contractor's figure itself may be misunderstood from the outset. To a layman, the difference between "We estimate the cost at" and "We hereby offer and tender the sum of" may not be significant, but if he has interpreted a probable-cost estimate as a binding tender he will have an unpleasant surprise at the end of the day.

Next to dispute over the nature of the contract, a common cause of argument is the customer's

ignorance of certain trade usages which builders often assume to be unquestionable. Among the more obvious are the calculation of daywork rates; the charging of travelling time, workshop time and haulage; the disposal of spoil from demolitions; and the allowance of credit for salvaged materials. Where there is no architect or surveyor to deal with such matters, there can be not only misunderstanding but unfounded accusations of bad faith. Since these are, if anything, even more offensive than allegations of inertia or incompetence the parties' relationship will break down irreparably unless the information gap can be bridged at an early stage.

Unfortunately there will be small hope of advice being sought until the customer is already facing the threat of an action, probably after querying an account and rejecting the builder's explanation. Even so, consultation with an expert can be worthwhile, since the small builder is not always faultlessly articulate when trying to justify something which he normally takes for granted. If the consultation does not completely set the complainant's mind at rest, it will at least give him a foundation on which to decide whether to contest the action, to pay up or to propose mediation or conciliation. Whether the builder will accept such a proposal will probably depend on how far the quarrel over payment has provoked peripheral arguments over such matters as quality of materials or workmanship. If the dispute is confined to a single issue — such as the number of hours worked — which need not call for expert evidence and could be settled under the small claims or summary cause procedures, he will be unlikely to agree to an alternative. It is a different matter where the situation has become complicated by the possibility of counterclaims, requiring expert evidence and presenting the risk of undesirable publicity. In such a case, the contractor would be well advised to look very seriously at an offer of mediation or conciliation or indeed to make that offer himself.

Preference order: (1) consultation
(2) mediation/conciliation.

Choice of intermediary

Whatever the nature of the dispute, the mediator, conciliator, consultant or negotiator needs to have the appropriate technical expertise and, in the first two capacities at least, a reputation for fair dealing. As with choosing an arbiter, it will be most satisfactory if both parties can rely on their own personal knowledge or that of their lawyers, although if a trade association's referral scheme is invoked they will probably have no voice in the matter.

As a *consultant*, an architect of experience is the obvious choice where the issue is essentially one of quality, and a quantity surveyor is equally obvious where the issue is essentially over the valuation of the work. Either may be suitable where the dispute concerns delay, architects having arguably most experience of the causes of delay and quantity surveyors having most experience in pricing the consequences.

In a *negotiator*, technical expertise is not enough: he must also have the skills of a practised bargainer, including that of keeping the ball in play for exactly the right length of time. The skills which serve a lawyer in adjusting missives or a quantity surveyor in negotiating contracts are appropriate. The former will do best when arguing with another lawyer about a legal, rather than a technical, point, e g over the propriety of implying a particular term. The surveyor will be essential if the other side is employing a surveyor of its own (as a builder well may) to handle the question of payment. Since that question is often inextricable from quality or delay, the quantity surveyor is probably the best general purpose negotiator. Architects are accustomed to having their intentions realised by firm enforcement of contract conditions: this is not a habit conducive to bargaining, and it is a rare architect who has brought that particular skill to the pitch expected in the other two professions.

The choice of a *mediator/conciliator* will almost certainly lie between architect, quantity surveyor and that rather less clearly identified profession of building surveyor. Although the latter title has historically described roles as disparate as those of Sir Christopher Wren and the builder's clerk, it will be given here to an individual who has had much the same technical training as an architect but without the element of design: he may have a very responsible position in the fields of contract administration or "troubleshooting".

Again, the quantity surveyor is the obvious choice where the root cause of the dispute is the price to be put upon the work, and — because of his familiarity with the acceptable reasons for delay and the valuation of its consequences — he is almost equally the best choice as intermediary in such disputes.

In the case of disputes over quality, the appointment is more debatable.

As a judge of quality, an architect is, at first sight, eminently suitable. He is accustomed to deciding the standards of quality appropriate to the function of the building and to the resources of money and time available, and to prescribing those standards with precision. He is accustomed to inspect the work in progress, compare it with the contract requirements and take appropriate action if it is disconform. All these are positive assets in a mediator or conciliator, as they are in an arbiter. However he is required by his professional code to enforce the obligations of a building contract upon both parties, yielding neither to persuasion by the builder nor pressure from his client. The habit of mind ingrained by that adjudicative tradition, while it is a wholly admirable quality in an arbiter, can be a positive handicap where the object of the exercise is compromise. It is a habit which the individual may be temperamentally capable of suppressing. But it has to be said — dangerous though such generalisations must be — that mediation or conciliation is most likely to succeed if conducted by someone more comfortable in the role of honest broker where give and take, so far from being improper, is going to be essential. Other things being equal, this points rather towards the surveyor, of either species.

For it has to be repeated, and that emphatically, that the parties do not come to a mediator or conciliator to be judged but to have their fences mended, and the success of the process is measurable by how far they come out of it in amity. They are, in fact, looking for what the earlier Scots lawyers called an "amicable composition" (Hunter, *Law of Arbitration in Scotland*, para 1.18). Unlike arbitration, none of the processes outlined above constitutes a bar to eventual resort to the courts: but the expectation is — or should be — that it is an alternative to litigation, not a preliminary to it. If that expectation is to be realised, certain precautions need to be taken by each party's lawyer.

He should explain to his client the exact nature of the particular process which is proposed, and be sure that it is acceptable: this is especially important where it is offered through a trade association's referral scheme. He should satisfy himself that his client is likely to stay with it to the end and accept the outcome; and he should at least attempt an intelligent guess at whether the other party genuinely wants an extracurial settlement. And above all he should try to make his client understand quite clearly that there are few less promising subjects for litigation than an informal building contract.

[For enlightenment on the complexities of the law regarding rescission and reparation (and much else) I am greatly indebted to Mr H D Sheldon.]

NEWS

Appreciation

Sir John Dick, MC, QC

Sir John Alexander Dick, MC, QC, who was Sheriff Principal of Glasgow and Strathkelvin from 1980 to 1986, died on 16 June aged 74.

A son of the manse, John Dick was born on 1 January 1920 and educated at Waid Academy, Anstruther and Edinburgh University. He entered the university in 1937 but, like many students of his generation, interrupted his studies to enlist in the armed forces. He was commissioned in the Royal Scots and served in Italy and Palestine. In 1944 he was awarded the MC for an act of bravery at a critical stage of the Italian campaign in which he sustained serious head injuries. On his release in 1946 he resumed his university career, graduating MA with first class honours in economics in 1947 and LLB with distinction in 1949. In the same year he was admitted to the Faculty of Advocates after devilling to Mr I H Shearer (later Lord Avonside).

In the Parliament House his acute intelligence and industry attracted a very large practice, and he appeared in many important litigations and inquiries in the 1950s and 1960s. He somehow found time to lecture in public law at Edinburgh University from 1953 to 1960, and he also gave thorough instruction in the ethics and practice of advocacy to a succession of fortunate devils until he took silk in 1963. In 1964 he notably conducted with the late Professor Campbell the public inquiry into the North of Scotland Hydro-Electric Board's proposal to harness the waters of Loch Fadafionn. He was appointed a sheriff in Edinburgh in 1969.

On the bench he displayed the same thoroughness and sense of fairness which had distinguished his career at the bar. Anyone who appeared before him in a civil case could be sure that the sheriff had already scrutinised the pleadings and researched the relevant law, generating a sheaf of typewritten notes with many manuscript additions. In court he was alert and equable, carefully noting every submission, however hopeless, for reproduction and rigorous analysis in the subsequent judgment.

It was not long before he was called on to undertake further duties. From 1972 to 1973 he was one of the first commissioners under the Terrorism (Northern Ireland) Order 1972. In 1978 he became Sheriff Principal of North Strathclyde, an office which, until October 1982, he continued to hold on a temporary basis after he was appointed Sheriff Principal of Glasgow and Strathkelvin in 1980. Thus for over two years he simultaneously discharged the office of sheriff principal in two sheriffdoms. In Glasgow he presided over the move from Ingram Street to the long-awaited new court house in Carlton Place. As sheriff principal he led his sheriffs by example and quickly earned the confidence of the legal profession in his sheriffdoms. As an appellate judge he was outstanding: his judgments were marked by complete mastery of law and principle and by meticulous attention to detail. He would have adorned greatly the Court of Session bench, elevation to which, it is widely believed, he was offered and declined because of the increasing deafness, a result of his war service, which led to his relatively early retirement. In 1987, the year after his retirement, he was knighted and Glasgow University awarded him the honorary degree of LLD.

He was for many years an elder of St Andrew's and St George's Church in Edinburgh, and his life was centred on his faith. Although he was an intensely private man, anyone who confided in him found that his sympathies were instantly engaged, and the advice he diffidently offered was shrewd and sympathetic. While he was deeply serious, he was by no means solemn: he had a sharp eye for the ridiculous, and many a conversation was punctuated by explosions of mirth when he was suddenly struck by some piece of absurdity or pretentiousness. A formidable golfer, he was a mainstay of the Scottish Bench and Bar team and a match for anyone the English Bench and Bar could produce from their much larger pool of players.

In 1951 he married Rosemary Sutherland. They had met in the office of Messrs Balfour & Manson, SSC when he was an apprentice and she was a secretary. In retirement they lived in North Berwick, where she sadly predeceased him. It was typical of him that when he knew his own death was imminent he gave instructions for a short and simple funeral service which included their favourite hymns.

— ◇ —

Appointment

Scottish Legal Services Ombudsman

The Secretary of State for Scotland, after consultation with the Lord President of the Court of Session, has appointed Mr Garry S Watson, CA as Scottish Legal Services Ombudsman to succeed Mr David W J Morrell who retired on 30 June.

Court

Rules of the Court of Session 1994

The price of the Act of Sederunt (Rules of the Court of Session 1994) 1994, published by HMSO, is £29.20 and not as stated at p 228 supra.

General

Research report on detention and voluntary attendance of suspects at police stations

A research report published by the Scottish Office into detention and voluntary attendance of suspects at police stations has found general satisfaction with the existing arrangements whereby the police may detain a suspect for up to six hours if they have reasonable grounds for suspecting that a person has committed an offence punishable by imprisonment. This view was held by groups of police, solicitors and procurators fiscal interviewed by the researchers.

The report, commissioned after concern by the Association of Chief Police Officers in Scotland that in some cases the six hour limit may prevent investigating officers from conducting inquiries effectively, shows that on balance the current arrangements work well and that both police and procurators fiscal are familiar with the procedures. In particular it demonstrates that the time constraint of six hours has not prevented investigating officers from collecting sufficient evidence to proceed with a case. Nor was any evidence found to suggest that existing arrangements are being applied unfairly or are being abused.

The Secretary of State, after considering the report's findings, has concluded that there is no need to change the present arrangements.

Taxation

Corporation tax: associated companies for small companies relief

The Inland Revenue have published a revised text of extra-statutory concession C9 which concerns the definition of an associated company for the purposes of the small companies' rate of corporation tax.

When companies are associated, the profit

limits for the small companies' rate and marginal relief are reduced. The concession has been revised because the existing text is in one respect too restrictive, and because one of the conditions relating to one part of the concession needs to be modified. The revised concession sets out the circumstances in which certain companies will not be treated as associated, in the following terms:

Section 13, ICTA 1988 (small companies' relief) contains rules which apply when one company is associated with one or more other companies. Broadly speaking, one company is associated with another if one of the two has control of the other, or both are under the control of the same person or persons. The rules about control are contained in ss 416 and 417, ICTA 1988. The provisions of this concession relate to the application of those rules only for the purpose of s 13.

The Revenue will not, by concession, treat one company as being under the control of another where the first company is only under the control of the second by taking into account fixed rate preference shares (as defined in s 95 (5), ICTA 1988) which a company possesses. Nor will the Revenue treat one company as associated with another where those companies are only under common control by taking into account fixed rate preference shares which another company possesses. In all cases, this part of the concession applies only when the company possessing the fixed rate preference shares is not a close company, and takes no part in the management or conduct of the company which issued the shares, or of the business of that company, and subscribed for the shares in the ordinary course of a business carried on by it which includes the provision of finance.

The Revenue will not, by concession, treat one company as being under the control of a loan creditor of that company where there is no past or present connection between the company and the loan creditor other than the loan or loans which cause it to be a loan creditor. Nor will the Revenue treat one company as associated with another where the first company is only associated with the second by being controlled by the same loan creditor provided there is no past or present connection between the companies other than the common loan creditor. In all cases, this part of the concession applies only when the loan creditor is a company which is not a close company, or is a bona fide commercial loan creditor.

The Revenue will not, by concession, treat one company as being associated with a trustee company (for example, a trustee company of a clearing bank) where the company is only associated with that trustee company because it is under its control by taking into account rights and/or powers the trustee company holds in trust provided there is no past or present connection between the company and the trustee company other than those rights and/or powers. In these circumstances, the Revenue will not, by concession, treat the trustee company as being associated with the other company. Nor will the Revenue treat one company as being associated with another because they are controlled by the same trustee by virtue of rights and/or powers held in trust by that trustee provided there is no past or present connection between the companies other than those rights and/or powers.

The Revenue will, by concession, treat the definition of a relative (in s 417 (4), ICTA 1988) for the purpose of s 13 as including only a husband or wife or child who is a minor. This part of the concession applies only in respect of companies where there is no substantial commercial interdependence between them.

◇

Capital gains tax: reinvestment rollover relief

The Financial Secretary to the Treasury has announced that the Government intends to introduce legislation in the next Finance Bill to correct a loophole in the rules for capital gains tax reinvestment rollover relief, which allow individuals and most trustees to defer capital gains tax on chargeable gains which they reinvest in a qualifying investment. This relief applies to disposals made on or after 30 November 1993.

The loophole identified enables taxpayers in certain circumstances to convert what is meant to be a tax deferral into an outright exemption. The main circumstances are where someone reinvests in shares bought from a spouse or where someone realises gains on two or more disposals and reinvests in shares whose market value is less than the total gains realised.

The Government intends to correct this defect in the next Finance Bill. The new rules will apply to disposals, acquisitions and other chargeable events occurring on or after 20 June 1994.

Under the new rules, the amount of any gains which can be rolled over into a qualifying investment will, in addition to the current restrictions, be restricted to the acquisition cost of the qualifying reinvestment, after any reductions in that cost due to gains already rolled over into that investment. The new rules will apply to all disposals and all acquisitions made on or after 20 June 1994. They will also apply to chargeable gains arising due to a failure of the conditions of the relief on or after 20 June 1994.

◇

Income tax: interest relief

The Inland Revenue have issued a revised text of extra-statutory concession A43, which relates to income tax relief for individuals who invest in partnerships, co-operatives, close companies, or employee controlled companies.

The concession, which will be applied to any cases which are currently open as well as to future cases, reads as follows:

Under ss 360-363 of the Income and Corporation Taxes Act 1988, income tax relief is available for interest paid by an individual on a loan taken out to invest in, or on lend to, a partnership, a co-operative, a close company, or an employee controlled company. The relief is subject to various conditions, and ceases to be available when those conditions are no longer met.

Relief is also reduced or withdrawn (following s 363) if the borrower recovers any capital from the business without using it to repay the loan — for example by selling or exchanging the interest or shares in that business. Strictly, therefore, relief ceases to be due where: (a) a partnership is incorporated into a co-operative, a close company, or an employee controlled company; or (b) shares in a co-operative, a close company, or an employee-controlled company are exchanged for, or replaced by, shares in any one of these kinds of company; or (c) there is a partnership reconstruction involving a merger or demerger.

Under the terms of this concession, relief for interest on a loan to an individual will not be discontinued in the three kinds of circumstances described above where, in relation to that individual, the conditions for relief would have been met if the loan had been a new loan taken out by that person to invest in the new business entity. The rules restricting or withdrawing relief where the borrower recovers any capital from the business continue to apply in the normal way.

— ◇ —

Obituary

On 25 June 1994, David Francis Simpson, WS, formerly a partner in the firm of Messrs Drummond, Johnstone and Grosset, WS, Cupar.

— ◇ —

Business change

Messrs Gray & Gray, solicitors, Peterhead, intimate that they have opened an office at 19 Bridge Street, Ellon, Aberdeenshire (tel 0358 724455; fax 0358 722506; DX 1351, Ellon).

— ◊ —

Parliamentary News

New Bills

HOUSE OF COMMONS

22 June 1994

Contaminated Land (Remediation)—To make provision for the improved clean up of contaminated land. (Private Member's Bill introduced by Mr Robert Ainsworth)

27 June 1994

Public Conveniences (No 2)—To secure a uniform provision of public lavatories by local authorities throughout the United Kingdom; to set certain minimum standards for such public lavatories; to require the provision of lavatories designed for persons with disabilities and the provision of nappy changing facilities; to make unlawful any discriminatory charging in respect of the use of local authority public lavatories; to make further provision in respect of turnstiles; and for connected purposes. (Private Member's Bill introduced by Mr Jon Owen Jones)

28 June 1994

Tampons (Safety)—To make provision for tampon packaging and advertisements for tampons to carry certain warnings and information, and to require the Secretary of State to make regulations for these purposes; to lay upon the Secretary of State duties with respect to research into, and publicity for tampons and health; and for connected purposes. (Private Member's Bill introduced by Ms Dawn Primarolo)

Progress of Bills

Coal Industry — Commons: Lords' amendments, 28 June 1994

Firearms (Amendment) — Lords: second reading, 29 June 1994.

Merchant Shipping (Salvage and Pollution) — Lords: third reading, 30 June 1994.

Questions answered

HOUSE OF COMMONS

22 June 1994

IMMIGRATION (EEA NATIONALS)

Mr Allen: To ask the Secretary of State for the Home Department what specific amount of capital or income has been set by the immigration and nationality department to satisfy the Department of a European economic area national's entitlement to residence under Council directive 90/364 EEC.

Mr Charles Wardle: No specific amounts are set, but in general we expect an applicant to have a sufficient level of income or capital to exceed the limits at which income support could be claimed.

PERSONAL INVESTMENT AUTHORITY

Mr Burns: To ask the Chancellor of the Exchequer if he will make a statement about the Personal Investment Authority.

Mr Nelson: The Securities and Investments Board is today announcing that it has decided to recognise the Personal Investment Authority as a self-regulating organisation, and as a self-regulating organisation for friendly societies under the Financial Services Act 1986.

The Treasury has given SIB leave under the FSA to recognise the PIA. That decision was reached after receiving two reports from the Director General of Fair Trading. Both reports concluded that the rules and guidance submitted by the PIA do not, and are not intended nor are likely to have, significantly anti-competitive effects. Having considered the DGFT's report, I have concluded that there is no impediment to the Treasury giving the leave sought by SIB. The DTI and the Friendly Societies Commission, as the prudential regulators for insurance companies and friendly societies respectively, have also certified that they are satisfied that the PIA may be recognised.

The PIA will regulate and supervise all types of retail financial services business covered by the FSA. This includes selling of life insurance and regulated collective investment schemes as well as independent financial advice. The PIA will aim for high standards of regulatory compliance so as to improve investor protection. It will start work as a regulator on 18 July.

SIB is today also giving notice of the revocation of recognition of two existing regulators, the Financial Intermediaries Managers and Brokers Regulatory Association, and the Life Assurance and Unit Trust Regulatory Organisation. The PIA will cover the parts of business which those SROs now regulate and SIB has concluded that it is undesirable for those SROs to continue to operate now that the PIA is to be recognised.

23 June 1994

WARRANT SALES

Mr McMaster: To ask the Secretary of State for Scotland what plans he has to abolish warrant sales as a means of collecting debt; and if he will make a statement.

Lord James Douglas-Hamilton: Warrant sales act as an ultimate sanction within a range of remedies available to the creditor for recovery of all types of debts. The system of warrant sales was reformed by the Debtors (Scotland) Act 1987. These reforms removed the most resented and harsh aspects of the procedure. The Government have no plans at present for further major reform of these arrangements.

27 June 1994

CRIMINAL JUSTICE

Mr Gallie: To ask the Secretary of State for Scotland what progress has been made with the review of the Scottish criminal justice system; and what conclusions he has reached on proposals for improving the delivery of justice in Scotland.

Mr Lang: I have today laid before Parliament and published a White Paper entitled "Firm and Fair" which sets out the Government's proposals for reform of the Scottish criminal justice system. The White Paper is the culmination of a wide ranging review of the Scottish criminal justice system and criminal legal aid, in which I have sought the views of all those with a genuine interest in the delivery of justice in Scotland. The response to the four consultation papers we issued was very encouraging. We have received a large number of thoughtful comments which have been carefully considered. The White Paper contains the Government's conclusions following that consideration.

The White Paper also reports on our consideration of those recommendations of the Royal Commission on Criminal Justice which were of relevance to Scotland and includes proposals on other aspects of the Scottish criminal justice system which were not part of the main review exercise.

The proposals in the White Paper seek to ensure that offenders are quickly identified, brought to account and punished and that all those who come into contact with the criminal justice system, whether as victims, witnesses or jurors, are dealt with fairly and sensitively. The proposals include action to tighten up bail procedures and to deal with people who commit offences while on bail, changes to pre-trial procedures, the operation of the jury system, the powers of the courts and appeals procedures.

On certain issues, I have concluded that there should be no change or that further work is necessary. One of the most controversial issues on which I consulted was the future of the not proven verdict. This provoked a healthy public debate. The clear weight of opinion was, however, in favour of retention and I have decided that the three verdicts, including not proven, should remain.

I also consulted on the need for change in the Appeal Court's consideration of appeals and the handling of alleged miscarriages of justice in Scotland, in the light of the recommendations of the Royal Commission on Criminal Justice for a new independent review authority for England and Wales. The response to the consultation was inconclusive and, given the complexity and importance of these related issues, I have decided to appoint an independent committee, which will include a senior member of the judiciary, to consider both these matters in the Scottish context and to report to me. I shall announce the membership and remit of the Committee soon.

The consultation exercise has been productive and worthwhile. I believe that the proposals contained in this White Paper will command widespread support. I also believe they will significantly improve the delivery of justice in Scotland. When legislation is required to implement the proposals contained in the White Paper it will be brought forward at the next available opportunity.

ARTICLES

Criminal Responsibility Under United Kingdom Offshore Safety Law

Eric C Brown,
Advocate.

This article considers the main features of the United Kingdom offshore safety law with respect to criminal responsibility and identifies some perceived weaknesses in the current legislation.

Introduction

The recent criminal proceedings in Aberdeen against both the operator and the owner of the Ocean Odyssey semi-submersible drilling installation have focused attention on the criminal responsibility of operators, owners and others under United Kingdom offshore safety law. The Odyssey case was the first to be taken in the High Court in Scotland in respect of offences allegedly committed by a company engaged in offshore oil and gas activity. It was not the first offshore prosecution to come before the High Court. In 1990 a toolpusher was acquitted after trial on a charge of culpable homicide in respect of an incident on another semi-submersible (*HM Advocate v Robb*, High Court at Aberdeen, August 1990, unreported).

The Odyssey prosecution related to an incident in September 1988. Two years later Lord Cullen reported on the Piper Alpha disaster. The United Kingdom offshore safety regime has since undergone fundamental changes including the establishment of the Offshore Safety Division (OSD) of the Health and Safety Executive as regulatory authority for offshore safety. The Offshore Installations (Safety Case) Regulations 1992 (SI 1992/2885) have been introduced and further changes in offshore regulations are proposed and under consideration. However, the underlying legislation remains the same and the statutory provisions which formed the basis for the Ocean Odyssey charges, namely the Offshore Installations (Mineral Workings) Act 1971 ("the 1971 Act") and the Health and Safety at Work etc Act 1974 ("the 1974 Act"), remain in force. It should also be noted that these provisions apply throughout Great Britain.

The evolution of United Kingdom offshore safety law

When exploration and production activity commenced in the North Sea in the 1960s, there was no offshore safety legislation. Licences to offshore areas were awarded under s 2 of the Petroleum (Production) Act 1934, the provisions of which were extended offshore by the Continental Shelf Act 1964. Section 1 (4) of the Continental Shelf Act stipulated that the model clauses required in licences by virtue of s 6 (1) (d) of the Petroleum Production Act 1934 had to include provision for the safety, health and welfare of persons employed on operations undertaken under authority of the licence. Provision was made in the model clauses to require the licensee to comply "with any instructions from time to time given by the Minister in writing, for securing the safety, health and welfare of persons employed in or about the licensed area": see model clause 26 in Sched 4 to the Petroleum (Production) (Seaward Areas) Regulations 1988 (SI 1988/1213). (This clause and s 1 (4) of the Continental Shelf Act 1964 ceased to have effect by virtue of s 3 of the Offshore Safety Act 1992.)

On 27 December 1965 the Sea Gem jack-up installation was lost off the English coast. The then Minister of Power appointed a tribunal to inquire into the causes of the accident and into the operation of the safety procedures applicable thereto. The tribunal report of 1967 (*Report of the Inquiry into the causes of the accident to the drilling rig Sea Gem* (HMSO, 1967)) observed that in 1964 the Minister of Power had instructed the licensee in writing to carry out operations in accordance with the safety, health and welfare provisions of the Institute of Petroleum Model Code of Safe Practice in the Petroleum Industry (pp 17-18). There was, however, no provision for enforcement of the licensee's obligations. As the tribunal report made clear, "The only sanction for ensuring the proper operation of the safety procedures is the revocation of the licence. There are no penal sanctions which can be invoked by anyone in this regard" (p 2).

The Offshore Installations (Mineral Workings) Act of 1971 gave effect to the recommendations contained in the Sea Gem report and established a framework for the regulation of offshore safety on installations. A broadly similar framework was created in respect of pipelines by the Petroleum and Submarine Pipelines Act of 1975 ("the 1975 Act"). A number of regulations have been made under both statutes. In the interim, the recommendations of the Robens Committee *Report on Safety and Health at Work* (Cmnd 5034, 1972) had led to the Health and Safety at Work etc Act 1974, s 84 (3) of which provided for its application outwith Great Britain by order in council. The principal, or prescribed, provisions of the 1974 Act were applied offshore by an order made in 1977 (see now the Health and Safety at Work Act 1974 (Application outside Great Britain) Order 1989 (SI 1989/840)). However regulations made under the 1974 Act apply offshore only if the regulations themselves expressly so provide (1974 Act, s 15 (9)).

There have in consequence been two separate lines of development in offshore safety legislation: "offshore legislation" under the 1971 and 1975 Acts on the one hand, and health and safety legislation under the 1974 Act which had offshore application on the other. The "offshore legislation" was effectively brought under the umbrella of the Health and Safety Act by the Offshore Safety Act of 1992, s 1, which gave the Secretary of State for Employment overall responsibility for the regulation of health and safety offshore. However, the characteristic features of the two types of legislation remain.

The maritime background to United Kingdom offshore safety legislation

The Sea Gem was a barge which had been converted into a self elevating jack-up. It was a mobile installation. Structural failure resulted in the collapse of one of the legs. The installation sank and 13 of the 32 persons on board lost their lives. The disaster was essentially marine in nature. In the late 1960s the UK legislature had had no previous experience of the offshore operational environment. The industry itself was relatively new to UK waters. It is therefore not surprising that some elements of the 1971 Act reflect both the circumstances of the Sea Gem's loss and the United Kingdom's historic involvement with the maritime environment.

Section 4 of the 1971 Act established the requirement for an offshore installation manager (OIM) in respect of every installation. The OIM was given extensive authority in respect of activities and persons on board. Certain responsibilities were placed upon him. His position was not unlike that of a marine captain. Furthermore, the legislation contemplated dangers which were essentially marine in nature. Section 5 (4) and (5) of the 1971 Act refers to operations or an emergency endangering "the seaworthiness or stability of the installation". The relevance of "seaworthiness or stability" to a fixed platform does not appear to have been considered. No reference is made in these provisions to other dangers which may place an offshore installation at risk such as a blowout, release of gas or other hydrocarbons, fire, explosion and loss of structural integrity.

There are other respects in which the legislation based on the 1971 Act does not adequately reflect the nature of offshore operations and the manner in which they are conducted. This applies, in particular, to the nature of the duties and to the identity of the duty holders.

Duties under the 1971 and 1974 Acts

On the United Kingdom continental shelf exploration and production activities are conducted by an operator approved, in respect of a particular licence, by the Secretary of State under model clause 24 in Sched 4 to the 1988 Regulations. There is no doubt that, as a matter of fact, the operator is in charge of operations on a fixed or mobile installation. However, no duties are incumbent on an operator under offshore legislation with the exception of duties under the Offshore Installations (Safety Case) Regulations 1992, which duties relate solely to compliance with the provisions of the Safety Case Regulations.

The primary duty holders under the 1971 Act and regulations made thereunder are the concession owner, the owner of the installation and the installation manager. In particular, it is the duty of the installation manager, and of the owner of the installation and of the concession owner, to ensure that the provisions of the Offshore Installations (Operational Safety, Health and Welfare) Regulations 1976 (SI 1976/1019) ("the 1976 Regulations") are complied with: reg 32 (1). In the event of any contravention of the 1976 Regulations, the installation manager, the concession owner and the owner of the installation are each guilty of an offence (reg 34 (1)). The concession owner is defined as being the person who has inter alia the right to exploit or explore for mineral resources: 1971 Act, s 12 (2). The concession owner is, in effect, the licensee, although the term "licensee" is not used in the 1971 Act or in regulations made thereunder. The owner of the installation is defined as the person in whose name the installation is registered, except where there is no registration (s 12 (1)). The installation manager is the person in charge of the installation and appointed in terms of s 4 (1) of the 1971 Act: ss 4 (8) and 12 (1).

In addition to his general authority over all persons on board in respect of safety, health, welfare and discipline (s 5 (2)), the OIM is given specific authority to take or to require to be taken any measures necessary or expedient to deal with an emergency or apprehended emergency: s 5 (5). Specific duties are imposed on the offshore installation manager. In particular, the OIM shall not permit the installation to be used in any manner, or permit any operation to be carried out on the installation, if the seaworthiness or stability of the installation is likely to be endangered by its use in that manner, or by the carrying out of the operation or by its being carried out in the manner proposed: s 5 (4), which also places a specific duty on the owner of an installation to ensure that the OIM complies with this provision. This duty formed the basis of one of the charges against the drilling contractor in the Ocean Odyssey prosecution. It is understood that this was the first time such a charge had been libelled in criminal proceedings.

Despite these provisions, problems remain with respect to responsibility for installations, particularly mobile drilling installations. On these vessels, operations are conducted by the vessel owner or "contractor" on behalf of the operator or "client". The operator will have his representative on board, who is known as the company man. His function is to supervise the work undertaken by the contractor's staff, under the instructions of the toolpusher, the contractor's senior drilling employee. There is a triangular network of relationships established: between the OIM and the toolpusher, between the toolpusher and the company man, and between the company man and the OIM. On some mobile drilling installations, the toolpusher will also be the OIM. On others, the OIM will be a mariner, who may have little experience or knowledge of drilling operations. Where the lines are drawn between the respective rights, duties and responsibilities of these parties may not be clear, particularly in an emergency situation. The legislation does not appear to have taken account of these issues, which have exercised the industry worldwide for many years.

Employers and employees are required to ensure that the employee complies with any duty or prohibition imposed upon him by the 1976 Regulations: reg 32 (2). "Employer" and "employee" are, however, not defined in the 1971 Act or in the 1976 Regulations. Other duties are incumbent on individuals. These include a duty on every person not to do anything likely to endanger the safety of himself or other persons on or near the installation or to render unsafe any equipment: reg 32 (3) (a).

The word "operator" does not appear in the 1971 Act or in the regulations made thereunder. However, one of the licensees is normally appointed as operator. In that event, the operator will be subject to the duties of a concession owner.

Duties under the Health and Safety at Work etc Act 1974 are incumbent on employers, employees and the self employed. These include:

(1) a duty on employers to ensure, so far as is reasonably practicable, the health, safety and welfare at work of all their employees (s 2 (1));

(2) a duty on employers to conduct their undertaking in such a way as to ensure, so far as is reasonably practicable, that persons not in their employment who may be affected thereby are not exposed to risks to their health or safety (s 3 (1));

(3) a duty on every employee to take reasonable care for the health and safety of himself and of other persons who may be affected by his actions or omissions at work (s 7 (a));

(4) a duty on self employed persons to conduct their undertaking in such a way as to ensure, so far as is reasonably practicable, that they and other persons who may be affected thereby are not exposed to risks to their health or safety (s 3 (2)).

"Employee" is defined as "an individual who works under a contract of employment" and related expressions are to be construed accordingly (s 53 (1)). There is no reference to the operator.

The operator as duty holder

It appears that, if a duty is to be established against an operator under the general provisions of the Health and Safety at Work etc Act 1974, it must be established that the operator is party to an employer/employee relationship, based on a contract of employment, in respect of at least one person on board. If there is no such person, no such contract and no such relationship, the operator is not an employer for purposes of the 1974 Act and is therefore not subject to the general provisions of the Act.

If this position is correct, it represents a failure on the part of the 1974 Act to take account of operational realities in certain industries, particularly the offshore industry. Comparatively few individuals working offshore are employees of the operator. Many are self employed or employed by one of the numerous contractors and subcontractors engaged on any particular installation.

The operator of an installation, particularly a mobile installation, may not have any employees on the installation. There may be "employees" on board engaged by a subsidiary or by an associated company of the operator. However, the engagement of such persons would not result in the creation of an employer/employee relationship between the operator and the "employee" based on a contract of employment. In particular circumstances, it may therefore not be possible to establish duties on the part of the operator under the Health and Safety at Work etc Act 1974.

In that event, it may be necessary to ascertain whether duties can be established against the operator under the "offshore legislation" of the 1971 Act and the regulations made thereunder.

One party and one party alone may be the licensee and therefore the "concession owner" in terms of the 1971 Act. This may be the case, but almost invariably licence interests in any particular block or development are divided among a large number of participating companies, none of whom may be the operator. The operator may be a joint venture company, distinct from but owned by some or all of the licensees and formed specifically for the purpose of "operating" the project in question. Alternatively, the operator may be engaged by the licensees on a contractual basis and have no pecuniary interest in the licence. It is therefore possible that, with respect to a particular installation, the operating company may not be "the concession owner". The operating company may also not be the owner of the installation, particularly where mobile vessels are involved.

There may therefore be some difficulty in establishing a duty under the "offshore legislation" in respect of the operator of a particular installation. If, at the same time, there is no employer/employee relationship for purposes of the 1974 Health and Safety at Work Act, the problem would be compounded. This issue is one of more than academic interest and is one which, it is suggested, should be addressed by amendment to and clarification of the legislation to reflect the practical and contractual realities of offshore operations.

Criminal liability of non-operating co-venturers

In the event of a breach of safety regulations, the authorities may consider, in an appropriate case, that the operator has been at fault. A prosecution may be sought. There may be no legal difficulties such as have been described above in establishing a duty on the operator. The way may then appear to be clear to proceed with charges under either the 1971 Act or the 1974 Act.

It may, however, be several years since the incident. The operator at the time of the incident may have pulled out of the United Kingdom sector of the North Sea and may no longer have a place of business in the UK. In that event, it may be impossible for the UK authorities to establish jurisdiction for the purposes of initiating proceedings. Alternatively, the operator may have gone into liquidation, making a prosecution of little practical significance. The question then arises as to whether, in the absence of the operator, the authorities are entitled to proceed against one of the other licensees at the time of the incident on the basis that liability under the 1971 Act attaches to "the concession owner", or whether that course is precluded on the basis that the other licensees, normally non-operating co-venturers, were not directly involved in the conduct of operations.

This question raises the issue of criminal liability of non-operating co-venturers, a matter

which has not yet been addressed by the courts. On one view, the definition of "concession owner" and the corresponding absence in offshore legislation of any reference to the operator, suggest that each and every licensee may be held accountable for breach of statutory provisions. The definition of "concession owner" in s 12 (2) of the 1971 Act does not ex facie allow any distinction to be drawn between a licensee which is the operator and a licensee which is not. A non-operating joint venture party, if a licensee, could, however, claim that operations on behalf of the joint venture or on behalf of the licensees were conducted by the operator and by the operator alone, as a result of which non-operators should escape criminal liability. Against such a claim, it could be argued by the authorities that in any joint venture the parties are acting in concert and that all participating parties are responsible for the actings of the operator, which are essentially actings on behalf of all the joint venture parties.

In a particular case it may be possible for the authorities to demonstrate that an operation or course of conduct was assented to, or condoned by, all the joint venture parties or licensees. Such a situation could arise where the matter was one that had been drawn to the attention of, or discussed by, the joint venture management committee, perhaps as a result of a previous incident involving similar circumstances. A fatal accident inquiry, a coroner's inquiry or a prosecution may have resulted in consequence of the previous incident. In such a case it could be argued by the prosecuting authorities that the co-venturers had been put on notice and should have taken positive steps to ensure the problem issues which had earlier been identified were dealt with by the operator and a subsequent and similar incident prevented. It is possible that by being aware of, but by condoning or by ignoring a course of action or activity conducted by the operator, a co-venturer might be unable to satisfy the requirements of a statutory defence in the event of criminal proceedings. Such considerations also raise important issues with respect to the civil liability of non-operating co-venturers, but these issues are outwith the scope of this paper.

Wider liability

Liability of individuals is not restricted to those on board installations who may have been directly involved in the events leading to an incident. Those with positions of responsibility onshore may find themselves being called to account in the criminal courts.

Where it is proved that any offence under the 1971 Act which has been committed by a body corporate has been committed with the consent or connivance of, or has been attributable to any neglect on the part of a director, manager, secretary or similar officer of the body corporate, or any person who was purporting to act in such capacity, that individual, as well as the body corporate, is guilty of the offence and is liable to be proceeded against and punished accordingly (1971 Act, s 9 (1)). There is a similar provision in s 37 (1) of the Health and Safety at Work Act 1974 in respect of offences under the 1974 Act committed by bodies corporate.

The question may then arise as to whether an individual is within the class of persons caught by these provisions. Each case will depend on its particular facts, on the duties, responsibilities and authority of the individual and on the part played by him in the organisation.

The provisions of s 37 (1) of the 1974 Act were considered in 1977 by the High Court of Justiciary, sitting as a court of appeal, in *Armour v Skeen*, 1977 SLT 71. The accused was the Director of Roads of Strathclyde Regional Council. A council employee was killed when he fell from a scaffold suspended from a bridge which was being repainted. The Crown had to prove that the statutory breach by the authority was attributable to neglect on the part of the accused and that he was a person who came within the categories set out in s 37 (1). Lord Wheatley stated that, having regard to the position of the accused in the organisation of the council and the duty which was imposed on him in connection with the provision of a general safety policy in respect of the work of his department, he had no difficulty in holding that the accused came within the ambit of the class of persons referred to in s 37 (1) (at pp 74-75).

In the *Armour* case, reference was made to *Tesco Supermarkets Ltd v Nattrass* [1972] AC 153, in which it was held that the manager of one of the stores within a large organisation was not a "manager" for the purposes of a provision similar to s 37 (1) found in the Trade Descriptions Act of 1968. In 1992 another similar provision under s 23 of the Fire Precautions Act 1971 was considered by the Court of Appeal (*R v Boal*, *The Times*, 16 March 1992). The court stated that the intended scope of the section was to fix with criminal liability only those who were in a position of real authority, the decision makers within the company who had both the power and the responsibility to decide corporate policy and strategy. It was to catch those responsible for putting proper procedures in place; it was not meant to strike at underlings. An individual who had responsibility only for the day to day running of a bookshop rather than enjoying any sort of governing role in regard to the affairs of the company itself was not such a person.

Even with the guidance which these reported decisions offer, it is difficult to assess where the line of statutory responsibility of company officers and senior employees will be drawn with respect to the conduct of offshore operations. The industry is not organised in the manner of a supermarket chain, with front line "managers" exercising little or no real authority with respect to the company's activities. On the contrary, this is a dynamic, diversified and international industry where many individuals hold positions of responsibility and exercise considerable authority delegated from above. The provisions of s 9 (1) of the 1971 Act and s 37 (1) of the 1974 Act may therefore cast a wide net.

Statutory defences

Section 9 (3) of the 1971 Act and reg 34 (4) of the 1976 Regulations provide defences to a corporate or individual accused. These relate to proof by the accused of the exercise of all due diligence by the accused and to the commission of the offence without the consent, connivance or wilful default of the accused.

The provisions of ss 2 and 3 of the 1974 Health and Safety at Work Act, which establish general duties on employers in respect of employees and persons other than employees respectively, impose a duty to ensure "so far as is reasonably practicable". Section 40 of the 1974 Act provides that it is for the accused to prove that it was not reasonably practicable to do more than was in fact done by the accused to satisfy the duty or requirement.

The duty on employees under s 7 (a) of the 1974 Act is one of "reasonable care", beyond which no provision is made.

Offences and penalties

Proceedings in respect of an offence or offences under the 1971 Act or the 1974 Act, or a combination of both, may be taken either at summary level or on indictment.

Summary proceedings are subject to a time bar. However, s 34 (1) of the 1974 Act provides that, in the event of proceedings at a coroner's inquest or at a fatal accident inquiry revealing a contravention of the relevant statutory provisions, summary proceedings may be commenced within three months of the conclusion of the inquest or inquiry. As the scope of the 1974 Act has been extended by the Offshore Safety Act of 1992 to include inter alia the 1971 Act and regulations made thereunder, any breach of the offshore legislation will be covered by the provisions of s 34 (1). Proceedings on indictment may be commenced at any time.

The holding of a coroner's inquest (in England), a fatal accident inquiry (in Scotland) or a public inquiry under the Offshore Installations (Public Inquiries) Regulations 1974 (SI 1974/338) is not a bar to subsequent criminal proceedings. With respect to Scotland, the examination of a witness at a fatal accident inquiry ("FAI") does not prevent criminal proceedings being taken against that witness (Fatal Accidents and Sudden Deaths Inquiry (Scotland) Act 1976, s 5 (1)). However, a witness at an FAI may not be compelled to answer any question tending to show that he is guilty of any crime or offence: s 5 (2). The determination of a sheriff at a fatal accident inquiry is not admissible in evidence and may not be founded on in any judicial proceedings of whatever nature, arising out of the death or out of any accident from which the death resulted: s 6 (3).

Proceedings for an offence under the 1971 Act may by s 9 (4) be taken, and the offence may be treated as having been committed, in any place in the United Kingdom. The effect of this provision is, for example, that an offence committed in the North Sea off the English coast could result in a prosecution in the sheriff court in Aberdeen.

The maximum penalty under the 1971 and the 1974 Acts, or regulations made thereunder, in respect of proceedings on indictment, is two years' imprisonment or an unlimited fine or both (1974 Act, s 33, as amended by the Offshore Safety Act 1992, s 4). In the event of a conviction of an individual on a charge of culpable homicide or manslaughter the maximum sentence is life imprisonment.

A charge of corporate culpable homicide or corporate manslaughter is competent in Scotland and England respectively. It should, however, be noted that the underlying substantive law with respect to this offence is not the same in both jurisdictions.

Conclusion

Safety is a key issue in the offshore industry. Most companies strive to achieve and to promote a good safety record. This in turn helps to market the company, not only within the industry, but also to the licensing authorities at home and abroad and to the public at large.

An offshore prosecution will attract publicity. If successful it may result in a substantial fine. However, the damage to a company's reputation may far exceed any financial penalty a court may impose. It is not only the company which may be called to account. Individuals may be held accountable. They include not only those directly involved in an incident, but also those who exercised, or failed to exercise, a measure of control

over the company's activities. In seeking to serve and to protect to company's interests, individuals must be aware of and satisfy the duties to which the company is subject. They must also be aware of and satisfy the duties placed upon them as individuals. In the criminal courts, ignorance of the law is no excuse.

At the same time, there is a need for the legislators to address some of the shortcomings of the existing law.

[This article was originally published in the *Oil and Gas Law and Taxation Review*, published by Sweet & Maxwell, and is reproduced with permission.]

Sharing Property in a Fluctuating Market

Alastair Bissett-Johnson,
Professor of Private Law, University of Dundee
and
Joe Thomson, Regius Professor of Law,
University of Glasgow.

This article explores the implications of the House of Lords decision in Wallis v Wallis, *1993 SLT 1348, on the effect of the Family Law (Scotland) Act 1985 on valuation and division of property in a fluctuating market. The authors suggest to practitioners the need to find imaginative ways of protecting clients who are out of occupation of the home from potential losses arising out of the decision. The vehicle, it is suggested, lies in the court's powers to make incidental orders under s 14 of the Act.*

Introduction

As a result of *Wallis* we now have been told definitively by the House of Lords (pace the criticisms of Dr Clive in 1992 SLT (News) 241) that where one spouse remains in occupation of the matrimonial home after separation, and the property rises in value prior to divorce, the "transfer value" of the spouse out of occupation has to be calculated at the date of separation even if the property is in joint names. We have also been told definitively that any post separation rise in value of the home is not a "special circumstance" within s 10 (6) of the Family Law (Scotland) Act 1985, even where the equity in the home more than doubles between separation and sale as in *Wallis*. However, the House of Lords felt that different considerations came into play in a property market undergoing substantial depreciation and we return to this later since the statements on this point by the House of Lords were less fully developed and may need clarification.

The post-*Wallis* situation

One effect of the decision may be to make practitioners reluctant to recommend to clients that their partners should remain in the home after separation, and instead to demand immediate sale. This is particularly likely to be the case in a rising property market. Judges may also be attracted to this reasoning and may be fortified in this belief if the husband is paying substantial child support payments under the Child Support Act 1991. They may feel that if the wife has custody of the children and the benefit of a child support order (which also contains a "carer's element") constituting a large share of the husband's income, and if "clean break" transfers attract no consideration under the Child Support Act, then any postponement of the husband's right to recoup his share in the home is not reasonable within the meaning of s 8 (2) of the Act. The husband in such a case might be losing the "opportunity cost" of being able to get back into the housing market and the opportunity, once lost, might never return. Though whether pressure for the sale of the home, arising from the interaction of the Child Support Act 1991 and the Family Law (Scotland) Act 1985, operates in the best interests of the child is another matter.

Incidental orders under s 14

(a) *On a rising market: interest*

Section 14 (2) (j) of the 1985 Act includes within the range of incidental orders: "an order as to the date from which any interest on any amount awarded shall run".

The width of this power only becomes clear when read in conjunction with the decision of the Inner House in *Geddes v Geddes*, 1993 SLT 494 that interest on capital sum payments can be backdated to a time such as the date of separation, the more important of the two "relevant dates" within s 10 (2) of the Act, and before the size of the award has been established. This was subject to two provisos indicated by the Lord President (Hope) (p 499I-J).

The first proviso was that the order must, in terms of s 8 (2) of the Act: (a) be justified by reference to s 9 principles; and (b) be reasonable having regard to the resources of the parties. The second proviso was that the award of the backdated order should be seen as an integral part of the order for financial provision and not something that is added in afterwards once all the exercises to arrive at this provision are complete. Both provisos should be borne in mind by practitioners to avoid allegations of error of judgment (or worse).

One of the examples specifically mentioned by Lord Hope was the case where one spouse has sole or exclusive occupation of the home and the interest is analogous to rent (pp 500L-501A). Thus the spouse out of occupation can be compensated by interest on the capital sum payment for any increase in value of the home in which the other spouse is living, unless property values are increasing so rapidly that no reasonable rate of interest can compensate for the rise. In the latter case, practitioners for spouses out of occupation ought to press strongly for the sale of the property.

These are not, however, the only cases where interest may be appropriate and one can think of examples where the use of a non-matrimonial asset creates for the owning spouse an advantage that is not otherwise taken into account under the principle enunciated in s 9 (1) (b). A third example lies in the "pension cases" (see Bissett-Johnson, 1993 SLT (News) 321), where the wife needs to be compensated for the postponement of her right to collect her share in her husband's occupational pension. In this case, however, compensation for the postponement of the right to share may also be effected by the alternative means of an uneven division relying on the "special circumstances" provisions of s 10 (6) of the 1985 Act (see *Bannon v Bannon*, 1993 SLT 999).

(b) *On a falling market: an expedient order under s 14 (2) (k)*

Section 14 (2) (k) of the 1985 Act perhaps opens up the greatest scope for a practitioner with a creative mind, since it encompasses any order which "is expedient to give effect to the principles set out in section 9 of this Act or to any order made under section 8 (2)".

The House of Lords was clearly concerned about whether a sale of property could be justified as "reasonable" within s 8 (2) of the Act if the sale was to be at a substantial loss (see Lord Keith in *Wallis* at p 1351K-L and Lord Jauncey at p 1352G). Whilst Lord Keith indicated (at p 1351L) that normal changes in value of property are to be expected, both their Lordships were clearly concerned about substantial downward changes in the value of property; Lord Jauncey gave the example of a house and contents whose value went down by a half (p 1352G). It was Lord Jauncey's view that in these circumstances both elements of s 8 (2) had to be satisfied and in some cases a sale might not be reasonable within s 8 (2) (b). It is submitted that it is helpful to define the term "loss" further to understand their Lordships' dicta with some precision, since making no order at all is a serious step to be reserved for very limited circumstances.

SHARING PROPERTY IN A FLUCTUATING MARKET

In recent years the decline in house prices has produced the unwelcome addition to the language of the words "negative equity", to describe a situation in which the sale of a house will leave the vendors with no capital but a present liabilty on their personal obligation to the lender. Even where the sale produces a small surplus, the expenses of sale can easily transform an apparent surplus into a deficit.

In some of these cases repossession by the lender is the only alternative. This may also apply where the value of particular property may have fallen more dramatically than other property and it may be unrealistic to expect the particular property's value to regain its value relative to property prices generally. In other cases, it may be possible to sit out the situation until the housing market generally has turned round and to turn a "negative equity" into a positive one. It is this case that their Lordships' dicta are most apt to describe.

Take the example of a house bought for £150,000 with a deposit of £50,000 and the remainder being raised on a standard security. If its value then falls between separation and divorce to £75,000 (Lord Jauncey's example), no rational spouse will wish to sell the matrimonial home if this can be avoided by riding out the depressed housing market. In this situation it may pay the spouses to have one of them live in the home rather than pay rent until the housing market has recovered. Once it has recovered then the home can be sold at a profit and each of the parties can go their chastened way with some hope of re-entering the housing market in a more modest way. The problem becomes one of either getting agreed minutes of settlement or, where this is not possible, a court order which avoids the risk of all the benefits of the risen housing market accruing to one spouse only, namely the spouse who continues to occupy the home. The answer may be in drafting terms or conditions in the agreement or court order which protect the interest of the non-occupying spouse. The terms and conditions in the court order could be justified under s 14 (2) (k).

Such terms or conditions must address the maintenance of the payments on the standard security together with any other necessary outgoings such as aliment between the spouses, less any notional rental element to be borne by the occupying spouse. Where the standard security is relatively small, the sums may roughly balance each other out. In the case where the sum outstanding to the lender is a large one, the position is more complex. The spouse in occupation may be unwilling to pay a notional rental element equal to the sums outstanding on the standard security and other outgoings. Any outgoings beyond the notional rental element will have to be shared between the spouses until the housing market improves. Equally, the lender may be reluctant to allow the transfer of title to one spouse if it is part of an agreement which purports to release the non-occupying spouse from their personal obligations under the standard security. The third party's rights cannot, of course, be prejudiced (see s 15 of the 1985 Act).

In this situation the non-occupying spouse will wish to be assured that, if the housing market picks up within a stipulated period, they will have a right to call for the sale of the property when it does. This right could be protected by the inclusion of some objective criteria such as two independent valuations that the sale would be likely to produce a stipulated percentage excess over liabilities relating to the property on its sale. In exchange for this, the party out of occupation may be willing to help contribute to expenditures which exceed the notional rental element accruing to the occupying spouse. Given the vagaries of the housing market it is unlikely that the imposition of interest pending sale under s 14 (2) (j) or postponing sale for a stipulated period would be an appropriate alternative way of compensating the non-occupying spouse.

In a case where the home has suffered a decline in value but there is still some (more than de minimis) equity in it, then it is submitted that there is a prima facie right to have the property sold. After all, if property prices have fallen generally then each spouse should be able to take advantage of the lower prices, provided that each has sufficient deposit and income to buy a modest property appropriate to their new family and financial circumstances. Indeed, Lord Jauncey admits that where the home is in joint names an action for division and sale outwith the 1985 Act would lie (see p 1352H).

It is suggested that in the case where the home is in the name of one spouse only and a modest surplus would accrue on sale, a similar view should prevail. It is submitted to deny that the sale and resulting division of surplus in such a case would not be reasonable to the non-occupying spouse within s 8 (2). In such a case postponing the sale will achieve little to benefit the party out of occupation since the matrimonial home and other alternative properties will, in general, be altering in value by comparable amounts.

Finally, it is submitted that the courts should be reluctant during a depressed housing market to give an inflated valuation to an occupational pension (usually the husband's) by using the "continuing service" basis of valuation whilst at the same time transferring the home to the other spouse (usually the wife) using the valuation arrived at under a depressed housing market. This not only leaves the husband "present cash poor" but may also leave the wife with a windfall profit when the housing market rebounds.

◆

NEWS

Appointments

New Court of Session judge
The Queen, on the recommendation of the Secretary of State for Scotland, has approved the appointment of Mr Brian Gill, QC, to be a Senator of the College of Justice with effect from 1 October 1994.

The Queen has accepted the resignation of Lord Cowie as a Senator of the College of Justice to take effect from 30 September 1994.

◇

New sheriff
The Queen, on the recommendation of the Secretary of State for Scotland, has approved the appointment of Mr Bruce Alexander Kerr, QC, to be an additional sheriff for the Sheriffdom of Glasgow and Strathkelvin with effect from 5 September 1994.

◇

Queen's Counsel
The Queen, on the recommendation of the Secretary of State for Scotland, to whom the names were submitted by the Lord Justice General, has been pleased to approve the rank and dignity of Queen's Counsel in Scotland being conferred on: Deirdre Margaret MacNeill, Andrew Michael Hajducki, James Alexander Peoples, Ian Ralph Abercrombie, advocates.

◇

Advocates depute
Mrs Elizabeth Jarvie resigns from the post of advocate depute with effect from 5 August 1994. The Lord Advocate has appointed Mr Craig Alexander Leslie Scott to be an advocate depute with effect from 8 August 1994.

◇

Scottish Episcopal Church
Miss Anne C McGavin, advocate, has been appointed Chancellor of the Diocese of Edinburgh by the Most Reverend Richard Holloway, Bishop of Edinburgh and Primus of the Scottish Episcopal Church.

— ◇ —

Court

Faculty of Advocates
Mr Leonard Wallace, BA (Open University), LLB (Edinburgh), Mr Ian Farquhar Maclean, LLB (Aberdeen), LLM (Cambridge), MSc (Edinburgh), Mrs Sarah Poyntell LaBudde or Wolffe, BA (Dartmouth, USA), LLB (Edinburgh), Mrs Lesley-Anne Purdie or Williamson, LLB (Aberdeen), Miss Jane Elizabeth Patrick, LLB (Aberdeen), Mr Jonathan Charles Lake, LLB (Edinburgh), Mr Peter Jonathan Brodie, LLB (Edinburgh), Mr Neil Christopher Kinnear, LLB (Aberdeen), Mrs Catherine May Forsyth or Phillips, LLB (Dundee), Mrs Dorothy Ruth Bain, LLB (Aberdeen), Mr Eric William Robertson, LLB (Edinburgh), Mr Murdo Angus Macleod, LLB (Aberdeen), Mr Francesco Lorenzo Pieri, LLB (Glasgow), Mr Pino Ernesto Gino Di Emidio, LLB (Glasgow), and Mr Roderick John MacLeod, LLB (Edinburgh), have been admitted to the Faculty of Advocates.

— ◇ —

Court of Session: sessions of court
The Lord President has directed under rules 10.1, 10.2 (2), 10.3 and 10.4 of the Rules of the Court of Session 1994 that the Court of Session shall be in session from 20 September 1994 to 25 September 1995, save for a vacation from 17 December 1994 to 4 January 1995, and that the ordinary terms of the Court of Session for the legal year 1994/1995 will be as follows: 20 September to 16 December 1994; 5 January to 24 March 1995; 25 April to 14 July 1995, and shall be extended to include every Wednesday and Thursday in vacation in 1994/1995.

Subject to rule 10.3 (3) of the Rules of the Court of Session 1994 no division, Lord Ordinary or vacation judge shall sit on the following days: 23 (afternoon), 26 and 27 December 1994; 1 and

2 January 1995; 10, 14 and 17 April 1995; 1 and 22 May 1995; and 18 September 1995.

This supersedes the intimation at 1994 SLT (News) 162.

Court of Session: directions

No 3 of 1994 (28 June 1994): Productions which may be sent by facsimile transmission
1. A production may not be sent to the court and lodged in process by facsimile transmission except as permitted under this direction.

2. Subject to para 3 below, where a motion mentioned in col 1 of the following table is enrolled by facsimile transmission, a document mentioned in col 2 of that table which is to be referred to solely in support of the motion may be sent by facsimile transmission with an inventory of productions.

Column 1	Column 2 Supporting document
1 Assessment of liability for expenses under or by virtue of the Legal Aid (Scotland) Act 1967 or the Legal Aid (Scotland) Act 1986	Minute of assessment
2 Commission to take evidence of witness	Medical certificate
3 Interim aliment	Wage certificate etc
4 To open confidential envelope	Copy of letter of intimation of motion to haver
5 Loosing, restriction or recall of arrestment or recall of inhibition	Copy of letter of intimation of motion

3. Where — (a) a motion to which para 2 applies is opposed, or (b) the court requests, the original of a document transmitted under para 1 above shall be lodged in process as a production.

4. This direction shall come into force on 5 September 1994.

No 4 of 1994 (28 June 1994): Motions
1. This direction does not apply to a motion under any of the following rules: rule 23.8 (motions by pursuer before calling or petitioner before first order); rule 23.9 (motions where caveat lodged); rule 23.10 (motions by defender or other person before calling).

2. Where, after calling, a motion is enrolled during a term, the provisions of the following timetable shall apply.

Time for enrolment		Latest time for opposition		Day of publication in the rolls	Day of court hearing
Monday	4 pm	Tuesday	12.30 pm	Tuesday	Wednesday
Tuesday	4 pm	Wednesday	12.30 pm	Wednesday	Thursday
Wednesday	4 pm	Thursday	12.30 pm	Thursday	Friday
Thursday	4 pm	Monday	12.30 pm	Monday	Tuesday
Friday	4 pm	Monday	12.30 pm	Monday	Tuesday

3. Where a motion is enrolled in session outwith a term or in vacation, the timetable in para 2 above shall apply subject to the following provisions: (a) there shall be no publication in the rolls of the motion; and (b) where a motion enrolled in a cause in the Inner House is one which — (i) may not be heard by the Lord Ordinary or the vacation judge; and (ii) the day for hearing the motion would fall outwith a term or in vacation, the motion should be put out for hearing in the single bills on the earliest available day in the following term of the court.

4. This direction shall come into force on 5 September 1994.

Court of Session: practice notes

No 3 of 1994 (28 June 1994): Revocation of previous practice notes
1. The practice notes listed in the schedule to this practice note are hereby revoked.

2. This practice note comes into force on the day that the new Rules of Court of Session in the Act of Sederunt (Rules of the Court of Session

1994) 1994 [SI 1994/1443] come into force, that is to say, on 5 September 1994.

Practice notes revoked by para 1 of this practice note: 28 January 1955 (Jury trials); 11 January 1957 (Motions); 7 May 1959 (Appeals to the House of Lords); 16 November 1961 (Walling); 20 March 1962 (Motions to ordain party to lodge account of expenses); 26 October 1962 (Lodging copies of closed record); 28 June 1963 (Lodging of issues and counter issues); 26 November 1963 (Late lodging of closed record); 15 July 1964 (Copies of productions for use of the court); 10 March 1966 (Up to date marriage certificate in certain consistorial actions); 1 June 1967 (By order (adjustment) roll); 18 July 1968 (Extract decree of divorce); 16 December 1968 (Adjustment roll); 13 November 1969 (Motions relating to interim custody and aliment; appeals and remits from inferior courts; remits to reporters in consistorial causes); 3 December 1969 (Hearings for petitions under the Trusts (Scotland) Act 1961); 16 January 1970 (Modification of expenses against assisted persons); 20 February 1970 (By order (adjustment) roll); 31 March 1970 (Vacation Court); 14 May 1970 (Bond of caution); 2 March 1972 (Shorthand writer to record objections); 5 May 1972 (Procedure roll); 4 January 1973 (Consistorial causes); 23 November 1973 (By order (adjustment) roll); 9 July 1974 (Fees and expenses of reporters in matters affecting children); 21 November 1974 (Fixing undefended proofs); 29 May 1975 (Proof forms); 29 May 1975 (Diets of proof and hearing); No 1 of 1976 (Fixing proofs in consistorial actions); No 5 of 1976 (Motion roll); No 6 of 1976, Defended consistorial causes — 4 January 1973; No 1 of 1977 (Diets of undefended proof in consistorial actions); No 2 of 1977 (Applications for undefended proofs in consistorial actions); 3 January 1980 (Inclusive fees in undefended divorce actions); 9 July 1980, Extracts department regulations; 30 October 1980, Remits to local authorities in consistorial causes; 26 March 1981 (Amendment of pleadings in reclaiming motions); 10 February 1983 (Curator ad litem in consistorial actions); 15 September 1983 (Return of medical records to health boards); 21 February 1986 (Applications for fiats); 6 November 1986, Applications for leave to appeal from employment appeal tribunal; No 2 of 1987, Fixing and allocation of diets of proof etc; No 3 of 1987, Fixing and allocation of diets of procedure roll hearings; No 1 of 1988, Children: supervision of access arrangements by social work department; No 3 of 1988, Fee fund dues; 22 September 1988 (Average waiting times for hearings); No 7 of 1988, Registration and enforcement of money judgments under s 4 of the Civil Jurisdiction and Judgments Act 1982; No 1 of 1989, Enrolment of motions; No 2 of 1989, Appendix in reclaiming motions and appeals from sheriff court; No 1 of 1990, Fixing and allocation of diets — Form 64; 22 March 1990, Commissions to take evidence and/or recover documents; No 6 of 1991, Warrants for diligence on the dependence of consistorial causes; No 8 of 1991, Transactions of business by post or facsimile; No 5 of 1992, Intimation on the walls of court; No 1 of 1993, Optional procedure — list of witnesses — Rule of Court 188L.

No 4 of 1994 (28 June 1994): Transaction of business by post or facsimile

Lodging documents by post

1. A step of process or a production may be lodged by post.

Fees

2.—(1) Where any item of business transacted by post requires payment of a fee, a cheque for the appropriate fee must be enclosed with the item, unless the person seeking to transact that item of business is an agent who holds a Court of Session account.

(2) No item of business which requires payment of a fee may be transacted by facsimile unless the person seeking to transact that item of business is an agent who holds a Court of Session account.

Signeting

3.—(1) A summons accompanied by the process, or an application for letters for arrestment or inhibition accompanied by relevant supporting documents, may be lodged for signeting by post.

(2) If the summons or letters are in order — (a) the summons, or (b) the letters of arrestment or inhibition and the relevant supporting documents, duly signeted will be returned by post to the sender.

(3) If there is a defect of a kind which cannot be remedied by a telephone call from the signet officer — (a) the summons and process, or (b) the application for letters of arrestment or inhibition and the relevant supporting documents, will be returned by post to the sender with a letter stating the reasons for their return.

Calling of summons

4.—(1) Where a summons is lodged for calling by post, there shall be enclosed with the summons (which shall have the certificate of service attached) the calling slip required by RCS 1994, rule 13.13 (4).

(2) If the summons is accepted for calling, the clerk of session will advise the agent by letter of the calling date.

(3) If there is a defect of a kind which may be dealt with by telephone, the clerk of session will telephone the agent for the pursuer. If the defect cannot be remedied by telephone the summons will be returned to the agent by post with a letter stating the reasons.

Entering appearance by post or facsimile
5.—(1) Appearance in an action under RCS 1994, rule 17.1 (1) may be made by post or facsimile.

(2) Where appearance is entered on behalf of a defender to an action by post or by facsimile, details of the cause reference number, parties to the action, date of calling and the names of counsel and agent(s) representing the defender (and in multi-defender cases which defender they represent) must be received in the general department not later than 4 pm on the last day for entering appearance.

Petitions and notes — warrant for intimation and service
6.—(1) Where a petition or note is lodged by post, it shall be accompanied by any motion, which is required under RCS 1994 to be enrolled, in accordance with RCS 1994, rule 23.2 (enrolment of motions).

(2) Where an interlocutor pronounced following the procedure in sub-para (1) above contains a warrant for intimation and service of the petition or note, a copy of the interlocutor will be transmitted by post to the agent who lodged the petition or note.

Walling of petitions and notes
7. Where a petition or note requires to be intimated on the walls of court, a copy of the first page of the petition or note may be transmitted by post or by facsimile to the petition department which will arrange for the petition or note to be walled.

Lodging of steps of process and productions by post
8.—(1) Productions lodged in process shall be numbered as sub-numbers of the number of process assigned to the inventory of productions (e g, in an inventory of productions no 15 of process; production 1 will be no 15/1 of process; production 2 will be no 15/2 of process, etc).

(2) A step of process or inventory of productions sent by post, must — (a) be received in the office of court not later than the last day for lodging it; and (b) if intimated, be marked accordingly.

(3) When a solicitor proposes to lodge an inventory of productions and accompanying productions by post, he must — (a) contact the appropriate section of the general department or the petition department, as the case may be, to ascer-tain from the clerk of session the relevant number of process; and (b) write the relevant number of process and the cause reference number on the inventory of productions and each production.

(4) Where a motion is required to be enrolled in respect of the lodgment of any document by post, the motion shall be sent with the document in accordance with para 9 below.

Enrolment of motions by post or facsimile transmission
9.—(1) A motion or notice of opposition to a motion enrolled by post or facsimile transmission shall be accompanied by — (a) any paper apart required under para 3 of practice note 10 December 1986 (Hearing of motions); and (b) any relevant document or step of process which may be transmitted with it in terms of this practice note or direction No 3 of 1994 (productions which may be sent by facsimile transmission).

(2) A motion or notice of opposition to a motion may be transmitted at any time of the day but must be received in the office of court at such time as shall comply with the latest times for enrolment and opposition set out in the table to direction No 4 of 1994 (Motions).

Cause reference numbers
10. Practitioners should ascertain from the general or petition department, as the case may be, the cause reference number of existing cases before enrolling a motion or lodging a document. The cause reference number is shown at the top of the summons returned for service in terms of para 3 (2) above or the copy interlocutor transmitted in terms of para 6 (2) above and should be noted for future use.

Transactions by facsimile transmission
11.—(1) Practitioners who intend to conduct business by facsimile transmission are reminded that fax machines can receive messages outwith the hours during which business is normally conducted. It follows, therefore, that there may be advantage in transmitting a message in the evening for the following day rather than waiting until the following day when the line may be busier.

(2) Practitioners who intend to conduct business by facsimile transmission should ensure that appropriate arrangements are made to deal expeditiously with fax transmissions from the Court of Session (e g, returned motions).

(3) It is unnecessary to send a hard copy of a fax message sent in terms of this practice note.

(4) The following are the fax numbers to be used for transacting business under this practice note: (a) General Department, 031-225 5496; and (b) Petition Department, 031-225 7233.

Date of commencement of this practice note
12. This practice note shall come into force on 5 September 1994.

No 5 of 1994 (28 June 1994): Fixing and allocation of proofs etc
1. Copies of form 6.2 (form for information for fixing diets in Outer House) and form 6.3 (form for information for fixing diets in Inner House) to be sent to the Keeper of the Rolls under RCS 1994, rule 6.2 (6) and rule 6.3 (2) respectively may be obtained from the Keeper's office.

2.—(1) Where there is an estimate that the length of a proof, jury trial or hearing will be not more than four days, the Keeper of the Rolls will normally allocate a diet of the length sought.

(2) Where there is an estimate that the length of a proof, jury trial or hearing will be more than four days or there is substantial variation in the estimates given by the parties, the Keeper of the Rolls will communicate with parties with a view to ascertaining a better estimate and fixing a diet.

3. This practice note comes into force on 5 September 1994.

No 6 of 1994 (28 June 1994): Hearing of motions
1. For para 1 of the practice note 10 December 1986 (Hearing of motions) there shall be substituted the following paragraph:— "1. All unopposed motions enrolled for hearing in the Outer House, other than those referred to in paragraph 9, shall *not*, in the first instance, require the appearance of counsel."

2. This practice note comes into force on 5 September 1994.

No 7 of 1994 (28 June 1994): Intimation on the walls of court
1.—(1) The information required for intimation of the presentation of a petition, note or other application on the walls of court must include (a) the nature of the application, (b) the name and address of the applicant, (c) the general purpose of the application, and (d) the name of the solicitor for the petitioner, or noter or other applicant.

(2) If the above information appears on the first page of the petition, note or other application, a copy of that page will be sufficient. If not, a separate typed slip must be prepared.

2. In accordance with para 7 of the practice note No 4 of 1994 (Transaction of business by post or facsimile) a copy of the first page of the petition, note or other application may be sent by post or facsimile transmission to the petition department. Where a separate typed slip is required, it may also be sent by such means.

3. On the day on which an interlocutor is pronounced ordering intimation on the walls of court of the petition, note or other application, as the case may be, a clerk of session in the petition department will be responsible for the walling of the petition, note or other application on the notice board at the entrance to the box corridor from the reception area at door 11.

4. A walling certificate shall not be required to be attached to the execution copy of a petition, note or other application or any certificate or intimation.

5. This practice note comes into force on 5 September 1994.

No 8 of 1994 (28 June 1994): Exchange of lists of witnesses
1. Subject to the provisions in RCS 1994, chap 43, part V (optional procedure in certain actions of damages) and chap 47 (commercial actions), not later than 28 days before the diet fixed for a proof or jury trial, each party shall — (a) give written intimation to every other party of a list containing the name, occupation (if known) and address of each person whom he intends to call as a witness; and (b) lodge a copy of that list in process.

2. A party who seeks to call as a witness a person not on his list intimated under para (1) may do so subject to such conditions, if any, as the court thinks fit.

3. This practice note comes into force on 5 September 1994.

No 9 of 1994 (28 June 1994): Value added tax in accounts for expenses
1. For the first paragraph of the preamble to the practice note 14 April 1973 (office of auditor of Court of Session: Value added tax etc), there shall be substituted the following paragraph: "RCS 1994, rule 42.12 (1) (value added tax) authorises solicitors to make an addition to fees, where appropriate, of such amount as is equal to the amount of value added tax."

2. This practice note comes into force on 5 September 1994.

— ◇ —

General

Small claims and summary cause forms: use of substitutes
From 1 April 1993, Scottish Courts Administration have allowed computer produced substitutes of small claims/summary cause forms to be accepted in sheriff courts.

Conditions for acceptance of substitute forms are laid out in a set of guidelines giving details on their production which is available on application to: Heather Hill, Organisation Branch, Scottish Courts Administration, 26-27 Royal Terrace, Edinburgh EH7 5AH.

◊

Glasgow High Court extension

The rt hon the Lord Fraser of Carmyllie, QC, Minister of State at the Scottish Office, carried out jointly with the rt hon Lord Ross, Lord Justice Clerk, a ground breaking ceremony to mark the start of construction on an extension to the justiciary buildings at the Saltmarket, Glasgow, on 11 July 1994.

The new extension will comprise three jury courts with witness and all other ancillary accommodation; judges', clerks' and macers' rooms; advocates depute and defence counsel rooms; procurator fiscals' offices; police cell accommodation; and public and staff restaurant facilities.

The new facilities are to be occupied and fully functional by the summer of 1997.

◊

Health and safety legislation consultation

The Health and Safety Commission (HSC) have published a discussion document on the rationalisation of provisions common to certain pieces of health and safety legislation. These common features include risk assessment, management of health and safety, information, training, and competence. The discussion document seeks views on possible ways to simplify and clarify this legislation and remove overlaps.

The discussion document explores ways in which the law could be made easier to understand. It invites views in particular on whether the law should be reorganised to remove duplication and inconsistency or whether HSC should produce new guidance to explain how similar and overlapping requirements relate to each other. Reform of legislation would not change what duty-holders have to do to comply with the law. It would present statutory requirements in a different way, with the aim of making them easier to understand and to comply with.

Respondents are also asked to comment on whether, if the regulations were expanded, all or part of them should confer a right of action in civil proceedings for breach of statutory duty, rather than relying on the right of action for damages based on negligence.

Responses should be sent to Ms C Bowen, Health and Safety Executive, Room 238, Baynards House, 1 Chepstow Place, Westbourne Grove, London W2 4TF, by the end of October 1994.

Rationalisation of risk assessment and other common provisions in health and safety legislation, DD194, is available free from HSE Books, PO Box 1999, Sudbury, Suffolk CO10 6FS (tel 0787 881165, fax 0787 313995).

◊

Sheriffs' Association

At the recent annual general meeting of the Sheriffs' Association, the following office bearers were elected: *President,* Sheriff G I W Shiach, Edinburgh; *vice president,* Sheriff J C McInnes, QC, Perth; *secretary/treasurer,* Sheriff J Douglas Allan, Lanark; *committee,* Sheriff C N Stoddart, Paisley, Sheriff R E G Younger, Stirling, Sheriff A G Johnston, Glasgow, Sheriff N McPartlin, Elgin, Sheriff A B Wilkinson, QC, Glasgow, Sheriff R J D Scott, Edinburgh, Sheriff R H Dickson, Airdrie, Sheriff J S Forbes, Dunfermline, Sheriff S A O Raeburn, QC, Glasgow.

—— ◊ ——

Taxation

Extra statutory concessions

The Inland Revenue have published a new edition of their booklet IR1, which contains an index, where the concessions are grouped under general subject headings; the full text of concessions still valid at 31 December 1993; the titles only of obsolete concessions.

The booklet is available free of charge to personal callers from any tax inquiry centre, tax office or the Public Inquiry Room, West Wing, Somerset House, Strand, London WC2R 1LB.

◊

Unitary taxation

The United States Supreme Court, in *Barclays Bank plc v Franchise Tax Board,* has upheld the constitutionality of the controversial California unitary tax laws which allowed California tax authorities to tax foreign owned companies on an apportioned share of the worldwide income of the group. This law was incompatible with the internationally accepted arms length principle and the British Government strongly opposed the imposition of world wide unitary tax on UK owned companies and supported Barclays throughout this litigation.

Legislation passed by California last September to modify its tax law should ensure that in future no UK owned company is exposed to damage there from the imposition of worldwide unitary tax. The British Government will be following closely the detailed regulations and the practical implementation of this law.

◇

Tax consequences of European Community insurance directives
The Financial Secretary to the Treasury, Stephen Dorrell, MP, has announced that legislation will be introduced in the next Finance Bill to change the tax legislation affecting insurance companies.

In reply to a Parliamentary question, Mr Dorrell said: "The third life and non-life insurance directives come into force on 1 July 1994. They are an important part of measures being taken to create a single market in financial services throughout the European Union. One effect of the directives is that insurance companies whose head office is in another member state of the European Union will not be subject to regulation and supervision by the Department of Trade and Industry under the Insurance Companies Act 1982. This will have the effect of taking these companies outside the tax rules which apply to insurance companies because those tax rules are based on provisions of the Insurance Companies Act which will no longer apply to them.

"As a result, we shall be introducing legislation in the next Finance Bill to change the definition of insurance company to ensure that all companies operating in the United Kingdom remain within the special tax rules for insurance companies. We shall also be amending provisions which give relief from tax where there is a transfer of insurance business sanctioned by a court in the United Kingdom so that they also apply where there is a transfer of United Kingdom insurance business sanctioned by the regulatory authorities in another member state.

"We will also introduce measures to prevent a loss of tax where there is a transfer of insurance business to a transferee who does not carry on that business in the United Kingdom so as to be within the charge to tax.

"Subject to their approval by Parliament, these measures will take effect from 1 July 1994, the date on which the third insurance directives come into force.

"I also wish to make it clear that, contrary to some reports, the coming into force of the third life assurance directive will of itself have no effect on the taxation of gains from life assurance policies. At my request, the Inland Revenue are currently conducting a review of life assurance taxation in the light of single market developments and this includes the taxation of policyholders. The Government will decide in due course in the light of that review whether changes to the taxation of gains from life assurance policies are necessary. Meanwhile, the existing rules on policyholder taxation remain in force, and the Inland Revenue will continue to certify policies as 'qualifying policies' where they meet the conditions laid down in the legislation."

◇

Benefits in kind: loans provided by employers
Regulations came into force on 6 July 1994 to change the "official rate" of interest for Swiss Franc loans from 5.7 per cent to 5.5 per cent. The change follows changes in rates of interest for loans in Swiss Francs.

◇

Mortgage interest relief at source (MIRAS) qualifying lenders: new arrangements
The Inland Revenue have published a register of mortgage lenders who have been given approval to operate the MIRAS (mortgage interest relief at source) scheme.

This register, the Register of Qualifying Lenders, is available for inspection at any tax inquiry centre and is also available for purchase, price £1.00 (post free), from: Inland Revenue, Library, Room 3A, New Wing, Somerset House, London WC2R 1LB, or Inland Revenue, FICO (Savings & Investments), Third Floor, St John's House, Merton Road, Bootle, Merseyside L69 9BB.

—— ◇ ——

Obituaries

On 19 June 1994, Harold Frank Ford, advocate, formerly sheriff substitute and sheriff at Forfar and Arbroath, and sheriff at Perth and Dunblane.

On 23 June 1994, William Fifield Irvine, solicitor, latterly procurator fiscal at Dumbarton and honorary sheriff.

On 20 June 1994, Adam Raeburn Napier, formerly senior partner of Curle Muir & Co, solicitors, Melrose; Cullen Kilshaw, solicitors, Galashiels; and Taylor, Bruce & Co, solicitors, Selkirk.

—— ◇ ——

Business changes

Faulds Gibson & Kennedy, Glasgow, intimate that with effect from 1 July 1994 their associate Francis Collins has been assumed as a partner.

Lawson, Coull & Duncan, solicitors, 136/138 Nethergate, Dundee, intimate the retiral from the partnership of their senior partner, Derek Grafton Lawson, with effect from 31 July 1994, to enable him to return to university to study for a Bachelor of Divinity degree. He will continue to be associated with the firm as a consultant.

Gerald Moran and Mrs Ann Moran announce that the firm of Turner MacFarlane Green & Co which carried on business as solicitors at Ashfield House, 402 Sauchiehall Street, Glasgow G2 3JQ, was dissolved on 28 June 1994. Mr and Mrs Moran will continue in practice as solicitors under the firm name Moran & Co from the same premises along with their son Timothy as associate. The telephone number is 041-332 4944 and the fax number is 041-332 4778. The DX number is 512224 — Glasgow Sandyford Place.

The partnership known as Turner MacFarlane Green & Co was dissolved on 28 June 1994. Marc Green (consultant), John Woods, Charles Harkins, Sheena Savage, Kevin Woods, all ex-partners or associates of the said firm, in conjunction with Keith Ross, commenced trading as "Green & Co" from premises at RWF House, 5 Renfield Street, Glasgow G2 5EZ. The above announce that they have now acquired from the judicial factor of the dissolved partnership the trading name and style of Turner MacFarlane Green and its constituents. As at 14 July 1994 therefore the above named persons will continue as a legal partnership trading under the name of Turner MacFarlane Green, RWF House, 5 Renfield Street, Glasgow G2 5EZ (tel 041-204 1777, fax 041-204 1771; DX GW 202 Glasgow).

W & J Burness, WS, announce that Shona Maclean has been assumed as a partner in their Glasgow office with effect from 1 August 1994.

— ◊ —

Parliamentary News

Royal Assent

5 July 1994

Parliamentary Commissioner Act 1994 (c 14).
Antarctic Act 1994 (c 15).
State Hospitals (Scotland) Act 1994 (c 16).
Chiropractors Act 1994 (c 17).
Social Security (Incapacity for Work) Act 1994 (c 18).
Local Government (Wales) Act 1994 (c 19).
Sunday Trading Act 1994 (c 20).

Coal Industry Act 1994 (c 21).
Vehicle Excise and Registration Act 1994 (c 22).
Value Added Tax Act 1994 (c 23).

New Bills

HOUSE OF COMMONS

29 June 1994

European Union (Accessions)—To amend the definition of "the Treaties" and "the Community Treaties" in s 1 (2) of the European Communities Act 1972 so as to include the treaty concerning the accession of the Kingdom of Norway, the Republic of Austria, the Republic of Finland and the Kingdom of Sweden to the European Union; and to approve that treaty for the purposes of s 6 of the European Parliamentary Elections Act 1978. (Government)

Regulation of Diet Industry—To regulate the diet industry; to bring all medicines relating to diets under control; and for connected purposes. (Private Member's Bill introduced by Mrs Alice Mahon)

6 July 1994

School Leavers Community Service—To amend s 22 of the Education Reform Act 1988 to introduce a mandatory requirement for the National Record of Achievement of every school leaver to include details of the school leaver's contribution to community service; and for connected purposes. (Private Member's Bill introduced by Mr Gyles Brandreth)

7 July 1994

Children Act 1989 (Prohibition of Corporal Punishment) Amendment—To amend the Children Act 1989 so as to ensure that corporal punishment is not used in childminding and daycare for young children. (Private Member's Bill introduced by Miss Joan Lestor)

11 July 1994

Unfair Dismissal (Insolvency of Employer)—To amend s 122 of the Employment Protection (Consolidation) Act 1978 so as to extend the awards of compensation for unfair dismissal which may be paid from the redundancy fund in the event of insolvency of the employer; and for connected purposes. (Private Member's Bill introduced by Mr Harry Cohen)

Road Traffic Reduction—To require the Secretary of State to draw up plans in order to achieve certain stated road traffic reduction targets and the discussion of those plans in Parliament; to require local authorities to draw up local traffic reduction plans; and for related purposes. (Private Member's Bill introduced by Mr Cynog Dafis)

12 July 1994

Trade Boycotts—To prohibit companies from giving information for the purposes of a trade boycott which has not been approved by United Nations or European Union agreement; and for connected purposes. (Private Member's Bill introduced by Mr Spencer Batiste)

Unfitness to Drive on Medical Grounds—To require medical practitioners to inform the Driver and Vehicle Licensing Agency in cases where they consider that their patients are unfit to drive on medical grounds. (Private Member's Bill introduced by Mr George Howarth)

Progress of Bills

Vehicle Excise and Registration — Commons: second reading, 4 July 1994.

Value Added Tax — Commons: second reading, 4 July 1994.

Land Drainage — Lords: third reading, 4 July 1994.

Police and Magistrates' Courts — Commons: remaining stages, 5 July 1994.

Education — Commons: remaining stages, 6 July 1994.

European Union (Accessions) — Commons: second reading, 11 July 1994, committee and remaining stages, 13 July 1994.

Criminal Justice and Public Order — Lords: report stage, 12 July 1994.

Questions answered

HOUSE OF COMMONS

28 June 1994

CONVEYANCING AND EXECUTRY SERVICES BOARD

Mr George Robertson: To ask the Secretary of State for Scotland if he has made a decision about the future of the Conveyancing and Executry Services Board; and what consultations he undertook before reaching his conclusions.

Mr Lang: My noble and learned Friend the Minister of State announced on 21 June that the suspension of the Scottish Conveyancing and Executry Services Board would continue for a further two years. After careful consideration, we had concluded that the housing market had not yet picked up sufficiently to provide worthwhile opportunities for qualified conveyancers. The decision will be reviewed in a year's time.

No formal consultation exercise was undertaken in reaching this decision. We did, however, take into account the representations we had received over the period since the board was suspended.

1 July 1994

DUMBARTON SHERIFF COURT

Mr McFall: To ask the Secretary of State for Scotland what plans he has for the future of Dumbarton sheriff court.

Mr Lang: A new site at Meadow Park in central Dumbarton has now been identified for the replacement sheriff court house and, subject to a satisfactory survey of the ground and completion of negotiations for its acquisition, detailed planning will start as soon as possible.

4 July 1994

HABITATS DIRECTIVE

Mr Kynoch: To ask the Secretary of State for Scotland what measures he proposes to introduce to implement the EC habitats directive 92/43/EEC; and if he will make a statement.

Sir Hector Monro: My right hon Friends the Secretaries of State for Scotland, for Wales and for the environment have today laid before Parliament a set of draft regulations which would, subject to approval by both Houses, give legislative effect to the directive in Great Britain.

The measures set out in the draft regulations build on our existing nature conservation legislation and provide increased protection on land and at sea for the most internationally important sites for nature conservation in Great Britain. They form part of the Government's wider action to promote nature conservation and biological diversity, as set out in "Biodiversity: The United Kingdom Action Plan", launched by the Prime Minister in January this year.

The draft regulations also reflect the comments made when the Government consulted a wide range of conservation, farming, fisheries, economic, recreational and other interests in the autumn of 1993 about implementation of the habitats directive. The 94 responses received in Scotland emphasised to the Government both the widespread support for the nature conservation objectives of the directive and the need to implement the directive in partnership with those who earn their living from our countryside and our sea.

The draft regulations apply to special protection areas designated under the EC wild birds directive and to special areas of conservation to be identified by the Government in accordance with the habitats directive. Together, these sites will contribute to a European network of sites of high biodiversity significance to be known as Natura 2000.

In brief, the regulations contain the following provisions. Duties are placed on Ministers and the statutory nature conservation agencies — for Scotland, Scottish Natural Heritage — to fulfil the requirements of the habitats directive. Duties are placed on other statutory authorities to address the requirements of the habitats directive in the exercise of their functions. New provisions build on those in the Wildlife and Countryside Act 1981 to give additional protection to Natura 2000 sites. Existing restrictions on potentially damaging operations may be toughened where necessary, and farmers and landowners will be compensated for any losses which they sustain because of this. Special nature conservation orders will give indefinite protection to the conservation interests of Natura 2000 sites from proposals to carry out damaging operations. In the last resort, Scottish Natural Heritage would be obliged to use its compulsory purchase powers to protect Natura 2000 sites from deterioration or where no satisfactory management agreements could be concluded following the making of a special nature conservation order. This power should seldom, if ever, be used given that SNH will be seeking to address the inappropriate management of land by the negotiation of voluntary management agreements. Some technical measures supplement the species protection provisions of the Wildlife and Countryside Act 1981. An innovative set of measures is proposed to secure the protection of Natura 2000 sites in the marine environment. Ministers and statutory authorities would be obliged to use their powers to protect the integrity of marine Natura 2000 sites. SNH would advise relevant authorities on the conservation objectives of marine Natura 2000 sites. Where desirable, the relevant authorities concerned would cooperate in drawing up a management scheme for the marine Natura 2000 site. Ministers would have reserve powers to ensure that management schemes were developed where necessary and to ensure these schemes effectively address the issues facing the site. Provisions are made to ensure that planning authorities, and other authorities giving consent for developments or operations potentially damaging to the integrity of Natura 2000 sites, cannot give consent to developments if they would damage the integrity of a Natura 2000 site. Authorities would be required to review, and where necessary modify or revoke, existing permissions whose implementation would be damaging to a Natura 2000 site, and compensatory provisions are established for developers who incur loss because of this. The Government will consider sympathetically requests from planning authorities for reimbursement of the costs of compensation necessarily incurred by them in revoking or modifying planning permissions under these regulations. Provisions governing simplified planning zones and enterprise zones are amended by the draft regulations so as not to give permission for developments damaging to the integrity of a Natura 2000 site. The General Permitted Development Order is being amended similarly following a separate consultation in the late summer of 1993.

Further minor measures will be introduced after the summer recess bringing the exercise by relevant authorities of powers under specific statutes into line with the requirements of the directive. The Government also expect in the autumn to consult owners, occupiers and other relevant interests on a draft list of proposed special areas of conservation. The Government believe this consultation to be important even though it is not required by the directive.

The Government intend, subject to the regulations coming into force, to issue a circular to the relevant authorities detailing the effect of the regulations.

The Government consider that the draft regulations set out before Parliament a balanced and effective range of measures to establish and protect Great Britain's valuable contribution to the Natura 2000 network.

12 July 1994

LEGAL AID

Mr McFall: To ask the Secretary of State for Scotland what instructions his department has given to consultants regarding a review of the functions of the Scottish Legal Aid Board; and if he will make it his policy to place a copy of any report in the library.

Lord James Douglas-Hamilton: In accordance with current practice, the Scottish Office Home and Health Department is at present seeking the views of interested parties on the quinquennial policy and financial management review of the Scottish Legal Aid Board. As part of that process, a small number of interviews with a range of interested individuals are being organised by the Scottish Office central research unit. Professor Alan Alexander, professor of local and public management at the University of Strathclyde, who is a member of the steering group set up to oversee the review, is providing assistance with the analysis of the results of these interviews. No further consultancy input to the review has yet been commissioned. My right hon friend will consider in due course how the results of the review should be publicised.

ARTICLES

Possession: Nine Tenths of the Law

Hamilton v McIntosh Donald Ltd, 1994 SLT 793

Robert Rennie,
University of Glasgow.

Professor Rennie considers the extent of the possession held sufficient to establish a prescriptive title in the Hamilton *case, and argues that the case raises a serious question over the use of a non domino disposition as a matter of land tenure policy.*

Positive prescription

All practitioners know the basis of positive prescription. There must be (a) a foundation writ which used to be termed "an ex facie valid irredeemable recorded title" (Conveyancing (Scotland) Act 1874, s 34; Conveyancing (Scotland) Act 1924, s 16), and which is now known as a deed which is "sufficient in respect of its terms to constitute in favour of that person a title to" the subjects (Prescription and Limitation (Scotland) Act 1973, s 1 (1) (b)); and (b) 10 years' possession following on that deed which must be continuous, open, peaceable and without judicial interruption (1973 Act, ss 1 (1) (a) and 2 (1) (a)).

I recall as a student the late Professor Halliday referring to positive prescription as the practitioner's friend, like a fairy godmother who swept all manner of mistakes and uncertainties under the carpet. Most practitioners look closely at the foundation writ to ensure that it includes the subjects and is ex facie valid but how many practitioners pay any attention to the actual question of possession? By and large practitioners assume possession has in fact been held openly, peaceably and without judicial interruption. Few practitioners take any cognisance of the nature of the possession required.

The *Hamilton* case

The question of possession was brought into sharp focus in the recent case of *Hamilton v McIntosh Donald Ltd*, 1994 SLT 212 (OH); 1994 SLT 793 (2nd Div). This was an action involving an area of land ("enclosure 1271") known as the Moss of Balquharn, part of an even larger area known as Portlethen Moss. The pursuer acquired a residual title to an area habile to include the Mains of Balquharn from the University Court of the University of Aberdeen. The various defenders had recorded titles to various parts of the moss. One of these dispositions was a convey-ance of enclosure 1271 recorded on 7 November 1950 which was a non domino. The defenders maintained that the disposition of 1950 was habile to convey the dominium utile and had been followed by prescriptive possession on the part of the defenders.

In the Outer House, the Lord Ordinary (Prosser) held that the defenders had established the necessary prescriptive possession and he repelled the pursuer's plea in law to the contrary. The pursuer appealed to the Inner House. The appeal was concerned only with the nature of the possession and all parties accepted Lord Prosser's summation at p 214I of what had to be decided: "The question is whether they have established the 10 year period required under the subsequent statutes. What one is looking for is any such 10 year period starting no earlier than 29 November 1962, and ending no later than 25 January 1991, when the present action was signeted and judicial interruption occurred."

Possession for the purposes of prescription must be possession asserted as if the possessor is owner, and after reviewing the evidence on the period from 1972 to 1987 the Lord Ordinary concluded at p 220I: "I am satisfied, looking at that period, that the survey by Mr Livingston in 1972, the taking of peat by contractors in 1976, the moving of the fence in 1981, the subsequent use of the new route to the triangular field, the further boreholes taken in 1982, and the surrender of land for the new junction in 1984, together with the subsequent use of that part of the land, are all to be seen as matters referable to a right of ownership."

The "subsequent use" of the land referred to by Lord Prosser was for shooting and dumping of waste.

The nature and extent of possession required

The Lord Ordinary was of the opinion that the evidence of shooting over the enclosure by certain parties and the dumping of waste on a restricted part of the enclosure were both significant acts of possession.

In the Inner House the Lord Justice Clerk had to accept that the evidence was sparse. The difficulty, of course, in relation to a landed estate or an area of moss or scrub is how anyone can be seen to possess it. It is easy to understand the concept of possession in relation to a semi-detached dwellinghouse. It is not so easy to understand the concept of possession in relation to subjects on which no buildings are erected. Thus, it is clear that the possession can only be as complete as the nature of the subject permits. In *Buchanan and Geils v Lord Advocate* (1882) 9 R 1218, Lord Mure at p 1230 referred to the foreshore as having been "in the occupation of the pursuer in every way that a foreshore admits of being used" (see also *Agnew v Lord Advocate* (1873) 11 M 309).

Similar problems arise in relation to the prescriptive possession of minerals (*Forbes v Livingstone* (1827) 6 S 167). It is for this reason that the Land Register are reluctant to issue land certificates for minerals with full indemnity. The possession of minerals is normally only established by continuous working. Obviously in connection with minerals, landed estates or the foreshore the nature of continuous possession required is relative. Gordon in his textbook on *Scottish Land Law*, at para 12-44, states: "What must be shown, with the aid of presumptions if need be, is a continuous series of acts, in which gaps are explicable as normal or natural. For example if the party in possession spends a lengthy holiday away from the subjects, but resumes acts of possession on his return, it will be possible to link the former acts with the latter and count the whole period. However, it will always be a matter of degree whether acts are considered to form a continuous series, or whether they are considered as occasional intrusions, tolerated by the true owner or not objected to because unknown."

The other factor which is relevant, apart from the nature of the possession, is the extent of the possession since it is, as the Lord Justice Clerk pointed out, a cardinal rule that the subject matter acquired by prescription can only be the same in extent as the subject matter possessed — tantum praescriptum quantum possessum. Thus in *Aitken's Trs v Caledonian Railway Co* (1904) 6 F 465, Lord Trayner stated at p 468: "I am not at present prepared to affirm — as contended for by the pursuers — that a proprietor having possession of a part of the foreshore for the prescriptive period necessarily thereby acquires the whole foreshore".

In the *Hamilton* case the Lord Ordinary accepted certain circumstantial evidence of possession despite the fact that it was accepted by the defenders that the onus of proving possession rested firmly with them. Of the evidence of possession already referred to, the Lord Ordinary thought that the most important evidence was the evidence of shooting and dumping and it was accepted in the case that the other elements of possession would not have been enough on their own.

The lesser acts of possession

An engineer who carried out a survey in relation to proposed roadworks gave evidence to the effect that the defenders had instructed him to carry out a survey of the whole moss to determine the depth of peat. The engineer stated that he had walked over the whole moss and had arranged for bores to be taken. The evidence was to the effect that the taking of the bores involved a team of two or three people involved for about a week. This appeared to the Inner House and to the Lord Ordinary to be a one off event with no follow up and not material possession for the purposes of prescription. The same was held to be the case in relation to the taking of peat in 1976. This work was carried out only for a short period of about three weeks. Evidence was also given to the effect that a fence cutting across enclosure 1271 had been constructed in 1981 in connection with the upgrading of a road to dual carriageway. Thereafter part of enclosure 1271 to the north of the fence was used as an access for animals from the remainder of a triangular field. The Lord Justice Clerk was of the view that this did constitute an assertion of ownership rights over part of enclosure 1271 to the north of the fence but he was not persuaded that such possession would have any bearing on the assertion of rights over the remaining part of that enclosure. Further boreholes were taken by the engineer in 1982 in relation to a proposed grade separated junction and possible housing development. A substantial number of bores were put down but again the Lord Justice Clerk was of the view that such acts of possession were transient and could not be regarded as material. Between 1984 and 1987 land was given up for the purposes of the grade separated junction. The Lord Justice Clerk was of the view that such a disposition of land constituted an act of possession involving an assertion of owner's rights but only in relation to the land actually surrendered. That, therefore, did not help in so far as the land retained was concerned.

Having read the judgment of the Lord Justice Clerk up to this point one might wonder how the Inner House came to hold that there had been sufficient possession. It was clearly the court's view that between 1972 and 1987 the acts of possession were held to be insufficient because there were considerable intervals between each act and the acts themselves were not assertive enough of ownership.

The shooting and dumping

The court then turned its attention to the evidence relating to shooting and dumping. The

POSSESSION: NINE TENTHS OF THE LAW

Lord Ordinary was satisfied that shooting had taken place with the consent of the possessors. Unfortunately the evidence here was sparse and, indeed, certain matters were not put to one of the defenders. Evidence was given by the son of a grieve or farm manager to the effect that he and his father had shot over the whole area of the moss mostly for rabbits and one or two pheasants. The evidence was to the effect that they went out "most weekends during the season". Evidence was also given that another party had shot pigeon, pheasants and rabbits. Whatever permissions were granted they do not appear to have been in the form of shooting leases, so that it was not contended that civil possession of any sort had been exercised on behalf of the defenders. However, the Lord Ordinary concluded that the father and son had authority from the defenders to shoot from 1970 up to 1979 and that the farm manager had apparently authority to permit other third parties to shoot. The court was satisfied that these shooting rights were exercised regularly.

So far as the dumping is concerned the evidence was to the effect that this had occurred off and on all the year round but almost every day in the spring of each year when stones were being removed from arable land. Materials had been dumped to the left of a track on part of enclosure 1271. The Lord Justice Clerk was satisfied that dumping occurred within one of these parts of the moss in contention. The Lord Justice Clerk accepted that dumping was localised and could not be said to have taken place over the whole extent of enclosure 1271.

The Lord Justice Clerk summed up the evidence in the following manner (at p 800I-L): "The critical question is whether the evidence as a whole discloses possession of a sufficient quantity and quality to indicate that the first defenders were asserting rights of ownership in plot 1271. I am bound to say that I regard this as a narrow question upon which my opinion has wavered during my consideration of the case. From the first defender's point of view the best evidence of possession is in the fact that shooting took place over plot 1271 from 1970 until at least 1979 when Mr McGregor, senior, died. This had involved the McGregors and Mr Johnstone going over the whole area of the moss, but the amount of game shot appears to have been very small, and shooting appears to have taken place mainly on Saturdays during the shooting season. Nevertheless, I regard the shooting as constituting a clear assertion of possession over nearly 10 years, and having regard to the nature of the shooting, I am of opinion that it can reasonably be regarded as

continuous. . . . As already indicated I am satisfied that they (the defenders) can rely on the dumping carried out by the McGregors but that was very localised and is not sufficient to support the proposition that the first defenders were asserting possession of the whole of plot 1271."

The extent of overall possession
His Lordship then went on to consider the circumstantial nature of all the evidence and came to the view that there was just enough evidence to entitle the Lord Ordinary to conclude that prescriptive possession on the part of the first defenders had been established. The starting point was the evidence in relation to the shootings and to that there could be added the evidence of dumping. The other actions in relation to the surveys, which were localised and transient, were weighed up with this and the court held that while they were not in themselves sufficient to evidence possession, they were circumstances pointing to some degree of possession in a limited sense. The same was apparently true of the taking of peat, albeit that it lasted for only three weeks. Taking all these factors together the Lord Justice Clerk was of the view that the Lord Ordinary had not erred in law.

The dissenting view
Lord Wylie basically agreed with the Lord Justice Clerk but Lord Murray dissented. Lord Murray assessed the evidence and eventually came to the view that it was insufficient. He stated: "On any view of the evidence which was led before the Lord Ordinary it is clear that the acts of possession on which the defenders had to rely were minimal in number and extent, no single one, with the possible exceptions of seasonal rough shooting and dumping, being continuous throughout the prescriptive period, nor affirming strongly the quality of an owner's possession of the whole" (p 801K-L).

Lord Murray referred to Rankine on *Landownership*. Rankine distinguished between casual possession and the type of possession entirely for the possessor with the intention to hold entirely for the possessor. Lord Murray took the view that to justify a circumstantial inference of continuity the acts of occupation would require to be connected in time, place and circumstance and also would require to be in such a manner as to indicate continuity of occupation rather than sporadic instances of occupation. Lord Murray pointed out that the actual parties who shot over the land were not the defenders who were then claiming ownership but other parties. Lord Murray pointed out that the evidence tended to suggest that the authority to shoot was not given by the defenders but by farm managers. Lord Murray, therefore, felt that whether or not the shooting was possession it was not the possession of those who were claiming the title. Lord Murray took the same view in relation to the question of the dumping. Again, it was not clear from the evidence that the dumping was actually done by the defenders. On that view Lord Murray came to the conclusion that there was insufficient evidence of possession although he, too, accepted that the issue was a narrow one.

Is the decision correct?
There are two preliminary points to be made about this decision:

(a) The Inner House were considering an appeal from the Lord Ordinary who had heard the evidence from the witnesses and came to the view that the evidence of possession was sufficient. In such cases there is always a natural reluctance on the part of the appellate court to interfere with a view which has been formed on the evidence by the judge who actually heard the evidence.

(b) In cases of this type the evidence of possession is not likely to be obvious and the decision is always bound to turn on the particular facts and circumstances.

It follows that there is no real principle of law flowing from the decision and it is therefore worthwhile to look at some authority on prescriptive possession. Montgomerie Bell states in relation to the extent and quality of possession required: "The possession, however, must be of the highest description of which the subject is capable" (*Lectures on Conveyancing* (3rd ed), p 707).

Rankine regards the possession of "visible corporeal subjects, such as land and houses" as being of an obvious nature and only admits of less obvious forms of possession in relation to minerals and incorporeal rights such as servitudes, salmon fishings and public privileges (*Land-ownership* (4th ed), p 48). Given the fact that the Inner House accepted that the evidence was sparse in the *Hamilton* case, it is difficult to see how the possession can have been "of the highest description", and to comply with the type of obvious possession required by Rankine one would perhaps have had to enclose the plot in question by a wall or fence. The case does however contain something of a warning to practitioners, especially those practitioners who have large agricultural or estate practices. It must be obvious that the owner of an estate extending to thousands of acres cannot be expected to pace

round the estate every week or month looking for evidence of possession by other parties. The question becomes even more acute when one considers the extent of land owned by foreign based interests.

There is no doubt that the evidence which was accepted in the *Hamilton* case was absolutely minimal. Indeed, both the Lord Ordinary and the Lord Justice Clerk began by discounting the various surveys, test bores and peat workings. Thereafter both judges went on to accept shooting and dumping as evidence of possession, notwithstanding the fact that the defenders were not the parties who shot or dumped and notwithstanding the fact that those who did shoot or dump were not the tenants of the defenders. It seems to have been tacitly accepted in the judgments that by some process an authority emanated from the defenders to farm managers and thereafter to other people. The Lord Justice Clerk and Lord Wylie then appear to have added back into the equation the surveys, the test bores and the peat cutting and come to the conclusion that this was enough to tip the scales in favour of the defenders. With respect, this seems rather an odd way to go about things. If these peripheral matters were not in themselves sufficient evidence of possession in the first place it is difficult to see how they can be added back to underline the possession "constituted by the shooting and the dumping".

The a non domino disposition and the registers
There must now be a serious question over the use of the a non domino disposition as a matter of land tenure policy. It is easy to see how a piece of scrub land could be made the subject of an a non domino disposition and then left for the prescriptive period. On the basis of the *Hamilton* decision there would be no requirement to fence off the area in an assertive manner. All that would apparently be required would be to shoot over the land or use it for casual dumping. How is the true owner to know that this is taking place? It may be accepted that where the subjects comprise an established shooting estate and the party claiming prescriptive possession has systematically let the shooting year in year out during the season there is sufficient evidence of possession, but it is difficult to accept that the casual type of shooting and dumping which was disclosed in the evidence in the *Hamilton* case can be regarded as sufficient.

Insofar as the title founding prescription is concerned there is no legal obligation on the keeper to advise the true owner of ground of the existence of an a non domino disposition affecting that ground. Indeed rules 17 (3) and 21 of the Land Registration (Scotland) Rules 1980 actually prohibit the keeper in a Land Register case from advising the true owner of the existence of an a non domino disposition which may have been registered to found a prescriptive title by possession. It may be that the keeper requires the presenter of a non domino title to confirm that attempts have been made to contact the true owner, but if that happens it is on an informal basis only.

It is understood that this case may go to the House of Lords. If so it will be interesting to see what their Lordships make of it. In the meantime landowners should be vigilant lest there be a land rush based on all manner of queer goings on in the middle of the night designed to establish possession.

Tracing, Constructive Trusts and Unjustified Enrichment

Southern Cross Commodities Ltd v Martin, 1991 SLT 83

Parker Hood,
University of Edinburgh.

The constructive trust has been an underdeveloped doctrine in Scots law, but Mr Hood argues that its value has been demonstrated in at least one recent case.

The application of the constructive trust in Scotland is somewhat uncertain. This has prompted one writer to remark that, whilst the constructive trust is part of Scots law in principle, it is rarely used in practice: see Gretton, "Unjust Enrichment in Scotland" [1991] JBL 108. Part of the reason for this uncertainty appears to be that Scotland has had a long standing system of unjustified enrichment, which has been used to deal with matters that, in England (which does not have such a long standing tradition), would be dealt with by constructive trusts — most notably the "knowing receipt" category of constructive trust, concerned with liability for, inter alia, knowingly receiving trust money, or money the subject of a fiduciary obligation, in breach of fiduciary duty for a person's own benefit: see for example, *Agip (Africa) Ltd v Jackson* [1990] Ch 265 (this point was not discussed on appeal: see [1991] Ch 547).

In Scots law, such a matter would be dealt with as a claim for unjustified enrichment (either in

recompense or repetition), and may involve issues of indirect enrichment: on this last matter, see Niall R Whitty, "Indirect Enrichment in Scots Law", 1994 JR 200, and Pt II in 1994 JR Pt 3, and Scottish Law Commission Discussion Paper No 95, "Recovery of Benefits Conferred Under Error of Law", Vol 1, at paras 3.118-123 on pp 181-186. This approach, based on unjustified enrichment rather than constructive trusts, has been approved by two noted English experts in the area: Professor Birks, in his article "Trusts in the Recovery of Misapplied Assets: Tracing, Trusts and Restitution", in E McKendrick (ed), *Commercial Aspects of Trusts and Fiduciary Obligations* (1992), chap 8; and the hon Mr Justice Millett, "Tracing the Proceeds of Fraud" (1991) 107 LQR 71, at p 82. Further, in Scots law, the constructive trust appears to have been confined, primarily, to cases of breach of fiduciary duty: the law concerning the application of constructive trusts in Scotland is set out in Wilson and Duncan, *Trusts, Trustees and Executors* (1978), at pp 78 et seq, and T B Smith's *Short Commentary on the Law of Scotland* at p 561.

Southern Cross Commodities

Where recovery of property which has been purchased with misappropriated money in breach of fiduciary duty is sought, it is first necessary to trace the money to the asset so purchased, and then to establish a valid cause of action — here, a claim for a constructive trust for breach of fiduciary duty — as tracing in itself does not allow recovery: on this last point, see Macdonald, "Restitution and Property Law", 1988 SLT (News) 81 at p 84; and Birks, supra, at p 157.

It is in this context — of the application of the constructive trust in relation to misapplied money in breach of fiduciary duty — that the fairly recent decision of Lord Milligan in *Southern Cross Commodities Property Ltd v Martin*, 1991 SLT 83, is of interest. The case, which was one of almost textbook averments, had all the hallmarks of an adventure novel, involving allegedly dishonest company officers in Australia, a Delaware corporation and land in Scotland; but, curiously, it has received very little attention in Scotland, although it has been referred to with approval in an English book on insolvency: see Rajani, "Equitable Assistance in the Search for Security" in Rajak (ed), *Insolvency Law: Theory & Practice* (1993), chap 2 at p 36.

Briefly stated, the case concerned a claim brought by an Australian private company (which had been wound up) and its liquidator against two officers of the company, who had allegedly misappropriated company money. It was contended that the individuals had breached their fiduciary duties and were constructive trustees with regard to the misapplied sums. These sums, it was said, had been channelled through a Delaware corporation, controlled by the two individuals, and used to purchase heritable property in Dunbartonshire, known as Arden House, in the name of the corporation (which was joined as a party).

The pursuers, by their court action, sought relief on three grounds. First, they sought a declarator that the pursuers were entitled to the heritable subjects. Secondly, the pursuers asked for an order that the title to the property be transferred to them. Thirdly, they required payment of the balance of the misapplied moneys (i e value surviving), after deducting the amount used to purchase the land.

In the course of his judgment, Lord Milligan, who accepted the submissions of the pursuers, laid down four relevant principles (at p 85A-D) relating to tracing and trust funds, which are of considerable importance and help to clarify the law:

(1) Where a person has mixed his own funds with trust funds, then the mixed funds are all treated as trust funds, except so far as that person can distinguish them.

(2) Where part of the mixed fund is used to acquire other property, that property, at the beneficiary's election, can be treated as trust property, at least up to the value of the trust's contribution to the mixed fund. (This, essentially, places the onus of proof on the trustee who has breached his duty to show which funds are his, but the problem of identification, discussed below, remains.)

(3) Where there is a dissipation of the balance of the mixed fund, the property acquired is to be treated as trust property, at least up to the value of the contribution of the trust property to the mixed fund.

(4) Where there is a wilful breach of trust, any profit on the property acquired accrues to the trust. (Cf the important recent Privy Council case of *Att Gen for Hong Kong v Reid* [1994] 1 AC 324, in which their Lordships advised that where a fiduciary had purchased heritable property in New Zealand, in breach of fiduciary duty, with money obtained through bribes in Hong Kong, the fiduciary was liable to pay the difference between the value of the property and the initial value, where the property had declined in value — the property being held on a constructive trust for the beneficiary.)

Applying these principles, Lord Milligan proceeded to pronounce (at p 85F-G) an interim

decree in the terms sought by the pursuers, referred to above, but superseded extract, pending the determination of a counterclaim in proceedings in England. His Lordship was not persuaded that questions of set off could be categorically excluded in relation to the interim decree for either the monetary sum or Arden House, having regard to his treating the Delaware corporation as, effectively, the first and second defenders jointly.

Contrast with the *Varsada* case

The *Southern Cross Commodities* case can be contrasted with another decision of Lord Milligan, also in 1990, which was not dissimilar, but in which a personal claim for value received was sought, rather than a constructive trust: *M & I Instrument Engineers Ltd v Varsada*, 1991 SLT 106.

In *Varsada*, V purchased a house for his mistress ("Mrs V"), in her name, for £42,140. He did so using money — £50,000 in cash — which he had tricked the pursuers into parting with on the false basis that he was the representative of a member of the Saudi Arabian Royal Family and that he was offering them the chance to invest in Saudi Arabia. Interestingly, after his release from prison, V went to live in the house, although it remained Mrs V's. In an action by the pursuers to recover the purchase price from Mrs V, Lord Milligan held (at p 109H-J) that, as Mrs V had benefited from someone else's fraud without giving any valuable consideration, she had to repay the £42,140 — there being no exception for bank notes or negotiable instruments. This decision is an application of the rule in *Clydesdale Bank v Paul* (1877) 4 R 626 and *Thomson v Clydesdale Bank* (1893) 20 R (HL) 59; [1893] AC 282, that a person cannot benefit from someone else's fraud, unless that person is both innocent of the fraud and gave valuable consideration. Whilst the *Varsada* case was categorised in the headnote as one of "restitution" (which, it is suggested, is a misapplication of the English term), it was probably a case of recompense, as Gretton, supra, at p 109, and the Law Commission paper, at para 3.8 (fn 3), note. (In relation to V, who was not worth suing, a claim could also have been brought in repetition: see *Royal Bank of Scotland plc v Watt*, 1991 SLT 138.)

Differences between the two cases

The most obvious difference is that, in the *Southern Cross Commodities* case, there was a proprietary claim for value surviving (Abden House and the remaining trust moneys) — although, arguably, a claim for recompense could have been brought, if it was thought worth doing; and in the *Varsada* case, it was a personal claim for value received: the purchase price of the house.

It is not known why the pursuers in *Varsada* did not want to claim the house: it may have been that the property had declined in value; or they did not want to go through the problems of selling it in a less than buoyant market; or they simply wanted their money back and felt that Mrs V was in a position to pay them.

Another possible difference was that in the *Southern Cross Commodities* case, the requisite fiduciary duty needed for a constructive trust was stronger than in the *Varsada* case. However, it is only necessary to have a fiduciary relationship at the outset; not every participant in the chain needs to be in a fiduciary relationship with the beneficiary: see *Re Diplock* [1948] Ch 465 (CA). And so, whilst Mrs V was not in a fiduciary relationship with the pursuers, it is strongly arguable that V was in such a relationship when he was "collecting" the money from the pursuers on the (albeit erroneous) basis that he would be investing it on their behalf in Saudi Arabia, as he was acting as their agent. It is possible for a person to be a fiduciary regarding part of their activities, but not others: see *New Zealand Netherlands Society "Oranje" Inc v Kuys* [1973] 1 WLR 1126, at p 1130, pcr Lord Wilberforce (PC). In this part of his activities, V was, it is suggested, a fiduciary to the pursuers — V was acting in a manner similar to a collecting bank (which is the agent of its customer), and was required to put the pursuers' interests ahead of his own (which he did not do). So, arguably, a constructive trust over the house could have been claimed, if desired.

Advantages/consequences of seeking a constructive trust

This difference in approach raises the question, why seek relief on the basis of constructive trust if a claim will lie in one of the categories of unjust enrichment? The trite answer is that where the defender is insolvent and there is an asset or fund over which a trust can be impressed (see Goode, *Principles of Corporate Insolvency Law*, at p 56), the pursuer (the beneficiary) will receive priority over any unsecured creditors — a priority which a personal claim in unjustified enrichment will not confer.

Normally, for a proprietary claim, or a claim involving a real right, over an asset to succeed, it needs to be an in specie one. In this connection, money poses a difficulty, as it is a fungible and cannot be the subject of a proprietary claim, unless it has been specifically earmarked and set

aside: see Bell's *Principles* (10th ed), at para 1333. And Scots law has not yet embraced the concept of the remedial constructive trust, based on unjustified enrichment, which confers a proprietary right over money. This concept is popular in the United States (*Re Barry* (1906) 147 Fed 208) and Canada (*Pettkus v Becker* (1980) 117 DLR (3d) 257 and *LAC Minerals Ltd v International Corona Resources Ltd* (1978) 61 DLR (4th) 14), and has crept into English law through the controversial decision in *Chase Manhattan Bank NA v Israel-British Bank (London) Ltd* [1981] Ch 105, a case which Macdonald argues does not apply in Scots law: see "Restitution and Property Law", supra. The case has also been criticised by Goff and Jones, *The Law of Restitution* (4th ed), at pp 131-132. (Cf *Re Goldcorp Exchange Ltd (In Receivership)* [1994] 3 WLR 199 (PC), at p 217, where the remedial constructive trust (or proprietary interest in unjustified enrichment) is referred to as "this important new branch of the law"; and at p 221, where the *Chase Manhattan* case, whilst not expressly approved of, is not disapproved of.)

However, as Burrows notes in his work, *The Law of Restitution*, at p 72, where there is a fund that can be traced, the courts have been sympathetic to the beneficiary and allowed him to follow the money into the offending fiduciary's bank account, under the principles elucidated by Lord Milligan earlier in this article; this is despite the fact that, technically, the money has not been earmarked or set aside and is an incorporeal moveable — being merely a book entry in the fiduciary's (current) account (unless the fiduciary has put the money in a specific account, which is unlikely), i e, it is suggested, it is something of a fiction.

Problems of identification of misapplied money

Nevertheless, the real difficulty for an aggrieved beneficiary will be not so much whether there is a right to trace and impose a constructive trust over the misapplied money, but, rather one of identification of the money — an asset purchased with the misapplied money poses less of a difficulty as it is readily identifiable. For example, if the fiduciary's bank account is overdrawn, there can be no tracing of the misappropriated money, and it does not matter whether the account was overdrawn at the time of each improper payment into it or whether the account subsequently became overdrawn, as there is now no fund to trace: see *Re Goldcorp Exchange Ltd (In Receivership)* and *Bishopgate Investment Management Ltd v Homan*, The Times, 14 July 1994.

Similarly, the operation of the rule in *Clayton's* case (*Devaynes v Noble* (1816) 1 Mer 572: see Burrows, supra at p 72) may present problems, particularly if there is a gap between the misappropriation and its discovery, as it could be argued that the misappropriated sum has been paid in and paid out, and that what is left in the account (which may be more or less than the misapplied sum) does not belong to the beneficiary, who would only have a personal claim along with other unsecured creditors. (Cf *Barlow Clowes International Ltd v Vaughan* [1992] 4 All ER 22, where it was held, in relation to a group of investors regarding a mixed fund in a bank account, that the rule in *Clayton's* case did not apply there, as it was intended to be a common investment fund, and the investors would share rateably in proportion to the amounts due to each investor; also, it was held that the rule will not apply where it would be impractical or lead to injustice.)

The most obvious problems, which are self evident, is if the fiduciary simply flees the jurisdiction with the money to a friendly country, or is hopelessly insolvent. Fortunately, none of these events appears to have occurred in the *Southern Cross Commodities* case.

Conclusion
The decision in *Southern Cross Commodities* shows that the constructive trust is still alive in Scotland. It provides guidance to pursuers (particularly liquidators) seeking to recover money, which has been misapplied in breach of fiduciary duty, and, not surprisingly, mixed with other moneys or used to purchase an asset. In view of the number of corporate collapses in recent years, amid allegations of misappropriation, the constructive trust, with its preliminary procedure of tracing, will continue to be a potent weapon. To this end, Lord Milligan is to be commended for clarifying and illuminating a somewhat obscure area of Scots law of significant practical importance.

NEWS

Appointments

Scottish Court Service
Michael Ewart, currently a deputy director of the Scottish Courts Administration, has been appointed chief executive of the new Scottish Court Service Agency following an open competition. Mr Ewart will take up appointment as chief executive designate from 1 September 1994 to lead the development of the new agency, which is to be launched on 3 April 1995. The appointment is for a four year term until September 1998.

Court

Greenock sheriff court
As of Monday, 8 August 1994, Greenock sheriff court has resumed its former location at Sheriff Court House, Nelson Street, Greenock. The new telephone number is 0475 787073.

New target waiting periods
Following consultation between the Government and the judiciary, the main targets for waiting periods for 1994-95 (the period between a trial or proof being requested or an appeal being received and the date assigned, expressed in weeks) are set out below. Similar targets applied in 1993-94 and national performance for that year is noted in the second column in the table.

	1993-94 Target	Performance
Criminal appeal business Summary prosecutions: Notes of appeal against sentence and stated cases (accused in custody)	4	4
Court of Session (a) Ordinary proofs	20	20
(b) Defended consistorial proofs	17	18
Sheriff courts (national average as at 31 March 1994) (a) Civil proofs/debates	12	11.6
(b) Summary criminal trials	12	15.2

In 1993-94 waiting periods of 12 weeks or less were achieved for civil debates/proofs in 81 per cent of sheriff courts.

Waiting periods of 12 weeks or less were achieved for summary criminal business in 72 per cent of sheriff courts.

Performance of individual sheriff courts at 31 March 1994 is set out in the table below.

Court	Civil proofs	(Weeks) Summary criminal trials
Hamilton	14	12
Glasgow	14	25
Inverness	13	11
Cupar	13	13
Dundee	13	16
Paisley	13	14
Dumbarton	12	10
Dunfermline	12	13
Peterhead	12	12
Stirling	12	12
Wick	12	12
Jedburgh	11	11
Kirkcudbright	11	11
Ayr	11	12
Kirkcaldy	11	11
Dingwall	10	10
Oban	10	11
Elgin	10	9
Haddington	10	13
Duns	10	10
Banff	10	10
Linlithgow	10	20
Stranraer	10	11
Falkirk	10	10
Forfar	10	10
Stornoway	10	10
Selkirk	10	10
Stonehaven	9	9
Dumfries	9	9
Peebles	9	10
Tain	9	10
Lanark	9	10
Arbroath	9	11
Aberdeen	9	13
Kilmarnock	9	16
Dunoon	8	8
Edinburgh	8	11
Alloa	8	8
Greenock	8	10
Perth	8	8
Portree	8	4
Rothesay	8	10
Airdrie	8	16
Lerwick	7	7
Campeltown	6	10
Dornoch	6	8
Lochmaddy	6	10
Fort William	6	14
Kirkwall	6	6

In addition, the sheriffs principal have agreed that sheriff court programmes should be designed to ensure that the number of trials adjourned due to lack of court time should not exceed 5 per cent of the total number set down, a target met in 83 per cent of sheriff courts.

Comparisons of the figures with those of 1992-93 shows that the performance standards in 1993-94 have been maintained. Twenty-two courts have reduced their waiting periods for summary criminal business since this time last year; 17 have increased and 10 remain the same. For civil proofs, 27 courts have reduced their waiting periods, 15 have increased and seven remain the same. This has been achieved against a growth rate in workload of 23.5 per cent for the Supreme Courts and 5.3 per cent for the sheriff courts.

◇

Witnesses with learning disabilities
A new explanatory leaflet for witnesses with learning disabilities, entitled "A Visit to Court", has been launched by the Crown Office and Procurator Fiscal Service.

The leaflet consists of cartoon style pictures, supplemented by short concise phrases, and symbols depicting key words. It informs witnesses with learning disabilities what they should expect to encounter from the moment they arrive in court, throughout the court proceedings, to the moment when the case ends and they depart. The last "frame" reassures witnesses that they can phone up next day to discover the outcome of their visit.

— ◇ —

Coming events

AIJA seminar
A seminar on current trends in cross border insolvency will be held from 30 September to 2 October 1994 in Windsor. For an application form please contact L Patterson, Bird Semple, Napier House, 27 Thistle Street, Edinburgh EH2 1BS.

— ◇ —

General

SSC Society
At the statutory meeting of the SSC Society held on 5 July 1994, Mrs Kathrine E C Mackie, partner of Gillam Mackie, SSC, was elected to serve as President of the society for the next three years, succeeding Mr A J Spencer Kennedy. The

other office bearers are Kenneth McGowan (*vice president*), Donald I S Reid (*treasurer*), Alistair R Brownlie (*secretary*), Ishbel J D McLaren (*librarian*), James A McGoogan (*fiscal*) and James T Aitken (*assistant secretary — social*). Council members are Robert Shiels, Alistair Duff, Denis Coffield, Mrs Margaret Neilson, Douglas Millar and John MacDonald.

The following have been recently admitted to membership of the society: Paul Burns, George Jamieson, Robert McCormack, Alistair McGregor, Michael McSherry, George More, Francis Mulholland, Francis Norton, Adrian Smith, Katrina Turner, James Taylor, Allan Crawford, Richard Godden, Richard Lobjoie, Lindy Patterson, George Pollock, Francis D'Ambrosio, Derek de Mayne Beaumont, Archibald MacCalman, John McMurdo, Leonard Murray, Lexy Plumtree, Donald Wright and Amanda Young.

◇

Observer National Mooting Competition

A team from Edinburgh University Law Faculty has won the Observer National Mooting Competition. The team of Ranald McPherson, senior counsel, and Holly Gunning, junior counsel, successfully negotiated five rounds of the competition, defeating teams from the University of Durham, Queen's University, Belfast, and Queen Mary and Westfield College, London, before defeating a team from Thames Valley University in the final. This is the first time that any Scottish team has won this competition. The achievement is particularly impressive since in all but one of the rounds concerned the problem mooted was one of English law. Edinburgh's victory means that next year's final will be arranged and hosted by Edinburgh University.

— ◇ —

Taxation

Income tax: self assessment

The Inland Revenue have published "Self Assessment — The New Current Year Basis of Assessment: A Guide for Inland Revenue Officers and Tax Practitioners", the first in a series of guides for taxpayers and practitioners which will explain the key features of the new system.

Tax offices will shortly be sending a free copy of the guide to each local tax practice they deal with. Extra copies — on paper or disk — can be ordered at £3 a copy from the Inland Revenue Library, Mid-Basement, Somerset House, Strand, London WC2R 1LB.

◇

Income tax: profit related pay

The Inland Revenue have published an extra-statutory concession relating to the treatment of "extraordinary items" in profit and loss accounts drawn up for the purposes of the tax relief for profit related pay. The text of the concession reads:

Under Sched 8 to the Income and Corporation Taxes Act 1988 a registrable profit related pay (PRP) scheme must provide for the preparation of a profit and loss account, drawn up in accordance with Sched 4 to the Companies Act 1985, for each profit period of the employment unit to be covered by the scheme. The Schedule also provides that, in preparing a profit and loss account for those purposes, certain items (including various categories of "extraordinary" items — para 19 (6) (g) to (k) of Sched 8 to the Income and Corporation Taxes Act 1988) may be either left out of account or taken into account, notwithstanding the requirements of Sched 4 to the Companies Act.

Notwithstanding the replacement of Statement of Standard Accounting Practice 6 (SSAP 6) by Financial Reporting Standard 3, the Inland Revenue will, by concession, be prepared to accept that items which might properly have been accounted for as "extraordinary" within the definition provided by SSAP 6 may continue to be taken into account, or left out of account, for the specific purposes of the PRP legislation, provided that the rules of the scheme specifically permit the items to be treated in that way.

This concession will apply to PRP profit and loss accounts for accounting periods ending on or after 22 June 1993.

◇

Charities: tax treatment of lotteries

The Paymaster General has announced that the Government intend to introduce legislation in the next Finance Bill to exempt from tax the income of lotteries run by charities. This follows advice that the current treatment by the Inland Revenue of income from a lottery operated by a subsidiary company on behalf of a charity, and covenanted to the charity, is incorrect where the lottery is a society lottery organised under s 5 of the Lotteries and Amusements Act 1976.

Income from small lotteries under s 3 of the Lotteries and Amusements Act 1976 will also be exempted.

Until the exemption comes into force the Inland Revenue will grant relief from tax on such income on a concessional basis.

Inquiries about the effect of the proposed

changes should be made, for charities in Scotland, to FICO (Scotland), Trinity Park House, South Trinity Road, Edinburgh EH5 3SD (tel 031-551 8643).

◇

Shares valuation

The Inland Revenue have published a leaflet explaining the work of the Shares Valuation Division (SVD), the part of the Capital Taxes Office which is responsible for the valuation of unquoted shares for tax purposes. The leaflet is available free of charge from tax inquiry centres and tax offices, and from the Capital Taxes Office.

◇

Corporation tax: small companies' relief

The Inland Revenue have published a statement of practice (SP 5/94) concerning holding companies and the corporation tax associated companies' rule for small companies' rate relief.

The statement sets out general circumstances in which companies which do no more than hold shares in one or more companies, all of which are 51 per cent subsidiaries of the holding company, are disregarded. It is, however, always open to a holding company whose circumstances do not fall within the terms of the statement to argue that, on the facts, it should also be disregarded. The statement reads:

Under s 13 (4) of the Income and Corporation Taxes Act 1988, a company which does not carry on any trade or business in an accounting period is disregarded in calculating the profits limits for the small companies' relief of any other company with which it is associated.

A holding company which does not carry on a trade, but which holds the shares in one or more companies which are its 51 per cent subsidiaries, may or may not be carrying on a business in respect of that holding. The Inland Revenue's view is that a company is not carrying on such a business in an accounting period if, throughout that period, *all* of the following apply: it has no assets other than shares in companies which are its 51 per cent subsidiaries; and it is not entitled to a deduction, as charges or management expenses, in respect of any outgoing; and it has no income or gains other than dividends which it has distributed in full to its shareholders and which are, or could be, the subject of a group income election under s 247 (1), or are foreign income dividends.

◇

Inland Revenue information powers: inquiry

The Government have announced the setting up of an independent inquiry into the Inland Revenue's power to call for the papers of tax accountants. Mr Philip Ely, a former President of the Law Society (of England and Wales), has been appointed with the following terms of reference: "To inquire into the power under s 20A of the Taxes Management Act 1970 of the Board of Inland Revenue to call for the papers of tax accountants; to consider in the light of developments since the report of the Keith Committee on Enforcement Powers of the Revenue Departments (Cmnd 8822) whether this power is suited to its purpose having regard to the need to ensure compliance with the law whilst respecting, as far as possible, client confidentiality; and to make recommendations, reporting by 17 October 1994."

Representations should be sent as soon as possible to Philip T Ely Esq, Paris Smith & Randall, Lansdowne House, Castle Lane, Southampton SO9 4FD.

◇

Double taxation
Spain
An exchange of notes has taken place with Spain amending the double taxation convention. The text will be published in due course.

United States
Regulations (SI 1994/1418) came into force on 16 June 1994 updating the rules relating to the UK taxation of dividends from United States sources.

— ◇ —

Obituary

On 14 July 1994, Ian Campbell MacArthur, DFC, WS, formerly senior partner in the firm of Messrs MacArthur & Co, solicitors, Inverness.

— ◇ —

Business changes

Messrs Carswell Kerr Mackay & Boyd, solicitors, Glasgow, intimate that, with effect from 29 July 1994, David M D Whyte has ceased to be a partner in the firm, and Alistair Macinnes, the remaining partner, intimates that, with effect from 1 August 1994, the practices of Messrs Carswell Kerr Mackay & Boyd and Messrs McLeish Thomson & Co, solicitors, Glasgow, have amalgamated. The firm name is now McLeish Carswell and the practice operates from 29 St Vincent Place, Glasgow G1 2DT (DX GW172). Telephone numbers are unchanged.

The partners are Miss Anne F Wilson and Kenneth B MacRae; consultants are Alexander Donaldson, Alistair Macinnes and Thomas A S Herd, and David G Robertson continues as assistant.

David M D Whyte, solicitor, Glasgow, intimates that following on the dissolution of Messrs Carswell Kerr Mackay & Boyd, solicitors, 50 Wellington Street, Glasgow G2 6EL (of which he has been one of the two constituent partners) on 29 July 1994, he has resumed practice on his own account with effect from 1 August 1994 at 147 Bath Street, Glasgow G2 4SQ (tel 041-221 4471; fax 041-221 3046; DX512400).

Dorman Jeffrey & Co, solicitors, Edinburgh, intimate that with effect from 1 July 1994 Douglas M Black, WS, and their associate Lorna A Sibbald have been assumed as partners in the firm. They also intimate that their assistant Susan A Hamilton has been appointed an associate.

Gardiner & Noble, solicitors, Ayr, intimate that with effect from 25 July 1994, they have moved to new premises at 25 Barns Street, Ayr KA7 1XB. The telephone number, fax number and DX number remain unchanged.

— ◊ —

Parliamentary News

Royal Assent

21 July 1994

Appropriation Act 1994 (c 24).
Land Drainage Act 1994 (c 25).
Trade Marks Act 1994 (c 26).
Inshore Fishing (Scotland) Act 1994 (c 27).
Merchant Shipping (Salvage and Pollution) Act 1994 (c 28).
Police and Magistrates' Courts Act 1994 (c 29).
Education Act 1994 (c 30).
Firearms (Amendment) Act 1994 (c 31).

New Bills

HOUSE OF COMMONS

13 July 1994

Data Protection—To make further provision for the retention, registration, use and disclosure of automatically processed information relating to individuals; to regulate the provision of services in respect of such information; to provide for a Data Protection Commissioner and a Data Protection Tribunal; to replace the Data Protection Act 1984; and for connected purposes. (Private Member's Bill introduced by Mr Harry Cohen)

War Pensioners (Equal Rights)—To review the effect of differential treatment of war disablement and war widow pensioners by local authorities; to bring forward means for equal treatment; and for connected purposes. (Private Member's Bill introduced by Mr Simon Hughes)

14 July 1994

Civil Rights (Disabled Persons) (Wales)—To prohibit in Wales, discrimination against disabled persons on the grounds of their disability; and for connected purposes. (Private Member's Bill introduced by Mr Barry Jones)

18 July 1994

Consolidated Fund (Appropriations)—To apply certain funds out of the Consolidated Fund to the service of the year ending on 31 March 1995. (Government)

19 July 1994

Civil Rights (Disabled Persons) (Northern Ireland)—To prohibit in Northern Ireland, discrimination against disabled persons on the grounds of their disability; and for connected purposes. (Private Member's Bill introduced by Rev Martin Smyth)

Control of Car Boot Sales—To regulate the holding of certain occasional sales; and for connected purposes. (Private Member's Bill introduced by Mr William Cash)

Environmental Claims—To prevent the making of false or unsupported environmental claims and similar claims relating to animal welfare in relation to goods or services; and for connected purposes. (Private Member's Bill introduced by Mr Alan Keen)

European Communities (Community Law)—To provide for the application of Community law within the United Kingdom to be supervised by Parliament. (Private Member's Bill introduced by Mr Bernard Jenkin)

20 July 1994

Civil Rights (Disabled Persons) Scotland—To prohibit in Scotland, discrimination against disabled persons on the ground of their disability; and for connected purposes. (Private Member's Bill introduced by Mr Gordon McMaster)

Progress of Bills

Drug Trafficking — Lords: third reading, 18 July 1994.

Criminal Justice and Public Order — Lords: third reading, 19 July 1994.

Sale of Supply of Goods — Lords: second reading, 22 July 1994.

European Union (Accessions) — Lords: second reading, 25 July 1994.

Marriage — Lords: second reading, 25 July 1994.

Questions answered

HOUSE OF COMMONS

12 July 1994

RESIDENCE QUALIFICATION

Mr Churchill: To ask the Secretary of State for Social Security for what reasons foreigners entering the United Kingdom immediately qualify for social security benefits; which other EC countries have a similar policy; and if he will now take steps to amend the recent United Kingdom situation so as to require a minimum of six months' residence to qualify for benefit.

Mr Burt: In general, income support, housing benefit and council tax benefit are not available to people who come from outside the European Economic Area. My right hon friend the Secretary of State announced yesterday new regulations which will reduce eligibility further. From 1 August claimants to these benefits will have to satisfy a habitual residence test, unless they are workers, refugees or given exceptional leave to remain in this country. The qualifying conditions for other social security benefits vary but are usually dependent on a contribution condition. Eligibility conditions for income related safety net benefits in other EEA countries vary widely, but most have a residence condition. The changes announced by my right hon Friend the Secretary of State, yesterday bring us into line with them.

13 July 1994

MONEY LAUNDERING

Mr Spellar: To ask the Secretary of State for the Home Department what arrangements have been made with the Governments of the Isle of Man and Jersey to harmonise procedures to prevent money laundering.

Mr Peter Lloyd: The Isle of Man and Jersey — and Guernsey — have all endorsed the 40 recommendations of the financial action task force against money laundering, established at the G7 summit in Paris in 1989, and have formally agreed to undergo an evaluation exercise, similar to that carried out by the task force in the United Kingdom in 1992, which will submit their anti-money-laundering systems to a thorough examination. They have all also issued anti-money-laundering notes for guidance to their financial institutions, similar to those issued in the United Kingdom. In addition, all three have criminalised drug money laundering in legislation modelled on the Drug Trafficking Offences Act 1986.

15 July 1994

PLANNING

Mr Kynoch: To ask the Secretary of State for Scotland when he plans to publish his consultation paper on the review of the Scottish planning system; and if he will make a statement.

Mr Lang: I have today published a consultation paper on the review of the Scottish planning system. Copies will be placed in the House Libraries.

Under the banner of the citizens charter, my general aim is to stimulate discussion on ways in which the effectiveness, efficiency and responsiveness of the system can be improved. This is the first step in a wide ranging review which will help to set the agenda for the development of the planning system in the years ahead.

The review will not address the underlying structure of the present system or the Government's proposals for local government reform in Scotland; its focus will be on matters of procedure and practice. In that context, my specific aim is to assess the adequacy of the decision making process in terms of its openness, fairness, consistency, speed and accountability to all interests; the extent to which current procedures help or hinder that process; the degree to which development plans and development control promote development and conservation objectives and in so doing add to the quality of the natural and built environment; and the adequacy of the arrangements for monitoring the decision making process and for measuring the achievement of objectives, targets and standards of service.

The consultation paper poses a number of questions to assist those who may wish to comment. However, there is no pre-determined agenda; the Government will welcome comments on any aspects of the system. Thereafter the outcome will be made public, and the Government will indicate how it proposes to take matters forward.

I should make it clear that no significant changes will be introduced until after the reorganised authorities are firmly in place. However, the review is designed to pave the way for any longer term changes that may be necessary to achieve the high standards now set by the Citizens' Charter. That means a more responsive and efficient system to give the public, developers and Government alike confidence in the plan making and decision making process, in the quality of the outcomes, and in the standard of service that is being provided.

19 July 1994

PRISON RULES

Mr Kynoch: To ask the Secretary of State for Scotland when he will introduce new rules for prisons and young offender institutions; and if he will make a statement.

Lord James Douglas-Hamilton: The new Prisons and Young Offenders Institutions (Scotland) Rules 1994, which were the subject of a wide ranging public consultation late last year, have been laid before this House today. They will come into force on 1 November. The revised rules not only pull together and update the Prison (Scotland) Rules 1952 and the Young Offenders (Scotland) Rules 1965, but also lift out of the old Prisons (Scotland) Standing Orders a number of matters which, because they concern prisoners' rights, more appropriately appear on the face of the rules so that they are subject to parliamentary and public scrutiny. They take account of the relevant European guidance, the European Convention on Human Rights and the European prison rules. They represent a fundamental and wide ranging overhaul of the rules governing the management of Scottish penal establishments, and are designed not merely to codify existing practice, but to introduce change.

The rules provide inter alia for the making of directions. While the latter have legislative force, they do not require to be formally laid before Parliament. Nevertheless, so that hon Members may see the detail of what is proposed, copies of the draft directions have been placed in the Library. In due course, the directions, like the rules, will be published.

21 July 1994

CRIMINAL INJURIES COMPENSATION

Mr Sheerman: To ask the Secretary of State for the Home Department what steps he is taking to ensure that the victims of violent crime will be given the right to appeal against decisions made under the reformed criminal injuries compensation scheme.

Mr Maclean: Applicants who are dissatisfied with the initial decision of the criminal injuries compensation authority have an unfettered right of appeal. The arrangements for considering appeals are described in paragraphs 32-37 of the White Paper "Compensating Victims of Violent Crime: Changes to the Criminal Injuries Compensating Scheme", Cm 2434.

Under these arrangements a dissatisfied applicant may request reconsideration of his case by the authority. This will be an internal review of the case conducted by a more senior member of the authority and may result in the original decision being confirmed, overturned or otherwise altered.

An applicant who remains dissatisfied after this review may appeal to an appeals panel. The panel, which is independent of the authority and Ministers, will be able to deal with the appeal on the papers or by offering the appellant an oral hearing at which he may present his case.

VAT

Mr Burns: To ask the Chancellor of the Exchequer when a fresh Treasury order will be laid before the House to update the payments on account scheme for VAT.

Mr Kenneth Clarke: The current annual cycle for the payments on account scheme runs from October to September. To avoid the timing difficulties caused by the move to a November Budget the scheme year will be realigned with the fiscal year to run from April to March.

The current scheme, which was intended to last for one year, will continue to the end of March 1995. The current VAT Payments on Account Order 1993 will therefore be replaced in time for the annual cycle beginning in April 1995.

This will mean that some business may be kept in the scheme for six months longer than expected, but the provisions for having payments reduced and for leaving the scheme where annual liability falls below £1.6 million will still apply in appropriate cases.

When the current order is replaced it will be amended to provide for automatic rolling forward of the scheme year in future without the need for a fresh statutory instrument.

Customs will conduct a review of the operation of the scheme. A consultation paper will be issued and all interested parties, including businesses in the scheme, will be offered the chance to participate in the consultation process.

The consultation paper will aim to address the concerns expressed by businesses about the scheme and to consider the scope for greater flexibility in its operation.

COUNCIL TAX

Mr Kynoch: To ask the Secretary of State for Scotland what proposals he has to make regulations which will prevent council tax payers from having to pay arrears of council tax when their property banding has been altered upwards due to an inaccuracy in the original list.

Mr Stewart: My right hon Friend proposes to make regulations later this year which will ensure that in future any increases in council tax banding resulting from the correction of an error in the original list will come into effect only from the date on which the list was altered.

Book Reviews

Nature Conservation Law

By Colin T Reid. 1994. Edinburgh: W Green. Paperback, £35. ISBN 0 414 00998 3.

While there are books which provide detailed coverage of particular areas of nature conservation law such as Howarth & Rodgers (eds), *Agriculture, Conservation and Land Use* (1992), and there are environmental law books which contain general introductory chapters on the subject, this is the first work to attempt a more comprehensive coverage and it is to be commended for that reason.

The author seeks to outline the legal framework of nature conservation law but does not attempt to deal with the practice or policy of nature conservation. While the task of studying the practice and policy of nature conservation would be considerable indeed, Colin Reid has undoubtedly made that task easier by producing this work.

The book deals with the law in Great Britain only: Northern Ireland is not covered for reasons of space despite the somewhat misleading statement by the publishers on the back cover that the author looks at the subject "from a United Kingdom perspective".

The work falls into three parts. The first part comprising chaps 1 and 2 covers the history and development of nature conservation law and the administrative structure of nature conservation. Chapter 1 includes interesting material on legal standing and legal approaches to nature conservation.

The second part (chaps 3-7), which forms the bulk of the book, contains the detailed provisions on the protection of species and wildlife habitats. Hunting and fishing provisions are dealt with in this part. The point of these provisions is that they are designed to ensure by means of, for example, close seasons that sufficient stocks of certain kinds of wildlife remain available for exploitation. While this may not be appealing to all conservationists, it has had the effect of conserving such species and accords with the contemporary rhetoric of sustainability. This part of the work concludes with a useful chapter, "European and International Aspects", which deals with measures including the Convention on International Trade in Endangered Species and the European Habitats and Species Directive.

Although the second part of the book is very thorough, it is at times little more than a catalogue of statutory provisions, as the author himself acknowledges in the preface. It is here that the reader begins to wish that Colin Reid had devoted himself in addition to considering the practice of nature conservation law. However, this criticism must be seen in the light of Colin Reid's very considerable achievement in bringing together in a readable form and explaining the diverse legislation relating to nature conservation.

The final part of the work deals effectively with a miscellany of provisions which impact on wildlife and the countryside, such as town and country planning, agricultural measures and pollution control measures.

Although the footnotes provide extensive references, a bibliography would have been a welcome feature to enable the reader to have easier access to the range of works referred to.

While a price of £35 may deter the potential student market, it is to be hoped that Colin Reid's very useful and interesting work will nonetheless encourage further study of this often neglected area of environmental law.

MARK POUSTIE,
University of Strathclyde.

ACT OF ADJOURNAL

ACT OF ADJOURNAL (CONSOLIDATION AMENDMENT) (MISCELLANEOUS) 1994

(SI 1994/1769) [1 JULY 1994]

The Lord Justice General, the Lord Justice Clerk, and the Lords Commissioners of Justiciary, under and by virtue of the powers conferred upon them by sections 282 and 457 of the Criminal Procedure (Scotland) Act 1975 (c 21), and of all other powers enabling them in that behalf, do hereby enact and declare:

Citation and commencement

1.—(1) This Act of Adjournal may be cited as the Act of Adjournal (Consolidation Amendment) (Miscellaneous) 1994 and shall come into force on 1st August 1994.

(2) This Act of Adjournal shall be inserted in the Books of Adjournal.

Amendment of Act of Adjournal (Consolidation) 1988

2.—(1) The Act of Adjournal (Consolidation) 1988 shall be amended in accordance with the following sub-paragraphs.

(2) In rule 73A (certificates in respect of documentary evidence)—

(a) in paragraph (1) (a) (ii), after the words "a person in" insert the words ", or who has been in,"; and

(b) in paragraph (1) (a) (iii), after the words "the person in" insert the words ", or who has been in,".

(3) In rule 122A (certificates in respect of documentary evidence)—

(a) after paragraph (1) (a) (i), omit the word "or";

(b) in paragraph (1) (a) (ii), after the words "a person in" insert the words ", or who has been in,"; and

(c) after paragraph (1) (a) (ii), for the word "and" substitute the word "or" and insert the following sub-paragraph:—

"(iii) the authorised representative of the person in, or who has been in, possession and control of the original of it or a copy of it; and".

(4) In Schedule 1, for Form 93 (form of certificate of authentication of document) substitute the form set out in the Schedule to this Act of Adjournal.

J A D HOPE, LORD JUSTICE GENERAL, *IPD*

SCHEDULE   Paragraph 2 (4)

FORM 93   **Rules 73A (1) and 122A (1)**

Form of certificate of authentication of document

I, (*insert name, address and title of office held*), being
the author
[*or*
the person in [*or* who was on (state when) in] possession and control]
[*or*
the authorised representative of (*insert name and address*) who [*or* which] is in [*or* who [*or* which] was on (state when) in] possession and control]
of
the original(s)
[*or*
a copy [*or* copies] of the original(s)]
[*or*
a copy [*or* copies] of a material part [*or* material parts] of the original(s)]
of the copy document [*or* documents listed and described below] on which this certificate is endorsed [*or* to which this certificate is attached]
hereby certify that
it is a true copy
[*or*
they are true copies]
of [*or* of part(s) of]
the original(s)
[*or*
the copy [*or* copies] of the original(s)]
[*or*
the copy [*or* copies] of the material part [*or* material parts] of the original(s)]
[of] which
I am the author
[*or*
is [*or* are] [*or* was] [*or* were] in my possession and control]
[*or*
is [*or* are] [*or* was] [*or* were] in the possession and control of (*name and address*) of whom [*or* which] I am the authorised representative].

Date: (*insert date*)   (*Signed*)
          (*Insert authorised capacity in which certificate signed*)

[*List and describe documents*]

ARTICLES

A Hooligan's Game — Played by Gentlemen

Alistair M Duff,
Henderson Boyd Jackson, WS,
Edinburgh.

In the first of his two articles Mr Duff criticises the inactivity of the prosecuting authorities in the face of violence on the rugby field, and describes a number of cases which featured a successful prosecution. In the second he collects the cases involving football and rugby players where a custodial sentence has been imposed.

This article will attempt to show that since the landmark case of *R v Billinghurst* [1978] Crim LR 553, in England, there has been a particular lack of criminal prosecutions for violent conduct on the rugby field and that it would appear that the appropriate sporting bodies, north and south of the border, have been left to regulate themselves and discipline players at their discretion. We will also very briefly look at the claims players could make under the Criminal Injuries Compensation Board and, from April 1994, the Criminal Injuries Compensation Authority.

The lack of action by the prosecuting authorities is primarily because the participants are not inclined to report the commission of offences to the police, yet of course it is open to other people to do so. Many players probably still accept the volenti non fit injuria argument and obviously it is in their hands to change this. The prosecuting authorities have never been keen to intervene.

It would certainly appear that players at the highest level of rugby are "above the law". The only convictions and prosecutions in Scotland have been concerned with club players where complaints have been made by the participants. The same is believed to be generally true in England.

Certainly players should accept the risks inherent in their sport, but they are not bound to accept the risk that fellow competitors might act in flagrant disregard of the rules and practice of their sport and commit assaults and other crimes. In any event consent is no defence to such actions: *Smart v HM Advocate*, 1975 SLT 65; 1975 JC 30. The difficulty of proving the necessary intent might have stopped assault charges being brought (see Gordon, *Criminal Law* (2nd ed), paras 29-30 and *Lord Advocate's Reference No 2 of 1992*, 1993 SLT 460 at p 464F-G; 1992 SCCR 960 at p 965D-F), but standing the five judge decision in *HM Advocate v Harris*, 1993 SLT 963; 1993 SCCR 559, charges along the lines of "reckless conduct causing injury" could be brought which would avoid having to prove such intent.

In England the judicial principles applying in the common law for criminal liability during sporting events were first stated in the case of *R v Bradshaw* (1878) 14 Cox CC 83. In this case the jury acquitted a footballer in a friendly game on a manslaughter charge which had arisen from the following circumstances: "Both players were running at considerable speed and on approaching each other the deceased kicked the ball beyond the prisoner and the prisoner, by way of charging the deceased, jumped in the air and struck him with his knee in the stomach. The two met, not directly but at an angle, and both fell. The prisoner got up unhurt but the deceased rose with difficulty and was led from the ground. He died next day after considerable suffering, the cause of death being a rupture of the intestine."

Bramwell LJ, in summing up the case to the jury, said: "The question for you to decide is whether the death of the deceased was caused by the unlawful act of the prisoner. There is no doubt that the prisoner has caused the death and the question is whether the act was unlawful. No rules of practice of any game whatever can make that lawful which is unlawful by the law of the land. . . . For instance, no persons can by agreement go out to fight with deadly weapons, doing by agreement what the law says shall not be done and thus shelter themselves from the consequences of their act. Therefore in one way you need not concern yourselves with the rules of football, but on the other hand, if a man is playing according to the rules of practice of the game and not going beyond it, it may be reasonable to infer that he is not actuated by any malicious motive or intention and that he is not acting in a manner which he knows will be likely to be productive of death or injury. But independent of the rules, if the prisoner intended to cause serious hurt to the deceased, or if he knew that, in charging as he did, he might produce serious injury and was indifferent and reckless as to whether he would produce serious injury or not, then the act would be unlawful. In either case he would be guilty of a criminal act and you must find him guilty."

Almost a century later, in the case of *R v Venna* [1976] QB 421, the court considered the mens rea for assault and whether recklessness was sufficient. The appellant was involved in a struggle with police officers who were attempting to arrest him. The appellant fell to the ground and then proceeded to lash out wildly with his legs. In doing so, he kicked the hand of one of the police officers, fracturing a bone. The appellant's story was that he was kicking out in an attempt to get up off the ground. The appellant was charged inter alia with assault occasioning actual bodily harm, contrary to s 47 of the Offences Against the Person Act 1861.

The judge directed the jury that they could find the appellant guilty if they found that he had lashed out with his feet "reckless as to who was there, not caring an iota as to whether he kicked somebody". The appellant was convicted and appealed. It was held by the appeal court that in order to secure the appellant's conviction on a charge of assault or battery it was not necessary to establish that he had kicked the police officer intentionally. The necessary mens rea was established by proof that he had done so recklessly.

The first rugby case to appear in England or Scotland was *R v Billinghurst*, supra, where in an off the ball incident Billinghurst punched the opposing scrum half in the face, fracturing his jaw in two places. The only issue in the case was consent. Evidence was given by the victim that on previous occasions he had been punched and had himself punched opponents on the rugby field and a defence witness, Mervyn Davies, a former Welsh rugby international player, stated that in the modern game of rugby, "punching is the rule rather than the exception"!

The judge directed the jury that rugby was a game of physical contact necessarily involving the use of force and that players are deemed to consent to force "of a kind which could reasonably be expected to happen during a game". He went on to direct them that a rugby player has no unlimited licence to use force and that "there must obviously be cases which cross the line of that to which a player is deemed to consent". The distinction which the jury might regard as decisive was that between force used in the course of play and force used outside the course of play. The judge told the jury that by their verdict they could set a standard for the future. The jury, by a majority of 11 to 1, convicted Billinghurst of inflicting grievous bodily harm. Billinghurst was treated as a man of previous good character and sentenced to nine months' imprisonment, suspended for two years. (No doubt he escaped actual imprisonment as this was stated to be the first case of its kind.)

In 1980 in the case of *R v Gingell* [1980] Crim LR 661, there was a prosecution against Gingell in Croydon Crown court for causing three fractures to the face of an opponent in a rugby tackle. An immediate custodial sentence of six months was imposed, but this was later reduced to two months by the Court of Appeal, because it was a first precedent. (See Edward Grayson, *Sport and the Law*, at p 135.) One might ask why he was not sentenced to a longer sentence as an exemplary sentence!

What is believed to be the first prosecution in Scotland for a rugby assault was reported in *The Scotsman* on 31 January 1980. Francis Vernall was fined £50 in Glasgow sheriff court after trial for assault by punching an opponent and breaking his jaw in two places. There had been a great deal of protest at the time by the victim's team, Glasgow University, who had been playing St Mungo's Academicals on 21 October 1978. After the incident the Academicals held an inquiry at the request of the university but wrote back saying they could see no justification for further action. The university were not satisfied and three months later the police charged Vernall.

This case has echoes of a later prosecution involving the Welsh international, David Bishop, who was sentenced in 1986. He punched an opponent on the ground, away from the ball, during a club match in South Wales and there was no move by his club to discipline him. The prosecuting authorities had no alternative but to proceed and the player pled guilty to a charge of common assault. The ultimate prison sentence of one month was varied on appeal by being suspended for one year. This was the first and is believed to be the only action against an international rugby player of the Home Unions.

Although he stands to be corrected, the writer has not come across any further prosecutions regarding international or top flight players; and despite recent incidents which it is thought could have given rise to prosecution, neither the Home Unions nor foreign boards seem to be policing matters internally. (Other prosecutions are described in the article following.)

In *The Scotsman* of 22 April 1978, it was reported that J McCluskey, QC (now Lord McCluskey), in May 1974 at the opening of the Biennial Congress of the European Union of Football Associations in Edinburgh, commented that wearing a football jersey did not put a person above the law. He commented that steps might have to be taken to curb football violence both on and off the field. He said that if it was an incident witnessed by thousands or even millions through television, unless the football authorities took effective steps to discipline the players to prevent such incidents, the time could come when those responsible for administering criminal law might have to step in. These comments would seem to apply equally to rugby. Notwithstanding these comments of almost 20 years ago, the prosecution authorities do not appear to be taking action despite the apparent increase in violence.

For example, (a) during the Wales/Scotland match of last season, Garin Jenkins threw punches at Derek Turnbull and despite the matter being reported to the South Wales police by an Edinburgh solicitor, there was no action; (b) during the All Blacks tour of Britain in 1993-94, Jamie Joseph committed alleged offences against Kyran Bracken and Philip De Glanville and again there was no action.

The 1993-94 season ended badly, culminating in the events in South Africa during June 1994 and obviously here it is the South African authorities who have failed to take the relevant action. The English player Jon Callard was kicked by the Eastern Province lock Elandre van der Bergh, who was duly sent off. In the same match Tim Rodber was sent off. The only action taken by the respective rugby authorities was to hold a disciplinary committee, which could hardly be said to be impartial. The result of the English hearing was that Rodber was not even banned for a game and the message which was apparently sent out by the rugby authorities involved appeared to be that they were not prepared to discipline players properly.

However, to be contrasted with this are two recent cases, one in England and one in Scotland, involving club players. In England, on 21 February 1994, Ian Russell, a Royal Navy training instructor, who had broken a civilian opponent's nose in six places during a match, was convicted of assault in what was believed to be the first occasion in which a military court martial dealt with such a case. Russell was given four months' detention and reduced in rank to able seaman. Both sentences were suspended for a year and he was ordered to pay £1,500 to the victim, Gary Curtis. The victim had reported the matter to the police, having been so severely injured by the punch and stamping that he needed two operations to repair the damage to his face. He said: "There are rules for the referee and there are what I call rules of the jungle, but that was so far beyond the rules of the jungle even. It was a horrible punch." (See *Sport and the Law Journal*, Vol 2, issue 1, Spring 1994.)

The Scottish case dealt with Scott McMillan, who was jailed for nine months for a head butt when he pled guilty at Haddington sheriff court on an amended indictment of assault to severe injury. The assault caused a bone injury in the victim's face which required surgical intervention

and the insertion of a metal plate. The sentence was upheld by the appeal court on 14 June 1994 (1994 GWD 26-1560). Temporary Sheriff Hamilton in his report to the High Court held that it was a deliberate assault off the ball and he commented: "It must be a rare occurrence to have a clear and accurate record of the commission of a crime. Such was the case here for a spectator at the match had been filming it and I was shown, as part of the presentation of the Crown, the narrative the recording made."

The sheriff held it was a premeditated attack resulting in severe injury and he said: "It would have been, in my opinion, altogether contrary to the public interest to have endorsed the view that because it had happened on the rugby field that made it less serious."

Lord Allanbridge, who sat with Lords Morison and MacLean said: "We have listened very carefully to all that has been said on behalf of the appellant. [Counsel] has put forward all that could be said on his behalf. We are quite satisfied that this was a case where the appellant ran forward in a rugby game and took a calculated and deliberate aim at another player whom he then head butted in the face, causing that player to suffer from the severe injuries which we have described. Such an assault is a very serious matter indeed whether or not it occurs in a rugby pitch or during any other such game. We fully endorse the decision of the sheriff to impose a custodial sentence in this case and we consider that he had little option but to do so in the public interest." (McMillan had one previous conviction for assault in June 1990 and had previously served a one year custodial sentence for offences involving dishonesty.)

The Criminal Injuries Compensation Board, which was created in 1964 to administer a compensations scheme for victims of violent crimes, do have jurisdiction to cover both field and crowd violence from sporting activities in appropriate circumstances. In their annual report there have been two specific mentions of sport as a separate item.

First, the CICB in their 16th report for the year ended 31 March 1980, at para 29, commented on referring to football violence: "Public attention has been focused recently upon the increasing pattern of mindless violence among both players and spectators . . . the phenomenon is not confined to professional soccer; amateur football, both association and rugby is by no means immune and there are disturbing signs that the cricket field has growing problems in this respect. . . . We are also getting more and more applications arising out of alleged crimes of violence on the field of play itself. There is little problem when there is a proved 'off the ball incident'. What raises far more difficulty is the alleged vicious or wild tackle. Here the alleged victim must prove either that there was an intention to injure him, as opposed to a mere over zealous desire to get the ball, or, and this is a very difficult matter in what is necessarily a heat of the moment situation, that the alleged assailant was guilty of recklessness within the meaning of *R v Venna* [1976] QB 421. . . . While there is now considerable public awareness of the existence and extent of football violence, we doubt whether the public is aware of the catastrophic effects which result in such criminal acts. The board frequently deals with cases of people scarred for life, sometimes with cases where people are seriously and permanently maimed and occasionally with cases of people who are killed. We welcome the efforts which the courts, the police and many sporting organisations are taking to attempt to lessen the number of such crimes."

The second and last mention by the CICB was in their 23rd report, for the year ended 31 March 1987. In para 37 under the heading "Violence connected with sport" they stated as follows: "In the last few years the board has received an increasing number of applications arising from violence among the players, particularly during rugby or football matches. A feature of applications from players is that in many such cases no report has been made to the police. Paragraph 6 (a) is a provision of the scheme which we have felt obliged to apply rigorously to applications by players who allege they were assaulted as opposed to being injured accidentally. In a sport in which bodily contact is a commonplace part of the game, the players consent to such contact even if, through unfortunate accident, injury, perhaps of a serious nature, may result. However, such players do not consent to being deliberately punched or kicked and such actions constitute an assault for which the board would award compensation. Assaults upon players bring the game into disrepute and the governing bodies of all such sports have made it plain that they intend to deal severely with offenders in such cases. It is extremely difficult for the board to decide whether a particular injury was caused by an assault as opposed to some negligent conduct, which may have constituted a foul, but would not be categorised as an assault by any reasonable person. It is all the more difficult since the events giving rise to such a claim are unlikely to be considered by a board member until long after the injury was sustained. We consider that it is in the interests of everyone that people who commit criminal offences on the playing fields should be prosecuted. Anyone who considers that an injury upon him was caused by a criminal offence, should draw the attention of the police to it. If he does not do so, he is unlikely to receive compensation from the board."

It would certainly appear that the board have shown the correct concern in the reports, but frankly, as has been stated already, it does not appear that players are reporting matters to the police, or indeed that the sporting authorities are dealing with matters sufficiently. Unfortunately the CICB do not keep relevant statistics for sporting awards as such, but certainly in Scotland it has been confirmed that over the last few years there have really only been a handful of such awards.

The old CICB, as of 1 April 1994, has become the Criminal Injuries Compensation Authority. Any claims lodged prior to that date will be dealt with by the old system but new claims will be dealt with under the new system. The general applicability to players has not changed, although the actual award of solatium is now based on a tariff system and there are now no awards made for wage loss.

In conclusion, following on from Lord McCluskey's words in 1974, it appears that especially at the highest level of the rugby game, the sporting bodies are not controlling their players and disciplining them accordingly. Surely criminal prosecutions should be brought in an effort to stop the violence which seems to be becoming more prevalent.

Postscript

Since the submission of the article at the beginning of July, there has been one high profile case concerning the prosecution of William Hardy in England arising out of the death of Seamus Lavelle. The prosecution for manslaughter against Mr Hardy, as reported in *The Times* of 12 July 1994, is believed to be the first of its kind after a death in the field of play during Rugby Union's 170 year history. Mr David Spence, prosecuting, said: "Towards the end of the match, Mr Hardy deliberately punched Mr Lavelle on the jaw. To use a boxing term it was an uppercut and impacted on the chin." The force of the blow caused Mr Lavelle, who was playing as a forward for Hendon, to lose consciousness. His knees buckled and as he fell backwards he was unable to prevent his head striking the ground. He died within two days.

William Hardy's defence was, as reported in

The Scotsman of 22 July 1994: "I threw a punch because I was receiving punches and thought I was likely to receive more. I did not mean to kill this man." Hardy stated he received two blows very close together from behind, which hit him on the back of his ear and he stated to the court: "I crouched and spun and threw a punch behind me. I thought I was going to get hit."

Stephen Batten, QC, defending, told the jury: "At the moment rugby does not have a very good name. We have seen on television thoroughly unpleasant moments and some people think it is high time something should be done about it, but there is a risk this case should be used to make an example. That would be wholly wrong." As reported in *The Scotsman* of 27 July, Hardy was acquitted.

Until full reports on this case are received, it can only be assumed that the jury accepted his defence of self defence, and in these circumstances the question of recklessness or intention it is thought would not come into it. It would obviously be interesting to look at the full case report when it is to hand.

An even more recent incident was reported in the press on Sunday, 24 July regarding the Springbok prop Johan Le Roux who blatantly bit the All Black captain, Sean Fitzpatrick's ear in a ruck. The South African management, having studied television pictures, sent Le Roux home in disgrace.

It was reported in *The Herald* on 26 July that the prop would be suspended until March 1996. The Rugby Union's judicial committee in Wellington, which handed down the suspension, said: "What Mr Le Roux did in this instance was clearly beyond anything that is acceptable on a rugby field."

It would appear that possibly because of the bad publicity rugby has been getting recently, action is, at long last, going to be taken in one form or another, but why not a criminal prosecution? — although the writer cannot comment on what is required in New Zealand for a prosecution for assault.

Summary of Criminal Prosecutions for Football and Rugby Violence

Culminating in Custodial Sentences

Alistair M Duff,
Henderson Boyd Jackson, WS,
Edinburgh.

It will be noted that all the football cases involve amateur players, and indeed all the rugby cases, with the exception of *R v Bishop*, involved club players. Interestingly enough, in all the cases, bar *Birkin* and *McMillan*, the accused appear to have been treated as people of good character — in essence, treated as first time offenders.

The football cases

There are five of these, which we shall deal with in chronological order:

(1) *R v Birkin* [1988] Crim LR 854. This arose out of an assault by one football player on another in an off the ball incident where the victim suffered a broken jaw. He was initially sentenced to eight months' imprisonment but the appeal court reduced this to six months, apparently taking into account the spur of the moment character of the offence. The appellant had been playing soccer when a member of the opposing team made a late tackle on him, which did not involve any direct violence. The appellant ran a few steps with the opponent after the tackle and then struck him a blow. (The appellant had several previous convictions including three for assault.)

(2) *R v Chapman* (1989) 11 Cr App R (S) 93. This case arose out of a Sunday football match. At the end of the day, after a jury trial, Chapman having pled guilty to unlawful wounding but not guilty to wounding with intent, the jury could not reach a verdict. He was sentenced on his original plea to 18 months' imprisonment in St Albans Crown court. On appeal this was reduced to 12 months to serve with the additional six months suspended. The victim had suffered a swelling and a laceration some three-four centimetres in length which required some five stitches.

(3) *R v Shervill* (1989) 11 Cr App R (S) 284. This incident arose out of a Sunday League football match in Swansea when the victim was kicked in the mouth whilst on the ground, requiring 13 stitches. The accused pled not guilty to wounding with intent, which was accepted by the court, but guilty to unlawful wounding. He was sentenced to six months' imprisonment at the

Crown court in Swansea. The appeal court reduced this to two months on the ground that it was an isolated incident. (It is not clear what is meant by this as in most of these cases the incident is an isolated case.)

(4) *R v Lincoln* (1990) 12 Cr App R (S) 250. This case arose out of an amateur football match between Hollingbury Old Boys and American Express Reserves. The appellant was convicted of assault occasioning actual bodily harm after a three day jury trial in Lewes Crown court. In the course of the match he struck an opposing player, fracturing the victim's jaw in two places. The victim required to have his jaw wired for six and a half weeks. The appellant was sentenced to four months' imprisonment but the appeal court reduced this to 28 days. As part of his plea of mitigation it was stated that only one blow was struck and it was on the spur of the moment and no doubt in the heat of the moment, and this appears to have been accepted by the appeal court.

(5) *R v Davies* [1991] Crim LR 70. The accused pled guilty to assault occasioning actually bodily harm during a soccer match. Matters became heated and a player on the opposing side came into collision with a player on the appellant's side. While the opposing player who had been involved in the collision was waiting for the subsequent free kick to be taken the appellant ran up and aimed a fist blow at his face which caused him to fall to the ground. The victim was later found to be suffering a fractured cheekbone which required an operation, and was absent from work for two weeks. A sentence of six months' imprisonment was imposed and, on appeal, the sentence was upheld. The appeal court considered that the blow struck in the present case did not arise out of the course of play, as did the blow in *Shervill*, and the appellant in that case admitted his responsibility when first interviewed by the police, whereas in this case the appellant denied striking the victim when first interviewed.

The rugby cases
(1) *R v Billinghurst* [1978] Crim LR 553. This is fully described in the article above at p 278.

(2) *R v Gingell* [1980] Crim LR 661; (1980) 2 Cr App R (S) 198. This is described in the article above at p 278.

(3) *R v Bishop*, 1986, unreported. See the article above at p 278.

(4) *R v Johnson* (1986) 8 Cr App R (S) 344. In this case at Cardiff Crown court the accused was charged with wounding with intent arising out of biting the lower lobe of an opposing player's ear,

tearing part of it away. This arose during a rugby match between two police teams (!), South Wales Police and Newport Police. The jury convicted him despite his defence at the trial that he was wearing a gumshield and it was not him! He was sentenced to six months' imprisonment and, on appeal, this was upheld.

(5) *R v Lloyd* [1989] Crim LR 513; (1989) 11 Cr App R (S) 36. This case involved a rugby match between Bishopton Rugby Football Club and Dings Crusaders and was heard at the Crown court in Bristol. The jury convicted the appellant of causing grievous bodily harm with intent. The injury suffered was caused by a kick resulting in a fractured cheekbone and the victim had to spend four days in hospital. The appellant was sentenced to 18 months' imprisonment and the appeal court upheld this. They seemed to be swayed by the fact that what the appellant did had nothing to do with rugby football and had nothing to do with the play in progress. They accepted the recorder's description that the blow was a vicious, barbaric act.

(6) *Ian Russell*, court martial, 21 February 1994, unreported. This is described in the article above at p 279.

(7) *McMillan v HM Advocate*, High Court of Justiciary appeal court, 14 June 1994, unreported (1994 GWD 26-1560). See the article above at p 279.

Ancient Legal Ban on Football in Scotland

Gordon M MacKay, FRCS,
and Archibald A McConnell, MRCPath,
Inverclyde Royal Hospital,
Greenock.

Two doctors raise another and (we hope) tongue in cheek matter of legal concern on the sporting field.

Following the recent increase in litigation in sport, and in particular football, we, as doctors with a passionate interest in sports medicine, are writing to you in fear and trepidation, as a consequence of our recent discovery while perusing some old Scots Acts of Parliament, in the second revised edition of *The Acts of the Parliament of Scotland, 1424-1707*, published by HMSO (1966).

But first it is necessary to explain the historical

background. In the early 15th century it seems that the youth of the nation were more interested in playing football than in practising more important skills such as archery, with the consequence that King James I arranged for an Act of Parliament banning football to be passed by the Parliament of Scotland at Perth on 26 May 1424, which was only a few days after he had been crowned at Scone on 21 May 1424. Perhaps the recent defeat of a large Scottish army at Hamildon Hill (in 1402) in Northumberland by Harry Percy, known as Hotspur (perhaps a portent of future football fame!) had made archery more immediately important than football. That football was indeed very popular amongst Scots youth is evidenced by the fact that just before the Battle at Beaugé (located between Tours and Angers) in 1421, at which the Earl of Buchan with a Scots army of 7,000 men defeated an English army and thus helped create the French nation with all that this implies for international football, the Scots indulged in a pre-battle game of football. There is no record of the score but it is assumed that the Scots fought with extra valour since they were aggravated by the interruption of their favourite sport.

The period following the return of James I from captivity in England saw the beginning of the practical statute law of Scotland, and one of the most important features of his law reforms

was that he ordered the laws to be promulgated in the vulgar tongue. The passage of 570 years means that it is necessary to provide a modern version of the Act which caused such consternation:

"Act 18. Of playing at the football.

"Item. it is decreed that the king forbids that any man [lit no man] play at the football under the penalty of four pence. to be summonsed to [appear before] the lord of the land as often as [i e every time] he is convicted, or to the sheriff of the land or his ministers if the lords will not punish such trespassers."

Ignorantia iuris neminem excusat, but since there is no requirement for mens rea in the statute and since the statute may be regarded as regulating the day to day functioning of society, then it is likely that the offence does not require mens rea but only actus reus.

Thus, as simple and probably underinsured medical doctors, while attempting to avoid the offside trap of negligence, we may be guilty of the handball offence of aiding and abetting criminal activities as specified in the above Act. It may only be the shinguards of desuetude which protect us from the criminal law. Can anyone set our minds at ease by proving that this Act has been repealed?

◆

NEWS

Appointments

Heriot-Watt University
Victor Craig, senior lecturer in industrial law at Heriot-Watt Business School, has been appointed to a personal professorship in the Department of Business Organisation.

— ◇ —

Court

Court of Session: practice note
No 10 of 1994 (12 August 1994): Revocations
The following practice notes are hereby revoked with effect from 5 September 1994:

No 3 of 1976 (signeting of summonses)

27 March 1986 (procedure for minutes of amendment).

— ◇ —

Coming events

Pensions law seminar
Stuart James, currently chairman of the Association of Pension Lawyers, will speak at a seminar held by the association's Scottish Group on the white paper, *Security, Equality, Choice: The Future for Pensions,* published in June. The legislation which will implement the white paper proposals will have major implications for the whole of the pensions industry in the UK. The seminar takes place on Monday, 12 September 1994 at 3.45 for 4.15 pm in the Copthorne hotel, Glasgow. The cost will be £10 for non-members. For members, there is no charge. Bookings should be addressed to Colin Browning, Scottish Life Assurance Co, 19 St Andrew Square, Edinburgh EH2 1YE.

— ◇ —

Taxation

Income tax: company cars
Legislation is to be introduced to counter tax avoidance by the availability of a cash alternative to a car: see Parliamentary News, below.

◇

Capital allowances: time limits for notification of expenditure
The Inland Revenue have issued a statement of practice (SP 6/94) which explains the general criteria the Board of Inland Revenue will apply in exercising their power under s 118 (5) of the Finance Act 1994 to extend the time limits for notification of expenditure on machinery and plant, contained in s 118 (3) and (4). Copies of the statement are available by sending a s a e to the Public Inquiry Room, West Wing, Somerset House, Strand, London WC2R 1LB.

◇

Corporation tax: Pay and File
The Inland Revenue have produced a new return form for companies to complete under the Pay and File system for assessing and collecting corporation tax. The new form CT200 (1994) will be issued about one month after the end of the company's accounting period. The form for making amended returns, form CT201, is also available.

Guidelines for production of substitute forms CT200 (1994) are available from Corporate Communications Office, Room 9/3A, North West Wing, Bush House, Aldwych, London WC2B 4PP, to whom applications for approval of such forms should be sent.

◇

Enterprise Investment Scheme: approved investment funds
The Inland Revenue have published guidelines which set out the principal criteria used in deciding whether to approve an investment fund for the purposes of tax relief under the Enterprise Investment Scheme. The guidelines also cover the procedures a fund manager should follow when applying for approval. They help ensure that the approval of investment funds is undertaken efficiently and consistently. The guidelines are available by application in writing to Brian Lodde, Inland Revenue, Company Tax Division, Room M22, West Wing, Somerset House, London WC2R 1LB (tel 071-438 6713; fax 071-438 6148).

— ◇ —

Business change

Peacock Johnston, solicitors, Glasgow and Beith, intimate that their assistant, Andrew S Pollock, has been assumed as a partner of the firm with effect from 1 July 1994.

— ◇ —

Parliamentary News

Questions answered
HOUSE OF COMMONS

21 July 1994

COMPANY CARS
Mr Burns: To ask the Chancellor of the Exchequer what is the practice of the Inland Revenue on the tax treatment of the offer of a cash alternative to a company car.

Mr Kenneth Clarke: Where an employee has a company car available for private use he or she is usually taxed on the benefit of the car. The employer pays class 1A national insurance contributions on the benefit.

However, a judgment by the House of Lords in 1969 means that in some circumstances, where the benefit of a car is freely convertible into cash, the benefit is taxable under the general income tax rules rather than the special provisions for company cars. In these special circumstances the employee pays tax on the cash which he or she could get, and the employer does not pay national insurance contributions.

Some employers are making arrangements designed specifically to bring company cars within the terms of this judgment to avoid Class 1A NICs and, in some cases, give a lower tax charge.

In order to remove further uncertainty and to prevent loss of revenues to the Exchequer and national insurance fund we intend to propose legislation in the next Finance Bill. The proposed legislation will ensure that where a car would otherwise be within the special income tax rules for company cars, and an alternative to the benefit of that car is offered, the mere fact that the alternative is offered will not make the benefit of the car chargeable to tax under the general income tax rules. The employee will then pay tax on what they actually get — car or cash. Employers will pay national insurance contributions as appropriate — class 1A on the benefit of a car or class 1 on cash.

We intend that this provision should apply from 6 April 1995.

ARTICLES

The Role of the District Court Clerk

June Hyslop,
Lecturer in Law,
University of Paisley.

Ms Hyslop discusses the scope of the duties and responsibilities of the district court clerk in the light of various decisions concerning the clerk's role.

District court clerks have a central role in the administration of lay justice, yet it can be argued that they are the Cinderellas of the criminal justice system. Very little has been written about what clerks actually do. The principal legislation is largely silent on what is involved, as are the standard legal textbooks. They have attracted little judicial attention, although during 1993 there were two cases which turned the spotlight on clerks and, in particular, their relationship with lay magistrates.

Until recently district court clerks received a fairly rudimentary training in addition to their degree and diploma studies despite the fact that many of them start off relatively inexperienced in criminal law (Bankowski, Hutton and McManus, *Lay Justice?*, pp 137-138). Training meant a short course coupled with several visits to court with a more experienced colleague before being thrown in at the deep end. However, that situation is changing and there is now increased recognition of the need for more formal training. In 1993 Napier University introduced a pilot distance learning course for clerks. The postgraduate certificate in district court practice and procedure is run by the Department of Accounting and Law on a modular basis over one academic year. To a large extent the course relies on written material prepared by Napier staff and a working party of practising district court clerks. Students are continuously assessed by submitting written coursework. They also sit an exam and undergo a workplace assessment. The first intake of students graduated this summer. This should lead to greater recognition of the work of district court clerks and a greater understanding of what they do. The clerks need to be skilled and effective court practitioners yet court work may make up a fairly small percentage of their total workload.

The clerk of court
The legally qualified clerk acts as both a check and a balance to the justice of the peace: a check on illegality by ensuring the law is observed and applied; a balance to the lay element provided by their legal knowledge and legal training.

The District Courts (Scotland) Act 1975 provides that it is the job of the local authority to appoint and employ "an officer to act as clerk of the district court for their area who shall also act as legal assessor in that court" (s 7). This includes the employment of depute clerks. Clerks can be full time or part time employees. In some areas there may be a number of clerks who attend the court on a rota basis, whilst in others one or two people have this responsibility. Some prefer to call themselves assessors rather than clerks. The Act does not make the distinction clear but in practice both roles are usually carried out by the same person. Clerking involves administering and organising the court and its business, whilst assessing relates to the provision of legal advice. In some courts both will be done by the same person whilst in others the tasks will be split. As the 1975 Act does not spell out in detail what the clerk actually does, the job is mainly a matter of common law and, it is submitted, common sense.

The silent partner?
The term "silent partner" is used in *Lay Justice?* (supra, at p 127) to describe the role of the clerk. However, that very much depends on the particular clerk of court. Some take a more active role in the proceedings than others. To a large extent it depends on the individual clerk, on the individual justice and on the working relationship between the two. It can depend on how experienced the justice is, or on the nature of the business before the court. A justice may rely more on the clerk when dealing with something for the first time. It can depend on how confident the justice is as an individual and as a judge. Obviously a new justice may look to the clerk for guidance on matters more frequently than an old hand but whatever the experience of the justice, or indeed the clerk, a good working relationship is essential. A magistrate should not be afraid to seek advice nor should the clerk shrink from giving advice where circumstances require it. This is easy to state but in practice it can be a difficult and delicate balancing act for both parties. The assessor and justice are part of a team in the district court, with each having a distinct role in the proceedings.

The role of the clerk
The clerk of court has a number of tasks, which can be categorised as the five As:

(1) Advance preparation. This entails checking over the complaints and related paperwork prior to court, and if necessary looking up the law and ensuring that appropriate source material is avail-

able for reference during court. A little time spent on advance preparation can save a lot of time in court for the clerk and the justice.

(2) Attending court and ensuring the justice attends. This means arriving in good time and meeting before court starts to consider the nature and volume of the day's business. The clerk also liaises with the others involved in court, e g procurators fiscal, defence agents, accused, witnesses, social workers, bar officers, etc.

(3) Advising justices on points of law, practice and procedure during court. This is central to the clerk's role and will be considered separately.

(4) Assisting the smooth running of the court by ordering the court business. This includes ensuring that accused and witnesses are present and called at the appropriate time, ensuring that the accused is identified, fixing new court dates, ensuring that bail undertakings are explained, accepted and signed by the accused and that he or she is given a copy, etc. The clerk generally makes sure that the court functions properly. Although the conduct of the proceedings is the responsibility of the justice, the clerk can help in this task by doing his or her job well.

(5) Administration during and after the sitting of the court. This involves checking the paperwork, complaints, penalty notices, schedules of previous convictions, driving licences, etc, noting the proceedings and outcome and ensuring that all persons involved are aware of the court's decision. If there is a trial both the clerk and the justice will take notes. The clerk also ensures that warrants and complaints are signed by the justice and that other essential paperwork relating to the business of the court is dealt with. Matters arising in court may have to be followed up. A report may have been sought by the justice and this will have to be obtained before the case next calls.

Also included under the heading of administration is responsibility for training justices. Although there is now greater provision for the national training of justices, in many courts it is still the clerk's responsibility to initiate training locally or at regional level. This responsibility includes ensuring justices are kept up to date with developments in the law as they affect the district court.

Points of law, practice and procedure
The clerk is not in court to usurp the role of the justice. The clerk is there as a safeguarder of the legality of the proceedings. In *Lay Justice?* the authors state that "the majority of justices were full of praise for the clerks. . . . The clerk seems to be a source of confidence for the justices"

(p 99). Decisions on matters of fact and law are for the justice, as are decisions on sentencing. The clerk is there to give advice on points of law, practice and procedure. While in court the clerk, like the justice, is on duty all the time; but it is not his or her job to give the justice a second opinion.

The *Handbook for Newly Appointed Justices of the Peace in Scotland* states that it is the clerk's duty to advise the justice on matters of law, practice and procedure either on request or on his or her own initiative to avoid mistakes being made, particularly in relation to technicalities of evidence and procedure. The *Handbook* goes on to say (at p 29): "Unless there is good reason for not doing so, justices should accept the clerk's advice on procedural and legal matters." This is because lay justices are not expected to be experts in the law of evidence or procedure and are entitled to rely on the advice of the legally qualified assessor.

Justice must be seen to be done
In the district court as in any other court it is important that justice is not only done but seen to be done and this has been stressed by the High Court in a number of appeal cases.

In the case of *Kelly v Rae*, 1916 2 SLT 246; 1917 JC 12, the magistrate expressed the view that the case was "not proven". The clerk of court then drew attention to an item of evidence and suggested that there should be a conviction. The accused was convicted and subsequently appealed. The court held that the clerk was entitled at any time prior to actual judgment to advise the magistrate with regard to any point which had been a matter of evidence.

Lord Dundas (at p 17) said: "I take it that a magistrate may at any time before actual judgment change his opinion, and I take it also that a Clerk of Court is entitled, and may be bound, to tender to the magistrate, if he does so timeously, any advice that occurs to him bearing on the decision of the case." The High Court approved this passage in the case of *McColligan v Normand*, 1993 SLT 1026; 1993 SCCR 330. This case involved a breach of the peace charge in the district court. At the end of the trial the justice said to the clerk, while still in court, "not proven". The clerk indicated that he and the justice should retire, which they did, and on his return the justice convicted the accused. On appeal it was held that at the time the justice made his remark, the stage of actual judgment had not yet been reached, and that the words were addressed to the assessor and not to the accused.

The case fell on the correct side of what may be a very narrow dividing line between the point at which the matter is open to intervention by the assessor and the point at which actual judgment has been pronounced.

A similar situation arose in the case of *Maxwell v Cardle*, 1993 SLT 1017; 1993 SCCR 15, where part of a conversation between the justice and the legal assessor was overheard prior to the guilty verdict being pronounced. The appellant stated that this showed that the justice was deciding the case on the basis of suppositions unrelated to the evidence. This was disputed by the justice who stated that the appellant had misunderstood what was being said. After a no case to answer submission had been repelled, but before the verdict was returned, the justice in consultation with the assessor allegedly said: "I think I'll return that not proven verdict you mentioned," and subsequently: "It doesn't really matter what I do in this case as the accused is coming up for these other matters referred to by the police, I'll just find him guilty." The High Court accepted the justice's assurance that she had decided the case solely on the evidence and stated that it was perfectly in order for a justice to consult with the assessor without resorting to an adjournment. However, discretion was required to ensure discussions on sensitive matters were not overheard. Lord Justice General Hope stated that the legal assessor was there to give legal advice whenever it was required and a justice should not feel inhibited from seeking advice at any stage when points of law or procedure arose, as it would be too disruptive to adjourn every time (1993 SLT, p 1018G). For a more detailed consideration of these cases see 1993 SLT (News) 291.

Points of law

There are a number of situations in the district court where the clerk may be called upon to give legal advice because points of law are involved, for example, where there are preliminary pleas to competency or relevancy; where there are objections during a trial; where questions of admissibility, sufficiency or corroboration of evidence arise; where a no case to answer submission is made, or where there is doubt about statutory interpretation.

Legal advice may not be necessary because an experienced justice may have faced a similar situation in the past and be very well aware of how to deal with the matter or may be quite clear in his or her own mind as to the correct course of action. If there is any doubt, however, advice should be sought. If necessary, the court should be adjourned to allow for proper consideration

and textbooks or statutes to be consulted. The no case to answer submission can cause particular difficulty because it is a legal concept, and the clerk's advice on such matters should not be rejected.

Practice and procedure

A clerk may also advise a justice on the practice of the particular court or of neighbouring courts in relation to sentencing and on the sentencing options which are available. The decision on sentencing, however, is the responsibility of the justice, not the clerk.

The clerk must ensure that proper procedures are followed in court and, on occasion, this may involve reminding the justice of the next step in the proceedings. To experienced magistrates the court routine is very familiar but it may not be so to newer recruits or to those who are unable to sit on a regular basis. In addition, there is always the possibility of some unusual procedural point cropping up while the court is sitting which might fox even an experienced clerk and require the assistance of Renton and Brown.

Common law and common sense

It has already been noted that the clerk's role is mainly a matter of common law and common sense and this can be illustrated by reference to case law. The High Court has set limits on the role of the clerk and has given some guidance as to what is and what is not appropriate.

First, the assessor must not have a personal interest in the case. An extreme example of this can be seen in *Smith v Robertson* (1827) 5 S 848, where a clerk of court in a JP court acted as an agent of one party and also as assessor for the proceedings. The agent for the other party agreed to this unusual state of affairs, but the High Court not surprisingly declared that this was unacceptable.

This case was decided in the days when the assessor was generally also in private practice which is no longer the position. It should be noted, however, that the fact that the clerk is an employee of a local authority does not mean that he or she cannot act as assessor in cases involving the authority. In the case of *City of Edinburgh District Council, Petrs*, 1990 SCCR 511, Lord Justice General Hope said (at p 517E-F): "I am not persuaded that this fact alone would be sufficient to create a suspicion of bias on his part in the mind of a reasonable man so as to invalidate the proceedings . . . the inference which I draw is that Parliament was satisfied that the clerk . . . could properly act as legal assessor in all cases which come before the district court, including those involving the local authority by whom he is appointed and employed."

Secondly, it is not the job of the assessor to conduct a defence for the accused — indeed it would be improper to do so. In the case of *Johannesson v Robertson*, 1945 JC 146, the accused sought an adjournment to obtain legal advice. The magistrate refused to adjourn and advised that the assessor, who was a solicitor, would look after the accused's interests. The High Court held that, while the magistrate could refuse the adjournment, he might have prejudiced the accused by advising that the assessor would look after her interests and that the effects of this could not be estimated. The conviction was quashed.

The *Johannesson* case also made it clear that it is improper for an assessor to cross examine witnesses and/or either party in any way. This was reinforced in the case of *Alexander v Boyd*, 1966 SLT 261; 1966 JC 24. After the accused had given evidence and had been cross examined and re-examined, the assessor cross examined the accused. There is some suggestion that he did so in an aggressive and sceptical manner. The Lord Justice Clerk accepted that the clerk's behaviour had been prejudicial to the accused and laid down broad rules, which are still relevant today. The assessor may put questions to witnesses to clarify matters which would otherwise be unclear, but must do so in a neutral and impartial manner; there must be no cross examination, no eliciting of new matter, particularly if it is hostile to the accused, and no questions which attack the credibility of the accused.

It is usual for some latitude to be given in the case of an unrepresented accused by the justice, the clerk and indeed the procurator fiscal. However the justice and the clerk must be careful not to stray beyond the bounds of assistance and into the realms of conducting the defence case.

A relationship between the fiscal and the clerk does not necessarily amount to improper conduct as both hold public office and are expected to act as responsible solicitors and carry out their public duty with integrity. In the case of *Laughland v Galloway*, 1968 SLT 272; 1968 JC 26, the clerk and the prosecutor were partners in the same legal firm. The High Court held that, unless there was some specific allegation, the court was entitled to assume that each would do their job properly. To do otherwise would make the administration of justice impossible. Again this was in the days when the fiscal and the clerk were not employees of the Crown and the local authority respectively and such a situation could not arise today. There might however be a situation where married or related solicitors were both involved in the same case and the same view would be taken.

Conclusion

The clerk's role is a demanding one. It requires a knowledge of substantive criminal law and of criminal procedure, of the law of evidence, and of sentencing decisions. It requires the ability to think and act quickly, often under pressure, and to communicate well verbally and in writing. It requires organisational and administrative skills and an understanding of human nature. In reality these skills are not dissimilar to the expertise required of any court practitioner.

[The author would like to thank Mrs Chris Ashton of Napier University for information about the postgraduate certificate in district court practice and procedure and for helpful comments on an earlier draft of this article.]

◆

NEWS

Appointments

Junior counsel

The following junior counsel appointments have been made by the Lord Advocate: Health and Safety Commission and Executive, Eric C Brown, advocate; Department of Trade and Industry (in Scotland) (energy matters), Eric C Brown, advocate; Scottish Office environment department (under exception of planning matters), Mr R G Clancy, advocate.

Court

Court of Session: practice note

No 11 of 1994 (18 August 1994): Petitions for the appointment of tutor dative

As from this date, a petition for the appointment of a tutor dative will require to seek service in common form on the Mental Welfare Commission for Scotland, 25 Drumsheugh Gardens, Edinburgh EH3 7RB.

Edinburgh sheriff court

Edinburgh sheriff court has moved to new premises at 27 Chambers Street, Edinburgh EH1 1LB. All civil, commissary and criminal business is now transacted there. The new DX numbers are: sheriff principal, regional sheriff clerk, criminal fines department: DX ED 308; civil department: DX ED 312; commissary office: DX ED 313. The new fax numbers are: sheriff principal, 031-225 2288; regional sheriff clerk, 031-225 4422; civil department, 031-225 8899; commissary office, 031-225 4605; criminal fines department, 031-225 6569.

— ◊ —

Coming events

LSA seminars

Legal Services Agency has organised the following seminars: 21 September 1994, Repairs, Improvements in the Law: Disputes in Rental Housing; 27 September 1994, Short Assured Tenancies under the "88" Act; 7 October 1994, New Maternity Rights and other Developments; 11 October 1994, Tenancy Agreements and Estate Transfer; 27 October 1994, Children's Hearings, Lawyers and the Courts; 3 November 1994, The Role of Company Secretaries and Directors in Voluntary Organisations; 8 December 1994, Disability Appeals Tribunals.

Further details are available from Susan Clark, LSA, 11th Floor, Fleming House, 134 Renfrew Street, Cowcaddens, Glasgow G3 6ST (tel 041-353 3354).

Socio-Legal Studies Association

The SLSA will hold a conference at the University of Edinburgh on 28 September 1994 at which the Scottish branch of the association will be launched. The conference will focus on the contribution made by socio-legal research to an understanding of legal practices, legal reform and legal policy in Scotland. Speakers include Alan Paterson on legal services, Mike Adler on criminal legal aid, Fran Wasoff on child support, Neil Hutton on sentencing and Tony Prosser on judicial review. There will also be workshop sessions on these topics. Further details and application forms are available from Mike Adler, SLSA Conference Organiser, Department of Social Policy, University of Edinburgh, Adam Ferguson Building, Edinburgh EH8.

◊

Opening of the new legal year

The red mass will be celebrated at St Mary's Cathedral, Broughton Street, Edinburgh, on Sunday, 9 October 1994, at 11.30 am, to mark the opening of the new law year. The principal concelebrant will be Archbishop Keith Patrick O'Brien. The preacher will be Father Francis Davidson, OSB. A cold buffet lunch will be provided after the mass in the King James Thistle hotel, Leith Street, Edinburgh. Members of the profession wishing to attend or to receive further information concerning the mass and/or the luncheon should contact Mrs Phil Kelly, John G Gray & Co, 24 York Place, Edinburgh EH1 3HL (DX ED 14) (tel 031-557 4452; fax 031-556 7677).

— ◊ —

General

Neighbourhood disputes in the criminal justice system

A report has been published by the Scottish Office Central Research Unit for the Home and Health Department following research to consider the characteristics of neighbourhood disputes coming to the attention of the police, and ways of dealing with these outside the criminal justice system.

The researchers found that criminal justice agencies in Dundee, the chosen study area, currently process a large number of neighbourhood disputes which, though often trivial in nature, can be complex and difficult to resolve and represent a significant drain on the resources of the police and other agencies. Most of the incidents of this kind reported to the police were relatively trivial and many were not strictly criminal matters at all. However, specific incidents were often symptoms of complex and long running disputes over issues such as noise, young people causing annoyance, car parking and property boundaries.

The researchers found general support amongst criminal justice personnel for the development of alternative methods of handling such disputes and, in particular, for the establishment of some form of community mediation scheme. They estimate that up to half of all disputes currently referred to the procurator fiscal each year in Dundee could be diverted to such a scheme.

The report is available from The Scottish Office Librarian, Room 1/44, New St Andrew's House, Edinburgh EH1 3TG, at a cost of £5.

◊

NEWS

Stamp Office opening hours

The Stamp Office public counter at 16 Picardy Place, Edinburgh, is now open from 9.30 am to 4 pm inclusive.

◇

Advocates Criminal Law Group

At the recent annual general meeting of the Advocates Criminal Law Group the following office bearers were elected for the year 1994/1995: *Chairman,* Leeona J Dorrian, QC; *vice chairman,* Andrew J Lamb, advocate; *secretary,* Robert B Anthony, advocate; *treasurer,* Simon Di Rollo, advocate.

◇

Companies House

New and reduced Companies House charges are to be introduced. These will be:

Incorporation and registration fees: Incorporation of a new company; change of name of a company incorporated in England, Wales or Scotland; registration of a branch of place of business of an overseas company; registration of a European Economic Interest Grouping; re-registration: for documents received at Companies House on or after 1 October 1994 — £20 (previously £50).

Filing fees: annual returns, for return dates (latest made up dates) on or after 1 October 1994 (applies to returns received on or after 20 September 1994) — £18 (previously £32); overseas company accounts, for accounts received at Companies House on or after 1 October 1994 — £18.

◇

ESPC opens in Stirling

A new branch of the Edinburgh Solicitors Property Centre is now open for business at 8-10 King Street, Stirling FK8 1BD. This brings the total number of centres in eastern central Scotland to five. Thirteen local firms have combined to establish this new showroom which is designed to display 1,000 properties throughout Central Region. The centre will be open six days a week: 9.30 am to 5.00 pm on weekdays and 10.00 am to 1.00 pm on Saturdays.

 —— ◇ ——

Taxation

Publication of internal guidance on tax

The Inland Revenue have announced plans for publishing the internal guidance used in local tax and collection offices. The manuals will be published progressively from the autumn of 1994 to the end of 1995. Until now the manuals have been treated as confidential to tax officials but they are being published as part of the Inland Revenue's response to the Government's Code of Practice on Access to Government Information. Arrangements for purchasing them will be announced when the first manuals are published.

◇

Business Economic Notes

The Inland Revenue have published a new business economic note entitled Insurance Brokers and Agents. This note includes information about the Financial Services Act 1986 and the payment and taxation of commission.

—— ◇ ——

Obituary

On 23 August 1994, John Alexander Dick Peddie, WS, formerly senior partner in the firm of Messrs Waddell, McIntosh & Peddie, WS, Edinburgh.

—— ◇ ——

Business changes

Messrs Brunton Miller, solicitors, announce that with effect from 19 September 1994 they have moved to new premises at Herbert House, 22 Herbert Street, Glasgow G20 6NB (tel 041-337 1199; fax 041-337 3300). The addresses, telephone and fax numbers of the branch offices at Helensburgh and Alexandria remain unchanged.

Murray Beith & Murray, WS, intimate that with effect from 1 September 1994 Richard Filleul has joined them as a partner in their personal law department.

L & L Lawrence, Glasgow and Edinburgh, intimate that their assistant Fiona Gemmell was appointed as an associate of the firm on 23 August 1994.

 —— ◇ ——

ACT OF SEDERUNT

ACT OF SEDERUNT (RULES OF THE COURT OF SESSION 1994 AMENDMENT NO 1) (COMMERCIAL ACTIONS) 1994

(SI 1994/2310) [25 AUGUST 1994]

The Lords of Council and Session, under and by virtue of the powers conferred on them by section 5 of the Court of Session Act 1988 (c 36) and of all other powers enabling them in that behalf, do hereby enact and declare:

Citation and commencement

1.—(1) This Act of Sederunt may be cited as the Act of Sederunt (Rules of the Court of Session 1994 Amendment No. 1) (Commercial Actions) 1994 and shall come into force on 20th September 1994.

(2) This Act of Sederunt shall be inserted in the Books of Sederunt.

Amendment of the Rules of the Court of Session

2.—(1) The Rules of the Court of Session 1994 shall be amended in accordance with the following sub-paragraphs.

(2) After rule 10.6 (Lord Ordinary in Exchequer Causes), insert the following rule:—

"*Hearing of commercial actions*

10.7. A commercial judge nominated under rule 47.2 (proceedings before commercial judge) may hear and determine a commercial action as defined by rule 47.1(2) when the court is in session or in vacation.".

(3) In rule 38.4 (leave to reclaim etc. in certain cases), after paragraph (5) insert the following paragraphs:—

"(6) An interlocutor granting or refusing a motion under rule 47.10(1) (appointing action to be a commercial action) may be reclaimed against only with the leave of the commercial judge within 14 days after the date on which the interlocutor was pronounced.

(7) An interlocutor pronounced on the Commercial Roll, other than a final interlocutor, may be reclaimed against only with the leave of the commercial judge within 14 days after the date on which the interlocutor was pronounced.".

(4) For chapter 47, substitute the following chapter:—

"CHAPTER 47

COMMERCIAL ACTIONS

Application and interpretation of this Chapter

47.1.—(1) This Chapter applies to a commercial action.

(2) In this Chapter —

"commercial action" means an action arising out of, or concerned with, any transaction or dispute of a commercial or business nature in which an election has been made under rule 47.3(1) or which has been transferred under rule 47.10;

"preliminary hearing" means a hearing under rule 47.11;

"procedural hearing" means a hearing under rule 47.12.

Procedures before commercial judge

47.2. All proceedings in the Outer House in a commercial action shall be brought before a judge of the court nominated by the Lord President as a commercial judge or, where a commercial judge is not available, any other judge of the court (including the vacation judge); and "commercial judge" shall be construed accordingly.

Election of procedure for commercial actions and form of summons

47.3.—(1) The pursuer may elect to adopt the procedure in this Chapter by bringing an action in which there are inserted the words "Commercial Action" immediately below the words "IN THE COURT OF SESSION" where they occur above the instance, and on the backing, of the summons and any copy of it.

(2) A summons in a commercial action shall —

(a) specify, in the form of conclusions, the orders sought;

(b) identify the parties to the action and the transaction or dispute from which the action arises;

(c) summarise the circumstances out of which the action arises; and

(d) set out the grounds on which the action proceeds.

(3) There shall be appended to a summons in a commercial action a schedule listing the documents founded on or adopted as incorporated in the summons.

Disapplication of certain rules

47.4.—(1) The requirement in rule 4.1(4) for a step of process to be folded lengthwise shall not apply in a commercial action.

(2) An open record shall not be made up in, and Chapter 22 (making up and closing records) shall not apply to, a commercial action unless otherwise ordered by the court.

(3) The following rules shall not apply to a commercial action:—

rule 6.2 (fixing and allocation of diets in Outer House),

rule 25.1(3) (form of counterclaim),

rule 25.2(2) (applications for warrants for diligence in counterclaims),

rule 36.3 (lodging productions).

Procedure in commercial actions

47.5. Subject to the provisions of this Chapter, the procedure in a commercial action shall be such as the commercial judge shall order or direct.

Defences

47.6.—(1) Defences in a commercial action shall be in the form of answers to the summons with any additional statement of facts or legal grounds on which it is intended to rely.

(2) There shall be appended to the defences in a commercial action a schedule listing the documents founded on or adopted as incorporated in the defences.

Counterclaims and third party notices

47.7.—(1) A party seeking to lodge a counterclaim or to serve a third party notice shall apply by motion to do so.

(2) The commercial judge shall, on a motion to lodge a counterclaim or to serve a third party notice, make such an order and give such directions as he thinks fit with regard to —

(a) the time within which a counterclaim may be lodged or a third party notice served and any answers lodged;

(b) where the motion is made before the preliminary hearing, a date for the preliminary hearing if it is to be a date other than the date referred to in rule 47.8(2); and

(c) any application for a warrant to use any form of diligence which would have been permitted under rule 13.6(c) (warrants for diligence in summons) had the warrant been sought in a summons in a separate action.

(3) Paragraphs (2) and (3) of rule 47.3 shall apply to the form of a counterclaim as they apply to the form of a summons.

Commercial Roll

47.8.—(1) All proceedings in an action in which an election has been made under rule 47.3(1) or which has been transferred under rule 47.10 shall, in the Outer House, be heard and determined on the Commercial Roll on such dates and at such times as shall be fixed by the commercial judge.

(2) A commercial action shall call on the Commercial Roll for a preliminary hearing within 14 days after defences have been lodged.

(3) The appearance of a commercial action on the Commercial Roll for a hearing on a specified date shall not affect the right of any party to apply by motion at any time under these Rules.

Withdrawal of action from Commercial Roll

47.9.—(1) At any time before or at the preliminary hearing, the commercial judge shall —

(a) on the motion of a party, withdraw a commercial action from the procedure in this Chapter and appoint it to proceed as an ordinary action where, having regard to —

(i) the likely need for detailed pleadings to enable justice to be done between the parties,

(ii) the length of time required for preparation of the action, or

(iii) any other relevant circumstances,

he is satisfied that the speedy and efficient determination of the action would not be served by the cause being dealt with as a commercial action; and

(b) on the motion of a party with the consent of all other parties, withdraw a commercial action from the Commercial Roll and appoint it to proceed as an ordinary action.

(2) If a motion to withdraw a commercial action from the Commercial Roll made before or renewed at a preliminary hearing is refused, no subsequent motion to withdraw the action from the Commercial Roll shall be considered except on special cause shown.

Transfer of action to Commercial Roll

47.10.—(1) In an action within the meaning of rule 47.1(2) (definition of commercial action) in which the pursuer has not made an election under rule 47.3(1), any party may apply by motion at any time to have the action appointed to be a commercial action on the Commercial Roll.

(2) A motion enrolled under paragraph (1) shall be heard by the commercial judge on such a date and at such a time as the Keeper of the Rolls shall fix in consultation with the commercial judge.

(3) Where an interlocutor is pronounced under paragraph (1) appointing an action to be a commercial action on the Commercial Roll, the action shall be put out by order for a preliminary hearing within 14 days —

(a) if defences have been lodged, after the date of that interlocutor; or

(b) if defences have not been lodged, after defences have been lodged.

Preliminary hearing

47.11.—(1) Unless a commercial action is withdrawn under rule 47.9 from the Commercial Roll then, at the preliminary hearing of a commercial action in which an election has been made under rule 47.3(1), the commercial judge —

(a) shall determine whether and to what extent and in what manner further specification of the claim and defences should be provided;

(b) may make an order in respect of any of the following matters:—

(i) detailed written pleadings to be made by a party either generally or restricted to particular issues;

(ii) a statement of facts to be made by one or more parties either generally or restricted to particular issues;

(iii) the allowing of an amendment by a party to his pleadings;

(iv) disclosure of the identity of witnesses and the existence and nature of documents relating to the action or authority to recover documents either generally or specifically;

(v) documents constituting, evidencing or relating to the subject-matter of the action or any invoices, correspondence or similar documents relating to it to be lodged in process within a specified period;

(vi) each party to lodge in process, and send to every other party, a list of witnesses;

(vii) reports of skilled persons or witness statements to be lodged in process;

(viii) affidavits concerned with any of the issues in the action to be lodged in process; and

(ix) the action to proceed to a hearing without any further preliminary procedure either in relation to the whole or any particular aspect of the action;

(c) may fix the period within which any such order shall be complied with;

(d) may continue the preliminary hearing to a date to be appointed by him; and

(e) may make such other order as he thinks fit for the speedy determination of the action.

(2) Where the commercial judge makes an order under paragraph (1) (b) (i) or (ii) or (c), he may ordain the pursuer to —

(a) make up a record; and

(b) lodge that record in process within such period as the commercial judge thinks fit.

(3) At the conclusion of the preliminary hearing, the court shall, unless it has made an order under paragraph (1) (b) (ix) (order to proceed without a further hearing), fix a date for a procedural hearing to determine further procedure.

(4) The date fixed under paragraph (3) for a procedural hearing shall not be extended except on special cause shown on a motion enrolled not less than 7 days before the date fixed for the procedural hearing.

Procedural hearing

47.12.—(1) Not less than 3 days before the date fixed under rule 47.11(3) for the procedural hearing, each party shall —

(a) lodge a written statement of his proposals for further procedure which shall, *inter alia*, state —

(i) whether he seeks to have the commercial action appointed to debate or to have the action sent to proof on the whole or any part of it; and

(ii) what the issues are which he considers should be sent to debate or proof;

(b) lodge a list of the witnesses he proposes to cite or call to give evidence, identifying the matters to which each witness will speak;

(c) lodge the reports of any skilled persons;

(d) where it is sought to have the action appointed to debate, lodge a note of argument consisting of concise numbered paragraphs stating the legal propositions on which it is proposed to submit that any preliminary plea should be sustained or repelled with reference to the principal authorities and statutory provisions to be founded on; and

(e) send a copy of any such written statement, lists, reports or note of argument, as the case may be, to every other party.

(2) At the procedural hearing, the commercial judge —

(a) shall determine whether the commercial action should be appointed to debate or sent to proof on the whole or any part of the action;

(b) where the action is appointed to debate or sent to proof, may order that written arguments on any question of law should be submitted;

(c) where the action is sent to proof, may determine whether evidence at the proof should be by oral evidence, the production of documents or affidavits on any issue;

(d) may determine, in the light of any witness statements, affidavits or reports produced, that proof is unnecessary on any issue;

(e) may direct that there should be consultation between skilled persons with a view to reaching agreement about any points held in common;

(f) without prejudice to Chapter 12 (assessors), may appoint an expert to examine, on behalf of the court, any reports of skilled persons or other evidence submitted and to report to the court within such period as the commercial judge may specify;

(g) may remit an issue to a person of skill;

(h) may direct that proof of the authenticity of a document or other formal matters may be dispensed with;

(i) if invited to do so by all parties, direct the action to be determined on the basis of written submissions, or such other material, without any oral hearing; and

(j) may continue the procedural hearing to a date to be appointed by him.

Debates

47.13. Chapter 28 (procedure roll) shall apply

to a debate ordered in a commercial action under rule 47.12(2) (a) as it applies to a cause appointed to the Procedure Roll.

Lodging of productions for proof
47.14.—(1) Any document not previously lodged required for any proof in a commercial action shall be lodged as a production not less than 7 days before the date fixed for the proof.

(2) No document may be lodged as a production after the date referred to in paragraph (1), even by agreement of all parties, unless the court is satisfied that any document sought to be lodged could not with reasonable diligence have been lodged in time.

Hearings for further procedure
46.15. At any time before final judgment, the commercial judge may, at his own instance or on the motion of any party, have a commercial action put out for hearing for further procedure; and the commercial judge may make such order as he thinks fit.

Failure to comply with rule or order of commercial judge
47.16. Any failure by a party to comply timeously with a provision in these Rules or any order made by the commercial judge in a commercial action shall entitle the judge, at his own instance —

(a) to refuse to extend any period for compliance with a provision in these Rules or an order of the court,

(b) to dismiss the action or counterclaim, as the case may be, in whole or in part,

(c) to grant decree in respect of all or any of the conclusions of the summons or counterclaim, as the case may be, or

(d) to make an award of expenses,
as he thinks fit.".

(5) In rule 73.2 (form of application for rectification of documents), for paragraph (2) substitute the following paragraph:—
"(2) An application to which this Chapter applies may be made —

(a) in an action to which Chapter 47 (commercial actions) applies, by summons or by a conclusion ancillary to other conclusions in the summons; or

(b) in any other action, by a conclusion ancillary to other conclusions in a summons.".

J A D HOPE, LORD PRESIDENT, *IPD*

[Acts of Sederunt are reproduced with the permission of the Controller of Her Majesty's Stationery Office.]

PRACTICE NOTE

No 12 of 1994 (3 September 1994): Commercial actions

Application and interpretation of Chapter 47: RCS 1994, rule 47.1
1. The actions to which the rules apply are intended to comprise all actions arising out of or concerned with any relationship of a commercial or business nature, whether contractual or not, and to include, but not be limited to —
    the construction of a commercial or mercantile document,
    the sale or hire purchase of goods,
    the export or import of merchandise,
    the carriage of goods by land, air or sea,
    insurance,
    banking,
    the provision of financial services,
    mercantile agency,
    mercantile usage or a custom of trade,
    a building, engineering or construction contract,
    a commercial lease.
Some Admiralty actions in personam, such as actions relating to or arising out of bills of lading, may also be suitable for treatment as commercial actions if they do not require the special facilities of Admiralty procedure in relation to defenders whose names are not known.

Commercial judge: RCS 1994, rule 47.2
2. The commercial judge may hear and determine a commercial action when the court is in session or in vacation: RCS 1994, rule 10.7. Although the court is in session or in vacation for about 50 weeks in the year, it is anticipated that during two weeks in April, the month of August and two weeks at Christmas and New Year, only interlocutory or incidental business will be dealt with; proofs and debates will not normally be heard during those times. The dates of these periods will be separately announced.

Election of procedure: RCS 1994, rule 47.3
3.—(1) The initial pleadings in a commercial action are expected to be in an abbreviated form; and while they should make clear what the subject matter of the cause is and the legal issues are, they should not be extended by lengthy recitals of contract documents, propositions of law or legal duties or similar material. Where damages are sought, a summary statement of a claim or a statement in the form of an account will normally be sufficient. Where it is sought to

obtain from the court a decision only on the construction of a document, it is permissible for the summons to contain an appropriate conclusion without a condescendence or pleas in law. The conclusion in such a case should specify the document the construction of which is in dispute and conclude for the construction contended for.

(2) Rule 47.3(3) is intended to require a party to produce with his summons the "core" or essential documents to establish the contract or transaction with which the cause is concerned. Under RCS 1994, rule 27.1(1) (a) documents founded on or adopted as incorporated in a summons must be lodged at the time the summons is lodged for calling.

(3) When the summons is lodged for signeting, a commercial action registration form (Form CA1), copies of which are available from the General Department, must be completed, lodged in process and a copy served with the summons.

Disapplication of certain rules: RCS 1994, rule 47.4

4. The ordinary rules of the Rules of the Court of Session 1994 apply to a commercial action to which Chapter 47 applies except insofar as specifically excluded under rule 47.4 or which are excluded by implication because of a provision in Chapter 47.

Procedure in commercial actions: RCS 1994, rule 47.5

5. The procedure in, and progress of, a commercial action is under the direct control of the commercial judge. He will be proactive.

Defences: RCS 1994, rule 47.6

6.—(1) In the first instance detailed averments are not required in the defences any more than in the summons and it is not necessary that each allegation should be admitted or denied provided that the extent of the dispute can be reasonably well identified. One of the objectives of the procedure is to make the extent of written pleadings subject to the control of the court.

(2) Under RCS 1994, rule 27.1(1) (b), documents founded on or adopted as incorporated in defences must be lodged at the time the defences are lodged.

(3) Defences must be lodged within seven days after the summons is lodged for calling: RCS 1994, rule 18.1(1).

(4) The defender's agent must complete the commercial action registration form (Form CA1) and lodge it in process, or complete the process copy, with the information required.

Counterclaims and third party notices: RCS 1994, rule 47.7

7. No counterclaim or the bringing in of a third party may be pursued without an order from the commercial judge.

Commercial roll: RCS 1994, rule 47.8

8. In the Outer House, an action, and all proceedings in it, in which an election has been made to adopt the procedure in Chapter 47 for commercial actions or which has been transferred under rule 47.10 to be dealt with as a commercial action, shall be heard and determined on the commercial roll.

Withdrawal of action from commercial roll: RCS 1994, rule 47.9

9. The object of this rule is to enable cases which are unsuitable for the commercial procedure to be removed from the commercial roll, but it should be understood that the commercial procedure is not to be regarded as limited to cases which are straightforward or simple or as excluding cases which involve the investigation of difficult and complicated facts.

Transfer of actions to commercial roll: RCS 1994, rule 47.10

10.—(1) An ordinary action which has not been brought as a commercial action under rule 47.3(1) may be transferred to the commercial roll as a commercial action on application by motion by any party (including the pursuer) to the commercial judge if it is an action within the meaning of a commercial action in rule 47.1(2).

(2) An interlocutor granting or refusing a motion to transfer an action to the commercial roll may be reclaimed against only with leave of the commercial judge within 14 days after the date of the interlocutor: RCS 1994, rule 38.4(6).

Preliminary hearing on commercial roll: RCS 1994, rule 47.11

11.—(1) The preliminary hearing of the commercial action is not a formality. It is intended that there should be a serious discussion of the issues in the cause and the steps necessary to resolve them, and counsel or solicitors appearing at the hearing will be expected to be aware of the issues and the principal contentions on each side and to be in a position to inform the court of them. In many commercial disputes, the parties will already be well aware of what their respective contentions are and those contentions may have been set out in correspondence or, for example, in a building contract in a formal claim or similar document. The court will expect to be informed of the position in that respect and may direct that no further pleading is required.

(2) In applying rule 47.11(3), the court will expect to set realistic time limits; but once established those time limits will be expected to be achieved and extension will only be granted in special circumstances. This emphasises the importance of ensuring that parties at the preliminary hearing are in a position to explain fully what will be required. Since it is part of the administration of commercial causes that wherever possible a commercial action should at all stages be heard before the same judge, it is important to avoid repeated appearances of the action on the commercial roll. For that reason it is necessary to try to give the court accurate information in order to enable the appropriate time limits for a particular case to be established in a manner which is both realistic and which does not prejudice the overall requirement that commercial actions should be dealt with expeditiously.

(3) The hearing of an action at a preliminary hearing will usually be heard in chambers. Those attending may be seated and wigs and gowns need not be worn.

Procedural hearing on commercial roll: RCS 1994, rule 47.12

12.—(1) The procedural hearing is also a serious hearing at which parties will be expected to be in a position to discuss realistically the issues involved in the action and the method of disposing of them. It should normally be expected that by the time of the procedural hearing the parties' positions will have been ascertained and identified and in consequence it is expected that, once a case has passed beyond the stage of a procedural hearing, it will not settle.

(2) This is one of the ways in which it is sought to meet the problem of ensuring that the judge is in a position to deal realistically with the procedure which he cannot do unless he is given information on which to proceed.

(3) Rule 47.12(2) is the kernel of the proposed procedure since it is intended to enable the court to direct what is really to happen.

(4) This hearing will also be heard in chambers in the same way as the preliminary hearing.

Debates: RCS 1994, rule 47.13

13. A debate in a commercial action is not heard on the procedure roll but on the commercial roll. The provisions of Chapter 28 of the RCS 1994 (procedure roll), however, do apply to a debate in a commercial action.

Lodging of productions: RCS 1994, rule 47.14

14. Before any proof or other hearing at which documents are to be referred to, parties shall, as

well as lodging their productions, prepare for the use of the court a working bundle in which the documents are arranged chronologically or in another appropriate order without multiple copies of the same document.

Hearings for further procedure: RCS 1994, rule 47.15

15. The commercial judge or a party may have a commercial action put out for a hearing other than a preliminary or procedural hearing to deal with a procedural or other matter which has arisen for which provision has not been made.

Failure to comply with rule or order of commercial judge: RCS 1994, rule 47.16

16. The purpose of this rule is to provide for discipline to ensure effective supervision of case management.

General

17.—(1) Arrangements will be made to ensure that at all appearances of an action in the commercial roll the same judge shall preside. Parties are expected to arrange that counsel or other persons having rights of audience responsible for the conduct of the case and authorised to take any necessary decision on questions of procedure should be available and shall appear at any calling in the commercial roll.

(2) Where any pleadings or other documents are to be adjusted, the party proposing adjustments shall do so by preparing a new copy of the document as adjusted in which the new material is indicated by underlining, sidelining, a difference in type face or other means.

(3) An interlocutor pronounced on the commercial roll, other than a final interlocutor, may be reclaimed against only with the leave of the commercial judge within 14 days after the date of the interlocutor: RCS 1994, rule 38.4(7).

Transitional provisions for old commercial actions

18. As the old rules under the RCS 1994 for commercial actions are replaced by new rules with new procedures, there will be no rules applicable to commercial actions commenced under the rules for commercial actions under the RCS 1965 or the old rules under the RCS 1994.

Accordingly, in relation to commercial actions commenced before 20 September 1994 in which a diet of proof or a diet for a hearing on the procedure roll has not been fixed, a notice will appear in the rolls of court on Thursday 29 September 1994 giving parties in each of the cases listed in the notice 28 days in which to apply to transfer such a case to the new commercial roll under rule 47.10. If in a particular case listed in the notice no such application is made within 28 days, the action will proceed as an ordinary action.

ARTICLES

Nervous Shock: Traumatised Fellow Workers and Bystanders

Dr James Blaikie,
Senior Lecturer in Law,
University of Aberdeen.

Dr Blaikie examines recent Scottish and English decisions on liability for nervous shock and considers the position of the fellow worker and the bystander who suffer psychiatric illness in consequence of witnessing the death or injury of a third party caused by the negligence of the defender.

Liability for nervous shock has been considered by the House of Lords in *Bourhill v Young*, 1943 SLT 105; 1942 SC (HL) 78; in *McLoughlin v O'Brian* [1983] 1 AC 410, and in *Alcock v Chief Constable of South Yorkshire Police* [1992] 1 AC 310. Two recent cases have raised important issues in relation to two categories of shocked pursuer, the fellow worker and the ordinary bystander, and it has fallen to the courts to apply the guidance laid down by the House of Lords in *Alcock*.

In *Robertson v Forth Road Bridge Joint Board (No 2)*, 1994 SLT 568, the two pursuers, Robertson and Rough, and a third man, Smith, were responsible for patrolling the Forth road bridge. On a day of gale force winds, Rough noticed a large piece of metal sheeting on the carriageway. Robertson and Smith arrived in a pickup truck, whereupon, assisted by Rough, they loaded the sheet on to the truck. Smith then sat on top of the metal sheet. The truck, driven by Robertson, and followed a few feet behind by a van driven by Rough, began the return journey to the south side of the bridge. A violent gust of wind caused the metal sheet and Smith to be thrown off the truck and over the side of the bridge. Smith landed on a girder below the level of the bridge and was found to be dead by other workmates a few minutes later. As a result of witnessing the accident both pursuers suffered nervous shock and post-traumatic stress disorder. The only issue in dispute between the parties was whether a workmate who suffers psychiatric injury in consequence of witnessing the death of a fellow worker caused by the negligence of their mutual employer is entitled to recover damages from that employer. Although Lord MacLean had upheld the relevancy of both pursuers' averments (see *Robertson v Forth Road Bridge Joint Board (No 1)*, 1994 SLT 566), Temporary Judge

J F Wheatley, QC, held that no duty of care was owed by the defenders to either pursuer. (It is understood that a reclaiming motion has been marked in this case.)

McFarlane v EE Caledonia Ltd [1994] 2 All ER 1, arose out of the explosions and fire on the Piper Alpha oil rig in the North Sea which resulted in the deaths of 164 men. The plaintiff, at the time of the disaster, was off duty on a support vessel, the *Tharos*, some 550 metres away from the rig. For two hours he witnessed the explosions and destruction of the rig before he was evacuated by helicopter. The closest he came to the fire was 100 metres when the support vessel moved towards the rig to fight the fire and to render assistance. The plaintiff brought an action against the owners and operators of the rig, claiming damages for the psychiatric illness which he had suffered as a result of the events he had witnessed. However the Court of Appeal held, principally, that as a mere bystander or witness of horrific events he was not, in the circumstances, entitled to recover. (Leave to appeal to the House of Lords was refused in this case.)

The decision in *Alcock*

Alcock arose out of the Hillsborough disaster in which due to negligent policing the overcrowding of a part of the stadium caused 95 spectators to be killed and over 400 to be injured. The 10 plaintiffs who appealed to the House of Lords were relatives, and in one case the fiancé, of the victims, though none was either a spouse or parent of a primary victim, and they claimed damages for psychiatric illness. Some were actually in the stadium at the time, another was outside and saw the scenes on television. Others were at home and saw live television broadcasts. Others, who were merely told about the disaster or heard reports on radio, saw recorded television pictures later that night, although in accordance with broadcasting guidelines no pictures of identifiable victims were shown. The main questions for the House of Lords were whether a plaintiff who was neither a spouse nor a parent of the primary victim of the tragedy could recover, whether the means by which the shock was caused could include viewing simultaneous television pictures, and whether the previous requirement of seeing the "immediate aftermath" of an accident should be modified to include the identification of a victim in a mortuary some hours later.

The House held that foreseeability of injury of the type which befell the particular plaintiff, on its own, was not enough to found liability but that, in addition, the plaintiff's proximity to the accident in which the primary victim was involved, or its immediate aftermath, had to be sufficiently close in both time and space, and his shock had to be suffered through seeing or hearing the accident or its immediate aftermath.

However, the condition of liability which was central to *Alcock*, and to *Robertson* and *McFarlane*, concerned the class of person to whom the wrong-doer owes a duty of care not to cause this type of injury. *Alcock* required that there be a close relationship between the trauma victim and the primary victim of the accident. The House stressed that there was neither logic nor virtue in laying down, as a matter of policy, categories of relationship within which claims might succeed and outwith which they would fail. What was important was not the mere title of the relationship but the actual ties of love and affection between the parties. It would be presumed, subject to contrary evidence, that such ties exist between spouses and parents and children (and between fiancées according to Lords Keith and Oliver). It would further be presumed, albeit rebuttably, that such ties would not be present as between siblings, other remote relatives and mere friends. Thus the mere fact of relationship, without evidence of particularly close ties of love or affection, was insufficient to sustain the claims of brothers, brothers in law or a grandfather. This issue was to be decided on a case by case basis, asking whether the degree of love and affection was such that the defendant should reasonably have foreseen the shock induced injury. Although, as Lord Oliver cautioned (at pp 415-416): "Obviously a claim for damages for psychiatric injury by a remote relative of the primary victim will factually require most cautious scrutiny and faces considerable evidentiary difficulties. Equally obviously, the foreseeability of such injury to such a person will be more difficult to establish than similar injury to a spouse or parent of the primary victim. But these are factual difficulties and I can see no logic and no policy reason for excluding claims by more remote relatives."

Alcock and the shocked bystander

Although *Alcock* did not specifically raise the problem of the mere bystander who suffers psychiatric illness caused by nervous shock resulting from witnessing a horrific accident, it seems clear from some of the speeches that such claims are not to be automatically excluded. In *McLoughlin*, Lord Wilberforce (at p 422) had contrasted the closest of family ties — parent and child, husband and wife — with that of the ordinary bystander, and noted that while the law, as it then stood, recognised the claims of the first, it denied the claim of the bystander: either on the basis that bystanders were assumed to have sufficient fortitude to enable them to endure the calamities of modern life, or that defendants could not be expected to compensate the world at large.

However, in *Alcock*, Lord Keith and Lord Ackner thought that while it might be very difficult to envisage the case of a stranger, who was not actively and foreseeably involved in a disaster or its aftermath, other than as a rescuer, suffering shock induced injury by mere observation, in circumstances which were reasonably foreseeable, such a bystander should not be entirely excluded, if "the circumstances of a catastrophe occurring very close to him were particularly horrific" (Lord Keith at p 397; also Lord Oliver at p 416). Lord Ackner postulated a petrol tanker careering out of control into a school in session and bursting into flames. Both he had Lord Oliver thought it possible to envisage a successful action by a passerby so shocked by the scene as to suffer psychiatric illness, if in the circumstances a reasonably strong-nerved person would have been so shocked. Although how a bystander could be regarded as foreseeably affected in such circumstances, when the House thought that injuries to relatives of the primary victims who were present in the stadium were not reasonably foreseeable by the defendant, is puzzling (see *Nasir* (1992) 55 MLR 705 at p 712). Lord Oliver further noted that the pursuer's claim in *Bourhill v Young* had not been dismissed in limine on the ground that she was no more than, at highest, a mere spectator.

Alcock and the shocked fellow worker

Alcock did not expressly discuss the fellow worker who suffers psychiatric illness by reason of witnessing physical injury to a colleague, understandably since the House of Lords was concerned with the claims of relatives and a fiancé, whose illnesses, they alleged, had been caused by the experiences inflicted on them as a result of the defendant's negligence. Certainly Lord Keith did not explore the possibility that fellow employees might be embraced by the relationships of "close friendship" of which he spoke. Lord Ackner thought that there could well be more remote relatives and friends whose relationship was so close and intimate that their love and affection for the primary victim was comparable to that of the normal spouse, parent or child of the victim. But, at best, Lord Ackner appears to indicate that the relationship between two employees would have to show a degree of love and affection comparable to that of the normal close family relative of the victim. On the other hand, Lord Oliver was ' probably discounting the claim of a fellow employee when he remarked that, in general, the likelihood of trauma of such a degree as to cause psychiatric illness would be less in the case of a friend or a brother in law than in that of a parent or fiancé.

However, in *Dooley v Cammell Laird & Co and Mersey Insulation Co Ltd* [1951] 1 Lloyd's Rep 271, the claim of a fellow worker was permitted. The plaintiff was in charge of a crane which was loading a ship with insulating materials. A defective sling gave way and the materials fell into the hold. The plaintiff knew that fellow workmen were in the hold. As a result of his fear that he might have killed them he was put into a state of apprehension and acute anxiety and thereby suffered nervous shock. Holding that he was entitled to recover, Donovan J remarked (at p 277): "if the driver of the crane concerned fears that the load may have fallen upon some of his fellow workmen, and that fear is not baseless or extravagant, then it is, I think, a consequence reasonably to have been foreseen that he may himself suffer a nervous shock".

In *Alcock* Lord Oliver placed *Dooley* in a category of case typified by the fact that the plaintiff has, to some degree, been personally involved in the accident out of which the action arises, either through the direct threat of bodily injury to himself (as in *Dulieu v White & Sons* [1901] 2 KB 669, where the plaintiff was put in fear for her safety when a runaway vehicle broke through the front of a public house where she worked), or in coming to the aid of others injured or threatened (as in *Chadwick v British Transport Commission* [1967] 2 All ER 945, where the plaintiff recovered damages for the nervous shock suffered by her late husband when he rescued and comforted victims of the Lewisham railway disaster), or where the defendant's negligence has put the plaintiff in the position of being, or thinking that he is, the involuntary cause of another's death or injury, and his illness stems from the shock of realising this (as in *Dooley*; *Galt v British Railways Board* (1983) 133 New LJ 870; *Wigg v British Railways Board* (1986) 136 New LJ 446; see also the Australian case of *Mount Isa Mines Ltd v Pusey* (1971) 45 ALJR 88, which was not cited in *Alcock*).

Lord Jauncey too, in *Alcock*, thought that *Dooley* was a very special case, of no assistance where, as in *Alcock*, the plaintiffs were not personally involved in the disaster. As Lord Oliver noted (at p 407), *Dooley* and cognate cases were not, in the context of *Alcock*, "particularly helpful . . . for they illustrate only a directness of relationship (and thus a duty) which is almost self-evident from a mere recital of the facts". And where the plaintiff is such a "participant" in the accident there is no need to establish the close relationship between plaintiff and primary victim which is normally necessary. Such cases were quite different from *Alcock*, in which the injury was caused by the grief and distress of witnessing an accident to another person in which the plaintiff was neither personally threatened nor directly involved, and where evidence of such a close relationship was vital.

How then was this guidance applied in *Robertson* and *McFarlane*?

The decision in *Robertson*

Treating the case before him as one in which the nervous shock arose out of what the defender's negligence did to a third party, and one therefore in which the relationship between the pursuer and third party has to be sufficiently proximate in order to meet the requirement of foreseeability of injury to the pursuer, the judge was satisfied that neither pursuer could claim sufficiently close ties of love and affection to the deceased to justify a claim for nervous shock. Rough had simply been a working colleague for a few years. Robertson and the deceased had spent the greater part of their working lives together and had gone out socially together from time to time. However, despite their genuine and understandable feelings about the deceased's death, their relationship with the deceased did not come within the terms of *Alcock*, namely of the sort that is found within the closest ties of friendship or family. The case was also "significantly different" from cases such as *Dooley* since the pursuers were not to be regarded as participants in the accident but merely as witnesses. Nor could the necessary proximity be established by the mere fact that the cause of the accident and the secondary victim were employer and employee, or that primary and secondary victims were fellow employees.

As to the possibility that an accident could be so horrific as to involve the ordinary bystander, the judge remarked that although *Alcock* had canvassed this possibility, no case on this basis had been successfully pled. And indeed, in *McFarlane*, a case very considerably more appalling than

Robertson, no liability on this basis was found. Accordingly, he did not think that a claim could be justified on the ground that the accident witnessed by the pursuers was so horrific that the ordinary bystander would foreseeably suffer nervous shock resulting in psychiatric injury.

The decision in *McFarlane*

The trial judge in *McFarlane* had held that the plaintiff in that case was a participant in the Piper Alpha disaster who had feared injury to himself, as distinct from someone who had been a passive and unwilling witness of injury caused to others. The significance of such a classification was noted by Lord Oliver in *Alcock* (p 408): "The fact that the defendant's negligent conduct has foreseeably put the plaintiff in the position of being an unwilling participant in the event establishes of itself a sufficiently proximate relationship between them and the principal question is whether, in the circumstances, injury of that type to that plaintiff was or was not reasonably foreseeable." However in the Court of Appeal, Stuart-Smith LJ, with whom McCowan and Ralph Gibson LJJ agreed, said that there were basically three situations in which a plaintiff may be a participant when he sustains psychiatric injury through fear of physical injury to himself: (i) where he is in the actual area of danger, but escapes physical injury by chance or good fortune; (ii) where he is not actually in danger, but because of the sudden and unexpected nature of the event he reasonably thinks that he is; (iii) where although he is not originally within the area of danger, he comes into it later as a rescuer.

The court held that the plaintiff did not come into either of the first two categories. The *Tharos* was never in actual danger; neither it nor anyone on board sustained any damage or injury. There was no credible evidence that the plaintiff was in genuine fear for his own safety, and, even if he had been, he could apparently have taken refuge in or behind a helicopter hangar. Nor did he come within the category of a rescuer, since he had rendered only minor assistance. And a defendant could not reasonably foresee that such a limited degree of involvement as a rescuer could give rise to psychiatric injury.

Nor was the court prepared to concede that as a bystander who had witnessed this horrific catastrophe at close range the defendants owed him a duty of care. There was no finding that it was reasonably foreseeable that a "man of ordinary fortitude and phlegm" would have been thus affected by what he saw, and, even if there had

been, the evidence of the plaintiff's history of depressive illness indicated that he was not such a man. That apart, the court's view of *Alcock* was that where shock is caused by fear of injury to others, as distinct from fear of injury to the participant, there must be a sufficiently close tie of love and affection between the plaintiff and the victim. As Stuart-Smith LJ concluded (at p 14): "In my judgment both as a matter of principle and policy the court should not extend the duty to those who are mere bystanders or witnesses of horrific events unless there is a sufficient degree of proximity, which requires both nearness in time and place and a close relationship of love and affection between plaintiff and victim."

Critique

Both *Robertson* and *McFarlane* illustrate the unsatisfactory state in which *Alcock* has left the law, despite the apparent flexibility which it gave to the classes of person who might successfully claim in respect of psychiatric illness caused by nervous shock. It seems that unless the fellow worker can be classified as a "participant" in the accident which precipitated his shock, he will be able to recover only if he can show ties of love and affection with the primary victim akin to those normally existing between close family members. Given the, albeit rebuttable, presumption that such ties do not exist as between siblings or, per a majority in *Alcock*, fiancées, it seems improbable that they will be held to exist as between fellow workers. However, just as Lord Ackner in *Alcock* distinguished degrees of brotherly love, ranging from Cain and Abel to Jonathan and David, so too there will be a wide spectrum of closeness between fellow workers. And it is certainly possible, although increasingly difficult in an age when recession and unemployment militate against the forming of long, close, working friendships, to envisage workers with qualitatively closer ties than were held to exist in *Robertson*: for example, two workers in a small, tight knit rural community, perhaps neighbours, who had known each other for many years, or two coal miners who over the years had faced common dangers underground. But it seems doubtful that such ties would be held as close as those to be found in normal family relationships. Although workmates may share a lengthy working relationship, as witness the 20 year personal friendship between Robertson and the deceased, typically they are not in each other's company for the time that normal family members are, nor do they share the confidences and intimacies to be found in such ties.

This apparent exclusion of the fellow worker who is not a participant in the accident seems the more unfortunate in face of the view in *Alcock* that the formal nature of a relationship was not important and that "the proper approach is to examine each case *on its own facts* [emphasis added] to see whether the claimant has established so close a relationship of love and affection as might reasonably be expected in the case of spouses or parents and children" (Lord Jauncey at p 421). *Robertson* too underlines the unfortunate consequences of the distinction between fellow workers, such as Dooley, who are classed as "participants" in an incident and those who are not. Thus if Robertson and Rough, rather than other workmates, had been the "rescuers" of the primary victim on the bridge, they could have shown proximity by mere foreseeability, without having to show close ties of love and affection. This seems to make the test of recovery depend on who got to the victim first, the "rescuers" or some other "non-participant". It points out too the significance of the judge's holding that the pursuers and the deceased were not members of a "team" engaged in a single operation, thus further denying force to the argument that they were "participants" (cf Lord MacLean in *Robertson (No 1)* who, in holding the pursuers' case relevant, noted (at p 568) that Robertson was "intimately involved" and that "all three were involved in the operation of transporting the metal sheet").

So far as the bystander is concerned *McFarlane* adds a condition for recovery which did not strike the judge in *Robertson*, nor indeed any of the House of Lords in *Alcock*, as necessary, namely that there should be a "sufficiently close tie of love and affection" between plaintiff and victim. This condition appears almost to deny the need for separate consideration of the bystander. The judgments of the House of Lords in both *McLoughlin* and *Alcock* treat the bystander in contradistinction to close family relationships, and indeed *Alcock* held that the only sufficiently close ties of love and affection were those between spouses, parents and children, and other comparable relationships. Surely, if the relationship between bystander and primary victim were that close, the plaintiff would be suing on the basis of that relationship, and not on the more difficult ground that he was a mere bystander. It is invidious enough to require that comparisons be drawn between two levels of family relationships, those where the necessary emotional ties are presumed to exist and those where they are not. But to require fellow workers and bystanders who merely witness disasters to establish the ties

which are to be found at the higher level of family relationships invites disbelief and does the law no credit. *McFarlane* too flies in the face of a number of clear dicta in *Alcock* to the effect that at least some bystanders would be able to recover.

Stuart-Smith LJ correctly points out the "great practical problems" involved in extending the duty of care to the bystander. Is it more horrific to see a petrol tanker running out of control on a school, or to see a child run over on a pedestrian crossing? Such matters are entirely subjective. Yet the distinction is of a piece with others which courts are obliged to draw in this area: for example, the distinction between the mother in *McLoughlin* who sees her family in an injured state in hospital two hours after a road accident and who is regarded as witnessing the "immediate aftermath", and the relative in *Alcock* who is doubted as witnessing even the "aftermath", far less the "immediate aftermath", when identifying a body eight hours after the disaster; the distinction between the sudden assault and the accumulation of separate assaults on the nervous system, which excludes shock caused by watching television pictures; the distinction between personally witnessing the death of a loved one, where recovery is permitted, and being told of the death by a third party, where it is not. However, these distinctions act as a filter to eliminate many nervous shock cases and so help to allay the "floodgates" fear which clearly lies behind the exclusion of a variety of shocked victims.

Ultimately such lines are drawn in the search for an answer to a more general issue, namely, the extent to which a person, himself outwith the area of physical impact, should have a legally protected right not to be caused psychiatric illness as a result of witnessing the danger into which others have been cast by the defender's negligence. It may certainly be that mere fellow workers and bystanders who suffer shock in the circumstances discussed ought, as a matter of policy, to be excluded from the class of persons entitled to recover. However, the reasoning in *Alcock*, *Robertson* and *McFarlane* in favour of the exclusion does not inspire confidence that the line is being drawn in the correct place.

NEWS

Appreciation

Clive Shenton, QC

The tragic death of Clive Shenton last month came as a stunning blow not only to his family but also to his many friends in the law, in politics and in the army. To write this gives some indication of the range of interests and the areas of life in which Clive was involved.

He was born in South Africa in 1946 and decided at an early age that the army would be his career. With typical determination he joined first the Black Watch and later on the Parachute Regiment and after a distinguished career reached the rank of major. However while in the army, he had on occasions to represent accused at army courts martial. This gave him an interest in the law, which he decided to further by taking a legal training in Scotland after which he entered the Faculty of Advocates in 1975.

At the bar he practised in both criminal and civil work and built up a wide circle of friends and a reputation for his reliability and his professional skill. In 1988 he received a commission to act as a temporary sheriff which continued up to his death. He also took steps to become a member of the English Bar and for a time lived in London and practised in the Middle Temple. However he chose to return to Scotland, where he found the lifestyle more congenial. In 1990 he became a Queen's Counsel here in Scotland.

From an early stage in his legal career Clive had been interested, and remained so to his death, in politics. He was a past chairman of the Edinburgh Central Conservative Association and also stood as Conservative candidate for the Dunfermline East constituency in 1983 and 1987.

Clive was a civilised and caring person whose life was rooted in his christian faith and whose interests among others spanned law and literature; the army and the arts; politics and pastimes such as riding. However he will be remembered by his many friends not just for these interests but for his warmth and his humanity; his directness and his great kindness to so many. To his parents and his sister Penny who survive him, and to his many friends who knew his true worth, his premature death has come as a heavy blow for it is indeed the loss of one who gave so much and had so much still to offer.

ALISTAIR McGREGOR.

— ◊ —

Appointments

Lands Tribunal for Scotland

The Lord President has re-appointed Mr Robin A Edwards, CBE, WS, as a part time legal member of the Lands Tribunal for Scotland for a further period of three years from 1 October 1994.

Court

Sheriffdoms: Grampian, Highland and Islands

Sessions for the disposal of civil business during 1995 will be as follows:

Aberdeen and Stonehaven: 9 January to 31 March; 1 May to 7 July; 4 September to 22 December.

Peterhead and Banff: 4 January to 31 March; 2 May to 30 June; 28 August to 22 December.

Elgin: 4 January to 31 March; 1 May to 3 July; 28 August to 18 December.

Kirkwall and Lerwick: 9 January to 24 March; 24 April to 7 July; 4 September to 22 December.

Inverness, Stornoway, Fort William, Portree, Lochmaddy, Dingwall, Tain, Dornoch and Wick: 5 January to 31 March; 1 May to 30 June; 28 August to 20 December.

Law reform

Scottish Law Commission: confiscation and forfeiture

The Scottish Law Commission in their *Report on Confiscation and Forfeiture* (Scot Law Com no 147; HMSO, £27.60), make recommendations for new legislation which would greatly extend the powers of the Scottish criminal courts to deprive criminals of the proceeds of their crimes and to forfeit property used in crime. The proposals take account of the United Kingdom's obligations under the 1990 Council of Europe Convention on Laundering, Search, Seizure and Confiscation of the Proceeds from Crime which came into force on 28 September 1993.

Confiscation of the proceeds of crime
Under the present law the courts' confiscation powers are limited to certain drug trafficking and terrorism related offences. The commission have

recommended that the confiscation powers be extended to all other cases in which a person has been convicted on indictment or on a summary complaint for an offence punishable by a fine or imprisonment above the normal limits for summary cases.

The new confiscation orders would catch not only the original proceeds of crime but also any other benefit an offender had obtained and any other property into which the property has been changed. Gifts to a third party or any other property that represented the gift would be taken into account.

A court would be entitled to require an offender to pay a sum not exceeding the amount of the benefit he had derived from the offence or, if less, the amount that might be realised from the property available to satisfy the order. Subsequent orders could also be made if (i) proceeds of the offence were discovered at a later date, (ii) there had been an increase in the benefit, or (iii) the realisable property either had increased in value or had proved insufficient to satisfy the order. Confiscation orders would be enforced in the same way as fines, with imprisonment as the sanction for failure to pay.

The law in terrorism related offences would not be affected. However, the existing provisions as to the confiscation of the proceeds of drug trafficking would be made identical, in all but a few respects.

Forfeiture of property used in crime
The specific powers of forfeiture available in relation to particular offences would be preserved, but the existing general power of forfeiture under the Criminal Procedure (Scotland) Act 1975 would be replaced with a completely new scheme, which would apply to any person convicted in the High Court or sheriff court, but not in the district court. A new "suspended forfeiture order" would be created which would be made as part of the sentence and which could be made in relation to heritable or moveable property, wherever situated. Forfeiture of the property would in general follow automatically after the lapse of a specific period — 60 days for moveable property, six months for heritable property — during which the accused could appeal.

A court could only make an order if the Crown applied for it and a court would have to be satisfied beyond reasonable doubt (i) that the property was in the accused's ownership, possession or control, either at the time of the offence or of his arrest, and (ii) that the property was or was intended to be used for the purpose of committing any offence.

Restraint orders
In cases where there are reasonable grounds for believing that a confiscation or forfeiture order might be made, the Crown would be able to apply for a restraint order to be made up to 28 days prior to the raising of proceedings, interdicting any person from dealing with property which might be required to satisfy such orders. If a restraint order were made, the court could in addition make an order inhibiting that person or granting warrant for arrestment or seizure of the property. Relevant orders would be registered in the appropriate property and personal registers. An administrator could be appointed to manage any property subject to restraint orders, which would also be protected from subsequent sequestration, liquidation or receivership.

Compensation orders
A court would be able to make compensation orders in addition to confiscation and forfeiture orders and could direct that the proceeds from the sale of forfeited property be directed first to the payment of the compensation order. Similar powers would exist for a person to be compensated out of the proceeds recovered under a confiscation order, where they had lost money or property.

Protection of third parties' rights
Third parties would be entitled to have recalled restraint orders affecting their interests and forfeiture orders affecting their property, unless it had been proved that they were aware of the intended use of the property. Compensation would also be available for those affected by such orders or whose property would be sold in order to satisfy a confiscation order. There would be constraints on the disposal of an accused's family home if it had been lawfully acquired.

International co-operation
Provisions would be made for the enforcement of Scottish orders in other jurisdictions and for enforcement of foreign orders in Scotland.

Death before sentence
Where an accused died before he was sentenced, the Court of Session would be empowered to forfeit such assets of a deceased as are proved beyond reasonable doubt to have been the proceeds of the offence.

In Vol 2 of the report, the commission have produced a draft Proceeds of Crime (Scotland) Bill, together with consequential amendments, in particular to the Criminal Justice (Scotland) Act 1987, to implement the proposals. The Government have already indicated that they will bring forward legislative proposals in this area at the earliest opportunity.

— ◇ —

Book Review

Textbook on Roman Law

By Andrew Borkowski. 1994. London: Blackstone Press Ltd. Paperback, £17.95. ISBN 1 85431 313 4.

An entirely new student textbook on Roman law is something of an event and an act of faith on the part both of the author and of the publishers. The Blackstone Press is to be congratulated on taking up this initiative when there is so much pressure to reduce the teaching of Roman law in favour of other apparently more modern subjects.

It may be said at once that the book has a number of things going for it. First, it has been written by an enthusiast who enjoys the subject and has enjoyed teaching it. He dedicates the book to "all students of Roman law at the University of Bristol for making the teaching of the subject a delightful experience". The implication is that the students also enjoyed his teaching and it is not difficult to see why. The author communicates his enthusiasm and enjoyment in his writing.

Secondly, the author writes well. He puts issues clearly but in general avoids oversimplification in so doing. He sets out the main points which a student should understand without glossing over the uncertainties in our knowledge of what the law was where there are uncertainties.

Thirdly, he takes opportunities throughout to refer to the continuing relevance of Roman ideas in modern law quite apart from his final chapter on Roman law and the modern world. For example, he notes that the French *Code Civil* uses some of the Roman tests of accession (p 180). At the same time he draws attention to the original social context of the law to aid understanding of the rules.

Fourthly, he includes many illustrative texts from the *Digest*. His approach here is almost the opposite of that of Lee's *Elements of Roman Law* which is essentially a commentary on Justinian's *Institutes*. Interestingly enough, however, his order of treatment largely follows that of the *Institutes*. The main divergences are that he deals with the law of actions before dealing with substantive law, very sensibly in the light of the importance of remedies in the Roman legal system, and that he deals with intestate succession before testate — which again is sensible even if it does not reflect the importance which the Roman lawyers seem to have attached to the latter.

Fifthly, as already noted, he devotes a separate chapter to the ways in which Roman law has exercised an influence on the modern world and more particularly on the law in the modern world. Special mention is made of the influence of Roman law on English law but he does deal briefly with the reception in Scotland (pp 340-341). The reviewer would encourage him to do more in a new edition and make his book one for British students.

On the negative side there are some mistakes or inaccuracies or suggestiones falsi. It is surely by a slip of the pen that it is said (on p 161) that a servitude was necessary to protect a view that was considered *un*remarkable — as the cross reference to para 6.2.4.2 makes clear. But, more seriously, it is not the case that slaves could only make contracts on behalf of their masters if so authorised (p 80) — this is one oversimplification. And is adstipulatio really a form of suretyship (p 282)? It is certainly an unusual use of suretyship to apply it to a case providing for an additional creditor. When an adiudicatio was inserted in the formula of an action, as in the action for division of common property, the action was for more than a declaration of rights (p 67). It is hardly true to say that Stair's *Institutions* were *modelled* on the *Institutes* of Justinian (p 341). Some revision of the text would be desirable, therefore, when the opportunity offers and some mention of the canon law might then be made in relation to the cognitio system and the reception of Roman law.

The author's desire to show the continuing relevance of Roman law has been cited above as one of the merits of the book. It is then something of a disappointment that he has put his main effort into describing Roman law as it was and has treated Roman law and the modern world as a postscript. His attitude is understandable, particularly in a book written primarily for English students of Roman law, and the approach can be defended given constraints of time and space, but when reference is made to the influence of Roman law on the modern law it is misleading to suggest that it was essentially the law as just dealt with in detail which had that influence. The reference to the Commentators adapting the law for practical use (p 339) is hardly enough. Perhaps what the reviewer would regard as a better balance could be achieved in a new edition.

W M GORDON,
University of Glasgow.

ARTICLES

The New Regime for Customs Appeals and Excise Appeals

Gavin McFarlane,
Director of Customs and Excise Services,
Titmuss Sainer Dechart,
London.

Dr McFarlane describes the expanded scope for appeals to the (now renamed) VAT and duties tribunal under the Finance Act 1994.

In the United States the subjects of customs law and excise law are strong specialities. Digests of American case law contain many pages of summaries of decisions on all aspects of these subjects, and across all levels of American court jurisdiction. The same is true of the major jurisdictions in mainland Europe, as is evidenced by the high proportion of cases from those states which find their way to the European Court of Justice. Yet within all the jurisdictions of the United Kingdom there is a paucity both of litigation and of reports on matters arising from some of the most complex legislation which affects British citizens. How has this situation come about, and how will it be affected by the deeply significant changes in both areas of practice which the Finance Act 1994 has brought about?

American case law spans two centuries of development, dealing with matters of importation, exportation and international trade which are virtually untouched by the jurisprudence of the various British jurisdictions. But there exists in the United States both an international trade court and a customs court. Groups of specialist lawyers have sprung up who practise before these courts, often exclusively in these areas. The same is true in European countries such as France, Italy, Holland, Belgium and Germany. In the last named country, the Finanzgericht produces a constant flow of cases which are taken to the European Court of Justice.

But search the law reports of Scotland, England and Wales this century, and few indeed are the reported cases on customs matters and excise matters which come to hand. Even quite basic matters such as what precisely is meant by an importation or an exportation have not been the subject of judicial interpretation. Interestingly, the reports of cases in the old Exchequer Court in London show that until the middle of the last century, there were regular reports of cases on customs and excise matters, at a time before the direct taxes administered by the Inland Revenue had achieved the position which they now occupy.

Over the last couple of decades a significant brake on the development of law in this area has been the prosecution driven approach of Customs and Excise. In many situations which involve what is in essence a commercial dispute between a business on the one hand and the department on the other, Customs and Excise will as a matter of course begin by exercising their information powers. Often they will go further and obtain a warrant to search premises, and so far as the jurisdiction of England and Wales is concerned, magistrates do not always carry out very searching questioning of those officers who swear oaths that reasonable grounds exist for suspecting that a serious customs offence has been committed. The very threat of a criminal investigation is often sufficient to deter a business from pursuing a legitimate civil dispute in commercial customs law.

Not only is a business disrupted by an investigation by the department, but it also creates a bad impression on employees, to say nothing of damaging a company's reputation in its trading sector. Customs and Excise are of course well aware of this. At the same time they will usually seize the goods which are the subject of the dispute, and are at present entitled to do so on what in many cases is the actual basis of the dispute, that the goods in question do not correspond with the importation documentation which has been lodged in respect of them. In other words if the importer believes that the goods are entitled to be imported at a duty rate of 5 per cent, but Customs and Excise consider that a higher rate applies, the fact that the documentation has been completed on the basis of the lower rate entitles them to seize the goods. What the correct rate may be is quite possibly something which can only be decided by a judge or chairman with considerable experience of commercial or customs law.

This was the very one sided situation which existed in the United Kingdom until recently; quite suddenly, a torrent of change swept in at the start of the 90s. First of all on 19 October 1992 the Council of the (then) European Community published as a regulation the Community Customs Code (Council Regulation 2913/92, OJ L302). This assembles in a single code the main provisions of customs legislation which previously had been scattered across a large number of regulations and directives. That fact alone had been sufficient to render customs law largely impenetrable to anyone unfamiliar with Community law or jurisdictions based on Roman law. But one of the most significant topics in the

Code was the establishment of a mandatory system for appeals within each member state. For all the other states of the Union, an appeals system was up and running by 1 January 1994. The United Kingdom obtained a derogation of one year, but despite that relaxation there are serious flaws in the UK's implementation of an appeals system for customs which will operate from the start of next year.

The situation was quite different on the excise side. Traditionally there had been a less tense relationship between trader and department, as those in the whisky industry would probably testify. Over the centuries a system of hands-on control had evolved, with large distilleries, brewers and tobacco interests frequently having an excise officer more or less permanently on their premises. In those circumstances it was scarcely surprising that warmer relationships sprang up than have generally proved to be the case in VAT and customs matters. The "in house" excise officer would often come to look on "his" trader as a kind of client for which he had accepted personal responsibility. If anything went wrong on the records or accounting side, the excise officer would regard it as his own responsibility to sort the matter out, and a reflection on himself if the matter failed to be resolved quickly.

Following a review of excise procedures, the system of hands-on personal control has been replaced by an audit based system. This has shifted responsibility for the accuracy of revenue declarations on to the business itself. Returns must now be made, as is the case with VAT, and assessments will be raised where returns are not made, or if made, Customs and Excise believe them to be inaccurate. Most of the minor criminal excise offences which can only be tried summarily have been decriminalised, and a range of civil penalties introduced in their place. By this means Customs and Excise intend dramatically to increase their excise revenue to an annual figure of £28.6 billion cited in their management plan for the years 1994 to 1997. As a quid pro quo for these administratively imposed civil penalties, they have been obliged to accept an appeals system. Thus the VAT tribunal has been extended to become the VAT and duties tribunal in order to cover the new appeals in excise and in customs.

A great deal of change in machinery and procedure has been brought about by the relevant sections of the Finance Act. Although major decriminalisation has been applied to excise, it has not yet come in on the customs side. But a system of civil penalties is clearly likely to come

in customs before many years have elapsed, and the appeal provisions as a whole have been drafted to dovetail with them. It is a complicated situation. An appeal to the new tribunal can only be initiated if the department has first reviewed a decision which it has made, or is assumed to have reviewed it. But there is no duty to review a decision unless Customs and Excise have first been required by notice in writing to carry out a review of the decision. And that requirement to conduct a review must have been made by a notice given within 45 days of written notice of the commissioners' decision or their assessment.

It is crucial to note that those decisions in respect of which a review may be requested and which in consequence are appealable are specifically set out in the Finance Act. These decisions are divided into those which are fully appealable, and capable of being allowed or dismissed, or those which are limited by being subject only to a form of judicial review. These are the basic decisions which are fully appealable: in connection with any customs duty or agricultural levy, (i) liability to a duty or levy; (ii) the rate of a duty or levy; (iii) the amount of a duty or levy, (iv) the liability of a particular person; (v) any entitlement to repayment, remission or drawback of any duty or levy (s 14 (1) (a)). An appeal may also be made against any liability to an excise duty or its amount. And the new penalties or the amount imposed may also be fully appealable.

These full appeals contrast very much with those more limited appeals in respect of ancillary matters. Here the appellate jurisdiction of the tribunals will be confined to the following powers: (a) to direct that a decision is to cease to have effect from a particular time; (b) to require Customs and Excise to carry out a further review of its original decision; (c) where a decision has been acted on or cannot be further reviewed, to declare the decision to have been unreasonable, and to give directions as to the steps to be taken to ensure that further instances of unreasonableness do not occur in future (s 14 (4)). But there is no provision for compensation after a successful appeal where an ancillary matter has been reviewed by a tribunal.

In the case of customs matters, those ancillary matters subject to limited judicial review are listed in Sched 5 to the Finance Act 1994. A number arise specifically under the Community Customs Code. These include decisions relating to (a) whether entry, unloading, transhipment or release of goods is to be allowed; (b) whether permission for examination of or taking samples from goods is to be granted; (c) the route to be used for the movement of goods; (d) whether procedures or formalities have been satisfied or complied with; (e) the designation or approval of any place or area; (f) the continuation, authorisation or approval of processing or other operations; (g) the warehousing or construction of a building; (h) requirements for the supply or furnishing of any document; (i) sampling of goods; (j) expenses incurred in the supply of information by or on behalf of the commissioners; (k) interest on any duty or levy; (l) the conditions subject to which any of the foregoing decisions have been made; (m) whether or not a person is obliged to give security for the fulfilment of a condition; (n) the time when any obligation is to be complied with; (o) the variation or revocation of any of the above decisions.

The 1994 Act then sets out an extremely wide selection of situations arising under specific sections of the Customs and Excise Management Act 1979. These provisions relate almost exclusively to the exercise of discretions by the department. The limited judicial review procedure built into these appeals therefore works in the following way when applied to a particular decision which may be appealed. If an appeal is brought, the tribunal may decide that the decision is to cease to have effect from a particular time, or that the commissioners must carry out a further review of the original decision, or it may make a declaration that the decision was unreasonable, and give directions to ensure that a repetition does not in future occur. On the other hand, the tribunal may dismiss the appeal.

Considerable difficulty will be caused by the imposition of a 45 day review period. Importers in particular will need to mount an immediate appeal if a dispute with Customs and Excise arises. There will be contracts to fulfil, and customers demanding their goods. This brings the question of seizure into sharp focus. As the law stands at present, the grounds on which goods have been seized as liable to forfeiture do not fall within the jurisdiction of the tribunals. This omission must be swiftly repaired in a future Finance Act. Customs and Excise cannot be allowed to operate a system of commercial blackmail at the ports and airports, particularly when they have failed to implement the recommendation of the Keith committee that access to the county court should be allowed. In fact they are under no legal obligation to set the matter down for court hearing at all.

The overlap between criminal and civil jurisdictions is very blurred in customs and excise law. The new tribunals must ensure that the department does not seek to place a dead hand on appeals by claiming that a criminal investigation is in progress, and that accordingly the tribunals cannot hear the case. A robust stance must be taken by the chairmen from the outset whenever a conflict arises, or they may find that they will have few live appeals to decide.

Re Charge Card Services Ltd and Guarantees

D P Sellar,
Lecturer in Private Law,
University of Edinburgh.

Mr Sellar explores an apparent limitation on the right of set off in Scots law which has implications in particular for commercial organisations acting as guarantors.

In a useful article published at 1991 SLT (News) 361, Mr A G Williamson considered the relevance to Scots law of the controversial English case of *Re Charge Card Services Ltd* [1987] Ch 150, a case which he graphically and justifiably described as having caused "in some cases panic among lending institutions in England". Put very briefly, Millet J decided in that case that it was conceptually impossible for a creditor having a right against a debtor under a contract (most obviously a cash deposit with a bank) to create a charge over that right in favour of the debtor himself. Such a charge is described by bankers and banking lawyers as a "charge back". Mr Williamson concluded that the decision "has little significance to the law of Scotland" (supra, p 363).

The purpose of this paper is to suggest that the position may be rather more difficult than Mr Williamson concluded. The problems arise in relation to guarantees and in particular to the received view of the guarantor's right of relief or indemnity from the principal debtor. The received view of the guarantor's right on the insolvency of the principal debtor may not in fact be as settled or as logical as the standard textbooks suggest.

It is unnecessary to rehearse the rather complicated detail of *Re Charge Card Services Ltd*, which arose out of the unique liquidation of a company operating credit card arrangements with retailers and card holders. It is sufficient to state the two general propositions of English law which

Millet J used to decide the dispute between the liquidator of the card company and a factoring company, to which the credit card company had sold the debts due to it by the card holders. The first proposition was (as stated above) that it was conceptually impossible for a creditor to create a charge back, even as an English equitable charge. The second proposition was that, in relation to set off on liquidation, a debtor of the insolvent company could "set off" a contingent right which he had against an obligation which would otherwise have been due to the company. A contingent right was held to include one whose existence, and not merely whose extent, was uncertain.

Having described *Re Charge Card Services Ltd* in considerably more detail, Mr Williamson made two general comments. The first was, as already stated, that the case "has little significance to the law of Scotland". This was because it was even clearer in Scots law that a charge back could not be created. A fixed security over a debt could be created only by an assignation in security and such an assignation to the debtor would discharge him.

Mr Williamson's second and more positive comment was that that case had now apparently brought "English law into line with Scots law". On insolvency Scots law had always extended the usual rules of set off so that "contingent debts might be set off against liquid debts". In other words, the lack of a charge back was of no practical significance.

The writer accepts Mr Williamson's rejection of a charge back, subject to a lingering doubt on the effect of a floating charge. It is not, however, accepted that the lack of a charge back is of no practical importance. This is because Mr Williamson's description of the Scots law of set off on insolvency, while generally correct, appears to be subject to a qualification which has serious practical implications. They relate especially to the lending institutions whose alarm Mr Williamson described. That qualification is that a guarantor may not always be allowed to set off the contingent right of relief (which he has against the principal debtor) against a separate obligation owed by the guarantor to the debtor. The guarantor's right of set off is excluded where the principal debtor has been wound up or sequestrated and the creditor ranks on, and receives a dividend from, the insolvent estate, recovering the balance from the guarantor (see *Anderson v Mackinnon* (1876) 3 R 608 and *Mackinnon v Monkhouse* (1881) 9 R 393, both of which involved accommodation parties to bills of exchange, who are in effect guarantors). This is the rule in insolvency against "double ranking" or "double proof" in English terminology. The principle behind the rule is, as the name suggests, to prevent the guaranteed debt receiving two dividends from the insolvent estate, which would be inequitable to the other creditors.

The reason why the basic rule is extended to exclude set off is clearly set out in the following statement of the Lord President (Inglis) in *Anderson v Mackinnon* (at p 614): "But the *right of retention depends on whether there is a debt due for which* [*the guarantor*] *is entitled to be* ranked on [the principal debtors'] estate. I am of the opinion that there is not, on the ground that it would be a double ranking for the same debt. The bills for £4,000 have been ranked on the estate of [the principal debtors] by [the creditors]. They have received a dividend, and when a *bankrupt estate pays a dividend it pays the debt*" [emphasis added].

The practical importance of this exception is increased by the fact that the rule against double ranking also applies to the very common form of guarantee which secures the whole principal obligation, subject only to a limit on the guarantor's liability. On the winding up, or sequestration, of the principal obligant the creditor under that form of guarantee may rank for the whole obligation on the insolvent estate and receive a dividend from it. The creditor may again recover the balance of the obligation from the guarantor up to the limit of his liability (see, for example, *Harvie's Trs v Bank of Scotland* (1885) 12 R 1141, especially per Lord President Inglis, at p 1145).

The practical importance of this exception to the guarantor's right of set off is seen in two common situations. The first is where each member of a group of companies gives cross guarantees of the indebtedness of the others, typically bank facilities. The member whose guarantee is called may also owe money to the member whose liabilities have been guaranteed.

The second common situation is where a bank gives a guarantee or related obligation, such as a performance bond. Bank guarantees are, for example, commonly given to obtain the release of diligence on the dependence of a court action. They also commonly secure deferred consideration in sale transactions. If the guarantee is called, the bank cannot simply apply any deposits of its customer (or any of his other credit balances) to reimburse itself. This "exposure" of banks has been keenly appreciated by eminent English banking lawyers, such as Peter Wood, who has also vigorously argued that a charge back can in fact be created in English law (see, for example, his admirable *English and International Set-Off*, paras 5.138 and 10.82, especially the former passage, in which he stresses the practical implications of the limitations of set off in relation to guarantees given by institutions). It is curious that there seems to be no express equivalent English authority to *Anderson v Mackinnon*. The cases such as *Re Oriental Commercial Bank* (1871) LR 7 Ch App 99, which is referred to by Mr Wood and was approved in *Barclays Bank Ltd v TOSG Trust Fund Ltd* [1984] AC 626 at p 637, all relate to a positive attempt to prove in the insolvency rather than to a defence of set off. The exclusion of set off is simply derived from the rule that set off requires the right to prove in the insolvent estate.

It is, therefore, hardly surprising that banks and other lending institutions which give guarantees protect themselves by requiring the client to place security of the bank's obligations with a different legal entity, if only a different company in the bank's group. The customer's right to that deposit is then charged in security of the bank's right of indemnity, as it is termed in English law. That cautious practice is also followed in Scotland, with the particular feature that the deposit can only be secured by an assignation in security or by a floating charge. It is quite clear that the guarantor's right of relief can be protected by an actual security. The common law rule against double ranking does not extend that far (see *Jamieson v Forrest* (1874) 2 R 701). There is, however, a rather obscure statutory restriction on the guarantor's right to secure his right of relief imposed by s 60 (2) of the Bankruptcy (Scotland) Act 1985, as applied to liquidations by rule 4.16 (1) (e) of the Insolvency (Scotland) Rules 1986. It is unnecessary to elaborate here on that rather difficult restriction.

There is, however, an irony in the extension of the rule against double ranking to deprive the guarantor of the usual right to set off contingent rights. The cases of *Anderson v Mackinnon* and *Mackinnon v Monkhouse* are far more doubtful authorities in relation to the extended rule than the later textbooks imply. These simply cite the two cases without qualification (see for example, *Green's Encyclopaedia of the Laws of Scotland*, Vol 3, para 402 (by J M Irvine); Lillie's *Mercantile Law of Scotland* (5th ed), p 248; Gow's *The Mercantile and Industrial Law of Scotland*, p 643; Gloag and Henderson, *Introduction to the Law of Scotland* (9th ed), para 21.17, and Wilson, *The Law of Scotland Relating to Debt* (2nd ed), para 13.10), subject to one exception dealt with below.

The doubt on the extended rule is very clearly

advanced by Lord Shand in his dissenting opinion in *Mackinnon v Monkhouse*. As already mentioned, the case was typically complicated, involving a number of accommodation bills of exchange. The main issue was whether the rule against double ranking applied where there was an informal agreement with creditors but no formal sequestration or equivalent English process. Lord Shand also dissented on the main issue. This paper is, however, concerned with his criticism of the reasoning in *Anderson v Mackinnon*, which is seen in the following passage (at p 408): "I think it right to say, however, that I am not satisfied of the soundness of the view to which effect was given in *Anderson v. Mackinnon*, or that according to our law of bankruptcy the *claim of retention depends upon whether the party retaining is entitled to make a claim and to rank as a creditor*" (emphasis added).

In support of his dissent, Lord Shand cited at p 409 the first footnote to Bell's *Commentaries* (5th ed), i, 348, which qualifies the statement in the text of the basic rule against double ranking. The footnote states: "It will be recollected, however, that the subject under discussion is only the claim of indemnification against the general fund. The cautioner may have security for his indemnification (1) by heritable security, (2) by pledge or other security on moveables, (3) *by retention or compensation*" (emphasis added).

It is significant that Lord Ardmillan in *Anderson v Mackinnon* (at p 617) relied on Bell's general statement in the text but did not refer to the footnote.

Returning to Lord Shand's dissent, his Lordship also referred to the case of *Christie v Keith* (1838) 16 S 1224, as an express application of the principle stated by Bell. That case is indeed directly in point and vouches Lord Shand's dissent. Again the case involved accommodation bills of exchange. All the members of the First Division emphasised the difficulty of the case, and Lord Mackenzie in effect dissented on this issue. The conclusion of the other three judges is, however, set out clearly in the following statement by Lord Corehouse at p 1234: "This is no double ranking on [the principal debtor's] estate; it is merely retaining as a pledge that which does not become part of [his] general estate, until the holder of the pledge be relieved."

It is therefore both surprising and significant that in *Anderson v Mackinnon* the case of *Christie v Keith* was neither cited by the court, nor apparently even cited to it.

Returning again to Lord Shand's dissent in *Mackinnon v Monkhouse*, his Lordship also cited the case of *Jamieson v Forrest* as supporting his approach, although it involved actual securities granted by a bankrupt to his cautioners, who were also his creditors in a separate debt. It is again surprising that the case was also not referred to in *Anderson v Mackinnon*, since it was a decision of the same First Division which decided the latter case in the following year. That omission may be explained to some extent by the fact that the Division in *Jamieson v Forrest* simply refused the reclaiming motion without delivering any opinions.

It is, however, significant that in the *Jamieson* case the Lord Ordinary (Gifford), when accepting that the cautioners could apply their securities first in satisfaction of their right of their right of relief, expressly approved the footnote in Bell's *Commentaries* which has been quoted above. Again, it is curious that the Lord Ordinary did not refer to the case of *Christie v Keith*.

The case of *Jamieson v Forrest* can, of course, be technically distinguished from, and reconciled with, that of *Anderson v Mackinnon*. As the sheriff pointed out at first instance in *Mackinnon v Monkhouse* (at p 396), the *Jamieson* case involved an actual security rather than a right of retention. It is, however, difficult to justify the distinction between the two rights. If payment of a dividend by the estate of the principal debtor extinguishes the principal debt so as to preclude retention or set off by the guarantor, it is legitimate to ask on what basis can a guarantor enforce his security. A security is an ancillary right which presupposes the existence of a principal obligation. It would seem more logical to distinguish between (1) a guarantor ranking on the estate of the principal obligant and (2) a guarantor exercising either of the "self help" remedies of retention or realising an actual security from the principal debtor, neither of which requires the positive step of ranking on the estate. That is the very distinction stated by Bell in his *Commentaries* and accepted in *Christie v Keith*, albeit with express hesitation.

As has already been mentioned, the difficulties with *Anderson v Mackinnon* have been neglected in the descriptions of guarantees in the later general textbooks. These difficulties have, however, been recognised in the larger works of Gloag and Irvine, *Law of Rights in Security*, pp 481 and 482, and Goudy, *Law of Bankruptcy in Scotland* (4th ed), p 572. The treatment in Gloag and Irvine is not wholly consistent, with the text accepting *Anderson v Mackinnon* and the footnote citing, without any express disapproval, both the decision in *Christie v Keith* and the dissent of Lord Shand in *Mackinnon v Monkhouse*. It is perhaps implicit that the two later cases have superseded *Christie v Keith*. Goudy, in turn, recognised the force of Lord Shand's dissent in *Mackinnon v Monkhouse*, but preferred the principle that retention requires the right to rank on the estate, which the rule against double ranking excludes. After Goudy the only further reference to these difficulties is one citation of the case of *Christie v Keith* by the late Professor Wilson (supra at para 13.10) as a possible qualification to *Anderson v Mackinnon*. The text simply states the received view.

Given that the cases of *Anderson v Mackinnon* and *Mackinnon v Monkhouse* have been accepted, and presumably acted upon, for over a century, it must be unlikely that either a larger court or the House of Lords would now overturn them, however doubtful their reasoning might be. This is particularly so given (1) the statutory restrictions of a guarantor's right to an actual security and (2) the general view of English law.

In any event, the difficulties with the rule against double ranking confirm the writer's suspicions about Scots common law in the second half of the 19th century. It seems to have been neither as settled, nor as based on clear general principles, as has traditionally been suggested. Equally, the extension of the rule against double ranking is an interesting example of the law diverging from the position set out by Bell.

The historical comment brings this paper to the rather more pressing implications for practitioners and their clients of *Re Charge Card Services Ltd* and the impossibility of creating charge backs. The conclusion of this paper is that Mr Williamson was too sanguine in his conclusion that Scots banking lawyers can simply ignore the case. While the law of set off, as extended in insolvency, will usually give the same protection as a charge back, there appears to be an important practical exception which arises from the received view of the extended rule against double ranking. Any practitioner acting for a guarantor, especially a bank, will have to advise on the basis that *Anderson v Mackinnon* will be applied. A challenge to that case would arise only if a guarantor were commercially unable to insist on an actual security to protect his right of relief.

Finally, Mr Williamson's paper cites several times the relatively recent Outer House case of *Mycroft, Petr*, 1983 SLT 342. That decision also raises a number of practical and difficult questions, which deserve further consideration but are beyond the scope of this paper.

◆

NEWS

Court

Ogden Tables: new edition

A revised (second) edition of the Ogden Tables, the popular name for the *Actuarial Tables with explanatory notes for use in Personal Injury and Fatal Accident Cases*, has been published by HMSO under the auspices of the Government Actuary's Department (price £5.95).

The tables, which suggest the appropriate multipliers to be employed in calculating future financial loss, have been revised in the light of changes in life expectancy and further tables have been added so that figures for men and women whose retirement ages are 60 and 65 are now available. Assistance is also given with contingencies other than mortality.

— ◊ —

Coming events

Crofting Law Group

The first annual general meeting and conference of the Crofting Law Group will be held in the George Hotel, George Street, Edinburgh, on Friday, 25 November 1994. After the a g m it is hoped to have lectures on the subjects of quotas, missives, valuations from both legal and practical aspects, recent cases, the Crofting (Scotland) Act 1993, succession and what advice to give crofters wishing to purchase the estate of their crofting landlord. In addition to the lectures, there will be a question and answer session. The cost of the conference is £115 per person which will cover coffees, teas, lunch and a set of the conference papers.

The conference is open to non-members of the group; anyone wishing to attend should contact the acting secretary of the group, Keith Graham, Scottish Land Court (tel 031-225 3595; DX ED 259).

◊

Muir Society

The Muir Society of Labour and Radical Lawyers are holding a Drugs and the Law Forum at Sloan's Restaurant, Argyll Arcade, Glasgow, on Wednesday, 5 October 1994 at 7.30 pm. Speakers include Fr Willy Slaven and Gerald Carroll, advocate.

— ◊ —

Law reform

Right to silence: consultation

The Secretary of State for Scotland has published a consultation paper seeking views on changes to Scots law on the right to silence, judicial examination, and evidence of previous convictions.

The paper proposes strengthening of judicial examination, and clarification of the law on silence at trial. It also seeks views on the removal, in certain circumstances, of restrictions on the prosecution's ability to tell the court about the accused's previous convictions. It proposes that there should be no change to the law on silence before trial. Responses are invited by 31 October.

— ◊ —

General

Sir Walter Scott's Courtroom Museum

Ettrick and Lauderdale District Council have opened Sir Walter Scott's former courtroom in Selkirk as a museum. Visitors enter through the former sheriff's robing room and then to the courtroom where an audio-visual presentation is given. The museum opens until the end of October and then from Easter. Admission is free.

— ◊ —

Taxation

Disclosure of information to DSS

The Financial Secretary to the Treasury has approved a minor extension in the information to be supplied by the Inland Revenue to the Department of Social Security. The information is the names and addresses of employers likely to be liable for payment of class 1A national insurance contributions (on company cars and fuel for use in those cars) so that outstanding liabilities to class 1A national insurance contributions may be more readily pursued by the DSS.

◊

End of year returns: waiver of penalties

The Inland Revenue have published a new extra-statutory concession to assist those persons who are required to make company returns or employers' and contractors' end of year returns to adjust to the new automatic penalty systems. These will take effect from October 1994 for late company returns and from May 1995 for late employers' and contractors' end of year returns. The text of the concession reads:

Under s 11 of the Taxes Management Act 1970 any company may be required to deliver a return within a specified time limit and, for returns required by notices served after 31 December 1993, automatic penalties are chargeable under s 94 TMA 1970, if that time limit is not met. Regulations under s 203 (2) and s 566 (1) ICTA 1988 require employers and contactors respectively to render their returns of sums deducted within 44 days of the end of the tax year, i e by 19 May. Automatic penalties will be chargeable under s 98A TMA 1970, in respect of returns for the year ended 5 April 1995 and subsequent years, where these returns are not received by the statutory filing date.

For a limited period the Inland Revenue do not propose to charge a penalty in the case of these returns received in their hands no later than 14 days from the statutory filing date. This concession applies only to those company returns having a statutory filing date under s 11 (4) TMA 1970 which is no later than 30 September 1995, and to employers' and contractors' returns for the year ended 5 April 1995. The concession does not apply to any other statutory date which may trigger higher or additional penalties under s 94 or 98A TMA 1970. This concession should not be regarded as an extension of the statutory time limits.

— ◇ —

Book Review

Sheriff's Ordinary Court Practice and Procedure

Second edition. By Duncan White. 1994. Edinburgh: Tolley. Paperback, £26.95. ISBN 0 85459 864 2.

As this book is intended to deal with the new Ordinary Cause Rules which came into effect on 1 January 1994, the title of the book appears to be rather inappropriate. Under the old sheriff court rules, the ordinary court was a court which we were all accustomed to attending for tablings and cases on the adjustment roll, continued adjustment roll and procedure roll. In some sheriff courts, motions were dealt with in the ordinary court. However, I would not regard the ordinary court as being synonymous with an ordinary civil action.

In arranging the chapters of this book, the author has followed to a large extent the arrangement of the new Ordinary Cause Rules and much of what is contained in the new rules is reproduced and re-expressed in this book. For example, in relation to the options hearing, which is perhaps one of the most important features of the new rules, the author tells us that it "is the first occasion on which the case is called in Court (apart from earlier Incidental Applications, if any)". The author tells us: "the Sheriff is required to secure expeditious progress of the case by ascertaining from parties the matters in dispute and any other relevant information. Parties are required to provide the Sheriff with such information as he may require". This is really just a synopsis of what the relevant provision of the new rules actually says and is not really likely to assist the reader particularly.

I think that sheriff court practitioners will be unlikely to find this particular book of much assistance. It might be of slightly more value to students, except that it appears to me that terms which are in common usage in the court are not really explained for the benefit of the student. For example, the author says under "preliminary pleas" that such a plea "is a plea-in-law by the pursuer, defender or third party, which, if sustained by the Sheriff, will render it unnecessary to consider, in whole or in part, the merits of the action". As the civil procedure lecturer at Glasgow University, I know at first hand how difficult it can be to explain such concepts to the students. Mr White goes on to say that the most common types of preliminary pleas are normally directed against (1) the competency of the action, or (2) the relevancy of the pleadings. However, Mr White does not explain what is meant by competency or relevancy in this context.

There is no table of cases, no doubt because no cases are cited. There is certainly room for a detailed treatment of the new Ordinary Cause Rules but except for the fact that this book reproduces the various forms contained in the new rules, I do not think that it is likely to find a very wide market.

DAVID C CLAPHAM, Solicitor, Glasgow.

— ◇ —

ARTICLES

Sharp Cases Make Good Law
Sharp v Thomson, 1994 GWD 19-1181

George L Gretton,
University of Edinburgh.

Professor Gretton argues that the decision in Sharp
v Thomson *was inevitable standing the principles of
Scots property law.*

Sharp v Thomson was decided in the Outer House
on 11 May 1994, and became instant news.
Photocopies of Lord Penrose's opinion multiplied
like rabbits. There was some hostile criticism.
Professor Robert Rennie, in a valuable article at
1994 SLT (News) 183, has doubted its
soundness. The case has been reclaimed, and the
decision of the Inner House is awaited with
interest. The issue is an important one both for
conveyancing and for insolvency law.

The facts in *Sharp* were rather unusual. Albyn
Construction Ltd concluded missives to feu
property to Mr and Mrs Thomson. The first
oddity is that whilst the missives were concluded
on 23 May 1989, entry was stated to be on 14
April 1989, i e before conclusion of missives. The
reason for this does not appear. The next oddity
is that no feu disposition was delivered to the
Thomsons until 9 August 1990, more than a year
later. It is unclear what the explanation was for
this most unusual delay. In normal conveyancing
practice the disposition or feu disposition is
delivered on the date of entry. The recording of
the feu disposition in the Sasine Register took
place on 21 August 1990. But on 10 August — i e
in the interval between the delivery of the feu
disposition and its recording — a floating charge
over the assets of Albyn crystallised. At this point
one must note yet another odd and unexplained
feature of the case. It is the norm when
purchasing heritable property from a company to
check whether there is a floating charge in place,
and, if there is, to obtain a certificate of non-
crystallisation from the chargeholder so as to
protect the purchaser from unexpected shocks of
this sort. As far as appears, no such steps were
taken. No adverse reflection is intended as to the
competency of the agents involved. There may be
good reasons for what happened. The point is
merely that this seems to have been a non-
standard transaction, and that the factual background to the case is obscure.

The question at issue was whether the
crystallisation of the floating charge, which
happened on 10 August, caught the property in
question. If by that date the property had passed

to the purchasers, then the charge could not
attach to it. Conversely, if the property still
belonged, on 10 August, to the company, then the
attachment would include the property, with
unhappy consequences for the purchasers. Lord
Penrose held that the charge did attach to the
property.

In the sale of heritable property, when does
ownership pass from the seller to the purchaser?
One could think of all sorts of potential answers.
It might be on conclusion of missives, or on
payment of the price, or on the transfer of
possession, or on the delivery of the disposition,
or on the recording of the disposition, and there
are other possibilities too. Or one might adopt the
English approach whereby ownership does not
necessarily pass at an exact given time, but, so to
speak, oozes across. No doubt there is much to be
said for all of these. But which approach has
actually been adopted by our law?

The idea that ownership passes on conclusion
of missives was suggested for the first and last
time by the unsuccessful party in *Gibson v Hunter
Home Designs Ltd*, 1976 SC 23; 1976 SLT 94.
The failure of that argument was not surprising.
The surprise was that such an unstatable case
could ever have reached the Outer House, let
alone the Inner House.

The view that ownership passes on delivery of
the disposition has more ammunition at its
disposal, in the shape of a variety of dicta.
Professor Rennie (above, p 188) concedes that
this view suffers from "illogicality" but he
nevertheless prefers it to what he calls the
"Reid/Gretton" school of thought, which is that
ownership passes on recording. As one of the
members of this school, the writer naturally
thinks that Lord Penrose's views are in essence
correct. But he would disclaim any suggestion of
originality: he is merely a dyed-in-the-wool
traditionalist.

The whole subject is a large one, as the length
of Lord Penrose's opinion indicates. There is a
valuable discussion in the shape of a debate
between Professor Reid and Mr Iain Doran at
1982 SLT (News) 149, 1985 SLT (News) 165
and 1985 SLT (News) 280. Professor Reid's
views are restated at Vol 18, paras 640-648 of the
Stair Memorial Encyclopaedia. The present note
will concentrate, briefly but with a sharp focus,
on just two issues, one an issue of feudal, and the
other of civil law.

Feudal law is hardly a popular subject. Indeed,
together with "mediaeval" and "Dickensian" it is
an all purpose term used for condemning the

SHARP CASES MAKE GOOD LAW

grubby and unwanted survivals of an obscure and barbarous past. Of course, most of feudal law has long since been abolished. But some parts remain, perhaps unloved, and perhaps unloveable, but law. It is a feudal principle that no one can acquire land without sasine. After the Registration Act 1617 the sasine had to be recorded. As a result of s 15 of the Titles to Land Consolidation (Scotland) Act 1868 the recording of the disposition or feu disposition itself has had the effect of a recorded sasine. Prior to the 1868 Act (or its predecessor the Titles to Land (Scotland) Act 1858) there was some debate as to whether a delivered disposition or feu disposition completed by sasine, but with no recording, was sufficient to pass the property. This debate was laid to rest by *Young v Leith* (1847) 9 D 932, a case to which Lord Penrose refers. As a decision of the whole court its authority is high. But in fact it was not necessary to rely on that case, because the situation in *Sharp* was a fortiori of *Young v Leith*. For in *Young v Leith* there had at least been sasine. In *Sharp* there had been no sasine. (Sasine today is obtained by recording.) If in *Young v Leith* there had been merely a delivered disposition, no one would have even thought the case worth litigating. Indeed, the law is that even an unsecured creditor can by diligence defeat the rights of a purchaser, and this even after delivery of the disposition: see the leading case of *Mitchell v Ferguson* (1781) Mor 10296.

Given *Young v Leith*, Lord Penrose had little choice. But what the unsuccessful party was seeking in *Sharp* was something more fundamental than an attempt to overturn the long settled interpretation of the 1617 Act. The unsuccessful party was asking the court to do that and more, namely to hold that the doctrine of sasine, round which feudal conveyancing revolves, and which much of the 19th century conveyancing legislation deals with, is in truth not part of the common law of Scotland. What is at issue here is something much more important than niceties of judicial precedent.

The other point is not a feudal one. Over the centuries, the feudal element in our land law has dwindled, while the Roman or civilian element has grown. As in all civilian systems, there exist certain real rights. Of these the chief is ownership, though there are others too, such as servitudes and rights in security. Now, nothing is better established than that a purchaser acquires no real right unless and until he records the disposition, or feu disposition, in his favour. Whatever else one may think of the dicta of Lord Emslie in *Gibson v Hunter Home Designs Ltd*, the

Lord President was surely right when he said that a purchaser's "acquisition of a real right to the subjects is dependent upon recording the disposition". It follows that until recording a purchaser does not have ownership, for if he had, he would have a real right, and he has no real right without recording. If Lord Penrose's decision were wrong, the curious consequence would seem to follow that ownership is not one of the real rights. On the contrary, it is submitted that in holding that ownership had not yet passed to the purchasers, Lord Penrose was correct. Any other decision would have put an axe to our system of property law.

There have been suggestions that the decision could upset conveyancing practice. My own view is the reverse, for conveyancing practice is based on the assumption that the law is as Lord Penrose states it. It has long been normal practice when buying heritable property from a company which has granted a floating charge to insist on a certificate of non-crystallisation. This of course is a document executed by the chargeholder assenting to the sale and confirming that the charge has not attached and will not do so for a certain period. If Lord Penrose's view were incorrect, this aspect of conveyancing practice would seem pointless to the extent that it covers the post-delivery period.

Lastly, there is another way of approaching the facts of *Sharp*. The Companies Act 1985, s 462 provides that a floating charge can be granted to cover "all or any part of the property . . . which may from time to time be comprised in its property and undertaking". This wording perhaps suggests that, for something to fall under a charge, it must not merely be the "property" of the company but also part of its "undertaking". Now, what does that mean? The floating charge is one of the mysteries of the cosmos, but it is tolerably clear that it was introduced to enable a company to grant a global floating hypothec over its business assets. Thus it is arguable that an asset will be exempt from such a charge if it is not an asset with which the company pursues its "undertaking", i e its business. If that is right, then it would seem to follow that this particular property, though still owned by the company, was no longer part of its "undertaking". It was no longer an asset with which the company "undertook" its business activities. This line of reasoning (which I owe to Mr Scott Wortley) may be sound or unsound. But at all events, it would have the merit of not pulling up by the roots the principles of Scots property law.

Housebreaking with Intent

HM Advocate v Forbes, 1994 SLT 861

Jenifer Ross,
Lecturer in Law,
University of Strathclyde.

Jenifer Ross argues that the Forbes case, which held that there is no crime known to Scots law of housebreaking with intent to rape, and that such intent is irrelevant to a charge of breach of the peace, creates an anomaly in the law and is difficult to justify in terms of policy.

Introduction

Which is more terrifying: to come upon someone in your home who appears intent on stealing whatever is of value there, or to come upon someone in your home who appears intent on raping or assaulting you? Perhaps this is a distinction without a difference: each situation is terrifying, and yet the law treats each of them differently. The former may amount to a specific crime in itself, but the latter not. If there was ever any doubt that housebreaking was a specific crime only when allied with an intent to steal, such a doubt has been removed by the recent case of *HM Advocate v Forbes*, 1994 SLT 861; 1994 SCCR 163 in which the High Court upheld a sheriff's finding that there was no crime known to Scots law of breaking into a house with intent to commit a crime unless with the intent to steal.

Decision

The accused was charged that he broke into a flat, stripped, prowled around the flat and made himself a hood out of a sweatshirt, with the intent of assaulting and raping a 14 year old girl who lived there. The sheriff upheld the accused's challenge to the relevancy of the charge, a decision which was confirmed by the High Court. In the sheriff court the Crown had argued that the charge was a relevant one of hamesucken, but this approach was abandoned in the High Court, and instead the Crown argued that to break into a house with intent to commit a crime was a crime in itself (p 863A), an argument which was rejected. Instead the High Court held that there was a relevant charge of breach of the peace (something which the accused conceded), but that any averment of the intent of the accused was irrelevant to a charge of breach of the peace (p 865B-C), and sent the case back to the sheriff court with a direction to amend.

Housebreaking

Housebreaking is an aggravation of theft (Hume, i, 98; Alison, i, 282; Macdonald (5th ed), p 24).

It is also an aggravation of assault to attack (or threaten) someone in their own home (Macdonald, p 118; Gordon (2nd ed), p 818). Housebreaking with intent to steal may also be charged as a crime, even although the accused has not reached the stage of a theft or an attempted theft. This was first established, according to Hume, in 1810 at a time when attempted theft was not a relevant charge. The "first express judgment" that it was a crime (Hume, i, 102, footnote 2) was in the case of *Charles Macqueen and Alexander Baillie* (1810) Hume, i, 102, where the accused were found guilty of housebreaking with intent to steal. Since then attempted theft has become a relevant charge (Criminal Procedure (Scotland) Act 1887, s 61, now Criminal Procedure (Scotland) Act 1975, ss 63 (1) and 312 (o), under which "Attempt to commit any indictable crime/offence punishable on complaint shall itself be an indictable crime/offence punishable on complaint"), but housebreaking with intent to steal remains a crime in itself (Macdonald, p 50; Gordon, p 542), as is attempted housebreaking with intent to steal (*Burns v Allan*, 1987 SCCR 449).

In *Forbes* the Crown, in order to make the argument that housebreaking with intent to commit a crime was itself a crime, sought to establish that housebreaking with intent to set fire to the premises had been accepted as a relevant charge in certain unreported cases at the beginning of this century (p 863A-C). The High Court, however, took the view that these cases were not authority for the Crown proposition since their facts could be said to have disclosed attempted fireraising and thus have amounted to relevant charges of attempted fireraising (p 864D-F). The court knew of no authority for a more general crime of housebreaking with intent to commit a crime (ibid; Gordon, p 542), preferring to view the crime of housebreaking with intent to steal as an exception to two principles that "It is not a crime for a person to enter another man's house", and that "Nor is it a crime for a person to form the intention of committing a crime" (p 864A).

Malicious mischief

While housebreaking is not a crime in itself, nevertheless in the course of breaking into the house, damage may be done which would amount to the common law crime of malicious mischief or the statutory crime of vandalism. Malicious mischief is the wilful destruction of or damage to another's property (Macdonald, p 84). Section 78 of the Criminal Justice (Scotland) Act 1980 makes it a summary offence wilfully or recklessly to destroy or damage any property belonging to another. While either of these charges may be relevant in the case where an intruder has damaged the premises as he made his entry, the social function of the crimes of malicious mischief and vandalism is not the protection of members of the public from fear for their safety but the protection of the property of the property owner. While the charge would be available, it is not truly relevant to the actual harm in issue in cases of intrusion into a person's house with a view to harming them.

Hamesucken

Hamesucken was an independent common law crime which, until the Criminal Procedure (Scotland) Act 1887, was a capital offence. It comprises an assault on the victim in their own home, the home having been entered for that purpose (Hume, chap 8; Alison, chap 6). The crime itself has not been formally abolished, and there has been some variance of opinion as to whether or not it still exists. Macdonald's view was that it "[was] no longer prosecuted as [a] separate crime(s) but . . . treated as aggravated assault" (Macdonald, p 118). Gordon (p 818) also takes the view that "it is not charged as a specific crime", as does Ferguson (*Offences Against the Person*, p 3) who states that "the nomen juris has fallen into desuetude". However, McCall Smith and Sheldon (*Scots Criminal Law*, p 147) state that while "The term hamesucken has been said to have fallen into disuse . . . it is still mentioned from time to time in the courts". Indeed *Greens Weekly Digest* reports an appeal against sentence on a conviction of hamesucken (*Brown v HM Advocate*, 1989 GWD 35-1604: my thanks to Dr Andrew Phillips for drawing this case to my attention).

In the sheriff court the Crown relied on the offence of hamesucken to establish a relevant charge (*Forbes*, p 862J). The difficulty with pursuing this line is that it appears from the authorities that the offence was restricted to situations where an actual assault had taken place (Hume, i, 320; Alison, i, 199). Although the writers seem to be clear about this (Alison stating at i, 199 that "The mere breaking into the house, without the personal violence, does not constitute the offence"), nevertheless it seems apparent that a major reason for requiring that some material harm had been caused (Hume, i, 320) is that the offence at the time was a capital one. The Crown in the sheriff court accordingly sought to assert that it was not necessary that an actual assault have taken place, an argument which the sheriff rejected. Although this point was not pursued

before them, the High Court indicated that they agreed with the sheriff that an assault was needed to establish hamesucken (p 862K), and further, although not going so far as to say that the crime no longer exists as a separate crime, they state that "The point is of academic interest only, as hamesucken is no longer charged as a specific crime". This case can therefore be taken as establishing that where someone is assaulted in their own home, it should be charged as aggravated assault, although this does not necessarily mean that the term will disappear altogether from legal usage.

Breach of the peace

The alleged behaviour however may amount to a relevant charge of breach of the peace. Both the sheriff at the trial and the Solicitor General before the High Court recalled an unnamed case in Glasgow in the 1980s, where the accused had been charged with breach of the peace by breaking into a house with the intention of committing a rape and had been convicted and sentenced to 10 years' imprisonment (*Forbes*, p 863G-H).

Breach of the peace is a notoriously spacious crime. Although the crime originated in behaviour which breached public order, it is now firmly established that a breach of the peace may take place within the confines of a private house, not only where the breach within the house has an effect outside it as where noise can be heard outside (*Ferguson v Carnochan* (1889) 2 White 278; *Matthews and Rodden v Linton* (1860) 3 Irv 570), but also where the breach is confined entirely within the private space (*McMillan v Normand*, 1989 SCCR 269). Nor is it necessary to prove that any member of the public was actually alarmed, annoyed, upset or disturbed so long as it can be shown that the accused's behaviour may reasonably be expected to cause such alarm etc (*Wilson v Brown*, 1982 SLT 361; 1982 SCCR 49).

It cannot be doubted that the alleged behaviour in *Forbes* might reasonably be expected to cause alarm. However, while holding that a relevant charge of breach of the peace was disclosed, the High Court also held that an averment about the intention of the accused was not relevant and should be deleted (*Forbes*, pp 864L-865B). The basis of this decision is that under Pt II of Sched 2 to the Summary Jurisdiction (Scotland) Act 1954 the standard charges for breach of the peace refer only to the accused's actings and not to any intent. Relying on *Ralston v HM Advocate*, 1989 SLT 474; 1988 SCCR 590 the court drew a distinction between the tendency of the acts to cause a breach of the peace and the intention or motive with which the acts were done, the latter being irrelevant. It is accepted as a general proposition, not just in relation to breach of the peace, but in relation to crime in general, that the motive of the accused is not relevant to guilt (*Lord Advocate's Reference (No 2 of 1992)*, 1993 SLT 460; 1982 SCCR 960). What is important is whether or not the accused has the required mental element for the immediate crime. In relation to breach of the peace the required mental element is that the actings be deliberate and voluntary, not that it was intended to bring about a disturbance or to cause alarm (*Butcher v Jessop*, 1989 SLT 593; 1989 SCCR 119; *Ralston v HM Advocate*, supra).

However, it is an equally widely accepted proposition that for certain crimes an intention to commit a further crime may act as an aggravating factor (Gordon, p 168, where the examples relate to assault). An obvious example of this is assault with intent to ravish. It is not a necessary part of the crime of assault that there be an intent to ravish: nevertheless it is relevant to include this where appropriate in a charge as an aggravating factor. While there may be no formal, or common, aggravations of breach of the peace, can it be the case that, at least so far as sentencing is concerned, the accused's intent to commit further crime is not relevant? Certainly someone who broke into a house because they were cold (and who would almost certainly be guilty of breach of the peace when confronted by the alarmed occupier) would be less terrifying than someone who broke in and made it clear that they intended to assault or rape the occupier. Even without its being considered as an aggravating factor, evincing an intent to rape someone must surely heighten the fear or alarm caused.

Even if this is couched in terms of motive rather than intent, it is submitted that whether or not the accused acted with intent to assault or rape must be relevant to the crime (and see Christie, *Breach of the Peace*, p 58, who suggests that "'bad' motive may well be an aggravating factor"). Although the most typical breach of the peace proceeds as a summary charge and is regarded as one of the less serious of common law crimes, it is not necessarily either of these. It may be prosecuted before a jury as in *Forbes* and the unnamed case referred to by the sheriff and Solicitor General. Like all common law crimes the sentence is restricted only according to the powers of the court before which the case is tried: in the case of a sheriff and jury trial, unless remitted to the High Court, the maximum sentence is three years.

To the extent that the crime of breach of peace concerns behaviour which causes alarm, it deals with the issues raised by this case. However, the primary social function of the crime of breach of the peace is the preservation of public order, and that cannot be seen as the major issue raised by behaviour of the sort alleged. The application of breach of the peace has been greatly extended, being described as "an almost limitless instrument of social control" (Christie, op cit, p 105). This is in the sense that the tendency of the crime seems to be to bring within its ambit anything capable of causing alarm, or capable of causing another to retaliate or commit a breach of the peace, thus in effect allowing the creation of new crime albeit under the umbrella of an already established one. Where the alarm that may be caused is individual and clearly capable of being classified within one of the other traditional interests of the criminal law than preservation of public order, use of this widest of crimes may not be the most appropriate way to deal with the behaviour involved.

Trespass

There is no common law offence of trespass. The nearest offences are the statutory offences created by the Trespass (Scotland) Act 1865 and the Civic Government (Scotland) Act 1982. Section 3 of the Trespass (Scotland) Act 1865 makes it a summary offence, inter alia, to occupy premises or land without the consent of the owner or legal occupier, and is obviously not appropriate for the form of behaviour being considered here. Section 57 of the Civic Government (Scotland) Act 1982 makes it a summary offence to be found on a building or other premises in circumstances in which it may reasonably be inferred that the accused intended to commit theft. The Crown does not have to establish that the accused intended to steal, but that there are circumstances from which it is reasonable to infer such. As with housebreaking at common law this offence is only committed where an intention to steal can be inferred, apparently being designed to prevent the major mischief identified as being associated with people entering premises without authority, while also relieving the prosecution of the burden of proving the mental element necessary for theft, attempted theft or housebreaking with intent to steal.

At the time of writing it is proposed to introduce additional trespass laws into Scots law, laws which fit neatly, if controversially, into the framework of English law, but which are complete innovations in the law of Scotland. These relate to trespass on land and in the open air. Clause 51 of the Criminal Justice and Public Order Bill introduces a new offence of trespass on land where damage or threats have occurred or there are six or more vehicles together. Clause 58 of the Bill introduces an offence of aggravated trespass which is committed where someone trespasses on land in the open air (other than a road) and intimidates, obstructs or disrupts those carrying out lawful activity there or near there. The purpose of these measures appears to be to give greater powers to move on travellers. While they may have implications for acts committed outdoors, they have no such implications for housebreaking.

Attempts
In 1983, after an intrusion into the Queen's bedroom in Buckingham Palace, the Home and Scottish Offices consulted on whether or not the law on trespass needed to be revised (SHHD *Consultation Paper on Trespass on Residential Premises* (1983)), considering the whole issue including the possibility of creating a new offence of housebreaking with intent to commit a crime (ibid, 5.6). Such a proposal would not be necessary in England where the Theft Act 1968, s 9 (1) (a) provides that the offence of burglary is committed where the accused enters a building with intent to commit the offences of stealing, grievous bodily harm, rape or unlawful damage. The maximum sentence on indictment for this offence is 14 years' imprisonment.

Within the Scottish consultation paper the necessity of creating such an offence was questioned, on the grounds that almost certainly by the time the person had broken into the premises an attempt at the crime would have taken place (ibid). Indeed this issue was raised in *Forbes*. The Lord Justice General left it as an open question whether the alleged facts might amount to an attempted rape: the crucial test being whether the accused's behaviour could be said to be such as "crosses the line separating preparation from perpetration" (*Coventry v Douglas*, 1944 JC 13; 1944 SLT 129, quoted in *Forbes* at p 864G). This area is a notably difficult one and while in some cases the line between preparation and perpetration can seem to be drawn very close to preparation ("acts more than preparatory acts to enter had begun": *Barrett v Allan*, 1986 SCCR 479 at p 481), in others it seems drawn much further along the spectrum towards perpetration ("some overt act, the consequences of which cannot be recalled by the accused, which goes towards the commission of the crime": *HM Advocate v Tannahill and Neilson*, 1944 SLT 118 at p 118; 1943 JC 150).

On the one hand it may be argued that breaking into a house, stripping down and prowling around in pursuit of a plan to assault or rape an occupant is more than merely preparatory to the crime of assault or rape, or even that simply breaking into the house in pursuit of such a plan is in itself sufficient to cross the line; on the other hand it might be argued that, until some more definite act unequivocally linked with the act of assault or rape itself is commenced, there is no attempt at assault or rape.

An added complication in the case of a charge of assault is that the existence of a crime of attempted assault has been questioned (Gordon, p 815; Ferguson, *Offences Against the Person*, p 1), but this is because almost any attempt at an assault will in itself amount to an assault, thus rendering the charge superfluous but not irrelevant. Because of the difficulties associated with the law of attempts, if it is felt that the behaviour under consideration here is sufficiently threatening in itself, it would not seem satisfactory to leave the law so that it is necessary to fit the behaviour precisely into the category of a legal attempt.

A statutory offence?
If it is accepted that it is inconsistent and inappropriate that housebreaking with intent to steal should be a crime but housebreaking with intent to assault or rape should not, there are two alternatives: to allow the former to fall into disuse, proceeding solely on charges of aggravated theft or attempted theft (and aggravated assault or rape or attempted rape, and perhaps attempted assault) or on charges of breach of the peace; or to create a new offence of housebreaking with intent to assault or intent to rape. If a statutory offence were to be created the question would arise as to what sort of offence would be appropriate. If the same approach were taken as in s 57 of the Civic Government (Scotland) Act 1982 then such an offence would not require the Crown to establish the intent to commit an assault or rape, but simply that there were reasonable grounds for inferring such an intent. With such a reduced burden of proof, such an offence could only reasonably be a summary offence. The fact that *Forbes* and its anonymous predecessor were considered to be serious enough to warrant solemn trial suggests that as a matter of public policy it should not be restricted to summary procedure. In that event, the usual position of Scots criminal law that the burden is on the prosecution to prove both the behavioural and the mental elements of the crime should stand.

Conclusion

The High Court refused to declare that housebreaking with intent to commit a crime is an offence (*Forbes*, p 864I-J), holding, with reference to Lord Justice Clerk Aitchison's famous dictum in *HM Advocate v Semple*, 1937 SLT 48 at p 51; 1937 JC 41 ("It may be reprehensible conduct; it may be injurious to private and public morality; it may be conduct which ought to be criminal conduct; but that will not make it a crime by the law of Scotland"), that it is best left to the legislature to create a new preventive crime. It might be thought that the court could have gone further: it is best left to the legislature to create a new crime. At the same time, the High Court was able to hold that the behaviour already fell within a criminal category. It has been argued here that while such behaviour can amount to breach of the peace, the High Court has unnecessarily restricted the remit of breach of the peace by holding that the intent with which the acts are carried out is irrelevant. It is also submitted that the crime of breach of the peace is in danger of being used as a catch all category for any anti-social behaviour which is found to be alarming. In effect the High Court can use what amounts to its declaratory power to declare that behaviour not previously considered criminal amounts to a crime, without having to use such a constitutionally explosive power explicitly and thus without having to justify its use.

Housebreaking with intent to steal appears to have been introduced as a means of getting round the absence of a charge of attempted theft. There seems no logical reason now, apart from easing the burden of proof on the Crown, why that crime should remain in isolation since attempted theft has been a relevant charge for over 100 years. To retain it in isolation suggests that the law considers the protection of property to be of greater importance than the protection of persons. The reason for retaining it as an offence is not primarily to prohibit behaviour which causes or might cause a breach of the peace (although that is a consequence of most crime), but as another (lesser) crime in the armoury of offences against property. Similarly, the harm caused by the alleged behaviour in the case under consideration is essentially a harm against the person. If housebreaking with intent to rape or intent to assault is to be a specific crime, it is preferable for Parliament to legislate to that effect. In the meantime there seems no reason not to take the intent with which the accused acted, which it has been argued is not necessarily the same as the motive, into account in a charge of breach of the peace.

♦

NEWS

General

Muir Society

At the general meeting of the Muir Society, the Organisation of Labour and Radical Lawyers in Scotland, on 10 August 1994 a new committee was appointed as follows: *Chair,* Peter Grant-Hutchison; *vice chair,* Tom Davidson; *secretary,* John McLaughlin; *treasurer,* Juliet Grant-Hutchison; *committee members,* Carol Thomson, Raj Jandoo, Graeme Henderson, Gerald Carroll. The society's honorary president is Mr Andrew Hardie, QC, Dean of Faculty.

Forthcoming events will include: 26 November 1994, Employment Law Dayschool. Topics include the Trade Union and Employment Rights Act 1993, sexual equality and the law, race discrimination and the law. (Sloan's restaurant at 10 am.) Membership fees for 1994-95 are £25 (trade union affiliation), £10 (ordinary membership), £5 (trainees) and £3 (students and unwaged). Full details of the above and information about further events can be obtained from John McLaughlin, c/o Faculty of Advocates, Parliament House, Edinburgh (tel 031-226 2881; fax 031-225 3642; DX ED302).

— ◇ —

Obituary

On 24 September 1994, Alexander Galloway, formerly deputy county clerk, Inverness-shire County Council.

— ◇ —

Book Review

The Law of Interdict

Second edition. By S Scott Robinson. 1994.
Edinburgh: Butterworths. Hardback, £45.
ISBN 0 406 01485 X.

This is an extremely useful book for the court practitioner. Its great strength is the range of coverage — everything from the matrimonial interdict to performers' rights. This means that some guidance is likely to be found no matter what the problem. There is a useful appendix of casenotes of interim interdict cases. Procedure is covered as well as substance.

The only thing which prevents this book from being a "great work" (which it does not seek to be) as well as a useful working tool (which it is) is the lack of depth in places. On p 70 there is no discussion of the (im?)possibility of restitutionary damages for trespass. On p 151, although it is the case that there was an injunction in *Kaye v Robertson, The Times*, 21 March 1990, it was expressly and clearly granted on the basis of the nominate tort of malicious falsehood and not for invasion of privacy. This could be made much more clear in the text. The text picks up *McMurdo v Ferguson*, 1993 SLT 193, but does not discuss the constitutional issue it raises.

Despite sections on passing off and on private international law there is no mention at all of *James Burrough Distilleries plc v Speymalt Whisky Distributors*, 1989 SLT 561, in which the double delict rule was applied against an application for interdict. The book does draw attention to the very important case of *Wilson v Shepherd*, 1913 SC 300 and does at least comment on *Leitch & Co v Leyden*, 1931 SC (HL) 1, an equally important case but one which in the modern era of retained title and "green" reusable products requires careful analysis.

No court practice will be without this valuable book.

WILLIAM J STEWART

◆

ACT OF SEDERUNT

ACT OF SEDERUNT (JUDICIAL FACTORS RULES) (AMENDMENT) 1994
(SI 1994/2354) [6 SEPTEMBER 1994]

The Lords of Council and Session, under and by virtue of the powers conferred on them by section 5 of the Judicial Factors (Scotland) Act 1880 (c 4) section 32 of the Sheriff Courts (Scotland) Act 1971 (c 58) and of all other powers enabling them in that behalf, having approved with modifications draft rules submitted to them by the Sheriff Court Rules Council in accordance with section 34 of the Sheriff Courts (Scotland) Act 1971, do hereby enact and declare:

Citation and commencement

1.—(1) This Act of Sederunt may be cited as the Act of Sederunt (Judicial Factors Rules) (Amendment) 1994 and shall come into force on 1st October 1994.

Amendment of the Act of Sederunt (Judicial Factors Rules) 1992

2.—(1) The Act of Sederunt (Judicial Factors Rules) 1992 shall be amended in accordance with the following sub-paragraphs.

(2) In rule 6 (intimation and service)—

(a) in paragraph (1) (a), for the words "a copy of the application" substitute the words "a notice in Form 7"; and

(b) after paragraph (2), insert the following paragraph:—

"(3) Before the first order in an application is pronounced, a copy of the application shall be lodged with the sheriff clerk, who may provide any interested party with further details of the application.".

(3) In the Schedule, after Form 6, insert the form set out in the Schedule to this Act of Sederunt.

J A D HOPE, LORD PRESIDENT, *IPD*

[Acts of Sederunt are reproduced with the permission of the Controller of Her Majesty's Stationery Office.]

ARTICLES

Who has "Interest" to Apply for Parental Rights?

Lillian Edwards,
Lecturer in Law,
University of Edinburgh.

Ms Edwards examines the difficulties caused by s 3 (1) of the Law Reform (Parent and Child) (Scotland) Act 1986 with particular reference to the decision in D v Grampian Regional Council, *1994 SLT 1038.*

Parental rights, according to current thinking, break down loosely into custody, access and guardianship. Applications can be made for any parental right either ancillary to the divorce process (Court of Session Act 1988, s 20 (1)) or as independent applications by virtue of the Law Reform (Parent and Child) (Scotland) Act 1986, s 3. While most awards of parental rights (typically sole custody awards) still arise in the context of the divorce process, s 3 is a flexible provision which is finding increasingly versatile use.

Section 3 (1) states that: "Any person claiming interest may make an application to the court for an order relating to parental rights and the court may make such order relating to parental rights as it thinks fit."

Section 3 (2) then provides that in determining a s 3 (1) application the courts shall regard the welfare of the child involved as the paramount consideration.

A number of recent cases have explored what "interest" is required to apply to the courts under s 3 (1). While the issue is procedural, the interpretation of the provision has a substantive, and somewhat unforeseen, impact on the welfare of the child, and on the processes by which the state attempts to guarantee the welfare of children whose natural parents have in some way failed to meet childcare standards.

Who can apply to the courts for an order relating to parental rights?

The straight answer to this from s 3 (1) is "any person claiming interest". The first case to interpret this provision after the 1986 Act came into force caused some immediate controversy. In *AB, Petr,* 1988 SLT 652, a girl aged 13 applied for access to her two natural sisters who had been adopted into another family. In the Outer House, Lord McCluskey took the view that only parents or persons claiming to be parents could apply for "parental rights" and so her application fell. This rather restrictive view was justified (i) by the long title of the 1986 Act which referred prominently to the rights and duties of parents, and (ii) by reference to the policy behind the adoption legislation, which, according to Lord McCluskey, was intended to sever completely any legal link between the adopted child and any natural relations of that child.

In the subsequent Outer House case of *M v Lothian Regional Council,* 1989 SLT 426, grandparents applied under s 3 to be appointed tutors to their grandson who was in the care of the local authority and subject to a supervision requirement of the children's panel. Without such an order, the grandparents, unlike natural parents, had no right to attend the children's hearing. Lord Cullen, the Lord Ordinary, rejected the restrictive interpretation of *AB* and replaced it with the simple statutory provision that title to sue was available to anyone with interest, whether or not a parent. While this result was widely greeted with approval, the matter remained technically in doubt, since although *M v Lothian* went up to the Inner House (1990 SLT 116), it was not appealed on this particular point.

The matter was clarified to some extent in the Inner House case of *F v F,* 1991 SLT 357, where the Lord President's judgment plainly supports Lord Cullen's approach. Here the children in question had already been freed for adoption by the local authority and so ties with the natural parents had already been severed by law. The paternal grandparents, who had had no locus to take part in the freeing for adoption proceedings, sought to apply for a custody order in respect of the children, since they felt a viable family home ought to take preference over care by foster parents who were now seeking a permanent adoption order. The natural father was in prison and the natural mother's whereabouts were unknown. Lord Hope giving the judgment of the court held that s 3 (1) allowed "any person claiming interest" to apply for parental rights and was not restricted to parents or persons with pre-existing parental rights. This rejected the limitations placed on the section in *AB, Petr.* However he also went further, observing that even if the children had actually been adopted, there would have been "no reason to restrict the scope of s 3 (1) of the 1986 Act so as to exclude persons such as the child's grandparents whose legal relationship with the child has ended as a consequence of the adoption" (p 361L).

It is worth stopping at this point to consider the issues of policy here. It is arguable that in both *M v Lothian* and in *F v F* a liberal policy on who has "interest" to apply for parental rights was in the

WHO HAS "INTEREST" TO APPLY FOR PARENTAL RIGHTS?

welfare of the children concerned. In both cases, grandparents maintained an interest in their blood descendants while the natural parents had largely dropped out of the picture. However in both cases also restrictive statutory rules, concerned with ensuring the confidentiality of family proceedings (in the first case, Children's Hearings Rules, and in the second, adoption legislation and procedure) made it impossible for the grandparents to oppose what the state was planning for their grandchildren through the normal channels which natural parents could have used. Their only alternative was to use s 3. In the circumstances, denial of title to sue would have seemed inequitable. If on the facts it was undesirable to grant the parental right applied for (which was perhaps the subtext in the first case of *AB, Petr*) this could be dealt with at the merits stage, where no order can be made unless justified by the welfare of the child. (And this is exactly what happened in *M v Lothian*, where in the end the grandparents, although allowed to apply under s 3, were unsuccessful in their quest to be tutors because their averments were not sufficient to demonstrate that it was in the child's welfare.)

What though of cases where there are good policy reasons why some classes of persons should not be entitled to sue at all? There are two obvious classes of persons that come to mind here. First, natural parents who have lost their rights as parents because their children have been adopted or freed for adoption (with or without the consent of the natural parents); secondly, parents whose parental rights have been removed by the local authority using a s 16 resolution for the assumption of parental rights under the Social Work (Scotland) Act 1968. In both cases parents have been divested of rights either because they have consented to do so or because in some way they have been found incapable of or unwilling to meet societal standards of reasonable parenting. The question then arises whether they should be allowed to go back to the courts to try to recover rights in some way equivalent to those they have already forfeited.

Parents whose parental rights have been removed by s 16 resolution

Under s 16 of the Social Work (Scotland) Act 1968, parental rights over a child can be assumed by resolution of the local authority. The effect is to remove the child compulsorily into care. The parent in respect of whom the resolution is passed is stripped of parental rights (with a few minor exceptions) and these rights vest instead in the local authority. Parent(s) so divested of rights may challenge the local authority within a month of

notice of the resolution having been passed by a counter notice if they wish (as seems likely) to have the matter adjudicated by a sheriff rather than left to administrative discretion. This procedure has been generally criticised (see the *Review of Scottish Child Care Law*, chap 11) as putting the onus on the family to vindicate its rights when it might be better if the local authority had to take its case to the courts in the first place.

Life was made even more difficult for parents divested of rights because of the so called *Beagley* principle. In the House of Lords case of *Beagley v Beagley*, 1984 SLT 202, it was clearly established that a person whose parental rights have been assumed under s 16 is divested of title to sue in relation to that child, including title to make an application for parental rights including custody or even access under statutory or common law provision. Such a parent was therefore constrained to follow the statutory procedures of the 1968 Act if he or she wished to contest the custody of the child. Effectively their only remedy was to ask the courts to rescind the s 16 resolution. Initially no statutory procedure existed within the 1968 Act to allow parents to contest any decision of the local authority to limit or curtail access, and so any such decision by the local authority could not be brought to the adjudication of the court, and remained wholly within administrative discretion. This obviously unfair situation was rectified by amendments to the 1968 Act made by the Health and Social Services and Social Security Adjudications Act 1983 (HASSASSA), s 7, which introduced provision for special statutory access orders in a new s 17B.

However since the introduction of the new provisions concerning applications for parental rights in s 3 (1), there has been a sustained and successful attack on the *Beagley* principle. In *Trainor v Trainor*, 1993 GWD 11-716, Sheriff Smith accepted that a mother of two children who had been taken into care under s 16 had a right to pursue a claim for custody under s 3 of the 1986 Act. She also had a right to oppose the custody action of the foster mother with whom the local authority had placed the children. Two arguments were adopted by the sheriff in favour of this rather radical development.

The first argument was that the introduction of s 3 (1) of the 1986 Act was intended to remedy and overrule the injustice found in *Beagley* and identified in the dissenting opinion therein. The injustice identified was (as discussed above) that parents who had been stripped of parental rights had no legal mechanism left by which they could force the local authority to consider granting access. But it is reasonably obvious that the parliamentary response to the injustice identified in *Beagley* was in fact the introduction of the 1983 HASSASSA amendments to the 1968 Act. Furthermore, the 1986 Act in toto was introduced primarily to end the legal second class status of illegitimate children. As a byproduct of this it was found desirable to restate the law relating to parental rights — who had them and who could get them. This was essentially a private law consolidation exercise and there is little evidence that the Scottish Law Commission (who drafted the Act) or Parliament had any thought then to child care law repercussions. (Although they have had subsequently — see *Report on Family Law* (Scot Law Com no 135), Draft Family Law (Scotland) Bill, cl 11 (4).) However some statement that s 3 (1) had superseded the *Beagley* principle was virtually essential if the decision not to apply the ratio in *Beagley* — a House of Lords decision — was to be justified at sheriff court level.

The second argument used to justify *Trainor* had at first sight more conviction. As noted above, there is clear authority now, particularly in *F v F*, that a blood relative whose legal ties to a child have been extinguished by adoption has "interest" to seek an order under s 3 in respect of that child. (There were also obiter dicta in the sheriff court case of *AB and CD v EF*, 1991 GWD 25-1420, that a natural father of an adopted child would hypothetically have title to sue for access under s 3.) The follow-up argument adopted by Sheriff Smith in *Trainor* was that if a parent who has been dispossessed of parental rights by adoption can have "interest" to sue under s 3, then surely a parent who has been divested of rights by s 16 assumption must have the same title to sue?

However this argument neglected to note the latent ambiguity in Lord Hope's remarks. Nowhere in *F v F* is there reference to allowing parents who have had their legal links to their children removed by adoption to sue for custody of them using s 3. That case concerned a s 3 petition by grandparents, and what remarks were made have to be taken in that context. Lord Hope made the following relevant dicta: "[An adoption order] achieves a complete severing of such legal relationships as are inconsistent with the consequences of the adoption. But that does not mean that the facts about natural relationships are altered, or that a person who can claim an interest on grounds related to the welfare of the child is disabled from applying for an order under s 3 (1) of the 1986 Act simply because he was previously related in law to the child" (pp 361L-362A).

Did Lord Hope intend to imply that the making of an adoption order (or freeing for adoption order) left the natural relationship of the child with *all* its blood relatives, including its parents, sufficiently intact that they might all claim to have "interest" to make a s 3 application? Or did he merely mean that the relationship with the non-parental relatives was conserved for these purposes? The obvious differentiation is that while a child may have been removed from parents, either by adoption or by s 16 as a result of fault or inadequacy on the part of the parent(s), there is generally no reason to suppose those problems necessarily extend to the rest of the blood family. This central problem of interpretation in Lord Hope's remarks remained largely unexplored in *Trainor* but proved to be of pivotal importance in the latest and most significant of the s 3 cases thus far, *D v Grampian Regional Council*, 1994 SLT 1038.

Parents whose parental rights have been removed by adoption orders: *D v Grampian*

D v Grampian goes some way towards settling the controversy as to who has "interest" explored inconclusively in the previous cases. In *D*, a mother of two children was divested of parental rights after a freeing for adoption order was made by the court. She opposed the freeing order but her consent was dispensed with under s 18 of the Adoption (Scotland) Act 1978. She then made a s 3 application to be awarded custody of her children. The case turned on whether she had "interest" to make this s 3 application.

By a 2:1 majority, the Second Division decided that she did. Both Lord Prosser and Lord Morison (writing separate opinions) felt that while not "everyone in the world" with an abstract interest in the welfare of the child would qualify as having "interest", in this case a natural mother certainly did. Lord Morison required there to be some interest personal to the claimant, which rendered him particularly qualified. Lord Prosser by contrast denied that "interest" was related to some personal characteristic in the applicant, but rather was an interest in the application itself, and its outcome. He felt that an applicant would truly have "interest" if on the granting of the order, the applicants would have gained rights with practical consequences.

Both Lords Morison and Prosser agreed that the principle in *Beagley*, which the natural mother needed to surmount if she was to be successful, had been superseded by the passing of s 3 (1). (The principle in *Beagley* was effectively restated to cover the natural parent who had lost rights and title after an adoption order, rather than by s 16 resolution, in *Borders Regional Council v M*, 1986 SLT 222.) Lord Prosser, in particular, building on his earlier definition of "interest", asserted that in s 3 (1) the concept of title to sue, which was what *Beagley* was concerned with, had been replaced or subsumed by the concept of "interest". Thus the *Beagley* principle could not operate to cut down the right of anyone who successfully met the test for interest — such as the natural mother D — just because under the old law she would not have had title to sue. Section 3 (1) was innovative in providing a new approach to title to sue, wholly independent of the prior rights of the applicant, on which the pre-1986 law had depended. Thus the statement of Lord Fraser in *Beagley* that the parent divested of rights did not retain an "outsider's" rights, had also been superseded, at least in relation to s 3 applications.

Some parts of the reasoning of Lords Morison and Prosser seem open to question on a purely analytical basis, particularly by contrast to the dissenting judgment of Lord McCluskey. Lord Prosser's requirements for "interest", are, with respect, meaningless. Any person who applies for custody of a child and wins, gains (or suffers) the practical consequences. They acquire parental rights over, and responsibilities towards, the child in question. It is impossible to see how this defines a class of "insider" applicants.

More importantly, as noted above, it is hard to believe that Parliament intended the relatively recent cases of *Beagley* and *Borders Regional Council* to be indirectly overruled by the new provisions of s 3 (1) without even some degree of explicit language to justify that assumption. On the contrary the only explicit language found in the 1986 Act relating to the interaction between adoption and parental rights is that "Nothing in this Act shall . . . affect the law relating to adoption of children" (s 9 (1) (b)). Both Lords Morison and Prosser argued that the *Beagley* principle was not part of the law of adoption but was rather about either the law of parental rights, or the relationship between parental rights and adoption. But this is pure semanticising. As Lord McCluskey commented, *Beagley* is part of the jurisprudence describing what the effect of an adoption order (or its equivalent) is. One of the attributes of such an order is, or was, that the divested parent loses the right to go to court and apply for a parental right over the relevant child. "If ss 18 and 12 of the Adoption (Scotland) Act 1978 are part of the law relating to adoption, as

they surely are, then judicial determinations as to their effect are also part of the law relating to adoption" (p 1043G).

In the end the arguments about what "interest" is, whether it is differentiable from title to sue, and whether it is lost by divested parents, are not linguistic ones but, as hinted at earlier, policy ones. In *Beagley*, Lord Fraser, speaking for the majority of the House of Lords, expressed the view that where parents have been divested of rights by social work or by the courts, they were reduced as it were, not to square one, but to square zero. They ended up with less right than strangers to apply for rights over their children. In *D v Grampian*, the majority felt that such parents should not be reduced to square zero. They should have another chance to invoke the ordinary jurisdiction of the courts. As Lord McCluskey pointed out, this is effectively to introduce an element of res judicata. These parents have already been through one court process (or had the chance of going to the courts, in the case of s 16) in which they have had a chance to defend themselves against the loss of parental rights. In cases like *D v Grampian*, the new action is really an attempt to re-fight old wars. It is interesting that now, at a time when confidence in social work departments is low, and respect for family autonomy as an ideology is on the ascendant, the climate of judicial opinion has shifted towards allowing these parents their second (and perhaps multiple) bite at the cherry, rather than on relying on social work and the courts to get it right the first time round.

As became evident in *F v F*, though, there are severe procedural problems if different types of actions in relation to the child are allowed to be competent. As in *F*, a child might simultaneously in one court be the subject of an adoption order and in another the subject of a custody dispute. Such actions may well involve different parties, different levels of admissible evidence and different types of proceedings (adoption proceedings are private, for example, while a custody action is debated publicly in the normal way). For these reasons it will be difficult to try to conjoin such multiple actions. Yet if this is not done there is a strong possibility that no one judge can be appraised of all the relevant evidence and can make a fully informed judgment on the welfare of the child.

The res judicata point is not the only problem raised by the *D v Grampian* judgment. An associated problem is what the implications will be for the stability of new adoptive families. Adoption has always before been regarded as permanent, and as giving the stability which is in the interests of the child. *D v Grampian* realises the problem that was the subtext in *AB, Petr.* It is all very well to say that a natural parent who has been divested of rights either through adoption or through a s 16 resolution is unlikely to win at the merits stage, where the test will be the welfare of the child (unless there has been a fundamental change of circumstances since the date of the original divestiture). However the mere fact that such an action may now be legitimately raised and would have to be fought on the merits may itself be highly disruptive, both to the adoptive family, the adopted child and the natural family. Any thorough adjudication of the merits will necessarily involve visits by social workers, the preparation of welfare reports, possibly interviews with the child to ascertain his wishes, the exposure of the child to alienating courtroom procedures, etc. It is very likely that all these procedures will have been gone through at least once before in the not too distant past. There are implications also for social work and judicial time, and legal aid costs, but the major concern must be for the welfare of the child in the face of possibly repeated attempts by natural parents to recover full or partial rights over their children.

The final concern must be for what will occur, unlikely as it may be, if a divested parent does succeed on the merits. Where rights have been removed by s 16, this is not a real problem. If a s 16 parent recovers full parental rights, the result will be the same as if a court had rescinded the s 16 resolution, as is possible under the current law. If the parent regains only partial parental rights, they will share parental responsibility with the local authority. Since any one holder of rights can exercise them without the consent of any other rights-holder (s 2 (4), 1986 Act) this need not raise practical difficulties.

But in the case of adoption the situation is much more complex. The effect of a conventional adoption order is not just to remove parental rights from the natural parent(s) but also to render the adopted child the legitimate child of the adoptive parents, and not the child of anyone else (Adoption (Scotland) Act 1978, s 39). In practical terms, this means that the adopted child has a right to be maintained by the adoptive parents and to succeed to them, and these rights will persist even if the child is returned after a s 3 application to the custody of his natural parents. On the other hand the child will not have succession or alimentary rights in relation to the natural parents. The child will still be registered as the child of his adoptive parents (and vice versa). There are other legal connections which will persist, even if the natural parents recover parental rights, move away and sever connections with the adoptive family. If the natural parents are only granted custody, there will still be an argument that the adoptive parents have rights as guardians. There are numerous possible legal nightmares. Of course these are not new nightmares. In real life, many adoption relationships already break down, especially of older or special needs children, and the problems described may already occur. There is also a possible solution in the shape of the re-adoption of the child (authorised by s 12 (7) of the 1978 Act, although this is rather a sledgehammer to crack a nut). But in the past at least there has been no formal legal procedure by which a competent adoption could effectively be fought over again and terminated in the courts.

Having made a number of rather negative comments about the decision in *D v Grampian*, it must be stressed that the majority were not unaware of these difficulties. Lord Prosser acknowledged that "there are genuine problems, both social and procedural, if divested parents retain a title based on their interest" (p 1048F). There is a similarly genuine problem in determining how wide title to sue for parental rights should be. As a society we are more receptive to ideas about "open adoption" than we were at the time of *Beagley*, for example, and there may be a need to provide a framework for applications for access to an adopted child (see Tizard, "Recent Developments in Adoption: social work policy and research outcomes" (1994) 6 JCL 50). (It is certainly competent to make such an order at the time of the adoption order itself — see s 12 (6) of the 1978 Act and recently *K, Petrs*, 1994 FamLB 82.) Lord Penrose, who heard *D v Grampian* at first instance (1994 SCLR 515) and reached the same conclusion as the Inner House, gave the example of a situation where the adoptive parents had died during infancy of an adopted child. In such circumstances, he felt it would be inequitable if the only persons who could not apply for parental rights over the child were to be the natural parents. But such circumstances are highly unusual, and in any case the remedy of re-adoption might here be more appropriate. Rather than artificially restraining the ambit of s 3 within case law, it may be that what are needed are specific amendments to the adoption legislation and Social Work (Scotland) Act 1968 which spell out exactly when and in what circumstances a person has a right to use s 3, and when the statutory schemes should be left in peace.

Local authorities

Finally it is worth noting that what is sauce for the goose is also sauce for the gander. Or, less metaphorically, if parents can subvert the statutory schemes by using s 3 then so can local authorities — as seen in *M v Dumfries and Galloway Regional Council*, 1991 SCLR 481. Here a girl was in the care of the local authority on a voluntary basis (under s 15 of the 1968 Act — that is, parents retaining all their parental rights). Her parents decided to take her home after she had been in care for about four years, and gave the legally appropriate notice required where a child has been in care over six months — that is, 28 days. The authority opposed this removal for a variety of reasons, not least that the girl had been making unproven allegations of sexual abuse against the father. The legal position under s 15 in such a case should have been that the authority had 28 days in which they could legally retain the child and investigate the case to assume parental rights under s 16 if they wished to keep her in care thereafter. There seem to have been difficulties with this. Instead the authority chose to fight the parents' warrant for delivery on the basis that it was an application for parental rights under s 3 and therefore subject to the welfare principle in s 3 (2). Sheriff Barr accepted this interpretation and found it not in the child's welfare to be returned to her parents.

While the actual decision here is probably unexceptionable, it is again an unfortunate precedent. The net result is that the child is retained de facto in the care of the local authority against the wishes of the parents but while the parents still have legal custody and all other rights. This could be very awkward if, for example, they chose to question the authority's right to make choices relating to medical treatment or education for the child. In such a situation too, it is doubtful if the local authority is legally empowered to regulate access by the parents. This problem has been recognised by the Scottish Law Commission and their recommendation is that local authorities should be constrained to follow the 1968 Act procedures and should not be able to take advantage of s 3 (*Report on Family Law*, paras 5.7 and 5.8).

Conclusions

At the moment it seems fair to say that:

(a) natural relatives, including natural parents, can apply for parental rights in respect of children using s 3, even where those children have been the subject of an adoption or freeing for adoption order;

(b) natural parents can short circuit the procedure of the Social Work (Scotland) Act 1968 by applying for parental rights in respect of their children using s 3, even where rights have been assumed by the local authority using a s 16 resolution; and

(c) local authorities themselves can currently use s 3 to apply for parental rights over children, or to resist attempts by parents to exercise their legitimate parental rights in respect of children in voluntary care.

NEWS

Appointments

Council on Tribunals

Mr Ian Penman, CB, a former civil servant and currently chairman of Viewpoint Housing Association, has been appointed by the Lord Chancellor and the Lord Advocate to be a member of the Council on Tribunals and of its Scottish Committee for a period of three years with effect from 1 October 1994.

Court

Sheriffdoms: South Strathclyde, Dumfries and Galloway

Sessions and vacation courts to be held during 1995 for the disposal of civil business will be as follows:

Spring session, 4 January to 13 April 1995; vacation court, 18 April 1995.

Summer session, 19 April to 14 July 1995; vacation courts, 18 and 19 July 1995.

Winter session, 20 July to 22 December 1995.

Law reform

Right to silence: consultation

The *Scots Law Times* has obtained a copy of the consultation paper, *The Right to Silence, Judicial Examination and Evidence of Previous Convictions* (see 1994 SLT (News) 311), which proposes changes to Scots law following upon research by the Scottish Office into the use of judicial examinations by prosecutors and the recent debate in England and Wales regarding the right to silence.

Judicial examinations

No change to the existing right to silence before trial is proposed. However, amendments are proposed to s 20A of the Criminal Procedure (Scotland) Act 1975 to allow questioning at judicial examinations designed to seek admissions and to remove the implied prohibition of questions, the answers to which may incriminate. This is intended to reduce the perceived artificial nature of questioning at examinations.

Views are further sought on whether an accused should be required to give notice of a special defence at a judicial examination. It is envisaged that such a rule would contain some flexibility to take account of defences, such as insanity, which may become apparent only at a later stage, and of possible later amendment of a charge in an indictment.

Further suggestions on how judicial examination can be improved and whether more should be done to explain to juries its purpose and the significance of silence at that stage are also sought.

Silence at trial

It is proposed that the case law governing when a judge can comment on an accused's silence at trial be restated in a statutory provision in order to reduce present uncertainties in its application, and that amendments be made to ss 141 and 346 of the 1975 Act to remove the prohibition against the Crown commenting on an accused's silence.

Previous convictions

Amendments are proposed to enable evidence to be led as to previous misconduct of an accused in any case in which the defence leads evidence impugning the character of the prosecutor or prosecution witness or seeking to establish the previous good character of an accused, although an accused has not himself given evidence, as presently required. The defence impugning the character of a deceased victim would be added as a ground for leading such evidence.

Views and comments should be sent not later than 31 October 1994 to Joanna Goodburn, The Scottish Office Home and Health Department, Room 313B, St Andrew's House, Edinburgh EH1 3DE.

— ◇ —

General

Extension of Land Register

The minister of state at the Scottish Office has made an order extending the Land Register of Scotland to the County of Fife from 1 April 1995, the target date previously projected. The counties next in line are Aberdeen and Kincardine, with a projected date of 1 April 1996 (see *Parliament House Book*, p J703).

— ◇ —

Taxation

Interest on unpaid tax and repayments

An Order of the Board of Inland Revenue was issued on 20 September 1994 specifying that in accordance with the relevant regulations the rate of interest charged on income tax paid late and paid in respect of tax overpaid has increased from 5.5 per cent to 6.25 per cent.

The rate of interest charged on inheritance tax paid late and paid in respect of inheritance tax overpaid has increased from 4 per cent to 5 per cent.

The rate of interest paid on overpaid corporation tax is 3.25 per cent.

The new rates will take effect from 6 October 1994 whether or not interest has already started to run from that date.

A new edition of the interest factor tables used to calculate repayment supplement and interest regarding investigation settlements has also been issued.

◇

Enterprise Investment Scheme

The Inland Revenue have published a guide to the Enterprise Investment Scheme. The booklet (IR137 in the Business Series) describes how the scheme works for investors wishing to subscribe for equity, and for companies intending to raise equity finance. It also explains how "Business Angels" can invest in a company under the scheme as well becoming involved in the management of the company. Copies are available from tax offices and tax inquiry centres.

◇

Foreign exchange gains and losses

The Financial Secretary to the Treasury has announced that the Government intend to introduce legislation to allow controlled foreign companies to continue to use currencies other than sterling for computing their taxable profits. As drafted, the new tax rules on exchange gains and losses would require certain profits to be computed by reference to sterling. These rules will be changed in the next Finance Bill to enable controlled foreign companies to compute all their profits by reference to the currency in which their accounts are prepared.

Some minor amendments will also be made at the same time to improve the operation of the new tax rules on exchange gains and losses and financial instruments.

— ◇ —

Obituaries

On 22 September 1994, Robert Dempster, formerly sole partner in and subsequently consultant to the firm of Messrs T J & W A Dykes, solicitors, Hamilton.

On 1 October 1994, Neil Gerard McNeill, solicitor, McNeill & Associates, Dubai.

— ◇ —

Business changes

Bennett & Robertson, solicitors, Edinburgh, intimate that with effect from 1 October 1994 they have assumed their associates Kenneth M C Gray and Julie G Macphail as partners of the firm.

— ◇ —

Book Reviews

The Succession (Scotland) Act 1964

Fourth edition. By Michael C Meston. 1993. Edinburgh: W Green. Paperback, £30. ISBN 0 414 01048 5.

Professor Meston's book on the Succession (Scotland) Act 1964 has long since achieved classic status. Much more than a mere commentary, it combines accurate and comprehensive statement of the current law of intestate succession (and, where relevant, aspects of wills also), critical analysis of its development, and suggestions for its reform. Its coverage is suitable for students and practitioners alike.

This edition broadly retains the structure and contents of the previous one, and makes some improvements. It of course discusses all relevant developments in the intervening 11 years, notably concerning unworthy heirs, illegitimacy, and age of legal capacity. A chapter has been added outlining and discussing the Scottish Law Commission's proposals for reform. The appendix now usefully includes the text, not only of the 1964 Act, but also of other germane statutes such as the Forfeiture Act 1982. The table of contents is helpfully expanded.

The law is stated as at January 1993, and in one respect changed significantly before publication — the author's addendum, anticipating the change, is itself outdated. The figures for prior rights are now £110,000 for dwellinghouse, £20,000 for furniture, and £30,000 or £50,000 for cash.

The standard of production is excellent, and there are very few printing errors. No one with any interest in the law of succession, whether as student or practitioner, should be without this book.

D R MACDONALD,
University of Dundee.

Tolley's Environmental Handbook

A Management Guide

Edited by Freshfields' Environmental Group. 1994. Croydon: Tolley Publishing Co Ltd. Paperback, £39.95. ISBN 0 85459 749 2.

Intended as a reference work for environmental managers and lawyers, this book brings together in a single volume a very diverse range of legal, policy and management subjects including chapters on environmental audits, environmental management, integrated pollution control, noise and waste management. There are no less than 30 chapters in all and they are arranged in alphabetical order after the first introductory chapters. It might have made more sense to group the chapters into broader subject categories such as management, pollution control and energy and power.

Although the breadth of the work is extensive, given that it is a work of less than 500 pages a matching depth of coverage obviously cannot be expected. Even so, the coverage of certain subjects leaves something to be desired. For example, the two pages of chap 13, "Environmental Insurance", a very important area, provide hardly any information at all, while chap 15, "Green Investment" which cannot be said to be a pressing daily issue for most environmental practitioners, merits no less than 16 pages.

There is a brief chapter on environmental law in Scotland by Professor Francis Lyall which does little more than provide a concise outline of the differences in the law in Scotland. However, it does not answer some basic questions which an environmental practitioner might ask. For example, it is not possible to establish from the information given in para 26.15 whether Her Majesty's Industrial Pollution Inspectorate or a river purification authority or both would be responsible for regulating a particular process subject to integrated pollution control which has, say, emissions to air, land and water. This is hardly satisfactory.

The chapter on Northern Ireland is welcome given that little space is usually devoted to environmental law there.

There are some signs that the book was prepared in a hurry. For example, in the Table of Cases we find *Docherty v Monifeth* (sic) *Town Council* and *Young (John) and Co v The Bankier Distillery Co (1983)* (sic) *20 Rettie 76*. In the Table of Statutory Instruments we find that the *Environmental Protection (Duty of Care) Regulations 1991* are listed as the *Environmental Protection (Duty of Care) Regulations 1992, SI 1992 No 2839*. One might have hoped that in a book which sets out to be a comprehensive work of reference more care had been devoted to getting such details right.

There is no doubt that despite its shortcomings this book has its uses as a work of reference. While it will not provide detailed answers for environmental practitioners, it should nonetheless assist them in identifying applicable laws and issues and should help them to ask the right questions.

MARK POUSTIE,
University of Strathclyde.

Insider Dealing
David Hume Institute Seminars

Edited by Hector L MacQueen. 1994.
Edinburgh: David Hume Institute.
Paperback, £3. ISBN 1 870482 37 9.

This occasional paper published by the David Hume Institute comprises revised copies of the three papers delivered at the seminar on "Insider Dealing" organised by the Institute. The seminar followed the passing of the Criminal Justice Act 1993, which introduced the new prohibitions with effect from 1 January 1994.

The main paper is by Alastair Brown, a criminal lawyer with the Crown Office. The main part of his paper is a discussion of the new provisions of the 1993 Act. Mr Brown fails, however, to address adequately any of the practical difficulties with these provisions which have been identified by responsible corporate finance professionals, including the Company Law Committee of the English Law Society. These difficulties arise particularly because the London Stock Exchange is based on a system of market makers (see the article by Mr Alcock, a former director of UBS Philips & Drew in [1994] 15 Co Law 67, and the relevant proceedings in *Hansard*). One serious problem arises from the fact that the "dealing offence" can be committed "through a professional intermediary". That could criminalise some perfectly legitimate corporate finance transactions, in which a merchant bank is involved, most obviously a "bought deal". The Government responded rather inadequately to these fears by introducing the appallingly vague defence that the use of "market information" could be legitimate, even if it was otherwise "inside information".

Mr Brown also includes certain comments on the Scottish cases of *HM Advocate v Mackie* and *HM Advocate v Styr*, 1994 SLT 5, which are at best very contentious, particularly those relating to Mr Mackie's defence. The statement that Mr Mackie's employers had a professional relationship with the company concerned seems simply incorrect. That company had London brokers. It is also important to appreciate that Mr Mackie's conviction has now, of course, been overturned (as the reviewer publicly predicted) and the *Styr* case also ended in an acquittal on a question of law.

In the second paper Professor Murray concentrates on the civil consequences of insider dealing, beginning with the old case of *Percival v Wright* [1902] Ch 421, and adopting largely the approach of Professor Gower in his *Principles of Modern*

Company law. Professor Murray goes on to deal with the United States authorities in which civil remedies have been developed, particularly the "windfall benefit" to the company.

It is interesting that Professor Murray approaches insider dealing from the perspective of breach of fiduciary duty. That is the basis of the United States legislation, which, contrary to popular belief, can be narrower than the 1993 Act. One difficulty with his paper relates to the discussion of the question of who is the counter party (and therefore the victim of insider dealing) in a Stock Exchange trade. Professor Murray appears to suggest that it may be Sepon Ltd, the Exchange's nominee under the present Talisman system. It is suggested that the other party in an ordinary transaction is in fact the market maker (see, in addition to Mr Alcock's article, the description of Talisman by Mr Abrahms in [1980] 1 Co Law 17).

The final paper by Professor Barry returns under the graphic title of "Witchcraft and Insider Dealing" to the economic effects of insider dealing. His principal theme is the confusion over the objections to insider dealing, referring particularly to the practical limits to the ideal of the "level playing field" in information. In relation to the 1993 Act, Professor Barry points to the risk (which has been highlighted in the media) that it may extend to analysts obtaining information from sources other than the company. That risk may, however, be exaggerated, since the Government has extended the definition of public information.

The papers are in fact interesting mainly because they show the very different perspectives from which the 1993 Act and the whole subject are seen. The papers are clearly worth the almost nominal price of £3.

D P SELLAR,
University of Edinburgh.

Bill Stewart, the Book Review Editor, is keen that books, and especially, books written with the practitioner in mind should be reviewed by practitioners. Accordingly, members of Faculty and solicitors who consider that they could competently review books, are invited to write with a note of their name and address, indicating upon what subjects they would be prepared to write reviews, to him c/o MacMillans, Solicitors, 78 Springfield Road, Glasgow G40 3ET.

◆

ACT OF SEDERUNT

ACT OF SEDERUNT (REGISTRATION APPEAL COURT) 1994

(SI 1994/2483) [22 SEPTEMBER 1994]

The Lords of Council and Session, under and by virtue of the powers conferred on them by section 57 of the Representation of the People Act 1983 (c 2) and of all other powers enabling them in that behalf, do hereby enact and declare:

Citation and commencement

1.—(1) This Act of Sederunt may be cited as the Act of Sederunt (Registration Appeal Court) 1994 and shall come into force on 1st October 1994.

(2) This Act of Sederunt shall be inserted in the Books of Sederunt.

Registration Appeal Court

2.—(1) The Court of three judges for hearing registration appeals under section 57 of the Representation of the People Act 1983 shall be the Honourable Lord Morison, the Right Honourable the Lord Morton of Shuna and the Honourable Lord Sutherland.

(2) The Act of Sederunt (Registration Appeal Court) 1990 is revoked.

J A D HOPE, LORD PRESIDENT, *IPD*

[Acts of Sederunt are reproduced with the permission of the Controller of Her Majesty's Stationery Office.]

ARTICLES

The Impact of the New Regulatory Framework on Scottish Charities

Dr Christine R Barker, Robert C Elliot and
Susan R Moody
Department of Law,
University of Dundee.

This article by the Charity Law Research Project team at the University of Dundee considers how the new regulatory framework is affecting charities operating in Scotland and their professional advisers.

The Law Reform (Miscellaneous Provisions) (Scotland) Act 1990 establishes a regulatory framework with particular functions for a new agency, the Scottish Charities Office, which was established as a division of the Crown Office in April 1992 in order to exercise powers of investigation and supervision on behalf of the Lord Advocate. Under the 1990 Act the Lord Advocate is given powers to carry out investigations into alleged mismanagement or misconduct, to suspend trustees and to bring actions in the Court of Session as well as the power to investigate bodies which represent themselves as charities. It is to the Scottish Charities Office that application for waivers of disqualification for criminal offences or bankruptcy is made. It does not have the dual advisory and investigative roles of the Charity Commission, and its investigative powers are essentially reactive, in response to complaints from members of the public. The Scottish Council for Voluntary Organisations (SCVO) and other bodies representing charities would have liked to see the establishment of an office with far more sweeping powers, more akin to those of the Charity Commission in England and Wales (Sime, "Issues relating to the Law, Regulation, Administration and Support of Charities in Scotland", 13 April 1993, SCVO).

The claims branch of the Inland Revenue continues to exercise a supervisory role in relation to tax abuse, and to receive copies of charities' accounts (although the Act does not make it a legal requirement to lodge accounts). Since the new legislation came into effect the Inland Revenue has for the first time in Scotland established a computerised list of all the recognised charitable bodies to which it has issued a charity number, although there is as yet no register of Scottish charities. Only a body recognised as a Scottish charity by the Inland Revenue (or one registered as a charity by the Charity Commission in England and Wales) may represent itself as a charity in Scotland.

As the reaction to the Duke of Edinburgh's recent Dimbleby lecture illustrates, charities are enjoying an increasingly high public profile. However, in Scotland for the first time they are receiving rather less welcome governmental attention as the subject of regulation at a time when the business sector is enjoying an increasing degree of deregulation. There may be good reasons for this apparently inconsistent governmental approach as charities receive substantial grants and tax privileges. The sheer size of the charitable sector makes it difficult for any government to ignore. There are more than 170,000 registered charities in England and Wales and 22,000 recognised charitable bodies in Scotland with a total income of approximately £16 billion in UK terms (of which approximately £2 billion is contributed by Scottish charities). These sums of money provide a considerable incentive to fraud and this aspect has been a major factor in the recent extension of regulatory control in both jurisdictions. Government has a particular interest in the charities field both because it is the major funder of the voluntary sector and because charities are central to its philosophy of privatisation. Increasingly, voluntary organisations are providing services, particularly in the field of social welfare and housing, which previously were managed directly by the Scottish Office and local authorities.

The effect of these changes on Scottish charities was the subject of a pilot study funded by the University of Dundee Research Initiative Fund and the Carnegie Trust. This project ran from April 1993 to November 1993 and is continuing in a more comprehensive form as the result of a grant from the Nuffield Foundation. The pilot study included semi-structured interviews with representatives of selected Scottish charities as well as open ended interviews with specialist charity lawyers, a charity accountant and an officer from the Inland Revenue's claims branch. The sample size was necessarily restricted as it was a pilot exercise, and tapped only the initial impact of the legislation, but the findings were nevertheless illuminating and are being borne out by our current research.

Among the main issues to emerge from these interviews were the following: (a) the ignorance of trustees and directors about the new regulatory framework; (b) that organisations not on the Inland Revenue's index continue to describe themselves as charities even though they are no

THE IMPACT OF THE NEW REGULATORY FRAMEWORK ON SCOTTISH CHARITIES

longer permitted to do so; (c) that the increased reliance of charities on their professional advisers gives rise to the possibility of professional negligence actions where the advisers have not kept their clients briefed on the implications of the new legal environment; (d) the development of charity law and management as a specialist field for lawyers, accountants and management consultants; (e) confusion about who are the trustees of charities and who are "persons concerned in the management and control" responsible inter alia for ensuring that proper accounting records are kept; and (f) confusion as to the role of the Scottish Charities Office.

A number of other problems came to light in the course of the pilot study. They included the new concept of "designated religious bodies" which are not exempt from the new legislation but need only meet certain requirements of it. The Order, the Charities (Designated Religious Bodies) (Scotland) Order 1993, listing the designated religious bodies came into force on 7 December 1993. It covers most of the main Christian denominations in Scotland, but excludes the Baptist Church on the basis of its devolved structure and other churches on the grounds that members do not meet the minimum target of 3,000. Furthermore, non-Christian religious bodies are not included in spite of their increasing role, particularly in the case of Muslims, in key areas of Scottish society. However, even those churches included in the "list" may find difficulty in meeting those parts of the legislation which apply to them. For example, the Church of Scotland would need to photocopy the first three chapters of Cox's *Practice and Procedure of the Church of Scotland* to supply an inquirer with legally required information as to its constitution!

As an earlier article has pointed out (Elliot, 1992 SLT (News) 270), the implementation of the provisions of the 1990 Act relating to the regulation of charities (Pt I, ss 1-15) has transformed the legal position of charities operating solely in Scotland. The legislation sets down specific accounting requirements which are contained in the Charities Accounts (Scotland) Regulations 1992. These came into force on 30 September 1992 and require any charity with an annual income of £25,000 or more to produce a statement of accounts which comprise a balance sheet, an income and expenditure account and a report on the activities of the charity. Where a charity's gross income is £100,000 or more, accounts must be professionally audited except where it is a company within the meaning of the Companies Act 1985, s 735 or an unregistered

company to which Pt VII of the 1985 Act applies. The accounts and the report must be supplied to any member of the public who requests them on payment of a fee to cover the cost of photocopying and postage.

The accounting aspects of the new regulatory framework have given rise to a number of problems and a considerable amount of confusion. For example, there was confusion amongst the interviewees about the date from which the new Accounting Regulations came into effect, as some charities assumed that it applied retrospectively, while others took the presumably correct view that the legislation implementing the regulations could not be retrospective and thus could only apply to the first full year's accounts after September 1992. Secondly, many small charities had used the term "audit" in their constitutions and had to incur the cost of a professional audit regardless of the level of their income or go to the expense of having their constitution rewritten. Thirdly, those charities which are not obliged to have a professional audit must have their accounts examined by an "independent examiner", but again there is confusion and uncertainty about who is qualified to act in this role. Fourthly, the Scottish Accounting Regulations were introduced before SORP2 was adopted by the Charity Commission as representing "best recommended practice" for accountants and auditors in England and Wales, and the mainly presentational differences between these accounting requirements seems likely to make charities operating throughout the whole of the UK produce two different sets of accounts.

Charities expressed their concern as to the disproportionate expense for small charities in particular in meeting the new accounting and reporting requirements, which has led to the winding up of some and for others the redrafting of constitutions. The new requirements are imposing additional administrative costs on charities operating in Scotland in spite of the fact that potential donors are strongly opposed to their money being diluted in this way. Obviously, criminal fraud by fundraisers and charity personnel needs to be curtailed, but that would appear to be better dealt with by making the criminal law more effective rather than increasing administrative costs for the innocent. This approach is very difficult to defend at a time when industry is being deregulated to make it more cost effective. On the other hand, there may be a need to build in checks against negligent mismanagement of charitable funds and encourage greater efficiency.

Set up with the aim of reducing the burden of regulation, the Charities and Voluntary Organisations Task Force published its report in July 1994. It contains a total of 189 proposals, of which 72 have been accepted in whole, in part or in principle, 60 are under review and 57 have been rejected. Those relating specifically to the Scottish legislation are among those "under review". The report points out that while the regulatory regime for charities in Scotland is weak and disjointed by comparison with the comprehensive regime operating in England and Wales, in some areas Scottish legislation is much more demanding than that operating in England and Wales. "The piecemeal nature of Scottish regulation and the lack of a support and information structure for charities inhibits the move towards self regulation of charities" (p 49).

The report recommends that the Scottish Office should initiate a review of the regulation of charities in Scotland with a view to: "(i) clarifying the role of the Scottish Charities Office; (ii) establishing a register of Scottish Charities; (iii) providing a central resource of consistent information and support; (iv) making fund raising controls consistent with those in England and Wales; (v) addressing cross-border issues affecting charities who operate nationally".

It further recommends that the Scottish Office should publish guidance on the role and responsibilities of the Independent Examiner. Although the recommendations are said to be "under review" by the Scottish Office, it has been made clear that there is no opportunity at present of primary legislation to implement some of the suggestions, but there is a willingness to examine the possibility of addressing concerns via secondary legislation and changes in administrative practice.

The team at Dundee would welcome the views of the legal profession and others on the new framework.

Recent Developments in English Law

The Demise of the Rule Against Perpetuities?

Robert C Elliot
Course Leader,
Qualifying English Law Degree,
University of Dundee.

Mr Elliot examines the background to the Law Commission's review of the Rule Against Perpetuities and considers some of the problems for conveyancers posed by the Law of Property (Miscellaneous Provisions) Act 1989.

The rule against perpetuities, together with its close relations the rules against accumulations, has blighted the lives of generations of English law students and provided a plethora of pitfalls for practitioners. However, thanks to the Law Commission's Consultation Paper no 133, *The Law of Trusts — The Rules Against Perpetuities and Excessive Accumulations* (1993), it may not be with us for very much longer.

There is an inherent irony in the whole situation as the rule against perpetuities was an attempt to solve the problem of land being tied up in trust settlements for centuries within the same extended families by means of ingenious legal devices, most notably the "shifting use" (e g "to A, B, C to the use of X for life, but if she marries a Scotsman to the use of Z and his heirs") and the "springing use" (e g "to A, B, C to the use of Y when he has graduated"), to ensure that the estate would not be sold by a future generation to settle gaming debts or finance a more self indulgent lifestyle. The religious and political upheavals of the 16th and 17th centuries alleviated the shortage of good agricultural land as a result of the forfeiture of the land of the losers, but after the restoration of the monarchy in 1660 and the return of relative political stability this problem became more acute, leading to the development of the modern rule against perpetuities shortly thereafter. Thus, the greatest achievement of English law, the family settlement trust, provoked a reaction in the form of one of the most complicated rules of "black letter law".

The rule itself may not appear at first sight to be particularly complicated as it essentially consists of two propositions: (1) any future interest in real or personal property is void from the outset if it may possibly vest, if at all, after the perpetuity period has expired; and (2) the perpetuity period consists of any life or lives in being when the future interest is created plus 21 years and the gestation period for babies in the womb. The lives in being for this purpose can be selected by the settlor and need not have any connection with the settlement; thus royal lives are sometimes used, as long as the number is not so great as to make it impossible to ascertain the death of the ultimate survivor as this would make the gift void for uncertainty.

However, complications arise from the numerous exceptions to the rule and special cases such as the application of the rule to the creation or exercise of powers of appointment. The 1925 property legislation was introduced to simplify the conveyancing process and provided an excellent opportunity to reform the rule, but it failed to address the issue, as all the Law of Property Act that year did in this area was abolish, by s 161, what was sometimes called the old rule against perpetuities, which was generally thought to be moribund until it was revived by the Court of Appeal in *Whitby v Mitchell* (1890) 44 Ch D 85; clarify the position of some rent-charges (s 162); and reduce the vesting age for children to 21 where a higher age had been selected in breach of the rule (s 163).

The Perpetuities and Accumulations Act 1964 modified the common law rule but did not abolish it, since its provisions can only be used where a gift made after 15 October 1964 would be void under common law. The increased complexity arising from the interaction of the Act with the common law was criticised by the Law Commission. It identified uncertainty (e g lives in being under s 3 (4) and (5)), inconsistency (e g lives in being identified differently by the Act and under common law), interference with commercial contracts (e g mineral options having to be exercised within 21 years), the overturning of the intention of the settlor by granting the property to unintended recipients, failure to take account of the fact that today trustees normally have wide powers of sale, prejudice to tax planning, and additional expense (e g in applying to the court for a variation of the terms of a trust), with the danger of encouraging investment in overseas property instead, as other major problems.

Unsurprisingly, the Law Commission indicated that its preferred option was either to abolish the rule without replacement or, if retained, to reform it. After the disastrous attempt to reform the rule in 1964, it is to be hoped that the final recommendation will be for total abolition, particularly as it has outlived its usefulness in an age of compulsory purchase; if unforeseen problems do arise the legislature or the judiciary could act to deal with them in a more satisfactory way.

Meanwhile, practitioners are having to come to terms with legislation arising from an earlier Law Commission report (Law Com no 164 (1987)) dealing with contractual formalities governing the disposition of an interest in land. This is the Law of Property (Miscellaneous Provisions) Act 1989. Section 1 alters the rules as to the requisite formalities for a conveyance executed on or after 31 July 1990, but it is s 2, affecting contracts entered into on or after 27 September 1989, which is of greater significance, as it replaces the provisions of s 40 of the LPA 1925, whereby oral conracts were valid but not directly enforceable.

The new rule is that if there is not a written agreement there is no contract at all, thus removing the doctrine of part performance from this area. This doctrine dates back to 1686 and was developed to combat fraud where, for example, a vendor orally agreed to sell land and allowed the purchaser into occupation, but then reclaimed the land after the purchaser had spent time and money improving it, on the ground that there was no enforceable contract. The doctrine enabled the courts to take into account acts referable to the alleged contract as evidence of the existence of an agreement, and to order specific performance of the contract. This doctrine created a number of problems, particularly as the approach of the courts to the application of this doctrine was inconsistent.

Similar problems arise under Scots law, where this situation is covered by rei interventus and homologation, but the approach of the courts is even more unpredictable: for example *Errol v Walker*, 1966 SLT 159; 1966 SC 93, is difficult to reconcile with *Mitchell v Stornoway Trustees*, 1936 SLT 509; 1936 SC (HL) 56.

However, reverting to the 1989 Act, since s 2 makes it plain that an oral agreement for the disposition of an interest in land cannot be a valid contract, the doctrine of performance can no longer apply as there can be no contract to be partly performed. This raises the question of how the courts will in future combat fraudsters taking advantage of non-compliance with the new formalities, although the Law Commission did suggest that they might use the doctrine of estoppel instead.

Some contracts do not need to be in writing and these exceptions are set out in s 2 (5). These are contracts to grant short leases (i e leases for a term not exceeding three years), contracts made in the course of a public auction and contracts regulated under the Financial Services Act 1986. Section 2 (5) also expressly excludes "the creation or operation of resulting, implied or constructive trusts". Furthermore, it was held in *Spiro v Glencown Properties Ltd* [1991] 2 WLR 931, that while an option agreement to purchase land had to comply with s 2, a notice exercising the option did not. Academic lawyers, as they did with the 1964 Act when that was introduced, have identified various areas of uncertainty needing judicial interpretation for clarification: e g can, as previously, a party enjoying the benefit of a term choose, if it has not been recorded, to waive that term and enforce the rest of the agreement, in view of the requirement in s 2 that all terms be recorded before a valid contract is made? It is to be hoped that the 1989 Act will not require amendment or replacement as a result of such difficulties as well!

NEWS

Appointment

International Bar Association
Professor J Ross Harper, CBE, has been elected President of the International Bar Association at its general meeting in Melbourne for a period of two years. Professor Harper is the second President to come from Scotland in a decade. Dr James Sutherland was the first Scottish IBA President.

General

Review of monetary penalties
The Scottish Office Central Research Unit have published *Monetary Penalties in Scotland* (HMSO, £13.95), a research based review by Linda Nicholson covering the nature and use, imposition and enforcement of, and default in relation to, such penalties. Current and possible future developments covered include improved enforcement procedures, supervised attendance orders, direct deductions from benefit, unitary fines, and the future for compensation orders.

Taxation

Capital gains tax: expenses incurred by personal representatives and corporate trustees
The Inland Revenue have issued the following statement of practice (SP 8/94, replacing statement of practice SP 7/81) on capital gains tax allowable expenditure for the costs of establishing title where personal representatives sell assets from a deceased person's estate, and for expenses incurred by corporate trustees:

Expenses incurred by personal representatives
Following discussion with representative bodies, the scale of expenses allowable under s 38 (1) (b) of the Taxation of Chargeable Gains Act 1992, for the costs of establishing title in computing the gains or losses of personal representatives on the sale of assets comprised in a deceased person's estate, has been revised. The Board of Inland Revenue will accept computations based either on this scale or on the *actual* allowable expenditure incurred.

The revised scale is as follows:

Gross value of estate	Allowable expenditure
A. Up to £40,000	1.75 per cent of the probable value of the assets sold by the personal representatives.
B. Between £40,001 and £70,000	A fixed amount of £700, to be divided between all the assets of the estate in proportion to the probate values and allowed in those proportions on assets sold by the personal representatives.
C. Between £70,001 and £300,000	One per cent of the probate value of the assets sold.
D. Between £300,001 and £400,000	A fixed amount of £3,000, to be divided as at (B) above.
E. Between £400,001 and £750,000	0.75 per cent of the probate value of the assets sold.

The scale does not extend to gross estates exceeding £750,000, where the allowable expenditure is to be negotiated according to the facts of the particular case by the inspector and the taxpayer.

The revised scale takes effect where death occurred after 5 April 1993.

Expenses incurred by corporate trustees
Following discussion with representative bodies, the Inland Revenue have agreed the following scale of allowable expenditure under ss 38 and 64 (1) (b) of the Taxation of Chargeable Gains Act 1992, for expenses incurred by corporate trustees in the administration of estates and trusts. The Board of Inland Revenue will accept computations based either on this scale or on the *actual* allowable expenditure incurred.

The scale is as follows:

(a) Transfers of assets to beneficiaries etc

    (i) Quoted stocks and shares

        (A) One beneficiary   £20.00 per holding

        (B) More than one beneficiary between   As (A), to be divided in equal shares between the
               whom a holding must be divided   beneficiaries

    (ii) Unquoted shares   As (i) above, with the addition of any exceptional
                                                   expenditure

    (iii) Other assets   As (i) above, with the addition of any exceptional
                                                   expenditure

(b) Actual disposals and acquisitions

    (i) Quoted stocks and shares   The investment fee as charged by the trustee

    (ii) Unquoted shares   As (i) above, plus actual valuation costs

    (iii) Other assets   The investment fee as charged by the trustee, subject
                                                   to a maximum of £60, plus actual valuation costs

Where a comprehensive annual management fee is charged, covering both the cost of administering the trust and the expenses of actual disposals and acquisitions, the investment fee for the purposes of (i), (ii) and (iii) above will be taken to be £0.25 per £100 on the sale or purchase moneys.

(c) Deemed disposals by trustees

    (i) Quoted stocks and shares   £6 per holding

    (ii) Unquoted shares   Actual valuation costs

    (iii) Other assets   Actual valuation costs

This scale takes effect for acquisitions and disposals, or deemed disposals, by corporate trustees after 5 April 1993.

— ◊ —

Business change

Dundas & Wilson, CS, announce that their associates Robin Jack (commercial property, based in Edinburgh) and Alastair Morrison (construction litigation, based in Glasgow) have been assumed as partners, and that Lyn Beattie (litigation) and Alistair McLean (construction litigation) have been appointed associates, both based in Edinburgh.

— ◊ —

Bill Stewart, the Book Review Editor, is keen that books, and especially, books written with the practitioner in mind should be reviewed by practitioners. Accordingly, members of Faculty and solicitors who consider that they could competently review books, are invited to write with a note of their name and address, indicating upon what subjects they would be prepared to write reviews, to him c/o MacMillans, Solicitors, 78 Springfield Road, Glasgow G40 3ET.

ARTICLES

Ultra Vires Swap Contracts and Unjustified Enrichment

Niall R Whitty
The author, a member of the Scottish Law Commission's staff, writes in a personal capacity.

Mr Whitty argues that the money paid to a local authority under an interest rate swap is recoverable in Scots law under the doctrine of recompense.

A. Introductory

Interest rate swap contracts were fully explained in W J Stewart, 1992 SLT (News) 315. Such contracts were held ultra vires local authorities and void in *Hazell v Hammersmith and Fulham LBC* [1992] 2 AC 1 (HL), which was followed by Lord Penrose in *Morgan Guaranty Trust Co of New York v Lothian Regional Council*, 1994 SCLR 213 (OH).

In relation, however, to a bank's right to recover money paid to a local authority under such a contract, English and Scots law have diverged. The bank's right was recognised in English law in *Westdeutsche Landesbank Girozentrale v Islington LBC*; *Kleinwort Benson Ltd v Sandwell BC* (1993) 91 LGR 323, varied [1994] 1 WLR 938 (CA) but was rejected in Scots law by Lord Penrose in *Morgan Guaranty*, whose decision has been reclaimed to an Inner House bench of five judges.

This article argues that the money paid to a local authority under an interest rate swap is recoverable in Scots law under the doctrine of recompense.

B. Recompense for recovery of money and the structure of unjustified enrichment

The *Morgan Guaranty* case raises fundamental questions as to the taxonomic structure of Scots enrichment law. Long criticised by our judges (e g *Buchanan v Stewart* (1874) 2 R 78, per Lord Neaves at p 81), that area of law is now recognised as unsatisfactory by professional bodies, academics and the Scottish Law Commission (see, e g Scot Law Com Discussion Paper no 95, *Recovery of Benefits Conferred Under Error of Law*; 1994 JR 127). In the absence of a comprehensive typology of cases and a secure taxonomy and analytic framework based thereon, the judges and practitioners are working blind. So in *Morgan Guaranty*, reference was made (1994 SCLR at p 221A) to "various ad hoc categories of authority" and the absence of authoritative discussion of the friction between the cases and (at p 225C) to "inconsistencies and incompatibilities

among the authorities which clearly were often based on partial citation of authority and which led to mutually incompatible results".

A benefit based structure?
For example the basis of the major divide between restitution and repetition on the one hand and recompense on the other — the most important boundary in Scots enrichment law — is shrouded in mystery. In *Morgan Guaranty* the benefit received by the defenders at the pursuers' expense was money. There is authority that repetition only and not recompense is available where the benefit received is money (e g *Royal Bank of Scotland plc v Watt*, 1991 SLT 138; *McIvor v Roy*, 1970 SLT (Sh Ct) 58 at p 60). Such a view is consonant with Birks' theory (1985 JR 227 at pp 233-238; (1985) 38 CLP 57 at pp 61-63) that the tripartite classification of the main obligations redressing unjustified enrichment depends on the type of benefit received, i e (1) repetition (money); (2) restitution (property); and (3) recompense (services or the product of services). This benefit based theory, however, overlooks the fact that recompense governs not only services but also some types of case where money or property is received by the defender, e g aliment paid in cash, or a benefit — goods or money — indirectly enriching the defender, or money misappropriated by the defender, or significantly for the *Morgan Guaranty* case, money paid to an incapax under a contract void for want of capacity (*Magistrates of Stonehaven v Kincardine County Council*, 1939 SLT 528; 1939 SC 760; *Bennett v Carse*, 1990 SLT 454 (OH); 1994 JR 127 at p 129, n 23).

A quantum based structure?
Perhaps more plausible is the theory that the tripartite classification is "quantum based", i e that it depends on the quantum or measure of recovery, the starting point of which in each case is (subject to equitable defences): (1) money received plus interest (repetition); (2) specific property received with its subsequent fruits and accessions or the value of all of these (restitution); and (3) a sum representing the extent of the defender's enrichment or quantum lucratus (recompense). But that theory does not explain all cases: see below.

A vitally important but largely unresearched question is, what is the relevant time for applying the measure of recovery? In repetition and restitution, the tempus inspiciendum is the time of receipt of the money or property but subject to equitable defences taking into account some post-receipt changes in value like change of position, or bona fide consumption (in Birks' terminology, "value received") (Scot Law Com DP no 95, Vol 2, paras 2.123-2.156). In the *Watt* case, it may have been assumed that in recompense the tempus inspiciendum is the time of the claim ("value surviving").

The measure of recovery in recompense
It is not possible here to answer the largely unresearched question of what measure of recovery is applied throughout the conglomerate category of recompense which covers such diverse typecases as: (1) P's intentional direct conferment of a benefit on D; (2) D's interference with P's rights; (3) P's claim as bona fide possessor for mistaken improvements to D's property; (4) P's payment of D's debt to X; and (5) other three party cases, e g indirect enrichment. The transfer cases in (1) include (a) P's services or expenditures benefiting D, usually where a transaction has failed (e g through nullity, voidability, or illegality) or its original cause has fallen away; (b) aliment provided by P to D in cash or kind; (c) P's expenditure on property owned in common with D; and (d) P's payment of money or transfer of property to D who, by reason of legal incapacity, is not bound by obligations of repetition or restitution. Ultra vires swaps belong to subcategory (d).

Birks' suggestion (1985) 38 CLP at p 65, that there are two measures — "value received" and "value surviving" — provides very useful analytic tools but in our law does not fit incapacity cases. Gloag, *Contract* (2nd ed), p 85 states that where money is paid to a minor incapax, recompense lies either (1) if the money "is still part of the minor's estate" (i e "value surviving") or (2) "has been expended in a manner profitable to him", i e in rem versum (an ambiguous phrase, cf *Henderson v Dawson* (1895) 22 R 895 at p 902, now rarely used). The second leg of Gloag's test differs from both "value received" and "value surviving".

Haphazard historical development?
A third theory assumes that to form a satisfactory basis for classification, "enrichment" in recompense must differ from "value received", e g "value surviving". It seems likely however that "value surviving" is not the measure in recompense for payment of another's debt; or aliment provided by a person who is not the alimentary obligant; or interference with the pursuer's property. On this theory, the measure of recovery in recompense is not uniform but a patchwork.

It would follow that the tripartite taxonomy has no satisfactory, rational basis. The scope of recompense must therefore be the product of

haphazard historical development. So recompense applies to indirect enrichment cases because it is the historical successor of the actio de in rem verso of the ius commune (see 1994 JR at p 201), and to recovery from an incapax of money paid to him because it is the historical successor of the civilian actio in quantum locupletior factus est. As to nonage, the development can be traced through J A C Thomas, "Minors and Contract: A comparative study", 1972 *Acta Juridica* 151 (explaining the Roman foundations); Stair, *Inst*, I vi 33; I viii 6; Bankton, *Inst*, I ix 41; Erskine, *Inst*, III i 11; and *Scott's Tr v Scott* (1887) 14 R 1043; as to mental disability, see Bankton, *Inst*, I ix 41; Gloag, p 93; as to juristic persons acting ultra vires, see *Sinclair v Brougham* [1914] AC 398 at pp 434-435, per Lord Dunedin; *Magistrates of Stonehaven v Kincardine CC*.

On this view, the court can apply recompense in the *Morgan Guaranty* case without deciding whether the taxonomy is quantum based or simply a haphazard patchwork produced by history, and can apply the two pronged measure of recovery (Gloag, p 85, quoted above). Only on the benefit based theory would recompense not apply.

C. Ultra vires and juristic persons
Meanings of "ultra vires" (private law)
Nowadays the courts emphasise that the private law concept of "ultra vires" should be confined to acts which are beyond the capacity of a juristic person; the term should not be loosely used to denote acts within its capacity but beyond the authority of its directors, partners or agents, or any act or activity which it cannot lawfully undertake: *James Finlay Corporation Ltd v R & R S Mearns*, 1987 SC 317; 1988 SLT 302 (OH). Further, "it is inappropriate to describe as *ultra vires* an act which is not null and void but which depends for its validity upon whether the other party to the transaction had knowledge of the unauthorised purpose for which it was being carried out": ibid at p 323 (p 306). Therefore, the concept of ultra vires should not apply to conveyances by trustees because the restrictions on their powers imposed by trust purposes are "a matter of obligation and not of capacity" (K G C Reid in *The Laws of Scotland, Stair Memorial Encyclopaedia*, Vol 18, para 599).

The doctrine of ultra vires operating as a type of "juridical incapacity" is mainly confined to common law systems (I England, "Restitution of Benefits Conferred Without Obligation" in P Schlechtriem (ed), *International Encyclopedia of Comparative Law*, Vol X, chap 5 (1991), para 5-113). In its typical way, Scots law has blended this common law doctrine with the civilian principle of recompense from a natural person who is incapax. Under the influence of European law, legislation (Companies Act 1985, ss 35, 35A and 35B, as inserted by the Companies Act 1989, s 108) has virtually abolished ultra vires in relation to companies incorporated under the Companies Acts, but it still applies to such bodies corporate as local authorities and statutory corporations.

In the case of unauthorised acts by a local authority, the role of the private law ultra vires doctrine is the protection of the general body of the local authority's tax and ratepayers (*Westdeutsche* (1993) 91 LGR at p 351), not the protection of the party transacting with the authority. The role of the public law concept of ultra vires, as applied in *Woolwich Equitable Building Society v IRC* [1993] AC 70 to recovery from a public authority, is in principle quite different. There its function is to protect not the general body of taxpayers but rather individual taxpayers transacting with government.

D. Repetition and restitution claims by or against an incapax

The main requirements of repetition of money paid by the pursuer (P) to the defender (D) are as follows: (1) P must have paid money to D; (2) except in certain compulsion cases, the payment must have undue (indebitum); (3) the orthodox view is that P must found on one or other of a number of specific grounds of repetition which, in the case of money paid for an existing cause (causa praeterita), include inter alia error or improper compulsion; and (4) there must be no equitable or other defence precluding decree of repetition.

The specific grounds of repetition
The field of obligations of repetition and restitution may be classified according to the specific grounds of recovery and related forms of action, but the mode of classification, long neglected, is controversial. The orthodox view is probably as follows: (a) condictio indebiti: payments and transfers made under error as to the payer's legal liability to the payee; (b) condictio causa data causa non secuta: payment or transfer on the assumption that a future event will occur which fails to materialise; (c) condictio ob turpem vel iniustam causam: payment or transfer for a shameful or illegal purpose; and (d) innominate actions of repetition and restitution, being the residual category of repetition and restitution equivalent to the condictio sine causa specialis of the ius commune, including condictio ob causam finitam (or ob non causam): payment on the basis

of the future continuation of a legal cause which later ceases.

In fact the foregoing classification is disputed. Critical are the scope and role of the condictio indebiti. On the orthodox view, it covers only error as in category (a). On another view, it is not confined to error but "should be seen as the claim to recover all transfers (made to discharge a debt or duty) which were not due" (R Evans-Jones and D McKenzie, 1994 JR 60 at p 75) and therefore comprehends not only (a), but also (c) and most cases of (d). On this view a condictio indebiti lies without proof of the payer's error, though his knowledge that the debt was undue is a defence. In the old law, when payment was made sine causa, error was presumed (*Carse v Carrick* (1778) Mor 2931 at p 2933), but nowadays the payer must aver and prove affirmatively that he paid in (excusable) error and what the error was: *Miller v Campbell*, 1991 GWD 26-1477 (Ex Div). The weight of authority favours the orthodox view: see Scot Law Com, DP no 95, Vol 1, Pt II; Vol 2, paras 2.7 and 2.30-2.41. In a fascinating article, du Plessis and Wicke, 1993 SLT (News) 303 argue (at p 305) that *Balfour v Smith and Logan* (1877) 4 R 454 shows that payments under doubt as to liability are treated as made under error. But in that case the payer was in doubt as to his liability, did not have his account books accessible for checking, was expressly assured by the recipient that the sum was indeed due, and paid on that footing.

Payments to or by an incapax
The condictio indebiti lies to recover money paid or property transferred under void obligations erroneously thought to be valid: Scot Law Com, DP no 95, Vol 2, paras 2.204-2.206, and excusable error as to the existence of the obligation has to be proved: ibid, paras 2.33-2.36.

Outside the condictio indebiti, the ground of the invalidity of an obligation may in some cases supply a policy reason for treating the enrichment as unjustified and redressible by repetition or restitution. For example, an enrichment claim by an incapax (natural or juristic person) for recovery of money or property is actionable by repetition or restitution (e g *General Property Investment Co v Matheson's Trs* (1888) 16 R 282; *Boyle v Woodypoint Caravans*, 1970 SLT (Sh Ct) 34). Knowledge of incapacity or ultra vires does not bar recovery; and error as to capacity or vires is not required: ibid. It seems to follow that the specific ground of recovery is simply the want of capacity or vires which renders the obligation void.

Haggarty v Scottish TGWU, 1955 SC 109, suggests that a condictio indebiti lies against an incapax for recovery of money or property paid or transferred in error if the incapax is a juristic person (or voluntary association such as a trade union) demanding the money ultra vires. This authority is difficult to reconcile with the *Stonehaven Magistrates* case considered below, which suggests that recompense is the relevant obligation and remedy.

E. Quantum lucratus as a measure of recovery reconciling doctrines of incapacity and unjustified enrichment?

There may be a good reason why the two pronged test of quantum lucratus (Gloag p 85, quoted above) should form the measure of recovery in recompense from an incapax of money, property or services furnished to him under a contract void through his incapacity. It is a means of reconciling two fundamental doctrines of the legal system. The first doctrine, that of incapacity, protects minors and mentally disabled adults by rendering some at least of their legal transactions null: it requires that the transactions of the incapax should not be enforced against him. (In this article, "minor" refers to persons whose acts are void for want of capacity through nonage: e g persons below 16 under the Age of Legal Capacity (Scotland) Act 1991, s 1 (1), and minors with curators acting alone or pupils before that Act.) The second doctrine, that of redressing unjustified enrichment, requires that the incapax should restore windfall benefits obtained under a contract void through incapacity.

To reconcile these doctrines, recompense lies if, but only if, the incapax either still retains the benefit received or it was profitably applied for him. Otherwise recovery from an incapax could in substance operate as an indirect means of enforcing the void transaction against him. It would for example be pointless for the law on personal incapacity to invalidate contracts of loan to minors if enrichment law were to allow the lender to recover the money in full. (This reasoning may seem inconsistent with *Colin Campbell Ltd v Pirie*, 1967 SLT (Sh Ct) 49 at p 53, but illegality differs from incapacity and ultra vires.) Gloag's two pronged test of quantum lucratus ensures that the doctrine of personal incapacity is not undermined. The Scottish Law Commission however have argued that quantum lucratus is over protective and arbitrary: *Report on the Legal Capacity and Responsibility of Minors and Pupils* (Scot Law Com no 110, 1987), paras 3.34-3.36.

Certainly not everyone would agree with the result that in a local authority swaps case (if the local authority is the net gainer in the swap) the measure of recovery in the bank's claim of recompense against the local authority is quantum lucratus while (if the bank is the net gainer in the swap) the measure of recovery in the local authority's claim of repetition against the bank is "value received" (even though subject to equitable deduction). But this is the consequence of applying to corporate bodies the special rules for the protection of an incapax natural person.

F. Juridical incapacity: ultra vires acts by local authorities

(1) The Stonehaven Magistrates case
In *Magistrates of Stonehaven v Kincardine CC*, the First Division held inter alia that a local authority which borrowed money under a purported contract of loan which was null because ultra vires the local authority's statutory powers, was under an obligation to recompense the "lender" by repaying the money in quantum locupletior.

The case is complicated because the very important decision on recompense and ultra vires loans was made in a kind of case within the case. The case arose out of a transfer of functions under the Local Government (Scotland) Act 1929, ss 2 (1), 6 and 21. That Act transferred certain highway authority functions from small burghs and district committees of the old county councils to reconstituted county councils; it transferred the outstanding roads liabilities of the old counties to the reconstituted county councils; it provided that the latter's expenditure on those functions should be apportioned between the small burghs and the county landward areas; and it enabled the reconstituted county councils to requisition sums from the small burghs to meet this expenditure.

A reconstituted county council (Kincardine) requisitioned a small burgh (Stonehaven) for payment of a sum to meet certain outstanding liabilities incurred by the district committees of the old county council before the date of the transfer of functions. Stonehaven paid the sum and then sought repayment on the ground that the requisition was unauthorised by law and illegal: see Stonehaven's pleas in law in 1939 SLT at p 532. The old county council had been empowered to levy rates year by year, or to borrow in accordance with certain statutory provisions, to meet the roads expenditure of their district committees. Instead of using those powers, Kincardine CC accumulated and carried forward defitis on their road accounts which were met by raising loans from the bank and issuing "short term mortgages". These were unauthorised by statute and thus ultra vires of Kincardine CC and illegally obtained: 1939 SC at p 763; 1939 SLT at p 529. So Stonehaven contended (wrongly as it turned out) that the deficits were therefore not liabilities within s 6 of the 1929 Act for which

Kincardine CC could requisition from Stonehaven under that Act and accordingly that Stonehaven were entitled to repayment.

In *Morgan Guaranty*, Lord Penrose observed (1994 SCLR at p 222C-D) that in *Magistrates of Stonehaven*, the pursuers in their plea in law did not refer to recompense but sought recovery on the basis that their payments to the county council had been illegally requisitioned. His conclusion that the decision was based on recompense was only tentative. Difficulty arises because the law on unjustified enrichment was relevant in the *Magistrates of Stonehaven* in two distinct issues representing different stages of the pursuers' argument.

The first was the main issue in the case, namely, whether Stonehaven could recover the requisitioned sums paid to Kincardine. It is not clear what "form of action", principle or doctrine (e g repetition/restitution, or recompense) was relied on. Perhaps the reason why Stonehaven pleaded "absence of statutory authority" or "illegal requisition" was that a condictio indebiti for error might have foundered on the error of law bar: cf *Bremner v Taylor* (1866) 3 SLR 24 (OH).

The answer to this main issue, however, depended on the answer to the second issue, namely, whether "the lender [a bank] from whom the old county council had borrowed ultra vires a sum of money which it used to defray road expenditure already incurred could recover that sum by legal process" (1939 SC at p 769; 1939 SLT at p 537), i e from the old county council. The principles of recompense were expounded by Lord President Normand not in his discussion of the main issue — Kincardine CC's liability to Stonehaven — but rather the issue in "the case within the case", namely Kincardine's liability to recompense the third party lender bank. As the Lord President explained at pp 768-769 (pp 536-537), if (as the court held) that sum was recoverable by recompense, then (1) it was a liability of the old Kincardine CC relating to roads administration as carried on by the district committees; therefore (2) it was a "liability" within the meaning of s 6 of the 1929 Act; therefore (3) the reconstituted Kincardine CC's requisition from Stonehaven of sums to meet that liability was lawful; therefore (4) the sums paid by Stonehaven to the reconstituted Kincardine CC were legally due; and therefore (5) the answer to the main issue was that Stonehaven could not recover those sums from the reconstituted Kincardine CC.

Stonehaven's payment had been due to Kincardine and therefore Kincardine were not thereby enriched. For a creditor is not enriched by receiving a payment discharging his debt. So no question of whether an enrichment was justified (i e no question of whether there was a specific ground of recovery or reason for reversing an enrichment, such as error, compulsion, incapacity or ultra vires) could logically arise. Accordingly the First Division did not, and did not need to, consider what would have been the specific ground of recovery if Stonehaven's payment had been undue.

In *Stonehaven Magistrates*, the question whether the doctrine of recompense should apply to a local authority borrowing ultra vires was not argued from the standpoint of policy but rather was taken for granted at p 770 (p 537) on the basis of Lord Dunedin's dicta in the English case of *Sinclair v Brougham* [1914] AC 398 at pp 434-435 drawing an analogy between the position of pupils liable under the actio in quantum locupletior factus est and juristic persons borrowing ultra vires. It is not self evident in policy terms that a principle (recompense quantum lucratus) designed for personal incapacity necessarily applies to juristic incapacity. However that must now be taken to be Scots law and it is a logical consequence of treating ultra vires as a form of juristic incapacity.

As regards the measure of recovery in *Stonehaven Magistrates*, it was observed that "the lender could have successfully sued the old county council for the money received by it *in quantum locupletior*. But, since it is common ground that the borrowing was for the purpose of meeting road liabilities properly incurred, it is obvious that the enrichment of the county council was exactly measured by the amount of the sums illegally borrowed": p 770 (p 538). This is consistent with the "in rem versum" prong of Gloag's two pronged test. "Value surviving" in the sense that the county council still had the money in its coffers at the date of the transfer of functions was not required (cf *Bell v Thomson* (1867) 6 M 64; *National Bank of Scotland v Lord Advocate* (1892) 30 SLR 579 (OH) at p 583).

(2) The Morgan Guaranty case

In the *Morgan Guaranty* case, the pursuer bank entered into an ultra vires swap agreement with the defender regional council under which the bank were liable for interest at variable rates on a notional sum of £10 million and the council were liable for interest at fixed rates on that sum: 1994 SCLR at p 215B. Payments were made between the parties resulting in a net excess of payments by the bank to the council of

£368,104.52. The bank concluded for payment of that amount. Lord Penrose rejected the bank's claim on two grounds.

(a) The meaning of "lucratus" or "enrichment". His Lordship distinguished *Stonehaven Magistrates* on the ground that the concept of "lucratus" or "enrichment" as used in that case and in *Cuthbertson v Lowes* (1870) 8 M 1073 was inapplicable: 1994 SCLR at pp 223E-224B. He characterised these as being cases in which one party performed his part of a purported contract which turned out to be ultra vires one or other of the parties or otherwise illegal and recovered by a remedy in quantum lucratus. (In fact recompense was not invoked in *Cuthbertson*, which depends on turpis causa, and the measure of recovery was not quantum lucratus but rather the market value of the goods as at the date of delivery: (1870) 8 M, at pp 1074-1075.) Lord Penrose said that the *Morgan Guaranty* case differed from those cases because, "having identified a nominal sum for the cross lending and borrowing, both parties were subject to interest rate movements in the money market reflected in the creation of debts inter se simply as a function of the nominal sum, the rates from time to time in being, and the passage of time. There was no other consideration and there was no other factor of importance in the working out of the parties' bargain. Once time had passed and rates had been determined the sums due inter se were fixed as a matter of calculation without further requirement of either party for performance of any obligation whatsoever. A decision that the swap agreements were ultra vires and void had no effect other than to limit the period for which the agreements would otherwise have been given effect between parties" (pp 223F-224A).

This reasoning is difficult to follow. The court's decision that the swap agreements were ultra vires and void was declaratory. It was not an executive decision or decree terminating the purported contract because that was void ab initio. Payments had been made under the void "contract" resulting in a net excess of payments by the bank to the council. It is hard to see why the council, which was in fact enriched by that excess, could not be treated as so enriched. It resulted from a performance by the bank of a purported obligation which had always been void. The two pronged test of quantum lucratus would be satisfied if the money were still in the council's purse or had been profitably applied.

(b) A heresy: error of law as a blight on all recovery. Lord Penrose's second ground for rejecting the bank's recompense claim was that "parties

proceeded upon an understanding of the local authority's capacity in law to conclude swap agreements. They were in error. Sums paid in faith of such a contract are, on authority, not recoverable" (p 225A-B). It is submitted however that the pursuers' error of law does not provide a defence to an enrichment claim based on a ground other than error.

First, the dicta in *Glasgow Corporation v Lord Advocate*, 1959 SC 203 at pp 232, 233; 1959 SLT 230 at p 245, and *Taylor v Wilson's Trs*, 1975 SC 146 at p 149; 1974 SLT 298 at pp 299-300, applied in *Morgan Guaranty* (at pp 224, 225) are irrelevant because in both of those cases the ground of recovery pleaded by the pursuer was error. The dicta should not be applied out of context to quite different grounds of recovery such as invalidity of a contract through ultra vires.

Secondly, *Magistrates of Stonehaven* provides authority that in a recompense claim for recovery of money paid under a contract void for incapacity, the payer's knowledge of the payee's incapacity does not bar recovery. In that case the third party lender could recover even though he "knew the statute law governing the County's power to borrow, and therefore he was aware that the transaction was ultra vires": p 769 (p 537). (See also ibid at p 770: "the lender's knowledge that the transaction is ultra vires is no bar to his claim".) If the payer's full knowledge of the incapacity does not bar recompense quantum lucratus from the incapax, then a fortiori the payer's erroneous assumption (whether of fact or law) that the recipient is capax cannot bar recovery. A payment under error as to invalidity through incapacity is more excusable than a payment in knowledge of invalidity through incapacity.

Thirdly, one (fictional) justification for the error of law bar is that a payer under error of law should be treated as if he did know the law and therefore as not paying under error (*Dixon v Monkland Canal Co* (1831) 5 W & S 445 at p 451). *Stonehaven Magistrates* holds that the payer's actual knowledge of the payee's contractual incapacity does not bar the payer's recompense claim for recovery. It necessarily follows that treating a payer under error of law as if he had knowledge of that incapacity cannot bar such a claim. If actual knowledge is no bar, a fortiori mere fictional knowledge cannot be a bar.

Fourthly, even if authorities on the condictio indebiti could be invoked, they would not have assisted the incapax local authority. A payer's erroneous belief that an invalid contract is legally valid does not bar a condictio indebiti (Scot Law Com DP no 95, Vol 1, para 2.53; *Haggarty v Scottish TGWU*). Even in trustees' claims for repetition of undue payments, where (contrary to the normal "private rights" rule of *Baird's Trs v Baird & Co* (1877) 4 R 1005) the trustees' error in interpretation of the trust deed does not found a claim (*Rowan's Trs v Rowan*, 1940 SC 30; 1940 SLT 34), nevertheless his error as to its validity does (*Armour v Glasgow Royal Infirmary*, 1909 SC 916; 1909 SLT 40 and 503; *Grant v Grant's Exrs*, 1994 SLT 163 (OH) at p 168J).

Fifthly, to hold that error of law provides a defence to enrichment claims would be to give it the same effect as the doctrine of turpis vel iniusta causa (illegality or contra bonos mores). There seems no warrant for this extensive interpretation of a much criticised doctrine either on principle or authority.

Sixthly, while English law can be an unsafe guide, the error of law rule derives from it. The English courts have rejected "the simple slogan: 'money paid under mistake of law cannot be recovered'", holding that the "essence of mistake of law is that it does not provide a basis of recovery: it is not that, without more, it provides a defence to a claim for money had and received": *Westdeutsche* (1993) 91 LGR at p 372, per Hobhouse J; *Woolwich* [1993] AC 70, obiter at pp 177H and 205A. It would be unfortunate if the scope of the error of law rule were wider with us than in its country of origin.

G. A cross-bearing on the English law

English law was not cited in *Morgan Guaranty*. Lord Dunedin's citation of civilian principles in *Sinclair v Brougham* has not affected the self sufficient way English law develops. The many restitution swaps cases in England show that the principles are unsettled and that there are at least two main differences of approach from Scots law.

First, English law seems to invoke the concepts of "total failure of consideration" and a new concept of "absence of consideration", neither of which are part of Scots law. Take three cases.

(1) At the time when the nullity of the swap is discovered and payments stop, the swap period has not elapsed; P has paid D but D had paid nothing. P obtains restitution under the doctrine of total failure of consideration.

(2) At that time, the swap period has not elapsed; P has paid more to D than D has paid to P. There has been no "total failure of consideration". In *Westdeutsche*, restitution was allowed on the basis of "absence of consideration". The

money was paid under a void contract and so was unsupported by good consideration. This has been much criticised as not disclosing a reason for reversing the enrichment (see Burrows (1993) 143 NLJ 480; Birks (1993) 23 Western Australian L Rev 195). It would for example reverse gifts and undermine the law on error, compulsion etc as grounds of recovery. On the other hand the judgments could be construed as restricted to void contracts, or contracts void for incapacity (ultra vires).

(3) At that time, the swap period has elapsed. On the "absence of consideration" ground there would be mutual restitution of benefits and set off. It has been argued however that there should be no restitution since inter alia both parties have got what they bargained for. To a Scots lawyer, this view seems suspect because it ignores the fact that one party is incapax and that the very policy underlying his incapacity is that he (or the council tax payers) must be protected against making a bad bargain.

An advantage of the Scottish grounds of error and incapacity is that they do not vary with the vagaries of consideration or the stage when the swap is discovered to be null.

Secondly, there is the common law/equity dualism of English law. In *Westdeutsche* it was held ([1994] 1 WLR at p 952) that where payment is made under a contract void for ultra vires, the legal property in the money passes to the payee but in equity the property remains with the payer. So Islington were fiduciaries bound in conscience to return the money to the bank which had "an equitable charge". This approach is inconsistent with the basic Scots doctrines of a unitary law (common law gaps and bars cannot be avoided by sidestepping into equity) and unitary ownership (trusts are contracts and — the dominium directum/utile dichotomy apart — two persons cannot simultaneously both be owners of the same subject). Moreover, this approach does not disclose a specific reason for redressing the enrichment. In principle, that reason is not supplied by the device of characterising the payee as a fiduciary (Birks, unpublished SPTL Conference Paper, 1994).

In *Barclays Bank plc v Glasgow City Council* [1993] QB 429, Hirst J said (at p 446) that ultimately "the House of Lords will be able to give one single decision which will be binding in both England and Scotland, and with no possibility of irreconcilability". It seems more likely however that each legal system can and should reach broadly the same result by its own route.

NEWS

Appointment

Parole Board for Scotland
The Secretary of State for Scotland, has appointed Mr Ian McNee as Chairman of the Parole Board for Scotland with effect from 1 January 1995, in succession to Mr Joseph Scott, who is retiring. Mr McNee, chairman of Macdonald Lindsay Pindar plc and formerly regional chairman of Lothian Region children's panel, has been a member of the board since 1989.

Court

Court of Session: sessions of court
The Lord President has directed under rules 10.3 (2) and 10.5 (2) of the Rules of the Court of Session 1994, additionally to the public holidays in the notice at 1994 SLT (News) 251, that subject to rule 10.3 (3), no Division of the Inner House, Lord Ordinary or vacation judge shall sit on the following days: 3 January 1995, and 8 May 1995 (VE Day).

Sheriffdoms: Tayside Central and Fife
Sessions and vacation courts to be held during 1995 for the disposal of civil business will be as follows:

Spring session, 4 January to 31 March; Summer session, 2 May to 30 June; Winter session, 28 August to 22 December.

Vacation courts: ordinary, summary cause and small claim courts will be held during vacation on the same days as during session.

Coming events

Hume Lecture 1994
Sir James Millar, chairman, Scottish Homes, will deliver the 1994 Hume Lecture, "A Flexible Housing System for the Global Market", at 5.30 pm on 30 November 1994 at the Wolfson Theatre, The Royal Society of Edinburgh, 22, 24 George Street, Edinburgh. Admission is free, but those wishing to attend are asked to contact Kathryn Mountain, The David Hume Institute, 21 George Square, Edinburgh EH8 9LD (tel 031-650 4633; fax 031-667 9111).

General

Will Aid
As most Scottish solicitors know already, Will Aid is taking place again in November. If anybody has any queries they can either phone the Will Aid central office number which is 0865 313102 or get in touch with Graeme Pagan, Hosack & Sutherland, DX Box OB 2, Oban; tel 0631 62308.

Income tax

Income tax: payments out of discretionary trusts
The Inland Revenue have published a revised version of extra statutory concession B18. The text of the concession reads:

UK resident trusts
A beneficiary may receive from trustees a payment to which s 687 (2), Income and Corporation Taxes Act (ICTA) 1988 applies. Where that payment is made out of the income of the trustees in respect of which, had he received it directly, the beneficiary would have been entitled to relief under ss 47, 48 or 123, ICTA 1988; or have been entitled to relief under the terms of a double taxation agreement; or not have been chargeable to UK tax, the beneficiary may claim those reliefs or, where he would not have been chargeable, repayment of the tax treated as deducted from the payment (or an appropriate proportion of it).

Relief will be granted to the extent that the payment is out of income which arose to the trustees not earlier than six years before the end of the year of assessment in which the payment was made, provided that the trustees have made trust returns for each year which are supported by the relevant income tax certificates and which give details of all sources of trust income and payments made to beneficiaries.

Non-resident trusts
A similar concession will operate where a beneficiary receives a payment from discretionary trustees which is not within s 687 (2), ICTA 1988 but is income arising from a foreign possession (e g where non-resident trustees exercise their discretion outside the UK).

Where a non-resident beneficiary receives such a payment out of income of the trustees in respect of which, had he received it directly, the beneficiary would have been liable to UK tax then he may claim relief under s 278, ICTA 1988 (if entitled); and may be treated as if he received that payment from a UK resident trust but claim credit only for UK tax actually paid by the trustees on income out of which the payment is made.

A UK beneficiary of a non-resident trust may claim credit for UK tax actually paid by the trustees on the income out of which the payment is made as if the payment were from a UK resident trust.

This treatment will only be available where the trustees make trust returns, supported by the relevant income tax certificates, giving details of all sources of trust income and payments made to beneficiaries; and pay tax at the rate applicable to trusts chargeable on the UK income of the trust under s 686, ICTA 1988.

No credit is given for tax treated as paid on income received by the trustees (for example foreign income dividends) which would not be available for set off under s 687 (2) if that section applied, and that tax is not repayable.

◇

Capital gains tax: definition of participator
The Inland Revenue have published a revised version of extra statutory concession D40 which limits the definition of "participator" for the purposes of s 96 of and para 8 of Sched 5 to the Taxation of Chargeable Gains Act 1992. The text of the concession reads:

Section 86 of and Sched 5 to the Taxation of Chargeable Gains Act 1992 provide for a charge to capital gains tax on settlors of certain non- or dual resident trusts arising on trust property which originated from the settlor. Paragraph 8 of the Schedule defines what property originates from the settlor and provides that property put into trust by certain companies is treated as originating from those who control the company in question. Paragraph 9 of the Schedule sets out conditions under which trusts created before 19 March 1991 may fall within the scope of the charge on the settlor, some of which may apply to companies controlled by defined persons.

Sections 87-88 charge UK resident beneficiaries to capital gains tax on certain capital payments received from non- or dual resident settlements. Section 96 is concerned with the application of these provisions to capital payments made by companies which are controlled by the trustees and capital payments received by certain non-resident companies.

For the purpose of determining who controls such companies "participator" is defined in s 417 (1) of the Income and Corporation Taxes Act

1988. In applying the provisions of paras 8 and 9 (11) of Sched 5 and s 96 a beneficiary of the trust, by concession, is not regarded as a participator in the company solely because of his status as beneficiary.

◇

Foreign exchange gains and losses
Following extensive consultations between the Inland Revenue and representatives of industry and commerce, the legislative package on foreign exchange gains and losses and financial instruments is in its finalised form, subject to the Government's decision that it should be implemented and parliamentary approval of regulations setting out detailed rules.

The package includes a number of important changes to the Government's original proposals to address concerns raised by the representatives of industry and commerce. In deciding whether the package should be implemented, the Government will take into account views on its broad acceptability to companies, which are, therefore, encouraged to make their views known. These should be sent, by 18 November 1994, to Jon Allen, Inland Revenue (Financial Institutions Division), Room 542, 22 Kingsway, London WC2B 6NR.

Copies of the finalised drafts of the regulations, an explanatory statement containing clarifications which have been given during the consultative process about the operation of the provisions, and a statement of practice on the application of the package to partnerships are available from the Public Inquiry Room, Room G1, West Wing, Somerset House, Strand, London WC2R 1LB.

— ◇ —

Business changes

Messrs Russel & Aitken intimate that with effect from 1 November 1994 they have acquired the goodwill and practice of Messrs McCosh & Holmes, WS, 8 Barclay Terrace, Edinburgh and that with effect from that date Edward Hasell McCosh, WS, will become an associate with Messrs Russel & Aitken at their Edinburgh office. The premises of McCosh & Holmes, WS, at 8 Barclay Terrace, Edinburgh, will close on 1 December 1994 and from that date the combined business will be conducted from Messrs Russel & Aitken's office at 27 Rutland Square, Edinburgh.

Dorman Jeffrey & Co intimate that, with effect from 1 October 1994, Mr Alan Masson, WS, has been appointed an associate with the firm.

Parliamentary News

New Bills

HOUSE OF COMMONS

18 October 1994

Deregulation of Trade Unions—To amend, and make provision for the amendment of, statutory provisions and rules of law affecting trade unions, and for purposes connected therewith. (Private Member's Bill introduced by Mr Tony Benn)

Residential Care Homes—To further regulate ownership, control and standards of private residential care homes; and for connected purposes. (Private Member's Bill introduced by Mrs Gwyneth Dunwoody)

Maximum wage—To fix the emoluments of chairpersons, chief executives and senior managers of private limited companies and public bodies so that their combined annual earnings do not exceed 20 times the average take home pay of their non-managerial employees save if their employees agree through a ballot of their non-managerial employees or through their union to permit salaries of their chairpersons, chief executives and senior managers to exceed a 20:1 ratio. (Private Member's Bill introduced by Mr Denis MacShane)

Questions answered

HOUSE OF COMMONS

17 October 1994

ENDOWMENT ASSURANCE

Mrs Ewing: To ask the Chancellor of the Exchequer what plans he has to introduce measures to permit, without loss of exemption of the policy proceeds from taxation, extension of existing policies of endowment assurance to provide cover against critical illness.

Sir George Young: The Inland Revenue is currently conducting a review of life assurance taxation which includes consideration of the way in which policyholders are taxed. The Government will decide in due course in the light of that review whether or not changes to the present rules on policyholder taxation should be introduced and whether or not existing policies will be affected by any changes. However, under present legislation, it is already possible in certain circumstances for critical illness cover to be added to the cover provided by an existing endowment policy without affecting the exemption of the proceeds from taxation at the higher rate. There is also no bar to policyholders taking out separate critical illness cover.

Book Reviews

Speech and Respect

(The Hamlyn Lectures)

By Richard Abel. 1994. London: Stevens/Sweet & Maxwell. Hardback, £28: ISBN 0 421 50210 X; Paperback, £17: ISBN 0 421 50220 7.

It cannot be said that this book must be on every practitioner's shelf. Nonetheless there are many practitioners who will find it a very refreshing, thought provoking — and it can be said with all respect due to the very many eminent predecessors in this series — and exciting book. So far as law students and law teachers are concerned the book represents four very "instant" and very lively seminars. The book is remarkable in being one of the very few that reiterates all sorts of "bad" words, albeit for scholarly purposes: the lyrics from a piece of modern music called "the Buck" are reproduced as an appendix — an appalling text that narrates a threat to someone's pet cat. Those who never want to make a remark like "Who are the Rolling Stones?" will find references to "2 Live Crew", "Niggaz with Attitude" and "Public Enemy". Many a crusty judge, if any there respectfully be, will have heard of one Madonna. It is a book of the global village and is populated by all the village people. Even Scotland has its clause of fame: "Glasgow 11-14 year olds could recognise an average of five brands." This was brands of cigarettes.

The strengths of this remarkable addition to this distinguished series of texts are: (1) it shows some respect for views which do not seem to be those of the author; contrary evidence is presented in the classic tradition of argument: it is eventually dismissed but it is honestly there and will not be overlooked. This makes the book especially useful for undergraduate teaching; (2) it has a very full bibliography; (3) the very extensive endnotes provide even more information and evidence.

It is in the end a very dangerous book. A moderate form of control over the ordinary speech of ordinary individuals is urged in order to prevent status inequality. The argument is sophisticated and all the more dangerous for that. There is no banning and burning. But there is indictment and degradation. Offenders must be easily complained against and will have to apologise or find another community. The complainer must be protected from the consequences of complaint. Simple liberal or market approaches are insufficient and must be remedied.

I could have said right at the start of this review what this book was justifying but I had already been intimidated in my use of speech by the text: "Conservatives denigrate the struggle for respect with the epithet 'political correctness' — a redundant tautology, since politics are omnipresent and all actors believe theirs are correct." The text sets out a subtle regime for telling those politically dominant some more things that they cannot say or else. The "or else" is that you will be called a "conservative", a purveyor of tautologies or you will have to go (what follows is a paraphrase of the text) to the social space remaining unregulated by any community — a speech frontier for the incurably disaffected (p 145). This place, the text has already explained, will not be your school, university, workplace, trade union, residential neighbourhood, library, shop, public transport, voluntary association, sports team, political party or religious congregation (p 144). The Glasgow smokers will have already discovered this exile to a social space if they have tried to have a fag in any of these places. Passive smoking has not been demonstrated to be good for anyone but Professor Abel's own text demonstrates that there are considerable benefits in people speaking their mind without having to do so before the uncomplaining audience of their own bathroom mirror. It is respectfully suggested that the lesson of democracy for the status victim, as Nelson Mandela could explain to Professor Abel, is not to tell everyone else to watch what they say — it is to get elected.

WILLIAM J STEWART.

The Laws of Scotland: Stair Memorial Encyclopaedia

Volume 18: Property
1993. Edinburgh: The Law Society of Scotland/Butterworths. ISBN 0 406 23718 2.

On St Andrew's Day 1981 Sir Thomas Smith announced the *Stair Memorial Encyclopaedia* in a lecture at the University of Aberdeen. The notion of Scots law as an aspect of national culture was reflected in his title "While One Hundred Remain . . ." — a reference to the Declaration of Arbroath. Any thought that T B Smith's distinctive approach to Scots law had a limited relevance and role must, of course, be considered in the context of an assessment of the extent and significance of his contribution and influence.

In demonstrating a measure of critical radicalism Vol 18 of the *Stair Memorial Encyclopaedia* manifests an important strand of what T B Smith was about. An assumption that one would be unlikely to find originality in the pages of a legal encyclopaedia does not hold for the volume under review. Principal author and co-ordinator Kenneth Reid is the architect of a unitary approach to the law of property which very probably charts the way for the future. Reid traces a process of bifurcation, commencing with the influential 19th century work of Bell, which left moveable and heritable property as separate subjects. Bell's departure from the approach of his teacher Hume (and, indeed, the work of Stair) led to the separation of conveyancing and a tendency to forget that the same fundamentals of property apply to both land and moveables.

Volume 18 is divided into two sections, the first being concerned with the general law applicable to property and the second with intellectual property. Kenneth Reid wrote much of the first section. This has a wide compass including both basic concepts, such as possession and the transfer of ownership, and particular aspects of property which justify special treatment, such as water. The general part includes valuable contributions by other specialists. These are: the feudal system, by George Gretton; servitudes, by A G M Duncan; corporeal moveables, by Professor W M Gordon; and the transfer of ownership under the Sale of Goods Act, by Alan Gamble.

The second section, on intellectual property — a very substantial contribution of over 400 pages — is largely written by principal author Dr Hector MacQueen. What will surely be a valuable and influential text on an area of considerable importance includes specialist contributions from Ian Lloyd (patents and data protection), Hamish Henderson (hallmarking) and Colin Tyre (taxation). With regard to trade marks, it could only be noted, at the time of writing of Vol 18, that all the relevant legislation was due to be replaced. The Trade Marks Act 1994 is now law and one assumes that paras 1261-1360, reserved in the text, will be taken up with a coverage of the new Act in the service material.

The *Stair Memorial Encyclopaedia* property volume demonstrates, at the optimum, the potential role of academic writers in contributing to legal development. Although neither the Scots nor the English legal system knows any systematic interrelation between juristic comment and judicial pronouncement in the French sense

BOOK REVIEWS

of la doctrine and la jurisprudence, there is probably an increasing tendency for case law to be, in part, informed by legal writings. In Scotland one has seen, relatively recently, in respect of reservation of title, the position contended for by two academic writers, in the pages of this publication, coming to prevail in the House of Lords. Modern writings may, of course, be an important indirect source of influence when their marshalling of authorities and arguments are adopted by counsel in submissions which are reflected in the court's opinion. It seems likely that the writings of academic lawyers involved in Vol 18 had this sort of role in the opinion of Lord Penrose in *Sharp v Thomson*, 1994 SLT 1068, in respect of the important issue of when ownership in heritable subjects passes in the context of the system involving (i) missives; (ii) execution and delivery of a disposition; and (iii) registration.

The volume under review reflects the very best of the *Stair Memorial Encyclopaedia's* excellence and it can hardly be doubted that its influence over Scots property law will be deep and sustained. The two principal authors — both recently appointed professor — and the contributing authors are to be congratulated on a volume of obvious quality which will almost certainly have lasting utility and influence.

D L CAREY MILLER,
University of Aberdeen.

Delictual Liability

By J M Thomson. 1994. Edinburgh: Butterworths. Paperback, £23.
ISBN 0 406 01024 2.

Students and practitioners of Scots private law have until recently lacked concise, user friendly resource books. In relation to delict, for example, the sole text before 1989 was Professor Walker's *Delict*, which not only presents a formidable challenge to the new law student but is also 15 years out of date and costly.

Professor Thomson's book is therefore a most welcome and timely addition to legal scholarship and complements Mr Stewart's *Delict* and *Casebook on Delict*. It is one of the few legal texts in this area which can be enjoyed as a book should be and read as a whole. The text is very up to date, including, for instance, *Nordic Oil v Berman*, 1993 SLT 1164, the first reported case in which judicial approval has been given to at least certain aspects of *Murphy v Brentwood* and *Kyle v P & J Stormonth Darling*, 1994 SLT 191; 1993 SCLR 18, where the Inner House affirmed the Lord Ordinary's decision in an action for the

loss of a right to proceed resulting from a solicitor's admitted negligence. The diagrammatic representation of certain cases is helpful, acknowledging that students assimilate information much more readily through the eye than the ear, something which much law teaching fails to grasp.

Professor Thomson allows himself the luxury, not given to the authors of standard texts, of developing particular areas. Readers will be especially interested in his imaginative interpretation of *Junior Books*, although not everyone will agree with his novel conclusion that the case is about wrongful interference with a contract. Given this approach it is not surprising that the book provides a very full account of the economic delicts, a difficult area for students. Quantum of damages is given fuller coverage than is traditional in textbooks on substantive law and this will certainly be welcomed by students, to whom McEwan and Paton may not be readily accessible.

Professor Thomson does the great service of extending the ambit of what is usually covered in tort and delict textbooks to include subjects of immense practical importance, such as the role of the Motor Insurers Bureau and subrogation, which are generally ignored in more standard works. It is essential that students understand how cases are likely to be dealt with in the real world and not just the very few unusual cases which appear in the law reports. He is also to be applauded for the attention which he pays to the social and economic contexts within which delictual liability is located.

This reviewer would have welcomed a more robust criticism of the legal concept of negligence as it has developed since 1932. Originally a daring and imaginative innovation shaped by Lords Atkin and Macmillan, it has suffered at the hands of their more timid judicial successors who have rendered it artificial and unnecessarily complex. The unsatisfactory state of the law in relation to economic loss and to nervous shock is particularly lamentable. Recalling the important roles played by Mrs Donoghue, Mrs Bourhill, Mrs Alexander and others in the development of delict, it is a pity that Professor Thomson has taken the traditional view that all litigants must be male.

There are inevitably a number of areas, such as nuisance and employers' liability, which Professor Thomson has clearly chosen not to explore as fully as he might. However, perhaps we can look forward to further exploration of some of these areas in future editions. Undoubtedly Professor Wilson, to whom this book is dedicated, and who did so much to promote the informed study of Scots private law, would have approved.

S R MOODY,
University of Dundee.

ARTICLES

Liability as Occupier to User of a Right of Way

John Blackie,
Professor of Law,
University of Strathclyde.

This article argues that there is no liability under the Occupiers' Liability (Scotland) Act 1960 on the part of the owner of the solum to someone injured by a dangerous feature of a right of way. It is prompted by certain considerations raised in the House of Lords decision McGeown v Northern Ireland Housing Executive [1994] 3 All ER 53, *relating to the English 1957 Act. The author suggests that the case of* Johnstone v Sweeney, 1985 SLT (Sh Ct) 2, *is wrongly decided on this point but that there are still in some circumstances duties at common law.*

In *Johnstone v Sweeney*, 1985 SLT (Sh Ct) 2, Sheriff Kelbie held that under the Occupiers' Liability (Scotland) Act 1960 there could be a duty on the part of the owner of the solum in appropriate circumstances to users of a public right of way. The House of Lords has now decided in *McGeown v Northern Ireland Housing Executive* [1994] 3 All ER 53, that in England and Northern Ireland there can be no such duty under the legislation applying there, the Occupiers Liability Act 1957, and this is so even if there was an invitation express or implied by the occupier to the injured person (Lord Browne-Wilkinson dissenting in part on this latter point). The opinion of the court is given by Lord Keith.

Johnstone is not referred to and despite presumably a slip of the pen reference by Lord Keith to the "British [sic] and Northern Irish Acts of 1957", nothing in the case relates directly to the position in Scotland. However, the decision contains reasoning some of which is relevant to a consideration of the position here. The facts were very simple. The plaintiff was injured on a path that formed the route to the house where she lived with her husband who rented the house. The point on the path at which she was injured was where it crossed a bit of land which remained as it were an island left still in the ownership of the defenders who had developed the estate, an island entirely surrounded by land that had been taken over by the local authority. The path at that point was a public right of way.

The reasoning of the House of Lords is very clear. (1) Prior to the 1957 Act there was no liability for "negligent non-feasance" by the owner of land to members of the public exercising a right of way. That was "the rule in *Gautret v Egerton* (1867) LR 2 CP 371". (2) Such a rule is "undoubtedly a sound and reasonable one" (per Lord Keith at p 59g), since otherwise it would place "an impossible burden" on the owner of the solum. (3) A person coming onto the premises as of right is not a "visitor" in terms of the English and Northern Irish legislation, unless the right is a legal right such as that of a policeman or a person going into a public park. These are, by contrast, specifically provided for in s 2 (6) of that legislation (approving dicta of Lord Denning MR in *Greenhalgh v British Railways Board* [1969] 2 QB 286 at pp 292-293). (4) It may be that the owner of land cannot be said ever to be occupier of land over which a right of way (whether public or private) passes, but it was not necessary to decide this (per Lord Keith at p 59j). (5) Even if the injured person was as an individual licensed or invited by the owner to use the way, as this person as the spouse of a tenant of one of the defenders' houses clearly was, that made no difference once it became a right of way. The reason given is a causal one, that once a person comes on a place as of right then he or she cannot be seen as coming there on some other basis (per Lord Keith at p 61h).

Some of these reasons particularly raise questions for Scots law. First, was there a rule in the common law prior to 1960 and if so would it survive the 1960 Act? Secondly, if the rule now certainly established as surviving under the English legislation of 1957 is seen as "undoubtedly a sound and reasonable one", what implications does that policy attitude have for interpreting the Scottish legislation? Thirdly, is the owner of land ever "an occupier" where a way runs over it?

The position at common law in Scotland prior to 1960

This raises the question whether the English "rule in *Gautret v Egerton*" was ever received and/or whether it existed in Scotland independently anyway. There appears to be no Scottish reference to *Gautret* prior to 1960. In *Johnstone* (above) Sheriff Kelbie said that prior to 1960 it would likewise have applied to make the pursuer's case irrelevant in Scotland (at p 4). There is, however, no Scottish case prior to 1960 directly concerned with injury to a user of a public right of way. An analogy with users of public parks, etc, who were considered people to whom there could be liability at common law (*Taylor v Glasgow Corporation*, 1922 SC (HL) 1), cannot be made. The one obiter dictum that has been taken recently as equiparating the position of the user of a right of way with such a person there as of right (*Plank v Magistrates of Stirling*, 1956 SLT 83 at p 93; 1956 SC 92 at pp 119-120, per Lord Mackintosh), referred to by A G M Duncan in the *Stair Memorial Encyclopaedia*, Vol 18, para 507) was almost certainly not meant to be taken in this way. There is attached to it a reference to the English Law Reform Committee's report (Cmnd 9305, pp 16-17). Lord Mackintosh must have been aware of the English rule, which is specifically mentioned at that point in that report. He should be taken as meaning that people there as of right are not categorisable as invitees, licensees or trespassers. The consequences of that promoted liability to, for example children in parks, but it could equally well promote non-liability to people using rights of way.

On the other hand some slight support for a liability to persons using rights of way perhaps emerges in pre-1960 Scottish cases dealing with pavements and roads not yet taken over by local authorities. It is established that there can be liability on the proprietor of the solum who has possession and control (*Baillie v Shearer's Judicial Factor* (1894) 21 R 498, per the Lord President (Robertson) at p 503; Lord Kinnear at p 512). This liability, it seems, can be jointly with the local authority at common law or on the basis of statute (*Carson v Magistrates of Kirkcaldy* (1901) 9 SLT 23; (1901) 5 F 18; *McClement v Magistrates of Kirkintilloch*, 1962 SLT (Notes) 91), so long as they also have some possession or control (*Black v Glasgow Corporation*, 1959 SLT 219 at p 223; 1959 SC 188 at p 192 per Lord President Clyde). There is authority, too, that a proprietor adjacent to a public footpath who widened it by throwing into it a strip along the front of his property could be liable if someone then using it was injured either by its state or by a danger arising from the way in which it was butted against the public footpath (*Laurie v Magistrates of Aberdeen*, 1911 2 SLT 231; 1911 SC 1226).

In none of these cases is the question directly addressed as to whether it made any difference that the footpath or road in question had become a public right of way. However, there are rather opaque dicta both ways. Since in Scotland the liability of a roads authority always comprehended non-feasance as well as misfeasance, it may be that it was assumed in those pavement and roads cases also involving private proprietors that essentially their liability was an ongoing one to the public just like a road authority's. There is also a dictum in *Laurie* by one judge stating that while there is no general duty to have any way for those crossing "in the exercise of a public or private right of way or by tolerance", yet, nonetheless, there is a "duty towards members of the public who enter his property either as of right or by tolerance . . . to refrain from exposing them to dangers which are or ought to be within his

own knowledge" (per Lord Skerrington at p 242; p 1245). On the other hand, in *Carson* the Lord Ordinary stated that in the case of a right of way the owner of the solum could be liable to members of the public using it, if the state of the danger was brought about by his own operations (per Lord Pearson at p 21). This is the English rule of no liability in *Gautret* since that rule does not apply to acts of misfeasance as opposed to non-feasance.

So it could have been argued both ways. The fact that there was no clear authority suggests at least that there was no "deeply entrenched rule" (cf *McGeown*, per Lord Keith describing the English rule).

The question of policy
Given the opinion of Lord Keith that the English rule is as a matter of policy correct, that factor could weigh in the balance if there is ambiguity in our law. Indeed, it suggests that if the law were still common law and the matter not decided for Scotland, he would hold there to be no duty of care capable of arising in respect of failure to protect, as it would not be just and reasonable to hold that there was proximity. The question therefore must be, is the 1960 Act worded in such a way as to avoid that approach? The answer, it is submitted, is that it is not.

The 1960 Act
When considering the 1960 Act it is worth stating at the outset that the First Report of the Law Reform Committee for Scotland (Cmnd 88, 1957), which prompted the Act, does not mention users of rights of way.

Unlike the English Act of 1957, which lists a category of people as those to whom there may be a duty, the Occupiers' Liability (Scotland) Act does not. The English Act expressly alters the common law only in respect of "visitors" (s 1 (1)). The 1960 Act expressly alters the common law in respect of "persons entering on the premises" (s 1 (1)). Thus, on a natural and ordinary reading of the words it would seem that there is a potential duty at least in some situations to users of rights of way and this is the view of Sheriff Kelbie in *Johnstone* (at p 5). This may be a natural meaning of the words. But rights of way are a technical legal concept and there is an alternative analysis that, unlike other people entering on premises as of right, such as policemen and children in public parks, users of rights of way are entering not on the premises but onto their own real right, the right of way itself. There is high authority that a public right of way or any other public right of that sort is a real right (Stair, I xv 4; Erskine, III iii 14; see K G C Reid, *Stair Memorial Encyclopaedia*, Vol 18, para 5).

The next question is: is the owner of the solum (assuming of course he has not let it to someone else, for example) an "occupier of premises" in respect of a right of way? An occupier of premises is defined as "a person occupying or having control of the premises" (s 1 (1)) and the duties he has are those that arise "by reason of his occupation or control" (ss 1 (1) and 2 (1)). In *Johnstone* the sheriff (at p 6) was of the view that this was satisfied as a matter of linguistic construction, on the ground that the owner of the solum could invite someone onto the way, and could use the land for any purpose consistent with non-obstruction of the way. However, Lord Keith's reference to a possible argument in England that there is no "occupation" of the way at least requires one to examine this. It is no longer the case that "there was never any doubt" in the English cases referred to that the defender was an "occupier" (cf Sheriff Kelbie in *Johnstone* at p 7). There was in fact a doubt in one of them (*Holden v White* [1982] QB 679; see *McGeown*, per Lord Keith at p 56), but the defender had already conceded the point so it could not be argued. Further, in holding in *McGeown* that the fact that the person using the way was also invited makes no difference suggests that the fact that the owner of the solum could invite someone to use the way (which they would be entitled to do anyway) is not relevant.

What then are the possible arguments that Lord Keith may have had in mind as suggesting that the proprietor of the solum is not the occupier where there is a right of way? It might be argued that at least with some rights of way he is not there and therefore not in possession. However, the Act specifically provides for "possession or control". Pre-1960 law is relevant to determining who is potentially liable (s 1 (2)). Even then, though, when the normal phrase used was "possession and control", it was held in cases dealing with the liability of proprietors of common stairs, where they had let all the flats, that actual presence was not necessary (see *Mellon v Henderson*, 1913 1 SLT 257 at p 258; 1913 SC 1207 at p 1210, per Lord Hunter). It might be argued that "possession or control" involves a power to exclude and this cannot be the case with a person on a right of way. A number of dicta from before 1960 to this effect are collected by Sheriff Kelbie in *Johnstone* (at p 5), e g *McIlwaine v Stewart's Trs*, 1914 2 SLT 127, per the Lord President at p 129; *Devlin v Jeffray's Trs* (1902) 10 SLT 375, per Lord Adam at p 376. However, the sheriff's argument in this respect is convincing, namely that they depend on the context, which was one of determining whether it was a landlord or a tenant who was the occupier of part

of a building or in other cases on considering whether there was any occupier at all (at p 6). Further, a right to exclude does not arise for example with cases of public parks, etc, and undoubtedly there are occupiers of these.

For all this, there is an argument that the proprietor is not with respect to a public right of way in "control" at all. He could be seen as it were as having handed over the keys to the public, even though he has retained a set for himself. An analogy is with where there is a building contractor on the site the owner is not liable for what the contractor does to or on it (see *Murdoch v A & R Scott*, 1956 SC 209), yet he will still have the right to enter on it and use it for his own purposes. This, taken together with the clearly established rule that the owner of the solum cannot be ordained to maintain the way and its corollary that members of the public do have a right to repair it (*Rodgers v Harvie* (1830) 8 S 611 at p 612 (interlocutor of the court)), is an argument which, it is submitted, would be of force in the light of Lord Keith's strong preference for a rule of no liability on policy grounds.

Duty of care or standard of care?

It must be emphasised that the duty which does not exist is a duty under the Occupiers' Liability (Scotland) Act 1960. In England they have no difficulty in holding that there is liability at common law on the ordinary principles of negligence for negligent acts done by the proprietor on his property. So carrying out activities in a negligent way, leaving concealed hazards and so on would all be actionable. The only relevance in England and Northern Ireland of the English 1957 Act to that sort of case is that in contexts other than public rights the injured person will be a "visitor" and base the claim on the 1957 Act. A generous view can be taken of what constitutes an act as opposed to an omission. A railway line crossing a public right of way (or being crossed by it) must be reasonably operated, and the act of operating the railway was held in one case to include reasonable fencing with a suitable stile at the point of crossing (*Thomas v British Railways Board* [1976] QB 912). If, as is argued above, users of public rights of way do not enter on to premises and the owners of the solum do not occupy the right of way, then likewise in Scotland it would be necessary to resort to general common law principles of negligence where it was a negligent doing of something. Just because the 1960 Act expressly states that occupiers do have a duty not only in respect of omissions but also in respect "of anything done there", does not mean that in cases falling outside the Act there is no such duty. The inclusion of acts as well as omissions in the Act was to deal with a particular mischief, namely that it had been held that unlike others "occupiers" could rely on the categories of invitee, licensee and trespasser to reduce what would otherwise have been their duty of care in respect of their acts. People other than occupiers could not thus limit their duty (see *Murdoch v A & R Scott*, above). So it follows that if it is the case that quoad public rights of way there is no liability under the 1960 Act, it does not mean that there is no liability in any context.

In *Johnstone v Sweeney* (above), although it was held, it is submitted wrongly, that there could be a duty under the 1960 Act, the content of that duty was stated not to extend to "a near passive failure to make the condition of the route safe" (per Sheriff Kelbie at p 7). The pursuer, who had slipped on some metal plates placed perhaps by a third party over an eroded gap, therefore in the end failed as her case was that there should have been warnings and handholds. The effect of holding that there is no duty capable of arising under the Occupiers' Liability (Scotland) Act 1960 would in practice be the same. But procedurally it is advantageous, since it forces the pursuer to focus on the fact that the ordinary right of way case will not succeed unless acts rather than omissions are pleaded.

The person encouraged onto the right of way by the owner of a solum

There certainly seems a manifest injustice in certain cases if the injured person was injured by an unsafe feature of the way that the owner of the solum had failed to ameliorate. These are cases where it is incidental to the injured person's being there that it is a public right of way. To take an extreme case: every year the owner has a house painter come up his garden path. Having been sued one year for failing to take reasonable steps to make it safe, he creates a public right of way by grant, and does not tell the painter, who is again injured. Is the law really unable to give the painter a remedy? Lord Browne-Wilkinson in *McGeown* suggested that there would be liability to those "who for purposes linked to the business of the owners of the soil, are encouraged, expressly or impliedly, to use facilities which the owner has provided" (at p 64). He referred to the fact that there can be public rights of way even over a shopping centre (*Cumbernauld and Kilsyth District Council v Dollar Land (Cumbernauld) Ltd*, 1993 SLT 1318). He suggested that the solution to this was to treat at least this class of people as invitees. That would make them after all "visitors" in terms of the English 1957 Act. There is, however, a difficulty. If the owner is not the "occupier" of the way, as argued above, then it cannot come under the Act. However, the law does recognise duties of affirmative action at common law in at least some classes of special relationship. Employers have protective duties to their workers with regard to the state of premises, even sometimes where the employer is not occupying the place where the worker is injured. Such a duty could thus be developed out of general common law principles based on a situation of proximity arising from a just and reasonable dependency on the owner's protection. That also has an attraction in that it could be developed incrementally and would not be limited to the very obviously deserving class mentioned as illustrative by Lord Browne-Wilkinson. It might for example cover the old lady next door whom the owner is in the habit of inviting to tea over a rutted path that happens to be a right of way.

◆

NEWS

Appointment

Junior counsel
The following junior counsel appointment has been made by the Lord Advocate: Department of Transport (in Scotland), Robert A McCreadie, advocate.

Law reform

The right to silence and related matters
The Scottish Law Commission recently submitted to the Scottish Office their comments on the Government's consultation paper entitled *The Right to Silence, Judicial Examination and Evidence of Previous Convictions* which was issued in September of this year.

Commissioners do not support the proposal

that, where there is a judicial examination, notice of a special defence should be given at the examination. Judicial examination usually takes place a very short time after the first appearance of the accused before the court. It may be very difficult for the accused's lawyer to carry out any worthwhile investigation in that short time. Also, any requirement to state a special defence at judicial examination might contravene the European Convention on Human Rights, which provides (art 6.3 (b)) that everyone charged with a criminal offence has the right "to have adequate time and facilities for the preparation of his defence".

The proposal for a clear statutory restatement of the law on silence at trial is superficially attractive, but commissioners doubt whether a satisfactory statutory formulation can readily be drafted. The consultation paper does not provide the terms of such a formulation. The commission would prefer to rely on the statements of the law by Scottish judges which are referred to in the consultation paper. The only significance of the accused's silence is that the prosecution evidence is uncontradicted. The commission do not see why it should be possible to draw adverse inferences where the accused has quite justifiably remained silent. Statutory provisions on the lines of those in the Criminal Justice and Public Order Bill might contravene art 6 of the European Convention on Human Rights. The European Commission of Human Rights has recently declared admissible an application complaining that the corresponding provisions for Northern Ireland violate art 6 (1) (the right to a fair trial) and art 6 (2) (the presumption of innocence).

The commission do not support the proposal that the prosecutor should be permitted to comment on an accused's silence at trial. In practice, the prosecutor is entitled to point out to the jury that the Crown evidence is uncontradicted. The commission think that the present arrangements are generally satisfactory.

— ◊ —

General

Financial services compliance deadline
The Law Society of Scotland have set the deadline for submission of all investment business exemption forms to the society as 5.00 pm on Wednesday, 30 November 1994.

— ◊ —

Taxation

Self assessment: guide for practitioners
The Inland Revenue have published the second in a series of guides for tax practitioners on key aspects of the self assessment system. Tax offices will shortly be sending a free copy of the guide — Self Assessment — the legal framework (SAT2) to each local tax practice they deal with. Extra copies — on paper or disk — can be ordered at £3 a copy from the Inland Revenue Library, New Wing, Somerset House, Strand, London WC2R 1LB.

◊

Capital gains tax: revised extra-statutory concessions
The Inland Revenue have published revised texts of a number of extra-statutory concessions concerning capital gains tax. The purpose of the revisions is to clarify the circumstances in which the concessions will be available. The text of the concessions reads as follows:

D15: Relief for the replacement of business assets: unincorporated associations
Rollover relief for the replacement of business assets extends, under s 158 (1) (e) of the Taxation of Chargeable Gains Act (TCGA) 1992, to unincorporated associations not established for profit whose activities are wholly or mainly carried on otherwise than for profit. In cases where the assets are held by a company in which at least 90 per cent of the shares are held by or on behalf of such an association or its members, the relief will be available provided the other conditions for it are satisfied.

D26: Relief for exchanges of joint interests in land
Where interests in land which is in the joint beneficial ownership of two or more persons are exchanged after 19 December 1984, and *either* a holding of land is held jointly, and, as a result of the exchange, each joint owner becomes sole owner of part of the land formerly owned jointly, *or* a number of separate holdings of land are held jointly, and, as a result of the exchange, each joint owner becomes sole owner of one or more holding, a relief along the lines of ss 247 and 248, TCGA 1992 (relief on compulsory acquisition of land) may be claimed to alleviate the charges to capital gains tax which would otherwise arise.

If the consideration received or deemed to be received for the interest relinquished is less than or equal to the consideration given or deemed to be given for the interest acquired, relief will be allowed on the lines of that provided by s 247 (2) and (5), TCGA 1992; where the consideration is greater, greater relief will be allowed on the lines of s 247 (3) and (5). For this purpose the interest relinquished will be treated as the "old land" and the interest acquired as the "new land". "Land" includes any interest in or right over land and "holding of land" includes an estate or interest in a holding of land, and is to be construed in accordance with s 243 (3), TCGA 1992.

Relief will not be allowed to the extent that the "new land" is, or becomes, a dwellinghouse or part of a dwellinghouse within the meaning of ss 222 to 226, TCGA 1992. However where individuals who are joint beneficial owners of dwellinghouses which are their respective residences become sole owners of those houses in consequence of an exchange of interests, concessionary relief may be claimed if, by virtue of ss 222 and 223, TCGA 1992, each gain accruing on a disposal of each dwellinghouse immediately after that exchange would be exempt. Each individual must undertake to accept for capital gains tax purposes that he or she is deemed to have acquired the other's interest in the dwellinghouse at the original base cost and on the original date on which that joint interest was acquired.

Where interests in land are exchanged after 29 October 1987; and this concession applies to that exchange; and there is a parallel exchange of interests in milk or potato quota associated with the land; and after the exchange each joint owner becomes sole owner of the part of the quota relating to the land he now owns; then this concession will apply to the exchange of interests in quota as it applies to the exchange of interests in the land.

For the purposes of this concession a married couple is treated as an individual, so that an exchange of interests which results in a married couple alone becoming joint owners of land or of a dwellinghouse will meet the terms of the concession.

D27: *Earn outs*

An agreement for the sale of shares or debentures in a company may create a right to an unascertainable element against the purchaser. Where the right is acquired by the vendor at the time of disposal and where it falls, under the agreement, to be satisfied wholly by the issue of shares or debentures, then, notwithstanding a concurrent right to consideration other than in the form of shares or debentures, the board is prepared to treat the right to shares or debentures in the hands of the vendor as a security within the meaning of s 132 (3) (b), TCGA 1992 issued by the purchasing company provided that: (a) the vendor so claims before his liability in respect of the sale of the shares or debentures is finally determined; and (b) as a consequence of it being

so treated, s 135, TCGA 1992 would apply to the disposal of the shares or debentures; and (c) any vendor who so claims undertakes to accept this treatment for all capital gains tax purposes.

In determining whether s 135, TCGA would apply, the board will have regard to the provisions of s 137 (1), TCGA 1992.

If a right falls to be treated as a security and subsequently is satisfied by shares or debentures issued to the vendor in accordance with the sale agreement by the purchasing company, the board will treat that issue as a conversion of securities falling to be dealt with in accordance with s 132, TCGA 1992.

Additionally, where, before 26 April 1988, a right was acquired under which the vendor could receive cash or some other alternative, and a maximum amount for the consideration was specified in the agreement, it will be possible to treat the consideration as if it were ascertainable in that maximum amount even though the cash alternative exists. If a vendor so claims, s 135, TCGA 1992 will — subject to s 137, TCGA — therefore be capable of applying to any shares or debentures issued to him by the purchasing company.

Where s 473 ICTA 1988 does not apply on an exchange of shares only because ss 126 to 136 TCGA would not have applied, then, if the taxpayer so claims, it may apply by concession if ss 126 to 136, TCGA 1992 would have applied by virtue of this concession, if it had been claimed. The vendor must claim the benefit of the extension to the concession before his trading profit or loss for the relevant chargeable period is finally determined, and must agree to accept this treatment for all tax purposes.

The concession will also be available in cases where the purchaser is itself subsequently purchased by another company not in the same group, and the vendor's rights against the purchaser are exchanged for similar rights against that other company; or where there is a subsequent variation in the terms of the original sale agreement; provided that in either case the conditions of the concession set out above were met before the change and would have been met if those new rights or the varied sale agreement had been the original rights or the original agreement.

D39: *Extensions of leases*

Where the extension of a lease other than under its original terms involves the surrender of the old lease and the grant of a new lease, a liability to capital gains tax may strictly arise. In an arms length transaction, the value, if any, of the new lease is taken into account as consideration for the disposal of the old lease.

In practice, however, the surrender of a lease before its expiry and the grant of a new lease for a longer term will not be regarded as a disposal or part disposal of the old lease where all the following conditions are met: the transaction is between unconnected parties bargaining at arms length; the transaction is not part of, or connected with, a larger scheme or series of transactions; a capital sum is not received by the lessee; the extent of the property in which the lessee has an interest under the new lease does not differ in any way from that to which the old lease related; the terms of the new lease (other than its duration and the amount of rent payable) do not differ from those of the old lease. For this purpose trivial differences will be ignored.

— ◇ —

Obituaries

On 22 October 1994, Ian Grant-Smith, WS, Grantown-on-Spey.

On 25 October 1994, William M MacPhail, formerly senior partner in and subsequently consultant to MacPhail & Co, solicitors, Glasgow.

— ◇ —

Business change

Duncan E Nicol, advocate intimates that he has resumed full time practice in Scotland. His clerk and deputy clerk are J K W Carvel and Nichola Graham (tel 031-226 2881; fax 031-225 3642) and his chambers are at Advocates Library, Parliament House, Edinburgh EH1 1RF (tel 031-226 5071). His mobile telephone number is 0831 410251.

— ◇ —

Parliamentary News

Progress of Bills

Criminal Justice and Public Order — Commons: consideration of Lords amendments, 20 October 1994. Lords: consideration of Commons amendments, 25 October 1994.

European Union (Accessions) — Lords: committee stage, 24 October 1994.

Deregulation and Contracting Out — Lords: third reading, 26 October 1994.

Marriage — Lords: third reading, 26 October 1994.

Local Government (etc) Scotland — Lords: third reading, 27 October 1994.

Sale and Supply of Goods — Lords: third reading, 27 October 1994.

— ◇ —

Book Review

Parent and Child

By A B Wilkinson and K McK Norrie. 1993. Edinburgh: W Green/Scottish Universities Law Institute. Hardback, £150. ISBN 0 414 01044 2.

Life is hard for the serious student of family law in the 90s. The first problem is the sheer breadth of the source material. Legislation, case law, multifarious reports of public, statutory and voluntary bodies, Law Commission memoranda, conference proceedings, local government charters, Scottish Office research documents and white papers all jostle for space on the overloaded bookshelves. The pages of the quality and not so quality press scream for attention, with daily accounts of ritual child abuse, surrogate mothers bearing triplets, lesbian fostering cases and children going to court to divorce their parents. Issues of law, families, medicine, life and death, are the stuff of soap operas, vox pop and serious documentaries. Aids and its consequences are everywhere.

Even in the traditional heartland of private law, the family law practitioner finds life becoming more complicated. Legislation such as the Child Support Act whose meaning cannot be even guessed at without full command of a dozen or more statutory instruments is a far cry from the former clarity of the Family Law (Scotland) Act 1985. The old certainties of maternity and paternity are deconstructed by the techniques that have taken us from Louise Brown to women old enough to be grandmothers giving virgin birth. The delegislation of divorce and the rise of conciliation lurk as uncertain possibilities. The meltdown of the nuclear family involves the family practitioner not just in the demarcated zones of aliment, custody and financial provision but also in the outlying suburbs of welfare, support, property law, housing and social work.

Having sketched these problems, where are the answers? A remarkable number of them are to be found in the new and most welcome *Parent and Child*. As has been noted elsewhere, it is remarkable that Scots law has survived since 1906 (when the last edition of Lord Fraser's classic work appeared under the editorship of James Clark) without an up to date, comprehensive and scholarly treatment of the law in this area. It is particularly interesting that this volume emerges at a time when child law, in the past perhaps the less interesting (and less lucrative) branch of family law compared to matrimonial law, has become arguably the central pivot of the law on families. As the stability and duration of marriage as the dominant feature of a family are ever more threatened, society and the state must place more and more emphasis on the regulation of the parent/child relationship. It is interesting that the political will to promote family values finds its most obvious form in the Child Support Act and the stigmatisation of single parenthood. In England, interest in the protection and welfare of children has culminated in the Children Act 1989. In Scotland we still await the consolidating and reforming legislation proposed by the Scottish Law Commission in 1992 (Scot Law Com Report no 135) for family law as a whole. Until that time a treatise such as *Parent and Child* is all the more valuable as a guide to the state of Scottish child law in its current transition between the logical corpus of statutory rules envisioned primarily by Eric Clive and the current piecemeal reality.

The transitional state of Scottish family law is well reflected in the volume at hand. Modern issues and concerns unthought of by Lord Fraser are dealt with in multiple new chapters; of particular note are sections on ante-natal issues, surrogate motherhood and assisted reproduction, DNA testing, and international custody disputes and child abduction. The growth of concern for the welfare of children and the responsibilities of the state as default parent are dealt with in three chapters which grapple admirably with the detail of modern child care law; much needed attention is paid to the important and neglected areas of the regulation of fostering and child minding as well as to the principal legislation in the Social Work (Scotland) Act 1968 under which children are taken into care either voluntarily or by assumption of parental rights. In particular chap 17 on compulsory measures of care and the children's hearings system is an extremely welcome and lucid addition to the rather thin collection of commentary available in this area to practitioners and academics alike. Sheriff Kearney's work remains the leading treatment to be consulted, but since its publication in 1987 the system has staggered through inter alia Cleveland, Orkney, Fife and the *Scotland's Children* white paper, and important case law has accumulated. The implications of *Sloan v B*, 1991 SLT 530, are manfully dealt with here. Unfortunately it is almost certain that in the near future at least parts of this chapter on place of safety orders will be rendered out of date following Lord Clyde's report.

Norrie and Wilkinson also maintain a firm grasp

on the historic basis of Scottish family law as well as on the more recent developments, and so the work as a whole is useful as a tool for fundamental research as well as for basic answer-hunting. For example, a full account is given of the institutional based law of minority and pupillarity, an appreciation of which is still essential to many difficult questions of children's and parental rights, despite the fact that the area of capacity at least in relation to contracts has been almost wholly reformed by the Age of Legal Capacity (Scotland) Act 1991.

Having stressed how well this work tackles the twin tasks of presenting an up to date view of modern child law and integrating an appreciation of the historic development of the law, it is perhaps reasonable to quibble a little at a few editorial decisions. Is it appropriate still in the 1990s to echo Stair and Erskine and begin with a comprehensive treatment of legitimacy and legitimation? Since 1986 these concepts have had little legal import and the Scottish Law Commission have recommended their abandonment as anachronistic (Scot Law Com no 135, para 17.4). Do we still need 31 close packed pages on this area? Or at least would it not be better to treat the topic under a head such as "the child's right not to be subject to discrimination on grounds of marital status of parents" (just as later, in very modern style, access is described as the child's right to contact)? Chapter 11 on aliment reveals a similar residual preference for the traditional arrangement of the law. It seems hard to justify a whole chapter on aliment, as against some three or four pages within on the new scheme under the Child Support Act 1991. Of course it may be that the authors have their doubts that the 1991 Act will remain on the statute book until its full implementation in 1996. In this kind of area the authors must wish forlornly for a political crystal ball. Nevertheless right now it is indubitable that for child law practitioners the Child Support Agency is far more of a headache than the old 1985 Act and perhaps the text should reflect this need.

These few points aside, this is a marvellous work which barely needs a review. Those who work in this area will already have purchased it, shaking their head only slightly at the exorbitant price of Scottish law books. A generation of students will be relieved to have Norrie and Wilkinson to consult alongside Clive on *Husband and Wife*. This reviewer hopes only that the economics of publishing will allow this work to stay up to date when the expected major changes in family law alluded to above finally arrive on the statute book.

LILIAN EDWARDS,
University of Edinburgh.

ARTICLES

The Commercial Agents (Council Directive) Regulations 1993

Ronald A J Herd,
Solicitor, Scotland
and England and Wales.

Mr Herd explains the effect of the regulations, which now cover many aspects of agency contracts and which as respects some provisions may not be contracted out of.

In general Scots law and English law have refrained from interference in the relationship between principal and agent and have only intervened to imply terms in accordance with the general principles of contract where express agreement between the parties is lacking. This situation changed on 1 January 1994 when the Commercial Agents (Council Directive) Regulations 1993 (SI 1993/3053) ("the regulations") came into force.

The regulations enact European Community Directive 86/653 on Commercial Agents ("the directive") in Great Britain under the powers conferred on the Secretary of State by s 2 (2) of the European Communities Act 1972. The directive is a harmonisation measure designed to create uniformity in the European Community. The regulations were laid before Parliament on 8 December 1993 and contain a number of substantive changes as against the draft issued by the Department of Trade and Industry in June 1993. The directive has clearly been influenced by those continental jurisdictions where the agency relationship has been regarded as nearer to that of status and the agent as deserving of protection from the law, akin to some extent to the protection given in recent decades in the United Kingdom to employees.

The European Commission's general thinking regarding the status of agents can be discerned from the Commission's Notice on Exclusive Dealing Contracts with Commercial Agents [1962] OJ 139/292, which dealt with the position of agents in relation to the competition provisions of art 85 (1) of the European Community Treaty. The notice states that agents are not in general akin to independent traders and regards them essentially as performing an auxiliary function akin to that of an employee. It provides that the principal and agent are not to be regarded as separate undertakings for the purposes of art 85 (1). It should be noted, however, that a new notice has been issued in draft form by the Commission which may reduce the number of agents to whom the provisions of art 85 (1) do not apply.

The regulations affect agency law in two ways, first by providing implied terms for the relationship where none have been agreed, a rule previously left to common law, and secondly by providing that some of the implied provisions shall apply to all agency contracts irrespective of the parties' express agreement. These provisions are generally protective of agents.

Applicability

The regulations apply to a "commercial agent" as defined in reg 2 (1). A commercial agent is a person who is: "a self employed intermediary who has continuing authority to negotiate the sale or purchase of goods on behalf of another person (the 'principal') or to negotiate and conclude the sale or purchase of goods on behalf of and in the name of that principal".

Regulation 2 (1) follows to a great extent the definition set out in art 1 (2) of the directive in defining a commercial agent in broader terms than the word "agent" would usually be understood in Scots or English law, and includes "agents" who do not have the authority to bind their principals. It has been argued that the definition, by using the words "self employed", excludes companies or partnerships acting as agents and that the regulations accordingly apply only to individuals. It is submitted that such an interpretation would unduly restrict the effect of the regulations and it should be assumed that the regulations will apply to companies and partnerships. The use of the words "self employed" ensures that employed sales representatives do not come within the scope of the regulations. Disputes may also arise as to the definition of "negotiate". There can be situations where a person is involved almost exclusively in marketing but may have some authority to discuss certain matters relating to a sale with a prospective customer on the principal's behalf. It is not possible to state with certainty whether such will be regarded by the courts as negotiation on the principal's behalf within reg 2 (1). The safest course for advisers is to assume that the regulations will be construed relatively widely by the courts and will be held to apply to such agents.

The definition of commercial agent specifically excludes officers of companies or associations with power to bind the company or association, partners acting on behalf of their partnership, or any persons acting as insolvency practitioners. Regulation 2 (2) follows art 2 (1) of the directive in exempting from the regulations the activities of the following: an agent who is unpaid; commercial agents operating on commodity exchanges; and the Crown Agents for Overseas Governments and Administrations. Regulation 2 (4), in conjunction with reg 2 (3) and the Schedule to the regulations, exempts from the regulations persons whose activities as agents are considered to be secondary. The Schedule provides a complicated definition of activities which are to be considered as secondary. An example of a transaction which is to be considered secondary is a sale to which the following conditions apply: (i) it is not normally negotiated individually and concluded on a commercial basis; (ii) the agent's activities are unlikely to lead to repeat business in the goods with the customer or other customers in that geographical area; and (iii) the agent does not expend its own resources in developing the market for the goods.

It appears likely from this provision that agents who are selling to consumers will not come within the provisions of the regulations. Paragraphs 3 and 4 of the Schedule set out eight criteria which can be used to give an indication as to whether or not an arrangement is to be considered as secondary under the Schedule. In particular, para 5 of the Schedule provides that the regulations do not apply to mail order catalogue agents for consumer goods and consumer credit agents.

The regulations apply only to the activities of agents in Great Britain. However the regulations do not apply where the parties agree that their relationship is to be governed by the law of another Community member state. The regulations also do not apply to agents operating outside the Community even though the parties choose to apply English or Scots law and the common law rules will continue to apply. Furthermore, if a British business appoints an agent to operate solely in another Community member state and the parties agree that English or Scots law is to govern the contract, the regulations do not apply and the relationship will be subject to the common law rules. This is an unsatisfactory anomaly which appears seriously to restrict the applicability of the regulations. However, the agent in such circumstances could argue that the directive is directly applicable and that it should have the protection offered by the directive against its British principal irrespective of the provisions of the regulations.

There are no transitional provisions. The regulations apply from 1 January 1994 to all agency relationships within their scope, irrespective of when the relationship commenced. The provisions of the regulations do not apply, however, to any rights or liabilities which have accrued before 1 January 1994.

The regulations are divided into parts which deal with the principal issues concerning the relationship between principal and commercial agent. The remainder of this article shall be split on the basis of the divisions in the regulations.

Rights and obligations

The duties of each party to the other are covered by Pt II of the regulations. Regulation 3 requires the commercial agent to look after the interests of its principal and act dutifully and in good faith. The duty to act in good faith is merely a broad restatement of the general principles which have been established in the law of agency by the courts of both Scotland and England. The regulation proceeds to elaborate on these general duties in reg 3 (2) by specifying that a commercial agent shall make proper efforts to negotiate and conclude transactions, communicate to its principal all necessary information available to it and comply with reasonable instructions given by its principal. The last of these duties is again no more than a restatement of an agent's duty at common law.

The parties may not derogate from the provisions of reg 3. However, reg 3 does not add a heavy burden to the implied duties imposed by law on agents as that term is understood by Scots and English law. The two principal changes are the restriction on the ability of the parties to exclude these duties and their application to sales agents and others who would not come within the legal definition of an agent as understood in Britain.

The duties applying to principals are set out in reg 4 which cannot be excluded or restricted by the parties. Regulation 4 (1) requires a principal to act dutifully and in good faith towards its commercial agent. Regulation 4 (2) (a) requires the principal to provide its commercial agent with the necessary documentation relating to the goods concerned. This presumably includes all appropriate sales materials and technical manuals. Disputes may, however, arise, where an agent is required to arrange transportation of goods which he sells in Britain to an overseas delivery point. It could be argued that all documentation required for such export must be supplied by the principal, whereas at present the provision of such documentation is often the agent's responsibility.

Article 4 (2) (b) of the directive is repeated almost verbatim in reg 4 (2) (b). The principal is under the very broad and ill defined duty of obtaining for its commercial agent the information necessary for the agent's performance of the agency contract. The principal must also

THE COMMERCIAL AGENTS (COUNCIL DIRECTIVE) REGULATIONS 1993

inform the commercial agent within a reasonable time if the principal anticipates that the volume of sales under the contract is likely to be lower than the volume which the commercial agent could have expected under normal circumstances. In many instances, however, the commercial agent is likely to know of any reduction in customer demand in advance of this coming to the principal's attention.

The final general duty upon the principal arises under reg 4 (3), in terms of which the principal must advise the commercial agent within a reasonable time whether he accepts or refuses a transaction or of any non-execution by the principal of a transaction which the commercial agent has procured for the principal. The provision is really a matter of commercial good manners, but it is important for an agent to know that a customer may be dissatisfied by the principal's refusal to supply or non-performance.

Remuneration

Many, if not most, agency contracts set out the commission which the agent is to receive. Nevertheless, a surprising number do not set down the level of commission unambiguously and it is not uncommon for a contract to specify that commission is to be agreed between the parties on a transaction by transaction basis. Where there is no agreement the courts have held that in the absence of any clear implication to the contrary the agent is entitled to reasonable remuneration. In the absence of agreement between the parties as to remuneration and without prejudice to any relevant statutory provisions regarding remuneration, reg 6 (1) provides that a commercial agent is entitled to such remuneration as is customarily given to commercial agents involved in selling the goods which are the subject of the agency in the location where the agency is to be carried out. In the absence of any customary practice the commercial agent is to receive reasonable remuneration taking into account all the aspects of the transaction. It is submitted that this adds little to the common law. In particular it offers no protection to an agent in a weak bargaining position against a principal who will only agree in the contract to a low level of commission.

Regulations 7 to 12 set out further provisions which are to apply to remuneration only if the commercial agent is remunerated wholly or partly by commission which is defined in the regulations as "any part of the Remuneration of a commercial agent which varies with the number or value of business transactions". Accordingly regs 7 to 12 do not apply, for example, to any periodic retainer paid by the principal to its agent.

Regulation 7 covers entitlement to commission in respect of transactions concluded during the agency contract. Paragraph 1 entitles an agent to commission on transactions concluded as a result of the agent's action or on a transaction which is concluded with a customer who was previously acquired by the commercial agent for transactions of the same kind even though the commercial agent has had no involvement in securing that particular sale. The agent's right to commission is further extended by reg 7 (2) which gives an agent that has exclusive rights to a particular geographical area or to specific customers the right to commission on all transactions in its area or with its assigned customers, whether or not it has had any input to the securing of the transaction. It is to be anticipated that those advising principals may wish to exclude contractually the right to receive commission on transactions in which the agent has not participated or provide that where an agent is to work in an area where the principal already has customers, commission is not payable on direct sales by the principal to customers of long standing.

Under reg 8 (a) a commercial agent is entitled to commission on transactions concluded after the agency terminates if the transaction is mainly attributable to the agent's efforts during the agency and was entered into within a reasonable period after termination. This provision is one which principals may wish to override in their agency contracts. It is suggested that a formal agency contract should specify a time limit within which a transaction must be entered into in order to qualify for commission. In the absence of such a limit disputes are bound to arise as to the definition of a reasonable time. Moreover the longer the time between termination of the agency and the transaction which is the subject of the claim for commission, the more involved will become the arguments as to whether or not the transaction is mainly attributable to the commercial agent's efforts.

A right to commission also arises under reg 8 (b) in respect of orders received before termination by the principal or the commercial agent from a third party, even if a binding contract is not concluded before termination, as long as the transaction is one which satisfies the requirements of reg 7, i e was concluded as a result of the commercial agent's actions, or with a customer acquired by the commercial agent or with a customer within the commercial agent's area of exclusivity. A transaction will frequently fall under both paras (a) and (b).

The apportionment of commission between a former agent and its successor is covered by reg 9. The new agent does not have any entitlement to commission for a transaction where the former agent is entitled to commission under the terms of the regulations. However the commission is to be shared between them if this is equitable in the circumstances. The question of what is equitable is likely to be a cause of disputes. It is advisable for those drafting agency agreements to make more detailed provision to regulate the conflicts which may arise under reg 9.

Having dealt with what commission is payable the regulations proceed to deal with the timing of payment in reg 10. Under reg 10 (1) commission is due as soon as and to the extent that the transaction has been executed by the principal or the third party or should have been executed by the principal. In using the word "execute" rather than a word such as "perform", the regulations are following the wording of art 10 of the directive. It has to be assumed that in this context "executed" means performance rather than merely entering into the contract. The wording of this regulation ensures that in the absence of agreement to the contrary the commercial agent receives commission even though the principal fails to perform its contract with the third party customer. Commission is also payable on part performance of the contract, thus if the customer pays an instalment to the principal on the contract being concluded commission will, in the absence of agreement to the contrary, be payable at that juncture on the value of the instalment paid.

As the provisions of reg 10 (1) may be overruled by the agreement of principal and agent, reg 10 provides a safeguard for the commercial agent in paras (2) and (3). Any attempt to derogate from the provisions of paras (2) and (3) is void. Under reg 10 (2) commission will be due at the latest when the third party executes its part of the contract or should have done so if the principal had performed its obligations under the contract. Thus the commercial agent is protected from the principal's delay in performance and from any failure to perform on the part of the third party customer. This means that payment will usually be due to the agent no later than the date when the customer pays or should pay under the contract. Regulation 10 (3) requires commission to be paid no later than the last day of the month following the end of the quarter during which payment became due. Thus reg 10 (3) now provides in all circumstances a final date by which commission must be paid to the agent.

The principal can only avoid paying commission if the circumstances listed in reg 11 (1) occur. Any contractual attempt to expand the circumstances where right to commission is extinguished

is void under reg 11 (3). The right to commission can be extinguished only if the contract between principal and third party will not be executed and this does not result from a reason for which the principal is to blame. Thus the agent may lose its commission if the contract is never performed due to a breach by the third party or force majeure. Under reg 11 (2) any commission which has already been paid shall be refunded if the commercial agent's right to it is extinguished.

Regulation 12 enables the agent to verify the level of commission payable, and any agreement to derogate from reg 12 is void. Regulation 12 (1) requires the principal to supply quarterly statements no later than the end of the month following the end of the quarter when commission becomes due, which accords with the time permitted for payment under reg 10 (3). The statement must set out the main components used in calculating commission. A commercial agent can demand under reg 12 (2) to be provided with all information available to the principal which the agent needs in order to check the amount of commission due to it, including extracts from the principal's accounts.

Formalities, conclusion and termination of the agency contract

Both commercial agent and principal are entitled under reg 13 to receive a signed written document setting out the terms of the contract between them. Any terms subsequently agreed are also to be set out in a signed document. Neither party can be bound by any purported waiver of this right.

Termination is dealt with by reg 15. Regulation 15 (1) restates the common law rule that an agency contract of indefinite duration may be terminated by either party on notice. Regulation 15 (2), however, sets out minimum required notice periods of one month in the first year of the contract, two months for the second year and three months thereafter. The parties are prohibited from agreeing shorter notice periods. It should be noted that under reg 14 if any agency contract is concluded for a fixed period and both parties continue to perform after the expiry of the fixed period it automatically becomes a contract for an indefinite period and the notice requirements of reg 15 (1) apply to it. In such circumstances the initial fixed period is to be included in calculating the length of the contract for the purpose of establishing the notice required. It should also be noted that these notice periods apply to both parties. Regulation 15 (3) provides that where longer notice periods are agreed the notice to be given by the principal must not be shorter than that required from the agent. Unless the parties agree to the contrary the period of notice must, under reg 15 (4), coincide with the end of a calendar month.

Regulation 16 mitigates the effect of reg 15 to a limited extent by providing that the regulations do not affect any rule of law which allows for termination without notice because of a failure of one party to perform its obligations under the agency contract or where exceptional circumstances arise. The second of these grounds is copied from the directive. It is submitted that it covers most of what is understood by force majeure and frustration in Scotland and England.

Regulations 17 and 18 provide that upon termination of the agency the commercial agent is to receive compensation or indemnification, as that concept is defined in the regulations. The principal and agent cannot derogate from the rules set out in regs 17 and 18 to the detriment of the agent before the agency contract expires, although they can agree a lower compromise figure after expiry of the agency.

Articles 17 and 18 of the directive permit member states to decide whether an agent is to be entitled to indemnification or compensation. When the government circulated its draft of the regulations it proposed that agents should be entitled only to compensation. When the regulations were laid before Parliament, however, reg 17 provided for both options.

In the absence of a provision in the agency contract electing for indemnification the agent is entitled to compensation only (reg 17 (2)). An agent cannot elect unilaterally for indemnification. The most radical aspect of reg 17 from the British perspective is the granting to the agent of rights to compensation or indemnification upon termination for whatever reason, even where a fixed term agency has merely expired by effluxion of time. The right to compensation or indemnification even arises when the contract terminates due to the death or retirement of the agent.

The right to indemnification is set out in paras 3 to 5 of reg 17. The right to compensation is dealt with by paras 6 and 7. In both cases the agent loses its rights if it does not notify the principal of its intention to seek compensation or indemnification within one year of termination of the contract.

The commercial agent is entitled to an indemnity where the principal continues after termination to derive substantial benefits either from customers who have been brought in by the agent or from existing customers who have increased their business with the principal because of the commercial agent's efforts. The indemnity to be paid is to be equitable in all the circumstances,

having particular regard to the commission which the agent has lost in relation to such customers. The indemnity is limited in value to one year's commission based on the average of either the last five years of the agency or, if the agency has lasted less than five years, the annual average over the period of the agency. The inclusion of this limit may be attractive to a principal in that its maximum liability will be immediately quantifiable on termination. The provision works to the detriment of agents whose commission earnings have grown from a small base over five years or less. The indemnity option may also be unattractive to agents who have little scope for attracting new customers or increasing business volumes as it will be argued by principals that such agents have not brought them increased business for which the agent should be rewarded on termination. However reg 17 (5) provides that an agent who has been granted an indemnity is not precluded from seeking damages in addition. Such damages should only be payable upon breach of contract by the principal, and would be expected to compensate for lost commission for the contractual notice period. It is arguable that any indemnity payable under the regulations should be deducted from such damages. It is questionable whether that is intended by reg 17 (5); but an agent receiving an indemnity under the regulations and damages for early termination is effectively being compensated twice compared to the common law damages payable on termination without notice or good reason.

Alternatively the agent is entitled to receive compensation for the damage it suffers on termination. Regulation 17 (7) states that such damage is deemed to occur particularly when termination takes place in circumstances where the agent is deprived of commission which it would have earned by proper performance of the agency while the principal receives substantial benefits from the agent's activities, or where the agent has not been able to amortise costs and expenses of performing the agency which were incurred on its principal's advice.

Regulation 18 limits the application of reg 17 by providing that no compensation or indemnity is payable: (1) where the principal has terminated the contract because of a default by the agent justifying immediate termination under statute or at common law, or (2) where the agent terminates the contract itself except if the termination by agent is justified by circumstances which can be attributed to the principal (effectively constructive termination by the principal) or where the agent has terminated because it is unreasonable for the agent to be required to continue to perform its obligations due to age, infirmity or illness, or (3) where the agent assigns its rights or duties under the contract to another person with the principal's consent.

In most cases it will not be simple for principals and their agents to judge whether indemnity or compensation will be more appropriate. It seems that indemnity may be preferable for the principal in some cases where there is the certainty of the maximum limit and where the calculation of the indemnity based on average commission paid in the last five years could benefit it if the level of business is very variable or is likely to build up from a low base. Furthermore, where an agent has not brought in new business either in the form of new customers or increased trade from existing ones, no indemnity will be payable. On the other hand, indemnity would appear to be payable on gross commission whereas compensation should be based on the agent's net loss, that is to say its loss of commission net of expenses. Although the regulations do not make this point explicitly, it is suggested that under the existing law of remedies this must be the case. It is also arguable that an agent is under a duty to mitigate its loss in respect of a claim for compensation but it is not clear whether this applies to an indemnity payment. Certainly, if an agent does not actually suffer any serious loss upon termination it would be financially better served by an indemnity rather than compensation.

It is accordingly difficult, especially at this early stage in the life of the regulations, to make any generalisations as to the situations in which indemnity or compensation will benefit a particular party. This issue may become the subject of heated discussion when agency contracts are being negotiated. However, it is likely that many agents will receive compensation by default because no election is agreed in the contract. There may be clear benefits for agents in particular circumstances and the decision between compensation and indemnity is one which should receive careful consideration at the time of appointment.

Restraint of trade clause
The provisions of a restraint of trade clause in an agency contract are already regulated at common law. Regulation 20 includes complementary rules in relation to contracts to which the regulations apply. Regulation 20 (3) specifically provides that reg 20 does not affect any other rule of law restricting the validity or enforceability of restraint of trade clauses. Under reg 20 (1) there are two requirements to be satisfied for a restraint of trade clause to be valid. First, the restraint must be concluded in writing. Secondly, it can relate only to the agent's geographical territory or

the group of customers and geographical area allocated to the agent and only to the types of goods covered by the agency. Such a clause can only be valid for up to two years beyond termination. It is submitted that this regulation adds little to the common law. However, the two year time limit provides an absolute time limit which makes it easier to advise parties on enforceability. Although the the common law requirement of reasonableness remains, the regulations do not include the provision which appeared in the draft of the regulations requiring that any restraint be reasonable from the point of view of the principal, agent and their customers.

Conclusion
It is impossible to gauge fully the effect of the regulations at this juncture. Some of the provisions do no more than restate the common law position. The provisions on termination and compensation/indemnity upon termination are however a major step. Furthermore, the regulations apply to a group of commercial businesses which do not fall within the existing legal definition of an agent. The regulations and the directive could be faulted for being slanted towards protection of agents without giving any recognition to the fact that some agents may be in a stronger financial position than their principals. Some principals may baulk at having to pay compensation to an agent who retires through old age or to an agent whom they have terminated on notice who, although not in default, has failed to meet the principal's expectations. Some businesses may now prefer to use other methods of marketing, most likely distributorship. However, there are disadvantages in using a distributor rather than an agent. A supplier can maintain much more control over an agent in important areas such as the price to be charged to the customer for its goods. A supplier can also retain closer control over the way goods are marketed by an agent and agents generally receive less commission than the mark up which a distributor can make. It is possible that some business may even choose to employ more sales representatives, but the costs involved in employing staff are likely to mitigate against this option.

The rules applied by the regulations are merely another consideration to be looked at alongside the other legal, commercial and financial considerations which must be balanced in selecting the marketing methods which are best suited to a particular business or product.

The regulations have some flaws. There are several issues upon which the regulations are unclear. Many of these difficulties can be overcome by well thought out drafting of agency contracts, being careful, of course, not to insert any provisions which fall foul of those parts of the regulations which may not be derogated from. The regulations have also failed fully to implement the directive in certain areas such as their applicability to agents working within the European Community (but outside Great Britain) for a British principal.

The regulations are a significant change to the law of agency and principal and, on occasion, agents may find that provisions with which they disagree are implied by default where the agency has been constituted by the minimum of formalities or apply irrespective of the terms of the contract. For these reasons, the provisions of the regulations will now be fundamental to the advice given by legal practitioners to their clients both in relation to existing agents and over proposed arrangements.

◆

NEWS

Court

Advocates' clerks
In order to accommodate the SSC Society Biennial Lecture the advocates' clerks' accommodation situated in the SSC upper library will be closed at 4.00 pm on 25 November 1994. A telephone answering service will be maintained for the last hour of the working day.

Coming events

Hume Lecture 1994
The speaker in the lecture "A Flexible Housing System for the Global Market" will be Sir James Mellon, not Sir James Miller as announced at 1994 SLT (News) 344.

General

Glasgow University Law Society
At the annual general meeting of the University of Glasgow Law Society, the following students were elected to office: *President,* Alistair R Aitken; *vice president,* Christopher G McKenna; *secretary,* Lesley-Anne Nicol; *treasurer,* Ali Murray; *assistant secretary,* Ruth Higgins; *diploma representative,* Alisdair S Matheson; *ordinary committee,* Eric Weir, Candice Sammeroff, John W Cush, Iain MacPhail, Colin Bole, Philip Curle; *first year representatives,* David J Milne, Laura M Anderson.

Taxation

New leaflet on open government
The Inland Revenue have published a new leaflet explaining the main commitments accepted by the Inland Revenue (and other Government departments) under the Government's code of practice on access to government information, and how they intend to meet them. It describes the information which will be made generally available and the Inland Revenue's policy on giving reasons for their decisions.

The leaflet entitled *Open Government* is available free of charge from any tax inquiry centre or tax office, or from the Public Inquiry Room, West Wing, Somerset House, London WC2R 1LB.

Income tax: benefits in kind: cheap loans
Regulations will come into force on 6 November 1994 to set the official rate of interest at 8 per cent from that date. This will bring the official rate of interest more closely into line with typical mortgage rates following their response to the rise in the bank base rate on 12 September 1994.

Capital gains tax: private residence relief
The Inland Revenue have published a new extra-statutory concession relating to private residence relief in certain cases where there is a delay by an owner occupier in taking up residence. This new concession replaces statement of practice D4, which is now withdrawn. The text of the concession reads as follows:

This concession applies: where an individual acquires land on which he has a house built, which he then uses as his only or main residence;

where an individual purchases an existing house and, before using it as his only or main residence, arranges for alterations or redecorations or completes the necessary steps for disposing of his previous residence.

In these circumstances, the period before the individual uses the house as his only or main residence will be treated as a period in which he so used it for the purposes of ss 223 (1) and 223 (2) (a), TCGA 1992, provided that this period is not more than one year. If there are good reasons for this period exceeding one year, which are outside the individual's control, it will be extended up to a maximum of two years.

Where the individual does not use the house as his only or main residence within the period allowed, no relief will be given for the period before it is so used. Where relief is given under this concession it will not affect any relief due on another qualifying property in respect of the same period.

— ◇ —

Obituary

On 27 October 1994, Ian Maxwell Ferguson, MC, WS, formerly consultant to Messrs Patrick & James, WS, Edinburgh.

— ◇ —

Business changes

Boyds, solicitors, Glasgow, intimate that with effect from 10 October 1994 Denis A Rodie has been assumed as a partner in the firm. In addition, with effect from 31 October 1994 the firm has moved office to Thistle House, 146 West Regent Street, Glasgow G2 2RZ. The telephone, fax and DX numbers remain unchanged.

Munro & Noble, solicitors, Inverness, intimate that with effect from 31 October 1994 Mr James H S Stewart has resigned from the partnership.

J B Soutter, Son & Main, solicitors, 63 Almada Street, Hamilton, intimate that David A Darroch has resigned from the firm with effect from 11 November 1994.

McClure Naismith Anderson & Gardiner, solicitors, Glasgow, Edinburgh and London, intimate that Mr Robin J M Morton resigned as a partner on 31 October 1994. He will continue to be associated with the firm as a consultant and in that capacity will be actively involved in liquor licensing matters. With effect from 1 November 1994 Valerie A Shand has been appointed an associate.

— ◇ —

Book Review

Money Laundering

Hume Papers on Public Policy, Vol 1, No 2. 1993. Edinburgh: Edinburgh University Press. Paperback, £9.95. ISBN 07486 04855.

The old truths still apply: "bad money drives out good". The constant theme in the five papers that make up this slim volume on money laundering is the need to protect the integrity of the banking profession and the financial sector. That integrity may have been taken for granted in the past but such complacency cannot now be tolerated.

Money laundering is the process by which criminals attempt to conceal the true origin and ownership of the proceeds of their criminal activities. If the laundering is done successfully, it allows the criminals to maintain control over those proceeds.

There are broadly three stages in the process: first, there is the placement stage when the dirty money is changed from the original cash form to another financial asset or by purchasing goods. That can be done in the same country or another. Secondly, there is the laundering stage when there are further attempts to conceal the criminal source of the proceeds. Thirdly, there is the integration where the funds are hidden in the legitimate financial system and assimilated with all the other assets in the system.

The various writers of these papers indicate the very considerable efforts internationally and domestically that have gone into providing a framework of policy and law to seek to deny the use of the banking and financial sectors to those involved in money laundering. That term was itself first used, it is believed, in a law case in the United States in 1982. Nearly all of the international obligations and domestic law reforms have occurred in recent years.

The useful bibliography to this volume outlines a substantial quantity of material: the volume itself is a most helpful introduction to the topic and easily lends itself to recommendation. Indeed in itself the collection of papers may prove to be influential for the various approaches arising out of money laundering begin to be focused properly.

ROBERT S SHIELS

ARTICLES

Protecting Reputations

Spring v Guardian Assurance [1994] 3 All ER 129

Douglas Brodie,
Simpson and Marwick Lecturer in Private Law,
University of Edinburgh.

It appears from the Spring *decision that the courts are developing an implied right of an employee to a reference from his employers, and at the same time allowing the possibility of a claim in negligence for information wrongly given. Dr Brodie examines the employment aspects of the decision.*

The central issue in the House of Lords decision in *Spring v Guardian Assurance* [1994] 3 All ER 129 was whether a duty of care in negligence was owed by an employer to a former employee with regard to the giving of a reference. By a majority of 4-1 their Lordships held that there was, with the case of *Hedley Byrne v Heller* [1964] AC 465 looming large in the speeches.

From the point of view of the development of delictual principle in general and recovery for pure economic loss in particular the most interesting feature of the case is the different views of the majority on the ratio of *Hedley Byrne*. Lord Goff, with whom Lord Lowry agreed on this point, took the view that liability under *Hedley Byrne* rested upon "an assumption or undertaking of responsibility by the defendant towards the plaintiff, coupled with reliance by the plaintiff on the exercise by the defendant of due care and skill" (at p 145). Applying this principle to the facts in *Spring* Lord Goff held that a duty of care was owed, a conclusion also reached by Lord Lowry who found the requisite degree of proximity by deploying the different route taken by the other judges in the majority. Nevertheless, according to Lords Goff and Lowry, the scope of *Hedley Byrne* is much wider than mis-statements and encompasses, inter alia, negligently provided services.

The attraction of this approach is that it offers a principled and unifying underpinning of both the law on negligent misrepresentation and cases which are more difficult to categorise such as *White v Jones* [1993] 3 All ER 481, *Ross v Caunters* [1980] Ch 297 and *Ministry of Housing and Local Government v Sharp* [1970] 2 QB 223 (assuming that a broad interpretation is given to the concept of reliance). The difficulty is that the principle, without further refinement, might be thought too all embracing as situations like the one in *Junior Books v Veitchi*, 1982 SLT 492, would also fall within it.

Lords Slynn and Woolf adopted a more general approach in *Spring* and, applying the standard tests for proximity, held that there was a duty of care. *Hedley Byrne* appears to have been viewed, certainly by Lord Slynn, simply as a case about negligent misrepresentation. It was perfectly reasonable to extend the benefit of that decision to someone to whom a statement was not communicated but who was nevertheless adversely affected by it.

It seems certain that *Spring* will be subject to critical appraisal in subsequent pure economic loss cases. However, in this article I wish to focus on the employment aspects of the case. It is clear from all the speeches that the importance of references, both to employers and employees, in the present day employment market is very much appreciated. *Spring* goes on to offer valuable discussion of the rights and duties to which the transmission of references gives rise.

Negligent misrepresentation

Spring tells us that the delictual obligation to take reasonable care in the compilation of a reference is owed not just by the employer or ex-employer but by anyone giving a reference in the business context. If, however, a social acquaintance acts as referee then it is likely that no duty will be owed — though this may not be true if the employee had asked him to act in this way. The obligation exists both during the currency of the employment relationship and after its termination; it would appear to exist irrespective of whether or not the employee had asked the referee to act. A broad notion of employment is embraced so that the obligation extends beyond those working under an employment contract to the self employed. In the course of compilation the referee may solicit information from a third party, but it seems that the latter does not owe a duty. This may lead to the drawing of difficult distinctions should it be thought that the third party has offered an opinion and not just information.

Where an employee succeeds in showing that loss has been incurred as a result of a reference which was negligently compiled it would be possible to recover damages on the basis that a chance of obtaining the job in question had been lost. Thus an employee might still be compensated even though he was not able to prove that he would have obtained the job.

Other rights of the employee

It had been accepted that in the absence of an

express term in the employment contract employees had no right to a reference, and this seems to have been assumed by the parties in the instant case. *Spring* suggests that the law, recognising the social importance of being able to obtain a reference, is moving in the direction of implying a term into employment contracts affording a right to a reference, at least in those sorts of employment where references are likely to be sought. Lord Slynn took the view that "even if there is no universal duty to do so it would seem to me that contracts may exist when it is necessary to imply such a duty" (at p 165g). Lord Woolf believed that there would be an implied term to give a reference in every employment contract where "the contract relates to an engagement of a class where it is the normal practice to require a reference from a previous employer before employment is offered . . . [and] . . . the employee cannot be expected to enter into that class of employment except on the basis that his employer will, on the request of another prospective employer made not later than a reasonable time after the termination of a former employment, provide a full and frank reference as to the employee" (at p 179a-b). The content of such a term would be that "during the continuance of the engagement or within a reasonable period thereafter, [the employer would] provide a reference at the request of a prospective employer which was based on facts revealed after making those reasonably careful inquiries which, in the circumstances, a reasonable employer would make" (at p 179c).

It might be asked whether there is any real value in such a right since if a reference is not given voluntarily it is less likely to be positive. Without risking a defamation or negligence action an employer can easily damn by faint praise. Against that such a right may assist in promoting a cultural change whereby employers are prepared to give a reference automatically.

The two employers
Prior to this decision it had been assumed that a duty of care would be owed by the giver of the reference to the recipient. One of their Lordships, Lord Goff, expressed a certain degree of doubt and thought the answer "may depend on the facts of the particular case before the court" (at p 147f). With the utmost respect it is hard to see why any doubt exists. The relationship would appear to be covered by *Hedley Byrne*: "the defendant giving advice or information was fully aware of the nature of the transaction which the plaintiff had in contemplation, knew that the advice or information would be communicated to

him directly or indirectly and knew that it was very likely that the plaintiff would rely on that advice or information in deciding whether or not to engage in the transaction in contemplation" (*Caparo Industries plc v Dickman* [1990] 1 All ER 568 at p 576c).

What if the reference is given on the basis that no liability will attach? This would presumably be intended to prevent the new employer from raising an action, but would it bind the employee suing in delict? The following dictum of Lord Goff in an earlier case is relevant at this juncture: "when C has a direct right of action in tort against A in respect of damages caused by A's breach of his duty to B, C's rights against A must be regulated by any provisions which controlled or limited B's rights against A" (*Leigh and Sillavan Ltd v Aliakmon Shipping Co Ltd* [1985] QB 350 at p 397). It seems reasonable to assume that such reasoning would be applied were the issue to arise in the context of an action of negligent misrepresentation over a reference.

An exemption clause might also exist directly between employee and employer: "This issue does not arise in the present case but it may be that employers can make it clear to the subject of the reference that they will only give one if he accepts that there will be a disclaimer of liability to him and to the recipient of the reference" (*Spring* at p 162h, per Lord Slynn).

In either situation the employee might, if the disclaimer was valid at common law, then argue that the Unfair Contract Terms Act applied. It would then be a question of whether the disclaimer was fair and reasonable. It is difficult to predict the outcome of such a judgment, but the relevant considerations will be similar to those involved in *Spring* in deciding whether it was just and reasonable to impose a duty of care. In deciding that question the court made much of the importance of accurate references to employees; indeed a bad reference could be as financially damaging as a serious physical injury. Moreover, employers derived a great deal of benefit from the exchange of references. One might then hazard the view that the defender would not be allowed the benefit of the exemption clause or at least that he could not rely on this with any degree of certainty.

How else might a referee protect himself? An action is unlikely to arise if the employee cannot obtain sight of the reference. What if the referee gives the reference on a confidential basis? Where the relationship is contractual, and in *Hedley Byrne* it seems to have been assumed that it would have been but for the absence of consideration, one could insert a confidentiality clause. If there is no express clause it is possible, but far from certain, that one would be implied. Even if the relationship is not contractual it is possible that since *Lord Advocate v The Scotsman Publications*, 1988 SLT 490, it would be subject to an obligation of confidentiality. What would be the remedy if the recipient were to breach the duty, however constituted, of confidentiality and the referee was forced to pay damages in a delictual action? There is an old authority to the effect that damages would only be nominal (*Weld-Blundell v Stephens* [1920] AC 956). A contemporary court might well take a different view given that the very essence of the duty breached was to guard against disclosure.

Defamation

Prior to *Spring* any employee dissatisfied by a reference would have been confined to a defamation action. Indeed one of the main arguments in the case was that to allow an action in negligence would adversely affect the overall coherence of the law by undermining the law of defamation. A defamation action is subject to the defence of qualified privilege and to overcome this the pursuer must prove malice. This is a heavy burden (*Spring* at p 156e, per Lord Slynn). Thus in *Spring* the plaintiff "was able to establish that one of his colleagues, who played a part in compiling the information on which the reference was based, had lied about interviewing him, but this was still insufficient to prove malice" (at p 172c).

Conclusions

From the point of view of the general law of delict the full significance of *Spring* remains to be seen. From the point of view of employment law *Spring* improves an employee's position with regard to references. Given the practical difficulties of obtaining evidence of a negligently prepared reference there will not necessarily be much litigation. The dicta in the case on the issue of a right to a reference are particularly noteworthy in the light of the significant number of recent cases on implied terms in employment contracts. They can be taken as further evidence of a current judicial willingness to add to the legal duties inherent in every employment contract. Lord Slynn took note of "the changes which have taken place in the employer/employee relationship, with far greater duties imposed on the employer than in the past, whether by statute or by judicial decision, to care for the physical, financial and even psychological welfare of the employee" (at p 161e). One suspects that further elaboration of

the rights and duties inherent in employment contracts will follow.

[I would like to thank Professor H L MacQueen for his critical comments on an earlier draft of this article.]

The Not Proven Verdict

Sir Nicholas Fairbairn, QC, MP

Sir Nicholas offers some typically robust comments on two of the subjects currently out to public consultation, the not proven verdict and the right to silence.

The not proven verdict has staggered out of the ring and the Lord Advocate has asked for comment. I have said it all before but I shall say it all again, because as Churchill said nothing repeated fewer than three times will be heard. I regret to say in passing that the reasons for the assaults upon it are that it is different and thoughtfully civilised. The question put to the jury by the court is this: "Do you find the charge proven or not proven?" It is not do you find the accused guilty or not guilty, though that may follow.

If the jury is satisfied beyond reasonable doubt that the Crown have proved their case, the proper verdict is proven and if not, not proven, but there may be and often are cases where the jury can go further and say that the accused is not guilty. If he can establish to their satisfaction for instance that he was in Iran, when the crime was committed in Bo'ness; or that he is not Donald Trump but Donald Duck; or that the "offensive weapons" he was carrying were his tool kit and he was on his way to mend Taggart's auntie's loo, he is entitled to a verdict of not guilty, i e innocence, not lack of sufficient proof.

At the other end of the spectrum logic requires a different approach. It would be obfusc and obtuse to say we find the case proven, but we do not find the accused guilty, so proven and guilty slide into guilty, leaving three verdicts, guilty, not guilty and not proven.

Not proven is not a let out verdict as is often claimed; it is the proper verdict where the jury are not satisfied beyond reasonable doubt but cannot say not guilty. For instance if you stab Taggart's auntie with a bread knife the jury may be in some doubt as to whether it was self defence or not, but you can hardly say not guilty as you did stab Taggart's auntie. In the absence of not proven, what are you to do? Not guilty does not describe the position, but not proven does. So what is wrong with a ranch of verdicts which provide for all situations? Nothing I can see, so I find the case against not proven, not proven. Long live "Not proven".

While I am considering old chestnuts falling out of fires, perhaps I may revert to the so-called "right" to silence. Of all the five billion odd people on earth — only one has the "right" to silence — the accused — on the absurd ground that he might incriminate himself. Well, first, why shouldn't he? If an accused falsely admits to a crime he didn't commit, so be it. It is prayed in aid that he might be flustered, anxious or in some way deluded as to his "rights" or predicament; but what of all the other witnesses, who can be called from the ends of the earth, who are much more likely to be flustered, anxious or deluded, but who have a motive if so inclined to stick the knife in the accused, charged say with killing a member of their family, raping their sister and mother, burning down their home or stealing their car and property? Why should the accused who has an interest to lie in his own favour have a "right" to silence, when those who have an interest to tell the truth, have no such "right"?

It is nonsensical and it is wrong. I am perfectly happy that alleged statements made in police custody should be inadmissible, because nothing is easier than to concoct, invent or falsify what an accused said whilst incommunicado of independent witnesses, but that is a very far cry from saying he should have a right not to tell us what he knows or what he claims to be the truth.

Let juries and the court scrutinise upon its worth and weight. But let us abolish the so-called "right" to silence and make all witnesses, accused or not, the same. Then justice will be done.

◆

NEWS

Appointment

Scottish Law Commission
The Lord Advocate has appointed Mr Niall R Whitty, MA, LLB, as a full time member of the Scottish Law Commission for a period of five years with effect from 1 January 1995. Mr Whitty has been on the legal staff of the commission since 1971. He succeeds Sheriff Iain Macphail, QC, who has completed his period of office and is returning to his post as a sheriff at Edinburgh.

— ◊ —

Court

Faculty of Advocates
Mr Geoff James Clarke, LLB (Edinburgh), Mr Alistair Macdonald Clark, LLB (Glasgow), PhD (Strathclyde), and Miss Rosemary McGuinness Guinnane, LLB (Glasgow), have been admitted to the Faculty of Advocates.

— ◊ —

Law reform

Scottish Law Commission: multi-party actions
The Scottish Law Commission have published a new discussion paper (*Multi-Party Actions: Court Proceedings and Funding* (no 98)), suggesting that a new court procedure is needed to provide effective remedies in situations where a number of people have the same or similar rights to raise a court action. Such situations may arise following, for example a North Sea oil rig explosion, illnesses suffered by a number of people who have all taken the same defective drug, or overcharging in the sale of goods or services. If one claimant's case is successfully pursued in court that will not necessarily help all the others; the person liable may refuse to pay up to the others who did not litigate and they may need to raise further actions themselves. In other countries, such as the USA, Canada and Australia, there are procedures for such "multi-party actions" where a number of cases can be advanced in a single litigation, the result of which is binding in all the cases. A similar procedure would seem to be desirable in Scotland, with special financial arrangements to meet at least part of the cost to the claimants of what might be complicated and expensive litigation.

The commission's proposals
The commission suggest new court procedures specifically designed for those multi-party actions where the issues — matters of fact or questions of law — are broadly similar and could be dealt with in a single litigation, without undue difficulty. The commission recognise that the cost of

litigating may deter some people from taking their claims to court and discuss how financial assistance might be provided from a contingency legal aid fund or a class action fund. The commission were not asked to consider changes in other important matters such as the legal principles which determine liability and how any compensation found due is calculated.

Possible new court procedures

The main aims of any new class action procedure should include that only those cases which are suitable for the new procedure are channelled into it; and that all those who have identical or similar claims know about the new procedure so that they can join in the litigation. Ideally, also, all the claimants ought to share at least some of the costs of litigating, if these are not borne by a public or other fund.

The commission propose that at an early stage in the litigation, but not before it starts, the court should decide whether the particular collection of claims is suitable for the proposed new class action procedure. A formal application would be made asking the court to decide whether the claims satisfy several specified criteria for "certification". These criteria are important since if they allow in unsuitable cases the new procedure may prove to be unmanageable; if suitable cases are not certified the procedure may be relatively unused and not worthwhile. The commission suggest four criteria for certification, all of which would need to be satisfied. First, that there are so many potential pursuers that it would be impracticable for all of them to sue together in a single conventional action. Secondly, that the potential pursuers are an identifiable class whose claims give rise to similar or common issues of fact or law. Thirdly, that a class action is preferable or superior to any other available procedure for the fair and efficient determination of the issues. Fourthly, that the representative pursuer will fairly and adequately protect the interests of the class in relation to those issues which are common to the class.

The commission suggest that if litigation is certified as a class action people who want to be covered by the court's final decision on the common issues should be required to say, by expressly "opting in", that they wish to be recognised as a member of the class. These people would need to know about the action so that they could decide if they wanted to opt in. The commission therefore invite views on when notices should be given to class members, what the form of the notice might be (such as newspaper or television advertisement?) and how the cost of the notice should be controlled and paid for. If there were a large number of possible class members, the cost of notice might be so large as to discourage people from ever starting a class action.

The commission further ask what special powers the judge might need to ensure that a Scottish class action is conducted fairly and with no avoidable delay, and whether there would have to be special rules with regard to abandonment of the action or settlement of the claims to regulate when the main claimant ("the representative pursuer") can drop out of the class action. It is possible that some defenders might attempt to make an abnormally good offer to the representative pursuer alone and he or she might accept that offer, do nothing to progress the litigation and leave the other members of the class in the lurch.

A class action might seek an award of damages for each of the members of the class, related to their own individual circumstances. The commission suggest that there should be other possibilities: for example the court might fix an amount due to the class as a whole, possibly on a more approximate basis than is usual in conventional litigation, and should say how that aggregate monetary award should be divided up among all the class members. In view of the number of members of the class and the difficulties of determining what each might be due on an exact calculation it might be that the division of the aggregate monetary award could be done on a rather rough and ready basis on the view that such an award is better than no award at all, which might be the alternative. Another possibility would be that the class action should determine only the common issues of fact or law, leaving the claimant to raise a separate action to determine what compensation was due to him or her.

How a new court procedure might be funded

It would be very unfair if the representative pursuer who raised the class action had to pay the main bulk of the cost himself. No-one would volunteer to be a representative pursuer if that was likely to happen. The commission therefore consider that special funding arrangements are needed.

Three possibilities are provisionally rejected. The first is to change the general rule that expenses follow success; that is, to restrict the court's discretion to make an award of expenses in favour of a party who is successful (such as the class of litigants). The second is to alter the law to allow a contingency fee agreement, as in the United States of America, which would give the lawyers for the class a share of the proceeds, if the class action was successful. The third would be to amend legal aid legislation to provide funding for the class. The commission noted the recent experience in England and Wales in large complex actions, particularly those in connection with tranquilliser drugs (benzodiazepines). It appears that this litigation has incurred very considerable legal aid expenditure, amounting to some £30m-35m, and none of the claims have actually reached the stage of a hearing of evidence. The Legal Aid Board, in England and Wales, has suggested that reforms are needed both of the legal aid system and of how these cases are dealt with by the courts.

The commission therefore invite views on the possible setting up of a contingency legal aid fund or a class action fund. These funds are similar in that each would be able to provide external funding for the class litigation and it would not be essential that applicants for funding should be means tested. They differ in the main source of their own funding. When fully operational the contingency legal aid fund would be partly or wholly drawn from contributions levied on successful class litigants in previous class actions. The class action fund might need to be financed from public funds.

The commission also suggest that the class members should not be free of any financial obligation to the representative pursuer if a decree for payment is obtained in the class action. The whole amount awarded should be paid into the court and the clerk of court would deduct a proportion of the legal expenses from each person's share before it was handed over.

The working party report
Published along with the discussion paper is a report by a working party which included lawyers experienced in multi-party actions. In their recommendations about court procedures and practices they suggest that court rules should be amended to avoid the need for parties raising very similar cases to repeat the pleadings in another summons; this other summons would be treated as the "master summons". They suggest also that there should be established arrangements for litigants to request a single judge to be allocated to take charge of all the stages of a multi-party action.

Invitation for views
Those who intend to comment may obtain copies of the discussion paper and working party report free of charge from the Scottish Law Commission, 140 Causewayside, Edinburgh EH9 1PR (tel 0131-668 2131). Views are invited by 30 April 1995.

◇

Committee on Appeals and Alleged Miscarriages of Justice

The Secretary of State for Scotland has announced the membership of an independent advisory committee to look into the current procedures surrounding appeals and alleged miscarriages of justice and to report on the need for and nature of any changes required to existing procedures. The committee is representative of the various relevant interests and the appointments have been made both on the basis of members' professional knowledge and expertise and the personal contribution they will be able to make.

The committee will be chaired by Professor Stewart R Sutherland, FBA, Principal and Vice Chancellor of Edinburgh University. The Rt Hon Lord Ross, Lord Justice Clerk, has agreed to serve as a member. The other members are: Derek Emslie, QC; Sheriff Gerald H Gordon, QC; Professor J Ross Harper; Professor Neil MacCormick, Edinburgh University; Andrew Normand, Regional Procurator Fiscal, Glasgow and Strathkelvin; Mrs Alison Paterson, Director, Victim Support, Scotland; and Leslie Sharp, Chief Constable, Strathclyde Police.

The terms of reference for the committee are as follows:

"(a) To examine the current criteria for consideration of appeals by the appeal court in Scotland: to consider possible changes to the statutory criteria contained in ss 228 and 442 of the Criminal Procedure (Scotland) Act 1975; and to make recommendations, having regard to the interests of justice, including the need for fairness to the appellant and the principle of finality in criminal proceedings.

"(b) To examine the current procedures under s 263 of the Criminal Procedure (Scotland) Act 1975 for referral of cases to the appeal court by the Secretary of State; to consider options for change to the procedures for considering alleged miscarriages of justice in Scotland; and to make recommendations on whether and what changes may be required to those procedures, having regard to the efficient use of resources throughout the criminal justice system; and to report before or by July 1996."

— ◇ —

NEWS

General

Licensing training package
The Patent Office, in association with the Licensing Executives Society, has launched a new training package addressing the legal and commercial aspects of product and technology licensing. The package is aimed at lawyers and their corporate clients. It consists of a video programme on 12 inch laser discs, and an accompanying 150 page workbook.

The complete training programme (discs and workbook) is available from the Patent Office at £1,200. For details, call 01633 814645.

Business changes

Balfour & Manson, Nightingale & Bell, Edinburgh, intimate the retiral of Ethel M Houston and Malcolm M Wylie as partners of the firm with effect from 1 November 1994.

Naftalin, Duncan & Co, 534 Sauchiehall Street, Glasgow, intimate the retiral of their consultant, Mrs Doreen P Sevitt Collins, with effect from 1 November 1994. On the same date their assistant, Mr Steven Kane, was appointed as an associate.

Simon John Black Hutchison, solicitor, Falkirk, intimates that, following the dissolution of the partnership of Hogg Hutchison, solicitors, Falkirk, he has set up on his own account trading as Hutchison, Solicitors, Ground Floor, 5 Manse Place, Falkirk FK1 1JN (tel 01324 633000; fax 01324 633005; DX FA 37).

Letter to the Editor

W & J Burness, WS,
Solicitors,
16 Hope Street,
Charlotte Square,
Edinburgh EH2 4DD
10 November 1994

Sir,
Professor Gretton's article "Sharp Cases Make Good Law" (1994 SLT (News) 313) calls for comment.

Justice does not appear to be served by an outcome which allows a holder of a floating charge not only the benefit of a sale of security subjects but the right, while benefiting from the first sale, also to benefit from the second sale of the same subjects to the exclusion of any benefit to the price-paid first purchaser.

When property is subject to a floating charge and a receiver is appointed then:

(1) the directors cease to be agents of the company with respect to the property; and

(2) the receiver becomes agent of the company; and

(3) the net proceeds of sale of the property are distributed first to the holders of prior ranking fixed securities created as such (i e not floating charges which have attached as fixed securities), secondly to preferential creditors and only then to the holder of the crystallised floating charge.

At no time does the holder of the crystallised floating charge have a power of sale. At no time can the subjects of the crystallised floating charge be sold by any person other than in the capacity of agent of the company. At no time therefore is there an alienation of the property by the company to the holder of the floating charge. There is merely a special dedication of the proceeds of a realisation which is carried out by means of a sale agreed and implemented on behalf of the company. This is what "attach as a fixed security" means. The statute creates, at this point, a fixed security whose efficacy (except against a good faith third party acquirer for value) is, like that of an English fixed equitable charge, not dependent upon the creation of a real right but upon its ability to attach to the proceeds of realisation of the secured subjects. The attachment serves its purpose adequately without being treated as a deemed registered standard security.

The implications of *Sharp* for the law of immoveable property have been much discussed but it also has implications for moveable property registered in a register, such as patents and trade marks. See Patents Act 1977, ss 31 and 33, and Trade Marks Act 1994, ss 22 and 25.

Within Great Britain it would appear that while the law of real rights in intellectual property is precisely the same for Scottish registered and English registered companies, the effect of insolvency law is to protect a purchaser from an English company but not (unless and until *Sharp* is overturned) a purchaser from a Scottish company. This flows from ss 117 and 120 of the Insolvency Act and their interaction with the general laws of England and Scotland respectively. Transfer of real rights in property situated outside the United Kingdom is, of course, governed by the law of the place but it is, nevertheless, helpful if the law of the incorporation of the transferor company recognises the alienation as effective in an insolvency. When a company is the proprietor of intellectual property registrations in the United Kingdom and abroad it is simply not possible for assignments of real rights to be perfected at or shortly after the payment of the purchase price.

There is a Community dimension to *Sharp*.

The event which causes a floating charge to attach to the same effect "as if the charge was a fixed security over the property to which it has attached" is the appointment of a receiver or the commencement of the winding up of the company. The first such event to occur terminates the ability of the directors to bind the company relative to the charged property, substituting the power of a receiver or liquidator. The crystallisation of a floating charge therefore automatically involves a "termination of office" for the purposes of art 2 (d) of the First Company Law Directive (68/151/EEC), even if not for every purpose. The "documents and particulars" bringing about the "termination of office" must, under art 3.4 of the directive, be "effected by publication in the National Gazette appointed for that purpose by the Member State".

Article 3.5 of the directive provides as follows: "The documents and particulars may be relied upon by the company as against third parties only after they have been published in accordance with Paragraph 4, unless the company proves that the third parties had knowledge thereof. However, with regard to transactions taking place before the sixteenth day following the publication, the documents in particular shall not be relied on as against third parties who proved that it was impossible for them to have knowledge thereof."

If the matter is viewed as a question of ostensible authority rather than property the decision in *Sharp v Thomson* can be seen to be incompatible with the obligations of the United Kingdom under the directive. A denial that the property had previously effectively been alienated from the company by the directors who were the receiver's predecessors as agents is an attempt by the company itself to rely upon the publishable document (the instrument of appointment of the receiver) to deny the efficacy of acts done on its behalf by the directors who were believed to be its agents, i e the execution and delivery of the disposition by the directors to the good faith purchaser. If the execution and delivery took place

before the execution of the instrument of appointment the attempted denial of the directors' agency is particularly extreme as it is an assertion of retrospective deprivation of capacity.

Neither denial is permitted by the directive if at the time of the purchaser's acting to his prejudice on the faith of the public record (at the Companies Office) the circumstances fall outside art 3.5. The alienation of the company's property by the directors on behalf of the company is required by Community law to be no more nor less effective than an alienation by agents of unchallengeable capacity. The disposition by the directors to the purchaser is required to be no more nor less reliable than it would have been had a receiver not been appointed. In other words it should be defeasible only if the holder of a competing writ wins the race to the Sasine Register or Land Registry.

There is nothing fundamentally inimical to Scots law in this proposition. It merely extends the historic Scottish concept of faith in the registers to embrace the Register of Companies. Nor, to anticipate an objection, does art 222 of the Treaty of Rome (Treaty not to prejudice "rules . . . governing the system of property ownership") present a difficulty, first because the matter concerns capacity not property, and secondly because in any event the provenance of art 222 indicates that it relates only to noninterference in the issue of state versus private ownership.

Yours faithfully,

J A McLean.

— ◇ —

Parliamentary News

Royal Assent

3 November 1994

Sale of Goods (Amendment) Act 1994 (c 32).
Criminal Justice and Public Order Act 1994 (c 33).
Marriage Act 1994 (c 34).
Sale and Supply of Goods Act 1994 (c 35).
Law of Property (Miscellaneous Provisions) Act 1994 (c 36).
Drug Trafficking Act 1994 (c 37).
European Union (Accessions) Act 1994 (c 38).
Local Government etc (Scotland) Act 1994 (c 39).
Deregulation and Contracting Out Act 1994 (c 40).

Questions answered

HOUSE OF COMMONS

28 October 1994

FAMILY LAW

Mr Salmond: To ask the Secretary of State for Scotland (1) what plans the Government have to bring Scottish child law in line with the principles set out in the UN convention on the rights of children;

(2) what action has been taken to consider whether law, policy and practice in Scotland concerned with juvenile justice and protection of children from violence are in full compliance with all provisions in the UN convention on the rights of the child.

Lord James Douglas-Hamilton: The principles of the UN convention underlie the proposals for child care policy and law set out in the White Paper "Scotland's Children", Cm 2286. We intend the children's hearings system to continue to play a crucial role in the care of children in Scotland and the White Paper contains proposals for strengthening that role. The necessary legislation is in the course of preparation and will be introduced when parliamentary time permits.

Mr Salmond: To ask the Secretary of State for Scotland what plans the Government have to introduce legislation in Scotland allowing for the exclusion of child abusers from the family home.

Lord James Douglas-Hamilton: The White Paper "Scotland's Children", Cm 2286, indicated the Government's intention to introduce an exclusion order for the protection of children. The necessary legislation is in the course of preparation and will be introduced when parliamentary time permits.

Mr Salmond: To ask the Secretary of State for Scotland what plans the Government have to implement the recommendations of the 1992 Scottish Law Commission report on family law; and when the legislation will be placed before the House.

Lord James Douglas-Hamilton: My right hon friend the Secretary of State plans to implement certain recommendations of the Scottish Law Commission report on family law, particularly those relating to parental responsibilities and rights. The necessary legislation is in the course of preparation and will be introduced when parliamentary time permits.

Mr Salmond: To ask the Secretary of State for Scotland what plans the Government have to implement the recommendations of Lord Clyde in his 1991 report on the Orkney child abuse inquiry; and when the legislation will be placed before the House.

Lord James Douglas-Hamilton: The proposals in the White Paper, "Scotland's Children", Cm 2286, reflect the recommendations of and consultations on Lord Clyde's report and other reports published from 1990 onwards. Many of Lord Clyde's recommendations related to social work practice and procedure, and action to implement these is in hand. Revised guidance on aspects of child protection is now at an advanced state of preparation. Other changes require legislation. This is in the course of preparation and will be introduced when parliamentary time permits.

Mr Salmond: To ask the Secretary of State for Scotland in what areas existing Scottish child law breaches the principles accepted by the British Government following its ratification of the UN convention on the rights of children.

Lord James Douglas-Hamilton: The welfare of the child is at the centre of the child care provisions of the Social Work (Scotland) Act 1968. This is in keeping with the principles of the UN convention. In ratifying the convention, the Government noted a detailed reservation on art 37 (d), which takes account of the operation of the children's hearing system in Scotland. The White Paper, "Scotland's Children", Cm 2286, proposed changes in policy and law which are consistent with the principles of the convention.

Mr Salmond: To ask the Secretary of State for Scotland what plans he has to bring forward proposals for statutory assistance to Scottish children aged 16 to 18 years who were in local authority care; and what comparison he has drawn with systems in force outside Scotland.

Lord James Douglas-Hamilton: Local authorities already have a statutory duty to provide assistance to young people under 18 if they have been in care immediately before school-leaving age. As was indicated in the White Paper, "Scotland's Children", Cm 2286, the Government propose to extend this duty to include young people aged 18 and to provide local authorities with a power to assist such young people under the age of 21 who meet the criteria of eligibility and need. These arrangements will stand satisfactory comparison with the other countries in the United Kingdom. The necessary legislation is in the course of preparation and will be introduced when parliamentary time permits.

3 November 1994

LICENSING LAWS

Mr Salmond: To ask the Secretary of State for Scotland what plans there are for extending licensing laws to allow shops to sell alcohol on a Sunday.

Lord James Douglas-Hamilton: Provisions permitting off-sale premises in Scotland to sell alcoholic liquor on Sundays between 12.30 pm and 10 pm are contained in s 22 of the Deregulation and Contracting Out Act 1994. An announcement about commencement of the provisions will be made shortly.

— ◇ —

Book Reviews

Divorce in the Sheriff Court

Fourth edition. By S A Bennett. 1994.
Edinburgh: W Green. Paperback, £25.
ISBN 0 414 01091 4.

The welcome fourth edition of Siggi Bennett's book has been produced to reflect the procedural changes in connection with introduction of new ordinary cause rules, to take account of the huge volume of decided cases predominantly in connection with the vexed question of financial provision on divorce, and to take account of the Scottish Law Commission *Report on Family Law* produced in 1992. Since its introduction in 1984 Mr Bennett's book has been recognised as a valuable introduction to sheriff court divorce.

Chapter 1 has been rewritten to take into account the volume of changes introduced by the new rules, and the remaining chapters of the book have been updated in respect of the new rules with developments in the substantive law being effected in an increased volume of footnotes. In Mr Bennett's original book chap 7, on financial provision, was 14 pages long; it is now some 25 pages long, reflecting primarily the incidence of reported cases. The text of that chapter is threatened on some occasions with being overwhelmed by the voluminous footnotes as a result of the variety and volume of new cases and the detail in which they are reported; there is an argument for saying that the text should be rewritten to take account of some of the more significant decisions, but to do so would interfere with the straightforward and clear way in which the principles are laid out in the text. The case list is full and includes a number of unreported cases.

The seven appendices take up as much of the book as the main text and continue to be valuable, not only for the specimen craves and pleas in law, but for the specimen writs which have been amended to take into account the changes in both style and content necessitated by the new rules; in particular the removal of separate counterclaim procedure is recognised by examples of defences which include craves. The appendices also help-

fully reproduce all of the ordinary cause forms relative to divorce actions and include for the first time a print of the draft Family Law (Scotland) Bill prepared by the Scottish Law Commission.

Mr Bennett's book continues to be an invaluable aid to sheriff court practitioners and as a starting point for those involved in divorce in the sheriff court, this book remains unsurpassed.

A M CUBIE,
Tilston MacLaurin,
Glasgow.

[*Editor's note:* The references to certain cases were inadvertently omitted from this work. These are as follows:

Crockett v Crockett, 30 June 1993, Extra Division;
McKenna v McKenna, 11 February 1992, Glasgow sheriff court;
Mainland v Mainland, 9 December 1991, Elgin sheriff court;
Nicoll v Nicoll, 24 March 1992, Edinburgh sheriff court;
Rae v Rae, 10 February 1992, Falkirk sheriff court;
Ranaldi v Ranaldi, 1994 SLT (Sh Ct) 25;
Shepherd v Shepherd, 25 February 1992, Aberdeen sheriff court.]

Property Offences

By A T H Smith. 1994. London: Sweet & Maxwell. Hardback, £115.
ISBN 0 420 47040 9.

Dr Smith's work, at 1,037 pages, is intended to be an extended account and analysis of the law of England as it relates to the protection of property through the criminal law. The author indicates in the preface that it has sometimes proved difficult to strike an even balance between reproducing without comment or explanation large quantities of legislation and sustained exposition and analysis of the principles underlying an area of the substantive law.

In the event Dr Smith's work has turned out to be an impressive example of sustained analysis over a large number of related topics. The book is likely to be of interest to various groups of lawyers because of the variety of issues raised under different headings: criminal lawyers in England will find the work to be essential but civil lawyers might well find that Dr Smith's endeavours in regard to cheques, creditors, bankruptcy and companies repay study by them.

ROBERT S SHIELS.

ARTICLES

Mother Knows Best
Or "When is a Presumption not a Presumption?"

Elaine E Sutherland,
Senior Lecturer in Private Law,
University of Glasgow.

Ms Sutherland discusses the recent decision in Brixey
v Lynas, *1994 SLT 847 and argues that, while it
may have been correct on its facts, it was in error in
accepting the maternal preference in cases concerning
custody of young children.*

Introduction

It is relatively rare for the Inner House to have
the opportunity to clarify the sometimes conflicting decisions emanating from the lower courts
on parental rights. Its clarification and guidance
can be invaluable (see, for example, *F v F*, 1991
SLT 357; *D v Grampian Regional Council*, 1994
SLT 1038). Sadly, this was not the case in the
recent decision in *Brixey v Lynas*, where, despite
its protestations to the contrary, it appears to have
condoned the resurrection of that old chestnut the
"maternal preference" in cases concerning the
custody of young children. Better known in the
USA as the tender years doctrine, it was widely
believed that this kind of gender stereotyping no
longer had a place in contemporary Scottish
jurisprudence.

At the outset, it is important to make clear that
it is not the actual decision in the present case
that is being criticised. Indeed, it can be argued
that the Division had sufficient other grounds on
which to justify its decision without having to
resort to the maternal preference. While it was at
pains to make clear that it was not stating any
general presumption applicable to all custody
cases, it is hard to view the statements made in
any other light.

Nor is this case without its positive aspects. A
number of factors which can quite properly be
taken into account in decisions relating to parental rights are considered. The case highlights the
fact that, regardless of the decision of the particular court, a child will usually remain where he
or she is pending the outcome of an appeal. Given
that the Scottish Law Commission's *Report on
Family Law* (Scot Law Com no 135, 1992) is still
awaiting implementation, perhaps this case could
not have come at a better time. The opportunity
to amend the commission's draft Bill to take
account of the decision remains a possibility. So
what happened in *Brixey v Lynas*?

The facts

The action arose out of a dispute between unmarried parents over the custody of their two year
old daughter, Kellianne. The parents met in 1990
while the father, Mr Lynas, was a 17 year old
schoolboy and the mother, Ms Brixey, was living
with her then partner and elder child, Natalie.
When Mr Lynas left school in July 1991, he
moved in with Ms Brixey and Natalie, her former
partner having apparently left the scene.
Kellianne was born in May 1992.

Ms Brixey, Mr Lynas and the two children
then went to live with Mr Lynas' parents in
Rutherglen. The relationship soon became
unhappy and Mr Lynas decided that it should
end. Arrangements were made for Ms Brixey and
the children to be collected by her mother and
taken to her mother's house near Inverness in
September 1992. Before that arrangement could
be fully implemented, Mr Lynas took Kellianne
away and concealed her whereabouts. At this
stage, Ms Brixey raised an action for delivery and
Mr Lynas raised an action for custody. Ms Brixey
obtained an interim order for delivery, Kellianne
was returned to her mother shortly afterwards,
and lived with her from that time onwards, first
at her mother's (the maternal grandmother's)
house, then in a two bedroomed house next door.

While the sheriff did not doubt the sincerity of
each parent's love for Kellianne or their ability to
look after her, he did not form a particularly
favourable impression of either of them. He
regarded them both as immature and felt that
neither of them had shown any great stability or
judgment in their lives. He was unimpressed by
Ms Brixey's behaviour in that there were allegations of frequenting public houses, getting drunk
occasionally, past consumption of cannabis, fondness for male company, and brief recent association with another man. The last two of these
points are interesting. In the light of the decision
in *Early v Early*, 1989 SLT 114 (affd 1990 SLT
221), it is clear that a mother's chance of obtaining custody will be improved if she is hetero-
sexual. It now seems clear that she must not be
too enthusiastic in her pursuit of her hetero-
sexuality. In any event, the sheriff rejected Mr
Lynas' contention that Ms Brixey's lifestyle
"endangered" Kellianne. On the other hand, he
found Mr Lynas to be weak and somewhat
priggish.

He found Kellianne to be happy, healthy and
well cared for with her mother and saw no reason
to think that she would be happier with one
family than the other. He noted that Mr Lynas
would have the help of his mother and family if
he obtained custody. In awarding custody to Mr

Lynas, the sheriff made the following observation (p 849C): "I have however come to the view that I should not deprive the child of the advantages which the accident of her paternity make available to her ... there is a better chance of the father providing a stable background and a successful future for the child than there is of the mother doing so."

Clearly, this statement was prompted by something other than Mr Lynas' character, which had so obviously failed to impress the sheriff; and he went on to say (p 849D): "there is a sense in which what I am saying represents an award of custody to the Lynas family or to Mrs Lynas [the respondent's mother] as much as to her father".

Ms Brixey appealed to the sheriff principal who recognised that he could only disturb the sheriff's decision if it could be demonstrated either that he had failed to take account of a significant factor or if he reached a conclusion that was so plainly wrong as to demonstrate that his discretion had not been properly exercised. In the event, the sheriff principal confirmed the original decision.

What did the Inner House decide and why?
From the point of view of the individuals involved, the significance of the Inner House's decision was that it overturned the decisions of the sheriff and the sheriff principal and awarded custody of Kellianne to her mother. For the present purpose, the significance of the decision lies in the basis on which it was taken.

The Inner House emphasised that the sheriff alone had the opportunity to see the individuals involved and to determine questions of reliability and credibility, and it repeated the limited circumstances in which the sheriff's original decision could be overturned. In determining what were the significant factors which the sheriff should have taken into account, the Division quite rightly felt that it could look at previous decisions on custody (p 849F-G). What it may have failed to do was to put the cases in the context of the time when they were decided. While previous decisions may be of enormous help in eliciting the principles on which the law is based, they are of little value if they turn on social mores which are out of line with those prevailing today.

The Division found itself in agreement with the sheriff insofar as he had taken account of the advantages of background and environment which the father and his family could provide (p 850A). While this factor may be relevant, it is important to remember that the relative affluence of the parties should not determine custody (*Casey v Casey*, 1989 SCLR 761 at pp 761 and

763; Clive, *The Law of Husband and Wife in Scotland* (3rd ed, 1992), at pp 543-544; Wilkinson and Norrie, *The Law Relating to Parent and Child* (1993), at pp 209-210). The difficulty is that the "better" role model or environment often seems to coincide with wealth.

Despite the relevance of the currently good environment offered by the father, the Division found that the sheriff had failed to take account of the fact that these circumstances might change and, in particular, that a young man of the respondent's age would be quite likely to leave his parents' home. The sheriff principal had confirmed the sheriff's view that, were circumstances to change, the matter could be brought back to the court. While this is undoubtedly correct, the Division acknowledged the difficulty in disturbing a decision on custody. While no member of the judiciary made the point, this has become even more important in the light of the recent curtailment of the availability of civil legal aid.

In a number of other respects, the Inner House felt that both the sheriff and the sheriff principal had failed to take account or, at least, sufficient account, of significant factors. While in some cases it acknowledged that this may have been because no submissions were made by the agents on these points, it felt entitled to consider them since the case involved the welfare of a child (p 850F).

One such consideration was the preservation of the status quo. Given that the sheriff had found Kellianne to be "happy, healthy and well cared for" (p 849J) with her mother, the Division felt that a case had been made out for preserving the status quo. It cited Wilkinson and Norrie (op cit), with approval, where the authors set out the case for the preservation of the status quo and warn against attaching undue weight to it. Sadly, the passage is tainted with echoes of maternal preference, but the warnings against undue weight being attached to the status quo and failing to take a long term view are points well made. In this case, not only did the status quo appear to be working well, it carried with it the advantages of continuing Kellianne's good relationship with her half sister, Natalie, as well as with her mother.

Had the Inner House confined its consideration of relevant factors to those discussed above, it is submitted that it would have had ample grounds for finding that the sheriff had failed to take significant factors into account and to reach the decision which it did reach, namely, awarding custody of Kellianne to her mother. Unfortunately, it devoted much of its attention to the maternal preference, a matter which, it is submitted, was quite properly not considered by the sheriff.

The maternal preference

In its discussion of the maternal preference, the Division cited Wilkinson and Norrie, and the cases mentioned therein, in support of the following proposition (p 849I): "it has been and remains the practice of the courts in Scotland to recognise as an important factor which has to be fully taken into account in a dispute concerning custody between the mother and father of a very young child, that during his or her infancy the child's need for the mother is stronger than the need for a father".

Nor does the Division confine the maternal preference to the child's infancy, since it later stresses a girl's needs for her mother's influence and care as she grows older (p 849L).

Two questions must be asked at this point. First, is the Division accurate in its view of the current state of Scots law? Secondly, should Scots law take this approach?

On the matter of the present state of the law, it is worth noting that, of the nine cases mentioned, four are over 40 years old and, even then, do not unanimously support the maternal preference (*McLean v Hardie*, 1927 SLT 340; 1927 SC 344; *McLean v McLean*, 1947 SLT 36; 1947 SC 79; *Brown v Brown*, 1948 SLT 129; 1948 SC 5; *Nicol v Nicol*, 1953 SLT (Notes) 67); one illustrates rejection of the maternal preference (*Whitecross v Whitecross*, 1977 SLT 225); one turns on a number of factors with only a passing reference to the maternal preference (*Jordan v Jordan*, 1983 SLT 539); one involves an award of custody to the father and firm rejection of the notion that the earlier award to the mother was "more in accordance with nature" (*Hannah v Hannah*, 1971 SLT (Notes) 42); one illustrates the unusual solution of awarding custody to the father and de facto care and control to the mother (*Robertson v Robertson*, 1981 SLT (Notes) 7); and one is English (*J v C* [1970] AC 668). This can hardly be seen as resounding support for the view that contemporary Scottish courts accept the maternal preference.

The Division made use of Wilkinson and Norrie as providing support for the maternal preference and it is indeed unfortunate that this excellent work should make its first appearance in the law reports apparently defending the indefensible. It is submitted that the quotations from the book are highly selective and taken out of context. Under the heading "Mother's Custody of Child of Tender Years" (pp 211-212), the authors provide a reasoned discussion of the

topic, opening with the sentence: "There is no settled rule of law that a child, even of tender years, should be in the custody of its mother."

In considering the criticism of some of the English cases which have accepted a degree of maternal preference, the authors make the point that "In the absence of a full survey, it is impossible to say whether Scottish decisions show, with any consistency, a similar pattern".

While the above quotations are, again, selective, they illustrate the point that the maternal preference does not find unqualified support from this source either.

In short, it is not the case that, prior to this decision, it "has been and remains the practice of the courts in Scotland" to accept the maternal preference when considering the custody of young, or indeed any, children. The Division was at pains to point out that (p 849I), despite clear statements in support of the maternal preference, "This priciple should not be regarded as creating any presumption in favour of the mother, nor, certainly, as a rule of law". When is a presumption not a presumption?

The second matter to consider here is whether or not Scots law should accept the notion of maternal preference. Certainly, the vast majority of children living with one parent live with their mother. On divorce, the mother is more likely to apply for custody than is the father. Why is this? It is submitted that this is a reflection of the practical arrangements parents choose to make, employment patterns and, to some extent, traditional views of parenting. Sometimes it amounts to no more than the fact that the woman is "left holding the baby". It would be interesting to find out how many men do not apply for custody or, at least, oppose the removal of their parental rights, because they believe that they have no hope of success, a view justified by this recent decision. None of this makes a case in support of a maternal preference.

The law as it stands makes quite clear that "In any proceedings relating to parental rights the court shall regard the welfare of the child involved as the paramount consideration" (Law Reform (Parent and Child) (Scotland) Act 1986, s 3 (2)).

In assessing "welfare" the courts have considered a number of factors but these factors are simply guiding principles extracted from past decisions. They are not intended to be an exhaustive or exclusive list, nor are they intended as a straitjacket. This point was reinforced by the Scottish Law Commission in its recent report, when it rejected the notion of providing a statutory checklist of factors (op cit, para 5.23). The point here is that the courts have considered all the factors which are relevant to welfare.

The commission did accept that one particular factor, the right of the child to express his or her own views, should be enshrined in statute (report, para 5.29; draft Bill, cl 12 (5) and (6)). However that is simply a recognition of the right of the child to do so, and not because these views can also be an indicator of welfare.

To accept the notion of maternal preference runs counter to the trend, at least until this recent decision, to look at the unique facts of each case and consider the applicants and the particular child as individuals, comparing what each applicant has to offer to the child. The importance of seeing each child as an individual was stressed in the *Report of the Inquiry into the Removal of Children from Orkney in February 1991* (27 October 1992, para 3.40) and acknowledged in the Government's statement of proposals for the future, *Scotland's Children: Proposals for Child Care Policy and Law* (Cm 2286 (1993), paras 2.6 and 2.7). To place any stress on a maternal preference is to diminish that recognition of the child's individual circumstances.

Furthermore, the United Nations Convention on the Rights of the Child, ratified by the United Kingdom in December 1991, makes quite clear that: "The States Parties to the present Convention shall respect and ensure the rights set forth in this Convention to each child within their jurisdiction *without discrimination of any kind, irrespective of the child's or his or her parent's* or legal guardian's race, colour, *sex*, language, religion, political or other opinion, national, ethnic or social origin, property, disability, birth or other status" (art 2, italics added).

One such right is the right of a child to live with his or her parents and to have the place of his or her residence determined if the parents are living apart (art 9). Thus, adopting a maternal preference would be arguably in breach of our international obligations.

Custody and appeals
It is worth noting that the sheriff in this case awarded custody to the father on 21 July 1993. Despite this, Kellianne remained with her mother throughout the ensuing 11 months of appeals. What this means is that, the sheriff having decided that the best interests of Kellianne were to be served by her living with her father, she nonetheless remained in the custody of her mother for almost a year. While it makes some sense to avoid a child being shuttled back and forwards in the course of a series of appeals, this does seem anomalous. In this case, it was clear that there was no concern (at least on the part of the court) about the well being of Kellianne while in her mother's care. Nonetheless, Kellianne's continuing to live with her mother and half sister could only have served to strengthen the case for preserving the status quo.

What should and can be done about this anomaly presents difficulties. If the child is to be moved fairly soon after each stage of the appeal process, the result could be highly disruptive for the child. One answer lies in increasing the speed with which cases involving children are dealt with, but such an approach is hardly likely to find favour with litigants in other cases or their agents. Perhaps the solution is to create a well staffed family court.

Conclusions
While there is occasional judicial authority supporting maternal preference in custody decisions in respect of young children, it is far from as widespread as the Inner House suggested. Furthermore, the acceptance of such a preference runs against the accepted principles of viewing each child as an individual and non-discrimination. That the Division should show such enthusiasm for this kind of prejudice is regrettable, but all is not lost.

There has been considerable regret that the Government has been so tardy in implementing the Scottish Law Commission's report, but this cloud of delay may have a silver lining. There is still time to amend the draft Bill to ensure that the maternal preference is laid to rest once and for all.

Bias in Industrial Tribunals

V Craig,
Heriot-Watt University.

Professor Craig considers the recent decision in Docherty v Strathkelvin District Council, *1994 SLT 1064, on the test for bias on the part of an industrial tribunal member, and suggests that the court's approach differs from that recently adopted by the House of Lords.*

The Second Division in *Docherty v Strathkelvin District Council*, 1994 SLT 1064, upheld an appeal by Strathkelvin against the decision of the employment appeal tribunal (EAT) that a member of the industrial tribunal which had dealt with the case had entered into a cross examination of Strathkelvin's witnesses designed to bring about a particular result. (The case was remitted to the EAT to deal with other matters with which this short note is not concerned.) However there appears to be a difference between the approach of the Second Division in *Docherty* and that of the House of Lords in *R v Gough* [1993] AC 646.

The basis of the appeal to the EAT by Strathkelvin insofar as it falls within the scope of this note was that (a) a question had arisen regarding a possible previous relationship and friendship between the appellant's agent and a tribunal member which the chairman ruled raised no difficulty and (b) during the course of the hearing it was alleged that a tribunal member in his questions to Strathkelvin's witnesses had displayed excessive aggression with the result that the tribunal had not approached the consideration of the case in a fair and unbiased manner and Strathkelvin had thereby suffered prejudice. The EAT, apparently dealing only with ground of appeal (b), while acknowledging the difficulty in such a case, concluded that the tribunal member had created the impression that he was not merely asking questions in order to elucidate evidence but had entered into cross examination of witnesses designed to bring about a particular result.

Strathkelvin's appeal to the Inner House was on two grounds, namely that the EAT had applied the wrong test and that in any event there was insufficient evidence for the EAT to arrive at the conclusion it did. Under reference to *Peter Simper & Co Ltd v Cooke* [1986] IRLR 19 (EAT) and *Telcon Metals Ltd v Henry*, EAT, 18 November 1987, unreported, the Second Division agreed that the test to be applied was an objective one and involved considering whether the reasonable observer, present at the hearing, not being a party or associated with a party to the proceedings but knowing the issues, would reasonably gain the impression of bias, but that the EAT had applied a subjective test by giving weight to the impressions actually produced on those who took part in, or were spectators of the proceedings. Indeed counsel for Strathkelvin accepted that the EAT had applied a subjective test, but contended that there was sufficient evidence to satisfy even the objective test. Having considered the affidavits and the chairman's notes on the objections taken by Strathkelvin's solicitor, the Second Division was of opinion that there was no sufficient material to justify the conclusion that there was bias or unfairness towards Strathkelvin.

Before commenting further on the decision of the Second Division it is worth noting that as recently as last year the House of Lords in the English appeal of *R v Gough* [1993] AC 646 — a decision to which, surprisingly, no reference is made in the decision of the Second Division — after an extensive review of the law and having canvassed the two competing tests, namely (1) whether a reasonable and fair-minded person sitting in the court and knowing all the relevant facts would have a reasonable suspicion that a fair hearing was not possible, or (2) whether there was a real danger of bias, concluded that the latter test was the correct one so that in all cases of apparent bias the test was the same, namely, whether in all the circumstances of the case, there appeared to be a real danger of bias concerning the member of the tribunal in question so that justice required that the decision did not stand.

Towards the end of his judgment Lord Goff of Chieveley emphasises that it is unnecessary to require that the court look at the matter through the eyes of the reasonable man, because the court personifies the reasonable man and that the court should think in terms of the "danger" or "possibility" of bias occurring or having occurred rather than its "likelihood" or "probability", concluding that "accordingly having ascertained the relevant circumstances the court should ask itself whether, having regard to those circumstances, there was a real danger of bias on behalf of the relevant tribunal member in the sense that he *might* unfairly regard with favour or disfavour the case of a party to the issue under consideration by him" (author's italics). In similar vein Lord Woolf opined that the role of the appeal court was to consider "whether there is a real danger of injustice . . . by examining all the material available and giving its conclusion on that material. If . . . having done so it [the appeal court] is satisfied that there is no danger of the alleged bias having created injustice the application to quash the decision should be dismissed".

The essence of the decision in *Gough* therefore appears to be that their Lordships preferred to apply the test of whether there is, or has been, a risk or possibility of bias creating injustice rather than the test of the reasonable and fair minded person sitting in the court in command of all the relevant facts. This is patently different from the approach of the Second Division in *Docherty* where, delivering the opinion of the court, the Lord Justice Clerk states (1994 SLT at p 1067E): "Having regard to what the tribunal chairman said and to what Mr Drummond and Mrs Campbell [two of Strathkelvin's witnesses] had stated in their affidavits, we are quite satisfied that there was no sufficient material to justify the conclusion that *there was* unfairness or bias on the part of the tribunal member", and later (at p 1067K): "When we have regard to the terms of the ground of appeal, the affidavits, and the chairman's comments, we are clearly of opinion that there was no sufficient material to justify the conclusion that *there was* bias or unfairness towards the respondents" (author's italics).

With respect, that suggests that the Second Division was more concerned to find evidence of actual bias, a test different from that endorsed by *Gough* which is whether there appeared to be a real danger or a possibility of bias. Indeed the Second Division's observations that neither of the two witnesses for Strathkelvin was forced to give answers which were untrue or to make concessions against their will suggests that that court was looking not just for evidence of bias but for evidence that it had been effective (which, incidentally, comes close to the subjective approach for which the decision of the EAT was criticised). It is respectfully submitted that in accordance with *Gough* once there is evidence of a danger of bias the effect of any bias (actual or apparent) is irrelevant and the decision of the inferior tribunal has to be quashed. Secondly *Gough* makes it plain that it is the appeal court, being the personification of the reasonable man, which must consider whether such a danger existed and not, as *Docherty* holds, the reasonable observer present at the hearing.

The approach of the EAT in *Docherty* equiparates with that of the EAT in England in *Greenaway Harrison Ltd v Wiles* [1994] IRLR 380. The case concerned a remark alleged to have been made by the chairman of an industrial tribunal at the conclusion of proceedings which had upheld the applicant's complaint, after the parties had been unable to respond to the tribunal's invitation to try to settle the matter over lunch. It was alleged the chairman remarked to the other members: "That will teach them not to settle when I tell them to". The EAT, having reminded itself of the test as expressed in *Gough*, considered the evidence and, assuming the remark had been made, could not find that there was a real danger of bias on the part of the chairman because the facts and the timing of the alleged remark made it clear that it could have been no more than a casual comment about the result.

The Second Division was to a point influenced by the nature of the tribunal being to an extent inquisitorial, and by the chairman's note which concluded that the member was entitled to put the questions as he did because one of the witnesses gave the impression that he did not understand the questions or was being evasive, and it may be that even if the Second Division had applied the *Gough* test to all the circumstances, including the nature of the tribunal's jurisdiction, it (or another appeal court) could have concluded that the evidence did not disclose a real danger of bias. That, however, is beside the point because the test which is applied ("reasonable observer test" or the "real danger test") determines the nature and the extent of the appeal court's inquiry and if one accepts that the latter is the correct test, the fact that the EAT in *Docherty* considered, inter alia, the impressions on witnesses and representatives as evidence of "real danger" — part of what Lord Woolf described as "all the material available" — should not, contrary to the decision of the Second Division, result in an error of law.

◆

NEWS

Coming events

Association of Pension Lawyers
The Scottish group of the Association of Pension Lawyers will hold a seminar on Tuesday, 6 December 1994 at 5.30 for 6 pm, on the implications of the *Vroege* case in relation to the entitlement of part time workers to membership of pension schemes. Andrew Holehouse of Shepherd & Wedderburn and Andy McKinnell of Sedgwick Noble Lowndes will speak. The seminar will be held at the offices of Shepherd & Wedderburn, WS, Saltire Court, 20 Castle Terrace, Edinburgh. The cost for non-members will be £10. All wishing to attend should book via

Colin Browning, Scottish Life Assurance Co, 19 St Andrew Square, Edinburgh EH2 1YE.

—— ◇ ——

General

Health and safety: pregnant workers
Regulations to implement the health and safety provisions of the Pregnant Workers Directive will come into effect on 1 December 1994.

The new regulations (SI 1994/2865) will apply to three groups of workers: those who are pregnant, those who have recently given birth, and those who are breastfeeding. They will require employers to assess risks to the health and safety of these three groups of workers; ensure that workers are not exposed to risks identified by the risk assessment, which would present a danger to their health or safety; and if a risk remains after taking whatever preventive action is reasonable, the employer should change the worker's hours or conditions of work to avoid the risk, or offer her alternative work, or if neither is possible, give her paid leave from work for as long as is necessary to protect her health and safety.

The Health and Safety Executive will be publishing guidance for employers on the known risks to new and expectant mothers and advice on what employers need to do to comply with the law. It should be available in mid-December.

— ◇ —

Taxation

Income tax: self assessment
The Inland Revenue have announced plans for public consultation on a new tax return to be issued in April 1997 with the introduction of self assessment. In response to taxpayers who want the new return and guidance notes to be tailored to their individual needs, a tax return has been developed which is split into separate schedules, each dealing with a particular area of tax and having its own notes on how to complete it.

The testing will involve asking taxpayers and advisers to complete working drafts of the new return and then giving the completed returns to staff to process. There will also be a series of workshops in November and December to explore the content and design of the new return and guidance.

Examples of the new tax return and guidance notes are contained in a consultation pack, available free of charge from the Public Inquiry Room, West Wing, Somerset House, London WC2R 1LB. Comments on the proposals should be returned by 16 December 1994 to Richard Steele, Tax Return Consultation, Room 318, South West Wing, Bush House, London WC2B 4RD.

◇

Income tax: benefits in kind: cheap loans
The Inland Revenue have published a draft clause which would amend the rules for taxing loans which replace cheap or interest free loans provided to employees by their employer.

In order to remove a possible obstacle to the provision of replacement loans to employees by arms length loans from subsidiaries of com-

mercial lenders, the clause would replace the rule which makes all replacement loans potentially taxable by new rules which focus more precisely on the potential for tax avoidance. The provision would apply from 6 April 1995.

The text of the draft provisions is available from the Public Inquiry Room, Room 41, West Wing, Somerset House, Strand, London WC2R 1LB.

◇

Pension schemes: loss of tax approval
The Financial Secretary to the Treasury has announced that the Government intend to introduce legislation in the next Finance Bill to discourage the exploitation of the pensions tax reliefs by certain approved occupational pension schemes.

Arrangements are now being encountered under which the trustees of some small self-administered occupational pension schemes have exploited the tax approval system. These arrangements involve initially taking advantage of the tax reliefs but then engineering loss of tax approval when access to the accumulated funds, in circumstances not allowed by the tax approval conditions, is desired by the scheme members or the sponsoring employer. An example is where the scheme wishes to lend all or a large part of its funds to the sponsoring employer.

In order to discourage the misuse of the tax approval system in this way a special 40 per cent tax charge will be levied on the value of funds held by these schemes at the time tax approval is withdrawn. This new tax charge will apply where tax approval ceases on or after 2 November 1994.

— ◇ —

Obituary

On 16 November 1994, Peter Ramsay, formerly regional solicitor, Scottish Gas.

— ◇ —

Business change

On 12 November 1994.

Steedman Ramage, WS, announce that Kenneth M Cumming, WS, has joined the firm as a partner from 12 November 1994.

— ◇ —

Book Review

Confessions

By David B Griffith. 1994. Edinburgh:
Butterworths. Paperback, £20.
ISBN 0 406 11543 5.

This work by Dr Griffith forms a welcome addition to the Butterworths Scottish Criminal Law and Practice series. The book is written in a clear, informative style and, not least because of its clarity and reference to up to date cases, will be of interest to both students and court practitioners. The author, we are told in the preface, "draws from his experience as a court practitioner". This is apparent from the style of writing. Seasoned criminal court practitioners will be familiar with some of the "terms of art" (e g "verballing") used. In a sense, it is a relief to see them because it is clear that the author has extensive practical experience with his subject matter.

The book is divided into six chapters, the longest by far of which concerns "The Admissibility of Confession Evidence". Obviously admissibility is at the very core of the problems and discussions concerning confession evidence and accordingly it is not surprising that so much of the book is devoted to this topic. This reviewer, in teaching evidence over a number of years, has found that students find the whole concept of confession evidence, and, in particular, where it is admissible, hard to grasp. If this is not clarified early on then those students who go on to be practitioners will inevitably still have a hazy grasp of the concept. Dr Griffith gives a very clear and coherent analysis of the historical development of the tests for the admissibility of confession evidence. This regrettably is where problems arise, because no matter how lucid the style of the author and how analytical his approach, the central problem remains unresolved. Dr Griffith discusses at length "the fairness test", but ultimately from his analysis it is perfectly apparent that there is no real definition of "fairness". It seems fairly apparent that "fairness" as far as judges are concerned is rather, as Carroll's Humpty Dumpty pointed out, "just what I choose it to mean — neither more nor less". That being the case, the position is unsatisfactory in the extreme. This is recognised by Dr Griffith, who early on in the book quotes Professor Maher to the effect that the fairness test is not much of a test if what it means cannot be known, and therefore "as part of the judicial technique puts a major hole in the desideratum of legality, that laws be clear and knowable".

The text compares the systems and procedures with other jurisdictions, particularly England both pre- and post-PACE, and ultimately it is hard to escape the conclusion that while the provisions of PACE might be difficult and cumbersome, if it has the benefit of a degree of clarity and "knowability" it is a more satisfactory state of affairs than presently obtains in Scotland.

It is perhaps not surprising to chart in the chapter concerning "Procedural Aspects", the many difficulties that have arisen with the manner of, and procedures for, admitting, or not, confession evidence. As is made very clear in this brief but informative chapter, there has been much change in the manner in which statements may be admitted, and if this reviewer's interpretation is correct then the changing procedural aspects being overlaid upon the changing basic test renders the whole situation opaque to say the least.

Dr Griffith concludes the book with a brief chapter on "The record of the extra judicial confession". He makes reference to the Thomson committee's recommendation in regard to tape recording (and the requirements incumbent upon the police in respect thereof) and also the possibility of future video recording of accused/witness statements in police stations and, indeed, at the locus.

Dr Griffith handles a difficult subject in a clear and robust manner, giving us in the process a very interesting book. Unusually for such a book it is best read from end to end rather than dipped into. While the book has a perfectly serviceable index and table of cases it would perhaps, not least standing the length of the chapter on the admissibility of confession evidence previously referred to, be useful in the old Walkers/Gloag and Henderson style, to have paragraph sub-headings at the very outset of each chapter in order that the user who is perhaps under pressure of time might more readily know the specific contents of the chapter.

This is a good book: indeed it is an enjoyable book. It should be of use to the student and practitioner alike and represents a useful contribution to this area of the law. Dr Griffith is to be thanked for letting us have the benefit of the fruits of his labour.

G P MacMillan,
MacMillans, Glasgow.

ACT OF SEDERUNT

ACT OF SEDERUNT (RULES OF THE COURT OF SESSION 1994 AMENDMENT NO 2) (HUMAN FERTILISATION AND EMBRYOLOGY) (PARENTAL ORDERS) 1994

(SI 1994/2806) [21 OCTOBER 1994]

The Lords of Council and Session, under and by virtue of the powers conferred on them by section 5 of the Court of Session Act 1988 (c 36), section 59 of the Adoption (Scotland) Act 1978 (c 28) as modified and applied in relation to parental orders under section 30 of the Human Fertilisation and Embryology Act 1990 (c 37) and applications for such orders by paragraph 15 of Schedule 1 to the Parental Orders (Human Fertilisation and Embryology) (Scotland) Regulations 1994 (SI 1994/2804) and of all other powers enabling them in that behalf, do hereby enact and declare:

Citation and commencement

1.—(1) This Act of Sederunt may be cited as the Act of Sederunt (Rules of the Court of Session 1994 Amendment No 2) (Human Fertilisation and Embryology) (Parental Orders) 1994 and shall come into force on the date of coming into force of the Parental Orders (Human Fertilisation and Embryology) (Scotland) Regulations 1994.

(2) This Act of Sederunt shall be inserted in the Books of Sederunt.

Amendment of the Rules of the Court of Session

2.—(1) The Rules of the Court of Session 1994 shall be amended in accordance with the following sub-paragraphs.

(2) After Chapter 80, insert Chapter 81 as set out in Schedule 1 to this Act of Sederunt.

(3) In the appendix, after Form 77.11, insert the forms in Schedule 2 to this Act of Sederunt.

J A D HOPE, LORD PRESIDENT, *IPD*

Paragraph 2 (2)

SCHEDULE 1
CHAPTER 81

APPLICATIONS FOR PARENTAL ORDERS UNDER THE HUMAN FERTILISATION AND EMBRYOLOGY ACT 1990

Application and interpretation of this Chapter

81.1.—(1) This Chapter applies to applications for parental orders under section 30 of the Human Fertilisation and Embryology Act 1990.

(2) In this Chapter, unless the context otherwise requires—

"the Act of 1978" means the Adoption (Scotland) Act 1978;

"the Act of 1990" means the Human Fertilisation and Embryology Act 1990;

"Her Majesty's Forces" means the Royal Navy, the regular armed forces as defined in section 225 of the Army Act 1955 (c 18), the regular air force as defined in section 223 of the Air Force Act 1955 (c 19) and the Queen Alexandra's Royal Naval Nursing Services;

"the Regulations" means the Parental Orders (Human Fertilisation and Embryology) (Scotland) Regulations 1994.

Disapplication of certain rules to this Chapter

81.2. Unless otherwise provided in this Chapter, the following rules shall not apply to a petition or note to which this Chapter applies:—

rule 14.5 (first order in petitions),

rule 14.6 (1) (d) (period of notice for lodging answers where service by advertisement),

rule 14.7 (intimation and service of petitions),

rule 14.8 (procedure where answers lodged),

rule 14.9 (unopposed petitions).

Confidentiality of documents in process

81.3. Unless the court otherwise directs, in any cause to which this Chapter applies—

(a) any document lodged in process, including a report by a reporting officer or a curator *ad litem*, shall be treated as confidential and open only to the court, the parties, the reporting officer and the curator *ad litem*; and

(b) a reporting officer or curator *ad litem* shall treat any information obtained by him in relation to the cause as confidential, and shall not disclose any such information to any person unless it is necessary for the proper execution of his duties.

Selection of reporting officer or curator *ad litem*

81.4. Where the court appoints a reporting officer or a curator *ad litem*, such person shall be selected from a panel established under the Curators ad Litem and Reporting Officers

(Panels) (Scotland) Regulations 1984 unless the court considers that it would be appropriate to appoint a person who is not on the panel.

Form of agreements to parental order

81.5.—(1) An agreement for the purposes of section 30 (5) of the Act of 1990 (agreement to parental order by a father who is not the husband of the female petitioner or by the woman who carried the child) shall be in Form 81.5.

(2) An agreement referred to in this rule which is executed furth of Scotland shall be witnessed—

(a) where it is executed in England, Wales or Northern Ireland, by a justice of the peace or commissioner for oaths;

(b) where it is executed furth of the United Kingdom—

(i) in the case of a person who is serving in Her Majesty's Forces, by an officer holding a commission in those forces; or

(ii) by a British consular official or any person authorised, by the law of the country where the agreement is executed, to administer an oath for any legal purpose.

Orders for evidence

81.6.—(1) In a cause to which this Chapter applies, the court may, before determining the cause, order—

(a) production of further documents (including affidavits); or

(b) parole evidence.

(2) A party may apply by motion for the evidence of a person to be received in evidence by affidavit; and the court may make such order as it thinks fit.

Expenses

81.7. In a cause to which this Chapter applies, the court may make such order as to expenses, including the expenses of a reporting officer, a curator *ad litem*, or any other person who attended a hearing, as it thinks fit.

Protection of identity of petitioners

81.8.—(1) Where a married couple, who seek to apply for a parental order, wish to prevent their identity being disclosed to any person whose agreement is required under section 30 (5) of the Act of 1990 (agreement to parental order by a father who is not the husband of the female petitioner or by the woman who carried the child), they may, before presenting a petition, apply by letter to the Deputy Principal Clerk for a serial number to be assigned to them.

(2) On receipt of such a letter, the Deputy Principal Clerk shall assign a serial number to the applicants and shall enter a note of it opposite the names of the applicants in a register of serial numbers.

(3) Where a serial number has been assigned under paragraph (2)—

(a) the record of the serial number and the persons to whom it applies shall be treated as confidential and disclosed only to the court;

(b) any agreement under section 30 (5) of the Act of 1990 shall not name or design the petitioners but shall refer to them by means of the serial number; and

(c) it shall be used to name or design the petitioners for all purposes connected with the petition.

Applications for a parental order

81.9.—(1) An application for a parental order shall be made by petition in Form 81.9.

(2) On presentation of the petition, there shall be lodged in process as productions—

(a) an extract of any entry in the register of births relating to the birth of the child;

(b) extracts of any entries in the register of births relating to the birth of each of the petitioners; and

(c) an extract of any entry in the register of marriages relating to the marriage of the petitioners.

Appointment of reporting officer and curator *ad litem*

81.10.—(1) On presentation of the petition, the court shall appoint—

(a) a reporting officer; and

(b) a curator *ad litem* where it appears desirable in order to safeguard the interests of the child.

(2) Where a curator *ad litem* is appointed under paragraph (1) and is not also the reporting officer, the court may order the reporting officer to make available to the curator *ad litem* any report or information in relation to the child.

(3) A married couple may, before presenting the petition, apply by letter to the Deputy Principal Clerk for appointment of a reporting officer.

(4) An application under paragraph (3) shall—

(a) set out the reasons for which the appointment is sought;

(b) not require to be intimated to any person;

(c) be accompanied by an interlocutor sheet; and

(d) be placed by the Deputy Principal Clerk before the Lord Ordinary for his decision.

(5) The Deputy Principal Clerk shall give written intimation to the applicant under paragraph (3) of the decision of the Lord Ordinary.

(6) The decision of the Lord Ordinary on an

application under paragraph (3) shall be final and not subject to review.

(7) The letter and the interlocutor sheet in an application under paragraph (3) shall be kept in the Petition Department and subsequently placed in the process of the petition.

Duties of reporting officer and curator *ad litem*

81.11.—(1) A reporting officer appointed under rule 81.10 (1) (a) shall, where appropriate—

(a) inquire into the facts and circumstances averred in the petition;

(b) ascertain whether the conditions in subsections (2) to (7) of section 30 of the Act of 1990 have been satisfied;

(c) witness any execution in Scotland of any agreement in Form 81.5 under section 30 (5) of the Act of 1990 (agreement to parental order by a father who is not the husband of the female petitioner or by the woman who carried the child), and investigate whether the agreement is given freely, unconditionally and with full understanding of what is involved;

(d) where a person whose agreement is required is furth of Scotland, confirm his views in writing, ensure that any agreement under section 30 (5) of the Act of 1990 is witnessed in accordance with rule 81.5 (2) and investigate whether the agreement is given freely, unconditionally and with full understanding of what is involved;

(e) ensure that each person whose agreement is required understands that in agreeing to the parental order he is giving up all future claims to the child and that all parental rights and duties will vest in the petitioners;

(f) investigate whether there are any other persons with a relevant interest and whether they should be informed of the petition;

(g) ascertain from any person whose agreement is required and who can be found whether alternatives to a parental order have been discussed with him;

(h) ensure that any person whose agreement is required is aware of the date (if known) of the hearing to determine the application if he wishes to appear, and confirm that any such person understands that he may withdraw his agreement at any time before a parental order is made;

(i) draw to the attention of the court any matter which may be of assistance; and

(j) prepare a report in relation to the exercise of his duties within such period as the court may specify.

(2) A curator *ad litem* appointed under rule 81.10 (1) (b) shall—

(a) safeguard generally the interests of the child;

(b) inquire, so far as he considers necessary, into the facts and circumstances averred in the petition;

(c) ascertain whether any money or other benefit has been received or agreed upon which is prohibited by section 30 (7) of the Act of 1990 (prohibition on gift or receipt of money or other benefit);

(d) establish that the petitioners understand that the nature and effect of a parental order is to transfer the parental rights and duties in relation to the child to the petitioners and make them responsible for the maintenance and upbringing of the child;

(e) ascertain whether the proposed parental order is likely to safeguard and promote the welfare of the child throughout his childhood;

(f) ascertain whether it may be in the interests of the child that the court should make a parental order subject to particular conditions including the making of special provision for the child;

(g) perform such other duties as appear to him to be necessary or as the court may require; and

(h) prepare a report in relation to the exercise of his duties within such period as the court may specify.

(3) The reporting officer shall, on completion of his report, send to the Deputy Principal Clerk—

(a) the report and a copy of it for each party; and

(b) any agreement for the purposes of section 30 (5) of the Act of 1990.

(4) The curator *ad litem* shall, on completion of his report, send the report and a copy of it for each party, to the Deputy Principal Clerk.

Hearing

81.12.—(1) On receipt of the reports referred to in rule 81.11, the Deputy Principal Clerk shall—

(a) cause the reports and any other documents to be lodged in process;

(b) give written intimation to each party of the lodging of those documents and make them available to each party; and

(c) within 7 days thereafter, cause—

(i) the petition to be put out on the By Order Roll before the Lord Ordinary; and

(ii) written intimation of the date of the hearing on the By Order Roll to be given to each party.

(2) At the hearing on the By Order Roll, the court—

(a) shall pronounce an interlocutor appointing the petition to a hearing to determine the petition; and

(b) may, in such interlocutor—

(i) order any person whose agreement is required to be given to attend the hearing;

(ii) order intimation of the date of the hearing to any person not mentioned in paragraph (3) (a), (b) or (c); and

(iii) order the reporting officer or curator *ad litem* to perform additional duties to assist the court in determining the petition.

(3) The petitioners shall intimate the date of the hearing ordered under paragraph (2) (a) in Form 81.12 to—

(a) every person whose whereabouts are known to them and whose agreement is required to be given;

(b) the reporting officer appointed under rule 81.10 (1) (a);

(c) any curator *ad litem* appointed under rule 81.10 (1) (b); and

(d) any person on whom intimation has been ordered under paragraph (2) (b) (ii).

(4) At the hearing ordered under paragraph (2) (a)—

(a) the petitioners, the reporting officer and, where one has been appointed, the curator *ad litem* shall, if required by the court, appear and may be represented;

(b) any person required by the court to attend the hearing shall appear and may be represented;

(c) any other person to whom intimation was made under paragraph (3) (a) or (d) may appear or be represented.

Supervision by or committal to care of local authority

81.13.—(1) Where the court refuses to make a parental order and considers—

(a) that the child should be placed under the supervision of a specified local authority, or

(b) that the child should be committed to the care of a specified local authority,

the court shall order intimation of the terms of the proposed order to be made to the local authority and give the local authority an opportunity to make representations.

(2) Any representations of the local authority shall be made by minute.

(3) On the expiry of the period allowed for answers to a minute under paragraph (2), the cause shall be put out on the By Order Roll before the Lord Ordinary for a hearing to determine the matter.

Applications for return, removal or prohibition of removal of child

81.14.—(1) An application under section 29 of the Act of 1978, as modified and applied in relation to applications for parental orders by Schedule 1 to the Regulations (order to return a child to, or not to remove a child from, the care

of the applicants), in relation to a breach of section 27 (1) of that Act as so modified and applied (restrictions on removal of child where application for parental order pending), or under section 27 (1) of that Act as so modified and applied for leave to remove a child, shall be made by note.

(2) Subject to paragraph (3), rule 81.2 (disapplication of certain rules to this Chapter) shall not apply to an application mentioned in paragraph (1) of this rule.

(3) An application mentioned in paragraph (1) shall not be intimated on the walls of the court or advertised.

Applications to amend, or revoke a direction in, a parental order

81.15.—(1) An application under paragraph 3 (1) of Schedule 1 to the Act of 1978, as modified and applied in relation to parental orders by Schedule 1 to the Regulations (amendment, or revocation of a direction in, a parental order), shall be made by petition.

(2) Subject to paragraph (3), rule 81.2 (disapplication of certain rules to this Chapter) shall not apply to an application mentioned in paragraph (1) of this rule.

(3) An application mentioned in paragraph (1) shall not be initimated on the walls of the court or advertised.

Registration of certified copy interlocutor

81.16. On the court pronouncing an interlocutor making—

(a) a parental order,

(b) an amendment to, or revocation of a direction in, a parental order, or

(c) a revocation of a parental order,

the clerk of court shall send a certified copy of that interlocutor to the Registrar General for Scotland in a sealed envelope marked "confidential".

Extract of order

81.17. An extract of a parental order shall not be issued except by order of the court on an application to it—

(a) where there is a petition for the parental order depending before the court, by motion in that process; or

(b) where there is no such petition depending before the court, by petition.

Procedure after intimation to Registrar General or issue of extract

81.18.—(1) After a certified copy of an interlocutor mentioned in rule 81.16 has been sent to the Registrar General for Scotland, the clerk of court or the Extractor, as the case may be, shall—

(a) place the whole process in an envelope bearing only—

(i) the name of the petitioners;

(ii) the full name of the child to whom the process relates; and

(iii) the date of the order; and

(b) seal the envelope and mark it "confidential".

(2) No person shall open a process referred to in paragraph (1) or inspect its contents within 100 years after the date of the parental order, except—

(a) the person in respect of whom the parental order was made after he has reached the age of 17 years;

(b) any other person or body entitled under section 45 (5) of the Act of 1978, as modified and applied in relation to parental orders and applications for such orders by Schedule 1 to the Regulations, to access to the registers and books kept under section 45 (4) of that Act, as so modified and applied, with the written authority of the person in respect of whom the parental order was made;

(c) by order of the court on an application made by petition presented by another court or authority (whether within the United Kingdom or not) having the power to make a parental order for the purpose of obtaining information in connection with an application to it for such an order;

(d) by order of the court on an application made by petition presented by any person; and

(e) a person who is authorised in writing by the Secretary of State to obtain information from the process for the purpose of research designed to improve the working of human fertilisation and embryology law and practice.

Paragraph 2 (3)

SCHEDULE 2

Rule 81.5 (1)   FORM 81.5

Form of agreement under section 30 (5) of the Human Fertilisation and Embryology Act 1990

IN THE COURT OF SESSION

in the PETITION of

[A.B.] (*designation and address*) and
[C.D.] (*designation and address*)
[*or serial number where one has been assigned*]

for

A Parental Order under the Human Fertilisation and Embryology Act 1990

in respect of

[E.F.] (*name as in birth certificate*)

I, (*name and address*) being the father of the child by virtue of section 28 of the Human Fertilisation and Embryology Act 1990 [*or otherwise*] [*or the woman who carried the child*] hereby state—

(1) That I understand that the effect of the parental order for which application has been made will be to deprive me permanently of parental rights and duties relating to the child and to vest them in the petitioners; and, in particular, I understand that, if an order is made, I shall have no right to see or get in touch with the child or to have him [*or her*] returned to me.

(2) That I understand that the court cannot make a parental order in relation to the child without my agreement and the agreement of the woman who carried the child [*or the father of the child, where he is not one of the petitioners*] unless the court dispenses with an agreement on the ground that the person concerned cannot be found or is incapable of giving agreement.

(3) That I understand that when the hearing of the petition to determine the application for a parental order in relation to the child is heard, this document may be used as evidence of my agreement to the making of the order unless I inform the court that I no longer agree.

(4) That I freely, and with full understanding of what is involved, agree unconditionally to the making of a parental order in relation to the child.

(5) That I have not received or given any money or benefit, other than for expenses reasonably incurred, for or in consideration of—

(a) the making of a parental order,

(b) the execution of this agreement,

(c) the handing over of the child to the petitioners, or

(d) the making of any arrangement with a view to the making of a parental order,

[other than (*state any money or other benefit given or received by authority of the court and specify such authority*)].

I have signed this agreement at (*place of signing*) on the day of

(*Signed by father of the child or woman who carried the child*)

This agreement was signed by   before me at on the   day of

(*Signed*)
Reporting Officer
[*or* Witness
(*full name and address*)]

Rule 81.9 (1)   FORM 81.9

Form of petition for parental order under section 30 of the Human Fertilisation and Embryology Act 1990

UNTO THE RIGHT HONOURABLE THE LORDS OF COUNCIL AND SESSION

PETITION

of

[A.B.] (*designation and address*) and
[C.D.] (*designation and address*)
[*or serial number where one has been assigned*]

Petitioners

for

A parental order under section 30 of the Human Fertilisation and Embryology Act 1990

in respect of

[E.F.] (*name as in birth certificate*)

HUMBLY SHEWETH:—

1. That the petitioners are married to each other, are domiciled in Scotland and reside at (*state full address*).

2. That the petitioners are respectively   and years of age.

3. That (*state name of child the subject of the petition*) is male [*or* female] and is   months old having been born on at

4. That the child was received into the home of the petitioners on

5. That the child was carried by a woman other than the female petitioner as the result of the placing in her of an embryo [*or* the placing in her of sperm and eggs] [*or* her artificial insemination].

6. That the gametes of (*state which petitioner or if both state both petitioners*) were used to bring about the creation of the embryo of the child.

7. That the child is not the subject of any other pending or completed court proceedings (*if the child is so subject give full details*).

[8. That (*state full name and address of the father of the child*), who is not the male petitioner, is the father of the child by virtue of section 28 of the Human Fertilisation and Embryology Act 1990 [*or otherwise*] and has freely and with full understanding of what is involved, agreed unconditionally to the making of the order sought.]

[[9.] That (*state full name and address of the woman who carried the child*), is the woman who carried the child and has freely and with full understanding of what is involved, agreed unconditionally to the making of the order sought.]

[10.] That no money or benefit, other than for expenses reasonably incurred, has been given or received by the petitioners for or in consideration of—
(a) the making of the order sought,
(b) any agreement required for the making of the order sought,
(c) the handing over of the child to the petitioners, or
(d) the making of any arrangements with a view to the making of the order,
[other than (*state any money or other benefit given or received by authority of the court and specify such authority*)].

[[11.] That the father of the child [and] [*or*] [the woman who carried the child] cannot be found (*state the efforts which have been made to find the person(s) concerned*) [*or* is [*or* are] incapable of giving agreement by reason of (*state reasons*)].]

MAY IT THEREFORE please your Lordships to dispense with intimation and to order notice of the petition to be served on such person or persons as the court thinks fit; to appoint a reporting officer and, if necessary, curator *ad litem*, to the child and direct them to report; [to dispense with the agreement of [the father of the child] [and] [*or*] [the woman who carried the child] [who cannot be found] [who is [*or* are] incapable of giving agreement];] on resuming consideration of this petition and the report by the reporting officer and the curator *ad litem*, if one is appointed, to make a parental order in their favour under section 30 of the Human Fertilisation and Embryology Act 1990 in respect of the child; to direct the Registrar General for Scotland to make an entry regarding the parental order in the Parental Order Register in the form prescribed by him giving   as the forename(s) and   as the surname of the child; and on proof to the satisfaction of the court in the course of the proceedings to follow hereon, to find that the child was born on the   day of   in the year   and is identical with the child to whom an entry numbered   and made on the   day of   in the year   , in the register of births for the registration district of   relates; and to direct the Registrar General for Scotland to cause such birth entry to be marked with the words "Parental Order" and to include the above mentioned date of birth in the entry recording the parental order in the manner indicated in that form; to pronounce such other or further orders or directions upon such matters,

including the expenses of this petition, as the court thinks fit.

ACCORDING TO JUSTICE ETC.

(*Signed*)

Solicitor [*or* Agent] for petitioners
(*Address*)

[*or* (*Signed*)
Counsel or other person having a right of audience]

Rule 81.12 (3)   FORM 81.12

Form of intimation of hearing of application for a parental order under section 30 of the Human Fertilisation and Embryology Act 1990

IN THE COURT OF SESSION

in

PETITION

of

[A.B.] (*designation and address*) and
[C.D.] (*designation and address*)
[*or serial number where one has been assigned*]

for

A Parental Order under section 30 of the Human Fertilisation and Embryology Act 1990

in respect of

[E.F.] (*name as in birth certificate*)

Date: (*date of posting or other method of intimation*)
To: (*name and address*)

TAKE NOTICE

1. That the hearing on this petition to determine the application for a parental order will come before the Lord Ordinary in the Court of Session, Parliament House, Edinburgh on the   day of   , at   o'clock and that you may then appear and be heard personally or by counsel or other person having a right of audience on the question whether a parental order should be made.

2. That you are [*not*] obliged to attend the hearing [unless you wish to do so].

3. That while the petition is pending you must not, except with the leave of the court, remove the child from the custody of the petitioners.

[4. That the court has been requested to dispense with your agreement to the making of an order on the ground[s] that (*specify ground(s)*).]

(*Signed*)

Messenger-at-Arms
[*or* Solicitor [*or* Agent] for petitioners]
(*Address*)

ARTICLES

Rewriting the European Convention on Human Rights

Wilson Finnie,
Senior Lecturer,
Department of Public Law,
University of Edinburgh.

Mr Finnie explains the radical changes, now awaiting implementation, by which the European Court of Human Rights hopes to deal with the ever increasing volume of cases brought before it.

I. Introduction

The 11th Protocol to the European Convention on Human Rights (ECHR) was opened for signature in Strasbourg on 11 May 1994. It will come into effect, if at all, one year after it is ratified by all the states which have ratified the main Convention, unanimity being necessary in view of the dramatic changes effected. Although it consists of only seven articles and an Appendix, one of those articles alone sweeps away Pts II to IV of the Convention (that is, almost everything except the substantive rights and freedoms set out in Pt I) and Protocol No 2 (concerning advisory opinions) and replaces them with a new Pt II setting up an entirely new "control mechanism" (in the jargon adopted in preliminary discussion of the issue). In what follows it is proposed to examine the reasons behind the changes, the debate over the options for change and, finally, the actual system prospectively chosen.

II. Is it broke enough to require fixing?

Both reasons of principle and practical considerations motivated the changes. They have in common that they result from dramatic changes in the years since the Convention was drafted and adopted over 40 years ago.

Looking first at issues of principle, the Convention was considered very radical at the time of its adoption in two principal ways. First, and perhaps most controversial, was the provision for a European Court of Human Rights. Britain, in particular (see G Marston, "The UK's Part in the Preparation of the ECHR" (1993) 42 ICLQ 796 at pp 803-805) was deeply opposed to this grant of power to a non-domestic body but other states to a greater or lesser degree also looked on the proposal with suspicion. Certainly, courts had existed before in international law, but this court was one to the jurisdiction of which the signatory states submitted in advance and not on an ad hoc, causuistic basis. In the end the compromise

arrived at was that, unlike the Commission which came into existence and began functioning as a natural consequence of ratification of the Convention, the court was to come into existence, if at all, only after eight of the states which had ratified the Convention made an additional declaration of acceptance of the court's jurisdiction. In the event this was not achieved until 1959. Presumably, suspicion of the court was also responsible for the curious provision that each member of the Council of Europe and not just those which had recognised the jurisdiction of the court (or even ratified the Convention) was entitled to elect a judge to the court.

Thus, the text of the Convention accurately reflects the perception of at least some states that the normal method of enforcement of the Convention was to be through the Commission and the Committee of Ministers, i e by a political decision. The court was only a possibility and was provided for by way of derogation from the norm. Contemporary reality is very different. By 1989 all Council of Europe states (except Lichtenstein, a then recent intrant) had ratified the Convention and all except Lichtenstein, Malta and Turkey had made a declaration under art 46. Partly as a result of Council of Europe negotiations with Turkey following its last military coup, between 1989 and the period of rapid increase in membership of the Council of Europe it had hardened into a convention (in the UK constitutional sense) that a state seeking membership of the Council must, as a condition, ratify the ECHR and make a declaration under art 46 (T Auchterlony, Address to European Community Studies Group, Europa Institute, University of Edinburgh on 11 October 1991, p 4). Most cases which go beyond the Commission go to the court and to a great extent the case law of the court defines the Convention's meaning whereas the decisions of the Committee of Ministers contribute nothing. Few would now argue that the Committee of Ministers either is or should be the "normal" route of enforcement and the court that of exception.

The second controversial innovation of the ECHR was its challenge to the traditional dogma that public international law does not confer rights on individuals. Thus, under art 25, a state ratifying the Convention can make an additional declaration that it recognises the competence of individuals and groups to petition the Commission alleging themselves to have been the victim of a violation of the Convention. Again the text of the ECHR reflects the daring innovatory nature of this provision. Again, it is facultative not integral to the Convention. Again, it is by way of exception to the normal rule that states enforce the Convention against each other. Finally, no attempt is made to give the individual the same standing in proceedings as states. Thus, the individual cannot refer a case to the court even if the Commission finds in his or her favour (though the 9th Protocol would alter the position here) and is not a full party to the proceedings even if the case is referred (though again the position of the individual has improved: see Muchlinksi, "Position of the Individual under ECHR Law and Contemporary International Law" (1983) 34 ICLQ 381.

The cumulative result of all this is that once again the text of the Convention fails to reflect reality. In practice inter-state applications, though not unknown, represent only a minuscule percentage of the workload of the court and Commission: almost the entire caseload is generated from individual petitions. Moreover, far from this being the facultative exception to the norm, there has again crystallised a convention that the acceptance of individual petitions is a condition of entry to the Council of Europe.

Equally important for practical reasons are the changes which have occurred in the Council of Europe and in the scale of the ECHR system. When the court came into existence the Council of Europe consisted of 15 states with a long (by world standards) common tradition (with recent aberration in the cases of Austria, Italy and West Germany) of liberalism, democracy and attachment to the rule of law. By the time of writing the Council consisted of 32 states with a combined population of over 500 million and looked likely to increase significantly further in size. Such provisions of the ECHR as those conferring jurisdiction on the plenary court become largely unmanageable with 32 judges.

Even more breathtaking than the increase in the scale of the Council is the increase in scale of the resort made to the Convention by the population of the "old" Council states. In the Commission's first year (1955) it received 138 applications, a figure which in 1958 fell to 96 before rising to 603 in 1971 and 1,961 in 1992. By that date "provisional files" were being opened following communications from the "new" states and a foretaste of what to expect can be seen in the 240 provisional files concerning Poland (figures from the annual *Survey of Activities* of the European Commission on Human Rights). In its Recommendation 1194 (1992) the Parliamentary Assembly expected "that the number of individual applications will increase disproportionately to the population of the new Member States as, contrary to older Member States, the Council of Europe's system for the protection of human rights constitutes for them an important element for the building-up of fundamental rights, democracy and the rule of law". The history of the court shows a similar (indeed even more dramatic) soaring activity. It decided no case until November 1961 and took until 1985 (26 years) to decide its first 100 cases. The second 100 took until 1989 (four and a half years) and the third only until 1991 (two years), while the fourth took only 15 months. The rate of referrals is rising inexorably.

These figures necessarily raise questions about the viability of the present system. Can it digest these ever larger numbers or, to put it another way, will it take ever longer to decide any given case? The general argument is that, sooner or later, the system will break down although the Commission pointed to its own rising productivity, argued that there was a common misperception of the delay actually involved and thought radical change not necessary (*Opinion of the Commission on Reform of the Judicial Control Mechanisms of the ECHR* (1993) 15 EHRR 359 at p 360). However, another point which must be borne in mind is that neither the judges nor the commissioners are full time salaried personnel. Yet in the case of the commissioners in particular the stage has been reached when they must be prepared to spend over 30 weeks a year in Strasbourg or preparing for meetings there (see van Dijk and van Hoof, *Theory and Practice of the ECHR* (2nd ed, 1991) pp 22-23). This must restrict the opportunities for employment in their home state and risk making the post of commissioner unattractive to potentially desirable candidates. Thus even if the present sytem could handle the numbers it might alienate the best candidates to operate it.

III. The genesis of Protocol No 11

If the major change effected by the new protocol is the merger of the court and the Commission in a new court, its entry into "official" discussion can be traced to the 8th meeting of the Committee of Experts for the Improvement of the Procedure under the European Convention on Human Rights ("DH-PR"), as narrated in *The Possibility of Merging the European Commission and European Court of Human Rights* (Report of DH-PR to the Steering Committee for Human Rights ("CDDH" Doc H (89) 2)). Merger was floated at political level for the first time by the Swiss delegation at the European Ministerial Conference on Human Rights held in Vienna in

1985 and by resolution the ministers directed DH-PR to bear the Swiss report in mind.

Following this the DH-PR began serious consideration of merger, whilst a two day academic seminar on the subject was held at the university of Neuchâtel (see (1987) 8 HRLJ Part I) and a recommendation followed a debate in the Parliamentary Assembly in October 1988. DH-PR reported to CDDH around the same time but its report was inconclusive and in January 1989 the Committee of Ministers decided to declassify and publish the report to stimulate debate. DH-PR was also asked to consider the detailed structure of a new court which it did in April 1990 (*Detailed Structure of a Possible Single Court Scheme*, reprinted in (1993) 15 EHRR 338). CDDH discussed the report but was unable to come to agreement.

The model envisaged by those in favour of merger (notably the then President (Wiarda), Vice President (Ganshof van der Meersch) and deputy registrar of the court (Petzold)) had a relatively unchanged role for the court but with the addition of a number of advocates general to assume the conciliatory function of the Commission and to suggest approaches to cases to the court (as do the advocates general in EC law) (see Petzold and Sharpe in F Matscher and H Petzold, *Protecting Human Rights: The European Dimension*, Carl Heymanns Verlag (1988) at p 471). This model (and indeed wholesale merger) was now radically challenged in proposals put forward at the same time by the Dutch and Swedish governments in an attempt to kickstart reform. Essentially they proposed to give legal force to the rulings of the Commission on the merits thus converting it into a first tier court, put individuals on the same footing as states and abolish the Committee of Ministers' role under art 32. The DH-PR was asked to assess the merits of these proposals and compare them with the merger proposal (their report is reprinted in (1993) 15 EHRR at p 345). Neither they nor the CDDH to whom they reported in March 1992 were able to reach consensus although the majority preferred the two tier system to merger. Seeking the opinion of the Commission and the court (reprinted in (1993) 15 EHRR at pp 359 and 363 respectively) also failed to deliver a clear consensus: the Commission split 2 to 1 in favour of the two tier system, whereas the court's members were in three groups: those who felt that more resources and better working conditions were all that were required, those who favoured a two tier system and those who favoured a single court (the last group being an overall minority).

In view of such dissensus the whole matter was referred for political decision to the Committee of Ministers in October 1992. Perhaps surprisingly in view of this history the result in May 1993 was a mandate to the CDDH to go for the most radical option, a single court assuming the jurisdiction of both the Commission and the Committee of Ministers under art 32. For good measure they were also told to consider whether the individual's right of application should remain optional. All this to be finalised by 30 September 1993 as a draft protocol! This was produced and with almost indecent haste the Heads of State and Government in Vienna in October mandated the Committee of Ministers to finalise the draft protocol. Following due consultation with Commission, court and Parliamentary Assembly the text was adopted on 20 April 1994.

IV. The new system

For reasons of space in what follows no attempt will be made to compare systematically the new and the old systems, though some changes will be flagged. References are to the *new* arts 19 to 51 as inserted by art 1 of Protocol No 11 unless otherwise stated. The Protocol is to enter into force on the first day of the month following the expiration of the period of a year since the date on which ratification by all Council members is achieved. During that year, however, the new judges may be elected and any other necessary steps taken to establish the new court (Protocol 11, art 4). Applications lying before the Commission at the date of entry into force are to be dealt with by the new court if the Commission has not ruled on admissibility and, provided it is done within a year, by the Commission if it has already ruled them admissible. In the latter case the old rules for referring the Commission's report to the court apply. Cases awaiting decision by the old court will be dealt with by the new and the Committee of Ministers likewise will deal with cases awaiting decision under art 32 at the date of entry into force (Protocol 11, art 5).

The new court retains the title of the old but "shall function on a permanent basis" (art 19). It is to consist of a number of judges equal to that of the High Contracting Parties: the former restriction on nationality is removed so that Lichtenstein need no longer turn to Canada for its judiciary! (art 20). Candidates for office must be of high moral character and either have the qualifications for domestic high judicial office or "be jurisconsults of recognised competence" (art 21). During their tenure of office judges must not engage in any activity incompatible with their independence or impartiality or with the demands of full time office. The court itself is to be the judge of this (art 21) and, in an innovation curiously described by the Explanatory Report on Protocol 11 as "added in order to ensure the independence of the Court", art 24 envisages (without specifying any mechanism) the dismissal of a judge provided a two thirds majority of the court decides he has ceased to fulfil the required conditions. The advocates general who featured so prominently in earlier drafts have disappeared. Instead a provision is made for the court to be assisted by "legal secretaries". Advocates general were intended to have two roles, assisting the court by doing a lot of preliminary research and thought for it and inheriting the conciliatory role of the Commission. It is difficult to resist the conclusion that their omission represents a diminution in the importance ascribed to conciliation (now arts 38 and 39), whilst provision is made for their other intended role via the "legal secretaries". Provision is also made for a registry (art 25).

The new procedure is characterised by the functioning of the court at four different levels: plenary, Grand Chamber, Chamber and Committee. The role of the plenary court is important but not adjudicatory. It elects its President and one or two Vice Presidents (who may be re-elected); it sets up the chambers for a fixed period of time; elects the presidents of Chambers (who may be re-elected); adopts the rules of court; and elects the registrar and deputy or deputies (art 26).

The closest parallel to the old plenary court is the Grand Chamber of 17 judges. This includes ex officio the President and Vice President of the court and the presidents of the chambers plus the judge elected in respect of the "defendant" state. The Grand Chamber may decide a case in two ways. Where a chamber is faced with a serious question affecting the interpretation of the Convention or is minded to decide contrary to precedent, and neither party to the case objects, it may (not, as before, must) relinquish jurisdiction in favour of the Grand Chamber (art 30). In this case the Grand Chamber acts as a court of first instance. Secondly, the Grand Chamber also acts as a court of appeal. Within three months of judgment by a chamber any party may request that the case be referred to the Grand Chamber. Such a request is heard by a panel of five members of the Grand Chamber which accepts the request if the case raises a serious question affecting the interpretation or application of the Convention or a serious issue of general importance. If the request is accepted a full

rehearing takes place (art 43). The other function ascribed to the Grand Chamber is the giving of advisory opinions (arts 31 (b), 47 and 48).

It is envisaged, however, in the explanatory report that the overwhelming majority of the court's work will not trouble the Grand Chamber but, even in admissible cases, go no further than the new chambers. Chambers are set up by the plenary court for a fixed time under an elected president (art 26). They consist of seven judges including the judge elected in respect of the "defendant" state (art 27). (Depending on the rules of court adopted this provision *could* lead to cases against some countries always being heard by the same court, that is the members of the chamber of which "their" judge is a member.) Even in the unlikely event that the 17 judges of the Grand Chamber exercise no other function there will thus already be enough judges to have two chambers at work permanently with a spare peripatetic judge to allow for illness. Finally, the chambers themselves appoint committees of three judges for a fixed time (art 27) to consider questions of admissibility.

Turning now to procedure, any high contracting party may refer to the court any alleged breach by another party (art 33) and the court may receive applications from any person, non-governmental organisation or group of individuals claiming to be the victim of a violation by a high contracting party (art 34). In cases before a chamber or Grand Chamber a high contracting party whose national is an applicant has a right to submit written pleadings and take part in hearings (art 36), whilst in the interest of the proper administration of justice the President of the Court may invite any high contracting party or person other than the applicant to make written submissions or take part (art 36 (2)) in oral proceedings. (This provision derives from the present rules of court.)

Although there is no mention of such in the text it is envisaged that as soon as an application is received it will be allocated to one judge as juge rapporteur. The criteria of admissibility in art 35 are unchanged. Committees, of which the juge rapporteur will be a member, may by unanimous vote declare individual applications inadmissible; there is no appeal (art 28). If no decision is taken under art 28 (and this must include all interstate cases) then a chamber decides on admissibility and merits, normally in separate decisions (art 29) or, exceptionally and with the consent of all parties, relinquishes jurisdiction in favour of the Grand Chamber (art 30). Whichever chamber takes the decision it will normally decide first on admissibility then (simultaneously) "pursue the examination of the case and if need be, undertake an investigation" and "place itself at the disposal of the parties concerned with a view to securing a friendly settlement of the matter on the basis of respect for human rights" (art 38). At any stage of the proceedings the chamber may find an application inadmissible and at any stage may strike it out for want of prosecution or because the matter has been resolved or if for any other reason the court is no longer justified in continuing to examine the application (art 37). If the decision was taken by a chamber there is the possibility of a rehearing by the Grand Chamber (art 43), the judgment of which is final (art 44). Judgments of a chamber become final when the parties declare they will not request a reference or when the panel of five Grand Chamber judges refuses a request or three months after the date of judgment (art 44). The high contracting parties agree to abide by the final judgment and its execution is supervised by the Committee of Ministers (art 46).

V. Conclusion

It is difficult to decide which is the more remark-able: the speed with which the issue of reform was given legal form following so many years of discussion and handwringing, or the decision to go for the most drastic modification of existing procedure on offer. Either way such decisiveness deserves success. That, however, is by no means guaranteed. It is as yet early days, admittedly, but so far only two states have ratified the Protocol and the pressures on the existing system are strengthening perceptibly. Even more difficult to pass judgment on is whether the reform will work. The obvious weak link is the system of reclaimer under art 43. There may be no point in increasing original jurisdiction capacity whilst creating a court of appeal because it is difficult to see that the highly motivated people who take their cases to Strasbourg will ever accept second best or accept that anything other than a Grand Chamber judgment is not second best. In that case everything hinges on how narrowly the appellate panels of five judges interpret art 43. Even if they do so narrowly there will still be a lot of judicial time and energy wasted on the quasi-appellate decisions on whether to allow appeals.

◆

NEWS

Court

Faculty of Advocates

Mr Angus Stewart, QC, has been elected Keeper of the Advocates Library in room of Mr Brian Gill, QC, who has been appointed a Senator of the College of Justice.

— ◊ —

General

Rate of interest on landed securities

The commissioners on the rate of interest on landed securities in Scotland have resolved that the rate of interest on such first class securities shall be 8.5 per cent per annum for the six months from and after the term of Martinmas (28 November) 1994.

— ◊ —

Taxation

Controlled foreign companies

The Inland Revenue have announced details of a new clearance procedure for companies which might be affected by changes to the controlled foreign companies legislation made by s 134 of the Finance Act 1994.

The Inland Revenue will be prepared to confirm, on the facts provided, that such a company will not be subject to a direction under the controlled foreign companies legislation, because it meets either the "exempt activities" or "motive" tests in s 748 of the Income and Corporation Taxes Act 1988. Clearance applications will be considered in respect of non-trading controlled foreign companies for accounting periods ending on or after 30 November 1993. Details of how to make an application and guidance on the information which the Inland

Revenue will require can be obtained by writing to: International Division 4/2, Room 311, Melbourne House, Aldwych, London WC2B 4LL (tel 071-438 6945).

Access to government information

The Inland Revenue have published two booklets containing internal guidance on the Enterprise Investment Scheme and Rent-a-Room. A third booklet on Employee Share Schemes will be published on 20 December. Copies of the booklets, priced at £4, £2 and £4 respectively, can be ordered from the Inland Revenue Library, New Wing, Somerset House, Strand, London WC2R 1LB.

Collection of tax: codes of practice

The Inland Revenue have published two codes of practice on collection of tax. The codes cover each step of the collection process, describing the practice and standards the Inland Revenue work to and explaining taxpayers' rights and responsibilities. The codes have been produced after consultation with representative bodies. One code is for individual taxpayers and the second is for employers and for contractors in the construction industry. Separate versions of the codes are available for Scotland.

The codes are available free from tax inquiry centres and tax offices.

Business changes

Carlton Gilruth, solicitors, 30 Whitehall Street, Dundee, announce the appointment of their senior associate Lesley Dron, as a partner with effect from 1 December 1994.

Messrs Burnside, advocates, 4 Queen's Terrace, Aberdeen, announce that with effect from 1 December, 1994, Alexander Kemp has been assumed as a partner of the firm. From that date the firm name has been changed to Burnside Kemp Fraser. The partners of the firm are David Melville Burnside, Alexander Kemp and Charles William Simpson Fraser. The firm's telephone number (0224) 624602, fax number (0224) 624011 and DX number, AB 78 remain unchanged.

Mary Crighton, Dundee, intimates that she will continue to practise from 10 Whitehall Street, Dundee, with effect from 1 November 1994 as a sole practitioner under the firm name of Calders, 10 Whitehill Street, Dundee DD1 4AQ (tel 0382 224391; fax 0382 202924; DX DD4).

Semple Fraser, WS, 130 St Vincent Street, Glasgow, intimate that with effect from 14 November 1994 Alison M Gow has been assumed as a partner. The firm also announce that Dawn Hamilton and June V Gilles have been appointed associates from 24 October 1994 and 1 November 1994 respectively.

Connons, solicitors, Stonehaven, announce that their assistant, Clare R Thomas, has been appointed as an associate of the firm with effect from 1 December 1994.

Parliamentary News

New Bills

HOUSE OF COMMONS

18 November 1994

European Communities (Finance)—To amend the definition of "the Treaties" and "the Community Treaties" in s 1 (2) of the European Communities Act 1972 so as to include the decision of 31 October 1994 of the Council on the Communities' system of own resources and so as to remove a spent provision. (Government)

22 November 1994

Health Authorities—To abolish regional health authorities, district health authorities and family health services authorities, require the establishment of health authorities and make provision in relation to health authorities and special health authorities and for connected purposes. (Government)

ACT OF SEDERUNT

ACT OF SEDERUNT (SHERIFF COURT PARENTAL ORDERS (HUMAN FERTILISATION AND EMBRYOLOGY) RULES) 1994

(SI 1994/2805) [21 OCTOBER 1994]

The Lords of Council and Session, under and by virtue of the powers conferred on them by section 32 of the Sheriff Courts (Scotland) Act 1971 (c 58), section 59 of the Adoption (Scotland) Act 1978 (c 28) as modified and applied in relation to parental orders under section 30 of the Human Fertilisation and Embryology Act 1990 (c 37) and applications for such orders by paragraph 15 of Schedule 1 to the Parental Orders (Human Fertilisation and Embryology) (Scotland) Regulations 1994 (SI 1994/2804), and of all other powers enabling them in that behalf, having approved, with modifications, draft rules submitted to them by the Sheriff Court Rules Council in accordance with section 34 of the said Act of 1971, do hereby enact and declare:

Citation and commencement

1.—(1) This Act of Sederunt may be cited as the Act of Sederunt (Sheriff Court Parental Orders (Human Fertilisation and Embryology) Rules) 1994 and shall come into force on the date of coming into force of the Parental Orders (Human Fertilisation and Embryology) (Scotland) Regulations 1994.

(2) This Act of Sederunt shall be inserted in the Books of Sederunt.

Sheriff court parental orders rules

2. The provisions of the Schedule to this Act of Sederunt shall have effect for the purpose of providing rules in relation to parental orders under section 30 of the Human Fertilisation and Embryology Act 1990 and applications for such orders.

J A D HOPE, LORD PRESIDENT, *IPD*

Paragraph 2   SCHEDULE

SHERIFF COURT PARENTAL ORDERS (HUMAN FERTILISATION AND EMBRYOLOGY) RULES

ARRANGEMENT OF RULES

1. Citation and application
2. Interpretation
3. Applications for parental order
4. Confidentiality of documents in process
5. Agreements to parental order
6. Orders for evidence
7. Expenses
8. Protection of identity of petitioners
9. Appointment of reporting officer and curator *ad litem*
10. Selection of reporting officer and curator *ad litem*
11. Duties of reporting officer and curator *ad litem*
12. Hearing
13. Supervision by or committal to care of local authority
14. Applications for return, removal or prohibition of removal of child
15. Applications to amend, or revoke a direction in, a parental order
16. Registration of certified copy interlocutor
17. Extract of order
18. Final procedure
    APPENDIX

Citation and application

1.—(1) These Rules may be cited as the Sheriff Court Parental Orders (Human Fertilisation and Embryology) Rules 1994.

(2) These Rules apply in relation to parental orders under section 30 of the Human Fertilisation and Embryology Act 1990 and applications for such orders.

Interpretation

2.—(1) In these Rules, unless the context otherwise requires—

"the Act of 1978" means the Adoption (Scotland) Act 1978;

"the Act of 1990" means the Human Fertilisation and Embryology Act 1990;

"Her Majesty's Forces" means the Royal Navy, the regular armed forces as defined in section 225 of the Army Act 1955 (c 18), the regular air force as defined in section 223 of the Air Force Act 1955 (c 19) and the Queen Alexandra's Royal Naval Nursing Services;

"the Regulations" means the Parental Orders (Human Fertilisation and Embryology) (Scotland) Regulations 1994.

(2) Unless the context otherwise requires, a reference to a specified rule or form is a reference to the rule or form in the Appendix so specified in these Rules; and a reference to a specified paragraph, sub-paragraph or head is a reference to that paragraph of the rule or form, that sub-paragraph of that paragraph or that head of that sub-paragraph, in which the reference occurs.

(3) Where there is a reference in these Rules to the use of a form, that form in the Appendix to these Rules, or a form substantially to the same effect, shall be used with such variation as circumstances may require.

ACT OF SEDERUNT (SHERIFF COURT (HUMAN FERTILISATION) RULES) 1994

Applications for parental order

3.—(1) An application for a parental order shall be made by petition in Form 1.

(2) On presentation of the petition, there shall be lodged in process as productions—

(a) an extract of any entry in the register of births relating to the birth of the child;

(b) extracts of any entries in the register of births relating to the birth of each of the petitioners;

(c) an extract of any entry in the register of marriages relating to the marriage of the petitioners; and

(d) any other document founded on by the petitioners in support of the terms of the petition.

Confidentiality of documents in process

4. Unless the sheriff otherwise directs—

(a) any document lodged in process, including a report by a reporting officer or a curator *ad litem*, shall be treated as confidential and open only to the sheriff, the parties, the reporting officer and the curator *ad litem*; and

(b) a reporting officer or curator *ad litem* shall treat any information obtained by him in relation to the cause as confidential, and shall not disclose any such information to any person unless it is necessary for the proper execution of his duties.

Agreements to parental order

5.—(1) An agreement for the purposes of section 30 (5) of the Act of 1990 (agreement to parental order by a father who is not the husband of the female petitioner or by the woman who carried the child) shall, if given in writing, be in Form 2.

(2) An agreement referred to in this rule which is executed furth of Scotland shall be witnessed—

(a) where it is executed in England, Wales or Northern Ireland, by a justice of the peace or commissioner for oaths; or

(b) where it is executed furth of the United Kingdom—

(i) in the case of a person who is serving in Her Majesty's Forces, by an officer holding a commission in those forces; or

(ii) by a British consular official or any person authorised, by the law of the country where the agreement is executed, to administer an oath for any legal purpose.

Orders for evidence

6.—(1) The sheriff may, before determining the cause, order—

(a) production of further documents (including affidavits); or

(b) parole evidence.

(2) A party may apply by motion for the evidence of a person to be received in evidence by affidavit; and the sheriff may make such order as he thinks fit.

Expenses

7. The sheriff may make such order as to expenses, including the expenses of a reporting officer, a curator *ad litem*, or any other person who attended a hearing, as he thinks fit.

Protection of identity of petitioners

8.—(1) Where a married couple, who seek to apply for a parental order, wish to prevent their identity being disclosed to any person whose agreement is required under section 30 (5) of the Act of 1990 (agreement to parental order by a father who is not the husband of the female petitioner or by the woman who carried the child), they may, before presenting a petition, apply to the sheriff clerk for a serial number to be assigned to them.

(2) On receipt of an application for a serial number, the sheriff clerk shall assign a serial number to the applicants and shall enter a note of it opposite the names of the applicants in a register of serial numbers.

(3) Where a serial number has been assigned under paragraph (2)—

(a) the record of the serial number and the persons to whom it applies shall be treated as confidential and disclosed only to the sheriff;

(b) any agreement under section 30 (5) of the Act of 1990 shall not name or design the petitioners but shall refer to them by means of the serial number; and

(c) it shall be used to name or design the petitioners for all purposes connected with the petition.

Appointment of reporting officer and curator *ad litem*

9.—(1) On presentation of the petition, the sheriff shall appoint—

(a) a reporting officer; and

(b) a curator *ad litem*.

(2) The sheriff shall, where it is practicable to do so, appoint the same person to be the curator *ad litem* and the reporting officer.

(3) Where a curator *ad litem* is not also the reporting officer, the sheriff may order the reporting officer to make available to the curator *ad litem* any report or information in relation to the child.

(4) A married couple may, before presenting the petition, apply to the sheriff for the appointment of a reporting officer.

(5) An application under paragraph (4) shall—

(a) be made by letter setting out the reasons for which the appointment is sought; and

(b) not require to be intimated to any person.

Selection of reporting officer and curator *ad litem*

10. The reporting officer and curator *ad litem* appointed by the sheriff shall be selected from a panel established under the Curators ad Litem and Reporting Officers (Panels) (Scotland) Regulations 1984 unless the sheriff considers that it would be appropriate to appoint a person who is not on the panel.

Duties of reporting officer and curator *ad litem*

11.—(1) A reporting officer appointed under rule 9 (1) (a) shall, where appropriate—

(a) inquire into the facts and circumstances averred in the petition;

(b) ascertain whether the conditions in sub-sections (2) to (7) of section 30 of the Act of 1990 have been satisfied;

(c) witness any execution in Scotland of any agreement in Form 2 under section 30 (5) of the Act of 1990 (agreement to parental order by a father who is not the husband of the female petitioner or by the woman who carried the child), and investigate whether the agreement is given freely, unconditionally and with full understanding of what is involved;

(d) where a person whose agreement is required is furth of Scotland, confirm his views in writing, ensure that any agreement under section 30 (5) of the Act of 1990 is witnessed in accordance with rule 5 (2) and investigate whether the agreement is given freely, unconditionally and with full understanding of what is involved;

(e) ensure that each person whose agreement is required understands that in agreeing to the parental order he is giving up all future claims to the child and that all parental rights and duties will vest in the petitioners;

(f) investigate whether there are any other persons with a relevant interest and whether they should be informed of the petition;

(g) ascertain from any person whose agreement is required and who can be found whether alternatives to a parental order have been discussed with him;

(h) ensure that any person whose agreement is required is aware of the date (if known) of the hearing to determine the application if he wishes to appear, and confirm that any such person understands that he may withdraw his agreement at any time before a parental order is made;

(i) draw to the attention of the court any matter which may be of assistance; and

(j) prepare a report in relation to the exercise of his duties within such period as the court may specify.

(2) A curator *ad litem* appointed under rule 9 (1) (b) shall—

(a) safeguard generally the interests of the child;

(b) inquire, so far as he considers necessary, into the facts and circumstances averred in the petition;

(c) ascertain whether any money or other benefit has been received or agreed upon which is prohibited by section 30 (7) of the Act of 1990 (prohibition on gift or receipt of money or other benefit);

(d) establish that the petitioners understand that the nature and effect of a parental order is to transfer the parental rights and duties in relation to the child to the petitioners and make them responsible for the maintenance and upbringing of the child;

(e) ascertain whether the proposed parental order is likely to safeguard and promote the welfare of the child throughout his childhood;

(f) ascertain whether it may be in the interests of the child that the court should make a parental order subject to particular conditions including the making of special provision for the child;

(g) perform such other duties as appear to him to be necessary or as the court may require; and

(h) prepare a report in relation to the exercise of his duties within such period as the court may specify.

(3) The reporting officer shall, on completion of his report, send to the sheriff clerk—

(a) the report and a copy of it for each party; and

(b) any agreement for the purposes of section 30 (5) of the Act of 1990.

(4) The curator *ad litem* shall, on completion of his report, send the report and a copy of it for each party, to the sheriff clerk.

Hearing

12.—(1) On receipt of the reports referred to in rule 11, the sheriff shall fix a hearing.

(2) The sheriff may—

(a) order any person whose agreement is required to be given to attend the hearing;

(b) order intimation of the date of the hearing to any person not mentioned in paragraph (3) (a), (b) or (c); and

(c) order the reporting officer or curator *ad litem* to perform additional duties to assist him in determining the petition.

(3) The petitioners shall intimate the date of the hearing in Form 3 by registered post or recorded delivery letter to—

(a) every person whose whereabouts are known to them and whose agreement is required to be given;

(b) the reporting officer appointed under rule 9 (1) (a);

(c) the curator *ad litem* appointed under rule 9 (1) (b); and

(d) any person on whom intimation has been ordered under paragraph (2) (b).

(4) At the hearing—

(a) the petitioners, the reporting officer and the curator *ad litem* shall, if required by the sheriff, appear and may be represented;

(b) any person required by the sheriff to attend the hearing shall appear and may be represented;

(c) any other person to whom intimation was made under paragraph (3) (a) or (d) may appear or be represented.

Supervision by or committal to care of local authority

13.—(1) Where the sheriff refuses to make a parental order and considers—

(a) that the child should be placed under the supervision of a specified local authority, or

(b) that the child should be committed to the care of a specified local authority,

the sheriff shall order intimation of the terms of the proposed order to be made to the local authority and give the local authority an opportunity to make representations.

(2) Any representations of the local authority shall be made by minute in the process of the petition for a parental order to which it relates.

(3) A minute under paragraph (2) shall include an appropriate crave and statements of facts.

(4) On receipt of the minute the sheriff shall order a hearing to be fixed and ordain the minuter to send a notice of such hearing in Form 4 and a copy of the minute by registered post or recorded delivery letter to the petitioners, the reporting office and the curator *ad litem* and to such other persons as the sheriff thinks fit.

Applications for return, removal or prohibition of removal of child

14.—(1) An application under section 29 of the Act of 1978, as modified and applied in relation to applications for parental orders by Schedule 1 to the Regulations (order to return a child to, or not to remove a child from, the care of the applicants), in relation to a breach of section 27 (1) of that Act as so modified and applied (restriction on removal of child where application for parental order pending), or under section 27 (1) of that Act as so modified and applied for leave to remove a child, shall be made by minute in the process of the petition for a parental order to which it relates.

(2) A minute under paragraph (1) shall include an appropriate crave and statement of facts.

(3) On receipt of the minute, the sheriff shall order a hearing to be fixed and ordain the minuter to send a notice of such hearing in Form 5 and a copy of the minute by registered post or recorded delivery letter to the reporting officer and the

curator *ad litem* and to such other persons as the sheriff thinks fit.

Applications to amend, or revoke a direction in, a parental order

15.—(1) An application under paragraph 3 (1) of Schedule 1 to the Act of 1978, as modified and applied in relation to parental orders by Schedule 1 to the Regulations (amendment, or revocation of a direction in, a parental order), shall be made by petition to the court which pronounced the order.

(2) The sheriff may order the petitioners to intimate the petition to such persons as the sheriff thinks fit.

Registration of certified copy interlocutor

16. On the sheriff pronouncing an interlocutor making—

(a) a parental order,

(b) an amendment to, or revocation of a direction in, a parental order, or

(c) a revocation of a parental order,

the sheriff clerk shall send a certified copy of that interlocutor to the Registrar General for Scotland in a sealed envelope marked "confidential".

Extract of order

17. An extract of a parental order shall not be issued except by order of the court on an application to it—

(a) where there is a petition for the parental order depending before the court, by motion in that process; or

(b) where there is no such petition depending before the court, by petition.

Final procedure

18.—(1) After a certified copy of an interlocutor mentioned in rule 16 has been sent to the Registrar General for Scotland, the sheriff clerk shall forthwith—

(a) place the whole process in an envelope bearing only—

(i) the name of the petitioners;

(ii) the full name of the child to whom the process relates; and

(iii) the date of the order; and

(b) seal the envelope and mark it "confidential".

(2) No person shall open a process referred to in paragraph (1) or inspect its contents within 100 years after the date of the parental order, except—

(a) the person in respect of whom the parental order was made after he has reached the age of 17 years;

(b) any other person or body entitled under section 45 (5) of the Act of 1978, as modified and applied in relation to parental orders and applications for such orders by Schedule 1 to the Regulations, to access to the registers and books kept under section 45 (4) of that Act, as so modified and applied, with the written authority of the person in respect of whom the parental order was made;

(c) by order of the court on an application made by petition presented by another court or authority (whether within the United Kingdom or not) having the power to make a parental order for the purpose of obtaining information in connection with an application to it for such an order;

(d) by order of the court on an application made by petition presented by any person; and

(e) a person who is authorised in writing by the Secretary of State to obtain information from the process for the purpose of research designed to improve the working of human fertilisation and embryology law and practice.

APPENDIX

Rule 3 (1)   FORM 1

Form of petition for parental order under section 30 of the Human Fertilisation and Embryology Act 1990

SHERIFFDOM OF (insert name of sheriffdom)
AT (insert place of sheriff court)

PETITION
of

[A.B.] (designation and address)

and

[C.D.] (designation and address)
[or serial number where one has been assigned]
Petitioners

for

A parental order under section 30 of the Human Fertilisation and Embryology Act 1990

in respect of

[E.F.] (name as in birth certificate)

The petitioners condescend as follows—

1. The petitioners are married to each other, are domiciled in Scotland and reside at (state full address).

2. The petitioners are respectively   and   years of age.

3. (State name of child, the subject of the petition) is male [or female] and is   months old having been born on   at

4. The child was received into the home of the petitioners on

5. The child was carried by a woman other than the female petitioner as the result of the placing in her of an embryo [or the placing in her of sperm and eggs] [or her artificial insemination].

6. The gametes of (state which petitioner or if both state both petitioners) were used to bring about the creation of the embryo of the child.

7. The child is not the subject of any other pending or completed court proceedings (if the child is so subject give full details).

[8. (State full name and address of the father of the child), who is not the male petitioner, is the father of the child by virtue of section 28 of the Human Fertilisation and Embryology Act 1990 [or otherwise] and has freely and with full understanding of what is involved, agreed unconditionally to the making of the order sought.]

[[9.] (State full name and address of the woman who carried the child), is the woman who carried the child and has freely

and with full understanding of what is involved, agreed unconditionally to the making of the order sought.]

[10.] No money or benefit, other than for expenses reasonably incurred, has been given or received by the petitioners for or in consideration of—

(a) the making of the order sought,
(b) any agreement required for the making of the order sought,
(c) the handing over of the child to the petitioners, or
(d) the making of any arrangements with a view to the making of the order,
[other than (state any money or other benefit given or received by authority of the court and specify such authority)].

[[11.] That the father of the child [and] [or] [the woman who carried the child] cannot be found (state the efforts which have been made to find the person(s) concerned) [or is [or are] incapable of giving agreement by reason of (state reasons)].]

The petitioners crave the court—

1. To order notice of the petition to be intimated to such person or persons as the court thinks fit.

2. To appoint a reporting officer and, if necessary, curator ad litem, to the child and direct them to report.

[3. To dispense with the agreement of [the father of the child] [and] [or] [the woman who carried the child] who cannot be found [or who is [or are] incapable of giving agreement].]

[4.] On resuming consideration of this petition and the report by the reporting officer and the curator ad litem, to make a parental order in their favour under section 30 of the Human Fertilisation and Embryology Act 1990 in respect of the child.

[5.] To direct the Registrar General for Scotland to make an entry regarding the parental order in the Parental Order Register in the form prescribed by him giving   as the forename(s) and   as the surname of the child; and upon proof to the satisfaction of the court in the course of the proceedings to follow hereon, to find that the child was born on the   day of   in the year   and is identical with the child to whom an entry numbered   and made on the   day of   in the year   , in the register of births for the registration district of   relates; and to direct the Registrar General for Scotland to cause such birth entry to be marked with the words "Parental Order" and to include the abovementioned date of birth in the entry recording the parental order in the manner indicated in that form.

[6.] To pronounce such other or further orders or directions upon such matters, including the expenses of this petition, as the court thinks fit.

(Signed)
Male petitioner

(Signed)
Female petitioner

[or (Signed)
Solicitor for petitioners
(Address)]

Rule 5 (1)   FORM 2

Form of agreement for parental order under section 30 (5) of the Human Fertilisation and Embryology Act 1990

in the
Petition
of

[A.B.] (designation and address)
and
[C.D.] (designation and address)
[or serial number where one has been assigned]

for

ACT OF SEDERUNT (SHERIFF COURT (HUMAN FERTILISATION) RULES) 1994

A Parental Order under the Human Fertilisation
and Embryology Act 1990

in respect of

[E.F.] (*name as in birth certificate*)

I, (*name and address*) being the father of the child by virtue of section 28 of the Human Fertilisation and Embryology Act 1990 [*or otherwise*] [*or the woman who carried the child*] hereby state—

(1) That I understand that the effect of the parental order for which application has been made will be to deprive me permanently of parental rights and duties relating to the child and to vest them in the petitioners; and, in particular, I understand that, if an order is made, I shall have no right to see or get in touch with the child or to have him [*or her*] returned to me.

(2) That I understand that the court cannot make a parental order in relation to the child without my agreement and the agreement of the woman who carried the child [*or the father of the child, where he is not one of the petitioners*] unless the court dispenses with an agreement on the ground that the person concerned cannot be found or is incapable of giving agreement.

(3) That I understand that when the hearing of the petition to determine the application for a parental order in relation to the child is heard, this document may be used as evidence of my agreement to the making of the order unless I inform the court that I no longer agree.

(4) That I freely, and with full understanding of what is involved, agree unconditionally to the making of a parental order in relation to the child.

(5) That I have not received or given any money or benefit, other than for expenses reasonably incurred, for or in consideration of—

(a) the making of a parental order,
(b) the execution of this agreement,
(c) the handing over of the child to the petitioners, or
(d) the making of any arrangements with a view to the making of a parental order,

[other than (*state any money or other benefit given or received by authority of the court and specify such authority*)].

I have signed this agreement at (*place of signing*) on the day of

(*Signed by father of the child or woman who carried the child*)

This agreement was signed by   before me at on the   day of

(*Signed*)
Reporting Officer
[*or* Witness
(*full name and address*)]

Rule 12 (3)   FORM 3

Form of intimation of diet of hearing of application for a parental order under section 30 of the Human Fertilisation and Embryology Act 1990

To: (*full name and address of person to whom this intimation is to be sent*)

You are given NOTICE that a hearing will take place at (*name of sheriff court*) Sheriff Court (*full address of court*) on (*date*) at (*time*) in relation to the child (*full name of child as given in the birth certificate*)

when the court will consider an application for a parental order under section 30 of the Human Fertilisation and Embryology Act 1990 in respect of the child.

You are [not] obliged to attend the hearing [unless you wish to do so].

If you do not attend this hearing the court may make an order as noted above.

[While the petition is pending you must not, except with the leave of the court, remove the child from the custody of the petitioners.]

[The court has been requested to dispense with your agreement to the making of an order on the ground[s] that (*specify ground(s)*).]

Date (*insert date*)

(*Signed*)
Male petitioner

(*Signed*)
Female petitioner

[*or* (*Signed*)
Solicitors for
petitioners
(*Address*)]

Rule 13 (4)   FORM 4

Form of intimation of diet of hearing of minute by local authority

To: (*full name and address of person to whom this intimation is to be sent*)

You are given NOTICE that a hearing will take place at (*name of sheriff court*) Sheriff Court (*full address of court*) on (*date*) at (*time*) in relation to the child (*full name of child as given in the birth certificate*)

when the court will consider representations made by minute under rule 13 of the Act of Sederunt (Sheriff Court Parental Orders (Human Fertilisation and Embryology) Rules) 1994 in respect of the child. A copy of the minute is attached.

You do not need to attend this hearing if you do not wish to be heard by the court.

Date (*insert date*)

(*Signed*)
Local Authority

[*or* (*Signed*)
Solicitor for Local
Authority
(*Address*)]

Rule 14 (3)   FORM 5

Form of intimation of diet of hearing of application under section 27 (1) or 29 of the Act of 1978 as modified and applied in relation to parental orders

To: (*full name and address of person to whom this intimation is to be sent*)

You are given NOTICE that a hearing will take place at (*name of sheriff court*) Sheriff Court (*full address of court*) on (date) at (*time*) in relation to the child (*full name of child as given in the birth certificate*)

when the court will consider a minute of application under rule 14 of the Act of Sederunt (Sheriff Court Parental Orders (Human Fertilisation and Embryology) Rules) 1994 in respect of the child. A copy of the application is attached.

You do not need to attend this hearing if you do not wish to be heard by the court.

Date (*insert date*)

(*Signed*)
Minuter

[*or* (*Signed*)
Solicitor for Minuter
(*Address*)]

[Acts of Sederunt are reproduced with the permission of the Controller of Her Majesty's Stationery Office.]

ARTICLES

Fees for Speculative Actions

A G McCulloch, SSC,
Drummond Miller, WS.

Mr McCulloch explores the potential for speculative actions, and suggests that on the basis on which they have been given statutory form, they are likely to be relatively little used.

The profession should by now be conversant with the terms of s 61A (a) of the Solicitors (Scotland) Act 1980, dealing with written agreements between solicitor and client relating to fees. This was introduced by s 36 of the Law Reform (Miscellaneous Provisions) (Scotland) Act 1990. Attention should be paid to subs (3) which is in the following terms: "A solicitor and his client may agree, in relation to a litigation undertaken on a speculative basis, that, in the event of the litigation being successful, the solicitor's fee shall be increased by such a percentage as may, subject to subsection (4), be agreed."

Subsection (4) indicates that the percentage increase referred to shall not exceed such limit as the court may, after consultation with the Law Society Council, prescribe by Act of Sederunt. The Act of Sederunt (Fees of Solicitors in Speculative Actions) 1992 (SI 1992/1879 in the sheriff court; SI 1992/1898 in the Court of Session) sets matters out in greater detail. The sheriff court Act of Sederunt came into effect on 24 August 1992 and is in the following terms:

"2.—(1) Where — (a) any work is undertaken by a solicitor in the conduct of litigation for a client; and (b) the solicitor and the client agree that the solicitor shall be entitled to a fee for the work only if the client is successful in the litigation; and (c) the agreement is that the solicitor's fee for all work in connection with the litigation is to be based on an account prepared as between party and party, the solicitor and client may agree that the fees element in that account, as hereinafter defined, shall be increased by a figure not exceeding 100 per cent."

By para 2 (2), the client is deemed to be successful in the litigation where "(a) the litigation has been concluded by the pronouncing of a decree by the court which, on the merits, is to any extent in his favour; (b) the client has accepted a sum of money in settlement of his claim in the litigation; or (c) the client has entered into a settlement of any other kind by which his claim in the litigation has been resolved to any extent in his favour".

There is a definition in para 2 (3) of "fees element", being all the fees in the solicitor's account of expenses for which any other party to the litigation has been found liable, taxed as between party and party or agreed, before the deduction of any award of expenses against the client", but by para 2 (4) one excludes "(a) any fees payable for copying papers and the proportion of any process fee and posts and incidents exigible thereon; (b) any discretionary fee allowed under Regulation 5 of the General Regulations set out in the Schedule to the Act of Sederunt (Fees of Solicitors in the Sheriff Court) 1989; and (c) any charges by the solicitor for his outlays".

The Court of Session details are now found in rule 41.14 of the Rules of the Court of Session 1994, replacing the former rule 350A, which came into effect on 17 August 1992.

Many people think that the speculative action is a new animal. That is not the case. What recent legislation has done is to recognise that there has existed for some time in Scotland a body of solicitors who are quite prepared to take on cases on a speculative basis; this legislation now seeks to reward the solicitors with higher fees than would otherwise have been allowed. We are not, however, talking about contingency fees. Many English writers have been confused, apparently because until very recently speculative actions have not been allowed at all in England. Neither have contingency fees, but they have tended to think that the two things are one and the same whereas in Scotland that is clearly not the case.

On one view, however, a speculative action might be considered in the same category as a contingency action, not least because whether or not one gets paid is "contingent" upon success. Following the rather unsatisfactory outcome of the Court of Session action of declarator brought by the Law Society of Scotland against Frank Lefevre, the matter has been re-affirmed by the court as making it illegal to charge a fee where the fee is calculated as a proportion of, and payable out of, the principal sum. It is the double headed aspect of the decision which highlights contingency fees. If, for example, it was just a proportion of the principal sum which was thought to be illegal then all settlements having regard to chap 10 of the Law Society's Table of Fees for Conveyancing and General Business (Extrajudicial Settlements) would have become illegal. It is a fact that under chap 10 a percentage is paid as a fee over and above the principal sum, and additional to it.

There are several different types of speculative actions. The most common one in the writer's experience is where a solicitor agrees that he will not charge a fee in the event that the action is unsuccessful, but the client still has to pay outlays. That could be extended slightly in Court of Session actions, or in sheriff court actions where counsel is used, because counsel is prepared quite often to undertake a case on a speculative basis and charge only if the action is successful. Different advocates have different views on speculative actions, but suffice to say at the present time that in the scheme for accounting for recovery of counsel's fees issued by the Law Society and the Faculty, speculative actions are one of the three exceptions to normal rules. Counsel can increase fees in the same way as solicitors, namely by up to 100 per cent, all as laid down by the Act of Sederunt (Fees of Advocates in Speculative Actions) 1992 (SI 1992/1897) with effect from 17 August 1992. This, therefore, is the most common type of speculative action. No win, no fee, but your outlays will be paid and therefore no out of pocket!

The second type would be where a solicitor agreed to underwrite the outlays necessarily incurred. It is the writer's view that as a solicitor has therefore increased his exposure in real terms he should be entitled to a higher fee than in the normal situation previously mentioned.

The final type of speculative action that the writer can think of is where the solicitor underwrites any liability that his client may have when awards of expenses are made against him. You might think that that would be a particularly courageous thing to do, but one has to bear in mind that legal aid regulations, and professional duties, impinge upon fee charging agreements or speculative actions. In the writer's opinion, the Law Society might find professional misconduct in not advising a client of the availability of legal aid, and instead taking the case on speculatively. If the action is lost the client, unless the solicitor underwrites the opponent's expenses, would be liable for a substantial bill to the opponent. One of the few benefits of the legal aid certificate is the right to modification of liability in expenses found in s 18 (2) of the Legal Aid (Scotland) Act 1986. In most cases at the end of the day the unsuccessful legally aided pursuer has his liability to pay the opponent's expenses modified, usually to nil. This means that for a person who would otherwise be eligible for legal aid to be put in no worse a position, having agreed for that solicitor act on a speculative basis, the solicitor must agree to underwrite any award of expenses made against the client. To the writer this is the most extreme form of speculative action and the one that is deserving of the highest percentage uplift.

It is interesting to note that the legislation does not appear to make it an essential element in acting speculatively that there be an agreement *in writing* with the client. Thus, taxation as between agent and client is competent in a speculative action, but only when there is no written fee charging agreement. The possibility of a percentage uplift where there is a fee charging agreement is an anomaly. Presumably in reaching the agreement with the client as to the fee to be charged, the fact that one is acting speculatively is taken into account, and thus a pretty high hourly rate will have been agreed with the client. A probability is that that would exceed whatever could be recovered where there is no fee charging agreement. In the latter circumstances all that can be recovered, having regard to the terms of the Act of Sederunt issued by the court, is an uplift of up to 100 per cent on the fees element of the award of judicial expenses made against the opponent.

There is nothing in the Act of Sederunt that allows any form of taxation or independent review of the percentage increase, unless there is no written fee charging agreement. It seems to be inevitable that unless market forces dictate otherwise, everybody is going to charge 100 per cent, regardless of the simplicity of the case, the risk taken by the solicitor, the amounts involved, the awkwardness of one's own client or any other matter. Perhaps clients will start looking at actions of reduction of charging agreements (apparently the only remedy), because at the present time there is nothing to stop a solicitor charging 100 per cent for each and every action. The gullible client will accept that; perhaps he will not fully understand what is involved.

It may help to envisage a situation where there is a fairly small claim, perhaps worth a total of £5,000. There falls some wage loss and, for the period that the client has been off work, there have been benefits paid. There is a CRU deduction. At the end of the day the client is left with, say, £3,000. You are acting speculatively with 100 per cent uplift. You prepare your judicial account for settlement by the other side. This case went to debate once where you were successful, but you did have to amend once, there was one day when the proof was discharged because one of your witnesses did not appear, and eventually it proceeded and was decided in your favour. The fees element of your account of expenses comes to, say, £4,000. You recover that from your opponent but you can increase this by 100 per cent. The bill to your client therefore is for a further £4,000, which is more than the whole of his principal sum. Is that fair and reasonable in all the circumstances?

Let us say, however, that you decided to enter into a fee charging agreement with your client.

You do not mention that you could act speculatively. You agree an hourly rate with him of, say, £120. All that you can recover from the other side by way of judicial expenses is, say, £60 per hour. If you now charge your client for your minute of amendment when in fact you are found liable for the other side's expenses, the discharged proof and a number of other matters, the account to your client will be substantial. Even if you recover certain judicial expenses there may still be a substantial shortfall. The probability is that your client's principal sum is again swallowed up. Consequently there is no benefit to your client in acting speculatively, if he is prepared to agree to a written fee charging agreement, but there is a benefit to you, as you are paid, win, lose or draw.

There are other problems which have been highlighted in discussions between solicitors in respect of fee charging agreements in speculative actions. The first is the obvious one where a large settlement is achieved but is inclusive of expenses. You are faced then with a dilemma. Your client is told that an offer of £100,000 inclusive of expenses has been received. How do you advise him? You might have to go back to the defenders and agree with them what the expenses element might be. In the Acts of Sederunt regarding speculative actions there is a definition of success, and clearly this type of settlement falls within that definition. The only basis upon which the solicitor can calculate the fees element is by reference to the fees in his account against the other party as either taxed or agreed. Defending solicitors may be willing to assist, but there again there will be many that might not.

Certain problems do not relate so much to the client in the street. Now that fee charging agreements are in force, and standing the basis upon which one can now charge one's own client, effectively a solicitor can charge whatever he likes to the client without regard to the table of fees. This is based upon the Act of Sederunt (Rules of the Court of Session Amendment No 3) (Taxation of Accounts) 1992 (SI 1992/1433; see now rule 42.7 of the 1994 Rules) and the Act of Sederunt (Solicitor and Client Accounts in the Sheriff Court) 1992 (SI 1992/1434), both of which came into effect on 20 July 1992. On this basis the solicitor can charge the client what he likes, as the auditor would allow a sum in respect of such work and outlays as may have been reasonably incurred and shall allow in respect of each item of work such sum as is merely *fair and reasonable having regard to all the circumstances* of the case. The auditor, in assessing what is fair and reasonable, has regard to seven pillars of wisdom. For completeness these are noted as follows, and can be found in para 4 of chap 1 of the Law Society

General Table, in Court of Session rule 347 (now rule 42.14) and in general regulation 5 of the Sheriff Court Table of Fees in the same or similar terms:

(1) The complexity of the litigation and the number or difficulty or novelty of the questions raised.

(2) The skill, labour, specialised knowledge, and responsibility involved.

(3) The time spent on an item of work, and the litigation, as a whole.

(4) The length, number and importance of any documents or any other papers prepared or perused.

(5) The place where and the circumstances (including the degree of expedition required) in which solicitors' work or any part of it has been done.

(6) The amount or value of any money or any property involved in the litigation.

(7) The importance of the litigation and the subject matter to the client.

Taxation as between solicitor and client has now been abolished if there exists a written fee charging agreement, but the same rules would in the writer's opinion still apply in an action brought by the solicitor for payment where the defender (client) claimed that the fee was not fair and reasonable. Some sheriffs have indicated that they might just remit the case to a man of skill (otherwise known as an auditor!) to assess the account and to report. Others have said that they would look at the whole matter and give their own opinion. In any event it is likely that they would have regard to the seven pillars of wisdom in deciding whether or not the fee was one that could be said to be fair and reasonable in the circumstances.

Is it possible to act for a defender in a speculative action? It is suggested that it is, having regard to para 2 (2) (a) of the Act of Sederunt. This indicates as a definition of success that the litigation has been concluded by the pronouncing of a decree by the court which, on the merits, is to any extent in his favour. Thus absolvitor, or dismissal, must be success and there could be room for a speculative fee charging agreement.

If anybody is going to charge on a speculative basis, and not enter into a fee charging agreement as such, merely coming to an agreement with the client to charge an uplift based upon the party and party expenses recovered, then some guidance as to the basis of such charging should be given, but until such matters come before the courts, auditors, or the Law Society, any guidance will by its very nature be speculation.

An indication has already been given of the different bases upon which the solicitor undertakes a speculative action (payment of outlays, or otherwise an indemnity against expenses), which must have an input into the percentage increase. The second factor has to be the complexity of the litigation itself. It is all too easy to act for the front seat passenger in a road traffic accident where no other car was involved. You sue the driver and you are almost guaranteed to succeed. However, in a medical negligence case are you going to act on a speculative basis? The client is going to want to know at an early stage. Presumably it would be possible to charge the client for work done in ingathering the evidence so that an informed view can be given. It has long been the position of the court that a solicitor is entitled to rely upon counsel's view on the prospects of success of a case, when deciding to act speculatively, and that must now be extended to solicitor advocates. However, it seems to the writer to be a good test for any solicitor, who should come to his decision fairly, having seen all the available preliminary evidence (see dicta of Lord President Normand in *X Insurance Co Ltd v A and B*, 1936 SC 225 at p 239; 1936 SLT 188 at p 195).

One still has to take into account the likely behaviour of one's own client! The client may be anxious to have several meetings with you, phone you on a regular basis, and generally take up a lot of your time. However, if in a speculative action all that you are recovering is an uplift on the party and party expenses recovered from the other side, it is unlikely that the other side would agree, or the auditor would allow, many of the meetings with the client, telephone calls, etc. Thus, work will be undertaken by you which would not be recoverable, and a substantial loss could be incurred even although an increase on party and party expenses of 100 per cent had been agreed.

There may well therefore be circumstances where an agreement in a speculative action that fees should be increased by a figure of 100 per cent will result in a lesser sum being paid than the solicitor would be paid on the normal basis of agent and client. This but highlights the growing gap between party and party accounts (judicial expenses) and agent and client accounts. Until the gap is abolished, perhaps by removing the Table of Fees and leaving all matters to the "fair and reasonable" test, then it is unlikely that much use will be made of speculative actions.

One has to wonder if the legislation dealing with speculative actions actually gives effect to the intention that solicitors should be compensated for the additional risk associated with undertaking speculative actions.

It has been expressed elsewhere that the legislation here is another example of the Government introducing change for the sake of change and results in no benefit to members of the public or profession. The writer does not necessarily share that view, but it has elements of truth. There are bound to be situations when clients who are outwith the legal aid financial limits, but cannot afford to litigate, are now assisted by the rules relating to speculative actions. That, however, pays scant regard to the number of actions that were frequently undertaken by members of the profession to the benefit of the public. Litigation was undertaken on the basis that remuneration at the end of the day would just be the judicial expenses ultimately awarded, and there would be little or no agent and client fee. The writer is unaware of any complaint by members of the public that the system of speculative actions as operated in Scotland prior to 1990 was unfair. One certainly hopes that the changes which the Government have made to the system will not result in injustice, but one fears that that is a possibility. Time will tell.

◆

NEWS

Appointments

Advocates depute
The Lord Advocate has appointed Mr Alan David Turnbull, advocate, to be an advocate depute with effect from 1 January 1995. Mrs Ann Paton, QC, resigns from the post of advocate depute with effect from 31 December 1994.

◇

Shrieval vacancies
There will shortly be vacancies for a resident sheriff in the Sheriffdom of Glasgow and Strathkelvin (at Glasgow), for a floating sheriff in the Sheriffdom of North Strathclyde (centred at Paisley), for a floating sheriff in the Sheriffdom of Tayside, Central and Fife (centred at Dundee), and for a floating sheriff to serve, where required, in all sheriffdoms. Advocates and solicitors of appropriate standing and experience who are interested in one or more of these appointments

are invited to write in confidence, enclosing their curriculum vitae, to the Director of the Scottish Courts Administration, 26-27 Royal Terrace, Edinburgh EH7 5AH, by 4 January 1995.

— ◊ —

Court

Sheriffdoms: Lothian and Borders
The Sheriff Principal of Lothian and Borders has prescribed the following sessions for the disposal of civil business in 1995: spring session, Thursday, 5 January to Saturday, 1 April; summer session, Monday, 1 May to Saturday, 1 July; winter session, Monday, 28 August to Wednesday, 20 December. Details of court holidays and vacation courts have been inserted in the appropriate act books of court.

— ◊ —

Coming events

Employment law course
The Robert Gordon University will offer for the first time in January 1995 a two year postgraduate diploma course (part time) in employment law and practice. This course will provide students with an extensive knowledge of employment law within the UK/European environment. Emphasis will be placed on the development of "best practice" skills.

Candidates holding a first degree in any discipline, and candidates with extensive workplace experience, but without a first degree, will be considered. Inquiries should be made to Richard Mays, School of Public Administration and Law, The Robert Gordon University, 352 King Street, Aberdeen AB9 2TQ (tel 0224 262900).

— ◊ —

General

Society of Advocates in Aberdeen
At the annual general meeting of the Society of Advocates in Aberdeen, the following office bearers were appointed for the year 1994-95: *President*, Frank H Lefevre, The Frank Lefevre Practice; *treasurer*, Melville F Watson, Storie, Cruden & Simpson.

◊

Dunfermline District Society of Solicitors
The following office bearers and members of the

Dean's council were elected at the annual general meeting: *Dean*, David A Harkess; *vice dean*, John R Bain; *secretary/treasurer*, Caroline J Flanagan; *librarian*, Craig Bennet; *council members*, Keith S Mason, Kyle A D Peddie, Douglas J C Thomson, Valerie Waddell, W Blair F Morgan, Paul K Donnachie, Douglas M Ferguson (Law Society Council Member).

◊

Review of solicitors' training
The Law Society of Scotland have circulated a consultation paper seeking views on the best means of achieving the transition between academic training and in-office pratice. The consultation follows a questionnaire on the Diploma in Legal Practice which disclosed a widely held view, among both trainees and employers, that the diploma is inadequate or only just adequate.

The consultation paper examines the whole range of options from a return to intending solicitors moving straight from their degree course to their traineeship, through a restructuring of the existing diploma, to establishing a joint venture with a university to provide a skills course on the Law Society's behalf, or even setting up the society's own law school. The points for and against each option are set out, with particular reference to the availability of funding (public or from within the profession), administrative and geographical problems, ease of establishing quality control and control over intake, all against the background of a "mission statement" setting out the areas in which someone wishing to become a solicitor should be trained prior to admission.

The areas identified for such training are: dealing with the client; handling the work; organising the workload; office/management skills; financial skills, and professional conduct. The consultation paper suggests, but requests views on the proposition, that entry to the profession can no longer be controlled by academic standards alone. It also asks whether the Law Society should introduce a system of authorisation before a firm is permitted to take on trainees, and whether, once the traineeship is completed, there should be a test of professional competence administered by the society prior to the grant of a full practising certificate.

Further suggestions concern the enhancement of the practice management course and restrictions on the ability of recently qualified solicitors to enter into partnership or establish their own business.

Responses on all question posed in the paper, and indeed on any other matters relevant to the training of solicitors, are invited by 28 February 1995, addressed to Lindsay Paterson, Deputy Secretary at the Law Society.

◇

Scottish Prisons Complaints Commission

The Scottish Prisons Complaints Commission opened for business to prisoners on 1 December 1994. The commission, which has been set up as a result of commitments made in the Citizen's Charter and in the Scottish Prison Service review of their complaints procedure, can receive applications from prisoners in Scottish prisons who have failed to obtain satisfaction from the internal grievance procedure.

Dr Jim McManus, formerly a senior lecturer in law at the University of Dundee, has been appointed by the Secretary of State to head the commission. He will be assisted initially by a deputy commissioner and by a personal secretary.

Only prisoners can make application to the commission. Before doing so they must exhaust the internal grievance procedure. Applications can cover any area for which SPS is responsible, though clinical judgments made by medical officers are for the moment excluded from the commission's jurisdiction. Equally, matters in relation to sentence, conviction and parole decision making are excluded from the commission's remit, as are matters which are the subject of legal proceedings. Otherwise everything is within the commission's jurisdiction. It can thus review decisions in relation to security categories of prisoners, decisions made in orderly rooms about discipline within the prison and decisions in relation to allocation of prisoners and any other matter within the prison.

After investigating applications in whatever way it considers appropriate the commission will report with recommendations to the Chief Executive of the Scottish Prison Service. The commissioner will also submit an annual report to the Secretary of State for Scotland detailing what he has done in the course of each year.

The commission is totally independent of SPS and is located at Government Buildings, Broomhouse Drive, Edinburgh. The commission is entitled to full and free access to all prison service establishments, personnel and documents.

◇

Supervised attendance order schemes

A research study published by the Scottish Office Central Research Unit describes an evaluation of the pilot supervised attendance order schemes. Based on analysis and monitoring of cases referred to the schemes, observation of the schemes themselves and interviews with court and scheme staff, sentencers and offenders, the report provides a detailed examination of the operation and impact of SAOs.

Whilst fewer SAOs had been made during the early stages of the pilot, schemes were effective in attracting cases. It is too early in the life of the schemes to make definitive statements about the impact of the SAO on custody rates for fine default; however, there was a significant reduction in such receptions in one court, Ayr, covered by the pilot schemes. The schemes were popular and credible with sentencers, courts and scheme staff and offenders; many offenders reported that they felt they had learned something from undertaking an SAO.

◇

Judicial examination procedure

A research report published by the Scottish Office into the use of the judicial examination procedure in Scotland found that the number of judicial examinations held has been falling in recent years and that procurators fiscal and advocates depute perceive the value of the current procedure to be limited.

The study found considerable variation between procurator fiscal offices in terms of the policies adopted for conducting judicial examinations. This variation tended to be related to local differences in both the practicalities and experiences of conducting examinations. For this reason, five of the nine procurators fiscal who were interviewed were against the introduction of standard policy guidance.

One of the main problems reported by procurators fiscal in conducting judicial examinations was the tendency for accused not to answer the questions put to them, particularly in relation to their line of defence. An examination of a sample of judicial examination transcripts from High Court trial cases found that the accused failed to make any comment about their defence in relation to three quarters of all charges. In many cases, the accused specifically stated that this was on the advice of their solicitor. Six procurators fiscal felt that judicial examinations which failed to elicit information about the accused's defence were of little value to them, either in preparing cases for prosecution or at the trial stage.

Interviews with advocates depute also found that the judicial examination procedure was perceived to be rarely valuable to the High Court trial process. They stated that they referred to transcripts in only a minority of trials, and that judicial examinations were crucial to securing a conviction in only a very small percentage of cases. However, they were keen to have judicial examinations conducted in all High Court cases in view of the fact that they could be of value.

The research report is published as part of the Central Research Unit series of research papers, and is available from the Scottish Office Library at a cost of £5.00.

—— ◊ ——

Taxation

Income tax: loss relief
The Inland Revenue have published two extra-statutory concessions concerning the calculation of relief for losses incurred in trades, professions and vocations. These concessions only apply where the trade, profession or vocation is treated for tax purposes as having commenced by 5 April 1994. Businesses which commenced more recently are subject to new statutory rules which give the same result as the application of these concessions. The text of the concessions reads as follows:

(1) Loss relief on accounts basis (A87)
This concession applies where: relief is claimed under s 380, ICTA 1988 (trading and other losses set against income generally) for losses sustained in tax years up to 1996-97 in trades, professions or vocations which commenced for tax purposes on or before 5 April 1994.

Relief under s 380 for these losses is in strictness available for the loss which arose in the tax year to 5 April. This means the results of two sets of accounts have to be apportioned unless the accounting date is 5 April. In practice, however, the Inland Revenue will allow relief for the loss of the year to the normal accounting date in the tax year — the "accounts basis".

For example, Sarah's accounting date is 31 December and she makes a loss of £5,000 in the year to 31.12.94. If she claims relief under s 380 on the accounts basis, the Inland Revenue will allow loss relief of £5,000 for 1994-95.

This concession does not apply to relief claimed under s 381, ICTA 1988 or to losses made: (a) in the first, second or third tax years of a new business; (b) in the fourth tax year of a new business if the assessment for the third year has been adjusted under s 62, ICTA 1988; (c) in any year immediately following a year for which relief under either s 380 or s 381 has been allowed on the strict basis of the loss of the year to 5 April; (d) in the year the business ceases; or (e) by a

partner where a partnership change has taken place, an election for continuation treatment is made under s 113 (2) ICTA 1988 and relief under s 381 could be claimed by any partner for that year.

These exclusions apply by reference to the year in which the loss was sustained, not the year for which loss relief is claimed. (Under s 380 (2), relief may be claimed against the income of the year following the year of loss.)

The loss must be calculated on the strict basis to 5 April in any case which falls within (a) to (e) above or where the claimant does not wish to take advantage of this concession.

(2) Cessation adjustment where loss relief has been allowed on accounts basis (A88)
This concession applies to trades, professions or vocations which commenced for tax purposes on or before 5 April 1994 and which: cease in business by 5 April 1997; or cease in business in the 1997-98 tax year if the Inland Revenue gives a direction under para 3 (2), Sched 20, FA 1994.

Where relief is claimed under s 380, ICTA 1988 (trading and other losses set against income generally) for the tax year in which the business ceases, it must be given for the loss for the period from 6 April to the date of cessation.

If s 380 relief has been allowed for the penultimate year on the accounts basis under ESC A87 the loss incurred after the accounting date in that year will fall into a gap and would not be relieved. Where this happens relief may be available under this concession, whether or not terminal loss relief (s 388, ICTA 1988) is claimed.

Loss relief will have been allowed under s 380 for one or more consecutive years preceding the year of cessation. The Inland Revenue will calculate the following in terms of tax: (a) the relief allowed for these years (up to a maximum of six years); (b) the relief which would have been given for the same years if the losses had been computed on the strict basis to 5 April each year; and (c) if terminal loss relief has been allowed, the amount (if any) which would no longer be due following the recomputation at (b).

The smaller of the two following amounts will be repaid for the year of cessation: the excess of (b) over (a) plus (c); or tax at the claimant's marginal rate for the year of cessation on the part of the penultimate year's loss which falls into the gap and which is not relieved under the terminal loss relief provisions.

The recomputation at (b) may create a loss for the year preceding the first of the consecutive years for which claims were made. Where this happens the Inland Revenue will accept a late claim under s 380 in respect of that year's loss, unless it is more than six years before the year of cessation.

◇

Double taxation treaties

The Financial Secretary to the Treasury has announced negotiating priorities for the United Kingdom's network of double taxation treaties.

Approval has been given for an Inland Revenue programme of negotiations covering the period to March 1996. This targets, in particular, the fastest developing economies offering greatest growth potential for United Kingdom business. These priorities have been determined following extensive consultation between the Inland Revenue and business, commercial and professional representative bodies and other government departments.

The programme allows for flexibility in responding to developments. The Inland Revenue welcome representations from interested parties on points they would like to see addressed in these negotiations, or on other matters relating to the negotiating programme or current treaty network.

Representations should be sent to: Peter Dennis, Inland Revenue, International Division, Strand Bridge House, 38-142 Strand, London WC2R 1HH.

— ◇ —

Obituary

On 1 December 1994, Alistair William Owen, formerly senior partner in and subsequently consultant to Messrs Adam & A C Brown, WS, Kirkcudbright.

— ◇ —

Parliamentary News

New Bills

23 November 1994

Channel Tunnel Rail Link—To provide for the construction, maintenance and operation of a railway between St Pancras in London and the Channel Tunnel portal at Castle Hill, Folkestone, Kent, together with associated works and of works which can be carried out in conjunction therewith; to provide for the improvement of the A2 at Cobham, in Kent, and of the M2 between junctions 1 and 4, together with associated works; to make provision with respect to compensation

in relation to the acquisition of blighted land; and for connected purposes. (Government)

24 November 1994

Children (Scotland)—To reform the law of Scotland relating to children, to the adoption of children and to young persons who as children have been looked after by local authorities; to make new provision as respects the relationship between parent and child and guardian and child in the law of Scotland; to make provision as respects residential establishments for children and as respects certain other residential establishments; and for connected purposes. (Government)

1 December 1994

Jobseekers—To provide for a jobseekers allowance and to make other provision to promote the employment of the unemployed and the assistance of persons without a settled way of life. (Government)

Progress of Bills

European Communities (Finance) — Commons: second reading, 28 November 1994; remaining stages, 7 and 8 December 1994.

Private International Law (Miscellaneous Provisions) — Lands: second reading, 6 December 1994.

War Crimes (Supplementary Provisions) — Lords: second reading, 7 December 1994.

Questions answered

HOUSE OF COMMONS

23 November 1994

NUISANCE LEGISLATION

Mr Kynoch: To ask the Secretary of State for Scotland, what conclusions the Government have reached in the light of the responses to their consultation paper "Contaminated Land Cleanup and Control" and the recent consultation exercise on the revision of Scotland's nuisance legislation; and if he will make a statement.

Mr Lang: The Government intend to replace the existing Scottish nuisance provisions in the Public Health (Scotland) Act 1897 with those of Pt III of the Environmental Protection Act 1990, which apply mainly to England and Wales. A clear majority of the 37 responses to our August consultation paper were in favour of such a change, which will usefully strengthen controls on nuisance in Scotland.

I hope to make a further announcement on the outcome of the contaminated land review shortly.

ACT OF SEDERUNT

ACT OF SEDERUNT (RULES OF THE COURT OF SESSION 1994 AMENDMENT NO 3) (MISCELLANEOUS) 1994

(SI 1994/2901) [10 NOVEMBER 1994]

The Lords of Council and Session, under and by virtue of the powers conferred on them by section 5 of the Court of Session Act 1988 (c 36), section 48 (1) of the Children Act 1975 (c 72), section 15 of the Presumption of Death (Scotland) Act 1977 (c 27), section 59 (1) of the Adoption Act 1978 (c 28), section 48 of the Civil Jurisdiction and Judgments Act 1982 (c 48), sections 114 (3), 204 (3) and 231 (3) of the Copyright, Designs and Patents Act 1988 (c 27), section 19 (3) of the Trade Marks Act 1994 (c 26), and of all other powers enabling them in that behalf, do hereby enact and declare:

Citation and commencement

1.—(1) This Act of Sederunt may be cited as the Act of Sederunt (Rules of the Court of Session 1994 Amendment No. 3) (Miscellaneous) 1994 and shall come into force on 5th December 1994.

(2) This Act of Sederunt shall be inserted in the Books of Sederunt.

Amendment of the Rules of the Court of Session

2.—(1) The Rules of the Court of Session 1994 shall be amended in accordance with the following sub-paragraphs.

(2) In rule 9.2 (retransmission of processes to Office of Court), for "—1 (1)", substitute "—(1)".

(3) In rule 10.2 (1) (sederunt days), after the words "rule 10.3 (1)", insert the words "or 10.4".

(4) In rule 16.12, for the word **"Excution"** in the heading, substitute the word **"Execution"**.

(5) In rule 23.10 (motions by defender or other person before calling), in paragraph (1), for the word "Clark", substitute the word "Clerk".

(6) In rule 24.2 (applications to amend pleadings), in paragraph (3) (a), after the words "have been lodged," where they first occur, insert the words "unless the court otherwise orders".

(7) In rule 35.4 (execution of commission and diligence for recovery of documents), in paragraph (12), for "(11)", substitute "(10)".

(8) In rule 36.6 (notices to admit and notices of non-admission), in paragraph (4), for "14", substitute "21".

(9) In Chapter 38 (reclaiming)—

(a) in rule 38.3 (reclaiming days), in paragraph (2) (b), for the word "expense", substitute the word "expenses";

(b) in rule 38.11 (reclaiming against decree by default), in paragraph (2), immediately before the words "to expenses", insert the word "as"; and

(c) in rule 38.16 (grounds of appeal in reclaiming motions), in paragraph (5), after the words "reclaiming motion", insert the words "with or without hearing parties as the court thinks fit".

(10) In Chapter 40 (appeals from inferior courts)—

(a) in rule 40.14 (grounds of appeal), in paragraph (5), after the words "refuse the appeal", insert the words "with or without hearing parties as the court thinks fit"; and

(b) in rule 40.17 (lodging of appendices in appeals), in paragraph (1), for the words "after the cause had", substitute the words "after the cause has".

(11) In Chapter 41 (appeals under statute)—

(a) in rule 41.17 (remit to reporter), in paragraph (3) (b), for the word "given", substitute the word "give";

(b) in rule 41.21 (orders for service and answers), in paragraph (2) (b), for the words "to every person", substitute the words "every person";

(c) for rules 41.23 to 41.25 (rules relating to Exchequer appeals), substitute the following rules:—

"Revenue appeals by stated case

41.23—(1) This rule applies to an appeal to the court as the Court of Exchequer in Scotland under any of the following provisions:—

(a) section 13 (1) of the Stamp Act 1891 (appeal from Commissioners of Inland Revenue);

(b) section 705A of the Income and Corporation Taxes Act 1988 (case for opinion of court from tribunal); and

(c) regulation 20 (1) of the General Commissioners (Jurisdiction and Procedure) Regulations 1994.

(2) Subject to paragraph (3), Part II (appeals by stated case etc.) shall apply to an appeal to which paragraph (1) applies.

(3) The following provisions of Part II shall not apply to an appeal to which this rules applies:—

rule 41.5 (applications for case),

rule 41.6 (additional questions by other parties),

rule 41.7 (consideration of application by tribunal),

rule 41.8 (procedure for ordaining tribunal to state a case),

rule 41.9 (preparation and issue of the case),

rule 41.10 (intimation of intention to proceed).

Revenue appeals from Special Commissioners

41.24.—(1) This rule applies to an appeal to the court under any of the following provisions:—

(a) section 56A of the Taxes Management Act 1970;

(b) section 225 of the Inheritance Tax Act 1984; and

(c) regulation 10 (1) of the Stamp Duty Reserve Tax Regulations 1986.

(2) Part III (appeals in Form 41.19) shall apply to an appeal to which paragraph (1) applies.

Appeals relating to penalties

41.25.—(1) This rule applies to an appeal to the court as the Court of Exchequer in Scotland under any of the following provisions:—

(a) section 53 (1) or 100C (4) of the Taxes Management Act 1970 (appeals from General or Special Commissioners in relation to penalties);

(b) an appeal against the amount of a penalty under section 100B (3) of the Taxes Management Act 1970;

(c) section 249 (3) or 251 (2) of the Inheritance Tax Act 1984 (appeals from Special Commissioners in relation to penalties); and

(d) paragraph 10 (3) of Schedule 12 to the Value Added Tax Act 1994 (appeal from VAT tribunal in relation to penalty).

(2) Part III (appeals in Form 41.19) shall apply to an appeal to which paragraph (1) (a), (c) or (d) applies.

(3) In relation to paragraph (1) (b)—

(a) Part II (appeals by stated case etc.) shall apply to an appeal from the General Commissioners; and

(b) Part III shall apply to an appeal from the Special Commissioners.

(4) Within 30 days after service on them of an appeal in Form 41.19, the Special Commissioners or the VAT Tribunal, as the case may be, shall—

(a) send six copies of a note of their findings and of the reasons for their decision to the Deputy Principal Clerk; and

(b) send a copy of that note to every party to the appeal.";

(d) in rule 41.26 (appeals relating to certain determinations of the Commissioners of Inland Revenue), in paragraph (4), after the word "solicitor", insert the words "in Scotland".

(12) In rule 42.10 (basis of charging), in paragraph (2), for the words "solicitor local to the party", substitute the words "local solicitor".

(13) In rule 49.2 (averments in certain family actions about other proceedings), in paragraph (3) (c) (ii), for the word "sub-paragraph", substitute the word "paragraph".

(14) In rule 50.5 (applications for variation or recall of decrees), in paragraph (4), for the words "paragraph (4)", substitute the words "paragraph (3)".

(15) In rule 51.13 (decrees for payment), in paragraph (1) (a), for the word "have" where it second occurs, substitute the word "has".

(16) In Chapter 55 (causes relating to intellectual property)—

(a) in rule 55.14 (appeals from Comptroller)—

(i) in the heading, after the word **"Appeals"**, insert the words **"and references"**;

(ii) in paragraph (1), after the words "a decision of", insert the words ", or a reference under the Copyright Act of 1988 from,";

(iii) in paragraph (2), after the words "an appeal", insert the words "or a reference";

(iv) in paragraph (3), after the words "an appeal", insert the words "or a reference";

(v) in paragraph (3) (a), after the words "the decision", insert the words "appealed against";

(vi) in paragraph (3) (b), after the words "the decision", insert the words "appealed against or the decision referring the proceedings to the court, as the case may be"; and

(vii) in paragraph (4), after the word "appeal", insert the words "or reference";

(b) for rule 55.17, substitute the following rule:—

"Intimation and service of applications under the Copyright Act of 1988 or the Trade Marks Act 1994 for orders for disposal of infringing matter

55.17. An application under section 114, 204 or 231 of the Copyright Act of 1988 (which provide for orders for disposal in respect of infringement of copyright, rights in performances and design rights), or section 19 of the Trade Marks Act 1994 (order as to disposal of infringing goods, material or articles), shall be made—

(a) in a cause depending before the court, by motion; or

(b) where there is no depending cause, by petition; and

the applicant shall intimate the motion to, or serve the petition on, as the case may be, all persons, so far as known to the applicant or reasonably ascertainable, having an interest in the copy, article, recording or other thing which is the subject of the application, including any person in whose favour an order could be made in respect of the copy, article, recording or other thing under any of the said sections of the Copyright Act of 1988 or section 19 of the said Act of 1994."; and

(c) after rule 55.18 (applications for leave to proceed), insert the following rule:—

"Appeals and references under the Trade Marks Act 1994

55.19.—(1) Subject to the following paragraphs of this rule, an appeal or reference under section 76 of the Trade Marks Act 1994 (appeal from registrar or reference from appointed person) shall be heard in the Outer House by the patents judge.

(2) In the application of Part III of Chapter 41 (appeals in Form 41.19) by virtue of rule 41.43 (appeals to Lord Ordinary) to an appeal or reference under paragraph (1) of this rule—

(a) for references to the Inner House there shall be substituted references to the patents judge; and

(b) the following paragraphs of this rule shall apply.

(3) Subject to paragraph (4), an appeal or reference shall be lodged in the General Department—

(a) in the case of a decision on a matter of procedure, within 14 days after the date of the decision appealed against; and

(b) in any other case, within 6 weeks after the date of the decision appealed against or the decision referring the proceedings to the court, as the case may be.

(4) Except with the leave of the court, no appeal or reference under this rule shall be entertained unless it has been lodged within the period specified in paragraph (3) or within such further period as the Comptroller may allow on an application made to him before the expiry of that period.

(5) Any determination by the Comptroller that a decision is on a matter of procedure shall be treated as being itself a decision on a matter of procedure.

(6) In the application of paragraph (1) of rule 41.21 (orders for service and answers), the order under that paragraph shall include a requirement to—

(a) intimate the appeal to the Comptroller; and

(b) serve the appeal on every other party to the proceedings before the Comptroller.

(7) On receiving intimation of the appeal, the Comptroller shall forthwith transmit to the Deputy Principal Clerk all the papers relating to the matter which is the subject of the appeal.

(8) A respondent who, not having appealed from the decision of the Comptroller, wishes to contend at the hearing of the appeal that the decision or the grounds of the decision should be varied shall—

(a) specify the grounds of that contention in his answers; and

(b) intimate those answers to the Comptroller and to every other party to the proceedings before the Comptroller.

(9) Intimation of the date of the hearing of the appeal shall be made to the Comptroller by the appellant not less than 7 days before that date, unless the court otherwise directs.

(10) An appeal under this rule shall be a re-hearing and the evidence led on appeal shall be the same as that led before the Comptroller; and, except with the leave of the court, no further evidence shall be led.".

(17) In rule 62.40 (enforcement in another Contracting State of Court of Session judgments etc.), in paragraph (3), for the word "of" where it second occurs, substitute the word "to".

(18) In Chapter 67 (applications under the Adoption (Scotland) Act 1978)—

(a) in rule 67.32 (procedure after intimation to Register General or issue of extract), in paragraph (1), for "67.29", substitute "67.30"; and

(b) in rule 67.41 (revocation or annulment of regulated adoptions), in paragraph (3), omit the comma after the word "adoption".

(19) In rule 70.5 (form of applications relating to international child abduction), in paragraph (1), for sub-paragraph (b), substitute the following sub-paragraph:—

"(b) there shall be produced with the petition and lodged as a production a certified or authorised copy of any relevant decision or agreement.".

(20) In rule 74.10 (form of petition for administration order), in paragraph (2) (f), after the words "winding up,", insert the word "of".

(21) In Chapter 76 (causes in relation to confiscation of proceeds of crime)—

(a) in rule 76.8 (incidental applications in an administration), in paragraph (2) (a), for "4 (1) (o)", substitute "14 (1) (o)"; and

(b) in rule 76.19 (application and interpretation of Part II of Chapter 76), for the word "act", substitute the word "Act".

(22) In the appendix—

(a) in the following forms, for the words "legal advice agency", substitute the words "local advice agency":—

Form 13.12

Form 35.4—A

Form 43.3

Form 43.13—B

Form 44.2—A

Form 44.3

Forms 49.8—A, 49.8—B, 49.8—C, 49.8—D, 49.8—E, 49.8—F, 49.8—G, 49.8—I, 49.8—J, 49.8—K, 49.8—L

Form 49.9

Forms 49.14—A, 49.14—C, 49.14—E, 49.14—F,

Form 49.37

Form 49.62—A

Form 50.2—B

Form 61.31

Form 62.9

Form 76.9;

(b) in Form 6.2, at the end, for the word "alternation", substitute the word "alteration";

(c) in Form 13.2—A

(i) to the left of the box drawn at the top of the form, insert the words "[*Insert the Royal Arms in Scotland*]";

(ii) centred below the words "IN THE COURT OF SESSION" on the first page, insert the words:

"SUMMONS

in the cause"; and

(iii) on the backing, centred below the word "Summons", insert the words "in the cause";

(d) in Form 13.2—B, in paragraph (17), for the words "or eighteen", substitute the words "of eighteen";

(e) in Form 14.4, to the left of the box drawn at the top of the form, insert the words "[*Insert the Royal Arms in Scotland*]";

(f) In Form 26.1—A, in the first alternative of the second paragraph, for the word "along" where it first occurs, substitute the word "alone";

(g) in Form 36.2—A—

(i) above the words "(*Name and address of pursuer*" in the first paragraph, insert the following—

"Date: (*insert date of service of citation*)";

(ii) in the second paragraph, after the words "[*or Agent*]", insert the word "for";

(iii) in the second paragraph, after the words "Messenger-at-Arms", insert the words "on the instructions of (*name of agent on whose behalf citation executed*)"; and

(iv) at the end of the second paragraph, after the words "a witness", insert the words "for the pursuer [*or as the case may be*]";

(h) in Form 44.2—B—

(i) in paragraph 3 of "PART B", for the word "instalment", substitute the word "instalments"; and

(ii) in the margin of "PART B", after the words "Delete whichever is", insert the words "not appropriate";

(i) In Form 49.29—A, after the words "specified in the", insert the words "attached schedule and being satisfied that on this evidence a motion for decree in terms of the conclusions of the";

(j) in Form 49.73—B—

(i) on page 2 of the form in the section headed "*Note on Section 4 opposite*", in the paragraph beginning with the words "MARRIAGE CERTIFICATE", for the words "Registrar nor", substitute the words "Registrar not"; and

(ii) on page 3 of the form, at the end of Section 4, after the words "space is", insert the word "not";

(k) in Form 62.40—A, in paragraph 4, for the words "in the sum or", substitute the words "in the sum of";

(l) in Form 62.42—A, in the heading, for the word **"of"**, substitute the word **"to"**;

(m) in Form 67.15, in paragraph 1, after the words "of an order freeing the child", insert "[E.F.]"; and

(n) in the form after Form 69.5 headed **"Form 64.15"**—

(i) for the words **"Form 64.15"**, substitute the words **"Form 69.15"**; and

(ii) for the words "Rule 64.15", substitute the words "Rule 69.15".

J A D HOPE, LORD PRESIDENT, *IPD*

APPENDIX

CASE NOTES ON EUROPEAN COURT DECISIONS RELATING TO THE JUDGMENTS CONVENTION

Edited by A E ANTON *and* P R BEAUMONT
University of Aberdeen

Overseas Union Insurance Ltd v New Hampshire Insurance Co (C-351/89) [1991] ECR I-3317.

(1) 1968 Convention, Art 21; 1982 Act, Sched 1, Art 21 — Lis pendens — Domicile of the parties — Discretion of court second seised.

Legal background

The Court was asked to interpret Art 21 of the Brussels Convention and the version applicable to this case (see para 12 below) did not contain the 1989 Accession Convention amendments. The implications of these amendments for this decision are considered in the comment.

Facts

In 1980 Overseas Union Insurance (OUI), a Singapore company registered in England as an overseas company, and two English insurance companies reinsured a proportion of New Hampshire Insurance Co's risk in relation to an insurance policy it had entered into with a French company in 1979. New Hampshire Insurance Co was incorporated in New Hampshire, USA, and registered as an overseas company in England and as a foreign company in France. After OUI and the two English insurance companies purported to avoid their respective insurance commitments in relation to New Hampshire Insurance Co it initiated proceedings against these companies in the French courts in 1987. The defenders in the French proceedings challenged the jurisdiction of those courts and in 1988 initiated proceedings in the English High Court against New Hampshire Insurance Co. The High Court granted a stay of the English proceedings on the basis of Art 21 of the Brussels Convention. On appeal the Court of Appeal decided to refer certain questions concerning Art 21 to the European Court. It was not in dispute that the French courts were first seised and that the proceedings in England and France involved the same cause of action and the same parties.

Law

The European Court (Sixth Chamber) said:

"In its first question the national court essentially seeks to establish whether Article 21 of the Convention applies irrespective of the domicile of the parties to the two sets of proceedings." [11]

"In order to answer that question it should be recalled that Article 21 of the Convention provides that:

" 'Where proceedings involving the same cause of action and between the same parties are brought in the courts of different Contracting States, any court other than the court first seised shall of its own motion decline jurisdiction in favour of that court.

" 'A court which would be required to decline jurisdiction may stay its proceedings if the jurisdiction of the other court is contested.' " [12]

"Thus, the wording of Article 21, unlike the wording of other provisions of the Convention, makes no reference to the domicile of the parties to the proceedings. Moreover, Article 21 does not draw any distinction between the various heads of jurisdiction provided for in the Convention. In particular, it does not provide for any derogation to cover a case where, in accordance with the provisions of Article 4 of the Convention, a court of a Contracting State exercises its jurisdiction by virtue of the law of that State over a defendant who is not domiciled in a Contracting State." [13]

"Consequently, it appears from the wording of Article 21 that it must be applied both where the jurisdiction of the court is determined by the Convention itself and where it is derived from the legislation of a Contracting State in accordance with Article 4 of the Convention." [14]

"The interpretation suggested by the wording is borne out by an examination of the aims of the Convention. In the judgment of 11 January 1990 in Case C-220/88 *Dumez France and Tracoba v Hessische Landesbank and Others* [1990] ECR I-49, the Court held that essentially the aim of the Convention was to promote the recognition and enforcement of judgments in States other than those in which they were delivered and that it was therefore indispensable to limit the risk of irreconcilable decisions, which is a reason for withholding recognition or an order for enforcement by virtue of Article 27 (3) of the Convention." [15]

"With regard in particular to Article 21, the Court observed in the judgment in [Case 144/86 *Gubisch Maschinenfabrik AG v Palumbo* [1987] ECR 4861] that the provision, together with Article 22 on related

A actions, is contained in Section 8 of Title II of the Convention, which is intended, in the interests of the proper administration of justice within the Community, to prevent parallel proceedings before the courts of different Contracting States and to avoid conflicts between decisions which might result therefrom. Those rules are therefore designed to preclude, insofar as possible and from the outset, the possibility of a situation arising such as that referred to in Article 27 (3), that is to say the non-recognition of a judgment on account of its irreconcilability with a judgment given in proceedings between the same B parties in the State in which recognition is sought. It follows that, in order to achieve those aims, Article 21 must be interpreted broadly so as to cover, in principle, all situations of lis pendens before courts in Contracting States, irrespective of the parties' domicile." [16]

"By its second and third questions, the national court essentially seeks to establish whether Article 21 of the Convention must be interpreted as meaning C that, if it does not decline jurisdiction, the court second seised may only stay its proceedings, or whether Article 21 permits or requires it to examine whether the court first seised has jurisdiction and, if so, to what extent." [19]

After referring to the Jenard Report the Sixth Chamber said:

"Moreover, it should be noted that in no case is the court second seised in a better position than the court D first seised to determine whether the latter has jurisdiction. Either the jurisdiction of the court first seised is determined directly by the rules of the Convention, which are common to both courts and may be interpreted and applied with the same authority by each of them, or it is derived, by virtue of Article 4 of the Convention, from the law of the State of the court first seised, in which case that court is undeniably better placed to rule on the question of its own jurisdiction." [23]

E "Moreover, the cases in which a court in a Contracting State may review the jurisdiction of a court in another Contracting State are set out exhaustively in Article 28 and the second paragraph of Article 34 of the Convention. Those cases are limited to the stage of recognition or enforcement and relate only to certain rules of special or exclusive jurisdiction having a mandatory or public policy nature. It follows that, apart from those limited exceptions, the Convention does not authorize the jurisdiction of a court to be F reviewed by a court in another Contracting State." [24]

"It therefore appears both from the wording of Article 21 and from the scheme of the Convention that the court second seised, . . . [may] stay the proceedings if the jurisdiction of the court first seised is contested. However, it cannot itself examine the jurisdiction of the court first seised." [25]

The Court (Sixth Chamber) ruled:

"(1) Article 21 of the [Brussels] Convention

G must be interpreted as applying irrespective of the domicile of the parties to the two sets of proceedings.

"(2) Without prejudice to the case where the court second seised has exclusive jurisdiction under the Convention and in particular under Article 16 thereof, Article 21 of the Convention must be interpreted as meaning that, where the jurisdiction of the court first seised is contested, the court second seised may, if it does not decline jurisdiction, only stay the proceedings and may H not itself examine the jurisdiction of the court first seised."

Comment

Article 21 of the Brussels Convention was amended by the 1989 Accession Convention. The court second seised is still required to decline jurisdiction if the jurisdiction of the court first seised is established. If, however, the latter's jurisdiction is not established then the amended version of Art 21 requires the court I second seised to sist its proceedings. This change removes the possibility of the court second seised declining jurisdiction while the jurisdiction of the court first seised has not been established. It does not, however, alter the substance of the Court's decision that Art 21 applies irrespective of where the parties to the proceedings are domiciled and that the court second seised cannot examine the jurisdiction of the court first seised.

Paragraph 14 of the judgment indicates that lis J pendens applies to actions in different Contracting States even where the basis for jurisdiction in one or both of the States is an exorbitant ground of jurisdiction preserved by Art 4 of the Brussels Convention in relation to parties who are not domiciled in a Contracting State. Thus an action in France brought by a French national (domiciled in part of the United States) against an American company on the basis of the nationality of the pursuer and an action brought by the American company against the same French K national in Scotland on the basis of the arrestment of his or her moveable property situated in Scotland would be subject to Art 21 of the Convention. It would not be possible for the Scottish courts to decline to exercise jurisdiction on the basis of forum non conveniens in favour of the appropriate courts in the United States.

L

Marc Rich and Co v Società Italiana Impianti (C-190/89) [1991] ECR I-3855.

(1) 1968 Convention, Art 1 (4); 1982 Act, Sched 1, Art 1 (4) — Scope of the Convention — Arbitration.

(2) Interpretation of the Convention — Use of reports — Jenard — Schlosser — Evrigenis and Kerameus — General principle of law — Legal certainty.

Legal background

Article 1 (4) of the Brussels Convention provides that:

"The Convention shall not apply to . . . (4) arbitration."

Facts

Marc Rich and Co, a Swiss company, entered into a contract with Società Italiana Impianti, an Italian company, for the purchase of a quantity of Iranian crude oil on f o b terms. Marc Rich contended that the contract included a clause providing for arbitration in London. On 6 February 1987 Marc Rich complained that the cargo was seriously contaminated with losses in excess of $7,000,000. On 18 February 1988, Impianti summoned Marc Rich to appear before a court in Genoa, Italy, in an action for a declaration that it was not liable to Marc Rich. Marc Rich contested the jurisdiction of the Italian court relying on the arbitration clause in the contract and itself commenced arbitration proceedings in London on 29 February 1988. As Impianti refused to take part in the arbitration proceedings Marc Rich commenced proceedings before the High Court in London for the appointment of an arbitrator. Impianti argued that the dispute came within the scope of the Brussels Convention, as it contended that the arbitration clause was not part of the contract, and that the dispute, therefore, should be adjudicated on in Italy. Marc Rich argued that as the case concerned arbitration it was excluded from the scope of the Brussels Convention by Art 1 (4). The High Court decided that the Convention was not applicable. On appeal, the Court of Appeal decided to refer questions to the European Court the first of which was as follows:

"Does the exception in Article 1 (4) of the Convention extend:

"(a) to any litigation or judgments and, if so,

"(b) to litigation or judgments where the initial existence of an arbitration agreement is in issue?"

Law

The European Court dealt only with the Court of Appeal's first question because the other questions were relevant only if the answer to the first question was negative.

"The purpose of the Convention, according to the preamble thereto, is to implement the provisions of Article 220 of the EEC Treaty [now EC Treaty] concerning the reciprocal recognition and enforcement of judgments of courts or tribunals. Pursuant to the fourth paragraph of Article 220, the Member States shall, so far as is necessary, enter into negotiations with each other with a view to securing for the benefit of their nationals the simplification of formalities governing the reciprocal recognition and enforcement of judgments of courts or tribunals and of arbitration awards." [15]

"In referring to decisions of courts and tribunals and to arbitration awards, Article 220 of the Treaty thus relates both to proceedings brought before national courts and tribunals which culminate in a judicial decision and to those commenced before private arbitrators which culminate in arbitral awards. However, it does not follow that the Convention, whose purpose is in particular the reciprocal recognition and enforcement of judicial decisions, must necessarily have attributed to it a wide field of application. Insofar as the Member States are called upon, by virtue of Article 220, to enter into negotiations 'so far as necessary', it is incumbent on them to determine the scope of any agreement concluded between them." [16]

After referring to p 13 of the Jenard Report the Court said:

"The international agreements, and in particular the New York Convention on the recognition and enforcement of foreign arbitral awards (New York, 10 June 1958, *United Nations Treaty Series*, Vol 330, p 3), lay down rules which must be respected not by the arbitrators themselves but by the courts of the Contracting States. Those rules relate, for example, to agreements whereby parties refer a dispute to arbitration and the recognition and enforcement of arbitral awards. It follows that, by excluding arbitration from the scope of the Convention on the ground that it was already covered by international conventions, the Contracting Parties intended to exclude arbitration in its entirety, including proceedings brought before national courts." [18]

"More particularly, it must be pointed out that the appointment of an arbitrator by a national court is a measure adopted by the State as part of the process of setting arbitration proceedings in motion. Such a measure therefore comes within the sphere of arbitration and is thus covered by the exclusion contained in Article 1 (4) of the Convention." [19]

"That interpretation is not affected by the fact that the international agreements in question have not been signed by all the Member States and do not cover all aspects of arbitration, in particular the procedure for the appointment of arbitrators." [20]

The Court then pointed out that its conclusion was corroborated by the Schlosser Report, p 93, on the 1978 Accession Convention, and by the Evrigenis and Kerameus Report. The Court then turned to address the question whether a preliminary issue concerning the existence or validity of an arbitration agreement affects the application of the Convention to the dispute in question.

"In order to determine whether a dispute falls within the scope of the Convention, reference must be made solely to the subject-matter of the dispute. If, by virtue of its subject-matter, such as the appointment of an arbitrator, a dispute falls outside the scope of the Convention, the existence of a preliminary issue which the court must resolve in order to determine the dispute cannot, whatever that issue may be, justify application of the Convention." [26]

"It would also be contrary to the principle of legal certainty, which is one of the objectives pursued by the Convention (see judgment in Case 38/81 *Effer v*

A *Kantner* [1982] ECR 825, paragraph 6) for the applicability of the exclusion laid down in Article 1 (4) of the Convention to vary according to the existence or otherwise of a preliminary issue, which might be raised at any time by the parties." [27]

"It follows that, in the case before the Court, the fact that a preliminary issue relates to the existence or validity of the arbitration agreement does not affect the exclusion from the scope of the Convention of a dispute concerning the appointment of an arbitrator." [28]

B

The Court ruled:

"Article 1 (4) of the Convention must be interpreted as meaning that the exclusion provided for therein extends to litigation pending before a national court concerning the appointment of an arbitrator, even if the existence or validity of an arbitration agreement is a preliminary issue in that litigation."

C

Comment

The European Court has pointed to the limited importance of Art 220 of the EC Treaty as an aid to interpretation of the Brussels Convention because Member States are free collectively to determine the scope of any agreement reached under that Article. The Court has given a judgment which is consistent with the reports of the experts on the original Brussels Convention of 1968 and on the Accession Conventions of 1978 and 1982. In particular, the Schlosser Report on the 1978 Accession Convention had clarified for the benefit of the United Kingdom that the Brussels Convention: "in no way restricts the freedom of the parties to submit disputes to arbitration. This applies even to proceedings for which the . . . Convention has established exclusive jurisdiction. The . . . Convention does not cover court proceedings which are ancillary to arbitration proceedings, for example the appointment or dismissal of arbitrators".

E (OJ 1979 C59/93).

The Court made use of a general principle of Community law, legal certainty, to support its view that the preliminary issue of whether or not the arbitration clause was part of the contract could not affect the applicability of the exclusion of arbitration from the scope of the Brussels Convention when the subject matter of the dispute is the appointment of an arbitrator.

F

Powell Duffryn plc v Petereit (C-214/89) [1992] ECR I-1745.

(1) 1968 Convention, Art 17; 1982 Act, Sched 1, Art 17; Sched 4, Art 17; Sched 8, Rule 5 — Prorogation — Agreement conferring jurisdiction in the statute of a company — Does Art 17 have an independent meaning? — Formal requirements — Particular legal relationship.

Legal background

G The relevant part of the version of Art 17 of the Brussels Convention applicable to this case, containing the amendments made by the 1978 Accession Convention but not those made by the 1989 Accession Convention, is as follows:

"If the parties, one or more of whom is domiciled in a Contracting State, have agreed that a court or the courts of a Contracting State are to have jurisdiction to settle any disputes which have arisen or which may arise in connection with a particular legal relationship, H that court or those courts shall have exclusive jurisdiction. Such an agreement conferring jurisdiction shall be either in writing or evidenced in writing or, in international trade or commerce, in a form which accords with practices in that trade or commerce of which the parties are or ought to have been aware."

Facts

In 1979 Powell Duffryn plc, an English company, subscribed for shares in IBM — Holding AG, a I German company. In 1980 at a general meeting of the German company the following clause was inserted into its statutes: "By subscribing for or acquiring shares or interim certificates the shareholder submits, with regard to all disputes between himself and the company or its organs, to the jurisdiction of the courts ordinarily competent to entertain suits concerning the company." In 1981 and 1982 the English company subscribed for further shares in the German company. In 1983 the German company was put into liquidation J and Mr Petereit, acting as liquidator, brought an action before the Landgericht Mainz claiming that Powell Duffryn had failed to make certain cash payments it owed to the German company and for recovery of dividends which he maintained had been wrongly paid to the English company. The Landgericht dismissed Powell Duffryn's plea of lack of jurisdiction. On appeal the Oberlandesgericht Koblenz decided to refer several questions on the interpretation of Art 17 of the Brussels Convention to K the European Court for a preliminary ruling.

Law

The European Court, assembled as a full Court of 13 judges, stated:

"The concept of 'agreement conferring jurisdiction' is decisive for the assignment, in derogation from the general rules on jurisdiction, of exclusive jurisdiction to the court of the Contracting State designated by the parties. Having regard to the objective and general L scheme of the Brussels Convention, and in order to ensure as far as possible the equality and uniformity of the rights and obligations arising out of the Convention for the Contracting States and persons concerned, therefore, it is important that the concept of 'agreement conferring jurisdiction' should not be interpreted simply as referring to the national law of one or other of the States concerned." [13]

"Accordingly, as the Court has held for similar reasons as regards, in particular, the concept of 'matters relating to a contract' and other concepts, referred to in Article 5 of the Convention, which serve as criteria for determining special jurisdiction (see the judgment in Case 34/82 *Peters v ZNAV* [1983] ECR 987 [1985 SLT (News) A8], paragraphs 9 and 10), the concept of 'agreement conferring jurisdiction' in Article 17 must be regarded as an independent concept." [14]

"In that connection, it must be recalled that, when it was requested to interpret that concept of 'matters relating to a contract', referred to in Article 5 of the Convention, the Court held that the obligations imposed on a person in his capacity as member of an association were to be considered to be contractual obligations, on the ground that membership of an association created between the members close links of the same kind as those which are created between the parties to a contract (see the judgment in Case 34/82 *Peters v ZNAV*, referred to above, paragraph 13)." [15]

"Similarly, the links between the shareholders of a company are comparable to those between the parties to a contract. The setting up of a company is the expression of the existence of a community of interests between the shareholders in the pursuit of a common objective. In order to achieve that objective each shareholder is assigned, as regards other shareholders and the organs of the company, rights and obligations set out in the company's statutes. It follows that, for the purposes of the application of the Brussels Convention, the company's statutes must be regarded as a contract covering both the relations between the shareholders and also the relations between them and the company they set up." [16]

"It follows that a clause conferring jurisdiction in the statutes of a company limited by shares is an agreement, within the meaning of Article 17 of the Brussels Convention, which is binding on all the shareholders." [17]

"It is immaterial that the shareholder against whom the clause conferring jurisdiction is invoked opposed the adoption of the clause or that he became a shareholder after the clause was adopted." [18]

"By becoming and by remaining a shareholder in a company, the shareholder agrees to be subject to all the provisions appearing in the statutes of the company and to the decisions adopted by the organs of the company, in accordance with the provisions of the applicable national law and the statutes, even if he does not agree with some of those provisions or decisions." [19]

"Any other interpretation of Article 17 of the Brussels Convention would lead to a multiplication of the heads of jurisdiction for disputes arising from the same legal and factual relationship between the company and its shareholders and would run counter to the principle of legal certainty." [20]

"When the company's statutes contain a clause conferring jurisdiction, every shareholder is deemed to be aware of that clause and actually to consent to the assignment of jurisdiction for which it provides, if the statutes are lodged in a place to which the shareholder

may have access, such as the seat of the company, or are contained in a public register." [28]

"Pursuant to Article 17 of the Brussels Convention, jurisdiction is conferred for the purpose of settling disputes which have arisen or which may arise 'in connection with a particular legal relationship'." [30]

"That requirement is intended to limit the scope of an agreement conferring jurisdiction solely to disputes which arise from the legal relationship in connection with which the agreement was entered into. Its purpose is to avoid a party being taken by surprise by the assignment of jurisdiction to a given forum as regards all disputes which may arise out of its relationship with the other party to the contract and stem from a relationship other than that in connection with which the agreement conferring jurisdiction was made." [31]

"In that regard, a clause conferring jurisdiction contained in a company's statutes satisfies that requirement if it relates to disputes which have arisen or which may arise in connection with the relationship between the company and its shareholders as such." [32]

"The question whether in the present case the clause conferring jurisdiction is to be regarded as having such an effect is a question of interpretation which is a matter for the national court to resolve." [33]

The European Court ruled:

"(1) A clause contained in the statutes of a company limited by shares and adopted in accordance with the provisions of the applicable national law and those statutes themselves conferring jurisdiction on a court of a Contracting State to settle disputes between that company and its shareholders constitutes an agreement conferring jurisdiction within the meaning of Article 17 of the Brussels Convention;

"(2) Irrespective of how shares are acquired, the formal requirements laid down in Article 17 must be considered to be complied with in regard to any shareholder if the clause conferring jurisdiction is contained in the statutes of the company and those statutes are lodged in a place to which the shareholder may have access or are contained in a public register;

"(3) The requirement that a dispute arise in connection with a particular legal relationship within the meaning of Article 17 is satisfied if the clause conferring jurisdiction contained in the statutes of a company may be interpreted as referring to the disputes between the company and its shareholders as such;

"(4) It is for the national court to interpret the clause conferring jurisdiction invoked before it in order to determine which disputes fall within its scope."

Comment

The crucial part of the Court's judgment is con-

A tained in paras 18 to 20. These paragraphs are all obiter because Powell Duffryn had voted in favour of the jurisdiction clause at the general meeting of the German company in 1980. Nevertheless, they represent the Court's response to the issue which divided academic opinion (see the Advocate General's opinion at p 1762) and on which the German Government had argued for the inapplicability of Art 17 (see p 1751). The thrust of the argument is that a shareholder who votes against a jurisdiction clause or did not take part in the vote has not "agreed" to that clause and there-

B fore there is no "agreement conferring jurisdiction" within the terms of Art 17. The Court followed the

rejection of this argument by the Commission (p 1752) and by Advocate General Tesauro. The latter G praised the Court for its "attention and sensitivity to the demands of international trade and more generally, to the actual functioning of the business world" (p 1760) in its avoidance of an excessively strict application of the requirement of consensus in Art 17. The Advocate General emphasises that a shareholder must be deemed to accept "all the rights and obligations flowing from the statutes" of the company. If a shareholder objects to a jurisdiction clause the only way to avoid being bound by it is to H sell the shares (see pp 1762-1765).

C

D

E

F

I

J

K

L

THE
SCOTS LAW TIMES

SHERIFF COURT
REPORTS

1994

EDINBURGH
PUBLISHED BY W GREEN, THE SCOTTISH LAW PUBLISHER
21 ALVA STREET

INDEX OF CASES

ACCORDING TO NAMES OF PARTIES

REPORTS OF CASES

DECIDED IN

THE SHERIFF COURTS OF SCOTLAND

1994

Edited by
DANIEL KELLY, LLB, *Advocate*

Note: **Cases in this volume may be cited 1994 SLT (Sh Ct)**

Thus: **Rochester Poster Services Ltd v A G Barr plc, 1994 SLT (Sh Ct) 2.**

Rochester Poster Services Ltd v A G Barr plc

SHERIFF COURT OF GLASGOW AND
STRATHKELVIN AT GLASGOW

SHERIFF PRINCIPAL N D MACLEOD, QC

17 MARCH 1993

Recompense — Payments in respect of use of portion of heritable subjects — Use of gable end of building for advertisement — Whether party occupying site liable to make payment in respect of occupation.

After the expiry of a lease of a site for advertising purposes, the advertisers continued to occupy the site for a period of 17 months. The owners of the site raised an action claiming payment from the occupiers of the site. After debate, the sheriff sustained the occupiers' pleas to the relevancy and specification and dismissed the action. The owners appealed to the sheriff principal, arguing that the law of recompense was applicable.

Held, that in the particular circumstances of occupation of land, there being a presumption of benefit and the occupier of land being required to pay a sum representing the value of that benefit, the remedy sought by the owners was one provided by Scots law (p 3C-E); and appeal *allowed.*

Stewart, *Restitution,* p 41, *approved.*

Action of payment

Rochester Poster Services Ltd raised an action of payment against A G Barr plc. Both parties had preliminary pleas to the relevancy and specification. After debate the sheriff (W G Stevenson, QC) sustained the defenders' plea and dismissed the action. The pursuers appealed to the sheriff principal.

On 17 March 1993 the sheriff principal *allowed* the appeal and *appointed* the cause to the procedure roll to consider the pursuers' preliminary plea.

THE SHERIFF PRINCIPAL (N D MACLEOD, QC).—This action relates to what the pleadings describe as "the brick chimney head located on and forming a continuation of the southmost gable wall of the building known as and forming 105 to 115 Union Street and 65 to 69 Gordon Street, Glasgow". That is no doubt an accurate but rather a prosaic description of a well known landmark in the centre of this city: the high gable end near the Central station that, for many many years, bore a large neon sign advertising "Barr's Irn Bru".

The defenders, apparently, originally leased the site for the advertisement from the British Railways Board. That was back in 1950. Latterly, they held the lease of it from British Transport Advertising Ltd who were, in 1990, succeeded by the pursuers. The lease expired at the end of 1992. Before it expired, negotia-

tions took place between the pursuers and the defenders with a view to the defenders taking a fresh lease. These negotiations broke down. It seems to be agreed that the defenders continued to occupy the site for a 17 month period beyond the date of the expiry of the lease. The pursuers now seek, by this action, payment from the defenders of £102,794.08 in respect of that period.

Both parties have pleas to the relevancy and specification of each other's pleadings, and the case came to debate before the sheriff. He pronounced the following interlocutor: "The sheriff, having heard parties' procurators on their preliminary pleas, dismisses the cause, on defenders' motion. Finds the pursuer liable to the defender in the expenses of the action, allows an account thereof to be given in and remits the same when lodged to auditor of court to tax and report thereon." In effect, the defenders' plea was sustained with the result that the action was dismissed. Against that disposal of the case the pursuers have appealed.

At the outset of the appeal the solicitor for the appellants informed me that, at the debate, the sheriff had advised her that he did not require to hear her in support of the pursuers' preliminary plea. In the result that plea remains undisposed of.

For the appellants, it was submitted that the sheriff had erred in his understanding of the law. It was argued that the circumstances of this case, involving the unauthorised use of property, took it into a specific branch of the law of recompense. The law governing it was that stated in *Glen v Roy* (1882) 10 R 239. Where a party was in unauthorised occupation of premises, "the presumption is that the party in possession is liable to pay the real worth of the subject occupied . . . the onus lying on him to show that he got it for less, or, . . . for nothing at all". The case of *Earl of Fife v Wilson* (1864) 3 M 323 was to similar effect: "He had possession. . . . He has had the article and must pay the price." A recent illustration of this particular branch of the law of recompense was the case of *Shetland Islands Council v BP Petroleum Development Ltd,* 1990 SLT 82. Where a party was in unauthorised occupation of property, the law implied an obligation to pay a reasonable sum. In their solicitor's submission the appellants' averments satisfied the requirements of the law: the respondents' occupation of the premises without the intention of its being gratuitous had been averred, and the reasonableness of the payment sought, with specification of the reason for arriving at it, had also been averred. The remedy sought was a remedy provided by the law. She moved that the appeal be allowed and the sheriff's interlocutor be recalled.

In my opinion, the appellants' solicitor is correct. In our law the use of another's property attracts the obligation to pay for its use. In the recently published work, Stewart on *Restitution,* at p 41, the learned author deals with this branch of the law in a paragraph entitled "Occupation of Premises". His comment, in my respectful view, admirably sets out the law:

"Occupation of premises is a benefit and it is usually the case that an owner can make money from his land. The Scots courts for a long time had no difficulty in finding that someone who lived on land had been enriched. In *Earl of Fife v Samuel Wilson*, possession on the basis of a lease which was later found not to exist was sufficient to allow the court to hold the possessor liable in an amount equal to the amount under the putative lease. Another benefit recognised in the law of Scotland is mere occupation of subjects. In *Glen v Roy* the defender was in occupation: applying *Young v Cockburn* the Lord Justice Clerk (Moncreiff) stated the law to be that there was a presumption that a person in occupation was presumed to pay the real worth of the subjects occupied which was the annual value unless the occupier could show that he was entitled to pay nothing or less. Despite the fact that the judgment states that the defender failed to prove he was not a tenant, the obligation is not contractual but is restitution of the use made of the land. The basis is that no reasonable man would say other than that the occupation of land was a benefit."

Recompense is an equitable remedy and each case, ultimately, turns on its own facts. In my opinion, in the circumstances encountered here, the sheriff was in error to dismiss the claim for lack of averment of quantum lucratus. In the particular circumstance of occupation of land, there appears to be a presumption of benefit; and the occupier of land is required to pay a sum representing the value of that benefit. Various formulae have been employed to ascertain the value of particular instances of occupation, for example, fair value (*Glen v Roy*), the rent paid in a pre-existing lease (*Earl of Fife*) and reasonable rent (*HMV Fields Properties Ltd v Skirt 'n' Slack Centre of London Ltd*, 1987 SLT 2). The value placed on the site in this case is described as reasonable, its reasonableness being demonstrated by reference to an annual "fee" discussed between parties during negotiations.

In my opinion the remedy sought by the appellants is one that appears to be provided by our law. In the absence of circumstances demonstrating a mutual intention that occupation of land should be enjoyed gratuitously, the owner of that land appears to be entitled to recover from the occupier a reasonable payment in respect of such occupation. The appellant's plea in law, in my opinion, invokes that principle.

The appellants have averred: "No agreement was reached between the parties to regulate the defenders' occupation of the premises. The defenders vacated the premises on 22 July 1991. The defenders have made no payments to the pursuers in respect of their occupation of the premises for the period 2 February 1990 to 22 July 1991. No agreement was entered into between the pursuers and the defenders which entitled the defenders to occupy the premises gratuitously. The pursuers did not intend the defenders to occupy the premises gratuitously. The defenders having occupied the premises between 2 February 1990 and 22 July 1991 and having failed to make a payment to

the pursuers in respect of their occupation, there being no agreement in existence between the pursuers and defenders which would entitle the defenders to occupy the premises gratuitously, the pursuers are entitled to recompense in respect of the defenders' occupation of the subjects" (art 3 of the condescendence).

They have also averred: "In the course of said negotiations referred to in cond 3 hereof, the defenders' agents prepared a draft minute of agreement between the pursuers and the defenders regulating the defenders' occupation of the premises. In terms of clause fourteenth of said draft minute of agreement in consideration of the right to have the sign and its associated works and services thereto located on the premises the defenders undertook to pay the pursuers an annual fee of £70,000, the first such payment being due in advance on 2 February 1990. Said draft minute of agreement is produced and incorporated herein brevitatis causa. In terms of said draft minute of agreement the defenders indicated that a fee of £70,000 per annum in respect of the occupation of the subjects was a reasonable rent for the premises. The said sum of £70,000 per annum does represent a reasonable rent for the defenders' occupation of the premises for the period from 2 February 1990 until 22 July 1991. The pursuers are entitled to recompense equivalent to a reasonable rent at said rate in respect of the defenders' occupation of the premises for said period which amounts to £102,794.08. This is the sum sued for" (art 4 of the condescendence).

In my opinion, the appellants have here sufficiently raised a recognisable claim and are entitled to be allowed to prove it.

Counsel for the respondents would have had me regard *Glen v Roy* as a case where the circumstances indicated a de facto lease. Certainly the interlocutor there reads: "the defender has failed to prove that he possessed the subjects in question otherwise than as tenant". But these words are immediately followed by the words "and is bound to account for the *fair value* of his occupation" (my italics). In the interlocutor the phrase "fair value" is preferred to the word "rent". It is clear from Lord Moncreiff's judgment that the evidence as to rent bore only upon Roy's assertion that he was under no obligation to pay. The circumstances, in my view, were not those of a de facto lease but rather circumstances giving rise to "the presumption of law . . . that . . . (Roy) . . . occupied as tenant, whether he actually paid rent or not, and whether there was a written lease or not". Lord Moncreiff referred to Roy as having "failed to prove that he was an occupant under no obligation to pay rent". The reference to "rent" is a somewhat loose reference, as is pointed out by Rankine on *Leases* (3rd ed), p 310.

Counsel for the respondents also submitted that the appellants' averments lacked averment of several of the elements necessary to support a claim for recompense. He referred in this connection to the general statement of the law of recompense in *Varney (Scotland) Ltd v Burgh of Lanark*, 1976 SLT 46; 1974

A SC 245. That was a case which, although concerned with the principle of recompense, was not concerned with the particular circumstance that has given rise to this claim, namely, the occupation of land. As the solicitor for the appellants put it, this circumstance seems to constitute a specific branch of the law of recompense.

In my view this court must recall the sheriff's interlocutor dismissing the action.

B Since the appellants are insisting on their plea to the relevancy and specification of the respondents' pleadings the cause will require to be appointed to the procedure roll, so that parties may decide on further procedure.

In response to counsel's motion I have sanctioned the employment of junior counsel. The appeal required consideration of an area of law not commonly encountered in practice, and one in which the authorities are not always clear. Also in response to counsel's motion I have put the case out for hearing
C on expenses.

Solicitors for Pursuers, Bird Semple Fyfe Ireland, Glasgow — Counsel for Defenders, Woolman; Solicitors, Tindal Oatts, Glasgow.

D

Cambridge Street Properties Ltd v City of Glasgow District Licensing Board

SHERIFF COURT OF GLASGOW AND
STRATHKELVIN AT GLASGOW

E SHERIFF PRINCIPAL N D MACLEOD, QC

6 APRIL 1993

Licensing — Appeal — Refusal by sheriff to allow adjustment — Refusal by sheriff of leave to appeal — Appeal to Court of Session permissible — Competency of appeal to sheriff principal — Sheriff Courts (Scotland) Act 1907 (7 Edw VII, c 51), s 27 — Licensing (Scotland) Act 1976 (c 66), s 39 (8).

Section 27 of the Sheriff Courts (Scotland) Act 1907
F provides a right of appeal against a sheriff's interlocutor to the sheriff principal with leave of the sheriff. Section 39 (8) of the Licensing (Scotland) Act 1976 permits a party to an appeal to the sheriff under the Act to appeal to the Court of Session if dissatisfied in point of law with a decision of the sheriff.

The holders of a public house licence which had been suspended by the local licensing board appealed to the sheriff by summary application against the suspension. The sheriff refused to allow an adjustment proposed by the applicants on the ground that it came

G too late and would have significantly widened the scope of inquiry at the imminent appeal. Leave to appeal was refused. The applicants appealed to the sheriff principal.

Held, (1) (the point not being disputed) that, the sheriff having refused leave to appeal, an appeal could not be taken under the 1907 Act (p 6B-C); (2) that the method of review being laid down in the 1976 Act, all other conventional modes of appeal were excluded (p 6C-D); and (3) that the power of the sheriff principal to entertain an appeal against an incompetent
H interlocutor did not extend to reviewing the exercise of a sheriff's discretion in a summary application (p 6H-I); and appeal *refused.*

Opinion, that the sheriff had been entitled to exercise his discretion in the way that he did (p 6J).

Opinion, provisionally, that the decision in *Brown v Hamilton District Council*, 1983 SLT 397, did not affect the sheriff principal's power and responsibility for the proper regulation of the conduct of judicial business within the sheriffdom (p 6E-F).   I

Summary application

Cambridge Street Properties Ltd and Audrey Mullen appealed to the sheriff against the suspension of their public house licence by City of Glasgow District Licensing Board. The Chief Constable of Strathclyde Police was the second respondent. The sheriff (F J Keane) refused to allow an adjustment proposed by the applicants. Leave to appeal was also refused. J
The applicants appealed to the sheriff principal.

On 6 April 1993 the sheriff principal *refused* the appeal.

THE SHERIFF PRINCIPAL (N D MACLEOD, QC).—This is an appeal in a summary application.

The appellants, whose public house licence has been suspended by the local licensing board, have appealed K
to the sheriff against the suspension. This appeal is one taken against the sheriff's refusal to allow adjustment which the sheriff considered was being made unduly late in the day having regard to the nature of the adjustment proposed. It was the sheriff's view that the adjustment proposed would have significantly widened the scope of inquiry at the hearing of the appeal which was due to take place in a few days' time. The appellants sought leave of the sheriff to appeal, but this has been refused.   L

In limine counsel for the second named respondent, the chief constable, objected to the appeal as being incompetent and moved that it be dismissed.

The Court of Session is empowered in terms of s 39 (9) of the Licensing (Scotland) Act 1976 to make rules for the conduct of proceedings under s 39. The appropriate Act of Sederunt (Act of Sederunt (Appeals under the Licensing (Scotland) Act 1976) 1977, as amended by the Act of Sederunt (Appeals under the Licensing (Scotland) Act 1976) (Amendment) 1979;

SI 1977/1622 and SI 1979/1520) regulates appeals
A procedure under that section; and reg 2 thereof is in
the following terms: "2. Any appeal to the sheriff
under section 39 of the 1976 Act against a decision of
a licensing board shall be made by way of initial writ
under the Sheriff Courts (Scotland) Acts 1907 and
1913 and such appeals shall be disposed of as a
summary application as defined in the said Acts."

The definition of a "summary application" is to be
found in the interpretation section, s 3, of the Sheriff
Courts (Scotland) Act 1907. It is in the following
B terms: "(p) 'Summary application' means and includes
all applications of a summary nature brought under
the common law jurisdiction of the sheriff, and all
applications, whether by appeal or otherwise, brought
under any Act of Parliament which provides, or,
according to any practice in the sheriff court, which
allows that the same shall be disposed of in a summary
manner, but which does not more particularly define
in what form the same shall be heard, tried, and
determined."

C Section 50 of the 1907 Act also refers to the disposal
of summary applications and the relevant part is as
follows: "50. In summary applications (where a
hearing is necessary) the sheriff shall appoint the
application to be heard at a diet to be fixed by him,
and at that or any subsequent diet (without record of
evidence unless the sheriff shall order a record) shall
summarily dispose of the matter and give his
judgment in writing".

That is the legislative background to appeals taken
D from a licensing board to the sheriff in a matter of this
kind.

As to the taking of appeals from the sheriff, s 39 (8)
of the Licensing (Scotland) Act 1976 is as follows:
"(8) If any party to an appeal to the sheriff under any
provision of this Act . . . is dissatisfied in point of law
with a decision of the sheriff, he may appeal therefrom
to the Court of Session within 28 days from the date
of that decision."

E Having regard to the fact that appeal to the sheriff
is by way of summary application, the second proviso
to s 50 of the Sheriff Courts (Scotland) Act 1907 is of
some relevance. It reads as follows: "Provided also
that nothing contained in this Act shall affect any right
of appeal provided by any Act of Parliament under
which a summary application is brought."

Sections 27 and 28 of the 1907 Act provide for
appeals to the sheriff principal and to the Court of
Session, but in the context of this appeal, it is notable
F that subs (2) of s 28 provides: "Nothing in this section
nor in section 27 of this Act contained shall affect any
right of appeal or exclusion of such right provided by
any Act of Parliament in force for the time being."

It is also to be noted, in this context, that the only
rules of the ordinary cause rules applicable to
summary applications are rules 1, 3, 4, 5 (3), 10 to 12
and 14 to 19; and they apply to a summary application
only insofar as they are not inconsistent with s 50 of
the 1907 Act. (See reg 5 of SI 1983/747, as amended
by SI 1988/1978.)

Counsel for the second named respondent, arguing
that the appeal was incompetent, drew attention first G
to the terms of s 39 (8) of the 1976 Act. In his submission its terms excluded appeal otherwise than to the
Court of Session. He drew particular attention to the
generality of the wording and submitted that the
wording would have been quite different if by "a
decision of the sheriff" had been meant only a decision
on the merits of an appeal. Its general terms, in his
submission, clearly indicated that appeal against
decisions in general was restricted in that way. It was
restricted in a way typical of such legislation. As H
authority for the proposition that s 39 (8) of the Act
provided a complete code of appeal he cited the case
of *Troc Sales Ltd v Kirkcaldy District Licensing Board*,
1982 SLT (Sh Ct) 77, and as an illustration of a
decision that was not a decision on the merits but had
been appealed to the Court of Session he referred me
to *Saleem v Hamilton District Licensing Board*, 1993
SLT 1092. Next, drawing attention to the terms of ss
27, 28 and 50 of the Sheriff Courts (Scotland) Act
1907, he submitted that the Act offered the appellants I
no conventional right or mode of appeal; and even if
such a right were necessarily implied, the interlocutor
in question was one that could competently be
appealed only with leave of the sheriff. Leave to
appeal had been refused. As to any common law power
in the sheriff principal to entertain appeal against
irregularity or incompetency of procedure he argued
that, in the light of the decision in *Brown v Hamilton
District Council*, 1983 SLT 397, asserting the exclusive jurisdiction of the Court of Session, no such J
power could be claimed; and cases like *Ladbrokes the
Bookmakers v Hamilton District Council*, 1977 SLT
(Sh Ct) 86 could no longer be relied on as good law.
In any event, in his submission, these were cases
dealing with the avoidance of decision, and in this case
there had been no such avoidance. Counsel finally
made reference to *Leitch v Scottish Legal Burial Society*
(1870) 9 M 40; *County Council of Roxburgh v
Dalrymple's Trs* (1894) 21 R 1063; and *Waddell v
Dumfries and Galloway Regional Council*, 1979 SLT K
(Sh Ct) 45. Cases involving finality clauses, he submitted, were also to be distinguished from cases such
as this where an avenue of appeal was provided by
statute.

The solicitor for the first named respondents
adopted counsel's argument and submissions.

For the appellants, senior counsel argued that
appeal was competent, objection to it should be
repelled and the court should proceed to deal with the L
merits of the appeal. The right of appeal prescribed in
s 39 (8) of the Act related, in his submission, only to
a decision on the merits or to a decision that was otherwise final. *Troc Sales Ltd* was an appeal to the sheriff
principal from a final decision and was therefore
clearly correct. The decision appealed against here
was not a final decision. It was an interlocutory
decision and a purely procedural one. The appellants
wished to argue that the sheriff's decision in this
matter was incompetent and appeal against an
incompetent interlocutor was competent: *Archer's Trs*

A *v Alexander & Sons* (1910) 27 Sh Ct Rep 11. There were numerous reported examples of sheriffs principal having entertained appeals in proceedings under the licensing legislation. The regularity of procedure was reviewed by the sheriffs principal in *Chief Constable of Strathclyde v Hamilton & District Bookmakers Club*, 1977 SLT (Sh Ct) 78; *Hutcheon v Hamilton District Licensing Board*, 1978 SLT (Sh Ct) 44; *Waddell v Dumfries and Galloway Regional Council*, 1979 SLT (Sh Ct) 45; and *Charles Watson (Scotland) Ltd v Glasgow District Licensing Board*, 1980 SLT (Sh Ct)

B 37. In his submission it was always competent for a party aggrieved by a sheriff's decision to appeal to the sheriff principal on the ground that the decision was irregular, and, as such, incompetent. That is what the appellant sought now to do.

It seems to be common ground that this appeal cannot be entertained as a conventional appeal. By conventional I mean an appeal in terms of s 27 of the Sheriff Courts (Scotland) Act 1907. It relates to an interlocutor of a kind that may be appealed only with

C leave of the sheriff. Here, the sheriff has refused leave.

The Licensing (Scotland) Act 1976 provides, in s 39 (8), specific provision for appeal against a decision of the sheriff and lays down the method of review. Where that is done, all other conventional modes of appeal are excluded by necessary implication: *Dodds v Ayr County Council*, 1954 SC 86; *Troc Sales Ltd v Kirkcaldy District Licensing Board* and the cases referred to therein.

D Since conventional modes of appeal are excluded, and since appeal is restricted to the Court of Session, the competence of this appeal depends entirely upon the sheriff principal's power to entertain appeal against an incompetent interlocutor, the power expressed in *Archer's Trs*.

Counsel for the second named respondent, with whose argument the agent for the first named respondent associated himself, argued that, since the decision

E of the House of Lords in *Brown v Hamilton District Council* in 1983 indicating that supervisory jurisdiction over inferior courts was vested exclusively in the Court of Session, the common law powers of the sheriff principal to rectify irregularity or incompetency in a sheriff's decision could no longer be invoked. The argument was not elaborated or answered in detail, and until I have had the benefit of full argument on the matter I shall remain in doubt on the point. I incline to the view that this (very par-

F ticular) power derived from the sheriff principal's responsibility at common law for the proper regulation of the conduct of judicial business within the sheriffdom was not within the contemplation of Lord Fraser whose speech provided the basis for the now well recognised procedures of judicial review.

Although I am of opinion that the power the appellants seek to invoke exists and would, in appropriate circumstances, entitle this court to grant the relief sought, I am of opinion that the circumstances of this case are not appropriate to the invoking of this power.

The appellants' contention is that the sheriff's decision not to allow further amendment was a purely

G procedural decision and therefore a decision of the kind subject to review by the sheriff principal. I think that contention misunderstands the true nature of the sheriff's decision.

Appeal to the sheriff is by summary application. In such applications the sheriff may deal with procedure so as to meet the justice of the case, and he may prescribe such procedure as he thinks requisite: *O'Donnell v Wilson*, 1910 SC 799 per Lord Salvesen at p 803, and *Park v Coltness Iron Co Ltd*, 1913 SC

H 1163 per Lord President Dunedin at p 1165. Procedure in summary applications is entrusted to the sheriff's discretion. Accordingly, in my opinion, the sheriff's decision not to allow further adjustment was not purely a matter of procedure, it was the exercise of this particular discretion. The sheriff principal's responsibility for the proper regulation of the conduct of judicial business does not extend to regulating a sheriff's exercise of a discretion.

The tests applicable to the exercise of a discretion I are well known. They are a matter of law. The sheriff's exercise of his discretion here might perhaps have been reviewed by the Court of Session, but not by invoking any power there may be in the sheriff principal to rectify irregularity or incompetency of procedure.

For these reasons I have sustained the respondents' objection to the competency of the appeal.

I should perhaps add that, had I proceeded to con- J sider the merits of the appeal, I should have been unable to hold that the sheriff's exercise of his discretion was wrong. In my opinion the sheriff was entitled to give the weight he did to the effect that adjustment would have upon the scope of the appeal and to its last minute timing.

As successful parties to the appeal the respondents are entitled to their expenses.

In view of the intricacy of the legal questions posed K by the appeal, I have sanctioned the employment of junior counsel by the appellants and by the second named respondents.

Counsel for Appellants, Henderson, QC; Solicitors, Brunton Miller, Glasgow — Solicitor for First Respondents, P Romano, City of Glasgow District Council — Counsel for Second Respondents, Peoples; Solicitor, J A Wilson. L

[This decision is under appeal to the Court of Session.]

Stroud v Stroud

SHERIFF COURT OF LOTHIAN AND
BORDERS AT EDINBURGH

SHERIFF PRINCIPAL C G B NICHOLSON, QC

14 APRIL 1993

*Process — Divorce — Decree in undefended action —
Appeal — Available forms of appeal — Ordinary appeal
or appeal after late appearance by defender in actions of
divorce and separation — Relevant considerations in
support of ordinary appeal — Sheriff Courts (Scotland)
Act 1907 (7 Edw VII, c 51), s 27 and Sched, rule 59B.*

In an action for divorce and ancillary orders no
notice of intention to defend or minute under ordinary
cause rule 34 was lodged by the defender. The pursuer
minuted for decree, which was granted. The defender
appealed to the sheriff principal but made no application to the sheriff to invoke rule 59B, which allows a
sheriff to make an order allowing a defender in an
action of divorce who has not lodged a notice of intention to defend or defences to appeal within 14 days of
the decree of divorce. The defender argued that
similar considerations could be taken into account in
an ordinary appeal to those which were appropriate
under rule 59B.

Held, that rule 59B provided a form of reponing
procedure to which different considerations applied
from what was required for an ordinary appeal to
succeed, and since no error on the part of the sheriff
had been demonstrated, the appeal had to fail (pp 8G-I
and 9B); and appeal *refused.*

Bangs v Bangs, Edinburgh sheriff court, 13
December 1984, unreported, and Macphail, *Sheriff
Court Practice,* para 22-44, *not followed.*

Action of divorce

Mrs Anne Buchanan Flockhart or Stroud raised an
action of divorce against Derek George Stroud. No
notice of intention to defend or minute having been
lodged, on 8 March 1993 the sheriff (N E D
Thomson) granted decree as craved. The defender
appealed to the sheriff principal.

On 14 April 1993 the sheriff principal *refused* the
appeal.

**THE SHERIFF PRINCIPAL (C G B
NICHOLSON, QC).**—The action to which this
appeal relates is one in which the pursuer seeks decree
of divorce, decree for payment of a periodical
allowance, decree for payment of a capital sum, and
sundry other ancillary orders. Warrant to cite the
defender was granted in December 1991, and it
appears that some time thereafter the pursuer's agents
gave an undertaking to the agents who were then
acting for the defender that they would not minute for
decree while negotiations on financial matters were
taking place. On that basis no notice of intention to
defend nor a minute under rule 34 of the ordinary

cause rules was lodged on behalf of the defender.
Some negotiations appear to have taken place thereafter, but they do not appear to have borne fruit and,
in August 1992, the defender's then agents withdrew
from acting, apparently on the basis that they were
unable to obtain instructions from the defender.

Towards the end of 1992 the defender for the first
time consulted his present solicitor and, on 1
December 1992, that solicitor received a letter from
the pursuer's solicitors stating that they were
instructed to proceed with the action as quickly as
possible. A few days later a motion for interim aliment
was lodged on behalf of the pursuer. It came before
the court on 8 December 1992 when it was continued
for one week since the defender's solicitor did not then
have information regarding the defender's financial
position. On 15 December the motion was again continued for one week for the same reason, with the
defender being ordained to lodge evidence of his
income. That order was not complied with and, on 22
December 1992, the pursuer was awarded interim
aliment at the rate of £65 per week. The defender's
solicitor intimated that decision to his client, but at
that stage he received no further instructions from the
defender.

Finally, in February 1993 the pursuer minuted for
an undefended decree in terms of the craves in the
initial writ. Prior to the papers and affidavits being
placed before the sheriff it appears that the sheriff
clerk telephoned the defender's solicitor's office to
inquire if they were still acting for the defender. The
sheriff clerk was told that there had been no involvement with the defender since January, and he then
proceeded to put the papers before the sheriff who, on
8 March 1993, granted decree as craved. The defender
has now appealed against that interlocutor.

In arguing that the appeal should be allowed the
solicitor for the defender submitted that there was
justification for the defender not having stated a
defence to the action in the fact that the undertaking
given to the defender's former solicitors about a year
ago had never been formally withdrawn. In that situation the defender was entitled to assume that the
pursuer would not minute for decree without giving
him notice of an intention to do so. In any event, the
defender had good grounds for challenging the pursuer's financial claims (though the nature of those
grounds was not specified), and the defender should
therefore be given an opportunity now to lodge a
minute under rule 34.

Before considering the nature, or the appropriate-
ness, of the foregoing submission I would observe that
in my view it must be questionable whether an undertaking given to former solicitors, which is around a
year old, and which was given in the expectation that
negotiations would take place, can now have any continuing force when negotiations have long since ceased
and when, in any event, the pursuer had indicated in
December 1992 that she was anxious to proceed with
the action as quickly as possible. Moreover, the decree
of 8 March did not come without any prior notice.

Notice was given, albeit by the sheriff clerk rather than on behalf of the pursuer, but no action was then taken on behalf of the defender. In my opinion the foregoing considerations substantially diminish the weight of the submissions which were advanced on behalf of the defender. However, I also consider that a much greater obstacle faces him in this appeal.

Although an undefended decree in an action for divorce may fall to be regarded as a decree in absence, at least for certain purposes (see *Paterson v Paterson*, 1958 SLT 205; 1958 SC 141), it is expressly excluded from the procedure of reponing as provided for in rule 28 of the ordinary cause rules. It therefore seems that the only remedy available to a defender against whom such a decree has passed is by way of an appeal. But, it appears, there are two possible avenues of appeal in such a case.

One is what might be termed a normal or traditional appeal against a final judgment under s 27 of the Sheriff Courts (Scotland) Act 1907, and I shall return in a moment to consider the nature of such an appeal. The other kind of appeal is the one provided under rule 59B of the ordinary cause rules. That rule, according to the headnote, deals expressly with "Late appearance by defender in actions of divorce and separation", and provides several remedies to such a defender including, in para (1) (c), the possibility of an appeal against a decree of divorce. In all cases, however, the remedy is at the discretion of the sheriff (by which must be meant the sheriff at first instance) who "may make an order" allowing the defender to seek one of the remedies provided for in the rule.

In the present case it is clear that the defender has not sought to invoke rule 59B since no application has been made to the sheriff; and in any event at the appeal hearing the solicitor for the defender expressly stated that he was not purporting to proceed under the rule, and was presenting the appeal in the normal way under s 27 of the 1907 Act. That, however, raises a question as to whether an appeal under s 27 is statable when, as I have indicated above, the appellant's submissions are in essence those which might normally be advanced in support of a reponing note and do not involve the slightest suggestion that the sheriff was in any way in error in pronouncing the interlocutor complained of.

In submitting that considerations appropriate to a reponing note can be taken into account in support of an ordinary appeal, the solicitor for the defender founded on a passage in Macphail, *Sheriff Court Practice*, where, at para 18-02, the learned author says that "An appeal is an application to a superior court . . . to reverse, vary or set aside the judgment . . . of an inferior court . . . on the ground that it was wrongly made or that as a matter of justice or law it requires to be corrected." The words "as a matter of justice" were founded on in particular.

Personally, I am not persuaded that words which appear to be a direct quotation from Halsbury's *Laws of England* (Vol 37, para 677) are necessarily the best guide to appeal practice in Scotland; but even if they

are a satisfactory guide, I am far from accepting that the words founded on in the present case have the effect of enabling an appellate court to allow an appeal simply on broadly equitable considerations, and without being able to find any error or misdirection in the judgment of the lower court.

Counsel for the pursuer's approach to this was, I think, to suggest that there must be a reason for the rule 59B procedure, and that reason must be to permit a form of appeal in which what I have called reponing note considerations can be advanced and considered. By contrast, such considerations are not appropriate in a conventional s 27 appeal which must proceed solely on the basis of seeking to show some error in the approach or in the decision of the inferior court. Upon that analysis, it was submitted, the defender could not succeed in the present appeal, though he might at least have had a presentable submission had he proceeded under rule 59B.

I have to say that I can see a lot of good sense in the distinction drawn by counsel for the pursuer since, on the one hand, it allows a defender in a divorce action a form of reponing process notwithstanding that in such an action decree is granted only after evidence has been considered, while at the same time it retains the traditional form of appeal (without leave of the sheriff) in cases where it can be asserted that the inferior court was in error. However, my attention was drawn to two authorities which appear at first sight to be at odds with that analysis. Both were brought to my attention by counsel for the pursuer.

The first is the case of *Reid v Reid*, 1960 SLT (Notes) 16, and the second is the unreported case of *Bangs v Bangs*, decided by Sheriff Principal O'Brien at Edinburgh on 13 December 1984, and referred to by Macphail in the footnote to para 22-44 of *Sheriff Court Practice*. In the case of *Reid* the First Division of the Court of Session recalled an interlocutor granting undefended decree of divorce, and allowed defences to be lodged. In the case of *Bangs* (the opinion in which I have been able to see) the sheriff principal refused an appeal against an undefended decree of divorce, but he did so on the facts of that particular case and not because, in the sheriff principal's opinion, such an appeal could never succeed except by showing error on the part of the inferior court. Indeed, at one point in his opinion the sheriff principal says: "Where a defender seeks to defend an action for the first time after an undefended decree has passed, I see no reason why the same considerations should not apply as in any other ordinary cause. In other words, he should be prepared to satisfy the sheriff principal (1) that he had good reason for not having entered the process at the proper time, and (2) that he has a prima facie defence."

In my opinion those two cases are distinguishable from the present case on the basis that they were decided before the existence of a rule such as now exists in rule 59B. On that basis I consider that the case of *Reid*, which was decided without any opinions being delivered, was very special and in no way binds

A me in my consideration of the two appeal procedures which are now available under rule 59B and under s 27 of the 1907 Act. So far as the case of *Bangs* is concerned, it too was concerned with normal appeal procedures and not with what is now rule 59B, and to that extent I consider that Macphail is wrong to refer to it in the part of his book which deals with the rule. Insofar as the passage which I have quoted above appears to support the view that an appeal (taken under s 27) can succeed if an appellant can establish reasonable excuse and a prima facie defence, I must

B take leave to differ from my learned predecessor. If what he says were correct, there would be no need for reponing procedures. Since such procedures do exist, that fact in my opinion confirms that something different will be required if an ordinary appeal is to succeed.

Since in the present case the defender has chosen to appeal in the ordinary way under s 27, and since he has not demonstrated any error on the part of the sheriff, it follows that this appeal must fail. It must also follow that the defender will be liable to the

C pursuer in the expenses of the appeal. Counsel for the pursuer sought certification of the appeal as suitable for his employment, but this was opposed on behalf of the defender. In my opinion the appeal raised issues of some difficulty, and I have therefore granted certification.

———————

Counsel for Pursuer, Mundy; Solicitors, Mackenzie & Dunn, SSC, Edinburgh — Solicitors for Defender, R J
D *Macleod & Co, Edinburgh.*

Stephen v Woodend Bowling
E # Club

SHERIFF COURT OF GRAMPIAN,
HIGHLAND AND ISLANDS AT ABERDEEN
SHERIFF PRINCIPAL R D IRELAND, QC
12 FEBRUARY 1993

Process — Appeal — Appeal from sheriff to sheriff principal — Competency — Application to sheriff whose decision "shall be final" — Decision that objection incom-
F *petent and irrelevant — Licensing (Scotland) Act 1976 (c 66), s 117 (2).*

Licensing — Application for certificate of registration of club — Objection by local residents that premises not suitable or convenient for sale of alcohol — Decision that objection incompetent and irrelevant — Competency of appeal — Licensing (Scotland) Act 1976 (c 66), s 117 (2).

Section 105 (6) of the Licensing (Scotland) Act 1976 provides that on an application for the grant of a certificate of registration in respect of a club, if objections are lodged and not withdrawn the sheriff shall hear

parties and may order such inquiry as he sees fit and thereafter shall grant or refuse the certificate. Section G 117 (2) provides that the decision of the sheriff shall be final.

A bowling club applied for a certificate of registration permitting it to serve alcohol to members and their guests. Objections by local residents, presented under para (d) of s 108, were to the effect that the situation of the club was not suitable or convenient for the purposes of a club which would be able to sell alcohol. The sheriff held that it was not a competent and relevant objection under para (d) that the premises H were not suitable for use to serve alcohol and granted a certificate. An objector lodged a note of appeal claiming that the sheriff's decision was wrong in law. The objector argued that the decision of the sheriff was of a purely procedural character which could competently be appealed.

Held, that the sheriff's decision was not procedural but was one on the merits and that no appeal to the sheriff principal was competent (p 11B-D); and appeal I *refused.*

Chief Constable of Strathclyde v Hamilton & District Bookmakers Club, 1977 SLT (Sh Ct) 79, *Ladbrokes the Bookmakers v Hamilton District Council,* 1977 SLT (Sh Ct) 86, and *Edinburgh North Constituency Association SNP Club v Thomas H Peck Ltd,* 1978 SLT (Sh Ct) 76, *considered* and *distinguished.*

———————

Application for certificate of registration of J
a club
Woodend Bowling Club applied for a certificate of registration under Pt VII of the Licensing (Scotland) Act 1976. Margaret Stephen and Marjory Hunter, local residents, lodged objections. After a hearing the sheriff (D Kelbie) granted a certificate. Miss Stephen lodged a note of appeal to the sheriff principal.

On 12 February 1993 the sheriff principal *refused* the appeal as incompetent.   K

THE SHERIFF PRINCIPAL (R D IRELAND, QC).—This is an appeal from an interlocutor of the sheriff granting a certificate of registration to the Woodend Bowling Club under Pt VII of the Licensing (Scotland) Act 1976 ("the Act") and dismissing the objections of Miss Margaret Stephen and Mrs Marjory Hunter. Miss Stephen has appealed.

Woodend Bowling Club has a clubhouse and L bowling green at 285 King's Gate, Aberdeen, and has been established there for many years. In 1992 the club applied for a certificate of registration under Pt VII of the Act. Such a certificate permits a club to serve alcoholic refreshment to members and their guests. Objections were lodged by a number of local residents, but in the end only the objections of Miss Stephen and Mrs Hunter were maintained. Section 105 (6) of the Act provides that "On an application for the grant of the certificate of registration in respect of any club . . . (b) if . . . objections are lodged and not withdrawn, the sheriff shall, as soon as may be, hear

A parties upon the application and objections and may order such inquiry as he thinks fit, and shall thereafter grant or refuse the certificate, and may award expenses against the unsuccessful party." Section 108 provides that "The sheriff shall not consider any objection to the grant . . . of a certificate of registration unless it is made on one or more of the following grounds". These words are followed by a series of paras (a) to (s). Miss Stephen's objection was presented by her solicitor as falling within para (d), namely "that the

B premises are, or the situation thereof is, not suitable or convenient for the purposes of a club". At the hearing before the sheriff Miss Stephen's solicitor argued that the situation of the club, which is in a residential area, was not suitable or convenient for the purposes of a registered club which would be able to serve alcohol.

The sheriff in the present case held that it was not a competent and relevant objection under para (d) of s 108 that the premises could be used to serve alcoholic refreshment. He contrasted the language of

C para (d), which uses the expression "suitable or convenient for the purposes of a club", with the ground for the refusal of an application for a licence under s 17 (1) (b) of the Act, which is that the premises "are not suitable or convenient for the sale of alcoholic liquor". The sheriff went on: "The selling of alcoholic refreshment in a registered club is always ancillary to the purposes of a club and therefore the objection has to be that the premises or the situation thereof are not suitable or convenient for the purposes of a club,

D whether or not alcoholic refreshment is to be available". On that ground he held that the objection did not fall within the terms of s 108 of the Act, and was therefore incompetent and irrelevant. Accordingly he granted a certificate under s 105 (6) (b). Miss Stephen's solicitor lodged a note of appeal claiming that the sheriff's decision was wrong in law.

Section 117 (2) of the Act provides that "The decision of the sheriff in dealing with an application for the grant of a certificate of registration . . . shall be

E final." Such a provision is to be found in many statutes concerned with licensing and related matters, and its general effect is to exclude an appeal from the decision of the sheriff, unless the decision is of a purely procedural character. At the appeal the solicitor on behalf of the appellant referred me to *Chief Constable of Strathclyde v Hamilton & District Bookmakers Club*, 1977 SLT (Sh Ct) 79 ("the *Hamilton Bookmakers* case"), and to *Edinburgh North Constituency Association SNP Club v Thomas H Peck Ltd*, 1978

F SLT (Sh Ct) 76 ("the *SNP Club* case").

In the *Hamilton Bookmakers* case an appeal to the sheriff principal was held to be competent. Sheriff Principal Robert Reid, QC, said at p 80: "In the present case the learned sheriff has not given any decision on the merits. The interlocutor appealed against is procedural in character and the issues raised concern the regularity of the procedure before the sheriff and the competency of his actings. Accordingly, I think that I can competently entertain the present appeal and any decision to which I may come

on the merits is one to which the finality clause would apply". In the *SNP Club* case Sheriff Principal Sir G Frederick O'Brien said at p 77: "Where the sheriff has dealt with matters of procedure only, or where he has left the merits untouched, as where he has held the matter before him to be incompetent, an appeal would appear to lie to the sheriff principal."

In order to find out what the sheriffs principal had in mind when they referred to "matters of procedure", "regularity" or "competency of procedure" or "a decision on the merits", it is useful to consider what happened in the cases with which they were dealing. H In the *Hamilton Bookmakers* case the chief constable lodged objections, alleging a number of contraventions of the licensing law, to an application for renewal of a club certificate. The statute required the sheriff, when objections were lodged, to hear parties on the application and objections, ordering such inquiry as he thought fit. The sheriff did not do that, but instead allowed the club to lodge answers to the chief constable's objections. In the answers the club admitted that there had been contraventions of the law, but I made averments about remedial measures which they had taken. The sheriff then allowed parties a proof of their averments. At that point the chief constable appealed to the sheriff principal. The sheriff principal held that the sheriff could not competently order a proof not, as the statute required, on the application and objections as originally submitted, but on the application, the objections and the club's answers to the objections. He allowed the appeal. "The averments sent to inquiry were not those in the application J and objections. . . . This is a different inquiry from that envisaged in [the Act], and one which might have a different result and a different liability in expenses. There is no statutory warrant for it, and I do not think it should have been ordered" (p 80).

In the *SNP Club* case objections had been lodged to an application for a certificate of registration. The sheriff appointed the application and objections to be heard on a stated date. When the case was called on that date the objector's solicitor was engaged in K another court. There being no appearance for the objectors, the sheriff repelled the objections and granted the application. On appeal the sheriff principal held that the absence of the objector's solicitor was in the circumstances excusable, and that it had been premature for the sheriff to treat the objections as withdrawn.

It was in these circumstances that in each case the sheriff principal held the appeal to be competent notwithstanding the finality clause. Each of the cases had L gone off the rails because of what the sheriff principal held to have been procedural error by the sheriff — in the *Hamilton Bookmakers* case the allowance of proof outwith the terms of the statute, and in the *SNP Club* case the failure to take account of objections which ought to have been treated as still before the court. A similar kind of procedural error was held to permit an appeal in *Ladbrokes The Bookmakers v Hamilton District Council*, 1977 SLT (Sh Ct) 86. In that case the applicants appealed to the sheriff against the refusal by

the licensing authority to renew a betting licence. The
A appeal was put out for a hearing on preliminary pleas.
Due to a misunderstanding the respondents failed to
attend the hearing, and the sheriff, in respect of the
non-appearance, sustained the appeal and granted the
licence, without dealing with the preliminary pleas.
The respondents appealed to the sheriff principal,
who held that the appeal was competent. He said at
p 87: "The learned sheriff . . . has not dealt either
with the preliminary pleas or with the merits of the
appeal but disposed of it in a manner which did not
B require him to exercise the jurisdiction conferred upon
him by statute. For this reason, his decision does not
fall to be treated as a final disposal . . . but — to use
the words of Lord Benholme in *Leitch* v. *Scottish Legal
Burial Society* (1879) 9 M. 40 — rather as an 'avoidance of judgment'."

In the present case there was no "avoidance of judgment". It is true that no evidence was led, but the
terms of s 105 (6) (b) do not require the sheriff to hear
evidence; he may do so "if he thinks fit". He was quite
C entitled to dispose of the application on preliminary
pleas and to hold, as he did, that "there is not relevantly stated in the objections a ground of objection
which can competently be made in terms of s 108".
There is nothing procedural about such a decision; it
was a decision on the merits. The sheriff was exercising the jurisdiction conferred upon him by s 105 (6)
(b), which was, after hearing parties on the application
and objections, to decide whether to grant or refuse
the certificate. When he made that decision, it was a
D decision covered by s 117 (2), and no appeal to the
sheriff principal is competent. I have accordingly
refused the appeal.

---

*Solicitors for Applicants, Aberdein Considine & Co,
Aberdeen — Solicitors for Objector, Adam Cochran,
Aberdeen.*

E

Cumming v Brown

SHERIFF COURT OF LOTHIAN AND
BORDERS AT EDINBURGH
SHERIFF PRINCIPAL C G B NICHOLSON, QC
F 23 JUNE 1993

*Heritable property — Sale — Missives — Breach —
Inability of purchasers to complete transaction — Seller
becoming entitled to resile in terms of missives — Purchasers subsequently offering to complete transaction —
Whether seller remained entitled to resile from contract.*

*Contract — Sale of heritage — Missives of sale — Breach
— Inability of purchasers to complete transaction —
Seller becoming entitled to resile in terms of missives —
Purchasers subsequently offering to complete transaction*

*— Whether seller remained entitled to resile from
contract.*
G

After missives were concluded for the sale and purchase of a house the purchasers became unable to
finance the transaction. The seller's solicitors wrote
calling upon the purchasers to implement the missives
failing which the seller would exercise his right to
resile from the contract. The purchasers' solicitors
finally wrote to intimate that they were able to complete the transaction but the seller's solicitors then
wrote to resile from the bargain. In an action for
implement of the missives, after a debate, the sheriff H
dismissed the action. The purchasers appealed to the
sheriff principal.

Held, that after effective tender of performance had
been made by the purchasers the seller was no longer
entitled to exercise his right to resile from the contract
(p 13J); and appeal *allowed.*

Action of implement
I
Andrew Francis Cumming and Rosemary Barrie
Flannigan raised an action for implement of missives
against Ian Wilson Brown. On 4 March 1993 the
sheriff dismissed the action. The purchasers appealed
to the sheriff principal.

On 23 June 1993 the sheriff principal *allowed* the
appeal, *ordained* the defender to implement the missives and *decerned* against the defender for payment of
£1,010 to the pursuers.
J

**THE SHERIFF PRINCIPAL (C G B
NICHOLSON, QC).**—This is an action for implement of missives of sale in respect of a house in Edinburgh. The pursuers were the prospective purchasers
of the house, and the defender was the seller. For convenience I refer hereafter to "the purchasers" and
"the seller" rather than to the pursuers and the
defender. After a debate the sheriff dismissed the
action and the purchasers have now appealed against K
that decision.

The facts of this case are not in dispute, and they are
as follows. On 25 February 1992 solicitors acting on
behalf of the purchasers sent an offer to purchase to
the estate agents who were then acting for the seller.
That offer provides that the purchase price is to be
£101,000 and that entry is to be given on 15 May
1992. It contains a large number of conditions, the
most important of which for present purposes is
no 14(a) which provides that the price will be payable L
on the date of entry in exchange for a valid and duly
executed disposition in favour of the purchaser.

On 2 March 1992 solicitors acting on behalf of the
seller sent a qualified acceptance to the solicitors
acting for the purchasers. So far as condition 14(a) of
the purchasers' offer is concerned, the only qualification is of no consequence for the present proceedings
since it merely related to an executed discharge. It is,
however, to be noted that the seller's qualified acceptance also contained certain conditions. For present

purposes the first of those is of significance, and it is in the following terms:

"It is an essential condition of this qualified acceptance and of any bargain following hereon that the full purchase price is paid within banking hours on the date of entry, failing which interest will be due by the purchaser to the seller at the rate of four per centum per annum above the base rate of the Bank of Scotland applicable to the period for which the said price is outstanding and that notwithstanding consignation and irrespective of whether actual physical entry is given to the purchaser. If the full purchase price, together with all interest due thereon, is not paid within four weeks of the said date of entry, the seller shall be entitled to resile from any bargain following hereon and to re-sell the subjects without penalty and without prejudice to the seller's right to interest and damages from the purchaser. Without prejudice to the foregoing generality, the said interest and damages shall include interest on the sale price, any decrease in the price of the property upon the re-sale of the property, additional rates and insurances, the whole estate agency, advertising costs and legal fees incurred in connection with the re-sale and VAT thereon and all other costs or losses incurred. No interest will be due nor will the seller be entitled to resile if a delay in settlement is caused solely through the fault of the seller or the seller's agents."

On 3 March 1992 the solicitors for the purchasers wrote to the solicitors for the seller agreeing the terms of the qualified acceptance and holding the bargain as concluded. It seems, however, that shortly thereafter it became apparent that the purchasers would be unable to secure the necessary finance to complete this transaction on account of their building society going into liquidation. This difficulty was brought to the notice of the seller's solicitors who, on 2 June 1992, wrote to express anxiety about the situation. Thereafter on 5 June 1992 the seller's solicitors wrote again calling upon the purchasers to implement their obligations within the time specified in the missives, failing which the seller would be entitled to exercise his rights in terms of the contract. On 16 June the purchasers' solicitor wrote to say that finance was then being organised with another building society, and asking the seller to bear with them for a matter of a week or two. On 20 July 1992 the purchasers' solicitors again wrote to the seller's solicitors saying that they expected to be in a position to complete the purchase on 27 July. They asked the seller's solicitors to send them a state for settlement showing the interest due by the purchasers for the period from 15 May. On 22 July a state for settlement was sent as requested. By 27 July matters had still not been resolved and the seller's solicitors again wrote to the solicitors for the purchasers. They recorded their client's distress and sought proposals for settlement by return. Finally, on 31 July 1992 the purchasers' solicitors wrote to say that they were then in a position to complete the transaction. However, this tender of payment was not accepted by the seller, and on 11 August 1992 his solicitors wrote to say "we hereby resile from the bargain concluded

between our respective clients by missives dated 25 February and 2 and 3 March 1992".

At the appeal hearing the solicitor for the seller did not seek to maintain that the letter of 31 July could not be treated as a valid and effective offer to conclude the transaction as at that date. His argument was essentially that, since there had been a material breach of contract on the part of the purchasers in respect that they had not paid the purchase price on the due date, the seller had thereby acquired a right to resile from the bargain which could be put into effect regardless of whether or not there was a subsequent attempt at completion of the transaction by the purchasers. For the purchasers the argument which was advanced was essentially that, while the seller could effectively have resiled from the bargain at any time prior to 31 July, the offer of payment made on that date had effectively brought that right to an end so that it could not be used at a later date.

Before considering the foregoing submissions in more detail I have to say that it is not clear to me that the case, as debated before the sheriff, was concentrated on the issue as I have just described it. Although it is not entirely clear from the sheriff's note, it seems that his attention was primarily directed to the question whether the seller had a right to resile from the contract rather than to the question whether, given the content and the nature of the letter of 31 July, he was still entitled to exercise that right 11 days later.

So that there can be no misunderstanding of the basis on which I have decided this case I think that it may be helpful if I were to set out what I understand to have been the positions adopted by the parties at the appeal hearing. This is of some importance since, as I understand it, those positions may have involved some concessions on matters of law, and may have involved not advancing certain arguments which could possibly have been available to one or other of the parties.

First, parties were agreed that the purchasers were in material breach of the contract when they failed to pay the purchase price by 12 June 1992. That date is four weeks after the agreed entry date, and takes account of the period of grace (albeit subject to the accrual of interest) provided for in the seller's first condition of sale which I have quoted above. There was accordingly no question as to the materiality of the breach.

Secondly, and as a corollary to that, it was accepted that, in terms of the contract, the seller acquired a right to resile which was effective from the date of the breach, that is to say from 12 June. It was, I think, further accepted that that right could be extinguished by personal bar; but no attempt was made to advance such a case. In particular it was not suggested that the seller had barred his right to resile by, for example, sending to the purchasers on 22 July a state for settlement showing the interest due to that date.

Finally, it was accepted on behalf of the seller that the letter of 31 July from the purchasers' solicitors

A falls to be treated as a valid and effective tender of performance by the purchasers of their obligations under the contract. Given that concession, and given the other points of argument which I have just summarised, the question for determination in this case is a sharp and narrow one: where one party to a contract has acquired a right to resile, does that right remain effective and exercisable notwithstanding a tender of performance by the other party?

B In seeking to persuade me to answer that question in the negative the solicitor for the purchasers made three broad submissions. First, and by reference to the mutuality principle, as at 31 July 1992 the missives were still in full force for the benefit of both parties notwithstanding the earlier failure in performance by the purchasers. Secondly, having tendered performance of their obligations on 31 July, the purchasers were entitled to demand performance by the seller of his obligations. And thirdly, having failed to exercise the right to resile by 31 July, the seller had lost that right and could not exercise it on 11 August. In
C support of the foregoing submissions the solicitor for the purchasers referred me to a number of cases and to several passages in Gloag on *Contract* and in McBryde on *Contract*. I shall return to some of them later.

For the moment it may be helpful to summarise the submissions which were advanced by the solicitor for the seller. They were, first, that the seller had acquired the right to resile under the express terms of
D the contract. From the moment when that right crystallised the contract was essentially different from what it had been before in that thereafter the seller had an option either to continue with the contract or to exercise his right to resile. That right to resile could be removed by the seller's own actings, for example by granting a waiver or by personal bar, but nothing of that sort applied in this case. The seller's right to resile could not be removed by any unilateral actings on the part of the purchasers, and he was accordingly
E entitled to exercise that right on 11 August notwithstanding the tender of performance by the purchasers on 31 July.

Solicitors for both parties were agreed that none of the authorities to which reference was made deals directly with circumstances such as those in the present case. Thus, some deal with what is sometimes referred to as anticipatory breach of contract (for example, *Gilfillan v Cadell and Grant* (1893) 1 SLT 387; (1893) 21 R 269; *Frost v Knight* (1872) LR 7 Ex
F 111), while others deal with what are sometimes referred to as continuing contracts (for example, *Lindley Catering Investments Ltd v Hibernian Football Club Ltd*, 1975 SLT (Notes) 56).

The solicitor for the seller submitted that cases such as those which I have just mentioned should be distinguished, and certainly the sheriff appears to have taken the view that no assistance is to be derived from cases dealing with anticipatory breach of contract. In my opinion, however, some guidance on general principles may be obtained from such cases notwithstanding that their circumstances are not directly in point. Thus, a right to claim damages under a con-
G tract, if not exercised, may not of itself prevent the other party from tendering performance of his obligations (see *Frost v Knight*, per Cockburn CJ at p 112), and a breach of contract may in certain circumstances be made good before a right to rescind has been exercised (see *Lindley Catering*, per Lord Thomson at p 57, second column). It also appears to be clear that, even in a continuing contract where one party has acquired a right to resile for the future, the exercise of that right will not affect performance by the other
H party where that has been tendered prior to the date when notice of rescission was given (*Dunford & Elliot v Macleod & Co* (1902) 10 SLT 90; (1902) 4 F 912).

Given what is said in the foregoing cases, and given that a right to resile is an option which can be exercised or not as the person having that right sees fit, I am unable to hold that a party who has not yet exercised that right can ignore a tender of performance by the other party and then purport to exercise the right thereafter. As is said by Gloag (p 620): "A party faced
I with a breach of contract which he regards as material would be well-advised in making a definite intimation to the defaulter that he regards the contract as at an end through his fault, and that he proposes to claim damages. If, in the absence of such intimation, the other party is led to act on the assumption that the contract is still in being, the right to reject may be barred."

In the present case it is accepted that the seller could
J validly and effectively have exercised his right to resile from the contract at any time between 12 June and 31 July. However, he did not do so, and in that situation effective tender of performance was made by the purchasers on the latter of these dates. That being the case, I do not consider that the seller remained entitled to exercise his right to resile thereafter, and no authority was brought to my notice (nor am I aware of any) which supports a contrary view.

It follows that in my opinion this appeal must
K succeed, and that the interlocutor of 4 March 1993 should be recalled. Parties were agreed that, if that were to be the outcome of the appeal, there would be no need for this case to proceed to proof, and that I should grant decree in favour of the purchasers in terms of their first and second craves. The first of those craves is for specific implement of the missives of sale, and the second is for payment of a sum of £1,010 which the purchasers will require to pay as stamp duty, that being a sum which they would not
L have required to pay had the transaction been completed prior to 18 August 1992. The solicitor for the seller accepted that decree for that sum should be granted in the event of the appeal being successful. The purchasers' third crave is for damages, but it was departed from both before the sheriff and before myself. It was also agreed that the expenses of the appeal should follow success.

Finally, I should add that the purchase price, as stated in the pursuers' first crave, is greater than that

A specified in the missives. I assume that the difference between the two figures reflects an amount of interest due by the pursuers. However, neither party addressed me on this, and I have therefore granted decree in terms of the first crave as stated.

B

Solicitors for Pursuers, Skene, Edwards & Garson, WS, Edinburgh — Solicitors for Defender, Bonar Mackenzie, WS, Edinburgh.

Armour v Anderson

SHERIFF COURT OF LOTHIAN AND BORDERS AT EDINBURGH

SHERIFF PRINCIPAL C G B NICHOLSON, QC

C 30 AUGUST 1993

Property — Cohabiting couple — Occupancy rights in dwellinghouse — Parties cohabiting for two years — Action raised 10 months after one party departed from the house — Whether parties a "cohabiting couple" in respect of whom orders might be made — Matrimonial Homes (Family Protection) (Scotland) Act 1981 (c 59), s 18 (3).

D Section 18 (3) of the Matrimonial Homes (Family Protection) (Scotland) Act 1981 extends to cohabiting couples provisions of the 1981 Act, including s 4 (relating to exclusion orders), where "both partners of a cohabiting couple are entitled, or permitted by a third party, to occupy the house where they are cohabiting".

After a couple had cohabited for two years, latterly in a house of which they were the joint tenants, one of them left the house to live elsewhere, and 10
E months later raised an action seeking an order suspending the other's occupancy rights in the house and an order for his summary ejection. Interim orders were granted by the sheriff. The defender appealed to the sheriff principal, arguing that such orders were incompetent, or in any event that they were neither necessary nor reasonable.

Held, (1) that each case had to be looked at by reference to its own facts and circumstances in order to see whether, at the date of an application, it could reason-
F ably be said that there was still in existence a cohabiting couple (p 15H); (2) that in the present case by the time that the action was raised the parties were no longer a cohabiting couple and therefore did not fall within the provisions of s 18 (3) of the 1981 Act (p 15I-L); and appeal allowed.

Opinion, that the appeal would have been refused on the merits since no basis had been shown for interfering with the discretion of the sheriff (p 16B).

Action

G Elizabeth Ann Armour raised an action against Alan Anderson seeking a variety of orders including an order suspending the defender's occupancy rights in a house and an order for his summary ejection. On 7 July 1993 the sheriff granted those orders ad interim. The defender appealed to the sheriff principal.

On 30 August 1993 the sheriff principal allowed the appeal.

H THE SHERIFF PRINCIPAL (C G B NICHOLSON, QC).—The parties to this action, who are not man and wife, cohabited together for a period in excess of two years, and did so latterly at a house in Rosewell of which they are joint tenants. They took up that tenancy in January 1992 and lived there together until about August of that year when the pursuer and the child of the association left, allegedly as a result of the defender's violent behaviour. Since that time the pursuer and the child have been residing with the pursuer's father at his
I home in Lasswade while the defender has continued to reside in the house in Rosewell.

In June 1993 the pursuer raised the present action in which she seeks a variety of orders. As well as conventional interdicts these include an order suspending the defender's occupancy rights in the house at Rosewell and an order for the summary ejection of the defender from that property. A motion to make those orders ad interim came before the sheriff on 7 July 1993 when the orders in question were granted. The
J defender has now appealed against that decision and, at the appeal as before the sheriff, the matters in dispute have been the order suspending occupancy rights and the ancillary order for summary ejection.

Both at first instance and at the appeal the solicitor for the defender challenged the making of those orders on two grounds. First, he submitted that in the circumstances of this case such orders are not competent; and secondly, he submitted that in any event
K they are not orders which are either necessary or reasonable. Unlike the sheriff, I find it convenient to deal first with the question of competency.

The Matrimonial Homes (Family Protection) (Scotland) Act 1981, which inter alia makes provision for the making of exclusion and ancillary orders, is primarily concerned with persons who are married to each other. However, by s 18 it does extend some of its provisions to cohabiting couples. In particular, by
L s 18 (3) it extends to such couples the provisions of s 4 (exclusion orders) where, inter alia, "both partners of a cohabiting couple are entitled, or permitted by a third party, to occupy the house where they are cohabiting". That is the provision which is relied on by the pursuer in the present action.

In submitting that the foregoing provision does not make the grant of an exclusion order competent in the present case the solicitor for the defender argued, first, that the use of the present tense in s 18 makes it plain that the section cannot apply in a case where a formerly cohabiting couple have ceased to be a cohabiting couple. As a secondary argument, he conceded that, notwithstanding the use of the present tense, the section could probably be invoked in circumstances where one partner had been forced to leave the home and had more or less immediately raised proceedings for an exclusion order. But, he submitted, it could no longer be used when, as in the present case, some 10 months had elapsed between the pursuer's departure from the house and the raising of the proceedings.

In response, the solicitor for the pursuer relied, as also did the sheriff, on the words which were added to s 4 of the Act by an amendment contained in the Law Reform (Miscellaneous Provisions) (Scotland) Act 1985. Those words, which qualify the right to apply for an exclusion order, state that such an application may be made "whether or not that spouse is in occupation at the time of the application". Given those words, and given that s 4 in its entirety is extended to cohabiting couples by s 18, it must follow, it was submitted, that an application by one partner of a cohabiting couple will be competent notwithstanding that, by the time of the application, that partner is no longer residing at the house in question. As I have observed, that submission was accepted by the sheriff when he rejected the challenge to the competency of making the orders in question.

I have to say that I have not found this an easy matter to determine, and my consideration of it has had to take place without the assistance of any relevant authority since it appears that there is none. Nor is the matter helped by the fact that s 18 itself is, to say the least, less than helpfully drafted. For a start, it is, as was pointed out by the defender's solicitor, drafted entirely in the present tense. So, of course, is the rest of the Act; but there is in my view a significant difference in the rest of the Act in that it is dealing with a continuing status, namely marriage, whereas s 18 is dealing with something which is not a status but a question of fact. Furthermore, while s 18 (2) provides a guide as to what is to be regarded as a cohabiting couple, it does so only for the purposes of subs (1), and no guidance whatever is given as to what will constitute a cohabiting couple for the purposes of subs (3), which is the subsection with which we are concerned in this case.

No doubt the added words in s 4 (1), to which I have referred above, may be of assistance in some cases, and in particular in the kind of case adumbrated by the defender's solicitor, where proceedings for an exclusion order are commenced within days of a partner of a cohabiting couple having to flee the former joint home. But I am by no means persuaded that those words have the effect of giving a former cohabiting partner a limitless entitlement to apply for orders of the kind permitted by s 18 (3). To take an extreme example, suppose that a former cohabiting partner were to leave the joint home and at some time thereafter set up in cohabitation with a new partner. Could she then competently seek an order under s 18 (3)? No doubt such an application would be most unlikely to succeed on its merits, but I also very much doubt whether it could ever be competent; and the reason for that would be that upon any view it could not be said that by the time of the application the original cohabitants were still a cohabiting couple.

The intervention of a new cohabitation with a new partner is of course a clear example of something which has brought a former cohabitation to an end, and the solicitor for the pursuer very fairly accepted that in such a case it would probably not be possible to invoke s 18 in relation to the former cohabitation. However, the example which I have given, albeit extreme, seems to me to demonstrate that, in the absence of any contrary indication in the statute itself, each case must be looked at by reference to its own facts and circumstances in order to see whether, at the date of an application, it can reasonably be said that there is still in existence a cohabiting couple. This is, in my opinion, the inevitable consequence of what I mentioned earlier, namely that marriage is a status which continues regardless until it is brought to an end by divorce, whereas, and by contrast, cohabitation does not involve any status and must simply be a question of fact.

Turning, then, to the present case, the first thing that strikes me is that there is no suggestion, either in the initial writ or in the affidavits, that the pursuer herself regards her cohabitation with the defender as anything other than at an end. She appears to be anxious to sever her connection with the defender, and that is, I think, confirmed by the fact that she also seeks in the initial writ a transfer of the defender's tenancy rights to herself. (That should, I think, be a crave for sole vesting under s 13 (9) of the Act rather than transfer, but that technicality is not an issue at this stage.) Moreover, as was founded on by the defender's solicitor, some 10 months have elapsed between the pursuer leaving the defender and the raising of the present proceedings. The solicitor for the pursuer explained that delay by saying that most of that period had been taken up in trying to persuade the housing association who own the house in question to evict the defender and to transfer the tenancy to the pursuer alone. That may be so but, if so, it seems to me to do no more than confirm that the parties to this action effectively ceased to be a cohabiting couple from the time, or from very shortly after the time, when the pursuer left the defender.

In the result, therefore, I have come to the conclusion that, certainly by the date when the present proceedings were commenced, the parties to this action could no longer be described as a cohabiting couple, and accordingly this case does not fall within the governing words of s 18 (3): "where both partners of a cohabiting couple are entitled . . . to occupy the house where they are cohabiting". I reach this conclusion with some hesitation and also with some regret because I suspect that, in doing so, I may not be reflecting the *intention* of the legislature when it enacted s 18. However, I can only proceed on the basis of what is actually said in the statute, and what it does say is, if anything, the exact opposite of what is con-

tended for by the pursuer in the present case. It would
A have been different if the subsection had said "where
both partners of a present or former cohabiting couple
are entitled . . . to occupy the house where they are
cohabiting or were formerly cohabiting"; but that is
not what is said, and I therefore conclude that I have
no alternative but to hold that the sheriff was wrong
to find that the present application is competent. The
appeal accordingly succeeds on that basis.

In those circumstances it is strictly unnecessary for
me to deal with the arguments which were presented
B on the merits of the application, and it may therefore
be sufficient for me simply to say that, had I reached
a different conclusion on the matter of competency, I
would have refused the appeal on this ground. My
reason for that is that a decision on a matter like this
is very much one for the discretion of the sheriff at
first instance, and nothing that was said to me by the
solicitor for the defender persuades me that the sheriff
committed any error in his approach such as would
have entitled me to review his decision.

C So far as expenses are concerned parties requested
me to find them to be expenses in the cause, and I have
given effect to that request.

————————

*Solicitors for Pursuer, Marshall Henderson & Whyte,
SSC, Edinburgh — Solicitors for Defender, Gilmore
Lewis, Edinburgh.*

D

GTW Holdings Ltd v Toet

SHERIFF COURT OF GLASGOW AND
STRATHKELVIN AT GLASGOW

SHERIFF PRINCIPAL N D MACLEOD, QC

E 4 MARCH 1993

*Recompense — Payments in respect of use of land —
Party occupying land — Whether liable to make payment
in respect of occupation.*

The heritable proprietors of a piece of ground raised
an action claiming payment from the occupiers of the
ground. In dismissing the action after debate the
sheriff held that the case was one of recompense but
F lacked the necessary averment of loss to the proprietors and profit by the occupiers. The proprietors
appealed to the sheriff principal.

Held, (1) that the use of another's property attracted
the obligation to pay for the use of it and accordingly
Scots law afforded the remedy sought by the proprietors (p 17A and F-G); (2) that the measure of
liability was the real worth and annual value of the
land possessed, which the pursuers had sufficiently
averred (p 17J-K); and appeal *allowed*.

————————

Action of payment

GTW Holdings Ltd raised an action of payment G
against Hendrick Toet and others. Both parties had
preliminary pleas to the relevancy and specification.
After debate the sheriff (W G Stevenson, QC) sustained the defenders' plea and dismissed the action.
The pursuers appealed to the sheriff principal.

On 4 March 1993 the sheriff principal *allowed* the
appeal and *appointed* the cause to the procedure roll to
consider the pursuers' preliminary plea.

THE SHERIFF PRINCIPAL (N D MACLEOD, H
QC).—The pursuers are heritable proprietors of a
certain piece of ground which has been occupied in
recent years by the defenders. In respect of that
occupation the pursuers are, by this action, claiming
payment from the defenders.

It is averred that: "The defenders have occupied the
said subjects without any title to do so . . . the pursuers have at no time indicated an intention either
expressly or impliedly that the defenders should enjoy I
possession gratuitously."

The defenders admit that. The pursuers also aver
that: "The pursuers as the owners of valuable heritable subjects have sought payment of the annual worth
of the said subjects in respect of the defenders' period
of possession or occupancy. . . . [They] . . . moder-
ately estimate that the annual worth of the said subjects for the period of five years prior to the raising of
this action was £1,500. Accordingly, the pursuers seek
recompense from the defenders in the sum of £7,500 J
which is the sum sued for."

The relative plea in law is as follows: "The
defenders having occupied valuable heritable subjects
belonging to the pursuers without title to do so and
there having been no intention on the part of the pursuers that they should do so gratuitously, the
defenders are bound to recompense the pursuers to the
extent of the annual worth of the subjects and the sum
sued for representing the annual worth of the said sub- K
jects for a period of five years decree should be granted
therefor as craved with expenses."

Both parties had pleas to the relevancy and specification of each other's pleadings and the case was thus
brought to debate before the sheriff. The sheriff, inter
alia, sustained the defenders' plea and dismissed the
action. Against that decision the pursuers have
appealed.

The sheriff was of the view that the case was one of L
recompense but that it lacked the necessary averment
of "grounds of loss to the pursuer and profit, quantum
lucratus, by the defender". The sheriff understood the
pursuers' pleadings to reflect a passage in Gloag on
Contract (2nd ed), at p 329, which was based, not upon
cases of recompense, but upon cases of implied
contract. It was the sheriff's view that because the
pursuers did not seem to have been aware for more
than five years that the defenders were occupying their
property a contract of tenancy could not be implied.
The sheriff also considered it significant that the

A pursuers were not trying to let the land. For these various reasons, he dismissed the action.

In my opinion the use of another's property attracts the obligation to pay for the use of it: see Stewart on *Restitution*, p 163. I am accordingly of the view that Scots law affords the remedy sought by the pursuers.

Cases such as *Varney (Scotland) Ltd v Burgh of Lanark*, 1976 SLT 46 and *Lawrence Building Co Ltd v Lanarkshire County Council*, 1977 SLT 110, although concerned with the principle of recompense,
B were not cases in which the circumstance giving rise to the action was the occupation of land.

That particular circumstance has come before our courts in a number of cases. These seem to me to justify the view that the use of another's property attracts the obligation to pay for the use of it. In *Earl of Fife v Wilson* (1864) 3 M 323, the position is succinctly stated: "He had possession. . . . He has had the article, and must pay the price." The position is more fully stated in *Glen v Roy* (1882) 10 R 239, as
C follows: "He admits that he was in occupation, and the presumption of law is that he occupied as tenant, whether he actually paid rent or not, and whether there was a written lease or not. The presumption is that the party in possession is liable to pay the real worth of the subjects occupied . . . an occupant, though no direct obligation to pay rent is proved, is bound to pay the annual value of the subject, the onus lying on him to show that he got it for less, or . . . for nothing at all."

D Stewart comments upon these cases in a paragraph entitled "Occupation of premises" (p 41). His comment seems to me admirably to set out the law relating to this particular circumstance: "Occupation of premises is a benefit and it is usually the case that an owner can make money from his land. The Scots courts for a long time had no difficulty in finding that someone who lived on land had been enriched. In *Earl of Fife v Samuel Wilson*, possession on the basis of a lease which was later found not to exist was sufficient
E to allow the court to hold the possessor liable in an amount equal to the amount under the putative lease. Another benefit recognised in the law of Scotland is mere occupation of subjects. In *Glen v Roy* the defender was in occupation: applying *Young v Cockburn* the Lord Justice-Clerk (Moncreiff) stated the law to be that there was a presumption that a person in occupation was presumed to pay the real worth of the subjects occupied which was the annual value unless the occupier could show that he was entitled to pay nothing or less. Despite the fact that the judgment
F states that the defender failed to prove he was not a tenant, the obligation is not contractual but is restitution of the use made of the land. The basis is that no reasonable man would say other than that the occupation of land was a benefit."

I am not concerned to analyse whether the remedy sought by the pursuers is properly ascribable to implied contract or to recompense. It is sufficient that it appears to be a remedy afforded by our law. In the absence of circumstances demonstrating a mutual intention that possession of land should be enjoyed

G gratuitously, the owner of that land is entitled to recover from the possessor a reasonable payment in respect of such possession. The pursuers' plea in law, in my opinion, correctly invokes that principle.

In the recent case *Shetland Islands Council v BP Petroleum Development*, 1990 SLT 82, Lord Cullen had occasion to consider *Glen v Roy*. The opinion he expressed is of import generally, and it is of particular import to the sheriff's view that the pre-existence of a tenancy is necessary to support an implied tenancy. Lord Cullen says at p 88K: "The implication of the
H relationship of landlord and tenant was derived as a matter of law from the fact that possession was conceded and accepted and not from evidence as to the parties' express or implied agreement upon particular terms. The evidence as to William Roy's payment of rent was potent, but in dispelling his case that he was an occupant under no obligation to pay. In those circumstances the use of the term 'rent' for the payment in which he was found liable may be somewhat loose, as Rankine on *Leases* observes at p. 310. The liability of an occupier in his position could be
I analysed as resting either on implied contract or on a quasi-contractual obligation of recompense."

It seems quite clear to me from a consideration of the reported cases dealing with the circumstance that presents itself in this case, that the implication of the relationship of landlord and tenant may derive from the mere fact of possession of land. Accordingly, the question of a pre-existing tenancy or of the landlord seeking to let the land, is a question of no necessary significance. Had there been a pre-existing tenancy or
J had the pursuers been seeking to let the land it might have been open to the court to have regard to that in the context of determining the real worth or annual value of the land.

In the cases, the occupation of land is regarded as a benefit, and the possessor's benefit is regarded as the owner's loss. The measure of liability — as Lord Clyde remarked in *HMV Fields Properties v Skirt 'n' Slack Centre of London*, 1987 SLT 2 at p 5L — is the "real worth" and "annual value" of the land possessed. The
K pursuers have averred their ownership of the land in question and the defenders' possession of it. It would be otiose to aver that the defenders were thereby enriched and that they, by the same measure, suffered loss. They have specifically claimed what they aver to be the annual worth of the land occupied.

In short, I am of the view that the remedy sought by the pursuers is one afforded by the law and that they have sufficiently pleaded it. I must therefore recall the sheriff's interlocutor dismissing the action.   L

The interlocutor complained of indicates that the sheriff not only sustained the defenders' plea to the relevancy but also sustained the pursuers' plea to the relevancy. The solicitors appearing at the appeal, who appeared also for parties at the debate, were agreed that the sheriff had made avizandum after hearing argument relating to the defenders' plea, and had not heard argument relating to the pursuers' plea. On the basis that the interlocutor is, in this respect, mistaken, I have appointed the cause to the procedure roll so

A that, as a preliminary matter, it may be ascertained whether the pursuers are insisting on their preliminary plea.

As successful party the pursuers are entitled to their expenses and I have accordingly found the defenders liable in that connection.

Solicitors for Pursuers, Macdonalds, Glasgow — Solicitors for Defenders, Archibald Sharp & Son, Glasgow.

B

Whiteaway Laidlaw Bank Ltd v Green

C SHERIFF COURT OF GRAMPIAN, HIGHLAND AND ISLANDS AT ABERDEEN

SHERIFF PRINCIPAL D J RISK, QC

15 JULY 1993

Process — Decree — Summary decree — Whether defence to action disclosed in defences — Whether likelihood of genuine defence — Sheriff Courts (Scotland) Act 1907 (7 Edw VII, c 51), Sched, rule 59A.

D _Cautionary obligations — Co-cautioners — Separate documents of guarantee covering liability for whole debt — Whether cautioners jointly and severally liable._

Agency — Creditor and cautioner — Co-cautioner alleging misrepresentation of cautioner inducing him to sign guarantee — Whether cautioner acting as agent of creditor — Whether guarantee enforceable by creditor.

A bank raised an action of payment against three alleged guarantors of a company which had borrowed money from them and which had subsequently been placed in liquidation. The bank sought summary decree against all three in terms of ordinary cause rule 59A. The motion was granted by the sheriff. One of the defenders appealed to the sheriff principal. The alleged guarantor argued that whereas the pleadings referred to one guarantee, the true position was that he had signed one document and the other two defenders had signed a second document, with the effect that the bank was not entitled to decree against all three defenders jointly and severally. He also maintained F that there was a further line of defence which had not yet appeared in the pleadings, that he had signed the guarantee at the request of the third defender acting as agent for the bank under the mistaken belief that he was signing a loan stock agreement and that the guarantee was reducible.

Held, (1) that the appellant had bound himself for the whole amount of the sums lent and that he had raised no maintainable defence (p 21I-K); and (2) that no facts had been suggested leading to the conclusion that the third defender was an agent of the bank and the proposed defence was unstatable (p 22G-H); and appeal _refused._   G

Opinion, that it was appropriate to be guided by the approach of the Court of Session to Rule of Court 89B in the application of Ordinary Cause Rule 59A (p 19I).

Action of payment

Whiteaway Laidlaw Bank Ltd raised an action of payment against Gordon F Green, James Morrison Ironside and Kevin John Ironside as guarantors of a H company which had borrowed money from the bank and which had since been placed in liquidation.

On 19 May 1993 the sheriff (D Bogie) granted the bank's motion for summary decree against all three defenders. The first defender appealed to the sheriff principal.

On 15 July 1993 the sheriff principal _refused_ the appeal.

I
THE SHERIFF PRINCIPAL (D J RISK, QC).—This is an action of payment by a bank against three persons who are alleged to be guarantors of a company which borrowed money from the pursuers and which subsequently was placed in liquidation. The case tabled on 17 February 1993. All three defenders lodged defences on 1 March. On 13 April the pursuers enrolled a motion for summary decree against all three defenders in terms of rule 59A of the Ordinary Cause Rules. On 14 April they lodged the J inventory of productions, no 12 of process. The motion called before the sheriff in the adjustment roll of 5 May and was continued until 19 May on which date the sheriff granted the pursuers' motion. Down to that date no party had adjusted any part of the pleadings. Against the interlocutor of 19 May the first defender alone has appealed.

When the appeal was marked the sheriff was requested to write, and did write, a note. Rule 59A confers upon the sheriff a measure of discretion with K the exercise of which an appellate tribunal would generally be slow to interfere. In this case, however, the sheriff's note fails to deal with significant areas of argument. Before me the appellant's solicitor attempted to develop certain material submissions of which the sheriff has made no mention. When I queried him he assured me that those submissions had in fact been deployed before the sheriff and the respondents' solicitor very fairly confirmed that that was the case. It may well be that the learned sheriff L gave careful consideration to those submissions and that he reached a sound conclusion thereanent, but in the absence of any indication of his reasoning I cannot presume that to be so. I have therefore felt obliged to deal with the matter de novo.

In art 2 of condescendence the pursuers aver that on or about 1 May 1992 they offered a loan facility to a company called Kevin Ironside (Cars) Ltd, to which I shall refer hereafter as "the company", and that the company accepted the offer on or about 6 May 1992.

They have produced and incorporated in the pleadings a letter, no 12/1 of process, dated 1 May 1992 and addressed to "The Directors, Kevin Ironside (Cars) Ltd". It reads inter alia: "we now have pleasure in offering a loan facility to you for the purpose of stocking used cars up to five years old for re-sale, subject to the undernoted terms and conditions:

"(1) The amount of the facility will be £25,000.

"(2) The facility is to be secured by the joint and several guarantee and indemnity in our standard form of the directors of the Company . . .

"(10) We reserve the right . . . to demand immediate repayment of the full outstanding balance under the facility if you are in default or breach of any of the terms and conditions of this offer letter or (in our complete discretion) any other circumstances arise whereby we consider our rights and interests are prejudiced or put in jeopardy."

On the last page of the letter there is a form of acceptance which reads:

"We have read the offer in your letter dated the 1st May 1992 (of which this is a copy) and hereby accept the offer on the terms and conditions contained therein.

"Signed for and on behalf of Kevin Ironside (Cars) Limited."

The form of acceptance is signed by each of the three defenders, each being designed as "Director" and each bearing to have signed on 6 May 1992. Below the form of acceptance there is printed a section headed "(Guarantors/Indemnifiers)" below which there again appear the signatures of each of the three defenders together with their home addresses and the date 6 May 1992. It is not, as I understand it, disputed that the first defender and appellant did in fact sign that document or that he was in fact a director of the company. Nevertheless, ans 2 for the first defender reads "Not known and not admitted".

In art 3 the pursuers aver: "The defenders guaranteed the prompt and complete performance by the said company of all its obligations in terms of the loan agreement. A copy of this guarantee will be produced, referred to for its terms and held to be repeated herein brevitatis causa." What they have in fact produced is two documents, nos 12/2 and 12/3 respectively. These are printed forms of guarantee and indemnity, each of which has space for the signature and designation of two guarantors and the signature and designation of two witnesses to the signature of each guarantor. Number 12/1 bears to have been signed by the first defender and appellant on 6 May 1992 in the presence of "J Green" and "Kerry Green", all of whom reside at the same address. No 12/3 bears to have been signed by the second and third defenders on 6 May 1992 in the presence of various witnesses. It is not disputed that the first defender and appellant did in fact sign no 12/2. Nevertheless, ans 3 for the first defender reads simply "Denied".

In art 4 the pursuers aver that in December 1992 they ascertained that the directors of the company had taken steps to put it into creditors' voluntary liquidation, that they considered that their rights and interests were prejudiced thereby and that they gave notice of immediate withdrawal of the loan facility. The sum due by the company to the pursuers was £25,195.84 and the company had failed to pay the said sum. The first defender and appellant answers "Not known and not admitted".

Rule 59A provides inter alia:

"(2) A pursuer may, at any time after the defender has lodged defences, apply by a written motion to the court — (a) to grant decree in terms of all or any of the craves of the initial writ . . . on the ground that there is no defence to the action or a part of it disclosed in the defences. . . .

"(4) After hearing a motion under this rule, the sheriff may, if he is satisfied that there is no defence to the action or to any part of it to which the motion relates — (a) grant summary decree against the defender in terms of the motion in whole or in part".

That rule was introduced on 4 May 1992 and I was not referred to any case in which it has been considered. In the Court of Session, however, Rule of Court 89B, which is in equivalent terms, has existed for several years and it is appropriate that sheriffs should be guided by that court's approach to that rule. In that regard I was referred to the cases of *McManus v Speirs Dick and Smith Ltd*, 1989 SLT 806, *Frimokar (UK) Ltd v Mobile Technical Plant (International) Ltd*, 1990 SLT 180, *Spink & Son Ltd v McColl*, 1992 SLT 470 and *Mitchell v H A T Contracting Services Ltd (No 2)*, 1993 SLT 734. *McManus* was a reparation action in which the family of a man who had died in 1987 sought damages against a company which had employed him between 1958 and 1975 upon the basis that they had negligently exposed him to asbestos dust. The defenders lodged what were little more than skeleton defences. In refusing summary decree the Lord Ordinary (Caplan) held that in the particular circumstances of the case it did not indicate any lack of candour on the part of the defenders that they could make no detailed averments concerning events so long in the past. In the course of his opinion he said at p 807I-J: "In my opinion the present case differs from the type of case where the courts will regard skeletal defences as wholly irrelevant. It is one thing to have a case where there is prima facie merit in the pursuers' case perhaps because of the production of a contract or on the basis of certain admissions by the defender. In such a situation the court may find it difficult to conclude that there is a genuine issue to try if the defenders fail to advance a plausible basis for a defence. In a position where the circumstances dictate that the defender should be able to articulate the true nature of the defence then the defender cannot hide behind skeletal answers and put the pursuer to proof simply to delay the conclusion of the case."

Mitchell was another reparation case in which the pursuer averred that each of two defenders was in breach of certain statutory safety regulations in respect of the breaking of a scaffolding board on which he was

A working. He sought summary decree against both defenders so as to limit the proof to quantum of damages. The temporary judge (R G McEwan, QC) granted the motion in respect of the owners of the off-shore installation where the accident had occurred but refused it in respect of the pursuer's employers. With regard to the latter he held that there was a serious issue of relevancy relating to the applicability of the regulations to them and that it was not appropriate to grant summary decree where such an issue remained unresolved. In the course of his opinion he said at p

B 737B: "It respectfully seems to me that the proper test for summary decree is set out by Lord Cullen in *Robinson v Thomson* [6 May 1986] . . .: 'Before grant-ing a motion for summary decree the court requires to be "satisfied that there is no defence to the action or any part of it to which the motion relates". I interpret "satisfied" in the same way as it has been interpreted in cases relating to interim damages, namely as requir-ing something more than probability but less than complete certainty. . . . The wording to which I refer

C also involves that the court should be able to identify a part of the case to which it is satisfied there is no defence.' I am also satisfied that if it unmistakably appears that there may be an issue of relevancy the matter must go to procedure roll and summary decree is inappropriate."

Frimokar was an action of payment for the price of goods sold and delivered by the pursuers to the defenders. In granting summary decree for all but a very small proportion of the sum sued for the Lord

D Ordinary (Caplan) at p 181K-182B described his approach as follows: "In my view Rule of Court 89B is largely aimed at the dilatory defence and the court is in effect given the power to inquire into the defender's capacity to present a defence which raises a real issue before allowing the normal protracted procedures of litigation to take their course. The summary decree hearing is different from a debate on preliminary pleas where the relevancy of a defence is

E tested purely on the pleadings. A hearing in a summary decree motion is more far reaching because the Rules of Court specifically admit material extran-eous to the pleadings such as affidavits or productions. Thus the court is concerned not only to test the relevancy of the defence but the authenticity of the defence. However, the reverse aspect of the matter is that the court is not confined to the pleadings as they stand at a particular time in testing whether or not there is a plausible defence. The defender's counsel is

F right in suggesting that if the court considered that there would be scope for improving a defence by amendment or addition to the pleadings then in terms of the Rules of Court it could be difficult to be satis-fied that there is no defence. The court is looking to see if the defenders can present a genuine issue not to test the articulation of that issue. However, I do not agree with the defenders' counsel if she is suggesting that this leaves it open for a defender who cannot at a particular time explain what the defence is to crave the indulgence of the court in case at a later stage the defender can think of something different or better.

The question of the defence must be tested at the time the motion is decided and it is for the defender, before G that stage, to be in a position to satisfy the court that there is the framework of a defence available."

In *Spink* the pursuers sued the defender for damages because he had sold to them two valuable vases which later turned out to have been stolen and were reclaimed by their true owner. Counsel for the defender argued inter alia that the court should not have regard to productions lodged which had not been agreed by the parties nor produced by order of the court and that, in any event, the defender was entitled H to put the pursuers to proof on the issue of whether the vases were the stolen vases. He also suggested that other lines of defence might be advanced in the future. The temporary judge (J M S Horsburgh, QC) granted summary decree. In the course of his opinion he said at p 472J: "In my view the purpose of rule 89B is to cut down attempts by defenders to delay the progress of unanswerable claims by exploiting procedural rules. To that extent it allows the court to go behind what is stated on averment to ascertain if there is material I available to support the defender's averments and to inquire into the defender's capacity to present a genuine defence raising a real issue. Summary decree procedure is more far reaching than a procedure roll hearing where relevancy is tested only by reference to the pleadings unless other documents are specifically incorporated into them or reference to them is other-wise agreed. The rule permits the consideration of material extraneous to the pleadings. Accordingly I do not regard as sound the defender's argument that J absence of agreement about the productions or refer-ence to them in the pleadings should prevent consider-ation of them. For the same reason I do not think it a sine qua non of their being considered that they should be produced by order of the court."

Having held that the documents produced showed that it was virtually certain that the pursuers would be able to prove that the vases were the stolen vases he continued at p 473A: "I am also of the view that rule 89B entitles the court to take account of not merely the K pleadings and documents lodged, but also the history of the case and any relevant background information available."

I respectfully agree with the opinions which I have cited above and consider that they should be applied mutatis mutandis in the application of rule 59A of the Ordinary Cause Rules. The purpose of that rule is to enable the sheriff to penetrate the form and examine the substance of the dispute between the parties. To L that end he is entitled to take account not only of the pleadings but also of any productions which are placed before him and of information given to him in the course of the respective submissions. He will look at the pleadings to see broadly what the case is about but he should not examine them with the rigour which would be applied at debate. That comment applies to both parties. Summary decree will not pass against a defender who appears to have the basis of a statable defence but who has expressed it badly; on the other hand summary decree will not be refused merely

because there is a drafting error or a lack of detail in
the pursuer's pleadings. There will be some cases in
which a defender is justified in stating a bald denial
and putting the pursuer to proof, but such cases do not
include those in which the pursuer's pleadings and
productions indicate that there is a prima facie case
calling for an answer, especially where the facts
founded upon by the pursuer are within the defender's
knowledge. Where the defence stated is manifestly
irrelevant and not capable of rectification by adjustment or amendment it would be appropriate to grant
summary decree. Conversely, it may be refused if the
pursuers' pleadings give rise to a genuine and substantial question of relevancy. Whether or not there is a
statable defence is a matter to be tested at the time
when the sheriff is hearing the motion.

I have earlier detailed the pursuers' averments and
the documents upon which they found. It is now a
matter of admission that the appellant was at the
material time a director of the company and that he
signed the acceptance of the facility letter no 12/1. He
cannot therefore be heard to dispute anything contained in art 2 of condescendence. Likewise, as a director of the company, it must be deemed to be within his
knowledge (a) whether or not the directors placed the
company in liquidation and (b) whether or not the
company was indebted to the pursuers in the sum
averred. He is not entitled to put the pursuers to proof
of the averments contained in art 4 of condescendence
on the basis of an answer "Not known and not admitted". The first point made by the solicitor for the
appellant was that the averments in art 3, which are
met with a denial, were factually incorrect. Article 3
and the pursuers' plea in law showed that the pursuers
were founding upon one guarantee granted by all three
defenders. The true position, as was obvious from the
pursuers' productions, was that the appellant had
signed one document, no 12/2, whereas the second and
third defenders had signed a different document, no
12/3. That being so there were two distinct contracts
and the pursuers were not entitled to decree against all
three defenders jointly and severally. The solicitor for
the appellant argued that it was important to the
appellant that he should not be found jointly and
severally liable along with the other defenders lest any
settlement which he might reach with the pursuers
could leave him liable to claims of relief by the other
two defenders. He submitted that the decision in
Morgan v Smart (1872) 10 M 610 indicated that where
guarantors gave separate guarantees they were not
jointly and severally liable. Standing the discrepancy
between the pursuers' averments and the documents
produced it was likely that they would lose any debate
which followed, and where there was a real question
of relevancy debate was the appropriate forum at
which to determine it.

The pursuers' solicitor submitted that it was not in
dispute that the appellant had signed a guarantee, no
12/2. The fact that the other two defenders had signed
a separate form did not affect their joint and several
obligation to the pursuers: each was bound for the
total amount of the company's indebtedness (Walker,

Principles of Scottish Private Law (3rd ed), p 426). She
distinguished *Morgan v Smart* on the ground that in
that case the two guarantees were for separate specified amounts which in aggregate covered the whole
debt. Since the defender admitted that he had signed
a guarantee the answer "Denied" was simply not good
enough.

In my opinion the submissions for the pursuers and
respondents are well founded. It is quite true that the
pursuers' averments refer to a guarantee whereas what
is produced is two separate documents. That is just
the sort of thing which one would expect to be tidied
up in the course of adjustment. It does not affect the
main thrust of the pursuers' case. There is not the
remotest likelihood that this point would be arguable
were the case ever to reach debate. What the pursuers
are saying in substance is that each of the three
defenders bound himself for the whole sum lent by the
pursuers to the company. It seems to me that the solicitor for the pursuers was probably right to argue that
there would be a right of relief among the defenders
per se even though they had bound themselves by
separate documents, but it is not strictly necessary to
decide that point. The admitted fact is that the appellant bound himself for the whole amount when he
signed no 12/2 of process. Whether or not he has a
right of relief against the other defenders is of no
interest to the pursuers. The theoretical possibility
that the appellant might reach a settlement with the
pursuers and then be pursued by the second and third
defenders simply does not arise: if the pursuers were
interested in any such arrangement they would not be
moving this motion. The case of *Morgan v Smart* gives
no support to the proposition argued on behalf of the
appellant. In that case a debt of £105 was guaranteed
by one cautioner to the extent of £70 and by another
to the extent of £35; in other words, each cautioner
was bound for a specified part of the total debt. That
is completely different from the situation here where
all three cautioners are liable for the entire debt. The
import of the decision in *Morgan* is not, as was argued
on behalf of the appellant, that if the obligations were
contained in separate documents there was no joint
and several liability, but that if each cautioner undertook liability for only part of the debt there was no
joint and several liability. In the instant case, reading
the pleadings along with the productions, it seems to
me that the pursuers have a prima facie claim against
the appellant to which he has disclosed no maintainable defence.

The appellant's agent went on to argue that he had
another line of defence which had not yet appeared in
his pleadings. That was that he had signed the guarantee no 12/2 at the request of the third defender who
had told him that his signature was required as a director of the company. The two men had met in the car
park at Aberdeen railway station where the appellant
had signed the document without reading it properly
and under the mistaken impression that he was
signing the stocking loan agreement. In obtaining the
appellant's signature the third defender had been
acting as an agent for the pursuers. The guarantee was
accordingly reducible.

In reply the pursuers' agent submitted that the third

A defender could not possibly be treated as an agent of the pursuers (Gloag & Henderson, *Introduction to the Law of Scotland* (9th ed), p 277; *Young v Clydesdale Bank Ltd* (1889) 17 R 231). In any event the appellant, having already signed the acceptance of the facility letter, no 12/1, must have known that he would be required to sign a guarantee. It was highly improbable that he had signed no 12/2 of process, which was witnessed by two persons having the same surname and address as himself, under any misapprehension as to

B its nature.

Once again I find myself in complete agreement with the submissions for the pursuers. It seems to me that the decision in *Young v Clydesdale Bank* is quite conclusive of the matter. The question before the court was whether a certain guarantee should be reduced, and one of the grounds upon which reduction was sought was that the cautioners had signed on the basis of a misrepresentation perpetrated by the debtor as to the nature of the obligation. It was held

C that in a question between the cautioners and the lender such misrepresentation was of no effect. Dealing with that point Lord Adam at p 243 said: "If that document had been read I do not believe that [the cautioners] would have signed it. It would have been known then that it was a very different document from what they were led to believe it was. But that being so, it does not follow that, although they did not know what they were signing, the bank are to be liable for that. I think every opportunity was given to them by

D the bank to read and examine it, and it was their duty to do so, and to ascertain the nature of the document they were signing. If David Young, relying upon his brother's statement, chose to sign the document without reading, or without looking at what he was signing in order to ascertain what was in it, the consequences must fall upon himself, the bank believing — as they were entitled to believe — that the cautioner knew perfectly well what he was signing. They gave their money on the faith of this document, and it

E appears to me that that being so, the bank was not and could not be affected by any fraud, or undue concealment in this matter, as far as I can see. Having given money on the faith of the document that had been signed by David Young, David Young must be responsible for the amount."

The Lord President (Inglis) at pp 247-248 said: "I do not doubt that the pursuer was under an error — and a very important error — as to the essence of the

F document which he subscribed. It is not enough to entitle him to a reduction of this obligation that that error was produced either by outside influence, for which the bank is in no way responsible, or by the negligence of the pursuer himself. I think the error was brought about by both of these means. I think in the first place that the pursuer was deceived — and grossly deceived — by his brother and his brother's cashier or clerk. The representations made by them were, I think, of a fraudulent character, and if the bank had been in any way answerable for these representations, I should have been inclined to pronounce

judgment against them. But there is no evidence what-

G ever that the bank were in the least degree aware of anything that had passed between the pursuer and his brother and his brother's clerk. All that was unknown to the bank."

In this case the third defender has nothing to do with the pursuers but he is a director of the debtor company. No facts were suggested which could possibly lead to the conclusion that the third defender was an agent of the pursuers. Accordingly I hold that this proposed, although as yet unpled, defence is also unstatable. As well as being legally unstatable I might H add that I consider it to be factually highly improbable. Having already signed no 12/1 of process I do not understand how the appellant could have thought that he was signing the same kind of document again or how he can express surprise at discovering that he has signed a guarantee. The appellant's signature to the guarantee no 12/2 is witnessed. Upon the appellant's narrative one would be interested to know whether the witnesses were present in the car at Aberdeen railway station or whether the appellant took the I document home and acknowledged his signature to them. Either way the scope for misunderstanding on the part of the appellant as to what he was signing seems distinctly limited.

On the whole matter I consider that neither the defence which now appears in the pleadings nor the defence which the appellant's agent has proposed to add has any substance. The pursuers are accordingly entitled to summary decree and I have refused the appeal. It was conceded that were the appeal to be J refused expenses should be awarded to the pursuers and respondents.

Solicitors for Pursuers, Mackie & Dewar, Aberdeen — Solicitors for First Defender, Raeburn, Christie & Co, Aberdeen.

[The rules on summary decrees are now contained in Chap

17 of the Ordinary Cause Rules 1993.] K

Smith v Greenhill

SHERIFF COURT OF LOTHIAN AND
BORDERS AT EDINBURGH L
SHERIFF PRINCIPAL C G B NICHOLSON, QC
27 AUGUST 1993

Parent and child — Declarator of paternity — Adverse inference to be drawn from failure of mother to provide sample for DNA testing — Whether presumption of paternity rebutted — Law Reform (Miscellaneous Provisions) (Scotland) Act 1990 (c 40), s 70 (2).

A man sought declarator that he was the father of a child and an award of access to her. The mother was married to another man and had two other children. After proof the sheriff, having concluded that both the pursuer and the defender's husband were having sexual relations with the mother at about the time of conception, refused the declarator. The pursuer appealed to the sheriff principal, arguing inter alia that, the defender having failed to provide a sample for DNA testing, the adverse inference to be drawn in terms of s 70 (2) of the Law Reform (Miscellaneous Provisions) (Scotland) Act 1990 rebutted the presumption of paternity.

Held, that s 70 (2) gave the court a discretion both as to whether to draw an adverse inference and as to the nature of any inference to be drawn, and since it had been established that either the pursuer or the defender's husband could have been the father of the child, the sheriff had been entitled to conclude that the presumption in favour of the husband had not been overcome (p 24F-G and J-K); and appeal *refused*.

Action of declarator

Anthony Martin Smith raised an action against Mrs Elaine Greenhill, seeking declarator that he was the father of the defender's child and an award of access to her. After proof the sheriff (R G Craik, QC) refused the declarator. The pursuer appealed to the sheriff principal.

On 27 August 1993 the sheriff principal *refused* the appeal.

THE SHERIFF PRINCIPAL (C G B NICHOLSON, QC).—This appeal concerns a dispute as to the paternity of a child, Jennifer, who was born to the defender on 25 February 1992. The pursuer is himself a married man and has two children from that marriage. The defender is also married, and has two children in addition to Jennifer. It appears that the pursuer and the defender first came to know each other towards the end of 1990, and in due course their relationship became an intimate one. According to the defender's pleadings, and her evidence, that relationship resulted in sexual intercourse on only one occasion in March 1991; but, according to the pursuer, the relationship was a sexual one from early in 1991 until about August of that year. In that situation the pursuer raised the present action in which he seeks a declarator that he is Jennifer's father, and an award of access to her.

After proof the sheriff found as a fact that the sexual relationship between the pursuer and the defender had endured for the period claimed by the pursuer, and as a result he concluded that the pursuer *could* be the father of Jennifer. However, he also found as a fact that at the time of conception, namely around May 1991, the defender and her husband were still living as man and wife and having sexual relations. In that situation he concluded that he could not be satisfied on a balance of probabilities that the pursuer had displaced the presumption in favour of the defender's husband being Jennifer's father, and he accordingly

refused the declarator which the pursuer was seeking. Although that, strictly speaking, made it unnecessary for him to consider the crave for access, the sheriff went on to state that he would not in any event have awarded access to the pursuer since he was not satisfied that such an award would be in Jennifer's interests. The pursuer has appealed against that decision, but at the commencement of the appeal hearing his solicitor advised me that he does not now seek to challenge the sheriff's conclusion on the matter of access. The appeal was therefore concerned solely with the matter of paternity.

In presenting the appeal the solicitor for the pursuer advanced two main submissions. They were, first, that the sheriff had failed correctly to adopt the test of the balance of probabilities and, secondly, that the sheriff had failed to draw the appropriate inference from the defender's refusal to comply with a request which had been made of her under s 70 of the Law Reform (Miscellaneous Provisions) (Scotland) Act 1990. I therefore turn to consider each of those submissions in turn.

[The sheriff principal considered and rejected the submission that the sheriff had not properly applied the balance of probabilities test in s 5 (4) of the Law Reform (Parent and Child) (Scotland) Act 1986 and continued:]

The second main submission advanced by the solicitor for the pursuer concerned the way in which the sheriff approached s 70 of the Law Reform (Miscellaneous Provisions) (Scotland) Act 1990. Introduced against the background of the general availability of DNA testing (which can effectively determine questions of paternity beyond reasonable doubt), that section provides, first, that in any civil proceedings to which the section applies the court may request a party to the proceedings to provide a sample for analysis and to consent to the taking of such sample from a child. In the present case it appears that, just before the commencement of the proof, the sheriff requested that the defender should consent to the taking of a sample from Jennifer, but that request was refused by the defender. By subs (2) s 70 deals with that situation as follows: "Where a party to whom a request under subsection (1) above has been made refuses or fails — (a) to provide or, as the case may be, to consent to the taking of, a sample . . . the court may draw from the refusal or failure such adverse inference, if any, in relation to the subject matter of the proceedings as seems to it to be appropriate."

In the present case the sheriff states that the adverse inference which he has drawn as a result of the defender's failure to comply with the request under the section is that she "is not telling the truth about the extent and duration of her relationship with the pursuer and that it is thus possible at least that the pursuer is the father of Jennifer". The solicitor for the pursuer submitted that, in approaching the matter in that way, the sheriff had restricted himself unduly, and had not properly applied the provisions of s 70 (2). If Parliament had intended that the subsection should only be used as a means of determining credibility, it need not have bothered to enact the subsection at all. Given the view reached by the sheriff in the present case as to the respective credibility of the pursuer and the defender, based simply on their evidence and that of the supporting witnesses, he could have reached exactly the same conclusion as to the nature and duration of the parties' sexual relationship without any reference to, or reliance on, s 70 (2); and in that situation he would have been bound, again without any aid from the subsection, to conclude that the pursuer *could* have been Jennifer's father. In that situation, it was submitted, the only proper construction of the subsection must be that, if it is to be invoked at all, it must go to rebut a presumption of paternity. If the sheriff here had approached the subsection in that way, he would, and should, have found that the defender's refusal to comply with the request was a significant factor tilting the balance of probabilities in the pursuer's favour.

In response on this point counsel for the defender submitted that the pursuer's solicitor was seeking to read more into s 70 (2) than is actually there, and to construe it as if it provided that a refusal should lead to a particular *conclusion* rather than merely enabling a court to draw an *inference*. Furthermore, it was submitted, the subsection does not even require the court to draw an inference, nor does it prescribe the inference that is to be drawn if the court is minded to draw one. The matter is entirely one for the discretion of the court and the only direction in the subsection is that, if the court is minded to draw an inference from refusal, that inference may be an adverse one.

On the foregoing basis, counsel went on by reference to well known authorities such as *G v G (Minors: Custody Appeal)* [1985] 1 WLR 647; [1985] 2 All ER 225, and *Britton v Central Regional Council*, 1986 SLT 207, to submit that no grounds had been established in the present appeal which would entitle me to review the sheriff's exercise of his direction. The sheriff here had plainly and correctly recognised that he had a discretion under the subsection, and he had proceeded to exercise that discretion in a manner which he regarded as appropriate. It was not a misuse of that discretion that he had not gone as far as the pursuer would have wished. In any event, given that the sheriff had found facts to support the possibility that the defender's husband could be Jennifer's father, it would have been unreasonable to found on s 70 (2) as justifying an inference, and therefore a conclusion, that he was not the father and that the pursuer was.

Before turning to my own view on the above matters I should just add that, in the course of the submissions, I was referred to several cases, some of them English, which I have not mentioned thus far. I was also referred by both parties to various definitions, culled from ever larger and more detailed versions of the *Oxford Dictionary*, in respect of words such as "inference", "adverse", and "presumption". I do not find them of assistance in determining this appeal, and I therefore do not propose to refer to them further.

In my opinion counsel for the defender is quite correct when he says that s 70 (2) of the 1990 Act gives the court a discretion where there is a refusal to provide, or to consent to the provision of, a sample. Moreover, that discretion is twofold. First of all, there is a discretion as to whether or not to draw any adverse inference at all. In the second place, even where a court decides to draw an inference, the nature of that inference is also at the discretion of the court. In those circumstances I consider that an appellate court will always be slow to interfere with the exercise of that discretion by the lower court unless it can be shown that that court has exercised the discretion in a way which is plainly wrong, or in a way which has led to an entirely unreasonable result. On the face of it, I agree with counsel for the defender that there does not appear to be anything in the sheriff's approach to the exercise of his discretion which comes near to satisfying that test.

I recognise, of course, that the pursuer's solicitor's position was that the sheriff had misconstrued the purpose of the subsection. In my opinion, however, the fallacy in his submission is to suppose that s 70 (2) must always lead to the same conclusion in cases where a court is minded to draw an adverse inference. That approach fails, I think, to recognise that the circumstances in which the subsection may come into play may be many and varied. In some instances where a man is seeking to establish that he is the father of a child there may be no other putative father in contention; and if, in such a case, the mother refuses a request under the section, it may be reasonable to draw the inference that she is falsely denying the paternity of the man in question. But, where there is a statutory presumption as to paternity to be overcome, and where, as in the present case, it is established that the woman was having sexual relations with her husband at the relevant time, it may be much more difficult, if not impossible, to draw an inference which leads to the rebuttal of the presumption and to a finding that a man other than the husband is the father of the child. No doubt this matter could have been put beyond doubt one way or the other if the defender in the present case had complied with the request that was made of her but, since she did not, I consider that the sheriff was well entitled to conclude that the furthest that he could go was to find that the pursuer could be the father, but equally that the father could be the defender's husband. In that situation, of course, the statutory presumption in favour of the husband could not be said to have been overcome.

For all of the foregoing reasons I have come to the conclusion that this appeal must be refused. It was a matter of agreement that expenses should follow success, and I have accordingly made an award against the pursuer.

Solicitors for Pursuer and Appellant, Cochran, Sayers & Cook, Edinburgh — Counsel for Defender and Respondent, Primrose; Solicitors, Allan McDougall & Co, SSC, Dalkeith.

Ranaldi v Ranaldi

^A SHERIFF COURT OF LOTHIAN AND
BORDERS AT EDINBURGH

SHERIFF R G CRAIK, QC

24 MARCH 1992

*Husband and wife — Divorce — Financial provision —
Capital sum — Matrimonial home — House purchased
before marriage — Family Law (Scotland) Act 1985
(c 37), s 10 (4).*

^B In an action of divorce the wife defender claimed a
capital sum. Her husband had purchased a house for
his previous wife and family. The defender argued
that the house had become matrimonial property as
defined by s 10 (4) of the Family Law (Scotland) Act
1985.

Held, that the house was not matrimonial property
but that the defender should be entitled to a capital
sum based on the enhancement value of the property
^C between the date of the marriage and the date of sepa-
ration (p 26F-I); and decree of divorce *granted* and
capital sum *awarded* to the defender.

———

Action of divorce

Guido Oreste Ranaldi raised an action of divorce
against Eileen Christine Abernethy or Ranaldi, who
inter alia claimed payment of a capital sum.

^D **Findings in fact**

The sheriff found the following facts admitted or
proved:

(1) The parties were married at Edinburgh on 5
November 1983. There are two children of the marriage, Richard Allan Ranaldi born 2 July 1982 and Julie
Kay Ranaldi born 23 July 1984. (2) After the marriage, the parties lived together at the pursuer's present
home at 31 Rosslyn Crescent, Pilrig, Edinburgh, until
^E in or about February 1990 when they separated. They
have not cohabited or had marital relations since. The
defender now resides with the children of the marriage
at 3F3, 2 Murieston Place, Edinburgh. (3) In its latter
stages, the marriage was unhappy. The defender
declined to sleep with the pursuer from about 1988
and declined to have sexual relations with him. In or
about November 1989, the defender formed an adul-
terous association with a Michael Moran, who was a
lodger in the parties' home. In or about the evening of
^F 3 February 1990, the pursuer returned to the parties'
home to find the defender in bed with said Michael
Moran. Said association is admitted by the defender.
A few days later, the defender left the matrimonial
home and the parties have not cohabited since. The
defender subsequently gave birth to a further child on
9 March 1991, of whom the pursuer is not the father.
(4) The said two children of the marriage presently
reside with the defender and have done so since
October 1990. They are presently happy in the
defender's care and well looked after by her. It is in
their best interests that the defender should be
awarded their custody. The pursuer has also looked
after said children in the past and it is in their best ^G
interests that he should continue to exercise regular
access to them. (5) The pursuer was previously
married and has a grown up family by that marriage.
He bought his present house at 31 Rosslyn Crescent,
aforesaid in or about 1966 as a family home for his
first family. The pursuer separated from his first wife
in or about 1970 and was divorced from her in or
about the middle of 1976. Shortly after his separation
from his first wife, the defender moved into the pursuer's home. Initially this was to assist him in looking ^H
after his children by his first marriage. After two years
or so however, the parties started to cohabit as man
and wife and continued to do so until they themselves
were married in 1983. (6) Throughout this period, the
pursuer took in boarders to augment the family
income. The defender assisted him in this enterprise
and cooked and cleaned for the lodgers. In about 1980,
she formalised the business by having the pursuer's
home registered as a guest house. She continued to
assist the pursuer in the administration of this busi- ^I
ness until the time of her departure from the family
home in or about February 1990. For part of this
period, the pursuer had jobs in the family cafe and also
as a cleaner. The bulk of the duties in caring for the
lodgers thus fell on the defender. (7) At the time of
the parties' marriage in 1983, the pursuer's home at
31 Rosslyn Crescent, aforesaid, was worth about
£38,000. As at the end of November 1989 (the effective date of separation of the parties), the said house
was worth about £85,000. (8) As at the effective date ^J
of separation, there was an accrued matrimonial debt
of about £14,000. This consisted of debts to the First
National Bank plc of about £9,170; to National
Provincial Building Society of £1,175; to Citybank
Savings of £2,220; to Lombard Tricity Finance of
about £250 and to Access of about £1,185. (9) For the
two tax years ending 5 April 1989 and 5 April 1990
respectively, the pursuer had taxable income from the
lodgers in the family home of £2,104 and £2,887
respectively. (10) The pursuer's present income ^K
position is that he receives £94 per week by way of
rent from three lodgers. He is also in receipt of income
support of £70 per week. He has a present liability of
£112 per week to service the accrued debt. This
explains why he is in receipt of the income support
figure. He also maintains a "Paymaster Account",
which is presently in debit to the extent of about
£1,865. The furniture and furnishings now in the pursuer's home were largely acquired before the parties'
marriage and the pursuer's "R" registered Ford ^L
Granada motor vehicle was worth about £500 at the
effective date of separation. (11) The defender is fully
occupied in looking after the two children of the
marriage. She is in receipt of benefit and child allowance for the support of herself and the children.

On 24 March 1992 the sheriff *granted* decree of
divorce, *awarded* custody of the children to the
defender, *awarded* access to the pursuer, *ordered* the
pursuer to pay a capital sum to the defender of
£16,000 on 1 October 1992 with interest at 15 per cent

per annum and *ordered* the pursuer to place his house
at 31 Rosslyn Crescent, Pilrig, Edinburgh, on the
market for sale.

THE SHERIFF (R G CRAIK, QC).—This is a
longstanding dispute between husband and wife
which originally embraced matters of custody, aliment
and interdict apart from the matters presently in contention. However, on the morning of the proof, parties
submitted a joint minute and made certain preliminary submissions which made it clear that the
present dispute between the parties is limited to
whether or not the pursuer should make payment of
a capital sum to the defender, in the event of divorce
being granted.

[The sheriff dealt with matters with which this
report is not concerned and continued:]

The solicitor for the defender's next submission was
that the former matrimonial home was "matrimonial
property" as defined by s 10 (4) of the Family Law
(Scotland) Act 1985 ("the 1985 Act"). Whether or not,
she argued, the home had originally been bought by
the pursuer as a family home for this family, it had
certainly become that family home. She cited the case
of *Buczynska v Buczynski*, 1989 SLT 558, in her
support. The solicitor for the pursuer replied that the
present property could not be so regarded. It had been
bought by the pursuer in 1966 as a family home for
his then wife and family. Section 10 (4) of the 1985
Act clearly envisaged that, to fall under the subsection,
the property would have to be acquired by the pursuer
for use by *the parties* as a family home. Clearly this
was not the case here. She cited the similar situation
discussed in the sheriff court case of *Maclellan v
Maclellan*, 1988 SCLR 399, as an illustration of a
situation where one of the parties had acquired
property before the marriage and there was no
evidence that it had been acquired for use as the matrimonial home. In that case the value of the property in
question was excluded as "matrimonial property".
However, the solicitor for the pursuer did concede
that the defender might be able to pray in aid the
terms of s 9 (1) (b) of the 1985 Act, in maintaining an
entitlement to a capital sum, since it could be said that
the pursuer had had the "economic advantage" of the
contributions by the defender in maintaining the
income from lodgers over the period of the marriage.
According to her, what should be looked at was not the
value of the home as at the relevant date (£85,000) but
the enhancement in value that there had been in the
property between the date of the marriage in 1983 and
the latter date (a figure of £47,000). If this were to be
the figure, she maintained, it would have to be subject
both to deduction of the matrimonial debt (£14,000)
and to an additional amount to enable the pursuer to
market the property and remove himself to another.

Having considered these submissions, I am of the
view that those of the solicitor for the pursuer are to
be preferred: In *Buczynska's* case, it appears that the
parties were cohabiting at the time that the matrimonial home was acquired and that they married
shortly thereafter, when the husband was free to do so.
It also appears that Lord Morton in that case did not
accept that the husband had necessarily acquired the
house purely as an investment. In the present case, the
matrimonial home was purchased years before the
defender even started to cohabit with the pursuer, and
in no way could it have been said to have been
acquired by the pursuer for use as a family home with
the defender and his second family. I thus conclude
that the house is not "matrimonial property" as
envisaged by s 10 (4) of the 1985 Act. However, I do
think that an award of a capital sum should be made
here. There was clear evidence that the defender
assisted the pursuer in the running of the boarding
house business and, indeed, that she had taken a major
part in that. The running of the business contributed
to the family income which enabled the mortgage on
the matrimonial home to be paid and the value of it
to become enhanced over the years. It would be
grossly unfair in my opinion for the pursuer to be able
to take total advantage of the property situation in
determining whether or not a capital sum ought to be
paid. I thus conclude that the defender should be
found entitled to such an award and that it should be
based on the enhancement value of the property
between the date of the marriage in 1983 and the effective date of separation in November 1989. This was
the approach taken by the Lord Ordinary in the case
of *Budge v Budge*, 1990 SLT 319. The only other relevant capital sum is the figure of £500 representing the
value of the pursuer's car at the relevant date.

I have thus taken the relevant enhancement value
figure which is £47,000. I have deducted the matrimonial debt from that (£14,000) and have made a
further allowance in the pursuer's favour of £1,500 to
enable him to meet the expenses of marketing, sale and
removal. I have added in the said figure of £500. This
leaves a net figure of £32,000 and, to reach the capital
sum awarded, I have merely divided this in two.

So far as expenses are concerned, the solicitor for the
defender contended that her client should be awarded
the expenses of the action. At the end of the day she
had not contested the matter of divorce and had been
successful in having her custody of the children confirmed and, as it transpires, has been awarded a substantial capital sum. The solicitor for the pursuer, on
the other hand, contended that an appropriate award
would be one of no expenses due to or by. Matters had
been in contention until the very last moment. The
pursuer was now to obtain his divorce on an undefended basis and, on any view, the defender's entitlement to a capital sum should be materially reduced
from the £50,000 that she counterclaimed for. Neither
party had found it necessary to insist on the craves for
interdict and the question of access had been agreed.
In my view, there has indeed been mixed success in
this action and an appropriate award of expenses
would be none to or due to or by either party. I have
provided accordingly.

*Solicitors for Pursuer, Morton Fraser Milligan, WS —
Solicitors for Defender, Shepherd & Wedderburn, WS.*

Stewart v The Royal Bank of Scotland plc

SHERIFF COURT OF GLASGOW AND
STRATHKELVIN AT GLASGOW

SHERIFF A B WILKINSON

23 JUNE 1992

Diligence — Arrestment — Decree against company — Service of arrestment at Scottish branch of bank — Whether pursuer entitled to have furthcoming to him sum held by bank at branch in England to credit of company.

Having obtained decree against a company, the pursuer served an arrestment on a bank at a branch in Glasgow. A sum was held to the credit of the company at a branch of the bank in Cheshire. A question arose in an action of furthcoming whether the pursuer was entitled to have that sum made furthcoming to him by virtue of the arrestment served in Glasgow. Expert evidence was led that under English law the duty of a bank in terms of the banking contract was to repay the balance at credit of the customer's account at the branch where the account was kept after due demand made there by the customer. There was no evidence of such demand having been made.

Held, (1) that the law governing the contract between the bank and the company was English law (p 28E-F); and (2) that the bank's liability to account was at its branch in Cheshire and therefore that liability had not been attached by the arrestment served in Glasgow (p 29D); and bank *assoilzied*.

Action of furthcoming

Robert Iain Stewart raised an action of furthcoming against The Royal Bank of Scotland plc and Country Produce Ltd seeking payment of a sum held by the bank in Cheshire to the credit of an account held by the company. An arrestment relating to the company had been served at the bank's branch in Buchanan Street, Glasgow.

The sheriff made the following findings:

Finds in fact: (1) The pursuer resides at 10 Merrick Gardens, Bearsden, Glasgow, and that the first defenders are a bank with their registered office at 36 St Andrew Square, Edinburgh, and a branch at 98 Buchanan Street, Glasgow. The whereabouts of the second defenders are unknown. No proceedings are pending before any other court involving the present cause of action and between the parties hereto, nor is there any agreement between the parties prorogating jurisdiction over the subject matter of the present cause to another court. (2) On 24 November 1989 and 31 January 1990 in an action in the sheriff court of the Sheriffdom of North Strathclyde at Dumbarton at the instance of the pursuer against the second defenders, the sheriff decerned against the second defenders for payment to the pursuer of the sum of £10,400 with interest at the rate of 15 per cent per annum from 2 December 1988 until payment together with £304.86 of expenses. Said decree was extracted on 28 February

1990. (3) On 22 November 1988 sheriff officers instructed by the pursuer served on the first defenders as arrestees a schedule of arrestment on the dependence by virtue of a warrant of the sheriff of North Strathclyde at Dumbarton of even date, that schedule of arrestment being delivered to the first defenders at their branch at 98 Buchanan Street, Glasgow. The formalities of service of an arrestment on the dependence were complied with. (4) By letter dated 18 January 1989 the first defenders wrote to agents acting for the pursuer informing them that they (the first defenders) regretted that, as the arrestment was on the dependence of an action, they were not at liberty to divulge any information at that stage. The letter went on to state "Your letter of 11-1-89 stated that the amount of the arrestment was £2,600. Please note that our records show the amount to be £10,600 more or less." By letter dated 26 February 1990 the first defenders further wrote to the pursuer's agent stating that the arrestment had attached the sum of £3,195.16 (plus interest). That letter went on to state: "To obtain these funds it will be necessary for you either to raise an action of furthcoming or, alternatively, provide us with a probative mandate in your favour signed by our customer authorising the release of the amount in question together with a letter from you confirming that on payment of the amount in question the arrestment may be regarded as having been withdrawn." These letters were sent and received in the ordinary course of business. (5) On 22 November 1988 there was at credit of an account in the name of the second defenders at the Sandbach, Cheshire branch of the first defenders the sum of £3,195.16. (6) On 22 November 1988 the second defenders maintained no account with the first defenders at any branch of the first defenders within Scotland and the only account maintained by them was the account referred to in finding in fact 5 above at the Sandbach, Cheshire branch. (7) The general rule of English law, applicable where no agreement to the contrary has been made, is that where a customer opens an account at a bank branch in England the contract between the bank and its customer is governed by English law. (8) Where the contract between a bank and its customer is governed by English law the primary duty imposed on the bank by English law is, in the absence of any express contractual provision as to repayment, to repay the balance at credit of the customer's account at the branch where the account is kept after due demand there by the customer. (9) Because of the risk of the bank's being called upon to pay the debt a second time, an English court would not grant a garnishee order against an English bank in relation to a debt situated at the bank's branch in Scotland. The proper course, in contemplation of English law, would be to have the English judgment recognised in Scotland and the appropriate steps taken to attach the debt there. Similarly, in contemplation of English law, the proper course in the case of a Scottish judgment against someone having a credit balance at an English branch of a Scottish bank would be to have the judgment recognised in England and appropriate steps taken to attach the debt there.

Finds in law: (1) The contract between the first
A defenders and the second defenders in respect of the
second defenders' account at the first defenders' Sandbach, Cheshire branch, is governed by English law. (2)
The obligation to account owed by the first defenders
to the second defenders in respect of the second
defenders' account at the first defenders' Sandbach,
Cheshire branch has not been attached by the arrestment used by the pursuer in the hands of the first
defenders at their branch at 98 Buchanan Street,
Glasgow. (3) The pursuer is not entitled to have made
B furthcoming to him any sum standing to the credit of
the second defenders' account at the first defenders'
Sandbach, Cheshire branch.

On 23 June 1992 the sheriff *assoilzied* the first
defenders.

THE SHERIFF (A B WILKINSON).—In an
attempt to attach funds of the common debtor the
pursuer used arrestments in the hands of the first
C defenders at their Buchanan Street, Glasgow branch.
There was no dispute that these arrestments had been
validly used. There were, however, no funds to the
credit of the common debtor in any account at the first
defenders' Buchanan Street, Glasgow branch or,
indeed, at any of their branches in Scotland. There
was, however, a sum to the credit of the common
debtor at an account kept by them at the first
defenders' branch in Sandbach, Cheshire. The question at issue is whether the pursuer is entitled to have
D that sum made furthcoming to him on the view that
the arrestments used in Glasgow either had attached
directly a debt owed by the first defenders in respect
of that sum or, alternatively, had attached an obligation of accounting owed by the first defenders to the
common debtor in respect of which, on a due accounting, that sum became payable.

There was evidence before me in affidavit form to
the effect that, in contemplation of English law, the
E law governing the contract of banker and customer as
between the first defenders and the common debtor
was the law of England and argument was addressed
to me to like effect. That is, however, in my opinion,
the wrong starting point. The law governing the contract must be determined in accordance with the international private law rules of Scots law. English law has
no part to play in that process. The point is not,
however, of importance in the result because the
English and Scottish rules of international private law
are not in conflict on this matter and they both indi-
F cate quite clearly that the law governing the contract
between the first defenders and the common debtor in
England is the law of England. The only Scottish
feature of that contract is that the first defenders are
a company registered in Scotland and have their head
office here. That is insufficient to give a Scottish
character to a contract whose every other connection
is with England. Among the authorities cited to me,
reference may be made to *James Miller & Partners v
Whitworth Street Estates* [1970] AC 583; *Libyan Arab
Foreign Bank v Bankers Trust Co* [1989] QB 728; and

to the dicta of Lord President Hope about the locality
of the account as an essential part of the contract G
between banker and customer in *Bank of Scotland v
Seitz*, 1990 SLT 584 at p 590. The conclusion that the
contract is governed by English law is, in my opinion,
beyond dispute.

The expert evidence on English law was that, in the
absence of any express provision as to repayment, the
duty of a bank in terms of the banking contract was to
repay the balance at credit of the customer's account
at the branch where the account was kept after due
demand made there by the customer. Reference was H
made to *Joachimson v Swiss Bank Corporation* [1921]
3 KB 110, from which it appears that the bank has no
obligation to repay until demand is actually made at
the branch. There is no evidence of any relevant
demand having been made in this case. The service at
the appropriate branch of an order nisi in English
garnishee proceedings might constitute such a demand
(*Joachimson v Swiss Bank Corporation*, supra at
pp 121, 126 and 131) but it is clear that that cannot
be said of a Scottish arrestment used in Scotland. It I
follows that any contention that the arrestment
attached a debt due and payable must be rejected. The
question remains, however, of whether an obligation
to account has been arrested. Such an obligation may
be attached in the hands of a banker by an English
garnishee order although no demand for payment has
been made (*Joachimson v Swiss Bank Corporation* at
p 131).

Of arrestment of an obligation to account Anton says
(*Private International Law* (1st ed), p 112): "It is J
essential, however, that the arrestee be subject to the
jurisdiction and that his liability is to account within
the jurisdiction". The first defenders are subject to the
jurisdiction. The question of liability to account
within the jurisdiction is more difficult. There is,
perhaps, a good deal to be said for the view that, as a
general rule, a person under a duty to account is liable
to make an accounting wherever the creditor finds him
and so requires. Just as the creditor in a loan can
demand repayment at any time and any place K
(*Joachimson v Swiss Bank Corporation* at p 119) so can
the creditor in an obligation to account demand an
accounting.

That that should be so consists with *McNairn v
McNairn*, 1959 SLT (Notes) 35, in which a debt
which had all the features of an English debt was
arrested in the hands of an English building society at
one of their Scottish branches and it was held that,
despite the foreign character of the debt, there was an L
obligation to account in Scotland which had been
validly arrested. The reason for holding that there was
an obligation to account in Scotland is, perhaps, not
fully explained but it seems that the fact that the building society carried on business in Scotland was
sufficient. The solicitor for the first defenders sought
to distinguish *McNairn v McNairn* on the ground that
the distinction between enforceability and prestability
had, so far as appeared from the report, not been
argued and had consequently become confused or
blurred. I think, however, that the true view may be,

not that *McNairn v McNairn* confuses or blurs that
A distinction, but that in obligations of accounting issues
of enforceability and prestability will tend to coalesce
at least to the extent that, unless reason can be shown
to the contrary, the obligation will generally be prest-
able in a place where jurisdiction can be founded
against the debtor. But there may be exceptions. Were
that not so it would be unnecessary, once jurisdiction
were established, to consider, as was done in *McNairn
v McNairn*, the place of accounting. Yet I doubt if the
fact that demand has to be made at a particular place
B before payment becomes due is of itself sufficient to
make that place the sole place of accounting. Although
in judicial proceedings a conclusion for accounting is
invariably combined with a conclusion for payment,
they are not necessarily inseparable. I see no inconsistency in a creditor's being free to require an accounting in one place and yet bound, if he seeks payment,
to make his demand for payment in another. The
highly localised character of banking contracts is,
however, sufficient, in my opinion, to constitute a
C specialty. That localised character is a feature of the
law of both Scotland and England (*Bank of Scotland v
Seitz*; *Joachimson v Swiss Banking Corporation*, supra).
It is based on the practical needs of banking and, in
particular, on the need to have in one place control of
the account and of the transactions, perhaps rapidly
changing, affecting it. The information necessary for
an accounting in a contract between banker and
customer is similarly and necessarily localised. That is
a point which was not before the court in *McNairn v
D McNairn* and on which it can be distinguished. There
may moreover be material differences between a building society deposit, which was at issue in *McNairn v
McNairn*, and the banking account at issue in this
case. I conclude that the first defenders' liability to
account was at Sandbach, Cheshire and therefore that
that liability has not been attached by the arrestment
used by the pursuer.

Where an obligation to account has been arrested on
the dependence of an action the party using the arrest-
E ment is entitled after final judgment to have the sum
due on an accounting made furthcoming towards satisfaction of any decree for payment in his favour. It
may, however, be questioned whether that principle
applies where the arrestee's obligation to make
payment is dependent on the making of a demand by
the common debtor and no such demand has been
made. If such a demand were required in Scotland, the
pursuer could no doubt, by virtue of his arrestment,
F come in place of the common debtor so as to make that
demand and, perhaps, the arrestment or the raising of
an action of furthcoming would in itself have that
effect; but there is no evidence that the pursuer has
made a demand at the place in England in which he
is required to do so and, indeed, it is difficult to see
how he could make such a demand in place of the
common debtor without resorting to English proceedings for enforcement. On the view I have taken that
the pursuer has failed to arrest the obligation to
account it is, however, unnecessary to decide these
questions.

I have reached these conclusions with some regret.
The pursuer has a remedy by means of registration of G
his judgment in England and enforcement there but,
in the circumstances of this case, that is a relatively
expensive and cumbersome procedure. There may be
much to be said for the ready enforcement of judgment debts throughout the United Kingdom, if not
throughout the European Community, and for the
protection in such cases of arrestees against the risk of
double jeopardy which is the substantial matter underlying the first defender's opposition to the pursuer's
claim. These are not, however, questions for me. It H
may also be questioned if the localised character of
banking contracts is a necessary doctrine in modern
conditions of automated accounting and electronic
communication, but that too is not a question for me.
The doctrine has been affirmed recently and any
modification of it is a matter for a higher court or for
legislation.

Solicitors for Pursuers, Alison Atack & Co, Bearsden I
— Solicitors for First Defenders, Brodies, WS,
Edinburgh.

Warners v Beveridge & Kellas, WS   J

SHERIFF COURT OF LOTHIAN AND
BORDERS AT EDINBURGH
SHERIFF PRINCIPAL C G B NICHOLSON, QC
15 NOVEMBER 1993

*Heritable property — Sale — Letter of obligation —
Undertaking to deliver clear search disclosing purchasers'
title provided that title recorded within 21 days of date of
settlement — Extent of qualification.* K

*Contract — Sale of heritage — Letter of obligation —
Undertaking to deliver clear search disclosing purchasers'
title provided that title recorded within 21 days of date of
settlement — Extent of qualification.*

In a house purchase transaction a firm of solicitors
undertook in a letter of obligation to deliver a clear
search within 12 months of settlement, which search
would disclose the purchasers' title, provided that title
was recorded within 21 days of settlement. L

A search which was produced revealed that the subjects were burdened by a hitherto undisclosed standard security. The debt secured was paid by the
purchasers' solicitors to clear the title and they then
claimed payment of that sum from the sellers' solicitors in terms of the letter of obligation. The sheriff
granted decree de plano. The defenders appealed to
the sheriff principal, arguing that on a proper construction of the letter of obligation, as the disposition
in favour of the purchasers had not been recorded

A until after 21 days from the date of the letter of obligation, there was no obligation on the defenders.

Held, that the undertaking granted was to deliver a search showing clear records, which search would disclose the purchasers' title provided it was recorded within the 21 day period (p 32B-C and G); and appeal *refused*.

Action of payment

B Messrs Warners, solicitors, raised an action of payment against Messrs Beveridge & Kellas, WS, founding on a letter of obligation granted by the defenders. On 10 August 1993, after debate, the sheriff (J A Farrell) granted decree de plano. The defenders appealed to the sheriff principal.

On 15 November 1993 the sheriff principal *refused* the appeal.

THE SHERIFF PRINCIPAL (C G B
C **NICHOLSON, QC).**—This appeal arises in an action between two firms of solicitors. In 1989 they were involved in a house purchase transaction involving certain subjects in Edinburgh. The pursuers acted for the purchasers, and the defenders acted for the sellers. The transaction was settled on 12 October 1989 and on that date the defenders sent to the pursuers a letter of obligation in terms of which they undertook: "(1) to deliver to you within 12 months from this date, Search for Incumbrances brought down in terms of
D the Memorandum adjusted between us and showing the Records to be clear in the Sasine and Personal Register in so far as affecting our client's Title, which Search will disclose your client's Title, provided your client's Title is recorded within 21 days from this date".

It is not in dispute that the purchasers' disposition was not recorded until 23 March 1990, that is to say substantially more than 21 days after the date of the letter of obligation.

E In due course the defenders produced a search which revealed that there was an undisclosed standard security on the register. That security had been granted by the seller of the property on 5 July 1989 and was recorded on 1 August 1989. In order to clear the title the debt due to the creditors in the standard security was paid by the pursuers who, in the present action, now claim the sum of £10,182.63 from the defenders in terms of the above obligation. On the
F authority of *Johnston v Little*, 1960 SLT 129, it is not in dispute that, if the above obligation is valid and enforceable, it gives rise to a debt due by the defenders themselves and not by their former clients.

After a debate the sheriff found in favour of the pursuers and granted decree de plano for the sum sued for. It is against that decision that the present appeal has been taken.

At the debate, and at the appeal hearing before myself, it was clear that the determination of this case turns on the words which I have quoted above, used

in the defenders' letter of obligation. Putting it shortly, the question before the sheriff and before G myself was whether the concluding words, namely "provided your client's title is recorded within 21 days from this date", apply to the obligation as a whole or merely to the words "which search will disclose your client's title". In his judgment issued after the debate the sheriff concluded, largely though not entirely as a matter of grammar and construction, that the words in question qualified the words "which search will disclose your client's title" but did not in any way qualify the main obligation contained in the letter. It was H upon that basis that he decided that the defenders were bound to pay to the pursuers the sum sued for.

In presenting the appeal counsel for the defenders began by explaining the significance of a letter of obligation. Putting it shortly, the need for such a letter arises from the fact that the up to date state of the records and registers can never be ascertained on the date when a conveyancing transaction falls to be settled. Normally, there will have been an interim search, but that may only take matters up to a point I considerably before the date of settlement. Consequently, there has to be some means whereby a purchaser can ensure that nothing will have happened thereafter which will adversely affect his title to the property. While this kind of assurance could be obtained by, for example, consigning the purchase price in joint names until a search has been brought up to date, such a course would create great practical difficulties both for the purchaser and the seller. For that reason it is common practice, though not obligatory, for a seller's solicitor to grant a letter of personal J obligation in terms similar to those used in the present case. However, as the textbooks make clear, any such obligation will not be lightly undertaken by a seller's solicitor, and he will normally try to take appropriate steps in the letter of obligation to limit the period of time for which he is to remain at risk.

Counsel then went on to submit that, for the foregoing reasons, a solicitor acting for a seller will normally seek to limit the period to be covered by the K search to one which will terminate on the date when the purchaser's disposition is recorded, and that in that regard he will normally provide in the letter of obligation that any such recording should take place within a very short period of time after the date when the transaction is settled. In that situation it was submitted that in the present case the closing words of the obligation granted by the defenders simply fixed a limitation of the extent of their potential liability, with the consequence that the purchasers for their part L would lose the protection offered by the obligation if they did not do what was required of them, namely to record their title within 21 days from the date of the letter of obligation. The purchasers had not complied with the time limit contained in the proviso, and consequently the obligation to provide a clear search fell and could not be enforced. This, it was submitted, was a construction of the obligation in this case which is open both on the grounds of normal practice and on the basis of the words and syntax actually used in the letter.

Counsel then went on to challenge the sheriff's
A interpretation of the obligation. In the first place, he
said, the sheriff's construction would defeat the object
of the search inasmuch as the purchasers wished to
have exhibited to them a document showing a clear
search, but could not achieve that if there was no
certain date (i e the date of recording the purchaser's
title) up to which the search should extend. In the
second place, counsel submitted, the sheriff's interpretation led to the consequence that, by delaying the
recording of their title, the purchasers could increase
B the risk undertaken by the defenders since the sellers
would be at risk until an unknown date of recording.
Finally, it was submitted, the searchers would not
know what to search for given that their search is for
the purchasers' deed and not up to a particular date.

In connection with the foregoing submissions
counsel made reference to passages in Halliday, *Conveyancing Law and Practice*, Vol II, pp 424 et seq, to
passages in McDonald, *Conveyancing Manual* (4th ed),
pp 372 et seq, and to an article entitled "Letters of
C Obligation" by G L F Henry, who was at the time
Professor of Conveyancing in the University of Edinburgh, and which is contained in (1959) 4 JLS 135.
Both Professor Halliday and Professor Henry give
examples of appropriate letters of obligation designed
to impose some limit on the risk undertaken by a
seller's solicitor, and I think that it is of interest to
compare what is said in those letters.

I turn first to the style suggested by Professor
Halliday (at p 426). It is in the following terms: "With
D reference to the settlement of the above transaction
today we hereby undertake to deliver (exhibit) a search
in the Property and Personal Registers continued
(obtained) in terms of the draft memorandum adjusted
between us and to clear the record of any deeds,
incumbrances or diligences disclosed by the continuation (search) prejudicial to the disposition in favour of
your client provided it is recorded within seven days
hereof but excluding any created by or against your
client."
E
I pause to observe that, prior to suggesting the above
formulation, Professor Halliday appears to indicate
that one of the objectives which that formulation will
achieve is to show that the obligation is being
expressed as conditional upon the disposition in
favour of the purchaser being recorded within seven
days.

Professor Henry, in the article to which I have
referred above, explains the need for a time limit rela-
F tive to the recording of a purchaser's title as being "in
order to prevent delay or failure to do so prolonging
unnecessarily the period of the search which the
seller's solicitor has obliged himself to exhibit or
deliver showing clear records". On that basis Professor Henry then goes on to set out two possible
forms of a letter ·of obligation, one of which he
describes as satisfactory, and the other of which he
describes as unsatisfactory.

The "satisfactory" form suggested by Professor
Henry is as follows: "With reference to the settlement

of this transaction today, we hereby undertake to
exhibit to you within four months from this date G
Search for Incumbrances in the Property and Personal
Registers brought down in terms of the draft Memorandum for Continuation of Search adjusted between
us and showing clear records which continuation will
disclose the disposition in favour of your client if it is
recorded within seven days from this date."

The "unsatisfactory" version set out by Professor
Henry is as follows: "With reference to the settlement
of this transaction today, we hereby undertake to
exhibit to you within four months from this date H
provided the Disposition in favour of your client is
recorded within seven days from this date Search for
Incumbrances in the Property and Personal Registers
brought down in terms of the draft Memorandum for
Continuation for Search adjusted between us and
showing clear records."

It is to be noted that the first of the foregoing styles,
being the one described by Professor Henry as satisfactory, is very similar in its terms to the letter of I
obligation in the present case.

Professor Henry goes on to explain the difference
between the two forms of letter. He says that the
difference is that in the first form of letter the purchaser is entitled to exhibition of a search showing
clear records although it may not disclose the disposition, but in the second the positioning of the proviso might in terms appear to deny the purchaser the
right to demand from the seller's solicitor any search
at all if the disposition is not recorded in time. In the J
present case, therefore, it seems that the defenders
may find some support for their position in the
approach adopted by Professor Halliday, but there is
nothing to offer them any comfort in the approach,
and the views, adopted by Professor Henry.

Given that letters of obligation can, as we have seen,
be expressed in a variety of ways, I have come to the
conclusion that the proper way to approach the letter
in this case is, first, to examine the letter itself in order
to try to construe it, just as one would any contractual K
document, according to its own terms and by reference
to its own grammar and syntax. Having done that, the
next stage, in my opinion, is to see whether that construction is one which does or does not make sense in
the context of a conveyancing transaction and in the
context of this transaction in particular. That does not
mean, of course, that what I have called the second
stage can displace a clear construction flowing from
the terms of the document itself: but it may serve to
confirm the correctness of that construction, or it may, L
if there is any possible ambiguity in the terms of
the document, be of assistance in resolving that
ambiguity. I therefore turn, first, to the terms of the
letter of obligation itself.

So far as that is concerned I am of opinion that the
words which are used cannot reasonably bear the construction which the defenders seek to place upon
them. As I read the words of the letter, what the
defenders are undertaking to do is to deliver a search
showing clear records with the letter then going on to

A say that that search will disclose the purchasers' title provided it is recorded within a certain time. In other words I consider that the letter fairly falls to be read as if it were two sentences with the first sentence ending with the words "as affecting our client's Title", and the second sentence continuing "That search will disclose your client's Title".

The meaning which is contended for by the defenders in this case would probably have been achieved if the letter had begun by saying: "Provided your client's title is recorded within 21 days from this

B date we undertake to deliver". Alternatively, the meaning contended for by the defenders could probably have been achieved by placing the proviso in the position where it appears in the "unsatisfactory" letter of obligation suggested by Professor Henry (see above). By placing the proviso at the end of the letter, however, I do not consider that it can properly be read as qualifying anything more than the phrase which immediately precedes it. I should add that I am reassured in my view as to the proper construction of

C this letter of obligation by the fact that Professor Henry, whom counsel for the defenders characterised as having been in his time the doyen of conveyancers, appears to attach the same construction to the "satisfactory" version of a letter of undertaking, that version being in very similar terms to the letter in the present case.

In my opinion the construction which I favour in this case is clear and unambiguous. However, as I indicated above, I think that it is proper to see if that

D construction makes sense in the context of a conveyancing transaction, and in the context of this transaction in particular.

So far as that is concerned, I think that it is true to say that a difficulty created by my favoured construction is that it does not of itself provide a date after which a seller's solicitor will no longer be at risk. But, neither does the construction advanced by the defenders in this case. That construction provides a date after which the obligation flies off altogether if

E the purchaser's title has not by then been recorded; but it does not state for how long a seller's solicitor is to be on risk if the purchaser *has* complied with the proviso.

I suppose that in practice the actual recording of a purchaser's title will effectively provide a date after which a seller's solicitor will no longer be exposed to risk, and it is therefore possible that, under the construction which I favour, difficult questions might

F have arisen if the seller in the present case had granted and recorded the offending standard security after the expiry of the 21 days but before the date when the purchasers eventually did record their title. It may be that in that event the defenders' period of risk could be held to have come to an end on the expiry of the period of 21 days. However, it is not necessary to express any concluded view on that point because in fact the security which is in issue here was granted and recorded prior to the date of settlement of the transaction and prior to the date of granting the letter of obligation.

In that situation I consider that the absence of a clearly expressed date beyond which the defenders G remained on risk is of little more than academic interest for present purposes. Upon any view it is clear that their period of risk covered the period between the date of the interim search and the date of settlement of the transaction, and that does not in my view present any difficulty for the construction of the letter of obligation which I regard as being clear and unambiguous.

For those reasons I am of opinion that the sheriff reached the correct conclusion in this case, and that H the appeal must fail. It was agreed that the expenses of the appeal should follow success, and that I should certify the appeal as suitable for the employment of junior counsel.

——————————

*Solicitors for Pursuers, Simpson & Marwick, WS —
Counsel for Defenders, Woolman; Solicitors, Party.*

I

Calder v Simpson

SHERIFFDOM OF GRAMPIAN, HIGHLAND
AND ISLANDS AT ABERDEEN

SHERIFF PRINCIPAL D J RISK, QC   J

30 SEPTEMBER 1993

*Damages — Award — Interim payment — Reparation —
Whether pursuer would succeed on question of liability
without any substantial finding of contributory negligence
— Meaning of "substantial" — Sheriff Courts (Scotland)
Act 1907 (7 Edw VII c 51), Sched, rule 147 (3).*

In an action of damages in respect of injuries sustained when the pursuer was struck by a car driven by the defender, the pursuer enrolled a motion seeking K interim damages. The pursuer averred that he had been crossing part of a dual carriageway when he had been struck by the defender's car, which had been travelling at excessive speed. The defender averred that he had been travelling at a lower speed, that the pursuer had run into his path and that there was a pedestrian crossing close by which the pursuer had failed to use. The sheriff found the pursuer entitled to interim damages. The defender appealed to the sheriff principal and argued that the sheriff had not been L entitled to be satisfied either that the pursuer would succeed as to liability or that there would be no substantial finding of contributory negligence.

Held, (1) that "substantial" meant of considerable amount (p 36C); and (2) that it could not be said that the pursuer would almost certainly succeed on the question of liability without any substantial finding of contributory negligence (p 36H-37D); and appeal *allowed.*

——————————

Action of damages

A　Alan Calder raised an action of damages against William Simpson. Defences having been lodged, the pursuer enrolled a motion for payment of interim damages.

On 30 June 1993 the temporary sheriff (W R W McMichael) found the pursuer entitled to payment of interim damages of £25,000. The defender appealed to the sheriff principal.

B　On 30 September 1993 the sheriff principal *allowed* the appeal and *appointed* the cause to the adjustment roll.

THE SHERIFF PRINCIPAL (D J RISK, QC).

—The pursuer seeks damages in respect of injuries which he sustained when he was struck by a motor car which was being driven by the defender. Defences having been lodged, the pursuer enrolled a motion for interim damages in terms of rule 147 of the Ordinary Cause Rules. By interlocutor of 30 June 1993 the C sheriff found the pursuer entitled to payment of interim damages in the sum of £25,000. The defender has now appealed. At the commencement of the appeal the defender's solicitor intimated that his submission would be that no award should have been made; if that submission were rejected he did not seek to challenge the sheriff's assessment of the sum which should be awarded.

Rule 147 (3) provides inter alia: "If after hearing the D parties on the motion the sheriff is satisfied either — (a) that the defender or defenders have admitted liability in the pursuer's action, or (b) that, if the action proceeded to proof, the pursuer would succeed in the action on the question of liability without any substantial finding of contributory negligence on his part . . . and would obtain decree for damages against the defender . . . the sheriff may, if he thinks fit, order the defender . . . to make interim payment to the pursuer". The wording of rule 147 (3) is in all material E respects identical to the wording of Rule of Court 89A (c) which is the corresponding rule in the Court of Session. I therefore agree with the defender's agent that opinions expressed in the Court of Session concerning the construction of Rule of Court 89A can be applied directly in the sheriff court to the construction of rule 147. Under reference to various such opinions the solicitor for the defender submitted that in this case the sheriff had not been entitled to be "satisfied" on the material to which he was entitled to have regard F either that the pursuer would succeed on the question of liability or, in any event, that there would be no substantial finding of contributory negligence.

Parties were not in dispute as to what was required before the court could be "satisfied" of any matter. They accepted the law as expressed by Lord Ross in *Reid v Planet Welding Equipment Ltd*, 1980 SLT (Notes) 7 at p 8: "When considering what is meant by the word 'satisfied' in this rule, I agree with Lord Maxwell that satisfaction in this context requires something less than complete certainty, yet more than

probability (*Douglas's Curator Bonis v Douglas and Another*, 1974 SLT (Notes) 67). In *Nelson v Duraplex* G *Industries Ltd*, 1975 SLT (Notes) 31, Lord Grieve expressed the view that to be satisfied that the pursuer would succeed on the question of liability, the court must be of opinion, on the information contained in the averments, that the pursuer would 'almost certainly' succeed on the question of liability at least to some extent. I respectfully agree with the approach described in these two cases". Accordingly, the sheriff had to ask himself, first, whether it was almost certain that the pursuer would succeed in establishing some H liability against the defender and, secondly, if so, whether it was almost certain that there would be no "substantial finding of contributory negligence".

As the pleadings now stand the pursuer avers that at the material time he was crossing Wellington Road, Aberdeen, from east to west near to the junction of that road with Polworth Road. He avers, "at the point where he decided to cross Wellington Road, Wellington Road is a dual carriageway which has a central reservation. The speed limit for motor cars travelling I in either direction on Wellington Road at the point where the pursuer chose to cross it was 30 mph. Prior to commencing to cross said road the pursuer looked to his right to check that there was no traffic travelling in a southward direction on Wellington Road. The said road was very quiet and there was no such traffic. Accordingly the pursuer commenced to cross the southbound carriageway of the said road. As the pursuer was more than halfway across the said southbound carriageway he suddenly became aware of a J motor vehicle travelling in a southbound direction on Wellington Road bearing down on him at an excessive speed of about 45 mph. The said motor vehicle . . . was being driven by the defender. The pursuer was unable to take avoiding action and the nearside of said vehicle struck him. . . . On 18 September 1991 at Aberdeen sheriff court the defender was found guilty of careless driving at the time of said accident." At a later point in art 2 of condescendence, when responding to certain of the defender's averments, the pursuer K adds: "When the police attended at the locus immediately after the accident the defender stated that he was travelling between 40 and 45 mph."

The defender admits that he was driving the car which struck the pursuer, that the collision occurred in the offside lane of the southbound carriageway and that he was convicted of careless driving. He denies that he was travelling at 45 mph and explains that his speed was approximately 35 mph. His general denial L must be taken to apply to the pursuer's averment concerning his alleged statement to the police immediately after the accident. He explains that for certain reasons it was normal for traffic at that point in Wellington Road to proceed in the offside lane and avers that the pursuer as a local resident ought to have known that. He describes the locus as being immediately to the south of what was for the defender a left-hand bend where mutual visibility was obscured by a high wall and buildings. He avers that 20 yards to the south of the point at which the pursuer was crossing

the road there was a pedestrian crossing which the
A pursuer had walked past. There was a barrier on the
central reservation intended to discourage pedestrians
from crossing other than at the pedestrian crossing.
When the defender came round the bend the pursuer
was still in the nearside lane of the carriageway but he
had run into the defender's path. Had he stood still the
defender would have passed him safely. The defender
maintains that the pursuer caused or materially contributed to the accident, first, by ignoring the pedestrian crossing and instead crossing the road at a place
B which was manifestly unsafe and, secondly, in
running into the path of the defender's car.

The sheriff gives his reasons for being satisfied that
the pursuer would succeed on the question of liability
as follows: "It was a matter of admission that the
defender when he came round the corner in Wellington Road to approach the pursuer where he stood was
exceeding the speed limit. It was admitted that he was
convicted of careless driving at the time of the accident. It seemed to me reasonable to suppose that the
C evidence of the defender's admission to police officers
anent his speed as averred would be led at the proof".
The defender's solicitor submitted that in the last sentence of that passage the sheriff had taken account of
an irrelevant consideration. At this stage in the case
only the parties' pleadings could be considered (*Reid
v J Smart & Co Ltd*, 1981 SLT (Notes) 20; *McCann
v Miller Insulation and Engineering Ltd*, 1986 SLT
147). The sheriff had fallen into the trap of relying on
evidence which might, when the time came, be dis-
D puted. The pursuer's agent on the other hand maintained that the sheriff had been entitled to have regard
to the averment that the defender had admitted a
speed of 45 mph.

On this point I have no doubt that the learned
sheriff misdirected himself. I reserve my opinion as to
whether there is an absolute prohibition against
looking beyond the pleadings when considering a
motion for interim damages. In *Reid v J Smart & Co
E Ltd* the Lord Ordinary was not asked to look at anything other than the pleadings, while in *McCann* what
the Lord Ordinary was asked to examine were medical
certificates prepared in circumstances of which the
defenders could not be expected to have knowledge. In
a case like the present one, however, if a pursuer's
averment that the defender had been convicted of careless driving were met with a denial and the pursuer
then produced an extract conviction at the hearing of
the motion for interim damages it would, I think, be
regrettable if the court could not at least ask the
F defender's solicitor for an explanation. I observe that
in *Reid v Planet Welding Equipment Ltd* the Lord
Ordinary (Ross) refers to an extract conviction as one
of the factors supporting his view that liability would
be established against the defender, and in *Herron
v Kennon*, 1986 SLT 260, the Lord Ordinary
(McDonald) also gave weight to an extract conviction,
even where the defender seems to have disputed the
matter. In *Duguid v Wilh Wilhelmsen Enterprises Ltd
A/S*, 1988 SLT 118, the Lord Ordinary (Morison)
reserved his opinion. Subject to that reservation I

agree that in most cases the court's attention must be
confined to the pleadings as they stand at the date of G
hearing the motion and where there is a disputed issue
of fact the court is not entitled to assume that one
version rather than the other will prevail. In this case
the sheriff appears to have assumed that the pursuer
will prove that the defender made the admission and
that the defender's speed at the material time was
about 45 mph. That was an assumption which he was
not entitled to make and, since it was a material factor
in his decision, that decision is flawed. It is accordingly necessary for me to consider the matter de novo. H

The factors which are not in dispute and which are
to my mind material are, that when the collision
occurred the defender was driving in the offside lane
of the southbound carriageway at a speed in excess of
the statutory limit, and that he was subsequently convicted of careless driving. Even on those limited facts
I have little difficulty in concluding that it is almost
certain that the pursuer will succeed in establishing
liability against the defender, at least to some extent.
In the course of reviewing the cases the solicitor for I
the defender pointed out that in *Nelson v Duraplex
Industries Ltd* and *Herron v Kennon* interim damages
had been refused even though the respective defenders
had been convicted of charges arising from the accidents. In each case, however, the Lord Ordinary indicated that he was satisfied that the pursuer would
succeed at least to some extent and only refused
interim damages because he was not satisfied that
there would be no substantial finding of contributory
negligence. A conviction is not conclusive of liability J
in a civil case but it creates a presumption which it is
for the defender to displace. In the circumstances of
this case I see little prospect that the defender will
succeed in discharging that onus.

In holding that he was satisfied that almost certainly
no substantial finding of contributory negligence
would be made against the pursuer the sheriff said:
"certainly he had a duty to take care for his own safety
and keep a good look out. It does not in my view help
him that he chose not to use the pedestrian crossing. K
By choosing to cross the road where he did he put
himself at risk. He cannot, however, in my view, be
blamed for reacting wrongly when the defender's
vehicle came upon him at speed. If it was impossible
as is averred for the defender proceeding southward in
Wellington Road to see a pedestrian such as the
pursuer crossing where he did then it seems to me that
his is by far the greater fault in travelling at a speed
which patently made no allowance for the presence of
a pedestrian such as the pursuer and which caused L
panic in him". It seems to me that the sheriff has
carried forward into his consideration of contributory
negligence the erroneous assumption about the
defender's speed, which he made when considering
the defender's liability and has compounded that error
by using the assumed speed to excuse the pursuer's
actings "in the agony of the moment". Once again,
therefore, his reasoning cannot be supported.

Before reverting to the pleadings it is necessary to
reach a view as to the meaning of "substantial". I was

greatly assisted by the solicitor for the defender's careful analysis of a number of cases in which various Lords Ordinary have considered the point, from which it appears that there are two distinct lines of thought. In *Nelson v Duraplex Industries Ltd* Lord Grieve said at p 33: "What meaning has to be given to the word 'substantial' in this context? Counsel for the pursuer suggested more than 50 per cent. I do not think one can approach the question that way. I am of opinion that 'substantial' has to be construed as 'of substance' in the sense of not being de minimis. After all, a finding of contributory negligence which does not appear high when expressed as a percentage and which was less than 50 per cent could have a very material effect on the amount recovered by a pursuer in the event of a tender being in process."

In *Noble v Noble*, 1979 SLT (Notes) 75, the case of *Nelson* was cited to Lord Cowie, who said at p 76: "In my opinion, however, there is no logical ground for rejecting Lord Grieve's decision on this matter and I respectfully agree with it and the reasoning behind it. I would only add that rule 89A introduced a new and unusual concept in actions of damages for personal injuries and one which was only intended to apply in very special circumstances. That being so it is my opinion that the provisions of the rule should be interpreted in the strictest possible way without detracting from what it was intended to achieve."

In *Herron v Kennon* Lord McDonald, when considering the conflicting views which had by then emerged, said at p 261K: "I do not find it necessary to resolve this difference of view in the present case, but I prefer the approach of Lords Grieve and Cowie".

The other view has its origins in the opinion of Lord Ross in *Reid v Planet Welding Equipment Ltd,* in which he declined to follow the views expressed in *Nelson v Duraplex Industries Ltd* and *Noble v Noble* and said at pp 8-9: "With the greatest respect to my brethren, however, I feel that they have given an unduly restrictive meaning to the word 'substantial' in this context. It is plain from the terms of rule 89A (1) (c) that the object of the rule was to permit interim payment of damages to be ordered even though liability was not admitted, and even though the court was satisfied that there would be some finding of contributory negligence . . . I cannot believe that rule 89A (1) (c) was intended to confine the power to award interim damages to cases of admitted liability or cases where there was a negligible or minimal finding of contributory negligence. On the interpretation favoured by my brethren anything which is not de minimis is substantial and thus a finding of contributory negligence to the extent of five per cent would presumably be a substantial finding of contributory negligence. In my opinion, the rule must be construed in a more liberal fashion. A more reasonable construction can be placed on the rule if 'substantial' is given another of its accepted meanings, viz. 'considerable or big'. . . . Accordingly, in this context, I am of opinion that the word 'substantial' means of considerable amount. To interpret the word in this way gives more content to rule 89A. . . . It may not be easy to fix the dividing line between substantial and slight findings of contributory negligence, and I certainly would not suggest that there are fixed percentages for substantial, slight or minimal. In the present case, however, where any finding of contributory negligence would almost certainly not exceed one-quarter, or at most one-third, I am of opinion that the finding of contributory negligence could not properly be described as substantial."

In *McNeill v Roche Products Ltd*, 1988 SLT 704, Lord Coulsfield in a passage at p 706A-E adopted and amplified the reasoning of Lord Ross in *Reid v Planet Welding* and rejected the reasoning of Lord Grieve in *Nelson v Duraplex Industries*, saying of the latter: "With the greatest of respect to those who have taken a different view there does not seem to me to be any satisfactory reason for adopting the construction of the Rule of Court which is more restrictive of the field of its operation. The purpose of the rule must, I think, be to benefit pursuers who are almost certainly going to be awarded damages by allowing them to obtain partial payment without suffering the inevitable delays of litigation. Provided that the sum awarded is moderate there seems to me to be ample room to allow awards to be made in the type of case envisaged by Lord Ross without giving rise to any material risk of injustice or prejudice to the defenders." In Macphail on *Sheriff Court Practice* at p 692, para 21.21 the learned author aligns himself with the broader interpretation favoured by Lord Ross.

Although the learned sheriff was referred to all of those cases he does not expressly commit himself to either view, but I think that it is to be implied from what he does say that he favoured the broader interpretation. If that was his view I agree with it. I find particularly persuasive the discussion by Lord Ross and Lord Coulsfield of the purpose of the rule. Any experienced reparation practitioner knows that at any given moment there are numerous cases pending before the courts in which it is obvious that the pursuer will eventually recover some damages but the action cannot be brought to a conclusion either because the defender, although having admitted liability, disputes the quantum of damages or because the defender alleges that the pursuer was to some extent himself at fault. Before there were rules allowing the award of interim damages the pursuer would receive nothing until every point had been settled by agreement or by a decision of the court. What must surely be the object of rule 89A in the Court of Session and rule 147 in the sheriff court is to enable such a pursuer to obtain some of his money at an early stage. If that is the case I cannot see that justice and equity require that he should not receive an interim award merely because the possibility exists that he may be found to blame to a very small extent, albeit one which cannot be disregarded as de minimis. In *Noble v Noble* Lord Cowie suggested that rule 89A was "only intended to apply in very special circumstances", but he gives no reason for that opinion and no example of what would amount to special circumstances. It seems to me, with respect, that the rule is intended to apply in the commonplace situation which I have described above. In the passage cited Lord Cowie was agreeing with the opinion of Lord Grieve in *Nelson v Duraplex Industries* but, again with respect, I do not find that opinion supported by persuasive reasoning. In the relevant passage, which I have quoted above, Lord Grieve refers to the effect on the damages ultimately recovered of a finding of contributory negligence coupled with a tender. I do not think that the possibility of a tender being lodged should play any part in the decision on an award of interim damages. On this point I agree with Lord Morison in *Duguid v Wilh Wilhelmsen* at p 119F: "In its consideration of the prospect of a finding of contributory negligence it is in my view not open to the court to have regard to any matters bearing on quantum of damages. A finding of contributory negligence is expressed in terms of the proportion of contributory negligence attributable to each of the parties in terms of s 1 of the Law Reform (Contributory Negligence) Act 1945. Such a finding is unaffected by the amount of damages to which the pursuer might be entitled. The words 'substantial finding of contributory negligence' cannot therefore refer to or be affected by the quantum of the claim."

Accordingly I hold that, in the words of Lord Ross in *Reid v Planet Welding Equipment*: "In this context . . . the word 'substantial' means of considerable amount". In reaching that view I have not overlooked the opinion of Lord Morison in *Duguid v Wilhelmsen* at p 119E where he seems to lean towards the restrictive interpretation but goes on to say: "It is quite inappropriate at this stage to attempt to determine any degree of contributory negligence even within a wide range; if the court considers that an award may be materially affected by a finding of contributory negligence that is sufficient to exclude the application of the rule."

Insofar as the Lord Ordinary is agreeing with the opinions of Lord Grieve and Lord Cowie I would, for the reasons given above, respectfully disagree. If his words are intended to go further and to convey that a court when considering an application for interim damages should not consider the degree of fault likely to lie upon the pursuer I would disagree upon the additional ground that so to hold appears to me to deprive the word "substantial" in the rule of any content.

I was referred to one further case which is not directly in point but which may be of marginal relevance. In *Kay v G P Inveresk Corporation*, 1988 SLT 711, the defenders had admitted liability but pled contributory negligence against the pursuer. The Lord Ordinary (Dervaird) held that in terms of rule 89A (1) (c) (i) he was entitled to make an award of interim damages whether or not any finding of contributory negligence against the pursuer would be "substantial" because the phrase "without any substantial finding of contributory negligence" applied only to subpara (ii). Nevertheless, in fixing the amount of interim damages he made allowance for the extent to which the plea of contributory negligence might succeed. It may well be

that the Lord Ordinary's decision came as a surprise to the draftsman of the rules but I find his logic irresistible. The question which then comes to mind is this: if the rule intends that a pursuer, against whom there may be a significant finding of contributory negligence, should be able to obtain interim damages from a defender who has admitted partial liability, why should a pursuer, against whom a small but not minimal finding of contributory negligence may be made, be prevented from recovering interim damages from a defender against whom the court is "satisfied" that liability will be established? Since the case of *Kay* is not in point I do not make it a ground of my decision, but insofar as it casts any light upon the issue it seems to me to fit better with the broad interpretation of "substantial".

It may be that the foregoing discussion is of academic interest only because, although I prefer the interpretation of "substantial" which is more favourable to the pursuer, I still cannot say that I am almost certain that he would succeed on the question of liability without any substantial finding of contributory negligence. The pursuer has to establish a negative proposition which is never an easy task. Each case must be decided on its own circumstances and in this case the only relevant circumstances are those which can legitimately be extracted from the pleadings. Where the pleadings raise disputed issues of fact they cannot be resolved at this stage. The pursuer avers that the defender's speed was 45 mph, while the defender avers that it was 35 mph; the pursuer avers that the pedestrian crossing was 120 feet south of the locus while the defender claims that it was only 60 feet. The pursuer avers that the defender would have had as much as 300 feet of visibility coming round the bend while the defender avers that he had virtually no visibility before he was upon the pursuer; the pursuer describes the barrier on the central reservation as a crash barrier whereas the defender avers that it was intended to deter pedestrians from crossing; and the pursuer avers that he was more than halfway across the carriageway when he became aware of the defender's motor car approaching whereas the defender avers that the pursuer was in the nearside lane where he would have been safe but ran into the offside lane and into the path of the car. The pursuer's agent invited me to carry out a kind of balancing exercise between the competing averments but I do not regard that as a proper approach. If at the end of the day the pursuer's version is preferred on all of those points there will at worst for him be a small finding of contributory negligence, but I cannot presume that he will succeed in proving all, or indeed any of them. If the defender's version is preferred the findings in fact will be that the pursuer chose to cross a main road ignoring a pedestrian crossing which was only 20 yards away, at a point where he could not see oncoming traffic and the drivers of oncoming traffic could not see him because of the high wall and where he had to circumnavigate a central barrier erected by the roads authority to prevent pedestrians from crossing, and that, being in the nearside lane when the

A defender's car approached in the offside lane at a speed of 35 mph, instead of standing still he ran into its path. The pursuer's agent referred to *Bingham's Motor Claims* (8th ed), pp 80 and 82 and to the cases of *Hurt v Murphy* and *Snow v Giddins* cited there as authority for holding that it was not contributory negligence either to cross a road where one's visibility was restricted, or to cross a road having ignored a nearby pedestrian crossing. Those cases were, of course, decided after proof. I can only reiterate that at this stage I cannot take any view as to what will be proved

B in the disputed areas and that each case must depend upon its own facts. In the present case if the defender were to prove all of his averments it is perfectly possible that a reasonable sheriff might take the view that the pursuer showed a negligent disregard for his own safety in crossing the road where he did and further in running from a place of safety into a position of danger. With regard to the latter point it is not legitimate to argue as the pursuer's agent did, or to hold as the sheriff did, that the pursuer's actings can

C be excused by the "agony rule". In the first place as the pleadings stand the pursuer's case is not that he ran into the offside lane in the agony of the moment but that he was already in the offside lane when the defender's car approached and, in any event, the level of emergency in which he was placed depends upon disputed facts concerning the defender's speed and the parties' mutual visibility. In those circumstances it would in my opinion be wrong to hold now that "any finding of contributory negligence would almost cer-

D tainly not exceed one quarter or at worst one third" (*Reid v Planet Welding Equipment* at p 9) or that it is "almost certain that any contribution of the pursuer will be a great deal less than the share of responsibility attributable to the defender" (*McNeill v Roche Products Ltd* at pp 705L-706A). I have therefore allowed the defender's appeal.

It was agreed that expenses should follow success and I have so ordered.

E

Solicitors for Pursuer, Raeburn, Christie & Co, Aberdeen — Solicitors for Defender, Tindal Oatts, Glasgow.

F # Cairney v Bulloch

SHERIFF COURT OF SOUTH STRATHCLYDE, DUMFRIES AND GALLOWAY AT AIRDRIE
SHERIFF PRINCIPAL J S MOWAT, QC
2 AUGUST 1993

Process — Citation — Service of writ — Purported service on defender — Interim hearing arranged by sheriff clerk — Whether attendance of defender's agent at interim hearing constituted appearance of defender which

G *remedied any defect of service on him — Sheriff Courts (Scotland) Act 1907 (7 Edw VII, c 51), Sched, rule 18.*

Rule 18 (1) of the ordinary cause rules, as amended prior to 1993, provides that a party who appears may not state any objection to the regularity of the service upon him and his appearance shall remedy any defect in the service.

A sheriff officer purported to serve an initial writ upon the defender. His agents wrote to the sheriff clerk pointing out alleged defects in service. The sheriff clerk advised parties' agents that an interim H hearing would be fixed and asked that they ensure that their firms be represented at it. At the hearing the sheriff considered that the citation was flawed but that the presence of the defender's agent at the hearing cured any defects in the citation. The defender appealed to the sheriff principal.

Held, that "appearance" in rule 18 meant the lodging of a notice of intention to defend and that the defender had effectively ignored the citation by not entering such a notice, and could not be held to have I accepted it by attending a hearing concerned with the question of its validity (p 39E-F and J); and appeal *allowed* and case *remitted* to sheriff.

Action

A sheriff officer purported to serve an initial writ upon Gary Bulloch in an action at the instance of Catherine Cairney. An interim hearing was fixed for J 17 June 1993 when the sheriff (I C Simpson) considered that the presence of the defender's agent at the hearing cured any defect in the citation. The defender appealed to the sheriff principal.

On 2 August 1993 the sheriff principal *allowed* the appeal and *remitted* the case for the sheriff to decide upon the validity of the service of the initial writ upon the defender.

K

THE SHERIFF PRINCIPAL (J S MOWAT, QC).—This is a note of appeal against an interlocutor of the sheriff dated 18 June 1993 in which, having heard parties on the pursuer's minute for decree, ex proprio motu he continued the cause to the procedure roll of 29 June 1993 at 10 am "in order that the defender might lodge a notice of intention to defend".

The solicitor for the defender and appellant explained that the appeal was concerned with whether L the sheriff was entitled to hold, as he did, that the attendance of the defender's agent at an interim hearing on 17 June constituted an appearance of the defender which, in terms of rule 18 of the ordinary court rules, remedied any defect in the service upon him. He explained that a sheriff officer had purported to serve the service copy initial writ on the defender, but that the defender's agents had taken the view that this attempted service was ineffective. They had written to the sheriff clerk on 24 February 1993 pointing out the defects on which they based this view and asking what the court's position would be if the pursuer were to attempt to minute for decree.

On 11 June 1993 the sheriff clerk depute wrote to the agents of each of the parties in the following terms: "I refer to the above case in which the pursuer's have [sic] now minuted for decree in absence. As the defender's position is that service of the Initial Writ was ineffective, an interim hearing was fixed for Thursday 17 June 1993 at 9.15 am. Please ensure your firm is represented at said hearing."

The defender's agents duly attended and presented their arguments in support of their position that the service had been ineffective. The sheriff's note showed that he appeared to accept that the citation in the case was flawed on the face of the service copy initial writ, but he accepted the argument for the pursuer that the presence of the defender's agent cured any defects in the citation. He had gone on to refuse the pursuer's minute for decree at that stage.

The solicitor for the appellant submitted that the sheriff had misdirected himself in law in holding that the presence of the defender's agent in the circumstances constituted the appearance of the defender in terms of rule 18. He argued (1) that there had been no appearance in terms of the rules of court and (2) that the hearing on 17 June was not a formal sitting of the court at which an appearance could be made.

His first argument was based on the ordinary court rules to be found in Sched 1 attached to the Sheriff Courts (Scotland) Act 1907 in their original form and also those substituted by SI 1983/747. In the 1983 version, rule 17 provided that any failure or irregularity in service could be cured by the sheriff allowing re-service upon the defender. Rule 18 (1), which was founded upon by the pursuer and by the sheriff reads: "A party who appears may not state any objection to the regularity of the service upon himself, and his appearance shall remedy any defect in the service."

The word "appearance" was not defined in the 1907 Act or in the 1983 rules. It was necessary to go back to the original rules and, in particular, to rule 22 thereof, which is headed "Appearance" and reads: "If a defender intends to state a defence he shall (except in a summary cause) before the expiry of the induciae, lodge with the sheriff clerk a notice of appearance in the following terms".

The first part of rule 13 was in similar terms to the present rule 18. He submitted that the word "appearance" in rule 13 must mean appearance as provided for in rule 22, i e the lodging of a notice of appearance. In the 1983 rules the provision for a notice of appearance disappeared and it was replaced by rule 33 which provided for a notice of intention to defend. Rule 18 (1) still used the word "appearance". The solicitor for the appellant argued that it should still have the same interpretation as in the original rules, i e the taking of the steps necessary to allow a defence to be stated. In the context of the 1983 rules that meant the lodging of a notice of intention to defend. Dobie on *Sheriff Court Practice* at p 139 and Fyfe on *The Law and Practice of the Sheriff Court* at p 155 both

equiparated appearance under the old rules with lodging a notice of appearance. The modern equivalent of a notice of appearance was a notice of intention to defend. No such notice had been lodged in this case. So no appearance had been made in terms of rule 18 (1) and the attendance at the hearing did not constitute such an appearance.

The second argument for the appellant was that the hearing on 17 June was not a formal calling at which an appearance in terms of rule 18 could be made. The interim hearing was an ad hoc procedure. The terms of the letter from the sheriff clerk suggested that there was to be an informal discussion as to the procedure to be followed if the service was defective.

If the defender's failure to lodge a notice of intention to defend led to the granting of a decree in absence it would mean that the attendance of the defender's agent on 17 June was an appearance for the purpose of ruling out any objection to the validity of the service, but was not an appearance which would prevent a decree in absence. That would be an absurd situation.

For these reasons, the solicitor for the appellant submitted that the appeal should be allowed and the matter remitted to the sheriff to decide on the validity of the service.

The solicitor for the pursuer and respondent pointed out that while the sheriff appeared to accept that the service had been irregular, he went on to indicate that he might have reached the wrong conclusion in the absence of any explanation from the sheriff officer concerned. Accordingly, if the appeal was allowed, there might have to be some form of proof in the matter.

He went on to argue that the appellant's contention that the defender's agents could attend the hearing without "appearing" was untenable. He referred to the case of *Thomson v Wiggins Teape Ltd*, 1981 SLT (Sh Ct) 85, in which the sheriff had held that by entering appearance the defenders had barred themselves from disputing the validity of an obviously defective citation. Sheriff Risk had said (at p 86) that the words of the rule in their natural meaning would apply to the circumstances of the case. The natural meaning of the word "appearance" was attendance at a hearing in the case. The sheriff had gone on to say (at p 88): "The proper course for a defender confronted with a defective citation is either to ignore it or to return it to the sender . . . and if the pursuers proceed to take decree in absence to have that decree reduced upon the ground of the bad citation".

Macphail on *Sheriff Court Practice*, at p 229, para 6-46, set out the procedure for challenging a decree in absence on the ground that citation was not validly effected.

The solicitor for the respondent argued that the absence of the notice of appearance did not mean that a notice of intention to defend was the only way in which a party could now appear. The rule must apply to any form of appearance including attendance at a hearing. Macphail dealt with the question of defective service at pp 213-214, para 6-04. He said that the due service of the initial writ apprised the defender of the nature of the proceedings against him and gave him an opportunity of lodging a notice of intention to defend. He went on to say that the rationale of rule 18 was that the purpose of citation was to convene a defender before the court "and, once he has in fact been convened and is before the court, it matters not how his appearance was secured". He referred in a footnote to the case of *Struthers v Magistrates of Kirkintilloch*, 1951 SLT (Notes) 77. Where agents appeared, that was still the appearance of the party.

The position of the interim hearing on 17 June was similar to a hearing on an interim interdict held before the expiry of the induciae. A party who attended or was represented at such a hearing could not be heard to say that he had not appeared because he had not yet lodged a notice of intention to defend.

In any event, it might be that the defender's appearance at the appeal itself cured any defect in the service. Macphail at p 214 said that the rule was applicable whether the defender appeared before the sheriff or at an appeal before the sheriff principal. The appeal should be refused.

In a short reply, the solicitor for the appellant pointed out that in the case of a hearing on an interim interdict, notice was contained in the warrant of citation itself. It was a different matter where the defender had not taken any of the actions required of him by the defective citation so as to comply with it.

I confess that I approach this appeal with the feeling that I should be slow to find that where a party's agent attends, at the request of the sheriff clerk, a hearing on the question of whether citation of that party has been validly executed, this should be construed as such an appearance by the party as to cure any defect in the service in terms of rule 18. I find it difficult to accept that the very act of attending court in order to argue that the service was invalid removes the right to object to it.

In that situation, I accept the submission of the solicitor for the appellant that, under the original Sched 1 to the 1907 Act, the appearance referred to in rule 13 was the method of appearance provided for in rule 22. I find it significant that in all the cases cited to me it was the lodging of a notice of appearance or entering appearance which cured any defect in service.

The question then comes to be whether the word "appearance" in rule 18 of the 1983 rules can mean anything less than the lodging of a notice of intention to defend which has replaced the lodging of a notice of appearance. I do not think that it does. The rationale of rule 18, it seems to me, is that a party cannot carry out the steps required of him by the citation if he is actively to defend the case and at the same time argue that the citation was not an effective notice to him of that requirement. In the case of *Struthers*, where it was said that the rationale of the rule was that "once he has in fact been convened before the court,

it matters not how his appearance was secured", the defenders had entered appearance. They had accordingly been convened before the court by means of the citation, even if it was a defective citation.

I consider that the situation was very different in the present case. In the first place the defender was not himself called upon to attend at the interim hearing, the purpose of which was to consider whether the citation was effective. It was his agents who were requested to attend because they had raised that question with the sheriff clerk. The attendance of the solicitors was not, in any sense, in answer to the citation itself so as to involve an acceptance that it had given due notice of the hearing. Secondly, the interim hearing did not appear to be concerned with the merits of the case. The letter from the sheriff clerk indicated that it was to discuss whether the citation had been effective, and if it was not, what procedure should follow as a result. The hearing itself was held in chambers. In these circumstances I consider there is considerable merit in the solicitor for the appellant's submission that it was not a diet of the court at which the attendance of the defender's agents could constitute an appearance of the defender himself in terms of rule 18.

For the reason given by the solicitor for the appellant in his reply, I do not consider that attendance at the hearing in this case can be equiparated with attendance at a hearing in relation to an interim interdict, which would represent compliance, to some extent, with the citation.

I consider that the defender effectively ignored the citation by not entering a notice of intention to defend and cannot be held to have accepted it by questioning its validity and complying with a request to attend, through his agents, a hearing concerned with that question.

For these reasons, I consider that the sheriff misdirected himself in law in holding that the "presence" of the defender's agents at the hearing on 17 June constituted the appearance of the defender in terms of rule 18 so curing any defect in the service upon him. I therefore allow the appeal and recall the interlocutor of 18 June 1993 and remit the cause to the sheriff to decide on the validity of the service upon the defender. I find the defender entitled to the expenses of the appeal.

Solicitors for Pursuer and Respondent, Trainor Alston, Coatbridge — Solicitors for Defender and Appellant, Robert Carty & Co, Cumbernauld.

International Factors Ltd v Ves Voltech Electronic Services Ltd

SHERIFF COURT OF NORTH
STRATHCLYDE AT KILMARNOCK
SHERIFF PRINCIPAL R C HAY, WS
12 AUGUST 1993

Company — Liquidator — Provisional liquidator — Provisional liquidator not advertising appointment and subsequently seeking recall — Whether court should grant recall — Payment of expenses incurred — Insolvency (Scotland) Rules 1986 (SI 1986/1015), rule 4.5 (3) — Act of Sederunt (Sheriff Court Company Insolvency Rules) 1986 (SI 1986/2297), rule 23 (5).

A provisional liquidator appointed to a company decided not to advertise his appointment as ordered by the court. After three months a note was lodged for the provisional liquidator seeking dismissal of the petition, recall of the appointment of the provisional liquidator and payment of his fees and outlays. The sheriff refused the craves of an amended note. The provisional liquidator appealed to the sheriff principal.

Held, (1) that the sheriff had erred in concentrating exclusively on the default by the provisional liquidator, that the matter was at large for the court and that the appointment of the provisional liquidator should be terminated and the petition dismissed (p 42E-G); but (2) that no order should be made for payment of the provisional liquidator's fees and outlays out of the property of the respondent company (p 42I-J); and appeal *allowed*, appointment of provisional liquidator *recalled* and petition *dismissed*.

Observed, that the provisional liquidator was an officer of the court and was required to comply with an order of the court and the statutory regulations governing his appointment; should advertisement of his appointment not be appropriate, he should immediately apply to the sheriff for dispensation from the requirement to advertise his appointment (p 42K-L).

Petition for liquidation
In a petition of International Factors Ltd for the liquidation of Ves Voltech Electronic Services Ltd, John Dickson Laurie was appointed as the provisional liquidator. A note was lodged seeking dismissal of the petition, recall of the appointment of the provisional liquidator and payment of his fees and outlays. On 28 May 1993 the sheriff refused the craves of an amended note. The provisional liquidator appealed to the sheriff principal.

On 12 August 1993 the sheriff principal *allowed* the appeal, *recalled* the appointment of the provisional liquidator and *dismissed* the petition.

THE SHERIFF PRINCIPAL (R C HAY, WS).—This is an appeal by the provisional liquidator and the petitioner company with leave of the sheriff against his interlocutor dated 28 May 1993 whereby he refused the craves of the amended note.

The petitioner company petitioned for the liquidation of the respondent company in respect of a debt constituted by decree of the sheriff at Ayr dated 22 June 1992 and extracted on 7 July 1992 for payment of £5,698.75 with interest and expenses. The respondents were charged on 28 July 1992. The petition was lodged at Kilmarnock sheriff court on 16 November 1992, and, on the motion of the petitioners, the provisional liquidator was appointed on 17 November 1992. The interlocutor appointed notice of the import of the petition and of the deliverance and of the particulars specified in the Act of Sederunt thereanent to be advertised once in the *Edinburgh Gazette* and *The Herald* newspaper.

The provisional liquidator took up the appointment. Having seen a business plan which was prepared by accountants for the respondent company, he formed the view that no dividend would be available to unsecured creditors, and that if advertisement took place the purposes of the business plan would be prejudiced and that this would be to the detriment of the respondents and their employees who numbered approximately 100. He therefore decided not to advertise his appointment as ordered by the court. He reported his views to the petitioners and obtained their consent.

Three months later, on 24 February 1993, a note was lodged for the provisional liquidator seeking dismissal of the petition, recall of his appointment, and payment of his fees and outlays as a result of the appointment. After sundry procedure, the sheriff refused the note on 14 April 1993. An appeal was marked and on 19 May 1993, on the motion of the solicitor now acting for the provisional liquidator and the petitioners, and of consent of the solicitor then appearing for the respondents, I allowed the note to be amended, allowed the appeal, and remitted to the sheriff to hear parties on the note as amended. Having heard parties, the sheriff, by interlocutor dated 28 May 1992, refused the craves of the amended note. Subsequently he granted leave to appeal.

The sheriff observes in his note that it appeared to him that the provisional liquidator carried out no functions between 17 November 1992 and 14 February 1993, apart from reporting to the petitioners. On appeal, the solicitor for the provisional liquidator and the petitioners has submitted that the sheriff may have misunderstood the activities of the provisional liquidator during this period. He stated that the provisional liquidator had investigated the position, and had reported to the petitioners with his views. He had then instructed his solicitors to seek his discharge and obtain leave of the court not to advertise. The solicitor for the petitioners did not suggest that the provisional liquidator had intromitted in any way with the property of the respondent company. He did not state at what stage the provisional liquidator had reported his views to the petitioners and obtained their agreement to the course he proposed. He did not indicate that the provisional liquidator had sought the views of any other creditor.

It is not clear to me why it should have taken three months to reach this stage, bearing in mind that the business plan which the provisional liquidator advised

A the petitioners to accept as offering the best prospect of payment had been circulated to all creditors by the accountants acting for the respondents on 19 October 1992.

The sheriff notes that in the meantime the petitioners had been achieving payment of their debt by means of payments made by debtors of the respondent company, and that during the dependence of this process the petitioners had been fully satisfied out of what might be regarded as the assets of the respondents. Payments to extinguish the respondents'
B indebtedness to certain other creditors had also been made, and the sheriff was prepared to draw the inference that these payments extinguished the indebtedness of the respondents to certain creditors who had intimated an interest in the instant process.

The solicitor for the petitioners stated to the sheriff that the provisional liquidator had reported to him that there was no list of the respondents' creditors nor of the amount of debts due to them. On appeal, the solicitor for the petitioners stated that he was unsure
C of the respondent company's current position. I found it surprising that this should be so.

The sheriff noted that part of the reason for the provisional liquidator not advertising his appointment had been cost, but that part of the reason had also been his view that by allowing the respondents to continue in business there was more chance of a successful result for all the creditors. On appeal, the solicitor for the petitioners stated that the provisional liquidator
D also bore in mind the interests of the respondents' employees whose jobs were likely to be put at risk if he advertised his appointment. The cost of advertising, while likely to have amounted to several hundreds of pounds, was not a decisive factor in the provisional liquidator's thinking or in his advice to the petitioners.

The solicitor for the petitioners submitted to the sheriff that if the petition was dismissed as craved, it would be open to any remaining creditors to petition
E for liquidation if they thought fit, and it would also be open to any liquidator subsequently appointed to challenge any of the payments already referred to.

The sheriff reiterated the view expressed in his earlier note, namely, that advertisement ordered by the court in a first deliverance is not an option for the provisional liquidator, but a duty, and that he is an officer appointed by the court in the interests of all creditors. I respectfully agree with that view of the provisional liquidator's status and duty.
F
The sheriff accepted that if, on the provisional liquidator making his initial investigation, it appeared that his appointment was unnecessary, or even harmful to the interests of creditors, he may be entitled to apply to the court for the termination of his appointment. He referred to the Insolvency (Scotland) Rules 1986, Pt IV, Chap I, rule 4.6 (1). In my respectful opinion, that rule clearly provides for termination of the appointment, but the decision to continue or to terminate the appointment remains one for the sheriff in the exercise of his discretion.

The sheriff concluded that, notwithstanding the entitlement of the provisional liquidator to seek ter- G mination of his appointment, he was not entitled to do nothing, far less deliberately not to advertise. He therefore took the view that the provisional liquidator and the petitioners were not entitled to the remedy craved since they were in default.

The remedies craved are: (a) dispensation from the requirement to advertise the appointment of the provisional liquidator; (b) termination of his appointment and a finding that he is entitled to payment from the respondent company's property of his fees and outlays H and his and the petitioners' law agents' fees and outlays; and (c) dismissal of the petition.

On appeal, the solicitor for the petitioners accepted that the sheriff's decision was one made in the exercise of his judicial discretion. He submitted that the sheriff had erred in the exercise of that discretion in respect that he failed to take into account (a) the risk to the respondent company of continuing the liquidation process; (b) the risk involved for the jobs of the company's 100 or so employees; (c) the difficulty for the I respondent company in having every banking transaction queried by their bankers; (d) the possibility that by continuing the liquidation process a viable company could be prevented from trading out of its difficulties; and (e) that so long as this liquidation process continued, other creditors were prevented from taking proceedings for liquidation.

In the solicitor for the petitioners' submission, if these considerations had been taken properly into account, the sheriff should have granted the craves of J the note at least to the extent of dismissing the petition. He argued that by concentrating his attention on the alleged default by the provisional liquidator in not advertising his appointment, the sheriff had erred in carrying out the so called "balancing exercise". The default, if such it was, was on the part of the provisional liquidator, and its consequences should not be visited on the petitioners or the respondents.

The solicitor for the petitioners did not concede that the petitioners had gained any unfair preference as a K result of these liquidation proceedings, but he reiterated his argument that it would remain open to any liquidator appointed in subsequent proceedings to challenge the payments made to the petitioners on the basis of unfair preference. In my opinion, that is a relevant consideration.

The solicitor for the petitioners invited me to allow the appeal and to grant the craves of the note, including in particular that for payment out of the property of the respondent company of the fees and outlays of L the provisional liquidator and his law agents. He submitted that rule 4.6 in Pt IV, Chap I of the Insolvency (Scotland) Rules 1986 was directory unless there were very cogent reasons not to direct that payment of these expenses be made from the property of the company. He referred to the decision of Harman J in *Re Walter L Jacobs & Co Ltd* (1987) 3 BCC 532, which proceeded on the interpretation of similar rules applying in England and Wales.

The solicitor for the petitioners' concluding submission was that if the provisional liquidator's failure to advertise his appointment was seen as properly outweighing all other considerations, I should invoke my dispensing power in terms of s 63 of the Bankruptcy (Scotland) Act 1985 as applied by rule 7.32 (1) of the Insolvency (Scotland) Rules 1986, and grant the provisional liquidator relief from his failure to advertise his appointment as ordered by the court, and thereafter dismiss the petition. In that event, however, he still maintained the crave for payment of the fees and outlays from the property of the respondent company. I understood that the question of the fees and outlays being awarded against the respondent company was regarded by the provisional liquidator and his law agents as being of primary importance.

In terms of rule 23 (5) of the Sheriff Court Company Insolvency Rules 1986 it was the duty of the provisional liquidator to intimate his appointment forthwith in the *Edinburgh Gazette* and *The Herald* newspaper as ordered by the sheriff on 17 November 1992. He decided unilaterally not to advertise his appointment as ordered, however. In my opinion, his reasons for deciding against advertisement may have been valid in commercial terms, but the provisional liquidator was not entitled to ignore the order of the court and then to delay for some three months before advising the court of his position and seeking dispensation from the requirement to advertise. The delay suggests to me a failure to recognise that a provisional liquidator is an officer appointed by the court in the interests of all creditors and subject to its control in terms of the relevant statutory provisions.

The first application to the sheriff on 24 February 1992 seeking dispensation and discharge was clearly inept in its form and it is not surprising that it was refused by the sheriff. I thought it right to allow the first note to be amended on the occasion of the first appeal, however, and the matter came before the sheriff in its amended form towards the end of May, that is, some six months after the appointment of the provisional liquidator.

I understand the learned sheriff's concern that his order had apparently been ignored by the provisional liquidator and that it was some three months before any attempt was made to seek dispensation from the requirement to advertise. As I understand his note, the sheriff concentrated exclusively on this default on the part of the provisional liquidator. His note does not indicate that he took into account any of the wider considerations to which reference has been made on appeal and which I consider to be valid. In the particular circumstances, I am driven to the view that there was a misdirection in the exercise of the sheriff's discretion to the extent that he visited on the petitioner and respondent companies the consequences of the provisional liquidator's failure to comply with the order of the court in the matter of advertisement. In reaching this view, I am conscious that the argument on the wider considerations may have been developed more fully on appeal than it was before the sheriff and that to that extent I have the advantage of the sheriff. However, I have come to the view that I may properly regard the matter as being at large on appeal, and I am

satisfied in the particular circumstances that the appointment of the provisional liquidator should now be terminated and the petition dismissed. To that extent, therefore, the appeal is allowed.

This leaves the question of liability for payment of the provisional liquidator's fees and expenses, and those of his law agents. In my opinion, this is a matter on which I have a discretion in terms of rule 4.5 (3) in Pt IV, Chap I of the Insolvency (Scotland) Rules 1986, and I propose to exercise that discretion so as to refuse payment of these expenses from the property of the respondent company.

As it appears to me, the only function performed by the provisional liquidator in this liquidation has been to consider the business plan prepared for the respondents (which was already in the petitioners' hands before they commenced these proceedings), to discuss it with the respondents, and then to advise the petitioners to accept it. He did not advertise his appointment despite the terms of the governing regulations and the order of the court. As I understand, he consulted with the petitioners about this position, but with no other creditor. He has not intromitted in any way with the property of the respondent company. In my opinion, these liquidation proceedings may not have been necessary in the first place, and have certainly proved to be abortive. In these circumstances, I consider that an exception properly falls to be made from the general application of the rules, and that no order should be made for payment of the provisional liquidator's fees and outlays or those of his law agents out of the property of the respondent company.

For the same reasons, no expenses are awarded in respect of this appeal.

In the course of his submissions on appeal, the solicitor for the petitioners stated that it was common practice for provisional liquidators not to advertise their appointment and to proceed as the provisional liquidator had done in this case. He indicated to me that, in his experience, this practice is commonly accepted by the courts. I was not previously aware of such a practice and I am bound to say that it is one of which I disapprove. In my opinion, a provisional liquidator is an officer appointed by the court to an office which is in the interests of all creditors, and he is required to comply with the orders of the court and the statutory regulations governing his appointment. I accept the possibility that there may be some cases in which for sound commercial reasons advertisement of the provisional liquidator's appointment might not be appropriate. In such cases, however, I consider that it would be the duty of the provisional liquidator to apply to the court immediately for dispensation from the requirement to advertise his appointment. The decision would then be one for the court. It is not a decision which can be taken unilaterally by a provisional liquidator, whether or not in consultation with any creditor or body of creditors.

Solicitors for Petitioners and Provisional Liquidator, Bennett & Robertson, Edinburgh.

Gribb v Gribb

A SHERIFF COURT OF TAYSIDE, CENTRAL
AND FIFE AT PERTH
SHERIFF J C McINNES, QC
29 MARCH 1994

*Husband and wife — Divorce — Financial provision —
Capital sum — Pension rights — Whether wife had
interest in widow's pension rights under husband's
occupational pension — Whether should be included in*
B *valuation of assets — Family Law (Scotland) Act 1985
(c 37), s 10 (5).*

In an action of divorce the wife pursuer sought the
transfer to her of her husband's interest in the matrimonial home. Its transfer was dependent upon
whether making such an order would amount to a fair
division of the capital assets. The husband argued that
the value placed on his wife's interest in his pension
scheme should be ignored.

C **Held,** that both parties' interests in the pension
scheme required to be taken into account
(pp 45K–46A); and order to transfer the defender's
interest in the matrimonial home to the pursuer
granted.

Brooks v Brooks, 1993 SLT 184, *Bannon v Bannon,*
1993 SLT 999, and *Welsh v Welsh,* 1994 SLT 828, *not
followed.*

D **Action of divorce**
Margaret Gribb raised an action of divorce against
William Gribb in which she sought transfer of the
defender's interest in the matrimonial home to her.

Facts
After a hearing the sheriff found the following facts
admitted or proved:

(1) Mr and Mrs Gribb were married at Glasgow on
28 March 1953. Mrs Gribb is aged 62, having been
E born on 13 June 1931. Mr Gribb is aged 65, having
been born on 9 October 1928. The three children of
their marriage are all over 25 years of age. [The sheriff
dealt with the history of the marriage and continued:]

(7) Prior to the marriage Mrs Gribb was employed
as a comptometer operator. She left that employment
prior to the birth of her elder daughter. When her
children were old enough she resumed employment.
She worked on a part time basis and later on an almost
full time basis with Sinclair and Collis, Perth, where
F she worked for about 13 years until she was made
redundant. Since 1988 Mrs Gribb has worked on a
part time basis, 10 hours per week, serving tea and
coffee at Tayside Health Board, Perth, where she
earns £35 per week. (8) Mrs Gribb receives £230.79
per annum from an occupational pension scheme. She
receives a state pension at the rate of 48p per week. Mr
Gribb voluntarily pays Mrs Gribb £40 per week as
aliment. (9) On divorce if Mrs Gribb were to be unemployed and receiving no periodical allowance or the
equivalent from Mr Gribb she would receive a retirement pension of about £54 per week. Mrs Gribb is

entitled to receive a full state retirement pension since
Mr Gribb has attained the age of 65. (10) Mr Gribb G
joined the Scottish prison service after the marriage.
He retired after 27 years' service. He has not worked
since then. He receives invalidity benefit because of a
nervous disorder. He suffers from tremors in his arms
and hands. He does not take medication.

(11) When Mr Gribb retired he received a lump sum
payment of £13,000 from the Scottish prison service
and a pension for the rest of his life which is linked
to the Retail Price Index. All or almost all of that sum
of £13,000 has been spent. He presently receives a H
pension of £529 per month gross, i e £495 per month
net. (12) Mr Gribb presently receives invalidity
benefit at the rate of £92 per week. That sum includes
an amount in respect of his wife. On divorce the
amount which he receives as invalidity benefit will
decrease, perhaps by about £30 per week. (13) In
terms of Mr Gribb's pension scheme the widow of a
deceased pensioner is entitled to a pension of 50 per
cent of the pension which her spouse would have
received. The interests of Mr and Mrs Gribb in that I
pension scheme were wholly acquired as a result of his
full time employment during the marriage. (14) As at
the relevant date for the purposes of this action the
total value of the interests of Mr and Mrs Gribb in Mr
Gribb's pension scheme is £100,800. Of that sum the
value of the interest of Mrs Gribb as the prospective
widow of Mr Gribb is £29,800. (15) The title to the
former matrimonial home at Ashgrove, Perth, was in
Mr Gribb's sole name. That property was sold. The
house at 78 Burghmuir Road, Perth, was purchased in J
June 1987 at a cost of £27,500. It is a three bedroom
house with a large garden. There is no mortgage in
respect of that property. Title to that property was
taken in joint names of Mr and Mrs Gribb. The value
of that house as at the relevant date was £52,000. It
has not been well maintained. Money requires to be
spent on it. (16) The contents of the house at 78
Burghmuir Road were valued in June 1991 at £6,195.
(17) The total value of the matrimonial property in
which Mr and Mrs Gribb had an interest or which was
owned by them as at the relevant date was £158,995, K
being the total of the sums of £100,800, £52,000 and
£6,195 mentioned above. There are no other capital
assets. If the value of the matrimonial property were
to be shared equally between Mr and Mrs Gribb, Mrs
Gribb would be entitled to receive £79,500. (18) The
matrimonial property of Mr and Mrs Gribb should be
shared fairly between Mr and Mrs Gribb. Unless
there are special circumstances that property should
be shared equally. Mrs Gribb would be content to
forego her claim for a capital sum if Mr Gribb were L
to be ordered to transfer to her his one half share in
78 Burghmuir Road, Perth. (19) It is reasonable
having regard to their resources that the one half pro
indiviso share owned by Mr Gribb in the matrimonial
home at 78 Burghmuir Road, Perth, be transferred to
Mrs Gribb. (20) In the event of divorce being granted
Mrs Gribb is likely to suffer serious financial hardship. It is reasonable having regard to the respective
resources of Mr and Mrs Gribb that an order be made
for the payment by Mr Gribb to her of a periodical
allowance of £30 per week.

On 29 March 1994 the sheriff *granted* decree of
A divorce and inter alia *ordered* the defender to transfer
to the pursuer his share in the matrimonial home.

THE SHERIFF (J C McINNES, QC).—This is a
defended action of divorce at the instance of Mrs
Gribb. There are capital assets, the division of which
is also in dispute. So far as the divorce is concerned I
am in no doubt that Mrs Gribb has proved that the
marriage has broken down because of the unreasonable behaviour of Mr Gribb. The evidence which I
B accepted is reflected in the findings in fact. Although
Mr Gribb denied many of Mrs Gribb's allegations as
to why the marriage had broken down he did not deny
that it had broken down. Evidence given by their two
daughters, Mrs Webb and Mrs Winton, left me in no
doubt that the marriage has broken down irretrievably
for the reasons which Mrs Gribb gave. There is no
reason to suppose that Mrs Gribb's behaviour caused
the breakdown of the marriage. Mr Gribb attributed
that breakdown to a lack of laughter and love. He
C regards himself as a sociable person. But almost all of
his social activities took place away from his family. I
am satisfied that Mrs Gribb is entitled to decree of
divorce. So far as the financial aspects of this action
are concerned a joint minute of admissions has been
entered into agreeing most of the matters which had
been in dispute.

In his closing submissions on behalf of Mrs Gribb,
her solicitor moved the court to grant decree in terms
of craves 1, 4 and 8. He made a motion, albeit almost
D as an afterthought, that an order for a periodical allowance be made in terms of crave 2. I shall return to the
matter of a periodical allowance later. He did not make
a motion that orders be made in terms of the other
craves of the writ. Crave 1 relates to divorce; crave 8
to expenses. Crave 4 seeks the transfer to Mrs Gribb
of Mr Gribb's interest in 78 Burghmuir Road, Perth.
He also moved the court to make an order that the contents of the house be transferred to her. No order is
sought to that effect in the writ. Crave 6 seeks an order
E that Mrs Gribb be granted the possession and use of
these contents in terms of the Matrimonial Homes
(Family Protection) (Scotland) Act 1981, s 3. However
any such order would cease to have effect on divorce.
An incidental order in similar terms which would
regulate the position after divorce could have been
sought (Family Law (Scotland) Act 1985, s 14 (2) (d)).
No such order has been craved. In his counterclaim
Mr Gribb seeks payment by Mrs Gribb of a capital
sum of £45,000 and an order for the sale of the
F property at 78 Burghmuir Road, Perth.

Whether or not an order for transfer of Mr Gribb's
interest in the matrimonial home should be made is
dependent upon whether the making of such an order
would amount to a fair division of the capital assets
which have been accumulated during the marriage and
prior to the relevant date, having regard to the terms
of the Family Law (Scotland) Act 1985. These assets
consist of the heritable property at 78 Burghmuir
Road, Perth, which is in the joint names of Mr and
Mrs Gribb, the contents of that house and the pension

scheme from which a pension is being paid to Mr
Gribb. There seems to have been no attempt to place G
a capital value on the modest occupational pension
which Mrs Gribb receives. At any rate there was no
evidence as to its value. For present purposes I intend
to ignore it.

Section 10 of the Family Law (Scotland) Act 1985
provides inter alia as follows:

"(1) In applying the principle set out in section 9 (1)
(a) of this Act [fair sharing of the matrimonial
property], the net value of the matrimonial property H
shall be taken to be shared fairly when it is shared
equally or in such other proportions as are justified by
special circumstances. . . .

"(4) Subject to subsection (5) below, in this section
and in section 11 of this Act 'the matrimonial
property' means all the property belonging to the
parties or either of them at the relevant date which was
acquired by them or him (otherwise than by way of
gift or succession from a third party) — . . . (b) during I
the marriage but before the relevant date.

"(5) The proportion of any rights or interests of
either party under a life policy or occupational
pension scheme or similar arrangement referable to
the period to which subsection (4) (b) refers shall be
taken to form part of the matrimonial property."

If the net value of the matrimonial property were to
be shared equally Mrs Gribb would be entitled to
property to the value of £79,500. The solicitor for Mr
Gribb argued that there should not be an equal divi- J
sion of that property. He argued that the value placed
on Mrs Gribb's interest in Mr Gribb's pension
scheme should be ignored on the basis of the following
decisions. In *Bannon v Bannon*, 1993 SLT 999, at
p 1003I-K, Lord Cameron of Lochbroom accepted
that a potential widow had an interest in such a
scheme but he went on to say: "I agree with Lord
Marnoch's view in *Brooks v Brooks* that since a
divorced wife would not be eligible to claim such
rights were they to come into being, they should not K
form part of the defender's interest for the purpose of
valuation. Until the parties' divorce, the pursuer's
interest is protected. The claim for a capital sum only
emerges upon divorce, when the pursuer's interest
flies off. That same interest could only become available after divorce if the defender remarried. Divorce is
the event which gives rise to the claim for a capital
sum. Accordingly thereafter the widow's interest
would reflect the interest of some party other than that
of the pursuer and the defender in this case. Insofar as L
the pursuer has any 'interest' under the police pension
scheme at the relevant date, it is extinguished upon
decree of divorce being pronounced and falls to be
disregarded."

In *Brooks v Brooks*, 1993 SLT 184, Lord Marnoch
assessed the prospective widow's rights in her husband's pension scheme at £15,000. He then deducted
that sum from the net value of the matrimonial
property as at the relevant date. Unfortunately he did
not go on to explain the basis upon which, having

A regard to the terms of the Act, he felt entitled to give effect to the submission of counsel for the defender that that deduction should be made. In *Welsh v Welsh*, 1994 SLT 828, Lord Osborne held that the value of a potential widow's pension should be disregarded on the basis that the wife's right at the relevant date was only a spes because the identity of the person entitled to the widow's benefits could not be known until the member of the pension scheme had died. Accordingly in his opinion the interest of the wife in that case was something less than an interest under an occupational

B pension scheme and so did not form part of the matrimonial property. What Lord Osborne said in relation to the terms of s 10 (5) of the Act was this: "It seems to me that the question which arises is whether the widow's pension element can be said to be a fund in which either party has any right or interest. In my opinion, it is not. . . . It appears to me plain that the identity of the person possessing an interest in that particular portion of the fund is incapable of ascertainment until the death of the defender. As at the

C relevant date, a wife of the defender could be seen as possessing only a spes in respect of this element of the fund. I do not think that that state of affairs can properly be described as possession of a right or interest" (at p 833E-G).

The first issue then is whether the pension to which Mrs Gribb is prospectively entitled as the potential widow of Mr Gribb is a "right" or "interest" in an occupational pension scheme. There is no doubt that this is such a scheme. But has she a "right" or

D "interest" in it? If Mr Gribb died on any day prior to decree of divorce being granted she would immediately become entitled to receive half the pension which he received prior to his death. The question as at the date of death of the pensioner is: "Did he leave a widow?" If the answer to that question is in the affirmative the trustees are required to pay an appropriate pension to her.

If Mr Gribb had died at any time before the date on

E which his interest in the scheme became an interest in possession he would in my opinion have had a greater interest than a spes as at the relevant date. His interest would have formed part of the matrimonial property. That is consistent with the decision in *Welsh*. I confess that I have difficulty expressing in principled form the reason why the interest of a spouse should be treated as neither "right" nor "interest" but merely as a spes.

F Section 10 of the Family Law (Scotland) Act 1985 requires that the matrimonial property be valued as at a date which, ex hypothesi, is a date prior to the date of the divorce. At that date the spouses must, of course, be alive and married to one another. At that time they have an interest in the matrimonial property as that phrase is defined in the Act. The proportion of any rights or interests of either of them under an occupational pension scheme referable to the period mentioned in s 10 (4) (b) is to be taken to form part of the matrimonial property. It is of course correct to say, as Lord Cameron does, that on divorce a spouse's

interest in the pension scheme flies off. If no provision had been made in the Act to take account of that fact G the spouse would lose that interest without compensation. Yet that is an interest which may well have been accumulated in circumstances (such as those in the instant case) in which a wife has remained at home to bring up a family while the husband worked. It is not obvious that the value of the spouse's interest should accrue to a second spouse. In this case that interest was wholly acquired during the marriage and prior to the relevant date.

Difficulty may be encountered giving effect to the H intention of the Act since in many cases the only substantial capital asset may be an interest in a pension scheme which may be inaccessible. There may be no other assets from which a capital sum could be paid. Whether that be so or not in a particular case, in my opinion what the Act requires is that account be taken of the value of an interest in a pension scheme accumulated since the date of the marriage and before the relevant date. The court is not required to have regard to what may occur after decree of divorce has I been granted. Indeed the attention of the court is directed to a period which must have terminated prior to the date when divorce may be granted. The "relevant date" is the date on which the parties ceased to cohabit or the date of service of the summons in the action of divorce, whichever is the earlier (s 10 (3) of the Act).

It could be that no value can be attached to an interest. That may happen where, for example, the J number of events which would have to occur before an interest vested and the improbability of their occurrence make the interest so remote that it is of no material value. But that would be a matter for evidence as to the value of the matrimonial property. It is not in itself a reason for defining such property so as to exclude an interest which is to be taken to form part of such property.

In the present case the interest of Mr Gribb in the occupational pension scheme is in possession. In the K case of Mrs Gribb, as at the relevant date, she had a contingent interest in that scheme, the contingency being that she survived her husband. On divorce she will cease to be his spouse and will lose that interest. I am in no doubt that as at the relevant date Mrs Gribb had that interest in the pension scheme. That is an interest which is not only capable of being valued, it has been valued for the purposes of the present case.

Of course Mrs Gribb might not have benefited from L that interest. She might have predeceased her husband. But a prospective pensioner whose interest is not in possession may die before he receives a pension. He may nonetheless have acquired a valuable asset, namely an interest in an occupational pension scheme, of which the court is required to take account in assessing the net value of matrimonial property. If the pension scheme so permitted he could assign for value or sell the right to receive the pension and so could his spouse in respect of her interest in that

A
scheme. In my opinion, as a matter of law, I am required to take account of the interests of each of Mr and Mrs Gribb in Mr Gribb's pension scheme.

The solicitor for the defender further argued that there should be a discount of the value of the interests in Mr Gribb's pension as there had been in the cases of *Muir v Muir*, 1989 SLT (Sh Ct) 20; 1989 SCLR 445 (where two fifths rather than one half was awarded) and *Carpenter v Carpenter*, 1990 SLT (Sh Ct) 68; 1990 SCLR 206 (where three eighths rather

B
than one half was awarded). Making the assumption, but not deciding, that Mrs Gribb should receive three eighths of the value of these interests she would receive £37,800. That sum plus one half of the value of the house and contents would amount to £66,897.50. The last mentioned sum would represent the value of assets which she could expect to receive if the matrimonial property were to be shared equally. If Mrs Gribb receives no more than the value of a one half share in the house she would receive only £26,000. That would not represent a fair sharing of

C
these assets. But, as I have noted, the pursuer's solicitor indicated that so far as capital was concerned his client would be content to receive the transfer of Mr Gribb's one half share in their house, even though that was less than the value of a one half share of the matrimonial property. In the foregoing circumstances the order to transfer that share could not be said to be unfair to Mr Gribb.

So far as the counterclaim is concerned I am of

D
opinion that it would be inappropriate to grant either of the craves. The sale of 78 Burghmuir Road would mean that both Mr and Mrs Gribb had to find alternative accommodation with all the cost which that would entail. If the house were to be sold for its agreed value following a transfer of the interest of Mr Gribb, Mrs Gribb could realise a significant amount of capital. If she were to reinvest that she could increase her income, but not by a very substantial amount. In that event she would probably have to pay rent for

E
alternative accommodation, which would reduce any advantage gained from the sale of the house to some extent. The sum of £45,000 claimed by Mr Gribb represents substantially more than half the value of the house and its contents. To make an order for a capital payment to Mr Gribb of that order, or indeed any order, would not be in accordance with the principles of the 1985 Act, if only because it would mean that the value of the interests in the pension scheme had been ignored and because it would, on any view, result in

F
Mr Gribb receiving an even more substantial share of the matrimonial property. I have concluded that Mrs Gribb is entitled to be absolved from the counterclaim.

So far as a periodical allowance is concerned it is averred by Mrs Gribb that she would suffer serious financial hardship if no order for payment of such allowance is made. The defender's solicitor conceded that Mrs Gribb may be entitled to a periodical allowance. The situation after divorce is likely to be that Mrs Gribb would receive a weekly pension of about

G
£54 per week in addition to her occupational pension unless the receipt of the latter causes an abatement of the former. Her total net income would be about £58.44 per week. Mr Gribb would receive about £62 per week plus his occupational pension which amounts to about £495 net per month or £114.23 net per week. He would therefore have a total income of perhaps about £168 net per week. That is a marked disparity. Mrs Gribb intends to live at 78 Burghmuir Road. That is a three bedroom house which requires to have money spent on its maintenance. While she

H
will not have to meet the cost of a mortgage in respect of that property it seems to me that she would suffer serious financial hardship if she were to live there with only the income from the pensions to which she is entitled. Her health is not good. It is deteriorating. She is of an age when she would find it difficult to find reasonably well paid work for which she is fit.

In my opinion an order for the transfer of Mr Gribb's interest in 78 Burghmuir Road is insufficient having regard to the resources of the parties to secure

I
the fair sharing of the net value of the matrimonial property and the avoidance of serious financial hardship for Mrs Gribb. I am of opinion that the making of an order for a periodical allowance is justified by the principles set out in s 9 of the 1985 Act and is reasonable having regard to the resources of Mr and Mrs Gribb. However on the transfer of his share in 78 Burghmuir Road Mr Gribb will have to obtain alternative accommodation for which he will presumably require to pay rent. Any order for payment of a

J
periodical allowance should take account of that. In all the circumstances of the case I consider that it is reasonable to make an order for the payment of a periodical allowance of £30 per week and that that allowance should be payable until the remarriage or death of Mrs Gribb.

Solicitors for Pursuer, A C Miller & Mackay, Perth — Solicitors for Defender, Miller Hendry, WS, Perth.   K

Kelly v Renfrew District Council

L

SHERIFF COURT OF NORTH STRATHCLYDE AT PAISLEY

SHERIFF PRINCIPAL R C HAY, WS

27 APRIL 1994

Process — Court fees — Dispute between pursuer and sheriff clerk about liability to pay fee — Whether sheriff had jurisdiction to resolve dispute — Civil Jurisdiction and Judgments Act 1982 (c 27), s 22 (4).

A *Jurisdiction — Sheriff court — Court fees — Dispute between pursuer and sheriff clerk about liability to pay fee — Whether sheriff had jurisdiction to resolve dispute — Civil Jurisdiction and Judgments Act 1982 (c 27), s 22 (4).*

Section 22 (4) of the Civil Jurisdiction and Judgments Act 1982 provides that where a court has jurisdiction in any proceedings by virtue of Sched 8 to that Act, "that court shall also have jurisdiction to determine any matter which — (a) is ancillary or incidental to the proceedings; or (b) requires to be determined for
B the purposes of a decision in the proceedings".

After an interim hearing was appointed in an action, the sheriff clerk sought payment from the pursuer of a fee of £53, founding on para 37 of the Schedule to the Sheriff Court Fees Amendment (No 2) Order 1993. The pursuer declined to pay. After a hearing, the sheriff held that he had no jurisdiction in any dispute over court fees. The pursuer appealed to the sheriff principal and, referring to s 22 (4) of the
C 1982 Act, submitted that the sheriff did have jurisdiction.

Held, (1) that the question of liability to pay the fee was a matter which was ancillary or incidental to proceedings in which the court had jurisdiction within s 22 (4) (a) (p 50D-E); (2) that a dispute about liability to pay a court fee for a step of process could be analysed as a question of the competency of that step and was a matter which properly fell to be determined by the court (p 50F-G); and appeal *allowed*.

D **Opinion,** that it was arguable that the dispute also fell within s 22 (4) (b) as a matter which required to be determined for the purposes of a decision in the proceedings (p 50E).

Observed, that it would be helpful if early action were taken to clarify those areas in the order which had given rise to doubt (p 50J).

———————————

E **Action**

Gerard Kelly raised an action against Renfrew District Council. The sheriff clerk sought payment of a fee of £53 in respect of the fixing of an interim hearing, which fee the pursuer declined to pay. After a hearing the sheriff (C N Stoddart) held that he had no jurisdiction in any dispute over fees. The pursuer appealed to the sheriff principal.

F On 27 April 1994 the sheriff principal *allowed* the appeal.

THE SHERIFF PRINCIPAL (R C HAY, WS).—This is an appeal by the pursuer with leave of the sheriff against his interlocutor dated 10 February 1994. In terms of that interlocutor the sheriff held that he had no jurisdiction to make an order in respect of a disputed court fee of £53 demanded by the sheriff clerk in terms of the table of fees in the Schedule to the Sheriff Court Fees Amendment (No 2) Order 1993, SI 1993/2957 (hereinafter "the 1993 Order").

The fee was demanded in terms of para 37 for fixing a hearing in connection with an interim order sought G by the pursuer.

The disputed issue of liability to pay the particular court fee has now been resolved by executive action and no question arises in that regard. However, the appeal raises a point of general importance, namely, whether a sheriff has jurisdiction to determine an issue of a disputed court fee in a process which is before the court.

The pursuer and appellant was represented by the H Vice-Dean of Faculty. By agreement the defenders, who had no interest in the point in issue, did not appear in the appeal.

The 1993 Order was made by the Secretary of State in exercise of his powers under s 2 of the Courts of Law Fees (Scotland) Act 1895, as substituted by s 4 of the Divorce Jurisdiction, Court Fees and Legal Aid (Scotland) Act 1983. The 1993 Order amends the Sheriff Court Fees Order 1985. The effect is to substitute a new table of court fees and to add para 9A I which specifies that certain new fees shall not apply to actions commenced before 1 January 1994.

The Vice-Dean of Faculty did not challenge the validity of the 1993 Order. He accepted that a sheriff has no power to enter on a judicial review of the vires of a statutory instrument. He drew a distinction, however, between questioning the validity of a statutory instrument, such as the 1993 Order, and determining its proper construction. The latter, he submitted, fell clearly within the jurisdiction of a sheriff. J

This argument was adduced before the sheriff. In his note, he points out that since the Act of 1895 was amended in 1983, all court fees have been fixed by the Secretary of State instead of, as formerly, by the Court of Session. The sheriff was referred to the historical survey of the process of fixing court fees set out by Lord Mackay in his opinion in *Carron Co v Hislop*, 1930 SC 1050 at pp 1071 et seq; 1930 SLT 689 at pp 702 et seq (a case further reported at 1931 SC (HL) K 75; 1931 SLT 312).

The Vice-Dean of Faculty submitted that it was clear from that case that the changes introduced in 1983 were not the first time that court fees had been regulated by a minister rather than by the Court of Session, and that, in any event, the regulation of court fees had never been within the province of the sheriff. In his submission, however, it matters not whether the table of fees is regulated by a minister or by the court, since the source of the authority in either case is L Parliament, which has provided the enabling powers in terms of the Act of 1895, as amended. Since it is a normal function of the courts to interpret both primary and subordinate legislation, a sheriff has a clear jurisdiction to determine questions arising incidentally in relation to payment of court fees under the 1993 Order.

The Vice-Dean of Faculty commented that in the *Carron Co* case the issue was one of vires, and the case was not concerned with any question of interpretation.

In his submission, therefore, the solicitor for the appellant had been correct in his submission to the sheriff that that case was of no particular assistance in relation to the question of jurisdiction.

The sheriff deemed it of significance, however, that in terms of the Act of Sederunt in issue in the *Carron Co* case, the sheriff clerk had specific power to seek a decree from the sheriff for the amount of an unpaid fee, whereas no such power was contained in the Act of Sederunt (Fees for Sheriff Court) 1982, which was the last occasion on which the Court of Session fixed sheriff court fees under the Act of 1895, nor subsequently. He then poses the question whether, in the absence of any specific provision for recovery of a disputed fee, resort must be had to the common law.

The sheriff goes on to discuss the consequences in the light of the submission by the appellant's solicitor that, given the ambiguities in the 1993 Order, it was quite likely that different sheriffs would come to differing views on similar points. He comments that, if a law of any kind is ambiguous, then it is inevitable that different interpretations will be made by judges of first instance. He goes on to say, and I respectfully agree, that this cannot be a reason for declining to interpret such a law.

The Vice-Dean of Faculty submitted that the absence of any specific provision for enforcement in the 1993 Order is significant. In his submission, the intended effect seems to be that if a fee properly sought by the sheriff clerk in terms of the 1993 Order is not paid, the next step of process will not take place, and that accordingly whether a fee is properly due becomes a question of the competency of the related step of process. As an issue of competency, it must be a matter for the sheriff to determine.

Having accepted that the possibility of differing judicial interpretations cannot be a reason for the court declining to interpret a piece of legislation, the sheriff goes on to say that the 1993 Order is unlike other rules of law upon which he is asked to adjudicate daily. It is, he says, a set of administrative regulations which control access to the courts for the litigant who wishes his case decided. He continues: "If there is a dispute between the sheriff clerk and the solicitor for the party as to whether a particular fee is payable, I take the view that such dispute is not justiciable before me, save perhaps in the context of an action between them. Apart from situations where he acts under statute in an administrative capacity, the sheriff decides issues between opposing parties; and only when parties seek to join issue in a competent form of process does the judicial function begin. The sheriff, in my view, does not (and ought not to) decide, by means of interpreting regulations dealing with court fees, which litigant comes before him and which does not. The doors of the court are open to all; and the judicial oath sworn by the sheriff on his installation obliges him to 'do right to *all* manner of people after the laws and usages of this realm, without fear or favour, affection or ill will'. The sheriff cannot (even indirectly) pick and choose the litigant he hears. For these reasons, I reject the proposition advanced by the solicitor for the appellant that to decide whether the fee in dispute is in fact payable is 'incidental' to my jurisdiction to hear Mr Kelly's case. In this context the very term 'incidental' suggests the existence before the sheriff of a justiciable issue incapable of resolution without some matter arising in the course thereof being itself resolved. That is not the situation in the present case."

The Vice-Dean of Faculty submitted that the sheriff was correct in his view that the 1993 Order provides a set of administrative regulations which control access to the court, but wrong in his view that it is different from other rules. In his submission, the first point must be to establish if there is a competent process. This is not necessarily an issue requiring to be raised by another party, since it is pars judicis to notice questions of competency. By saying that the doors of the court are open to all, the sheriff stated the proposition too widely. The proposition should be that the doors of the court are open to all who come in the way the court requires, and the sheriff is perfectly entitled to insist that the correct procedures are followed. Payment of the appropriate fee is as much an incident of the correct procedure as is the correct form of initial writ, defences or other document. On that basis, the Vice-Dean of Faculty submitted, the sheriff does decide which litigants come before him, and which do not.

He went on to submit that in the instant case the sheriff was wrong in his view that to decide the issue of a disputed court fee was not "incidental" to his jurisdiction to hear the pursuer's case, and also in his view of what "incidental" means in this context. In the learned Vice-Dean's submission, there was in the instant case a justiciable issue between the pursuer and the defender, but if the pursuer was not permitted to come to court except on payment of the fee sought by the sheriff clerk, the justiciable issue could not be determined until the issue of whether the fee was properly due had been resolved. The issue of the disputed fee was therefore "incidental" to the justiciable issue before the court.

The sheriff goes on to discuss the duty of the sheriff clerk in cases where there is a dispute as to the fee payable. He notes that the Act of Sederunt (Fees for Sheriff Court) 1982 contained a provision that, prior to payment of the appropriate fee, the sheriff clerk was not required to do any act, including the acceptance of any writ, in connection with the matter to which the fee related. That provision has not been carried forward into subsequent regulations made by the Secretary of State. The sheriff comments that he must construe its absence from current regulations as bestowing no more than a discretion in the hands of the sheriff clerk to carry out without fee a function for which a fee is prima facie payable.

The Vice-Dean of Faculty doubted whether, on a sound construction of the statutory provisions, either pre- or post-1982, the sheriff clerk has any discretion whether or not to demand a fee. In his submission, the 1993 Order gives no indication that the sheriff clerk has any discretion in the matter.

The sheriff refers to Notes for Guidance of Sheriff Clerks on the 1993 Order, which I understand to have been prepared by Scottish Courts Administration, and which have apparently been circulated by the Law Society of Scotland to their members. He regarded para 7.5 of the guidance notes as recognising that the sheriff clerk has a discretion. This certainly appears to be the view of the author of the guidance notes in relation to refunding fees in certain circumstances and not seeking payment of a fee when a new diet of proof, debate or hearing has to be fixed following the discharge of the original diet because of illness. In the learned Vice-Dean's submission, however, there is no warrant in the 1993 Order for this view. In any event, he argued, the guidance notes have no status when it comes to a question of interpretation of the statutory instrument by the court, and the question is solely for the court. If, however, the sheriff is well founded in his view, and the sheriff clerk does have a discretion, this leads to the highly unsatisfactory situation that the duty of interpretation is being left to the sheriff clerk, but with no obvious means being provided for review of his decision.

The sheriff refers in his note to the possibility of judicial review of the sheriff clerk's decision by the Court of Session. The learned Vice-Dean of Faculty accepted that this would be a possibility if a discretion was indeed given to the sheriff clerk acting in his administrative capacity. He argued, however, that this course could only become available if the sheriff clerk's exercise of his duties in relation to charging court fees was independent of any control by the sheriff.

The Vice-Dean of Faculty summarised his argument under two main propositions. These were, first, that the sheriff has, as part of his inherent jurisdiction, power to determine all issues which arise in the process before him, and, secondly, that determination of whether a particular court fee is payable is such an issue.

In relation to the first point he began, as did the solicitor for the appellant before the sheriff, with the proposition stated in Erskine, *An Institute of the Law of Scotland* (Nicolson ed, 1871), I ii 8, as follows: "In all grants of jurisdiction, whether civil or criminal, supreme or inferior, every power is understood to be conferred without which the jurisdiction cannot be explicated. . . . By this rule a judge may determine incidentally questions which fall not under his original cognisance, where, without that power, he could not pronounce a definitive judgment in the action which is properly insisted in before him."

The Vice-Dean of Faculty also referred to Macphail, *Sheriff Court Practice*, at paras 2-05 and 2-06 in relation to the inherent jurisdiction of the sheriff, para 2-09 in relation to matters which are pars judicis, and para 2-14 in relation to the proposition that it is pars judicis to notice questions of competency notwithstanding the absence of a plea.

The learned Vice-Dean then referred to the provisions of s 22 (4) of the Civil Jurisdiction and Judgments Act 1982. He accepted that this provision was not cited before the sheriff. Section 22 (4) is in Pt III of the Act, dealing with jurisdiction in Scotland, and provides as follows: "Where a court has jurisdiction in any proceedings by virtue of Schedule 8, that court shall also have jurisdiction to determine any matter which — (a) is ancillary or incidental to the proceedings; or (b) requires to be determined for the purposes of a decision in the proceedings".

The Vice-Dean of Faculty submitted that s 22 (4) is an express statutory recognition of the common law position. That being so, he found it unnecessary to review the line of authority cited before the sheriff (*Thomson v City of Edinburgh District Council*, 1982 SLT (Land Ct) 39, and *Glasgow Corporation v Flint*, 1966 SC 108). In his submission, the sheriff has a plain jurisdiction in terms of s 22 (4) to determine any incidental matter in the process coming before him, and this must include any question of liability to pay a disputed court fee.

He went on to consider the consequences of failure to pay a fee demanded by the sheriff clerk, and pointed out that there is no express provision enabling the sheriff clerk to enforce payment. He postulated three possibilities in the event of refusal to pay a fee demanded: (i) the sheriff clerk gives up the demand — a course which seems in general terms to be unlikely; or (ii) the sheriff clerk declares that the next step of process will not take place — a situation which causes an immediate difficulty when there is a dispute about whether the fee is properly due; or (iii) the sheriff clerk brings the matter before the sheriff.

In the learned Vice-Dean's submission, the situation in which the sheriff clerk seeks payment of a fee in terms of the 1993 Order and a solicitor argues that the fee is not properly payable can be analysed as a bona fide dispute, not on a question of the competency of the action in general, but on a question of the competency of the particular step of process in respect of which the fee is demanded. He drew an analogy with a dispute about the application of rules of court to a step of procedure, and argued that if there is a bona fide dispute on the interpretation or application of a procedural rule in a particular instance, the appropriate course is to argue the point before the judge or sheriff. He argued that there is no reason in principle to draw a distinction in this respect between rules governing procedure and rules prescribing the fees to be paid for procedure. Both sets of rules control access to the court and if there is a dispute as to whether something has to be done so that the cause may proceed, that is a preliminary matter which the court should determine.

In this connection, the Vice-Dean of Faculty referred to the recent case of *Muir v Muir*, 1994 SCLR 182, in which Sheriff A L Stewart held that a motion was incompetent in respect that no fee had been paid. In that case, he submitted, a dispute about a fee demanded by the sheriff clerk had been properly

referred to the sheriff and judicially determined as a
A   question of competency.

In conclusion, I was invited to find that the learned
sheriff had misdirected himself in holding that he had
no jurisdiction to determine the question of the disputed fee, and to allow the appeal on that basis, but
to make no further order as liability to pay the particular fee was no longer in issue. Finally, I was
invited to sist the cause of new.

I am conscious that, absent a contradictor before the
B   sheriff, and again on appeal, no counter argument to
that advanced for the appellant has been heard by the
court. Obviously, it would have been of assistance in
a matter of such general importance if the contrary
view had been argued. I am indebted to the learned
Vice-Dean of Faculty, however, for his comprehensive
and helpful submissions, and on the whole matter I
find his arguments persuasive.

In the passage from his note cited above, the learned
sheriff has stated his reasons for rejecting the argu-
C   ment that to decide whether the fee in dispute was in
fact payable was "incidental" to his jurisdiction to
hear the appellant's case. "In this context," he says,
"the very term 'incidental' suggests the existence
before the sheriff of a justiciable issue incapable of
resolution without some matter arising in the course
thereof being itself resolved. That is not the situation
in the present case."

In so holding, the learned sheriff has, in my
D   respectful opinion, misdirected himself. It is unfortunate that his attention was not directed to the provisions of s 22 (4) of the Civil Jurisdiction and
Judgments Act 1982.

I am satisfied that the dispute about liability to pay
the fee sought by the sheriff clerk arose in the course
of proceedings brought by the appellant against the
defenders in which the court had jurisdiction by virtue
of Sched 8 to the Civil Jurisdiction and Judgments Act
1982. In my opinion, the question of liability to pay
E   the court fee was a matter which was ancillary or
incidental to these proceedings in terms of s 22 (4) (a)
of the Act. It is also, I think, arguable that it was a
matter which required to be determined for the purposes of a decision in the proceedings in terms of s 22
(4) (b), on the basis that until the question of liability
to pay the fee had been determined a decision could
not be reached in the proceedings to which that question was ancillary or incidental.

I agree with the proposition advanced by the Vice-
F   Dean of Faculty that a dispute about liability to pay
a court fee for a particular step of process can be
analysed as a question of the competency of that particular step of process, and that as such it is a matter
which properly falls to be determined by the court. In
my opinion, there is no reason in principle to draw a
distinction in this respect between rules governing
procedure and rules prescribing the fees to be paid for
steps in procedure. Both sets of rules control access to
the court and I am of the opinion that if a dispute
arises in relation to either set of rules it raises a ques-

tion of the competency of the particular step of process
which is ancillary or incidental to the proceedings   G
before the court and which properly falls to be determined by the court by way of interpretation of the rule
in question.

For these reasons, I am of the view that the learned
sheriff did have jurisdiction to determine the issue of
the disputed court fee. It follows that the appeal will
be allowed and the interlocutor of the sheriff complained of will be recalled to that extent. No question
of expenses arises.

The detailed provisions of the table of fees in the   H
1993 Order were not considered to any extent in the
course of the appeal and I am therefore unable to
express any concluded view. I think it right to
comment, however, that I see considerable force in the
views tentatively expressed by the learned sheriff
anent possible difficulties in interpretation of the term
"hearing" used in para 37. I can also envisage the possibility of doubt about the meaning and application in
certain circumstances of para 39 in relation to the use   I
of the term "minute".

I therefore support the view expressed by the
learned sheriff that disputes about liability to pay
court fees for particular steps in process or for lodging
particular papers are likely to arise with some frequency. The determination of these questions will
take up court time and will tend to add to the cost of
procedure generally. It is also possible, given the
imprecise way in which some of the provisions are
expressed, that such questions will be determined in   J
different ways by different sheriffs at first instance and
that appeals to sheriffs principal will follow. I agree
with the learned sheriff that wrangling about court
fees does not advance the cause of justice to the litigant; nor does it assist the work of the courts. Accordingly, I share the sheriff's view that it would be
helpful if those competent to do so considered taking
early action to clarify those areas in the 1993 Order
which have given rise to doubt.

K

*Counsel for Pursuer and Appellant, Macfadyen, QC;
Solicitors, Pattison & Sim, Paisley — No appearance for
Defenders and Respondents.*

L

City of Edinburgh District Council v Robbin

SHERIFF COURT OF LOTHIAN AND BORDERS AT EDINBURGH

SHERIFF PRINCIPAL C G B NICHOLSON, QC

4 OCTOBER 1993

Process — Appeal — Appeal from sheriff to sheriff principal — Competency — Incidental interlocutor in summary cause — Sheriff Courts (Scotland) Act 1971 (c 58), s 38.

Process — Summary cause — Incidental interlocutor — Competency of appeal against incidental interlocutor — Sheriff Courts (Scotland) Act 1971 (c 58), s 38.

Process — Consignation — Action for recovery of possession of heritable property — No pecuniary crave — Whether order for consignation competent.

A local authority raised a summary cause action for the recovery of a house from their tenant following his non-payment of rent. The tenant admitted that rent had not been paid but stated a defence that he was entitled not to pay it on account of the local authority's failure to carry out essential repairs. The sheriff ordered the tenant to consign a sum for the unpaid rent. When the tenant appealed to the sheriff principal the sheriff refused to state a case on the basis that his interlocutor was neither a final judgment nor an incompetent interlocutor.

Held, that, in summary cause procedure, s 38 of the Sheriff Courts (Scotland) Act 1971 and rule 81 of the Summary Cause Rules excluded an appeal against an incidental interlocutor and the appeal was therefore incompetent (p 52I-J); and appeal *refused.*

Macphail, *Sheriff Court Practice,* para 24-175, *followed; City of Glasgow District Council v McAleer,* 1992 SLT (Sh Ct) 41, *not followed.*

Opinion, that the order for consignation was incompetent since there was no crave for payment of money (p 53I-K).

Observed, that any general practice of using the recovery of possession procedure as a device to secure payment of rent arrears was inappropriate (pp 53L-54A).

Action for recovery of possession of heritable property

The City of Edinburgh District Council raised a summary cause action against Alexander Robbin for recovery of possession of heritable property let to him. The action was defended. On 7 May 1993 the sheriff (J A Farrell) ordered the defender to consign the sum of £1,263 in respect of the allegedly unpaid rent. The defender marked an appeal to the sheriff principal. However, the sheriff refused to state a case on the ground that an appeal was not competent in the circumstances. The sheriff principal thereafter put the appeal out for hearing.

On 4 October 1993 the sheriff principal *refused* the appeal as incompetent.

THE SHERIFF PRINCIPAL (C G B NICHOLSON, QC).—This appeal has been taken in a summary cause action for recovery of possession of heritable property. The pursuers are a local authority and the defender is the tenant of one of their houses. The action has been raised under s 47 of the Housing (Scotland) Act 1987 and, although the summons avers that the defender has arrears of rent amounting to £848.25, it is to be noted that the action is solely for recovery of possession of the house in question and does not contain any crave for payment of the allegedly unpaid rent. So far as appears from the summons, the amount of unpaid rent is stated simply to establish the ground under Pt I of Sched 3 to the 1987 Act by virtue of which recovery of possession is sought.

When the action first called in court on 7 May 1993 the defender admitted that rent had not been paid to the pursuers, but he stated a defence to the effect that he was entitled not to pay it on account of the pursuers' failure to carry out essential repairs to the house. After that defence had been noted by the sheriff the pursuers' solicitor then moved the court to order the defender to consign a sum of £1,263 into the hands of the sheriff clerk within seven days. (It appears to be common ground that that sum represents the whole accrued arrears of rent as at 7 May 1993.) The sheriff granted the motion and the defender thereupon marked an appeal and requested the sheriff to state a case.

The sheriff refused to do so and, instead, issued a brief note in which he expresses the opinion that his interlocutor is not a final judgment nor is it an incompetent interlocutor. In those circumstances he concluded that the defender is without the right of appeal. Notwithstanding the sheriff's refusal to state a case I put the appeal out for hearing, and at that stage two factors of significance emerged. The first was that the pursuers indicated that they did not propose to challenge the competency of the appeal; and the second was that both parties indicated that they were anxious to have any decision regarding the competency of the order for consignation. Without at that stage forming any concluded view myself as to the competency of the appeal, I considered that it would be inappropriate to hear parties regarding the order for consignation without at least giving the sheriff the opportunity to explain the considerations which had led him to make that order. Accordingly, I adjourned the appeal hearing and, without prejudice to any final decision regarding the competency of the appeal, I invited the sheriff to prepare a note in relation to the order for consignation. Unfortunately the sheriff did not find it possible to assist on this matter. His note states: "I do not have a note of what was said on behalf of parties on 7 May. I do have a recollection of what was said but, at this distance in time, that is not something upon which I would consider it proper to rely." In that situation questions relating to the competency of the order for consignation are effectively at large for me.

However, such questions will only arise properly before me if I can be satisfied that the present appeal is itself competent. I have already observed that it was a matter of concession on the part of the pursuers that the appeal *is* competent, but counsel for the pursuers very fairly and properly accepted that I could not be bound by that concession. While a court may be obliged to go along with a concession on a matter of fact it can never be obliged by virtue of a concession to be incompetent. I therefore turn now to consider the competency of the present appeal.

Provision is made for appeals on summary causes by s 38 of the Sheriff Courts (Scotland) Act 1971. That section provides: "In the case of — (a) any summary cause an appeal shall lie to the sheriff principal on any point of law from the final judgment of the sheriff . . . but save as aforesaid an interlocutor of the sheriff . . . in any such cause shall not be subject to review."

Counsel for the defender accepted, as I think he was bound to do, that the foregoing provision does not provide for an appeal against what may be termed an incidental interlocutor; and, indeed, that view is confirmed by the terms of rule 81 of the Summary Cause Rules which, by making reference to findings in fact and certain other matters, is clearly designed only for appeals against final judgments. However, counsel submitted that any restriction on appeals is always subject to an overriding power in an appellate court to recall an interlocutor that is incompetent. For a general review of the authorities supporting that proposition counsel referred me to the decision of Sheriff Principal (as he then was) Caplan in *VAG Finance v Smith*, 1988 SLT (Sh Ct) 59; and for an illustration of the proposition being applied in the context of summary cause procedure he referred me to the decision of Sheriff Principal MacLeod in *City of Glasgow District Council v McAleer*, 1992 SLT (Sh Ct) 41. Counsel also referred me to a passage in Macphail, *Sheriff Court Practice*, para 24-175, which suggests that there is no common law right of appeal in summary cause procedure; but that view is expressed on the authority of an unreported decision by Sheriff Principal Bell, sitting at Aberdeen, which Sheriff Principal MacLeod, in *McAleer*, expressly declined to follow. There is thus a conflict of authority on this matter.

For my part I am prepared to accept that in certain circumstances appellate courts have a common law power to review incompetent interlocutors even where such a review is not expressly provided for by statute. Thus, under ordinary sheriff court procedure, an incompetent interlocutor may be open to review without leave notwithstanding the restrictions on appeals contained in ss 27 and 28 of the Sheriff Courts (Scotland) Act 1907. But, in my opinion, there is a fundamental difference between ordinary cause procedure and summary cause procedure, and that is that ordinary cause procedure makes provision for the taking of appeals against interlocutors other than those containing a final judgment whereas summary cause procedure makes no such provision. That means that, where an appeal is taken without leave against an allegedly incompetent interlocutor under ordinary procedure, that appeal will take place under well established procedural rules and practices. By contrast, if there is to be an appeal against an allegedly incompetent interlocutor under summary cause procedure, it will be necessary to invent the procedure as one goes along. The statute itself, and the Summary Cause Rules, make no provision for any procedure other than that by way of stated case, and it must at least be questionable, for example, whether a sheriff principal has any power to require a sheriff to write a note regarding an interlocutor which is said to be incompetent. Indeed, the sheriff in the present case plainly entertained considerable doubts on that point.

Counsel for the defender sought to submit that the test should be whether the statute uses express words which would exclude a common law right of appeal against an incompetent interlocutor. However, having considered this matter as best I can, I have come to the conclusion, albeit with reluctance, that the test must be whether the statute uses words which render such an appeal possible. So far as s 38 of the 1971 Act and rule 81 of the Summary Cause Rules are concerned, I am of opinion that, so far from rendering possible an appeal against an incidental interlocutor, they positively exclude it by making provision only for an appeal against a final judgment.

As I have said, I have reached the foregoing conclusions with reluctance, and that is in part because I am in sympathy with the observations made by Sheriff Principal MacLeod in *McAleer*, and in particular with what he says (at p 42) about the distorting effect that will be caused if an incompetent interlocutor cannot be corrected by appeal procedure. Regretfully, however, I am unable to agree with the sheriff principal's final decision on the matter. I have also reached my conclusions with reluctance because there can be no doubt that the unavailability of an appeal against an incompetent interlocutor may create injustice for one or other of the parties: and that may well be the situation in the present case. Finally, I have to say that I have also reached my conclusions with reluctance because the consequence of those conclusions is that there is now a difference of opinion on this matter as between two of the six current sheriffs principal. However, given the plain words used in s 38 of the 1971 Act and the absence of any provision for an appeal procedure other than that set out in rule 81, I consider that I am bound to take a different view from that taken by Sheriff Principal MacLeod. In that situation it is perhaps to be hoped that the Court of Session may have an early opportunity to give a definitive ruling on this matter. It is also to be hoped that, if that ruling were to support the view which I have expressed above, Parliament might then find an early opportunity to correct a provision which can be productive of injustice. No doubt Parliament sought to exclude incidental appeals under summary cause pro-

A cedure for the best of reasons, namely to keep that procedure as simple and straightforward as possible. However, if the view which I have formed is correct, there can be little doubt that those good intentions may in certain circumstances produce undesirable and even unjust results.

While what I have said thus far effectively disposes of this appeal, I think that it is desirable that I should briefly state my views regarding the competency of the order for consignation notwithstanding that in the circumstances any such views must be regarded as B obiter. I take this course for several reasons. First, I do so simply as a courtesy to counsel who addressed me on this matter with care and clarity. Secondly, I do so in order that my views on this matter may be known in the event that there should be any further appeal in this case. And thirdly, I do so because, in light of something which was said to me by counsel for the pursuers (and to which I refer in detail later), I consider that this matter raises an issue of some general importance for cases where local authorities take C actions for the recovery of possession of houses or other properties let by them.

On this branch of the appeal the submission advanced by counsel for the defender was a simple and straightforward one. It was that, while courts have in certain circumstances a discretionary power to order a party to an action to consign a sum of money in the hands of the clerk of court, that power can competently be exercised only in cases where the other D party has a crave which may ultimately be satisfied by the payment to him by the clerk of court of all or part of the money so consigned. In the absence of any such crave (as in the present case) there can be no competent basis for ordering consignation since, whatever the outcome of the case, there could be no lawful ground upon which the clerk of court would be entitled to hand over all or part of the consigned money to the other party. As a subsidiary to the foregoing submissions counsel also argued that it was incompetent, as was done here, to order consignation of a E sum greater than the only sum mentioned in the pleadings. In support of the foregoing submissions counsel referred me to Macphail, paras 11-44 and 11-48 to 50, and to Dobie, *Sheriff Court Practice*, p 163. He also referred to several of the cases cited by those authors but did so in order to show that they are examples of consignation having been ordered where there was a pecuniary crave or conclusion: none of them supported the view that consignation could competently F be ordered where there is no such crave. Among the cases referred to were *Cohen & Sons v Jamieson*, 1963 SLT 35; 1963 SC 289; *Mackenzie v Balerno Paper Mill Co* (1883) 10 R 1147; and *Littlejohn v Reynolds* (1890) 6 Sh Ct Rep 321.

In response, counsel for the pursuers submitted that consignation is always a matter for the discretion of the court, and that it matters not whether or not there is a pecuniary crave in the action. In the present case there is in any event an admitted averment about unpaid rent, and that provided a sufficient basis for

the sheriff to make the order for consignation. Counsel founded on the cases to which I have referred above G as illustrating the discretionary nature of orders for consignation. He also went on (and this raises the issue of general importance to which I referred above) to advise me that it is normal practice for the present pursuers to seek, and to be granted, orders for consignation in cases like the present one where defenders admit that rent is unpaid but seek to defend an action for recovery of possession on the ground that essential repairs or maintenance have not been carried out. The experience of the pursuers, it was said, is that in such H cases defenders often do not attend court to lead evidence at the diets fixed for proof, and simply use the stated defence as a device to put off the day when decree will be granted against them. An order for consignation is a useful remedy against such delaying tactics since in most instances consignation is not effected within the time allowed, and decree for recovery of possession can then be obtained without delay.

I shall return in a moment to this account of general I practice, but for the present I have to say that I have no hesitation in holding that the submissions advanced by counsel for the defender are to be preferred to those advanced by counsel for the pursuers. In my opinion the only competent purpose to be served by consignation is to ensure that money or property, all or part of which is ultimately likely to be found due and payable to the pursuer, can be preserved safely in the hands of the clerk of court until the extent of the pursuer's entitlement has been judicially determined. But J that, in my opinion, clearly requires that the pursuer must have a crave which can ultimately be satisfied by payment to him of all or part of the money or property so held by the clerk of court. In my opinion consignation cannot be competent where, at the end of the day, a pursuer can have no lawful basis for seeking payment to him of any consigned money. In the present case the pursuers have no crave for payment of a sum of money. They make averments about unpaid rent but, in the context of the 1987 Act, K unpaid rent is but one of several grounds justifying the taking of proceedings for recovery of possession under the Schedule to the Act. In the result, therefore, the pursuers could never lawfully — at least in the context of the present proceedings — seek decree for payment to them by the defender of any sum of money, and it follows from that, in my opinion, that the order for consignation in this case was not competent.

I return now to the general practice of which I was L told by counsel for the pursuers. If what he said is accurate, then it is something which causes me considerable anxiety. Quite apart from the fact, as I have now held, that such orders for consignation are incompetent, I am concerned that an apparently routine practice of seeking orders for consignation in all cases where a defence of a particular character is stated may preclude the proper consideration of the circumstances of individual cases and may put quite improper pressure on at least some defenders. The practice is one which lends some support to the apparently widely held view that some local authorities may inappropriately use the recovery of possession procedure simply as a device to secure payment of rent arrears (see my own comments in *City of Edinburgh District Council v Stirling*, 1993 SCLR 587). I am frankly surprised if it be the case that sheriffs regularly go along with such a practice but, if that is the case, I hope that it will cease in future.

There remains the question of expenses. Notwithstanding that I have dismissed this appeal as incompetent, I consider that the defender did not act unreasonably in bringing the appeal given, first, that there was, and is, a conflict of authority regarding the competency of such an appeal and, secondly, that I have at the end of the day supported his view as to the competency of the order for consignation. In those circumstances I consider that the appropriate course is to find no expenses due to or by either party in respect of the appeal. I have also certified the whole appeal as suitable for the employment of counsel.

Counsel for Pursuers and Respondents, Armstrong; Solicitor, W Blyth, SSC, Director of Administration, City of Edinburgh District Council — Counsel for Defender and Appellant, Sutherland; Solicitors, Legal Services Agency, Glasgow.

Worth v Worth

SHERIFF COURT OF LOTHIAN AND BORDERS AT EDINBURGH

SHERIFF N E D THOMSON

18 NOVEMBER 1993

Husband and wife — Divorce — Financial provision — Minute of agreement on financial provision — Party seeking to set aside minute as not fair and reasonable at time it was entered into — Pension rights not taken into account in minute — Whether minute should be set aside — Family Law (Scotland) Act 1985 (c 37), s 16 (1).

Section 16 (1) of the Family Law (Scotland) Act 1985 provides inter alia that where the parties to a marriage have entered into an agreement as to financial provision to be made on divorce, the court may make an order setting aside or varying the agreement or any of its terms where the agreement was not fair and reasonable at the time it was entered into.

After consulting a solicitor, a husband and wife entered into a minute of agreement the terms of which they had previously agreed regarding inter alia a settlement of all financial claims. In a subsequent action of divorce the wife defender sought to have the minute of agreement set aside in terms of s 16 (1) of the Family Law (Scotland) Act 1985, inter alia on the ground that the minute failed to take account of the parties' pension provisions. Neither party had been aware at the time of signing the agreement of the sig-

nificance of pension rights, and their solicitor had not raised the subject with them.

Held, that the minute of agreement did not fairly reflect the actual value of the parties' property or the defender's fair entitlement to it, for the defender had been entitled to a share of the value of the pursuer's pension rights (p 56K-L); and minute *set aside* to the extent that it discharged all the defender's capital claims against the pursuer.

Action of divorce

John Worth raised an action of divorce against Sandra McLean Fraser or Worth. The defender sought to have set aside a minute of agreement between the parties settling financial provision on their separation.

Facts

The sheriff found the following facts established:

(1) The parties were married at Edinburgh on 1 December 1978. (2) There are two children of the marriage, namely, Kevin Alexander Worth, born 14 June 1980 and Gary Worth, born on 28 June 1982. (3) The parties and their children lived together in Edinburgh, latterly at 47 Durham Road South. (4) The parties bought this house in August 1987 for £41,000 with the help of a mortgage for £31,000 from the Northern Rock Building Society. (5) The purchase was carried through on their behalf by Mr Murdo Tait, solicitor, Haddington, whose wife was a work colleague of the defender. (6) The defender worked with British Telecom; the pursuer worked as a milkman. (7) Relations between the parties deteriorated, and in February 1988 the defender left the pursuer. (8) When she did so, she set in train a financial settlement which she agreed with the pursuer. They agreed inter alia that title in the matrimonial home be transferred to the pursuer's sole name and that the equity they owned in the matrimonial home was £10,000. (9) The defender asked Mr Tait to contact the pursuer to confirm the terms they had agreed. (10) Mr Tait did so, and met the parties separately and together. He emphasised that if they felt there was any conflict of interest between them, existing or likely to arise, they should seek separate representation. Neither party wished to be separately represented.

(11) Mr Tait inquired if there was any property other than the house, shareholdings and a life policy which they felt should be taken into account in reaching a financial settlement, and was told that there was none. (12) Neither party was aware that a value could be placed on each other's pension rights or that such rights could be regarded as property. (13) Mr Tait was aware of these matters, but did not consider it appropriate to mention them to the parties. (14) Mr Tait proceeded to draw up a minute of agreement between the parties which the parties duly signed. (15) This agreement provided inter alia, that the defender accepted its financial provision in full and final settle-

ment of all claims present and future which she might have against the pursuer whether on divorce or otherwise. (16) This agreement was entered into freely by both parties on 10 August 1988. (17) In implement of the agreement the pursuer duly paid the defender £6,800 in August 1988. (18) As at February 1988 the value of the pursuer's pension rights for the purposes of s 10 (5) of the Family Law (Scotland) Act 1985 was £6,100 and the value of the defender's pension rights for these purposes was £1,700.

On 18 November 1993 the sheriff *set aside* the minute of agreement to the extent that the defenders therein discharged all capital claims against the pursuer.

THE SHERIFF (N E D THOMSON).—The parties consented to divorce after more than two years' separation. They also consented to each having custody of one of their children, and this indeed appeared to be in the children's best interests.

The only matters in dispute between them were whether or not the minute of agreement which they entered into in August 1988 was fair and reasonable, and what was the relevant date for valuing the matrimonial property.

[The sheriff considered the question of "the relevant date" and continued:]

Section 16 (1) of the Family Law (Scotland) Act 1985 provides inter alia that where the parties to a marriage have entered into an agreement as to financial provision to be made on divorce, the court may make an order setting it aside or varying the agreement or any of its terms where the agreement was not fair and reasonable at the time it was entered into.

In granting what appears to be a discretionary power to the court, Parliament has not provided any guidance as to its exercise; nor has it indicated how the questions of fairness and reasonableness are to be approached. I accordingly think that this power should not be too readily exercised, and, if exercised, should only be exercised in the light of the full circumstances at the time.

For the defender her solicitor moved me to exercise this power and to set aside the minute of agreement entered into between the parties in August 1988 as being, in terms of her third plea in law, "unfair to the defender", and put forward three grounds for my so doing — that the same solicitor had acted for both parties in drawing up the agreement, that the parties' house had not been revalued, and that the value of their pension provisions had not been brought into the reckoning.

I should say that the first of these three grounds presented little difficulty. The defender's solicitor founded strongly on the Solicitors (Scotland) Practice Rules 1986. These rules do not have statutory force, but bear the authority of the Law Society of Scotland and the approval of the Lord President, and are commonly observed throughout the profession. They provide inter alia a general rule that "a solicitor shall not act for two or more parties whose interests conflict". This is clearly a sound rule of practice. It also appears to me that in a breakdown of marriage where parties' financial interests do not conflict and where they both have confidence in the same solicitor it is equally sound practice that the same solicitor should indeed act for both parties in effecting a financial settlement. Otherwise, positions may become entrenched and delay, worry, expense and animosity may result. Here, so far from there being a conflict of interest, parties came to Mr Tait, the solicitor, with an agreement they had already worked out between themselves. He was the defender's choice, being already known to her as the husband of one of her working place colleagues and having already acted for both parties together in the purchase of their matrimonial home. I should say that it was clear from Mr Tait's evidence that the defender was the driving force in the preparation of this minute — the pursuer, he said, was "fairly mute"; and, as the defender said herself, she wanted the whole thing over and done with as soon as possible. Nevertheless, it was clear that Mr Tait had counselled parties more than once that they should take separate advice if they believed there might be conflict; and not only was she not "denied the benefit of separate legal advice", as she averred on record, but it was clear that she had in fact written to Mr Tait to say that she did not want to take separate advice. Mr Tait said that he saw his role as that of "honest broker" between the parties, and I think that was indeed an apt description. I accordingly find no substance in the defender's first ground of complaint.

Mr Tait said that he was in effect presented with a fait accompli and asked to put it into legal form. Nevertheless, he went through the heads of their agreement with parties to satisfy himself that they were indeed agreed. As regards the matrimonial home, on which the defender's second ground of complaint was based, Mr Tait had of course acted for the parties when they purchased it, and was as well aware as they were that it had been bought by them in August 1987 for £41,000 with the help of a £31,000 mortgage. For the defender, her solicitor submitted that Mr Tait should have advised the parties to have their house valued of new and sold; and she led evidence from a chartered surveyor, Mr Batts, that in his opinion its value in April 1988 would have been £50,000 and in October 1989, £60,000. However, another surveyor, Mr Scott, called by the pursuer, said that in his opinion its value at May 1988 would have been £42,500 and in September 1989, £46,000. Bearing in mind that the parties separated not in April or May but in February 1988; that Mr Scott was unshakeable and rather more impressive than Mr Batts; that if the house had been valued, prepared for marketing and sold in February 1988 the cost of valuation, marketing and sale might well have approximated the amount of its increase in value in the six months between August 1987 and February 1988 — this latter consideration appearing to have weighed strongly with Mr Tait — I do not think he can be faulted for having accepted the parties' own approach to the matter, that £10,000 be taken to be their joint equity in the matrimonial home.

A

The third ground of complaint was of more substance, however. The defender complained that the parties' pension rights had not been valued, that she had not even been advised that she or the pursuer had pension rights capable of valuation for the purpose of a separation agreement, and that if they had been taken into consideration there would have been a substantial balance in her favour, which she had not received.

B

The question, however, is whether the absence of any mention of pension rights in the minute of agreement was not fair and reasonable at the time when the agreement was entered into in August 1988. It may be said that nothing is more firmly implanted in human nature than a concept of fair dealing as far as one's own interests are concerned: where a person is aggrieved by a perceived unfairness to him or her a cry of "It's not fair!" will very readily be heard. Here, however, there was not a whisper of unfairness from either party till several years after the agreement, when the defender had learned about the provision of the 1985 Act regarding pensions. The reason why she had not complained before was, of course, that in common with, I imagine, the vast majority of the population of Scotland, she had had no idea that pension rights could be regarded as matrimonial property. In the understanding of both parties, pensions were something that happened in the distant future when retirement age was reached. A feeling of unfairness in this subjective sense through absence of pension rights from the agreement was completely absent from either party at the time it was entered into. It was quite clear that both parties had been wholly happy with the agreement at that time.

C

D

Mr Tait did, of course, know about the legislation relating to pensions, but frankly admitted that he had not concerned himself with this question. There appeared to have been a number of reasons for this — partly because the Act with its esoteric provision about pension rights had only come into force relatively recently, partly because both parties were young, partly because he believed that the defender's pension as a British Telecom employee would not amount to very much and that the pursuer's pension as a milkman would also not amount to very much, and partly because obtaining actuarial valuations was an expensive business. At any rate, Mr Tait appeared to have received a negative reply when, having discussed the various heads of their agreement with the parties, he finally asked if they had any other property than what they had already disclosed. As I have already remarked, neither party had any idea that pension rights could be looked upon as property. It was accordingly not surprising that he should have received a negative reply. What was surprising was that the defender nevertheless averred that the pursuer "did not disclose that he subscribed to an occupational pension scheme". This averment has a suggestion of

E

F

deliberate concealment about it, but it was perfectly clear that there was no question of concealment, trickery or unfair pressure being brought to bear upon either party by the other or by Mr Tait. Unfairness in this sense also was completely absent from the agreement.

G

In all the circumstances it is difficult to say that it was unreasonable of Mr Tait not to investigate the parties' pension rights; and, on the face of it, I would hesitate to describe the minute of agreement as unreasonable. But I also have to consider whether it can be described as "unfair" — which Parliament must have intended to be taken as a different concept from "unreasonable". In so doing, I think that not only external factors such as concealment, trickery or pressure may be considered, but also that the intrinsic fairness or otherwise of the agreement must be considered. Although neither party thought subjectively that the agreement was unfair at the time, I think that unfairness also has to be considered objectively; and that it is not just a question of what was in but also what was not in the agreement which may determine the matter.

H

I

Was there, then, unfairness in an objective sense? Now it can be said that when they entered into the agreement the parties were in error as regards the value of their matrimonial property since part of its value — their pension rights — had not been recognised by them; and that as a general principle in contract, error as to value has never been regarded as ground for avoiding an agreement. Part of the matrimonial property in a separation agreement might have been a china jug which the parties had bought at a jumble sale for £1. If it had gone to one of them under the agreement, and four years later it had turned out that, quite unbeknown to them at the time, it was in fact an unusual antique properly valued at £1,000, it does not necessarily follow that the other party could have the agreement set aside as having been unfair at the time — however much he or she could have complained afterwards about bad luck.

J

K

But general principles of contract as between buyer and seller do not necessarily apply here. In my opinion Parliament has provided that in the particular type of contract as between husband and wife dealt with in s 16 (1) of the Act, unfairness or unreasonableness either within it or surrounding is enough to set it aside. Further, I do not think it can properly be said that the parties were in error as to the value of their pension rights when they were not aware that valuable pension rights existed at all. Error, ignorance of the law and back luck do not really come into it. What cannot be escaped is the fact that the agreement does not fairly reflect the actual value of the parties' property or the defender's fair entitlement to it, for the defender was in law, and thus presumably in fairness, entitled to a share of the value of the pursuer's pension rights.

L

Although reluctant in the whole circumstances to exercise my discretion in the defender's favour, I think I have to do so, particularly since Mr Tait conceded

A that he should have canvassed the question of pension rights but did not do so.

I accordingly set aside the minute of agreement to the extent that the defender discharges all capital claims. Parties were agreed that the value of the pursuer's pension rights at the relevant date was £6,100 and that the value of the defender's was £1,700. Since each was entitled to one half of the other's, it follows that there is a balance in favour of the defender of £2,200 and I accordingly grant decree for payment by the pursuer of this sum to the defender.

B

Solicitors for Pursuer, Stuart & Stuart WS, Edinburgh — Solicitors for Defender, P H Young & Co, Bo'ness.

C # Milne v Milne

SHERIFF COURT OF GRAMPIAN, HIGHLAND AND ISLANDS AT ABERDEEN

SHERIFF PRINCIPAL D J RISK, QC

7 FEBRUARY 1994

Heritable property — Common property — Division and sale — Husband and wife — Needs of wife and children residing in house — No offer of alternative accommoda-
D *tion — Matrimonial Homes (Family Protection) (Scotland) Act 1981 (c 59), s 19.*

Husband and wife — Occupancy rights — Action of division or sale — Needs of wife and children residing in house — No offer of alternative accommodation — Matrimonial Homes (Family Protection) (Scotland) Act 1981 (c 59), s 19.

A husband raised an action of division or sale against his wife in respect of the matrimonial home of which
E the parties were equal pro indiviso proprietors. The defender sought refusal of a grant of decree, in terms of s 19 of the Matrimonial Homes (Family Protection) (Scotland) Act 1981. She had lived in the home for 18 years and continued to live there with two younger children of the marriage. The defender could not afford to purchase another property. No offer of suitable alternative accommodation was made.

Held, (1) that the defender required to aver circumstances which put s 19 in issue, but it was sufficient
F to constitute a relevant defence that the defender required to continue to occupy the matrimonial home along with a child or children (p 60J-K); (2) that to remove the defender from the matrimonial home would cause major disruption to herself and the youngest child of the marriage and it was unclear what alternative accommodation she could find, with the result that the pursuer had failed to discharge the onus upon him (p 61B-D); and decree *refused.*

Authorites *reviewed.*

Action of division or sale

G James Gordon Milne raised an action of division or sale against his wife, Muriel Margaret Murray or Milne. A proof was heard before the sheriff (D J Risk, QC), who at the date of judgment had taken up appointment as sheriff principal.

Findings in fact

The sheriff principal found the following facts admitted or proved:

(1) The parties are husband and wife, having been married on 27 March 1967. They are equal pro
H indiviso proprietors of subjects known as 51 Cranford Road, Aberdeen by virtue of a disposition in their favour dated 27 January and recorded 6 March 1975. (2) There are three children of the marriage. From 1975 until December 1990 the parties and the children lived in family in the said house. In December 1990 the pursuer left the matrimonial home. Since then the parties have not lived together. (3) The house is a granite terraced house containing on the ground and first floors two public rooms, three bedrooms, a
I kitchen and a bathroom. The loft space is floored and lined and divided into two rooms and a shower cabinet. The rooms are fitted with velux windows. Access to the loft is by Ramsay or Slingsby type ladder. There is a double garage. The value of the subjects is somewhat in excess of £100,000. The mortgage had been paid off prior to the pursuer's departure. The house is not subject to any security in favour of any third party. (4) The defender lives in the said
J house with the two younger children of the marriage. Andrew is over 16 years of age and a student. Christopher, who was born on 13 April 1981, is a pupil at Broomhill primary school which is a short distance from the house. In August 1993 it is expected that he will become a pupil at Harlaw Academy which is a considerably greater distance from the house. The defender, Andrew and Christopher each occupy one of the bedrooms in the house. (5) The defender is a clerical officer employed at Aberdeen Royal infirmary. She has a net monthly salary of approximately £425. In
K addition she has a part time job at a hotel from which she earns approximately £55 per month. The pursuer pays aliment for the defender and Christopher amounting in total to £260 per month. The defender has savings of approximately £10,000. (6) The pursuer lives in a two bedroomed flat for which he pays rent of £200 per month. The eldest child of the marriage formerly lived with him but has since moved to a flat of his own. The pursuer is employed as a telephone engineer at a net monthly salary approaching £1,000.
L (7) The pursuer wishes to have the house at 51 Cranford Road sold and the proceeds divided between himself and the defender. He is willing to accept 40 or 45 per cent of the price as his share although he would be entitled to 50 per cent. His intention would be to use his share of the proceeds to purchase another house. (8) The defender wishes to continue to live in the house with Andrew and Christopher. She regards it as her and the children's home. It is situated in an attractive and convenient part of Aberdeen. Were the house to be sold and the proceeds divided she does not

consider that she would be able to acquire comparable
A property. (9) Neither party has made any offer of alternative accommodation to the other. Neither party has
offered to buy the other's share in the former
matrimonial home. The evidence does not establish
what alternative accommodation could be purchased
by either party for about £50,000.

On 7 February 1994 the sheriff principal *refused*
decree.

B **THE SHERIFF PRINCIPAL (D J RISK,
QC).**—This is an action of division and sale at the
instance of a husband against a wife in respect of the
house which was the matrimonial home and of which
the parties are equal pro indiviso proprietors. The
parties themselves were the only witnesses to give evidence at the proof. There was no dispute upon the
material matters of fact and no question of credibility
arose.

The defence is based upon s 19 of the Matrimonial
C Homes (Family Protection) (Scotland) Act 1981.
When the record was closed on 13 November 1992 the
defender had a preliminary plea outstanding. The
interlocutor of that date allowing proof omitted to deal
with the plea. At the commencement of the proof the
defender's agent agreed that it should have been
repelled and I proceeded to repel it. The pursuer had
tabled no preliminary pleas.

Section 19 of the 1981 Act provides: "Where a
D spouse brings an action for the division and sale of a
matrimonial home which the spouses own in common,
the court, after having regard to all the circumstances
of the cases including — (a) the matters specified in
paragraphs (a) to (d) of section 3 (3) of this Act; and
(b) whether the spouse bringing the action offers or
has offered to make available to the other spouse any
suitable alternative accommodation, may refuse to
grant decree in that action or may postpone the granting of decree for such period as it may consider
E reasonable in the circumstances or may grant decree
subject to such conditions as it may prescribe."

Of the parts of s 3 (3) referred to, para (d) has no
bearing upon this case. The other matters are "(a) the
conduct of the spouses in relation to each other and
otherwise; (b) the respective needs and financial
resources of the spouses; and (c) the needs of any child
of the family".

Section 19 has been the subject of judicial construc-
F tion and comment in a number of cases to which I was
referred in closing submissions. Put briefly, the contention for the pursuer was that he was entitled to the
declarator sought unless the defender made out the
statutory defence. It was up to the defender to establish by averment and evidence that there was something out of the ordinary which made it necessary for
her to remain in the subjects. The pursuer's agent submitted that this case was on all fours with *Berry v
Berry,* 1988 SLT 650; 1988 SCLR 296. The
defender's agent on the other hand argued that the
onus was on the pursuer to show that it was reasonable

to grant declarator or, to put it another way, that the
defender was being unreasonable in refusing to agree G
to the sale of the subjects. He referred to the cases of
Crow v Crow, 1986 SLT 270, *Hall v Hall,* 1987 SCLR
38; 1987 SLT (Sh Ct) 15 (in which only the judgment
of the sheriff principal is reported) and *Rae v Rae,*
1991 SLT 454.

From the cases cited it appears that the courts have
not yet made any systematic analysis of the relationship between the principles derived from (a) the
common law relating to the co-proprietors of heritable
property, (b) s 19 of the Matrimonial Homes (Family H
Protection) (Scotland) Act 1981, and (c) the orders
relating to property rights and capital payments which
a court may make on divorce in terms of the Family
Law (Scotland) Act 1985. Three of the cases cited deal
with questions of competency, relevancy or procedure
in actions of division and sale at a time when actions
of divorce were pending. Only in *Hall* did a court
make a decision after proof and only in *Hall* was there
no divorce action current. It appears from the reports
that the decision in *Hall* was not brought to the atten- I
tion of the Lord Ordinary in *Berry* or of the court in
Rae. Accordingly, in considering whether in this case
any assistance can be derived from the earlier decisions, it is necessary to establish precisely what issue
was being decided in each case and to read any opinions expressed by the respective judges in the context
thereof.

In *Crow,* a divorce action based upon two years'
separation and consent was pending. In an action of
division and sale brought by the husband, the wife J
sought postponement of decree until the 18th birthday
of the youngest child of the marriage, which date
would have been long after the granting of decree of
divorce. The husband pled that it was incompetent
under s 19 of the 1981 Act to postpone decree to a date
later than the date of decree of divorce. After debate
the Lord Ordinary (Wylie) repelled that plea. The
ratio of that case therefore has no application to the
instant case. What may be of some interest is the view
expressed by the Lord Ordinary in his opinion (at K
p 271I-J) regarding the terms of s 19: "These provisions ex facie confer very wide discretionary powers.
. . . The section is concerned with the situation in
which the spouses are joint owners of the matrimonial
home and the court has to balance the interest of the
spouse who wishes to dispose of the property against
the interest of the other spouse in relation to the needs
of that spouse and in relation also to 'the needs of any
child of the family'". He did not require to consider,
and did not consider, what either party would require L
to aver to make a relevant case or what weight, if any,
would be given to the circumstances referred to in
paras (a) and (b) of s 19 of the 1981 Act.

In *Hall v Hall* the parties were living under the same
roof although occupying separate bedrooms and had
no plans to raise an action of divorce. In an action for
division and sale at the instance of the husband the
sheriff (D B Smith) refused decree and his decision
was affirmed by the sheriff principal (Caplan, QC). As
the sheriff observed at 1987 SCLR, p 40: "Parliament

A seems to have laid down no real guidance as to how the court is to exercise its discretion. The injunction to have regard to all the circumstances results in every case in a decision on its own facts", but the reasoning which led him to his decision is instructive. He had begun the hearing (as I would have done myself) with the view that it was for the defender to put forward some argument against the pursuer's claim, but he had been persuaded that that view was wrong: "The objective of the 1981 Act is, inter alia, to give some sort of security in the matrimonial home to the spouse who

B in strict law has no legal title to it. If one approaches a case such as this with that objective in view it appears clear that it is not for the defender to state or prove any reason why he or she does not wish to surrender the new right created in his or her favour by the 1981 Act: it is for the spouse who wishes to sell to satisfy the court that all the circumstances conduce to the sale of the matrimonial home. . . . Having regard to all the circumstances of the case, I am satisfied that I should exercise my discretion against grant-

C ing decree" (at p 41).

The sheriff's reasoning was approved by the sheriff principal at pp 42-43; 1987 SLT (Sh Ct), p 17; where he said: "Section 19 of the Act does not in its terms state that in applying it the court should pay regard to the occupancy rights of the defending spouse. However, the paramount purpose of the Act is to establish occupancy rights in the matrimonial home and to protect against undue disturbance of such

D rights. . . . Thus although the section makes no direct reference to occupancy rights, the whole tenor of the Act indicates that the restriction on right to division and sale which section 19 imposes is intended to protect the occupancy rights of the defending spouse. The Act does not specify the test the court is to apply in deciding a section 19 issue, although it does set out certain of the factors to be taken into consideration. If a non-entitled spouse was in occupation of the matrimonial home and refused to consent to a sale by

E the entitled spouse, then the latter could apply to the court under section 7 (1) for a dispensing order if, inter alia, 'such consent is unreasonably withheld'. Thus, in the normal case, if there is no specialty such as mental disability or minority, the occupancy rights of the non-entitled spouse could only be defeated if it could be shown that consent to the sale of the matrimonial home was being unreasonably withheld. This section can give some guidance to a judge applying the less definite provisions of section 19. In the

F first place, the Act could not have intended that an entitled spouse with a joint interest in the matrimonial home should have less protection for occupancy rights than a non-entitled spouse. Accordingly, the reasonableness of displacing the defending spouse should properly be taken into account in deciding a section 19 case. Secondly, in relation to a section 7 (1) application the onus must clearly be on the applicant spouse to show that consent is being unreasonably withheld. Thus, if in an application aimed against a non-entitled spouse the onus rests on the pursuer to show that protection of occupancy should be lifted, it would be

G curiously inconsistent if the same did not apply in relation to section 19. The pattern imposed by the legislation is that, prima facie a spouse has a right to continue to occupy the matrimonial home and that it is for the spouse seeking to disturb such right to show that it is reasonable to do so. Thus, in my view, the learned sheriff was right when he decided that it is not for the defender to convince him that she should be allowed to continue in her home but rather for the pursuer to show that it is fair and reasonably necessary to disturb her."

H The case also contains some guidance as to what constitutes an offer of suitable alternative accommodation in terms of s 19 (b) of the 1981 Act.

In *Berry v Berry* cross actions of divorce were in dependence when the wife raised an action of division and sale in respect of the matrimonial home in which the husband was then residing. The husband pled that decree should be refused or at least postponed until the determination of the actions of divorce. The Lord

I Ordinary (Sutherland) held that the defence was irrelevant and granted decree de plano. From the Lord Ordinary's summary of the arguments it appears that the principal thrust of the submission for the defender was that, since the questions of the parties' conduct towards each other and their financial resources were to be explored in the course of the divorce actions, it was inappropriate that division and sale would take place prior thereto. That argument was rejected, and the submission for the pursuer that the court should only be concerned with whether or not there were cir-

J cumstances relating to the right of occupancy of the matrimonial home which should delay the division and sale of the property to which the pursuer would otherwise be entitled was upheld. The Lord Ordinary said at 1988 SLT, p 65: "There is no doubt that the pursuer would be entitled in normal circumstances to the declarator which she seeks and the only reason for preventing such declarator being granted would be if there were circumstances averred which showed that it was necessary for the defender to have continued

K occupancy of the matrimonial home at least until the time of the divorce".

He also held that, having regard to the substantial financial resources of the defender as disclosed in the pleadings in the divorce actions, he would have no difficulty in finding alternative accommodation and that it was not relevant to consider whether the pursuer had offered an alternative. It is unfortunate that the attention of the Lord Ordinary was not drawn to *Hall* since, although the circumstances of the two

L cases are entirely different, the Lord Ordinary's approach to the construction of s 19 seems at first sight to be different from that adopted by the sheriff and the sheriff principal in the earlier case.

The question which concerned the Extra Division of the Inner House in *Rae v Rae* was whether a sheriff court action of division and sale raised by a husband should be sisted pending resolution of a divorce action raised by the wife in the Court of Session. It appeared from the wife's pleadings in the action of division and

A sale that she was living in the matrimonial home along with her daughter, that it was also used as an occasional residence for the student son of the marriage, and that no suitable alternative accommodation had been suggested. In the divorce action she was seeking transfer of her husband's title to his share of the matrimonial home. The sheriff (in my respectful view erroneously) thought himself to be bound by the opinion of the Lord Ordinary in *Berry* and refused a sist. His decision was reversed by the Inner House which distinguished *Berry* upon the grounds that (1)
B the wife had no alternative accommodation for herself and the children or the means to acquire such, and (2) the action of divorce contained a conclusion for transfer of property and not merely for payment of money. It was held that it would be highly prejudicial to the wife to allow an action to proceed to decree which could deprive her of her potential right to a transfer of title, and deprive her of a home in the interim. No question was raised concerning the Lord Ordinary's interpretation of s 19 in *Berry* and no reference was
C made to *Hall*.

I have examined the foregoing cases at perhaps tedious length in an attempt to deduce therefrom a principled approached to s 19. Unfortunately each decision seems to depend very much upon its own circumstances and the three Court of Session cases have the added complication of concurrent divorce proceedings in the background. What can be said is that in *Crow* the relevancy of a defence that the defender was
D living in the subjects with her then 10 year old child, that she had no alternative accommodation, that she had claimed a capital sum in the divorce proceedings was not challenged and that the Lord Ordinary expressed the view that what the court had to do in respect of s 19 was to balance the respective interests of the spouses, while in *Rae* it is implicit in the grounds on which the Inner House distinguished *Berry* that it was a relevant defence for the wife to aver that she and her daughter and occasionally her own
E son were residing in the matrimonial home, that they had no alternative accommodation and that a transfer of property had been sought in the divorce action. Neither case addresses directly whether it is for the pursuer in an action of division and sale to show that it is reasonable that decree should be granted or, on the contrary, for the defender to show that having regard to the provisions of s 19 of the 1981 Act it would be unreasonable to grant decree. In *Berry* the language used by the Lord Ordinary suggests that he
F tended to the former view, although from the summary of the arguments it does not appear that he had to apply his mind to the kind of considerations which are mentioned in *Crow* and *Rae* and which were adjudicated upon in *Hall*. It seems to me that the ratio of *Berry* was just that the defender's averments in that case did not raise any matter upon which a court could have exercised the discretion created by s 19. When the Lord Ordinary said (1988 SLT, at pp 651L-652A): "the only reason for preventing such declarator being granted would be if there were circumstances *averred* [emphasis supplied] which showed that it was neces-

G sary for the defender to have continued occupancy of the matrimonial home at least until the time of the divorce", he must be taken to have been referring to the pleadings in the case before him; he did not purport to be giving consideration to all of the circumstances referred to in s 19 and, by reference, s 3 (3) of the 1981 Act.

Section 19 receives its most detailed consideration in *Hall v Hall*. Apparently no preliminary pleas were tabled and the case was decided after proof. Both the sheriff and the sheriff principal noted that s 19
H required the court to exercise a discretion and that Parliament had given no indication of the test to be applied in exercising that discretion. I find the reasoning of the sheriff and sheriff principal, which I have cited at length above, persuasive. In particular, I agree that Parliament cannot possibly have intended that a non-entitled spouse to whom s 7 would apply should be in a stronger position than a co-proprietor to whom s 19 applies. So far as the onus of proof is concerned, the question will not often arise after evidence has been led, but the actual words of s 19 seem to me to
I be quite neutral; the section does not say either that the court shall only grant decree if it considers it reasonable to do so, or that it shall be a defence for the defender to establish that it would not be reasonable to grant decree; it merely says that the court shall take account of certain circumstances and exercise a discretion. Nevertheless it respectfully seems to me that the approach of the sheriff and the sheriff principal in *Hall* is a sound and practical one.

J In the light of the foregoing discussion I would tentatively advance the following propositions: (1) where an action of division and sale is raised it is for the defender to put s 19 in issue by averring circumstances upon which a reasonable court would be entitled to exercise its discretion by refusing or postponing decree (*Berry*); (2) it is sufficient to constitute a relevant defence that the defender requires to continue to occupy the matrimonial home along with a child or children (*Crow, Rae*); and (3) once proof has
K taken place the court must take account of such facts as have been established and are relevant in terms of s 19 and apply its discretion thereto. There may be an onus on the pursuer but there is no onus on the defender (*Hall*).

Turning to the circumstances of the instant case, the defender avers that she lives in the former matrimonial home with the two younger children of the marriage and that if she were forced to remove therefrom she would find it difficult to obtain accommodation of a
L comparable standard. From the evidence it appears that the house was the family home from 1975 until December 1990. From the defender's point of view, it is clearly quite unreasonable that she and the children should be required to leave what has been their home for 18 years. No evidence was led of the cost of acquiring alternative accommodation but it is self evident that half of the value of one house, even with the addition of the defender's savings, will not purchase an equivalent house and the defender's income is not such to enable her to service a loan of any size. Accord-

A ingly, under reference to s 3 (3) (b) and (c), the needs and financial resources of the defender and the needs of the children and in particular of the youngest child of the family are factors tending to suggest that the defender should be allowed to remain in the house. A further factor tending to the same conclusion is that the pursuer has made no offer of suitable alternative accommodation (s 19 (b)). From the pursuer's point of view, however, it is quite unreasonable that he should be deprived of the use of capital in excess of £50,000 — which, so far as the evidence reveals is his only sub-

B stantial asset — which is tied up in the heritage. He has, however, been able to obtain alternative accommodation for himself and he has no current responsibility to provide accommodation for any of the children. His resources are sufficient to enable him to maintain himself in his present accommodation and, since the mortgage has been paid off, he has no ongoing liability in respect of the former matrimonial home. Weighing up the competing considerations in the light of my understanding of the law as explained

C above, it seems to me that the balance comes down decisively in favour of the defender. To remove now from the matrimonial home would cause major disruption to the lives of herself and the youngest child of the marriage. It is unclear what alternative accommodation she could find. Those potential problems outweigh the hardship to the pursuer in being prevented from turning his heritable property into cash. I am able to reach that view simply upon a consideration of the evidence. So far as any question of

D onus of proof is concerned, I hold that there is no onus on the defender and that whatever onus is upon the pursuer has not been discharged. I have accordingly refused decree. I have done so by granting decree of dismissal rather than of absolvitor. That is because in the fullness of time circumstances may change to such an extent that an action of division and sale by the pursuer would be successful and I would not wish this decision to be cited as res judicata.

E *Solicitors for Pursuer, Cohen & Co, Aberdeen — Solicitors for Defender, Peterkins, Aberdeen.*

G # Scottish & Newcastle plc v Harvey-Rutherford

SHERIFF COURT OF NORTH STRATHCLYDE AT GREENOCK
SHERIFF PRINCIPAL R C HAY, WS
5 NOVEMBER 1993

Bankruptcy — Sequestration — Procedure — Copy of petition for sequestration to be sent to Accountant in Bankruptcy on day presented to court — Both petition H *and copy sent on same day — Whether requirement complied with — Bankruptcy (Scotland) Act 1985 (c 66), s 5 (6).*

Section 5 (6) of the Bankruptcy (Scotland) Act 1985 provides that on the day a petition for sequestration is presented, the petitioner shall send a copy of the petition to the Accountant in Bankruptcy.

A copy of a petition for sequestration was sent to the Accountant in Bankruptcy on the same day that the I initial writ was sent to the sheriff clerk. The sheriff refused to award sequestration and dismissed the petition on the basis that the provisions of s 5 (6) had not been complied with inasmuch as the copy of the petition had been sent to the accountant not on the day that the petition had been presented but on the previous day. The pursuers appealed to the sheriff principal.

Held, that the requirement to send a copy of the petition to the Accountant in Bankruptcy had been J fulfilled on the day that the petition was presented to the court (pp 62L-63A); and appeal *allowed.*

Opinion, that as a matter of good practice it would be helpful if it was averred in petitions for sequestration that intimation would be made to the Accountant in Bankruptcy and a copy of the intimation should thereafter be lodged with the execution of citation of the debtors (p 62K-L).

K ## Petition for sequestration
Scottish & Newcastle plc raised a petition for sequestration of the estate of Mrs Georgina E W Harvey-Rutherford. On 13 August 1993 the sheriff (Sir S S T Young) refused to award sequestration and dismissed the petition. The pursuers appealed to the sheriff principal.

On 5 November 1993 the sheriff principal *allowed* L the appeal and *remitted* the case to the sheriff to proceed as accords.

THE SHERIFF PRINCIPAL (R C HAY, WS).
—This is an appeal by the pursuers against the interlocutor of the sheriff dated 13 August 1993, whereby he refused sequestration of the defender's estates. The solicitor for the defender stated that the position had changed since the date of the sheriff's interlocutor, and that the defender was now not resisting sequestration. He was prepared to concede the appeal, but

withdrew the concession when the solicitor for the pursuers stated that he wished to argue a point of statutory interpretation which he considered to be of general importance.

As the sheriff has recorded in his note, the petition was presented at Greenock sheriff court on 27 July 1993. Warrant to cite the debtor was granted on 28 July 1993. On 13 August 1993, the sheriff, having heard a local agent acting for the pursuers' principal agent, and the solicitor for the defender, refused sequestration. He did so on the basis that the pursuers had not complied with the provisions of s 5 (6) of the Bankruptcy (Scotland) Act 1985, as amended by the Bankruptcy (Scotland) Act 1993.

Section 5 (6), as amended, provides as follows:

"(6) The petitioner shall, on the day the petition for sequestration is presented under this section, send a copy of the petition to the Accountant in Bankruptcy."

There was no averment in the petition, and nothing in the productions lodged with it, to indicate that there had been compliance with this provision. The local agent appearing for the pursuers was given the opportunity to seek further instructions and returned with a faxed copy of a letter dated 26 July 1993 sent by the principal agents to the Accountant in Bankruptcy. A copy of that letter has since been lodged. The letter states: "We enclose herewith copy Sequestration Petition and relevant Inventory of Productions which we are about to raise".

In the opinion of the sheriff, it was clear that the pursuers' principal agents had failed to comply with the provisions of s 5 (6) inasmuch as they had sent the copy of the petition to the Accountant in Bankruptcy, not on the day the petition was presented, but on the previous day. In these circumstances, the solicitor for the defender submitted that the sheriff could not be satisfied that the provisions of s 5 (6) had been complied with, and that sequestration could not competently be awarded. This submission found favour with the sheriff, who refused to award sequestration, and dismissed the petition with no expenses being awarded to or by either party.

In his note, the sheriff considered the provisions of s 5 (6), as amended. He did not find it obvious why it should be important that a copy of the petition for sequestration should be sent to the Accountant in Bankruptcy on the day the petition was presented, but he recognised that, in amending the terms of s 5 (6) with effect from 1 April 1993, Parliament had provided that this should be done and, further, in amending s 12 (3), had explicitly directed the court that it must be satisfied that the provisions of s 5 (6) had been complied with. The sheriff was not satisfied that there had been compliance with s 5 (6) and accordingly decided that he could not competently award sequestration.

On appeal, the solicitor for the pursuers founded on the provisions of s 7 of the Interpretation Act 1978, which was not cited before the sheriff. Section 7 provides as follows:

"Where an Act authorises or requires any document to be served by post (whether the expression 'serve' or the expression 'give' or 'send' or any other expression is used), then, unless the contrary intention appears, the service is deemed to be effected by properly addressing, pre-paying and posting a letter containing the document and, unless the contrary is proved, to have been effected at the time at which the letter would be delivered in the ordinary course of post."

It was not in dispute that the pursuers' principal agents subscribed to the Rutland document exchange scheme and the letter dated 26 July 1993 addressed to the Accountant in Bankruptcy had been sent to him by that means. The solicitor for the pursuers submitted that in the circumstances this amounted to prepaid postal transmission which complied with the requirements of s 7 of the 1978 Act. It was not in dispute for the purposes of the appeal that the use of the document exchange system was equivalent to the use of the general postal service.

The solicitor for the pursuers stated that both the letter to the Accountant in Bankruptcy and the letter to the sheriff clerk, sending the initial writ, productions and fee, were sent by Rutland Exchange on the same day, 26 July 1993, and would therefore be received in normal course on the following day, 27 July 1993. On that basis, the petition was presented to the sheriff clerk on 27 July 1993, and was received by the Accountant in Bankruptcy on the same day. In these circumstances, the solicitor submitted, the effect of applying s 7 of the 1978 Act was that service of the copy petition on the Accountant in Bankruptcy complied with the provisions of s 5 (6) of the 1985 Act, as amended.

The solicitor for the defender maintained his position that the duty to send a copy of the petition to the Accountant in Bankruptcy could not arise until the petition was presented to the court, and that the intimation to the Accountant in Bankruptcy was one day early and therefore ineffective. In his submission, "presentation" extended to and included granting the warrant to cite the debtor, and could not be complete until it was known that the cause would proceed. I do not find that argument persuasive.

In my opinion, the pursuers' principal agents were remiss in not adverting to the provisions of s 5 (6) of the 1985 Act, as amended, either in the initial writ or when lodging the execution of citation of the defender. As a matter of good practice, I consider that it would be helpful if in such petitions it was averred that intimation of the petition will be made to the Accountant in Bankruptcy in terms of s 5 (6), and that a copy of that intimation should thereafter be lodged with the execution of citation of the debtor.

The essential point arising in this appeal, however, is whether there has been compliance with the provisions of s 5 (6). In the light of the provisions of s 7 of the 1978 Act, I am satisfied that there has been such compliance. In my opinion, the requirement to "send" a copy of the petition to the Accountant in Bankruptcy was fulfilled on 27 July 1993. On that date the petition was presented to the court when it

A was received by the sheriff clerk. It was received on the same day by the Accountant in Bankruptcy. Unfortunately, the terms of s 7 of the 1978 Act were not brought to the learned sheriff's attention.

The solicitor for the pursuers briefly addressed a subsidiary argument in relation to the possible exercise by the sheriff of the dispensing power in terms of s 63 of the 1985 Act, as amended. The sheriff does not mention this question in his note and it is not clear to what extent, if any, it was addressed before him. In the circumstances, I do not require to consider the point
B further. The exercise of the dispensing power would have been a matter within the sheriff's discretion.

For the reasons stated, I allow the appeal and recall the interlocutor of the sheriff complained of.

While the point taken for the pursuers may be of some general interest to practitioners who have occasion to present petitions for sequestration by some form of post, the defender's solicitor was prepared at the outset to concede the appeal. For that reason,
C taken with the consideration that the appeal has been successful on the basis of a point which could have been but was not argued before the learned sheriff, I make no finding of expenses to or by either party in respect of the appeal.

The cause is remitted to the sheriff's procedure roll of 12 November 1993, to proceed as accords.

D *Solicitors for Pursuers, Macdonalds, Glasgow; Solicitors for Defender, Neill Clerk, Gourock.*

Eurocopy Rentals Ltd v McCann Fordyce

E SHERIFF COURT OF NORTH STRATHCLYDE AT DUMBARTON

SHERIFF PRINCIPAL R C HAY, WS

7 APRIL 1994

Contract — Termination — Lease of photocopier — Clause allowing suppliers to take possession of copier "and this agreement will thereon be terminated" — Purported termination of agreement by letter — Whether effective — Whether termination at common law rele-
F *vantly averred.*

Parties to a contract for the lease of a photocopier agreed that in specified circumstances the suppliers would be entitled to enter the premises at which the copier was installed and take possession of it "and this agreement will be thereon terminated". The suppliers wrote to the hirers of the copier, warning them that their continued failure to make payment of quarterly rentals due in terms of the contract would be regarded as repudiation of the agreement which would lead to the suppliers terminating it, as they subsequently pur-

ported to do. In response to an action of payment based on the termination formula, the hirers argued
G that the suppliers were entitled to terminate the contract only when they took possession of the copier, which they had not averred. After debate the sheriff held that the contract had been validly terminated by the suppliers, and that they had also sufficiently averred a case for damages at common law. The hirers appealed to the sheriff principal.

Held, (1) that the clause in the agreement fell to be interpreted strictly and, in dubio, contra proferentem,
H and since the suppliers had not followed the agreed termination procedures their averments relating to termination were irrelevant (p 68F-G and H-I); (2) that the suppliers had not relevantly averred termination at common law by means of an accepted repudiation (p 68J); and appeal *allowed* and action against first defenders *dismissed.*

Action of payment
I Eurocopy Rentals Ltd raised an action of payment against (first) Messrs McCann Fordyce and (second) Eurocopy (GB) plc. After a hearing involving the pursuers and first defenders, on 8 September 1993, the sheriff (C K Higgins) allowed a proof before answer. The first defenders appealed to the sheriff principal.

On 7 April 1994 the sheriff principal *allowed* the appeal and *dismissed* the action against the first defenders.
J

THE SHERIFF PRINCIPAL (R C HAY, WS).—This is an appeal by the first named defenders, with leave of the sheriff, in an action for payment in the sum of £122,792.94. The appeal is against the interlocutor of the sheriff dated 8 September 1993, issued following debate, and in terms of which he repelled the first and fourth pleas in law for the pursuers, and quoad ultra allowed proof before answer. The pursuers' first plea in law related to a contractual claim for
K payment averred in art 4 of condescendence, and the fourth was a plea of personal bar. By interlocutor dated 8 November 1993, the sheriff found the pursuers liable to the first named defenders in the expenses of the debate.

The second named defenders did not take part in the debate. The sheriff records that with consent of all parties they were allowed to withdraw, while maintaining both their interest in the action and their whole pleas. They did not take part in the appeal.
L

There is no cross appeal by the pursuers. The appeal has therefore been restricted to the two points on which the sheriff upheld the argument for the pursuers, namely, that the contract had been validly terminated by the pursuers, and that they had sufficiently averred a case on damages at common law.

The pursuers aver that, by an agreement dated 15 and 28 February 1990, they agreed to lease to the first named defenders a photocopier for an initial period of seven years at a quarterly rental of £4,501.80 based on

A an agreed price of 25.01 p per copy and an agreed monthly copy volume of 6,000. The pursuers refer to the agreement for its terms which are held to be incorporated brevitatis causa. A copy of the documents is in process. It will be convenient to refer to this document as "the agreement".

The pursuers go on to aver that in breach of the agreement the first named defenders failed to maintain the agreed quarterly payments. On 3 September 1991 the pursuers wrote to the first named defenders,

B warning them that their continued failure to make payment would be regarded as repudiation of the agreement which would lead to the pursuers terminating it. The letter is referred to for its terms and held to be incorporated brevitatis causa. A copy of it is in process. The pursuers go on to aver that the first named defenders ignored the warning and failed to make any further payment, and that the pursuers accordingly terminated the agreement on 10 September 1991, as provided for in terms of cl 10 (a)

C thereof.

The first named defenders admit having executed a document purporting to hire a photocopier on the terms averred by the pursuers, and admit not having paid the sums which the pursuers claim. They make detailed averments about the circumstances in which they entered into negotiations with a salesman which resulted in the photocopier being delivered to them. They aver that they were induced to enter into the agreement by reason of misrepresentation on the part

D of employees of a company, Purdie & Kirkpatrick Ltd.

The agreement is on what appears to be a standard printed form headed "Supplying & Servicing". On the front of the form there is a series of boxes in which various details have been typed. On one side are details of the first named defenders, and on the other details of a photocopier and of copy volumes and prices. Under the boxes there is a series of five printed sentences which bear to set out terms of agreement. Two of these contain references to Purdie &

E Kirkpatrick Ltd.

The back of the form is entirely printed. It is headed: "This Agreement made between the Supplier and the Customer is subject to the conditions overleaf and following". There then follows a series of 17 clauses setting out detailed conditions. In terms of cl 1, the "Supplier" is the pursuers, and the "Customer", by reference to the front of the form, is the first named defenders.

F Clause 3 (c) reserves to the supplier the right to vary the agreed price (as defined by cl 1 and the related typed entry on the front of the form) at any time, reserving to the customer a right to terminate the agreement if the agreed price is increased by more than 15 per cent per annum, unless such increase is justified by an equivalent increase in the supplier's costs.

Clause 8 (b) gives the supplier a monopoly in the provision of supplies. In terms of the fifth sentence printed on the front of the form, all consumables and

parts for the equipment are to be purchased from Purdie & Kirkpatrick Ltd.   G

Clause 9 makes provision for payment of the copy charges quarterly in advance.

Clause 10 is headed "Termination" and is the clause with which this appeal is principally concerned. Clause 10 (a) is in the following terms: "In the event of the Customer (being a company) going into liquidation or a receiver, Administrative Receiver or Administrator, judicial factor or other similar officer being appointed over the whole or any part of the H assets of the Customer or in the event of the Customer (being an individual or partnership) becoming bankrupt or committing an act of bankruptcy or being the subject of a receiving order or being sequestrated or being apparently insolvent or notour bankrupt or granting any trust deed or entering into any composition or similar arrangement with his creditors, or the Customer failing to comply in any respect with any of these conditions or circumstance [sic] arising which render in the sole opinion of the Supplier any I of the foregoing likely to occur then the Supplier will be entitled without notice to enter the premises at which the Copier is installed and to take possession thereof and this agreement will be thereon terminated. The Customer hereby expressly and irrevocably empowers authorises and mandates the Supplier to make such entry and take possession as aforesaid".

Clause 10 (b) provides that termination of the agreement will not discharge any pre-existing liability of the customer to the supplier and that the supplier will be J entitled to recover damages from the customer. A formula for the calculation of such damages is set out. The pursuers initially sought to recover damages from the first named defenders in terms of cl 10 (b), but their averments in art 4 of condescendence were held by the sheriff to be irrelevant when he repelled the pursuers' first plea in law. This has not been challenged on appeal.

Counsel for the first named defenders submitted K that, by averring in art 3 of condescendence that these defenders were in breach of the agreement by failing to maintain the quarterly payments, and that in consequence the pursuers terminated the contract in terms of cl 10 (a), the pursuers' case is perilled on breach of contract.

In terms of cl 10 (a) of the agreement, the pursuers were entitled to enter the first named defenders' premises and to remove the photocopier. In counsel's submission, the pursuers were entitled to terminate L the contract in terms of cl 10 (a) only when they took possession of the photocopier. There is no averment that they did so, or of what happened to the photocopier.

Counsel for the first named defenders argued that, not only was it clear from the ordinary grammatical construction of cl 10 (a) that the pursuers must take possession of the photocopier for the agreement to be terminated, but that this was also clear from the terms of cl 10 (b), which sets out a formula for calculation of damages based on the "Termination Date". This, he argued, has to be a specific date which will be clear to all parties, and not one which exists only in the mind of the supplier. In his submission, this can only be the date on which the photocopier is removed in terms of cl 10 (a). Accordingly, for the pursuers' pleadings to be relevant, they would have to aver a date on which they took possession of the photocopier. Absent such an averment, the pursuers cannot relevantly plead that the agreement was terminated in terms of cl 10 (a). Counsel submitted that the pursuers, having contracted for a particular method of termination, were bound by their agreement, were not entitled to resort to any alternative method of termination, and should not be permitted by the court to do so, since this would involve the court rewriting the contract.

The pursuers aver in art 3 of the condescendence that the defenders having ignored the warning in the letter dated 3 September 1991, and having failed to make any further payment, the pursuers terminated the agreement on 10 September 1991 "as provided for in terms of cl 10 (a)". In the submission of counsel for the first named defenders, the pursuers were not entitled in terms of the agreement to proceed in this way, and the procedure which they adopted did not conform to the provisions of cl 10 (a). The agreement is in a standard form provided by the pursuers themselves, and should be construed strictly and contra proferentem.

Counsel referred to *Arnhold & Co Ltd v Att Gen of Hong Kong* (1989) 47 BLR 129 at p 133. That was a building case decided in the High Court of Hong Kong in which it was held that the contra proferentem principle fell to be applied to the interpretation of provisions on liquidated damages in a printed form of contract. Applying that principle, the clause in question was held to be void for uncertainty.

Counsel also referred to *Northern Regional Health Authority v Derek Crouch Construction Co Ltd* [1984] 2 All ER 175 ([1984] QB 644; [1984] 2 WLR 676), a case in which the question was whether the court could substitute its procedures for arbitration provisions in the contract. The Court of Appeal came to the view that it could not substitute its procedure for that chosen by the parties. Dunn LJ said at p 184: "Where parties have agreed on machinery . . . for the resolution of disputes, it is not for the court to intervene and replace its own process for the contractual machinery agreed by the parties". Browne-Wilkinson LJ said, at p 186: "in an action based on contract the court can only enforce the agreement between the parties: it has no power to modify that agreement in any way. Therefore, if the parties have agreed on a specified machinery for establishing their obligations, the court cannot substitute a different machinery. . . . In no circumstances would the court have power to revise such certificate or opinion solely on the ground that the court would have reached a different conclusion, since to do so would be to interfere with the agreement of the parties".

In the instant case, counsel for the first named defenders argued, the parties had agreed a particular machinery for termination of the contract. The contract fell to be interpreted strictly and contra proferentem, and the pursuers must be held to the agreed machinery for termination if they are to rely, as they seek to do, on the provisions of cl 10 (a).

Counsel also referred to *D & J McDougall Ltd v Argyll and Bute District Council*, 1987 SLT 7, in which the Lord Ordinary followed *Northern Regional Health Authority*.

I was also referred to an unreported judgment of Sheriff Veal at Forfar in the case of *Eurocopy Rentals Ltd v Tayside Health Board and Eurocopy (Great Britain) Ltd*, issued on 10 September 1993, that is, after the date of the interlocutor under appeal. That case concerned the interpretation of a supplying and servicing agreement which appears to have been in terms identical to those in the agreement. The sheriff held that the contract fell to be interpreted strictly and contra proferentem quoad the pursuers. He found that they had not followed the procedure for termination of the contract provided in cl 10 (a). The action was dismissed.

In the instant case, the sheriff, having supported the attack by counsel for the first defenders on cl 10 (b) of the agreement, says, at p 14 of his note: "However cl 10 (a) does not express itself as in any way exclusive and while it narrates a number of circumstances entitling the pursuers to enter upon the defenders' premises and seize the copier, it does not state or even imply that only in the circumstances or following upon the occurrence of the events set out therein is the agreement to be viewed as terminated. Counsel for the pursuers is in my view right in arguing that the suggestion that the agreement can be terminated only if and when the pursuers take physical possession of the copier is an unrealistically strict interpretation. It is also extremely unlikely that the parties would provide for termination of an agreement such as this only by means of such a crude and unsophisticated method. In my view the real thrust of cl 10 (a) is to set out clearly the circumstances in which the pursuers may enter upon the defenders' premises and take possession of the copier, action which would otherwise be wholly unlawful. I am supported in this view by the final sentence of cl 10 (a) which is effectively a warrant by the defenders to the pursuers so to enter upon their premises."

Counsel for the first named defenders accepted that the cases of *Northern Regional Health Authority* and *D & J McDougall Ltd*, supra, had not been cited to the sheriff. He submitted that the lack of such citation may have led to the sheriff reaching his view that the provisions of cl 10 (a) in relation to termination were not exclusive. Counsel accepted that it was theoretically possible for the agreement to be terminated on other grounds, but argued that in the circumstances termination had to be in terms of cl 10 (a). In his submission, it matters not that the pursuers may have been unwise in restricting themselves by the terms in which cl 10 (a) is framed; the question for the court is what the parties have agreed, and cl 10 (a) should be given its plain meaning.

A Counsel for the first named defenders submitted that termination has to be on a date which is certain, and that without the event of taking possession of the photocopier it is impossible to ascertain the termination date. In his submission, the purpose of cl 10 (a) is to ensure commercial certainty, as well as to provide contractual machinery enabling the pursuers to take possession of the photocopier, and to terminate the contract.

B Counsel then referred to the letter dated 3 September 1991 from the pursuers to the first named defenders, and bearing to be signed by their senior litigation assistant. The letter states in terms that these defenders are in breach of cl 9 (a) of the agreement in respect that their payments are in arrears. It does not refer to cl 10 (a). In counsel's submission, however, the reference to cl 9 (a) indicates that the pursuers were stating a reason which would justify termination in terms of cl 10 (a). The letter goes on to give these defenders seven days in which to pay the arrears. It continues: "If we have not received the payment of C arrears within the 7 day period, we will have no alternative but to regard your refusal of payment as repudiation of our contract. As a result of your repudiation the Agreement will terminate automatically. Our equipment will be uplifted and the above claim for agreed damages, which includes the arrears, will become due." The reference to "agreed damages" appears to arise from the terms of cl 10 (b).

In art 3 of condescendence, after referring to the D letter, the pursuers aver that: "The defenders ignored said warning and failed to make any further payment. The pursuers accordingly terminated the agreement on 10 September 1991, as provided for in cl 10 (a) thereof."

Counsel for the first named defenders argued that cl 10 (a) does not provide for termination of the contract as averred by the pursuers, even in the event of repudiation. The mode of termination averred by the pursuers is wholly different from the contractual pro-E visions of cl 10 (a). In his submission, it follows that the pursuers' case is wholly irrelevant.

Counsel for these defenders then addressed a subsidiary argument that, even if his argument that the effect of cl 10 (a) was to provide exclusive machinery for termination was wrong, and if the pursuers were entitled to claim that they had terminated the contract at common law, nevertheless their averments to that end were irrelevant and would not provide a relevant basis for a claim for damages at common law.

F This argument was based on the terms of the letter dated 3 September 1991. In counsel's submission, the proposition that failure to make payment would be regarded by the pursuers as repudiation of the agreement terminating the contract automatically is wrong in law and therefore irrelevant. A contract cannot terminate by repudiation alone. He referred to *Howard v Pickford Tool Co Ltd* [1951] 1 KB 417, where, at p 421, Asquith LJ said: "An unaccepted repudiation is a thing writ in water and of no value to anybody: it confers no legal rights of any sort or kind. Therefore

a declaration that the defendants had repudiated their contract with the plaintiff would be entirely valueless G to the plaintiff if it appeared at the same time . . . that it was not accepted." In counsel's submission, this is apt to describe the case sought to be made by the pursuers in art 3 of condescendence.

In the instant case, counsel argued, if the pursuers seek to claim any right to terminate the agreement otherwise than in terms of cl 10 (a), they have not averred it. The assertion in the letter dated 3 September 1991, which is adopted into the pursuers' pleadings, that the agreement would terminate auto- H matically is wrong in law, and so therefore is the averment in art 3 of condescendence that the pursuers terminated the agreement in terms of cl 10 (a). Counsel submitted that, having regard to the terms of cl 10 (a), the agreement could not terminate on the basis expressed in the letter dated 3 September 1991 on which the pursuers found. The action should therefore be dismissed as irrelevant.

Finally, counsel for the first named defenders sub- I mitted that, even if he was wrong on all these points, the pursuers had not relevantly averred a claim for damages at common law. The cl 10 (b) formula averred in art 4 of condescendence has been held by the sheriff to be irrelevant. In art 5 of condescendence, the pursuers aver that in any event the sum sued for represents a reasonable pre-estimate of their loss arising naturally and directly from the first named defenders' breach of contract. Counsel for these defenders submitted that this averment seems to anticipate the possibility of the formula set out in cl 10 J (b) for the calculation of damages being unsuccessful. However, the pursuers go on to aver a calculation which reflects the cl 10 (b) formula, but which does not suggest the existence of an actual, present loss. The averments appear to be an estimate of possible future losses.

Counsel accepted that the pursuers' second plea in law refers to "loss and damage by reason of the first named defenders' said breach of contract", but argued K that there are no averments to support a claim for damages at common law. He also submitted that there is no crave in respect of such a claim, since the terms of the first crave with its conclusion for interest from the date of citation are appropriate to a contractual claim.

The sheriff was satisfied that the pursuers had open to them a claim for damages at common law. He understood that counsel for the first named defenders accepted this. On appeal, however, counsel has stated, L and I accept, that his acquiescence was limited to the situation in which the contract had been properly terminated.

In counsel's submission, the sheriff erred in his view that a claim for damages at common law is available to the pursuers. He argued that the averments in art 5 of condescendence are not relevant to a common law claim for damages. The cl 10 (b) formula is as inoperable and unenforceable in relation to a claim at common law as it is in contractual terms. There are no averments setting out a common law claim for damages in terms of actual, as distinct from pre-estimated, losses. Counsel for the first named defenders therefore invited me to sustain the appeal, to sustain the first plea in law for these defenders and to dismiss the action as irrelevant so far as laid against them.

In reply, counsel for the pursuers invited me to sustain the sheriff's interlocutor. In his submission, the argument for the first named defenders that, without repossession of the photocopier, the provisions of cl 10 (a) and (b) could not be invoked, was misconceived. He argued that it was appropriate now to look simply at the common law position.

Counsel for the pursuers maintained his argument that the contractual provisions for termination were not exclusive and submitted that the sheriff had expressed a correct view on this point. In his submission, the provisions of cl 10 (a) in relation to termination should be read as the precursor to the formula provisions in cl 10 (b) and it would only be on the clearest language that the proposition, that the pursuers had given away their right to terminate the agreement in any other fashion, would be justified. He posed the question whether the pursuers would be in the position of having no remedy if the equipment had been lost by theft or fire. However, this possibility seems to be covered by the insurance provisions of cl 7.

Counsel for the pursuers accepted that the right to terminate a contract arises when one party accepts a repudiatory breach of contract by the other, acceptance of the repudiation being essential. He referred to *White & Carter (Councils) Ltd v McGregor*, 1962 SLT 9; 1962 SC (HL) 1. He went on to argue, however, that the right to terminate the contract at common law remains, notwithstanding the terms of the agreement, and that it would require the clearest words, expressed in the contract, if the argument on exclusivity maintained by the first named defenders was to be accepted.

In counsel's submission, the numbering of the provisions for termination as 10 (a) and (b) suggests that both parts are intimately connected and should be read together. He pointed out that cl 10 (b) provides that termination will not discharge any pre-existing liability. If, therefore, the position is that cl 10 (a) is not exclusive, the sheriff has reached a correct conclusion. In particular, he submitted, the sheriff was correct in his view that the real thrust of cl 10 (a) is to set out clearly the circumstances in which the pursuers may enter upon the defenders' premises and take possession of the photocopier.

Counsel for the pursuers accepted that, contrary to what is asserted in the letter dated 3 September 1991, the contract could not terminate automatically. He argued, however, that it is necessary to look at the letter in context. It refers to "your repudiation", that is, the failure by the first named defenders to make the contractual payments, which put them in breach of contract. In counsel's submission, the writer of the letter was saying that, if the arrears were paid, the pursuers would not accept the repudiation by the first named defenders. However, if the arrears were not paid within seven days, the agreement would terminate without further ado, and this was the intended meaning in the context of the phrase "will terminate automatically".

In counsel's submission, the only matter which properly attracts criticism is the use of the phrase "the Agreement will terminate automatically"; but even construing the letter on the contra proferentem principle, he argued, the criticism cannot succeed because there is no ambiguity. It followed that the sheriff was correct in his view that the pursuers "deemed the agreement terminated as at 10 September 1991".

Turning to the question of damages, counsel for the pursuers supported the sheriff's view that the pursuers have "adequate averments regarding their claim for damages at common law arising from the defenders' alleged breach of contract to justify the matter proceeding to proof before answer". Counsel referred to *Bell Brothers (HP) Ltd v Aitken*, 1939 SC 577; 1939 SLT 453, a case involving a hire purchase contract on a motor vehicle, where, at p 587 (p 462), Lord President Normand said: "it is nevertheless true that the first thing to be ascertained in assessing damages for breach is what would have been received under the contract if it had been carried out, and what would have been received under the contract in this case is just the total amount of the hire. It is irrelevant to consider whether the total amount of the hire corresponded to the market value of the article, or even whether it was grossly excessive. The total hire was the consideration stipulated for, and the question, whether the hirer is in breach, is what loss has been suffered by the owner . . . through the failure to carry out the contract and to pay the stipulated hire".

In counsel's submission, the pursuers had clearly averred in art 3 of condescendence that the first named defenders were in arrears of payment in terms of the agreement. He conceded that art 4 of condescendence is framed in terms appropriate to a cl 10 (b) claim. These averments were held by the sheriff to be irrelevant when he repelled the pursuers' first plea in law. Counsel for the pursuers submitted, however, that the averments in art 5 of condescendence relevantly set out the pursuers' claim for damages based on arrears of payments and future loss and conform to the principles enunciated by the Lord President in *Bell Brothers (HP) Ltd*.

So far as the claim for interest in terms of the first crave was concerned, counsel argued that it was entirely within the court's discretion to decide from what date interest should run. In his submission, the claim for damages at common law was not so irrelevant as to exclude proof before answer simply because the crave was expressed in a form appropriate to a contractual claim.

In reply, counsel for the first named defenders submitted that nothing said by counsel for the pursuers had met his arguments. The pursuers are bound by

A their averments on record, and the only case made in termination of the agreement is in art 3 of condescendence, where it is averred that the pursuers terminated the agreement "as provided for in terms of cl 10 (a) thereof".

In counsel's submission, the argument that the provisions of cl 10 (a) refer only to termination for the purposes of cl 10 (b) is not well founded. Clause 10 (a) is not tied in to cl 10 (b). The former provides the mechanics for any termination, and the latter the results, provided always that cl 10 (b) can apply only
B when the agreement has been properly terminated in terms of cl 10 (a). In his submission, cl 10 (a) is unqualified in its terms and covers exclusively all classes of termination of the agreement. The pursuers have therefore given up any right to terminate the contract otherwise than in terms of cl 10 (a).

Counsel for the first named defenders argued that the concession by counsel for the pursuers that there was no such thing as automatic termination of the con-
C tract was fatal to his case, because the letter dated 3 September 1991, adopted into the pursuers' pleadings, was written on the basis that there would be "automatic termination" of the agreement. In art 3 of condescendence, the pursuers refer to the terms of the letter, and then aver that "accordingly" they terminated the agreement "as provided for in terms of cl 10 (a) thereof". The word "accordingly" must refer back to the terms of the letter.

Counsel argued that the sheriff's view that the pur-
D suers "deemed the agreement terminated" was as strange a concept as that of "automatic termination". In his submission, there was no averment of any event following the letter which would constitute acceptance of a repudiation of the contract, and no averment of what, if anything, happened on 10 September 1991. He argued that in these circumstances there could not be termination of the agreement at common law.

In a brief reply, counsel for the pursuers pointed out
E that the letter dated 3 September 1991 does not refer to cl 10 (a) of the agreement. He maintained his argument that the letter should be interpreted as an acceptance by the pursuers of the first named defenders' repudiation of the contract by failing to make the quarterly payments, and that it was effective to that end.

In my opinion, the arguments of counsel for the first named defenders are to be preferred. It follows that I respectfully dissent from the view expressed by the
F learned sheriff that cl 10 (a) of the agreement is not exclusive, and that its real thrust is to give warrant to the pursuers to enter upon the first named defenders' premises to take possession of the photocopier. In my respectful opinion, the sheriff was not well founded in his view that the pursuers were entitled to deem the agreement to be terminated when their letter dated 3 September 1991 was not followed by payment of the sums they claimed.

In my opinion, the provisions of cl 10 (a) in the pursuers' printed terms of contract, on which they rely in their averments on record, fall to be interpreted strictly, and in dubio, contra proferentem. G

I respectfully differ from the learned sheriff's view that the argument that the agreement can be terminated only if and when the pursuers take physical possession of the photocopier is unrealistically strict. The sheriff refers to this as being a "crude and unsophisticated method of termination", and in his opinion it was extremely unlikely that the parties would provide for termination exclusively in such a way. With respect, however, it seems to me that, for whatever reason, this is the procedure for termination H agreed by the parties. As it appears to me, the sheriff has acquiesced in a method of termination for which there is no basis in the agreement or at common law. In my respectful opinion, he has misdirected himself by effectively rewriting the contractual provisions for termination.

I am of the view that the pursuers did not follow the termination procedures provided in cl 10 (a). It follows that the averments in art 3 of condescendence that the pursuers terminated the agreement on 10 September 1991 as provided for in terms of cl 10 (a) are wrong in law and therefore irrelevant. The question is one of interpretation of the terms of contract agreed by the parties and I am satisfied that the agreement falls to be interpreted strictly and, in dubio, contra proferentem. In my opinion the cl 10 (a) provisions for termination proposed by the pursuers and accepted by the first named defenders properly fall to be interpreted as exclusive of any other method of termination. J

I am also of the view that, even if the pursuers were entitled to determine the agreement otherwise than in terms of cl 10 (a), they have not relevantly averred termination at common law by means of an accepted repudiation of the contract. It follows that, in my opinion, a claim for damages at common law is not available to the pursuers. If such a claim had been available, however, I would have agreed with the learned sheriff's view that the averments in art 5 of K condescendence are sufficient to enable the claim to proceed to proof before answer. In the event, this does not arise.

In my opinion, the present action must fail. I shall therefore allow the appeal, recall the interlocutor of the sheriff complained of, sustain the first plea in law for the first named defenders, and dismiss the action so far as laid against them.

———

L

Counsel for Pursuers, Cheyne; Solicitors, Macdonalds, Glasgow — Counsel for First Defenders, Howie; Solicitors, Bishop and Robertson Chalmers, Glasgow — No appearance for Second Defenders.

McMeechan v Uniroyal
Engelbert Tyres Ltd

SHERIFF COURT OF LOTHIAN AND
BORDERS AT EDINBURGH

SHERIFF PRINCIPAL C G B NICHOLSON, QC

5 MAY 1994

*Reparation — Negligence — Master and servant —
Breach of statutory duty — Fencing of machinery —
Defence that machinery not in motion or use at the time
— Whether required to be pled — Factories Act 1961 (9
& 10 Eliz II, c 34), ss 14 and 16.*

*Process — Reparation — Personal injuries — Defenders
founding without averment on qualification of statutory
duty — Whether fair notice given of line of defence —
Factories Act 1961 (9 & 10 Eliz II, c 34), ss 14 and 16.*

Section 14 of the Factories Act 1961 provides inter
alia that every dangerous part of any machinery shall
be securely fenced. Section 16 provides inter alia that
all such fencing shall be constantly maintained and
kept in position while the parts required to be fenced
are in motion or use.

In an action of damages the pursuer claimed, inter
alia, that there had been a breach of s 14 (1) of the
1961 Act. After proof, the sheriff found in favour of
the pursuer on that part of his case but also found that
the blades on the machine were not in motion or use
and, by reference to s 16, assoilzied the defenders. The
pursuer appealed, contending that the defenders had
not given proper and fair notice of a line of defence
that the machinery was not in motion or use at the
time of the accident.

Held, that s 16 of the Act, being a limitation on the
duty imposed under s 14 of which cognisance ought
to have been taken by the pursuer, was a matter which
the sheriff was entitled to take account of in reaching
his decision (p 71G); and appeal *refused*.

Nimmo v Alexander Cowan & Sons, 1967 SLT 277,
distinguished.

Observed, that the defenders would have required
to plead that part of s 16 providing an exception where
dangerous parts were necessarily exposed for certain
purposes (p 71D-E).

Action of damages

Robert McMeechan raised a summary cause action
seeking an award of damages from Uniroyal Engelbert
Tyres Ltd. After proof, the sheriff (A M Bell) assoilzied the defenders. The pursuer appealed to the sheriff
principal.

On 5 May 1994 the sheriff principal *refused* the
appeal.

**THE SHERIFF PRINCIPAL (C G B
NICHOLSON, QC).**—This appeal arises in a summary cause action in which the pursuer seeks an award
of damages from his employers in respect of an injury
which he sustained in the course of his employment in

September 1991. Although the point in issue at the
appeal was a fairly short one relative to pleading and
fair notice, it is necessary, in order to set the scene, to
begin by saying a little about the facts of the case and
about the pleadings.

The injury sustained by the pursuer occurred when
his hand came into contact with a blade on a wire
cutting machine. As appears from the sheriff's findings in fact the machine had jammed shortly before
the accident, and the pursuer, together with a fellow
employee, had stopped the machine in order to enable
them to clear the jam. The pursuer removed the guard
which was guarding the blades and was leaning over
the machine to feed the wire into the blades while at
the same time operating a foot pedal to inch the blades
forward. As he was doing so a light over the machine
suddenly went out. The surprise occasioned by this
caused the pursuer to jerk his hand so as to bring it
into contact with the blades.

The pursuer's case in respect of the foregoing
accident is set in a full and detailed statement of claim,
and the defenders' case is set out in an equally full and
detailed statement of defence. Both of these documents were drafted by very experienced solicitors.

In the statement of claim as originally drafted the
pursuer made several cases of fault against the
defenders both at common law and under statute. In
particular he claimed that there had been a breach of
s 14 (1) of the Factories Act 1961. So far as relevant
that section provides: "Every dangerous part of any
machinery . . . shall be securely fenced unless it is in
such a position or of such construction as to be as safe
to every person employed or working on the premises
as it would be if securely fenced."

The defenders for their part averred that they had
fulfilled all duties incumbent on them both at common
law and under statute, and asserted that the accident
had been caused wholly, or at least partly, by the pursuer's own fault. Shortly before the date fixed for the
proof the pursuer's solicitors lodged an incidental
application which sought to enlarge the case against
the defenders by adding a reference to s 14 (2) of the
1961 Act and by adding a case of defective lighting
under s 5 of that Act. On the day before the proof the
defenders intimated an incidental application which
contained averments to answer those of the pursuer in
relation to ss 5 and 14 (2). Additionally, that incidental
application sought to introduce an averment in the
following terms: "Furthermore, the machinery was
not in motion or in use at or immediately prior to the
accident. Reference is made to s 16 of said Act."

Section 16 of the 1961 Act is in the following terms:
"All fencing or other safeguards provided in pur-
suance of the foregoing provisions of this Part of this
Act shall be of substantial construction, and constantly
maintained and kept in position while the parts
required to be fenced or safeguarded are in motion or
use, except when any such parts are necessarily
exposed for examination and for any lubrication or
adjustment shown by the examination to be immediately necessary".

At the commencement of the proof no objection was

taken to those parts of the defenders' incidental application which dealt with ss 5 and 14 (2) of the Act, but objection was taken to the introduction of the two sentences which I have quoted above on the ground that their introduction at such a late stage would be prejudicial to the pursuer in that there had been no opportunity to investigate the matters raised under s 16 or to put them to the pursuer himself. What happened thereafter is not, through no fault on his part, immediately clear from the sheriff's note, but I was advised by the defenders' solicitor, who had represented the defenders at the proof, that what happened was that he offered to withdraw the two sentences in question from the incidental application on the basis that they were not strictly necessary in the defenders' pleadings since they did no more than refer to a point of law. At the end of the day that seems to have been what happened, and the proof then proceeded without these sentences forming part of the defenders' pleadings.

The consequences of excluding those two sentences from the defenders' pleadings form the subject matter of the present appeal, but, before coming to that, I should narrate briefly the decision which was reached by the sheriff after proof. He rejected the pursuer's case of fault at common law, and his statutory case under s 5 of the 1961 Act; and that part of his decision was not challenged on appeal. So far as the statutory case under s 14 (1) is concerned, the sheriff concluded that the blades on the machine in question were a "dangerous part" within the meaning of the subsection, and that they had not been "securely fenced" at the relevant time. Prima facie, therefore, the sheriff found in favour of the pursuer on that part of his case, and, if that were to be the end of the matter, the defenders do not now dispute that the sheriff was entitled to reach that conclusion. However, the sheriff also found as a fact that, at the time of the accident, the blades on the machine were not in motion or use and, by reference to s 16 of the Act, he proceeded to assoilzie the defenders. The question whether the sheriff was in the circumstances entitled to have regard to s 16 formed the subject matter of the appeal.

In his stated case the sheriff posed two questions for my determination. The first was: whether the sheriff erred in law by disregarding failure by the defenders and respondents to give proper and fair notice to the pursuer and appellant of a line of defence that the machinery involved in the accident to the pursuer and appellant was not in motion or use at the time of said accident. The second question was: whether the sheriff erred in law in determining the liability of the defenders and respondents to make reparation to the pursuer and appellant in terms of s 14 of the Factories Act 1961 by reference to s 16 of the said Act.

I have to say that it is not immediately clear whether the second of the foregoing questions is intended to put in issue the question whether, as a matter of law, s 16 of the Act, as applied to the facts of the present case, affected or modified any liability otherwise attaching to the defenders under s 14, or whether it really does no more than to restate the first question in a slightly different way. Happily, it is unnecessary to consider that uncertainty further since the appel-

lant's position at the appeal was that the appeal would stand or fall by the answer to the first question. In other words it was accepted on behalf of the pursuer that, if I were to conclude that the sheriff had been entitled to have regard to s 16 notwithstanding that at the end of the day there was no averment relating to that section in the defenders' pleadings, then the appeal must fail. Conversely, it was accepted by the solicitor for the defenders that, if I were to conclude that the sheriff had erred by having regard to s 16, then the appeal must succeed, and in that event the pursuer would be entitled to an award of damages in a sum of £750, that being the sum which, as the sheriff says in his note, he would have awarded had he found in the pursuer's favour.

The solicitors on both sides of the appeal presented their submissions with great care and in considerable detail. At the end of the day, however, I think that those submissions can be set out quite shortly. The solicitor for the pursuer and appellant submitted that the averments which the defenders had sought to introduce in the incidental application presented on the day of the proof, but which were then withdrawn, did much more than merely raise a point of law which did not require to be mentioned in the pleadings. Fundamentally, the averments in question involved a crucial averment of fact, namely that at the time of the accident the blades which caused the accident were not "in motion or use". Our system of pleading requires that all essential facts should be averred in the pleadings with candour so that fair notice is given to the other party of all relevant matters which are to be proved and founded on. Reference was made in that regard to *Ellon Castle Estates Co Ltd v Macdonald*, 1975 SLT (Notes) 66 and to *Lossie Hydraulic Co v Ecosse Transport*, 1980 SLT (Sh Ct) 94. A failure to give fair notice in the manner desiderated by the foregoing authorities is prejudicial in that it denies to the other party an opportunity to examine the evidence relative to the averment in question and to consider his position in the light of that examination.

The pursuer's solicitor then went on to submit that there is no dilution of the requirement to give fair notice just because an action is proceeding, like the present one, as a summary cause rather than as an ordinary cause. Reference was made in that connection to *Lochgorm Warehouses v Roy*, 1981 SLT (Sh Ct) 45; *Roofcare Ltd v Gillies*, 1984 SLT (Sh Ct) 8; and *McInnes v Alginate Industries Ltd*, 1980 SLT (Sh Ct) 114. In all the circumstances, it was submitted, the defenders ought timeously to have made averments along the lines of those contained in, but ultimately withdrawn from, their incidental application; and in the absence of such averments, it was submitted, the sheriff had erred in giving consideration to the question whether the blades had been in motion or use at the time of the accident and in taking s 16 of the 1961 Act into account.

In response the solicitor for the defenders submitted that the issue here is not one of fair notice. Sections 12 to 16 of the 1961 Act together form a single code and ought to be read together (per Lord Hailsham LC in *F E Callow (Engineers) Ltd v Johnson* [1970] 3 All

ER 639 at p 641). In that context s 16 is to be read as
A defining the extent of the duty imposed under s 14 and
as introducing exceptions as to when the duty under
s 14 need not be carried out (per Lynskey J in *Smith
v Morris Motors Ltd* [1949] 2 All ER 715 at p 718).
Looking at ss 14 and 16 together, it was submitted, it
is clear that the reference in s 16 to "motion or use"
simply defines the extent of the duty imposed under
s 14. In that situation it was for the pursuer, in
presenting his case under s 14, to take cognisance of
the limit imposed by s 16, and it was not for the
defenders to pray that limit in aid in their pleadings.
B Consequently, even though the averments relating to
motion or use and to s 16 had been withdrawn from
the incidental application, and thus did not figure in
the defenders' pleadings, the sheriff had been fully
entitled to consider the evidence as to motion or use
and to consider whether the extent of the duty under
s 14 had been restricted by virtue of the provisions of
s 16.

In concluding that he could properly take account of
C s 16, notwithstanding that there were no averments by
the defenders directed to the applicability of that
section, the sheriff appears to have proceeded on the
basis contended for by the solicitor for the defenders,
namely that, at least in its first part, the section does
no more than to define the extent of the duty imposed
under s 14. For that reason he concluded that he was
entitled to have regard to s 16 even in the absence of
averments relating to it.

As the sheriff says, the difficulty with s 16 is that,
D within a single section, it does at least two things in
that it defines the extent of the duty under s 14 while
at the same time providing an exception to that duty.
In that regard my decision in the present case has not
been made easier by the fact that, very properly and
very frankly, the solicitors on both sides each made
certain concessions with regard to the section. The
solicitor for the pursuer conceded that, in the context
of this part of the 1961 Act, s 14 might well have been
prefaced by the words "Subject to section 16 of this
Act", and that, had that been so, he would have had
E difficulty in advancing any submissions against the
sheriff's judgment. Equally, the solicitor for the
defenders conceded that, had he been seeking to
invoke the latter part of s 16 which provides an exception where dangerous parts are necessarily exposed for
certain purposes, he would have been obliged by our
rules of pleading and fair notice to make specific averments to that effect.

It therefore appears that the issue in the present case
falls somewhere in the middle between these two posi-
F tions. I have not found it easy to reach a decision on
that issue, not least because there does not appear to
be any authority in point. The solicitors for the parties
referred me to several cases, both English and Scottish, where consideration has been given to the terms
of s 16. However, none of these cases was concerned
with questions of pleading and fair notice and, indeed,
in most of them it is impossible to tell from the reports
whether s 16 was put in issue by the pursuer (plaintiff)
or by the defenders (defendants).

On balance, however, I have come to the conclusion

that the view contended for by the solicitor for the
defenders is to be preferred to that contended for by G
the solicitor for the pursuer. That is to say, in my
opinion the provision in s 16 relating to "in motion or
use" properly falls to be regarded as a limitation on
the scope and extent of the duty imposed under s 14
and, as such, is something of which cognisance ought
to be taken by any pursuer who is seeking to assert that
there has been a breach of s 14. In reaching that conclusion I am conscious that a different approach has
been taken upon the highest authority in relation to
reasonable practicability (*Nimmo v Alexander Cowan
& Sons*, 1967 SLT 277; 1967 SC (HL) 79). However, H
I consider that that case can be distinguished from the
present one on two grounds. First, it was concerned
with onus of proof rather than with questions of pleading and fair notice. Admittedly, that may be a fine distinction. But, secondly, and more importantly in my
view, the majority decision in *Nimmo* was reached
largely upon a consideration of the respective means of
knowledge and spheres of responsibility of the parties;
and it was largely upon that basis that it was decided
that it was for the defenders to aver and prove that a I
working place had been made as safe as was reasonably
practicable. In my opinion the question whether a part
of a machine was in motion or use at the time of an
accident is in a very different category. That is a
simple question of fact regarding which a pursuer will
normally be in as good a position as a defender to
provide an answer, and for that reason I do not consider that the decision in the present case need necessarily be influenced by the decision in *Nimmo*.

On the whole matter I am of opinion that ss 14 and J
16 (at least insofar as the latter section deals with
motion or use) ought properly to be regarded as
together defining the nature and extent of the duty
which is primarily imposed under s 14. That approach
appears to me to have the general support of the
House of Lords in the case of *Callow* and of the
English Court of Appeal in *Smith*. Furthermore, it is
an approach which appears to me to be consistent with
the manner in which the two sections are framed, and
in particular with the fact that s 16 begins by expressly K
referring back to the earlier provisions (including s 14)
of that Part of the Act. For those reasons, therefore,
I consider that in the present case the sheriff was
entitled to take account of s 16 in reaching his
decision, and to hold that the pursuer must fail on
account of the fact that, at the material time, the
blades of the machine were not in motion or use.

On the whole matter, accordingly, I have answered
the first question in the stated case in the negative and
I have refused the appeal. As noted earlier, it is L
unnecessary for me to answer the second question in
the stated case. On the matter of expenses it was
agreed that the expenses of the appeal should follow
success, and I have therefore awarded them in favour
of the defenders.

---

*Solicitors for Pursuer, Robin Thompson & Partners —
Solicitors for Defenders, McClure, Naismith, Anderson
& Gardiner.*

MacRitchie v MacRitchie

A SHERIFF COURT OF GRAMPIAN,
HIGHLAND AND ISLANDS AT STORNOWAY
SHERIFF PRINCIPAL D J RISK, QC
31 JANUARY 1994

Husband and wife — Divorce — Financial provision — Capital sum — Meaning of "matrimonial property" — Refund of income tax after relevant date — Family Law (Scotland) Act 1985 (c 37), s 10 (4).

B   In an action of divorce the wife pursuer sought a capital sum which was directed against a refund of income tax overpaid by the defender and attributable to the period before but received after the relevant date. The sheriff held that the claim for a refund was not matrimonial property. The pursuer appealed to the sheriff principal.

Held, that the proper test was whether at the relevant date the defender had a right to the money which C he ultimately received, and as he had, the outstanding claim against the Inland Revenue was matrimonial property (p 73G-H); and appeal *allowed.*

Action of divorce

Lynn Hyslop Paterson or MacRitchie raised an action of divorce against Colin MacRitchie and claimed payment of a capital sum. The sheriff (D Booker-Milburn) held that a tax refund paid to the D defender after the relevant date was not matrimonial property. The pursuer appealed to the sheriff principal.

On 31 January 1994 the sheriff principal *allowed* the appeal and *awarded* the pursuer a capital sum of £1,500.

THE SHERIFF PRINCIPAL (D J RISK, QC).—
This is an action of divorce in which the pursuer E sought custody of the children of the marriage together with awards of aliment, periodical allowance and capital payment. The defender lodged a rule 34 minute challenging the amounts of the sums craved. After a hearing at which evidence was led the sheriff made awards of aliment and periodical allowance which have not been challenged. He refused the crave for a capital payment. The pursuer has appealed against that refusal.

F   Parties were agreed that "the relevant date" for the purposes of s 10 (3) of the Family Law (Scotland) Act 1985 was 30 October 1990. The pursuer's claim for a capital sum was directed against a refund of overpaid tax amounting to £4,156.81 which was received by the defender on or about 17 December 1992, i e more than two years after the relevant date. The refund related to overpayments in the tax years 1986-87, 1987-88, 1988-89, 1989-90 and 1990-91. Parties were agreed that out of the total sum refunded £3,000 could be regarded as attributable to overpayments prior to the relevant date. It was also agreed that if that sum was regarded as matrimonial property the pursuer was entitled to one half thereof.

G   The matter which was in dispute was whether the portion of the tax refund attributable to the period prior to the relevant date fell within the definition of "the matrimonial property" set out in s 10 (4) of the 1985 Act. The sheriff held that it did not. In his note he said: "What has been proved is that the defender received certain tax rebates in respect of the tax years (1986-1991) amounting in total to £4,157.81. Notification was dated 17.12.92. It would appear that this H payment is in respect of tax deducted from the defender's income during these years which, once the defender got round to his tax returns, turned out to be overdeductions. The payment is *income* and was not received until well after the relevant date. In my opinion it does not form part of the matrimonial property at the relevant date".

The pursuer's agent submitted that the tax refund was merely the postponed payment of money which I the defender had earned prior to the relevant date. Had the defender received the money when he earned it, it would undoubtedly have formed part of the matrimonial property. If it ceased to be matrimonial property simply because payment did not take place until after the relevant date there would be a loophole in the law: an unscrupulous spouse who foresaw the breakdown of his marriage could deliberately arrange his affairs in such a way as to make overpayments of tax prior to the relevant date and thus defeat or reduce any claim against him for capital payment. The situa- J tion was analogous to cases in which a spouse had received damages after the relevant date in respect of injuries sustained prior to the relevant date: *Petrie v Petrie*, 1988 SCLR 390 (Sh Ct); *Skarpaas v Skarpaas*, 1991 SLT (Sh Ct) 15.

The defender's solicitor submitted that had tax not been overpaid the money would have come to the defender over a period of years as part of his income and in all probability would have been spent by the K relevant date. Unless it could be assumed that the money would have been saved it could not be treated as matrimonial property for the purpose of awarding a capital sum.

It does not appear from the learned sheriff's note that he was referred to any cases or indeed that he was asked to consider in any detail the provisions of s 10 of the 1985 Act. His observation that the tax repayment constituted income in the hands of the defender and that it was received after the relevant date is L accurate, but, with respect, it does not answer the question of whether it constituted matrimonial property. Section 10 (4) of the Family Law (Scotland) Act 1985 provides: "Subject to subsection (5) below, in this section . . . of this Act 'the matrimonial property' means all the property belonging to the parties or either of them at the relevant date which was acquired by them or him (otherwise than by way of gift or succession from a third party) . . . (b) during the marriage but before the relevant date."

That definition is apt to cover heritable property,
corporeal moveable property and cash. Once gift and
succession have been excluded, in the majority of cases
matrimonial property is derived from the income of
the parties or one or other of them. If income has been
saved and then used to purchase a motor car there is
no doubt that the car is part of the matrimonial
property. If the relevant date occurred while the
money was still being saved and before a purchase was
possible there would be no logic or justice in holding
that the money was not matrimonial property.
Stripping the matter down to its barest essentials, it
seems to me that if at the relevant date a spouse has
an unopened pay packet in his pocket its contents fall
within the description of property belonging to that
spouse acquired by him during the marriage but
before the relevant date. It is accordingly matrimonial
property as well as being his income for the week.

As well as items which have a physical existence, the
definition in s 10 (4) extends to such property as sums
deposited with banks. In such a situation the spouse
does not have physical possession of the money and
the bank does not have identifiable banknotes
attributed to the individual account. The spouse's
property consists of the right to require the bank to
pay the appropriate sum on demand or at the expiry
of a contractual period of notice. The same principle
would apply to money lent by one of the spouses to a
third party. A right to payment which exists at the
relevant date is matrimonial property even if payment
is not demanded or made until after the relevant date.

There are other indications in s 10 of the 1985 Act
that in identifying the matrimonial property the court
has to look beyond what is in the actual possession of
the spouses at the relevant date. Section 10 (2) provides inter alia: "The net value of the matrimonial
property shall be the value of the property at the relevant date after deduction of any debts incurred by the
parties or either of them . . . which are outstanding
at that date."

In other words there has to be a balancing of
accounts with the parties' creditors before the matrimonial property available for division is identified. If,
for example, at the relevant date a spouse had money
upon which he was liable to pay income tax but upon
which he had not yet paid that tax, the sum due to the
Inland Revenue would have to be deducted before the
amount of the matrimonial property was known.
Section 10 (5) goes on to provide that the interests of
parties in life assurance policies and pension schemes
form part of the matrimonial property. Life policies
and pension policies may have a surrender value but
it is well established that for the purposes of the
Family Law (Scotland) Act 1985 that is not the basis
upon which they are valued: actuarial calculations are
used to give a capital value to a benefit which cannot
be claimed until some time in the future and which in
some cases may never produce a capital sum.

Reverting to the present case I consider that the
sheriff erred in holding that the fact that the money
paid by the Inland Revenue was the defender's income

prevented it from being matrimonial property and that
in looking to the date upon which it was actually paid
he applied the wrong test. The proper question is
whether at the relevant date the defender had a right
to the money which he ultimately received. In my
opinion he had. It was money which he had earned.
He was liable to pay income tax but, because he had
failed to make tax returns, the Inland Revenue
deducted tax at an excessive rate. In effect the
defender was making a compulsory, interest free
investment in the Inland Revenue. All that he had to
do in order to realise his "investment" was to submit
the relevant returns. Once he had done that the
application of the relevant tax statutes to the figures
produced the sum due by way of repayment. Just as
the defender would have been entitled to deduct from
the matrimonial property an outstanding claim by the
Inland Revenue, so it seems to me he must add in to
the matrimonial property a valid outstanding claim by
him against the Inland Revenue.

I have reached my decision principally upon a consideration of the terms of s 10 of the 1985 Act. So far
as there is any assistance to be derived from the cases
on damages they seem to me to support the view
which I have reached. *Petrie v Petrie* is in fact of no
assistance since the sheriff (who happened to be
myself) successfully avoided the question which arises
in this case. In *Skarpaas v Skarpaas*, the defender sustained an accident after the marriage but before the
relevant date in respect of which he was awarded
damages after the relevant date. Of this the sheriff said
(at 1991 SLT (Sh Ct), p 18H): "I consider that the
first question to be answered is whether the defender's
award of damages, or any part thereof, is 'matrimonial
property' at all. In my opinion a substantial proportion of the award is indeed matrimonial property.
The accident occurred during the course of the
marriage and it gave rise to a claim for damages. A
claim for damages is itself an asset which may be
assigned. . . . Although the claim was not quantified
until after the relevant date and payment was not
made until later still, I am satisfied that the claim itself
is matrimonial property".

The defender appealed to the sheriff principal who
adhered to the view of the sheriff on that point, saying
(at p 20F): "the solicitor for the defender argued that
from the date of the accident the defender had an
assignable claim to damages but that that claim had no
value until it was either settled or decree was granted.
There was a potential asset only, which might even
turn out to be a liability in the event of the defender
losing his action and becoming liable in expenses. At
the relevant date there was only a possibility of
damages which was not then capable of valuation. On
this point I agree with the sheriff's reasoning when he
holds that the claim itself was matrimonial property
although not quantified until after the relevant date. It
cannot be said that prior to the relevant date the claim
necessarily had no value at all, and no doubt a
potential assignee after considering the available evidence would have been prepared to make him an offer
for it. I therefore reject this first argument".

The case was subsequently appealed to the Court of Session (1993 SLT 343) but by that stage the defender had conceded the claim for damages did form part of the matrimonial property. It seems to me that what was said by the sheriff and sheriff principal in *Skarpaas*, supra, with regard to a claim for damages, which is full of uncertainties regarding both liability and quantification, applies if anything more strongly to a claim for repayment of overpaid tax where the amount of tax due is fixed by statute and the refund of overpayment automatically follows the submission of a proper tax return. The point of similarity is that both the claim for damages and the claim for refund of overpaid tax were valuable rights which came into existence before the relevant date but which were not converted into money until after that date. In each case, in my view, the claim is matrimonial property.

For the foregoing reasons I have allowed the appeal and awarded to the pursuer the agreed capital sum of £1,500. It was agreed that the expenses of the appeal should follow success but that the loser should be found liable as an assisted person. I have so ordered.

Solicitors for Pursuer and Appellant, Allen & Co, Inverness — Solicitors for Defender and Respondent, MacDonald, MacIver & Co, Stornoway.

Murie McDougall Ltd v Sinclair

SHERIFF COURT OF NORTH STRATHCLYDE AT DUMBARTON

SHERIFF J T FITZSIMONS

13 JUNE 1994

Loan — Consumer credit — Application for time order to reduce monthly payments due in respect of regulated agreement — Whether power to make order restricted to arrears — Whether just to make time order — Whether power to vary contractual interest rate — Consumer Credit Act 1974 (c 39), ss 129 and 136.

Section 129 of the Consumer Credit Act 1974 permits the court, "if it appears to the court just to do so", to make a "time order" providing for the payment of "any sum owed . . . by such instalments, payable at such times, as the court . . . considers reasonable". By s 136 the court may include in an order made by it under the Act "such provision as it considers just for amending any agreement or security in consequence of a term of the order".

After the debtor under a credit agreement ceased to make payments the creditor served a default notice and, the debtor having granted a standard security over property, raised an action of declarator and ejec-

tion. The debtor applied for a time order under s 129 of the Consumer Credit Act 1974. The creditor questioned the competency of the application, the debtor having failed to respond to a notice of default served in relation to the standard security. The debtor claimed to have £163 per month free after meeting other commitments and sought a time order substituting £160 per month for the contractual instalments of £60 per week. Such instalments, given the contractual rate of interest of 27.1 per cent APR, would have taken over 40 years to pay off the loan. The debtor sought a further order under s 136 reducing the interest rate to 10.95 per cent, which he claimed was the average rate charged by High Street banks at the relevant time. The loan would then have taken 13 years to pay off as against the original four.

Held, (1) that the court had a wide discretionary power under s 129 and there were no time limits on applications for the exercise of such powers, and the application was therefore competent (pp 76L-77B); (2) that the pursuers having demanded payment of the whole sum due under the agreement, it was open to the court to treat that sum as "any sum owed" in terms of s 129 (p 79K-L); (3) that the repayment period which would be required by granting the application could not be regarded as just since the creditor would have to wait for payment of the debt for an inordinate period and the agreement might have extended beyond the debtor's lifetime (p 80E-F); (4) that s 136 could only come into play when a time order was made and could not be used to make a just order where one could not otherwise exist (p 80F-H); (5) that neither singly nor in combination did s 129 or s 136 give the court power to vary the contractual interest rate (pp 80L-81D); and application *refused.*

Opinion, (1) that the terms of s 129 (1) permitted a court to make a time order without the necessity of a specific application from the debtor (p 77A); and (2) that as the pursuers specialised in high risk lending, undertaking risks which banks would not, it would not have been just to reduce the interest rate to the figure contended for as the average rate of interest being charged by banks (p 81F and I).

Action of declarator and ejection

Murie McDougall Ltd raised an action of declarator and ejection against John Sinclair. The defender applied for a time order under s 129 of the Consumer Credit Act 1974. The case came before the sheriff for a hearing.

On 13 June 1994 the sheriff *refused* the application.

THE SHERIFF (J T FITZSIMONS).—This interlocutor relates to an application by the defender during the progress of an action raised by the pursuers under the Conveyancing and Feudal Reform (Scotland) Act 1970 (hereinafter referred to as the 1970 Act). In the action the pursuers seek declarator that the defender is in default in respect of payments due

in terms of a standard security by him in favour of the
A pursuers dated 21 May 1992 and recorded in the Land
Register of Scotland on 25 May 1992. The heritable
property concerned is situated at 18 Langfaulds Crescent, Faifley, within the jurisdiction of this court, and
the pursuers seek a declarator that they are entitled to
enter into possession of the said subjects, and an order
ordaining the defender to vacate. The standard security is stated to have been granted in respect of a sum
of money advanced to the defender by the pursuers in
terms of a credit agreement, and the balance outstanding as at the date of raising of the action is stated
B to be £11,820.39.

The cause tabled on 15 April 1993, and was thereafter sisted for legal aid purposes. The sist was recalled
on 12 August 1993, and defences ordered. On 9
November 1993 the defender lodged the present application. Following upon sundry procedure the application called before me for a hearing on 11 February
1994. Unfortunately due to pressure of court business
the hearing required to be continued over a number of
C days, and submissions were not completed until 16
May 1994.

It is not in dispute that the pursuers and the
defender entered into a credit agreement regulated by
the Consumer Credit Act 1974 (hereinafter referred to
as the 1974 Act). In terms of the agreement dated 21
May 1992, the defender agreed to repay to the pursuers the total sum of £12,480.00 (being an advance of
£8,000.00, plus interest of £4,480.00) over a period of
208 weeks at the rate of £60.00 per week. The interest
D rate was fixed at 27.1 per cent APR (annual percentage
rate), and the same rate of interest applies to arrears.
In terms of cl 3 of the agreement the pursuers are
entitled to demand earlier repayment of the balance of
the loan in the event, inter alia, of any amount payable
being overdue for more than 14 days. Earlier payment
may be demanded by the service on the defender of a
default notice in terms of the 1974 Act, and failure to
comply with the terms of the notice results in the
whole of the remaining balance becoming payable
E immediately.

Also on 21 May 1992 the defender granted a standard security over his property at 18 Langfaulds Crescent, Faifley, in favour of the pursuers "in security of
all monies due by the Borrower to the Lender now or
at any future time under any agreement between
them". The said standard security was registered on
25 May 1992, subject to a prior charge relating to a
standard security in favour of the National Home
Loans Corporation plc, registered on 11 June 1991
F (the first mortgage).

The defender maintained the payments initially, but
by September 1992 he was in arrears and penalty
interest was being applied. No payments have been
made since 28 October 1992. Following upon correspondence with the Citizens' Advice Bureau, acting on
behalf of the defender, the pursuers served a default
notice under s 87 (1) of the 1974 Act, dated 17
December 1992. The notice required the defender to
bring payments up to date together with penalty
interest by 28 December 1992, failing which the pur-

suers intended inter alia to demand earlier payment of
the sum of £8,753.83 (allowing for a rebate) by 31 G
December 1992. No action was taken by the defender
and on 13 January 1993 the pursuers' solicitors wrote
to the defender intimating that unless the outstanding
balance of £11,820.39 was paid within 10 days an
action of ejection would be raised. On 19 January 1993
the pursuers' solicitors served a notice of default on
the defender under the 1970 Act.

It is my understanding that the above matters were
not in dispute. In the defences to the action the
defender takes issue with alleged defects in the setting H
up of the credit agreement and the standard security.
In addition the solicitor for the defender in submissions on the application referred to certain alleged
ambiguities relating to the content of the notices
served on the defender under the 1970 and 1974 Acts.
For the most part, however, these matters were not
germane to the issue before me, and for the purposes
of the present application it was accepted that the
various documents were in proper form, and that the
notices had been properly served.   I

The solicitor for the defender went on to explain
that the defender had taken out the loan to repay existing debts. He had responded to an advertisement
offering a loan designed to consolidate outstanding
debts, and had made an error of judgment in not
approaching his existing lender. At the time of the
agreement he had been employed as a taxi driver, but
had been made redundant around July 1992. Thereafter he was reliant upon state benefit in the form of
income support plus payment of the interest on his J
first mortgage only. He had managed to maintain payments on the present agreement until around September 1992, but found that he could not afford to
keep up the commitment apart from two further payments in October. The defender's financial position
improved however when he became a self employed
taxi driver in May 1993, with a gross monthly income
of around £1,200.00. I was informed that the
defender, a single man with no family, after deduction
of tax, national insurance and all other essential out- K
goings including his first mortgage now had a net dis-
posable income of £163.00 per month. He was willing
to pay £160.00 per month to the pursuers in respect
of the present agreement. A schedule giving the
detailed figures of average monthly income and expenditure was produced. The pursuers did not dispute the
figures.

These are the circumstances in which the present
application has been brought. In terms of the applica- L
tion the defender asks the court to make a time order
under s 129 of the 1974 Act reducing the monthly
payments due in respect of the regulated agreement to
£160.00 per calendar month. In addition the defender
applies for an order under s 136 of the said Act to
reduce the interest rate chargeable from an annual percentage rate of 27.1 per cent to 10.95 per cent. In the
course of submissions I allowed the defender, there
being no objection, to amend the crave of the application by insertion of a reference to s 127 of the 1974
Act. However at the conclusion of the hearing the soli-

citor for the defender intimated that he was not at this
stage of the action seeking any order in terms of s 127.

Competency of the application

At the outset of the hearing the solicitor for the
pursuer raised a question regarding the competency of
the application. He pointed out that the pursuers had
raised the present action on the basis of a notice of
default served on the defender in terms of s 21 of the
1970 Act. Once such a notice had been served the
defender, as debtor, was entitled under s 22 to object
to the notice by way of application to the court, if he
considered himself aggrieved by any requirement of
the notice. However s 22 (1) required that any such
application be made within 14 days of service of the
notice. If such an application had been made the pursuers would have been entitled to make a counter
application seeking any of the remedies conferred on
them as creditors by the 1970 Act. The court would
then have had power to set aside the notice, in whole
or in part, or vary or uphold it, or to grant any remedy
to the pursuers as craved in the counter application.
Thus the court would have been in a position to deal
with the matter within a fairly short time span, due to
the initial time limit imposed.

The solicitor for the pursuers recognised that the
present application by the defender had been made
under the 1974 Act, not the 1970 Act. Nevertheless,
he submitted, the two Acts should be read together
and the 1974 Act should not be regarded as overriding
the time limit imposed by the 1970 Act for submission
of applications following upon service of a notice of
default. It was not disputed that the present application came well outside that time limit, and it should
therefore be dismissed as incompetent.

In reply, the solicitor for the defender stressed that
the pursuers had served two notices on the defender
in the present case: a default notice under the 1974
Act dated 17 December 1992, and a notice of default
under the 1970 Act, dated 19 January 1993. It was
accepted that the defender had not responded to the
latter notice, quite simply because he did not
challenge the terms of that notice. The defender did
not dispute that he was in default under the standard
security, nor does he now dispute the sum claimed by
the pursuers as being outstanding. The present
application was not therefore made under s 22 of the
1970 Act, but was an application under s 129 of the
1974 Act.

Section 129 provides:

"129.—(1) Subject to subsection (3) below, if it
appears to the court just to do so — (a) on an application for an enforcement order; or (b) on an application
made by a debtor or hirer under this paragraph after
service on him of — (i) a default notice, or (ii) a notice
under section 76 (1) or 98 (1); or (c) in an action
brought by a creditor or owner to enforce a regulated
agreement or any security, or recover possession of
any goods or land to which a regulated agreement
relates, the court may make an order under this section
(a 'time order').

"(2) A time order shall provide for one or both of the
following, as the court considers just — (a) the
payment by the debtor or hirer or any surety of any
sum owed under a regulated agreement or a security
by such instalments, payable at such times, as the
court, having regard to the means of the debtor or
hirer and any surety, considers reasonable; (b) the
remedying by the debtor or hirer of any breach of a
regulated agreement (other than non-payment of
money) within such period as the court may specify.

"(3) Where in Scotland a time to pay direction or a
time to pay order has been made in relation to a debt,
it shall not thereafter be competent to make a time
order in relation to the same debt."

Having regard to those provisions, submitted the
defender's solicitor, the application was competent, in
that it was an application under s 129 (1) (c) made in
an action which had been brought by the pursuers, as
creditors, to enforce a regulated agreement secured by
a standard security over the defender's home. The
court was therefore empowered to make a time order
under subs (1). In the present application the defender
invited the court to do so, and to make provision under
subs (2) (a) for the payment of all the sums outstanding
by reasonable instalments other than those provided
for in the agreement. No time limits for the making of
such applications were specified in the 1974 Act, and
the unqualified nature of the words "in an action"
indicated that a time order could be applied for at any
point during the progress of a cause.

Neither the 1974 Act nor the sheriff court rules
make provision for specific procedures regarding
applications for time orders. However by way of
guidance the solicitor for the defender referred me to
a letter from the secretary of the Sheriff Court Rules
Council published in SCOLAG, May 1991, Issue
no 176. The letter in question expresses the view that
an application for a time order may be made by motion
in the course of an ordinary cause, by way of summary
application where no cause has been raised, or by
application post-decree provided no time to pay direction or time to pay order has previously been made (cf
subs (3)).

I find myself in full agreement with the observations
in the said letter, and in my view the solicitor for the
defender's submission is well founded. Section 129 of
the 1974 Act serves in my view a much wider purpose
than s 22 of the 1970 Act. The latter section allows the
debtor to object to the notice of default within a specified time limit. Thus he can mount a challenge to the
notice, and in the course of dealing with the challenge
the court may inter alia vary the notice. Section 129
is much wider in scope, and does not require the
debtor to challenge the terms of any notice or to
contest the sums claimed by the creditor as owing.
The use of the words "just" and "reasonable"
throughout the section makes it clear that the court is
being given a wide discretionary power to allow
payment of any sum owed by reasonable instalments.
The debtor may well, as in the present case, accept
fully that he is in default, yet invite the court to exer-

cise the discretionary power in order to alleviate his current financially straitened circumstances. Time limits on applications for the exercise of such powers would in my view be inimical to the concept inherent in s 129. Indeed it seems to me that the very wide terms of subs (1) (a) and (c), when compared with subs (1) (b), indicate that the court may in cases such as the present make a time order without the necessity of a specific application from the debtor.

I am in no doubt that the time limit referred to in s 22 of the 1970 Act has no relevance to the application before me under the 1974 Act. It is not in dispute that the present action falls within the terms of s 129 (1) (c), and the court is being invited to make a time order of the type envisaged by subs (2) (a). In those circumstances the application is competently before the court by motion during the progress of the action.

Merits of the application

Turning to the merits of the application, the solicitor for the defender submitted that in view of the defender's current financial position he could not reasonably be expected, as was conceded by the pursuers, to pay any more than £160.00 by way of monthly instalments. Indeed this was the sum the defender was offering to pay despite his having only £163.00 per month surplus after covering all his essential commitments including his first mortgage. Section 129 (2) (a) required the court to have regard to the means of the debtor, and the defender was therefore in his current situation asking the court to make a time order substituting instalments of £160.00 per month for the contractual instalments of £60.00 per week.

On the other hand the solicitor for the defender recognised that s 129 did not empower the court to vary the contractual rate of interest, and that at the contractual rate of 27.1 per cent by far the greatest proportion of the monthly payment of £160.00 would go towards interest. In those circumstances it would take an inordinate length of time for the debt to be paid off, exceeding 40 years and very probably not in the debtor's lifetime. The solicitor for the defender readily conceded that it would be unjust and unreasonable for the pursuers to be required to wait for such an inordinate length of time for full repayment of the debt. It could not therefore be regarded as just for the court to make a time order in respect of the moneys outstanding at the instalments requested, were that time order to stand on its own.

However, submitted the solicitor for the defender, the time order need not stand on its own, because the court was given further powers by s 136 of the 1974 Act to amend any agreement in consequence of a term of a time order.

Section 136 provides:

"136. The court may in an order made by it under this Act include such provision as it considers just for amending any agreement or security in consequence of a term of the order."

This section, argued the solicitor for the defender,

gave very wide power to vary a regulated agreement provided the variation was in consequence of a time order. In the present case, the defender sought such an order under s 136 to vary the agreement by substituting an APR of 10.95 per cent for the contractual rate of 27.1 per cent. If such an order were made, the outstanding debt would be paid off at £160.00 per month over a period of around 10.5 years beyond the contractual term of four years. In the context of a second mortgage, such periods for repayment were not unknown and not unreasonable.

The solicitor for the defender went on to indicate that the figure for APR of 10.95 per cent was being suggested because it represented the general level of interest rates which would have been charged by reputable banks on a second mortgage at around the time of the present agreement. In support of this contention he referred to three letters from well known banks in answer to a query by him as to the interest rate applicable in May 1992 on a second mortgage of £8,000.00 repayable over four years, and secured over a house in which the equity was well in excess of the amount being borrowed. The Bank of Scotland indicated that their rate of interest would have been 10.69 per cent as of May 1992, provided they held the initial mortgage. Clydesdale Bank indicated that their APR would have been 10.95 per cent at that time. The TSB Bank could not supply figures for APR but indicated that the variable interest rate for mortgages would have been 10.65 per cent.

These letters indicated, in the solicitor's submission, that the contractual rate of interest in the present case was nearly three times the average interest rate applying at the time. He was well aware that the pursuers, in search of their own funding, did not have access to the same financial markets as banks, and were justified in charging higher rates of interest in view of the higher risk involved. However in the present case the risk was diminished by the security on the defender's home, and it was reasonable that a rate of interest reflecting the average figure current at the time should now be substituted for the figure in the agreement.

The solicitor for the defender turned next, in anticipation of the pursuers' submissions, to the interpretation of the words "any sum owed" in s 129 (2) (a). In this context he referred me to a number of English cases dealing with the question as to whether the words in question restrict the powers available under s 129 to arrears actually owed by the debtor at the time of the application. Such a restrictive interpretation would, it was conceded, prevent the court from using s 136 to vary the interest rate applying to the agreement. The absurd situation would then arise in which the court might consider a time order to be justified, but if it were restricted to arrears the defender would in order to avoid repossession require to pay substantially increased monthly instalments in the form of payments towards the arrears in addition to the contractual monthly payments. Such a scenario was against the spirit of the legislation, and was easily obviated by a proper interpretation of the words "any

A   sum owed". Those words meant the total amount outstanding, not only arrears but principal and contractual interest and penalty interest past and future. In support of his argument the solicitor prayed in aid the case of *Jenkins v Cedar Holdings Ltd*, Sheffield county court, 10 August 1987, unreported, in which HH Judge Cotton on appeal took the view that the powers in ss 129 and 136 were wide enough to allow the registrar to vary instalments and reduce the rate of interest in the agreement between the parties. The solicitor for the defender also relied upon the final

B   paragraph of Dillon LJ's judgment in *First National Bank plc v Syed* [1991] 2 All ER 250, in which he said: "Moreover the remedy of a time order under the section would seem to be directed at rescheduling the whole of the indebtedness under the regulated agreement, the principal which has become presently payable as a result of default as well as the arrears and current interest".

  I was also referred to a number of cases which had taken a similar approach: *Cedar Holdings Ltd v*
C   *Thompson* [1993] CCLR 7; *Cedar Holdings Ltd v Aguinaldo*, Bow county court, 25 March 1992, unreported; *Wimbledon and South Western Finance plc v Winning*, Oxford county court, 19 June 1992, unreported; and *Premier Portfolio Ltd v Morris*, Bradford county court, 11 June 1993, unreported.

  The solicitor for the defender also very properly referred me to a case which was against him, namely *Ashbroom Facilities Ltd v Bodley* [1992] CCLR 31, in
D   which HH Judge Wooton held that a time order must refer to sums actually owing, that is arrears, at the time the matter came before the registrar. The only power was to make an instalment order relating to those arrears, and s 136 provided no authority for the rewriting of the agreement in such circumstances. Not surprisingly I was invited not to follow that reasoning, and to hold that s 136 was indeed available to vary the contractual rate of interest. That course would be justified in the present case, because the debtor was
E   now in a position to make sizeable payments and to pay the debt within a reasonable time if the interest rate was reduced to a reasonable level. If the defender was not given this opportunity he would be rendered homeless. He was single, had no relatives, and the local authority would have no duty to provide housing since he was single and not in priority need. The defender had suffered bad luck and had made ill advised decisions, but the court was in a position to do justice to him by allowing him to retain his home while at the same time ensuring that the pursuers
F   received an adequate return on their money. The situation the defender now found himself in was just the type of situation envisaged by s 129, and the purpose of s 136 was to provide an overriding power to a court which considered a time order to be justified, to take such further action as it considered just to amend the agreement between the parties in order to give effect to the time order.

  In his reply on behalf of the pursuers their solicitor also referred me to a number of English cases. In addi-

tion to *Ashbroom Facilities Ltd v Bodley*, he relied on two cases in particular, namely *First National Bank plc* G *v Colman*, Leicester county court, 6 October 1992, unreported and *First National Bank plc v Holgate*, Nelson county court, 30 October 1989, unreported. *Colman* stressed the requirement to have regard to the interests of both creditor and debtor, and held that s 129 was designed to allow the court to go no further than allowing the debtor more time to pay. In *Holgate* the registrar specifically refused to follow *Jenkins v Cedar Holdings* and rejected the proposition that s 136 allowed the court to rewrite an agreement with respect H to contractual interest. The same view was taken in *First National Bank plc v Shah and Fatima*, Rochdale county court, 21 May 1993, unreported, in which the court endorsed the commentary on s 136 by the editors of Goode on *Consumer Credit Legislation*, at para 280-1. This commentary and the line of cases made it clear, submitted the pursuers' solicitor, that what the defender in the present case was asking the court to do was not within the scope of s 129 or 136. He was not merely seeking relief in respect of pay- I ments due, but was asking the court to rewrite the agreement with the effect that the original four year agreement would continue for around 13 years, and at an unreasonably reduced rate of interest.

  The solicitor for the pursuers invited me to take the view that s 129 was intended to deal with the situation where there has been a build up of arrears, and the debtor seeks relief in that respect. The court may then provide that relief through a time order, by allowing payment of the arrears by reasonable instalments J running alongside the contractual payments. Alternatively the court might take the view that s 129 was not restricted to arrears. In that event the court would have power to regulate the amount and method of instalment payments in respect of the total sums outstanding, and s 136 could be used to extend the contractual period in consequence. It was going too far however to interpret s 136 as giving the court power to vary fundamental terms such as the agreed rate of interest under the agreement. This was particularly so K since s 137 provided the court with a very wide power to reopen any credit agreement it found to be extortionate "so as to do justice between the parties", a power which the defender was not seeking to invoke, at this stage in the action at any rate. The power under s 136 must be viewed as merely an ancillary power to the powers contained in inter alia s 129, and did not provide the court with an unfettered discretion to rewrite agreements.

  In the event that I was not with him on the inter- L pretation of the legislation, the solicitor for the pursuers turned to the question of whether it would be just and reasonable to grant the orders sought. It was accepted that the defender could not reasonably be expected to pay more than the amount offered in view of his means. However justice had to be maintained between the parties, and it was entirely unjust to expect the pursuers to wait for around 13 years for their return on an agreement with an original four year span and in the end of the day also to receive a much

A reduced return. The solicitor for the defender had produced letters regarding interest rates from three banks, only one of which referred to an APR. The pursuers were not prepared to accept these figures as indicating an average APR of 10.95 per cent at the time of the agreement. The solicitor for the pursuers suggested that the figure was more likely to have been around 15 per cent, although he produced no evidence in support.

B Moreover, the pursuers' solicitor argued, the defender in producing such figures was not comparing like with like. If he had wished to obtain a loan based on bank rates, he could have approached a bank. He did not do so because he was aware that he was a high risk, and was consolidating other outstanding debts. Instead he sought a loan from the pursuers, who are lenders specialising in lending to high risk individuals. The solicitor described the pursuers as "lenders of last resort" for borrowers who are normally unable to obtain funds from other sources such as banks or building societies, or from what the solicitor referred

C to as "secondary tier lenders" such as First National Bank. The pursuers obtained their funds through brokers, and were required to fulfil their obligations to their sources of finance. The maintenance of those obligations was geared to their receiving the return through the expected payments coming from agreements such as that negotiated with the defender. The pursuers were engaged in high risk lending, and the rate of interest reflected that risk, the type of risk which banks would not contemplate. The defender

D had entered into the agreement freely, and it had not been shown in the present proceedings that it would be just to allow him to have that agreement rewritten for his benefit alone.

Conclusion

I am grateful to both solicitors for their very careful submissions, and full reference to English case law dealing with the interpretation of the statutory provisions. My own researches have confirmed the

E absence of any reported Scottish authority on the matter. The English cases referred to cannot be regarded as authoritative in any way, the majority having been decided at county court or district judge level, and are not in any event binding on me. *First National Bank plc v Seyd* was decided at Court of Appeal level, but the case was not concerned at all with the crucial issue in the present case, namely the construction of s 136 and its relationship with s 129. The passage referred to by the solicitor for the

F defender would appear to be no more than an obiter remark, but insofar as it indicates that s 129 is not necessarily restricted to arrears, and that it allows for rescheduling of payments I entirely agree, as will be explained below. However if the passage is intended to indicate that s 129 in itself contains the power to open up and rewrite an agreement, with regard for instance to the contractual interest rate, then I respectfully disagree.

I do not propose to rehearse the cases in detail, nor do I consider that anything is to be gained by attempt-

ing to distinguish the various cases on their facts, as the solicitor for the defender sought to do in his final G reply to the solicitor for the pursuers. The English cases referred to are of value only insofar as they provide guidance on the interpretation of the statutory provisions, and although I do not follow the reasoning in any particular case in full I consider, as will be seen, that the line of cases relied upon by the pursuers most accurately reflect the proper principles to be applied in terms of the legislation.

Dealing first with the words "any sum owed", as used in s 129, one cannot in my view lay down as a H matter of law that the phrase applies only to arrears accumulated under a regulated agreement. The phrase clearly relates to any sum owed at the time when the court is considering the matter, but what sums are owed at that time will depend on the circumstances of the particular case. There may well be cases in which arrears have accumulated, but the loan has not been "called in" by the creditor. In such circumstances the court might well take the view that only the arrears are owed at that particular time. An entirely different situ- I ation obtains however when, as in the present case, the creditor has served notices of default in respect of both the agreement and the standard security, and has thereafter raised an action for possession of the security subjects based on that default.

The initial writ in the present action specifies the "balance outstanding" as being the total sums due in terms of the agreement. In the course of his submission the solicitor for the defender made reference J to alleged ambiguities and inconsistencies in the terms of the notices served on the defender under the 1970 and 1974 Acts. I fail to detect any inconsistencies such as would affect the issue before me. Be that as it may, whatever else is contained in the said notices the default notice under the 1974 Act specifies the pursuers' intended course of action in the event of the defender not bringing payments up to date, namely to demand payment of all the sums outstanding in terms of the agreement, less a rebate. By not making pay- K ments as required, the defender has now lost any entitlement to a rebate, and the full outstanding sum referred to in the notice is now specified in the writ as the basis of the action. The pursuers have therefore in my view placed the whole indebtedness of the defender under the agreement before the court, and cannot now claim that any time order granted by the court must be restricted to arrears. The total sums outstanding on the agreement consisting of principal plus contractual and penalty interest, constitute the sums L owed in the circumstances of this case and may therefore be made the subject of a time order in terms of s 129. As I understand the position the total sums outstanding are now in excess of £12,000.00.

I turn now to consideration of the making of a time order in the circumstances of the present case. Section 129 empowers the court to order payment by instalments, of such amounts and at such times, as are reasonable having regard to the means of the debtor. However that power may be exercised by the making

of a time order only if it appears, or is considered, just
A to do so, and in deciding what is just in the context of
any particular case the positions of both creditor and
debtor must be taken into account by the court.
Section 129 undoubtedly allows the court to exercise
a wide discretion, but a discretion which must be exercised within the confines of the specific powers conferred on the court by the wording of the section. That
wording is perfectly clear. The specific power is to
provide for payment of the sums owed in terms of the
agreement by instalments which are within the dis-
B cretion of the court in respect of both amount and frequency. The section therefore allows for rescheduling
of the payment of the debt, to allow the debtor more
time to pay either at the contractual or reduced instalments. A time order means what it says, and the
section specifies what the court may do in respect of
giving relief by allowing further time to pay. Section
129 however provides no power beyond that to amend
or modify an agreement, and in particular does not
allow the court to modify contractual interest rates
C under the agreement. As it was put in *First National
Bank plc v Colman:* "Section 129 is mechanical. It
provides a debtor with relief in that it suspends his
obligation to make payments as and when required to
do so contractually. It gives him more time. To that
extent, but not otherwise, it alters the contractual
rights and obligations between creditor and debtor."

I entirely agree that this is the type of relief contemplated by the section, and find myself in general agreement with the interpretation of s 129 and its
D relationship with s 136, as expressed in the above case
and in similar terms in *First National Bank plc v
Holgate* and *First National Bank plc v Shah and
Fatima.*

In the present case I am in no doubt that in view of
the means and commitments of the defender he could
not reasonably be expected to pay monthly instalments of more than the £160.00 being offered. If it
were possible on the basis of such instalments to do
E justice to the parties by extending the repayment
period I might well have been prepared to take such
a course. However the repayment period required in
such circumstances, standing the interest rate applying under the agreement, could not possibly be
regarded as just. It could not be considered just that
the pursuers be expected to wait for payment of the
debt for the inordinate period which would be
required to fulfil the agreement. Indeed it would not
be in the interests of the defender in my view to allow
F the agreement to extend probably beyond his lifetime.
As indicated above, this aspect of the case is not in
dispute, and the solicitor for the defender conceded
that it would not be just to make a time order in such
circumstances without a further order under s 136
reducing the contractual interest rate.

In my view that concession, quite properly made in
the circumstances, is fatal to the defender's application. Before a time order can be made it must be considered just, and an order which is not considered just,
and cannot therefore be made, cannot be turned into

a just order by reference to a section of the Act which
can only come into play when a time order is made. G
An amending order under s 136 may be made only in
an order made by the court under the 1974 Act, in the
context of the present case under s 129. It seems to me
to be entirely illogical for the defender to concede that
a time order cannot be justified in terms of s 129, but
then to proceed to invoke powers allegedly available
under s 136 but powers which can be used by the
court only in consequence of a term of a time order
made under s 129. If such powers are available only in
consequence of a time order, they cannot exist without H
an existing time order.

If my reasoning on this matter is considered to be
flawed, I am in any event of the view that even were
I to make a time order I would not under s 136 have
the power contended for by the defender, to rewrite
the agreement in respect of the contractual interest. In
this context I refer to *First National Bank plc v
Holgate*, in which it was said: "I am bound to say that
it seems to me to be an extraordinary situation that
after a freely negotiated loan and mortgage, a defen- I
dant is allowed . . . to come along to a court and say
'I cannot now pay the amount I agreed to pay, but I
would be able to pay something under the agreement
provided the rate of interest was reduced to a figure
which fitted my ability to pay' . . . there is no doubt
whatever that the court could make an order whereby
payment of the arrears could be made over a longer
period of time commensurate with the means of the
debtor and so extend the period of the agreement. I am
being asked to go much further than this and, because J
the defendant cannot keep up with payments to meet
the interest, vary the rate of interest. Section 136 however, in my opinion only gives me power to amend an
agreement in consequence of the term of the order.
The order I am being asked to make is a time order.
How this can be extended to an order reducing the
rate of interest I do not know, and I am bound to disagree entirely with those who decided the case of
Cedar Holdings v Jenkins. Applications to vary the
terms of the agreement in relation to interest are con- K
tained in the extortionate credit bargain sections of the
Act. In those circumstances if a court found a credit
bargain to be extortionate, it could reopen an agreement so as to do justice between the parties. One
wonders if those provisions are completely and utterly
irrelevant if a defendant can do what this defendant is
asking me to do and as it were alter the entire terms
of a freely negotiated agreement, by what I may
describe as the 'back door'."

I quote this passage at length because I find myself L
in agreement with the reasoning contained therein. As
indicated above, I am of the view that s 129 is intended
to allow a debtor relief in terms of the amount,
number and frequency of payments. It is not intended
to deal with the fundamental rights or obligations
under the agreement, and in particular it does not give
the court power to reduce a debtor's liability as distinct from allowing him further time to settle that liability. Section 136 provides the court with no more
than an ancillary power to amend the agreement, exer-

cisable only in consequence of a term of the time order. It thus allows the court to give effect to the practicalities of the time order, by for instance amending the agreement in respect of the length of the contractual repayment period. The power under s 136 cannot however be utilised to reduce a debtor's liability under the agreement, since a time order itself cannot make such provision. To reduce the contractual rate of interest would be going far beyond, in my view, the intention of s 136, and would provide the debtor with a fundamentally different and supplementary form of relief from that contemplated by s 129. The debtor would be given not only an extension of time but a reduction in liability.

In the present case the defender seeks a very substantial reduction in his liability under the agreement, and he attempts to reach that objective by arguing that s 136 allows such a course of action as result of a time order. However what he is really saying is that he requires an order under s 136 reducing his overall liability, not as a consequence of a time order but as a precondition since otherwise the time order could not be made. He is thereby in effect making the validity of the time order under s 129 dependent upon, and therefore a consequence of, an order under s 136, which seems to me to invert the relationship between the two sections. I reject the contention by the defender that s 136, in combination with a time order, allows the court to rewrite the agreement between himself and the pursuers by reducing the contractual rate of interest.

Finally, had I taken the view that I had the power to open up and rewrite the agreement to the extent desiderated by the defender, I would not on the information before me have considered it just to do so. I use the word "information" advisedly because I was being asked to decide the matter on the basis of ex parte statements not all of which were a matter of agreement. In particular the figures as to rates of interest provided by the defender in the form of letters from banks, and the inferences to be drawn therefrom, were in dispute. Had I considered the matter to be crucial to my decision I would have required a proof on that issue. However I do not consider that to be necessary, not only because of my interpretation of the legislation as given above, but because even taking the highest inferences contended for by the solicitor for the defenders, as to the average rate of interest being charged by High Street banks, I am not persuaded that it would be just to reduce the rate of interest to that figure or indeed any comparable figure and to extend the period of the loan in consequence. There is a world of difference between lenders of the status of banks and building societies, and lenders such as the pursuers who specialise in high risk lending. High risks inevitably entail high interest rates. The mortgage in the present case is not only a second mortgage but a second mortgage with a high risk, and the agreement was entered into in that knowledge. I have to assume for the purposes of the present application, despite certain matters alluded to in defences, that the agreement was entered into freely and in full know-

ledge of the rate of interest applying. I am not dealing in this application with any allegations regarding an extortionate credit bargain, although it seems to me that the solicitor for the defender came perilously close to suggesting that when using the comparison of bank rates. His principal objective however, as I understand it, in using these comparisons was to demonstrate that the pursuers would receive a reasonable return on their money at the average rate of 10.95 per cent suggested in the application.

Section 136 amendments require to be based on what the court considers just, and I cannot regard the amendments proposed by the defender as doing justice between the parties. I fully appreciate the difficulties in which the defender finds himself, and accept the almost inevitable consequences to him of my decision as outlined by his solicitor. However I must have regard to, and try to balance, the interests of each party. I do not regard it as being just arbitrarily to reduce the rate of interest to coincide with what the defender can afford to pay, and that in essence is what I am being asked to do. I do not regard it as just on the information before me to force the lenders to wait for around three times the agreed period for their money while at the same time reducing the rate of interest to around one third of that originally agreed. It seems to me that the defender simply wishes to have a freely negotiated agreement changed to fit in with his ability to pay. If he wishes to claim that the agreement should be reopened on the basis of an extortionate interest rate, a remedy is available under s 137 etc. He cannot in my view by invoking s 136 obtain that remedy by the "back door".

For all the reasons given I am not prepared to make any order in terms of s 129 or 136, as craved by the defender. I have therefore dismissed the application, and have continued the cause for consideration of further procedure, and to hear submissions on expenses.

Solicitors for Pursuers, Turner, MacFarlane, Green & Co, Glasgow — Solicitors for Defender, Legal Services Agency Ltd, Glasgow.

INDEX OF CASES

ACCORDING TO SUBJECT MATTER

THE
SCOTS LAW TIMES

THE SCOTTISH LAND COURT
AND
THE LANDS TRIBUNAL
FOR SCOTLAND

1994

EDINBURGH
PUBLISHED BY W GREEN, THE SCOTTISH LAW PUBLISHER
21 ALVA STREET

INDEX OF CASES

ACCORDING TO NAMES OF PARTIES

★ signifies case reported in note form.

REPORTS OF CASES

DECIDED IN

THE SCOTTISH LAND COURT
AND
THE LANDS TRIBUNAL
FOR SCOTLAND

1994

Note: Cases in these Reports may be cited:
1994 SLT (Land Ct) or 1994 SLT (Lands Tr) as appropriate.

Thus: Clydebank District Council v Keeper of the Registers of Scotland, 1994
SLT (Lands Tr) 2.
Broadland Properties Estates Ltd v Mann, 1994 SLT (Land Ct) 7.

A ## Clydebank District Council v Keeper of the Registers of Scotland

LANDS TRIBUNAL FOR SCOTLAND

SHERIFF A C HORSFALL, QC,
R A EDWARDS, WS

29 JUNE 1993

B *Landlord and tenant — Public sector housing — Tenants' rights — Purchase of dwellinghouse — Discount on market value — Repayment of discount on early disposal — Disposal by executor of deceased owner — Whether discount repayable on subsequent disposal — Housing (Scotland) Act 1987 (c 26), ss 72 and 73.*

By the Housing (Scotland) Act 1987 a public sector tenant is given the right to purchase the house of which he is the tenant at a discount on its market value. Section 72 of the Act provides that in certain C circumstances the purchaser or any of his successors in title shall be liable to repay to the landlord all or part of that discount if he disposes of the house within a period of three years from the date of the conclusion of missives for the sale by the landlord. By s 73 there shall be no liability to make such a repayment where the disposal is made, inter alia, by the executor of a deceased owner acting in that capacity.

A district council tenant having died shortly after D purchasing his house, his executor sold it. Although none of the discount had been repaid and the period of three years had not expired, the Keeper of the Registers thereupon amended the Land Register by cancelling the registration of a standard security which had been granted in favour of the district council for the amount of the discount. The council appealed, arguing that such a disposal did not prevent a liability to repay discount arising on a subsequent disposal within the three year period.

E **Held,** that the sale of the house by the deceased's executor terminated the liability to repay to the council a proportion of the statutory discount on the purchase price of the house, and the keeper accordingly acted correctly in cancelling the entry in the Land Register relating to the standard security for the amount of the discount (pp 4A-B and D-F and 6L).

Appeal against decision of the Keeper of the
F ### Registers of Scotland

Clydebank District Council appealed to the Lands Tribunal for Scotland against a decision of the Keeper of the Registers of Scotland to amend the Land Register for Scotland by cancelling the registration of a standard security over subjects at 8 McKenzie Avenue, Clydebank. It was agreed between the parties, in a joint minute, that the sole issue between them to be determined by the tribunal was the interpretation of ss 72 and 73 of the Housing (Scotland) Act 1987 insofar as those statutory provisions related to the facts outlined in the appeal.

On 29 June 1993 the tribunal *pronounced* an order G *finding* (first) that the sale of the subjects by the executor of the deceased owner discharged the obligations arising from the standard security granted by the deceased in respect of the liability to repay discount, and (second) that the entry in the register relating to the standard security was properly cancelled.

The opinion attached to the tribunal's order was in the following terms:

THE TRIBUNAL.—This is an appeal by Clyde- H bank District Council under s 25 of the Land Registration (Scotland) Act 1979 arising out of the action of the Keeper of the Registers in amending the land register by cancelling the registration of a heritable security, following the sale of the house which was subject to that security.

The house had been bought from the council by the tenant, Mr John Girvan, under the tenants' rights legislation contained in Pt III of the Housing (Scot- I land) Act 1987, which confers on a tenant whose landlord is a public authority the right to purchase his house at a discount on its market value. By s 72 the Act provides that in certain circumstances, if the tenant who has purchased his house, or any of his successors in title, sells or otherwise disposes of the house within a period of three years, he shall then be liable to repay all or part of the discount. The period of three years runs from the date when missives for the sale of the house are concluded by the service by the tenant under s 66 of a notice of acceptance of the land- J lord's offer to sell.

The landlord may, and commonly does, secure his right to that repayment by requiring the purchaser to grant a standard security for the amount of the discount. That was done in this case, the security being registered in January 1991. The termination date of the security was stated to be 13 August 1993, that being three years from the date of the conclusion of missives. K

In February 1991 Mr Girvan died, and his executor sold the house, the disposition being registered on 5 November 1991. Although there had been no repayment of any part of the discount, the keeper thereupon amended the register by cancelling the registration of the security. He claims that he was entitled to do so, because, on his interpretation of ss 72 and 73 of the 1987 Act, the liability to repay discount came to an end when a house bought under the tenants' rights legislation was sold by the executor of the deceased L owner. The council do not accept that that liability then came to an end, and they dispute the keeper's right to cancel the registration of the security before 13 August 1993 or the date of receipt of a formal discharge of the security, if that should come sooner.

It is agreed between the parties that the sole matter to be determined by the tribunal is the proper construction to be put on ss 72 and 73 of the 1987 Act insofar as their provisions relate to the facts outlined in the appeal.

The relevant parts of those sections are:

A   "72.—(1) A person who has purchased a house in exercise of a right to purchase under section 61, or any of his successors in title, who sells or otherwise disposes of the house (except as provided for in section 73) before the expiry of three years from the date of service of a notice of acceptance by the tenant under section 66 shall be liable to repay to the landlord, in accordance with subsection (3), a proportion of the difference between the market value determined, in respect of the house, under section 62 (2) and the price B   at which the house was so purchased. . . .

"(2) Subsection (1) applies to the disposal of part of a house except in a case where — (a) it is a disposal by one of the parties to the original sale to one of the other parties; or (b) the remainder of the house continues to be the only or principal home of the person disposing of the part. . . .

"(4) Where as regards a house or part of a house there is, within the period mentioned in subsection (1), more than one disposal to which that subsection C   would (apart from the provisions of this subsection) apply, that subsection shall apply only in relation to the first such disposal of the house, or part. . . .

"73.—(1) There shall be no liability to make a repayment under section 72 (1) where the disposal is made — (a) by the executor of the deceased owner acting in that capacity; or (b) as a result of a compulsory purchase order; or (c) in the circumstances specified in subsection (2).

"(2) The circumstances mentioned in subsection (1) D   (c) are that the disposal — (a) is to a member of the owner's family who has lived with him for a period of 12 months before the disposal; and (b) is for no consideration: Provided that, if the disponee disposes of the house before the expiry of the three year period mentioned in section 72 (1), the provisions of that section will apply to him as if this was the first disposal and he was the original purchaser."

The keeper's case may be summarised in this way, that, since subs (4) of s 72 provided that the liability E   to repay should only arise on the occasion of the first of two or more disposals within the three year period, and since the disposal by Mr Girvan's executor was a first disposal, it alone could result in such a liability. However, since s 73 (1) (a) provided that there should be no liability where the disposal was by the executor of a deceased owner, no such liability had then arisen and it could not now arise in the future. Accordingly, in the keeper's view, the reference to the security for that liability must now be removed.

F   On behalf of the council it was submitted that to interpret the provisions of those two sections in that way was to ignore the words in brackets in subs (1) of s 72. Before subs (4) of that section could apply, there must have been a disposal to which subs (1) would apply were it not for the provisions of subs (4). But for subs (1) to apply the house must have been disposed of "except as provided for in section 73" — to quote the words which appears in brackets in subs (1). The exceptions stated in that section included the case where the disposal was made by the executor of the deceased owner acting in that capacity. Since the

present case was covered by that exception, it was submitted that there had not yet been a disposal to which G   the provisions of subs (1) of s 72 would apply were it not for the provisions of subs (4). Accordingly, the latter subsection did not yet apply and the liability to repay discount might still arise.

It was submitted that support for the interpretation which produced that result was to be found in the history of these provisions. A tenant's right to buy a public sector house at a discount on its market value was introduced by the Tenants' Rights, Etc (Scotland) Act 1980. In that Act the provision for the recovery of H   discount on an early resale was contained in s 6, which provided:

"(1) A person who has purchased a dwelling-house in exercise of a right to purchase under section 1 of this Act, or any of his successors in title, who sells or otherwise disposes of the dwelling-house (otherwise than in the capacity of executor of the deceased owner or as a result of an order for compulsory purchase) before the expiry of five years from the date of service of a notice of acceptance by the tenant under section I   2 (6) of this Act shall be liable to repay to the landlord a proportion of the discount. . . .

"(2) Subsection (1) above applies to the disposal of part of a dwelling-house except in a case where — (a) it is a disposal by one of the parties to the original sale to one of the other parties; or (b) the remainder of the dwelling-house continues to be the only or principal home of the person disposing of the part. . . .

"(4) Where there is more than one disposal within the period mentioned in subsection (1) above, this J   section applies only in relation to the first disposal."

Since that reference in subs (4) covered *any* disposal within the prescribed period, the effect of those provisions was plainly that, even if the first disposal within that period did not give rise to a liability to repay discount, because it was by an executor or as the result of a compulsory purchase order, there could be no liability to repay discount on any subsequent disposal within that period.

However, subs (4) was soon amended, by s 40 of and K   para 42 of Sched 3 to the Local Government (Miscellaneous Provisions) (Scotland) Act 1981. As then amended, it was in approximately the same terms as subs (4) of s 72 of the 1987 Act, the slight differences in the use of words not being such as could affect the meaning. Instead of the reference in subs (4) of s 6 of the 1980 Act being simply to more than one disposal within the prescribed period, it became a reference to more than one disposal to which subs (1) would (apart from the provisions of subs (4)) apply, and the pro- L   vision that the section should apply only in relation to the first disposal was replaced by a provision that subs (1) should apply only in relation to the first "such" disposal.

The effect of those amendments was clearly to change the existing position so that in future there might be a disposal within the prescribed period which would give rise to a liability to repay discount, notwithstanding that it had been preceded by a disposal which did not give rise to that liability. On behalf of the council it was submitted that that would

A be so in the case where the first disposal was by the deceased owner's executor or as a result of a compulsory purchase. In such a case, while there would be no liability on the occasion of that first disposal, there would be such a liability if the disponee should then go on to dispose of the house before the expiry of the prescribed period.

However, in the tribunal's opinion, an intention that the amendment should have that result would be inconsistent with the way in which the third exception from liability was subsequently added to those originally specified in s 6 (1). That is the exception which
B is now referred to in para (c) of subs (1) of s 73, and which is described in detail in subs (2) of that section.

That exception was added by s 12 of and paras 7 and 8 of Sched 1 to the Housing (Scotland) Act 1986. Subsection (1) of s 6 of the 1980 Act was amended so that for the words "otherwise than in the capacity of executor of the deceased owner or as a result of an order for compulsory purchase" there were substituted the words "except as provided for in section
C 6A of this Act". The effect of that amendment was to change the wording of s 6 (1) of the 1980 Act so that those parts of it which are relevant for the purposes of this appeal were to the same effect as the provisions which are now contained in s 72 (1) of the 1987 Act. A new section, s 6A, was then inserted, the terms of which were identical with those of s 73 of the 1987 Act. In particular, it contained in subs (2) the proviso which is now the proviso to subs (2) of s 73 of the 1987 Act. That provided specifically that in the one case where the first disposal was to a member of the
D owner's family for no consideration a liability to repay discount should arise where that person then disposed of the house before the expiry of the prescribed period.

If it had been intended that the earlier amendment of s 6 (4) of the 1980 Act should have the result that, where a first disposal was covered by one of the two original exceptions in s 6 (1), discount would nevertheless be repayable on a second, non-excepted, disposal within the prescribed period, there would have been
E no need for the proviso to s 6A (2), since that earlier amendment would apply equally in the case of the new exception and would have the same result.

The most probable reason therefore for the inclusion of the proviso is that the earlier amendment had not been intended to have that result in the case of the first two of the exceptions, nor in the case of those exceptions was it believed that it had had that result. Only in the case of the third, newly added exception was it intended that a liability to repay discount might
F still arise despite the fact that there had already been a disposal of a kind mentioned in s 73 which did not give rise to that liability.

The argument that that must have been what was intended is persuasive. The two original exceptions have this in common, that in each case the first disposal is the result of something outwith the control of the owner, that being his own death in the first case and the making of a compulsory purchase order in the second. It might be thought reasonable that in those cases the liability to repay discount should then come to an end and should not transmit to the purchaser

from the executor or to the authority which had acquired the house by compulsory purchase. In the G case of the third exception, however, there would be an obvious danger of abuse, since a tenant who had purchased his house could at once give it to a member of his own family on the understanding that it was to be immediately resold for the benefit of the donor. Were it not for the proviso the obligation to repay discount could in that way be easily evaded.

A further consideration is this, that if, when the third exception was added by the 1986 Act, it was believed by the draftsman that a disponee from an H executor and an authority which had acquired the subjects by compulsory purchase were indeed to be liable to repay discount if the house was again disposed of within the prescribed period, one might have expected him to take advantage of the opportunity to express that more clearly and simply, by making the proviso to subs (2) apply to the whole of s 73.

In any event, it seems to the tribunal to be inherently improbable that by the amendment introduced by the 1981 Act Parliament should have been intended to make such a radical change as would be involved if I the council's interpretation were correct. A clue to what might have been the intention behind that amendment may be gleaned from the commentary on subs (4) of s 6 of the 1980 Act contained in *Current Law Statutes* for that year. The very brief comment made there (by Mr Himsworth) was as follows: "Subs. (4): *'disposal.'* This is presumably intended not to include the 'excepted' disposals under subs. (2). Could it not be argued, however, that a 'second disposal' preceded by a 'first disposal' to which subs. (1) does not apply J would not attract liability to repay discount?"

A possible explanation for the amendment made in 1981 is that it was intended to deal with an unforeseen consequence of the drafting of subs (4) of s 6 of the 1980 Act, in respect that in 1980, when subs (2) was incorporated into s 6 by a parliamentary amendment, the draftsman failed to introduce a corresponding, consequential amendment into subs (4). The problem to which Mr Himsworth's commentary somewhat cryptically alludes would seem to have been this. As K originally drafted, s 6 (4) provided that the obligation to repay discount should only occur on the occasion of the first disposal of the house. Because of the definition of "dwellinghouse" in s 82 of the 1980 Act, that would apply not only in the case of a disposal of a whole house, but also in the case of a disposal of part of a house. However, subs (2) of s 6 of the 1980 Act then introduced two excepted cases where the obligation to repay discount would not arise, namely where that disposal either took place between the parties to the original sale or left the person disposing of the L property still in occupation of the remainder of the house. The effect of s 6 as finally set out in the 1980 Act would therefore be seen to be that, while a disposal of part of the house would not trigger the repayment of discount in those excepted cases, it would, or might, be read as also precluding the operation of the discount repayment obligation in relation to a subsequent disposal of such a house falling within the prescribed period. The potential for abuse would be, for example, that if a husband and wife purchased a public sector house jointly, and then agreed to transfer

A full ownership to one or other of them, who subsequently disposed of the house, it would be possible to argue that that disposal was not a first disposal but a second disposal, and that because of the terms of subs (4) the obligation to repay discount would not apply. The amendment may therefore have been introduced to avoid that particular abuse by providing that, while a disposal of a kind covered by subs (2) would not itself trigger the discount repayment obligation at that stage, it would not preclude the future triggering of the obligation.

B The intention of the Act is clear in its application to the ordinary case of a tenant who has purchased his house with the benefit of a discount and subsequently resells it. In providing for such discounts Parliament set out to promote home ownership, not to provide an opportunity for tenants to make a quick profit at the public expense. Section 72 therefore aims to discourage a quick sale of discounted property at its market price, by requiring from a purchaser who resells within a three year period the repayment of the whole or part of the discount.

C The difficulty with which the tribunal is concerned arises, not in that ordinary case, but because of the reference in s 72 (1) to "any successors in title" of the original purchaser. Those words do not have any defined or accepted meaning. They could refer either to singular successors or to successors by inheritance, or indeed to both. It seems probable, however, that the words are intended to apply to singular successors, in order to make it possible for a public authority which has sold a house to the tenant at a discount, to claim

D back that discount from a singular successor, if the discount should not be repaid, as it ought to be, on the resale by the original purchaser. There would be nothing unreasonable in such a result, particularly if an intending purchaser was put on his guard, by the registration of a standard security, that there was an outstanding liability to repay discount. It is less likely, however, that the intention would be that a liability for the repayment of discount should arise on a sale following a disposal by an executor after the death of the owner, or following a disposal by the owner

E himself as a result of a compulsory purchase order. In neither case would there have been any failure, on the first disposal of the house, to make a repayment which ought then to have been made, since in each case the disposal would not have been by the owner's voluntary act and would have been covered by a specific exemption. That being so, there would appear to be no good reason why the liability to repay discount should subsequently be revived if either the disponee from the executor or the authority which had acquired

F the house by compulsory purchase should resell it within the statutory period. Indeed, it would make no kind of sense to provide that a disposal by an executor was not to give rise to a liability to repay discount, although such a disposal would secure the value of that discount for the deceased's estate, but yet to intend that a subsequent disposal by the disponee from the executor should give rise to that liability. The same could be said of the exemption from liability in the case of a forced disposal resulting from compulsory purchase.

That the words "successors in title" were not

intended to mean successors by inheritance is borne out to some extent by the terms of the report in G *Hansard* for 11 June 1980 (Vol 986, col 680) of the debate on the 1980 Bill in the House of Commons. Furthermore, to give the words "successors in title" the meaning of successors by inheritance would have the result that, while on the original purchaser's death a sale of his house by his executor would not attract liability to repay discount, a sale by his heir would attract such a liability. There is no apparent reason for such a distinction and it is therefore unlikely that it was intended. It is more likely that what was intended H was that in all cases the death of the owner would put an end to the liability to repay discount.

In the tribunal's opinion, s 72 is to be regarded as the "lead provision", which sets out the main framework of the provisions for the repayment of discount. If it were not for the words in brackets in s 72 (1), discount would be repayable not only where there was a sale by the former tenant, but also where there was a sale by an executor of the former tenant. The effect of the words in brackets, however, is that such a case, I and the case of a house acquired by compulsory purchase, is dealt with separately, and the provisions applying to the one type of case cannot thereafter be applied to the other.

Given that the 1980 Act in its original form did not have the result for which the council now contend, the tribunal cannot accept that the 1981 amendment could have been intended to reverse the position or that it has in fact done so. Section 72 is to be regarded as dealing with, and dealing only with, cases other than J those with which s 73 is designed to deal. The provisions of s 72 (4) accordingly only have relevance to cases arising under s 72. As has already been suggested, there are such cases to which the provisions of s 72 (4) might be applicable, these being the cases covered by s 72 (2). In all cases other than those two excepted cases and the case provided for in s 73 (2) (a) and (b) the tribunal is satisfied that the Act continues to have the same effect as that which undoubtedly resulted under s 6 of the 1980 Act, although in reach- K ing that conclusion the tribunal has followed a line of reasoning rather different from that which was put forward on behalf of the keeper.

The conclusion to which the tribunal has come is at first sight contrary to the view taken by Watchman on *The Housing (Scotland) Act 1987,* at p 167. In his comment on subs (4) of s 72 the author states initially that "Liability to repay discount only arises on the first disposal within the three year period and does not L apply to subsequent disposals within that period." However, he then goes on to state that it should be noted that "where there is an 'exempt disposal' followed by a 'non-exempt' disposal within the three year period . . . the first disponee will face liability to repay discount". The terms "exempt disposal" and "non-exempt" disposal are not, however, terms used by the Act itself. It is possible that by "exempt disposal" the author was referring to the cases which Mr Himsworth described as "excepted" cases, that is, the two cases described in s 72 (2) of the Act. The passage referred to goes on to make a cryptic reference, in brackets, to a subs (3) of s 73. There is no such subsection. It is difficult in all the circumstances to understand just what the author may have been intending to say, or by what process of thought he arrived at his view. The passage referred to therefore provides doubtful support for the council's case.

The conclusion to which the tribunal has come is also contrary to an opinion expressed obiter by the sheriff principal in *Jack's Exrx v Falkirk District Council*, 16 April 1990, unreported (1990 GWD 23-1290). The sheriff principal's decision was subsequently appealed to the Second Division of the Court of Session (whose decision is reported at 1992 SLT 5). In that case a tenant had exercised her right in terms of s 61 of the Act to purchase a house let by a local authority. Missives had been entered into whereby the local authority had contracted to sell the house to the tenant. The missives provided that the tenant would require to repay a proportion of the discount in accordance with s 72 (1) of the Act, and made it a material condition that the tenant should grant a standard security containing a clause of ranking. The tenant died before delivery of the disposition. Her executrix raised an action against the local authority seeking delivery of an executed disposition and seeking a declarator that no discount would be repayable by the executrix in the event of the sale by her of the subjects. The sheriff at first instance granted decree in terms of both craves, but on appeal the sheriff principal assoilzied the local authority from the second crave and dismissed the first crave. The executrix appealed to the Court of Session, which disposed of the appeal on the limited ground that the tenant had not been an owner within the meaning of the Act. The opinion expressed obiter by the sheriff principal was not commented upon and did not form part of the ratio of the decision. It was argued that as the Second Division would have the judgment of the sheriff principal in front of them, they would, if they considered that the opinion expressed obiter was incorrect, have felt bound to correct the sheriff principal on this matter. Such an implication is plainly unsound. We do not know the extent to which the arguments put to the sheriff principal were similar to the arguments put to the tribunal in this case, and the sheriff principal's opinion is not of course binding on the tribunal.

The tribunal was also referred to an opinion expressed by Professor Cusine in an article at (1991) 36 JLS 186. However, that article is of limited assistance. Professor Cusine was there concerned only with the question whether the proviso at the end of s 73 applied to the case where the first disposal was by the executor of a deceased owner and the disponee then disposed of the house before the expiry of the three year period. If the proviso applied not only to subs (2) but to the whole section, then it would be because of the operation of the proviso that the discount would be repayable by the disponee. While expressing the opinion, with which the tribunal agrees, that the proviso did not apply to the whole section, so that in those circumstances the discount would not be repayable in terms of it, Professor

Cusine did not consider the question whether it might be repayable because of other provisions in the Act. In particular, he did not consider the question now raised regarding the interpretation of subss (1) and (4) of s 72.

It should also be noted that, when expressing the opinion that s 6 of the 1980 Act could have been construed as meaning that a purchaser from an executor would be liable to repay discount if he resold the subjects within the statutory period, Professor Cusine appears to attach no significance to the provisions of subs (4) of that section, to which indeed he makes no reference. His conclusion, that the subsequent change in wording was to put it beyond doubt that on the death of the tenant, or following on a compulsory purchase order, the discount ceased to be repayable, is based on the opinion that that had been left in doubt by the 1980 Act. It is difficult to understand how he could have been of that opinion if he had considered the effect of s 6 (4) of that Act.

The right to buy conferred by the Tenants' Rights, Etc (Scotland) Act 1980 on tenants in Scotland of public sector landlords was conferred on such tenants in England by the Housing Act 1980. The relevant provisions of that Act were superseded by those of the Housing Act 1985. On behalf of the council it was submitted that there could be no reason to suppose that it was intended that the effect of the Scottish legislation should be different from that of the English, and it was submitted that the council's interpretation of the Scottish Act was consistent with the construction which should be put on the equivalent provisions in the English legislation. However, the submissions on this matter were limited to directing the tribunal to comments made by the annotators in *Current Law Statutes*. The solicitor for the council sought to put a certain gloss on those comments, but the tribunal is not satisfied that the comments concerned bear the meanings put on them, and there was no evidence put before the tribunal of the way in which the English provisions had been interpreted or applied in practice. In any event, given the difference in the property law applying in the two jurisdictions, and the fact that the structure and language of the Scottish and English Acts is different in many respects, the tribunal has not found that the English legislation affords any useful guidance in the interpretation of the Scottish Act.

Under s 25 of the 1979 Act an appeal to the tribunal lies on any question of fact or law arising from anything done or omitted to be done by the keeper under the Act. It is common ground that in such an appeal the tribunal has no power to order the keeper to make changes in the register, but may only answer the question raised by the appeal. The tribunal accordingly finds that in terms of ss 72 and 73 of the 1987 Act the sale of the subjects by Mr Girvan's executor terminated the liability to repay to the council a proportion of the statutory discount on the purchase price of the house, and finds accordingly that the keeper acted correctly in cancelling the entry in the Land Register relating to the standard security for the amount of the discount.

A *Solicitor for Appellants, S B Brown, Clydebank District Council — Counsel for Respondent, Dewar; Solicitor, R Brodie, Solicitor to the Secretary of State for Scotland.*

Broadland Properties Estates
B # Ltd v Mann

SCOTTISH LAND COURT

LORD PHILIP, D D McDIARMID,
D M MACDONALD, J KINLOCH

24 AUGUST 1993

Landlord and tenant — Agricultural holding — Rent properly payable — Milk quota — Allocated quota — Whether allocated quota should be taken into account in determining rent — Whether capable of being tenant's
C *improvement — Agriculture Act 1986 (c 49), s 16 — Agricultural Holdings (Scotland) Act 1991 (c 55), s 13 (5).*

The landlords of three holdings appealed against an award of a statutory arbiter appointed by the Secretary of State for Scotland to determine the rent payable for those holdings. The tenant of the three holdings held both allocated milk quota and transferred milk quota, and had himself borne the cost of the transferred quota. The arbiter considered in respect of the allo-
D cated quota that as the quota would not have been awarded but for improvements carried out by the tenant, any value attributable to that quota fell to be disregarded.

Held, (1) that an allocated milk quota could not in itself be regarded as a tenant's improvement (p 9K-L); and (2) that the effect of s 16 of the Agriculture Act 1986 was that in determining the rent properly payable for the holdings an allocated quota required to be taken into account (p 9F-H).

E

Observations, on the documents and information to be presented to the court in respect of holdings sought to be used as comparables (p 10G-J).

Appeal from decision of arbiter

Broadland Properties Estates Ltd appealed to the Land Court against the award of Kenneth Farquhar Shaw MacKenzie, the arbiter appointed to determine
F the rent for the holdings of Castleton, Corrachie and Muiralehouse, of which the respondent Alistair Huntly Mann was tenant. The landlords' first and second grounds of appeal were that the arbiter had erred in law in leaving the entire milk quota out of account in his determination of the rent and that the allocated quota should have been taken into account. The court held a preliminary debate on these two grounds of appeal.

On 24 August 1993 the court *found* that the arbiter had erred in leaving the entire milk quota out of

account in his determination of the rent and that the allocated quota should have been taken into account in G his determination of the rent.

The note appended to the court's order was as follows:

THE COURT.—In this application the landlord applicants, Broadland Properties Estates Ltd, appeal under s 61 (2) of the Agricultural Holdings (Scotland) Act 1991 against a rental award of an arbiter, Mr Kenneth Farquhar Shaw MacKenzie, FRICS, in an arbitration under s 13 of the 1991 Act to determine H the rent payable from Whitsunday 1992 in respect of the combined holdings of Castleton, Corrachie and Muiralehouse, of which the respondent Alistair Huntly Mann is tenant.

Although the three holdings are held on three separate leases, they are farmed as a single dairy farm and together form "the holding" in terms of art 12 of the European Community Council Regulation 857/84 to which the "reference quantity" or milk quota applies. The parties have agreed that the holding I should be rented as a single holding and the arbiter has proceeded on that basis. The parties have expressed the wish that we should proceed in the same way. For the purposes of the determination of the particular issues raised in the hearing to which this note relates, we are prepared to accede to this request, but in the procedure which must inevitably follow this decision, we will require to be persuaded of the propriety of this approach in a situation in which the three holdings are held on three separate leases whose terms may differ J from one another.

Following parties lodging their statements of case and before making his award, the arbiter held a hearing at which oral evidence was led. He carried out inspections of the combined holding and of the comparables and issued proposed findings. Thereafter he issued his award on 22 November 1992 fixing the rent for the combined holding for the period from Whitsunday 1992 at the sum of £16,430 per annum.

The landlords' grounds of appeal are in the follow- K ing terms: "(i) the arbiter erred in law in leaving the entire milk quota out of account in his determination of the rent; (ii) the allocated quota should have been taken into account; (iii) the landlords also appeal against the amount of the award and request the Land Court to fix the rent in the sum for which the landlords contended before the arbiter, taking the rental value of allocated quota into account; (iv) even if the Land Court find against the landlords on grounds of appeal (i) and (ii) supra, the landlords nonetheless L appeal against the amount of the arbiter's award in respect that the rent fixed was too low and request the court to fix a new rent at a sum greater than that awarded by the arbiter. In particular, the arbiter failed to take proper account of the landlords' representations on his proposed findings, of the extent of the additions provided by the landlords and of comparables submitted on the landlords' behalf. He was not entitled to make an allowance in respect of the non-residence of the tenant at Upper Manbeen nor to disregard the provision in the Muiralehouse

lease requiring the landlords to provide a milk
house''.

The tenant Mr Mann has also appealed against the
arbiter's determination on grounds concerned with the
amount of the award, expenses and procedure.

A preliminary hearing was held in Edinburgh on 20
April 1993 in order to determine the appropriate procedure for disposing of the various grounds of appeal.
In this case the arbiter has endeavoured to comply
with the provisions of the Agricultural Holdings
(Specification of Forms) (Scotland) Order 1983 and to
set out his findings and the material on which they
were based. In certain previous cases involving
appeals against arbiters' rental awards, the form and
content of the arbiters' awards have fallen far short of
the requirements of the provisions of the 1983 Order,
with the result that, without hearing evidence, the
court had insufficient material before it to enable it to
make its own determination of rent. In those cases the
court had no alternative but to hear the cases de novo.

It should be borne in mind that s 61 (2) of the 1991
Act provides for an appeal against the award of an
arbiter in rental arbitrations rather than a rehearing.
In the light of that provision, it will normally be
appropriate for appeals to be presented by way of
argument directed at the arbiter's findings. It will
generally only be appropriate for the court to hear
further evidence when the court is satisfied that it will
require to determine the rent for itself, but is unable
to do so in accordance with the provisions of s 13 of
the 1991 Act, because of a successful attack on, or the
absence of, findings in fact recorded in the arbiter's
award on material considerations such as comparables
and tenant's improvements. With this in mind we
ordered that the landlords' grounds of appeal (i) and
(ii), which were concerned with the arbiter's failure to
take into account the allocated milk quota in respect
of the holding, should be dealt with first and separately. Once these grounds of appeal have been dealt
with the court may more readily be able to determine
what, if any, further evidence may require to be led.

This decision is therefore concerned only with the
extent to which the arbiter should have taken milk
quota into account in determining the rental value of
the holdings.

It is helpful at the outset to place the present legislation relating to milk quotas in this country in its
historical context. In 1968 the European Economic
Community introduced an intervention system for
butter and skimmed milk powder under which an
intervention agency, designated by each member state,
was obliged to buy in, at a guaranteed price, all butter
and skimmed milk powder offered to it by producers
in the member state, provided it was of a required
standard. This system led to surpluses in production
for which the Community was obliged to pay at the
guaranteed price. Those surpluses led to an undesirable drain on EC funds. Remedial measures were
needed. European Community Council Regulations
856/84, 857/84 and 1371/84 were introduced in order
to limit the production of milk and milk products to
a pre-determined "reference quantity". This was done

by imposing a levy on quantities of milk and milk
products delivered or sold in any year in excess of a
fixed production level, the "reference quantity". It
became incumbent on each member state to make
regulations for carrying the Community law into
effect in its own territory. This was done in the United
Kingdom initially by means of the Dairy Produce
Quotas Regulations 1984 which fixed upon the production level attained by individual producers in the
year commencing April 1983, and imposed the levy on
quantities of milk and milk products delivered or sold
in any one year in excess of 91 per cent of that production level. That percentage of the production level
attained in 1983 is called in the United Kingdom a
"quota". Payment of levy was not triggered unless a
national quota fixed for the whole of the United
Kingdom was exceeded in any year. In such an event
the levy was imposed on individual producers in
respect of the net overproduction attained by each
producer measured by reference to the individual
quotas held by each producer.

The 1984 Regulations were followed by the Dairy
Produce Quotas Regulations 1986 which dealt with
the transfer of quotas from one producer to another by
virtue of the changes in occupation of the land to
which the quota applied. Following upon the introduction of these regulations, it became possible in
certain circumstances to trade in quotas and a market
in milk quotas came into being. A distinction came to
be made between "allocated quota" and "transferred
quota". This distinction was recognised in the Agriculture Act 1986. In para 2 (1) (a) of Sched 2 to that
Act allocated quota is defined as the milk quota allocated to a tenant in terms of the relevant regulations
in relation to a holding consisting of or including his
tenancy. Transferred quota, on the other hand, is
defined by para 2 (2) of the Schedule as milk quota
transferred to him by virtue of the transfer to him of
the whole or part of the holding.

Section 16 of the 1986 Act gives certain specific
directions to arbiters who are dealing with references
under various statutory provisions and contains the
following provisions:

"(2) This section applies where an arbiter or the
Scottish Land Court is dealing with a reference under
— (a) section 6 of the 1886 Act; (b) section 32 (7) of
the 1911 Act; (c) section 13 of the 1991 Act; or (d)
section 5 (3) of the 1955 Act, (determination of rent)
and the tenant has milk quota, including transferred
quota by virtue of a transaction the cost of which was
borne wholly or partly by him, registered as his in
relation to a holding consisting of or including the
tenancy.

"(3) Where this section applies, the arbiter or, as the
case may be, the Land Court shall disregard any
increase in the rental value of the tenancy which is due
to — (a) where the tenancy comprises the holding, the
proportion of the transferred quota which reflects the
proportion of the cost of the transaction borne by the
tenant; (b) where such transferred quota affects part
only of the tenancy, that proportion of so much of the
transferred quota as would fall to be apportioned to

the tenancy under the 1986 Regulations, on a change of occupation of the tenancy.

"(4) For the purposes of determining whether transferred quota has been acquired by virtue of a transaction the cost of which was borne wholly or partly by the tenant any payment by a tenant when he was granted a lease, or when a lease was assigned to him, shall be disregarded."

In this case the tenant, Mr Mann, has both allocated quota and transferred quota. It is common ground that he holds the transferred quota by virtue of a transaction, the cost of which was borne by him. That transferred quota is registered in relation to the holding which consists of the tenancy.

In his award, the arbiter dealt with the question as to how milk quota should be treated in the assessment of rental and his reasoning is, we think, fairly summarised by the following extracts from his award:

"Section 13 (5) contemplates a causal connection between the improvement carried out and the increase in rental value. If it had not been for the improvements carried out by the tenant no viable dairying operation would have been carried on in the base year. From this it follows that no milk quota would have been allocated to the holding. There is thus a direct causal connection between the improvements carried out by the tenant and the allocation of quota and because of that connection I am directed by s 13 (5) to disregard any increase in rental value attributable to the improvements, and this must include any value which would otherwise attach to the milk quota which reflects the increase in production brought about by the improvements. . . . I therefore conclude that without the efforts of the tenant, in terms of the provision of fixed equipment by him, no quota would have been attached to the unit. I therefore also conclude that no part of the milk quota falls to be included in any calculation of the rent. The result of this is that the hypothetical tenant would be offering for a cropping and stock farm."

The determination of grounds of appeal (i) and (ii) turns upon the correct construction of s 16 of the 1986 Act. Subsection (1) provides that para 1 and the other provisions of Sched 2 referred to in para 1 are to have effect for the interpretation of s 16. Paragraphs 1 and 2 of the Schedule differentiate between "allocated quota" and "transferred quota" and provide definitions of each, to which we have already made reference.

Subsection (2) of s 16 provides that s 16 will apply in a rental arbitration when "the tenant has milk quota, including transferred quota by virtue of a transaction, the cost of which was borne wholly or partly by him, registered as his in relation to a holding consisting of or including the tenancy". The use of the words "milk quota including transferred quota" indicates that the possession by the tenant of both allocated and transferred quota was in the contemplation of Parliament in that subsection.

It having thus been made clear that the section is intended to apply to arbitrations in which the tenant has both allocated and transferred quota, subs (3) (a) then goes on to direct the arbiter or the Land Court, where the tenancy comprises the holding, to disregard any increase in the rental value of the tenancy which is due to the proportion of the *transferred quota* (our emphasis) which reflects the proportion of the cost of the transaction borne by the tenant. So if the tenant has paid for the whole of the transferred quota, any increase in rental value due to all of the transferred quota must be disregarded.

Against the background of subss (1) and (2) the direction to the arbiter to disregard any increase in value due to transferred quota, carries the clear implication that he is *not* directed to disregard allocated quota, and must therefore have regard to allocated quota in a rent determination.

The arbiter considered that this construction of s 16 could not be maintained in the face of the provisions of s 13 (5) of the 1991 Act. His view was that the principle which that subsection enshrined, and which had remained unchanged from previous legislation, was that a tenant should not be rented on the contribution which he had made by his skill and provision of capital to the productive capacity of the holding. Parliament could not have intended by the enactment of s 16 of the 1986 Act to cut across that principle. As the quota could not have been acquired without the tenant's improvements, so the argument ran, the arbiter was obliged to disregard it. This argument was supported by counsel for the tenant by reference to diverse principles of statutory interpretation.

We cannot agree with the arbiter's approach. Section 7 (2) of the 1949 Act and its successor, s 13 (5) of the 1991 Act, direct the arbiter to leave out of account any increase in the rental value of the holding which is due to *improvements* (our emphasis) so far as they have been executed wholly or partly at the expense of the tenant. It was accepted by the arbiter, correctly in our opinion, that milk quota was not itself an improvement within the meaning of the Agricultural Holdings Acts. In our opinion the two sections to which we refer apply to improvements executed by the tenant on the holding, wholly or partly at his expense, in the way that all the improvements listed in Scheds 3, 4 and 5 to the 1991 Act require to be. Without exception, all the improvements listed in those Schedules are works which a tenant carries out on the holding. As was argued by counsel for the landlords, allocated milk quota cannot itself be said to have been executed on the holding at the tenant's expense and is not itself a tenant's improvement. Accordingly, it cannot be construed as falling within the scope of the provisions relating to the disregard of tenant's improvements contained in s 7 (2) of the 1949 Act or s 13 (5) of the 1991 Act. Any effect therefore which allocated quota may have in increasing the rental value of the farm cannot be disregarded by virtue of these provisions. Similarly, as we have already found, any effect which allocated quota may have in increasing rental value is not to be disregarded under the provisions of the 1986 Act. We therefore conclude that the arbiter must *not* disregard any increase in the rental value which is due to allocated quota.

In passing the 1986 Act Parliament has decided that transferred quota which has been paid for by the tenant should be disregarded in the calculation of rental value because the landlord has played no part in its acquisition. So far as allocated quota is concerned Parliament has approached it from the point of view that both landlord and tenant have contributed to its allocation. The tenant's contribution is taken account of by the provisions of Sched 2 relating to compensation of the tenant at outgo. The provisions of Sched 2 apply only to tenants to the extent to which their efforts have contributed to the attachment of quota to the tenancy: see para 2 of that Schedule. During the currency of the tenancy the tenant's contribution is taken account of by disregarding any increase in rental value due to the tenant's improvements themselves.

In the course of argument counsel for the landlords made reference to milk quota in a way which suggested that milk quota would be a separate and identifiable item for renting, and that an arbiter in determining rent might, for example, value quota at so many pence per litre. Although counsel appeared ultimately to dissociate himself from such a suggestion, we wish to make it clear that it is premature to assume that this suggestion represents the correct treatment of milk quota in the assessment of rent in arbitrations under s 13 of the 1991 Act. It can be argued that milk quota is merely a statutory device designed to achieve a political result which, as the tenant himself says in his statement of case, may or may not have an effect on the farm's profitability. Output may be diminished as a result of the imposition of quota, or in some cases, for example, where a quota has been bought in, output may be increased. At the same time the effect of the allocation of quota is to limit the ability of other producers to compete in the milk market. These are all factors to which arbiters may have to have regard. But if the arbiter considers that the transferred quota for which the tenant has himself paid is having the effect of increasing the rental value he must disregard the increase to that extent. In the light of all these considerations, the correct treatment of milk quota in the assessment of rent will be a matter to be addressed by the parties in argument before us at a subsequent hearing.

Having concluded that the arbiter must not disregard any increase in rental which is due to allocated quota held by the tenant in respect of the holding, it is necessary for the court to fix a further hearing to enable the grounds of appeal and cross appeal which raise the issue of quantum of rent to be dealt with in the light of this decision.

The court anticipates that the parties will wish at the subsequent hearing to rely on comparables in support of their arguments on quantum of rental. We wish to draw to the attention of parties that it is necessary for the court to have certain information and documents lodged before a holding can be used as a comparable. If this information and the documents are not available, the court may be unable to use the holding in question as a comparable. In these circumstances parties should ensure that when referring to a holding as a comparable, the following information and documents are presented to the court:

(1) The lease of the tenant's holding and any subsequent minutes of agreement relating to that lease including any relevant partnership agreement.

(2) A plan of the holding, if possible, based on an ordnance survey map showing field numbers and acreages.

(3) A description of all the tenant's improvements to the holding and a plan clearly identifying these improvements.

(4) Any improvements carried out by the landlord, together with details of the total cost of these improvements and the grant aid received thereon.

(5) A sketch plan showing the steading buildings and, if appropriate, marking thereon any tenant's improvements to these buildings.

(6) A brief description of the accommodation of the dwellinghouse, a note of its last available rateable value or council tax banding and details of any improvements carried out by the tenant.

(7) Where the comparable offered is a holding let on the open market, then the particulars of let of that holding together with details of the total number and full range of offers received (with any relevant conditions attached to particular offers) must also be lodged.

Section 13 (5) of the 1991 Act requires the court to disregard any increase in the rental value of the holding which is due to tenant's improvements. The arbiter's award contains no definitive list as to what the tenant's improvements were on the three holdings, and, as we understand it, there is no agreement between the parties on the matter. It therefore appears to us that at the subsequent hearing the court will require to satisfy itself as to the precise extent of the tenant's improvements and any grant aid paid on the landlord's provisions.

At the same time as fixing a hearing for the determination of the quantum of rent, we propose to fix a brief preliminary hearing at an earlier date at which parties may address us on the form the subsequent hearing should take. In particular we would wish to be addressed on the nature and extent of the subject matter in respect of which they consider it necessary for further evidence to be led, the comparables the parties propose to rely upon, and the propriety of renting the three holdings as one holding.

Counsel for Landlords, Scott, QC; Solicitors, Snell & Co, WS, Edinburgh — Counsel for Tenant, Simpson; Solicitors, Munro & Noble, Inverness.

(NOTE)

A # Fernie v Strathclyde Regional Council

LANDS TRIBUNAL FOR SCOTLAND

SHERIFF A C HORSFALL, QC;
T FINLAYSON, FRICS

29 SEPTEMBER 1989

B *Landlord and tenant — Public sector housing — Tenants' rights — Purchase of dwellinghouse — Notice of refusal — Statement as ground of refusal that tenancy not secure for one reason — Statement before tribunal of additional reason why tenancy not secure — Competency — Housing (Scotland) Act 1987 (c 26), ss 61 and 68 (3) and (4).*

Section 61 of the Housing (Scotland) Act 1987 provides that a public sector tenant whose tenancy is "secure" is given the right to purchase the house which he occupies. Under Sched 2 to the Act certain tenancies are excluded from being secure. Section 68 C (3) provides that a landlord's notice of refusal shall specify the grounds on which the landlord disputes the tenant's right to purchase.

On an application to the Lands Tribunal under s 68 (4) for a finding that a tenant had a right to purchase the house which he occupied, the landlord sought to put forward a reason why the tenancy was not secure which had not been stated as a ground of refusal in the notice of refusal of the application to purchase. The D applicant argued that the landlord was barred by the terms of the Act from subsequently adding a new ground of refusal.

Held, that in an application under s 68 (4) the tribunal was not restricted to deciding whether a ground of refusal which had been stated in the notice of refusal was valid, but could competently consider other reasons why the tenant had no right to purchase.

E Mr James Fernie, 3 Glen Maree Cottages, Cochno Road, Duntocher, applied to the Lands Tribunal for Scotland for a finding in terms of s 68 (4) of the Housing (Scotland) Act 1987 that he had a right to purchase the house known as 3 Glen Maree Cottages, of which he was the tenant. The landlord, Strathclyde Regional Council, had refused an application by the tenant on the ground specified in para 8 of Sched 2 to the Act. At the hearing before the tribunal the landlord sought to add a further ground of objection under F para 1 of Sched 2. In allowing this move, while granting the tenant's application, the tribunal said:

"In their notice of refusal of Mr Fernie's application to purchase the house the council specified only one ground on which they disputed his right to do so. That was stated to be because 'the dwelling house forms part of or is within the curtilage of a building which is held mainly by the Landlord for purposes other than housing accommodation and consists of accommodation other than housing accommodation'. That, in effect, invokes the exclusion in para 8 of the

Schedule. The building whose curtilage is referred to by the council is a building within the waterworks. G

"At the hearing before the tribunal the solicitor for the council asked to be allowed to invoke in addition the exclusion provision in para 1 of the Schedule, and to state a second ground on which the council disputed Mr Fernie's right to purchase the house. That ground was that Mr Fernie was an employee of the council, and that it was an implied condition of his contract of employment that he should occupy the house for the better performance of his duties. The council's intention to ask that they should be allowed to state that H new ground had been intimated to Mr Fernie's solicitor about 12 days before the hearing.

"The solicitor who appeared for Mr Fernie initially opposed as incompetent any attempt by the council at this stage to add what he called a new ground of refusal. He submitted that, in terms of s 68 (3) of the Act, the whole grounds on which a landlord disputed a tenant's right to purchase must be specified within the same period of one month within which the landlord was required to serve the notice of refusal, and I that they could not be added to thereafter. By subs (3) it was provided that the notice should specify the grounds of refusal. Accordingly, in his submission, a landlord was barred from adding at a later date grounds which had only occurred to him subsequently. In the tribunal's opinion, however, the provision in subs (3) is not a bar to matters being considered which were not stated as grounds of refusal in the notice. In terms of s 68 (4) what the tribunal has to do, on an application to it under that section, is to J decide whether the tenant has a right to purchase the house under s 61. The tribunal is not therefore restricted to deciding only whether a ground of refusal which was originally stated was valid. It can consider other reasons why the tenant has no right to purchase, although, if they were not reasons which were in the landlord's mind when he refused the application, they were not grounds of refusal and cannot become such subsequently. When an application has been refused by a landlord, the tenant must of course be told why K it has been refused, so that he can decide whether he has a good ground of appeal against the refusal. But once he has appealed, he can only be prejudiced by the stating of an additional reason why he has no right to purchase, if the position is that, had he known of it in the first place, he would not have appealed, or if it results in his being prejudiced by having to meet a new case for which he is not prepared. The former prejudice can be dealt with by an appropriate award of expenses and the latter by an adjournment and an L award of any expenses occasioned thereby.

"It was not in fact claimed that Mr Fernie had suffered any prejudice as a result of the belated statement of a fresh reason why the council disputed his right to purchase the house, and the tribunal accordingly allowed the amendment of the council's case, subject to Mr Fernie's solicitor retaining the right to ask for an adjournment should he think fit. In the event, however, he did not find that necessary."

A *Solicitors for Applicant, Walker, Laird, Herron & Harper, Johnstone — Solicitor for Respondents, J G Donnelly.*

[This decision has been reported by request.]

Bisset v Secretary of State for Scotland

B

LANDS TRIBUNAL FOR SCOTLAND

SHERIFF A C HORSFALL, QC;
W HALL, FRICS; A R MACLEARY, FRICS

23 JANUARY 1991

Compulsory powers — Purchase — Compensation — Purchase of part of land of hotel for road construction — Whether severance loss — Nature of claim for loss of profit — Validity of claim for personal disruption —
C *Extraordinary costs of replacing house — Land Compensation (Scotland) Act 1963 (c 51), s 12 (2) — Land Compensation (Scotland) Act 1973 (c 56), ss 34 and 35.*

A substantial part of the grounds of a roadside hotel was acquired for the improvement of the road. The land acquired was part of land used for the hotel car park, for the dwellinghouse of the claimant, the owner of the hotel, and garden ground, for various other buildings including a unit for staff accommodation, and as woodland, and was separated from the hotel by
D the road. Part of the car park was left in the claimant's ownership. The claimant submitted claims for loss of land and buildings, loss of profit from the commencement of the road works, the amount of additional incidental costs to the hotel, the personal disruption caused to him and his family and for the extraordinary costs in connection with building a new dwellinghouse. The acquiring authority submitted that the car park loss was met by determining the open market value of the lost land in accordance with s 12 (2) of the
E Land Compensation (Scotland) Act 1963, and that there was no severance loss to the hotel, and opposed the claims for personal disruption and for the costs in connection with the new dwellinghouse. It accepted the claim for loss of profit but at a lesser amount and only from the date when the claimant moved from the acquired land.

Held, (1) that there was a severance loss to the hotel which could be valued at £10,000 (p 16B-E); (2) that the loss of profit was injurious affection by the execution of the works and compensation should be paid
F from the vesting date (pp 17G-K and 18G-I); (3) that there was no authority to support the claim for personal disturbance (p 20G-H); and (4) the claimant had received value for money as far as the extraordinary costs were incurred (p 21A-C).

Reference to determine compensation

Mr Jack Arthur Bisset, Inverbeg Hotel, Inverbeg, Dunbartonshire, referred to the Lands Tribunal for Scotland the question of compensation payable after

the compulsory acquisition of ground at the Inverbeg Hotel, Inverbeg, Dunbartonshire.   G

On 23 January 1991 the tribunal *pronounced* an order *determining* the compensation to be £194,915, with in addition a surveyor's fee calculated in accordance with Ryde's scale.

The opinion attached to the tribunal's order was in the following terms:

THE TRIBUNAL.—This reference is to determine a claim for compensation in connection with the H compulsory acquisition of 1,663 sq m or thereby of land east of the A82 consisting of part of the Inverbeg Hotel car park, woodland, a dwellinghouse and garden ground. Inverbeg Hotel, Inverbeg, Dunbartonshire, belongs to Mr J A Bisset, who is also the sole proprietor of the hotel business.

The land, designated plot 234, was acquired for improving the A82 by the London-Carlisle-Glasgow-Inverness Trunk Road (A82) North of Luss to Hollybank Improvement (excluding Luss to Camus-Nan- I Clais Stage 1) Compulsory Purchase Order, which was made on 4 February 1985. The date of vesting was 9 May 1986.

The dispute relates to the compensation for the loss of part of the car park; the loss of hotel business due to the road works; the additional incidental costs to the hotel; the disruption caused to Mr Bisset and his family, and the extraordinary costs in connection with the replacement house. The value of the original house and the land pertaining to it has been agreed in J the sum of £37,000. The claim for all losses (including land and buildings) is £514,112, and the acquiring authority propose £121,500.

The details of the claim and the acquiring authority's answers, with its description in brackets, are as follows:

	Claimant	Acquiring authority	
(a) Loss of land and buildings			
(i) domestic properties	£37,000	£37,000	
(ii) car park area — reduction in capital value	£4,000	—	K
(iii) car park area — construction cost	£68,000	—	
(car park land)	—	£1,800	
(b) Loss of business			
foregone gross profit from April 1985 to April 1990	£376,392	—	
(loss of gross profit from 1 July 1988 to 30 April 1991 — percentage due to SDD's road scheme)	—	£78,541	L
(c) Additional incidental costs (Rule 6 minor elements)			
(i) cost of pressure water pump to maintain hotel frontage £350 less 50% for residual value	£175	£175	
(ii) costs of external painting to the hotel	£4,465	£2,332	
(iii) costs of window cleaning	£600	£300	
(iv) sweeping of car park	£300	£300	
(v) cost of survey of condition and re-inspection	£1,200	£716	

A
(d) Disturbance caused to Mr
    Bisset and his family
    (i) living in house adjacent to
        blasting and pecker works   £5,000   —
    (ii) disruption to access to new
        house, disruption to water
        and electrical services   £1,000   —

(e) Extraordinary costs of
    replacement house
    (i) architects' fees on equivalent
        house 12.5% of £40,000   £5,000   —

B
    (ii) legal fees in obtaining
        servitude rights of access
        over new road and through
        underpass   £3,000   —
    (iii) cost of planning application
        fees to district council   £53   —
    (iv) additional cost of slates as
        distinct from concrete
        roofing tiles   £1,280   —
    (v) additional foundation costs
        because of site levels, poor
        subsoil conditions and high
        water table   £3,000   —

C
    (vi) additional costs due to
        earlier entry being required   £1,980   —
    (vii) cost of new electrical supply £1,074   —
    (viii) cost of re-siting calor gas tank £350   —
                                       ————————
                                       £514,112 say £121,500

The claimant was represented at the hearing by
counsel who led in evidence the following witnesses:
the claimant, Mr J A Bisset; Mr N S Clark, the
present chef at the Inverbeg Hotel; Mr J B Fraser,
D director of the Loch Lomond, Stirling and Trossachs
Tourist Board; Mr M B Paul, chartered surveyor; and
Mr A Sturgess, chartered accountant. The Secretary
of State was represented by counsel, who led in evidence the following: Mr G Murdoch, resident consulting engineer; Mr D Mustard, principal engineer,
Roads Directorate, Scottish Development Department; Mr P Low, principal, Accountancy Services,
the Scottish Office; and Mr J S Anderson, chartered
surveyor, principal valuer in the district valuer's
E office, Dumbarton.

Inverbeg Hotel is situated on the west side of the
A82 trunk road from Glasgow to Inverness. Inverbeg
is approximately 5 km north of Luss and 7 km south
of Tarbet. It is situated at the entrance to Glen
Douglas and on the opposite side of Loch Lomond
from Rowardennan, with which it is linked by ferry in
the summer.

Prior to 1988 the hotel was located at the roadside
F of the A82. It consisted of the hotel, a car park, woodland, a dwellinghouse and garden ground, together
with a garden shed, woodshed, workshop, garage
building and an accommodation unit for staff. The
hotel was separated from the car park and the other
land and buildings by the A82.

The A82 is a busy trunk road, and because of the
topography along the shore of Loch Lomond it was
twisting and ill suited for modern traffic conditions.
Traffic on the road was congested and slow moving.
As a roadside inn the hotel is dependent for custom on
the traffic using the A82. For many years there had
been proposals to improve the road.   G

The programme for the improvement of the existing
A82 to a higher standard and for the realignment of
the single carriageway provided for the renewal of the
whole of the road from Auchendennan to Tarbet in
eight sections. Six of these have been completed, and
one, the Luss bypass, is under construction. Construction of the final section from Hollybank to Tarbet will
commence at some time after April 1991.

The two sections covered by the compulsory pur- H
chase order which are relevant to the acquisition of
plot 234 are the Camus-Nan-Clais to Hollybank
improvement and the Luss to Camus-Nan-Clais
improvement. Together these two sections of roadworks comprise the scheme for the purpose of assessing compensation.

Construction of the Camus-Nan-Clais to Hollybank
section, of 4.4 km, commenced in April 1985 and was
completed in July 1987. This was the first phase of the
scheme, and it was the first of the eight sections of I
roadworks on which construction was commenced. At
its nearest point, this section of roadworks was 1.5 km
north of Inverbeg.

Construction of the Luss to Camus-Nan-Clais
section, of 6.3 km, was commenced in January 1988
and the contract was completed in December 1989.
This was the second phase of the scheme, and it was
the section which involved the reconstruction and
realignment of the A82 in the immediate vicinity of J
the hotel.

Both phases involved the construction of a new road
of 7.3 m wide with a 1 m marginal strip and 2.5 m
wide soft verges on each side. The first phase cost
£8.76m and the second £11.8m.

The first phase involved the excavation of 445,000
cubic metres of rock, of which 225,000 cubic metres
were transported by barge to form marine embankments for the second phase. One hundred and forty
thousand cubic metres of rock were taken by lorry to K
these embankments past the hotel. At the peak period
a loaded truck passed the hotel southbound on the old
A82 every four minutes, with an empty truck travelling northwards at the same frequency. All unsuitable
spoil was taken to three tipping areas to the north and
none was taken via Inverbeg.

The second phase involved the excavation of
108,000 cubic metres of rock by blasting. At the
Inverbeg cut, which is adjacent to the hotel, 18,500 L
cubic metres of rock were removed by hydraulic
breaker. After initial blasting in this area Mr Bisset
complained to the Health and Safety Executive. As a
result the blasting was discontinued.

During the second phase the contractors, Messrs
Shanks and McEwan, operated from a compound
located about 150 m north of the hotel. This was a
private arrangement entered into between the
contractors and the landowner.

The new road has been designed as a clearway, with

no parking being allowed on the verges. It has a design capacity of between 10,000 and 13,000 vehicles per day and will cater for traffic travelling at speeds approaching the legal limit.

Prior to the upgrading of the carriageway the old A82 experienced traffic flows of between 2,000 to 3,000 vehicles a day in the winter and 8,000 to 9,000 vehicles a day in the summer, with as many as 12,000 vehicles a day at weekends. This level of use meant that at busy periods traffic would be slow moving at speeds often less than 30 mph. The poor quality of the carriageway and the state of congestion experienced on it meant that it was unpopular with road users. The advent of major roadworks further exacerbated the problem. Whatever other reasons may have contributed, it is clear that the level of traffic fell below forecast volumes from 1985 onwards. In contrast the rebuilt A9 was exceeding projected volumes during this period.

Before the scheme commenced the hotel car park extended to 1,355 sq m of which some 1,130 sq m was owned by Mr Bisset and the remaining 225 sq m, for which no rent was paid, was used with the permission of the owners, Luss Estates Ltd. After the land comprising plot 234 had been acquired and the roadworks completed, the car park, including the Luss Estates land, extended to 930 sq m. The remaining car park was therefore some 69 per cent of its original size. It was also of an awkward shape.

On the basis of properly set out car parking spaces the land retained is capable of accommodating a maximum number of 30 vehicles on the 930 sq m, at 31 sq m of land per vehicle. On a pro rata basis the original car park might therefore have been expected to hold not more than 44 vehicles. However, the pre-scheme car park was square in shape as against the L shape of the remaining car park. For that reason it was more efficient in terms of the total number of vehicles it was able to contain. The evidence of Mr Bisset was that the original car parking area could hold 72 or 73 vehicles at the maximum, but in the tribunal's opinion that is substantially overstated. In any event, in the pre-scheme car park there were 12 spaces reserved in connection with a boat hiring business which has now been discontinued.

The hotel has 14 bedrooms and can accommodate 28 people. As well as a large bar, it has a 60 seat dining room. It is heavily dependent on passing trade and attracts custom from United Kingdom and international tourists using the A82, but it is also patronised by local day trippers. In that sector it has been successful in establishing repeat business.

According to the standards for parking specified in the Strathclyde Regional Council Guidelines for Development Roads 1986 the planning requirements for the hotel are as follows:

28 beds at 1 space per 2.5 beds	=	12 spaces
20 staff at 1 space per 3 staff	=	7 spaces
200 sq m bar space at 1 space per 10 sq m bar space	=	20 spaces
		39 spaces

Mr Bisset contended that, since the hotel is so dependent on food and liquor sales, and since it has dining facilities in excess of those normally expected for a hotel with 14 bedrooms, the operational need for car parking spaces for the hotel business is in excess of that which is required for planning purposes. He estimated that 90 per cent of the hotel's patrons came by car.

The turnover of the hotel for the year ending 30 April 1984 was £404,968 and for 1985 £425,172. The average of these two years is £415,070. The turnover for the following years and the corresponding figures adjusted by the retail price index, assuming no growth in trade, are:

	Actual	Anticipated
1986	£384,979	£437,494
1987	£356,888	£450,307
1988	£363,575	£470,901
1989	£352,894	£501,104
5 months to 30.9.89	£163,069	£322,629
7 months to 30.4.90	£122,307	£215,086

The loss of gross profit for the relevant years is as follows:

1987	£26,015
1988	£32,929
1989	£38,580
5 months to 30.9.90	£46,678
7 months to 30.4.90	£23,698

The earth moving operations resulted in the deposit of mud on the roadway and elsewhere. That was exacerbated by the wet weather which characterised the summer of 1988. The mud or dust was carried into the hotel premises. Because the contractors were using the hotel car park for access to the roadworks, mud was also deposited there. Mr Bisset arranged to have the hotel elevations cleaned with a pressure hose and to have the car park swept of mud and other debris. The windows of the hotel had to be cleaned at frequent intervals. Mr Bisset, on the advice of Mr Paul, arranged for a structural survey to be undertaken before blasting commenced. A follow up survey to determine whether any consequential damage had occurred has not been instructed and no such damage is alleged.

The second phase of the scheme was under construction from January 1988 to December 1989. The works in the vicinity of the hotel, including the work on the Inverbeg cut, continued for a period of six months from the beginning of 1988. In spite of the vesting declaration on 9 May 1986 Mr Bisset was allowed to stay on in his original house until July 1988, when he moved into his new house. The new A82 was opened in August 1989, and the access road into the hotel was completed in December 1989. From 14 August to 20 October 1989 access to the hotel was by a temporary route, by the Glen Douglas Road.

The work in the vicinity of the hotel included topsoil removal and, initially, blasting to remove the hill in front of the hotel. Blasting was carried out each day from Monday to Friday at 4 pm. After representa-

A tions were made about the blasting, the work of rock cutting was carried out by means of a hydraulic breaker. The use of such a breaker causes loud and repetitive noise. Mr Bisset was still in occupation of his original house and in close proximity to the area in which the breaker was working. Water and electricity supplies to the new house were cut on a number of occasions and access restricted.

B Mr Bisset received planning permission for the erection of a new house at Inverbeg to replace the house which was acquired. The new house, which was completed in July 1988, is on land owned by Mr Bisset between the new A82 and Loch Lomond. One of the conditions attaching to the planning permission restricted the occupancy of the house in a way which is more accurately set out in a minute of the agreement entered into between Mr Bisset and the planning authority in terms of s 50 of the Town and Country Planning (Scotland) Act 1972. Therein it is provided that: "Occupancy of the dwellinghouse to be erected in accordance with the said Planning Permission shall C be restricted to the Second Party (Mr Bisset), his spouse and their heirs or a person who, by virtue of his or her employment or other direct interest in the economic activity of the area . . . has a need to reside within the said area." The planning agreement also allows for public access across part of the land on which the house stands and makes other provision regarding vehicle access from the A82.

The cost of the house which has been constructed was £111,000. There was only one possible site on D which the house could have been built, and because the site had inherent difficulties, both practical and planning, the cost was alleged to be inflated by £15,882.

Decision
This is a case which involves s 61 of the Lands Clauses Consolidation (Scotland) Act 1845, which states: "In estimating the purchase money or compensation to be paid by the promoters of the undertaking E . . . regard shall be had not only to the value of the land to be purchased or taken by the promoters of the undertaking, but also to the damage, if any, to be sustained by the owner of the lands by reason of the severing of the lands taken from the other lands of such owner, or otherwise injuriously affecting such land by the exercise of the powers of this or the special Act".

In terms of s 12 (2) of the Land Compensation (Scotland) Act 1963 "The value of land shall . . . be taken F to be the amount which the land if sold in the open market by a willing seller might be expected to realise".

The tribunal now turns to the various headings of claim which have been submitted.

Loss of land and buildings
The value of the domestic part of the land acquired has been agreed, as already stated, at £37,000.

That does not include the area of the car park which was acquired. Mr Anderson proposes £1,800 for this, based on a net usable area of 360 sq m at £5 per sq m. G Mr Bisset does not place a specific value on this land, but considers that the claim should be dealt with by reference to the capital cost of acquiring an area of land to replace that taken. That cost is £4,000, being the rent of £500 per year to be charged, capitalised at 8 years' purchase. To that will be added the cost of preparing the new car park, based on an estimate from contractors of £62,000. This is, in effect, the cost of what is considered an equivalent reinstatement to provide a total of about 60 car spaces. H

The basis of equivalent reinstatement is not, however, pressed by Mr Bisset, as it is accepted that there is a general demand for car parking. The claim on record refers to a reduction in value which, in relation to its effect on the hotel, appears to be the relevant approach in the absence of any challenge to the £1,800 proposed by the district valuer. As already stated, the hotel had parking spaces for about 70 cars, although these were nearly all on the other side of the busy main road. The acquisition has left a car park of I awkward shape, which has been shown diagrammatically by Mr Bisset to allow, at the most, 34 car spaces, if the land belonging to Luss Estates is included, and also if the part of the solum of the former A82 in front of the hotel is included.

Mr Anderson, correctly, had considered the severance effect of the loss of car parking, but came to the conclusion that the remaining car park was sufficient for the hotel and that there was therefore no diminution of value of the hotel. The tribunal have J inspected the hotel and car park and do not agree with that conclusion.

There was a suggestion by Mr Anderson that, as is averred on record, any adverse effect on the hotel would be compensated by the betterment arising from the relocation of the main road and by reduced maintenance costs. No quantification of this, however, was presented by Mr Anderson, as would be necessary in view of the terms of s 110 of the Roads (Scotland) Act K 1984, if a set off was to be applied. No betterment can be collected from an owner who benefits from public works but has no land taken from him, and any deduction from compensation due to an owner who has land taken has to be specifically established.

It was submitted by counsel for the Secretary of State that, if the tribunal did not agree with Mr Anderson, there was no evidence about the reduction in value of the hotel which would enable the tribunal to determine any particular figure. There are, L however, two propositions before the tribunal: first, that there has been no diminution of value, and, secondly, that the diminution should be measured by the cost of replacing the lost car parking space, that cost being £4,000 for the land and £62,000 for the necessary work.

The £62,000 is the rounding up of a 1990 estimate of £61,987 to excavate, and dispose to a tip off-site, all unsuitable material, infill to required levels, including provision of materials, supply and lay all sub-base and

black top materials, and provide necessary drainage to
A the existing system. The site which is proposed
extends to about 900 sq m additional to the car park
which remains after the acquisition. The cost was said
to be high because of boggy conditions. The net area
which was lost was 360 sq m, and the tribunal considers that only the replacement of such an area, as far
as practicable, should be taken into account.

The larger area is available from Luss Estates on a
10 year lease at a rent of £500 a year, but Mr Bisset
said that the scheme was not acceptable if he had to
B pay £62,000 for the work. The scheme may not therefore go ahead.

From our inspection an extension to the east of the
existing Luss Estates area could restore the regular
shape of the car park and provide an area equivalent
to that which formerly existed. The costs of preparing
this would be substantially less than £62,000 because
of the discount back to the vesting date, the smaller
area and the fact that the proposed standard is higher
than existed at the vesting date. The tribunal is of the
C opinion that a purchaser intending to acquire the hotel
would make some discount for the restricted parking.
He would take into account the facts set out above,
including the costs of providing extra space, which he
might estimate at just over £18,000. He may, of
course, decide that there is no solution and accept that
the hotel's business may be reduced because of the
inadequate parking.

It is common practice, in valuing subjects with a
liability, to deduct a purchaser's allowance for the cost
D of meeting that liability. That was done in the case of
*McLaren's Discretionary Trustee v Secretary of State for
Scotland*, 1987 SLT (Lands Tr) 25, in which it was
held that the burden of future expenditure on maintenance and renewal of agreed accommodation works
forming part of the retained land fell to be compensated as injurious affection under rule 2 rather than as
consequential loss under rule 6, but having regard to
the likely costs as indicative of reduced value. It was
further held that the district valuer's allowance of a sum
E related to prime costs agreed to by other proprietors
reasonably reflected that diminution in value.

The tribunal comes to the conclusion that the reduction in value due to the severance of part of the car
park would be £10,000.

Loss of business
Because of the disruption by the roadworks it is
claimed that there has been a loss of business amount-
F ing to £376,392, being the gross profit excluding
wages from 1 April 1985, when the roadworks started,
to 30 April 1990. This is calculated by taking the turnover figures for the years ending 30 April 1984 and
1985 and averaging these. The resultant figure of
£415,070 is used as the base for the claim. By adjusting that for inflation and comparing the result with
what was actually achieved in each year, the difference
in the gross profit excluding wages is said to be the
measure of the loss. The calculations on that basis
assume that turnover would have been static in real
terms.

Mr Anderson accepted that the business had been
affected by the disruption caused by the roadworks, G
but only from 1 July 1988, which was the actual date
of displacement, when it was agreed that Mr Bisset
would remove from his house. His proposal is
£78,541. His figures are based on an analysis carried
out by Mr Low. The substantial difference between
the claim and the proposal is caused by several factors.
The first is the period of loss, although Mr Anderson
extends that period to 30 April 1991. The second is
that the exclusion of wages was not considered the
proper basis, and Mr Low's calculation is based on the H
gross profit including wages. Other differences
between his calculations and those of Mr Bisset are his
use of the retail price index instead of a straight 5 per
cent per annum increase; the use of actual figures
rather than a conversion to 1990 prices, and an
allowance for a higher ratio of wages to turnover in the
year ending 30 April 1990. Mr Anderson then
discounts the actual losses because he does not consider that they were entirely due to the roadworks. He
also discounts the losses for the fact that statutory I
interest would accrue from the vesting date on the
whole compensation, so that, if the loss were not
discounted, Mr Bisset would obtain a double benefit.

The claim for compensation for loss of business has
been presented as a claim for disturbance, at least in
its general sense, including damage, loss and expenses,
and it was accepted as such by counsel for the Secretary of State. In assessing it, the first thing to be
decided is when the loss should be held to have commenced. In the amended closed record it is averred J
that Mr Bisset suffered a loss of business from the date
of service of the notice of vesting, which was 7 April
1986, and it is further averred that since the date of
vesting, on 9 May of the same year, the turnover of the
hotel had fallen and Mr Bisset lost profits as a result.
However, counsel for Mr Bisset submitted that the
date when the loss should be held to have commenced
should be earlier than the date of vesting and should
be when the business first started to suffer from the
effects of the whole roadworks covered by the scheme, K
that being when the first phase was begun on 1 April
1985. For support for that submission he relied on the
decisions in *Smith v Strathclyde Regional Council*,
1982 SLT (Lands Tr) 2, and *City of Aberdeen District
Council v Sim*, 1983 SLT 250. In the submission of
counsel for the Secretary of State, the commencing
date for the loss due to disturbance should be 1 July
1988, which was the date of Mr Bisset's actual
physical dispossession. The purpose of compensation L
for disturbance was to put a proprietor in the same
position as if he had not been physically dispossessed
of his land. Accordingly, it was submitted, disturbance
necessarily involved dispossession in the sense of
physical dispossession or displacement, and for there
to be a right to compensation there must be a causal
connection between the alleged loss and the physical
dispossession. It was accepted that there might be
circumstances in which certain losses or types of
expenditure incurred before the date of physical dispossession could be allowed, but that could only be

where there was the necessary causal connection.

A There had been such a connection in *Smith* and *City of Aberdeen District Council,* but here, it was submitted, there was no connection between Mr Bisset's physical dispossession and any losses caused by the roadworks either during the first phase of the scheme or during the second phase in the period prior to that dispossession on 1 July 1988. By that date the first phase was complete. Any loss suffered by Mr Bisset during that phase would therefore have been suffered even if no land had been taken from him, just as it was

B suffered by other local residents who had no right to compensation. As far as that phase was concerned, the date of vesting had no relevance, since the position was the same both before and after that date. With regard to the second phase, it was submitted that the position was similar up to the date of physical dispossession, and that any loss of profits before that must be regarded as having resulted from something other than the acquisition. For further support for the contention that to be compensatable any disturbance

C must result from physical dispossession or displacement, counsel for the Secretary of State referred to the terms of s 34 of the Land Compensation (Scotland) Act 1973.

In *Venables v Department of Agriculture for Scotland,* 1932 SLT 411; 1932 SC 573, the Lord Justice Clerk (Alness) stated, at 1932 SLT, p 415: "The sound principle would seem to be that the person dispossessed should get compensation for all loss occasioned to him by reason of his dispossession." The tests which

D should be applied were held to be those stated by Romer LJ in *Harvey v Crawley Development Corporation* [1957] 1 QB 485, at p 494, where he said: "any loss sustained by a dispossessed owner (at all events one who occupies his house) which flows from a compulsory acquisition may properly be regarded as the subject of compensation for disturbance, provided first, that it is not too remote and, secondly, that it is the natural and reasonable consequence of the dispossession of the owner". In both these cases the dis-

E turbance consisted of the simple loss and the expenses caused by physical displacement. In *Smith* the tribunal held that the consequences of dispossession should be considered in a causal rather than a temporal sense. That was approved by the Court of Session in *City of Aberdeen District Council.* The Court of Appeal in *Prasad v Wolverhampton Borough Council* [1983] Ch 333 confirmed the causal meaning of consequence and likewise approved the tribunal's reasoning in *Smith.*

F Counsel for the Secretary of State submitted that until the date of displacement Mr Bisset was in no different position from other owners of land who had not had land taken from them and therefore were not entitled to compensation. The difference, however, is that Mr Bisset, by having land taken, is entitled to compensation on a different basis from those who are equally affected by the road scheme but have not had land taken. The latter have their own right to statutory compensation either under s 6 of the Railways Clauses Consolidation (Scotland) Act 1845, for loss resulting

from the execution of the works, or Pt I of the Land Compensation (Scotland) Act 1973 for depreciation in G value caused by the subsequent use of the works.

In this case the statutory compensation to Mr Bisset allows a claim for loss of profits. The loss of profits agreed by Mr Anderson to be due to the Scottish Development Department's road scheme, as contained in the compulsory purchase order, was not caused by the physical displacement of Mr Bisset from his house and plot of land. It was due to the exercise of compulsory purchase powers and the execution of the road works. It is an injurious affection loss affecting the H land which was not taken but which was held with the acquired land. Mr Bisset was not physically displaced from his hotel.

In our opinion, the provisions of s 34 of the 1973 Act do not support the view that compensation for loss of business by the hotel is only due in respect of the loss incurred after the date of Mr Bisset's physical displacement. Those provisions are concerned with disturbance payments to persons without compen- I satable interests but who are in lawful possession of the land. It is specifically provided that to be entitled to such a payment the person must be "displaced" from the land. That is entirely logical, since such a person's interest is not affected by vesting per se, and there is no purchase price to be determined in respect of his interest. In terms of s 35 the amount of the disturbance payment is to be equal to the reasonable expenses of removing from the land from which the person is displaced and, if he was carrying on a trade J or business on the land, the loss sustained by reason of the disturbance of that trade or business. That is what may be described as pure disturbance, and it is provided that it must be consequent, in the causal sense, upon the person having to quit the land, that is, upon his displacement from it. It should also be noted that, in terms of s 34 (5), it is from the date of displacement that interest runs on such a disturbance payment. Those provisions accordingly provide no support for the proposition that compensation for loss K of profits due to injurious affection can only arise from the date of physical displacement.

On the whole matter, therefore, we do not accept the submission of counsel for the Secretary of State that Mr Bisset can only have a right to compensation for the hotel's loss of profits from the date of his own physical displacement. The question then is from what other date compensation for loss of profits is due.

In *Venables* the Lord Justice Clerk referred to the L following passage from Cripps on *Compensation* (7th ed), at p 172: "The loss to an owner, whose lands are acquired or have been taken, omitting all question of injury to adjoining lands, includes not only the actual value of such lands but all damage directly consequent on the taking thereof under statutory powers." His Lordship also referred to a passage in the opinion of Lord Kinnear in *Lanarkshire and Dumbartonshire Railway Co v Main* (1895) 22 R 912 at p 919: "it is a well-settled rule in the construction of the Lands Clauses Act that when lands have been taken in the exercise of powers of compulsory purchase, the owner or occupier, as the case may be, is entitled not only to the market value of his interest but to full compensation for all the loss which he may sustain by being deprived of his land". From his judgment it is clear that the Lord Justice Clerk accepted and approved these statements, which both relate the loss to the taking of the land.

All compensation payable for the acquisition of an interest in land is part of the purchase price for the interest. Where the vesting procedure is applied the interest is taken at the vesting date. The purchase price has to be determined at that date, which is therefore the valuation date: see *Renfrew's Trs v Glasgow Corporation*, 1972 SLT (Lands Tr) 2, and *Ware v Edinburgh District Council*, 1976 SLT (Lands Tr) 21. The purchase price consists of the market value of the land, together with any losses due to severance and injurious affection, and any other damage, loss or expense consequent on the taking of the land under statutory powers. The owner, in determining his selling price, is entitled, in terms of s 61, to have these items taken into account. The valuer has therefore to consider, at the valuation date, what losses are foreseeable, so that the purchase price can be determined. The practice has grown, particularly in vesting cases, of waiting until the damage, loss or expense has occurred, and of then using that after-knowledge to assist in the assessment of the purchase price at the valuation date. That is in accordance with the principle in *Bwllfa and Merthyr Dare Steam Collieries Ltd v Pontypridd Waterworks Co* [1903] AC 426.

In the present case the assessment has been delayed until the loss of profits has become known, although some attempt had been made earlier to forecast them. Mr Anderson had estimated the pre-contract loss at £6,000, the loss during the contract at £14,000 and the post-contract loss at £10,000.

As stated above, the compensation for loss of profits is accepted by Mr Anderson as being due because of the Scottish Development Department's road scheme, and he concedes that there were losses due to that from 1 April 1985 when the contract began. Injurious affection, as referred to in ss 48 and 61 of the 1845 Act, consists of the loss, on the land not taken, occasioned by both the construction and the subsequent use of the works: see Cripps' *Compulsory Acquisition of Land* (11th ed), at para 4-260. No claim, however, is here made for any adverse effect of the subsequent use of the road.

Mr Anderson's approach to the losses is in accordance with Cripps at paras 4-277, 4-278 and 4-283, where it is made clear that losses due to injurious affection such as occurred at Inverbeg are admissible. As Mr Anderson's assessment of loss is based on the scheme, he clearly has not limited it to the works which took place on the relatively short length of road built on Mr Bisset's plot of land. Taking the scheme into account means that he has invoked s 41 of the Land Compensation (Scotland) Act 1973, which provides that compensation for injurious affection of land

retained by the person whose other land has been taken shall be assessed by reference to the whole of the works and not only the part situated on the land taken from him. In subs (2) of that section "compensation for injurious affection" is stated to mean compensation for injurious affection under s 61 of the 1845 Act, and that, as already stated, includes such losses.

It is conceded by Mr Anderson that the road works were causing a loss of profits even before the vesting date, and also in the period from the vesting date until 30 April 1991. That loss from the vesting date was occasioned by Mr Bisset's land being taken by the Secretary of State at that date in order to enable the whole scheme to be programmed and constructed. It could be foreseen at the valuation date that such loss would take place. That was therefore required to be taken into account in determining the purchase price at the date of valuation. Any determination of other losses or expenses which were consequent on the taking of the land by compulsory powers would likewise take into account what happened at a particular time.

For those reasons we are satisfied that compensation for loss of profits due to the roadworks should run from the vesting date.

The next matter to be decided is whether wages should be excluded from the calculations of gross profit. It would be accepted normally that a loss of turnover would be matched by a reduction of purchases, consumables and wages, and that the measure of a loss of business should therefore be by reference to the gross profit. However, Mr Bisset submits that there is a minimum staff level necessary to operate the hotel, and it is implicit in his claim that this was the position in 1984-85. As the turnover dropped, he claimed that his wage bill did not reduce substantially and his loss was therefore aggravated beyond the normal gross profit margins. Yet an analysis produced by Mr Low showed that in the years from 1985 to 1989 the actual gross profit, including wages, ranged from 30.21 per cent to 34.45 per cent of turnover. The respective percentages of wages to turnover ranged from 19.89 per cent to 21.37 per cent. These percentages do not bear out Mr Bisset's contention. In the year ending 1990 there was an apparent increase in the percentage of wages to turnover. Mr Low identified an element of administrative wages in the figures and he adjusted for that. He accepted, however, that there was a 10 per cent tolerance which could be added to the loss of gross profit. This was added to the gross profit for the period up to 30 April 1990 and increased the total by £7,038.

The tribunal determines that the proper measure of the loss should be the gross profit including wages. Mr Low's adjustment to the 1989-90 year is also accepted.

Mr Low's figures were used as a basis by Mr Anderson, and he applied his two sets of discounting referred to above. He adopted his own estimate after 30 September 1989 because the main road and the permanent access to the hotel had been opened by then.

Starting from the vesting date in May 1986 the first loss of gross profit is for the year ending 30 April 1987 and then for the following years up to 30 April 1989. That is followed by the five months up to the opening of the road in October 1989.

Mr Bisset has asked for 100 per cent of these figures during the whole period. Mr Anderson proposes that the loss should be assessed as follows: 60 per cent for 1987; 70 per cent for 1988; 85 per cent for 1989 and 100 per cent for the period from 1 May 1989 to 30 September 1989. A summary of his reasons for the reductions is as follows: the A82 was becoming a busy, accident prone stretch of road, and the A9 was becoming a more popular alternative access to the north; the weather in the summers of the years involved was not particularly good; bedroom occupancy rose only slightly in the period 1984-1989, and, finally, there was possible competition from the Duck Bay Marina and the Lomond Castle Hotel. Those reasons were disputed by Mr Bisset.

The tribunal is not convinced that those factors made a contribution to the losses incurred. The A82 is accepted as being a very busy, narrow road, but there was some evidence that three hotels on that road had increased their turnover in real terms during the period 1986-1989. The claim is submitted on the basis of no growth in real terms. The claimed losses are, therefore, only to maintain the business in real terms as it was in 1983-84 and 1984-85. The summers of those years would be affected by the difficult road conditions and also by the earlier road construction further south. The Scottish summer weather is notoriously unreliable but that does not appear to have affected the other establishments referred to above. It was stated that 1985 was the wettest year since 1879, yet the loss in that summer produced the lowest drop in gross profit, and, of course, was before the vesting date. The movement of traffic has already been itemised and the amounts of material passing the hotel recorded. The contractor's compound was only 150 m away from the hotel, the blasting took place in an area south of the car park, and from 8 August to 26 November 1989, a temporary access was used for the hotel.

It is clear that there was considerable disruption to the hotel during the whole period from May 1986 to November 1989. As there is no firm evidence that there was any other cause of the losses, the tribunal determines that the full losses should be allowed for that period. Thus the figures for the years ending 30 April 1987, 1988 and 1989, and for the five months to 30 September 1989, which are determined, are respectively £26,015, £32,929, £38,580 and £51,346, giving a total of £148,870. Although the claim was only for the period up to 30 April 1990, Mr Anderson considered that there could still be a loss up to 30 April 1991, and he has conceded that. Mr Low had assessed the gross profit loss for the seven months to 30 April 1990 at £26,068, which is close to Mr Anderson's subjective estimate of £28,000. Mr Anderson, however, only allows 80 per cent for the period to 31 December 1989 and 60 per cent up to 30 April 1990. Applying his estimate of £4,000 per month for the year to 30 April 1991, he discounts that by 70 per cent. The gross profit/loss which he calculates is therefore £31,200, which exceeds the £25,274 claimed for the final period.

The tribunal accepts Mr Anderson's figures for the period from 30 September 1989 to 30 April 1991.

These losses were calculated by using the actual yearly losses compared with the anticipated figures, allowing for inflation, which should have been attained if the business had remained static. Statutory interest will accrue from the vesting date, and Mr Anderson, correctly in the tribunal's opinion, discounts the losses back to the vesting date. That was not disputed by Mr Bisset, and the tribunal therefore accepts the calculations involved in that. They have the following effect on the above figures for the appropriate years, so that they become as follows: for 1987 £24,506; 1988 £28,088; 1989 £30,285; to 30 September 1989 £37,803. The remaining period up to 30 April 1990 is discounted to £21,433.

The total figure for loss of business is therefore determined at £142,115.

Additional incidental costs and disruption

The acquiring authority describes these as "rule 6 minor elements".

(1) The cost of equipment for pressure washing the building frontage is agreed at £175.

(2) The cost of painting the hotel after the road works were completed is accepted in principle by Mr Anderson, but he considered that, as painting was an ongoing charge, only 50 per cent should be allowed. However, after hearing the evidence, Mr Anderson was prepared to allow £2,332, which was above 50 per cent of the actual cost. The tribunal accepts that as reasonable.

(3) The cost of window cleaning was estimated by Mr Bisset at £600. Mr Anderson considered that, as the hotel was close to the road prior to the new road works, window cleaning would be necessary in any event. He allowed one half of that, namely £300, and the tribunal accepts that as reasonable.

(4) £300 for cleaning the car park was agreed.

(5) The surveyor who had been instructed to survey the condition of the hotel building prior to the road works had submitted a fee of £716. That is accepted by Mr Anderson. A claim had been made for a further fee, but the surveyor has not been instructed to re-survey, and, as already stated, no claim has been lodged for damage and it appears unlikely that it will be necessary. The tribunal therefore determines the claim at £716.

The total under this heading was rounded off by Mr Anderson at £4,000, although the actual figure was £3,823. £4,000 is accordingly determined by the tribunal.

Disturbance caused to Mr Bisset and his family

A The first part of this claim is for £5,000 for the blasting and breaking of rock close to Mr Bisset's original house. That took place in 1988. The second part is for £1,000 in respect of disruption to the access and the water and electricity supplies to the new house.

The claim was opposed by counsel for the Secretary of State on the ground that it was for disturbance or inconvenience to the person, which was not an incident of land but was a purely personal matter. To
B be compensatable, it was submitted, any damage, disruption or disturbance must be a direct consequence of the compulsory acquisition and must result in some loss of value to Mr Bisset's land, so that thereby it caused damage to an interest in land. This claim, by contrast, was for something akin to solatium in a claim for damages for personal injury.

Counsel for Mr Bisset submitted, however, that personal disturbance was covered by the words "dis-
C turbance or any other matter not directly based on the value of land" in rule 6 for the assessment of compensation in terms of the 1963 Act.

In *Venables* it was held that the tenant of a sporting estate, which had been acquired under compulsory powers, was entitled to full compensation for all loss resulting to him from his dispossession, and so was entitled to compensation for any loss occasioned by the removal or by the disposal of livestock, implements and other property on the estate. That loss,
D however, was entirely the pecuniary or material loss which the claimant had sustained by being deprived of his land — see per the Lord Justice Clerk (Alness) at 1932 SLT, p 413 and Lord Ormidale at p 415. As it was put by Lord Anderson, at p 417: "the determining consideration would seem to be whether the claimant, by reason of dispossession, has been put to expense".

In *Nisbet Hamilton v The Commissioners of Northern Lighthouses* (1886) 13 R 710, the claim was in respect
E of damage which it was apprehended would be done to the amenity of a mansion house and to the feuing prospects of the estate by the use of a foghorn which might be installed at a lighthouse which was to be built on a nearby island. Land on the island had been compulsorily acquired from the claimant for the building of the lighthouse. Although it was not for identical reasons that a majority of their Lordships in the Second Division held that the claim could not be maintained, there was agreement that for there to be
F a right to compensation the injury in question must be an injury which affected property, and that such damage as might be caused by the sound of a foghorn would be of the nature of a personal nuisance to the proprietrix of the estate rather than an injury to her property. Although Lord Rutherfurd Clark dissented, it was on another ground, and he accepted that for there to be a right to compensation the injury must be to land. The ratio of the decision was similar in *Caledonian Railway Co v Ogilvie* (1852) 2 Macq 600, in which the House of Lords held that a landowner was not entitled to compensation where the injury was caused by the placing of a railway level crossing on a public road near the entrance to his property, since
G that was a personal inconvenience rather than an injury to the property. That has been the basis of a long line of decisions. In every case the loss for which compensation has been allowed has been a loss of value or some other loss or expense which could be quantified in money terms, and which the owner sustained by being deprived of his land.

While counsel for the Secretary of State submitted, for the reasons already stated, that in law this was not a valid claim, no authority was adduced, and no real
H argument was presented, to the contrary. There would appear to be no reported cases in Scotland in which such claims for personal disturbance have been admitted, and there is a considerable weight of authority against them. The tribunal, accordingly, is not prepared, as at present advised, to introduce such a category of compensation.

Extraordinary costs in connection with the new house
I The tribunal now turns to the last part of the claim, which relates to extraordinary costs in connection with the house which Mr Bisset has built to replace the accommodation which was on the plot of land acquired. The house which was acquired is included in the value of £37,000 already stated as agreed. Mr Bisset received planning permission to erect the new house, and the position regarding the s 50 agreement has already been set out. Mr Bisset makes a claim of just under £16,000 for the items under this head. The
J whole claim is rejected by Mr Anderson, since he considers that Mr Bisset has got value for money in the new house, and that the claim is not established otherwise.

As a matter of principle, the existence in s 12 of the Land Compensation (Scotland) Act 1963 of rule 5, which provides for compensation on the basis of the cost of equivalent reinstatement, does not mean that anything in the nature of reinstatement must be disregarded where rule 5 does not apply: see Leach on
K *Disturbance on Compulsory Purchase* (3rd ed), para 35. The unproductive part of the cost of a new building on a new site has been allowed: see *John I Fearn (Agricultural) Ltd v British Electricity Authority* (1952) 3 P & CR 94.

Prior to the tribunal considering the items which are claimed, the following comments on the house which has been built appear appropriate. It is on a unique site, which normally would not have been likely to
L obtain planning permission for house building. The circumstances of the acquisition would appear to have had a considerable influence on the grant of such permission, as is evidenced by the terms of the s 50 agreement. To erect a house on this site would have involved any prospective owner in additional costs compared with a standard site. These would have included additional architect's fees, the legal expenses of obtaining servitude rights of access through the underpass constructed by the acquiring authority, the cost of planning application fees and the legal fees for

a minute of waiver. These are all items which have been claimed. As far as the additional cost of slates is concerned, that was the result of a planning condition for a high amenity site. The additional foundation costs and the cost of the electricity supply and the calor gas tank are all related to the value of the site if the land had had to be purchased. These costs will now be reflected in the value of the site and therefore in our opinion are not reimbursable. As already stated, the site is a unique one and obviously of considerable value. However, the value could not be realised unless a purchaser was prepared to meet the cost of obtaining and implementing planning permission as well as the cost of providing services and access, together with the cost of obtaining any necessary servitude. These costs would be taken into account by a purchaser in making his offer for the site. Conversely, the expenditure once made would enhance the value of the land to that extent. Mr Bisset has made that expenditure and thus has the benefit of that increased value. The onus is on him to establish that the expenditure did not enhance the value. This has not been done, and the tribunal accordingly finds that he has received value for money. Accordingly, the tribunal makes no award in respect of these items under this heading of expenditure. That leaves a sum of £1,980 for additional costs associated with overtime working to finish the new house earlier than had been arranged, in order to give entry to the road contractors. Mr Bisset was under the impression that he could stay in his original house until the end of July 1988, but he was asked to vacate it on 1 July. In the event, he did not have to move until nearer the end of the month, so that the expenditure was in fact unnecessary. The tribunal is not satisfied that the expenditure could not have been avoided by prior consultation, and in the tribunal's opinion it is too remote from the acquisition. We do not therefore accept it.

The result of all the determinations is as follows:

Section 12 (2)	£38,800
Severance	£10,000
Section 12 (6) loss of gross profit	£142,115
Minor elements	£4,000
	£194,915

In addition a surveyor's fee in accordance with Ryde's scale will be payable by the acquiring authority.

Counsel for Claimant, Brodie, QC; Solicitors, McGrigor Donald, Edinburgh — Counsel for Respondent, Campbell, QC; Solicitor, R Brodie, Solicitor to the Secretary of State for Scotland.

Bisset v Secretary of State for Scotland (No 2)

LANDS TRIBUNAL FOR SCOTLAND

SHERIFF A C HORSFALL, QC;
W HALL, FRICS; A R MACLEARY, FRICS

12 APRIL 1991

Expenses — Award — Tender — Compulsory purchase compensation — Award slightly less than sum tendered — Acquiring authority in evidence supporting lower figure than awarded, omitting head of claim found justified — Authority prepared to allow other sum disallowed by tribunal — Whether special reasons for not finding claimant liable in expenses — Land Compensation (Scotland) Act 1963 (c 51), s 11 (1).

The owner of an hotel, part of the land of which had been compulsorily acquired for road widening, sought compensation of £514,112, made up of various elements. After a hearing the tribunal awarded £194,915. The acquiring authority had previously made an unconditional offer of £200,000. In evidence the authority supported a lower figure on the basis that a claim for loss of profits could only arise from the date of physical dispossession, on which point the tribunal found against the authority. The authority had however been prepared to allow a sum of £6,253 which the tribunal did not include in its award. The claimant argued that these factors, together with the small margin by which the award fell short of the offer, constituted special reasons for not finding him liable in expenses in terms of s 11 (1) of the Land Compensation (Scotland) Act 1963. The acquiring authority sought a finding of no expenses due prior to the date of the offer in view of a delay in quantifying the loss of profits claim and a late amendment substantially increasing certain sums claimed.

Held, (1) that none of the factors founded on by the claimant constituted special reasons in terms of s 11 (1) (pp 22F-G and 22I-23A); and (2) that the factors founded on by the authority had not added materially to the expense of the proceedings, and that the claimant was entitled to his expenses to the date of the offer (p 23H-J).

Reference to determine compensation

Mr Jack Arthur Bisset, Inverbeg Hotel, Inverbeg, Dunbartonshire, referred to the Lands Tribunal for Scotland the question of compensation payable after the compulsory acquisition of ground at the Inverbeg Hotel, Inverbeg, Dunbartonshire.

On 23 January 1991 the tribunal *pronounced* an order *determining* the compensation to be £194,915, with in addition a surveyor's fee calculated in accordance with Ryde's scale. (Reported 1994 SLT (Lands Tr) 12.)

On 12 April 1991, following a second hearing, the

tribunal *pronounced* an order *finding* the acquiring authority liable to the claimant in his expenses up to the date of their lodging of an unconditional offer, *finding* the claimant liable to the acquiring authority in their expenses after that date, both on the Court of Session scale, *certifying* the case as appropriate for the employment of counsel and *certifying* the expert witnesses.

The note attached to this order was in the following terms:

THE TRIBUNAL.—The compensation claimed by Mr Bisset was £514,112. On 18 May 1990, in the course of the proceedings before the tribunal, an unconditional offer of £200,000, together with a surveyor's fee, was made on behalf of the Secretary of State and was lodged with the clerk of tribunal. In the event the tribunal awarded £194,915, together with a surveyor's fee.

Section 11 (1) of the Land Compensation (Scotland) Act 1963 provides that where "(a) the acquiring authority have made an unconditional offer in writing of any sum as compensation to any claimant and the sum awarded by the Lands Tribunal to that claimant does not exceed the sum offered . . . the Lands Tribunal shall, unless for special reasons it thinks proper not to do so, order the claimant to bear his own expenses and to pay the expenses of the acquiring authority so far as they were incurred after the offer was made".

In terms of that provision, since the award was of less than the offer, the tribunal must order Mr Bisset to bear his own expenses and to pay the Secretary of State's expenses so far as they were incurred after 18 May 1990, unless it can hold that there are here special reasons why it should not do so.

On behalf of Mr Bisset it was submitted that special reasons could be found in certain features of the case. The first was in the nature of some of the evidence given on behalf of the Secretary of State. The second was in the fact that the award had only fallen short of the offer because the tribunal had failed to include an item of compensation which the Secretary of State's principal witness had been prepared to allow. The witness was Mr J S Anderson, the principal valuer in the district valuer's office, Dumbarton. It was to Mr Anderson's evidence that the first of the alleged special reasons also related.

The criticism of Mr Anderson's evidence was that, although he must have been fully aware that an offer of compensation had been lodged for the sum of £200,000, he nevertheless spoke in evidence to £121,500 on the basis that a claim for disturbance can only arise from the date of physical dispossession, which occurred on 1 July 1988. If the tribunal held that all disturbance to trade should be taken into account from the date of vesting, then he spoke to £168,500.

We cannot agree, however, that that could be regarded as a special reason in terms of s 11 (1) of the

Act. The fact that that evidence, led on behalf of the Secretary of State, was designed to secure an award much lower than the compensation already offered could not be said to have resulted in the proceedings being prolonged or in any additional expense having been needlessly incurred. In particular, it could hardly have played a part in Mr Bisset's decision not to accept the offer, either when it was lodged or at a later stage in the proceedings, and it was not suggested that it had done so. If anything, the fact that the Secretary of State was still pressing for a substantially smaller award might be expected to have served as an incentive to accept the offer. In any event, it was up to Mr Bisset to consider the offer as it stood and from his own point of view, and not in the context of the evidence of Mr Anderson.

In the £168,500, which was the appropriate figure following the tribunal's decision that loss to trade ran from the vesting date, Mr Anderson was prepared to allow, but the tribunal did not include in its award, the sum of £6,253 in respect of loss of gross profit due to the road works before the date of vesting of the land acquired from Mr Bisset. It was submitted on Mr Bisset's behalf that it would be inequitable, the loss having been conceded by Mr Anderson, that it should nevertheless be disallowed by the tribunal, with the result that the total award was brought below the offer, which it would otherwise have exceeded.

In the end of the day, however, this pre-vesting loss was not conceded. On behalf of the Secretary of State counsel at the debate on expenses stated that in his opinion, as a matter of law, Mr Anderson should not have conceded a loss prior to the date of vesting, and that he was in error in so doing. It should be observed that even in the amended closed record Mr Bisset refers only to loss of profits since the date of vesting. From that and the presentation of his case it became clear that, although he produced figures for the pre-vesting period, Mr Bisset was not relying on a claim for that period. In the circumstances, the tribunal was in no way bound by the fact that Mr Anderson would himself have allowed the pre-vesting loss. To have allowed it would have been inconsistent with what the tribunal held was the proper approach, and when comparing the offer with the award for the purpose of determining liability for expenses, the tribunal is not obliged to regard Mr Anderson's view as a material factor.

Another factor which it was suggested might constitute a special reason within the meaning of s 11 (1) was that the award had fallen short of the offer by a very small margin, of between only 2 and 3 per cent. Counsel also submitted that it could be argued that there had here been undercompensation as a result of the "device" adopted by the tribunal of discounting the loss back to the date of vesting and valuation, and of then allowing only simple interest from that date. That method brings out a smaller capital sum than if there had been no discounting back. However, far from being a device, it is the only way in which the true gross profit loss can properly be calculated. Since

Mr Bisset must receive statutory simple interest on the loss of profit from the date of vesting, the loss has to be discounted back to that date, on the same simple interest basis, in order to arrive at the actual loss. That, accordingly, cannot be regarded as a special reason for not giving its normal effect to the fact that the award is less than the sum offered. Neither, in our opinion, is it a special reason that the award is so close to the offer.

During the course of the hearing the question was raised, whether the offer was of as much as £200,000, and so was greater than the award, only because in its quantification a sum had erroneously been included for the pre-vesting loss of profits, even though the Secretary of State's position was that that was not a valid item of claim. There was no indication that Mr Bisset had requested details of the offer in respect of each head of claim: cf Cripps, *Compulsory Acquisition of Land* (11th ed), para 3-234. We do not think, however, that, in deciding whether special reasons exist, we can attempt to speculate on the composition of the £200,000, assuming that to be competent. That is particularly so in view of counsel's statement that the amount of the offer was not a summation of various detailed figures, but was a "broad" figure, based on a broad axe estimate. When comparing it with the award, we must therefore simply take the £200,000 as it stands and look at it as a whole.

Accordingly, we do not find in the case anything in the way of special reasons which would justify an exception to the general rule set out in s 11 (1) of the Act. We therefore order that Mr Bisset should bear his own expenses and should pay the Secretary of State's expenses so far as they were incurred after 18 May 1990.

With regard to expenses before that date, it is not in dispute that the tribunal may deal with these in such manner as in its discretion it thinks fit, in accordance with rule 33 (1) of its own rules and having regard to the general principles relating to awards of expenses. These include the general principle that expenses should follow success: see *McLaren's Tr v Secretary of State for Scotland*, 1989 SLT 83 and *Pepys v London Transport Executive* [1975] 1 WLR 234. Counsel for the Secretary of State accepted that the normal rule was to award a successful claimant his expenses up to the date of an unconditional offer. He also accepted that the onus was therefore on him to show that there were here special circumstances to justify his motion that the tribunal should make no order in respect of the expenses before that date.

He submitted that there were a number of such circumstances. First, there was the delay in quantifying the claim until the actual loss of profits had become known. Then there had been a delay in producing accounts. Earlier offers for a settlement of the claim had therefore to be made on the basis of the best information available. The unconditional offer had been made as soon as was possible after receipt of the accounts for the year to 30 April 1989, which were not produced until 3 May 1990. It had therefore been virtually impossible to negotiate a reasonable settlement at any time before the lodging of the unconditional offer. Lastly, a fundamental change in the basis of the claim had been made by a minute of amendment received on 22 August 1990. Intimation of the intention to amend had been made only a few days after the offer of 18 May 1990. That had resulted in the discharge, on 29 May 1990, of the original hearing, which had been fixed for 31 May 1990.

In our opinion, however, these factors do not justify a departure from the normal rule. As has already been observed in the tribunal's decision, the practice has grown, particularly in vesting cases, of waiting until a loss has occurred, and of then using that after-knowledge to assist in the assessment of the purchase price at the valuation date. That is a practice which has obvious advantages, even though it may result in further information coming in at intervals while a claim is being pursued. We are not satisfied that that added materially to the expenses of the proceedings before the tribunal in the period before 18 May 1990, or that those expenses were increased by such delays as there were in producing accounts.

While the minute of amendment resulted in large increases in certain of the sums claimed, it did not, in our opinion, make a fundamental change in the basis of the claim that it should affect liability for pre-amendment expenses. In view of the date when the amendment was made, the consequent expenses, including those of the discharged diet of 31 May 1990, are covered by the order regarding those expenses incurred after 18 May 1990. We accordingly find Mr Bisset entitled to his expenses before that date in the usual way.

Parties were agreed that the case should be certified as suitable for the employment of senior counsel, and that is clearly appropriate. On joint motion we have certified as expert witnesses James Stewart Anderson, Peter Low, Michael Paul and Andrew Sturges.

————————

Counsel for Claimant, Brodie, QC; Solicitors, McGrigor Donald, Edinburgh — Counsel for Acquiring Authority, Moynihan; Solicitor, R Brodie, Solicitor to the Secretary of State for Scotland.

Ashbourne Homes plc v Assessor for Central Region

A

LANDS TRIBUNAL FOR SCOTLAND
SHERIFF A C HORSFALL, QC;
A R MACLEARY, FRICS; J DEVINE, FRICS
16 DECEMBER 1992

B

Valuation — Appeal — Application to valuation appeal committee to refer appeal to Lands Tribunal — Appeal to Lands Tribunal against committee's decision not to refer — Valuation Appeal Committee Procedure (Scotland) Regulations 1984 (SI 1984/1506), reg 4 (3) (d) — Valuation for Rating (Decapitalisation Rate) (Scotland) Regulations 1990 (SI 1990/505), reg 2 (3).

Ratepayers who had appealed against the assessment of a nursing home applied to the valuation appeal committee to refer the appeal to the Lands Tribunal. The assessor opposed the application. The committee decided not to refer the appeal. The ratepayers

C appealed to the tribunal against that decision on the ground specified in reg 4 (3) (d) of the Valuation Appeal Committee Procedure (Scotland) Regulations 1984, namely that the case raised "a fundamental or general issue likely to be used as a precedent in other cases". The principal issue was as to whether the nursing home was a "hospital" within the meaning of reg 2 (3) of the Valuation for Rating (Decapitalisation Rate) (Scotland) Regulations 1990, and as to what therefore was the decapitalisation rate to be applied to

D it in a valuation using the contractor's principle. The ratepayers claimed that the nursing home had been valued in accordance with a scheme of valuation for nursing homes throughout Scotland, which had been agreed between the Scottish assessors and which was based on general cost information relating to subjects other than nursing homes. Any decision in the case would therefore be likely to be of general importance and to be used as a precedent.

Held, that an examination of the factors which had
E a bearing on the question whether a particular nursing home was a hospital, appeared to raise general issues which would be likely to be used as a precedent in other cases (p 27C-E); and appeal *upheld*.

Reference of disputed valuation
Ashbourne Homes plc appealed against a decision of the valuation appeal committee not to refer to the
F Lands Tribunal an appeal against the entry made in the valuation roll by the Assessor for Central Region in respect of a nursing home at Dalnair House, Croftamie.

On 16 December 1992 the tribunal *pronounced* an order *upholding* the appeal.

The opinion attached to the tribunal's order was in the following terms:

THE TRIBUNAL.—Ashbourne Homes plc are the

owners and occupiers of a nursing home at Dalnair
House, Croftamie, in Central Region. The subjects G were entered in the valuation roll with effect from 1 April 1990 at a net annual value of £106,000.

An appeal was lodged against that entry, and the case was cited for hearing before the valuation appeal committee. The ratepayers then applied to the committee for the appeal to be referred to the Lands Tribunal. In written representations on the application the assessor expressed the opinion that a referral to the tribunal was unnecessary. The committee subsequently declined to refer the appeal. The rate- H payers have now appealed to the tribunal against that decision.

The appeal is in terms of subs (3BA) of s 1 of the Lands Tribunal Act 1949. The subsection is in the following terms: "The Lands Tribunal for Scotland may also determine any appeal against the decision of a valuation appeal committee not to refer to the Tribunal any appeal or complaint made to the committee and, where the Tribunal upholds such an appeal, the appeal or complaint made to the com- I mittee shall, for the purposes of this section, be regarded as having been referred by the committee to the Tribunal for determination under subsection (3A) above."

The grounds on which a valuation appeal committee may refer an appeal to the Lands Tribunal are set out in reg 4 (3) of the Valuation Appeal Committee Procedure (Scotland) Regulations 1984. That regulation specifies five categories of ground for referring an J appeal to the tribunal. The regulation provides that, if it appears to the committee that the case comes into one or more of those categories, it shall refer the appeal to the tribunal. One of the grounds is that contained in para (d) of reg 4 (3), namely, that the case raises a fundamental or general issue likely to be used as a precedent in other cases.

The ratepayers claimed that this case came within that category for the reasons set out in a letter dated 5 June 1992 from their agents to the secretary of the K committee. In the letter it was stated:

"The grounds on which this application is made are as follows:

"*Fundamental or general issues — Regulation 4 (3) (d)*

"It is understood that the assessor has derived the assessment for nursing homes in accordance with cost information which has been 'collated' on a national basis with other regional assessors, to which a decapitalisation rate has been applied. It is our further L understanding that costs relating to homes other than nursing homes have been used to arrive at the assessor's valuation rate per square metre.

"In the first instance, the basic rate per square metre adopted for nursing [homes] is being questioned on the basis that nursing homes form a particular class of subject within the general grouping of homes. This contention is supported by the statutory controls specifically for nursing homes which put certan obligations on the operator of the nursing home,

A different from that of other homes. Such provisions also include the physical requirements within a nursing home. Nursing homes are governed by the Nursing Homes Registration (Scotland) Act 1938 and the Nursing Homes Registration (Scotland) Regulations 1988.

"As a result of this contention, the actual cost to be used to determine an appropriate valuation rate will also affect the valuation of nursing homes elsewhere in Scotland.

B "Furthermore, the decapitalisation rate which should be applied to the appropriate costs is governed by the Valuation for Rating (Decapitalisation Rate) (Scotland) Regulations 1990, and 6 per cent has been adopted by assessors throughout Scotland. In certain circumstances, the regulations permit a lower decapitalisation rate to be used, subject to certain statutory definitions. It is our further contention that nursing homes fall within the statutory definition of hospital contained within the 1990 Regulations and, as such, the lower decapitalisation rate of 4 per cent should be C applied to nursing homes.

"The issues, therefore, in this case involve valuation principles which will be applied to similar situations elsewhere in Scotland. It is our understanding that the general valuation of nursing homes throughout Scotland is based on recommendations which have been given by the Assessors' Association to the various assessors in Scotland and certainly from our discussions there has been a similarity of application, one region with another."

D The assessor's observations on that statement of reasons were set out in a letter to the secretary of the committee dated 29 June 1992, and were as follows:

"(1) There are 17 nursing homes in the valuation roll for Central Region.

"(2) The valuations of these nursing homes are arrived at on the contractor's principle using cost information gathered both from within Central Region and elsewhere in Scotland and employing a E statutory decapitalisation rate of 6 per cent.

"(3) A total of seven appeals have been lodged since the 1990 revaluation in respect of nursing homes with six being either withdrawn or settled on the basis of the valuation method adopted. Four of the latter six were dealt with by professional agents.

"(4) The case does not raise a fundamental or general issue likely to be used as a precedent in other cases as envisaged in reg 4 (3) (d). There are no other F cases outstanding in Central Region where it could be said any 'precedent' has already been created.

"(5) Regardless of the foregoing, the matters of cost levels and the choice of decapitalisation rate in terms of the Valuation for Rating (Decapitalisation Rate) (Scotland) Regulations 1990 are not beyond the scope of the valuation appeal committee."

In answer to those observations the ratepayers' agents made further representations in a letter to the secretary of the committee dated 22 September 1992, in which they stated, among other things:

"Maternity home, sanatorium, nursing home, convalescent home, hospice, rest home, hostel etc are G some examples of the use to which properties can be used within the general term 'home' but each has a specific purpose and criteria to meet to enable the property to be used for that particular purpose. All have been statutorily defined as to their particular meaning with such definitions having already been accepted for rating and valuation purposes. The specific criteria governing nursing homes make them a readily identifiable subject distinct from other types of homes, especially as nursing homes and their H operators require to be registered with the Local Health Board in accordance with certain statutory conditions, laid down within the Nursing Homes Registration (Scotland) Act 1938 and the Nursing Homes Registration (Scotland) Regulations 1988. In addition, due to the statutory requirement to provide certain services and facilities all support the view that nursing homes are a particular category of subject for valuation purposes. . . .

"There are many nursing homes situated through- I out Scotland with the appellants currently operating nursing homes in Grampian, Central, Lothian and Strathclyde Regions. The issues in this case involve valuation aspects which have been applied to all nursing homes throughout Scotland as a result of the valuation scheme adopted by assessors for the purposes of the 1990 revaluation and, with this valuation scheme having been derived from a national data base provided by the various regional assessors. If, at the end of the day, following a full appeal hearing, the J data base upon which the valuation scheme is derived is proved to be suspect, then it would appear as though all nursing home valuations are similarly affected."

When stating their reasons for refusing the application, the committee dealt not only with the ground of referral contained in para (d) of reg 4 (3), but also with the grounds contained in paras (a), (b) and (c), although these had not been founded on, or even referred to, by the ratepayers. They also stated that K they did not regard para (e) as relevant. With regard to the ground contained in para (d), the committee stated: "While the Nursing Regulations are comparatively new, no doubt any extra costs would receive expression in allowances. Costs would presumably be a question of fact and not of law which would provide a precedent for other appeals."

The principal issue in the appeal against the valuation of these subjects will be whether they are a "hospital" within the meaning of reg 2 (3) of the L Valuation for Rating (Decapitalisation Rate) (Scotland) Regulations 1990. That arises because of the fixing by those regulations of a standard decapitalisation rate of 6 per cent for all lands and heritages valued in accordance with the contractor's principle other than those specified in reg 4 (a). That prescribes a lower rate, of 4 per cent, in the case of any lands and heritages consisting of any church property, an educational establishment or a hospital. Such subjects are defined in reg 2, which provides, in para (3), that

A "hospital" means "any lands and heritages constructed or adapted wholly or mainly either — (a) for the reception or treatment of persons suffering from any illness, injury or infirmity; or (b) as a maternity home; and used for such a purpose".

That definition encompasses a number of ways in which subjects might qualify as a hospital. Since treatment is stated as an alternative to reception, it is not necessary that any treatment should be provided. Similarly, it is not necessary that the persons received into the nursing home should be suffering from an B illness or injury. It is enough that they should be suffering from an infirmity.

Although, as already stated, the principal issue in this case is whether the subjects are a hospital, the committee's statement of their reasons for refusing the application makes no mention of that issue. Accordingly, if the tribunal were restricted to a consideration of the committee's reasons, those reasons could not be regarded as supporting the decision.

C On behalf of the ratepayers counsel referred to, but did not rehearse, certain of the arguments which he had presented in their recent appeals in respect of two nursing homes in Strathclyde Region (see *Ashbourne Homes plc v Assessor for Strathclyde Region*, 9 July 1992, unreported (1993 GWD 3-206)). He went on, however, to present further arguments which had not been put forward in the earlier appeals. He also put before the tribunal further material in addition to that which had been before the committee in the present D case. His principal submission was that the factors which might establish that this nursing home was a hospital within the meaning of reg 2 (3) were likely to have a general application. Although what had to be decided must always be whether the particular nursing home which was the subject of appeal was a hospital, the reasons for which it was held that it was or was not a hospital were likely to serve as important precedents in relation to all other nursing homes. From the earlier appeals it appeared that the number in Strathclyde E Region was over 50. The information provided by the assessor in the present case showed that in Central Region the number whose position might be affected was 17. There were many others in Grampian Region. All of these had been valued using a uniform method of valuation which had been decided on by the Assessors' Association for application to nursing homes throughout Scotland. It did not appear that any attempt was made to decide whether some might in fact qualify as hospitals, and it was significant that the Central Regional Assessor had not stated what tests he F applied in order to determine whether any particular nursing home was a hospital. Although appeals in respect of many nursing homes had been settled on the basis that they were not hospitals, it did not follow that that was because it was accepted that they were not hospitals. It could hardly be the position that no nursing home in the whole of Scotland was for the reception of persons who were infirm. The true reason why it had not previously been contended that a nursing home was a hospital was likely to be that hospitals were liable for rates, whereas nursing homes

were not. It might not therefore be considered to be in the ratepayers' interest to establish that a nursing G home was a hospital.

Reference was also made to the details set out in part 1 of the Lothian Health Board's list of registered nursing homes in that region. It listed 62 establishments. All had been valued using a decapitalisation rate of 6 per cent, yet it appeared from the descriptions of their facilities that many might be hospitals within the meaning of reg 2 (3). Whatever the differences between them with regard to other factors, the factors which might be relevant to the decision whether they H were hospitals were in many cases the same.

The tribunal was also referred to the definition of "nursing home" in s 10 (3) of the Nursing Homes Registration (Scotland) Act 1938 (as amended). That defines "nursing home" as "any premises used, or intended to be used, for the reception of, and the provision of nursing for, persons suffering from any sickness, injury or infirmity". It was submitted that since that was a more restrictive definition than in the 1990 I Regulations, any premises registered under the 1938 Act were likely to come within the definition of "hospital" in the regulations.

Accordingly, it was submitted, a decision in favour of the ratepayers in this case might have the effect of requiring a re-assessment of over 100 nursing homes in Scotland. It could reasonably be held, therefore, that the decision was likely to be used as a precedent in other cases.
J
On behalf of the assessor it was submitted that what premises were called was not conclusive of the category into which they came for the purpose of valuation. The assessor was only concerned with the position in fact, and what he must look at was the actual use to which premises were put. Whereas premises might satisfy the definition of "nursing home" in the 1938 Act merely by being intended to be used for the purposes specified, that would not be sufficient to determine their character for valuation. In K the 1990 Regulations it was specifically provided that, to constitute a hospital, not only must lands and heritages be constructed or adapted wholly or mainly for the purposes specified, but they must be used for such a purpose. Furthermore, nursing homes could vary considerably in character. There were two homes owned by Ashbourne Homes on the Lothian Health Board's list of registered nursing homes, but the categories of patient for which they were registered were different and they differed in the services which L they provided. All nursing homes were not therefore the same, and any particular subjects which were so described must be looked at individually. It was not therefore possible to have a decision which was of general application or which set a precedent which could be applied to other premises which were set up as a nursing home. There was no difference between the position in this case and that in the recent cases brought by the same appellants against Strathclyde Regional Assessor. The appeal should therefore be refused.

A In the tribunal's opinion, there are sufficient grounds for upholding this appeal. From the material put before the tribunal and the submissions made, it appears that, far from this being a case of the ratepayers seeking to have subjects valued on a particular basis simply because they are called a nursing home, it may be the assessor who is attempting to do so. It is claimed, and this is not disputed, that assessors throughout Scotland have valued nursing homes in accordance with a general scheme which has been agreed between members of the Assessors' Associa-

B tion. The valuations have been arrived at using the contractor's principle and by applying the standard decapitalisation rate of 6 per cent. If the uses made of a nursing home were such that it satisfied the definition of a hospital in the regulations which prescribe the decapitalisation rates, the appropriate rate would be 4 per cent. The ratepayers believe, and again this is not disputed, that no nursing home has been valued using the lower rate, and they believe that that is because assessors have made no attempt to study the

C particular uses to which each home is put in order to determine whether it should be treated as a hospital. It appears that that has been accepted by those who operate nursing homes because, as things stand at present, it is to their advantage to accept it.

However, whatever may be their reasons for wishing to do so, Ashbourne Homes are entitled to challenge the application of a standard scheme which, they allege, assumes that all nursing homes are not hospitals within the meaning of the regulation. If the

D ratepayers are correct in their submission that a nursing home qualifies as a hospital if it is constructed or adapted mainly for the reception of persons suffering from any infirmity, and is used for that purpose, it would certainly be odd that no nursing home in Scotland should qualify as a hospital on that basis, even if it was only for the reception of persons suffering from the infirmities of old age. The descriptions of the categories of patient for which the various nursing homes in Lothian Region are registered would

E suggest that some at least might qualify as hospitals on that basis. An examination of the factors which have a bearing on the question whether a particular nursing home is a hospital, would therefore appear to raise general issues which would be likely to be used as a precedent in other cases. For those reasons the tribunal upholds the appeal.

F *Counsel for Appellants, McGhie, QC, instructed by Montagu Evans, Chartered Surveyors, Glasgow — Counsel for Respondent, Liddle.*

Philips v MacPhail

G

SCOTTISH LAND COURT

D M MACDONALD

8 JUNE 1993

Landlord and tenant — Cottar — House built on croft land for applicant's late grandfather — Applicant living in subjects from time to time before acquiring local authority tenancy — No clear consent by landlord — No right of succession to cottar subjects — Crofters (Scotland) Act 1955 (3 & 4 Eliz II, c 21), s 28 (4).

H

The applicant claimed cottar rights to a hut erected on croft land for her grandfather following the destruction of his croft house. The applicant was unable to show any more than tolerance by the landlord of the presence of the hut and certainly not his "clear consent" found to be necessary in the case of *Duke of Argyll's Trs v MacNeill*, 1983 SLT (Land Ct) 35. The applicant had no right of succession to whatever right her grandfather might have had; she had in any event

I taken up residence on another property and had therefore ceased to occupy the subjects she claimed to be cottar subjects.

Held, that the subjects of the application were not a cottar subject within s 28 (4) of the Crofters (Scotland) Act 1955 (pp 29K-30B).

Application

J Mrs V Philips applied to the Land Court for an order declaring that she was the cottar of subjects known as Eagles Hut, Acharacle, and as such entitled to purchase these subjects from the landlord respondents, Mr and Mrs John Angus MacPhail.

On 8 June 1993 the divisional court *pronounced* an order *dismissing* the application and *finding* the applicant liable for the expenses incurred by the landlord respondents.

K

The note appended to the order of the court was in the following terms:

THE COURT.—At the hearing of this application at Acharacle on 18 May 1993, the applicant was represented by her solicitor and the landlords by Mr John Angus MacPhail, on his own behalf and on behalf of his wife, the joint landlord. The remaining respondents were not present or represented.

L The applicant gave evidence that Eagles Hut was built for her grandfather about 50 years previously. He had formerly lived at Sanna but his house there had been burnt down and the crofters gifted him a piece of land at Achnaha and helped him to build a small house there. He remained in the house until his death in 1955 and thereafter her parents visited the house with her for two weeks each year in summer. Her father had paid rates over the house which became known as Eagles Hut from the time they were asked of him, and thereafter community charge. She came to live in the hut at Easter 1989 with her youngest son. Her husband carried out any necessary repairs although the house had no electricity or mains water supply and no toilet. She was dependent on a sink outside the hut for water, and heating was by means of gas. She conceded that the property required work to bring it up to standard as a dwellinghouse but it was in fair condition in 1989. She had added a caravan beside the hut about 18 years previously and the crofters had assisted her in putting it there. She felt that they would not have done so if the ground had not belonged to her and her husband.

She had known the MacPhails since they had moved to live at Achnaha some 15 years previously and her mother had been friendly with them. The MacPhails made no objection to the applicant's presence on the property and the first she knew about any challenge to her supposed right was when they asked her to remove the caravan in about 1990. She had received a letter from the MacPhails in May 1992 asking her to remove the hut and the caravan from its present site. She herself moved into a council house at 9 Pier Road, Kilchoan, in January 1992 but had occupied Eagles Hut as a dwellinghouse between March 1991 and January 1992. She did not consider that she required the MacPhails' consent to remain in Eagles Hut because it was her own place and she had had the crofters' consent. She conceded that if she were successful in her application she would need to do a lot of work on the hut, and the caravan required demolition.

The reason why she had "delayed to make the application" was that she had applied for legal aid. She considered that the MacPhails had acquiesced to her occupation of the site and also considered that she was a cottar because she stayed there. She accepted that the MacPhails had a title to the land but she did not consider that Mr Gibb, the previous proprietor, was entitled to sell the piece of land given to her grandfather. She should have been notified about this.

At some time in March 1991 or 1992, Mr MacPhail had assisted her in repairing a gas cylinder supply for the hut.

Cross examined by Mr MacPhail, the applicant agreed that her mother had been known prior to her marriage to Laurence Eagle as Annie Taylor and that she had been adopted by the applicant's grandfather David Cunningham who had a croft in Sanna. Her grandfather had signed away the croft because he could not read or write and did not know what he was doing. When she came to live in Achnaha in the spring of 1989 with her son, she used to sleep in the caravan and used the hut as a classroom to teach her son for three months. She denied that she moved out of the hut in September 1990, although she lived in the nearby house of a Miss Henderson at times. She stayed in the hut for six weeks during the summer of 1991, then moved into Miss Henderson's house. She still considered Eagles Hut to be her residence and went every day to it. She thought that the hut had been built by her grandfather together with the adjoining crofters and could not confirm or deny if the hut had been built by a Mr MacCallum. She conceded that there was a demolition order over the hut and assumed that Mr MacPhail had been at the back of this, although Mr MacPhail denied that he had been.

Re-examined by her solicitor, the applicant asserted that Eagles Hut had been her permanent residence between 1989 and 1992. Although she lived in the house of Miss Henderson nearby for a short time, she nevertheless visited the hut daily.

Mr Anthony John Thain then gave evidence on behalf of Mr MacPhail. The witness stated that he lived about 50 m from the hut and caravan in a property he had bought in October 1988. From his observation, the hut was used as a temporary classroom in 1989 and the caravan provided sleeping accommodation. It was his impression that the applicant resided in Miss Henderson's house until she moved to Kilchoan. The hut and caravan were in poor condition, the caravan now being a total wreck and the hut having deteriorated to the extent to which it could not now be brought up to a proper standard. However, this was a lay opinion.

Mr Malcolm Hugh MacMillan, 63 Carraig, Kilchoan, then gave evidence on behalf of Mr MacPhail. He knew of a similar situation of a hut being built in the area as temporary accommodation for a distressed crofter. He quoted a case in the 1950s where a hut was erected on common grazings at Portuick by public subscription to accommodate a widow until she obtained other accommodation in the 1960s. The hut had then been demolished and the site cleared. He was not of the opinion that this conferred cottar status, such houses being known as "poor houses". There was no right of succession to them and he was of the opinion that Eagles Hut was in a similar situation.

Giving evidence on his own behalf and on behalf of his wife, the joint landlord, Mr MacPhail, stated that the man in charge of the funds and purchase of materials for Eagles Hut had been Campbell Mackenzie, merchant in Kilchoan. The hut was actually built by a Hugh MacCallum who was paid by Mr Mackenzie. It had been erected on common grazings within an old stackyard pertaining to the croft 116 Achnaha then tenanted by a Duncan Henderson. The hut was originally known as "Old Davie's Hut" and the landlord's consent had not been sought for its erection. After David Cunningham died in 1955, the Eagle and Philips families, including the applicant, had returned on holiday. Nobody objected to them having two weeks there in the summer.

Mrs Philips had made the point that he had not objected to her presence with her younger son in 1989 when she came to stay at the hut. However, he was hardly going to turn them out in midwinter. She had then lived for 18 months with Miss Henderson until she got a council house and it was thought that she would move out of the hut. She had written to Mr Gibb, the then joint landlord, on 31 July 1990 claiming to be the owner of Eagles Hut and the ground on which it was erected. Mr Gibb had made a non-committal reply but had indicated that he thought that the hut was erected as a temporary expedient and that following David Cunningham's death, the intention would have been to dismantle the hut. Mr MacPhail then referred to the limitations of the hut in the way of water and electricity supplies and sanitation and claimed that no effort had been made during the previous 15 or 16 years to provide proper sanitation, although during the summer up to eight people lived in the hut at one time. He considered there was no particular significance in the fact that rates had been paid for the hut because rates were payable over caravans. The applicant was never known as a cottar. He quoted para 11.03 of McCuish and Flyn on *Crofting Law*, in which it was stated that there was no right of succession to a cottar's subject and that any person who obtained the occupancy of a cottar's subject following upon the death of an existing cottar, must do so by permission of the landowner or landlord. In his opinion, the applicant was by definition a squatter occupying subjects without legal right and in the face of the landowner.

Cross examined by the applicant's solicitor, Mr MacPhail strongly denied that he had acquiesced in the applicant's occupation of the Eagles Hut, although he felt he could hardly turn her out of it. He also asserted that she had lived at Miss Henderson's house although she may have occupied Eagles Hut for some periods during the summer. He himself had taken the applicant's furniture to Miss Henderson's and she had moved it on to Pier Road, Kilchoan, where her family were now living. He considered there was no significance in the fact that rates demand notices, etc, were addressed to the applicant at Eagles Hut. This did not indicate that it was her dwellinghouse.

The applicant's son, Stephen Neil Philips, aged 23, gave evidence that he had stayed in the hut for a total of approximately six to nine months between 1989 and 1992. He had used a sofa as a bed and the hut contained a cooker and the necessary cooking utensils. He slept in the caravan during the holidays only.

Summing up for the applicant, her solicitor claimed that the applicant conformed to the definition of a cottar as occupying a dwellinghouse within the crofting counties. The fact that bills for the community charge and local rates had been payable indicated that Eagles Hut was a dwellinghouse. He felt that she must have had the landlord's consent, because although he had denied acquiescence to her presence there, this could be implied. She was in a direct relationship with Mr MacPhail as a landowner and was therefore a cottar in terms of the legislation. The solicitor claimed that temporary use of the subjects was not detrimental to her title and quoted in support of this *McAlister v Gray*, 1938 SLCR 3. The only objection to her occupation of the subjects by Mr MacPhail had come in the form of a letter dated 19 May 1992. In conclusion he moved for the expenses of the application.

Summing up, Mr MacPhail claimed that the applicant had never been an occupier of the subjects concerned and therefore she could never have been the occupier as a cottar thereof. Furthermore, the subjects themselves had never been a dwellinghouse apart from a poor house for a destitute crofter. Mrs Philips was not a blood relation of David Cunningham and therefore she could have no right of succession. She was in fact a squatter and had not lived in the property since September 1990. She had made no attempt to find out whether she had any legal right to the subjects. No rent was paid — and the reason he had not objected to the Philips' use of the hut was that they had not been resident there since he became owner of the ground. In conclusion, he moved for the expenses of the application.

Decision

The history of Eagles Hut may be briefly summarised. It was erected by or on behalf of one David Cunningham whose own house had been destroyed by fire, in or around 1942. The ground on which it was built was described in para 2 of the statement of facts as being "gifted by the then crofters of Achnaha". David Cunningham lived in Eagles Hut until his death in 1955, after which the property was occupied for various periods by Laurence Eagle, the applicant's father, and by the applicant and various members of her family. The applicant now claims to be the cottar of the subjects.

Section 28 (4) of the Crofters (Scotland) Act 1955 defines cottar thus: "the occupier of a dwelling-house situate in the crofting counties with or without land who pays no rent, or the tenant from year to year of a dwelling-house situate as aforesaid who resides therein and who pays therefor an annual rent not exceeding six pounds in money, whether with or without garden ground but without arable or pasture land". This is a fairly broad definition, but it is one which has been qualified or restricted by various decisions by this court over the years.

First and foremost, cottar status is dependent on the attitude of the landlord. In *Duke of Argyll's Trs v MacNeill*, 1983 SLT (Land Ct) 35 at p 37 the court held: "To acquire cottar's status (and in the absence of a right of succession this status strictly attaches more to the occupant than to the house), there must be both knowledge and also clear consent to the occupancy on the part of the landlords. A squatter in a former cottar's residence does not acquire cottar status until the landlord consents." The evidence in the present application is that Mrs Philips' occupation was at best tolerated and at worst actively opposed by the previous and present landlords. She received no encouragement when she wrote to Mr Gibb, the previous joint landlord on 31 July 1990, and was directly asked by the present landlord and respondent, Mr MacPhail, to remove Eagles Hut (letter of 19 July 1992). This indicated that far from there being "clear consent" on the landlord's part to the presence of the applicant in Eagles Hut, there was active opposition. It is simply not sufficient for Mrs Philips to claim that Mr MacPhail tolerated Eagles Hut and her occupation of it and that following from this she could claim to

be a cottar tenant. We accept Mr MacPhail's evidence
A that he refrained for a while from upsetting the status
quo from motives of humanity, an attitude which
changed when Mrs Philips obtained the tenancy of a
council house. Mere toleration falls far short of the
clear consent which the full court held to be necessary
in the case just referred to.

We therefore find that Eagles Hut is not a cottar
subject and accordingly dismiss the application. It
goes without saying that the remains of the caravan
located beside the hut is not part of a cottar subject
B either.

We conclude by considering certain other issues
which, although not necessarily relevant to our
decision, are relevant to the application.

The applicant seemed to be claiming some right of
succession from her grandfather's occupation of
Eagles Hut. This is misconceived. Even had it been
shown that David Cunningham was a cottar in his
own right, this would not have assisted the applicant.
C In *MacInnes v Strathcona*, 1925 SLCR 39 at p 47 the
court explained the rule: "We are of the opinion that
the appellant's case fails on the pure question of law
that under the statute no right to succeed is given to,
or can be inferred in favour of, the heir-at-law of a
cottar . . . whereas the Statute is careful to provide for
the succession to a crofter or landholder of his heirs
and successors and also confers rights of assignation
and bequest, there is an entire absence of any such
provisions in the case of a cottar." In actual fact,
D David Cunningham fell clearly within the description
of squatter, given by the court in *Duke of Argyll's Trs
v MacNeill*, supra, at p 37: "It appears therefore that
a squatter is a person permitted not by the landlord
but by the crofter, to whom he is often related, to
build a house on the crofter's land, or it may be, the
common grazings." It was somewhat naive of Mrs
Philips to claim that the crofters had "given" the land
to David Cunningham, because of course they had no
right or title to do so, being merely tenants of the land.
E However, it would not be fatal to the applicant's case
that her grandfather was a mere squatter for, as the
court stated in *Sutherland v Earl of Ronaldsay*, 1920
SLCR 17 at p 19: "Indeed the definition of a cottar
takes no account of the method of acquiring possession
but only deals with the attributes or qualities of the
subject occupation." As we have shown, however, the
applicant's occupation of Eagles Hut lacks at least one
vital attribute — namely, the "clear consent" of the
landlord.

F   Finally, we consider the issue of occupation. There
were sharp differences of opinion as to the length of
time the applicant and her family were in physical
occupation of Eagles Hut. This is not a matter of conclusive importance either way — for example, in
Macvicar v Cameron, 1931 SLCR 63 at p 68 the court
stated, albeit obiter: "We are doubtful if the circumstances of this case would justify a finding to the effect
that the Applicant had forfeited any right as a cottar
in respect of his ceasing to reside in the cottage, but
as it is not necessary to decide the point we reserve our

opinion." What does appear to be of greater importance than the fact of possession is that in 1991 Mrs G
Philips acquired the council house in which she now
lives, which as from that time must be considered as
her normal residence. In *Baikie v Baikie*, 1925 SLCR
42 at p 44 the following comment by the court is relevant to the present application: "Assuming for the
moment that the Applicant's position was that he
became a cottar upon his ceasing to be a crofter, the
Court is of the opinion that he could not be properly
described as a cottar because he was not the occupier
of the dwellinghouse within the meaning of the defini- H
tion. He was never in that sense at any time the occupier. When he left the holding he took up his
residence on a farm a considerable distance away.
Further, as it has not been shown that the site of the
house was taken out of the holding during the Applicant's tenancy of the holding, the necessary conclusion
is that when he quitted the holding as a result of the
notice of the removal he quitted the possession of the
whole holding including the house site."

There seems little doubt that the applicant, having I
quitted her hut as a residence, if indeed it was ever her
residence, looks upon the property as a possible
holiday house, although we use the word "possible"
advisedly. The building is in very poor condition and
it is not hard to see why the landlord wishes this
eyesore to be removed, nor why the local authority
have decreed that it should be demolished as failing to
reach a tolerable standard.

As to the matter of expenses, the landlord respondents have succeeded in defeating the applicant's J
challenge which would have restricted their title to
their own property. Following the normal rule of
expenses following success, we therefore find the
applicant liable to them in expenses. These will be
restricted to the expenses of answering the application, as moved for in para 5 of the answers submitted
on the MacPhails' behalf by their solicitor. We find no
expenses due to or by any other party.

                                                              K

*Solicitors for Applicant, Macarthur Stewart & Co,
Fort William — For Respondents, Party.*

[The definition of "cottar" in s 28 (4) of the 1955 Act has
been re-enacted as s 12 (5) of the Crofters (Scotland) Act
1993.]

                                                              L

McLoughlin's Curator Bonis v Motherwell District Council

LANDS TRIBUNAL FOR SCOTLAND

SHERIFF A C HORSFALL, QC;
A R MACLEARY, FRICS

10 DECEMBER 1992

Landlord and tenant — Public sector housing — Tenants' rights — Purchase of dwellinghouse — Tenant incapax and permanently hospitalised — Whether tenancy secure — Whether house tenant's only or principal home — Whether tenant in occupation — Whether tenancy abandoned — Whether application to purchase could be made by curator bonis — Whether curator bonis could occupy on behalf of an incapax — Housing (Scotland) Act 1987 (c 26), ss 44 (1) (b) and 61 (2) (c).

An application to purchase a local authority house was made by the curator bonis of the tenant, who had been admitted to hospital almost five months previously. The nature of the tenant's illness was such that he could not return to his home, which he had occupied on his own. The curator wished to preserve the tenant's estate by exercising a right to add a valuable asset to it. The district council, as landlord, refused the application on the grounds that the tenant was not in occupation of the house and that the tenancy was not a secure tenancy, as the house was not the tenant's only or principal home. They also disputed the curator's right to make the application to purchase on the grounds that s 61 (1) of the Housing (Scotland) Act 1987 provides that only a tenant has the right to do so, that by the time of the application the council had already acquired the right to regain possession through non-payment of rent and that an order of the sheriff authorising the curator to buy the house had not been granted at the time of the application and in any event only related to the house "presently tenanted by" the incapax. The council then commenced proceedings to recover possession on the ground that the tenancy had been abandoned. After his appointment, the curator bonis paid the rent, which had been in arrears, and otherwise carried out those actions necessary to meet the obligations of the tenancy.

Held, (1) that as the council only initiated steps to recover possession after the curator's application, the tribunal was not barred from entertaining the application, the date as at which the tribunal had to decide whether the right to purchase existed being the date of the application, even though the council might have taken action sooner (p 33D-E); (2) that an application to purchase could be made on behalf of a tenant by a curator bonis (p 33F); (3) that the curator did not need any special powers at the time of the application to purchase but only at the time he served on the landlord a notice of acceptance of the offer to sell (p 33J); (4) that the tenancy had not been abandoned or terminated, and the house was "presently tenanted by" the incapax through his curator in terms of the sheriff's order (pp 33K and 34F-G); but (5) that the tenancy

was not secure, as the house was no longer the tenant's only or principal home within s 44 (1) (b) (p 34E-F); and (6) that "occupation" in s 61 (2) (c) meant actual physical occupation and the tenant did not satisfy the condition that immediately prior to the date of service of the application to purchase he had been in occupation of the house for not less than two years (pp 34K-35A); and application *refused.*

Matheson v Western Isles Islands Council, 1992 SLT (Lands Tr) 107, *distinguished.*

Application under the Housing (Scotland) Act 1987

S J R Wight, the curator bonis of Thomas McLoughlin, applied to the Lands Tribunal for Scotland under s 68 (4) of the 1987 Act, for a finding that he had a right, under s 61 of the Act, to buy on behalf of the incapax the local authority house in which the incapax formerly resided prior to his admission to hospital some five months before the date of the application.

On 10 December 1992 the tribunal *pronounced* an order *refusing* the application and *finding* the applicant liable to the respondents in their expenses of the application on the sheriff court scale, as the same, failing agreement, should be taxed by the auditor of Hamilton sheriff court.

The opinion attached to the tribunal's order was in the following terms:

THE TRIBUNAL.—This is an application by a curator bonis under s 68 (4) of the Housing (Scotland) Act 1987 for a finding that he has a right under s 61 of the Act to buy a local authority house in which the incapax formerly resided. The incapax is Mr Thomas McLoughlin. His curator is Mr S J R Wight. The landlords are Motherwell District Council. The application to buy the house was made by the curator on 2 September and was refused on 26 September 1991. The council refused the application on the grounds that the tenant was not in occupation of the house and that the tenancy was not a secure tenancy because the house was not then the tenant's only or principal home.

At the hearing Mr McLoughlin's curator was represented by his solicitor. Both the curator and his solicitor gave evidence. The council were represented by their solicitor, and evidence was given on their behalf by Mr David Shaw, an assistant finance officer of the council, and Mr Stuart Forrester, a housing officer.

The evidence disclosed that Mr McLoughlin has not lived in the house since 10 April 1991, when he was admitted to hospital. He has remained in hospital since that date. He is 79 years of age and is suffering from severe Parkinson's disease, dementia and incontinence of urine. It is agreed that he will never be able to return to live in the house. The curator does not therefore wish to buy it for occupation by Mr McLoughlin. He wishes to buy it because of the gain

to Mr McLoughlin's estate. In October 1991 the
A house was valued, with vacant possession, at £23,500.
Since Mr McLoughlin had been the tenant for over 30
years, he would be entitled, if he could buy the house,
to do so at the maximum statutory discount of 60 per
cent of its market value. The curator proposes, if he
is found to be entitled to buy the house, to retain it for
the three years required in order to avoid a liability to
repay part of the discount in terms of s 72 of the Act.
During that time he hopes to be able to let the house
furnished. He has been advised that, provided various
B things were done to put the house in a fit state for
letting, it could command a monthly rent in the region
of £300. The curator has sought the authority of the
court to deal with the house in that way, and by a
decree of the sheriff at Hamilton dated 17 September
1992 he has been authorised to buy it, with power to
lease it and then to sell it after three years.

Since April 1991 there has been nobody living in the
house, but it is still in the condition in which it was
while Mr McLoughlin resided there. Indeed, much of
C Mr McLoughlin's clothing and the personal posses-
sions of himself and his late wife are still in the house.
It contains the same furnishings as it did while he
lived there. Although those furnishings are very old
and somewhat sparse, the house is therefore capable of
being occupied, notwithstanding that, before it could
be used for furnished letting, it would need to be
thoroughly cleaned and redecorated and much of the
furniture and such things as the cooker would have to
be replaced. The applicant's solicitor, as solicitor to
the curatory, has insured the property, and he visits it
D at reasonably regular intervals in order to check its
security and to collect mail. Once this summer he has
had the garden tidied up. If he has not done more than
is necessary in order to avoid complaints from the
council and from neighbours, that is because he could
not justify spending more pending a decision on the
curator's right to buy the house.

Since Mr McLoughlin was admitted to hospital the
rent of the house has not been paid regularly, and at
times the payments have been very much in arrears.
E Although various payments were made until about the
beginning of June 1991, nothing was paid between
then and early in September 1991, when the arrears
amounted to approximately £220. Although these
were then paid, there were no further payments until
the beginning of March 1992, when approximately
£500 was paid. That brought the payments almost up
to date at that time. What has happened since then was
not gone into and is not apparently regarded as
relevant.

F
Having refused the application to buy the house, by
the notice of refusal served on 26 September 1991, the
council decided to treat the tenancy as having been
abandoned and to regain possession in terms of the
provisions of s 50 of the Act. That provides that a
landlord may terminate a secure tenancy, and may
take possession of the house, if he is satisfied that it is
unoccupied and that the tenant does not intend to
occupy it as his home. On 10 October 1991 a notice
stating that the council had reason to believe that these
things were so was served on the curator in terms of

subs (1) of s 50. In view, however, of the fact that the
curator had already applied to the tribunal for a G
finding that he had a right to buy the house, the
council have agreed to take no further steps in terms
of s 50 until the tribunal's decision is known.

On behalf of the curator it was submitted, with
regard to the tenant's right to buy, that Mr
McLoughlin's tenancy, being a secure tenancy, could
only be brought to an end in one of the ways provided
by s 46 of the Act. The only way which the council
claimed could apply was that provided by s 50 (2).
That, however, only applied where a house was H
unoccupied. Here it should be held that the house was
still occupied and that it had not been abandoned. In
that respect the position in the present case was
similar to that in *Matheson v Western Isles Islands
Council*, 1992 SLT (Lands Tr) 107, the decision in
which should be followed. Furthermore, by demanding and accepting rent the council had recognised that
the tenancy still existed, and they were thereby barred
from claiming that it had been terminated by abandonment.
I

With regard to the curator's right to make the
application, it was submitted that a distinction must
be drawn between having a power under the Trusts
(Scotland) Act 1921 to buy heritage and having a right
under the 1987 Act to present an application to purchase. Paragraph (ee) of s 4 (1) of the 1921 Act dealt
only with the power to carry through a purchase of
heritage. That stage had not yet been reached. In any
event, in terms of subs (1) of s 2 of the Trusts (Scotland) Act 1961 the validity of a transaction under J
which the curator purported to do an act in terms of
para (ee) was not challengeable by the council, and in
terms of subs (3) of that section it would be open to
the curator to obtain a consent to his act from the
Accountant of Court. As a general rule a curator stood
in place of his ward and had the same rights. If there
had been any doubt as to the curator's power to make
an application to purchase, that had been cured by the
authority which had subsequently been granted by the
sheriff.
K

On behalf of the council it was submitted that Mr
McLoughlin had no right to purchase the house. That
right applied to tenants in secure tenancies. In terms
of s 44 (1) (b) of the 1987 Act a tenancy was only
secure if the house was the tenant's only or principal home. By the time when the application to purchase was made it was a hospital which was Mr
McLoughlin's only home. Furthermore, he did not
satisfy the requirement of s 61 (2) (c) that he should
have been in occupation of a local authority house for L
not less than two years immediately prior to the date
of service of the application to purchase. By that date
he had been in hospital for almost five months, and he
could not be said to have been at the same time in
occupation of the house. On the relevant date he was
in breach of his tenancy agreement, and in particular
of his obligations to pay rent and to occupy the subjects of let. Since he had no intention of re-occupying
the house, it should be treated as having been abandoned. As a result the council had already acquired
an established right to regain possession in terms of

s 50 (2). It could not therefore be held that Mr McLoughlin still had a right to purchase, and it was accordingly ultra vires of the tribunal to entertain the present application.

It was submitted further that a curator had no power or right to present an application to purchase. Under the tenants' rights legislation only a tenant might do so. Such an act was not covered by any general power conferred by the Judicial Factors or Trusts Acts, and the deficiency could not be cured by an order of the sheriff obtained subsequently. The order was not retrospective and could not give the curator a right to do what he had no right to do at the time. In any event, the order gave authority to purchase only the house "presently tenanted by" the incapax. If the house had by then been abandoned, there was no house presently tenanted by him and the order was therefore ineffectual.

The decision in *Matheson*, it was submitted, could be distinguished. The question of abandonment had not been raised, and it had been accepted by the tribunal that it was still possible that the tenant would return to live in the house. She was not incapax and the application to purchase was not by a curator. To the extent to which it could not be distinguished, it was submitted that *Matheson* had been wrongly decided. The council's refusal to sell should therefore be upheld.

In the tribunal's opinion, it is not barred from entertaining this application by the fact that the council, as landlords, have already taken the first step towards repossessing the house in accordance with the provisions of s 50 (2) of the 1987 Act. That step was taken only after the curator had applied to purchase the house, after the council had refused the application, and after the curator had appealed against the refusal by applying to the tribunal for a finding that he had a right to purchase the house. The date as at which the tribunal must decide whether he had that right is the date of service of the application to purchase. If it is held that he had such a right at that time, that cannot be altered by the fact that the council have subsequently initiated action to terminate the tenancy. Nor can it be altered by the fact that the council might have been able to take such action sooner but failed to do so.

The council dispute the curator's right to make the application to purchase the house. They do so on the ground that s 61 (1) of the 1987 Act provides that only a tenant shall have the right to do so, and the curator is not a tenant. However, as far as the provisions of the 1987 Act are concerned, we see no reason why an application to purchase a house on behalf of a tenant who is incapax should not be made by his curator, provided that the curator has the necessary powers by virtue of his office of curator.

It is not accepted by the council that he had such powers at the relevant date, which was the date of service of the application to purchase. He had been appointed as curator in July 1991. The actual date was not stated, but it was between one and two months before the date of the application. It would appear that he was appointed with the usual powers. These included a power in terms of s 4 (1) (ee) of the Trusts (Scotland) Act 1921 to acquire with funds of the trust estate any interest in residential accommodation if that was reasonably required to enable him to provide a suitable residence for occupation by the incapax, but they did not include a power to purchase heritage for the purpose for which the curator wishes to purchase it in this case. The curator obtained such power just over a year after the date of service of the application to purchase the house.

In the tribunal's opinion, however, there was a distinction to be drawn between the curator's power to make an application to purchase under the 1987 Act and any powers which he might need to obtain in terms of s 4 (6) of the Judicial Factors (Scotland) Act 1880 in order to carry through the purchase. As appears from the terms of s 63 (1) of the 1987 Act, an application to purchase does no more than to give notice that the tenant seeks to exercise his right to purchase and to give certain other essential information. It is a necessary preliminary rather than part of the actual process of buying the property. The first step in that process takes place when the landlord serves a notice containing an offer to sell. The tenant need not accept that offer. As the opening words of ss 65 and 66 make clear, it is only if the tenant still wishes to exercise his right to purchase that the matter is taken further. If he still wishes to exercise his right, he will serve on the landlord a notice of acceptance of the offer, and in terms of s 66 (2) a contract of sale is then constituted. Until that stage is reached the tenant's estate, if he is incapax, is placed under no liability. It is therefore sufficient that the curator should have obtained special power to make the purchase before he serves on the landlord a notice of acceptance of the offer to sell.

With regard to the effect of the power which the curator obtained, the tribunal does not accept that the sheriff's order was ineffectual because it gave authority to purchase only the house "presently tenanted by" the incapax, but that when the order was made the tenancy had been abandoned, so that there was no house "presently tenanted by" the incapax. For reasons which are stated later the tribunal is satisfied that that was not the position, but that there was then a house "presently tenanted by the incapax" through his curator.

It should, however, be noted that the purchase which the curator wishes to make is not a transaction under which he purports to do an act of the description specified in para (ee) of s 4 (1) of the Trusts (Scotland) Act 1921. The provisions of s 2 (1) of the Trusts (Scotland) Act 1961 cannot therefore apply so as to bar the council from challenging the validity of the transaction. Furthermore s 2 (1) bars challenge only on the ground that the act in question is at variance with the terms or purposes of the trust. That is not the basis of the challenge in this case.

A tenant's right to purchase a public sector house is conferred by s 61 of the 1987 Act. Subsection (2) of that section provides that the section applies to every house let under a secure tenancy where certain conditions are satisfied. The requirements for a secure

tenancy are set out in s 44. One of these is the requirement contained in subs (1) (b), that the house is the
tenant's only or principal home. One of the conditions
which must then be satisfied if the tenant is to have
a right to purchase the house is that contained in s 61
(2) (c), which requires that immediately prior to the
date of service of an application to purchase the tenant
should have been for not less than two years in occupation of a house or of a succession of houses provided
by a public sector landlord. The principal issues in
this case are whether, during the period of almost five
months before the date of the application to purchase,
the house was Mr McLoughlin's only or principal
home and whether he was then in occupation of the
house.

In order that a house may be regarded as having
been a person's only or principal home at a particular
date it is not necessary that he should have resided
there during any arbitrary period within which that
date fell. On the other hand, a house is not a person's
home simply because he is its tenant. A home is where
a person has a settled abode, his connection with
which has a degree of permanence, and to which he
will return after periods of absence. That is so whether
a house is a person's only home or his principal home.
When the application to purchase this house was
served, Mr McLoughlin had ceased to live there. In
the joint minute lodged in September 1992 it is agreed
that, in view of his medical condition, severe Parkinson's desease, dementia and incontinence of urine, and
his deteriorated condition both physically and
mentally over the past year, he will never be able to
return to live in the house. That is stated in the
present tense. It therefore relates to the position
approximately a year after the date of the application
to purchase the house, and one of the reasons which
it states, why Mr McLoughlin will never be able to
return to live there, is "his deteriorated condition both
physically and mentally over the past year". Nothing,
however, was made of that. It is not now suggested
that he would have been fit to return to live at 41
Glencalder Crescent in September 1991 or that there
was any possibility then that he might have done so.
Indeed, it was clear from the evidence of Mr Wight
that his only motive in applying to purchase the house
was to preserve Mr McLoughlin's estate by exercising
a right to add a valuable asset to it. The house was not
to be purchased as a home to which Mr McLoughlin
might one day return. In these circumstances the
tribunal is of the opinion that the house cannot reasonably be held to have been Mr McLoughlin's only or
principal home at the relevant date. At that time his
tenancy was not therefore secure.

That conclusion is not based on the view that the
tenancy had been abandoned or had been terminated
for non-payment of rent. After Mr McLoughlin's
admission to hospital, the relative or relatives who
were involved clearly wished to maintain the tenancy,
as did the curator once he had been appointed. For a
short time after Mr McLoughlin's admission payments were made towards the rent. Although there
was then a gap of several months when nothing was
paid, the payments were brought up to date by the

curator at about the time when he applied to purchase
the house. The receipt of that payment was not
recorded on the council's computer records until 6
September 1991, a few days after the service of the
application, but it may well have been sent at the same
time as, or even before, the application was made. In
any event, the council accepted the payment.

The remaining question is whether Mr McLoughlin
can be said to have remained in occupation of the
house after his admission to hospital, and so to have
satisfied the condition in s 61 (2) (c) that immediately
prior to the date of service of the application to purchase he should have been for not less than two years
in occupation of a house or of a succession of houses
provided by a public sector landlord. Admittedly he
was not then in physical occupation of the house, but
it was submitted on behalf of the curator that what was
meant by "occupation" in s 61 (2) (c) was no more
than legal occupation, in the sense of having the right
to occupy. Since the tenancy agreement had not been
terminated, the right to occupy remained, and, after
the curator was appointed, he became the occupier in
place of Mr McLoughlin and on his behalf.

For support for that submission the tribunal was
referred to the meaning given to the word "occupation" in the case of *Matheson*. In the tribunal's
opinion, however, the occupation referred to in s 61
(2) (c) is something different from the occupation
which a person may be said to enjoy because as the
tenant under missives of let he has the right to occupy
a house, whether or not he in fact exercises that right.
Subsection (10) of s 61 provides that in that section
(and in s 62) references to occupation of a house
include occupation by various persons other than
tenants. These persons include any person occupying
the house rent free or as the spouse of a tenant or of
any such person. If certain other requirements are
satisfied, such references also include occupation by
the child or the spouse of a child of a tenant or of a
person occupying the house rent free, and occupation
by a member of the family of a tenant or a person
occupying the house rent free, other than a spouse or
child or child's spouse. From that it seems clear that
what is meant by "occupation" in s 61 is occupation
in the physical sense of actually residing in the house
rather than in the sense of merely having the right to
reside there by virtue of being the tenant.

That interpretation is borne out by the terms of
ss 49 and 50 of the Act, under which a local authority
landlord may take action to repossess a house which he
has reasonable grounds for believing to be unoccupied. To be entitled to repossess it, it is enough
that the landlord is satisfied that the house is unoccupied and that the tenant does not intend to occupy
it as his home, that is, in the physical sense of residing
in it.

For those reasons Mr McLoughlin did not satisfy
the condition that immediately prior to the date of
service of the application to purchase he should have
been for not less than two years in occupation of a
house or of a succession of houses provided by a public
sector landlord. His occupation of such a house came

A to an end in April 1991, almost five months before his curator applied to purchase the house on his behalf.

The position is therefore very different from that in *Matheson*, in which the application to purchase the house was by the tenant herself and not by a curator bonis. Mrs Matheson still regarded the house as her home, to which, if she could, she would return. It was found as a fact that she could still do so, provided that there was some other member of her family living there who was able to give her a hand, and it was found that it was not impossible that that might still B occur. In the circumstances it was held that, although Mrs Matheson had been in hospital for a considerable period, interrupted only by one brief stay of two weeks at home, she could still be said to be in occupation of the house. That, however, is not the case here.

The tribunal accordingly finds that the curator has no right to purchase Mr McLoughlin's house on his behalf. It was accepted that in the event of the tribunal so finding the council should be entitled to an award of their expenses, but it was intimated that in that C event the curator would wish to be heard on the question of modification under the provisions of the legal aid scheme. That matter therefore remains to be dealt with.

Solicitors for Applicant, Freeland McFadzean, Wishaw — Solicitor for Respondents, E Smith, Motherwell District Council.

D

Mackay v Lord Burton

LANDS TRIBUNAL FOR SCOTLAND
SHERIFF A C HORSFALL, QC;
R A EDWARDS, WS
E 13 APRIL 1993

Heritable property — Land obligations — Variation of — Servitude of access — Access restricted to existing use — Application by benefited proprietors to extend right of access — Whether servitude of access a separate interest in land — Whether restriction a separate obligation — Whether benefited proprietors burdened by restriction — Competency of application — Conveyancing and Feudal Reform (Scotland) Act 1970 (c 35), s 1 (3).

F In terms of s 1 (3) of the Conveyancing and Feudal Reform (Scotland) Act 1970 the Lands Tribunal for Scotland may vary or discharge a land obligation on the application of any person who in relation to the obligation is a burdened proprietor. "Burdened proprietor" means a proprietor of an interest in land upon whom, by virtue of his being such proprietor, the obligation is binding. "Interest in land" means any estate or interest in land which is capable of being owned or held as a separate interest and to which a title may be recorded in the Register of Sasines.

A disposition of agricultural land created a servitude right of access by the existing roads for all necessary G and usual agricultural purposes, but only to the extent to which the roads were then so used. Subsequently, parts of the land were sold for residential development. The owners of certain parts applied to the tribunal to vary the obligation so as to permit access for normal and necessary domestic purposes to all dwellinghouses situated or to be erected upon the subjects. Although they were benefited proprietors in relation to the obligation, the applicants claimed that they were at the same time burdened proprietors, being burdened by the restriction on their right, which H they submitted constituted a separate interest in land.

Held, (1) that a servitude was not an interest in land which was capable of being held as a separate interest (pp 37L-38A); (2) that the applicants' right of access was not a right which was then burdened by a restriction on it, but was a restricted right, and the applicants were not therefore burdened proprietors (p 38B-D); and application *dismissed* as incompetent.

I

Application for variation of land obligation

Thomas Charles Mackay, Dalreoch, Lower Dunain, Inverness, and others applied to the Lands Tribunal for Scotland in terms of s 1 of the Conveyancing and Feudal Reform (Scotland) Act 1970 for the variation of a land obligation affecting subjects at Dalreoch.

On 13 April 1993 the tribunal *pronounced* an order *dismissing* the application as incompetent.   J

The opinion annexed to the tribunal's order was in the following terms:

THE TRIBUNAL.—Thomas Charles Mackay, Elizabeth Dunbar Mackay and William Mackay, as partners of the firm of Messrs T Mackay, and James Fraser and Mrs Dorothy Wendy Fraser have applied to the tribunal under s 1 (3) of the Conveyancing and Feudal Reform (Scotland) Act 1970 for a variation of a land obligation created by a disposition by the K respondent, the rt hon Michael Evan Victor, Baron Burton, in favour of Mrs Jessie Ann Fraser, dated 7 October 1981 and recorded in the Division of the General Register of Sasines for the County of Inverness on 29 January 1982. The subjects conveyed by that disposition were the former croft at Dalreoch, Lower Dunain, Inverness. Prior to the granting of the disposition they were part of the farm of Lower Dunain on the respondent's estate of Dochfour.

In the application to the tribunal the subjects con-   L veyed to Mrs Jessie Ann Fraser are described as "the land burdened by" the land obligation, although by that obligation it was on Mrs Jessie Ann Fraser, as disponee of the subjects, that a right was conferred. In the disposition the right was described as "a heritable and irredeemable servitude right and privilege to use for all necessary and usual agricultural purposes the existing roads leading to the subjects . . . but that only to the extent to which the same are at present so used".

Subsequent to the granting of that disposition the
A subjects were divided into a number of parts. The
applicants are all heritable proprietors of certain of the
individual parts of the subjects as thus divided. They
do not between them own the whole of the subjects,
the remaining parts of which belong respectively to a
Mrs Helen Wood and a Miss Mairi Cameron. However, there can be no objection to the fact that Mrs
Wood and Miss Cameron are not parties to the
application, which has been duly served upon them in
terms of s 2 (1) of the Act.

B   The application is to have the obligation varied to
the extent of permitting all necessary and reasonable
access for usual domestic purposes to any dwellinghouses situated or to be erected upon the subjects.
What the applicants seek is described in slightly different terms in cond 3 of the closed record, where they
submit "that the land obligation should be varied to
permit access for normal and necessary domestic purposes to all dwellinghouses situated or to be erected
upon the subjects, conform to existing and future
C planning permissions". However, for present purposes the difference is not material and was not
founded upon.

Pleas to the competency of the application have
been stated in the following terms: "(1) The applicants
as benefited proprietors in respect of the land obligation in question having no title to make the application, the application should be refused"; and "(2) The
applicants' interests in land not being subject to the
land obligation referred to in para 2 of the application,
D the application should be refused." When the parties
were heard in debate on those pleas both parties were
represented by counsel.

In terms of s 1 (2) of the Act, a land obligation, for
the purposes of that section and s 2 of the Act, is "an
obligation relating to land which is enforceable by a
proprietor of an interest in land, by virtue of his being
such proprietor, and which is binding upon a proprietor of another interest in that land, or of an
E interest in other land, by virtue of his being such
proprietor".

It is not in dispute between the parties that in terms
of that definition a servitude is a land obligation. Nor
is it in dispute that when this obligation was imposed
its purpose and its effect were to create a servitude
right of access over the respondent's lands in favour of
the proprietor of the subjects which were disponed. In
relation to the obligation Mrs Jessie Ann Fraser was
therefore a benefited proprietor, and the applicants are
F now benefited proprietors as her successors.

In terms of s 1 (3) of the Act the tribunal may vary
or discharge a land obligation on the application of any
person who in relation to the obligation is a burdened
proprietor. For the purposes of that section it is
provided by subs (6) of s 2 that "burdened proprietor", in relation to a land obligation, means a proprietor of an interest in land upon whom, by virtue of
his being such proprietor, the obligation is binding.
"Benefited proprietor", in relation to such an obligation, means a proprietor of an interest in land who is

entitled, by virtue of his being such proprietor, to
enforce the obligation. In terms of the same subsection G
"interest in land" means any estate or interest in land
which is capable of being owned or held as a separate
interest and to which a title may be recorded in the
Register of Sasines.

From those definitions it might appear that only
Lord Burton was a burdened proprietor in relation to
this obligation and accordingly that only he could
apply to the tribunal for it to be varied or discharged.
However, on behalf of the applicants it was submitted
that where a title conferred a right of access, but the   H
terms of the title restricted that right, the benefited
proprietor whose right was thus restricted was at the
same time a burdened proprietor, being burdened by
that restriction. That being so, it was competent for
him to apply for the obligation to be varied so as to
remove or reduce the restriction and thereby to
remove or reduce the burden on him. Having regard
to the definitions of "burdened proprietor" and
"interest in land" in s 2 (6) of the Act, it was accepted
that it was essential to the validity of that argument   I
that a servitude right of access should be an interest in
land which was capable of being owned or held as a
separate interest, and of which the person entitled to
exercise the right could therefore be said to be the proprietor.

It was accepted that there was no precedent for that
proposition, but it was argued that there was no reason
in principle why it should not be so. The fact that a
servitude might be created in a feudal grant separate
from the grant of the dominant tenement satisfied the   J
part of the definition of "interest in land" which
required that it must be capable of being "held" as a
separate interest. The fact that a deed of servitude
could be recorded separately satisfied the other part of
the definition, which required that it must be an
interest to which a title might be recorded in the
Register of Sasines.

With regard to the requirement of s 1 (2) that the
obligation must be binding upon the proprietor of   K
another interest in the same land, or of an interest in
other land, counsel submitted that this servitude was
binding upon both parties. It was binding on the
respondent as proprietor of the servient tenement.
Given the restrictive language of the servitude, it was
also binding upon the applicants, insofar as they were
bound to observe the restrictions on their right. If they
were to seek to use the right in a way which was more
extensive than that provided for in the disposition,
they could be interdicted from doing so.   L

It was submitted that that interpretation did no
violence to the wording of the legislation, and that it
was important to keep in mind the overall purpose of
the Act, which was to provide for changes in circumstances. There would inevitably be cases where a party
in right of a restricted servitude would find that with
the passage of time it had become unduly restrictive.
It was consistent with the objectives of the Act that
that party should then be able to apply to the tribunal
for the restrictions to be relaxed.

The contention that the applicants were at the one time benefited and burdened proprietors in relation to the same obligation was described by counsel for Lord Burton as the merest casuistry. It was agreed that the matter hinged on whether a servitude of access was a separate interest in land. It was submitted, however, that a servitude was inseparable from the dominant tenement which it had been conceived to benefit. While there was no doubt that in conveyancing practice it was competent to present for recording in the Sasines Register, as a deed separate from any other deed, a deed of servitude which contained a new, express grant of servitude right in favour of the dominant tenement therein specified, that did not make the servitude a separate interest in land. For statements of the characteristics of servitudes counsel referred to Halliday's *Conveyancing Law and Practice in Scotland*, Vol II, at para 20-02, and to Rankine on *Land-ownership*, at p 413. It was submitted that on those authorities it was clear that it was not possible to separate a servitude from the dominant tenement. It ceased to exist on the dominant tenement ceasing to exist, and it would cease to exist confusione if the same person became proprietor of both the dominant and the servient tenements. It could not therefore be considered to be a separate interest in land, and the applicants could not therefore be treated as burdened proprietors within the meaning of the Act. Furthermore, if the variation sought were to be granted, the effect would be to increase the degree of access and thereby to increase the burden on the servient tenement. That had never been regarded as permissible: see *Irvine Knitters Ltd v North Ayrshire Co-operative Society Ltd*, 1978 SC 109 at p 121; 1978 SLT 105 at p 112; and *Carstairs v Spence*, 1924 SC 380 at p 385; 1924 SLT 300 at p 304. In any event, since the applicants were not burdened proprietors the application should be refused as incompetent.

The background to this application is that Dalreoch croft was sold to Mrs Jessie Ann Fraser by order of the Scottish Land Court. The order of the court directed that it should be conveyed "with a right of access as at present in use". That order was made in 1978. In the disposition, which was granted in 1981, the right was accordingly described as a right to use for all necessary and usual agricultural purposes the existing roads leading to the subjects conveyed and forming part of any other portion of the Dochfour estate, but that only to the extent to which the same were at that time so used. It must have been accepted that that was in accordance with the court order and no doubt it satisfied the needs of the disponee at that time. Subsequently, in 1991, it was agreed that the right of access to be enjoyed by the original disponee's son and daughter in law, Mr and Mrs James Fraser, who were her successors in title, should be subject to what was termed an "exception", by which they might also use the right for usual domestic access to and from a bungalow which they had built on part of the subjects in 1982. Since then Mr and Mrs Fraser have conveyed part of the subjects to the firm of Messrs T Mackay. Mrs Wood and Miss Cameron own parts of the sub-

jects, and a Mr and Mrs Anderson are potential purchasers under missives of a plot on which they wish to build a house. It appears that yet other developments may be envisaged.

It is for those reasons that the applicants wish the right of access to the subjects to be varied in the manner sought, so as to permit all necessary and reasonable access for usual domestic purposes to any dwellinghouses situated or to be erected upon the subjects.

The applicants are faced with the apparent difficulty that under the Act it is only on the application of a person who, in relation to the obligation, is a burdened proprietor that the tribunal may vary a land obligation, and it may only vary the obligation in relation to the interest in land in respect of which the application is made. Furthermore, for the purposes of the Act that interest must be capable of being owned or held as a separate interest, to which a title may be recorded.

No authority could be cited for the propositions that a servitude by itself can be held as a separate interest in land, or that it is an interest to which a title may be recorded. All authority is to the contrary. In Halliday's *Conveyancing Law and Practice in Scotland*, Vol II, at para 20-02, the learned author's summary of the characteristics of servitudes includes these statements:

"(1) A servitude is *jus in re aliena* and can be created only over one property in favour of another owned by a different person.

"(2) A servitude is a right annexed to the dominant tenement, is inseparable from it and cannot be communicated to any person not connected with the dominant tenement.

"(3) A servitude right exists for the benefit of the dominant tenement: it cannot be used for the benefit of another property even although it also belongs to the owner of the dominant tenement."

In Rankine on *Land-ownership*, at p 413, it is stated that "real or predial servitudes, or servitudes simply, are certain conventional rights known to the law, in virtue of which the owner, as such, of one tenement possesses certain privileges as against the owner, as such, of a neighbouring tenement; or altering the stand point, they are certain conventional real burdens known to the law, in virtue of which the latter owner is subjected to certain restraints in favour of the former. The first-mentioned tenement is termed the dominant, the other the servient, tenement; and their owners are called, for shortness, the dominant and servient owner respectively".

From those statements it is abundantly clear that a servitude cannot have a separate, independent existence. The fact that a deed of servitude can be recorded separately from any other deed does not support the contrary view. That is a matter of conveyancing procedure only. It does not follow that the servitude so created is "held" or is "capable of being owned or held" as a separate interest in land.

It was conceded that it was only by establishing that

a servitude was a separate interest in land that the applicants could bring themselves within the definition of burdened proprietors, who alone might apply to the tribunal for the variation of a land obligation. If they could establish that the servitude of access was a separate interest in land, they could go on to say that the land obligation which they wished to have varied was the restriction on the use which could be made of that servitude. In relation to that obligation they would then be the burdened proprietors, since they were burdened by the restriction. That line of reasoning involves treating a servitude of access as a right which in itself is necessarily unrestricted, but which may then be limited by specific restrictions which, in relation to that right, are therefore land obligations.

In the tribunal's opinion that involves a misconception. The applicants have not been granted a right and at the same time been made subject to a corresponding obligation to observe certain restrictions on their right. What they have been granted is a restricted right, which only goes so far and to which there are limits. A right of access is not a "natural right", as that term is used by the institutional writers, in the sense that (a) the law regards the right as being a normal and reasonable restriction on property which needs no special justification and (b) it does not require to be constituted expressly or by implication. It is a conventional right, granted in this case by the 1981 disposition. Where such a conventional grant is to be made, it is necessary to consider in each case, as a matter of normal conveyancing practice, just what should be the extent of the right; for example, whether it should be a right of vehicular or only of pedestrian access. In the present case, the disposition creating the servitude was drawn in a way which limited the right to the right of access enjoyed by the original disponee at the date of the granting of the disposition. There was no reason why it should not have done so. In *Carstairs v Spence*, the Lord President (Clyde) stated, at 1924 SC, p 386; 1924 SLT, p 304: "Private ways constituted by writing may undoubtedly be made subject to close restriction with reference to the purposes of the traffic which is carried by them." His Lordship added that such restrictions were rigorously enforced.

Accordingly, if this right of access is properly to be regarded as one the extent of which is limited, rather than one which is in itself limitless in extent and which is then made subject to a restriction on the use which the applicants may make of it, that being a restriction which can then be treated as a separate land obligation, it follows that there is here no obligation which the tribunal may competently vary on an application by the persons who enjoy the benefit of the right of access.

In relation to the applicants this servitude is essentially a right, not an obligation. As an obligation it is upon Lord Burton that the servitude is binding. It is of the essence of any positive servitude, as this is, that it should require the servient proprietor simply to suffer something to be done on his land. That rule, expressed in the maxim servitus in faciendo consistere

nequit, is firmly based on institutional authority, as is the principle that the proprietor of the dominant tenement may not do anything to increase the burden on the servient tenement: see *Irvine Knitters*, at p 121 (p 112), and *Carstairs v Spence*, at p 385 (p 304). In his summary of the characteristics of servitudes, to which we have already referred, Professor Halliday states: "(6) The burden on the servient tenement may not be increased beyond the extent of the right granted or acquired by prescription." See also Bell's *Principles of the Law of Scotland*, para 988. If the tribunal were to grant the application, the additional and more extensive rights of access over the road which leads to the subjects, and in particular a right of access to any new buildings placed thereon, would in the tribunal's opinion, clearly increase the burden on the respondent as proprietor of the servient tenement. It is at best doubtful that such a result was contemplated by the legislature when framing the provisions of the 1970 Act. On behalf of Lord Burton it was submitted that, had it been contemplated, the Act would surely have made provision for the awarding of compensation to the servient as well as to the dominant proprietor. As things are, in terms of s 1 (4) of the Act an award of compensation may only be made to a benefited proprietor. There is some force in that submission, although if one were to accept the applicants' argument that they are also burdened proprietors in relation to the servitude, it would be logical to regard Lord Burton as being also a benefited proprietor and, as such, a person to whom an award of compensation could competently be made. However, counsel for the applicants did not go so far as to suggest that Lord Burton was to be regarded as a benefited proprietor, and, as the legislation is framed, the tribunal does not believe that it could competently make an award of compensation in his favour. In any event, having regard to the general principle in the case of conventional servitudes that the burden on the servient tenement should not be increased, the tribunal is of the opinion that for it to do so in the absence of clear statutory authority would amount to an improper use of the power to vary land obligations.

It may be desirable that a person who has the benefit of a conventional servitude of access should be able to obtain an extension or enlargement of that servitude where that is justified by changes in circumstances. However, for the reasons already stated, that is not something which the tribunal has power to order under s 1 (3) of the Act on the application of such a benefited proprietor. If he is to have a remedy, he must seek it on other grounds and in another forum.

The tribunal accordingly sustains the first and third pleas in law for Lord Burton and dismisses the application as incompetent.

Counsel for Applicants, J D Campbell; Solicitors, Sutherland & Co, Inverness — Counsel for Respondent, Hodge; Solicitors, Tods Murray, WS, Edinburgh.

INDEX OF CASES

ACCORDING TO SUBJECT MATTER

★ signifies case reported in note form.

THE
SCOTS LAW TIMES

LYON COURT
REPORTS

1994

EDINBURGH
PUBLISHED BY W GREEN, THE SCOTTISH LAW PUBLISHER
21 ALVA STREET

INDEX OF CASES

ACCORDING TO NAMES OF PARTIES

REPORTS OF CASES

DECIDED IN

THE LYON COURT

1994

Reported by
Sir C H AGNEW OF LOCHNAW, *Advocate*,
Rothesay Herald of Arms

Note: **Cases in this volume may be cited 1994 SLT (Lyon Ct)**

Thus: **MacDonald of Keppoch, Petitioner (No 2), 1994 SLT (Lyon Ct) 2.**

SCOTS LAW TIMES 1994

LYON COURT REPORTS

A
MacDonald of Keppoch, Petitioner (No 2)

COURT OF THE LORD LYON

27 AUGUST 1990

B
Heraldry — Petition for confirmation of arms — Succession to arms — Proof of extinction of stirpes with prior claims — Presumption non apparentibus non existentibus presumuntur — Traditional Gaelic sloinneadh (oral genealogy retained by members of family) — Weight to be given where evidence showed that traditional descent required some correction — Weight to be given to document, only evidence of existence of person, which showed that person to have died without issue — Evidence of tanist nomination of heir to name and arms.

C
Heraldry — Petition for confirmation of arms — Succession to arms — Proof of legitimacy — Weight to be given to statements in birth, death and marriage registers and census records — Presumptions in regard to legitimacy of ancestor long dead — Onus of proof where legitimacy of ancestor put in issue — Whether "any one of his children" meant lawful children when used in commercial contract.

D
Evidence — Petition for confirmation of arms — Succession to arms — Proof of extinction of stirpes with prior claims — Traditional Gaelic sloinneadh (oral genealogy retained by members of family) — Weight to be given where evidence showed that traditional descent required some correction.

Parent and child — Legitimacy — Presumptions in regard to legitimacy of ancestor long dead — Onus of proof where legitimacy of ancestor put in issue — Whether "any one of his children" meant lawful children when used in commercial contract.

E
A petitioner to the Lord Lyon prayed that the plain undifferenced arms of MacDonald of Keppoch should be confirmed to him as tanist heir of his great uncle, whose father was the heir male of Chichester, 21st and last chief of the MacDonalds of Keppoch who died in 1848. The petitioner's great uncle, who was the tanist heir of his elder brother, had verbally nominated the petitioner's father and then the petitioner to succeed him as chief of MacDonald of Keppoch in a family ceremony before witnesses. The petitioner claimed descent from Donald Gorm (died circa 1697), fourth son of Alasdair Buidhe, 14th chief, and relied upon

F
the family sloinneadh or Gaelic oral genealogy to prove a link over two generations in that pedigree. To extinguish the descendants of the 16th chief, the petitioner relied upon the printed family histories of the Clan Donald and the presumption non apparentibus non existentibus presumuntur. Evidence was led to prove that the other descendants of Alasdair Buidhe who had a prior claim to the chiefship, were extinguished. The Lord Advocate entered process in the public interest to put in issue (a) the legitimacy of the petitioner's great grandfather born circa 1832, and (b) the attribution of Donald Gorm as fourth son of

G
Alasdair Buidhe, the Lord Advocate maintaining that he was probably the brother of Alasdair Buidhe.

Held, (1) that the evidence of printed family histories together with the presumption non apparentibus non existentibus presumuntur was sufficient to extinguish the descendants of the 16th chief (*Macnab of Macnab, Petr*, 1957 SLT (Lyon Ct) 2, *applied*) (p 4L); (2) that, as the only evidence of the existence of Alexander, another son of Alasdair Buidhe, 14th
H
chief, was a document that also extinguished him, the petitioner was entitled to rely on that document to prove the extinction (*Earl of Rosscommon's Claim* (1828) 6 Cl & F 79, *followed*) (p 4E-F); (3) that a familial statement in a census return that the petitioner's grandfather was the son of the person making the return was sufficient to raise a rebuttable presumption that the former was legitimate (p 9K); (4) that the respondent had failed to discharge the onus of proof on him to establish that the petitioner's grandfather was illegitimate (p 11C); (5) that the oral evidence of
I
witnesses at a verbal nomination by the petitioner's great uncle of the petitioner's father as tanist heir to the name and arms of MacDonald of Keppoch was sufficient to prove the nomination (p 7L); but (6) that to be of significant weight a sloinneadh or traditional genealogy had to be kept in the correct form, and not require emendation, and as the petitioner's sloinneadh required emendation it could not be relied upon as the only evidence to prove a link in his pedigree connection to Donald Gorm, fourth son of Alasdair Buidhe
J
(pp 6A-B and 11J-L); and petition *refused* in hoc statu.

Observed, (1) that where the precise form of the arms of MacDonald of Keppoch were not known, that would fall to be determined by the Lord Lyon after he had decided who was in right of them (p 3L); (2) that while lawful children might be the appropriate interpretation of the word "child" in relation to testaments and wills, it was not safe to assume that such an interpretation would be appropriate in relation to a commercial contract such as a lease (*Hay v Duthie's
K
Trs*, 1956 SLT 346, *commented on*) (p 9A); and (3) that while in point of form it might be thought somewhat unusual to find in fact that something had not been proved, this manner of proceeding was not without precedent (*Stewart Mackenzie v Fraser-Mackenzie*, 1920 2 SLT 295, *referred to*) (p 12A-G).

Petition for confirmation of arms

L
Ranald Alasdair MacDonald of Keppoch presented a petition to the Lord Lyon King of Arms "(primo) to officially recognise the petitioner in the name Ranald Alasdair MacDonald of Keppoch, Chief of the Name and Arms of MacDonald of Keppoch and of the Honourable Clanranald of Keppoch, Mac-'ic-Raonuill and (secundo) to grant warrant to the Lyon Clerk to prepare letters patent maintaining, ratifying and confirming unto the petitioner and his heirs male, Chiefs of the Name and Arms of MacDonald of Keppoch and of the Honourable Clanranald of Keppoch such arms

A for MacDonald of Keppoch with supporters, standard and pinsel as may be found suitable and according to the law of arms". After sundry procedure (reported 1989 SLT (Lyon Ct) 2), the Lord Advocate entered process to oppose the petition in the public interest. The facts of the petition are set out in the note appended to the interlocutor of the Lord Lyon King of Arms.

A proof before answer was held before the Lord Lyon on 2 to 5 and 9 April 1990.

B **Cases referred to**
Brook's Executrix v James, 1971 SC (HL) 77; (sub nom *James v McLennan*) 1971 SLT 162.
Campbell v Campbell (1866) 4 M 867.
Hay v Duthie's Trustees, 1956 SLT 345; 1956 SC 51.
Macnab of Macnab, Petitioner, 1957 SLT (Lyon Ct) 2.
Macpherson v Reid's Trustees (1876) 4 R 132.
Rosscommon's (Earl of) Claim (1828) 6 Cl & F 97.
Roxburghe (Duke of) v Ker (1822) 6 Pat 820.
Smith v Dick (1869) 8 M 31.
C *Stewart Mackenzie v Fraser-Mackenzie*, 1920 2 SLT 295; 1920 SC 805.

Textbooks referred to
Dickson, *Evidence* (3rd ed), Vol 1, p 27.
Fraser, *Parent and Child* (3rd ed), p 22.
Walker and Walker, *Evidence*, p 63.

On 27 August 1990 the Lord Lyon *pronounced* the following interlocutor:

D The Lord Lyon King of Arms having considered the closed record and productions and taken proof and heard counsel for the petitioner and the Lord Advocate, finds in fact:

(1) That the petitioner, born Glasgow, 19 February 1930, is the eldest son of Donald MacDonald and his wife Margaret MacCormack. (2) That the said Donald MacDonald died in Glasgow 4 December 1977, was the fourth son of Collin MacDonald and his wife Margaret Gillies. (3) That Alexander MacDonald,
E eldest son of the said Collin MacDonald did, while in life, nominate his younger brother Huntly MacDonald, the third son of the said Collin MacDonald, to succeed him in the chiefship of the undifferenced arms of MacDonald of Keppoch. (4) That Alexander MacDonald, second son of Collin MacDonald, has issue, a son Collin MacDonald. (5) That the said Huntly MacDonald did, while in life, nominate his younger brother Donald MacDonald, the petitioner's father, to succeed him in the chiefship
F and undifferenced arms of MacDonald of Keppoch. (6) That the said Collin MacDonald was the second son, but eventual heir male, of Alexander (known as Alasdair Raonuill) MacDonald and his wife Margaret Cameron. (7) That the said Alexander MacDonald was the eldest son of Ranald (known as Raonuill) MacDonald, crofter in Brackletter, cattle drover and dealer, and his wife Margaret Ross. (8) That the said Ranald MacDonald was the elder son of Donald (known as Domhnaill) MacDonald and his wife Margaret Kennedy. (9) That Alexander MacDonald of

Inverroy Mor was the elder son of Donald Gorm MacDonald of Inverroy Mor. (10) That Donald Gorm G MacDonald of Inverroy Mor was the fourth son of Alexander Buy MacDonald 14th chief.

(11) That no heirs male of the body exist of Allan MacDonald, of Archibald MacDonald 15th chief and of Alexander MacDonald, the first, second and third sons respectively of Alexander Buy MacDonald 14th chief. (12) That it has not been proved that Donald MacDonald was the son and heir male of Ranald MacDonald. (13) That it has not been proved that the said Ranald MacDonald was the son and heir male of H Donald MacDonald. (14) That it has not been proved that Donald MacDonald was the son and heir male of Alexander MacDonald of Inverroy Mor. (15) That the undifferenced ensigns armorial of MacDonald of Keppoch have not been recorded in the Public Register of All Arms and Bearings in Scotland by anyone with the surname "MacDonald of Keppoch". (16) That armorial bearings were recorded in the Public Register of All Arms and Bearings in Scotland (Vol 1, Folio 228), of date 25 May 1761 in name of I John Michie, and the first quartering of those armorial bearings was recorded for the petitioner "as being descended from MacDonald of Keppoch".

Finds in law

(1) That the petitioner is not entitled to be recognised in the name Ranald Alasdair MacDonald of Keppoch, Chief of the Name and Arms of MacDonald of Keppoch nor is he entitled to Letters Patent confirming unto him and his heirs male the undifferenced J Armorial Bearings of MacDonald of Keppoch.

Repels the three pleas in law for the petitioner and sustains the plea in law for the respondent.

In hoc statu refuses the prayer of the petitioner.

The note appended to the interlocutor was in the following terms:

THE LORD LYON KING OF ARMS (INNES K **OF EDINGIGHT).**—This is a petition by Ranald Alasdair MacDonald to be officially recognised in the name Ranald Alasdair MacDonald of Keppoch, chief of the name and arms of MacDonald of Keppoch and of the honourable Clanranald of Keppoch, Mac-'ic-Raonuill and to be confirmed in such undifferenced armorial bearings of MacDonald of Keppoch with supporters, standard and pinsel as might be found suitable and according to the laws of arms. The undifferenced arms of MacDonald of Keppoch have L not been matriculated in the Public Register of All Arms and Bearings in Scotland for any person bearing the name "MacDonald of Keppoch". There is a recording of armorial bearings in that register (Vol 1, folio 228) of 25 May 1761 in name of John Michie where the first quartering was recorded for that petitioner "as being descended of MacDonald of Keppoch". The appropriate form of the undifferenced arms of MacDonald of Keppoch would fall to be determined by Lyon after he had decided who was in right of them.

A   In order to succeed in his claim to the undifferenced arms of MacDonald of Keppoch the petitioner must show first, that the right to the chiefship or headship of the house of MacDonald of Keppoch descends to the heir male and secondly, that the petitioner is the heir male of Alexander Buy MacDonald, 14th chief.

B   The evidence of Mr Norman H MacDonald, author of *The Clan Ranald of Lochaber — a History of the MacDonalds or MacDonells of Keppoch*, indicated that the right to the chiefship of the MacDonalds of Keppoch passed to lawful heirs male. None of the other witnesses expressed a contrary view. It is significant that no 16 on the pedigree chart, the sister of Alexander MacDonald, 13th chief, was passed over in favour of Alexander Buy following the murder of the 13th chief. Counsel for the Lord Advocate accepted that the succession to the chiefship of this family is confined to heirs male. I am accordingly of the opinion that the succession to the chiefship of this family is confined to lawful heirs male.

C   According to received accounts of the clan the male issue of Alexander Buy by his first wife were Allan, Archibald, 15th chief, and Alexander.

Allan was shown to have been party to the murder of Alexander MacDonald, 13th chief. After the murder he fled from the district and there were rumours that he had descendants in Nova Scotia and there was another tradition that he was killed without issue. It is clear, however, that with regard to the chiefship he was passed over in favour of Archibald, D   15th chief on the death of Alexander Buy, 14th chief, in 1669.

Alexander does not appear in any of the listings of the chiefly family prepared in the 17th century and may be presumed to have died young. With regard to the extinction of Alexander MacDonald there is one further aspect to be considered and that is that the only document that shows he existed (i e the published work *The Clan Donald*, Vol III, p 421) also extin- E   guishes him. It would appear that the opinion expressed in the *Earl of Rosscommon's Claim* allows the view to be taken that if a source raises or estab- lishes the existence of a person and also extinguishes that person the whole source may be relied upon: "but with respect to S. F. Dillon it may be said that he was no party, and therefore that evidence cannot affect this case. But though he was no party, he was cognizant of the evidence, for he was present during the whole investigation, and though he was no actual party, yet, F   standing by, I think he must be taken as if he was a party. Now where is the evidence that there existed any such persons as those four sons, from one of whom he claims to derive his descent? There is no evi- dence whatsoever, except the pedigree, and the pedigree states them to have died without issue. The very evidence which proves their existence proves their deaths without issue; for the whole document must be taken together, and not a part of it, so that there is no evidence on the part of the Crown that there were such persons, except this pedigree, and this shows them to have died without issue".

G   Archibald, 15th chief, had four sons — Coll MacDonald "of the Cows", Ranald MacDonald of Tirnadris, Alexander MacDonald of Gaskmore, and Angus Odhar MacDonald.

For the extinction of the male descendants of Coll MacDonald, 16th chief, Coll of the Cows, the peti- tioner relies almost entirely on printed sources — *The Clan Donald* (by the Rev A Macdonald, Minister of Killearnan, and the Rev A Macdonald, Minister of Kiltarlity, 3 vols, 1896, hereinafter referred to as *The Clan Donald*), *The Clan Ranald of Lochaber* (by H   Norman H MacDonald, 1971) and *Clan Donald* (by Donald J MacDonald of Castleton, 1978). *The Clan Donald* narrates the descent down to Richard MacDonald and concludes by stating "It may be suffi- cient merely to say that the family continues to be worthily represented in Lochaber until a few years ago" (Vol II, p 671). In Castleton's *Clan Donald* it is stated that "Richard died of yellow fever in 1819, while serving with his regiment in Jamaica. He also had never married, and the succession fell upon his I   cousin Chichester, son of Alexander, the 'Big Major'. Of Chichester, 21st chief, little is known beyond the meagre facts that he lived in Glasgow and Greenock, served in the Glengarry Fencibles for a short time, and died in 1848. He had two sons who went to Canada. Neither of them married, and both predeceased their father, being killed in action while serving in the army. Chichester also had a brother John, and a sister Janet, a nun, both of whom are recorded as having died of cholera in Montreal in 1832. John, who thus J   predeceased Chichester by many years, does not appear to have left any issue" (p 385). It appears that in 1921 a search was made in records in Canada to trace the two sons of Chichester and that no evidence of the existence of descendants of Alexander was found. In Norman H MacDonald's *The Clan Ranald of Lochaber* (published 19 years ago) it is stated "Charles died at Greenock in 1848 and with him the male line of Keppoch from Coll of the Cows would appear to have become extinct" (p 51). Norman H K   MacDonald admitted in the course of his evidence that in preparing his book he had to some extent drawn on the work of Josephine M MacDonell (*The MacDonells of Keppoch and Gargavoch*, 1931), and of Dr Angus MacDonald in Taunton. There has been considerable interest in this chiefship in recent years and the present claim has received a certain amount of pub- licity. It was advertised in *The Scotsman* newspaper (11 December 1986) and in *The Oban Times* news- paper (11 December 1986) and there also appeared in *The Oban Times* newspaper a letter of 29 March 1976 L   from Mrs Ann MacDonell concerning the chiefship. This court has relied on the presumption *non apparentibus non existentibus presumuntur* in some- what analogous circumstances in *Macnab of Macnab, Petr*, and as no answers or counterclaim have been lodged by any male descendant of Coll MacDonald I am of the opinion that the petitioner can rely on this presumption and I accordingly find that the male descendants of Coll MacDonald have been satisfac- torily extinguished.

Ranald Mor MacDonald of Tirnadris, the second son of Archibald MacDonald, 15th chief, had three sons. The eldest son Archibald died in 1729 aged 35 leaving a son Donald who was shown to have been executed at Kennington in 1746 (the accounts of his execution in the *Gentleman's Magazine*, 1746, pp 173-174, 400-401, and *Scots Magazine*, August 1746, pp 396-397, describe him as a nephew of Keppoch: this relationship to Keppoch was through his mother Margaret, daughter of Coll MacDonald, 16th chief, and sister of 17th chief). The second son of Ranald was Donald, who was executed at Carlisle in 1746. Donald had a son Ranald, who died young at Douai while training for the priesthood. The extinction of the male line of Donald is further indicated by the fact that the family tack of Corriechoille passed to the Delafour branch, a junior branch. With regard to Donald the extinction of his male line is indicated by the printed accounts of the family and by the fact that the tack of Tirnadris also passed to the Delafour line.

The third and youngest son of Ranald MacDonald was Alexander MacDonald of Delafour who married Rachel Macpherson, the heiress of Delafour, who had a son Donald and two daughters, Sarah who married Charles Robertson in Perth, and Katherine who married Alexander McDonell, son of Ranald mac Ian vic Donald Gorm of Inverroy. The extinction of Donald is prima facie established from an entry in the Register of Testaments, Commissariot of Edinburgh, recorded 27 January 1784 where it states "The Testament Dative . . . of Donald McDonald late of Dilafour . . . who died abroad upon" (date blank) ". . . faithfully made and given up by Charles Robertson, Shoemaker in Perth, husband to and in name and behalf of Sarah McDonald his spouse . . . sister germain of the said defunct". As Donald's nearest kin was his sister Sarah, I am of the opinion that the Delafour line may be accepted as being extinct in the male line.

Alexander MacDonald, the third son of Archibald MacDonald, 15th chief, had two stepsons, Thomas Leslie and Alexander Leslie. It appears he did have a son by his wife but researches carried out over a period of time by an experienced researcher under the direction of counsel skilled in heraldic and peerage law have produced no evidence of his existence in late life nor of any male descendants. In these circumstances I am of the opinion that it may be reasonably assumed that there are no male descendants of Alexander MacDonald.

Archibald MacDonald, 15th chief, had a fourth son Angus Odhar who married Marjorie Shaw, who had two husbands prior to marrying Angus Odhar. Angus Odhar married relatively late in life: there is a letter of 17 May 1704 from Coll MacDonald, 16th chief, to his agent stating that "The Bearer Angus McDonald my youngest brother being latelie married". The only evidence of issue of this marriage is found in the papers of Father Andrew MacDonell at Fort Augustus wherein a daughter "Isabel" is mentioned. No evidence has been found to show that there were male descendants of this marriage.

The extinction of the male lines of Ranald, Alexander and Angus are supported by the presumption non apparentibus non existentibus presumuntur. They are also supported to some small extent by the statement made in the *Collected Works of George Borrow, A Tour of Scotland* (1924) at p 562. "The young man said that his uncle was the proper Cean Cinne or Chief of the Macdonell's, that he was an old man and lived far off". This statement appears to have been made at Roy Bridge in 1858 and indicates that there was at that time a tradition in the Roy Bridge area that the chief of the Macdonells was in the area. George Borrow described the man who made the statement as "a stout young man with a red beard" and also that he was called Macdonell. Mrs Ann MacDonell in her evidence indicated that her husband had told her that his grandfather, Donald MacDonald known as "Donald the Drover" had red hair and it may have been he who spoke to George Borrow in 1858. The evidence of Mrs Ann MacDonell was also to the effect that the local tradition was that the line of Ranald MacDonald of Tirnadris was extinct in the male line. I am therefore of the opinion that the male line descendants of Archibald MacDonald, 15th chief, may be regarded as having been satisfactorily extinguished.

The petitioner claims that the chiefship is to be looked for among the descendants of Donald Gorm, younger brother of Archibald, 15th chief, and son of Alexander Buy, 14th chief. The petitioner's case for this starts with the sloinneadh of Donald the Drover. It was established that a sloinneadh is a traditional patronymic genealogy, and is a genealogy of the male line only and is most likely to be preserved if it is a claim to chiefly ancestry. It is more usually remembered when a family stays in one place and is frequently lost when the family move away from that place. Mrs Ann MacDonell gave to Mr Hugh Peskett a handwritten note of the sloinneadh with annotated translation which were both produced as evidence. A copy of the letter of Mrs Ann MacDonell of 29 March 1976 to *The Oban Times* referring to the sloinneadh was also produced. The sloinneadh of Donald the Drover is as follows: "Domhnall mac Alasdair mhic Dhomhnaill mhic Raonuill mhic Dhomhnaill mhic Dhomhnaill Ghuirm" (translated Donald, son of Alexander, son of Donald, son of Ranald, son of Donald, son of Donald Gorm). Donald the Drover was the grandfather of John MacDonell the husband of Mrs Ann MacDonell, a witness in this case. There is some doubt as to whether Donald was a drover or not; his father Alexander certainly was a drover and the more correct description of Donald from the Gaelic may have been "son of the drover" rather than "the drover". Mrs Ann MacDonell in her evidence and in her letter to *The Oban Times* of 1976 indicated that according to local tradition Donald Gorm, the head of the sloinneadh, was a stepbrother of Archibald, 15th chief, and that she was of the opinion that Donald Gorm was designated "of Clianaig" but she also indicated that it had never occurred to her that the same person might have held both Inverroy Mor and

A Clianaig. Her evidence was also to the effect that
Donald Gorm was traditionally regarded as a son of
the 14th chief. The evidence of Mr Peskett was that
the start or earliest person of a sloinneadh was always
accurately known and that the later generations were
correctly known but that omissions and slippages were
often found in the earlier generations. It is the petitioner's contention that Alexander was omitted from
the sloinneadh and falls to be inserted where shown on
the pedigree chart. This court has always taken due
cognisance of Gaelic genealogies derived from oral and
B traditional sources but it must be said that where it has
been shown that such a traditional genealogy requires
adjustment or amendment in any part the weight to be
given to it may be considerably lessened. It has been
satisfactorily proved that Ranald MacDonald and
Alexander MacDonald were brothers and that Ranald
was the elder brother. It appears that Mrs Ann
MacDonell was unaware of these facts in 1976 when
she wrote to *The Oban Times*.

C The petitioner contends that the position of Donald
Gorm in the Keppoch genealogy has been wrongly
stated by the main printed source *The Clan Donald*. In
that work (Vol III, pp 421 and 458) Donald, son of
Alexander Buy is designated "of Clianaig", and a
Donald Gorm of the previous generation, a brother of
Alexander Buy, is described as "of Inverroy" (Vol III,
pp 420 and 456). This statement was repeated in *Clan
Donald* (by MacDonald of Castleton, pp 373, 378 and
379) and in *Clan Ranald of Lochaber* (Norman H
D MacDonald, pp 15, 19 and 21). It is the petitioner's
contention that all these printed works are in error,
that they cite no authority for the statements made in
relation to this part of the genealogy and that when
these statements are disregarded the correct position
of Donald Gorm in the genealogy becomes clear. A
series of significant documents for the period
1665-1697 were referred to. The first document was a
Privy Council order of 29 June 1665 for commission
for apprehension of "Alan McDonald, sone to the
E tutour of Kepoch; Donald McDonald brother to the
said Alan". The second document was an Act of
Adjournal from the McIntosh Muniments of 24 July
1671 naming "Archibald Mcdonold in Kipoch,
Donald Gorme Mcdonold in Inneroymore, Angus
Mcdonold in Murlaggan". The third document was a
Privy Council protection of August 1672 for inter alia
"Archibald McDonald, Donald McDonald of Inneroy
and Eneas McDonald of Muirlagan" (Eneas being
Gaelic for Angus). The fourth document was a com-
F plaint to the Privy Council of 23 November 1676 by
Archibald, Earl of Argyle, against inter alia "Donald
Gorume, and Allan McDonald, Keapoch's brethren,
and John McDonald his son, Allan and Angus
McDonald, his brethren". While the first two names
in this last document can probably be satisfactorily
identified, the usefulness of this document is much
reduced by the fact that the identities of the last three
names are not at all clear, and in relation to this document, Mr Peskett was frank enough to suggest that it
should be disregarded as the person who had drafted
it was not consistently accurate. The fifth document

G was a commission of the Privy Council of 20 September 1681 for fire and sword against inter alia
"Archbold McDonald in Keapoch, Donald Gorme in
Innereimoir". The sixth document was a horning of
14 June 1697 against a list of the men of Keppoch
including "Alister McDonald alias McCoill guerm
principall possessor of Inverroy moir". Mr Peskett
stated in his evidence that he had fully searched
the Register of the Privy Council, the Gordon
Muniments, the McIntosh Muniments (which from
their undisturbed state did not appear to have been
H searched by anyone prior to his search) and that all the
references to the name Donald Gorm had been
mentioned in his report.

Counsel for the respondent drew the court's attention to *Antiquarian Notes* by Dr C Fraser-Mackintosh
which, in a passage regarding the inhabitants of Brae
in Lochaber, stated: "Under the circumstances, so
honourable to the Mackintoshes and their tenants, it
may interest at least the latter to know the names of
some of the chief tenants in 1655, held bound for
I their subtenants, cotters, descendants. . . . There were
the minors (Alexander and Ranald) Macdonell of
Keppoch, sons of Donald Glas, and their uncle
Alexander MacDonald Buidhe, their 'pretended'
tutor", then it lists a number of names, and included
amongst these was "Donald Gorme Macdonald for
Inverroy More". The weight of this evidence is not
great as it is essentially hearsay evidence and the
source of the evidence was not given. On balance it is
outweighed by the later primary sources of evidence
J from the Privy Council records, court records and
muniment records and by the negative research evidence of Mr Peskett and indeed as a result of these
researches it may well have been the case that if a
Donald Gorme existed in 1665 he was by the period
1670-97 long dead. Counsel for the respondent also
raised a significant point with regard to the commission for apprehension of 1665 and the Act of
Adjournal and that was that it would be highly
unlikely, if not impossible, for the two Donald
K MacDonalds in these documents to be the same
person because Donald MacDonald, brother to Allan,
had already been decerned and denounced a rebel in
1665 and that a more reasonable interpretation of the
two documents would be that in 1665 the Crown had
attempted to apprehend certain members of the family
and in the later document were against the remaining
(i e those who had not been apprehended) members of
the family. It may well be that some of those mentioned in the first document were apprehended but it
L would not be safe to assume, given the conditions to
be found in the Highlands at that time, that they were
and that the same names would not appear in a similar
document some years later. In the introduction to Vol
IV of the Third Series of the *Register of the Privy
Council, 1673-1676*, Professor P Hume Brown stated:
"Again we have the same measures taken for the
suppression of crime throughout the whole Highland
country and with the same futile result. . . . In 1671,
it had been enacted that all Highland droves should be
in possession of certificates and passes before they

were allowed to drive their cattle into the low country.
A The Act had been more than once renewed, but it continued to remain a dead letter" (pp xxii and xxiii). In the introduction to Vol VIII of the *Register of the Privy Council of Scotland, 1683-1684*, Professor P Hume Brown observed: "If there was improvement on the Borders, the same cannot be said of the Highlands and Western Islands. In the present volume we have the same monotonous record of lawlessness and of the abortive measures taken to check it" (p xiv), and he gives an entry for 19 July 1683: "List of thieves and
B broken men within the shires of Stirling and Perth who had been denounced by the commission for these districts, and who had failed to appear when summoned" (p xv). It is clear from these references that Acts of Parliament were regularly re-enacted and that criminals frequently failed to appear when summoned and fresh commissions were issued in respect of such. It was, therefore, quite likely that the same names would appear in similar documents at that period.

C I am of the opinion that the series of documents for the period 1665-1697 should not be considered singly but must be taken together and considered with the negative research evidence of Mr Peskett with regard to the existence of a Donald Gorm of Inverroy Mor. It is also significant that Mr Peskett, Mrs Ann MacDonell and Mr Norman MacDonald all indicated that *The Clan Donald* was in parts unreliable and inaccurate. I am of the opinion that the primary sources from the Privy Council records and from muniment
D collections are to be relied on much more heavily than the printed *The Clan Donald* which does not support the statements contained in it by reference to appropriate authorities. I think it has been established on a balance of probabilities that Donald Gorm falls to be regarded as son of Alexander Buy, 14th chief, and not as a younger brother of that chief. It was the authors of *The Clan Donald* who first asserted (Vol III, p 421) that Donald Gorm had the designation "of Clianaig". This was probably followed by the genealo-
E gist Father Andrew. It is not easy to decide how much weight should be given to Father Andrew's work on the family of MacDonald of Keppoch as it would appear that when writing on this branch of the MacDonald family he relied to some extent on the work of the authors of *The Clan Donald* and that his interest was concentrated on MacDonald priests and MacDonald bards and the lines of descent that concerned such priests and bards. It does appear, however, that his work in certain areas was relied
F upon by Lord Lyon Grant and Lord Lyon Innes of Learney and therefore was in some respects regarded as valuable by those Lyons. I do not think it would be safe to give significant weight to his genealogies regarding this branch of the family. Mrs Ann MacDonell indicated in her evidence a stirpes called "Donald Gorm, Clianaig". It was established that in an address by Archibald MacDonald of Keppoch, 15th chief, to the Marquess of Huntly of 1682 (wherein a number of MacDonalds made a commitment to the Marquess of Huntly) there appeared a Donald MacDonald of Clianaig (that is in the Gordon

lands and not in the Mackintosh lands). References to other MacDonald tacksmen were also found; to a G Donald of Clianaig in 1691, a Ranald younger of Clianaig 1712, and an Alexander of Clianaig in 1714. One would not expect to find a mention of MacDonald of Clianaig in the long list of the men of Keppoch of 1697 as that was a Mackintosh document. The possibility was raised of members of this family holding tacks from both Gordon and Mackintosh landlords. Counsel for the respondent suggested that it would be likely that a person would hold of one landlord rather than of two or more, but Mr Peskett was H of the opposite opinion and he was supported in that view by Mr Norman H MacDonald who, although he could not recall an example of someone holding a tack from both his chief and another chief or lesser landowner, could see no reason against it "if it were agreeable to the chief". The evidence on the matter of exactly who those designated "Clianaig" were was not such that it would be safe to reach any definite decision on the matter.

The horning of 14 June 1697 giving the list of the I men of Keppoch, including "Alister McDonald alias McCoill guerm principall possessor of Inverroy moir", establishes that Donald Gorm of Inverroy Mor was dead by 1697 and that his eldest son Alexander had succeeded him in the tack. It would also appear that the succession of Inverroy subsequently was not to the son of Alexander but to his brother John, as is shown from the inscription on the memorial erected at Cille Choirill by Alexander McDonell, grandson of John, for his wife (who died in 1768), where he J described himself as "Ranald Mack Ian vic Conil-Gorm MacDonell of Inverroy". The wording of the inscription is corroborated by the existence of a tack of 1724 of the lands of Inverroy Mor by Lachlan MacIntosh of that Ilk in favour of John McDonald of Inverroy and Ranald McDonald his eldest lawful son.

The immediate ancestry of the petitioner falls to be considered next. It has been satisfactorily proved that the petitioner is the heir male of his father Donald K MacDonald who was the fourth son of Collin MacDonald, and that Alexander MacDonald second son of Collin MacDonald was shown to have left a son Collin MacDonald upon whom this petition (which contains in stat 14 the assertion that the succession to the chiefship "devolved by tanist nomination from Alexander, eldest son of the said Collin Macdonald on the said Huntly MacDonald elder brother of the Petitioner's father the said Donald MacDonald and that the said Huntly MacDonald nominated the Peti- L tioner's father the said Donald MacDonald to be his tanist heir in the said name, arms and chiefship as MacDonald of Keppoch, Chief of the Honourable Clanranald of Keppoch") has been served. No answers or objections have been lodged by Collin MacDonald following such service. Counsel for the respondent indicated that he accepted that the nominations were effectively made by Alexander MacDonald and by Huntly MacDonald and I am of the opinion that it has been proved that these nominations were effectively made.

A It has been satisfactorily proved that Collin MacDonald was the second son, but eventual heir male, of Alexander MacDonald and that Ranald MacDonald was the elder son and heir male of Donald MacDonald.

One of the key points in the pedigree is the matter of the legitimacy of Alexander MacDonald which the respondent has put in issue. Counsel for the petitioner endeavoured to establish that there was a presumption in favour of the legitimacy of Alexander MacDonald B and accordingly there was an onus upon the respondent to displace that presumption. It was suggested that the onus could arise in two ways: first, where people are reputed to be husband and wife there is a presumption in favour of legitimacy, and secondly, where the person claimed to be illegitimate has long been dead and the question of his status has only recently been raised then the descendants of that person are entitled to the presumption of legitimacy in relation to their ancestor. It was conceded by the petitioner that a presumption of legitimacy could not arise C under the first category based on Ranald MacDonald and Margaret Ross having cohabited with habit and repute as man and wife because virtually no evidence could be produced concerning the marriage, and if Margaret Ross did in fact die in childbirth at an early stage of the marriage (a tradition spoken to by two of the witnesses) no evidence of cohabitation with habit and repute for the necessary period could be forthcoming. The petitioner's position is that he cannot prove how the marriage was constituted: no evidence is to be D found in statutory records nor in parish records and evidence was led to show that there were gaps in the records and there were at the relative period three forms of irregular marriage. The petitioner contended that no evidence was produced to establish that Alexander was ever treated as illegitimate and that in such circumstances the party raising the question of his legitimacy, after a period of nearly 100 years, has the onus of proving the illegitimacy.

E Various authorities were referred to in support of that contention. W G Dickson stated: "Where the legal presumption is in favour of one party's plea, the party maintaining the opposite must prove it, although involving a negative. Thus, one who alleges that a person is not sane must prove it, the presumption being in favour of sanity; and, similarly, the party who alleges that a person is not legitimate, must displace the presumption of legitimacy" (*A Treatise on the Law of Evidence* (1887), Vol 1, p 27, para 27), and F A G and N M L Walker stated: "It has been said that there is a presumption of legitimacy but it is thought that this arises only where the person concerned has been accorded the status of legitimacy during his lifetime, or where one of the presumptions associated with an undisputed marriage applies" (*The Law of Evidence in Scotland* (1964), p 63). Both authorities appear to base their statements on *Campbell v Campbell*. In *The Law of Parent and Child*, p 22, Fraser stated: "The possession of the status of legitimacy throws the *onus probandi* upon the party challenging it; and a person is said to possess it when

he is held and reputed to be the child of the husband and the wife." In support of his statement Fraser G refers to *Duke of Roxburghe v Ker* (1822) 6 Pat at p 830, where Lord Eldon observed: "I think that the presumption is to be made in favour of legitimacy, especially of a person who existed 200 or 300 years ago, if upon looking through the transactions of the family descended from him, and the family connected with him, there has been no cogent evidence to show that one branch of the family did not consider another branch of the family as springing from an illegitimate source; but instead of doing so, took one another as H individuals coming from a pure source." The circumstances obtaining in the *Campbell* case are not present in this case. In *Campbell* the main issue was whether the parties who had by cohabitation with habit and repute been held to be man and wife would pass the status of legitimacy to their child. As there is no evidence before this court of the father and mother of Alexander having constituted a marriage by cohabitation with habit and repute I do not think the opinions of the consulted judges, nor the actual decisions, in I that case are of much assistance in the present case.

There is one aspect of *Campbell*, however, that does require to be considered and that is the petitioner's contention that the succession to the croft at Brackletter by Alexander (shown by the evidence of the information on the census return of 1861 (where Alexander MacDonald is described as "Head of Family" there and also as "Crofter")) is to be regarded as analogous to the prior services of Glenfalloch and his ancestor William John Lamb Campbell: "There J can be no doubt that, in the proceedings of service such as those here in dependence, a prior service of the claimant or his ancestor is good evidence of propinquity. The verdict of an inquest in a service proceeds on open and edictal notice to the public, and is a solemn act, which not only declares, but confers on the party served, the status there asserted and ascertained; and such verdict exhibited in the shape of a formal retour, is admissible evidence against all and sundry while unreduced" (Lord Justice Clerk, Lord Neaves and Lord Mure, p 923). K

In the conditions of let relating to the croft the following clause is to be found in cl 9: "The tenant is bound not to sublet or assign his lease without permission, in writing, of the proprietor. The tack is to go to the lawful heirs-male of his own body, according to seniority in the first instance; failing them, to the heirs-male by the same rule, without division; and failing them, to his nearest male heir whatsoever, on his finding security for punctual payment of five years' rents; but the tenant is allowed notwithstand- L ing, by a regular deed under his hand, to select any one of his children that he may incline, in preference to another, to succeed him in the lease."

It was argued by the petitioner that as Alexander had succeeded to the croft under the conditions of let he must be regarded as having been a legitimate child of his father, and that the words "any one of his children" in the conditions of let should be regarded as having the meaning "any one of his legitimate children" because it has been held in Court of Session

A decisions that the word "children" primarily means lawful issue only (*Hay v Duthies' Trs*, 1956 SC at p 514; 1956 SLT at p 347). While this is the appropriate interpretation of the word "child" in relation to testaments and wills, I do not think it would be safe to assume that such an interpretation would be appropriate in relation to a commercial contract such as a lease. With regard to the analysis of Mr Peskett entitled "Succession of Crofters at Brackletter 1806-1861" (The Crofters of Brackletter-Succession Recorded in Rentals and Censuses), it was suggested that this docu-

B ment showed that the succession to all the Brackletter crofts was to widows and heirs, but I am of the opinion that it would not be safe to draw such a conclusion from this document as in relation to some of the crofts one has a clear indication that succession has been to heirs and in relation to others that that might not necessarily have been the case. From the analysis a clear indication cannot be taken that the succession always went to lawful heirs male. The petitioner is not, I think, in a position to rely on the succession to the tack of the croft being evidence of the lawful

C propinquity between Alexander and his father and therefore the analogy between the succession to the croft and the service of heirs is not of assistance.

Lord Justice Clerk Moncrieff expressed the opinion that "There is an undoubted presumption in favour of legitimacy. There is also a presumption in favour of a status enjoyed by common reputation. The onus of proof lies on the party impugning" (*Smith v Dick* (1869) 8 M at p 33), and that opinion regarding status

D enjoyed by common reputation was approved of by Lord Guest: "It is true that in that case there was a divided reputation and therefore no reliance could be placed on the presumption. But the expression of opinion by the Lord Justice-Clerk is, in my view, sound" (*Brooks's Exrx v James*, 1971 SC (HL) at p 84; 1971 SLT at p 166). In my view, however, the petitioner has not been able to establish a common reputation from the evidence of the witnesses called. The evidence of the petitioner and of his brother Hughie to the effect that their father used to refer to "Grannie

E Ross" is of little weight as they are not disinterested parties, and furthermore "Ross" would have been a great grandmother of their father and not a grandmother. The hearsay evidence of Clementine MacArthur is of very little weight. No weight can be attached to the fact that Mrs Ann MacDonell was unaware of, or had not heard of, any problems regarding the legitimacy of Alexander until she saw censuses and other extracts. The taking over of the croft by Alexander has already been shown to be of no help in

F this context. The only piece of evidence that is of some weight is Mrs Ann MacDonell's statement in her letter to *The Oban Times* in 1976 to the effect that Alexander and Donald were "first cousins, agreed by both sides of the family". In the light of Lord Eldon's comment in *Roxburghe v Ker* ("There has been no cogent evidence to show that one branch of the family did not consider another branch of the family as springing from an illegitimate source; but instead of doing so, took one another as individuals coming from a pure source") already referred to, this evidence is relevant. Mrs Ann MacDonell is not herself a cousin

of Alexander but her husband John MacDonell is. However, in my view the evidence is not sufficient of G itself to establish a presumption that Alexander enjoyed a legitimate status by common reputation.

The petitioner argued that the extract from the records for the censuses of Scotland for 31 March 1851 for Brackletter established that a familial statement was made by Ranald MacDonald to the effect that Alexander was his lawful son. With regard to the evidence of Mr Peskett regarding the taking of censuses, frequent references were made to what the head of household might have said to the enumerator. H It is, however, clear from an official publication that the information provided by heads of households was not given to enumerators verbally but that the "Householder's Schedule" was completed and the completed schedule was called for on Monday 31 March 1851. The form of the "Householder's Schedule" is at p 111 of *Guides to Official Sources, No 2, Census Reports of Great Britain 1801-1931* (HMSO, 1951). It is in my view significant that the head of the schedule starts with the words "LIST of the I MEMBERS of the FAMILY". In the first column the person completing the schedule is instructed to "Write after the Name of Head of the Family the Names of his Wife, Children", and at the bottom of the schedule appear the following words: "The foregoing is a true Return concerning all the Members of this Family. Witness my Hand." It is also significant that in the "General Instruction" it is stated "Persons who refuse to give CORRECT information, incur a Penalty of Five Pounds" (*Census Reports*, p 110). £5 J was a significant sum of money in 1851. I am satisfied that the extract from the census records sufficiently summarises the familial statement that was made by Ranald MacDonald to the effect that his son was Alexander MacDonald. The word "Un." (for "Unmarried") does appear in the column headed "Condition as to Marriage". The significance of the use of this word will be considered later in this opinion but I do not think it undermines the fundamental nature of the statement as to parenthood made K by Ranald MacDonald. I am of the opinion that the familial statement of Ranald is sufficient to give rise to the rebuttable presumption that Alexander MacDonald was legitimate and that the onus of proving that he was not legitimate is on the respondent, the standard of proof being on a balance of probabilities.

In considering the evidence relating to the legitimacy of Alexander it is probably convenient to consider a number of adminicles of evidence which in my L opinion were of no value. The question of succession to the croft at Brackletter: this is neutral pointing neither to the legitimacy nor to the illegitimacy of Alexander. The fact that Alexander appears from census returns of 1841 and 1851 to be staying with his father Ranald is also neutral because it has been established that in Scots law the father of an illegitimate son had the right to custody of such son if he was willing to pay for the child's upkeep. The fact that Alexander bore his father's surname is also neutral because the evidence of Mrs Ann MacDonell was to the effect that an illegitimate son could bear the father's surname if A the father accepted paternity. The use of the patronymic "Alasdair Raonuill" is also neutral because according to Mrs Ann MacDonell and Mr Norman MacDonald neither legitimacy nor illegitimacy could be inferred from the use of such a name. The evidence with regard to the "List of Cotters in the Island of Tiree — 14 July 1846", where it appeared that a widow was described as "unmarried", was also of no assistance because the only options that were given were "married" or "unmarried" and, presumably, B those gathering the statistics were only interested in these two categories and were not interested in ascertaining whether people had been previously married.

Counsel for the respondent submitted that no evidence was produced that showed that Ranald MacDonald was ever married. The rebuttable presumption of the legitimacy of Alexander having been established by the petitioner, the onus is on the respondent to show that Ranald was not married and that Alexander was illegitimate. As has already been C mentioned, it is certainly the case that no entry could be shown for the marriage of Ranald in a parochial marriage register, nor for a baptism of Alexander in a parochial register of baptisms. It would appear that after a long period of time that in relation to this marriage and birth there is a clear penuria testium. Mr Peskett showed that the registers were incomplete at the relative period and that a number of Catholic families refrained from recording baptisms, etc, and there was no system of compulsory registration of D births, deaths and marriages until the passing of the Registration of Births, Deaths and Marriages (Scotland) Act 1854.

Difficulties were raised for the petitioner by the inclusion of the word "unmarried" in the column headed "Condition as to Marriage" in the extract of the census for Brackletter of 1851. In the schedule completed "by the Head of the Family" for the 1851 census the relevant column is headed "Condition" E and below that word appeared the instructions "Write 'Married', 'Widower', 'Widow', or 'Unmarried', against the names of all Persons except Young Children" (*Census Reports of Great Britain 1801-1931*, p 111). I think it is to a certain degree significant that in the general instructions attached to the schedule is included a table headed "Examples of the Mode of Filling up the Return" (*Census Reports*, p 110), and that of the 14 examples given in the "Condition" column not one example of "Widower" is shown, and F that eight of the 14 examples are "Unmarried". It must also be kept in mind that a penalty of £5 might be incurred by refusing to give correct information, and that penalty would almost certainly have deterred informants from giving incorrect information. Evidence was led regarding the difficulties that might have arisen if the informant was not fully bilingual in Gaelic and in English. It may have been the case that there was no satisfactory equivalent in Gaelic of the English word "widower". *A Pronouncing and Etymological Dictionary of thè Gaelic Language* by Malcolm Maclennan for "widower" in English gives

"aonrachdan", and in the Gaelic section the root of that word is translated as "alone, solitary, singular". G Mrs Ann MacDonell, who studied Gaelic at Glasgow University for two years, indicated that she did not know of a single Gaelic word for "widower" and indicated a possible Gaelic phrase which translated into English as "he never married". That phrase, however, is not helpful in relation to the essential meaning of the word "widower" (ie that a man was married at some time). Help may, or may not, have been given by the enumerator but in relation to censuses which were completed within a very short period of time it may H well have been the case that enumerators may not have had time to read through every householder's schedule very carefully. It would not in my opinion be safe to take the view that "unmarried" as shown in the census extract necessarily implies that Ranald had never married, particularly in the face of the signed statement in the same deed that Alexander was his son.

The extract certificate of death of Ranald MacDonald must be considered next. The informant I was Alexander MacDonald who is described in the certificate as "son", and below the father's name appears the word "Single". The entry in the register of deaths is evidence of the death only: "Every extract (but not extracts from parochial registers under section 47 of this Act) and every abbreviated certificate of birth, in either case duly authenticated as aforesaid, shall be sufficient evidence of the birth, death or marriage as the case may be" (Registration of Births, Deaths and Marriages (Scotland) Act 1965, s 41 (3)). This Act does not, however, preclude what appears on J these certificates from being treated as adminicles of evidence and such statements have been received by the courts as being relevant adminicles of evidence as to how people regarded themselves and how people regarded members of their family. Lord Guest observed: "I am more impressed, however, by the evidence of common reputation. There is no doubt that William M'Innes regarded himself legitimate, as appears on his marriage certificate" (*Brooks's Exrx v James*, 1971 SC (HL) at p 84; 1971 SLT at p 165). K There is no doubt that the words "son" and "single" are incompatible. Column 1 of the entry in the register indicates that what is to be given after the name and rank or profession is "Whether single, married or widowed". The informant was not given the option "Widower" (unlike the schedule between 1854-1860 which sought "Condition, married or single, widower or widow" — *Vital Registration*, G T Bisset, p 226). It is generally appreciated by educated persons that a widower may be described as "widowed", but persons L of limited education would probably not know this and might well answer "single" if "widower" was not given as an option. It is possible that the local registrar gave the informant advice on this subject. It was shown that the registrar, Donald McAuley, was an educated person, a school teacher who was born in South Uist, a Gaelic speaking area, and was very probably bilingual. No evidence was, however, produced regarding the use of the word "Widowed" in relation to deceased men in the registry district of Lochaber at the period in question. Mr Peskett admitted that he

A had not analysed the usage of such words as "widowed" and "single" when the informant was a son or daughter, and he indicated that it could be done "but would take a lot of time". It may be that a comprehensive analysis of the entries in the register of deaths for Lochaber for the period 1860-67 would yield crucial information. The severe difficulties raised for the petitioner by the word "Single" in the death certificate of Ranald are to some extent contradicted by the indication in the certificate of death of Alexander by his son, Ranald MacDonald, the infor-

B mant, that Ranald regarded his lawful paternal grandmother as having been Margaret Ross because the information he gave with regard to the name and maiden surname of the mother of the deceased Alexander MacDonald was "Margaret MacDonald, m.s. Ross (Deceased)". The information given in relation to the deceased's parentage can reasonably be regarded as indicating the opinion of the informant with regard to the family tradition on the matter.

C On the matter of the legitimacy of Alexander MacDonald I am of the opinion that, weighing together the inferences that may be drawn from the proved facts, the matter has been left in even scales and that the respondent on whom lies the onus of proof, has failed to prove that Alexander MacDonald was illegitimate.

The petitioner requires to establish that Donald MacDonald was the son and heir male of Ranald MacDonald, that Ranald MacDonald was the son and
D heir male of Donald MacDonald and that Donald MacDonald was the son and heir male of Alexander MacDonald of Inverroy Mor. Much reliance is placed by the petitioner on the sloinneadh and on the statement alleged to have been made by Donald the Drover to George Borrow that his uncle was the chief, and the petitioner argues that by making this statement to George Borrow, Donald the Drover was confirming the sloinneadh. The statement of Donald the Drover was not an independent source of evidence but
E might be regarded as corroborating the sloinneadh. The only independent corroboration is to be found in Clementine MacArthur's hearsay evidence in her affidavit to the effect that her grand-aunt Miss Cameron told her that Alexander Raonuill was recognised as chief. With regard to the weight that is to be given to family tradition and the sloinneadh, reference was made to the Lord President's observations in *Macpherson v Reid's Trs* (1876) 4 R at p 138: "There is no doubt that in questions of pedigree, family tradition, if it have a relevant bearing on the question at
F issue, is admissible in evidence. But on the other hand, it is equally clear that the gossip of the locality in which the family is planted is quite inadmissible; and it appears to me that every question like that now before us must be tested by the consideration whether the information which is sought to be given in evidence belongs to the one class or the other. Family tradition is not only admissible in evidence, but if it be a well established and constant family tradition it may be very important and valuable evidence. But, then, to make a family tradition, you must have the

fact intended to be proved — as, for example, the rela-
G tion of father and son between two persons — shewn to have been matter of belief within the family, and handed down from one generation to another"; and: "By direct testimony I do not mean the testimony of the witness in the box, but the statement of deceased members of the family, made seriously and deliberately to the person who is put in the box; whereas, according to the law of Scotland, we admit such statements repeated at second hand, if they have been made by persons who, though not members of the family,
H have special means of knowledge. I think our rule in this respect is a rational and intelligible rule. It is quite possible that though in the general case members of the family will have the best means of knowledge, there may be members of the family who, from accidental circumstances, know very little about the family pedigree and lineage; whereas, on the other hand, there may be confidential servants who have been a long time in the family, or very intimate friends, who have much more peculiar means of knowledge and of hearing the family traditions than
I members of the family who may be absent and out of the country or otherwise estranged. I think it is the means of knowledge, therefore, that ought to be the test of the value of any statement made by a deceased person and repeated in the witness-box. Both laws equally exclude, I apprehend, anything like common gossip; that is to say, talk between persons who have no special means of knowledge whatever."

With regard to the sloinneadh it has not been estab-
J lished that it was kept in correct form without emendation, and in view of the length of time it was purportedly kept I am of the opinion that if it is to be of any significant weight it must have been kept in correct form and in a form that required no emendation. I do not think that Clementine MacArthur's hearsay evidence is sufficient to reinforce the sloinneadh to the requisite degree. More cogent evidence is required than is provided by the sloinneadh. There is no documentary evidence to prove that Donald was
K the son of Ranald or that Ranald was the son of Donald or that Donald was the son of Alexander of Inverroy Mor, nor to say whether Donald or Archibald was the elder of the two alleged brothers. The evidence of Father Andrew relating to Donald is of very doubtful weight if it is indeed relevant. The petitioner has been unable to produce any evidence with regard to possession of a house or land by any member of these three generations. Name patterns are of no assistance in relation to these three generations.
L I am of the opinion that on the balance of probabilities the evidence of the petitioner is not sufficient to establish that Donald MacDonald was the son and heir male of Ranald MacDonald, that Ranald MacDonald was the son and heir male of Donald and that Donald was the son and heir male of Alexander MacDonald of Inverroy Mor.

Counsel for the petitioner suggested that the case should be continued if the evidence in relation to any part of the claim was found to be insufficient or inadequate. It is certainly common practice in this court that when there is only a petitioner, and there is no respondent, a case may be continued so that further evidence may be obtained. When there is a respondent I do not think that that is an appropriate course to follow. The prayer of the petition shall be refused in hoc statu. In point of form it might be thought somewhat unusual to find in fact that certain matters have not been proved. This manner of proceeding is not without precedent — finding in fact 14 ("that it has not been proved that the respondent, Mrs Fraser-Mackenzie, is a stranger in blood to the family of Mackenzie of Kintail") in *Stewart Mackenzie v Fraser Mackenzie*.

I shall refuse the prayer of the petitioner in hoc statu.

———

Counsel for Petitioner, Rothesay Herald of Arms (Agnew of Lochnaw); Solicitors, D A Brittain — Counsel for Lord Advocate, McNeill; Solicitor, I Dean, Crown Agent.

INDEX OF CASES

ACCORDING TO SUBJECT MATTER